PROFESSIONAL

Microsoft® SQL Server® 2014 Integration Services

PROFESSIONAL

Microsoft® SQL Server® 2014 Integration Services

Brian Knight
Devin Knight
Jessica M. Moss
Mike Davis
Chris Rock

A Wiley Brand

Professional Microsoft® SQL Server® 2014 Integration Services

Published by
John Wiley & Sons, Inc.
10475 Crosspoint Boulevard
Indianapolis, IN 46256
www.wiley.com

Published simultaneously in Canada

ISBN: 978-1-118-85087-9
ISBN: 978-1-118-85090-9 (ebk)
ISBN: 978-1-118-85085-5 (ebk)

Manufactured in the United States of America

10 9 8 7 6 5 4

Library of Congress Control Number: 2014930406

To my great team and work family at Pragmatic Works

—Brian Knight

Proverbs 3:5-6

—Devin Knight

For Rich: Thank you for your support.

—Jessica M. Moss

To my kids, Gabriel and Sydney — they are the light of my life.

—Mike Davis

To the three girls in my life that mean more than anything to me, Tammy, Calista, and Callie

—Chris Rock

ABOUT THE AUTHORS

BRIAN KNIGHT, SQL Server MVP, MCITP, MCSE, MCDBA, is the owner and founder of Pragmatic Works. He is also the cofounder of BIDN.com, SQLServerCentral.com, and SQLShare.com. He runs the local SQL Server users group in Jacksonville (JSSUG). Brian is a contributing columnist at several technical magazines. He is the author of a dozen SQL Server books. Brian has spoken at conferences like PASS, SQL Connections, and TechEd, SQL Saturdays, Code Camps, and many pyramid scheme motivational sessions. His blog can be found at `http://www.bidn.com`. Brian lives in Jacksonville, Florida, where he enjoys his kids and running marathons.

DEVIN KNIGHT, SQL Server MVP, is the Training Director at Pragmatic Works. This is the sixth SQL Server book that he has authored. Devin has spoken at past conferences like PASS Summit, PASS Business Analytics Conference, SQL Saturdays, and Code Camps and is a contributing member to the PASS Business Intelligence Virtual Chapter. Making his home in Jacksonville, Florida, Devin is the Vice President of the local users' group (JSSUG). His blog can be found at `http://www.devinknightsql.com`.

JESSICA M. MOSS is a well-known practitioner, author, and speaker of Microsoft SQL Server business intelligence and has received a Microsoft MVP award for the past 6 years. She has created numerous data warehouse and business intelligence solutions for companies in different industries and has delivered training courses on Integration Services, Reporting Services, and Analysis Services. Jessica has authored technical content for multiple magazines, websites, and books, including the Wrox book *Professional Microsoft SQL Server 2012 Integration Services*, and has spoken internationally at conferences such as the PASS Community Summit, SharePoint Connections, and the SQLTeach International Conference. As a strong proponent of developing user-to-user community relations, Jessica actively participates in local user groups and code camps in central Virginia. In addition, Jessica volunteers her time to help educate people through the PASS organization.

MIKE DAVIS, MCTS, MCITP, is the Managing Project Lead at Pragmatic Works. This book is his fifth on the subject of Business Intelligence and specifically Integration Services. He has worked with SQL Server for over a decade and has led many successful Business Intelligence projects with his clients. Mike is an experienced speaker and has presented at many events such as several SQL Server User Groups, Code Camps, SQL Saturday events, and the PASS Summit. Mike is an active member at his local user group (JSSUG) in Jacksonville, Florida. In his spare time he likes to play darts and guitar. You can also find him on twitter `@MikeDavisSQL`, and his blog on `MikeDavisSQL.com`.

CHRIS ROCK is a software developer and program manager for Pragmatic Works. He started developing software using VB6 and SQL Server 6.5 in 1998 and has been using SSIS since its inception. Chris has spoken at many local SQL Saturday and Code Camp events in Florida. When he's not writing code, Chris enjoys training cats to speak English. He blogs at `http://rocksthoughts.com`.

ABOUT THE TECHNICAL EDITOR

MICHAEL MCINTYRE recently progressed into the role of Consulting Sales Engineer with Pragmatic Works, coordinating solutions and engagements that utilize the Microsoft BI stack for customers with a variety of BI needs. Previously with Pragmatic Works, he was a BI Software Support Engineer focusing on ETL within SQL Server Integration Services. This transition provided the opportunity to relocate to Salem, New Hampshire, from Jacksonville, Florida. Michael spends his free time with his wife and 3-year-old daughter and enjoys keeping up with and "tinkering" with mobile technologies

CREDITS

EXECUTIVE EDITOR
Robert Elliot

SENIOR PROJECT EDITOR
Kevin Kent

TECHNICAL EDITOR
Michael McIntyre

PRODUCTION EDITOR
Christine Mugnolo

EDITORIAL MANAGER
Mary Beth Wakefield

ASSOCIATE DIRECTOR OF MARKETING
David Mayhew

MARKETING MANAGER
Ashley Zurcher

BUSINESS MANAGER
Amy Knies

VICE PRESIDENT AND EXECUTIVE GROUP PUBLISHER
Richard Swadley

ASSOCIATE PUBLISHER
Jim Minatel

PROJECT COORDINATOR, COVER
Todd Klemme

PROOFREADER
Nancy Carrasco

TECHNICAL PROOFREADERS
Steve Wake
Stephen Wynkoop

INDEXER
Johnna VanHoose Dinse

COVER DESIGNER
Wiley

COVER IMAGE
©Mark Evans/iStockphoto.com

ACKNOWLEDGMENTS

THANKS to everyone who made this book possible. As always, I owe a huge debt to my wife, Jenn, for putting up with my late nights, and to my children, Colton, Liam, Camille, and John, for being so patient with their tired dad who has always overextended. Thanks to Kevin Kent and my tech editor Michael McIntyre for keeping me in my place. Thanks also to the makers of Guinness for providing my special juice that helped me power through the book. Thanks for all the user group leaders out there who work so hard to help others become proficient in technology. You make a huge difference!

—Brian Knight

I MUST GIVE THANKS to God; without God in my life, I would not have such blessings. Thanks to my wife, Erin, who has had amazing patience during the late nights of writing and editing. To our three children, Collin, Justin, and Lana, who have sacrificed time away from daddy. Finally, I would like to thank my Fierljeppen mentor, Bart Helmholt, for showing me the extreme sport of Canal Jumping. The sport of Canal Jumping has always been a dream of mine, and I look forward to accomplishing my ultimate goal of Dutch Champion Canal Jumper.

—Devin Knight

THANK you to everyone for your support throughout the book writing process. Specifically, I would like to thank my coauthors and editors: Brian Knight, Devin Knight, Mike Davis, Chris Rock, Kevin Kent, and Bob Elliott. Your passion and dedication still astound me on a regular basis. Thank you to Rich, who helped me through the late nights, and my family, for putting up with my regular disappearances to write. Also, thank you to the many others that have helped me in my career, but are too numerous to name.

—Jessica M. Moss

THANKS to my Pragmatic Works Team for their support in this book. Thank you to Brian Knight for giving me the opportunity of a lifetime. Thank you to Adam Jorgensen for pushing me. Thank you to the Wiley team, especially Kevin and Bob. Thank you to the technical editor and technical proofreaders for their help in making this book great. Thank you to my mother for raising me to be the man I am today. Thank you to my kids for being awesome and putting up with all the writing time. And finally, thank you to the Flying Spaghetti Monster for showing me the way of logic and reasoning.

—Mike Davis

THANKS to everyone who made this book possible. First and foremost, I want to thank my colleague Tyler Ryan. His help made parts of this book possible, and I couldn't have completed the book without his help. I want to thank my wife, Tammy, and my two girls, Calista and Callie. Without you I wouldn't have tried so hard to achieve the goals I've reached in my life. Finally, thanks to Brian Knight again for giving me the opportunity to contribute to this book.

—Chris Rock

CONTENTS

INTRODUCTION

THE MOST IMPORTANT BUSINESS INTELLIGENCE TOOL in the Microsoft Swiss Army knife of tools is SQL Server Integration Services (SSIS). This is because the other tools would be nothing without the cleansing and movement of data into a presentable format. The product can extract, transform, and load (ETL) data astonishingly fast. A 2010 benchmark showed movement of more than a terabyte an hour with SSIS! If you're new to SSIS, you've picked a fantastic field to become involved in. The one consistent skill needed in today's technical job market is ETL. If a company wants to establish a partnership with another company, it'll need to communicate data back and forth between the two companies. If your company wants to launch new products, it'll need a way to integrate those products into its website and catalog. All of these types of tasks are going to require the skill set you are developing and will learn in this book.

Companies that had never used SQL Server before are now allowing it in their environment because SSIS is such an easy-to-use and cost-effective way to move data. SSIS competes with the largest ETL tools on the market like Informatica, DataStage, and Ab Initio at a tiny fraction of the price. SQL Server 2014 now offers more components that you use to make your life even easier and the performance scales to a level never seen on the SQL Server platform.

The best thing about SSIS is its price tag: free with your SQL Server purchase. Many ETL vendors charge hundreds of thousands of dollars, if not millions, for what you will see in this book. SSIS is also a great platform for you to expand and integrate into, which many ETL vendors do not offer. Once you get past the initial learning curve, you'll be amazed with the power of the tool, and it can take weeks off your time to market. This author team has trained hundreds of people over the years, and you'll find that the learning curve of SSIS is shallow relative to competing platforms. In SQL Server 2012, the product matured to its third major envisioning. In that release the focus was on scalability, management, and more advanced data cleansing. In SQL Server 2014 an incremental change has happened so new content focuses on patterns in SSIS.

WHO THIS BOOK IS FOR

Because we have used SSIS since the beta stages of SQL Server 2005 and through its evolution into its current form, the idea of writing this book was quite compelling. If you've never used SSIS before, we spend the first chapters focusing on lowering your learning curve on this product. If you've used SSIS in the past, we've added more patterns and best practices to this SQL Server 2014 version of the book to take your skills to the next level. If you're an SSIS 2005 or 2008 user, luckily the interface has not drastically changed, so you'll want to focus on advanced data cleansing and administration, which has gone through a drastic overhaul.

This book is intended for developers, DBAs, and casual users who hope to use SSIS for transforming data, creating a workflow, or maintaining their SQL Server. This book is a professional book, meaning that the authors assume that you know the basics of how to query a SQL Server and have some rudimentary programming skills. Not many programming skills will be needed or assumed, but it will help with your advancement. No skills in the prior release of SSIS are required, but we do reference it throughout the book when we call attention to feature enhancements.

WHAT THIS BOOK COVERS

Whether you're new to SSIS or an experienced SSIS developer, there's something for you in this book. This book takes you from the architecture and basics of SSIS all the way through to developing hard-core SSIS solutions to solve many of the industry's common business scenarios. The book is tutorial based, meaning that it teaches you through simple examples.

By the time you complete this book, you'll know how to load and synchronize database systems using SSIS by using some of the new SQL Server 2014 features. You'll also know how to load data warehouses, which is a very hot and specialized skill. Even in warehousing, you'll find features in the new 2014 release that you'll wonder how you lived without like the Data Quality Services integration and CDC integration!

HOW THIS BOOK IS STRUCTURED

After discussing the architecture of SSIS, we'll start with the basics by introducing the fundamental concepts of SSIS: the Data Flow and Control Flow. We'll then build through the various other features, including the warehousing and scripting, and proceed to advanced topics like programming and extending the engine. SSIS is a very feature-rich product, and it took a lot to cover the product:

Chapter 1, "Welcome to SQL Server Integration Services," introduces the concepts that we're going to discuss throughout the remainder of this book. We talk about the SSIS architecture and give a brief overview of what you can do with SSIS.

Chapter 2, "The SSIS Tools," shows you how to quickly learn how to import and export data by using the Import and Export Wizard and then takes you on a tour of the SQL Server Data Tools (SSDT).

Chapter 3, "SSIS Tasks," goes into each of the tasks that are available to you in SSIS. These tasks are the building blocks for your SSIS workflow and are much like LEGO block programming.

Chapter 4, "The Data Flow," dives into the Data Flow components in SSIS. These components are where typical ETL developers will spend 75 percent of their time when loading a database.

Chapter 5, "Using Variables, Parameters, and Expressions," instructs you how to use the obscure expression language in SSIS by showing you many example use cases and how to solve them through the language. We also cover in the chapter a new concept of parameters and parameterization of a package.

Chapter 6, "Containers," covers how to use containers to do looping in SSIS and describes how to configure each of the basic transforms.

Chapter 7, "Joining Data," focuses on how to join systems together, whether those systems are two flat files or database platforms. Much of the chapter is spent showing the Lookup Transform.

Now that you know how to configure most of the tasks and transforms, **Chapter 8, "Creating an End-to-End Package,"** puts it all together with a large example that lets you try out your SSIS experience.

Chapter 9, "Scripting in SSIS," shows you some of the ways you can use the Script task in SSIS.

Chapter 10, "Advanced Data Cleansing in SSIS," walks through common patterns in data cleansing and how to accomplish them in SSIS. The chapter also covers Data Quality Services (DQS) and how to integrate it into SSIS.

Chapter 11, "Incremental Loads in SSIS," shows you common patterns you can use to incrementally refresh your data. It also shows you how to use and integrate Change Data Capture (CDC) into SSIS.

Chapter 12, "Loading a Data Warehouse," covers how to load a data warehouse from the ground up through example. Even smaller companies now are finding that to compete they need to make their data work for them by employing a data warehouse. In this chapter we show how to load dimension and fact tables and some of the common issues.

Chapter 13, "Using the Relational Engine," discusses other features in the SQL Server arsenal that can help you build robust and high-performance ETL solutions. The SQL Server relational database engine has many features that were designed with data loading in mind, and as such the engine and SSIS form a perfect marriage to extract, load, and transform your data.

Chapter 14, "Accessing Heterogenous Data," shows you how to connect to systems other than SQL Server like Excel, XML, and web services.

Chapter 15, "Reliability and Scalability," demonstrates how to scale SSIS and make it more reliable. You can use the features in this chapter to show you how to make the package restartable if a problem occurs.

Chapter 16, "Understanding and Tuning the Data Flow Engine," explains the architecture of the SSIS Data Flow engine in detail and how to tune your SSIS packages for maximum efficiency.

Chapter 17, "SSIS Software Development Life Cycle," introduces a software development life cycle methodology to you. It speaks to how SSIS can integrate with Visual Studio Team System.

Chapter 18, "Error and Event Handling," discusses how to handle problems with SSIS with error and event handling.

Chapter 19, "Programming and Extending SSIS," shows the SSIS object model and how to use it to extend SSIS. The chapter goes through creating your own task, and then . . .

Chapter 20, "Adding a User Interface to Your Component," adds a user interface to the discussion.

Chapter 21, "External Management and WMI Task Implementation," walks through creating an application that interfaces with the SSIS to manage the environment. It also discusses the WMI set of tasks.

Chapter 22, "Administering SSIS," shows you how to deploy and administer the packages that you've worked so hard to develop. Much of the work in SSIS in SQL Server 2014 has gone into modifying the way you deploy and administer SSIS packages.

Appendix A, "SSIS Crib Notes," provides solutions to common problems and a cheat sheet for the SSIS expression language.

Appendix B, "SSIS Internal Views and Stored Procedures," gives you a listing and way to use common stored procedures in the SSIS catalog.

Appendix C, "Interviewing for an ETL Developer Position, "is your interview coach to help you ace an interview where SSIS is part of your job description.

WHAT YOU NEED TO USE THIS BOOK

To follow this book, you will only need to have SQL Server 2014 and the Integration Services component installed. You'll need a machine that can support the minimum hardware requirements to run SQL Server 2014. You'll also want to have the AdventureWorks and AdventureWorksDW databases installed. You can find the versions of these databases we used for this book on the Wrox website (`www.wrox.com`). If you download the AdventureWorks databases from CodePlex, they will have a version number at the end of the database names. Make sure that you rename the database to take this version off the name.

CONVENTIONS

To help you get the most from the text and keep track of what's happening, we've used a number of conventions throughout the book.

> **WARNING** *Warnings hold important, not-to-be-forgotten information that is directly relevant to the surrounding text.*

> **NOTE** *Notes indicate notes, tips, hints, tricks, and asides to the current discussion.*

As for styles in the text:

- We *highlight* new terms and important words when we introduce them.
- We show keyboard strokes like this: Ctrl+A.
- We show filenames, URLs, and code within the text like so: `persistence.properties`.
- We present code in two different ways:

```
We use a monofont type with no highlighting for most code examples.
```

```
We use bold to emphasize code that's particularly important in the present
context.
```

SOURCE CODE

As you work through the examples in this book, you may choose either to type in all the code manually, or to use the source code files that accompany the book. All the source code used in this book is available for download at `www.wrox.com`. Specifically for this book, the code download is on the Download Code tab at:

```
www.wrox.com/go/prossis2014
```

> **NOTE** *Because many books have similar titles, you may find it easiest to search by ISBN; this book's ISBN is 978-1-118-85087-9.*

Once you download the code, just decompress it with your favorite compression tool. Alternately, you can go to the main Wrox code download page at `www.wrox.com/dynamic/books/download.aspx` to see the code available for this book and all other Wrox books.

Don't forget. You will also find and be able to download the versions of the AdventureWorks and AdventureWorksDW databases that we used for this book at `www.wrox.com`.

ERRATA

We make every effort to ensure that there are no errors in the text or in the code. However, no one is perfect, and mistakes do occur. If you find an error in one of our books, like a spelling mistake or faulty piece of code, we would be very grateful for your feedback. By sending in errata, you may save another reader hours of frustration, and at the same time, you will be helping us provide even higher quality information.

To find the errata page for this book, go to:

```
www.wrox.com/go/prossis2014
```

And click the Errata link. On this page you can view all errata that has been submitted for this book and posted by Wrox editors.

If you don't spot "your" error on the Book Errata page, go to `www.wrox.com/contact/techsupport.shtml` and complete the form there to send us the error you have found. We'll check the information and, if appropriate, post a message to the book's errata page and fix the problem in subsequent editions of the book.

P2P.WROX.COM

For author and peer discussion, join the P2P forums at `http://p2p.wrox.com`. The forums are a web-based system for you to post messages relating to Wrox books and related technologies and interact with other readers and technology users. The forums offer a subscription feature to e-mail you topics of interest of your choosing when new posts are made to the forums. Wrox authors, editors, other industry experts, and your fellow readers are present on these forums.

At `http://p2p.wrox.com`, you will find a number of different forums that will help you, not only as you read this book, but also as you develop your own applications. To join the forums, just follow these steps:

1. Go to `http://p2p.wrox.com` and click the Register link.
2. Read the terms of use and click Agree.
3. Complete the required information to join, as well as any optional information you wish to provide, and click Submit.
4. You will receive an e-mail with information describing how to verify your account and complete the joining process.

> **NOTE** *You can read messages in the forums without joining P2P, but in order to post your own messages, you must join.*

Once you join, you can post new messages and respond to messages other users post. You can read messages at any time on the web. If you would like to have new messages from a particular forum e-mailed to you, click the Subscribe to this Forum icon by the forum name in the forum listing.

For more information about how to use the Wrox P2P, be sure to read the P2P FAQs for answers to questions about how the forum software works, as well as many common questions specific to P2P and Wrox books. To read the FAQs, click the FAQ link on any P2P page.

1

Welcome to SQL Server Integration Services

WHAT'S IN THIS CHAPTER?

- What's new to this version of SSIS
- Exploring tools you'll be using in SSIS
- Overview of the SSIS architecture
- Considering your licensing options around BI with SQL Server

SQL Server Integration Services (SSIS) is the anchor in a growing suite of products that make up the Microsoft SQL Server Business Intelligence (BI) platform. What makes SSIS so important is without the data movement and cleansing features that SSIS brings to the table, the other SQL Server BI products can't operate. What's the point of a cube, for example, with bad or inconsistent data? In its simplest form, SSIS is an enterprise-level, in-memory ETL tool. However, SSIS is not just a fancy wrapper around an import wizard. In a drag-and-drop development environment, ETL developers can snap together intricate workflows and out-of-the-box data-cleansing flows that rival custom coding and expensive million-dollar, third-party tools. The best thing about SSIS is that you have already paid for it when you license SQL Server.

When we put together the first edition of this book, we were blown away by the new architecture and capabilities of SSIS. SSIS was a big change from the Data Transformation Services (DTS) product that it replaced, and there was much to learn. Since the first edition of SSIS, we have collectively racked up many years of experience converting older DTS packages and mind-sets over to using it, and trust us when we say that no one who has made the change is asking to go back. We've learned some things, too.

While SQL Server 2012 was a large jump forward for SSIS, SQL Server 2014 has some very small iterative changes. When we wrote this book, we dug deeply to mine the decades of cumulative experience working with this product, adding our collective knowledge back into these pages. We hope you will agree that the result makes your experience with SSIS a more productive one. This chapter starts from the beginning by providing an overview of SSIS, describing where it fits within the BI product platform and ETL development in general.

SQL SERVER SSIS HISTORICAL OVERVIEW

In SQL Server 7.0, Microsoft had a small team of developers work on a very understated feature of SQL Server called Data Transformation Services (DTS). DTS was the backbone of the Import/Export Wizard, and its primary purpose was to transform data from almost any OLE DB–compliant data source to almost any destination. It also had the ability to execute programs and run scripts, making workflow a minor feature.

By the time that SQL Server 2000 was released, DTS had a strong following of DBAs and maybe a few developers. Microsoft included in the release new features like the Dynamic Properties Task that enabled you to alter the package dynamically at runtime. Even though DTS utilized extensive logging along with simple and complex multiphase data pumps, usability studies still showed that developers had to create elaborate scripts to extend DTS to get what they wanted done. A typical use case was enabling DTS to load data conditionally based on the existence of a file. To accomplish this in DTS, you had to use the ActiveX Script Task to code a solution using the file system object in VBScript. The problem with that was DTS lacked some of the common components needed to support typical ETL processes. Although it was powerful if you knew how to write scripting code, most DBAs didn't have this type of scripting experience (or time).

After five years, Microsoft released the much-touted SQL Server 2005 and SSIS, which was no longer an understated feature like DTS. With the SQL Server 2008 release, SSIS was given extra scalability features to help it appeal more to the enterprise. This is entirely appropriate because so much has been added to SSIS. Microsoft made a huge investment in usability, with simple enhancements to the toolbox that allow newer users to ramp up easier. The main focus of the newest release of SQL Server is on the management and deployment of SSIS.

WHAT'S NEW IN SSIS

The scope of the SQL Server 2014 release of SSIS resembles the scope of the SQL Server 2008 R2 release. With the last release of SQL Server 2008 R2, the Microsoft SSIS team did very incremental changes after a very large SQL Server 2008 release. In SQL Server 2012 release, Microsoft had focused on SSIS manageability, making it easier to deploy and execute. Also added in 2012 are robust new data cleansing components that help you standardize and detect data anomalies. Furthermore, improvements to the development tools will help make SSIS developers more productive and help new developers get up to speed more easily. The SQL Server 2014 release uses a newer version of Visual Studio but all in all, it will feel much like SQL Server 2012. You will find new components in SQL Server 2014 SSIS, but they will have to be downloaded from sites like CodePlex from the product team and will eventually be rolled into the core product at a future release.

TOOLS OF THE TRADE

Most of this book will assume that you know nothing about previous releases of SQL Server SSIS. Instead, it takes a fresh look at SQL Server SSIS. The learning curve can be considered steep at first, but once you figure out the basics, you'll be creating complex packages in no time. To provide an idea of how easy SSIS is to use, the following section looks at a staple tool in the ETL world: the Import and Export Wizard.

Import and Export Wizard

If you need to move data quickly from almost any OLE DB–compliant data source or flat file to a destination, you can use the SSIS Import and Export Wizard (shown in Figure 1-1). In fact, many SSIS packages are born this way, but most packages you wish to keep in a BI solution should not be created with the wizard. The wizard provides a quick way to move data and perform very light transformations of data but does not create packages that use best practices. The wizard is available in all editions of SQL Server except the Local Database edition and Express. It enables you to persist the logic of the data movement into a package file. The basic concept of an import/export wizard has not changed substantially from the days of DTS. You still have the option to check all the tables you want to transfer. In addition, however, you can also encapsulate the entire transfer of data into a single transaction.

Where do you find the wizard? It depends. If you just need to perform a quick import or export, access the wizard directly from the Start menu by navigating to Start ⇨ Microsoft SQL Server "2014" ⇨ Import and Export Data. The other option is to open a project in the SSIS development environment and select Project ⇨ SSIS Import and Export Wizard. We cover this in detail in Chapter 2. Before we get into all the mechanics for that, see Figure 1-1 for an example of the wizard that has bulk loaded tables.

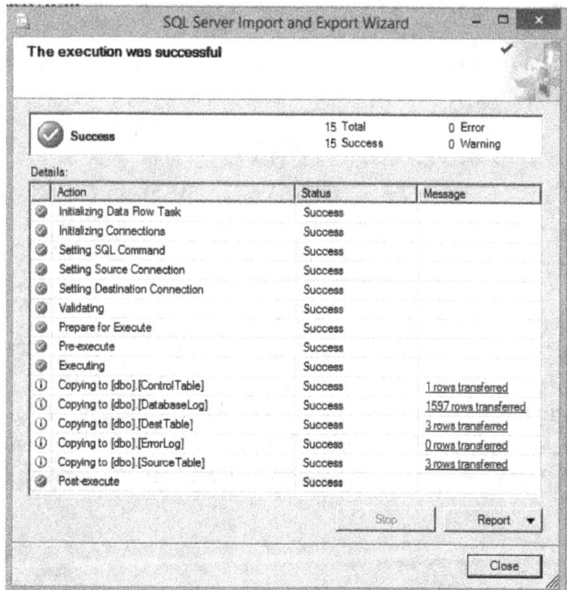

FIGURE 1-1

The SQL Server Data Tools Experience

The SQL Server Data Tools (SSDT) was previously called Business Intelligence Development Studio (BIDS) in SQL Server 2008, and it is the central environment in which you'll spend most of your time as an SSIS developer. SSDT is just a specialized use of the familiar Visual Studio development environment. In SQL Server 2014, SSDT no longer installs when you install SQL Server. Instead, you'll have to download and install the SQL Server Data Tools (Business Intelligence for Visual Studio) from the Microsoft website. At the time of this publication, SQL Server 2014 can use the Visual Studio 2012 and 2013 versions to design SSIS packages. Visual Studio can host many different project types, from Console applications to Class Libraries and Windows applications. Although you may see many project types when you create a project, SSDT actually contains project templates for only Analysis Services, Integration Services, Report Server, and variants thereof. SSIS in particular uses a BI project type called an Integration Services project (see Figure 1-2), which provides a development design surface with a completely ETL-based set of tools in the Toolbox window.

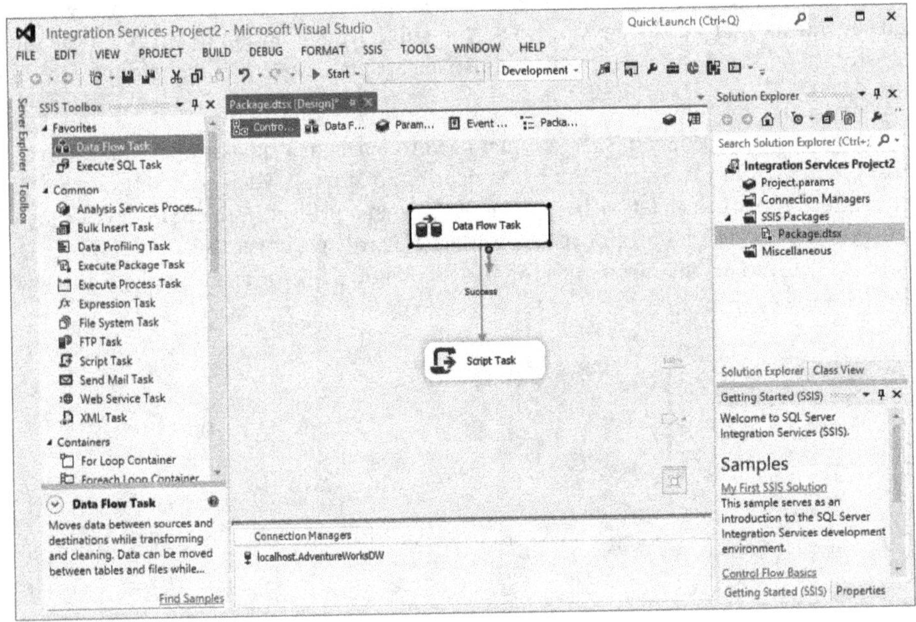

FIGURE 1-2

This development environment is similar to the legacy DTS Designer, but the approach is completely different. Most important, this is a collaborative development environment just like any Visual Studio development effort, with full source code management, version control, and multi-user project management. SSIS solutions are developed just like all other .NET development solutions, including being persisted to files — in this case, XML file structures with a .DSTX file extension.

You can even develop within the SSDT environment without a connection to a SQL Server instance using the offline mode. Once your solution is complete, it can be built and deployed to one or multiple target SQL servers. These changes from DTS to SSIS are crucial to establishing the discipline and best practices of existing software development methodologies as you develop business intelligence solutions. We'll discuss this SSDT development interface in more detail in Chapter 2.

SSIS ARCHITECTURE

Microsoft has truly established SSIS as a major player in the extraction, transformation, and loading (ETL) market. Not only is the SSIS technology a complete code rewrite from SQL Server 2000 DTS, it now rivals other third-party ETL tools that can cost hundreds of thousands of dollars depending on how you scale the software — and it is included free with the purchase of SQL Server 2014. Free always sounds great, but most free products can take you only so far if the feature set is minimal or the toolset has usability, scalability, or enterprise performance limitations. SSIS, however, is the real deal, satisfying typical ETL requirements with an architecture that has evolved dramatically from earlier incarnations. At the time of this publication, SSIS held the world speed record of loading more than 2 terabytes in a single hour.

Packages

A core component of SSIS is the notion of a *package*. A package best parallels an executable program that you can write that contains workflow and business logic. Essentially, a package is a collection of tasks snapped together to execute in an orderly fashion. A package is also a unit of execution and development, much like a .NET developer creates programs or DLL files. Precedence constraints are used to connect the tasks together and manage the order in which they execute, based on what happens in each task or based on rules defined by the package developer. The package is brought together into a .DTSX file that is actually an XML-structured file with collections of properties. Just like other .NET projects, the file-based code is marked up using the development environment and can then be saved and deployed to a SQL Server.

Don't worry; you won't have to know how to write this type of XML to create a package. That's what the designer is for. The point here is that the SSIS package is an XML-structured file, much like .RDL files are to Reporting Services. Of course, there is much more to packages than that, and you'll explore the other elements of packages, such as event handlers, later in this chapter.

Control Flow

The brain of a package is its *Control Flow*, which orchestrates the order of execution for all its components. The components consist of tasks and containers and are controlled by *precedence constraints*, discussed later in this chapter. For example, Figure 1-3 shows three tasks that are tied together with two precedence constraints.

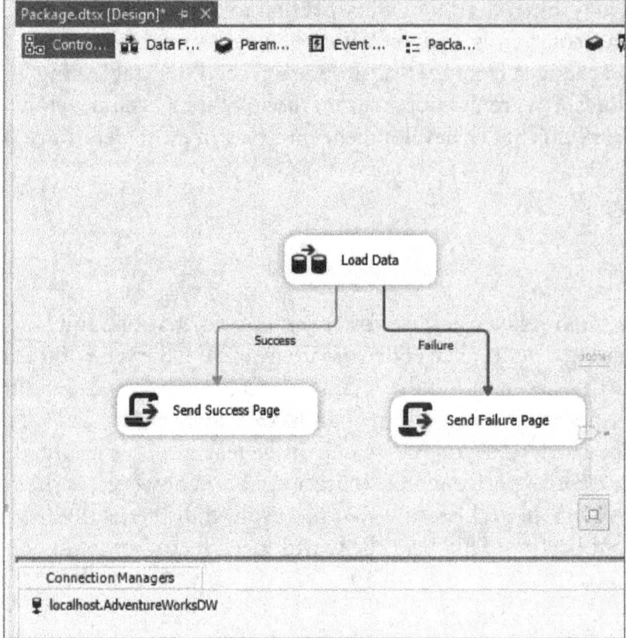

FIGURE 1-3

Tasks

A *task* can best be described as an individual unit of work. Tasks provide functionality to your package, in much the same way that a method does in a programming language. However, in SSIS, you aren't coding the methods; rather, you are dragging and dropping them onto a design surface and configuring them. You can develop your own tasks, but here are the current ETL tasks available to you out of the box:

- **Analysis Services Execute DDL Task:** Executes a DDL Task in Analysis Services. For example, this can create, drop, or alter a cube (Enterprise and Developer Editions only).
- **Analysis Services Processing Task:** This task processes a SQL Server Analysis Services cube, dimension, or mining model.
- **Bulk Insert Task:** Loads data into a table by using the `BULK INSERT` SQL command.
- **CDC Control Task:** Maintains and interacts with the change data capture (CDC) feature from SQL Server.
- **Data Flow Task:** This very specialized task loads and transforms data into an OLE DB and ADO.NET destination.
- **Data Mining Query Task:** Allows you to run predictive queries against your Analysis Services data-mining models.
- **Data Profiling Task:** This exciting task enables the examination of data; it replaces your ad hoc data profiling techniques.

- **Execute Package Task:** Allows you to execute a package from within a package, making your SSIS packages modular.
- **Execute Process Task:** Executes a program external to your package, such as one to split your extract file into many files before processing the individual files.
- **Execute SQL Task:** Executes a SQL statement or stored procedure.
- **Expression Task:** Sets a variable to an expression at runtime.
- **File System Task:** This task can handle directory operations such as creating, renaming, or deleting a directory. It can also manage file operations such as moving, copying, or deleting files.
- **FTP Task:** Sends or receives files from an FTP site.
- **Message Queue Task:** Sends or receives messages from a Microsoft Message Queue (MSMQ).
- **Script Task:** This task enables you to perform .NET-based scripting in the Visual Studio Tools for Applications programming environment.
- **Send Mail Task:** Sends a mail message through SMTP.
- **Web Service Task:** Executes a method on a web service.
- **WMI Data Reader Task:** This task can run WQL queries against the Windows Management Instrumentation. This enables you to read the event log, get a list of applications that are installed, or determine hardware that is installed, to name a few examples.
- **WMI Event Watcher Task:** This task empowers SSIS to wait for and respond to certain WMI events that occur in the operating system.
- **XML Task:** Parses or processes an XML file. It can merge, split, or reformat an XML file.

Also included are a whole set of DBA-oriented tasks that enable you to create packages that can be used to maintain your SQL Server environment. These tasks perform functions such as transferring your SQL Server databases, backing up your database, or shrinking the database. Each of the available tasks is described in Chapter 3 in much more detail, and you will see them in other examples throughout the book.

Tasks are extensible, and you can create your own custom tasks in .NET if you need a workflow item that doesn't exist or if you have a common scripting function that can benefit from reuse in your package development. To learn more about this topic, see Chapter 19.

> **NOTE** *There's a thriving ecosystem of third-party components that are available for SSIS. If you are looking for a task or Data Flow component that doesn't exist out of the box, be sure to first search online before creating your own. Some examples of these components include support for SFTP, SalesForce.com communication, SharePoint integration, and compression of files to name just a few.*

Precedence Constraints

Precedence constraints are package components that direct tasks to execute in a given order. In fact, precedence constraints are the connectors that not only link tasks together but also define the workflow of your SSIS package. A constraint controls the execution of the two linked tasks by executing the destination task based upon the final state of the prior task and business rules that are defined using special expressions. The expression language embedded in SSIS essentially replaces the need to control workflow using script-based methodologies that enable and disable tasks, as was used in the DTS legacy solution. With expressions, you can direct the workflow of your SSIS package based on all manner of given conditions. You'll look at many examples of using these constraints throughout this book.

To set up a precedence constraint between two tasks, you must set the constraint value; optionally, you can set an expression. The following sections provide a brief overview of the differences between the two.

Constraint values define how the package will react when the prior task of two linked tasks completes an execution. The options define whether the destination task of two linked tasks should execute based solely on how the prior task completes. Three constraint values are possible:

- **Success:** A task that's chained to another task with this constraint will execute only if the prior task completes successfully. These precedence constraints are colored green.
- **Completion:** A task that's chained to another task with this constraint will execute if the prior task completes, whether or not the prior task succeeds or fails. These precedence constraints are colored blue.
- **Failure:** A task that's chained to another task with this constraint will execute only if the prior task fails to complete. This type of constraint is usually used to notify an operator of a failed event. These precedence constraints are colored red.

You can also conditionally tie tasks together by writing logic on a precedence constraint. This is done by placing an SSIS expression language (resembles C#) on the precedence constraint. For example, you might specify that a task should run only at the end of each month. To do this, you would add an expression that evaluated the runtime of the package to determine if the next step should be run. Much more about writing expressions can be found in Chapter 5.

Containers

Containers are core units in the SSIS architecture for grouping tasks together logically into units of work. Besides providing visual consistency, containers enable you to define variables and event handlers (these are discussed in a moment) within the scope of the container, instead of the package. There are four types of containers in SSIS:

- **Task Host Container:** Not a visible element that you'll find in the Toolbox, but rather an abstract concept like an interface.
- **Sequence Container:** Allows you to group tasks into logical subject areas. Within the development environment, you can then collapse or expand this container for usability.
- **For Loop Container:** Loops through a series of tasks until a condition is met.
- **Foreach Loop Container:** Loops through a series of files or records in a data set, and then executes the tasks in the container for each record in the collection.

Because containers are so integral to SSIS development, Chapter 6 is devoted to them. As you read through the book, you'll see many real-world examples that demonstrate how to use each of these container types for typical ETL development tasks.

Data Flow

The core strength of SSIS is its capability to extract data into the server's memory, transform it, and write it out to an alternative destination. If the Control Flow is the brains of SSIS, then the Data Flow would be its heart. The in-memory architecture is what helps SSIS scale and what makes SSIS run faster than staging data and running stored procedures. Data sources are the conduit for these data pipelines, and they are represented by connections that can be used by sources or destinations once they've been defined. A data source uses connections that are OLE DB–compliant and ADO .NET data sources such as SQL Server, Oracle, DB2, or even nontraditional data sources, such as Analysis Services and Outlook. The data sources can be in scope to a single SSIS package or shared across multiple packages in a project.

All the characteristics of the connection are defined in the Connection Manager. The Connection Manager dialog options vary according to the type of connection you're trying to configure. Figure 1-4 shows you what a typical connection to SQL Server would look like.

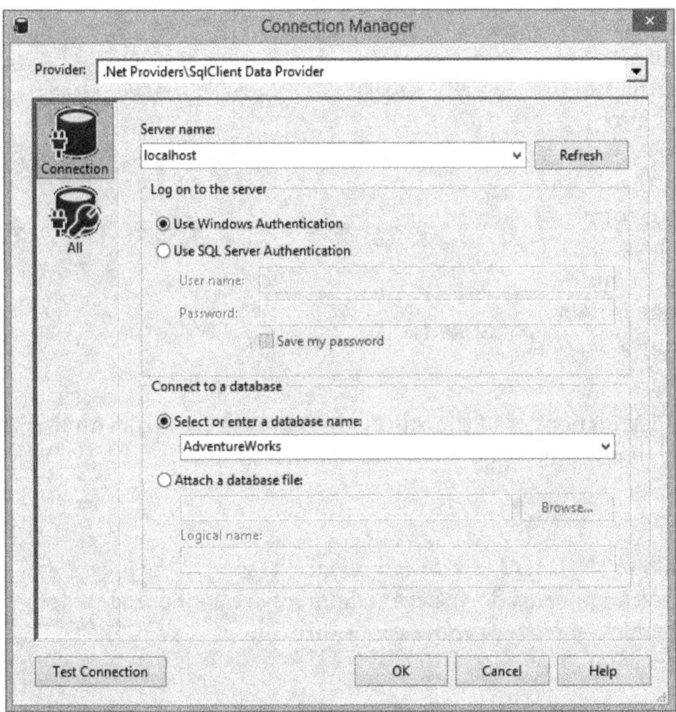

FIGURE 1-4

Connection Managers are used to centralize connection strings to data sources and to abstract them from the SSIS packages themselves. They can be shared across multiple packages in a project or isolated to a single package. Connection Managers also allow you to externalize the configuration of them at runtime by your DBA with a configuration file or parameters (which we'll describe in Chapter 22). SSIS will not use the connection until you begin to instantiate it in the package. This provides the ultimate in lightweight development portability for SSIS.

You learned earlier that the Data Flow Task is simply another executable task in the package. The Data Flow Task is the pipeline mechanism that moves data from source to destination. However, in the case of SSIS, you have much more control of what happens from start to finish. In fact, you have a set of out-of-the-box transformation components that you snap together to clean and manipulate the data while it is in the data pipeline.

One confusing thing for new SSIS developers is that once you drag and drop a Data Flow Task in the Control Flow, it spawns a new Data Flow design surface with its own new tab in the SSDT user interface. Each Data Flow Task has its own design surface that you can access by double-clicking the Data Flow Task or by clicking the Data Flow tab and selecting the name of the Data Flow Task from the drop-down list. Just as the Control Flow handles the main workflow of the package, the Data Flow handles the transformation of data in memory. Almost anything that manipulates data falls into the Data Flow category. As data moves through each step of the Data Flow, the data changes, based on what the transform does. For example, in Figure 1-5, a new column is derived using the Derived Column Transformation, and that new column is then available to subsequent transformations or to the destination.

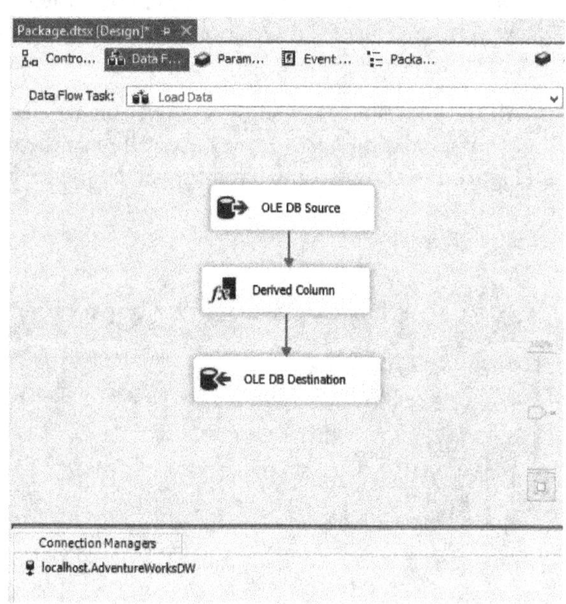

FIGURE 1-5

In this section, each of the sources, destinations, and transformations are covered from an overview perspective. These areas are covered in much more detail in later chapters.

Sources

A *source* is a component that you add to the Data Flow design surface to specify the location of the source data that will send data to components downstream. Sources are configured to use Connection Managers in order to enable the reuse of connections throughout your package. SSIS provides eight out-of-the-box sources:

- **OLE DB Source:** Connects to nearly any OLE DB data source, such as SQL Server, Access, Oracle, or DB2, to name just a few.

- **Excel Source:** Specializes in receiving data from Excel spreadsheets. This source also makes it easy to run SQL queries against your Excel spreadsheet to narrow the scope of the data that you wish to pass through the flow.
- **Flat File Source:** Connects to a delimited or fixed-width file.
- **Raw File Source:** Produces a specialized binary file format for data that is in transit; it is especially quick to read by SSIS. This component is one of the only components that does not use a Connection Manager.
- **Xml Source:** Retrieves data from an XML document. This source does not use a Connection Manager to configure it.
- **ADO.NET Source:** This source is just like the OLE DB Source but only for ADO.NET-based sources. The internal implementation uses an ADO.NET `DataReader` as the source. The ADO.NET connection is much like the one you see in the .NET Framework when hand-coding a connection and retrieval from a database.
- **CDC Source:** Reads data out of a table that has change data capture (CDC) enabled. Used to retrieve only rows that have changed over a duration of time.
- **ODBC Source:** Reads data out of table by using an ODBC provider instead of OLE DB. When you are given the choice between OLE DB and ODBC, it is still recommended in SSIS packages that you use OLE DB.

If the source components included in SSIS do not provide the functionality required for your solution, you can write code to connect to any data source that is accessible from a .NET application. One method is to use the Script Component to create a source stream using the existing .NET libraries. This method is more practical for single-use applications. If you need to reuse a custom source in multiple packages, you can develop one by using the SSIS .NET API and object model.

Transformations

Transformations are key components within the Data Flow that allow changes to the data within the data pipeline. You can use transformations to split, divert, and remerge data in the data pipeline. Data can also be validated, cleansed, and rejected using specific rules. For example, you may want your dimension data to be sorted and validated. This can be easily accomplished by dropping a Sort and a Lookup Transformation onto the Data Flow design surface and configuring them.

Transformation components in the SSIS Data Flow affect data in the data pipe in memory. Because this process is done in memory, it can be much faster than loading the data into a staging environment and updating the staging system with stored procedures. Here's a complete list of transformations and their purposes:

- **Aggregate:** Aggregates data from transformation or source.
- **Audit:** Exposes auditing information from the package to the data pipe, such as when the package was run and by whom.
- **CDC Splitter:** After data has been read out of a table with CDC enabled, this transform sends data that should be inserted, updated, and deleted down different paths.

- **Character Map:** Makes common string data changes for you, such as changing data from lowercase to uppercase.
- **Conditional Split:** Splits the data based on certain conditions being met. For example, this transformation could be instructed to send data down a different path if the State column is equal to Florida.
- **Copy Column:** Adds a copy of a column to the transformation output. You can later transform the copy, keeping the original for auditing purposes.
- **Data Conversion:** Converts a column's data type to another data type.
- **Data Mining Query:** Performs a data-mining query against Analysis Services.
- **Derived Column:** Creates a new derived column calculated from an expression.
- **DQS Cleansing:** Performs advanced data cleansing using the Data Quality Services engine.
- **Export Column:** Exports a column from the Data Flow to the file system. For example, you can use this transformation to write a column that contains an image to a file.
- **Fuzzy Grouping:** Performs data cleansing by finding rows that are likely duplicates.
- **Fuzzy Lookup:** Matches and standardizes data based on fuzzy logic. For example, this can transform the name Jon to John.
- **Import Column:** Reads data from a file and adds it to a Data Flow.
- **Lookup:** Performs a lookup on data to be used later in a transformation. For example, you can use this transformation to look up a city based on the zip code.
- **Merge:** Merges two sorted data sets into a single data set in a Data Flow.
- **Merge Join:** Merges two data sets into a single data set using a `join` function.
- **Multicast:** Sends a copy of the data to an additional path in the workflow.
- **OLE DB Command:** Executes an OLE DB command for each row in the Data Flow.
- **Percentage Sampling:** Captures a sampling of the data from the Data Flow by using a percentage of the Data Flow's total rows.
- **Pivot:** Pivots the data on a column into a more nonrelational form. Pivoting a table means that you can slice the data in multiple ways, much like in OLAP and Excel.
- **Row Count:** Stores the row count from the Data Flow into a variable.
- **Row Sampling:** Captures a sampling of the data from the Data Flow by using a row count of the Data Flow's total rows.
- **Script Component:** Uses a script to transform the data. For example, you can use this to apply specialized business logic to your Data Flow.
- **Slowly Changing Dimension:** Coordinates the conditional insert or update of data in a slowly changing dimension.
- **Sort:** Sorts the data in the Data Flow by a given column.
- **Term Extraction:** Looks up a noun or adjective in text data.

- **Term Lookup:** Looks up terms extracted from text and references the value from a reference table.
- **Union All:** Merges multiple data sets into a single data set.
- **Unpivot:** Unpivots the data from a non-normalized format to a relational format.

Destinations

Inside the Data Flow, destinations consume the data after the data pipe leaves the last transformation components. The flexible architecture can send the data to nearly any OLE DB–compliant, flat file, or ADO.NET data source. Like sources, destinations are also managed through the Connection Manager. The following destinations are available to you in SSIS:

- **ADO.NET Destination:** Exposes data to other external processes, such as a .NET application.
- **Data Mining Model Training:** Trains an Analysis Services mining model by passing data from the Data Flow to the destination.
- **Data Reader Destination:** Allows the ADO.NET `DataReader` interface to consume data, similar to the ADO.NET Destination.
- **Dimension Processing:** Loads and processes an Analysis Services dimension. It can perform a full, update, or incremental refresh of the dimension.
- **Excel Destination:** Outputs data from the Data Flow to an Excel spreadsheet.
- **Flat File Destination:** Enables you to write data to a comma-delimited or fixed-width file.
- **ODBC Destination:** Outputs data to an ODBC data connection like SQL Server, DB2, or Oracle.
- **OLE DB Destination:** Outputs data to an OLE DB data connection like SQL Server, Oracle, or Access.
- **Partition Processing:** Enables you to perform incremental, full, or update processing of an Analysis Services partition.
- **Raw File Destination:** Outputs data in a binary format that can be used later as a Raw File Source. It's usually used as an intermediate persistence mechanism.
- **Recordset Destination:** Writes the records to an ADO record set. Once written, to an object variable, it can be looped over a variety of ways in SSIS like a Script Task or a Foreach Loop Container.
- **SQL Server Compact Edition Destination:** Inserts data into a SQL Server running the Compact Edition of the product on a mobile device or PC.
- **SQL Server Destination:** The destination that you use to write data to SQL Server. This destination has many limitations, such as the ability to only write to the SQL Server where the SSIS package is executing. For example, if you're running a package to copy data from Server 1 to Server 2, the package must run on Server 2. This destination is there largely for backwards compatibility and should not be used.

Variables

Variables are another vital component of the SSIS architecture. SSIS variables can be set to evaluate to an expression at runtime. You can also set variables to be set in the Control Flow with either a Script Task or an Expression Task. Variables in SSIS have become the method of exchange between many tasks and transformations, making the scoping of variables much more important. By default, SSIS variables exist within a package scope, but they can be scoped to different levels within a package as mentioned earlier in the "Containers" section.

Parameters

Parameters behave much like variables but with a few main exceptions. Parameters, like variables, can make a package dynamic. The largest difference between them is that parameters can be set outside the package easily and can be designated as values that must be passed in for the package to start, much like a stored procedure input parameter. Parameters replace the capabilities of Configurations in previous releases of SQL Server.

Error Handling and Logging

In SSIS, you can control error handling in several places, depending on whether you are handling task or Data Flow errors. For task errors, package events are exposed in the user interface, and each event can have its own event-handler design surface. This design surface is yet another area where you can define workflow, in addition to the Control Flow and Data Flow surfaces you've already learned about. Using the event-handler design surface in SSIS, you can specify a series of tasks to be performed if a given event happens for a task in the task flow.

Some event handlers can help you develop packages that can self-fix problems. For example, the `OnError` error handler triggers an event whenever an error occurs anywhere in scope. The scope can be the entire package or an individual task or container. Event handlers are represented as a workflow, much like the Control Flow workflow in SSIS. An ideal use for an event handler would be to notify an operator if any component fails inside the package. (You will learn much more about event handlers in Chapter 18.) You can also use the precedence constraints directly on the task flow design surface to direct workflow when a task fails to complete or it evaluates to an expression that forces the workflow to change.

Logging has also been improved in SSIS in this latest release. Logging is now enabled by default, and packages are easier to troubleshoot. More than a dozen events can be simply selected within each task or package for logging. You can also choose to enable partial logging for one task and enable much more detailed logging for another task, such as billing. Some of the examples of events that can be monitored are `OnError`, `OnPostValidate`, `OnProgress`, and `OnWarning`, to name just a few. The logs can be written to nearly any connection: SQL Profiler, text files, SQL Server, the Windows Event log, or an XML file. You'll see some examples of this in Chapter 18.

EDITIONS OF SQL SERVER

The available features in SSIS and SQL Server vary according to what edition of SQL Server you're using. Of course, the more high-end the edition of SQL Server, the more features are available. In order from high-end to low-end, the following is a partial list of SQL Server editions:

- **SQL Server Enterprise Edition:** This edition of SQL Server is for large enterprises that need high availability and more advanced features in SQL Server and business intelligence. For example, there is no limit on processors or RAM in this edition. You're bound only by the number of processors and the amount of RAM that the OS can handle. Microsoft will also continue to support Developer Edition, which enables developers to create SQL Server solutions at a much reduced price. Ultimately, if you're trying to scale your solution into terabytes of data storage in SQL Server then Enterprise Edition is the right choice for you.
- **SQL Server Business Intelligence Edition:** This edition includes all the features of Standard Edition and also includes additional data cleansing features like Data Quality Services, which helps you create business rules that SSIS consumes. It also has many SharePoint integration features outside of SSIS and some scalability features. You can scale all the BI features other than the database engine to the OS maximum of cores with this edition.
- **SQL Server Standard Edition:** This edition of SQL Server now offers even more value than before. For example, you can create a highly available system in Standard Edition by using clustering, database mirroring, and integrated 64-bit support. Like Enterprise Edition in SQL Server 2012, it also offers unlimited RAM. Thus, you can scale it as high as your physical hardware and OS will allow. However, there is a cap of four processors with this edition.

As for SSIS, you'll have to use at least the Standard Edition to receive the bulk of the SSIS features. In the Express Edition, only the Import and Export Wizard is available. BI Edition gives you access to items like Data Quality Services and the DQS Cleansing Transformation. You need to upgrade to the higher editions in order to see some features in SSIS. For example, the following advanced transformations are available only with Enterprise Edition:

- Analysis Services Partition Processing Destination
- Analysis Services Dimension Processing Destination
- CDC Source, Destination, Splitter Transformation, and CDC Control Task
- Data Mining Training Destination
- Data Mining Query Component
- Fuzzy Grouping
- Fuzzy Lookup
- Term Extraction
- Term Lookup

Half of these transformations are used in servicing Analysis Services. Along those same lines, one task is available only in Enterprise Edition: the Data Mining Query Task.

SUMMARY

In this chapter, you were introduced to the historical legacy and the exciting capabilities of the SQL Server Integration Services (SSIS) platform. You looked at where SSIS fits into the business intelligence (BI) platform for SQL Server, and then dove into an overview of the SSIS architecture.

Within the architecture, we stayed up at 20,000 feet to ensure that you have a good understanding of how SSIS works and the core parts of the architecture. You learned about the core components of tasks, Data Flows, transformations, event handlers, containers, and variables — all crucial concepts that you'll be dealing with daily in SSIS. Packages are executable programs in SSIS that contain a collection of tasks. Tasks are individual units of work that are chained together with precedence constraints. Lastly, transformations are the Data Flow items that change the data to the form you request, such as sorting the data.

The next chapter describes some of the tools and wizards you have at your disposal to expedite tasks in SSIS. Chapter 3 dives deeply into the various tasks in the SSIS Toolbox that you can use to create SSIS workflows. In Chapter 4, you'll learn about Data Flow Task and examine the data components that are available for use within the Data Flow pipeline to perform the transformations in ETL.

The SSIS Tools

WHAT'S IN THIS CHAPTER?

- Working with the Import and Export Wizard
- Using the SQL Server Data Tools application
- Examining the windows used to create packages
- Utilizing Management Studio to administer your packages

As with any Microsoft product, SQL Server ships with a myriad of wizards and tools to make your life easier and reduce your time to market. In this chapter you will learn about some of the tools of the trade that are available to you and how to create your first basic package. These wizards make transporting data and deploying your packages much easier and can save you hours of work in the long run, but they're only a starting point in most cases. In the first part of this chapter, you'll look at the Import and Export Wizard, which enables you to create a package for importing or exporting data quickly with minimal transformations. As a matter of fact, you may run this tool in your day-to-day work without even knowing that SSIS is the back end for the wizard. The latter part of this chapter explores other, more powerful, tools that are available to you, such as SQL Server Data Tools (SSDT). By the time this chapter is complete, you will have created your first SSIS package.

IMPORT AND EXPORT WIZARD

The Import and Export Wizard is the easiest method to move data from sources like Oracle, DB2, SQL Server, Excel, and text files to nearly any destination, and it is available across all versions of SQL Server — even those that don't include SSIS. This wizard uses SSIS as a framework and can optionally save a package as its output prior to executing. The package it produces may not be the most elegant, but it can eliminate a lot of tedious package development work and it provides the building blocks that are necessary for building the remainder of the package. Oftentimes as an SSIS developer, you'll want to relegate the grunt work and heavy lifting to the wizard when you want to just move data for a onetime load, and then do the more complex coding yourself.

As with any of the SSIS tools, there are numerous ways to open the tool. To open the Import and Export Wizard, right-click the database you want to import data from or export data to in SQL Server Management Studio and select Tasks ⇨ Import Data (or Export Data based on what task you're performing). You can also open the wizard by right-clicking the SSIS Packages folder in SSDT and selecting SSIS Import and Export Wizard. Another common way to open it is from the Start menu under SQL Server 2014, where it's called Import and Export Data. The last way to open the wizard is by typing **dtswizard.exe** at the command line or Run prompt. Regardless of whether you need to import or export data, the first few screens in the wizard look very similar.

When the wizard appears, you'll see the typical Microsoft wizard welcome screen. Click Next to begin specifying the source connection. If you had opened the wizard from Management Studio by selecting Export Data, this screen is pre-populated. In this screen you specify where your data is coming from in the Source dropdown box. Once you select the source, the rest of the options on the dialog may vary based on the type of connection. The default source is .Net Framework Data Provider for Odbc. Out of the box, you have ODBC and OLE DB sources that connect to SQL Server, Oracle, and Access. You can also use text files, Excel files, and XML files. Traditionally, the SQL Native Client is the provider used in SSIS because it gives additional functionality during design time. Change the data source to use the SQL Server Native Client 11.0 provider.

For SQL Server, you must enter the server name, as well as the user name and password you'd like to use. If you're going to connect with your Windows account, simply select Use Windows Authentication. Windows Authentication will pass your Windows local or domain credentials into the data source. Lastly, choose a database to which you want to connect. For most of the examples in this book, you'll use the AdventureWorksDW database or a variation of that DW database, shown in Figure 2-1. This database can be downloaded at `www.wrox.com`.

NOTE *Additional sources such as Sybase and DB2 are also available if you install the vendor's OLE DB providers. You can download the OLE DB provider for DB2 free if you're using Enterprise Edition by going to the SQL Server Feature Pack on the Microsoft website. (As of this writing, the SQL Server 2014 Feature Pack has not be released. However, the SQL 2012 Feature Pack will work for 2014 as well.)*

NOTE *In 2011, Microsoft released information regarding the appropriate provider types to use for new development. It was recommended that any new development should be done with ODBC providers rather than OLE DB. This rule should only be followed for home grown applications for now. SSIS developers should continue using OLE DB because ODBC does not have full feature parity yet to complete some ordinary tasks.*

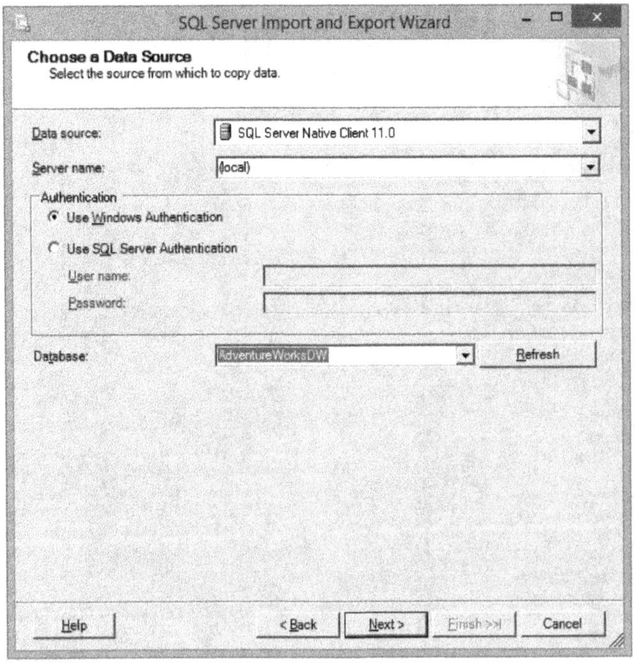

FIGURE 2-1

After you click Next, you are taken to the next screen in the wizard, where you specify the destination for your data. The properties for this screen are identical to those for the previous screen with the exception of the database. Change the Destination provider to SQL Server Native Client 11.0, then select TempDB from the Database dropdown. This will create and load the tables into a temporary space, which will disappear once you restart your instance of SQL Server. Click Next again to be taken to the Specify Table Copy or Query screen (see Figure 2-2). Here, if you select "Copy data from one or more tables or views," you can simply check the tables you want. If you select "Write a query to specify the data to transfer," you can write an ad hoc query (after clicking Next) that defines where to select the data from, or what stored procedure to use to retrieve your data.

For the purpose of this example, select "Copy data from one or more tables or views" and click Next. This takes you to the Select Source Tables and Views screen, where you can check the tables or views that you want to transfer to the destination (see Figure 2-3). For this tutorial, check a couple of tables such as FactResellerSales and FactInternetSales in the AdventureWorksDW database.

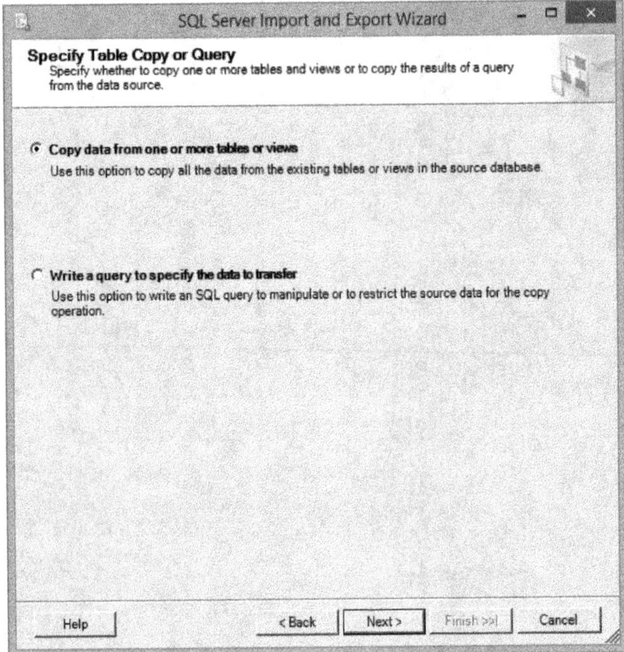

FIGURE 2-2

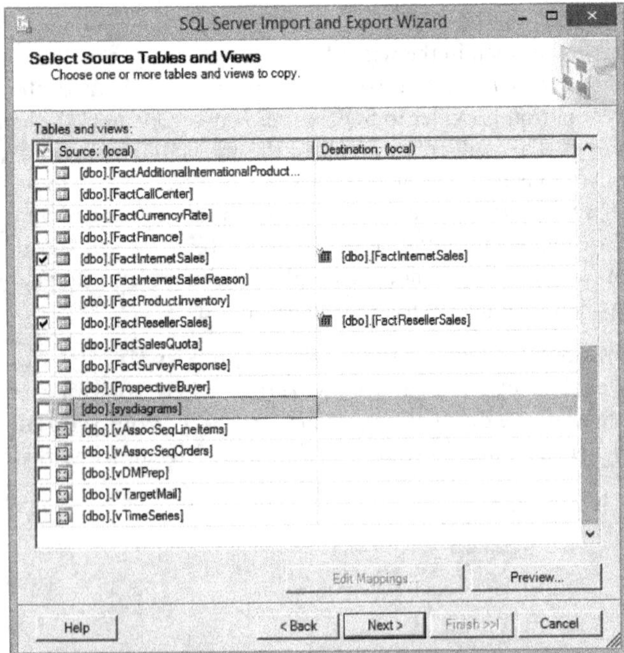

FIGURE 2-3

If you wish, you can click the Edit buttons to access the Column Mappings dialog for each table (see Figure 2-4). Here you can change the mapping between each source and destination column. For example, if you want the ProductKey column to go to the ProductKey2 column on the destination, simply select the Destination cell for the ProductKey column and point it to the new column, or select <ignore> to ignore the column altogether.

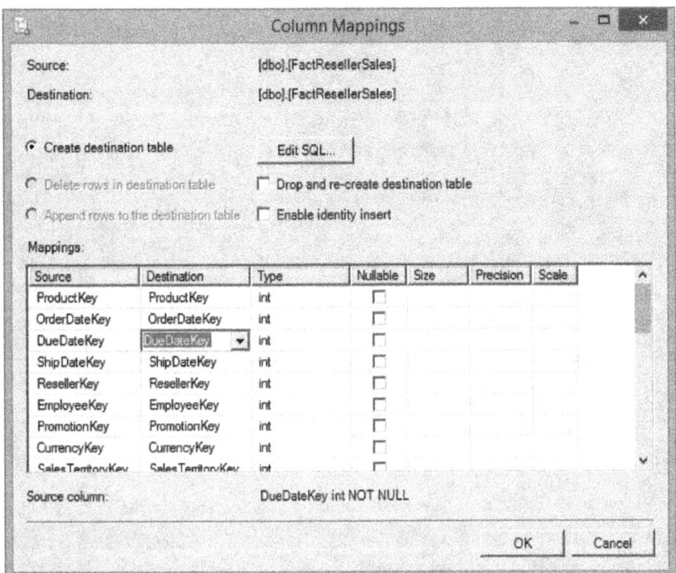

FIGURE 2-4

Note that because you're moving the data to a new database that doesn't already contain the FactInternetSales table, the "Create destination table" option is one of the few options enabled by default. This will create the table on the destination before populating it with data from the source. If the table already existed, the data will append existing records but you could specify that all rows in the destination table should be deleted before populating it.

Finally, you can check the "Enable identity insert" option if the table into which you are moving data has an identity column. If the table does have an identity column, the wizard automatically enables this option. If you don't have the option enabled and you try to move data into an identity column, the wizard will fail to execute.

For the purpose of this example, don't change any of the settings in this screen. Click OK to apply the settings from the Column Mappings dialog and then click Next to proceed.

If no errors are found, you are taken to the Save and Run Package screen (Figure 2-5). Here you can specify whether you want the package to execute only once, or whether you'd like to save the package for later use. As shown earlier, it isn't necessary to execute the package here. You can uncheck Run Immediately and just save the package for later modification and execution.

For this example, check the options for Run Immediately, Save SSIS Package, and File System. This collection of options will execute the package and save it as a `.dtsx` file to your computer. You learn more about where to save your SSIS packages later in this chapter. Note that if you save the package to SQL Server or to the file system, you're saving the package with the Package Deployment Model. We'll discuss more about the package deployment model in Chapter 22.

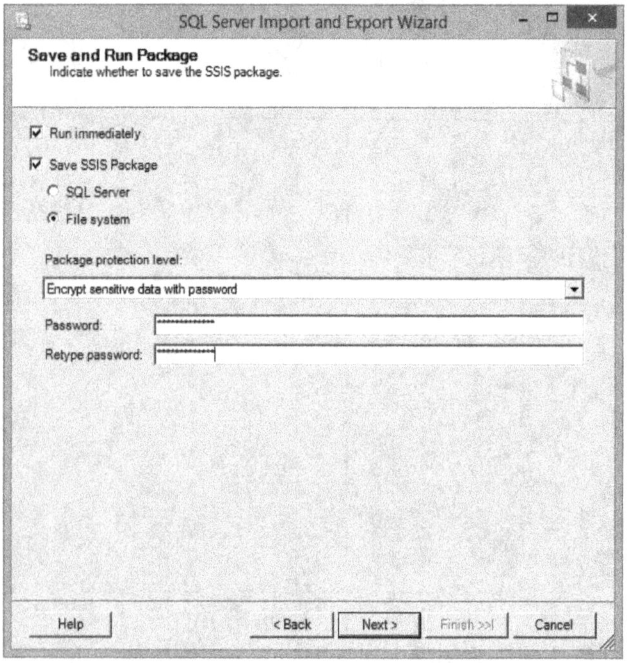

FIGURE 2-5

In this screen, you're also asked how you wish to protect the sensitive data in your package. SSIS packages are essentially large XML files behind the scenes, and encryption of sensitive data, such as passwords, is critical to ensuring that no one sees that information by opening the XML manually. Again, you learn more about this later in this chapter, so for now just change the Package Protection Level property to "Encrypt sensitive data with password" to protect your sensitive data with a password, and give the dialog a password (as shown in Figure 2-5).

You are then taken to the Save SSIS Package screen, where you can type the name of the package and the location to which you want to save it (see Figure 2-6).

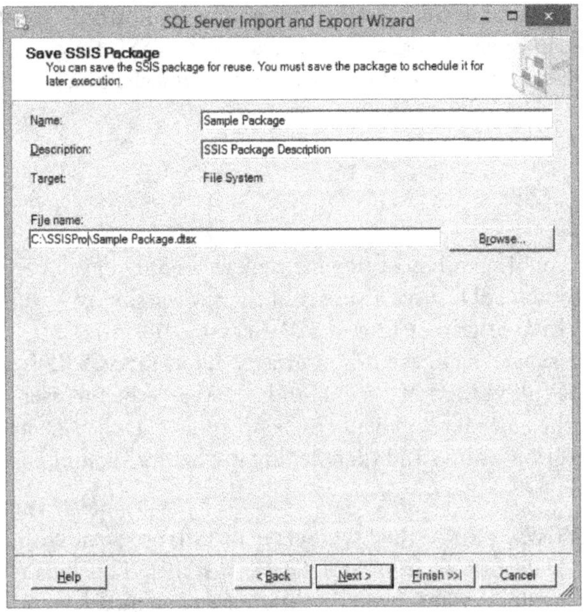

FIGURE 2-6

Click Next and confirm what tasks you wish the wizard to perform. The package will then execute when you click Finish, and you'll see the page shown in Figure 2-7. Any errors are displayed in the Message column. You can also see how many rows were copied over in this column, and you can double-click an entry that failed to see why, in the event that there are errors during execution.

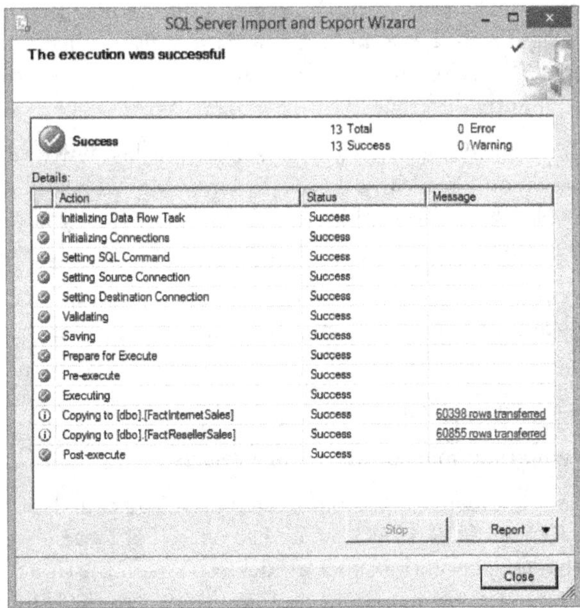

FIGURE 2-7

After the wizard executes, the package can be found in the location that you have specified, but the default is the My Documents directory. You can open the package that executed in SSDT by creating a project in SSDT and copying and pasting the package into the project or by right-clicking on Packages and selecting Add Existing Package.

SQL SERVER DATA TOOLS

The SQL Server Data Tools (SSDT) is where you'll spend most of your time as an SSIS developer. It is where you create and deploy your SSIS projects. SSDT uses a subset of the full version of Visual Studio 2013. If you have the full version of Visual Studio 2013 and SQL Server 2014 installed, you can create business intelligence projects there as well as in the full interface, but as far as SSIS is concerned, there's no added value in using the full version of Visual Studio. Either way, the user experience is the same. In SQL Server 2014, the SSIS development environment is detached from SQL Server, so you can develop your SSIS solution offline and then deploy it wherever you like in a single click.

In prior versions of Integration Services, SSDT was part of the SQL Server installation, but with the release of SQL Server 2014, SSDT has been decoupled from SQL Server installer. This means to develop new SSIS packages you must go download SSDT from the Microsoft download site. The benefit of this change is that developers will now see more frequent enhancements to the development environment. Use a search engine with the term "SQL Server Data Tools for Visual Studio 2013" to find the most recent release.

After you download and install SSDT you'll find SSDT in the root of the Microsoft SQL Server 2014 program group from the Start menu. Once you start SSDT, you are taken to the Start Page, an example of which is shown in Figure 2-8, before you open or create your first project. You can open more windows (you learn about these various windows in a moment) by clicking their corresponding icon in the upper-right corner of SSDT or under the View menu. Please note that some of the screenshots in this book, such as Figures 2-8, 2-9, and 2-10, were shot using Visual Studio 2012, which also works with SQL Server 2014. You may also choose to use Visual Studio 2013 if you prefer, and the screenshot may be slightly different.

The Start Page contains key information about your SSDT environment, such as the last few projects that you had open (under the Recent Projects section). You can also see the latest MSDN news under the Get Started section from the Latest News box. By clicking the Latest News box, you can also set the RSS feed that you're consuming as well.

The Visual Studio environment is that it gives you full access to the Visual Studio feature set, such as debugging, automatic integration with source code control systems, and integrated help. It is a familiar environment for developers and makes deployments easy.

The starting point for SSIS is to create a solution and project.

- A **solution** is a container in Visual Studio that holds one or many projects.
- A **project** in SSIS is a container of one or many packages and related files. You can also create projects for Analysis Services, Reporting Services, C#, and so on. All of these projects can be bundled together with a single solution, so a C# developer is in the same environment as an SSIS developer. Make sure you put packages that belong together into a single project since the project is the unit of deployment in SQL Server 2014.

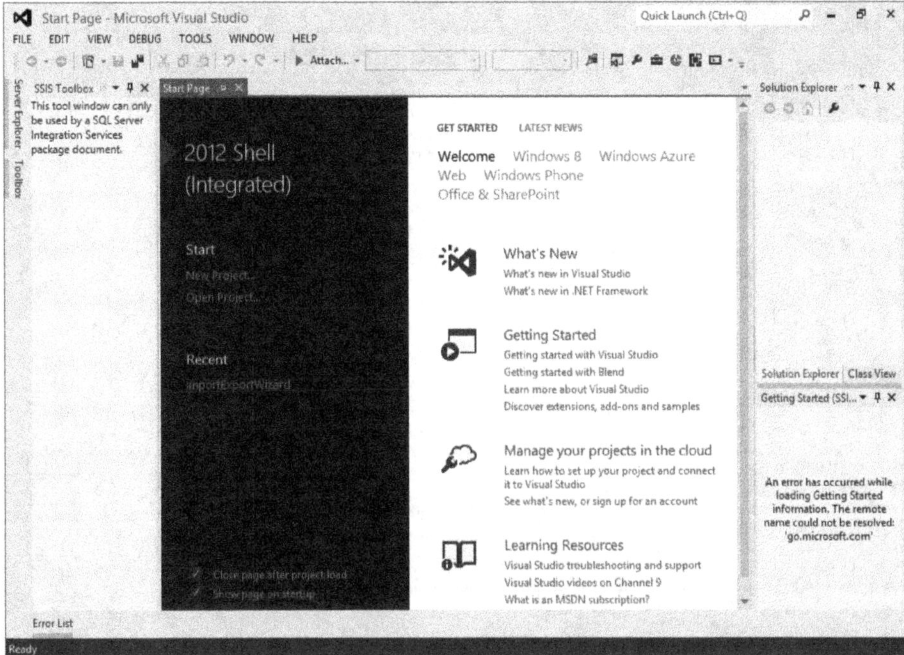

FIGURE 2-8

To start a new SSIS project, you first need to open SSDT and select File ➪ New ➪ Project. Note a series of new templates (shown in Figure 2-9) in your template list now that you've installed SSDT for Visual Studio 2013. From the Installed Templates pane on the left, select Integration Services and then select Integration Services Project. Name your project and solution whatever you like (I named the solution ProSSISSolution and the project ProSSISProject). Also shown in Figure 2-9 is another type of SSIS project called the Integration Services Import Project Wizard, which is used to bring packages into a project from another deployed project. Click OK at this point to create the solution, the project, and your first package.

Typically, you want to align your projects into solutions that fit the business requirement that you're trying to meet. For example, you may be assigned to a business project for the creation of a data warehouse. That warehouse project would probably have ETL, an SSAS cube, and Reporting Services reports. You could place all of these into a single solution so you could manage them from a unified interface. Note that once you begin work in Visual Studio, if your solution contains only a single project, the solution will be hidden by default. If you want to always see the solution name, go to Tools ➪ Options and check Always Show Solution from the Projects and Solutions group (shown in Figure 2-10). If you're doing any type of source control, this option should always be turned on so you can check in the solution easily. Otherwise, once a second project is added to the solution, you'll see the solution and both projects under the solution.

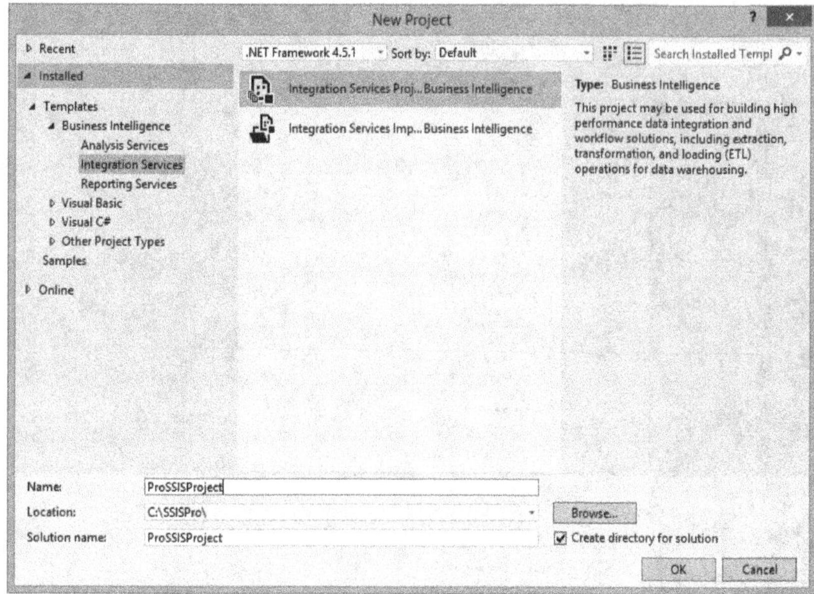

FIGURE 2-9

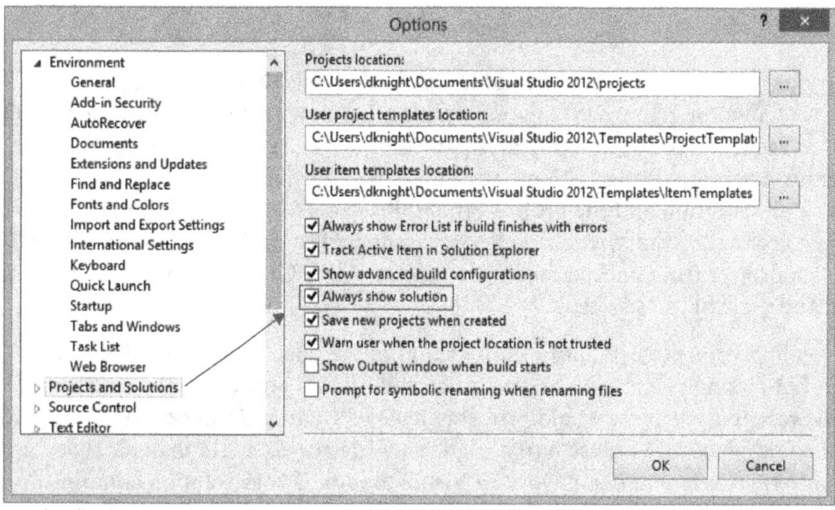

FIGURE 2-10

THE SOLUTION EXPLORER WINDOW

The Solution Explorer window is where you can find all your created SSIS packages, project connection managers, project parameters, and any other miscellaneous files needed for the project, such as installation documents. As mentioned earlier, a solution is a container that holds a series of projects. Each project holds a myriad of objects for whatever type of project you're working on.

Once you create a solution, you can store many projects inside of it. For example, you may have a solution that has your VB.NET application and all the SSIS packages that support that application. In this case, you would have two projects: one for VB and another for SSIS contained within the single solution.

After creating a new project, your Solution Explorer window will contain a series of empty folders. Figure 2-11 shows a partially filled Solution Explorer. In this screenshot, there's a solution named ProSSISSolution with two projects: SSASProject and ProSSISProject. Inside that project are two SSIS packages.

To create a new project inside an existing open solution, right-click the solution name in the Solution Explorer window and select Add ⇨ New Project. To add a new item to your project in the folder, right-click the folder that holds the type of item that you wish to add and select New Connection Manager or New SSIS Package. You can also drag or copy and paste files into the project if they are of a similar type, like `.dtsx` files.

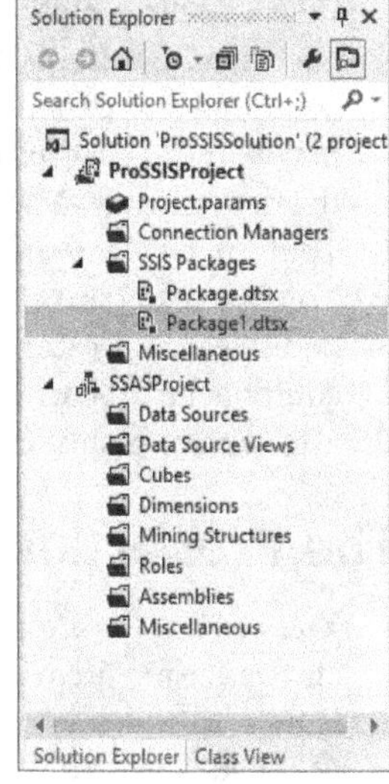

FIGURE 2-11

If you look in the directory that contains your solution and project files, you'll see all the files that are represented in the Solution Explorer window. Some of the base files you may see will have the following extensions:

- `.dtsx`: An SSIS package, which uses its legacy extension from the early beta cycles of SQL Server 2005 when SSIS was still called DTS
- `.conmgr`: A connection manager that can be shared across any package in the entire project
- `.sln`: A solution file that contains one or more projects
- `.dtproj`: An SSIS project file
- `.params`: An SSIS project parameter file

If you copy any file that does not match the `.params`, `.conmgr`, or `.dtsx` extension, it will be placed in the Miscellaneous folder. This folder is used to hold any files that describe the installation of the package, such as Word documents or requirements documents. You can put anything you like in that folder, and it can potentially all be checked into a source control system like Team Foundation Server (TFS) or SourceSafe with the code. You'll learn more about source control systems in Chapter 17.

The SSIS Toolbox

The SSIS Toolbox contains all the items that you can use in the particular tab's design pane at any given point in time. For example, the Control Flow tab has a list of tasks (a partial list is shown in Figure 2-12). This list may grow depending on what custom tasks are installed, and the list will be completely different when you're in a different tab, such as the Data Flow tab. All the tasks shown in Figure 2-12 are covered in Chapter 3 in much more detail.

In the Control Flow tab, the Toolbox is organized into tabs such as Favorites, Common, Containers, and Other Tasks. These tabs can be collapsed and expanded for usability. As you use the Toolbox, you may want to customize your view by removing tasks or tabs from the default view. You can move or customize the list of items in your Toolbox by right-clicking on a given component (refer to Figure 2-12). You can also reset the entire Toolbox to its defaults by right-clicking and selecting Restore Toolbox Defaults. As you install third-party components, those tasks will now automatically appear in the Toolbox after you refresh the Toolbox or when you reopen SSDT.

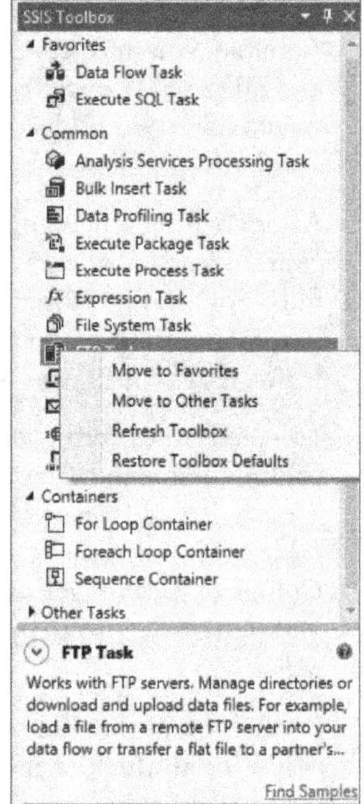

FIGURE 2-12

The Properties Windows

You can use the Properties window (shown in Figure 2-13) to customize any item that you have selected in the Control Flow or Data Flow tabs. For example, if you select a task in the design pane of those tabs, you'll be shown a list of properties to configure, such as the task's name and what query it's going to use. The view varies widely based on what item you have selected. Figure 2-13 shows the properties of the Execute Process task you created earlier in this chapter.

Most tasks can be configured through the user interface of the tasks or by going to the Properties pane when the task is selected. Note that the Properties pane may contain some advanced properties not shown in the user interface for the component. To edit the properties for the package, simply select the design pane in the background. If the Properties pane is closed, you can press F4 to reopen it or select the Properties Window button under View.

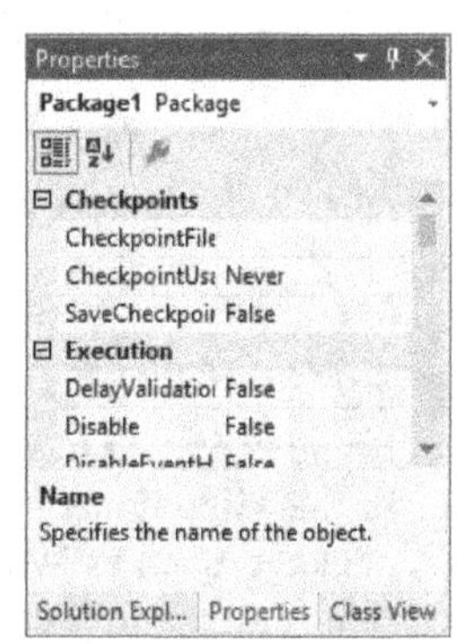

FIGURE 2-13

THE SSIS PACKAGE DESIGNER

The SSIS Package Designer contains the design panes that you use to create an SSIS package. This tool contains all the items you need to move data or create a workflow with minimal or no code. The great thing about SSIS is that it is like programming with building blocks. The Package Designer contains five tabs: Control Flow, Data Flow, Parameters, Event Handlers, and Package Explorer. One additional tab, Progress, also appears when you execute packages. This Progress tab is renamed to Execution Results after the package stops running and you click Stop.

This chapter focuses on exploring the Control Flow tab, and the bulk of the next chapter dives into details about this tab. In SSIS, the Control Flow contains tasks and the workflow of the package and is separated from most of the movement of data in the Data Flow tab. This usability feature gives you greater control when creating and editing packages. The task that binds the Control Flow and Data Flow together is the Data Flow Task, which you study in depth over the next two chapters.

Understanding the difference between the Control Flow and Data Flow tabs represents one of the largest learning curves for a new SSIS developer. The easiest way to keep them straight is to think of the Data Flow tab as simply a way to configure the Data Flow Task. This separation gives you a huge amount of power when configuring the task. The other way to differentiate the two tabs is that the Control Flow tab handles the workflow of the package and ties the tasks together, whereas the Data Flow tab handles a data load.

Control Flow

The Control Flow contains the workflow parts of the package, which include the tasks, containers, and precedence constraints. SSIS has introduced the new concept of containers, which was briefly discussed in Chapter 1 and is covered in detail in Chapter 6. In the Control Flow tab, you can click and drag a task from the SSIS Toolbox into the Control Flow design pane. Once you have a task created, you can double-click the task to configure it. Until the task is configured, you may see a yellow warning or red error indicator on the task.

FIGURE 2-14

After you configure the task, you can link it to other tasks by using precedence constraints. Once you click the task, you'll notice a green arrow pointing down from it, as shown in Figure 2-14.

For example, to create an On Success precedence constraint, click the green arrow coming out of the task and drag it to the task you wish to link to the first task. In Figure 2-15, you can see the On Success precedence constraint between an Execute Process task called EPR - Run Notepad and an Execute Process task called EPR - Run Calc.

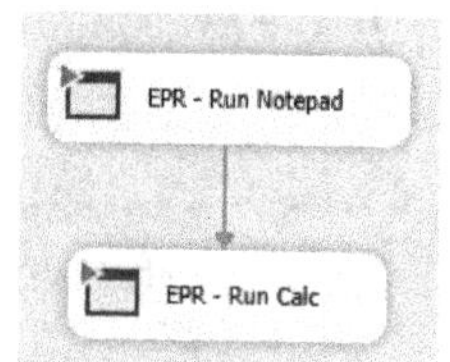

FIGURE 2-15

In the Data Flow tab, when you click a source or a transformation, you'll also see a blue and red arrow pointing down, enabling you to quickly direct your good (blue) or bad (red) data to a separate output. Therefore, if you run a formula that returns an error in the Data Flow, that single row could be outputted to a different table, and then all other rows could continue down the proper path.

In the Control Flow, though, you need to use a different approach. If you want the next task to execute only if the first task has failed, create a precedence constraint as shown earlier for the On Success constraint. After the constraint is created, double-click the constraint arrow. You'll be taken to the Precedence Constraint Editor (see Figure 2-16).

Use this editor to set what type of constraint you'll be using. Three options are available in the Value dropdown field: Success, Failure, or Completion. A success constraint will fire the second task or container only when the first task or container succeeds. A failure constraint executes the second task or container only when the first task fails. The last scenario is a completion constraint, which will execute the second task or container whether the first task succeeds or fails.

In SSIS, you have the option to add a logical `AND` or `OR` when a task has multiple constraints. In the Precedence Constraint Editor in SSIS, you can configure the task to execute only if the group of predecessor tasks has completed (`AND`), or if any one of the predecessor tasks has completed (`OR`).

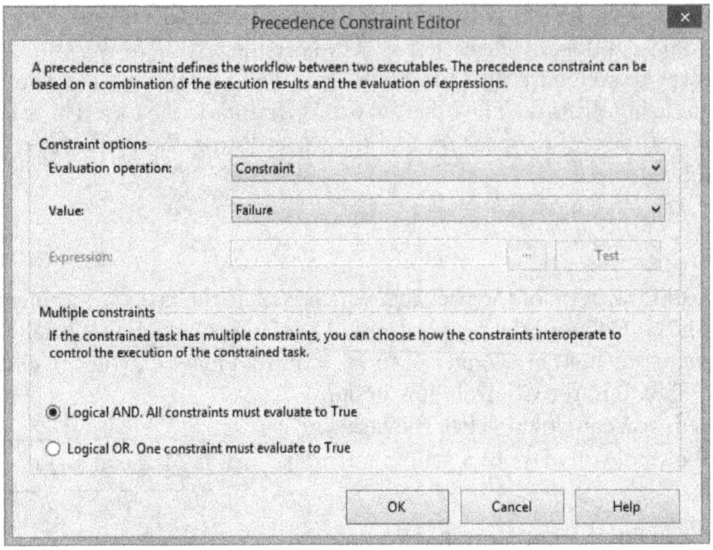

FIGURE 2-16

If a constraint is a logical AND, the precedence constraint line is solid. If it is set to OR, the line is dotted. This is useful if you want to be notified when any one of the tasks fails by using the logical OR constraint.

In the Evaluation Operation dropdown, you can edit how the task will be evaluated:

- **Constraint:** Evaluates the success, failure, or completion of the predecessor task or tasks
- **Expression:** Evaluates the success of a customized condition that is programmed using an expression
- **Expression and Constraint:** Evaluates both the expression and the constraint before moving to the next task
- **Expression or Constraint:** Determines whether either the expression or the constraint has been successfully met before moving to the next task

If you select Expression or one of its variants as your option, you'll be able to type an expression in the Expression box. An expression is usually used to evaluate a variable before proceeding to the next task. For example, if you want to ensure that `InputFileVariable` variable is equal to the `Variable2` variable, you would use the following syntax in the Expression box:

```
@InputFileVariable == @Variable2
```

You can also single-click the constraint and use the Properties window on the right to set these properties, if you prefer not to use the editor.

Now that you know more about constraints, it's a good time to look at a scenario and how the constraints apply to your environment. The example shown in Figure 2-17 demonstrates how flexible precedence constraints can be. The first Script Task runs a script to determine whether the file exists. An expression on the precedence constraint coming out of the Script Task determines whether the answer returned from the script is set to true or false. If the file exists, then Task A is run; otherwise, Task B is run. After that, note that regardless of whether Task A or B is run, the Archive Script Task always runs because of the Logical Or constraint. Finally, if the Sequence Container succeeds, then Task C is run, and if it does not, then the Alert Script Task is run.

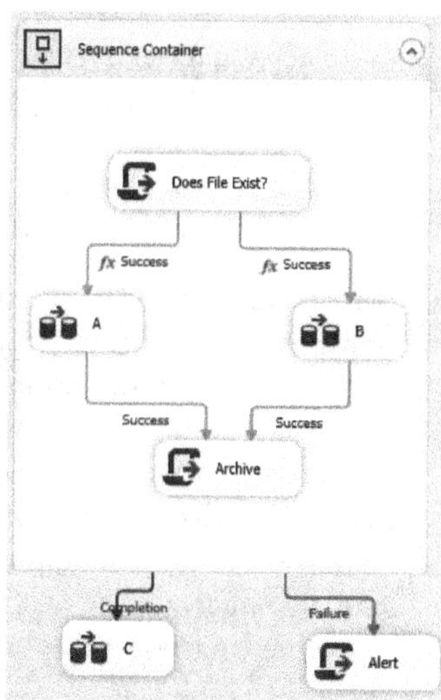

FIGURE 2-17

You may have noticed that in Figure 2-17, I added the names of the precedence constraints (success, failure, completion) to each of the arrows. This may be necessary for those who are color-blind (and is required for this book because it's printed in black and white). To do this in SSDT, select Tools ➪ Options, and then check "Show precedence constraint labels" under the Business Intelligence Designers ➪ Integration Services Designers tab, as shown in Figure 2-18.

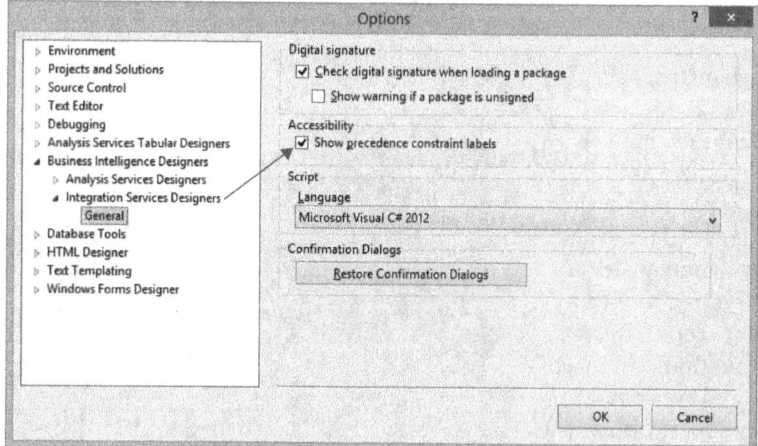

FIGURE 2-18

Task Grouping

A very nice usability feature in SSIS is the capability to group tasks or transforms logically in *containers*. For example, if you have a group of tasks that create and purge the staging environment, you can group them together so that your package is not cluttered visually. For example, in Figure 2-19 there are two tasks to load data and send a message. To group them, select both tasks by clicking one task and holding the Ctrl key down while you select the second task. Then, right-click the tasks and select Group.

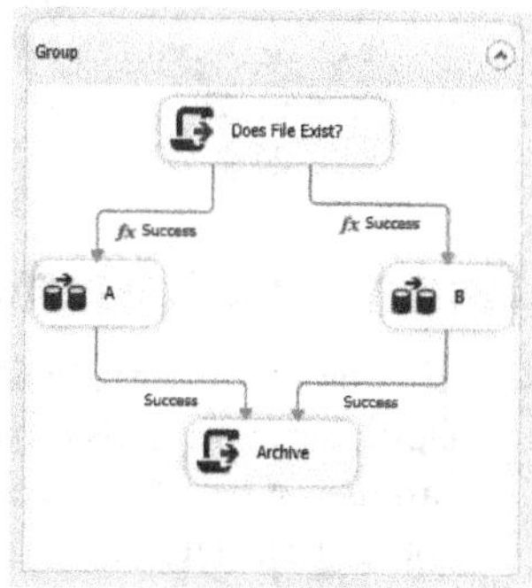

FIGURE 2-19

> **NOTE** *Groups and containers are not the same. Groups are a usability feature to bring together components. Containers on the other hand allow you to pass properties into them. You can read more about groups, containers, and their differences in Chapter 6.*

After you have the two tasks grouped, you'll see a box container around them. A group is not the same as a container. It only gives you a usability feature to bring tasks together. They don't share properties like transactions. To rename the group, simply double-click the container and type the new name over the old one. You can also collapse the group so that your package isn't cluttered. To do this, just click the arrows that are pointing downward in the group. Once collapsed, your grouping will look like Figure 2-20. You can also ungroup the tasks by right-clicking the group and selecting Ungroup.

FIGURE 2-20

This same type of group can be created in the Data Flow tab to logically group sources, transformations, and destinations together. You'll learn more about containers in Chapter 6.

Annotation

Annotations are a key part of any package, and a good developer won't fail to include them. An *annotation* is a comment that you place in your package to help others and yourself understand what is happening in the package. To add an annotation, right-click where you want to place the comment, select Add Annotation, and begin typing. You can resize the box if you need more room. It is a good idea to always add an annotation to your package that shows the title and version of your package. Most SSIS developers also add a version history annotation note to the package, so that they can see what has changed in the package between releases and who performed the change. You can see an example of this in Figure 2-21.

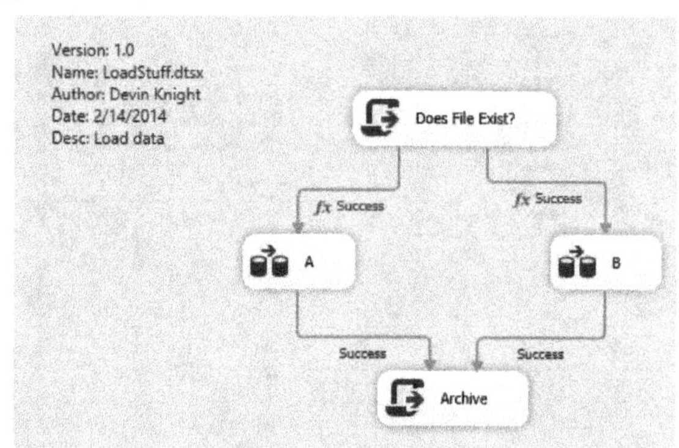

FIGURE 2-21

Connection Managers

You may have already noticed the Connection Managers tab at the bottom of your Package Designer pane. This tab contains a list of connections that both Control Flow and Data Flow Tasks can use. Whether the connection is an FTP address or a connection to an Analysis Services server, you'll see a reference to it here. These connections can be referenced as either sources or targets in any of the operations, and they can connect to relational or Analysis Services databases, flat files, or other data sources. They're also used in many of the SSIS tasks.

When you create a new package, no connections are defined. You can create a connection by right-clicking in the Connections area and choosing the appropriate data connection type. Once the connection is created, you can rename it to fit your naming conventions or to better describe what is contained in the connection. Nearly any task or transformation that uses data or references a file will require a Connection Manager. Figure 2-22 shows a few connections: two to relational databases (AdventureWorksDW and Stage), an SMTP reference, and a directory.

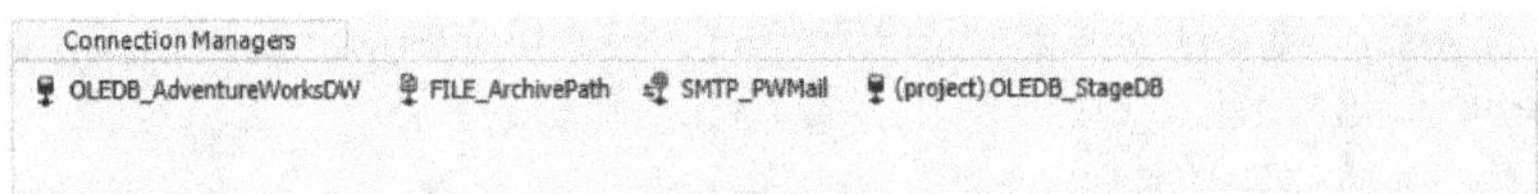

FIGURE 2-22

Notice the two Connection Managers that refer to the AdventureWorksDW database and the staging database. The one with a database icon is a local Connection Manager that can be seen only inside the current package. The Connection Manager with (project) in front is a project connection that can be seen in any package. Any local Connection Manager can be converted to a project connection by right-clicking it and selecting Convert to Project Connection. Note that we have used a naming convention so the designer can easily recognize what type of connection it is.

Variables

Variables are a powerful piece of the SSIS architecture; they enable you to dynamically control the package at runtime, much like you do in any .NET language. There are two types of variables: system and user. *System variables* are those built into SSIS, such as a package name or the package's start time; *user variables* are created by the SSIS developer. Variables can also have varying scope, with the default scope being the entire package. They can also be set to be in the scope of a container, a task, or an event handler inside the package.

One of the optional design-time windows can display a list of variables. To access the Variables window, right-click in the design pane and select Variables, or select Variables from the SSIS menu. The Variables window (shown in Figure 2-23) will appear in the bottom of SSDT by default. Also by default, you will see only the user variables; to see the system variables as well, click Grid Options and then select the Show System Variables icon in the top of the window. To add a new variable, click the Add Variable icon in the Variables window and type the variable name.

Variables

Name	Scope	Data type	Value	Expression
CancelEvent	Package	Int32	0	
ContainerStartTime	Package	DateTime	10/21/2013 7:03 AM	
CreationDate	Package	DateTime	10/19/2013 8:18 PM	
CreatorComputer...	Package	String	SQL2014	
CreatorName	Package	String	SQL2014\dknight	
ExecutionInstance...	Package	String	{F3DB97AE-8FCB-408F-A460-...	
FailedConfigurati...	Package	String		
IgnoreConfigurati...	Package	Boolean	False	
InteractiveMode	Package	Boolean	False	
LastModifiedProd...	Package	String	11.0.3369.0	
LocaleID	Package	Int32	English (United States)	

FIGURE 2-23

When you click the Add Variable icon, whatever task or container you select at the time will be the scope for the variable. Once the scope was set for a variable in the past SQL Server 2005 and 2008 releases, it could not be changed. Now a nice little feature in 2014 is you can change the variable scope at any time. Some of the additional columns are the Namespace and Raise Event on Variable Change properties. Lastly, you can select a variable and go to the Properties pane to see extended properties on the variable. We discuss these properties in more depth in Chapter 3.

You'll find yourself regularly using system variables throughout your package for auditing or error handling. Some of the package-scoped system variables that you may find interesting for auditing purposes are listed in the following table.

VARIABLE NAME	DATA TYPE	DESCRIPTION
`CreationDate`	DateTime	Date when the package was created
`InteractiveMode`	Boolean	Indicates how the package was executed. If the package was executed from SSDT, this would be set to true. If it was executed from a SQL Server Agent job, it would be set to false.
`MachineName`	String	Computer on which the package is running
`PackageID`	String	Globally unique identifier (GUID) for the package
`PackageName`	String	Name of the package
`StartTime`	DateTime	Time when the package started
`UserName`	String	User who started the package
`VersionBuild`	Int32	Version of the package

Variables are discussed in greater detail in each chapter. For a full list of system variables, please refer to Books Online under "System Variables."

Data Flow

Most of your time in SSIS is spent in the Data Flow tab. When you add a Data Flow Task to the Control Flow design surface, a subsequent Data Flow is created in the Data Flow tab. Whereas a package has a single Control Flow, it can have many Data Flows. You can expand the Data Flow by double-clicking the task or by going to the Data Flow tab and selecting the appropriate Data Flow Task from the top dropdown box (shown in Figure 2-24). In the Data Flow, the key components are sources, destinations transformations (which appear in the SSIS Toolbox), and paths. Unlike in the Control Flow, where tasks and containers are connected by precedence constraints that define the package's execution workflow; in the Data Flow, sources, transformations, and destinations are connected by paths that define the flow of data between these components. As you make a connection, the metadata (information about the columns and their data types) becomes available to the next component in the Data Flow path. Everything after the source is performed in memory with a very few exceptions.

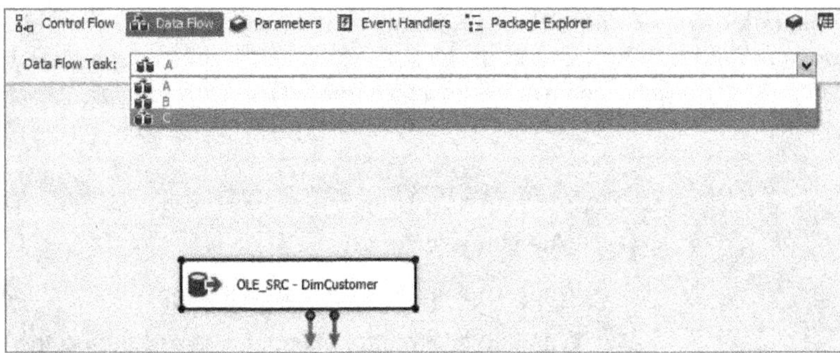

FIGURE 2-24

When you first start defining the Data Flow, you add a source component to connect to a data source, and then a destination to go to. The transformations (also known as transforms throughout this book) modify the data before it is written to the destination. As the data flows through the path from transform to transform, the data changes based on what transform you have selected. This entire process is covered in much more detail in Chapter 4.

Parameters

The Parameters tab enables you to create input parameters for a package. These are different from variables in that they can easily be passed in from a DBA or a job. If you're familiar with SQL Server 2005 or 2008 SSIS, these best resemble configuration files and are indeed replacements for configuration files and tables. You can find parameters in the list of tabs in SSIS. This tab identifies project level parameters but you can also have parameters that are specific to individual packages. Parameters can be made secure by setting the Sensitive property to True, as shown in Figure 2-25, and they can be used to override nearly any property in SSIS. Some parameters can also be set to Required by setting the corresponding property to True, meaning the package won't run without passing in this parameter. Using parameters will be discussed in more detail in Chapter 5.

Control Flow | Data Flow | Parameters | Event Handlers | Package Explorer

Name	Data type	Value	Sensitive	Required	Description
pServerName	String	localhost	False	False	
pServerPW	String		True	False	

FIGURE 2-25

Event Handlers

The Event Handlers tab enables you to create workflows to handle errors, warnings, or completion in tasks, containers, or packages. For example, if you want to trap any errors and have them e-mailed to you, you could create an `OnError` event handler that is scoped to the entire package and configure it to send a message out to an operator.

You can configure the event handler's scope under the Executable dropdown box. An executable can be a package, a Foreach Loop container, a For Loop container, a Sequence container, or a task. In the Event Handler box, you can specify the event you wish to monitor. The events you can select are described in the following table:

EVENT	WHEN EVENT IS RAISED
`OnError`	When an error occurs
`OnExecStatusChanged`	When an executable's status changes
`OnInformation`	When an informational event is raised during the validation and execution of an executable
`OnPostExecute`	When an executable completes
`OnPostValidate`	When an executable's validation is complete
`OnPreExecute`	Before an executable runs
`OnPreValidate`	Before an executable's validation begins
`OnProgress`	When measurable progress has happened on an executable
`OnQueryCancel`	When a query has been instructed to cancel
`OnTaskFailed`	When a task fails
`OnVariableValueChanged`	When a variable is changed at runtime
`OnWarning`	When a warning occurs in your package

Event handlers are critically important to developing a package that is "self-healing" — that is, it can correct its own problems. The key events to handle are `OnError`, `OnWarning`, `OnPreExecute`, and `OnPostExecute`. You will learn more about event handlers in Chapter 18.

Package Explorer

The final tab in the SSIS Package Designer is the Package Explorer tab, shown in Figure 2-26. This tab consolidates all the design panes into a single view, and lists all the tasks, connections, containers, event handlers, variables, and transforms in your package. You can double-click any item here to configure it easily. You can also modify the properties for the item in the Properties window on the right after selecting the item you wish to modify.

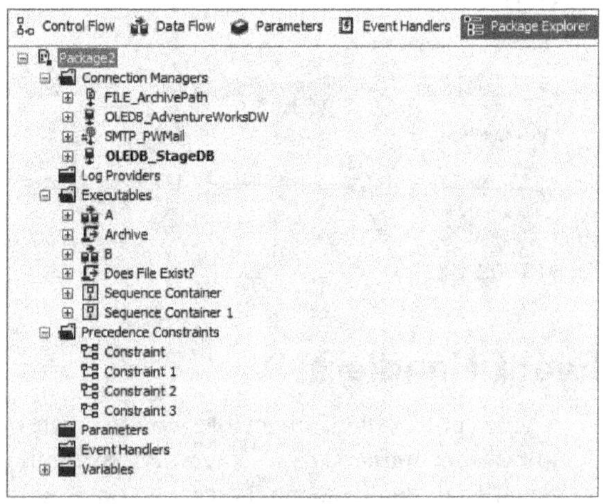

FIGURE 2-26

This tab is useful if you have a task that is throwing an error and you can't find it to remove or fix it. This problem happens sometimes when you have tasks that accidentally fall behind a container or another task.

Executing a Package

When you want to execute a package, you can click the Play icon on the toolbar, or press F5, or choose Debug ➪ Start. You can also execute packages by right-clicking the package in Solution Explorer and selecting Execute Package. This last technique may be a better habit to get into because clicking the Play button initiates a build, and if your packages are in a solution that has multiple projects, it may also deploy SSRS reports or SSAS cubes if those projects are included in the solution. This puts the design environment into execution mode, opens several new windows, enables several new menu and toolbar items, and begins to execute the package. When the package finishes running, SSDT doesn't immediately go back to design mode but rather stays in execution mode to allow you to inspect any runtime variables or view any execution output. This also means that you can't make some changes to the objects within the package. You may already be familiar with this concept from executing .NET projects.

To return to design mode, you must click the Stop icon on the debugging toolbar, or press Shift+F5, or choose Debug ➪ Stop Debugging.

MANAGEMENT STUDIO

SSIS delineates between the SSIS developer and the administrator. SQL Server Management Studio is where administrators do most of their work — executing, securing, and updating packages. From the Management Studio interface, the administrator is not able to design packages, however. This function is reserved for SSDT only.

You can open SQL Server Management Studio under the Microsoft SQL Server program group on the Start menu. Then, in the Object Browser pane (which can be opened from the View menu if it's closed), select Connect ➪ Database Engine. Type your SQL Server instance name and click Connect. If you receive an error, you may want to jump ahead to Chapter 22, which explains how to correct connectivity issues. There's also an SSIS service you can connect to, but this is for packages running in legacy mode. You'll learn much more about this in Chapter 22 as well.

SUMMARY

This chapter provided an overview of the main SSIS wizards and core tools. The Import and Export Wizard is a quick way to create a package that does a simple import or export of data. The wizard is capable of producing a package that can be run multiple times.

You were then taken on a tour of the SQL Server Data Tools (SSDT), which is where you'll be spending most of your time as you develop packages. You looked at the key parts of the interface. Don't worry if you don't yet understand all the components of SSIS. Now that you have been exposed to the basic concepts, you'll dive deeper into SSIS as you look at each component.

Now that you've gotten your feet wet, it's time to explore the real power of SSIS, which lies in the multitude of tasks you can use in your packages. You will learn about some of the more common ones in Chapter 3, and containers are covered in depth in Chapter 6.

3

SSIS Tasks

WHAT'S IN THIS CHAPTER?

- Working with the Task Editor
- Extending SSIS with scripting tasks
- Using data preparation tasks
- Integration into the database with the RDMS tasks
- Performing common DBA tasks with the DBA tasks in SSIS

WROX.COM CODE DOWNLOADS FOR THIS CHAPTER

You can find the wrox.com code downloads for this chapter at `http://www.wrox.com/go/prossis2014` on the Download Code tab.

SSIS tasks are the foundation of the Control Flow in SSIS. When you are on the Control Flow design surface in SSDT, the SSIS Toolbox is populated with a set of task components that can be connected together to represent a workflow for your package. You'll also learn later in Chapter 18 how tasks can also react to failures in the package in the Event Handler tab.

A *task* is a discrete unit of work that can perform typical actions required by an ETL process, from moving a file and preparing data sources to sending e-mail confirmations when everything is complete. This is most evident in the fact that the Data Flow is tied to the Control Flow with a specific Data Flow Task. More advanced tasks enable you to perform actions like executing SQL commands, sending mail, running VB or C# code, and accessing web services. The SSIS Toolbox contains a large list of out-of-the-box tasks that you can use for ETL package development. Most of the tasks are covered in this chapter, with some in less detail because they are covered in other chapters. Two exceptions are the Looping and Sequence Containers, which are covered separately in Chapter 6. This chapter introduces you to most of the tasks you'll be using on a frequent basis and provides some examples that demonstrate how to use them. This material is reinforced as you read through the rest of the book, because each of these tasks is used in at least one further example in subsequent chapters.

SSIS TASK OBJECTS

Tasks are component-based, small units of work that can be sequenced in an SSIS package Control Flow or in the Event Handlers tab. To add a task to a package, click and drag it from the SSIS Toolbox onto the design surface. If you don't see the SSIS Toolbox, you can open it by clicking SSIS Toolbox under the SSIS menu in SSDT. Once you drag the task over, you can then double-click the task's icon in the design pane to configure it. You may immediately see a red or yellow warning on the task until you configure any required properties. Setup requirements vary depending upon the task. You may also need to provide a database connection, external mail server connection, or the name of an external package to complete the task's configuration.

Using the Task Editor

To configure a task you need to access the Task Editor. To do so, double-click directly on the task's icon in the Control Flow design surface or right-click the task and select the Edit option in the pop-up menu. In either case, generally you'll see a Task Editor dialog appear (generally, because not all tasks have a Task Editor to configure). The Task Editor provides a specialized interface that enables configuration of the task's properties. Each task has different property and setup requirements, but the Task Editor always employs a consistent design that makes it easy to follow. Figure 3-1 shows an example of a typical Task Editor dialog to help get you oriented.

Each Task Editor contains a few generic properties such as its Name and Description. Try to select a meaningful name that best represents what the task is doing. Otherwise, your error log will be tough to read later. Each tab of the Task Editor varies according to what you select in the previous tab. Familiarizing yourself with this dialog will make configuring new tasks much easier.

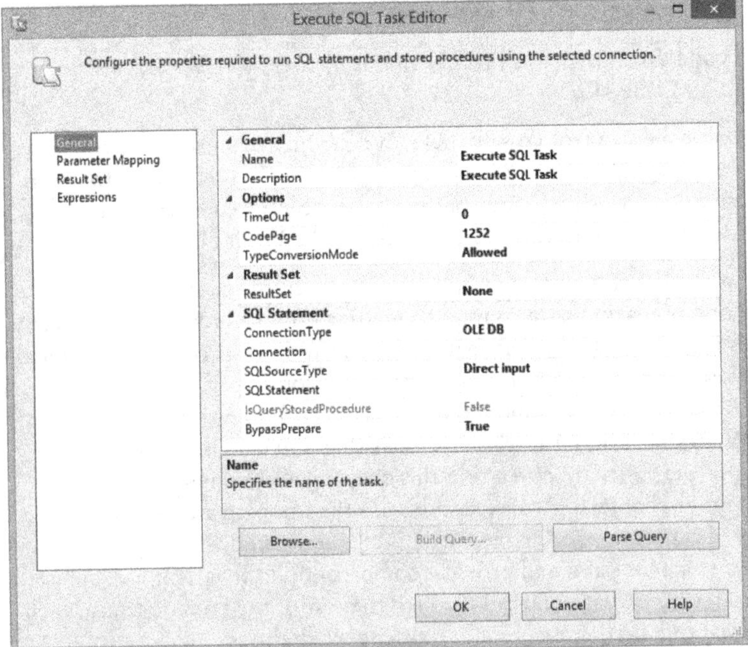

FIGURE 3-1

The Task Editor Expressions Tab

SSIS uses a concept of setting the value of most task properties to a dynamic expression that is evaluated at runtime. This way, you can dynamically configure packages at runtime, replacing the Dynamic Properties Task and scripting-based configuration of the legacy DTS object model. Common to all the tasks is an Expressions tab in each of the editors that exposes the properties you can set dynamically at runtime with an expression. The expression can be a constant value, an expression, or an SSIS variable that is either a scalar constant or an expression. With this capability, you could read a series of variables from a configuration file (these are discussed later) and then dynamically set properties of any SSIS task. We provide many examples of using expressions throughout this book. Chapter 5 is dedicated to variables and expressions, and explains how to use them in SSIS.

For a basic understanding of the Expressions tab within each task, click the ellipsis (...) button next to the Expressions option in the Expressions tab of any of the Task Editors. This will take you to the Property Expressions Editor, where you can set properties within a task — either directly by providing the actual expression or indirectly by providing the variable that evaluates to the result of an expression. To create a new one, select the property you wish to set from the Property column and then type the expression into the Expression column. Optionally, you can also select the ellipsis button in the Expression column to open Expression Builder, where you can create an expression using a visual UI. You'll see this capability in most of the SSIS tasks.

LOOPING AND SEQUENCE TASKS

First up in the SSIS Toolbox are three container tasks: For Loop, Foreach, and Sequence. These are all Control Flow Tasks that simplify the process of repeated processing of a set of logic. In legacy DTS, looping constructs were not intuitive. If you wanted this type of Control Flow logic, you had to set properties on the tasks directly using code in the ActiveX Scripting Tasks. To achieve the same thing in SSIS, you only need to add one of these containers to your Control Flow and define what is being used to enumerate the loop. Again, these containers are covered in detail in Chapter 6, so they are only briefly covered here.

SCRIPT TASK (.NET)

The Script Task enables you to access the Microsoft Visual Studio Tools for Applications (VSTA) environment to write and execute scripts using the VB and C# languages. Using this task, you can create additional logic that the canned SSIS tasks can't accomplish.

Scripting now is almost a misnomer because the latest SSIS edition solidifies the connection to the full .NET 4.0 libraries for both VB and C#. The latest addition to SSIS of the VSTA environment and the Script Task, in general, also offer these extra functional advantages:

- A coding environment with the advantage of IntelliSense
- An integrated Visual Studio design environment within SSIS
- An easy-to-use methodology for passing parameters into the script
- The capability to add breakpoints to your code for testing and debugging purposes
- The automatic compiling of your script into binary format for increased speed

The Script Task is configured through the Script tab in the Script Task Editor (shown in Figure 3-2). The `ScriptLanguage` property is where you select the .NET language you want to use in the task. Notice that the default language is set to C#, so if you are coding in VB.NET, don't whiz through these settings when setting up your Script Tasks.

The `EntryPoint` property enables you to provide an alternative function to call initially when the `ScriptMain` class is instantiated. Typically, you'll leave this set to the default `Main()` function. The `ReadOnlyVariables` and `ReadWriteVariables` properties enable you to pass SSIS variables into the script as a listing of variable names separated by commas. While this is not the only way to pass variables into a script, it is the easiest. Having these variables provides a significant advantage when coding. You only need to refer to them by ordinal position or by name in the Variable collection to be able to access their values without worrying about locking, unlocking, or blocking variables during read and write actions. Just make sure that any variables you wish to write back to in the script code are listed in the `ReadWriteVariables` property; otherwise, you'll get an error in the script. There are alternative methods for altering variables that aren't provided in these collections during setup; these are demonstrated in Chapter 9, which covers scripting.

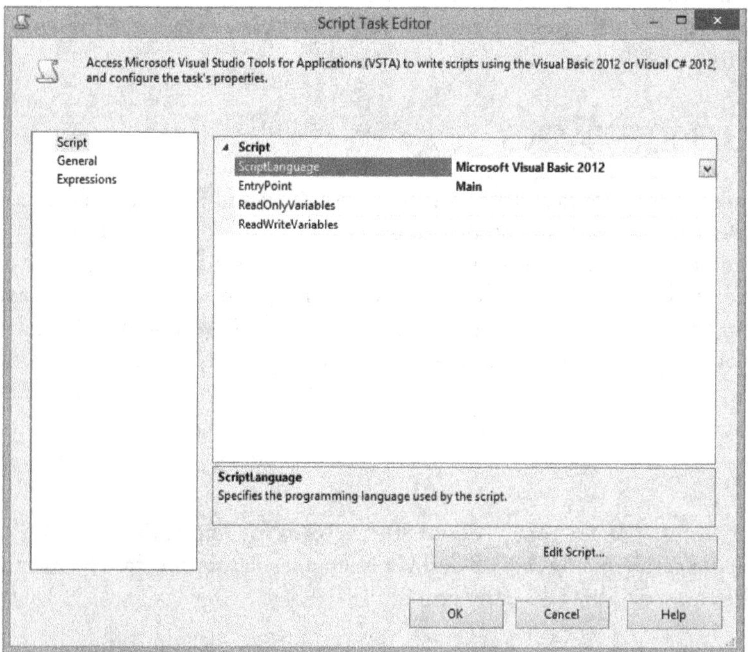

FIGURE 3-2

When you click the actionable Edit Script button, the Visual Studio Tools for Applications environment opens to allow coding directly in the class `ScriptMain`. In this IDE, you have access to all the advanced debugging tactics, breakpoints, and IntelliSense found in the Visual Studio environment. If you create a package with a variable named `myValue` containing the string `"Hello World"`, and set up the Script Task as shown in Figure 3-3, the following example shows you how to write code that uses the passed-in `myValue` variable:

C#

```
public void Main()
{
if(Dts.Variables.Contains("User::MyValue"))
{
System.Windows.Forms.MessageBox.Show("MyValue=" + Dts.Variables
["User::MyValue"].Value.ToString());
}
Dts.TaskResult = (int)ScriptResults.Success;
}
```

VB

```
Public Sub Main()
If Dts.Variables.Contains("User::MyValue") = True Then
System.Windows.Forms.MessageBox.Show("myValue=" & Dts.Variables
("User::MyValue").Value.ToString())
End If
Dts.TaskResult = ScriptResults.Success
End Sub
```

First, the script (Figure 3-3) checks for the existence of the variable, and then pops up a message box with the famous message “Hello World.”

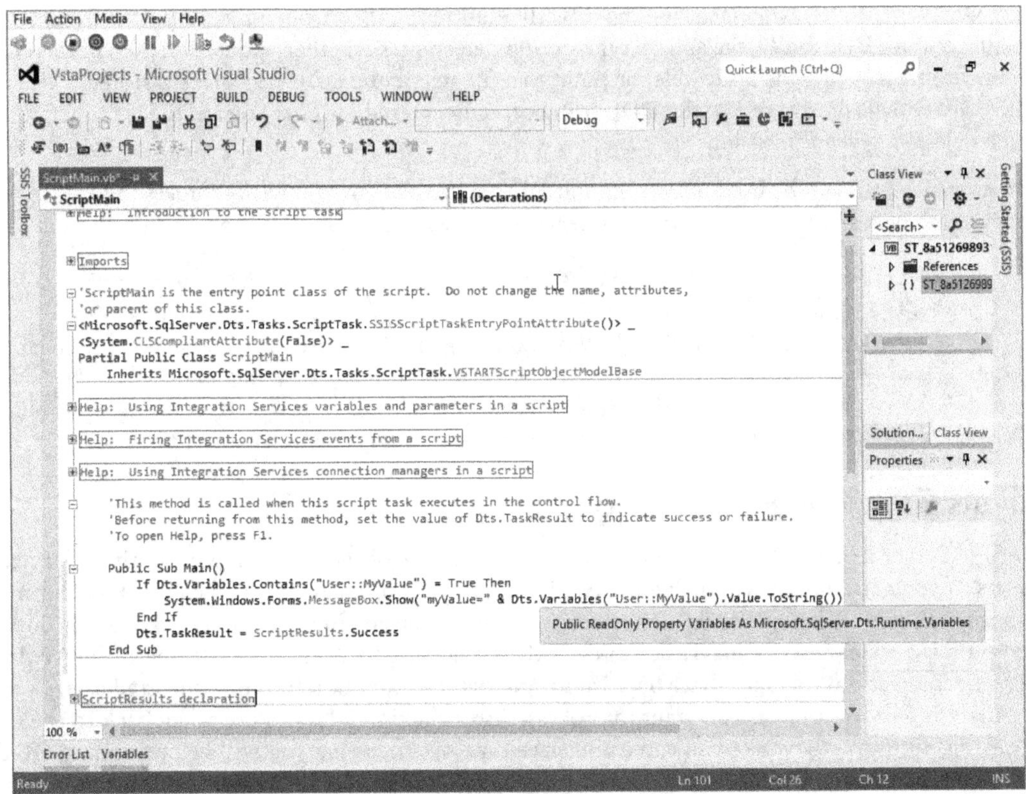

FIGURE 3-3

This is just a very simple example of the Script Task in action. We've created an entire chapter to dive into the details and provide specific use cases for both the Script Task and the Data Flow version called the Script Component, so see Chapter 9 for more information.

ANALYSIS SERVICES TASKS

The Analysis Services tasks are provided in the SSIS environment to deal with generating and updating cubes and working with data mining projects in SQL Server Analysis Services only. Three tasks can be used for Analysis Services in SSIS: the Analysis Services Execute DDL Task, the Processing Task, and the Data Mining Task. To review the tasks in this section, you need to have installed the sample Analysis Services databases from Microsoft SQL Server.

Analysis Services Execute DDL Task

The SQL Server Analysis Services Execute DDL Task is the Analysis Services equivalent of the Execute SQL Task, but it is limited in scope to issuing Data Definition Language statements. The task simply executes a DDL statement against an Analysis Services system. Typically, you would use DDL statements to create a cube, a dimension, or any other online analytical processing (OLAP) object.

To configure the task, go to the DDL tab and select the Connection Manager that you wish to execute the DDL statement against in the Connection option. Then in the SourceType property, select whether the DDL statement will be directly inputted, pulled from a file, or pulled from a variable option. Essentially, the source type option determines whether you need to key in the DDL statement directly, provide a variable, or point to a file where the DDL statement is stored. Figure 3-4 shows an example of the DDL being directly entered into the SourceDirect property, which deletes a given dimension.

Note that this task can be used only to submit DDL statements. If you wish to query cubes to retrieve data, you need to use the Analysis Services Processing or Data Mining Tasks.

> **NOTE** *You can easily find XMLA statements by going to Management Studio and scripting a given action. In the example just mentioned, you can open Management Studio and delete the dimension, but instead of clicking OK, click the Script icon.*

Analysis Services Processing Task

The SQL Server Analysis Services Processing Task takes care of the processing of Analysis Services objects. If you are familiar with using the Analysis Service projects in SSDT, then you'll be familiar with the task of processing a cube, dimension, or mining object. Configuration of the task is done in the Analysis Services Processing Task Editor in the Processing Settings tab. First, select the Analysis Services Connection Manager that you wish to process. Next, click the Add button and select the Analysis Services objects you want to process. After clicking OK, you are taken back to the Processing Settings tab, where you can change the type of processing you will be performing. To do this, right-click each object and select the process option you want. The options vary according to the type of object.

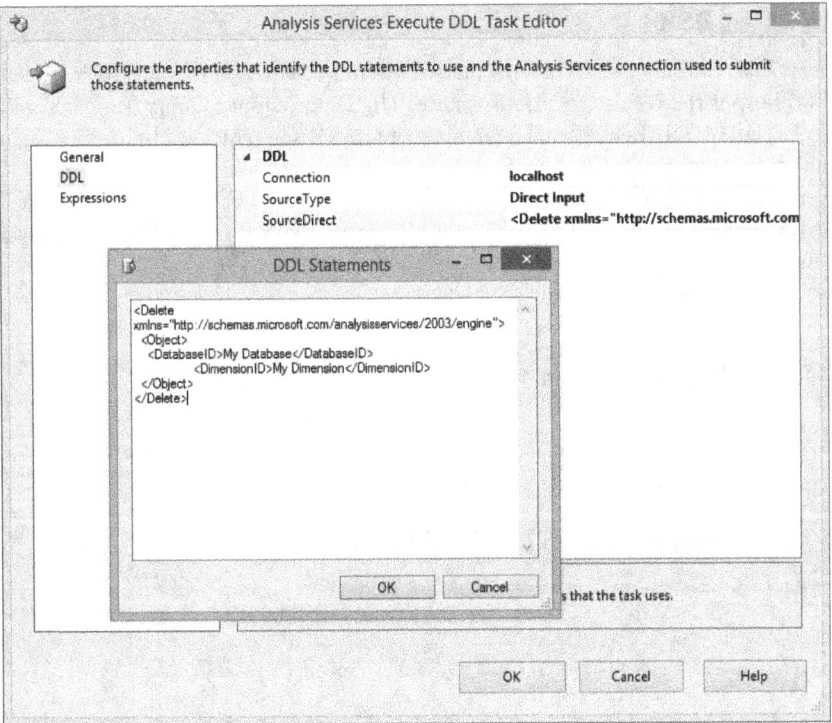

FIGURE 3-4

If you click Impact Analysis, analysis is performed on the selected objects, showing you the objects that will be affected by the processing. The Change Settings button enables you to configure the batch settings for the task. For example, here you can specify whether you want the objects to be processed in sequential order or in parallel and how you want errors handled.

To get a feel for how this SSIS task works, you need to download and deploy the AdventureWorks Analysis Services SSAS project from `www.wrox.com`. This will deploy the cube and a set of dimensions that you'll want to process periodically as new data is loaded into the warehouse. In SSIS, you can process the deployed cube using the Analysis Services Processing Task. Connect to the Analysis Services server that you deployed to, and in the Processing Settings tab select the Employee Cube and the Sales Territory dimension to process.

The Analysis Services Processing Task can then be run to reprocess the existing dimension and employee cube. These SSIS tasks enable you to periodically update your warehouse structures based on events that can be processed using an event captured by the Message Queue Task, which we cover later in the "Message Queue Task" section of this chapter.

Data Mining Query Task

The Data Mining Query Task enables you to run predictive queries against your Analysis Services data-mining models and output the results to a data source. The Data Mining Query Task is similar to the Analysis Service Execute DDL Task in that you can execute subsequent mining queries against a processed mining model in Analysis Server. The Task Editor enables configuration to a source Analysis Services server and can output the results in any ADO.NET or OLE DB Data Source. An example of the Data Mining Task configured to run a mining query against a predefined Employee Dimensional Mining model is shown in Figure 3-5.

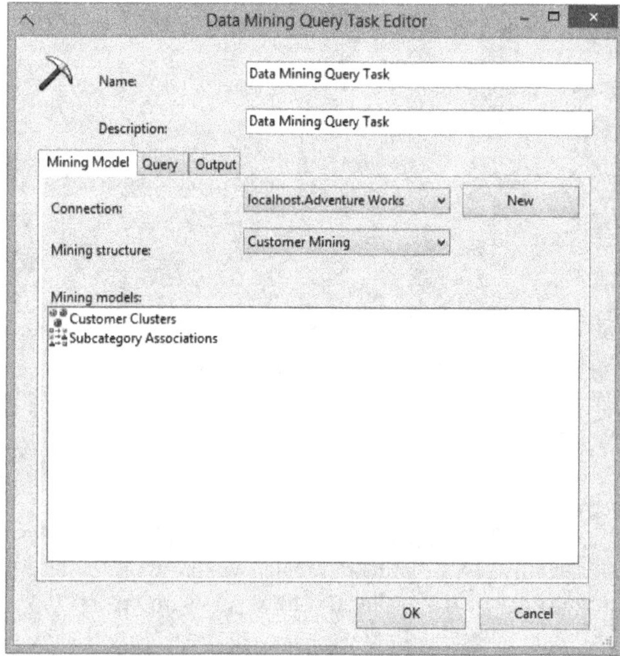

FIGURE 3-5

This task would be used to run predictive queries based on built-in prediction models in Analysis Services. The query uses a Data Mining Extension to T-SQL called DMX. If you are not fluent in DMX, don't worry, the Query tab in this task will walk you through building one. However, first you need a mining structure to query against. In the Analysis Service server, a deployed data mining model would look like the highlighted decision tree model in Figure 3-6.

The results of the prediction query can be set to return single or multi-row results and can be saved to table structures for further analysis. These results can be useful for additional SSIS packages that can integrate the predictive results into further Data Flows, but before we can step any further into these capabilities, let's first go over the Data Flow Task itself.

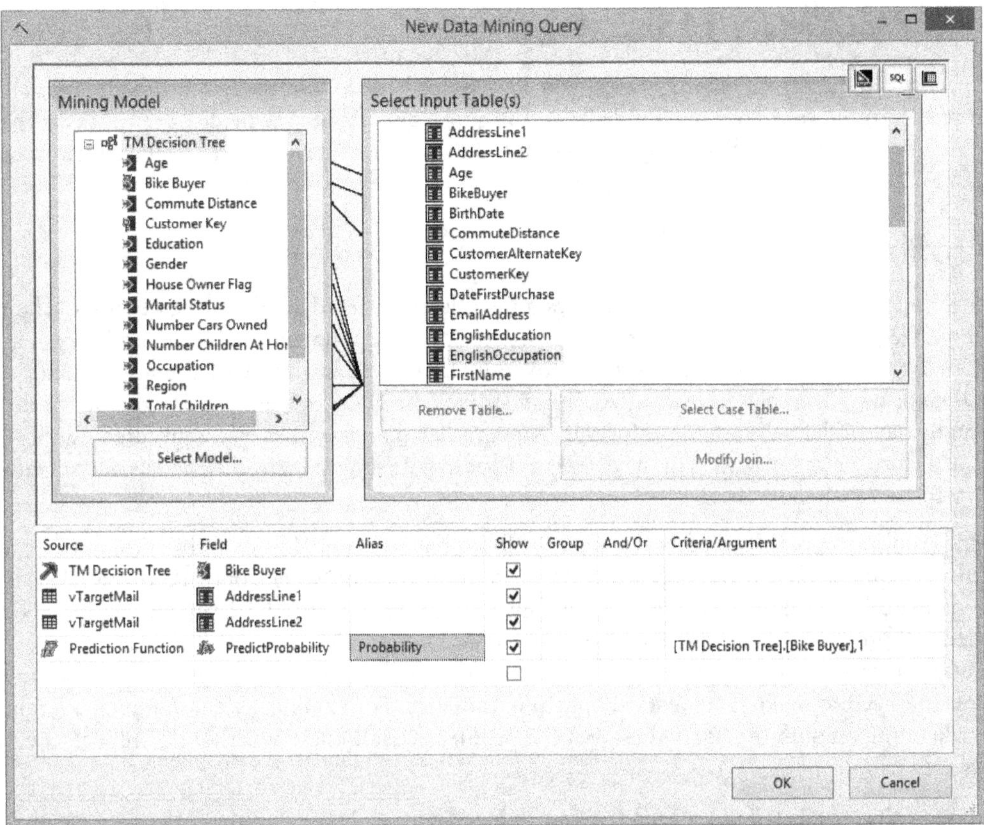

FIGURE 3-6

DATA FLOW TASK

The most important task in SSIS is the Data Flow Task. The SSIS Data Flow Task can be selected directly from the SSDT Toolbox, and then the source and destinations are defined within the task. The Data Flow Task isn't merely a mapping transform for input and output columns. This task has its own design surface like the Control Flow, where you can arrange task-like components called *transforms* to manipulate data as it flows in a pipeline from the source to a destination. The Data Flow, as you can imagine, is the heart of SSIS, because it encapsulates all the data transformation aspects of ETL.

Data Flows can split the data in the pipeline based on a data element and handle each stream separately. In the Data Flow, the header line of the file can be split off and examined separately from the detail lines. As the pipeline exits the data-cleansing process, the streams can be sent to separate destinations or converged to a final combined destination. Note that you may have several different Data Flows within an SSIS package. For each of the Data Flow Tasks you add to the control surface, you'll have a corresponding Data Flow surface. This task is so important and such an integral part of moving data in SSIS that it is covered in detail in Chapter 4.

DATA PREPARATION TASKS

Before processing data from other systems, you sometimes have to first retrieve it or validate the content to determine your level of confidence in the data's quality. SSIS provides a set of tasks that can be used to retrieve data files using the files and folders available in the file system, or it can reach out using FTP and web service protocols. The following sections explore these tasks in SSIS.

Data Profiler

Data profiling is the process of examining data and collecting metadata about the quality of the data, about frequency of statistical patterns, interdependencies, uniqueness, and redundancy. This type of analytical activity is important for the overall quality and health of an operational data store (ODS) or data warehouse. In fact, you've most likely been doing this activity whether or not you actually have a defined tool to perform it. Now, rather than use a set of complicated queries or rely on a third-party product, you have a Data Profiling Task as part of the SSIS development environment.

The Data Profiling Task is located in the SSIS Toolbox, but you probably shouldn't attempt to use the results to make an automated workflow decision in the SSIS package Control Flow. Rather, it is more of an ad hoc tool for placement in a design-time package that will be run manually outside of a scheduled process. In fact, the task doesn't have built-in conditional workflow logic, but technically you can use XPath queries on the results. The profiler can only report on statistics in the data; you still need to make judgments about these statistics. For example, a column may contain an overwhelming amount of NULL values, but the profiler doesn't know whether this reflects a valid business scenario.

You can view the structured output file that is produced by the Data Profiling Task in a special Data Profiler Viewer that provides drill-downs back to the detail level. To access this viewer, select SQL Server ➪ Integration Services from the Start menu. Once the tool is loaded, use the Open button to browse to the output file that will be generated by the Data Profiling Task. Figure 3-7 shows an example of an analysis of the DimCustomer table in the AdventureWorksDW database. You can see here that the majority of the rows in the MiddleName column are null.

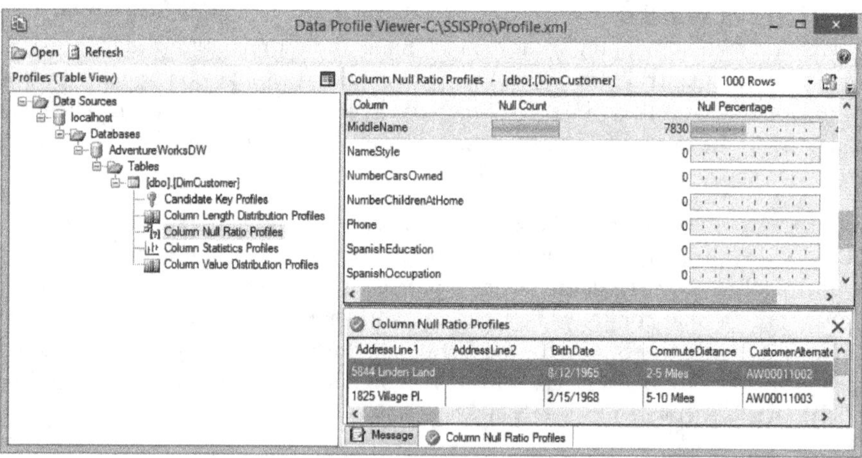

FIGURE 3-7

The task provides a set of defined profile request types that can be modified like the other tasks in specific properties. The following list describes the different request types and how you can use them to profile your data:

- **Candidate Key Profile Request:** The profile request will examine a column or set of columns to determine the likelihood of there being a unique candidate key for the data set. Use this to determine whether you have duplicate key values or whether it is possible to build a natural key with the data.
- **Column Length Distribution Profile:** This profile request enables you to analyze the statistical profile of all the data in a column, with the percentage of incidence for each length. You can use this to help you determine whether your data column length settings are set correctly or to look for bad data in attributes that are known to be one fixed size.
- **Column Null Ratio Profile Request:** This profile request looks at the ratio of `NULL` values in a column. Use this to determine whether you have a data quality problem in your source system for critical data elements.
- **Column Pattern Profile Request:** This profile request enables you to apply regular expressions to a string column to determine the pass/fail ratio across all the rows. Use this to evaluate business data using business formatting rules.
- **Column Statistics Profile Request:** This profile request can analyze all the rows and provide statistical information about the unique values across the entire source. This can help you find low incidence values that may indicate bad data. For example, a finding of only one color type in a set of 1 million rows may indicate that you have a bad color attribute value.
- **Functional Dependency Profile Request:** This is one of two profile requests that enable you to examine relationships between tables and columns to look for discrepancies within a known dependency. For example, you can use this request to find countries with incorrect currency codes.
- **Value Inclusion Profile Request:** This profile request tests to determine whether the values in one column are all included in a separate lookup or dimension table. Use this to test foreign key relationships.

There are two ways to activate these profiles. The first is to click the Quick Profile button on the Data Profiling Task Editor. This creates a set of profiles to run against the same table. You can also skip the quick profile option and create the profiles one by one. Either way you can navigate to the Profile Requests table to configure the request and add regular expressions or other parameter values to the task properties. Figure 3-8 shows the Data Profiling Task Editor with all the requests defined for the DimCustomer table.

For each profile request type, the lower section of the editor for the Request Properties will change to accept the configurable values. Note that the ConnectionManager property must be set to an ADO.NET-based Connection Manager, like the one here connected to AdventureWorksDW. Moreover, you must create this connection prior to attempting to configure this task, but this is a minor inconvenience for such a powerful and welcome addition to the SSIS toolset, which rivals more expensive ETL tools.

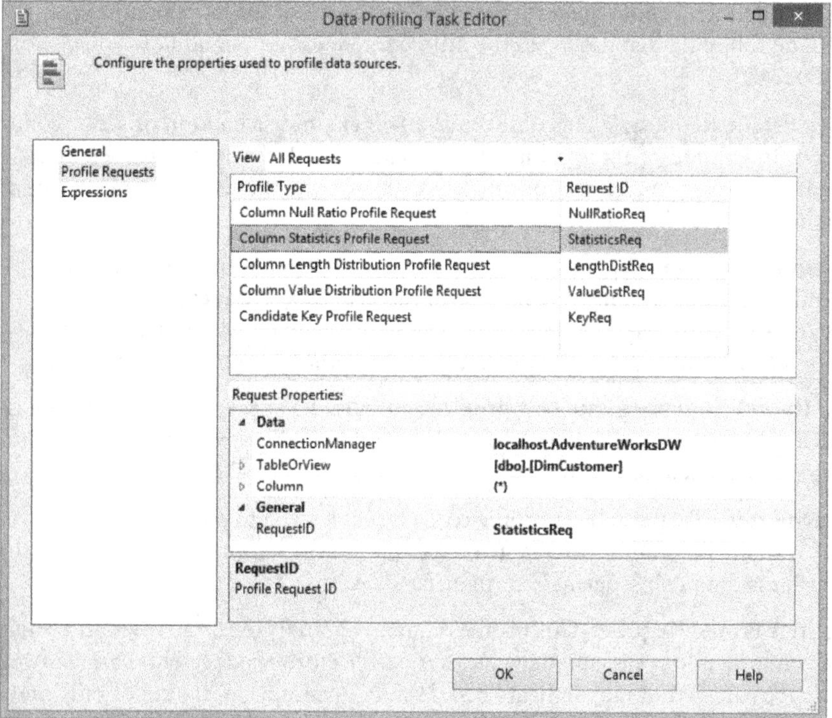

FIGURE 3-8

File System Task

The File System Task is a configurable GUI component that performs file operations available in the `System.IO.File` .NET class. If you are used to coding in VBScript, this is an out-of-the-box replacement for the VBScript utility classes that you used to write using the COM-based `FileSystemObject`. In either case, the File System Task can perform basic file operations such as the following:

- **Copy Directory:** Copies all files from one directory to another. You must provide the source and destination directories.
- **Copy File:** Copies a specific file. You must provide the source and destination filename.
- **Create Directory:** Creates a directory. You must provide the source directory name and indicate whether the task should fail if the destination directory already exists.
- **Delete Directory:** Deletes a directory. You must provide the source directory to delete.
- **Delete Directory Content:** Deletes all files in a source directory
- **Delete File:** Deletes a specifically provided source file
- **Move Directory:** Moves a provided source directory to a destination directory. You must indicate whether the task should fail if the destination directory already exists.

- **Move File:** Moves a specific provided source file to a destination. You must indicate whether the task should fail if the destination file already exists.
- **Rename File:** Moves a specific provided source file to a destination by changing the name. You must indicate whether the task should fail if the destination file already exists.
- **Set Attributes:** Sets Hidden, Read-Only, Archive, or System attributes on a provided source file.

One benefit that may not be apparent in these functional descriptions is that the creation of directory structures does not have to be made recursively. For example, you may create the path named `c:\ssis\tasks\my file system task\` using the Create Directory form of the File System Task by simply providing the path. You don't have to create each part of the directory separately, as you did in the DTS legacy product. This capability greatly reduces the typical file operation coding to a simple configuration task for directory operations. However, don't assume that you can do the same with a file-level operation. If you attempt to rename a file from `c:\ssis\` to `c:\ssis\my archive\` and the folder `\my archive\` doesn't exist, you will get an error that the path is not found.

Another feature of this task that may not be apparent is that it is written for a single operation. This is by design. If you need to iterate over a series of files or directories, the File System Task can be simply placed within a Looping Container. By keeping the task granular and singularly focused, it is simplified and easily reused.

Most of the properties in this task are set in the General tab of the File System Task Editor (see Figure 3-9). The contents of this tab may vary widely according to what you set in the Operation property. These options correspond to specific file operations that the task can perform. Once the option is set, you may be prompted to complete other properties not shown in this figure.

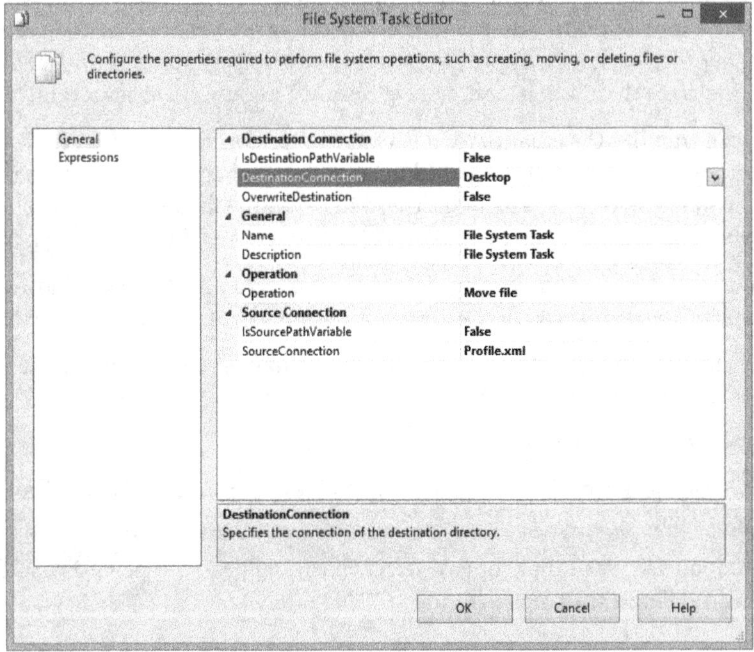

FIGURE 3-9

In this case, the Operation property is set to Move file, which should move a file from a working source path to an archive destination path. The IsDestinationPathVariable property enables you to specify whether the destination path will be set to an SSIS variable or use a Connection Manager. If this is set to true, the dynamic property DestinationVariable sets the destination path to a variable. If it is set to false, then the DestinationConnection option will be available so you can select the Connection Manager that contains your file or directory. These same properties exist for the source connection in the bottom of the tab. The OverwriteDestination option, set to false by default, specifies whether the task will overwrite the destination file or directory if it already exists. To get an idea of how you configure this task, see the example in the next section.

Archiving a File

Consider a typical use of the File System Task for an ETL process from a mainframe system. To automate a nightly data load, the process would look like this:

1. A file or series of similar files would be generated from a mainframe or other source system and dumped to a network drive.
2. An SSIS package would start on a schedule to poll a directory looking for files to process. If any files were found, they would be moved into a staging or working directory.
3. The data would be extracted out of the file(s).
4. The file(s) would then be archived to another directory.

In legacy DTS packages, each of these steps would require some coding in the ActiveX Script Task. You would have to write one task in VBScript to poll the directory to determine whether the file arrived. Another script would pick up the file and move it to another directory. The last script would archive the file. Even worse, the ActiveX scripts had to use the code-and-paste method of code reuse to perform the same function in other packages. Typically, this led to various states of unfinished code that was better in some packages than others and most certainly a nightmare to maintain.

In SSIS, the File System Task can simplify the creation of a package by performing these ETL file-based requirements. We'll postpone the task of polling until later in this chapter when we get to the WMI Event Watcher Task. The iteration of files is also discussed in detail in Chapter 6. However, you can use what you know about the File System Task to move the file to an archive directory.

1. Create a new project named Tasks and a package in `c:\ProSSIS\Tasks\FileSystemTask` or download the complete code from `www.wrox.com/go/prossis2014`.
2. Create a subdirectory called `c:\ProSSIS\Tasks\FileSystemTask\Archive`, and create a dummy file called `myfile.txt` in `c:\ProSSIS\Tasks\FileSystemTask`.
3. Add a File System Task into the Control Flow.
4. In the new task, change the operation to Move File. Select <New Connection> from the SourceConnection dropdown.
5. When the File Connection Manager Editor opens, select Existing File and type **C:\ProSSIS\Tasks\FileSystemTask\MyFile.txt** for your file.

6. For the DestinationConnection property, select the <New Connection> option and choose Existing Folder when the File Connection Manager Editor reopens. This time type **C:\ProSSIS\Tasks\FileSystemTask\Archive** for the path name.
7. Now run the SSIS package. You'll see the file `myfile.txt` move into the archive directory.
8. If you want to rename the file as you move it to a date-based filename, you need to specify the full filename in the variable and use the Rename File option of the File System Task. That achieves the movement of the file and a new filename in one task. The filename can also be dynamically set using a variable as an expression.

For examples of how you can rename this file using a dynamically generated name as you archive, see Chapter 5.

FTP Task

The SSIS FTP Task enables the use of the File Transfer Protocol (FTP) in your package development tasks. This task now exposes more FTP command capability, enabling you to create or remove local and remote directories and files. Another change from the legacy DTS FTP Task is the capability to use FTP in passive mode. This solves the problem that DTS had in communicating with FTP servers when the firewalls filtered the incoming data port connection to the server.

The General tab in the FTP Task Editor is where you specify the FTP Connection Manager for the FTP site you wish to access. If you haven't specified one, follow these steps:

1. Select <New Connection...> under the FTPConnection property. This will open the FTP Connection Manager, where you can configure the FTP connection. In Figure 3-10, the Server Name property contains the FTP address for the FTP server. The Server Port property is set to 21, which is the default port for most FTP sites. You can change this if necessary. The other important option to note here is the "Use passive mode" checkbox.
2. Once you have the FTP connection configured, move to the File Transfer tab. The IsRemotePathVariable and IsLocalPathVariable properties allow the paths to be set to an optional variable. Using variables enables you to set these values dynamically at runtime. The RemotePath property sets the directory or files for the remote FTP system.

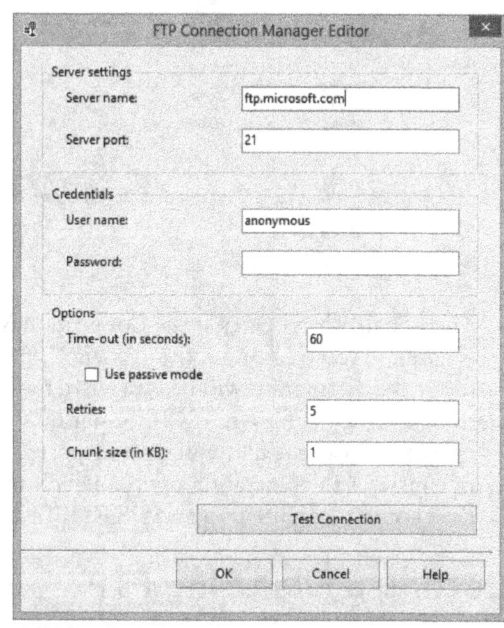

FIGURE 3-10

3. Once the FTPConnection property from the General tab has been selected, you can browse to the actual remote file system to select the remote path or file by clicking the ellipsis in the Remote Path property. You'll see a dialog similar to the one shown in Figure 3-11 for browsing the FTP remote paths (and files if you choose Receive files for the Operation property).

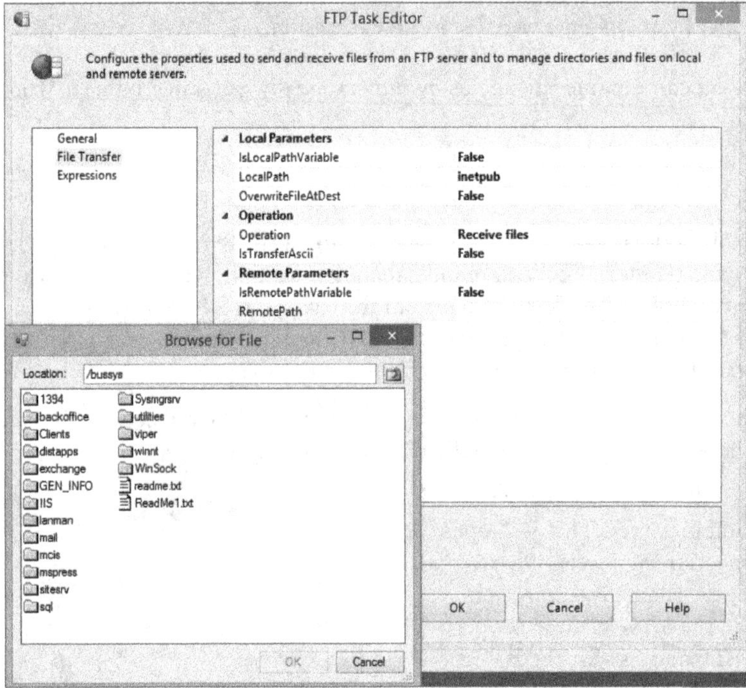

FIGURE 3-11

The LocalPath property is the Connection Manager that contains a directory on the SSIS side that is going to receive or send the files via FTP. The OverwriteFileAtDest option specifies whether the file at the destination will be overwritten if a conflict exists. Like many FTP clients, you can specify transporting the files in ASCII format by setting the IsTransferAscii option to true. If you set this option to false, the files will be transported in a default binary format. The most important option, of course, is the Operation option, which specifies what type of action you want to perform. In the next section, you'll set up an SSIS FTP Task to get a file from an FTP server like `Microsoft.com`.

Getting a File Using FTP

To build an SSIS package that can use FTP to retrieve a file from an FTP server, follow these steps:

1. Create a directory called `c:\prossis\tasks\ftptask\` or copy the code from `www.wrox.com/go/prossis2014`.

2. Create a new project and package in this folder and add an FTP Task to the Control Flow work surface.
3. Double-click the FTP Task to open the editor, and set it up.
4. In the General tab, select <New connection...> for the FTPConnection dropdown. This will open the FTP Connection Editor. Set the Server Name option to `ftp.microsoft.com` and click Test Connection (refer to Figure 3-10).
5. Click OK to go back to the FTP Task Editor.
6. Go to the File Transfer tab and set it up to resemble Figure 3-12. Select Receive files for the operation.
7. For the RemotePath property, click the ellipsis to browse to the `/bussys/readme.txt` folder on the remote path.
8. For the Local Path option, set the IsLocalPathVariable property to true and select <New Variable ...> to create a new variable named LocalPath that is set to the value of `c:\Prossis\Tasks\ftptask\`.
9. For the OverwriteFileAtDest property, select True. The final task should look like Figure 3-12.

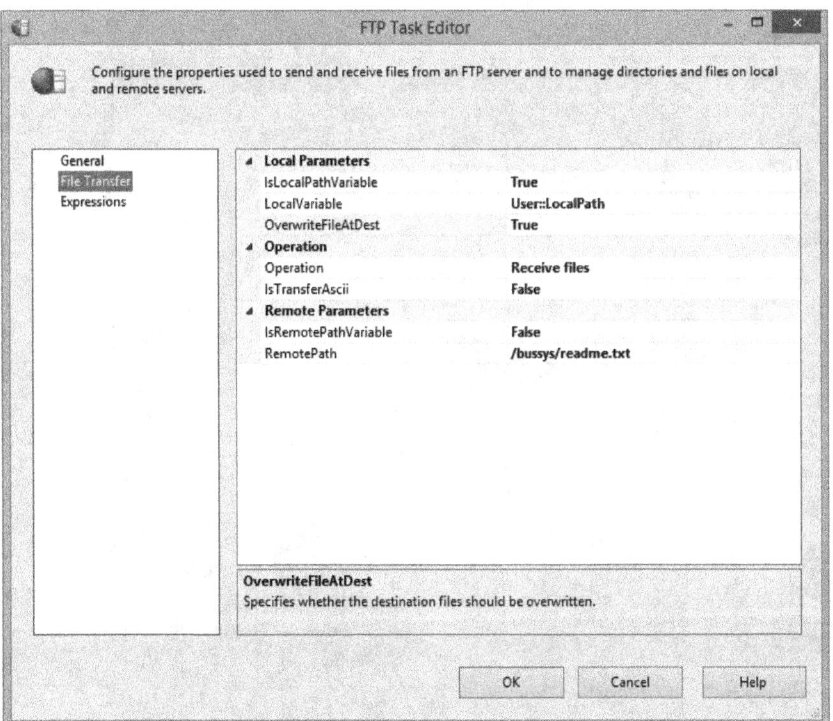

FIGURE 3-12

If you run the package, you'll see that the file is downloaded from the FTP site at Microsoft to your local file system. In a real-world scenario, you would probably download the file, load it into a SQL Server, and then archive it. This complete scenario is discussed in detail in Chapter 8.

Web Service Task

The Web Service Task in SSIS is used to retrieve XML-based result sets by executing a method on a web service. Just like the other tasks we've separated out into the Data Preparation Task category for this chapter, this task only retrieves the data; it doesn't yet address the need to navigate through the data, or extract sections of the resulting documents. Web services are a big part of advancing service-oriented architectures, and they can be used in SSIS to provide real-time validation of data in your ETL processes or to maintain lookup or dimensional data.

The task requires creation of an HTTP Connection Manager to a specific HTTP endpoint on a website or to a specific Web Services Description Language (WSDL) file on a website. Because of this HTTP connection, keep in mind that the task may not work for some locked-down server environments. If the HTTP Connection Manager doesn't point to a WSDL file on the site, a local version must be provided. The WSDL file provides a standard XML-formatted list of available methods that can be called in the web service. The WSDL file also provides information about what type of parameters can be used and what results can be expected in return. Figure 3-13 shows how you can configure the HTTP Connection Manager to access a web service called USZIP at `www.webservicex.net/uszip.asmx`.

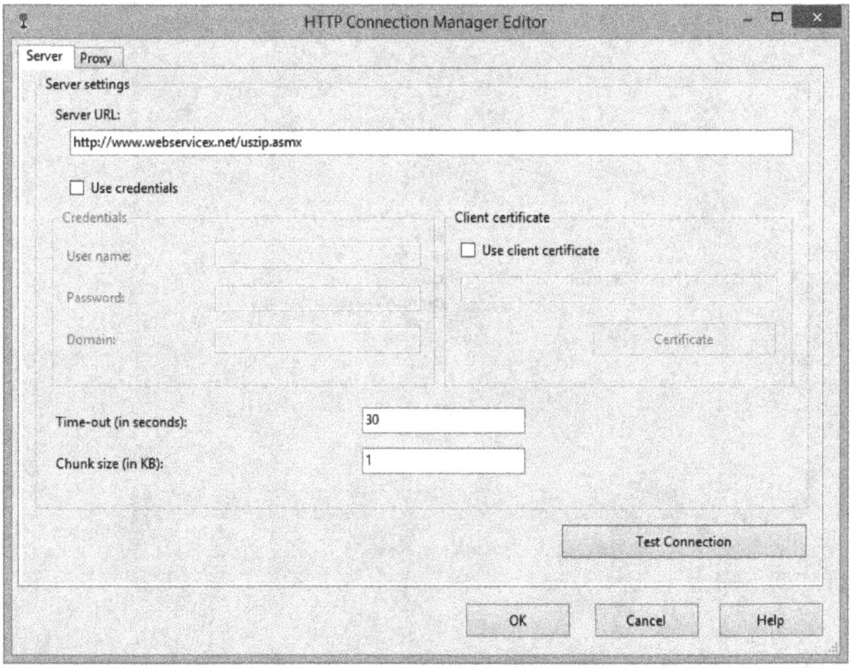

FIGURE 3-13

This is a simplistic HTTP Connection Manager setup. In this case, no special proxy, credentials, or certificate setup is required. If you are using secure, corporate web services, this undoubtedly will not be the case.

The General Tab

The General tab on the Web Service Task is where you set the HttpConnection property of the task to the HTTP Connection Manager that you have already created or alternatively create at the same time by selecting the <New Connection...> option in the property. In Figure 3-14, the value for the WSDL parameter file has been provided. This indicates to the Connection Manager that the definitions of the web service can be obtained remotely. In this case, you are not required to provide a local version of the WSDL file as well. This property is required only if you don't provide the WSDL parameter in the Connection Manager. If this is the case, simply provide the local filename and click the Download WSDL button to have the task, at design time, reach out to the HTTP endpoint and retrieve a copy of the WSDL file for you.

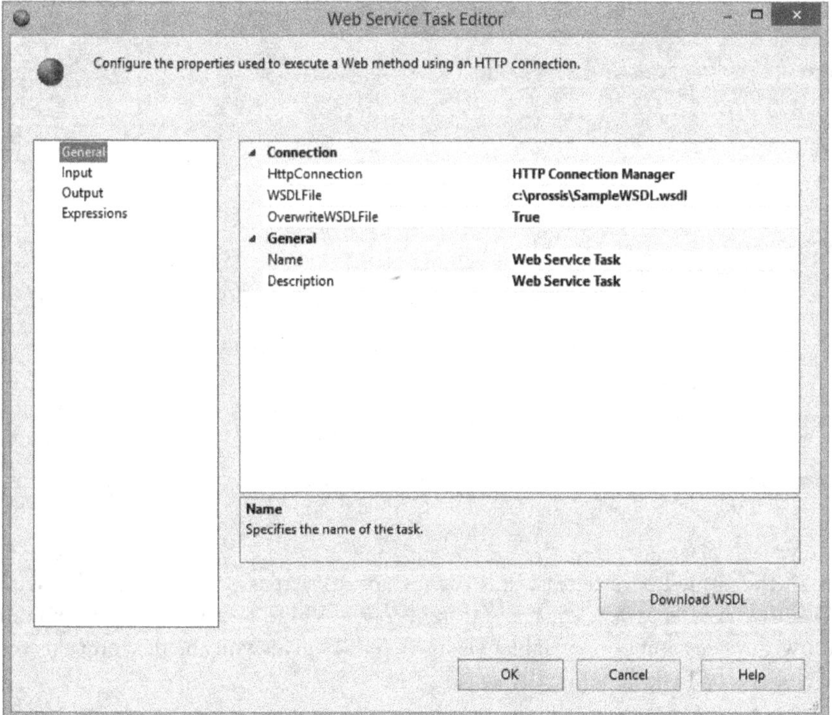

FIGURE 3-14

The Input Tab

The next step is to define the input that you want to retrieve from the web service. It makes sense that if you have defined the web service in the General tab, you now need to specify the web method that you want to access for the input to the task. The Web Service Task makes this easy by using the WSDL file to provide a dropdown in the Input tab where you can specify the method, as shown in Figure 3-15. If you get an error trying to access the Input tab, consider downloading the WSDL file directly onto your computer.

After you select a web method, such as GetInfoByAreaCode, the Web Service Task uses the WSDL to set up the interface for you to provide how the input parameters will be fed into the task. You can choose to set up hardcoded values as shown in Figure 3-15 or you can fill these parameters with variables.

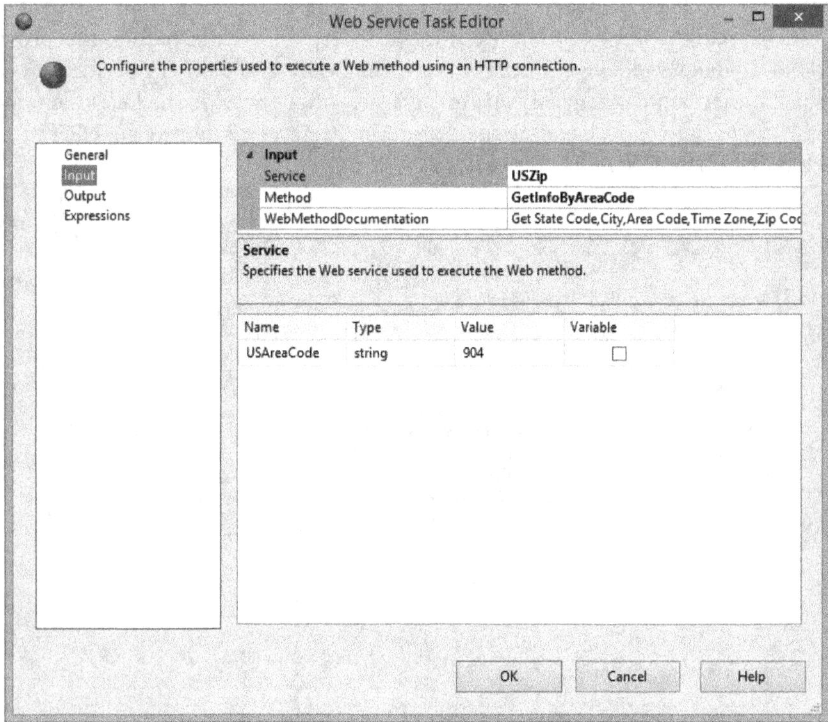

FIGURE 3-15

You can see here that all the named parameters, in this case only USAreaCode, are provided with the expected data types. If you select the Variable option here, the Value column would morph into a dropdown list to allow the selection of a variable. Using variables gives you the flexibility to send something into the Web Service Task dynamically at runtime.

The Output Tab

The remaining tab is the Output tab. Here you have only two options in this task. The resulting retrieval from the web service method can be stored in a file or in a variable. The output is in XML format, so if you choose to save in a variable, select a data type of string. In this example, we'll set the OutputType property to a file connection, and then set the location of the file to a spot on the local file system.

Running the Web Service Task using this configuration will result in calling the web method `GetInfoByZipCode` on the web service USZip and retrieving data into an XML file that looks like this:

```
<?xml version="1.0" encoding="utf-16"?>
<NewDataSet xmlns="">
<Table>
<CITY>Saint Augustine</CITY>
<STATE>FL</STATE>
<ZIP>32084</ZIP>
<AREA_CODE>904</AREA_CODE>
<TIME_ZONE>E</TIME_ZONE>
</Table>
<Table>
<CITY>Jacksonville</CITY>
<STATE>FL</STATE>
<ZIP>32226</ZIP>
<AREA_CODE>904</AREA_CODE>
<TIME_ZONE>E</TIME_ZONE>
</Table>
<Table>
<CITY>Macclenny</CITY>
<STATE>FL</STATE>
<ZIP>32063</ZIP>
<AREA_CODE>904</AREA_CODE>
<TIME_ZONE>E</TIME_ZONE>
</Table>
</NewDataSet>
```

Retrieving data into a file is good, but using it in an SSIS package is even better. The next example demonstrates how you would use the XML Task to retrieve this same zip code data and use it in a Data Flow.

Retrieving Data Using the Web Service Task and XML Source Component

In this example, you'll configure the data retrieved from the Web Service Task to be read through the XML source in the Data Flow. Don't worry if the Data Flow is a little confusing at this time. You'll see much more about it in the next chapter.

1. Set up a project and package in the directory `c:\ProSSIS\tasks\websvc` or download the complete package from `www.wrox.com/go/prossis2014`.
2. Drop a Web Service Task onto the Control Flow design surface and configure the task to use the GetInfoByZipCode method on the web service USZip as shown in the preceding section.
3. Go to the Output tab and set the OutputType to store the results of the web service method to a file of your choosing, such as `C:\ProSSIS\Tasks\WebSVC\Output.xml`.
4. Drop a Data Flow Task onto the Control Flow design surface and connect the Web Service Task to the Data Flow.
5. In the Data Flow, drop an XML source component on the design surface.

If the XML source contained schema information, you could select the Use Inline Schema option — the Data Access Mode should be set to "XML file location" — and you'd be done. However, you've seen the data we are getting from the web service, and no schema is provided. Therefore, you need to generate an XML Schema Definition language file so that SSIS can predict and validate data types and lengths.

NOTE *Here's a little trick that will save you some time. To demonstrate the Web Service Task initially, you set the XML output to go to a file. This was not by accident. Having a concrete file gives you a basis to create an XSD, and you can do it right from the design-time XML Source Component. Just provide the path to the physical XML file you downloaded earlier and click the Generate XSD button. Now you should have an XSD file that looks similar to this:*

```
<?xml version="1.0"?>
<xs:schema attributeFormDefault="unqualified" elementFormDefault=
    "qualified"
xmlns:xs="http://www.w3.org/2001/XMLSchema">
<xs:element name="NewDataSet">
<xs:complexType>
<xs:sequence>
<xs:element minOccurs="0" maxOccurs="unbounded" name="Table">
<xs:complexType>
<xs:sequence>
<xs:element minOccurs="0" name="CITY" type="xs:string" />
<xs:element minOccurs="0" name="STATE" type="xs:string" />
<xs:element minOccurs="0" name="ZIP" type="xs:unsignedShort" />
<xs:element minOccurs="0" name="AREA_CODE" type=
    "xs:unsignedShort" />
<xs:element minOccurs="0" name="TIME_ZONE" type="xs:string" />
</xs:sequence>
</xs:complexType>
</xs:element>
</xs:sequence>
</xs:complexType>
</xs:element>
</xs:schema>
```

Notice that the XSD generator is not perfect. It can only predict a data type based on what it sees in the data. Not to give the generator anthropomorphic qualities, but the `ZIP` *and* `AREA_CODE` *data elements "look" like numeric values to the generator. You should always examine the XSD that is created and edit it accordingly. Change the sequence element lines for* `ZIP` *and* `AREA_CODE` *to look like this:*

```
<xs:element minOccurs="0" name="ZIP" type="xs:string " />
<xs:element minOccurs="0" name="AREA_CODE" type=" xs:string" />
```

Now if you refresh the XML Source and select the Columns tab, as shown in Figure 3-16, you should be able to see the columns extracted from the physical XML file.

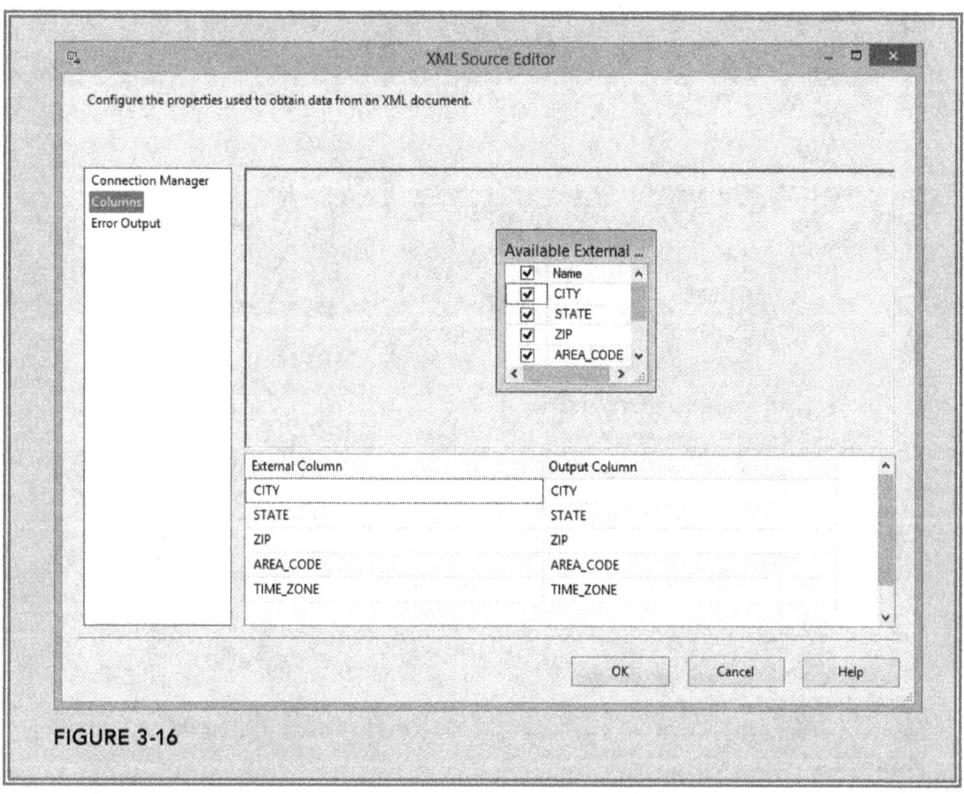

FIGURE 3-16

6. To complete the package, add a Flat File Destination to dump the data into a comma-separated file (CSV file).
7. Connect the output pipeline of the XML source to the Flat File Destination.
8. Click the New button next to the Connection Manager dropdown box to create a new Flat File Connection Manager. Place the file somewhere in the `C:\ProSSIS\Tasks\WebSVC` directory and call it whatever you'd like, as shown in Figure 3-17.
9. Click OK to go back to the Flat File Destination and then click the Mappings tab to confirm that the columns map appropriately (straight arrows between the left and right). If you save and run the package, it will download the XML file into a variable, and then export the columns and rows to a flat file.

This is hardly a robust example, but it demonstrates that the Web Service Task makes retrieving data from a web service a very simple point-and-click task. However, the Web Service Task can retrieve only the results of a web service call. You may find that you need to prepare, extract, or validate your XML files before running them through your ETL processes. This is where the XML Task comes in.

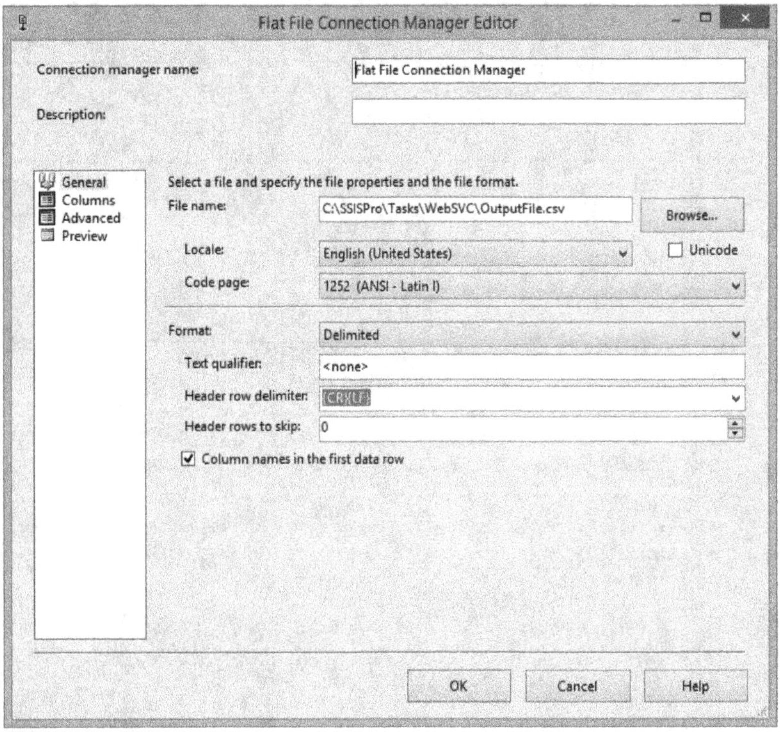

FIGURE 3-17

XML Task

The XML Task is used when you need to validate, modify, extract, or even create files in an XML format. Earlier we used a Web Service Task to retrieve data in an XML-formatted web service response. In terms of validating this type of XML result, the WSDL that you copy down locally is your contract with the web service, which will break if the XML contents of the results change. In other situations, you may be provided with XML data from a third-party source outside of a contractual relationship. In these cases, it is a good practice to validate the XML file against the schema definition before processing the file. This provides an opportunity to handle the issue programmatically.

If you look at the task in Figure 3-18, the editor looks simple. There are two tabs: only one for General configuration and the obligatory Expressions tab.

The current OperationType is set in this example to the Diff operation. This option is one of the more involved operations and requires two XML sources, one as the Input and the other as the Second Operand. However, these properties change based on the selection you make for the OperationType property. The options are as follows:

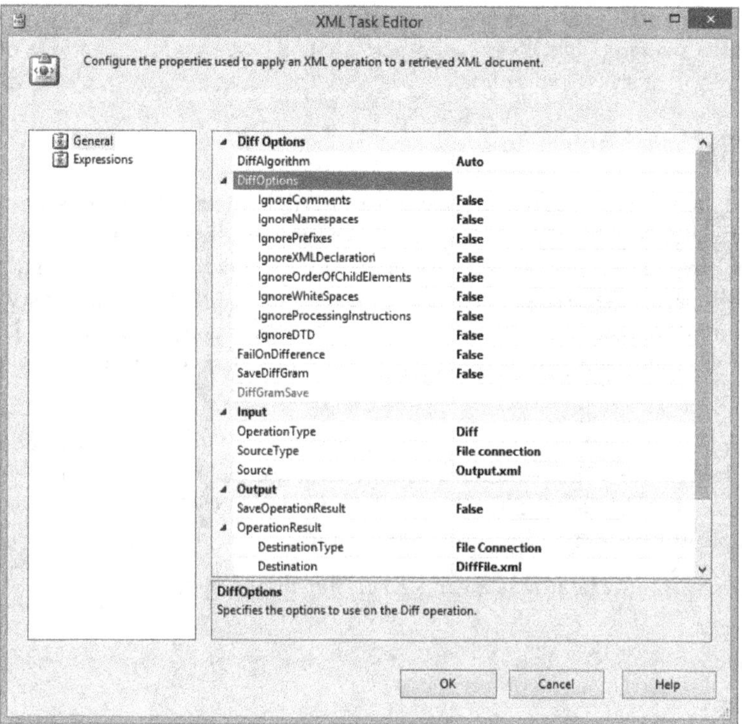

FIGURE 3-18

- **Validate:** This option allows for the schema validation of an XML file against Document Type Definition (DTD) or XML Schema Definition (XSD) binding control documents. You can use this option to ensure that a provided XML file adheres to your expected document format.
- **XSLT:** The Extensible Stylesheet Language Transformations (XSLT) are a subset of the XML language that enables transformation of XML data. You might use this operation at the end of an ETL process to take the resulting data and transform it to meet a presentation format.
- **XPATH:** This option uses the XML Path Language and allows the extraction of sections or specific nodes from the structure of the XML document. You might use this option to extract data from the XML document prior to using the content. For example, you might want to pull out only the orders for a specific customer from an XML file.
- **Merge:** This option allows for the merging of two XML documents with the same structure. You might use this option to combine the results of two extracts from disparate systems into one document.
- **Diff:** This option uses difference algorithms to compare two XML documents to produce a third document called an *XML Diffgram* that contains the differences between them. Use this option with another XML Task using the Patch option to produce a smaller subset of data to insert into your data store. An example use of this task is extracting only the prices that have changed from a new price sheet in XML format.
- **Patch:** This option applies the results of a Diff operation to an XML document to create a new XML document.

As you might expect, you can configure the task to use either a file source or a variable. The option to input the XML directly is also available, but it's not as practical. The best way to get an idea of how this task can be used is to look at a few examples.

Validating an XML File

First up is a basic use case that demonstrates how to validate the internal schema format of an XML file. To make sure you are clear on what the XML Task does for you, the validation is not about whether the XML file is properly formed but about whether it contains the proper internal elements. If an XML file is malformed, then simply attempting to load the XML file in the task will generate an error. However, if a missing node is defined within the XSD contract, the XML Task Validation option will inform you that the XML file provided doesn't meet the conditions of the XSD validation.

For this example, we'll borrow the information from the XML and XSD files in the Web Service Task example. Recall that we had an XSD that validated a string node for `City`, `State`, `Zip`, `Area_Code`, and `Time_Zone`. (See the Web Service Task example to view the XSD format.) You can download this complete example at `www.wrox.com/go/prossis2014`.

We'll use three files to exercise this task. The first is a valid XML file named `MyGetZipsData.xml` that looks like this:

```
<?xml version="1.0" encoding="utf-16"?>
<NewDataSet xmlns="">
<Table>
<CITY>Saint Augustine</CITY>
<STATE>FL</STATE>
<ZIP>32084</ZIP>
<AREA_CODE>904</AREA_CODE>
<TIME_ZONE>E</TIME_ZONE>
</Table>
</NewDataSet>
```

The second file is an invalid XML file named `MyGetZipsData_Bad.xml`. This file has an improperly named node `<CITYZ>` that doesn't match the XSD specification:

```
<?xml version="1.0" encoding="utf-16"?>
<NewDataSet xmlns="">
<Table>
<CITYZ>Saint Augustine</CITYZ>
<STATE>FL</STATE>
<ZIP>32084</ZIP>
<AREA_CODE>904</AREA_CODE>
<TIME_ZONE>E</TIME_ZONE>
</Table>
</NewDataSet>
```

The last file is a malformed XML file named `MyGetZipsData_ReallyBad.xml`. This file has an empty `<Table>` node and is not a valid XML format:

```
<?xml version="1.0" encoding="utf-16"?>
<NewDataSet xmlns="">
<Table></Table>
<CITY>Saint Augustine</CITY>
```

```
<STATE>FL</STATE>
<ZIP>32084</ZIP>
<AREA_CODE>904</AREA_CODE>
<TIME_ZONE>E</TIME_ZONE>
</Table>
</NewDataSet>
```

For this example, follow these steps:

1. Create a package and add a new XML Task to the Control Flow surface.
2. Select the OperationType of Validate, set the Input Source Type to a new file connection, and browse to select the MyGetZipsData.xml file.
3. Expand the OperationResult property in the Output section to configure an additional text file to capture the results of the validation. The result values are only true or false, so you only need a simple text file to see how this works. Typically, you store the result in a variable, so you can test the results to determine the next action to take after validation.
4. Set the OverwriteDestination property to True to allow the result to be overwritten in each run of the task.
5. In the Second Operand, you'll need to create another file connection to the XSD file. This will be used for validation of the schema.
6. Create another file connection using an existing file that points to this XSD file.
7. Finally, set the validation type to XSD, as we are using an XSD file to validate the XML. The editor at this point should look like Figure 3-19.

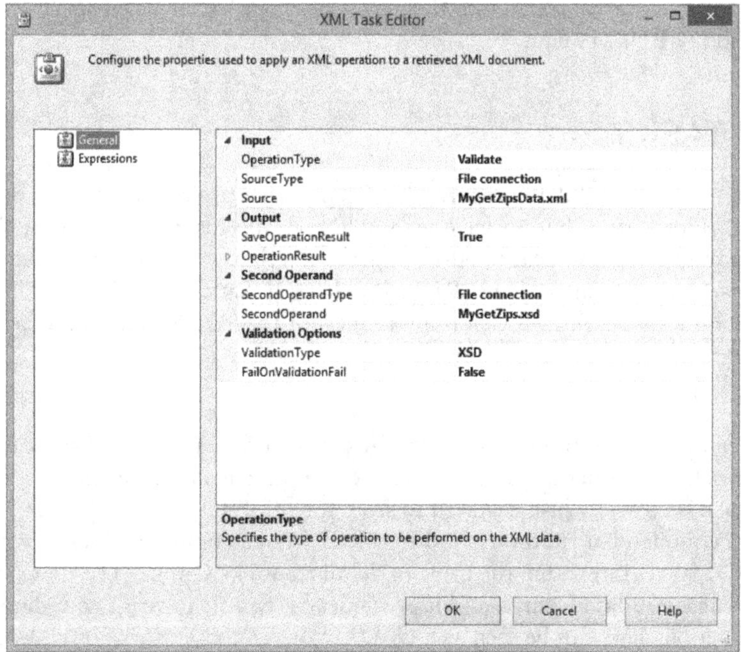

FIGURE 3-19

This completes the happy path use case. If you execute this task, it should execute successfully, and the results file should contain the value of `true` to indicate that the XML file contains the correct schema as defined by the XSD file. Now on to the true test:

8. Change the source to a new connection for the `MyGetZipsData_Bad.xml` file.
9. Execute the task again. This time, although the task completes successfully, the result file contains the value of `false` to indicate a bad schema. This is really the whole point of the Validation option.
10. Finally, change the source to create a new connection to the poorly formatted XML file `MyGetZipsData_ReallyBad.xml` to see what happens. In this case, the task actually fails — even though the Validation option's FailOnValidationFail property is set to False. This is because the validation didn't fail — the loading of the XML file failed. The error message indicates the problem accurately:

```
[XML Task] Error: An error occurred with the following error message:
"The 'NewDataSet' start tag on line 2 does not match the end tag of
 'Table'. Line 9, position 5.".
[XML Task] Error: An error occurred with the following error message: "Root
element is missing.".
```

Just be aware of the difference between validating the schema and validating the XML file itself when designing your package Control Flows, and set up accordingly. You need to have a Control Flow for the failure of the task and for the successful completion with a failure result.

This is just one example demonstrating how you can use the XML Task for SSIS development. There are obviously several other uses for this task that are highly legitimate and useful for preparing data to feed into your SSIS ETL package Data Flows. The next section turns to another set of data preparation tasks, which we have separated into their own category, as they deal specifically with retrieval and preparation of RDBMS data.

RDBMS SERVER TASKS

These tasks could also be considered data preparation tasks, as they are responsible for bringing data sources into the ETL processes, but we have separated the Bulk Insert Task and the Execute SQL Task into this separate category because of the expectation that you will be working with data from relational database management systems (RDBMS) like SQL Server, Oracle, and DB2. The exception to this is the Bulk Insert Task, which is a wrapper for the SQL Server bulk-copy process.

Bulk Insert Task

The Bulk Insert Task enables you to insert data from a text or flat file into a SQL Server database table in the same high-octane manner as using a `BULK INSERT` statement or the `bcp.exe` command-line tool. In fact, the task is basically just a wizard to store the information needed to create and execute a bulk copying command at runtime (similar to BCP from a command line). If you aren't familiar with using BCP, you can research the topic in detail in Books Online. The downside of the Bulk Insert Task is its strict data format, and it precludes being able to work with data in a Data Flow within one action. This can be seen as a disadvantage in that it does not allow any transformations to occur to the data in flight, but not all ETL processes are efficiently modified in the Data Flow. In high-volume extracts, you may be better served by loading the initial extract down in a staging table and extracting data in discrete chunks for processing within specific Data Flows. The Bulk Insert Task has no ability to transform data, and this trade-off in functionality gives you the fastest way to load data from a text file into a SQL Server database.

When you add a Bulk Insert Task to your Control Flow, follow these steps:

1. Open the Bulk Insert Task Editor to configure it. As in most tasks, use the General tab to name and describe the task. Make sure you name it something that describes its unit of work, like **Prepare Staging**. This will be helpful later when you deploy the package and troubleshoot problems.

   The next tab, Connection, is the most important. This tab enables you to specify the source and destination for the data.

2. Select the destination from the Connection dropdown in the Destination Connection group.
3. Specify a destination table from the next dropdown, below the destination connection.
4. While you're specifying connections, go to the bottom to specify the source connection's filename in the File dropdown. Both the source and the destination connections use the Connection Manager. If you haven't already created the shared connections, you'll be prompted to create them in either case by selecting <New Connection ...>.

> **NOTE** *Both the source and the optional format file must be relative to the destination SQL Server, because the operation occurs there when a Bulk Insert Task is used. If you are using a network file location, use the UNC path* (`\\MachineName\ShareName\FileName.csv`) *to the source or format file.*

5. After you specify the connections, you need to provide file specifications for the format of file you're importing. If you created the file using the BCP utility, you can use the `-f` option to create a format file as well. The Bulk Insert Task can then use the BCP format file to determine how the file is formatted, or you can select the column and row delimiters in the Format property of the task. The two options are:
   - **Use File:** This uses the BCP format (`.fmt`) file.
   - **Specify:** This enables you to select the file delimiters. The available delimiters are New Line ({CR}{LF}), Carriage Return ({CR}), Line Feed ({LF}), Semicolon (;), Comma (,), Tab, or Vertical Bar (|). Note that the defaults are for the row to be {CR}{LF} delimited, and the column tab-delimited.
6. In the Options tab of the Bulk Insert Task Editor, you can use some lesser-known options:
   - **Code page:** You can specify the code page for the source file. You will rarely want to change the code page from RAW, which is the default. Using RAW is the fastest data-loading option because no code page conversion takes place.
   - **OEM:** You should use this when copying from one SQL Server to another.

- **ACP:** This converts non-Unicode data to the ANSI code page of the SQL Server you are loading the data into, or you can specify a specific code page mapping.
- **DataFileType:** Specifies the type of the source file. Options here include char, native, widechar, and widenative. Generally, files you receive will be the default option, char, but in some cases, you may see a file with a native format.

A file (`myzips_native.txt`) in native format was created from SQL Server by using the `bcp.exe` program with the `-n` (native) switch and supplied with the download from `www.wrox.com/go/prossis2014`. You'll see how to import it later in an example.

You can also use the Options tab to specify the first and last row to copy if you want only a sampling of the rows. This is commonly used to set the first row to two (2) when you want to skip a header row. The BatchSize option indicates how many records will be written to SQL Server before committing the batch. A BatchSize of 0 (the default) means that all the records will be written to SQL Server in a single batch. If you have more than 100,000 records, then you may want to adjust this setting to 50,000 or another number based on how many you want to commit at a time. The adjustment may vary based on the width of your file.

The Options dropdown contains five options that you can enable/disable:

- **Check Constraints:** This option checks table and column constraints before committing the record. It is the only option enabled by default.
- **Keep Nulls:** By selecting this option, the Bulk Insert Task will replace any empty columns in the source file with `NULL`s in SQL Server.
- **Enable Identity Insert:** Enable this option if your destination table has an identity column into which you're inserting. Otherwise, you will receive an error.
- **Table Lock:** This option creates a SQL Server lock on the target table, preventing inserts and updates other than the records you are inserting. This option speeds up your process but may cause a production outage, as others are blocked from modifying the table. If you check this option, SSIS will not have to compete for locks to insert massive amounts of data into the target table. Set this option only if you're certain that no other process will be competing with your task for table access.
- **Fire Triggers:** By default, the Bulk Insert Task ignores triggers for maximum speed. When you check this option, the task will no longer ignore triggers and will instead fire the insert triggers for the table into which you're inserting.

There are a few other options you can set in the Options tab. The SortedData option specifies what column you wish to sort by while inserting the data. This option defaults to sort nothing, which equals `false`. If you need to set this option, type the column name that you wish to sort. The MaxErrors option specifies how many errors are acceptable before the task is stopped with an error. Each row that does not insert is considered an error; by default, if a single row has a problem, the entire task fails.

> **NOTE** *The Bulk Insert Task does not log error-causing rows. If you want bad records to be written to an error file or table, it's better to use the Data Flow Task.*

Using the Bulk Insert Task

Take time out briefly to exercise the Bulk Insert Task with a typical data load by following these steps:

1. Create a new package called BulkInsertTask.dtsx. If you haven't already downloaded the code files for this chapter from `www.wrox.com/go/prossis2014`, do so. Then extract the file for this chapter named `myzips.csv`.
2. Create a table in the AdventureWorksDW database using SQL Management Studio or the tool of your choice to store postal code information (code file `Ch03SQL.txt`):

    ```
    CREATE TABLE PROSSIS_ZIPCODE (
    ZipCode CHAR(5),
    State CHAR(2),
    ZipName VARCHAR(16)
    )
    ```

3. Back in your new package, drag the Bulk Insert Task onto the Control Flow design pane. Notice that the task has a red icon on it, indicating that it hasn't been configured yet.
4. Double-click the task to open the editor. In the General tab, provide the name **Load Zip Codes** for the Name option and **Loads zip codes from a flat file** for the description.
5. Click the Connection tab. From the Connection dropdown box, select<New connection ...>. This will open the Configure OLE DB Connection Manager dialog.
6. Now, you're going to create a connection to the AdventureWorksDW database that can be reused throughout this chapter. Click New to add a new Connection Manager. For the Server Name option, select the server that contains your AdventureWorksDW database. For the database, select the AdventureWorksDW database.
7. Click OK to go back to the previous screen, and click OK again to return to the Bulk Insert Task Editor.

    You'll now see that the Connection Manager you just created has been transposed into the Connection dropdown box.

8. Now you need to define the destination. For the DestinationTable option, select the [dbo].[PROSSIS_ZIPCODE] table. For the first attempt, you'll import a comma-delimited version of the zip codes. This simulates importing a file that would have been dumped out of another SQL Server (with the same table name) using this `bcp` command:

    ```
    bcp AdventureWorksDW.dbo.prossis_zipcode out
        c:\ProSSIS\tasks\bulkInsertTask\myzips.csv
    -c -t, -T
    ```

9. Leave the remaining options set to the defaults. The RowDelimiter property option will be {CR}{LF} (a carriage return) and the ColumnDelimiter property should be set to Comma {,}.

10. For the File option, again select <New connection ...> to create a new Connection Manager. This will open the File Connection Manager Editor.

11. For the Usage Type, select Existing File. Then point to `myZips.csv` for the File option. Click OK to return to the editor. Your final Bulk Insert Task Editor screen should look similar to Figure 3-20.

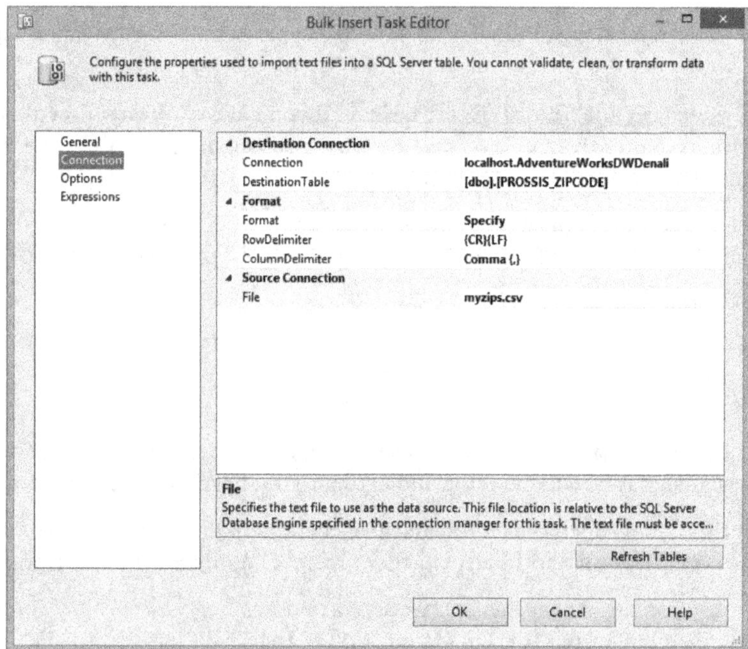

FIGURE 3-20

If you open the `myzips.csv` file, you'll notice there is no header row with the column names before the data. If you had a column header and needed to skip it, you would go to the Options tab and change the FirstRow option to 2. This would start the import process on the second row, instead of the first, which is the default.

12. You should be able to run the package now. When it executes, the table will be populated with all the postal codes from the import file. You can verify this by selecting all the rows from the PROSSIS_ZIPS table.

As you can see, the Bulk Insert Task is a useful tool to load staging files quickly, but you may need to further process the file. One reason is because this task provides no opportunity to divert the data into a transformation workflow to examine the quality of the data. Another reason is that you have to import character-based data to avoid raising errors during the loading process. The Bulk Insert Task handles errors in an all-or-nothing manner. If a single row fails to insert, then your task may fail (based on your setting for the maximum number of allowed errors). These problems can be easily solved by using a Data Flow Task if the data is unreliable.

Execute SQL Task

The Execute SQL Task is one of the most widely used tasks in SSIS for interacting with an RDBMS Data Source. The Execute SQL Task is used for all sorts of things, including truncating a staging data table prior to importing, retrieving row counts to determine the next step in a workflow, or calling stored procedures to perform business logic against sets of staged data. This task is also used to retrieve information from a database repository. The Execute SQL Task is also found in the legacy DTS product, but the SSIS version provides a better configuration editor and methods to map stored procedure parameters to read back result and output values.

This section introduces you to all the possible ways to configure this task by working through the different ways you can use it. You'll work through how to execute parameterized SQL statements or execute batches of SQL statements, how to capture single-row and multiple-row results, and how to execute stored procedures.

Executing a Parameterized SQL Statement

The task can execute a SQL command in two basic ways: by executing inline SQL statements or by executing stored procedures. The resulting action can also result in the need to perform one of two options: accepting return values in parameters or a result set. You can get an idea of how the task can be configured to do these combinations in the General tab of the Execute SQL Task Editor, shown in Figure 3-21. Here, the Execute SQL Task is set to perform an Update operation on the DimProduct table using an inline SQL statement with a variable-based parameter. This is the easiest use of the Execute SQL Task because you don't need to configure the Result Set tab properties.

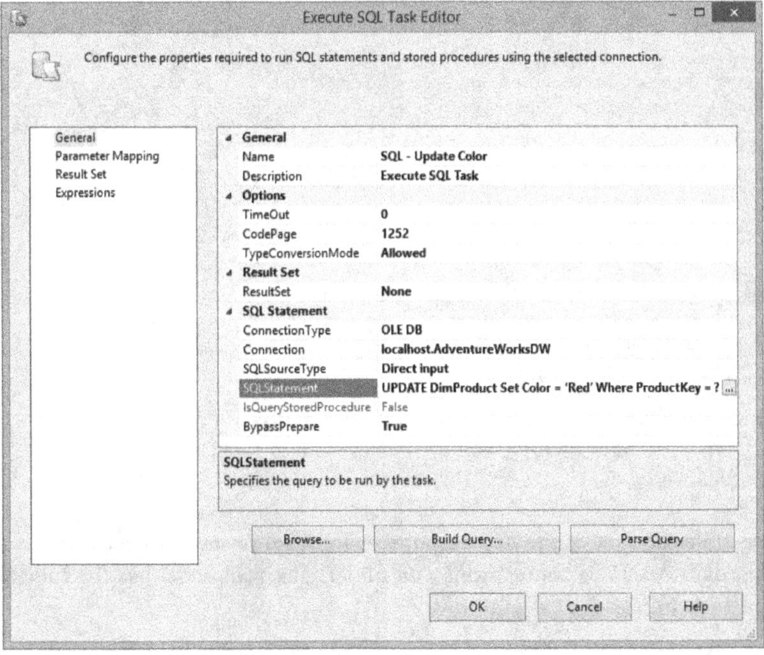

FIGURE 3-21

Notice in Figure 3-21 that the General tab contains the core properties of the task. Here the task is configured to point to an OLE DB connection. The other options for the ConnectionType include ODBC, ADO, ADO.NET, SQLMOBILE, and even EXCEL connections. The catch to all this connection flexibility is that the Execute SQL Task behaves differently depending upon the underlying data provider. For example, the SQLStatement property in Figure 3-21 shows a directly inputted T-SQL statement with a question mark in the statement. The full statement is here:

```
UPDATE DimProduct Set Color = 'Red' Where ProductKey = ?
```

This `?`, which indicates that a parameter is required, is classic ODBC parameter marking and is used in most of the other providers — with the exception of the ADO.NET provider, which uses named parameters. This matters, because in the task, you need to configure the parameters to the SQL statement in the Parameter Mapping tab, as shown in Figure 3-22.

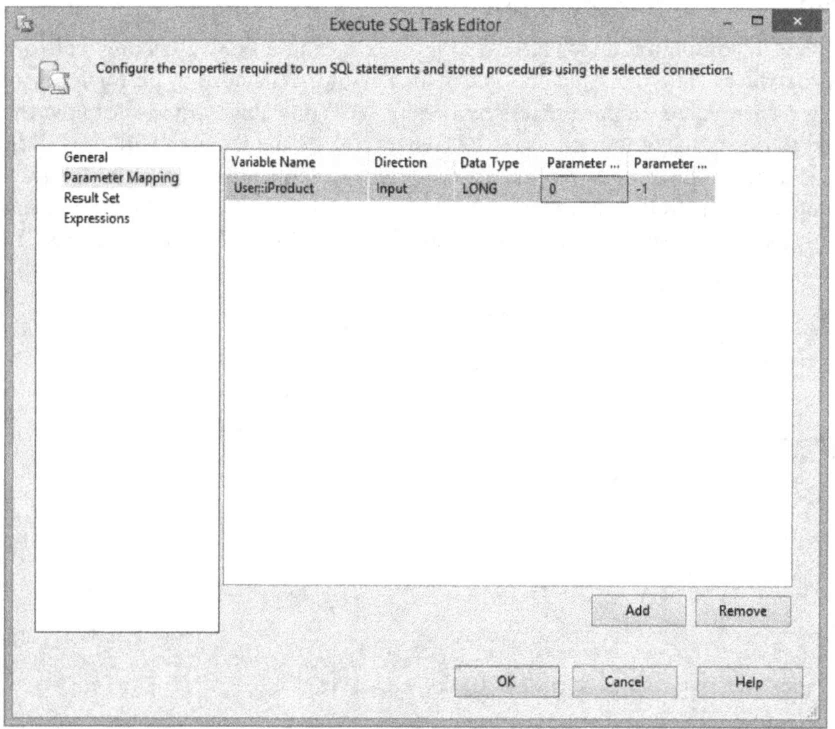

FIGURE 3-22

Here the parameter mapping collection maps the first parameter [ordinal position of zero (0)] to a user variable. When mapping parameters to connections and underlying providers, use the following table to set up this tab in the Task Editor:

IF USING CONNECTION OF TYPE	PARAMETER MARKER TO USE	PARAMETER NAME TO USE
ADO	?	Param1, Param2, ...
ADO.NET	@<Real Param Name>	@<Real Param Name>
ODBC	?	1, 2, 3 (note ordinal starts at 1)
OLEDB and EXCEL	?	0, 1, 2, 3 (note ordinal starts at 0)

Because we are using an OLE DB provider here, the parameter marker is ?, and the parameter is using the zero-based ordinal position. The other mapping you would have needed to do here is for the data type of the parameter. These data types also vary according to your underlying provider. SSIS is very specific about how you map data types, so you may need to experiment or check Books Online for the mapping equivalents for your parameters and provider. We'll cover many of the common issues in this regard throughout this section, but for this initial example, we mapped the System::ContainerStartTime to the OLE DB data type of DATE. At this point, the Execute SQL Task with this simple update statement could be executed, and the ModifyDate would be updated in the database with a current datetime value.

A variation of this example would be a case in which the statement can be dynamically generated at runtime and simply fired into the Connection Manager. The SQLSourceType property on the General tab allows for three different types of SQL statement resolution: either directly input (as we did), via a variable, or from a file connection. Another way to build the SQL statement is to use the Build Query action button. This brings up a Query-By-Example (QBE) tool that helps you build a query by clicking the tables and establishing the relationships. The variable-based option is also straightforward. Typically, you define a variable that is resolved from an expression. Setting the SQLSourceType property in the Execute SQL Task to Variable enables you to select the variable that will resolve to the SQL statement that you want the task to execute.

The other option, using a file connection, warrants a little more discussion.

Executing a Batch of SQL Statements

If you use the File Connection option of the Execute SQL Task's SQLSourceType property, typically you are doing so to execute a batch of SQL statements. All you need to do is have the file that contains the batch of SQL statements available to the SSIS package during runtime. Set up a File Connection to point to the batch file you need to run. Make sure that your SQL batch follows a few rules. Some of these rules are typical SQL rules, like using a GO command between statements, but others are specific to the SSIS Execute SQL Task. Use these rules as a guide for executing a batch of SQL statements:

- Use GO statements between each distinct command. Note that some providers allow you to use the semicolon (;) as a command delimiter.
- If there are multiple parameterized statements in the batch, all parameters must match in type and order.
- Only one statement can return a result, and it must be the first statement.

- If the batch returns a result, then the columns must match the same number and properly named result columns for the Execute SQL Task. If the two don't match and you have subsequent `UPDATE` or `DELETE` statements in the batch, these will execute even though the results don't bind, and an error results. The batch is sent to SQL Server to execute and behaves the same way.

Returning results is something that we haven't explored in the Execute SQL Task, so let's look at some examples that do this in SSIS.

Capturing Singleton Results

On the General tab of the Execute SQL Task, you can set up the task to capture the type of result that you expect to have returned by configuring the ResultSet property. This property can be set to return nothing, or None, a singleton result set, a multi-line result, or an XML-formatted string. Any setting other than None requires configuration of the Result Set tab on the editor. In the Result Set tab, you are defining the binding of returned values into a finite set of SSIS variables. For most data type bindings, this is not an issue. You select the SSIS variable data type that most closely matches that of your provider. The issues that arise from this activity are caused by invalid casting that occurs as data in the Tabular Data Stream (TDS) from the underlying provider collides with the variable data types to which they are being assigned. This casting happens internally within the Execute SQL Task, and you don't have control over it as you would in a Script Task. Before you assume that it is just a simple data type–assignment issue, you need to understand that SSIS is the lowest common denominator when it comes to being able to bind to data types from all the possible data providers. For example, SSIS doesn't have a currency or decimal data type. The only thing close is the `double` data type, which is the type that must be used for real, numeric, current, decimal, float, and other similar data types.

The next example sets up a simple inline SQL statement that returns a single row (or singleton result) to show both the normal cases and the exception cases for configuring the Execute SQL Task and handling these binding issues. First, we'll use a simple T-SQL statement against the AdventureWorks database that looks like this (code file `Ch03SQL.txt`):

```
SELECT TOP 1
CarrierTrackingNumber,
LineTotal,
OrderQty,
UnitPrice
From Sales.SalesOrderDetail
```

We've chosen this odd result set because of the multiple data types in the SalesOrderDetail table. These data types provide an opportunity to highlight some of the solutions to difficulties with mapping these data types in the Execute SQL Task that we've been helping folks with since the first release of SSIS.

To capture these columns from this table, you need to create some variables in the package. Then these variables will be mapped one-for-one to the result columns. Some of the mappings are simple. The CarrierTrackingNumber can be easily mapped to a string variable data type with either nvarchar or varchar data types in the Execute SQL Task. The OrderQty field, which is using the smallint SQL Server data type, needs to be mapped to an int16 SSIS data type. Failure to map the data type correctly will result in an error like this:

```
[Execute SQL Task] Error: An error occurred while assigning a value to variable
"OrderQty": "The type of the value being assigned to variable "User::OrderQty"
differs from the current variable type. Variables may not change type during
execution. Variable types are strict, except for variables of type Object."
```

The other two values, for the SQL Server UnitPrice (money) and LineTotal (numeric) columns, are more difficult. The closest equivalent variable data type in SSIS is a double data type.

Now the parameters can simply be mapped in the Execute SQL Task Result Set tab, as shown in Figure 3-23. The Result Name property maps to the column name in your SQL statement or its ordinal position (starting at 0).

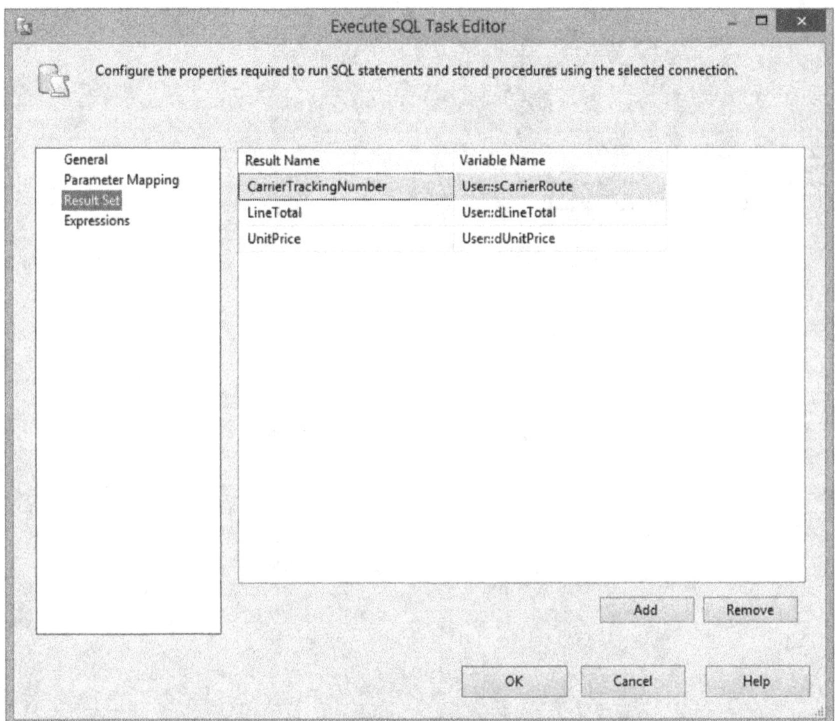

FIGURE 3-23

Just use the Add and Remove buttons to put the result elements in the order that they should be returned, name them according to the provider requirements, and get the right data types, and you'll be fine. If these are in the incorrect order, or if the data types can't be cast by the Execute SQL Task from the TDS into the corresponding variable data type, you will get a binding error. This should give you a general guide to using the Execute SQL Task for capturing singleton results.

Multi-Row Results

Typically, you capture multi-row results from a database as a recordset or an XML file (particularly between SQL Server Data Sources) to use in another Script Task for analysis or decision-making purposes, to provide an enumerator in a Foreach or Looping Task, or to feed into a Data Flow Task for processing. Set up the SQLSourceType and SQLStatement properties to call either an inline SQL statement or a stored procedure. In either case, you would set the ResultSet property in the General tab to Full Result Set, and the Result Set tab is set up to capture the results. The only difference from capturing a singleton result is that you need to capture the entire result into a variable, rather than map each column. The data type you should use to capture the results varies according to what you are capturing. The XML file can be captured in either a string or an object data type. The recordset can only be captured in a variable with the object data type. An example of the Execute SQL Task configured to create an object data type to store the results of a selection of rows from the Sales. SalesOrderDetail table is shown in Figure 3-24. Note that the Result Set tab shows the capturing of these rows with the required zero-ordinal position.

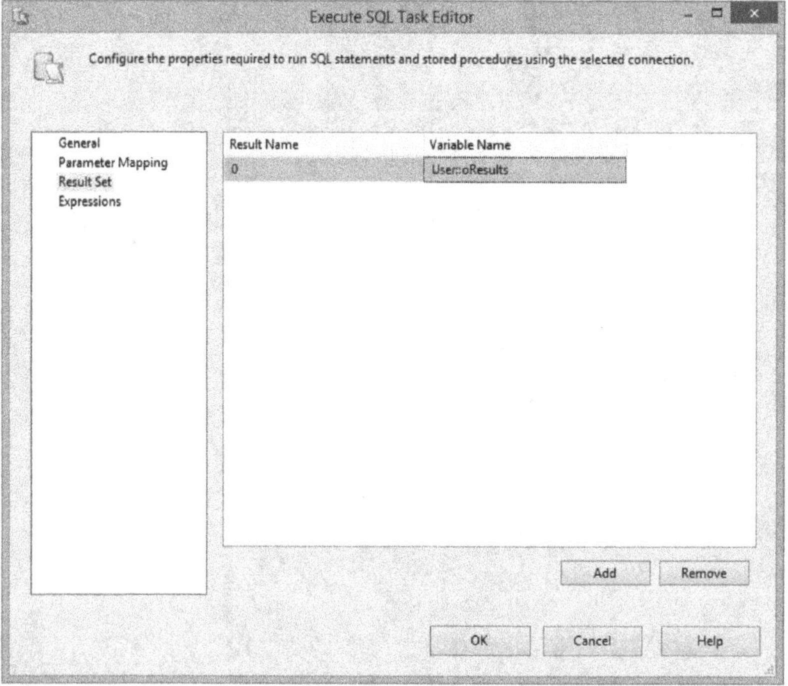

FIGURE 3-24

Once the recordset is stored as a variable, you can do things like "shred" the recordset. The term *shredding* means iterating through the recordset one row at a time in a Foreach Loop operation. For each iteration, you can capture the variables from, and perform an operation on, each row. Figure 3-25 shows how the Foreach Loop Container would look using the variable-based recordset. This container is covered in detail in Chapter 6.

Another way to use the variable-based recordset is to use it to feed a data transform. To do this, just create a Source Script Transform in a Data Flow and add to it the columns that you want to realize from the stored recordset and pass in the recordset variable. Then add code (code file `Ch03SQL.txt`) similar to the following to turn the column data from the recordset into the output stream (to save time and space, only two columns are being realized in the recordset):

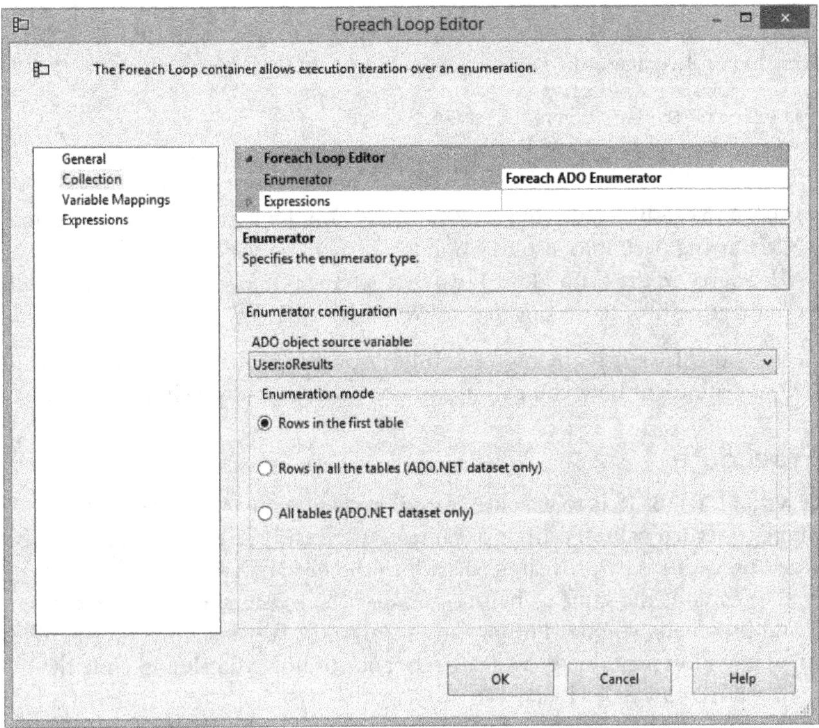

FIGURE 3-25

C#

```
public override void CreateNewOutputRows()
{
System.Data.OleDb.OleDbDataAdapter oleDA =
new System.Data.OleDb.OleDbDataAdapter();
System.Data.DataTable dT = new System.Data.DataTable();
oleDA.Fill(dT, Variables.RecordSetResult);
foreach (DataRow dr in dT.Rows)
{
Output0Buffer.AddRow();
//by Name
Output0Buffer.CarrierTrackingNumber =
dr["CarrierTrackingNumber"].ToString();
//by Ordinal
Output0Buffer.UnitPrice = System.Convert.ToDecimal(dr[6]);
}
}
```

VB

```
Public Overrides Sub CreateNewOutputRows()
Dim oleDA As New System.Data.OleDb.OleDbDataAdapter()
Dim dT As New System.Data.DataTable()
Dim row As System.Data.DataRow
oleDA.Fill(dt, Variables.RecordSetResult)
```

```
For Each row In dT.Rows
Output0Buffer.AddRow()
Output0Buffer.CarrierTrackingNumber = _
row("CarrierTrackingNumber").ToString()
Output0Buffer.UnitPrice = System.Convert.ToDecimal(row(6))
Next
End Sub
```

The XML version of capturing the result in a string is even easier. You don't need to use the Script Component to turn the XML string back into a source of data. Instead, use the out-of-the-box component called the XML Source in the Data Flow. It can accept a variable as the source of the data. (Review the example demonstrating how to do this in the "Web Service Task" section of this chapter.)

You can see that the Execute SQL Task is really quite useful at executing inline SQL statements and retrieving results, so now take a look at how you can use stored procedures as well in this task.

Executing a Stored Procedure

Another way to interact with an RDBMS is to execute stored procedures that can perform operations on a data source to return values, output parameters, or results. Set up the SSIS Execute SQL Task to execute stored procedures by providing the call to the proc name in the General tab's SQLStatement property. The catch is the same as before. Because the Execute SQL Task sits on top of several different data providers, you need to pay attention to the way each provider handles the stored procedure call. The following table provides a reference to how you should code the SQLStatement property in the Execute SQL Task:

IF USING CONNECTION TYPE	AND ISQUERYSTOREDPROCEDURE	CODE THE SQL STATEMENT PROPERTY LIKE THIS
OLEDB and EXCEL	N/A	`EXEC usp_StoredProc ?, ?`
ODBC	N/A	`{call usp_StoredProc (?, ?)}`
ADO	false	`EXEC usp_StoredProc ?, ?`
ADO	true	`usp_StoredProc`
ADO.NET	false	`EXEC usp_StoredProc @Parm1, @Parm2`
ADO.NET	true	`usp_StoredProc @Parm1, @Parm2`

Returning to the earlier example in which you used an inline SQL statement to update the modified date in the sales order detail, create a T-SQL stored procedure that does the same thing (code file `Ch03SQL.txt`):

```
CREATE PROCEDURE usp_UpdatePersonAddressModifyDate(
@MODIFIED_DATE DATETIME
)
AS
BEGIN
Update Person.Address
Set ModifiedDate = @MODIFIED_DATE
where AddressId = 1
END
```

In the online downloads for this chapter, we've created a package that demonstrates how to call this procedure using both the OLE DB and the ADO.NET Connection Managers. In the General tab (shown in Figure 3-26), the SQLStatement property is set up as prescribed earlier in the guide, with the `?` parameter markers for the one input parameter. Note also that the IsQueryStoredProcedure property is not enabled. You can't set this property for the OLE DB provider. However, this property would be enabled in the ADO.NET version of the Execute SQL Task to execute this same procedure. If you set the IsQueryStoredProcedure for the ADO.NET version to true, the SQLStatement property would also need to change. Remove the execute command and the parameter markers to look like this: `Usp_UpdatePersonAddressModifyDate`. In this mode, the Execute SQL Task will actually build the complete execution statement using the parameter listing that you'd provide in the Parameter Mapping tab of the Task Editor.

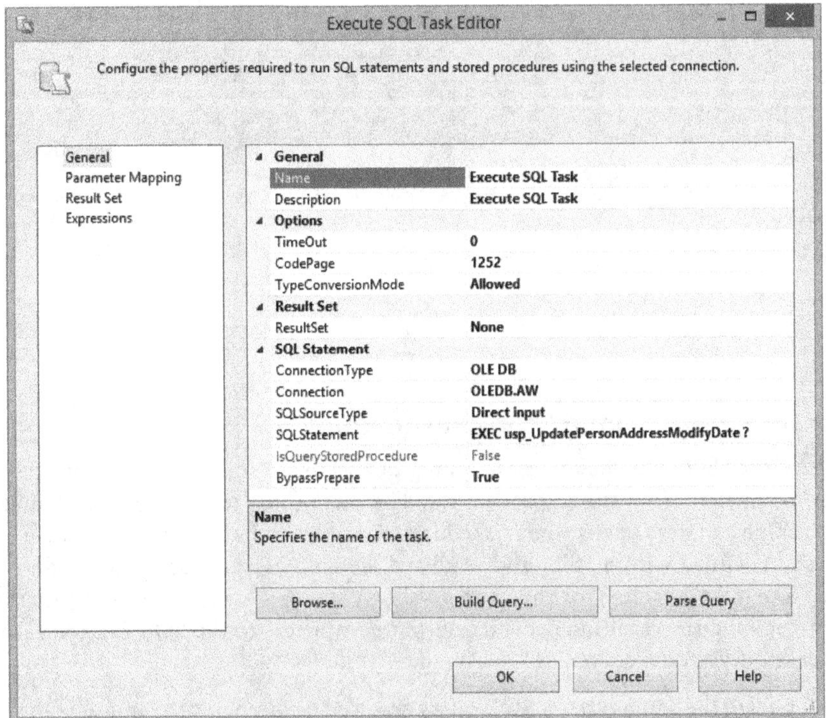

FIGURE 3-26

The Parameter Mapping tab of the Task Editor varies according to the underlying provider set on the Execute SQL Task, as shown in Figure 3-27.

For brevity, this figure just shows an OLE DB connection with parameters. With ADO.NET connections though, the parameter names follow the same rules you used when applying parameters to inline SQL statements earlier in this chapter by changing the Parameter Name option to @MODIFIED_DATE, for example.

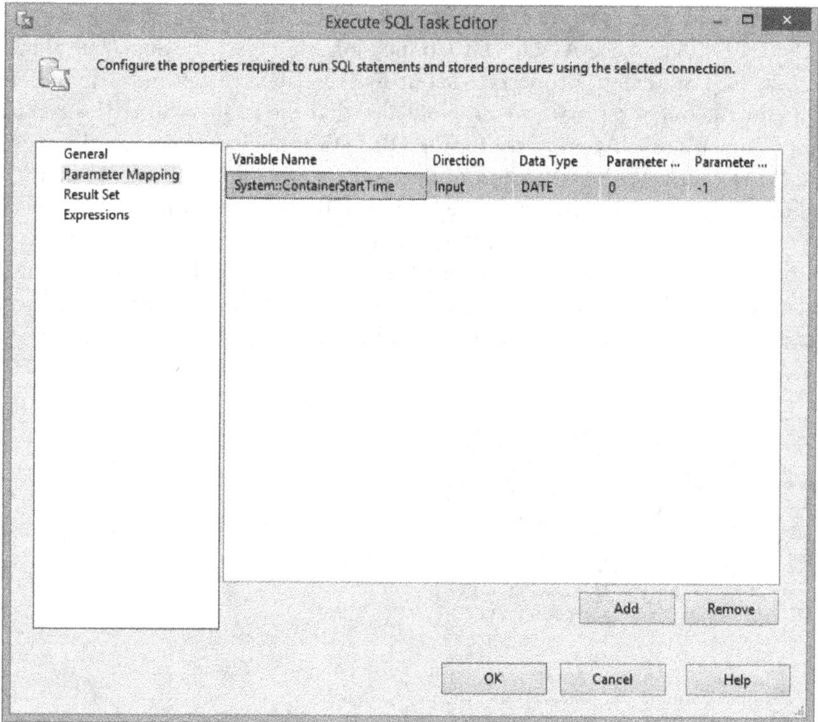

FIGURE 3-27

Retrieving Output Parameters from a Stored Procedure

Mapping input parameters for SQL statements is one thing, but there are some issues to consider when handling output parameters from stored procedures. The main thing to remember is that all retrieved output or return parameters have to be pushed into variables to have any downstream use. The variable types are defined within SSIS, and you have the same issues that we covered in the section "Capturing Singleton Results" for this task. In short, you have to be able to choose the correct variables when you bind the resulting provider output parameters to the SSIS variables, so that you can get a successful type conversion.

As an example, we'll duplicate the same type of SQL query we used earlier with the inline SQL statement to capture a singleton result, but here you'll use a stored procedure object instead. Put the following stored procedure in the AdventureWorks database (code file Ch03SQL.txt):

```
CREATE PROCEDURE usp_GetTop1SalesOrderDetail
(
@CARRIER_TRACKING_NUMBER nvarchar(25) OUTPUT,
@LINE_TOTAL numeric(38,6) OUTPUT,
@ORDER_QTY smallint OUTPUT,
@UNIT_PRICE money OUTPUT
)
AS
BEGIN
```

```
SELECT TOP 1
@CARRIER_TRACKING_NUMBER = CarrierTrackingNumber,
@LINE_TOTAL = LineTotal,
@ORDER_QTY = OrderQty,
@UNIT_PRICE = UnitPrice
From Sales.SalesOrderDetail
END
```

In this contrived example, the stored procedure will provide four different output parameters that you can use to learn how to set up the output parameter bindings. (Integer values are consistent and easy to map across almost all providers, so there is no need to demonstrate that in this example.) One difference between returning singleton output parameters and a singleton row is that in the General tab of the Execute SQL Task, the ResultSet property is set to None, as no row should be returned to capture. Instead, the Parameters in the Parameter Mapping tab will be set to the Direction of Output and the Data Types mapped based on the provider.

To get the defined SQL Server data type parameters to match the SSIS variables, you need to set up the parameters with these mappings:

PARAMETER NAME	SQL SERVER DATA TYPE	SSIS DATA TYPE
@CARRIER_TRACKING_NUMBER	nvarchar	string
@LINE_TOTAL	numeric	double
@ORDER_QTY	smallint	int16
@UNIT_PRICE	money	double

You might assume that you would still have an issue with this binding, because, if you recall, you attempted to return a single-rowset from an inline SQL statement with these same data types and ended up with all types of binding and casting errors. You had to change your inline statement to cast these values to get them to bind. You don't have to do this when binding to parameters, because this casting occurs outside of the Tabular Data Stream. When binding parameters (as opposed to columns in a data stream), the numeric data type will bind directly to the double, so you won't get the error that you would get if the same data were being bound from a rowset. We're not quite sure why this is the case, but fortunately stored procedures don't have to be altered in order to use them in SSIS because of output parameter binding issues.

The remaining task to complete the parameter setup is to provide the correct placeholder for the parameter. Figure 3-28 is an example of the completed parameter setup for the procedure in OLE DB.

At this point, you have looked at every scenario concerning binding to parameters and result sets. Stored procedures can also return multi-row results, but there is really no difference in how you handle these rows from a stored procedure and an inline SQL statement. We covered multi-row scenarios earlier in this section on the Execute SQL Task. Now we will move away from tasks in the RDBMS world and into tasks that involve other controlling external processes such as other packages or applications in the operating system.

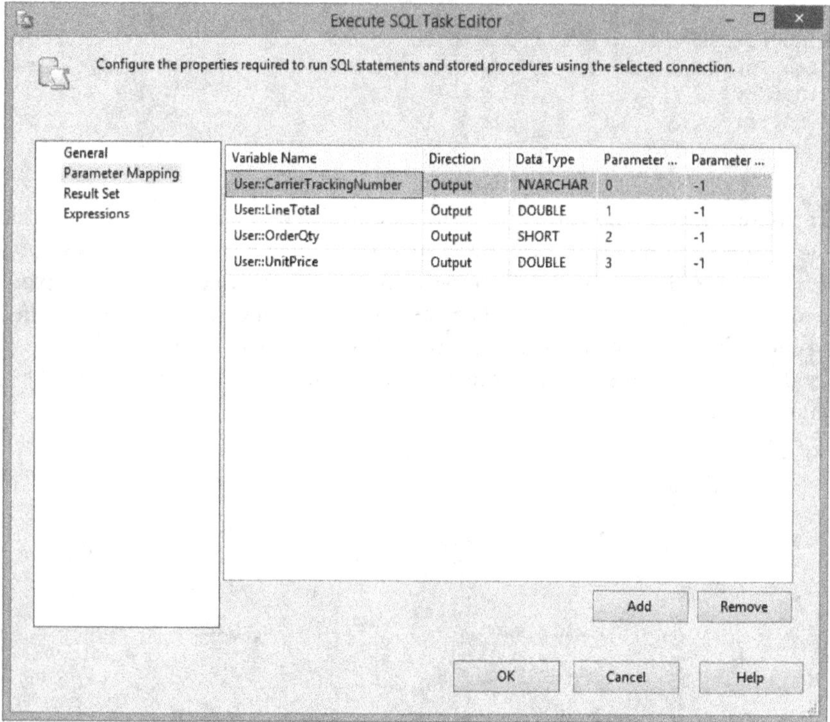

FIGURE 3-28

WORKFLOW TASKS

So far, we've been focused on tasks that are occurring within the immediate realm of ETL processing. You've looked at tasks for creating control structures, preparing data, and performing RDBMS operations. This section looks at being able to control other processes and applications in the operating system. Here we sidestep a bit from typical ETL definitions into things that can be more enterprise application integration (EAI) oriented. SSIS packages can also be organized to execute other packages or to call external programs that zip up files or send e-mail alerts, and even put messages directly into application queues for processing.

Execute Package Task

The Execute Package Task enables you to build SSIS solutions called *parent packages* that execute other packages called *child packages*. You'll find that this capability is an indispensable part of your SSIS development as your packages begin to grow. Separating packages into discrete functional workflows enables shorter development and testing cycles and facilitates best development practices. Though the Execute Package Task has been around since the legacy DTS, several improvements have simplified the task:

- **The child packages can be run as either in-process or out-of-process executables.** In the Package tab of the Execute Package Task Editor is the ExecuteOutOfProcess property; set to the default value of false, it will execute the package in its own process and memory space. A big difference in this release of the task compared to its 2008 or 2005 predecessor is that you execute packages within a project to make migrating the code from development to QA much easier.

- **The task enables you to easily map parameters in the parent package to the child packages now too.**

The majority of configurable properties are in the Package tab of the Execute Package Task Editor. The first option provides the location of the child package. The ReferenceType option can be either External or Project References. This means you can point to a package inside your current project or outside the project to a SQL Server or file system. The best (easiest) option is to refer to a package in a project, as this option will easily "repoint" the reference as you migrate to production. If you point to an External Reference, you'll need to create a Connection Manager that won't automatically repoint as you migrate your packages from development to production. The configured tab will look like Figure 3-29.

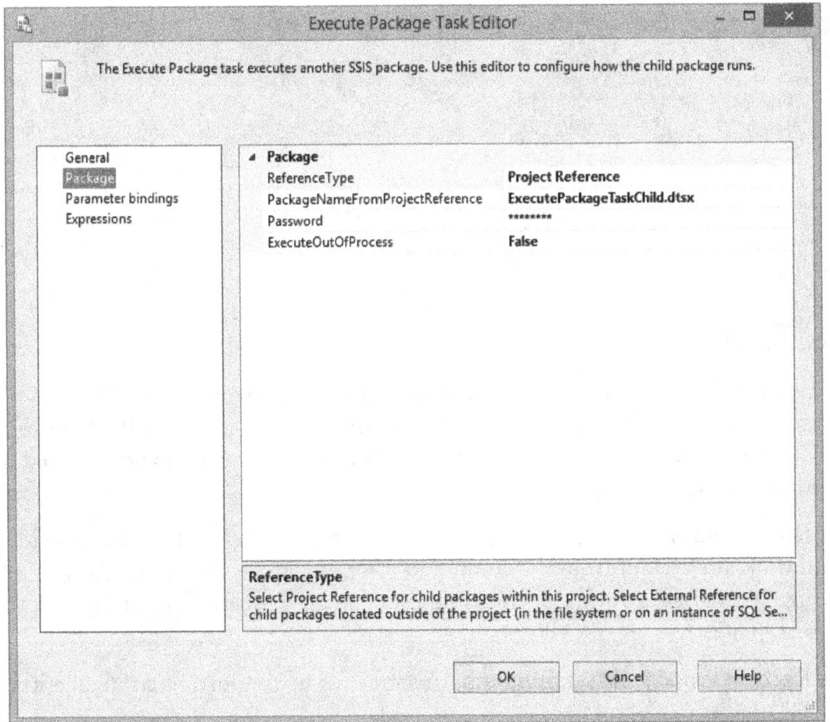

FIGURE 3-29

Next, go to the Parameter Bindings tab to pass parameters into the child package. First, select any parameters in the child package from its dropdown box, and then map them to a parameter or variable in the parent package. Parameters will only work here with Project Referenced packages. You can see an example of this in Figure 3-30, or download the entire example from `www.wrox.com/go/prossis2014`.

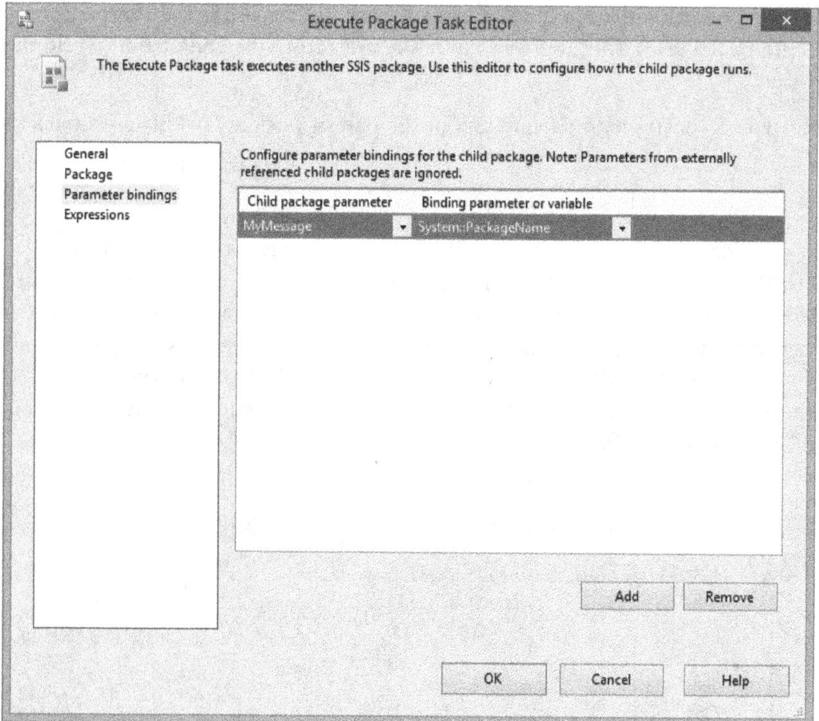

FIGURE 3-30

Execute Process Task

The Execute Process Task will execute a Windows or console application inside of the Control Flow. You'll find great uses for this task to run command-line-based programs and utilities prior to performing other ETL tasks. The most common example would have to be unzipping packed or encrypted data files with a command-line tool.

You can store any errors resulting from the execution of the task into a variable that can be read later and logged. In addition, any output from the command file can also be written to a variable for logging purposes. Figure 3-31 shows a sample of using the Execute Process Task to expand a compressed `customers.zip` file.

The Process tab in the Execute Process Task Editor contains most of the important configuration items for this task:

- **RequireFullFileName property:** Tells the task whether it needs the full path to execute the command. If the file is not found at the full path or in the PATH environment variables of the machine, the task will fail. Typically, a full path is used only if you want to explicitly identify the executable you want to run. However, if the file exists in the `System32` directory, you wouldn't normally have to type the full path to the file because this path is automatically known to a typical Windows system.

- **Executable property:** Identifies the path and filename for the executable you want to run. Be careful not to provide any parameters or optional switches in this property that would be passed to the executable. Use the Arguments property to set these types of options separately. For example, Figure 3-31 shows that the task will execute `expand.exe` and pass in the cabinet from which you want to extract and where you'd like it to be extracted.
- **WorkingDirectory option:** Contains the path from which the executable or command file will work.
- **StandardInputVariable parameter:** This is the variable you want to pass into the process as an argument. Use this property if you want to dynamically provide a parameter to the executable based on a variable.
- **StandardOutputVariable parameter:** You can also capture the result of the execution by setting the property StandardOutputVariable to a variable.
- **StandardErrorVariable property:** Any errors that occurred from the execution can be captured in the variable you provide in this property.

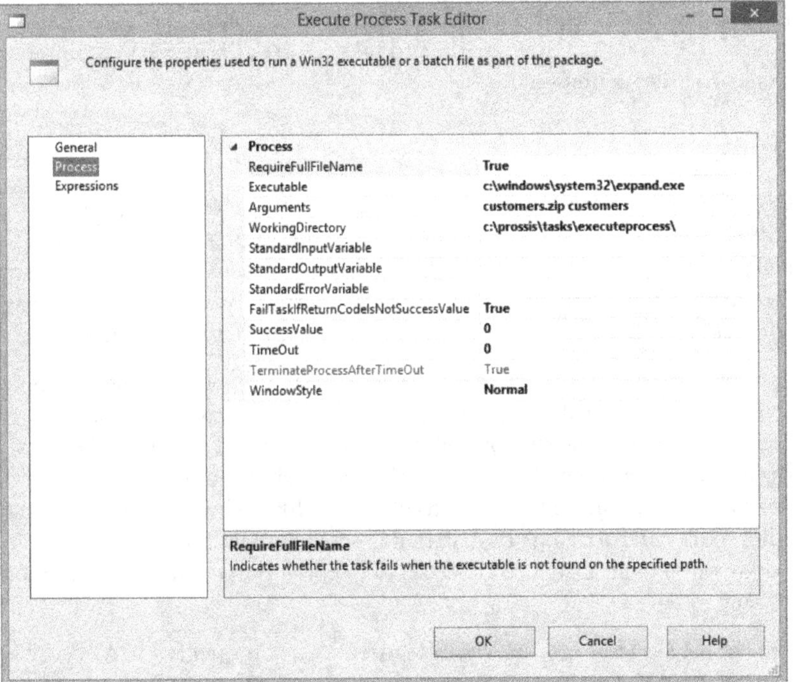

FIGURE 3-31

These variable values can be used to send back to a scripting component to log or can be used in a precedence constraint that checks the length of the variables to determine whether you should go to the next task. This provides the logical functionality of looping back and trying again if the result of the execution of the `expand.exe` program was a sharing violation or another similar error.

Other options in the Process tab include:

- **FailTaskIfReturnCodeIsNotSuccessValue property:** Another option for validating the task.
- **SuccessValue option:** The Execute Process Task will fail if the exit code passed from the program is different from the value provided in the SuccessValue option. The default value of 0 indicates that the task was successful in executing the process.
- **Timeout/TerminateProcessAfterTimeOut properties:** The Timeout property determines the number of seconds that must elapse before the program is considered a runaway process. A value of 0, which is the default, means the process can run for an infinite amount of time. This property is used in conjunction with the TerminateProcessAfterTimeOut property, which, if set to true, terminates the process after the timeout has been exceeded.
- **WindowStyle option:** This can set the executable to be run minimized, maximized, hidden, or normal. If this is set to any option other than hidden, users will be able to see any windows that potentially pop up and may interact with them during runtime. Typically, these are set to hidden once a package is fully tested.

With the Execute Process Task, you can continue to use command-line or out-of-processes executables to organize work for ETL tasks. Now it's time to take a look at how SSIS can interact and integrate with your enterprise messaging bus.

Message Queue Task

The Message Queue Task enables you to send or receive messages from Microsoft Message Queuing (MSMQ) right out of the box. For integration with other messaging systems like IBM's MQ Series or Tibco's Rendezveus, you need to either code to a library within a Script Task, create a custom component, or execute T-SQL statements to a SQL Server Service Broker queue. Messaging architectures are created to ensure reliable communication between two disparate subsystems.

A message can be a string, a file, or a variable. The main benefit to using this task is the capability to make packages communicate with each other at runtime. You can use this to scale out your packages, having multiple packages executing in parallel, with each loading a subset of the data, and then checking in with the parent package after they reach certain checkpoints. You can also use this task for enterprise-level information integration to do things like deliver dashboard-level information using XML files to an enterprise bus or distribute report content files across your network. Satellite offices or any other subscriber to those services could pull content from the queue for application-level processing.

The task is straightforward. In the General tab, shown in Figure 3-32, you specify the MSMQ Connection Manager under the MSMQConnection property. Then, you specify whether you want to send or receive a message under the Message option. In this tab, you can also specify whether you want to use the legacy Windows 2000 version of MSMQ; this option is set to false by default.

The bulk of the configuration is under the Send or Receive tab (the one you see varies according to the Message option you selected in the General tab). If you're on the Receive tab, you can configure the task to remove the message from the queue after it has been read. You can also set the timeout properties here, to control whether the task will produce an error if it experiences a timeout.

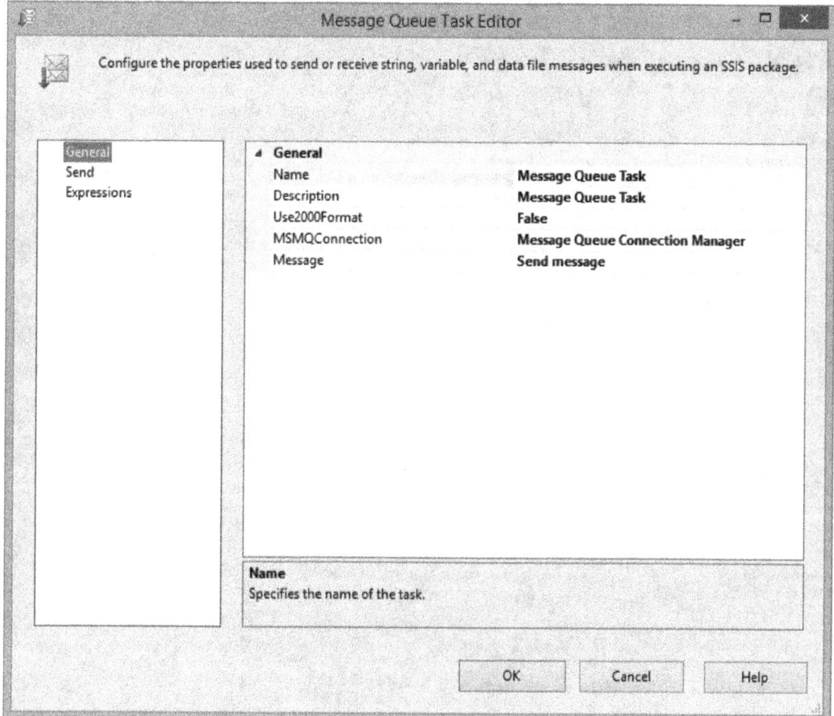

FIGURE 3-32

Regardless of whether you're sending or receiving messages, you can select the type of the message under the MessageType option. You can either send or receive a string message, a variable, or a data file. Additionally, if you're receiving a message, you can immediately store the message you receive in a package variable by setting String Message to Variable and then specifying a variable in the Variable option.

Send Mail Task

The Send Mail Task provides a configurable SSIS task for sending e-mail messages via SMTP. In legacy DTS packages, you had to send messages out through MAPI, which meant installing Outlook on the server on which the package was running. That is now no longer a requirement. Most of the configuration options are set in the Mail tab (shown in Figure 3-33) of the Send Mail Task Editor. The SmtpConnection property is where you either create a new or select an existing SMTP Connection Manager.

Most of the configuration options will depend upon your specific SMTP connection. One option of special interest is the MessageSourceType property, which specifies whether the message source will be provided from a file or a variable or be directly inputted into the MessageSource property. Typically, the best practice is to use a variable-based approach to set the MessageSource property.

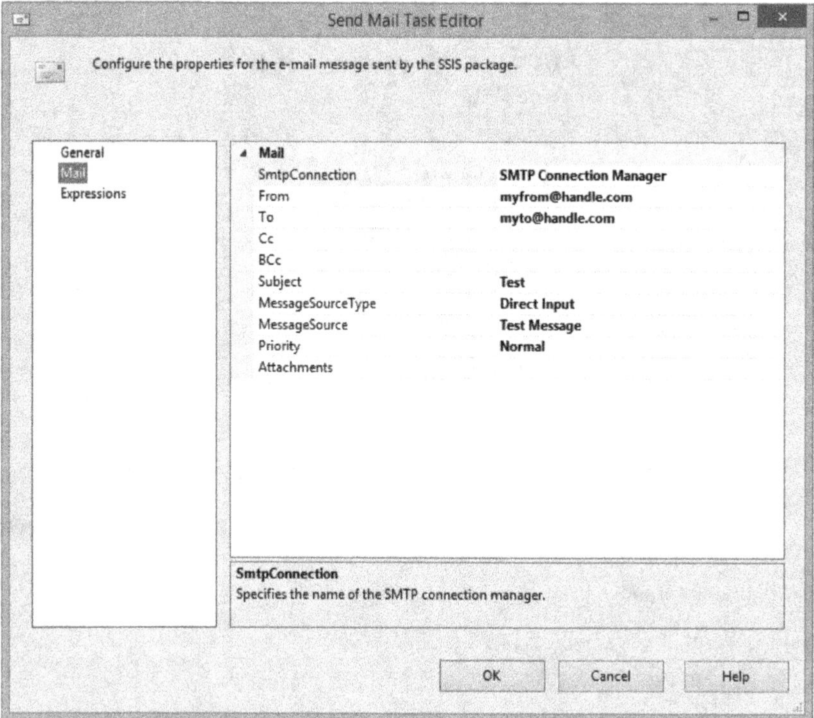

FIGURE 3-33

WMI Data Reader Task

Windows Management Instrumentation (WMI) is one of the best-kept secrets in Windows. WMI enables you to manage Windows servers and workstations through a scripting interface similar to running a T-SQL query. The WMI Data Reader Task enables you to interface with this environment by writing WQL queries (the query language for WMI) against the server or workstation (to look at the Application event log, for example). The output of this query can be written to a file or variable for later consumption. Following are some applications for which you could use the WMI Data Reader Task:

- Read the event log looking for a given error.
- Query the list of applications that are running.
- Query to see how much RAM is available at package execution for debugging.
- Determine the amount of free space on a hard drive.

To get started, you first need to set up a WMI Connection Manager in the Connection Manager Editor. Connection requirements vary, but Figure 3-34 shows an example of a WMI connection for a typical standalone workstation.

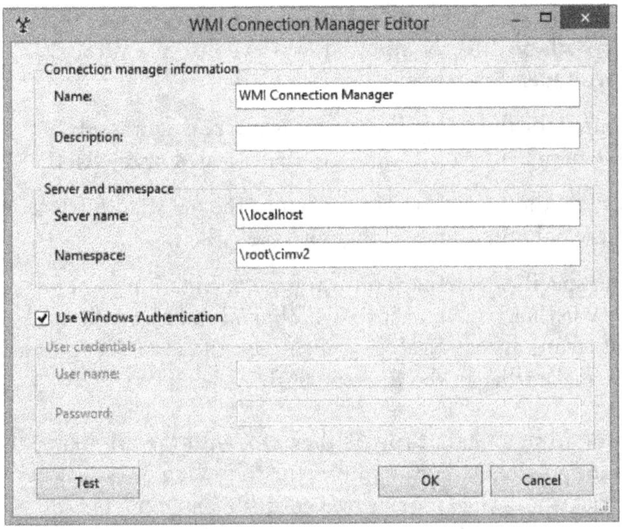

FIGURE 3-34

Notice here that the Use Windows Authentication option has been set. WMI typically requires a higher level of security authorization because you are able to query OS-level data. With a WMI connection, you can configure the WMI Data Reader Task Editor using the WMI Options tab shown in Figure 3-35.

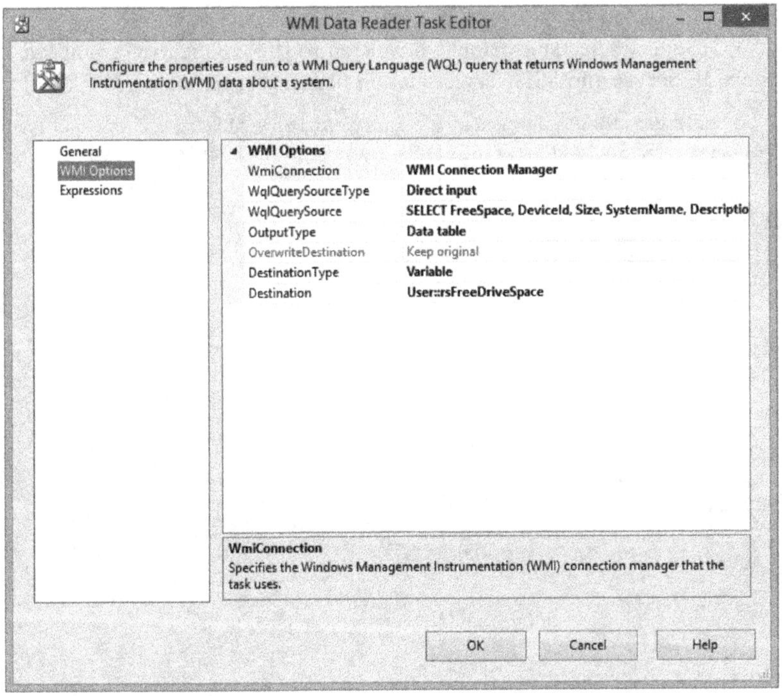

FIGURE 3-35

- **WmiConnection/WqlQuerySourceType:** First, you set the WMIConnection, and then determine whether the WMI query will be directly inputted, retrieved from a variable, or retrieved from a file, and set the WqlQuerySourceType.
- **WqlQuerySource:** Specifies the source for the query that you wish to run against the connection. This may be a variable name, a text filename, or a hardcoded query itself.
- **OutputType:** This option specifies whether you want the output of the query to retrieve just the values from the query or also the column names along with the values.
- **OverwriteDestination:** This option specifies whether you want the destination to be overwritten each time it is run, or whether you want it to just append to any configured destination. If you save the output to an object variable, you can use the same technique of shredding a recordset that you learned earlier in the Execute SQL Task.

WQL queries look like SQL queries, and for all practical purposes they are, with the difference that you are retrieving data sets from the operating systems. For example, the following query selects the free space, the name, and a few other metrics about the C: drive (see code file `Ch03SQL.txt`):

```
SELECT FreeSpace, DeviceId, Size, SystemName, Description FROM Win32_LogicalDisk
WHERE DeviceID = 'C:'
```

The output of this type of query would look like this in a table:

```
Description, Local Fixed Disk
DeviceID, C:
FreeSpace, 32110985216
Size, 60003381248
SystemName, BKNIGHT
```

The following example of a WQL query selects information written to the Application event log after a certain date about the SQL Server and SSIS services (code file `Ch03SQL.txt`):

```
SELECT * FROM Win32_NTLogEvent WHERE LogFile = 'Application' AND
(SourceName='SQLISService' OR SourceName='SQLISPackage') AND TimeGenerated>
'20050117'
```

The results would look like this:

```
0
BKNIGHT
12289
1073819649
3
System.String[]
Application
3738
SQLISPackage
20050430174924.000000-240
20050430174924.000000-240
Information
BKNIGHT\Brian Knight
0
```

Typically, the WMI Data Reader Task is used in SQL Server administration packages to gather operational-type data from the SQL Server environments. However, the WMI Event Watcher Task has some interesting uses for ETL processes that you'll look at next.

WMI Event Watcher Task

The WMI Event Watcher Task empowers SSIS to wait for and respond to certain WMI events that occur in the operating system. The task operates in much the same way as the WMI Data Reader Task operates. The following are some of the useful things you can do with this task:

- Watch a directory for a certain file to be written.
- Wait for a given service to start.
- Wait for the memory of a server to reach a certain level before executing the rest of the package or before transferring files to the server.
- Watch for the CPU to be free.

To illustrate the last example of polling to determine when the CPU is less than 50 percent utilized, you could have the WMI Event Watcher Task look for an event with this WQL code:

```
SELECT * from __InstanceModificationEvent WITHIN 2 WHERE TargetInstance ISA
'Win32_Processor' and TargetInstance.LoadPercentage < 50
```

The next section looks at a direct application of this WMI Event Watcher Task to give you a better idea of how to configure it and what it can do.

Polling a Directory for the Delivery of a File

One very practical use of the WMI Event Watcher for ETL processing is to provide a buffer between the time when an SSIS job starts and the time when a file is actually delivered to a folder location. If there is a window of variability in file delivery and an SSIS package starts on a onetime schedule, then it is possible to miss processing the file for the day. By using a WMI Event Watcher, you can set up your SSIS packages to poll a folder location for a set period of time until a file is detected. If you have this type of challenge, a better solution may be a ForEach Loop Container scheduled to run periodically, but you'll learn more about that in Chapter 6. To set up a task to perform this automated action, open the WMI Options tab of the WMI Event Watcher Task Editor (see Figure 3-36). Notice that this WMI Task is completely different from the WMI Data Reader Task.

This WMI Event Watcher Task provides properties such as the AfterEvent option, which specifies whether the task should succeed, fail, or keep querying if the condition is met. You also need to provide a length of time after which the WMI Event Watcher stops watching by setting the Timeout property. The timeout value is in seconds. The default of zero (0) indicates that there is no timeout. Outside of your development activities, be very careful with leaving this setting on zero (0). The WMI Event Watcher could leave your SSIS package running indefinitely.

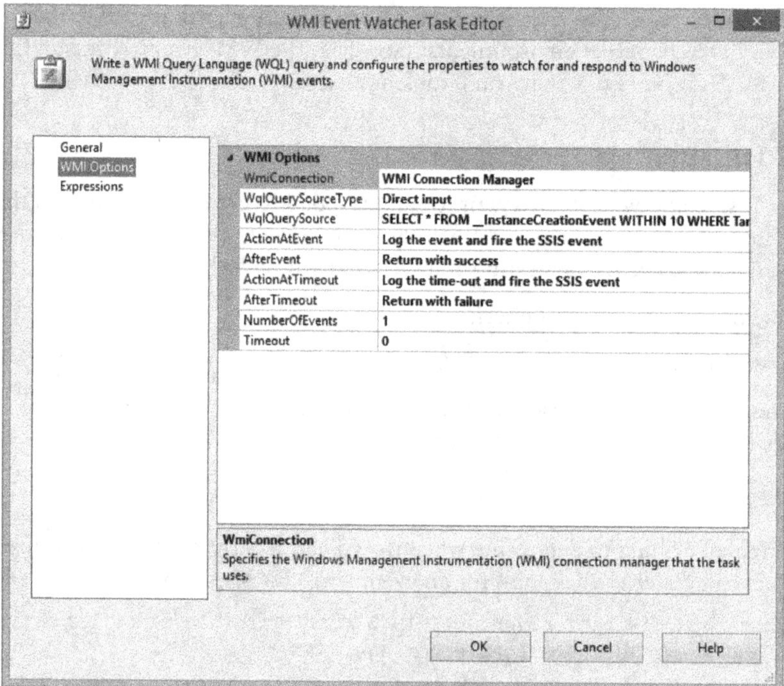

FIGURE 3-36

You can also configure what happens when a timeout occurs under the ActionAtTimeout and AfterTimeout settings. The NumberOfEvents option configures the number of events to watch for. You can use this setting to look for more than one file before you start processing.

The WqlQuerySource for the File Watcher Configuration for this WMI Task would look like this code:

```
SELECT * FROM __InstanceCreationEvent WITHIN 10
WHERE TargetInstance ISA "CIM_DirectoryContainsFile"
AND TargetInstance.GroupComponent = "Win32_Directory.Name=\"c:\\\\ProSSIS\""
```

If you run this task with no files in the `c:\ProSSIS\` directory, the task will remain yellow as the watcher continuously waits for an event to be raised. If you copy a file into the directory, the task will turn green and complete successfully. This is a great addition that is less resource-intensive than the legacy DTS version of iterating in a For loop until the file is found. As you can see, there are some major improvements in the capabilities to control workflow in SSIS.

SMO ADMINISTRATION TASKS

The last section of this chapter is reserved for a set of tasks that are convenient for copying or moving schema and data-level information. The SQL Management Objects (SMO) model allows developers to interact with DBA functions programmatically. These rarely used tasks are used by DBAs to synchronize systems. Because they aren't used as often, they're covered only at a high level. These tasks can do the following:

- Move or copy entire databases. This can be accomplished by detaching the database and moving the files (faster) or by moving the schema and content (slower).
- Transfer error messages from one server to another.
- Move or copy selected or entire SQL Agent jobs.
- Move or copy server-level or database-level logins.
- Move or copy objects such as tables, views, stored procedures, functions, defaults, user-defined data types, partition functions, partition schemas, schemas (or roles), SQL assemblies, user-defined aggregates, user-defined types, and XML schemas. These objects can be copied over by selecting all, by individually selecting each desired object type, or even by selecting individual objects themselves.
- Move or copy master stored procedures between two servers.

Transfer Database Task

The Transfer Database Task has, as you would expect, a source and destination connection and a database property. The other properties address how the transfer should take place. Figure 3-37 is an example of the Transfer Database Task filled out to copy a development database on the same server as a QA instance.

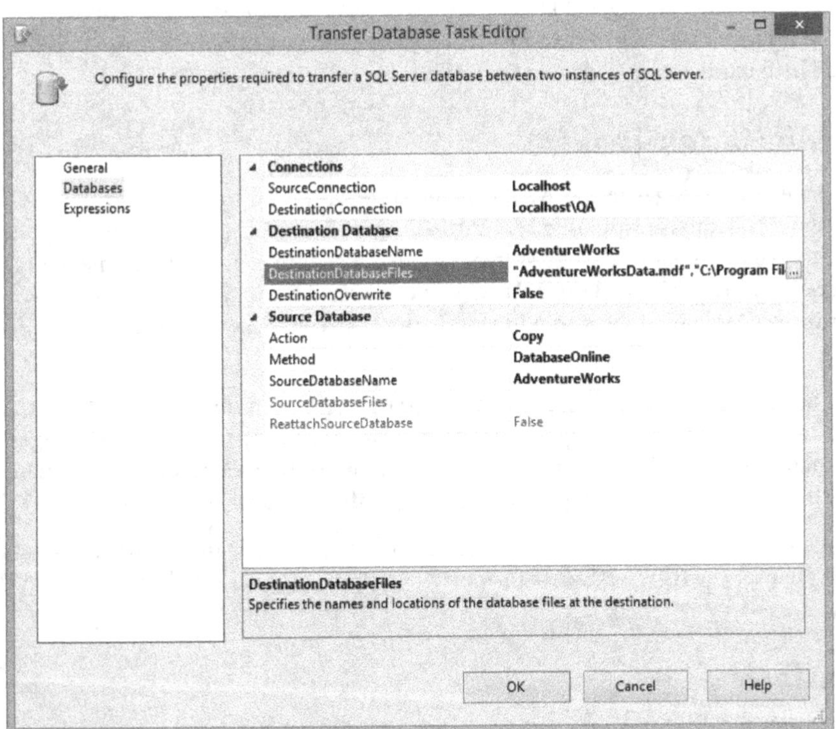

FIGURE 3-37

Notice that the destination and source are set to the same server. For this copy to work, the DestinationDatabaseFiles property has to be set to new `mdf` and `ldf` filenames. The property is set by default to the SourceDatabaseFiles property. To set the new destination database filenames, click the ellipsis, and then change the Destination File or Destination Folder properties.

You can set the Method property to DatabaseOnline or DatabaseOffline. If the option is set to DatabaseOffline, the database is detached copied over and then reattached to both systems. This is a much faster process than with DatabaseOnline, but it comes at a cost of making the database inaccessible.

The Action property controls whether the task should copy or move the source database. The Method property controls whether the database should be copied while the source database is kept online, using SQL Server Management Objects (SMO), or by detaching the database, moving the files, and then reattaching the database. The DestinationOverwrite property controls whether the creation of the destination database should be allowed to overwrite. This includes deleting the database in the destination if it is found. This is useful in cases where you want to copy a database from production into a quality-control or production test environment, and the new database should replace any existing similar database. The last property is the ReattachSourceDatabase, which specifies what action should be taken upon failure of the copy. Use this property if you have a package running on a schedule that takes a production database offline to copy it, and you need to guarantee that the database goes back online even if the copy fails.

What's really great about the Transfer Database Task is that the logins, roles, object permissions, and even the data can be transferred as well. This task may in some instances be too big of a hammer. You may find it more advantageous to just transfer specific sets of objects from one database to another. The next five tasks give you that capability.

Transfer Error Messages Task

If you are using custom error messages in the sys.messages table, you need to remember to copy these over when you move a database from one server to another. In the past, you needed to code a cursor-based script to fire the sp_addmessage system stored procedure to move these messages around — and you needed to remember to do it. Now you can create a package that moves your database with the Transfer Database Task and add this Transfer Error Messages Task to move the messages as well.

One thing you'll find in this task that you'll see in the rest of the SMO administration tasks is the opportunity to select the specific things that you want to transfer. The properties ErrorMessagesList and ErrorMessageLanguagesList in the Messages tab are examples of this selective-type UI. If you click the ellipsis, you'll get a dialog in which you can select specific messages to transfer.

Generally, unless you are performing a one-off update, you should set the TransferAllErrorMessages property to true, and then set the IfObjectExists property to skip messages that already exist in the destination database.

Transfer Logins Task

The Transfer Logins Task (shown in Figure 3-38) focuses only on the security aspects of your databases. With this task you can transfer the logins from one database and have them corrected at the destination.

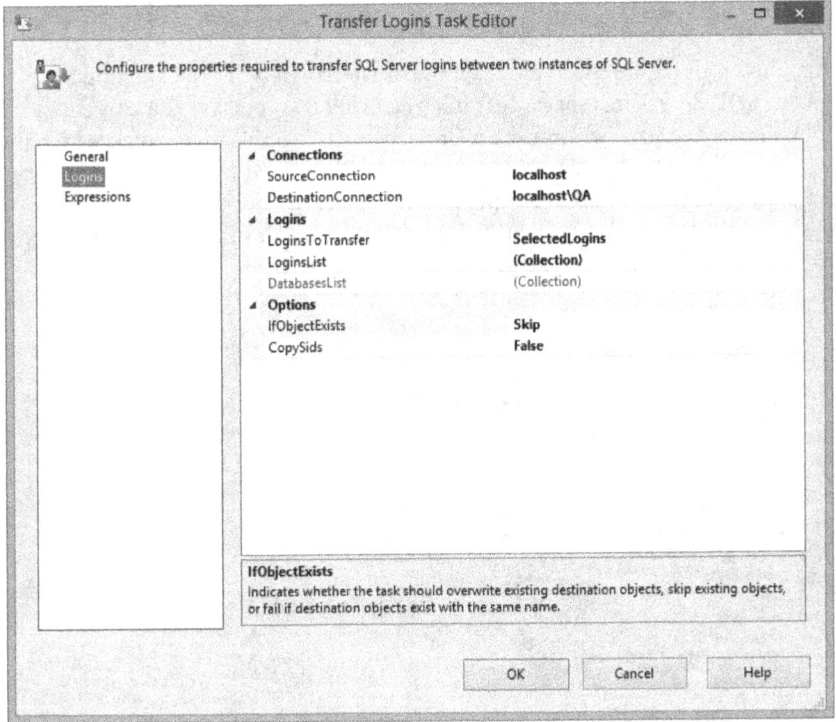

FIGURE 3-38

Of course, you'll have your obligatory source and destination connection properties in this editor. You also have the option to move logins from all databases or selected databases, or you can select individual logins to transfer. Make this choice in the LoginsToTransfer property; the default is SelectedLogins. The partner properties to LoginsToTransfer are LoginsList and DatabasesList. One will be activated based on your choice of logins to transfer.

Two last properties to cover relate to what you want the transfer logins process to do if it encounters an existing login in the destination. If you want the login to be replaced, set the IfObjectExists property to Overwrite. Other options are to fail the task or to skip that login. The long-awaited option to resolve unmatched user security IDs is found in the property CopySids, and can be true or false.

Transfer Master Stored Procedures Task

This task is used to transfer master stored procedures. If you need to transfer your own stored procedure, use the Transfer SQL Server Objects Task instead. To use this task, set the source and destination connections, and then set the property TransferAllStoredProcedures to true or false. If you set this property to false, you'll be able to select individual master stored procedures to transfer. The remaining property, IfObjectExists, enables you to select what action should take place if a transferring object exists in the destination. The options are to Overwrite, FailTask, or Skip.

Transfer Jobs Task

The Transfer Jobs Task (shown in Figure 3-39) aids you in transferring any of the existing SQL Server Agent jobs between SQL Server instances. Just like the other SMO tasks, you can either select to transfer all jobs to synchronize two instances or use the task to selectively pick which jobs you want to move to another instance. You can also select in the IfObjectExists property how the task should react if the job is already there. One important option is the EnableJobsAtDestination property, which turns the jobs after they've been transferred. This default property is false by default, meaning the jobs transfer but will not be functioning until enabled.

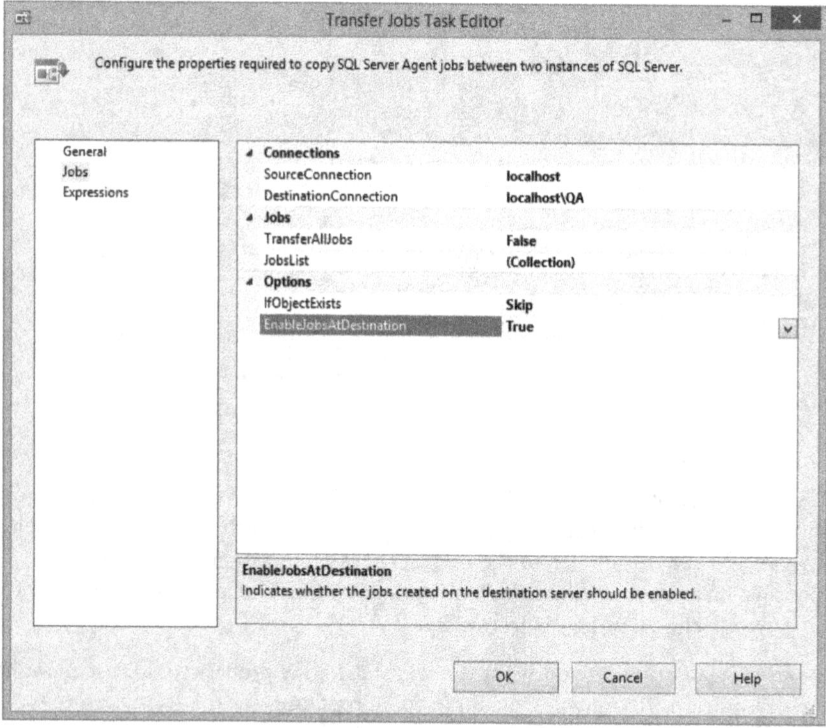

FIGURE 3-39

Transfer SQL Server Objects Task

The Transfer SQL Server Objects Task is the most flexible of the Transfer tasks. This task is capable of transferring all types of database objects. To use this task, set the properties to connect to a source and destination database; if the properties aren't visible, expand the Connection category. Some may be hidden until categories are expanded.

This task exists for those instances when selective object copying is needed, which is why this is not called the Transfer Database Task. You specifically have to set the property CopyData to true to get the bulk transfers of data. The property CopyAllObjects means that only the tables, views, stored procedures, defaults, rules, and UDFs will be transferred. If you want the table indexes, triggers, primary keys, foreign keys, full-text indexes, or extended properties, you have to select these individually. By expanding the ObjectsToCopy category, you expose properties that allow individual selection of tables, views, and other programmable objects. The security options give you some of the same capabilities as the Transfer Database Task. You can transfer database users, roles, logins, and object-level permissions by selecting true for these properties.

The power of this task lies in its flexibility, as it can be customized and used in packages to move only specific items, for example, during the promotion of objects from one environment to another, or to be less discriminate and copy all tables, views, and other database objects, with or without the data.

SUMMARY

This chapter attempted to stick with the everyday nuts-and-bolts uses of the SSIS tasks. Throughout the chapter, you looked at each task, learned how to configure it, and looked at an example of the task in action. In fact, you saw a number of examples that demonstrated how to use these tasks in real-world ETL and EAI applications. In Chapter 6, you'll circle back to look at the Control Flow again to explore containers, which enable you to loop through tasks. In the next chapter, you'll cover the Data Flow Task and dive deeper into configuring Data Flow, and learn about all the transformations that are available in this task.

The Data Flow

WHAT'S IN THIS CHAPTER?

- Learn about the SSIS Data Flow architecture
- Reading data out of sources
- Loading data into destinations
- Transforming data with common transformations

WROX.COM CODE DOWNLOADS FOR THIS CHAPTER

You can find the wrox.com code downloads for this chapter at `www.wrox.com/go/prossis2014` on the Download Code tab.

In the last chapter you were introduced to the Control Flow tab through tasks. In this chapter, you'll continue along those lines with an exploration of the Data Flow tab, which is where you will spend most of your time as an SSIS developer. The Data Flow Task is where the bulk of your data heavy lifting occurs in SSIS. This chapter walks you through the transformations in the Data Flow Task, demonstrating how they can help you move and clean your data. You'll notice a few components (the CDC ones) aren't covered in this chapter. Those needed more coverage than this chapter had room for and are covered in Chapter 11.

UNDERSTANDING THE DATA FLOW

The SSIS Data Flow is implemented as a logical pipeline, where data flows from one or more sources, through whatever transformations are needed to cleanse and reshape it for its new purpose, and into one or more destinations. The Data Flow does its work primarily in memory, which gives SSIS its strength, allowing the Data Flow to perform faster than any ELT type environment (in most cases) where the data is first loaded into a staging environment and then cleansed with a SQL statement.

One of the toughest concepts to understand for a new SSIS developer is the difference between the Control Flow and the Data Flow tabs. Chapter 2 explains this further, but just to restate a piece of that concept, the Control Flow tab controls the workflow of the package and the order in which each task will execute. Each task in the Control Flow has a user interface to configure the task, with the exception of the Data Flow Task. The Data Flow Task is configured in the Data Flow tab. Once you drag a Data Flow Task onto the Control Flow tab and double-click it to configure it, you're immediately taken to the Data Flow tab.

The Data Flow is made up of three components that are discussed in this chapter: sources, transformations (also known as transforms), and destinations. These three components make up the fundamentals of ETL. Sources extract data out of flat files, OLE DB databases, and other locations; transformations process the data once it has been pulled out; and destinations write the data to its final location.

Much of this ETL processing is done in memory, which is what gives SSIS its speed. It is much faster to apply business rules to your data in memory using a transformation than to have to constantly update a staging table. Because of this, though, your SSIS server will potentially need a large amount of memory, depending on the size of the file you are processing.

Data flows out of a source in memory buffers that are 10 megabytes in size or 10,000 rows (whichever comes first) by default. As the first transformation is working on those 10,000 rows, the next buffer of 10,000 rows is being processed at the source. This architecture limits the consumption of memory by SSIS and, in most cases, means that if you had 5 transforms dragged over, 50,000 rows will be worked on at the same time in memory. This can change only if you have asynchronous components like the Aggregate or Sort Transforms, which cause a full block of the pipeline.

DATA VIEWERS

Data viewers are a very important feature in SSIS for debugging your Data Flow pipeline. They enable you to view data at points in time at runtime. If you place a data viewer before and after the Aggregate Transformation, for example, you can see the data flowing into the transformation at runtime and what it looks like after the transformation happens. Once you deploy your package and run it on the server as a job or with the service, the data viewers do not show because they are only a debug feature within SQL Server Data Tools (SSDT).

To place a data viewer in your pipeline, right-click one of the paths (red or blue arrows leaving a transformation or source) and select Enable Data Viewer.

Once you run the package, you'll see the data viewers open and populate with data when the package gets to that path in the pipeline that it's attached to. The package will not proceed until you click the green play button (>). You can also copy the data into a viewer like Excel or Notepad for further investigation by clicking Copy Data. The data viewer displays up to 10,000 rows by default, so you may have to click the > button multiple times in order to go through all the data.

After adding more and more data viewers, you may want to remove them eventually to speed up your development execution. You can remove them by right-clicking the path that has the data viewer and selecting Disable Data Viewer.

SOURCES

A *source* in the SSIS Data Flow is where you specify the location of your source data. Most sources will point to a Connection Manager in SSIS. By pointing to a Connection Manager, you can reuse connections throughout your package, because you need only change the connection in one place.

SOURCE ASSISTANT AND DESTINATION ASSISTANT

The Source Assistant and Destination Assistant are two components designed to remove the complexity of configuring a source or a destination in the Data Flow. The components determine what drivers you have installed and show you only the applicable drivers. It also simplifies the selection of a valid connection manager based on the database platform you select that you wish to connect to.

In the Source Assistant or Destination Assistant (the Source Assistant is shown in Figure 4-1), only the data providers that you have installed are actually shown. Once you select how you want to connect, you'll see a list of Connection Managers on the right that you can use to connect to your selected source. You can also create a new Connection Manager from the same area on the right. If you uncheck the "Show only installed source types" option, you'll see other providers like DB2 or Oracle for which you may not have the right software installed.

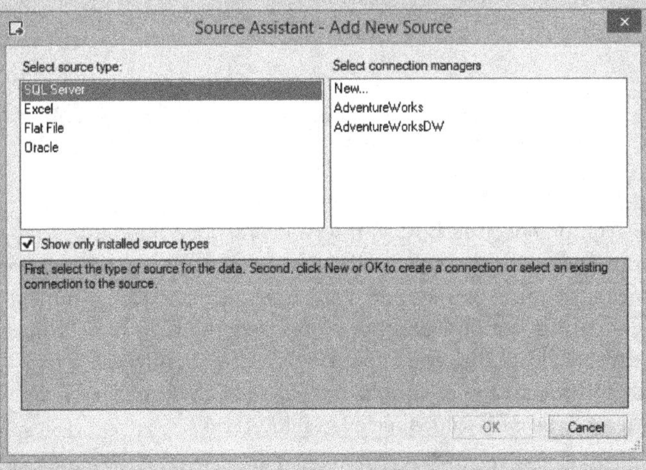

FIGURE 4-1

OLE DB Source

The OLE DB Source is the most common type of source, and it can point to any OLE DB–compliant Data Source such as SQL Server, Oracle, or DB2. To configure the OLE DB Source, double-click the source once you have added it to the design pane in the Data Flow tab. In the Connection Manager page of the OLE DB Source Editor (see Figure 4-2), select the Connection Manager of your OLE DB Source from the OLE DB Connection Manager dropdown box. You can also add a new Connection Manager in the editor by clicking the New button.

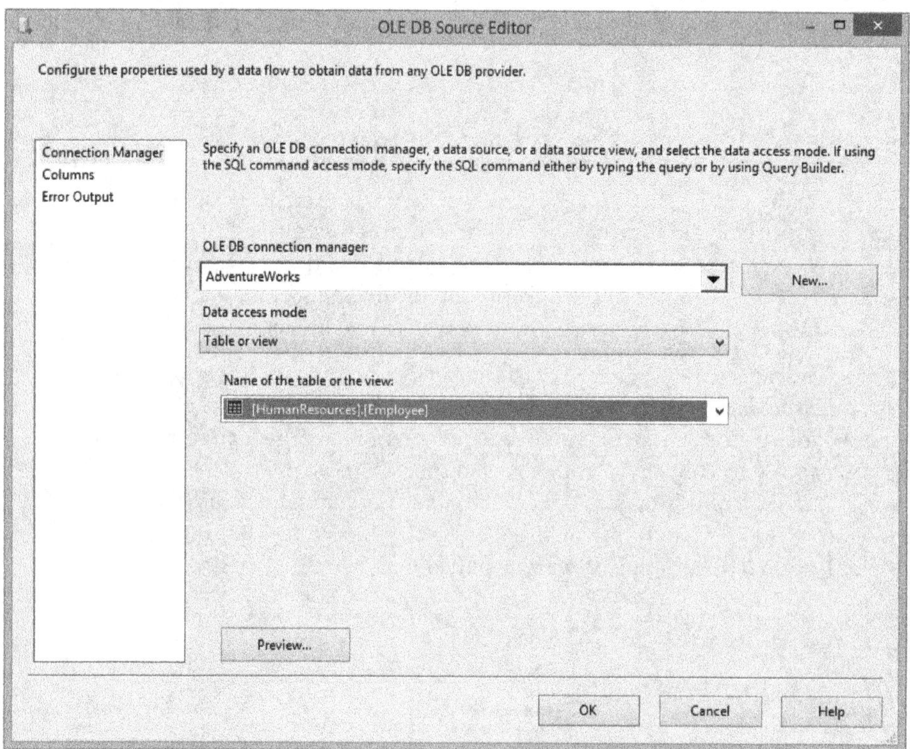

FIGURE 4-2

The "Data access mode" option specifies how you wish to retrieve the data. Your options here are Table/View or SQL Command, or you can pull either from a package variable. Once you select the data access mode, you need the table or view, or you can type a query. For multiple reasons that will be explained momentarily, it is a best practice to retrieve the data from a query. This query can also be a stored procedure. Additionally, you can pass parameters into the query by substituting a question mark (?) for where the parameter should be and then clicking the Parameters button. You'll learn more about parameterization of your queries in Chapter 5.

As with most sources, you can go to the Columns page to set columns that you wish to output to the Data Flow, as shown in Figure 4-3. Simply check the columns you wish to output, and you can then assign the name you want to send down the Data Flow in the Output column. Select only the columns that you want to use, because the smaller the data set, the better the performance you will get.

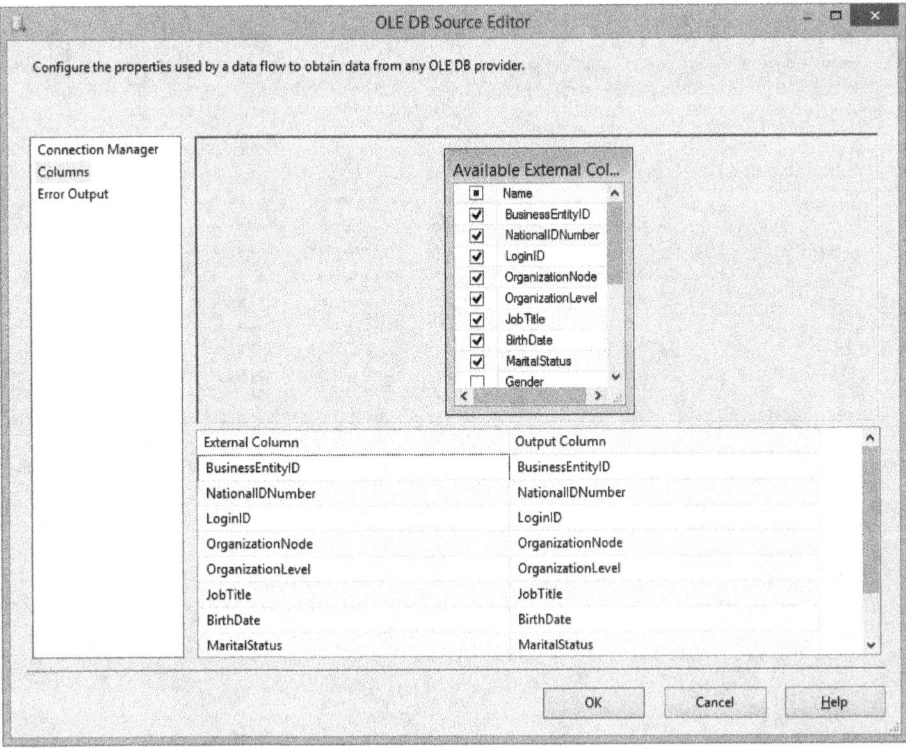

FIGURE 4-3

From a performance perspective, this is a case where it's better to have typed the query in the Connection Manager page rather than to have selected a table. Selecting a table to pull data from essentially selects all columns and all rows from the target table, transporting all that data across the network. Then, going to the Columns page and unchecking the unnecessary columns applies a client-side filter on the data, which is not nearly as efficient as selecting only the necessary columns in the SQL query. This is also gentler on the amount of buffers you fill as well.

Optionally, you can go to the Error Output page (shown in Figure 4-4) and specify how you wish to handle rows that have errors. For example, you may wish to output any rows that have a data type conversion issue to a different path in the Data Flow. On each column, you can specify that if an error occurs, you wish the row to be ignored, be redirected, or fail. If you choose to ignore failures, the column for that row will be set to NULL. If you redirect the row, the row will be sent down the red path in the Data Flow coming out of the OLE DB Source.

The Truncation column specifies what to do if data truncation occurs. A truncation error would happen, for example, if you try to place 200 characters of data into a column in the Data Flow that supports only 100. You have the same options available to you for Truncation as you do for the Error option. By default, if an error occurs with data types or truncation, an error will occur, causing the entire Data Flow to fail.

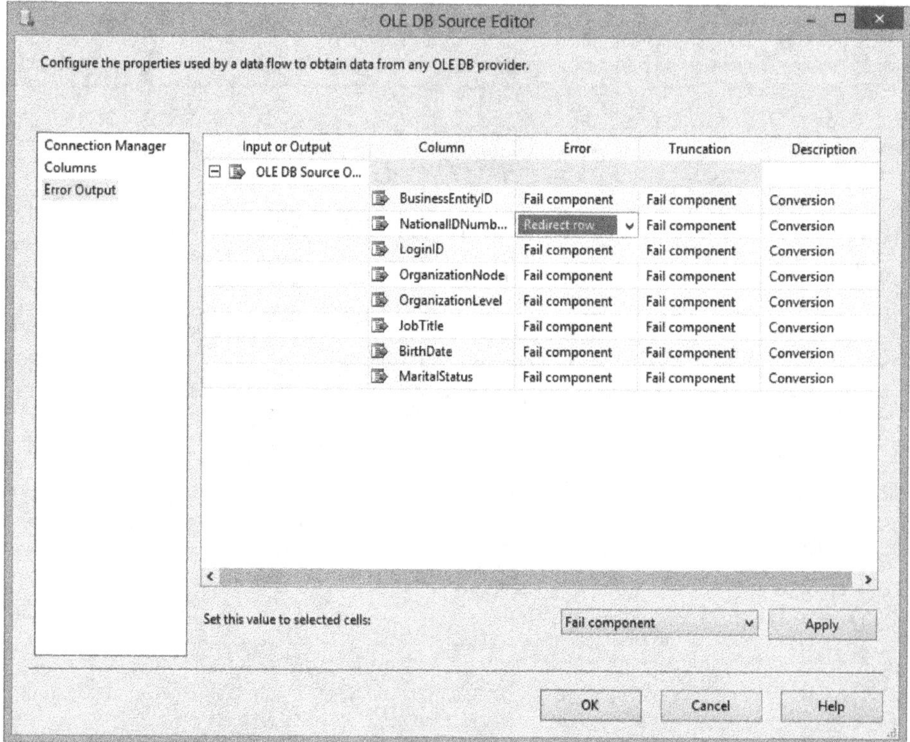

FIGURE 4-4

Excel Source

The Excel Source is a source component that points to an Excel spreadsheet, just like it sounds. Once you point to an Excel Connection Manager, you can select the sheet from the "Name of the Excel sheet" dropdown box, or you can run a query by changing the Data Access Mode. This source treats Excel just like a database, where an Excel sheet is the table and the workbook is the database. If you do not see a list of sheets in the dropdown box, you may have a 64-bit machine that needs the ACE driver installed or you need to run the package in 32-bit mode. How to do this is documented in the next section in this chapter.

SSIS supports Excel data types, but it may not support them the way you wish by default. For example, the default format in Excel is General. If you right-click a column and select Format Cells, you'll find that most of the columns in your Excel spreadsheet have probably been set to General. SSIS translates this general format as a Unicode string data type. In SQL Server, Unicode translates into nvarchar, which is probably not what you want. If you have a Unicode data type in SSIS and you try to insert it into a varchar column, it will potentially fail. The solution is to place a Data Conversion Transformation between the source and the destination in order to change the Excel data types. You can read more about Data Conversion Transformations later in this chapter.

Excel 64-Bit Scenarios

If you are connecting to an Excel 2007 spreadsheet or later, ensure that you select the proper Excel version when creating the Excel Connection Manager. You will not be able to connect to an Excel 2007, Excel 2010, or Excel 2013 spreadsheet otherwise. Additionally, the default Excel driver is a 32-bit driver only, and your packages have to run in 32-bit mode when using Excel connectivity. In the designer, you would receive the following error message if you do not have the correct driver installed:

```
The 'Microsoft.ACE.OLEDB.12.0' provider is not registered on the local machine.
```

To fix this, simply locate this driver on the Microsoft site and you'll be able to run packages with an Excel source in 64-bit.

Flat File Source

The Flat File Source provides a data source for connections such as text files or data that's delimited. Flat File Sources are typically comma- or tab-delimited files, or they could be fixed-width or ragged-right. A fixed-width file is typically received from the mainframe or government entities and has fixed start and stop points for each column. This method enables a fast load, but it takes longer at design time for the developer to map each column. You specify a Flat File Source the same way you specify an OLE DB Source. Once you add it to your Data Flow pane, you point it to a Connection Manager connection that is a flat file or a multi-flat file. Next, from the Columns tab, you specify which columns you want to be presented to the Data Flow. All the specifications for the flat file, such as delimiter type, were previously set in the Flat File Connection Manager.

In this example, you'll create a Connection Manager that points to a file called `FactSales.csv`, which you can download from this book's website at `www.wrox.com/go/prossis2014`. The file has a date column, a few string columns, integer columns, and a currency column. Because of the variety of data types it includes, this example presents an interesting case study for learning how to configure a Flat File Connection Manager.

First, right-click in the Connection Manager area of the Package Designer and select New Flat File Connection Manager. This will open the Flat File Connection Manager Editor, as shown in Figure 4-5. Name the Connection Manager **Fact Sales** and point it to wherever you placed the `FactSales.csv` file. Check the "Column names in the first data row" option, which specifies that the first row of the file contains a header row with the column names.

Another important option is the "Text qualifier" option. Although there isn't one for this file, sometimes your comma-delimited files may require that you have a text qualifier. A text qualifier places a character around each column of data to show that any comma delimiter inside that symbol should be ignored. For example, if you had the most common text qualifier of double-quotes around your data, a row may look like the following, whereby there are only three columns even though the commas may indicate five:

```
"Knight,Brian", 123, "Jacksonville, FL"
```

In the Columns page of the Connection Manager, you can specify what will delimit each column in the flat file if you chose a delimited file. The row delimiter specifies what will indicate a new row. The default option is a carriage return followed by a line feed. The Connection Manager's file is automatically scanned to determine the column delimiter and, as shown in Figure 4-6, use a tab delimiter for the example file.

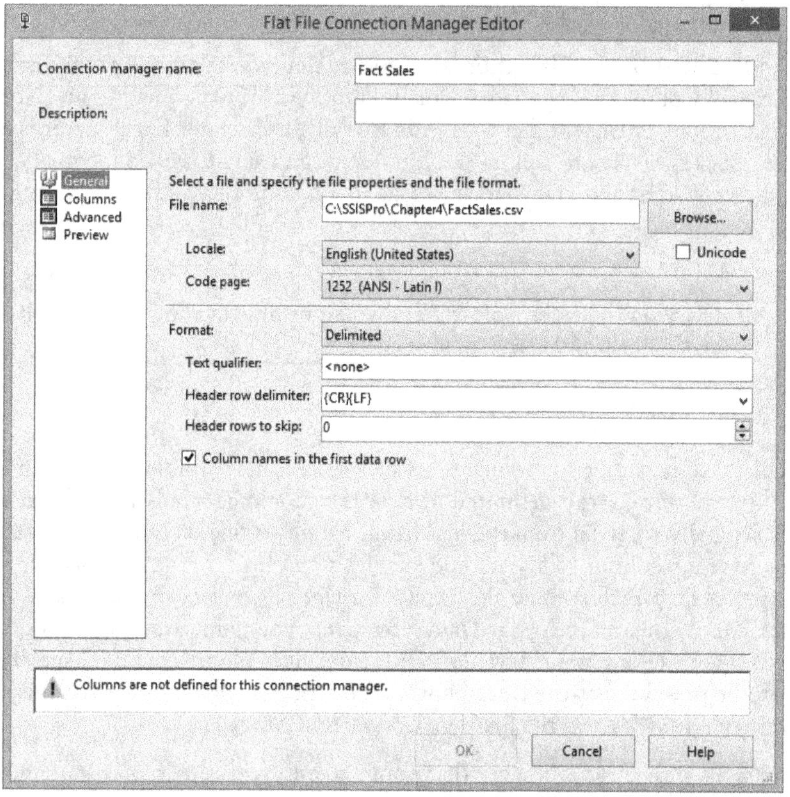

FIGURE 4-5

> **NOTE** *Often, once you make a major change to your header delimiter or your text qualifier, you'll have to click the Reset Columns button. Doing so requeries the file in order to obtain the new column names. If you click this option, though, all your metadata in the Advanced page will be recreated as well, and you may lose a sizable amount of work.*

The Advanced page of the Connection Manager is the most important feature in the Connection Manager. In this tab, you specify the data type for each column in the flat file and the name of the column, as shown in Figure 4-7. This column name and data type will be later sent to the Data Flow. If you need to change the data types or names, you can always come back to the Connection Manager, but be aware that you need to open the Flat File Source again to refresh the metadata.

> **NOTE** *Making a change to the Connection Manager's data types or columns requires that you refresh any Data Flow Task using that Connection Manager. To do so, open the Flat File Source Editor, which will prompt you to refresh the metadata of the Data Flow. Answer yes, and the metadata will be corrected throughout the Data Flow.*

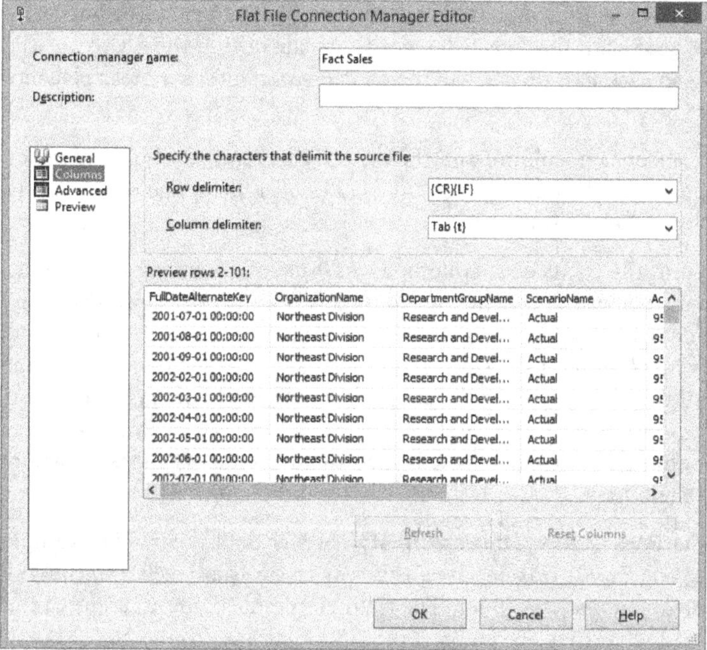

FIGURE 4-6

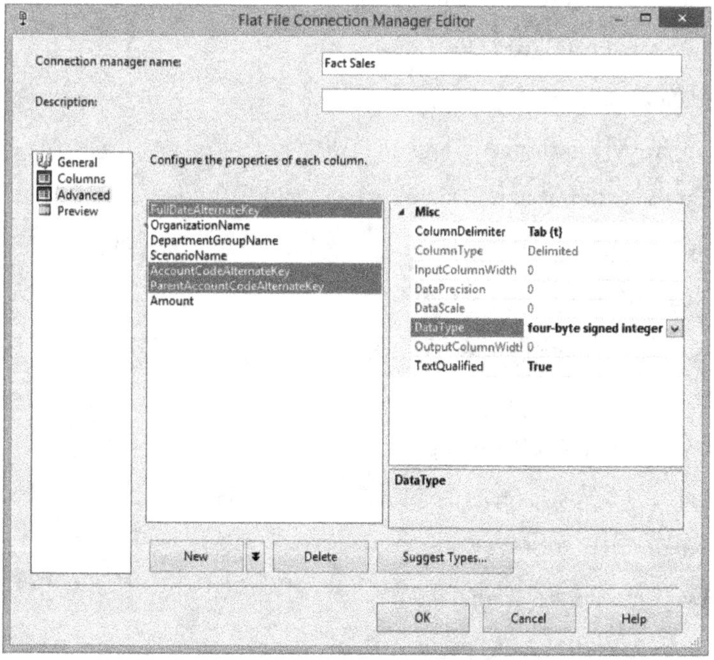

FIGURE 4-7

If you don't want to specify the data type for each individual column, you can click the Suggest Types button on this page to have SSIS scan the first 100 records (by default) in the file to guess the appropriate data types. Generally speaking, it does a bad job at guessing, but it's a great place to start if you have a lot of columns.

If you prefer to do this manually, select each column and then specify its data type. You can also hold down the Ctrl key or Shift key and select multiple columns at once and change the data types or column length for multiple columns at the same time.

A Flat File Connection Manager initially treats each column as a 50-character string by default. Leaving this default behavior harms performance when you have a true integer column that you're trying to insert into SQL Server, or if your column contains more data than 50 characters of data. The settings you make in the Advanced page of the Connection Manager are the most important work you can do to ensure that all the data types for the columns are properly defined. You should also keep the data types as small as possible. For example, if you have a zip code column that's only 9 digits in length, define it as a 9-character string. This will save an additional 41 bytes in memory multiplied by however many rows you have.

A frustrating point with SSIS sometimes is how it deals with SQL Server data types. For example, a varchar maps in SSIS to a string column. It was designed this way to translate well into the .NET development world and to provide an agnostic product. The following table contains some of the common SQL Server data types and what they are mapped into in a Flat File Connection Manager.

SQL SERVER DATA TYPE	CONNECTION MANAGER DATA TYPE
Bigint	Eight-byte signed integer [DT_I8]
Binary	Byte stream [DT_BYTES]
Bit	Boolean [DT_BOOL]
Tinyint	Single-byte unsigned integer [DT_UI1]
Datetime	Database timestamp [DT_DBTIMESTAMP]
Decimal	Numeric [DT_NUMERIC]
Real	Float [DT_R4]
Int	Four-byte signed integer [DT_I4]
Image	Image [DT_IMAGE]
Nvarchar or nchar	Unicode string [DT_WSTR]
Ntext	Unicode text stream [DT_NTEXT]
Numeric	Numeric [DT_NUMERIC]
Smallint	Two-byte signed integer [DT_I2]
Text	Text stream [DT_TEXT]
Timestamp	Byte stream [DT_BYTES]

Uniqueidentifier	Unique identifier [DT_GUID]
Varbinary	Byte stream [DT_BYTES]
Varchar or char	String [DT_STR]
Xml	Unicode string [DT_WSTR]

FastParse Option

By default, SSIS issues a contract between the Flat File Source and a Data Flow. It states that the source component must validate any numeric or date column. For example, if you have a flat file in which a given column is set to a four-byte integer, every row must first go through a short validation routine to ensure that it is truly an integer and that no character data has passed through. On date columns, a quick check is done to ensure that every date is indeed a valid in-range date.

This validation is fast but it does require approximately 20 to 30 percent more time to validate that contract. To set the FastParse property, go into the Data Flow Task for which you're using a Flat File Source. Right-click the Flat File Source and select Show Advanced Editor. From there, select the Input and Output Properties tab, and choose any number or date column under Flat File Output ➪ Output Columns tree. In the right pane, change the FastParse property to True, as shown in Figure 4-8.

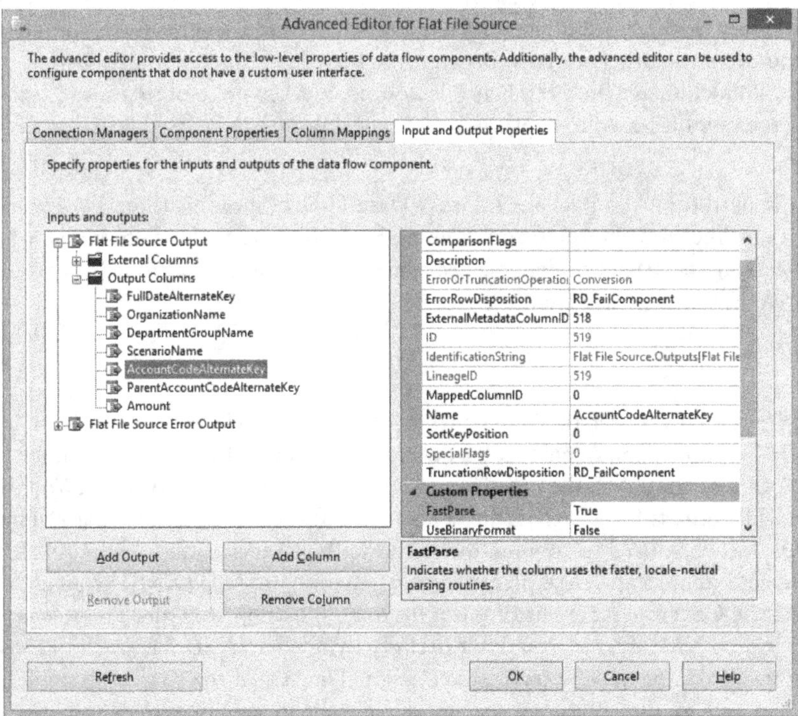

FIGURE 4-8

MultiFlatFile Connection Manager

If you know that you want to process a series of flat files in a Data Flow, or you want to refer to many files in the Control Flow, you can optionally use the MultiFlatFile or "Multiple Flat File Connection Manager." The Multiple Flat File Connection Manager refers to a list of files for copying or moving, or it may hold a series of SQL scripts to execute, similar to the File Connection Manager. The Multiple Flat File Connection Manager gives you the same view as a Flat File Connection Manager, but it enables you to point to multiple files. In either case, you can point to a list of files by placing a vertical bar (|) between each filename:

```
C:\Projects\011305c.dat|C:\Projects\053105c.dat
```

In the Data Flow, the Multiple Flat File Connection Manager reacts by combining the total number of records from all the files that you have pointed to, appearing like a single merged file. Using this option will initiate the Data Flow process only once for the files whereas the Foreach Loop container will initiate the process once per file being processed. In either case, the metadata from the file must match in order to use them in the Data Flow. Most developers lean toward using Foreach Loop Containers because it's easier to make them dynamic. With these Multiple File or Multiple Flat File Connection Managers, you have to parse your file list and add the vertical bar between them. If you use Foreach Loop Containers, that is taken care of for you.

Raw File Source

The Raw File Source is a specialized type of file that is optimized for reading data quickly from SSIS. A Raw File Source is created by a Raw File Destination (discussed later in this chapter). You can't add columns to the Raw File Source, but you can remove unused columns from the source in much the same way you do in the other sources. Because the Raw File Source requires little translation, it can load data much faster than the Flat File Source, but the price of this speed is little flexibility. Typically, you see raw files used to capture data at checkpoints to be used later in case of a package failure.

These sources are typically used for cross-package or cross-Data Flow communication. For example, if you have a Data Flow that takes four hours to run, you might wish to stage the data to a raw file halfway through the processing in case a problem occurs. Then, the second Data Flow Task would continue the remaining two hours of processing.

XML Source

The XML source is a powerful SSIS source that can use a local or remote (via HTTP or UNC) XML file as the source. This source component is a bit different from the OLE DB Source in its configuration. First, you point to the XML file locally on your machine or at a UNC path. You can also point to a remote HTTP address for an XML file. This is useful for interaction with a vendor. This source is also very useful when used in conjunction with the Web Service Task or the XML Task. Once you point the data item to an XML file, you must generate an XSD (XML Schema Definition) file by clicking the Generate XSD button or point to an existing XSD file. The schema definition can also be an in-line XML file, so you don't necessarily need an XSD file. Each of these cases may vary based on the XML that you're trying to connect. The rest of the source resembles other sources; for example, you can filter the columns you don't want to see down the chain.

ADO.NET Source

The ADO.NET Source enables you to make a .NET provider a source and make it available for consumption inside the package. The source uses an ADO.NET Connection Manager to connect to the provider. The Data Flow is based on OLE DB, so for best performance, using the OLE DB Source is preferred. However, some providers might require that you use the ADO.NET source. Its interface is identical in appearance to the OLE DB Source, but it does require an ADO.NET Connection Manager.

DESTINATIONS

Inside the Data Flow, *destinations* accept the data from the Data Sources and from the transformations. The architecture can send the data to nearly any OLE DB–compliant Data Source, a flat file, or Analysis Services, to name just a few. Like sources, destinations are managed through Connection Managers. The configuration difference between sources and destinations is that in destinations, you have a Mappings page (shown in Figure 4-9), where you specify how the inputted data from the Data Flow maps to the destination. As shown in the Mappings page in this figure, the columns are automatically mapped based on column names, but they don't necessarily have to be exactly lined up. You can also choose to ignore given columns, such as when you're inserting into a table that has an identity column, and you don't want to inherit the value from the source table.

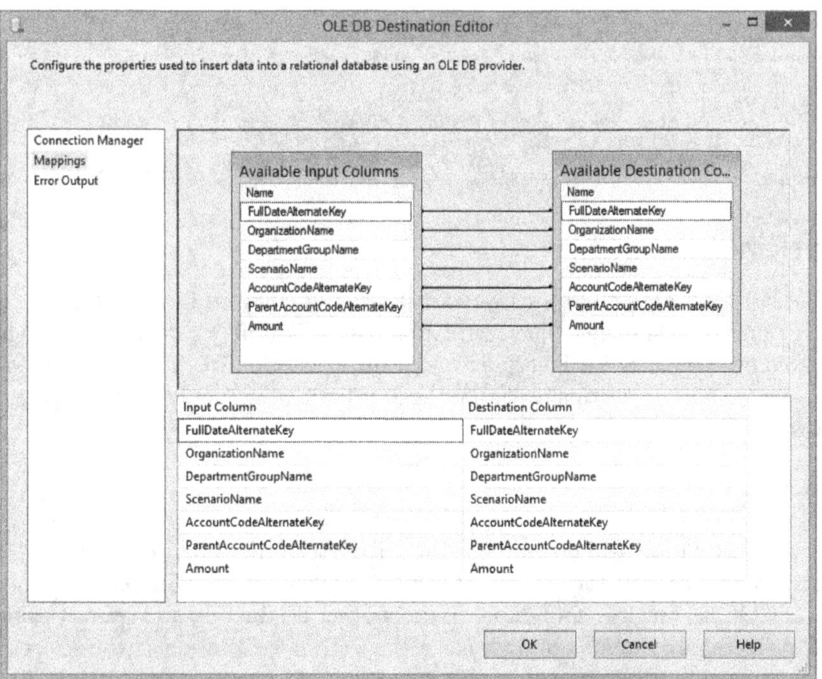

FIGURE 4-9

In SQL Server 2014, you can start by configuring the destination first, but it would lack the metadata you need. So, you will really want to connect to a Data Flow path. To do this, select the source or a transformation and drag the blue arrow to the destination. If you want to output bad data or data that has had an error to a destination, you would drag the red arrow to that destination. If you try to configure the destination before attaching it to the transformation or source, you will see the error in Figure 4-10. In SQL Server 2014, you can still proceed and edit the component, but it won't be as meaningful without the live metadata.

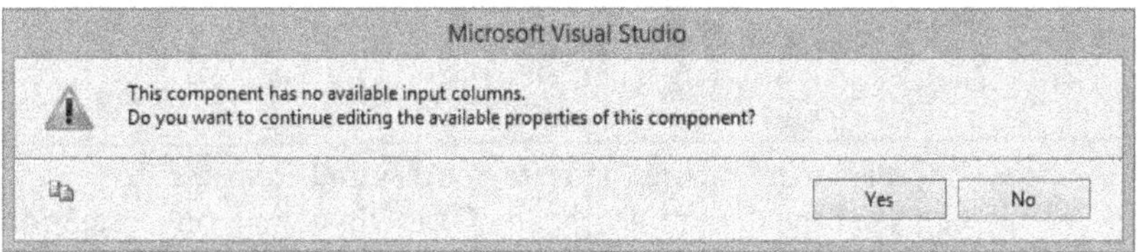
Microsoft Visual Studio
This component has no available input columns.
Do you want to continue editing the available properties of this component?
Yes
No

FIGURE 4-10

Excel Destination

The Excel Destination is identical to the Excel Source except that it accepts data rather than sends data. To use it, first select the Excel Connection Manager from the Connection Manager page, and then specify the worksheet into which you wish to load data.

WARNING *The big caveat with the Excel Destination is that unlike the Flat File Destination, an Excel spreadsheet must already exist with the sheet into which you wish to copy data. If the spreadsheet doesn't exist, you will receive an error. To work around this issue, you can create a blank spreadsheet to use as your template, and then use the File System Task to copy the file over.*

Flat File Destination

The commonly used Flat File Destination sends data to a flat file, and it can be fixed-width or delimited based on the Connection Manager. The destination uses a Flat File Connection Manager. You can also add a custom header to the file by typing it into the Header option in the Connection Manager page. Lastly, you can specify on this page that the destination file should be overwritten each time the Data Flow is run.

OLE DB Destination

Your most commonly used destination will probably be the OLE DB Destination (see Figure 4-11). It can write data from the source or transformation to OLE DB–compliant Data Sources such as Oracle, DB2, Access, and SQL Server. It is configured like any other destination and source, using OLE DB Connection Managers. A dynamic option it has is the Data Access Mode. If you select Table or View - Fast Load, or its variable equivalent, several options will be available, such as Table Lock. This Fast Load option is available only for SQL Server database instances and turns on a bulk load option in SQL Server instead of a row-by-row operation.

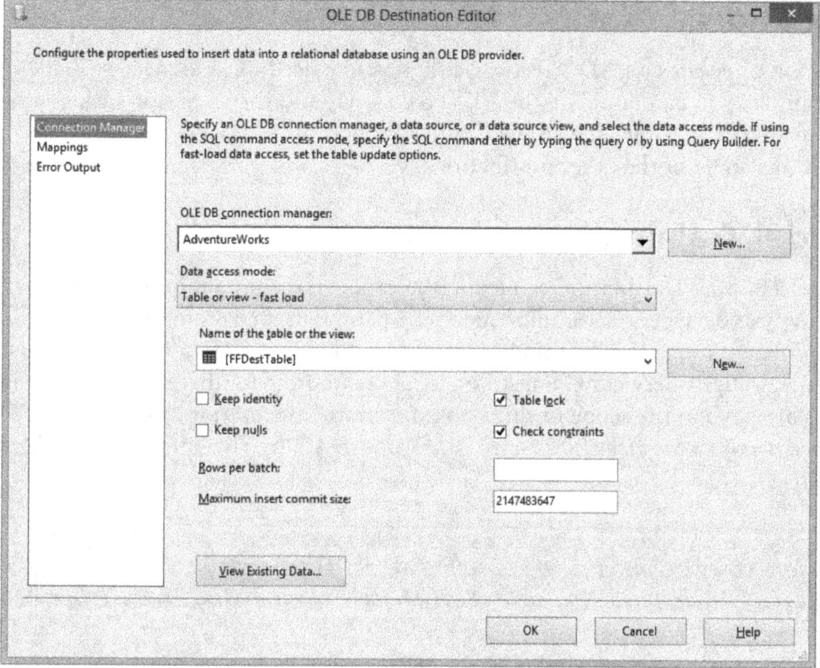

FIGURE 4-11

A few options of note here are Rows Per Batch, which specifies how many rows are in each batch sent to the destination, and Maximum Insert Commit Size, which specifies how large the batch size will be prior to issuing a commit statement. The Table Lock option places a lock on the destination table to speed up the load. As you can imagine, this causes grief for your users if they are trying to read from the table at the same time. Another important option is Keep Identity, which enables you to insert into a column that has the identity property set on it. Generally speaking, you can improve performance by setting Max Insert Commit Size to a number like 10,000, but that number will vary according to column width.

New users commonly ask what the difference is between the fast load and the normal load (table or view option) for the OLE DB Destination. The Fast Load option specifies that SSIS will load data in bulk into the OLE DB Destination's target table. Because this is a bulk operation, error handling via a redirection or ignoring data errors is not allowed. If you require this level of error handling, you need to turn off bulk loading of the data by selecting Table or View for the Data Access Mode option. Doing so will allow you to redirect your errors down the red line, but it causes a slowdown of the load by a factor of at least four.

Raw File Destination

The Raw File Destination is an especially speedy Data Destination that does not use a Connection Manager to configure. Instead, you point to the file on the server in the editor. This destination is written to typically as an intermediate point for partially transformed data. Once written to, other packages can read the data in by using the Raw File Source. The file is written in native format, so it is very fast.

Recordset Destination

The Recordset Destination populates an ADO recordset that can be used outside the transformation. For example, you can populate the ADO recordset, and then a Script Task could read that recordset by reading a variable later in the Control Flow. This type of destination does not support an error output like some of the other destinations.

Data Mining Model Training

The Data Mining Model Training Destination can train (the process of a data mining algorithm learning the data) an Analysis Services data mining model by passing it data from the Data Flow. You can train multiple mining models from a single destination and Data Flow. To use this destination, you select an Analysis Services Connection Manager and the mining model. Analysis Services mining models are beyond the scope of this book; for more information, please see *Professional SQL Server Analysis Services 2012 with MDX and DAX* by Sivakumar Harinath and his coauthors (Wrox, 2012).

> **NOTE** *The data you pass into the Data Mining Model Training Destination must be presorted. To do this, you use the Sort Transformation, discussed later in this chapter.*

DataReader Destination

The DataReader Destination provides a way to extend SSIS Data Flows to external packages or programs that can use the DataReader interface, such as a .NET application. When you configure this destination, ensure that its name is something that's easy to recognize later in your program, because you will be calling that name later. After you have configured the name and basic properties, check the columns you'd like outputted to the destination in the Input Columns tab.

Dimension and Partition Processing

The Dimension Processing Destination loads and processes an Analysis Services dimension. You have the option to perform full, incremental, or update processing. To configure the destination, select the Analysis Services Connection Manager that contains the dimension you would like to process on the Connection Manager page of the Dimension Processing Destination Editor. You will then see a list of dimensions and fact tables in the box. Select the dimension you want to load and process, and from the Mappings page, map the data from the Data Flow to the selected dimension. Lastly, you can configure how you would like to handle errors, such as unknown keys, in the Advanced page. Generally, the default options are fine for this page unless you have special error-handling needs. The Partition Processing Destination has identical options, but it processes an Analysis Services partition instead of a dimension.

COMMON TRANSFORMATIONS

Transformations or transforms are key components to the Data Flow that transform the data to a desired format as you move from step to step. For example, you may want a sampling of your data to be sorted and aggregated. Three transformations can accomplish this task for you: one to take a random sampling of the data, one to sort, and another to aggregate. The nicest thing about transformations in SSIS is that they occur in-memory and no longer require elaborate scripting as in SQL Server 2000 DTS. As you add a transformation, the data is altered and passed down the path in the Data Flow. Also, because this is done in-memory, you no longer have to create staging tables to perform most functions. When dealing with very large data sets, though, you may still choose to create staging tables.

You set up the transformation by dragging it onto the Data Flow tab design area. Then, click the source or transformation you'd like to connect it to, and drag the green arrow to the target transformation or destination. If you drag the red arrow, then rows that fail to transform will be directed to that target. After you have the transformation connected, you can double-click it to configure it.

Synchronous versus Asynchronous Transformations

Transformations are divided into two main categories: *synchronous* and *asynchronous*. In SSIS, you want to ideally use all synchronous components. Synchronous transformations are components such as the Derived Column and Data Conversion Transformations, where rows flow into memory buffers in the transformation, and the same buffers come out. No rows are held, and typically these transformations perform very quickly, with minimal impact to your Data Flow.

Asynchronous transformations can cause a block in your Data Flow and slow down your runtime. There are two types of asynchronous transformations: partially blocking and fully blocking.

- **Partially blocking transformations**, such as the Union All, create new memory buffers for the output of the transformation.
- **Fully blocking transformations**, such as the Sort and Aggregate Transformations, do the same thing but cause a full block of the data. In order to sort the data, SSIS must first see every single row of the data. If you have a 100MB file, then you may require 200MB of RAM in order to process the Data Flow because of a fully blocking transformation. These fully blocking transformations represent the single largest slowdown in SSIS and should be considered carefully in terms of any architecture decisions you must make.

> **NOTE** *Chapter 16 covers these concepts in much more depth.*

Aggregate

The fully blocking asynchronous Aggregate Transformation allows you to aggregate data from the Data Flow to apply certain T-SQL functions that are done in a `GROUP BY` statement, such as Average, Minimum, Maximum, and Count. For example, in Figure 4-12, you can see that the data is grouped together on the ProductKey column, and then the SalesAmount column is summed. Lastly, for every ProductKey, the maximum OrderDateKey is aggregated. This produces four new columns that can be consumed down the path, or future actions can be performed on them and the other columns dropped at that time.

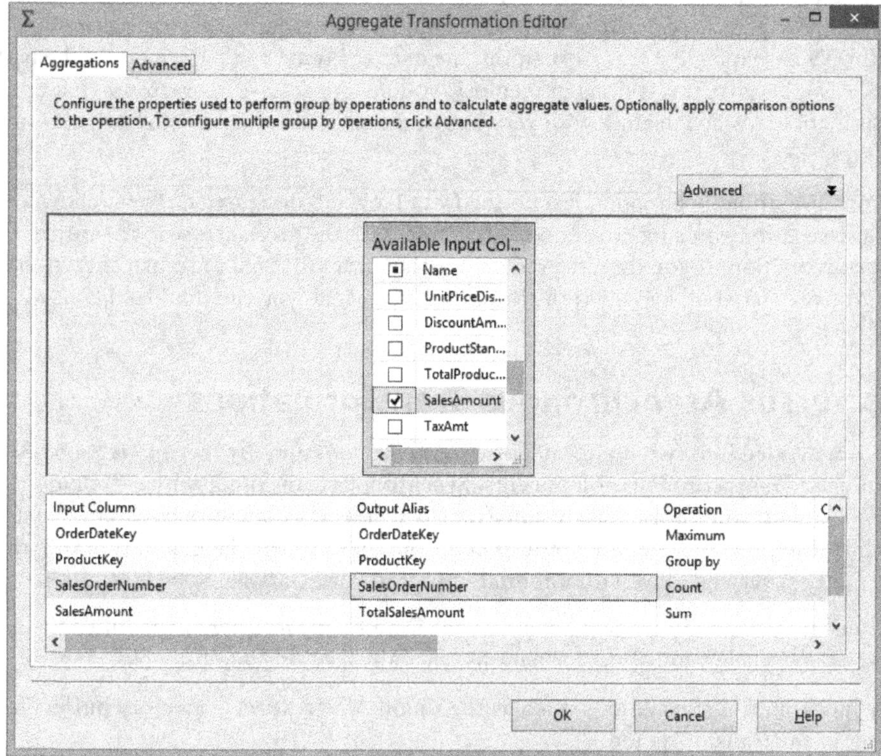

FIGURE 4-12

The Aggregate Transformation is configured in the Aggregate Transformation Editor (see Figure 4-12). To do so, first check the column on which you wish to perform the action. After checking the column, the input column will be filled below in the grid. Optionally, type an alias in the Output Alias column that you wish to give the column when it is outputted to the next transformation or destination. For example, if the column currently holds the total money per customer, you might change the name of the column that's outputted from SalesAmount to TotalCustomerSaleAmt. This will make it easier for you to recognize what the column represents along the data path. The most important option is Operation. For this option, you can select the following:

- **Group By:** Breaks the data set into groups by the column you specify
- **Average:** Averages the selected column's numeric data
- **Count:** Counts the records in a group
- **Count Distinct:** Counts the distinct non-NULL values in a group

- **Minimum:** Returns the minimum numeric value in the group
- **Maximum:** Returns the maximum numeric value in the group
- **Sum:** Returns sum of the selected column's numeric data in the group

You can click the Advanced tab to see options that enable you to configure multiple outputs from the transformation. After you click Advanced, you can type a new Aggregation Name to create a new output. You will then be able to check the columns you'd like to aggregate again as if it were a new transformation. This can be used to roll up the same input data different ways.

In the Advanced tab, the "Key scale" option sets an approximate number of keys. The default is Unspecified, which optimizes the transformation's cache to the appropriate level. For example, setting this to Low will optimize the transform to write 500,000 keys. Setting it to Medium will optimize it for 5,000,000 keys, and High will optimize the transform for 25,000,000 keys. You can also set the exact number of keys by using the "Number of keys" option.

The "Count distinct scale" option will optionally set the amount of distinct values that can be written by the transformation. The default value is Unspecified, but if you set it to Low, the transformation will be optimized to write 500,000 distinct values. Setting the option to Medium will set it to 5,000,000 values, and High will optimize the transformation to 25,000,000. The Auto Extend Factor specifies to what factor your memory can be extended by the transformation. The default option is 25 percent, but you can specify another setting to keep your RAM from getting away from you.

Conditional Split

The Conditional Split Transformation is a fantastic way to add complex logic to your Data Flow. This transformation enables you to send the data from a single data path to various outputs or paths based on conditions that use the SSIS expression language. For example, you could configure the transformation to send all products with sales that have a quantity greater than 500 to one path, and products that have more than 50 sales down another path. Lastly, if neither condition is met, the sales would go down a third path, called "Small Sale," which essentially acts as an `ELSE` statement in T-SQL. This exact situation is shown in Figure 4-13. You can drag and drop the column or expression code snippets from the tree in the top-right panel. After you complete the condition, you need to name it something logical, rather than the default name of Case 1. You'll use this case name later in the Data Flow. You also can configure the "Default output name," which will output any data that does not fit any case. Each case in the transform and the default output name will show as a green line in the Data Flow and will be annotated with the name you typed in.

You can also conditionally read string data by using SSIS expressions, such as the following example, which reads the first letter of the City column:

```
SUBSTRING(City,1,1) == "F"
```

You can learn much more about the expression language in Chapter 5. Once you connect the transformation to the next transformation in the path or destination, you'll see a pop-up dialog that lets you select which case you wish to flow down this path, as shown in Figure 4-14. In this figure, you can see three cases. The "Large Sale" condition can go down one path, "Medium Sales" down another, and the default "Small Sales" down the last path. After you complete the configuration of the first case, you can create a path for each case in the conditional split.

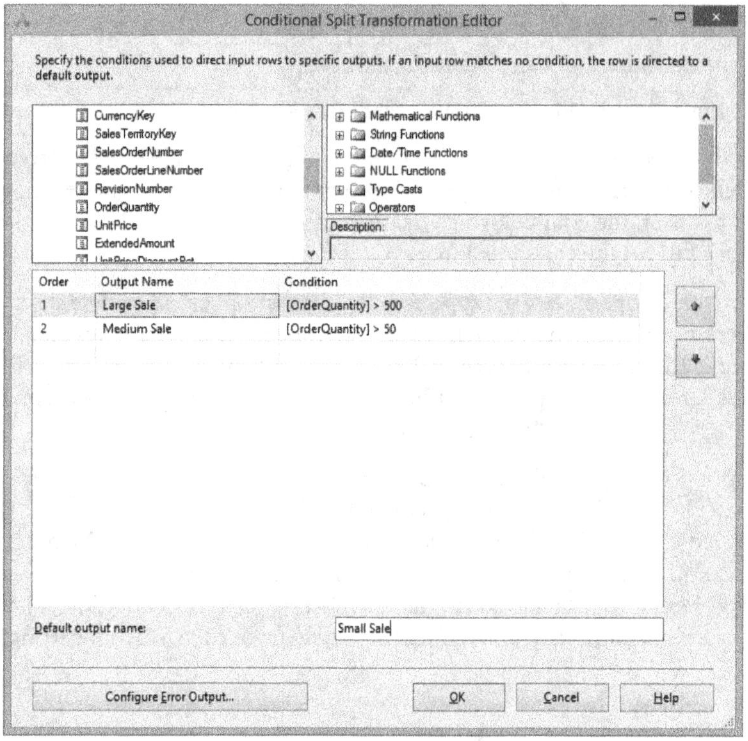

FIGURE 4-13

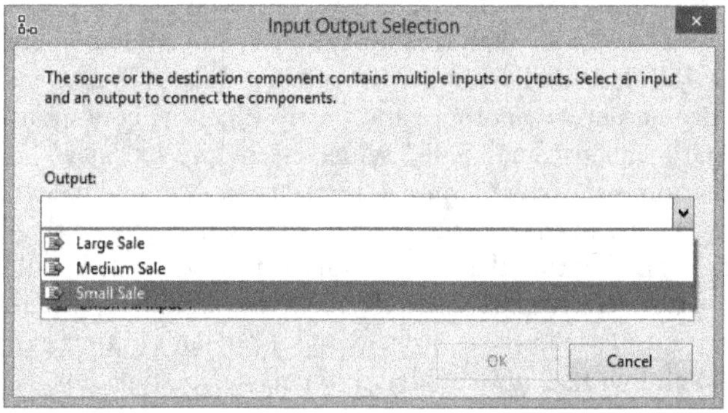

FIGURE 4-14

A much more detailed example of the Conditional Split Transformation is given in Chapter 8.

Data Conversion

The Data Conversion Transformation performs a similar function to the `CONVERT` or `CAST` functions in T-SQL. This transformation is configured in the Data Conversion Transformation Editor (see Figure 4-15), where you check each column that you wish to convert and then specify to what you wish to convert it under the Data Type column. The Output Alias is the column name you want to assign to the column after it is transformed. If you don't assign it a new name, it will later be displayed as Data Conversion: ColumnName in the Data Flow. This same logic can also be accomplished in a Derived Column Transform, but this component provides a simpler UI.

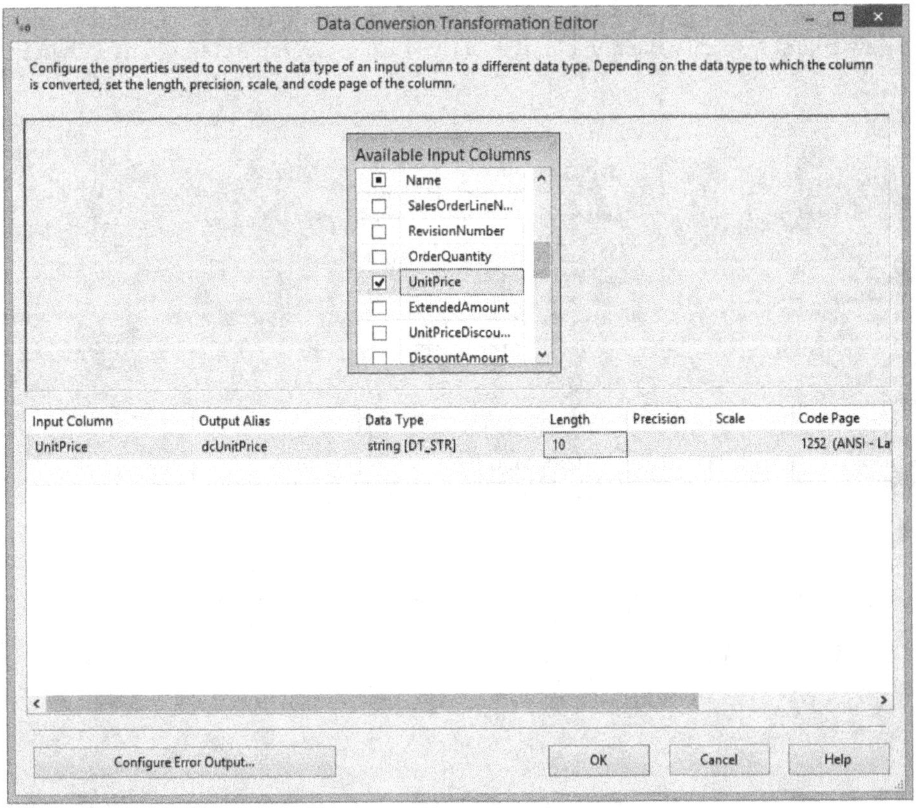

FIGURE 4-15

Derived Column

The Derived Column Transformation creates a new column that is calculated (derived) from the output of another column or set of columns. It is one of the most important transformations in your Data Flow arsenal. You may wish to use this transformation, for example, to multiply the quantity of orders by the cost of the order to derive the total cost of the order, as shown in Figure 4-16. You can also use it to find out the current date or to fill in the blanks in the data by using the `ISNULL` function. This is one of the top five transformations that you will find yourself using to alleviate the need for T-SQL scripting in the package.

To configure this transformation, drag the column or variable into the Expression column, as shown in Figure 4-16. Then add any functions to it. You can find a list of functions in the top-right corner of the Derived Column Transformation Editor. You must then specify, in the Derived Column dropdown box, whether you want the output to replace an existing column in the Data Flow or create a new column. As shown in Figure 4-16, the first derived column expression is doing an in-place update of the OrderQuantity column. The expression states that if the OrderQuantity column is null, then convert it to 0; otherwise, keep the existing data in the OrderQuantity column. If you create a new column, specify the name in the Derived Column Name column, as shown in the VAT column.

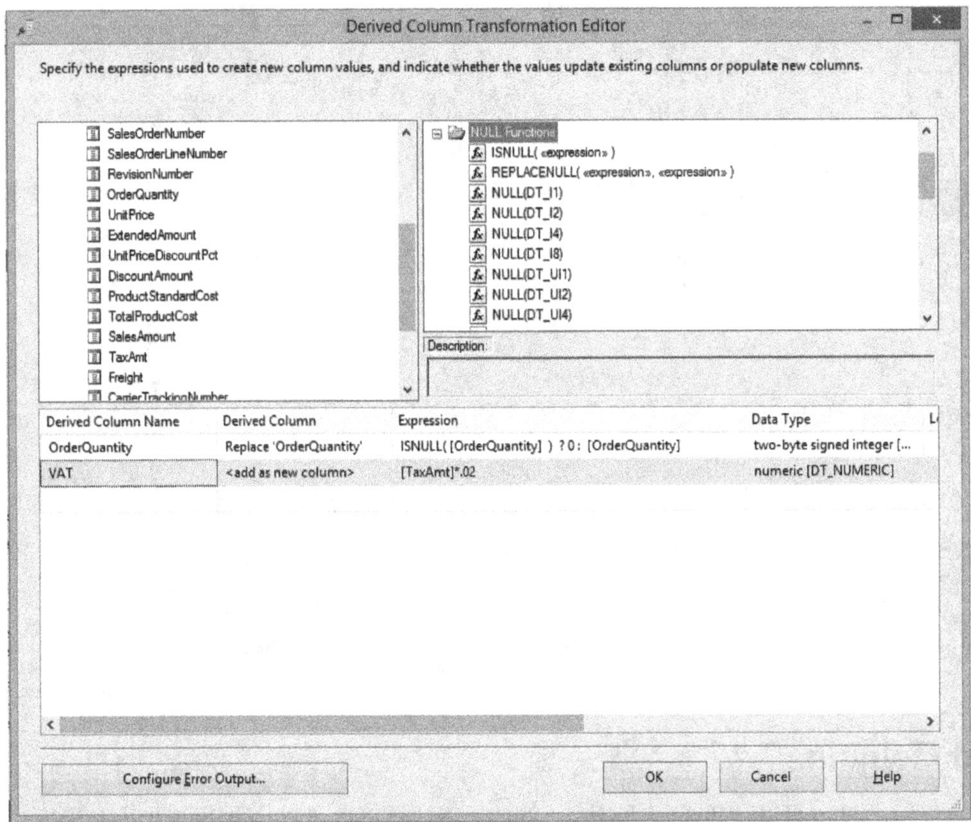

FIGURE 4-16

You'll find all the available functions for the expression language in the top-right pane of the editor. There are no hidden or secret expressions in this C# variant expression language. We use the expression language much more throughout this and future chapters so don't worry too much about the details of the language yet.

Some common expressions can be found in the following table:

EXAMPLE EXPRESSION	DESCRIPTION
SUBSTRING(ZipCode, 1,5)	Captures the first 5 numbers of a zip code
ISNULL(Name) ? "NA" : Name	If the Name column is NULL, replace with the value of NA. Otherwise, keep the Name column as is.
UPPER(FirstName)	Uppercases the FirstName column
(DT_WSTR, 3)CompanyID + Name	Converts the CompanyID column to a string and appends it to the Name column

Lookup

The Lookup Transformation performs what equates to an `INNER JOIN` on the Data Flow and a second data set. The second data set can be an OLE DB table or a cached file, which is loaded in the Cache Transformation. After you perform the lookup, you can retrieve additional columns from the second column. If no match is found, an error occurs by default. You can later choose, using the Configure Error Output button, to ignore the failure (setting any additional columns retrieved from the reference table to `NULL`) or redirect the rows down the second nonmatched green path.

> **NOTE** *This is a very detailed transformation; it is covered in much more depth in Chapter 7 and again in Chapter 8.*

Cache

The Cache Transformation enables you to load a cache file on disk in the Data Flow. This cache file is later used for fast lookups in a Lookup Transformation. The Cache Transformation can be used to populate a cache file in the Data Flow as a transformation, and then be immediately used, or it can be used as a destination and then used by another package or Data Flow in the same package.

The cache file that's created enables you to perform lookups against large data sets from a raw file. It also enables you to share the same lookup cache across many Data Flows or packages.

> **NOTE** *This transformation is covered in much more detail in Chapter 7.*

Row Count

The Row Count Transformation provides the capability to count rows in a stream that is directed to its input source. This transformation must place that count into a variable that could be used in the Control Flow — for insertion into an audit table, for example. This transformation is useful for tasks that require knowing "how many?" It is especially valuable because you don't physically have to commit stream data to a physical table to retrieve the count, and it can act as a destination, terminating your data stream. If you need to know how many rows are split during the Conditional Split Transformation, direct the output of each side of the split to a separate Row Count Transformation. Each Row Count Transformation is designed for an input stream and will output a row count into a Long (integer) or compatible data type. You can then use this variable to log information into storage, to build e-mail messages, or to conditionally run steps in your packages.

For this transformation, all you really need to provide in terms of configuration is the name of the variable to store the count of the input stream. You will now simulate a row count situation in a package. You could use this type of logic to implement conditional execution of any task, but for simplicity you'll conditionally execute a Script Task that does nothing.

1. Create an SSIS package named Row Count Example. Add a Data Flow Task to the Control Flow design surface.
2. In the Control Flow tab, add a variable named **iRowCount**. Ensure that the variable is package scoped and of type Int32. If you don't know how to add a variable, select Variable from the SSIS menu and click the Add Variable button.
3. Create a Connection Manager that connects to the AdventureWorks database. Add an OLE DB Data Source to the Data Flow design surface. Configure the source to point to your AdventureWorks database's Connection Manager and the table [ErrorLog].
4. Add a Row Count Transformation Task to the Data Flow tab. Open the Advanced Editor. Select the variable named User::iRowCount as the Variable property. Your editor should resemble Figure 4-17.
5. Return to the Control Flow tab and add a Script Task. This task won't really perform any action. It will be used to show the conditional capability to perform steps based on the value returned by the Row Count Transformation.
6. Connect the Data Flow Task to the Script Task.
7. Right-click the arrow connecting the Data Flow and Script Tasks. Select the Edit menu. In the Precedence Constraint Editor, change the Evaluation Operation to Expression. Set the Expression to @iRowCount>0.

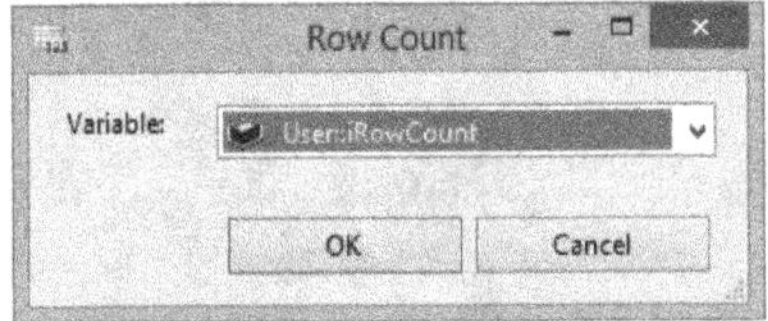

FIGURE 4-17

When you run the package, you'll see that the Script Task is not executed. If you are curious, insert a row into the [ErrorLog] table and rerun the package or change the source table that has data. You'll see that the Script Task will show a green checkmark, indicating that it was executed. An example of what your package may look like is shown in Figure 4-18. In this screenshot, no rows were transformed, so the Script Task never executed.

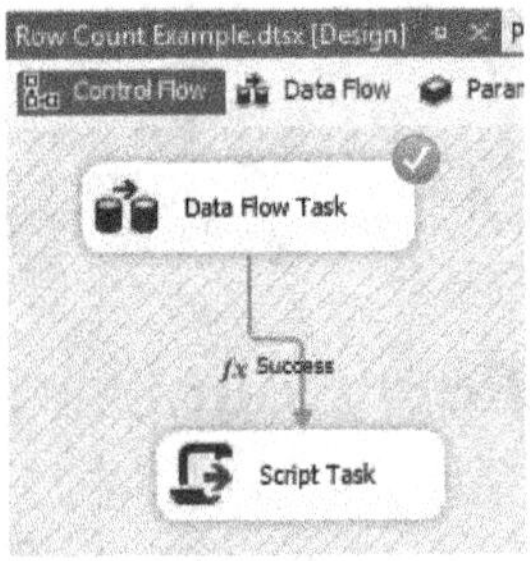

FIGURE 4-18

Script Component

The Script Component enables you to write custom .NET scripts as transformations, sources, or destinations. Once you drag the component over, it will ask you if you want it to be a source, transformation, or destination. Some of the things you can do with this transformation include the following:

- Create a custom transformation that would use a .NET assembly to validate credit card numbers or mailing addresses.
- Validate data and skip records that don't seem reasonable. For example, you can use it in a human resource recruitment system to pull out candidates that don't match the salary requirement at a job code level.
- Read from a proprietary system for which no standard provider exists.
- Write a custom component to integrate with a third-party vendor.

Scripts used as sources can support multiple outputs, and you have the option of precompiling the scripts for runtime efficiency.

> **NOTE** *You can learn much more about the Script Component in Chapter 9.*

Slowly Changing Dimension

The Slowly Changing Dimension (SCD) Transformation provides a great head start in helping to solve a common, classic changing-dimension problem that occurs in the outer edge of your data model — the dimension or lookup tables. The changing-dimension issue in online transaction and analytical processing database designs is too big to cover in this chapter, but a brief overview should help you understand the value of service the SCD Transformation provides.

A dimension table contains a set of discrete values with a description and often other measurable attributes such as price, weight, or sales territory. The classic problem is what to do in your dimension data when an attribute in a row changes — particularly when you are loading data automatically through an ETL process. This transformation can shave days off of your development time in relation to creating the load manually through T-SQL, but it can add time because of how it queries your destination and how it updates with the OLE DB Command Transform (row by row).

> **NOTE** *Loading data warehouses is covered in Chapter 12.*

Sort

The Sort Transformation is a fully blocking asynchronous transformation that enables you to sort data based on any column in the path. This is probably one of the top ten transformations you will use on a regular basis because some of the other transformations require sorted data, and you're reading data from a system that does not allow you to perform an ORDER BY clause or is not pre-sorted. To configure it, open the Sort Transformation Editor after it is connected to the path and check the column that you wish to sort by. Then, uncheck any column you don't want passed through to the path from the Pass Through column. By default, every column will be passed through the pipeline. You can see this in Figure 4-19, where the user is sorting by the Name column and passing all other columns in the path as output.

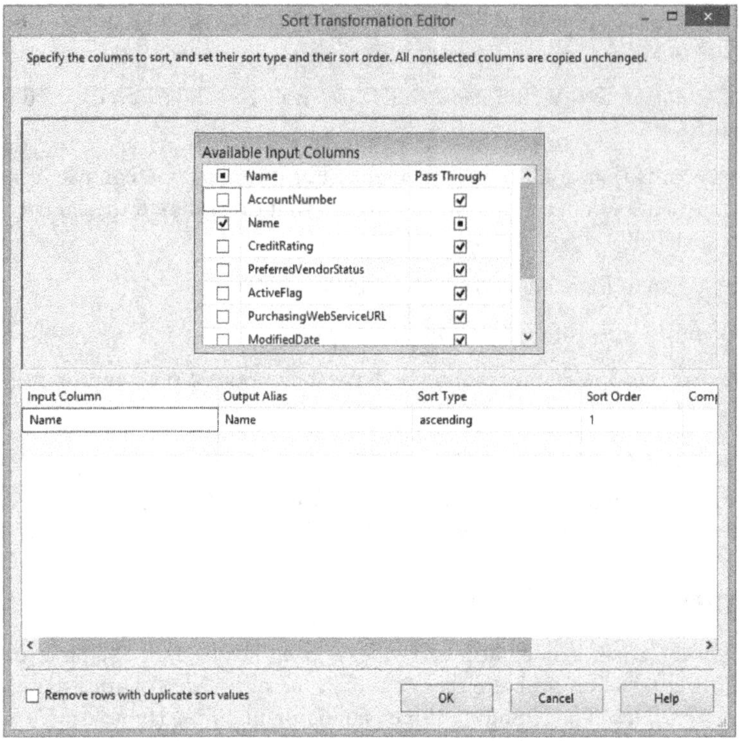

FIGURE 4-19

In the bottom grid, you can specify the alias that you wish to output and whether you want to sort in ascending or descending order. The Sort Order column shows which column will be sorted on first, second, third, and so on. You can optionally check the Remove Rows with Duplicate Sort Values option to "Remove rows that have duplicate sort values." This is a great way to do rudimentary de-duplication of your data. If a second value comes in that matches your same sort key, it is ignored and the row is dropped.

> **NOTE** *Because this is an asynchronous transformation, it will slow down your Data Flow immensely. Use it only when you have to, and use it sparingly.*

As mentioned previously, avoid using the Sort Transformation when possible, because of speed. However, some transformations, like the Merge Join and Merge, require the data to be sorted. If you place an `ORDER BY` statement in the OLE DB Source, SSIS is not aware of the `ORDER BY` statement because it could just have easily been in a stored procedure.

If you have an `ORDER BY` clause in your T-SQL statement in the OLE DB Source or the ADO .NET Source, you can notify SSIS that the data is already sorted, obviating the need for the Sort Transformation in the Advanced Editor. After ordering the data in your SQL statement, right-click the source and select Advanced Editor. From the Input and Output Properties tab, select OLE DB Source Output. In the Properties pane, change the IsSorted property to True.

Then, under Output Columns, select the column you are ordering on in your SQL statement, and change the SortKeyPosition to 1 if you're sorting only by a single column ascending, as shown in Figure 4-20. If you have multiple columns, you could change this SortKeyPosition value to the column position in the `ORDER BY` statement starting at 1. A value of -1 will sort the data in descending order.

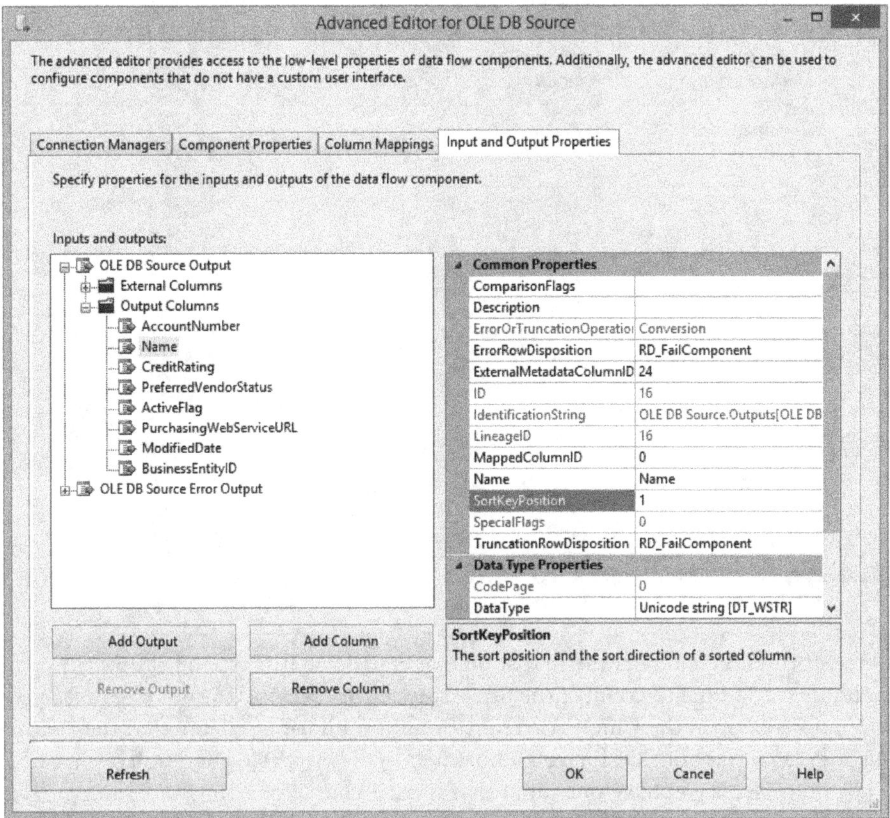

FIGURE 4-20

Union All

The Union All Transformation works much the same way as the Merge Transformation, but it does not require sorted data. It takes the outputs from multiple sources or transformations and combines them into a single result set. For example, in Figure 4-21, the user combines the data from three sources into a single output using the Union All Transformation. Notice that the City column is called something different in each source and that all are now merged in this transformation into a single column. Think of the Union All as essentially stacking the data on top of each other, much like the T-SQL `UNION` operator does.

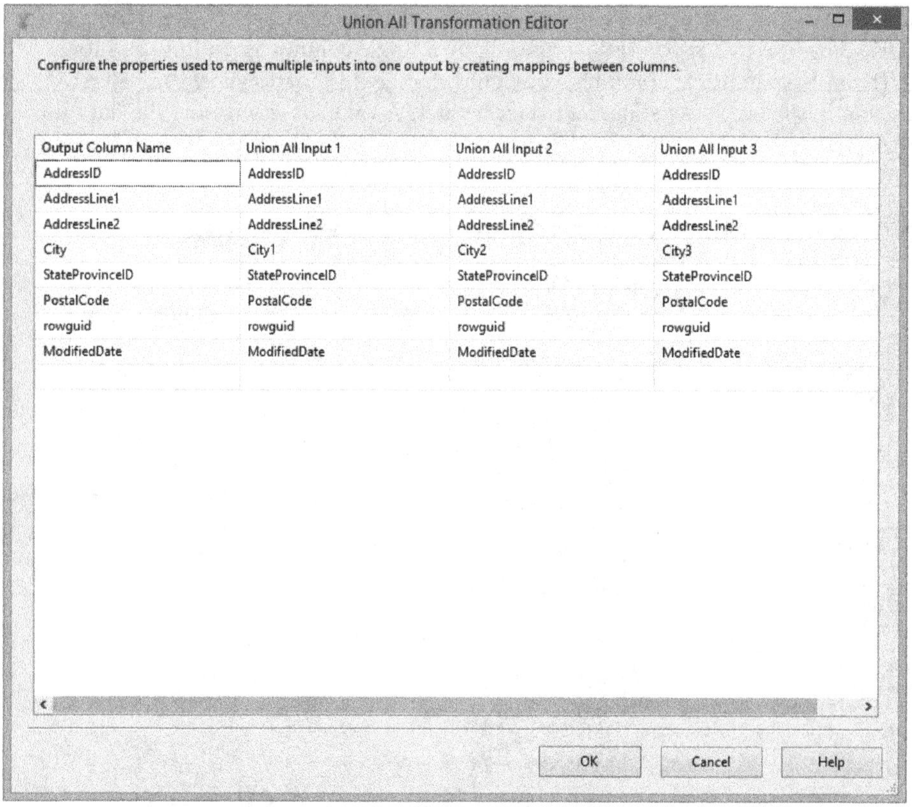

Union All Transformation Editor

Configure the properties used to merge multiple inputs into one output by creating mappings between columns.

Output Column Name	Union All Input 1	Union All Input 2	Union All Input 3
AddressID	AddressID	AddressID	AddressID
AddressLine1	AddressLine1	AddressLine1	AddressLine1
AddressLine2	AddressLine2	AddressLine2	AddressLine2
City	City1	City2	City3
StateProvinceID	StateProvinceID	StateProvinceID	StateProvinceID
PostalCode	PostalCode	PostalCode	PostalCode
rowguid	rowguid	rowguid	rowguid
ModifiedDate	ModifiedDate	ModifiedDate	ModifiedDate

OK Cancel Help

FIGURE 4-21

To configure the transformation, connect the first source or transformation to the Union All Transformation, and then continue to connect the other sources or transformations to it until you are done. You can optionally open the Union All Transformation Editor to ensure that the columns map correctly, but SSIS takes care of that for you automatically. The transformation fixes minor metadata issues. For example, if you have one input that is a 20-character string and another that is 50 characters, the output of this from the Union All Transformation will be the longer 50-character column. You need to open the Union All Transformation Editor only if the column names from one of the transformations that feed the Union All Transformation have different column names.

OTHER TRANSFORMATIONS

There are many more transformations you can use to complete your more complex Data Flow. Some of these transformations like the Audit and Case Transformations can be used in lieu of a Derived Column Transformation because they have a simpler UI. Others serve a purpose that's specialized.

Audit

The Audit Transformation allows you to add auditing data to your Data Flow. Because of acts such as HIPPA and Sarbanes-Oxley (SOX) governing audits, you often must be able to track who inserted data into a table and when. This transformation helps you with that function. The task is easy to configure. For example, to track what task inserted data into the table, you can add those columns to the Data Flow path with this transformation. The functionality in the Audit Transformation can be achieved with a Derived Column Transformation, but the Audit Transformation provides an easier interface.

All other columns are passed through to the path as an output, and any auditing item you add will also be added to the path. Simply select the type of data you want to audit in the Audit Type column (shown in Figure 4-22), and then name the column that will be outputted to the flow. Following are some of the available options:

- **Execution instance GUID:** GUID that identifies the execution instance of the package
- **Package ID:** Unique ID for the package
- **Package name:** Name of the package
- **Version ID:** Version GUID of the package
- **Execution start time:** Time the package began
- **Machine name:** Machine on which the package ran
- **User name:** User who started the package
- **Task name:** Data Flow Task name that holds the Audit Task
- **Task ID:** Unique identifier for the Data Flow Task that holds the Audit Task

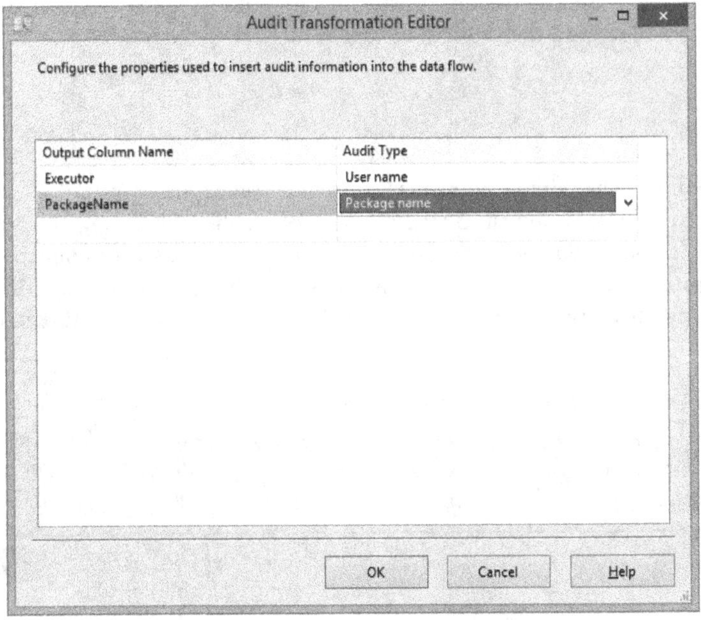

FIGURE 4-22

Character Map

The Character Map Transformation (shown in Figure 4-23) performs common character translations in the flow. This simple transformation can be configured in a single tab. To do so, check the columns you wish to transform. Then, select whether you want this modified column to be added as a new column or whether you want to update the original column. You can give the column a new name under the Output Alias column. Lastly, select the operation you wish to perform on the inputted column. The available operation types are as follows:

- **Byte Reversal:** Reverses the order of the bytes. For example, for the data `0x1234 0x9876`, the result is `0x4321 0x6789`. This uses the same behavior as LCMapString with the LCMAP_BYTEREV option.
- **Full Width:** Converts the half-width character type to full width
- **Half Width:** Converts the full-width character type to half width
- **Hiragana:** Converts the Katakana style of Japanese characters to Hiragana
- **Katakana:** Converts the Hiragana style of Japanese characters to Katakana
- **Linguistic Casing:** Applies the regional linguistic rules for casing
- **Lowercase:** Changes all letters in the input to lowercase
- **Traditional Chinese:** Converts the simplified Chinese characters to traditional Chinese
- **Simplified Chinese:** Converts the traditional Chinese characters to simplified Chinese
- **Uppercase:** Changes all letters in the input to uppercase

In Figure 4-23, you can see that two columns are being transformed — both to uppercase. For the TaskName input, a new column is added, and the original is kept. The PackageName column is replaced in-line.

Copy Column

The Copy Column Transformation is a very simple transformation that copies the output of a column to a clone of itself. This is useful if you wish to create a copy of a column before you perform some elaborate transformations. You could then keep the original value as your control subject and the copy as the modified column. To configure this transformation, go to the Copy Column Transformation Editor and check the column you want to clone. Then assign a name to the new column.

> **NOTE** *The Derived Column Transformation will allow you to transform the data from a column to a new column, but the UI in the Copy Column Transformation is simpler for some.*

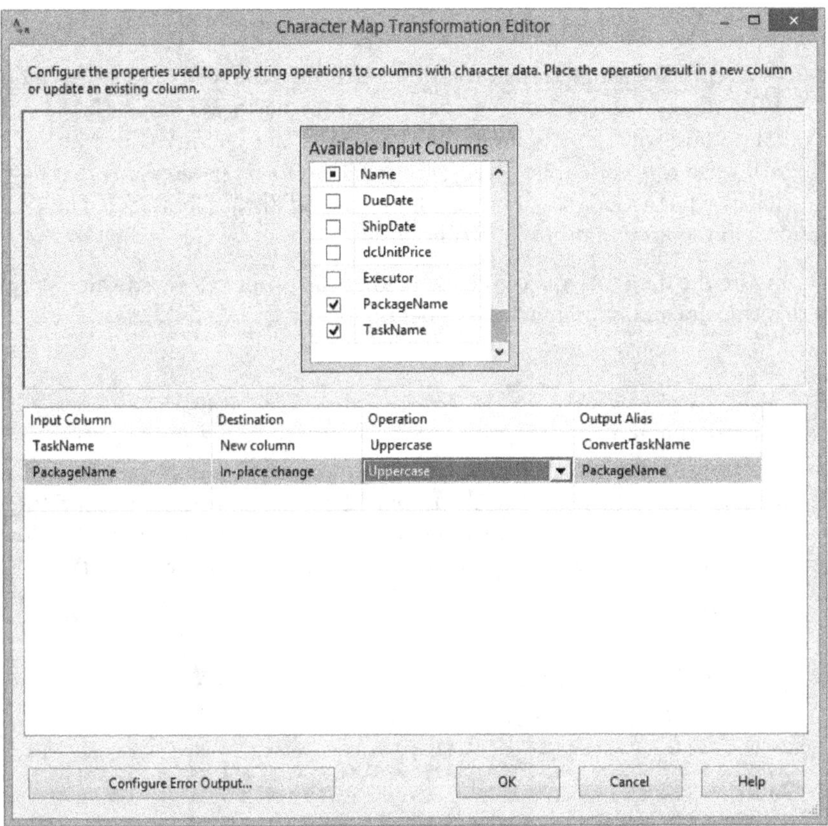

FIGURE 4-23

Data Mining Query

The Data Mining Query Transformation typically is used to fill in gaps in your data or predict a new column for your Data Flow. This transformation runs a Data Mining Extensions (DMX) query against an SSAS data-mining model, and adds the output to the Data Flow. It also can optionally add columns, such as the probability of a certain condition being true. A few great scenarios for this transformation would be the following:

- You could take columns, such as number of children, household income, and marital income, to predict a new column that states whether the person owns a house or not.
- You could predict what customers would want to buy based on their shopping cart items.
- You could fill the gaps in your data where customers didn't enter all the fields in a questionnaire.

The possibilities are endless with this transformation.

DQS Cleansing

The Data Quality Services (DQS) Cleansing Transformation performs advanced data cleansing on data flowing through it. With this transformation, you can have your business analyst (BA) create a series of business rules that declare what good data looks like in the Data Quality Client (included in SQL Server). The BA will use a tool called the Data Quality Client to create domains that define data in your company, such as what a Company Name column should always look like. The DQS Cleansing Transformation can then use that business rule.

This transformation will score the data for you and tell you what the proper cleansed value should be. Chapter 10 covers this transformation in much more detail.

Export Column

The Export Column Transformation is a transformation that exports data to a file from the Data Flow. Unlike the other transformations, the Export Column Transformation doesn't need a destination to create the file. To configure it, go to the Export Column Transformation Editor, shown in Figure 4-24. Select the column that contains the file from the Extract Column dropdown box. Select the column that contains the path and filename to send the files to in the File Path Column dropdown box.

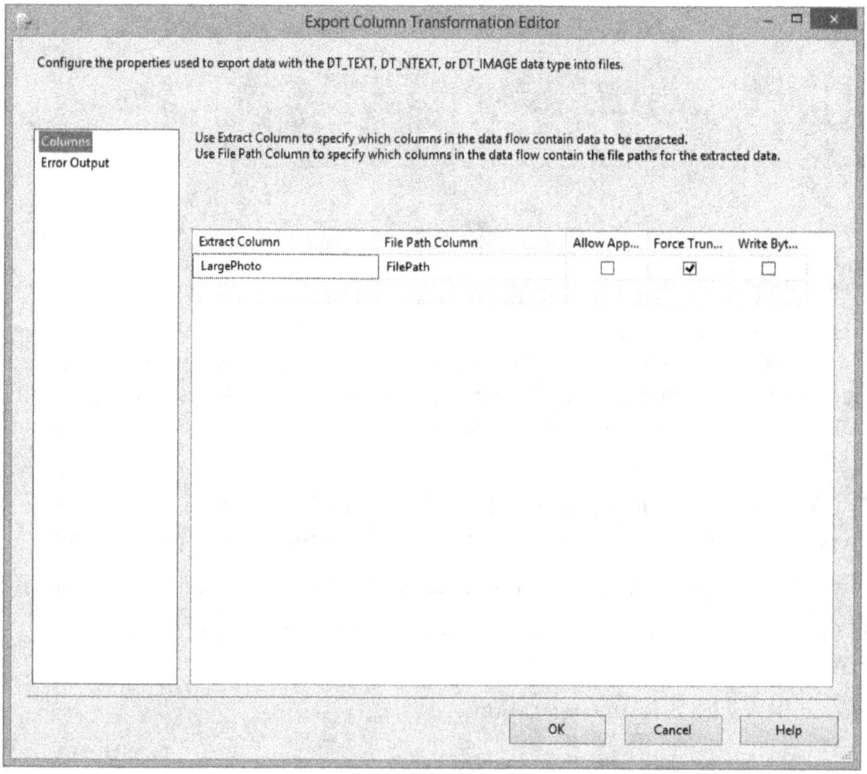

FIGURE 4-24

The other options specify where the file will be overwritten or dropped. The Allow Append checkbox specifies whether the output should be appended to the existing file, if one exists. If you check Force Truncate, the existing file will be overwritten if it exists. The Write BOM option specifies whether a byte-order mark is written to the file if it is a DT_NTEXT or DT_WSTR data type.

If you do not check the Append or Truncate options and the file exists, the package will fail if the error isn't handled. The following error is a subset of the complete error you would receive:

```
Error: 0xC02090A6 at Data Flow Task, Export Column [61]: Opening the file
"wheel_small.tif" for writing failed. The file exists and cannot be
overwritten. If the AllowAppend property is FALSE and the ForceTruncate
property is set to FALSE, the existence of the file will cause this failure.
```

The Export Column Transformation Task is used to extract blob-type data from fields in a database and create files in their original formats to be stored in a file system or viewed by a format viewer, such as Microsoft Word or Microsoft Paint. The trick to understanding the Export Column Transformation is that it requires an input stream field that contains digitized document data, and another field that can be used for a fully qualified path. The Export Column Transformation will convert the digitized data into a physical file on the file system for each row in the input stream using the fully qualified path.

In the following example, you'll use existing data in the AdventureWorksDW database to output some stored documents from the database back to file storage. The database has a table named DimProduct that contains a file path and a field containing an embedded Microsoft Word document. Pull these documents out of the database and save them into a directory on the file system.

1. Create a directory with an easy name like `c:\ProSSIS\Chapter4\Export` that you can use when exporting these pictures.
2. Create a new SSIS project and package named **Export Column Example.dtsx**. Add a Data Flow Task to the Control Flow design surface.
3. On the Data Flow design surface, add an OLE DB Data Source configured to the AdventureWorksDW database table DimProduct.
4. Add a Derived Column Transformation Task to the Data Flow design surface. Connect the output of the OLE DB data to the task.
5. Create a Derived Column Name named FilePath. Use the Derived Column setting of <add as new column>. To derive a new filename, just use the primary key for the filename and add your path to it. To do this, set the expression to the following:

```
"c:\\ProSSIS\\Chapter4\\Export\\" + (DT_WSTR,50)ProductKey + ".gif"
```

> **NOTE** *The \\ is required in the expressions editor instead of \ because of its use as an escape sequence.*

6. Add an Export Column Transformation Task to the Data Flow design surface. Connect the output of the Derived Column Task to the Export Column Transformation Task, which will

consume the input stream and separate all the fields into two usable categories: fields that can possibly be in digitized data formats, and fields that can possibly be used as filenames.

7. Set the Extract Column equal to the [LargePhoto] field, since this contains the embedded GIF image. Set the File Path Column equal to the field name [FilePath]. This field is the one that you derived in the Derived Column Task.
8. Check the Force Truncate option to rewrite the files if they exist. (This will enable you to run the package again without an error if the files already exist.)
9. Run the package and check the contents of the directory. You should see a list of image files in primary key sequence.

Fuzzy Lookup

If you have done some work in the world of extract, transfer, and load (ETL) processes, then you've run into the proverbial crossroads of handling bad data. The test data is staged, but all attempts to retrieve a foreign key from a dimension table result in no matches for a number of rows. This is the crossroads of bad data. At this point, you have a finite set of options. You could create a set of hand-coded complex lookup functions using SQL Sound-Ex, full-text searching, or distance-based word calculation formulas. This strategy is time-consuming to create and test, complicated to implement, and dependent on a given language, and it isn't always consistent or reusable (not to mention that everyone after you will be scared to alter the code for fear of breaking it). You could just give up and divert the row for manual processing by subject matter experts (that's a way to make some new friends). You could just add the new data to the lookup tables and retrieve the new keys. If you just add the data, the foreign key retrieval issue is solved, but you could be adding an entry into the dimension table that skews data-mining results downstream. This is what we like to call a *lazy-add*. This is a descriptive, not a technical, term. A lazy-add would import a misspelled job title like "prasedent" into the dimension table when there is already an entry of "president." It was added, but it was lazy.

The Fuzzy Lookup and Fuzzy Grouping Transformations add one more road to take at the crossroads of bad data. These transformations allow the addition of a step to the process that is easy to use, consistent, scalable, and reusable, and they will reduce your unmatched rows significantly — maybe even altogether. If you've already allowed bad data in your dimension tables, or you are just starting a new ETL process, you'll want to put the Fuzzy Grouping Transformation to work on your data to find data redundancy. This transformation can examine the contents of a suspect field in a staged or committed table and provide possible groupings of similar words based on provided tolerances. This matching information can then be used to clean up that table. Fuzzy Grouping is discussed later in this chapter.

If you are correcting data during an ETL process, use the Fuzzy Lookup Transformation — my suggestion is to do so *only* after attempting to perform a regular lookup on the field. This best practice is recommended because Fuzzy Lookups don't come cheap. They build specialized indexes of the input stream and the reference data for comparison purposes. You can store them for efficiency, but these indexes can use up some disk space or take up some memory if you choose to rebuild them on each run. Storing matches made by the Fuzzy Lookups over time in a translation or pre-dimension table is a great design. Regular Lookup Transformations can first be run against this lookup table and then divert only those items in the Data Flow that can't be matched to a Fuzzy Lookup. This technique uses Lookup Transformations and translation tables to find matches using `INNER JOINs`. Fuzzy Lookups whittle the remaining unknowns down if similar matches can be found with a high level of confidence. Finally, if your last resort is to have the item diverted to a subject matter expert, you can save that decision into the translation table so that the ETL process can match it next time in the first iteration.

Using the Fuzzy Lookup Transformation requires an input stream of at least one field that is a string. Internally, the transformation has to be configured to connect to a reference table that will be used for comparison. The output to this transformation will be a set of columns containing the following:

- **Input and Pass-Through Field Names and Values:** This column contains the name and value of the text input provided to the Fuzzy Lookup Transformation or passed through during the lookup.
- **Reference Field Name and Value:** This column contains the name and value(s) of the matched results from the reference table.
- **Similarity:** This column contains a number between 0 and 1 representing similarity to the matched row and column. Similarity is a threshold that you set when configuring the Fuzzy Lookup Task. The closer this number is to 1, the closer the two text fields must match.
- **Confidence:** This column contains a number between 0 and 1 representing confidence of the match relative to the set of matched results. Confidence is different from similarity, because it is not calculated by examining just one word against another but rather by comparing the chosen word match against all the other possible matches. For example, the value of Knight Brian may have a low similarity threshold but a high confidence that it matches to Brian Knight. Confidence gets better the more accurately your reference data represents your subject domain, and it can change based on the sample of the data coming into the ETL process.

  The Fuzzy Lookup Transformation Editor has three configuration tabs.

- **Reference Table:** This tab (shown in Figure 4-25) sets up the OLE DB Connection to the source of the reference data. The Fuzzy Lookup takes this reference data and builds a token-based index (which is actually a table) out of it before it can begin to compare items. This tab contains the options to save that index or use an existing index from a previous process. There is also an option to maintain the index, which will detect changes from run to run and keep the index current. Note that if you are processing large amounts of potential data, this index table can grow large.

  There are a few additional settings in this tab that are of interest. The default option to set is the "Generate new index" option. By setting this, a table will be created on the reference table's Connection Manager each time the transformation is run, and that table will be populated with loads of data as mentioned earlier in this section. The creation and loading of the table can be an expensive process. This table is removed after the transformation is complete.

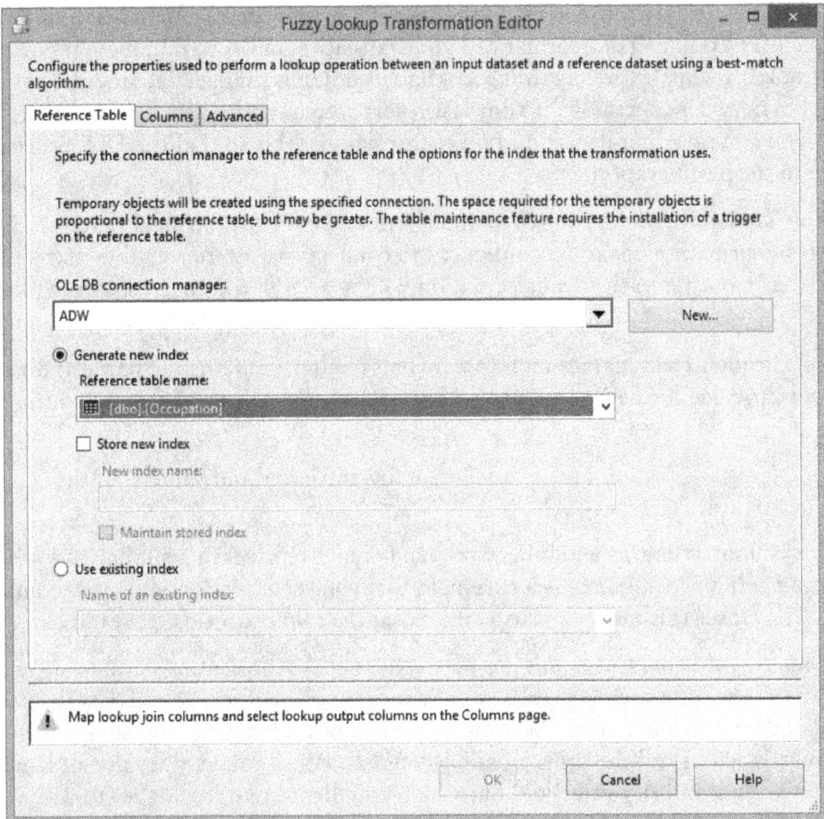

FIGURE 4-25

Alternatively, you can select the "Store new index" option, which will instantiate the table and not drop it. You can then reuse that table from other Data Flows or other Data Flows from other packages and over multiple days. As you can imagine, by doing this your index table becomes stale soon after its creation. There are stored procedures you can run to refresh it in SQL, or you can click the "Maintain stored index" checkbox to create a trigger on the underlying reference table to automatically maintain the index table. This is available only with SQL Server reference tables, and it may slow down your insert, update, and delete statements to that table.

- **Columns:** This tab allows mapping of the one text field in the input stream to the field in the reference table for comparison. Drag and drop a field from the Available Input Column onto the matching field in the Available Lookup Column. You can also click the two fields to be compared and right-click to create a relationship. Another neat feature is the capability to add the foreign key of the lookup table to the output stream. To do this, just click that field in the Available Input Columns.
- **Advanced:** This tab contains the settings that control the fuzzy logic algorithms. You can set the maximum number of matches to output per incoming row. The default is set to 1, which means pull the best record out of the reference table if it meets the similarity

threshold. Incrementing this setting higher than this may generate more results that you'll have to sift through, but it may be required if there are too many closely matching strings in your domain data. A slider controls the Similarity threshold. It is recommended that you start this setting at .71 when experimenting and move up or down as you review the results. This setting is normally determined based on a businessperson's review of the data, not the developer's review. If a row cannot be found that's similar enough, the columns that you checked in the Columns tab will be set to NULL. The token delimiters can also be set if, for example, you don't want the comparison process to break incoming strings up by a period (.) or spaces. The default for this setting is all common delimiters. Figure 4-26 shows an example of an Advanced tab.

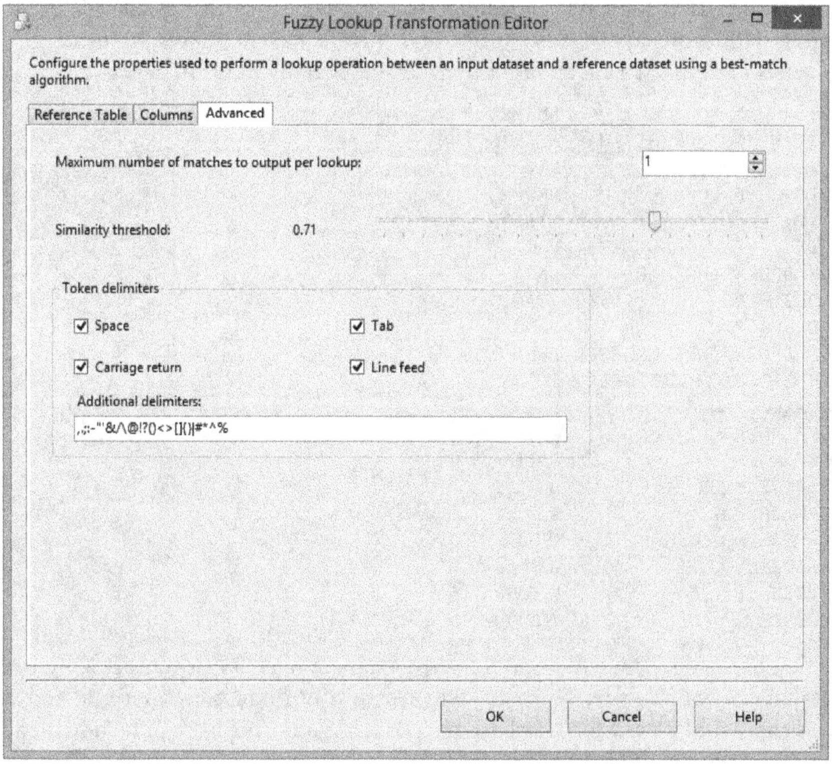

FIGURE 4-26

It's important to not use Fuzzy Lookup as your primary Lookup Transformation for lookups because of the performance overhead; the Fuzzy Lookup transformation is significantly slower than the Lookup transformation. Always try an exact match using a Lookup Transformation and then redirect nonmatches to the Fuzzy Lookup if you need that level of lookup. Additionally, the Fuzzy Lookup Transformation does require the BI or Enterprise Edition of SQL Server.

Although this transformation neatly packages some highly complex logic in an easy-to-use component, the results won't be perfect. You'll need to spend some time experimenting with the configurable settings and monitoring the results. To that end, the following short example puts the Fuzzy Lookup Transformation to work by setting up a small table of occupation titles that will represent your dimension table. You will then import a set of person records that requires a lookup on the occupation to your dimension table. Not all will match, of course. The Fuzzy Lookup Transformation will be employed to find matches, and you will experiment with the settings to learn about its capabilities.

1. Use the following data (code file `FuzzyExample.txt`) for this next example. This file can also be downloaded from `www.wrox.com/go/prossis2014` and saved to `c:\ProSSIS\Chapter4\FuzzyExample.txt`. The data represents employee information that you are going to import. Notice that some of the occupation titles are cut off in the text file because of the positioning within the layout. Also notice that this file has an uneven right margin. Both of these issues are typical ETL situations that are especially painful.

```
EMPID TITLE                      LNAME
00001 EXECUTIVE VICE PRESIDEN    WASHINGTON
00002 EXEC VICE PRES             PIZUR
00003 EXECUTIVE VP               BROWN
00005 EXEC VP                    MILLER
00006 EXECUTIVE VICE PRASIDENS   WAMI
00007 FIELDS OPERATION MGR       SKY
00008 FLDS OPS MGR               JEAN
00009 FIELDS OPS MGR             GANDI
00010 FIELDS OPERATIONS MANAG    HINSON
00011 BUSINESS OFFICE MANAGER    BROWN
00012 BUS OFFICE MANAGER         GREEN
00013 BUS OFF MANAGER            GATES
00014 BUS OFF MGR                HALE
00015 BUS OFFICE MNGR            SMITH
00016 BUS OFFICE MGR             AI
00017 X-RAY TECHNOLOGIST         CHIN
00018 XRAY TECHNOLOGIST          ABULA
00019 XRAY TECH                  HOGAN
00020 X-RAY TECH                 ROBERSON
```

2. Run the following SQL code (code file `FuzzyExampleInsert.sql`) in AdventureWorksDW or another database of your choice. This code will create your dimension table and add the accepted entries that will be used for reference purposes. Again, this file can be downloaded from `www.wrox.com/go/prossis2014`:

```
CREATE TABLE [Occupation](
[OccupationID] [smallint] IDENTITY(1,1) NOT NULL,
[OccupationLabel] [varchar] (50) NOT NULL
CONSTRAINT [PK_Occupation_OccupationID] PRIMARY KEY CLUSTERED
(
[OccupationID] ASC
) ON [PRIMARY]
) ON [PRIMARY]
GO
INSERT INTO [Occupation] Select 'EXEC VICE PRES'
INSERT INTO [Occupation] Select 'FIELDS OPS MGR'
INSERT INTO [Occupation] Select 'BUS OFFICE MGR'
INSERT INTO [Occupation] Select 'X-RAY TECH'
```

3. Create a new SSIS package and drop a Data Flow Task on the Control Flow design surface and click the Data Flow tab.

4. Add a Flat File Connection to the Connection Manager. Name it **Extract,** and then set the filename to `c:\projects\Chapter4\fuzzyexample.txt`. Set the Format property to Delimited, and set the option to pull the column names from the first data row, as shown in Figure 4-27.

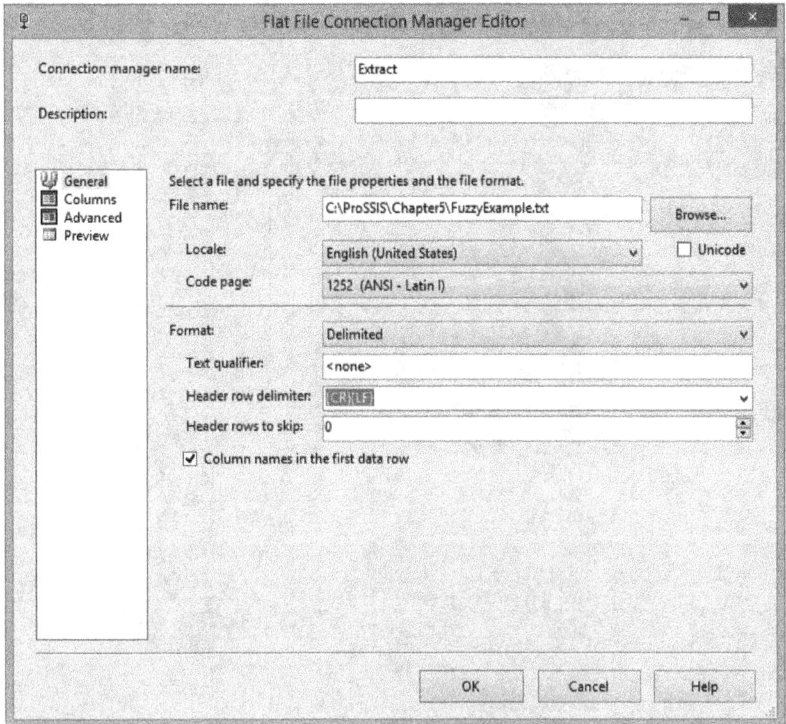

FIGURE 4-27

5. Click the Columns tab to confirm it is properly configured and showing three columns. Click the Advanced tab and ensure the OuputColumnWidth property for the TITLE field is set to 50 characters in length. Save the connection.

6. Add a Flat File Source to the Data Flow surface and configure it to use the Extract connection.

7. Add a Fuzzy Lookup Transformation to the Data Flow design surface. Connect the output of the Flat File Source to the Fuzzy Lookup, and connect the output of the Fuzzy Lookup to the OLE DB Destination.

8. Open the Fuzzy Lookup Transformation Editor. Set the OLE DB Connection Manager in the Reference tab to use the AdventureWorksDW database connection and the Occupation table. Set up the Columns tab by connecting the input to the reference table columns as in Figure 4-28, dragging the Title column to the OccupationLabel column on the right. Set up the Advanced tab with a Similarity threshold of 50 (0.50).

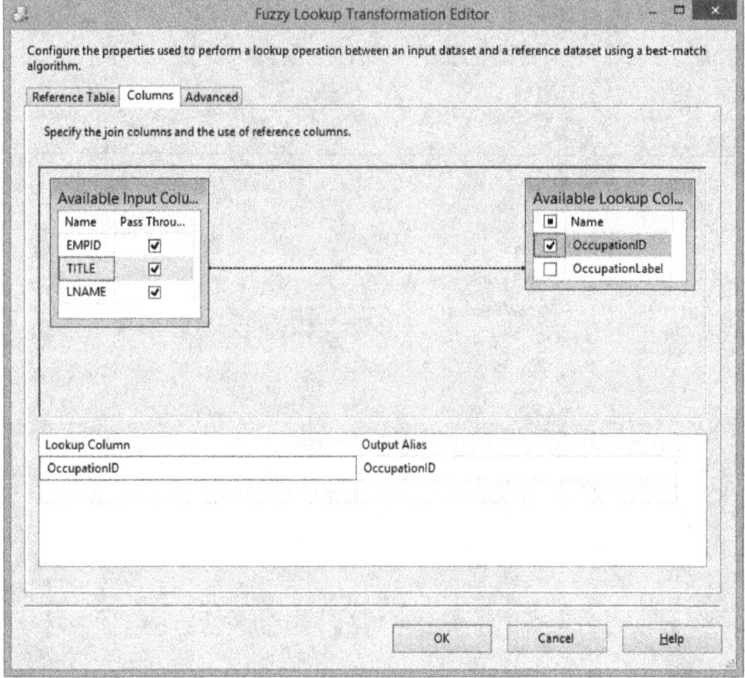

FIGURE 4-28

9. Open the editor for the OLE DB Destination. Set the OLE DB connection to the AdventureWorksDW database. Click New to create a new table to store the results. Change the table name in the DDL statement that is presented to you to create the [FuzzyResults] table. Click the Mappings tab, accept the defaults, and save.

10. Add a Data Viewer of type grid to the Data Flow between the Fuzzy Lookup and the OLE DB Destination.

Run the package. Your results at the Data View should resemble those in Figure 4-29. Notice that the logic has matched most of the items at a 50 percent similarity threshold — and you have the foreign key OccupationID added to your input for free! Had you used a strict `INNER JOIN` or Lookup Transformation, you would have made only three matches, a dismal hit ratio. These items can be seen in the Fuzzy Lookup output, where the values are 1 for similarity and confidence. A few of the columns are set to NULL now, because the row like Executive VP wasn't 50 percent similar to the Exec Vice Pres value. You would typically send those NULL records with a conditional split to a table for manual inspection.

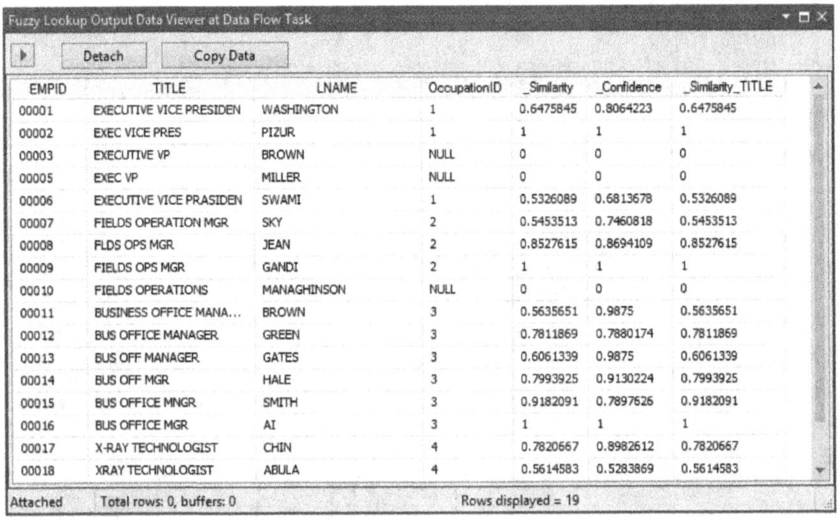

Fuzzy Lookup Output Data Viewer at Data Flow Task

Detach | Copy Data

EMPID	TITLE	LNAME	OccupationID	_Similarity	_Confidence	_Similarity_TITLE
00001	EXECUTIVE VICE PRESIDEN	WASHINGTON	1	0.6475845	0.8064223	0.6475845
00002	EXEC VICE PRES	PIZUR	1	1	1	1
00003	EXECUTIVE VP	BROWN	NULL	0	0	0
00005	EXEC VP	MILLER	NULL	0	0	0
00006	EXECUTIVE VICE PRASIDEN	SWAMI	1	0.5326089	0.6813678	0.5326089
00007	FIELDS OPERATION MGR	SKY	2	0.5453513	0.7460818	0.5453513
00008	FLDS OPS MGR	JEAN	2	0.8527615	0.8694109	0.8527615
00009	FIELDS OPS MGR	GANDI	2	1	1	1
00010	FIELDS OPERATIONS	MANAGHINSON	NULL	0	0	0
00011	BUSINESS OFFICE MANA...	BROWN	3	0.5635651	0.9875	0.5635651
00012	BUS OFFICE MANAGER	GREEN	3	0.7811869	0.7880174	0.7811869
00013	BUS OFF MANAGER	GATES	3	0.6061339	0.9875	0.6061339
00014	BUS OFF MGR	HALE	3	0.7993925	0.9130224	0.7993925
00015	BUS OFFICE MNGR	SMITH	3	0.9182091	0.7897626	0.9182091
00016	BUS OFFICE MGR	AI	3	1	1	1
00017	X-RAY TECHNOLOGIST	CHIN	4	0.7820667	0.8982612	0.7820667
00018	XRAY TECHNOLOGIST	ABULA	4	0.5614583	0.5283869	0.5614583

Attached | Total rows: 0, buffers: 0 | Rows displayed = 19

FIGURE 4-29

Fuzzy Grouping

In the previous section, you learned about situations where bad data creeps into your dimension tables. The blame was placed on the "lazy-add" ETL processes that add data to dimension tables to avoid rejecting rows when there are no natural key matches. Processes like these are responsible for state abbreviations like "XX" and entries that look to the human eye like duplicates but are stored as two separate entries. The occupation titles "X-Ray Tech" and "XRay Tech" are good examples of duplicates that humans can recognize but computers have a harder time with.

The Fuzzy Grouping Transformation can look through a list of similar text and group the results using the same logic as the Fuzzy Lookup. You can use these groupings in a transformation table to clean up source and destination data or to crunch fact tables into more meaningful results without altering the underlying data. The Fuzzy Group Transformation also expects an input stream of text, and it requires a connection to an OLE DB Data Source because it creates in that source a set of structures to use during analysis of the input stream.

The Fuzzy Lookup Editor has three configuration tabs:

- **Connection Manager:** This tab sets the OLE DB connection that the transform will use to write the storage tables that it needs.
- **Columns:** This tab displays the Available Input Columns and allows the selection of any or all input columns for fuzzy grouping analysis. Figure 4-30 shows a completed Columns tab.

  Each column selected is analyzed and grouped into logical matches, resulting in a new column representing that group match for each data row. Each column can also be selected for Pass-Through — meaning the data is not analyzed, but it is available in the output stream. You can choose the names of any of the output columns: Group Output Alias, Output Alias, Clean Match, and Similarity Alias Score column.

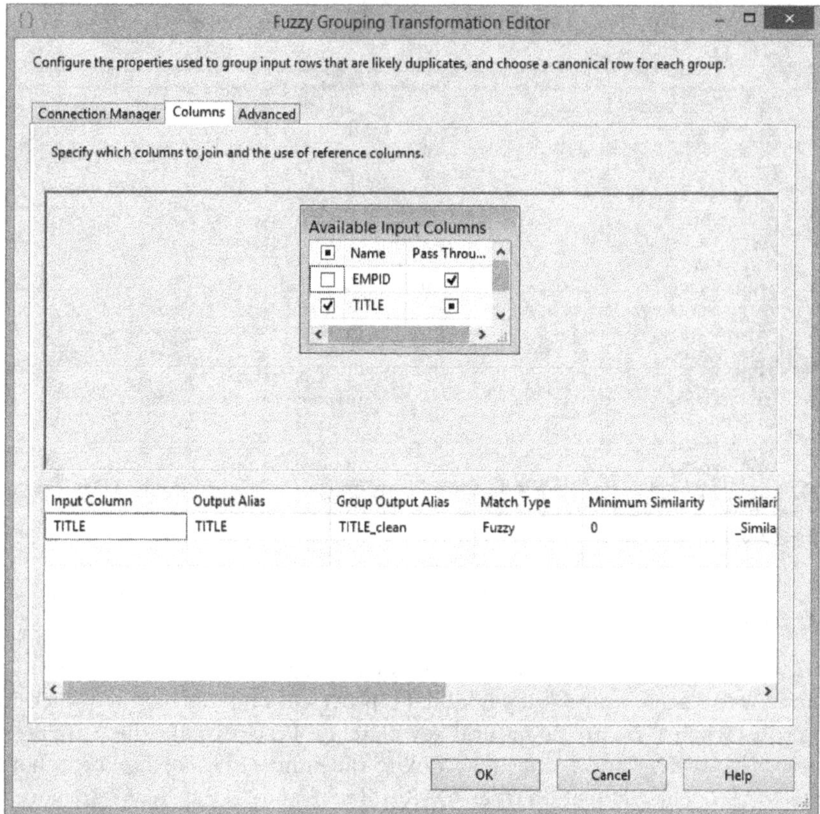

FIGURE 4-30

The minimum similarity evaluation is available at the column level if you select more than one column.

The numerals option (which is not visible in Figure 4-30 but can be found by scrolling to the right) enables configuration of the significance of numbers in the input stream when grouping text logically. The options are leading numbers, trailing numbers, leading and trailing numbers, or neither leading nor trailing numbers. This option needs to be considered when comparing addresses or similar types of information.

Comparison flags provide the same options to ignore or pay attention to case, kana type, nonspacing characters, character width, symbols, and punctuation.

- **Advanced:** This tab contains the settings controlling the fuzzy logic algorithms that assign groupings to text in the input stream. You can set the names of the three additional fields that are added automatically to the output of this transformation. These fields are named _key_in, _key_out, and _score by default. A slider controls the Similarity threshold. The recommended initial setting for this transformation is 0.5, which can be adjusted up or down as you review the results. The token delimiters can also be set if, for example, you don't want the comparison process to break incoming strings up by a period (.) or spaces. The default for this setting is all common delimiters. Figure 4-31 shows a completed Advanced tab.

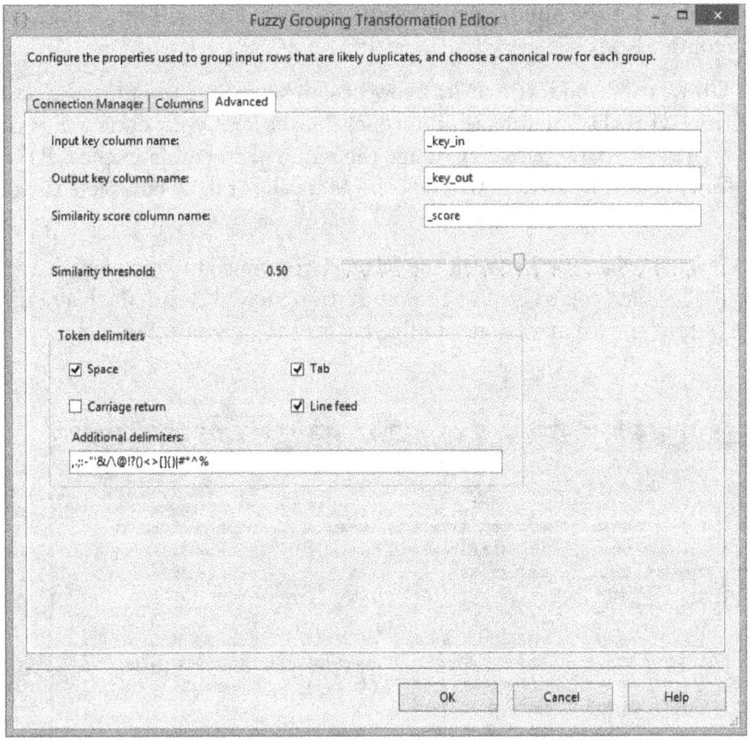

FIGURE 4-31

Suppose you are tasked with creating a brand-new occupations table using the employee occupations text file you imported in the Fuzzy Lookup example. Using only this data, you need to create a new employee occupations table with occupation titles that can serve as natural keys and that best represent this sample. You can use the Fuzzy Grouping Transformation to develop the groupings for the dimension table, like this:

1. Create a new SSIS project named Fuzzy Grouping Example. Drop a Data Flow Task on the Control Flow design surface and click the Data Flow tab.
2. Add a Flat File Connection to the Connection Manager. Name it **Extract**. Set the filename to `c:\ProSSIS\Chapter4\FuzzyExample.txt`. (Use the `FuzzyExample.txt` file from the Fuzzy Lookup example with the same configuration.) Save the connection.
3. Add a Flat File Source to the Data Flow surface and configure it to use the Employee Data connection.
4. Add a Fuzzy Grouping Transformation to the Data Flow design surface. Connect the output of the Flat File Source to the Fuzzy Lookup.
5. Open the Fuzzy Grouping Editor and set the OLE DB Connection Manager to a new AdventureWorksDW connection.
6. In the Columns tab, select the Title column in the Available Input Columns. Accept the other defaults.

7. In the Advanced tab, set the Similarity threshold to 0.50. This will be your starting point for similarity comparisons.

8. Add an OLE DB Destination to the Data Flow design surface. Configure the destination to use the AdventureWorksDW database or another database of your choice. For the Name of Table or View, click the New button. Change the name of the table in the CREATE table statement to [**FuzzyGroupingResults**]. Click the Mappings tab to complete the task and then save it.

9. Add a Data Viewer in the pipe between the Fuzzy Grouping Transformation and the OLE DB Destination. Set the type to grid so that you can review the data at this point. Run the package. The output shown at various similarity thresholds would look similar to Figure 4-32.

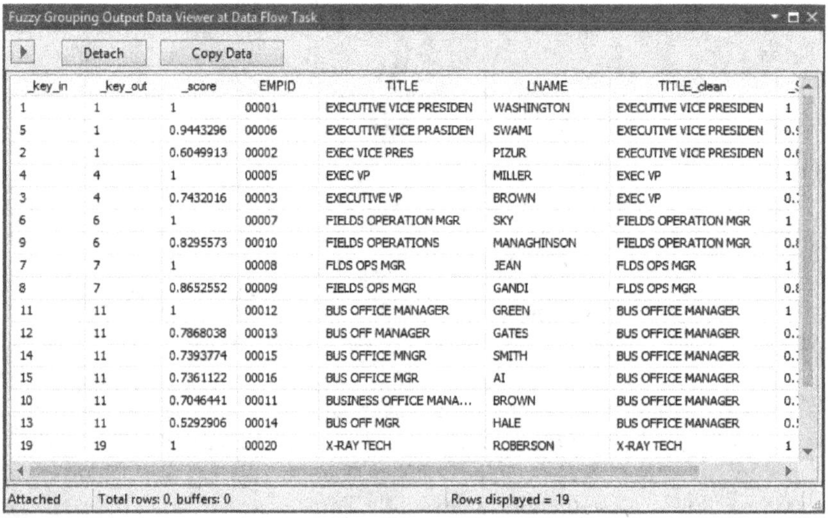

Fuzzy Grouping Output Data Viewer at Data Flow Task

Detach | Copy Data

_key_in	_key_out	_score	EMPID	TITLE	LNAME	TITLE_clean	_s
1	1	1	00001	EXECUTIVE VICE PRESIDEN	WASHINGTON	EXECUTIVE VICE PRESIDEN	1
5	1	0.9443296	00006	EXECUTIVE VICE PRASIDEN	SWAMI	EXECUTIVE VICE PRESIDEN	0.9
2	1	0.6049913	00002	EXEC VICE PRES	PIZUR	EXECUTIVE VICE PRESIDEN	0.6
4	4	1	00005	EXEC VP	MILLER	EXEC VP	1
3	4	0.7432016	00003	EXECUTIVE VP	BROWN	EXEC VP	0.
6	6	1	00007	FIELDS OPERATION MGR	SKY	FIELDS OPERATION MGR	1
9	6	0.8295573	00010	FIELDS OPERATIONS	MANAGHINSON	FIELDS OPERATION MGR	0.8
7	7	1	00008	FLDS OPS MGR	JEAN	FLDS OPS MGR	1
8	7	0.8652552	00009	FIELDS OPS MGR	GANDI	FLDS OPS MGR	0.8
11	11	1	00012	BUS OFFICE MANAGER	GREEN	BUS OFFICE MANAGER	1
12	11	0.7868038	00013	BUS OFF MANAGER	GATES	BUS OFFICE MANAGER	0.
14	11	0.7393774	00015	BUS OFFICE MNGR	SMITH	BUS OFFICE MANAGER	0.
15	11	0.7361122	00016	BUS OFFICE MGR	AI	BUS OFFICE MANAGER	0.
10	11	0.7046441	00011	BUSINESS OFFICE MANA...	BROWN	BUS OFFICE MANAGER	0.
13	11	0.5292906	00014	BUS OFF MGR	HALE	BUS OFFICE MANAGER	0.
19	19	1	00020	X-RAY TECH	ROBERSON	X-RAY TECH	1

Attached | Total rows: 0, buffers: 0 | Rows displayed = 19

FIGURE 4-32

Now you can look at these results and see more logical groupings and a few issues even at the lowest level of similarity. The title of "X-Ray Tech" is similar to the title "X-Ray Technologist." The title "Executive Vice Presiden" isn't a complete title, and really should be grouped with "Exec VP," but this is pretty good for about five minutes of work.

To build a dimension table from this output, look at the two fields in the Data View named _key_in and _key_out. If these two values match, then the grouped value is the "best" representative candidate for the natural key in a dimension table. Separate the rows in the stream using a Conditional Split Transformation where these two values match, and use an OLE Command Transformation to insert the values in the dimension table. Remember that the more data, the better the grouping.

The output of the Fuzzy Grouping Transformation is also a good basis for a translation table in your ETL processes. By saving both the original value and the Fuzzy Grouping value — with a little subject matter expert editing — you can use a Lookup Transformation and this table to provide much better foreign key lookup results. You'll be able to improve on this with the Slowly Changing Dimension Transformation later in the chapter.

Import Column

The Import Column Transformation is a partner to the Export Column Transformation. These transformations do the work of translating physical files from system file storage paths into database blob-type fields, and vice versa. The trick to understanding the Import Column Transformation is knowing that its input source requires at least one column that is the fully qualified path to the file you are going to store in the database, and you need a destination column name for the output of the resulting blob and file path string. This transformation also has to be configured using the Advanced Editor. The Advanced Editor is not intuitive, or wizard-like in appearance — hence the name "Advanced" (which, incidentally, you will be once you figure it out). In the editor, you won't be able to merge two incoming column sources into the full file path; therefore, if your source data for the file paths have the filename separate from the file path, you should use the Merge Transformations to concatenate the columns before connecting that stream to the Import Column Transformation.

In the following example, you'll import some images into your AdventureWorksDW database. Create a new SSIS package. Transformations live in the Data Flow tab, so add a Data Flow Task to the Control Flow, and then add an Import Column Transformation to the Data Flow surface. To keep this easy, you will complete the following short tasks:

1. Find a small GIF file and copy it three times into `c:\ProSSIS\Chapter4\import` (or just copy and paste the files from the Export Column example). Change the filenames to `1.gif`, `2.gif`, and `3.gif`.

2. Create a text file with the following content and save it in `c:\ProSSIS\Chapter4` as `filelist.txt`:

   ```
   C:\import\1.Gif
   C:\import\2.Gif
   C:\import\3.Gif
   ```

3. Run the following SQL script in AdventureWorks to create a storage location for the image files:

   ```
   CREATE TABLE dbo.tblmyImages
   (
   [StoredFilePath] [varchar](50) NOT NULL,
   [ProdPicture] image
   )
   ```

4. You are going to use the `filelist.txt` file as your input stream for the files that you need to load into your database, so add a Flat File Source to your Data Flow surface and configure it to read one column from your `filelist.txt` flat file. Rename this column **ImageFilePath**.

Take advantage of the opportunity to open the Advanced Editor on the Flat File Source by clicking the Show Advanced Editor link in the property window or by right-clicking the transformation and selecting Advanced Editor, which looks quite a bit different from the Advanced Editor for a source. Note the difference between this editor and the normal Flat File Editor. The Advanced Editor is stripped down to the core of the Data Flow component — no custom wizards, just an interface sitting directly over the object properties themselves. It is possible to mess these properties up beyond recognition, but even in the worst case you can just drop and recreate the component. Look particularly at the Input and Output Properties of the Advanced Editor.

You didn't have to use the Advanced Editor to set up the import of the `filelist.txt` file. However, looking at how the Advanced Editor displays the information will be very helpful when you configure the Import Column Transformation. Notice that you have an External Columns (Input) and Output Columns collection, with one node in each collection named ImageFilePath. This reflects the fact that your connection describes a field called ImageFilePath and that this transformation simply outputs data with the same field name.

Connect the Flat File Source to the Import Column Transformation. Open the Advanced Editor for the Import Column Transformation and click the Input Columns tab. The input stream for this task is the output stream for the flat file. Select the one available column, move to the Input and Output Properties tab, and expand these nodes. This time you don't have much help. An example of this editor is shown in Figure 4-33.

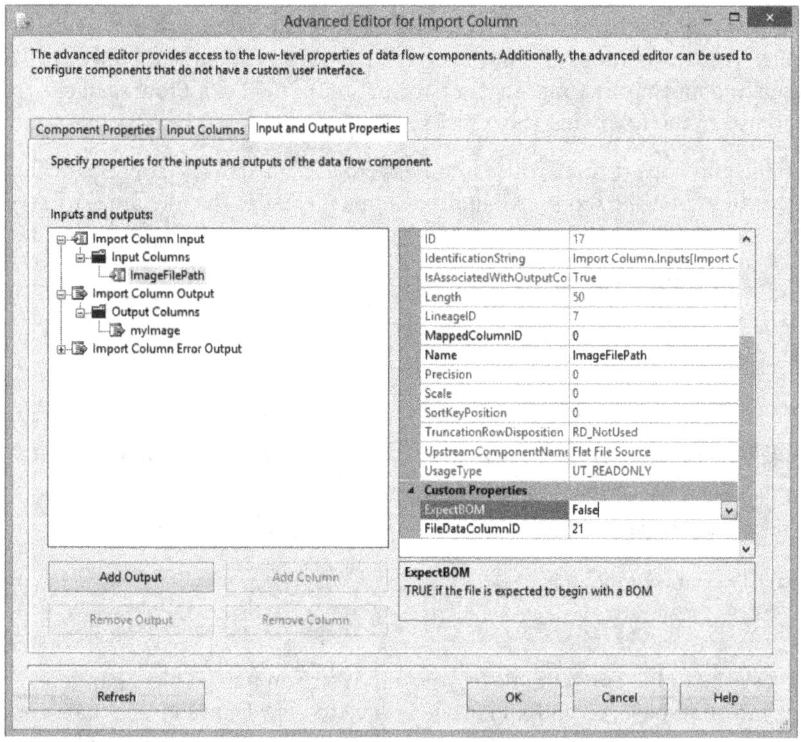

FIGURE 4-33

The Input Columns collection has a column named ImageFilePath, but there are no output columns. On the Flat File Source, you could ignore some of the inputs. In the Import Column Transformation, all inputs have to be re-output. In fact, if you don't map an output, you'll get the following error:

```
Validation error. Data Flow Task: Import Column [1]: The "input column
"ImageFilePath" (164)" references output column ID 0, and that column is not
found on the output.
```

Add an output column by clicking the Output Columns folder icon and click the Add Column button. Name the column **myImage**. Notice that the DataType property is [DT_IMAGE] by default. That is because this transformation produces image outputs. You can also pass DT_TEXT, DT_NTEXT, or DT_IMAGE types as outputs from this task. Your last task is to connect the input to the output. Note the output column's ID property for `myImage`. This ID needs to be updated in the FileDataColumnID property of the input column ImageFilePath. If you fail to link the output column, you'll get the following error:

```
Validation error. Data Flow Task: Import Column [1]: The "output column
"myImage" (207)" is not referenced by any input column. Each output column
must be referenced by exactly one input column.
```

The Advanced Editor for each of the different transformations has a similar layout but may have other properties available. Another property of interest in this task is Expect BOM, which you would set to True if you expect a byte-order mark at the beginning of the file path (not for this example). A completed editor resembles Figure 4-33.

Complete this example by adding an OLE Destination to the Data Flow design surface. Connect the data from the Import Column to the OLE Destination. Configure the OLE Destination to the AdventureWorksDW database and to the tblmyImages structure that was created for database storage. Click the Mappings setting. Notice that you have two available input columns from the Import Column Task. One is the full path and the other will be the file as type DT_IMAGE. Connect the input and destination columns to complete the transform. Go ahead and run it.

Take a look at the destination table to see the results:

```
FullFileName          Document
--------------------- -----------------------
C:\import\images\1.JPG 0xFFD8FFE120EE457869660000494492A00...
C:\import\images\2.JPG 0xFFD8FFE125FE457869660000494492A00...
C:\import\images\3.JPG 0xFFD8FFE1269B457869660000494492A00...
(3 row(s) affected)
```

Merge

The Merge Transformation can merge data from two paths into a single output. This transformation is useful when you wish to break out your Data Flow into a path that handles certain errors and then merge it back into the main Data Flow downstream after the errors have been handled. It's also useful if you wish to merge data from two Data Sources.

This transformation is similar to the Union All Transformation, but the Merge Transformation has some restrictions that may cause you to lean toward using Union All:

- The data must be sorted before the Merge Transformation. You can do this by using the Sort Transformation prior to the merge or by specifying an `ORDER BY` clause in the source connection.
- The metadata must be the same between both paths. For example, the CustomerID column can't be a numeric column in one path and a character column in another path.
- If you have more than two paths, you should choose the Union All Transformation.

To configure the transformation, ensure that the data is sorted exactly the same on both paths and drag the path onto the transform. You'll be asked if the path you want to merge is Merge Input 1 or 2. If this is the first path you're connecting to the transformation, select Merge Input 1. Next, connect the second path into the transformation. The transformation will automatically configure itself. Essentially, it maps each of the columns to the column from the other path, and you have the option to ignore a certain column's data.

Merge Join

One of the overriding themes of SSIS is that you shouldn't have to write any code to create your transformation. This transformation will merge the output of two inputs and perform an `INNER` or `OUTER` join on the data. An example of when this would be useful is if you have a front-end web system in one data stream that has a review of a product in it, and you have an inventory product system in another data stream with the product data. You could merge join the two data inputs and output the review and product information into a single path.

> **NOTE** *If both inputs are in the same database, then it would be faster to perform a join at the OLE DB Source level, rather than use a transformation through T-SQL. This transformation is useful when you have two different Data Sources you wish to merge, or when you don't want to write your own join code.*

To configure the Merge Join Transformation, connect your two inputs into the Merge Join Transformation, and then select what represents the right and left join as you connect each input. Open the Merge Join Transformation Editor and verify the linkage between the two tables. You can see an example of this in Figure 4-34. You can right-click the arrow to delete a linkage or drag a column from the left input onto the right input to create a new linkage if one is missing. Lastly, check each of the columns you want to be passed as output to the path and select the type of join you wish to make (`LEFT`, `INNER`, or `FULL`).

Multicast

The Multicast Transformation, as the name implies, can send a single data input to multiple output paths easily. You may want to use this transformation to send a path to multiple destinations sliced in different ways. To configure this transformation, simply connect it to your input, and then drag the output path from the Multicast Transformation onto your next destination or transformation. After you connect the Multicast Transformation to your first destination or transformation, you can keep connecting it to other transformations or destinations. There is nothing to configure in the Multicast Transformation Editor other than the names of the outputs.

> **NOTE** *The Multicast Transformation is similar to the Conditional Split Transformation in that both transformations send data to multiple outputs. The Multicast will send all the rows down every output path, whereas the Conditional Split will conditionally send each row down exactly one output path.*

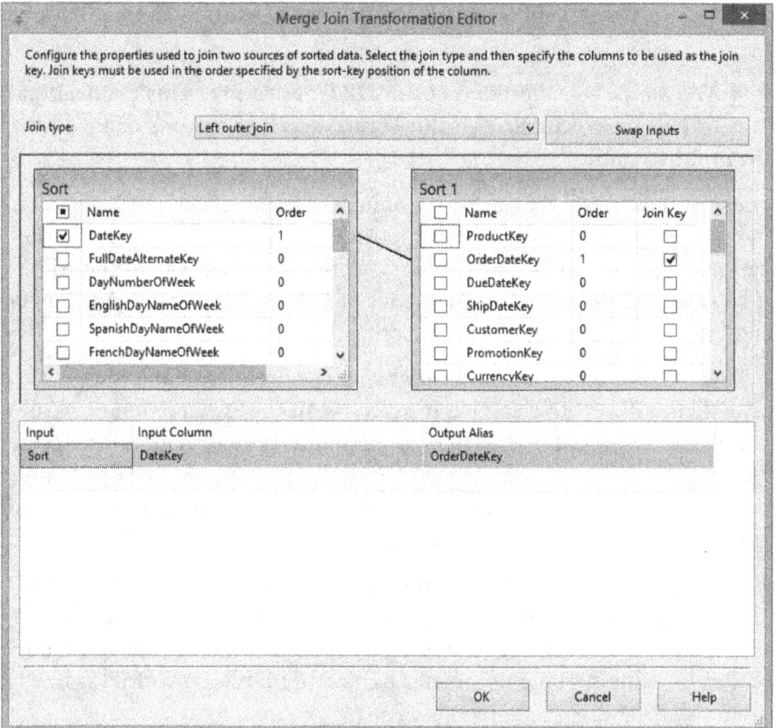

FIGURE 4-34

OLE DB Command

The OLE DB Command Transformation is a component designed to execute a SQL statement for each row in an input stream. This task is analogous to an ADO Command object being created, prepared, and executed for each row of a result set. The input stream provides the data for parameters that can be set into the SQL statement, which is either an in-line statement or a stored procedure call. If you're like us, just hearing the words "for each row" in the context of SQL makes us think of two other words: performance degradation. This involves firing an update, insert, or delete statement, prepared or unprepared some unknown number of times.

This doesn't mean there are no good reasons to use this transformation — you'll actually be doing a few in this chapter. Just understand the impact and think about your use of this transformation. Pay specific attention to the volume of input rows that will be fed into it. Weigh the performance and scalability aspects during your design phases against a solution that would cache the stream into a temporary table and use set-based logic instead.

To use the OLE DB Command Transformation, you basically need to determine how to set up the connection where the SQL statement will be run, provide the SQL statement to be executed, and configure the mapping of any parameters in the input stream to the SQL statement. Take a look at the settings for the OLE DB Command Transformation by opening its editor. The OLE DB

Command Transformation is another component that uses the Advanced Editor. There are four tabs in the editor:

- **Connection Manager:** Allows the selection of an OLE DB Connection. This connection is where the SQL statement will be executed. This doesn't have to be the same connection that is used to provide the input stream.
- **Component Properties:** Here you can set the SQL Command statement to be executed in the SQLCommand property, and set the amount of time to allow for a timeout in the CommandTimeout property, in seconds. The property works the same way as the ADO Command object. The value for the CommandTimeout of 0 indicates no timeout. You can also name the task and provide a description in this tab.
- **Column Mappings:** This tab displays columns available in the input stream and the destination columns, which will be the parameters available in the SQL command. You can map the columns by clicking a column in the input columns and dragging it onto the matching destination parameter. It is a one-to-one mapping, so if you need to use a value for two parameters, you need use a Derived Column Transformation to duplicate the column in the input stream prior to configuring the columns in this transformation.
- **Input and Output Properties:** Most of the time you'll be able to map your parameters in the Column Mappings tab. However, if the OLE DB provider doesn't provide support for deriving parameter information (parameter refreshing), you have to come here to manually set up your output columns using specific parameter names and DBParamInfoFlags.

This transformation should be avoided whenever possible. It's a better practice to land the data into a staging table using an OLE DB Destination and perform an update with a set-based process in the Control Flow with an Execute SQL Task. The Execute SQL Task's statement would look something like this if you loaded a table called stg_TransactionHistoryUpdate and were trying to do a bulk update:

```
BEGIN TRAN
update CDCTransactionHistory
    SET TransactionDate = b.TransactionDate,
        ActualCost = b.ActualCost
FROM CDCTransactionHistory CDC
    INNER JOIN [stg_TransactionHistoryUpdate] b
ON CDC.TransactionID = b.TransactionID
GO
TRUNCATE TABLE [stg_TransactionHistoryUpdate]
COMMIT
```

If you have 2,000 rows running through the transformation, the stored procedure or command will be executed 2,000 times. It might be more efficient to process these transactions in a SQL batch, but then you would have to stage the data and code the batch transaction. The main problem with this transformation is performance.

Percentage and Row Sampling

The Percentage Sampling and Row Sampling Transformations enable you to take the data from the source and randomly select a subset of data. The transformation produces two outputs that you can select. One output is the data that was randomly selected, and the other is the data that was not selected. You can use this to send a subset of data to a development or test server. The most useful application of this transformation is to train a data-mining model. You can use one output path to train your data-mining model, and the sampling to validate the model.

To configure the transformation, select the percentage or number of rows you wish to be sampled. As you can guess, the Percentage Sampling Transformation enables you to select the percentage of rows, and the Row Sampling Transformation enables you to specify how many rows you wish to be outputted randomly. Next, you can optionally name each of the outputs from the transformation. The last option is to specify the seed that will randomize the data. If you select a seed and run the transformation multiple times, the same data will be outputted to the destination. If you uncheck this option, which is the default, the seed will be automatically incremented by one at runtime, and you will see random data each time.

Pivot Transform

Do you ever get the feeling that pivot tables are the modern-day Rosetta Stone for translating data to your business owners? You store it relationally, but they ask for it in a format that requires you to write a complex case statement to generate. Well, not anymore. Now you can use an SSIS transformation to generate the results. A *pivot table* is a result of cross-tabulated columns generated by summarizing data from a row format.

Typically, a Pivot Transformation is generated using the following input columns:

- **Pivot Key:** A pivot column is the element of input data to "pivot." The word "pivot" is another way of saying "to create a column for each unique instance of." However, this data must be under control. Think about creating columns in a table. You wouldn't create 1,000 uniquely named columns in a table, so for best results when choosing a data element to pivot, pick an element that can be run through a `GROUP BY` statement that will generate 15 or fewer columns. If you are dealing with dates, use something like a `DATENAME` function to convert to the month or day of the year.
- **Set Key:** Set key creates one column and places all the unique values for all rows into this column. Just like any `GROUP BY` statement, some of the data is needed to define the group (row), whereas other data is just along for the ride.
- **Pivot Value:** These columns are aggregations for data that provide the results in the matrix between the row columns and the pivot columns.

The Pivot Transformation can accept an input stream, use your definitions of the preceding columns, and generate a pivot table output. It helps if you are familiar with your input needs and format your data prior to this transformation. Aggregate the data using `GROUP BY` statements. Pay special attention to sorting by row columns — this can significantly alter your results.

To set your expectations properly, you have to define each of your literal pivot columns. A common misconception, and source of confusion, is approaching the Pivot Transformation with the idea that you can simply set the pivot column to pivot by the month of the purchase date column, and the transformation should automatically build 12 pivot columns with the month of the year for you. It will not. It is your task to create an output column for each month of the year. If you are using colors as your pivot column, you need to add an output column for every possible color. For example, if columns are set up for blue, green, and yellow, and the color red appears in the input source, then the Pivot Transformation will fail. Therefore, plan ahead and know the possible pivots that can result from your choice of a pivot column or provide for an error output for data that doesn't match your expected pivot values.

In this example, you'll use some of the AdventureWorks product and transactional history to generate a quick pivot table to show product quantities sold by month. This is a typical upper-management request, and you can cover all the options with this example. AdventureWorks Management wants a listing of each product with the total quantity of transactions by month for the year 2003.

First identify the pivot column. The month of the year looks like the data that is driving the creation of the pivot columns. The row data columns will be the product name and the product number. The value field will be the total number of transactions for the product in a matrix by month. Now you are ready to set up the Pivot Transformation:

1. Create a new SSIS project named **Pivot Example**. Add a Data Flow Task to the Control Flow design surface.
2. Add an OLE DB Source to the Data Flow design surface. Configure the connection to the AdventureWorks database. Set the Data Access Mode to SQL Command. Add the following SQL statement (code file `PivotExample.sql`) to the SQL Command text box:

```
SELECT p.[Name] as ProductName, p.ProductNumber,
datename(mm, t.TransactionDate) as TransMonth,
sum(t.quantity) as TotQuantity
FROM production.product p
INNER JOIN production.transactionhistory t
ON t.productid = p.productid
WHERE t.transactiondate between '01/01/03' and '12/31/03'
GROUP BY p.[name], p.productnumber, datename(mm,t.transactiondate)
ORDER BY productname, datename(mm, t.transactiondate)
```

3. Add the Pivot Transformation and connect the output of the OLE DB Source to the input of the transformation. Open the transformation to edit it.
4. Select TransMonth for the Pivot Key. This is the column that represents your columns. Change the Set Key property to ProductName. This is the column that will show on the rows, and your earlier query must be sorting by this column. Lastly, type the values of [December],[November],[October],[September] in the "Generate pivot output columns from values" area and check the Ignore option above this text box. Once complete, click the Generate Columns Now button. The final screen looks like Figure 4-35.

> **NOTE** *The output columns are generated in exactly the same order that they appear on the output columns collection.*

5. To finish the example, add an OLE DB Destination. Configure to the AdventureWorks connection. Connect the Pivot Default Output to the input of the OLE DB Destination. Click the New button to alter the `CREATE TABLE` statement to build a table named PivotTable.

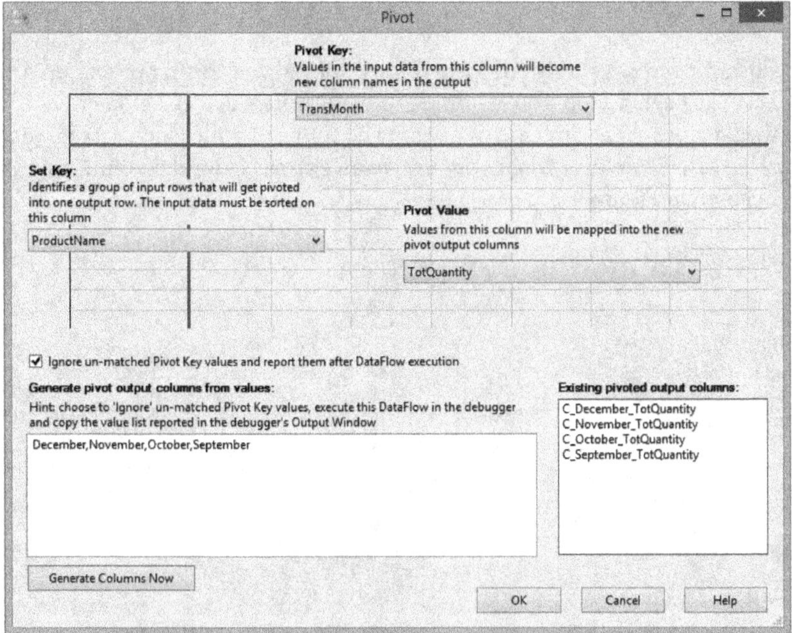

FIGURE 4-35

6. Add a Data Viewer in the pipe between the PIVOT and the OLE DB destination and run the package. You'll see the data in a pivot table in the Data Viewer, as shown in the partial results in Figure 4-36.

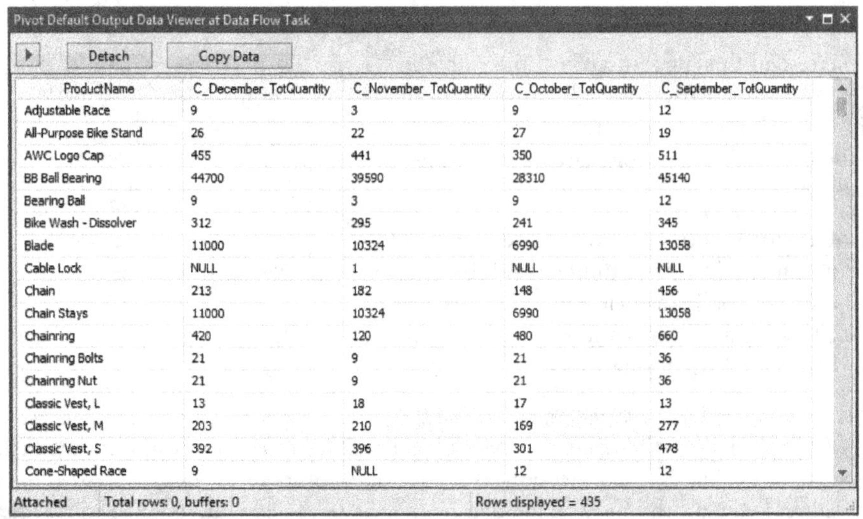

ProductName	C_December_TotQuantity	C_November_TotQuantity	C_October_TotQuantity	C_September_TotQuantity
Adjustable Race	9	3	9	12
All-Purpose Bike Stand	26	22	27	19
AWC Logo Cap	455	441	350	511
BB Ball Bearing	44700	39590	28310	45140
Bearing Ball	9	3	9	12
Bike Wash - Dissolver	312	295	241	345
Blade	11000	10324	6990	13058
Cable Lock	NULL	1	NULL	NULL
Chain	213	182	148	456
Chain Stays	11000	10324	6990	13058
Chainring	420	120	480	660
Chainring Bolts	21	9	21	36
Chainring Nut	21	9	21	36
Classic Vest, L	13	18	17	13
Classic Vest, M	203	210	169	277
Classic Vest, S	392	396	301	478
Cone-Shaped Race	9	NULL	12	12

FIGURE 4-36

Unpivot

As you know, mainframe screens rarely conform to any normalized form. For example, a screen may show a Bill To Customer, a Ship To Customer, and a Dedicated To Customer field. Typically, the Data Source would store these three fields as three columns in a file (such as a virtual storage access system, or VSAM). Therefore, when you receive an extract from the mainframe you may have three columns, as shown in Figure 4-37.

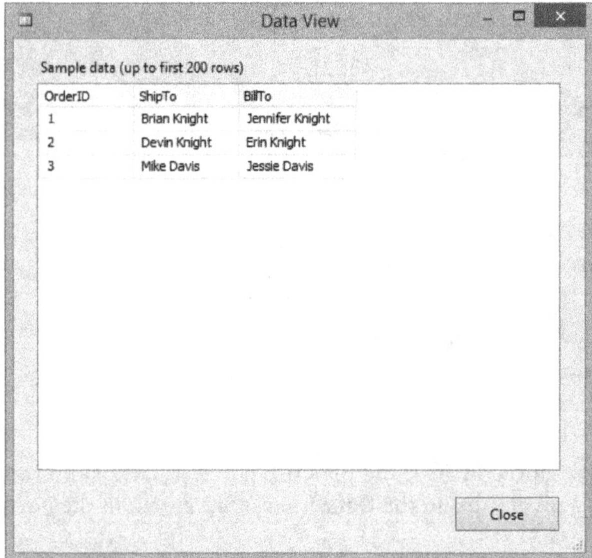

OrderID	ShipTo	BillTo
1	Brian Knight	Jennifer Knight
2	Devin Knight	Erin Knight
3	Mike Davis	Jessie Davis

FIGURE 4-37

Your goal is to load this file into a Customer table in SQL Server. You want a row for each customer in each column, for a total of six rows in the Customer table, as shown in the CustomerName and OrderID columns in Figure 4-38.

Unpivot Output Data Viewer at Data Flow Task

Detach | Copy Data

OriginalColumn	CustomerName	OrderID
BillTo	Jennifer Knight	1
ShipTo	Brian Knight	1
BillTo	Erin Knight	2
ShipTo	Devin Knight	2
BillTo	Jessie Davis	3
ShipTo	Mike Davis	3

Attached | Total rows: 0, buffers: 0 | Rows displayed =

FIGURE 4-38

The Unpivot Transformation is a way to accomplish this business requirement. In this example, you'll be shown how to use the Unpivot Transformation to create rows in the Data Flow from columns and shown how it is the opposite of the Pivot Transformation.

Your first step is to create a new package and drag a new Data Flow Task onto the Control Flow. From the Data Flow tab, configure the task. For this example, create a Flat File Connection Manager that points to `UnPivotExample.csv`, which looks like Figure 4-39 and can be downloaded from `www.wrox.com/go/prossis2014`. Name the Connection Manager **FF Extract**, and make the first row a header row. The file is comma-delimited, so you will want to specify the delimiter on the Columns page.

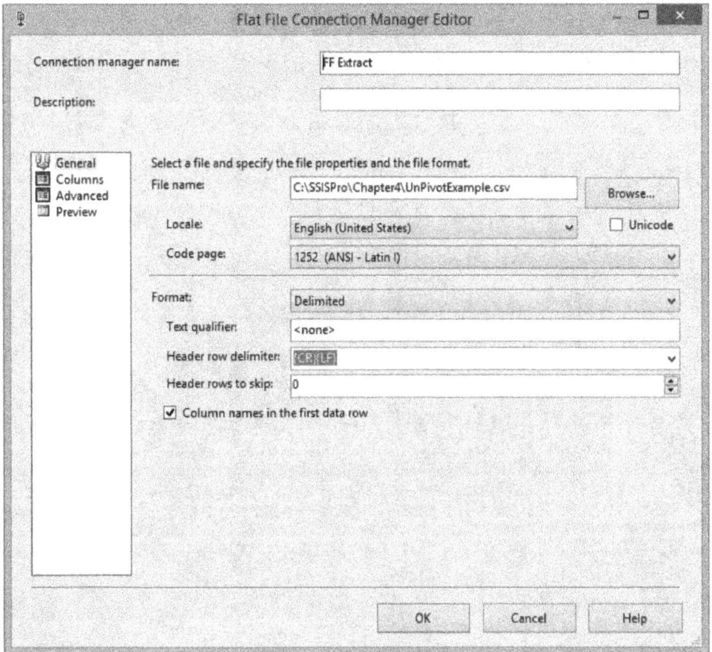

FIGURE 4-39

Once the Connection Manager is created, add a new Flat File Source and rename it "Mainframe Data." Point the connection to the Pivot Source Connection Manager. Ensure that all the columns are checked in the Columns page on the source and click OK to go back to the Data Flow.

The next step is the most important step. You need to unpivot the data and make each column into a row in the Data Flow. You can do this by dragging an Unpivot Transformation onto the Data Flow and connecting it to the source. In this example, you want to unpivot the BillTo and ShipTo columns, and the OrderID column will just be passed through for each row. To do this, check each column you wish to unpivot, as shown in Figure 4-40, and check Pass Through for the OrderID column.

As you check each column that you wish to unpivot on, the column will be added to the grid below (shown in Figure 4-40). You'll then need to type **CustomerName** for the Destination Column property for each row in the grid. This will write the data from each of the two columns into a single column called CustomerName. Optionally, you can also type **Original Column** for the Pivot Key Column Name property. By doing this, each row that's written by the transformation will have an additional column called Original Column. This new column will state where the data came from.

The Pivot Transformation will take care of columns that have NULL values. For example, if your ShipTo column for OrderID 1 had a NULL value, that column will not be written as a row. You may wish to handle empty string values though, which will create blank rows in the Data Flow. To throw these records out, you can use a Conditional Split Transformation. In this transformation, you can create one condition for your good data that you wish to keep with the following code, which accepts only rows with actual data:

```
ISNULL(CustomerName) == FALSE && TRIM(CustomerName) != ""
```

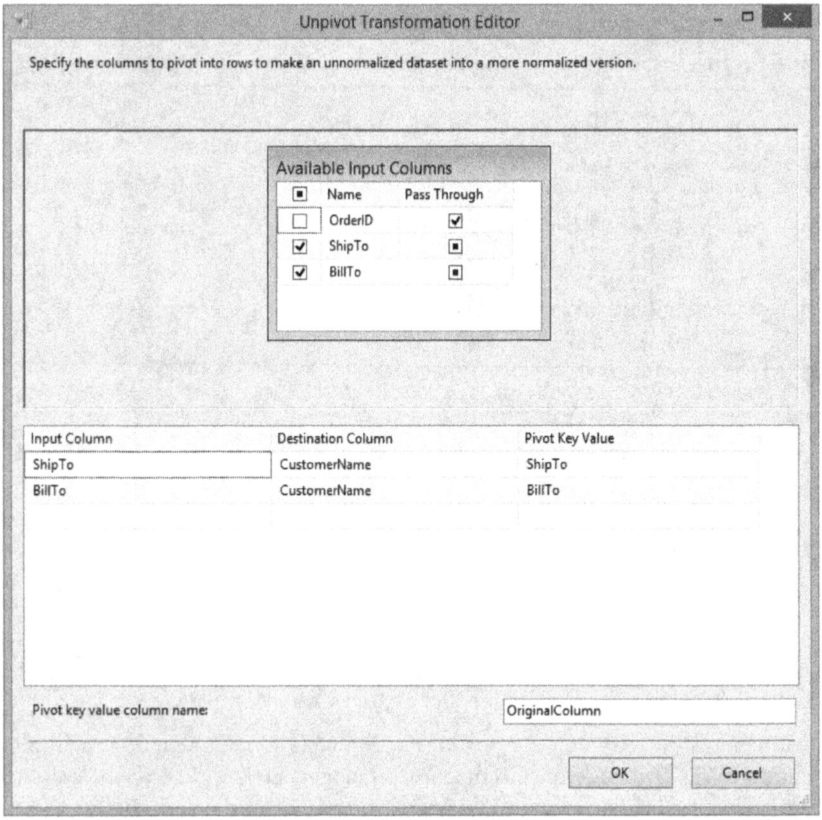

FIGURE 4-40

The default (else) condition handles empty strings and NULL customers and in this example is called NULL Customer. After this, you're ready to send the data to the destination of your choice. The simplest example is to send the data to a new SQL Server table in the AdventureWorks database.

Execute the package. You'll see that the Valid Customer output goes to the customer table, and the NULL data condition is just thrown out. You could also place a data viewer prior to the OLE DB Destination to see the data interactively.

Term Extraction

If you have ever done some word and phrase analysis on websites for better search engine placement, you are familiar with the job that this transformation performs. The Term Extraction Transformation is a tool to mine free-flowing text for English word and phrase frequency. You can feed any text-based input stream into the transformation and it will output two columns: a text phrase and a statistical value for the phrase relative to the total input stream. The statistical values or scores that can be calculated can be as simple as a count of the frequency of the words and phrases, or they can be a little more complicated, such as the result of a formula named the TFIDF score. The TFIDF acronym stands for Term Frequency and Inverse Document Frequency, and it is a formula designed to balance the frequency of the distinct words and phrases relative to the total text sampled. If you're interested, here's the formula:

```
TDIDF (of term or phrase) = (frequency of term) * log((# rows in sample)/ (#
rows with term or phrase))
```

The results generated by the Term Extraction Transformation are based on internal algorithms and statistical models that are encapsulated in the component. You can't alter or gain any insight into this logic by examining the code. However, some of the core rules about how the logic breaks apart the text to determine word and phrase boundaries are documented in Books Online. What you can do is tweak some external settings and make adjustments to the extraction behavior by examining the resulting output. Because text extraction is domain-specific, the transformation also provides the capability to store terms and phrases that you have predetermined are noisy or insignificant in your final results. You can then automatically remove these items from future extractions. Within just a few testing iterations, you can have the transformation producing meaningful results.

Before you write this transformation off as a cool utility that you'll never use, consider this: How useful would it be to query into something like a customer service memo field stored in your data warehouse and generate some statistics about the comments being made? This is the type of usage for which the Term Extraction Transformation is perfectly suited. The trick to understanding how to use the component is to remember that it has one input. That input must be either a NULL-terminated ANSI (DT_WSTR) or a Unicode (DT_NTEXT) string. If your input stream is not one of these two types, you can use the Data Conversion Transformation to convert it. Because this transformation can best be learned by playing around with all the settings, the next example puts this transformation to work doing exactly what was proposed earlier — mining some customer service memo fields.

Assume you have a set of comment fields from a customer service database for an appliance manufacturer. In this field, the customer service representative records a note that summarizes his or her contact with the customer. For simplicity's sake, you'll create these comment fields in a text file and analyze them in the Term Extraction Transformation.

1. Create the customer service text file using the following text (you can download the code file `custsvc.txt` from `www.wrox.com/go/prossis2014`). Save it as `c:\ProSSIS\Chapter4\custsvc.txt`.

    ```
    Ice maker in freezer stopped working model XX-YY3
    Door to refrigerator is coming off model XX-1
    Ice maker is making a funny noise XX-YY3
    Handle on fridge falling off model XX-Z1
    Freezer is not getting cold enough XX-1
    Ice maker grinding sound fridge XX-YY3
    Customer asking how to get the ice maker to work model XX-YY3
    Customer complaining about dent in side panel model XX-Z1
    Dent in model XX-Z1
    Customer wants to exchange model XX-Z1 because of dent in door
    Handle is wiggling model XX-Z1
    ```

2. Create a new SSIS package named TermExtractionExample. Add a Data Flow Task to the Control Flow design surface.

3. Create a Flat File connection to `c:\ProSSIS\Chapter4\custsvc.txt`. Uncheck "Column names in first data row". Change the output column named in the Advanced tab to **CustSvcNote**. Change OutputColumnWidth to 100 to account for the length of the field. Change the data type to DT_WSTR.

4. Add a Flat File Source to the Data Flow design surface. Configure the source to use the Flat File connection.

5. Add a Term Extraction Transformation to the Data Flow design surface. Connect the output of the Flat File Source to its input. Open the Term Extraction Transformation Editor. Figure 4-41 shows the available input columns from the input stream and the two default-named output columns. You can change the named output columns if you wish. Only one input column can be chosen. Click the column CustSvcNote, as this is the column that is converted to a Unicode string. If you click the unconverted column, you'll see a validation error like the following:

```
The input column can only have DT_WSTR or DT_NTEXT as its data type.
```

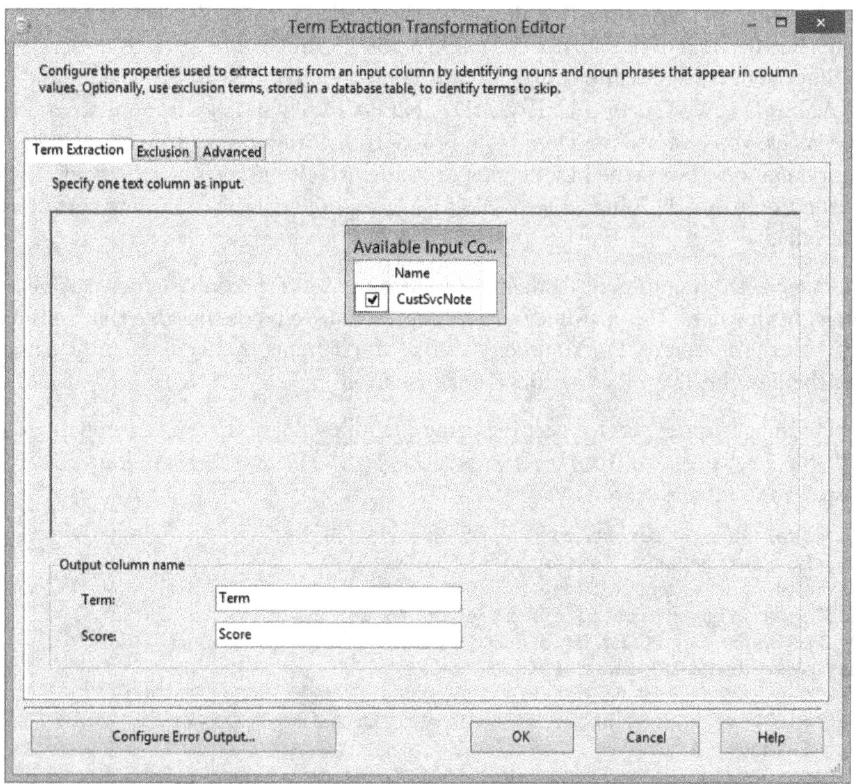

FIGURE 4-41

6. Even though we're not going to set these tabs, the Exclusion tab enables you to specify noise words for the Term Extraction to ignore. The Advanced tab enables you to control

how many times the word must appear before you output it as evidence. Close the Term Extraction Transformation Editor. Ignore the cautionary warnings about rows sent to error outputs. You didn't configure an error location where bad rows should be saved, but it's not necessary for this example.

7. Add an OLE DB Destination to the Data Flow. Connect the output of the Term Extraction Task to the OLE DB Destination. Configure the OLE DB Destination to use your AdventureWorks connection.

8. Click the New button to configure the Name of Table or View property. A window will come up with a `CREATE TABLE` DDL statement. Notice that the data types are a Unicode text field and a double. Alter the statement to read as follows:

```
CREATE TABLE TermResults (
[Term] NVARCHAR(128),
[Score] DOUBLE PRECISION
)
```

9. When you click OK, the new table TermResults will be created in the AdventureWorks database. Click the Mappings tab to confirm the mapping between the Term Extraction outputs of Term and Score to the table TermResults.

10. Add a data viewer by right-clicking the Data Flow between the Term Extraction Transformation and the OLE DB Destination. Set the type to grid and accept the defaults.

11. Run the package.

The package will stop on the data viewer that is shown in Figure 4-42 to enable you to view the results of the Term Extraction Transformation. You should see a list of terms and an associated score for each word. Because you accepted all of the Term Extraction settings, the default score is a simple count of frequency. Stop the package, open the Term Extraction Transformation Editor, and view the Advanced tab.

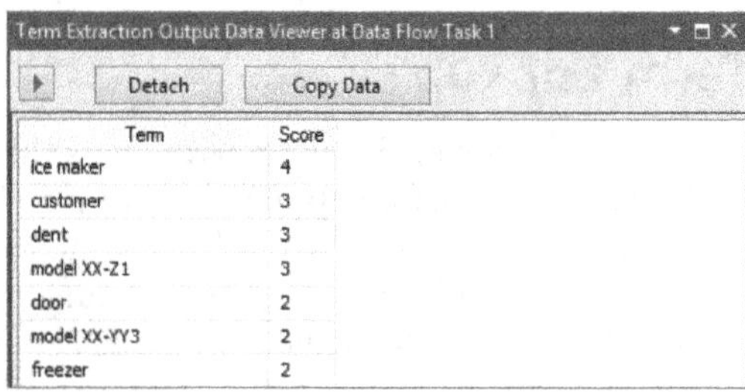

FIGURE 4-42

The Advanced tab, which allows for some configuration of the task, is divided into four categories:

- **Term Type:** Settings that control how the input stream should be broken into bits called *tokens*. The Noun Term Type focuses the transformation on nouns only, Noun Phrases extracts noun phrases, and Noun and Noun Phrases extracts both.
- **Score Type:** Choose to analyze words either by frequency or by a weighted frequency.
- **Parameters:** Frequency threshold is the minimum number of times a word or phrase must appear in tokens. Maximum length of term is the maximum number of words that should be combined together for evaluation.
- **Options:** Check this option to consider case sensitivity or leave it unchecked to disregard.

This is where the work really starts. How you set the transformation up greatly affects the results you'll see. Figure 4-43 shows an example of the results using each of the different Term Type (noun) settings combined with the different score types [Tascam Digital Interface (TDIF)].

Currently, using a combination of these statistics, you can report that customer service is logging a high percentage of calls concerning the terms "model,""model XX-Z1,""model XX-YY3,""ice maker,""dent," and "customer." From this, one can assume that there may be some issues with models XX-Z1 and XX-YY3 that your client needs to look into.

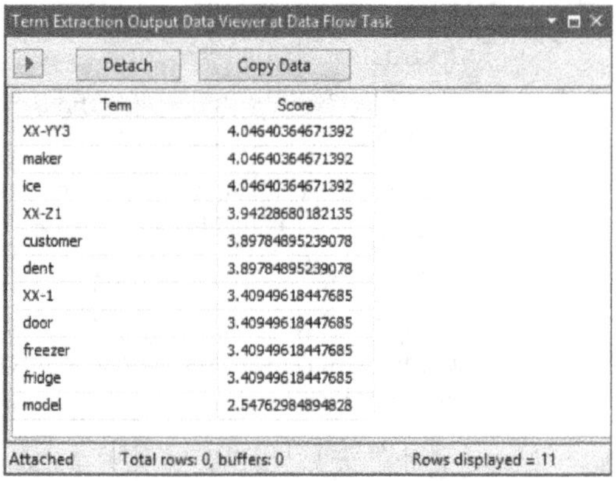

Term Extraction Output Data Viewer at Data Flow Task

Detach | Copy Data

Term	Score
XX-YY3	4.04640364671392
maker	4.04640364671392
ice	4.04640364671392
XX-Z1	3.94228680182135
customer	3.89784895239078
dent	3.89784895239078
XX-1	3.40949618447685
door	3.40949618447685
freezer	3.40949618447685
fridge	3.40949618447685
model	2.54762984894828

Attached | Total rows: 0, buffers: 0 | Rows displayed = 11

FIGURE 4-43

In evaluating this data, you might determine that over time some words are just not relevant to the analysis. In this example, the words "model" and "customer" serve no purpose and only dampen the scores for other words. To remove these words from your analysis, take advantage of the exclusion features in the Term Extraction Transformation by adding these words to a table.

To really make sense of that word list, you need to add some human intervention and the next transformation — Term Lookup.

Term Lookup

The Term Lookup Transformation uses the same algorithms and statistical models as the Term Extraction Transformation to break up an incoming stream into noun or noun phrase tokens, but it is designed to compare those tokens to a stored word list and output a matching list of terms and phrases with simple frequency counts. Now a strategy for working with both term-based transformations should become clear. Periodically use the Term Extraction Transformation to mine the text data and generate lists of statistical phrases. Store these phrases in a word list, along with phrases that you think the term extraction process should identify. Remove any phrases that you don't want identified. Use the Term Lookup Transformation to reprocess the text input to generate your final statistics. This way, you are generating statistics on known phrases of importance. A real-world application of this would be to pull out all the customer service notes that had a given set of terms or that mention a competitor's name.

You can use results from the Term Extraction example by removing the word "model" from the [TermExclusions] table for future Term Extractions. You would then want to review all the terms stored in the [TermResults] table, sort them out, remove the duplicates, and add back terms that make sense to your subject matter experts reading the text. Because you want to generate some statistics about which model numbers are causing customer service calls but you don't want to restrict your extractions to only occurrences of the model number in conjunction with the word "model," remove phrases combining the word "model" and the model number. The final [TermResults] table looks like a dictionary, resembling something like the following:

```
term
--------
dent
door
freezer
ice
ice maker
maker
XX-1
XX-YY3
XX-Z1
```

Using a copy of the package you built in the Extraction example, exchange the Term Extraction Transformation for a Term Lookup Transformation and change the OLE DB Destination to output to a table [TermReport].

Open the Term Lookup Transformation Editor. It should look similar to Figure 4-44. In the Reference Table tab, change the Reference Table Name option to **TermResults**. In the Term Lookup tab, map the ConvCustSvrNote column to the Term column on the right. Check the ConvCustSvrNote as a pass-through column. Three basic tabs are used to set up this task (in the Term Lookup Transformation Editor):

- **Reference Table:** This is where you configure the connection to the reference table. The Term Lookup Task should be used to validate each tokenized term that it finds in the input stream.
- **Term Lookup:** After selecting the lookup table, you map the field from the input stream to the reference table for matching.
- **Advanced:** This tab has one setting to check whether the matching is case sensitive.

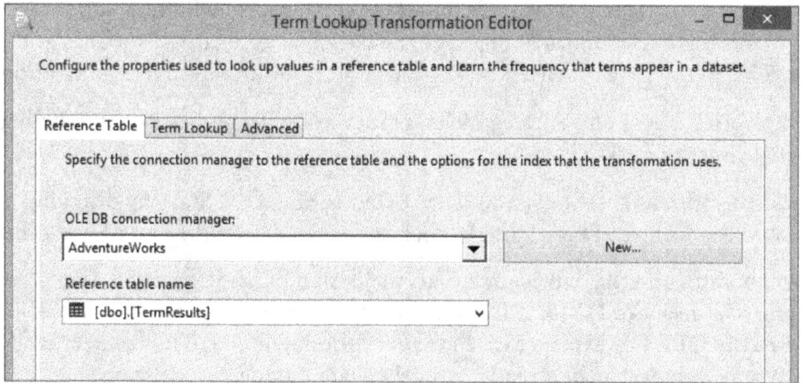

FIGURE 4-44

The result of running this package is a list of phrases that you are expecting from your stored word list. A sample of the first six rows is displayed in the following code. Notice that this result set doesn't summarize the findings. You are just given a blow-by-blow report on the number of terms in the word list that were found for each row of the customer service notes. In this text sample, it is just a coincidence that each term appears only once in each note.

```
term         Frequency    ConvCustSvcNote
-----        ---------    ------------------------------------------
freezer              1    ice maker in freezer stopped working model XX-YY3
ice maker            1    ice maker in freezer stopped working model XX-YY3
XX-YY3               1    ice maker in freezer stopped working model XX-YY3
Door                 1    door to refrigerator is coming off model XX-1
XX-1                 1    door to refrigerator is coming off model XX-1
ice maker            1    ice maker is making a funny noise XX-YY3
(Only first six rows of resultset are displayed)
```

To complete the report, you could add an Aggregate Transformation between the Term Lookup Transformation and the OLE DB Destination. Set up the Aggregate Transformation to ignore the ConvCustSvcNote column, group by the Term column, and summarize the Frequency Column. Connect the Aggregate Transformation to the OLE DB Destination and remap the columns in the OLE DB Destination.

Although this is a very rudimentary example, you can start to see the possibilities of using SSIS for very raw and unstructured Data Sources like this customer service comment data. In a short period of time, you have pulled some meaningful results from the data. Already you can provide the intelligence that model XX-Z1 is generating 45 percent of your sample calls and that 36 percent of your customer calls are related to the ice maker. Pretty cool results from what is considered unstructured data. This transformation is often used for advanced text mining.

DATA FLOW EXAMPLE

Now you can practice what you have learned in this chapter, pulling together some of the transformations and connections to create a small ETL process. This process will pull transactional data from the AdventureWorks database and then massage the data by aggregating, sorting, and calculating new columns. This extract may be used by another vendor or an internal organization.

Please note that this example uses a Sort and Aggregate Transformation. In reality it would be better to use T-SQL to replace that functionality.

1. Create a new package and rename it `AdventureWorksExtract.dtsx`. Start by dragging a Data Flow Task onto the Control Flow. Double-click the task to open the Data Flow tab.
2. In the Data Flow tab, drag an OLE DB Source onto the design pane. Right-click the source and rename it **TransactionHistory**. Double-click it to open the editor. Click the New button next to the OLE DB Connection Manager dropdown box. The connection to the AdventureWorks database may already be in the Data Connections list on the left. If it is, select it and click OK. Otherwise, click New to add a new connection to the AdventureWorks database on any server.
3. When you click OK, you'll be taken back to the OLE DB Source Editor. Ensure that the Data Access Mode option is set to SQL Command. Type the following query for the command, as shown in Figure 4-45 or as follows:

```
SELECT ProductID, Quantity, ActualCost from
Production.TransactionHistoryArchive
```

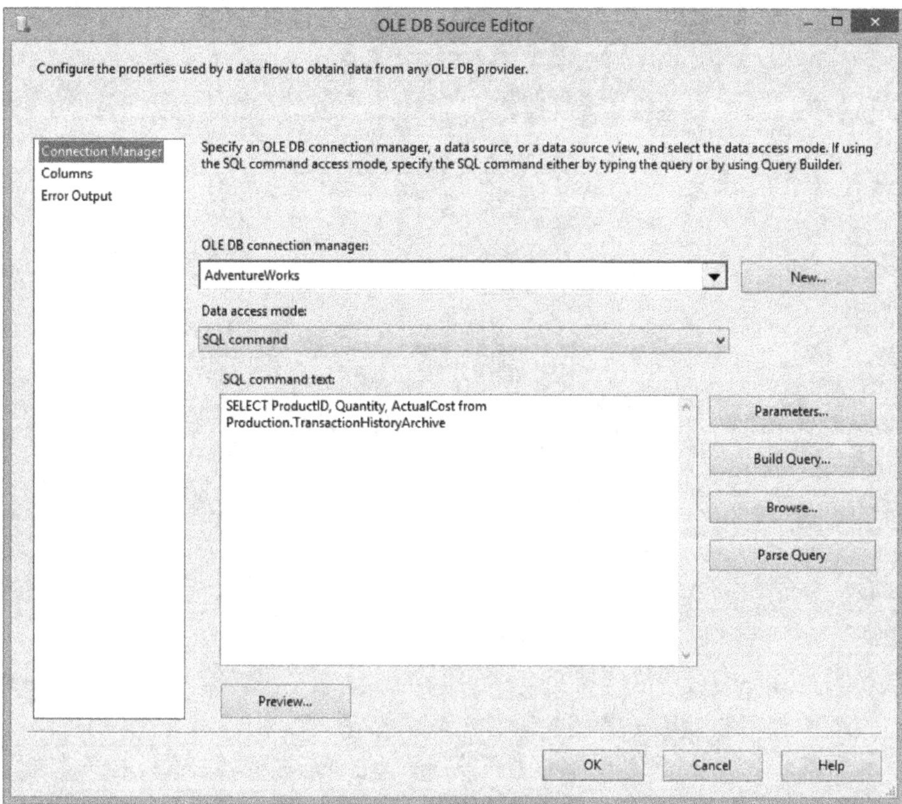

FIGURE 4-45

4. Drag a Derived Column Transformation onto the Data Flow, right-click it, and select Rename. Rename the transform **Calculate Total Cost**. Click the TransactionHistory OLE DB Source and drag the green arrow (the data path) onto the Derived Column Transformation.

5. Double-click the Derived Column Transformation to open the editor (shown in Figure 4-46). For the Expression column, type the following code or drag and drop the column names from the upper-left box: **[Quantity]*** **[ActualCost]**. The Derived Column should have the <add as a new column> option selected, and type **TotalCost** for the Derived Column Name option. Click OK to exit the editor.

6. Drag an Aggregate Transformation onto the Data Flow and rename it **Aggregate Data**. Drag the blue arrow from the Derived Column Transformation onto this transformation. Double-click the Aggregate Transformation to open its editor (shown in Figure 4-47). Select the ProductID column and note that it is transposed into the bottom section. The ProductID column should have Group By for the Operation column. Next, check the Quantity and TotalCost columns and set the operation of both of these columns to Sum. Click OK to exit the editor.

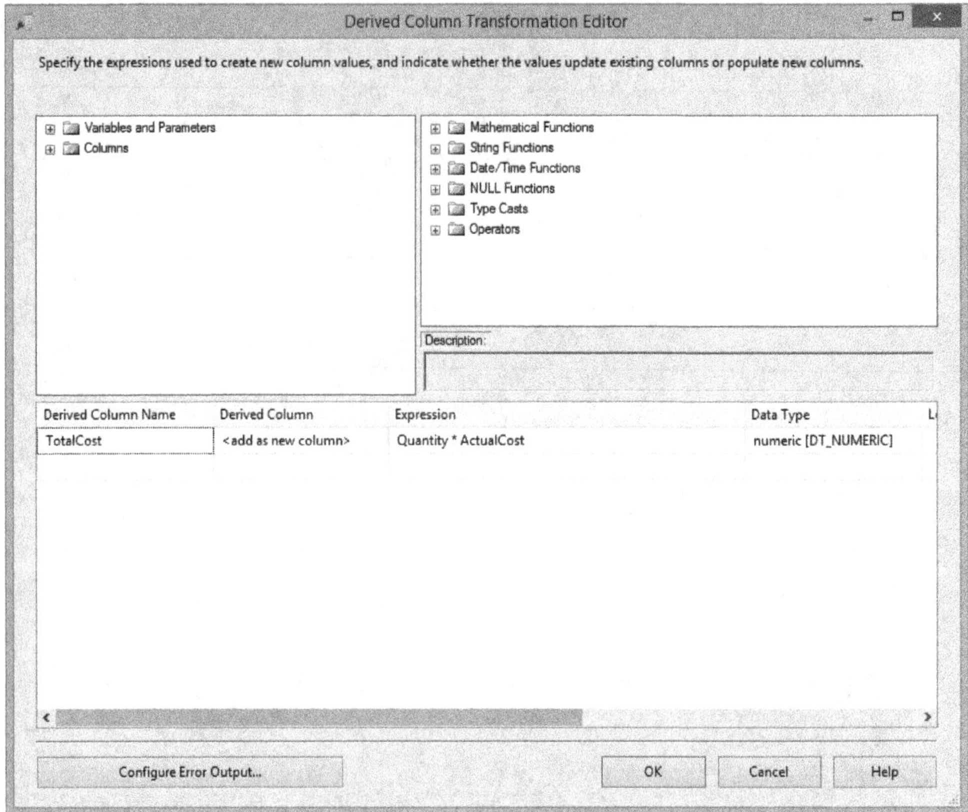

FIGURE 4-46

7. Drag a Sort Transformation onto the Data Flow and rename it **Sort by Quantity**. Connect the Aggregate Transformation to this transformation by the blue arrow as in the preceding step. Double-click the Sort Transformation to configure it in the editor. You can sort by the most popular products by checking the Quantity column and selecting Descending for the Sort Type dropdown box. Click OK to exit the editor.

8. You have now done enough massaging of the data and are ready to export the data to a flat file that can be consumed by another vendor. Drag a Flat File Destination onto the Data Flow. Connect it to the Sort Transformation by using the blue arrow as shown in the last few steps. Rename the Flat File Destination **Vendor Extract**.

9. Double-click the destination to open the Flat File Destination Editor. You're going to output the data to a new Connection Manager, so click New. When prompted for the Flat File Format, select Delimited. Name the Connection Manager **Vendor Extract** also, and type whatever description you'd like. If you have the directory, point the File Name option to `C:\ProSSIS\Chapter4\VendorExtract.csv` (make sure this directory is created before proceeding). Check the "Column names in the first data row" option. Your final screen should look like Figure 4-48. Click OK to go back to the Flat File Destination Editor.

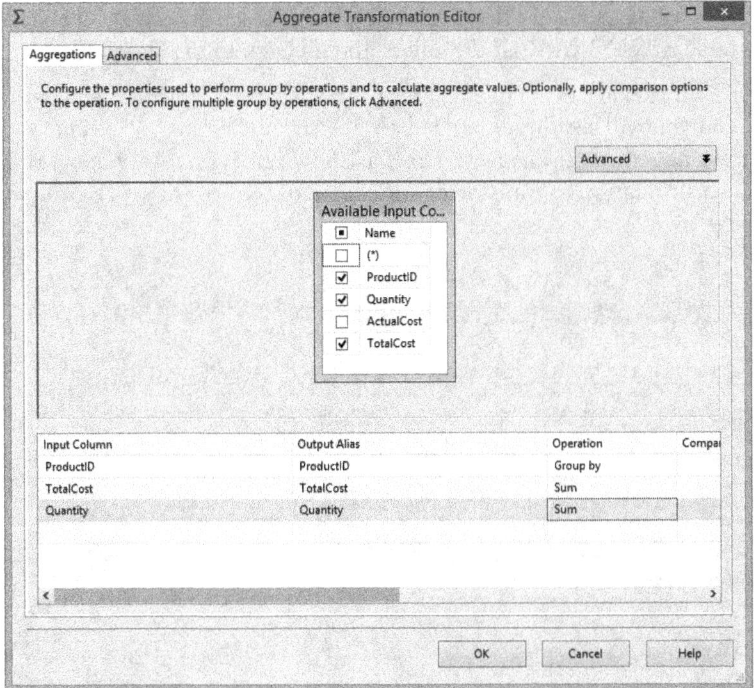

FIGURE 4-47

FIGURE 4-48

10. From the Mappings page, ensure that each column in the Inputs table is mapped to the Destination table. Click OK to exit the editor and go back to the Data Flow.

Now your first larger ETL package is complete! This package is very typical of what you'll be doing daily inside of SSIS, and you will see this expanded on greatly, in Chapter 8. Execute the package. You should see the rows flow through the Data Flow, as shown in Figure 4-49. Note that as the data flows from transformation to transformation, you can see how many records were passed through.

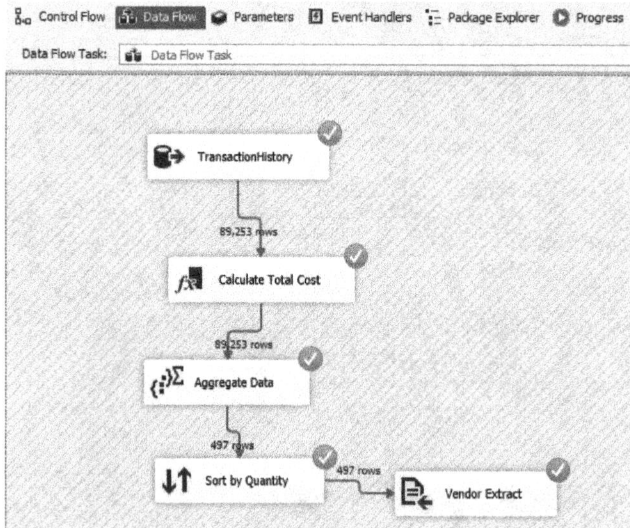

FIGURE 4-49

SUMMARY

The SSIS Data Flow moves data from a variety of sources and then transforms the data in memory prior to landing the data into a destination. Because it is in memory, it has superior speed to loading data into a table and performing a number of T-SQL transformations. In this chapter you learned about the common sources, destinations, and transformations used in the SSIS Data Flow. In the next chapter, you learn how to make SSIS dynamic by using variables and expressions.

5

Using Variables, Parameters, and Expressions

WHAT'S IN THIS CHAPTER?

- Reviewing variables, parameters, and expressions
- Using data types for variables and parameters
- Creating variables and parameters
- Expression syntax and usage
- Expression examples

WROX.COM DOWNLOADS FOR THIS CHAPTER

You can find the wrox.com code downloads for this chapter at `www.wrox.com/go/prossis2014` on the Download Code tab.

If you have used SSIS packages for any involved ETL processes, you have inevitably encountered the need for dynamic capabilities. A *dynamic package* can reconfigure itself at runtime to do things like run certain steps conditionally, create a series of auto-generated filenames for export, or retrieve and set send-to addresses on an alert e-mail from a data table. Because dynamic changes are fairly common occurrences, developers and architects turn to expressions as they begin rolling out SSIS projects in their development shops.

This chapter attempts to provide a solid information base to get you up to speed on expressions. Here we will consolidate the common questions, answers, and best practices about expressions that we've heard and explained since the first release of SSIS. The good news is that expressions are easy to use and impressively powerful. As you read this chapter, you will not only gain an understanding about how expressions work but also gain some insight into how you can use variables and parameters to set up expressions on your current SSIS project.

DYNAMIC PACKAGE OBJECTS

SSIS includes multiple objects that can be used to create dynamic packages. Figure 5-1 provides a graphical description of this model in SSIS. SSIS can dynamically set a property in a task or component using an expression, which can be built using a set of building blocks, including variables, parameters, functions, literals, and more. When the package is run, the expression is evaluated and used in the property as each task or component is accessed.

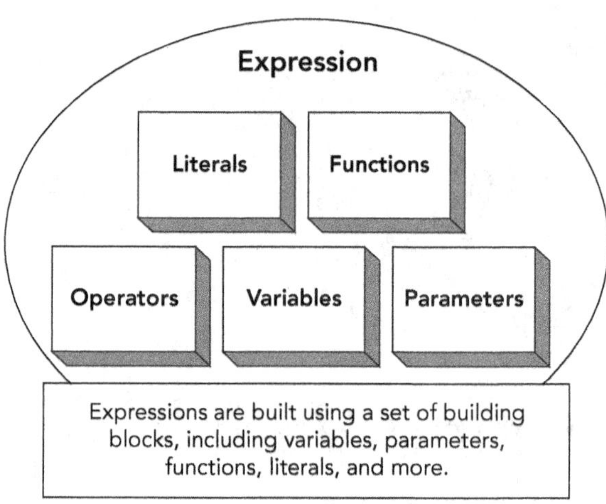

FIGURE 5-1

Variable Overview

Variables are a key feature in the SSIS package development process. This object contains a value that can be hardcoded, dynamically set once, or modified multiple times throughout the execution of the package. Principally, variables provide a method for objects in a package to communicate with each other. Similar to their use in programming languages, variables are used in specific types of logic, such as iterating through a loop, concatenating multiple values together to create a file directory, or passing an array between objects.

Parameter Overview

Parameters were first introduced in SQL Server 2012. While similar to a variable in that a parameter can store information and be used in an expression, it has a few different properties and uses that you will want to understand. As demonstrated in Figure 5-2, parameters are set externally. The parameter can then be used in an expression to affect different properties in the package.

SSIS uses two types of parameters: *project parameters* and *package parameters*. Project parameters are created at the project level and can be used in all packages that are included in that project. On the other hand, package parameters are created at the package level and can be used only in that package. Project parameters are best used for values that are shared among packages, such as e-mail addresses for error messages. Package parameters are best used for values specific to that package, such as directory locations.

When using the project deployment model (discussed in depth in Chapter 22), parameters are the best choices to replace package configurations to create a dynamic and more flexible SSIS solution. Using the Required property of the parameter, you can also necessitate the caller of the package to pass in a value for the parameter. If you want to set the value of a property from outside the package, either required or not, parameters are the object to use. On the other hand, if you want to create or store values only within a package, variables are the object to use.

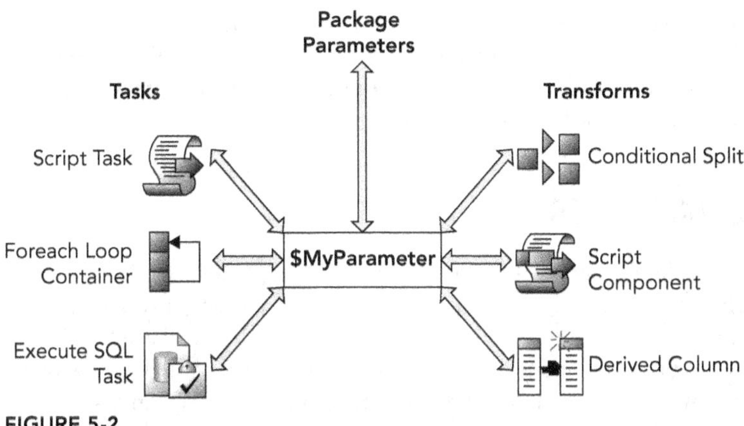

FIGURE 5-2

Expression Overview

Expressions are the key to understanding how to create dynamic packages in SSIS. One way to think about expressions is to compare them to the familiar model of a spreadsheet cell in a program like Microsoft Excel. A spreadsheet cell can hold a literal value, a reference to another cell on the spreadsheet, or functions ranging from simple to complex arrangements. In each instance, the result is a resolved value displayed in the cell. Figure 5-3 shows these same capabilities of the expression, which can hold literal values, identifiers available to the operation (references to variables or columns), or functions (built-in or user-defined). The difference in the SSIS world is that these values can be substituted directly into properties of the package model, providing powerful and dynamic workflow and operational functionalities.

Similarity of Expressions to Microsoft Excel Cells

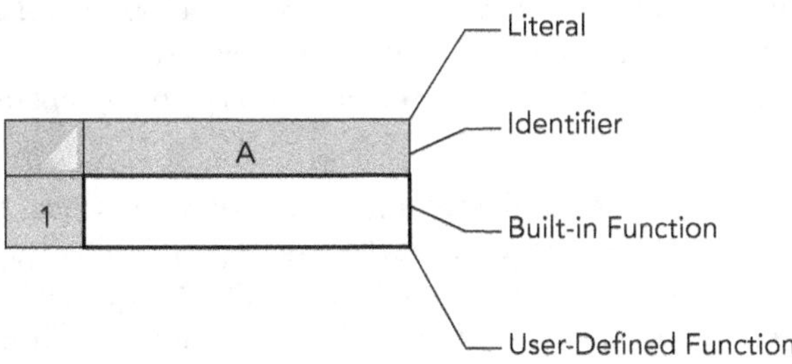

FIGURE 5-3

Starting with SQL Server 2012, it is easy to see when an expression has been set on a property within an object. *Expression adorners* are special icons that are placed on top of the object icon if the object has an expression. This indicator makes it easier to understand why the package seems to be doing something behind the scenes that you weren't expecting!

If you understand these visual analogies explaining how expressions, parameters, and variables fit into the SSIS picture, then you are almost ready to dig into the details of how to build an expression. First, however, it's time to take a look at some of the details about data types, variables, and parameters that cause many of the issues for SSIS package developers.

UNDERSTANDING DATA TYPES

In SSIS, you must pay attention to data types, whether the data is coming from your Data Flow, is stored in variables, or is included in expressions. Failure to do so will cause a lot of frustration because the syntax checker will complain about incompatible data types when you are building expressions. If your Data Flow contains incompatible data types, your packages will raise either warnings or errors (if implicit conversions are made). This will happen even if the conversion is between Unicode and non-Unicode character sets. Comparison operations also are subject to either hard or soft errors during implicit conversion. Bad data type decisions can have a serious impact on performance. This seemingly simple topic causes significant grief for SSIS developers who haven't yet learned the specifics of data types and how they are converted. The following sections provide a brief overview of how to resolve common data type conversion issues, beginning with a primer on SSIS data types.

SSIS Data Types

If you research the topic of "Integration Services Data Types" in Books Online, you'll first notice that the data types are named much differently than similar types found in .NET or T-SQL. This nomenclature is troublesome for most new users. The following table provides a matrix between SSIS data types and a typical SQL Server set of data types. You'll need this table to map between Data Flow columns and variable or parameters data types. The .NET managed types are important only if you are using Script component, CLR, or .NET-based coding to manipulate your Data Flows.

The following table is just for SQL Server. To do a similar analysis for your own data source, look at the mapping files that can be found in this directory: `C:\Program Files\Microsoft SQL Server\120\DTS\MappingFiles\`. If you're familiar with OLE DB data types, you'll understand these SSIS data type enumerations, because they are similar. However, there is more going on than just naming differences.

First, SSIS supports some data types that may not be familiar at all, nor are they applicable to SQL Server — namely, most of the unsigned integer types and a few of the date types. You'll also notice the availability of the separate date-only (`DT_DBDATE`) and time-only (`DT_DBTIME`) types, which prior to SQL Server 2008 were available only for RDBMS databases like DB2 and ORACLE. With the introduction of similar data types in the SQL Server 2008 engine, they are also applicable in SSIS. Finally, notice the arrow "⇨" in the table, which indicates that these data types are converted to other SSIS data types in Data Flow operations that may be opportunities for performance enhancements.

SSIS DATA TYPE	SQL SERVER DATA TYPE	.NET MANAGED TYPE
DT_WSTR	nvarchar, nchar	System.String
DT_STR ⇨ DT_WSTR	varchar, char	
DT_TEXT ⇨ DT_WSTR	text	
DT_NTEXT ⇨ DT_WSTR	ntext, sql_variant, xml	
DT_BYTES	binary, varbinary	Array of System.Byte
DT_IMAGE ⇨ DT_BYTES	timestamp, image	
DT_DBTIMESTAMP	smalldatetime, datetime	System.DateTime
DT_DBTIMESTAMP2 ⇨ DT_DBTIMESTAMP	datetime	
DT_DBDATE ⇨ DT_DBTIMESTAMP	date	
DT_DATE ⇨ DT_DBTIMESTAMP		
DT_FILETIME ⇨ DT_DBTIMESTAMP		
DT_DBDATETIMESTAMPOFFSET	datetimeoffset	
DT_DBTIME2	time	System.TimeSpan
DT_DBTIME ⇨ DT_DBTIME2		
DT_NUMERIC	numeric	System.Decimal
DT_DECIMAL ⇨ DT_NUMERIC	decimal	
DT_GUID	uniqueidentifier	System.Guid
DT_I1		System.SByte
DT_I2	smallint	System.Int16
DT_CY	smallmoney, money	System.Currency
DT_I4	int	System.Int32

continues

(continued)

SSIS DATA TYPE	SQL SERVER DATA TYPE	.NET MANAGED TYPE
DT_I8	bigint	System.Int64
DT_BOOL ⇨ DT_I4	bit	System.Boolean
DT_R4	real	System.Single
DT_R8	float	System.Double
DT_UI1	tinyint	System.Byte
DT_UI2	int	System.UInt16
DT_UI4	bigint	System.UInt32
DT_UI8	numeric	System.UInt64

Date and Time Type Support

SQL Server 2008 included new data types for separate date and time values and an additional time zone-based data type compliant with the ISO 8601 standard. SSIS has always had these data type enumerations for the other RDBMS sources, but as of SQL Server 2008, these can also be used for SQL Server as well, including `DT_DBTIMESTAMP2` and `DT_DBTIME2`, added for more precision, and `DT_DBTIMESTAMPOFFSET`, added for the ISO `DateTimeOffset` SQL Server data type.

A common mistake made in SSIS packages is the improper selection of an SSIS date data type. For some reason, `DT_DBDATE` and `DT_DATE` are often used for date types in Data Flow components, but improper use of these types can result in overflow errors or the removal of the time element from the date values. SSIS data types provide a larger net for processing incoming values than you may have in your destination data source. It is your responsibility to manage the downcasting or conversion operations. Make sure you are familiar with the data type mappings in the mapping file for your data source and destination, and the specific conversion behavior of each type. A good start would be the date/time types, because there are many rules regarding their conversion, as evidenced by the large section about them in Books Online. You can find these conversion rules for date/time data types under the topic "Integration Services Data Types" found here: `http://msdn.microsoft.com/en-us/library/ms141036(v=SQL.120).aspx`.

How Wrong Data Types and Sizes Can Affect Performance

If you've been working with SSIS for a while, you know that it can use serious memory resources and sometimes be slower than you expect. That's because the Data Flow components do most of their work in memory. This can be good because it eliminates the most time-consuming I/O operations. However, because SSIS uses memory buffers to accomplish this, the number of rows that can be loaded into a buffer is directly related to the width of the row. The narrower the row, the more rows that can be processed per buffer.

If you are defining the data types of a large input source, pick your data types carefully, so that you are not using the default 50 characters per column for a text file, or the suggested data types of the Connection Manager, when you do not need this extra safety cushion. Also, be aware that there are some trade-offs when selecting specific data types if they require any conversion as the data is being loaded into the buffers.

Data conversion is a fact of life, and you'll have to pay for it somewhere in the ETL process. These general guidelines can give you a start:

- **Convert only when necessary.** Don't convert columns from a data source that will be dropped from the data stream. Each conversion costs something.
- **Convert to the closest type for your destination source using the mapping files.** If a value is converted to a nonsupported data type, you'll incur an additional conversion internal to SSIS to the mapped data type.
- **Convert using the closest size and precision.** Don't import all columns as 50-character data columns if you are working with a fixed or reliable file format with columns that don't require as much space.
- **Evaluate the option to convert after the fact.** Remember that SSIS is still an ETL tool and sometimes it is more efficient to stage the data and convert it using set-based methods.

The bottom line is that data type issues can be critical in high-volume scenarios, so plan with these guidelines in mind.

Unicode and Non-Unicode Conversion Issues

One aspect of ETL package development that you might not be used to is the default use of Unicode data types in SSIS packages. Not only is this the default import behavior, but all the string functions in SSIS expect Unicode strings as input. Unicode is a great choice if you're unsure of the incoming data for handling data from import files with special characters, but if you're not familiar with using this character set, it can be confusing at first. At the very least, using Unicode requires an additional step that is frequently missed, resulting in errors. For a typical demonstration, create a package that imports an Excel data source into a table defined with non-Unicode fields, or download the samples from `www.wrox.com`. Excel data is imported as Unicode by default, so the mapping step in the destination component complains that the data is not compatible, as shown in Figure 5-4.

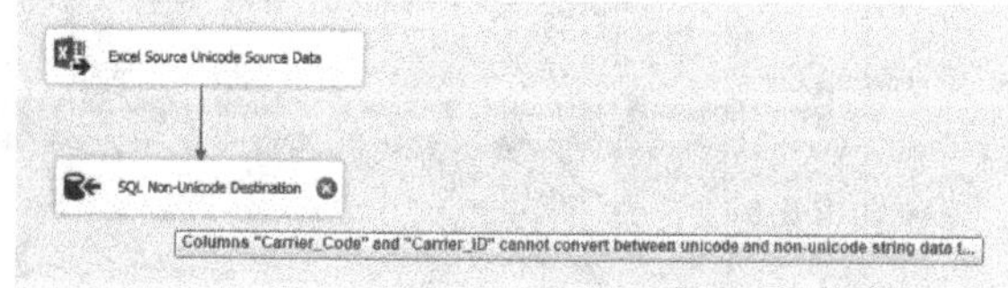

FIGURE 5-4

> **NOTE** *You may experience some data being replaced by NULLs when importing Excel files using the Excel Connection Manager. This typically occurs when numeric and text data is stored within one column. One solution is to update the extended properties section of the connection string to look like this:*
>
> ```
> Extended Properties="EXCEL 14.0;HDR=YES;IMEX=1"
> ```

At first, you might assume that all you need to do is change the source data type to match the non-Unicode destination. Using the SQL conversion table as a guide, right click on the source, select the Show Advanced Editor option, and change the column type to `DT_STR` to match the destination SQL Server `varchar` data type. Now you'll find that the same error from Figure 5-4 is occurring on both the source and the destination components. As discussed earlier in this section, SSIS requires purposeful conversion and casting operations. To complete the task, you need to add only a Data Conversion Transformation to convert the `DT_WSTR` and `DT_R8` data types to `DT_STR` and `DT_CY`, respectively. The Data Conversion Transformation should look similar to Figure 5-5.

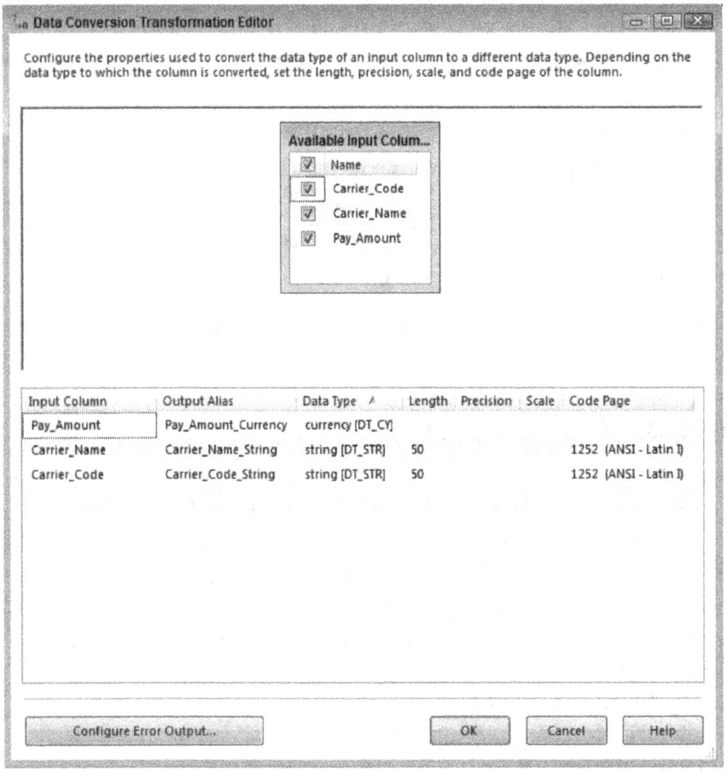

FIGURE 5-5

Notice in this Data Conversion Transformation that the data types and lengths are changed to truncate and convert the incoming string to match the destination source. Also, notice the Code Page setting that auto-defaults to 1252 for ANSI Latin 1. The Code Page setting varies according to the source of the Unicode data you are working with. If you are working with international data sources, you may need to change this to interpret incoming Unicode data correctly.

This type casting operation is a good, simple example of how SSIS packages handle data of differing types. However, within expressions it is not necessary to bring in the conversion component to cast between different types. You can simply use casting operators to change the data types within the expression.

Casting in SSIS Expressions

If you want to experience the developer's equivalent of poking your eye out, forget to put a casting operator in your Data Flow expressions. SSIS is tightly tied to data types and requires *casting*, which simply defines the data type for a value or expression. If you forget to use casting or choose the wrong data type, the package may fail or cause errors when trying to insert that column into the final destination.

While you can run into some frustrating issues if you don't do it, the need for casting is not always intuitive. For example, the result of any string function defaults to the Unicode `string` type. If you are attempting to store that value in a non-Unicode column, you need to cast. Conversely, if you are storing the value in a variable, you don't need to cast. (That's because the data types in variable definitions allow only Unicode; more about that later in the section "Defining Variables.")

The good news is that casting is easy. In the expression language, this looks just like a .NET primitive cast. The new data type is provided in parentheses right next to the value to be converted. A simple example is casting a 2-byte signed integer to a 4-byte signed integer:

```
(DT_I4)32
```

Of course, not all the casting operators are this simple. Some require additional parameters when specific precision, lengths, or code pages have to be considered to perform the operation. These operators are listed in the following table:

CASTING OPERATOR	ADDITIONAL PARAMETERS
DT_STR(<<length>>, <<code_page>>)	length — Final string length code_page — Unicode character set
DT_WSTR(<<length>>)	length — Final string length
DT_NUMERIC(<<precision>>, <<scale>>)	precision — Max number of digits scale — Number of digits after decimal
DT_DECIMAL(<<scale>>)	scale — Number of digits after decimal
DT_BYTES(<<length>>)	length — Number of final bytes
DT_TEXT(<<code_page>>)	code_page — Unicode character set

Casting causes the most obvious trouble during comparison operations and logical expressions. Remember that all operands in comparison operations must evaluate to a compatible data type. The same rule applies to complex or compound logical expressions. In this case, the entire expression must return a consistent data type, which may require casting sections of the expression that may not readily appear to need casting. This is similar to the situation that you have in T-SQL programming when you attempt to use a number in a `where` clause for a numeric column, or when using a `case` statement that needs to return columns of different types. In the `where` predicate, both the condition and the column must be convertible into a compatible type. For the `case` statement, each column must be cast to the same variant data type. Later in the chapter, you'll look at examples in which you need to pay attention to casting when using comparison and logical expressions.

A less obvious issue with casting can occur when data becomes truncated during casting. For example, casting Unicode double-byte data to non-Unicode data can result in lost characters. Significant digits can be lost in forced casting from unsigned to signed types or within types like 32-bit integers to 16-bit integers. These errors underscore the importance of wiring up the error outputs in the Data Flow components that have them. Before you look at that, however, look at the following section about variables and parameters and how they are used in dynamic SSIS package development.

USING VARIABLES AND PARAMETERS

Variables and parameters are the glue holding dynamic package development together. As discussed earlier, both of these objects are used to move values between package components. They are no different from variables in any programming environment. Variables in SSIS packages are scoped, or can be accessed, either within the package level or to a specific package component. Parameters can be scoped to either the package or project level.

Defining Variables

Variables can be created, deleted, renamed, and have their data types changed, as long as the package is in design mode. Once the package is validated and in runtime mode, the variable definition is locked; only the value of the variable can change. This is by design, so that the package is more declarative and type-safe. Creating a new variable is done through a designer that defines the scope of the variable depending upon how it is accessed. As mentioned earlier, variables can be scoped either to the package or to a specific component in the package. If the variable is scoped at a component level, only the component or its subcomponents have access to the variable. The following important tips can keep you out of trouble when dealing with variables:

- **Variables are case sensitive.** When you refer to a variable in a script task or an expression, pay attention to the case of the name. Different shops have their own rules, but typically variables are named using camel-case style.
- **Variables can hide other variable values higher in the hierarchy.** It is a good practice to not name variables similarly. This is a standard readability programming issue. If you have one variable outside a task and one inside the task, name them using identifiers like "inner" or "outer" to differentiate them.

A variable can be created by right-clicking the design surface of the package in which you need it. The Variables dialog enables you to create, edit, and delete variables. Figure 5-6 shows an example of two variables created within two scope levels: the Data Flow Task and the package.

Name	Scope	Data type	Value	Expression
BaseSelect	02Scope Package	String	SELECT AddressLine1, AddressLine2, City, StateProvinceCode...	
SelectSQL	Data Flow Task	String	SELECT AddressLine1, AddressLine2, City, StateProvinceCode...	@[UserVar::BaseSelect] + "'" + @[User...
SelectSQL_ExpDateParm	Data Flow Task	String	2000-1-12 0:0:0	(DT_WSTR, 4) DATEPART("yyyy", @[UserV...
SelectSQL_UserDateParm	Data Flow Task	DateTime	1/12/2000	

FIGURE 5-6

However, the Variables window does not expose all the capabilities of the variables. By selecting a variable and pressing F4, you will see the Properties window for the SelectSQL variable, as shown in Figure 5-7.

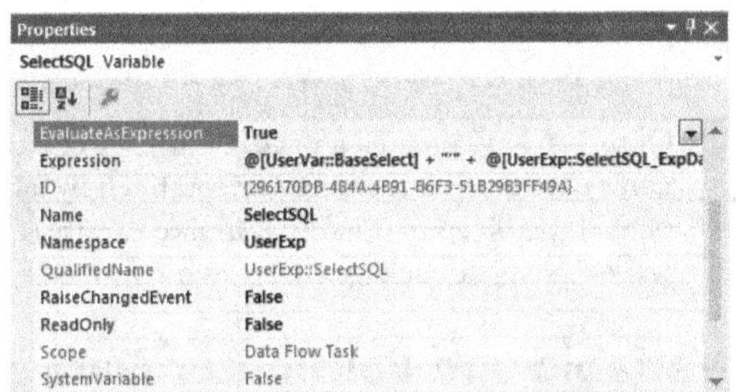

FIGURE 5-7

The reason for displaying the Properties window for the `SelectSQL` variable is to point out the `EvaluateAsExpression` and `Expression` properties. The value of a variable either can be a literal value or can be defined dynamically. By setting the `EvaluateAsExpression` property to `True`, the variable takes on a dynamic quality that is defined by the expression provided in the `Expression` property. The `SelectSQL` variable is actually holding the result of a formula that concatenates the string value of the base select statement stored in the `BaseSelect` variable and a user-provided date parameter. The point often missed by beginning SSIS developers is that these variables can be used to store expressions that can be reused throughout the package. Rather than recreate the expression all over the package, you can create an expression in a variable and then plug it in where needed. This greatly improves package maintainability by centralizing the expression definition. You'll see an example that shows how to create an expression-based variable later in this chapter.

As an alternative to using expressions, variables can also be set programmatically using the script tasks. Refer to Chapter 9 for examples describing how this is accomplished.

Defining Parameters

An exciting addition to the Integration Services family is the concept of parameters. Like variables, parameters store information, but they can be set in a variety of ways: package default, project default, or execution values. Using any method, the value stored in the parameter can be used in any expression to set a package property or variable. The parameter is initially created in the package or project.

To create a package parameter, select the Parameters tab in the design window and click the first icon on the toolbar. You can enter all the information shown in Figure 5-8. If you set the Required property, you force the setting of the parameter value to occur at runtime. If you set the Sensitive property, you tell Integration Services to encrypt the value in the catalog. To create a project parameter, right-click on the Project.params node in the Solution Explorer and select the Open option. This will open a similar view to the package parameters view.

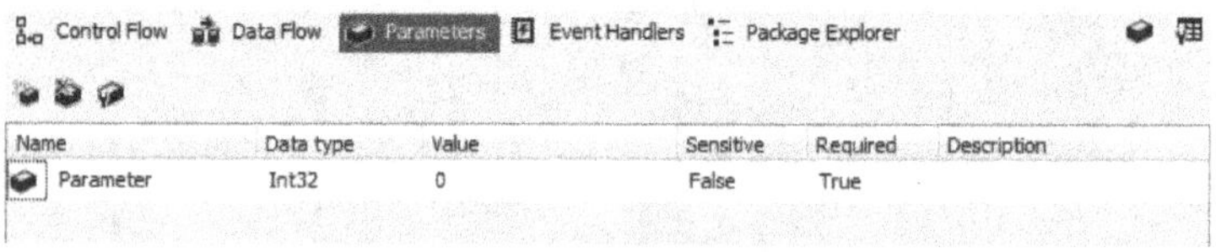

Name	Data type	Value	Sensitive	Required	Description
Parameter	Int32	0	False	True	

FIGURE 5-8

Once you have created a package or project parameter, you can use it to set other values. Parameter names are case sensitive and are prefixed by a dollar sign and either "Project" or "Package" depending on its type. Keep in mind that unlike variables, parameters cannot be changed by an expression. You'll walk through a package that uses a parameter to create expressions later in this chapter.

Variable and Parameter Data Types

You may have noticed that the data types available for variable definition are a little different from the SSIS variables that were discussed earlier in this chapter. For example, the value type for string variable storage is `String` instead of `DT_WSTR` or `DT_STR`. Admittedly, this is confusing. Why does SSIS use what looks like a generalized managed type in the variable definition and yet a more specific set of data types in the Data Flows? The answer lies in the implementation of variables within the SSIS engine. Variables can be set from outside of the package, so they are implemented in SSIS as COM variants. This enables the SSIS engine to use some late binding to resolve to the variable value within the package. However, note that this variant data type is not available anywhere within your control as an SSIS programmer. Variants are only an internal implementation in SSIS. Use the following table to help map the variable data types to SSIS Data Flow data types:

VARIABLE DATA TYPE	SSIS DATA TYPE	DESCRIPTION
`Boolean`	`DT_BOOL`	Boolean value. Either `True` or `False`. Be careful setting these data types in code because the expression language and .NET languages define these differently.
`Byte`	`DT_UI1`	A 1-byte unsigned int. (Note this is not a byte array.)

VARIABLE DATA TYPE	SSIS DATA TYPE	DESCRIPTION
Char	DT_UI2	A single character
DateTime	DT_DBTIMESTAMP	A date-time structure that accommodates year, month, hour, minute, second, and fractional seconds
DBNull	N/A	A declarative NULL value
Double	DT_R8	A double-precision, floating-point value
Int16	DT_I2	A 2-byte signed integer
Int32	DT_I4	A 4-byte signed integer
Int64	DT_I8	An 8-byte signed integer
Object	N/A	An object reference. Typically used to store data sets or large object structures
SByte	DT_I1	A 1-byte, signed integer
Single	DT_R4	A single-precision, floating-point value
String	DT_WSTR	Unicode string value
UInt32	DT_UI4	A 4-byte unsigned integer
UInt64	DT_UI8	An 8-byte unsigned integer

For most of the data types, there is ample representation. Typically, the only significant issues with variable data types are related to the date/time and string data types. The only options are the higher capacity data types. This is not a big deal from a storage perspective, because variable declaration is rather finite. You won't have too many variables defined in a package. If a package requires a string data type, note in the preceding table that the default data type for strings is the Unicode version; if you put values into a variable of the string data type, you need to convert for non-Unicode values.

This seems like a lot of preliminary information to go over before diving into creating an expression, but with a basic understanding of these core concepts, you will avoid most of the typical issues that SSIS developers encounter. Now you can use this knowledge to dive into the expression language and some sample uses of expressions in SSIS.

WORKING WITH EXPRESSIONS

The language used to build expressions can be a bit disorienting at first. If you started out as a programmer, you will be comfortable switching between Visual Basic, C#, and T-SQL. The key to being proficient in building expressions is understanding that the syntax of this new scripting language is a combination of all these different languages.

C#-Like? Close, but Not Completely

Why not write the expression language in T-SQL or a .NET-compliant language? The answer is mostly related to marketing: expressions should reflect the multiplatform capability to operating on more than just SQL Server databases. Remember that expressions can be used on data from other RDBMS sources, like Oracle, DB2, and even data from XML files. However, the technical explanation is that the SSIS and SQL Server core engines are written in native code, so any extension of the expression language to use .NET functions would incur the performance impact of loading the CLR and the memory management systems. The expression language without .NET integration can be optimized for the custom memory management required for pumping large row sets through Data Flow operations. As the SSIS product matures, you'll see the SSIS team add more expression enhancements to expand on the existing functions. Meanwhile, let's look at some of the pitfalls of using the expression language.

The expression language is marketed as having a heavily C#-like syntax, and for the most part that is true. However, you can't just put on your C# hat and start working, because some peculiarities are mixed into the scripting language. The language is heavily C#-like when it comes to using logical and comparison operators, but it leans toward a Visual Basic flavor and sometimes a little T-SQL for functions. For example, notice that the following common operators are undeniably from a C# lineage:

EXPRESSION OPERATOR	DESCRIPTION
`||`	Logical OR operation
`&&`	Logical AND operation
`==`	Comparison of two expressions to determine equivalency
`!=`	Comparison of two expressions to determine inequality
`? :`	Conditional operator

The conditional operator may be new to you, but it is especially important for creating compound expressions. In earlier releases of SSIS, the availability of this operator wasn't readily intuitive. If you aren't used to this C-style ternary operator, it is equivalent to similar `IF..THEN..ELSE..` or `IIF(<Condition>, <True Action>, <False Action>)` constructs.

The following functions look more like Visual Basic script or T-SQL language functions than C#:

EXPRESSION FUNCTION	DESCRIPTION	C# EQUIVALENT
`POWER()`	Raise numeric to a power	`Pow()`
`LOWER()`	Convert to lowercase	`ToLower()`
`GETDATE()`	Return current date	`Now()`

This makes things interesting because you can't just plug in a C# function without ensuring that there isn't an SSIS expression function to perform the same operation that is named differently. However, if you make this type of mistake, don't worry. Either the expression turns red, or you'll immediately get a descriptive error instructing you that the function is not recognized upon attempting to save. A quick look in Books Online can help resolve these types of function syntax differences.

In some instances, the function you are looking for can be drastically different and cause some frustration. For example, if you are used to coding in C#, it may not be intuitive to look for the `GETDATE()` function to return the current date. The `GETDATE()` function is typically something one would expect from a T-SQL language construct. Thankfully, it performs like a T-SQL function should to return the current date. This is not always the case. Some functions look like T-SQL functions but behave differently:

EXPRESSION FUNCTION	DESCRIPTION	DIFFERENCE
`DATEPART()`	Parses date part from a date	Requires quotes around the date part
`ISNULL()`	Tests an expression for `NULL`	Doesn't allow a default value

This departure from the T-SQL standard can leave you scratching your head when the expression doesn't compile. The biggest complaint about this function is that you have to use composite `DATEPART()` functions to get to any date part other than month, day, or year. This is a common task for naming files for archiving. Nor does the `ISNULL()` function work like the T-SQL function. It returns either `True` or `False` to test a value for existence of `NULL`. You can't substitute a default value as you would in T-SQL.

These slight variations in the expression language between full-scale implementations of T-SQL, C#, or Visual Basic syntaxes do cause some initial confusion and frustration, but these differences are minor in the grand scheme of things. Later in this chapter, you'll find a list of expressions that you can cut and paste to emulate many of the functions that are not immediately available in the expression language.

The Expression Builder

Several locations in the SSIS development environment allow the creation of an expression. Whether you are in the Variables window or within any property expression editor, ultimately the expression is created within a user interface called the Expression Builder. This user interface maintains easy references to both system- and user-based variables and provides access to expression functions and operators. The most important feature of the Expression Builder is the capability it provides to test an expression — that is, to see the evaluated value — by clicking the Evaluate Expression button. This is especially helpful as you learn the syntax of the expression language. By dragging and dropping variables and operators onto the expression workspace, you can see how to format expressions properly. Inside Data Flow components, typically a specific expression builder includes additional elements related to the Data Flow. In Figure 5-9, you can see that the user interface for the Derived Column Transformation includes a folder named Columns to allow expressions to be built with data from the Data Flow.

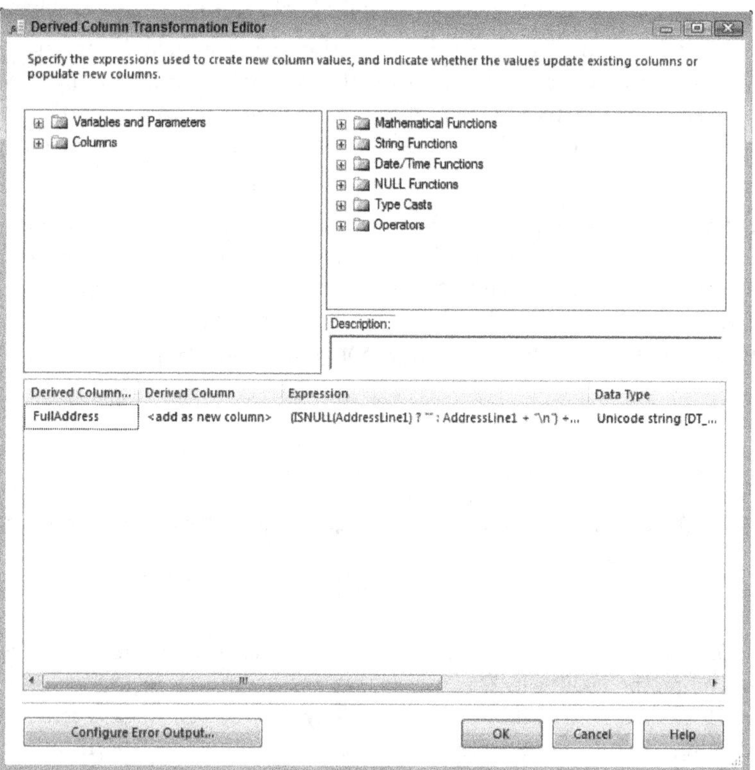

FIGURE 5-9

The only downside in the Data Flow component versions of the Expression Builder is that you don't have the option to see the results of evaluating the expression to determine whether you coded the expression properly. The reason is because you can't see the data from the Data Flow, because this information is not available without running the package.

This brings up a point about maintainability. If you have an involved expression that can be realized independently from data from the data stream, you should build the expression outside of the Data Flow component and simply plug it in as a variable. However, in some cases you have no choice but to build the expression at the Data Flow component level. If so, one of the best practices that we recommend is to create one variable at the package level called `MyExpressionTest`. This variable gives you a quick jumping off point to build and test expressions to ensure that the syntax is coded correctly. Simply access the Variables property window and click the ellipsis beside the expression property, and the Expression Builder pops up. Use this technique to experiment with some of the basic syntax of the expression language in the next section.

Syntax Basics

Building an expression in SSIS requires an understanding of the syntax details of the expression language. Each of the following sections dives into an aspect of the expression syntax and explores the typical issues encountered with it, including their resolution.

Equivalence Operator

This binary operator, which is used to compare two values, seems to create some problems for SSIS developers who are not used to using the double equal sign syntax (==). Forgetting to use the double equal sign in a comparison operation can produce head-scratching results. For example, consider a precedence operation that tests a variable value to determine whether the value is equal to `True`, but the expression is written with a single equal sign. Imagine that the variable is set by a previous script task that checks whether a file is available to process.

```
@[User::MyBooleanValue] = True
```

The expression is evaluated, and `@MyBooleanValue` is assigned the value of `True`. This overwrites any previous value for the variable. The precedence constraint succeeds, the value is `True`, and the tasks continue to run with a green light. If you aren't used to using the double equal sign syntax, this will come back to bite you, which is why we have discussed this operator by itself at the front of the syntax section.

String Concatenation

There are many uses for building strings within an expression. Strings are built to represent a SQL statement that can be executed against a database, to provide information in the body of an e-mail message, or to build file paths for file processing. Building strings is a core task that you have to be able to do for any development effort. In SSIS the concatenation operator is the plus (+) sign. Here is an example that you can quickly put together in the Expression Builder and test:

```
"The Server [" + LOWER( @[System::MachineName]) + "] is running this package"
```

This returns the following string:

```
The Server [myserver] is running this package
```

If you need to build a string for a file path, use the concatenation operator to build the fully qualified path with the addition of an escape character to add the backslashes. Later in this chapter, the section "String Literals" covers all the common escape characters that you'll need for string building. A file path expression would look like this:

```
"c:\\mysourcefiles\\" + @myFolder + "\\" + @myFile
```

Note that strings are built using double quotes (`""`), not single quotes (`''`) as you might see in T-SQL; it's important to ensure that the strings are all Unicode or all non-Unicode. A previous limitation of 4,000 characters for an expression has been removed from Integration Services. Feel free to make strings as long as you desire!

Line Continuation

There are two reasons to use line continuation characters in SSIS expressions. One is to make the expression easier to troubleshoot later, and the other is to format output for e-mail or diagnostic use. Unfortunately, the expression language does not support the use of comments, but you can use the hard returns to help the expression look more organized. In the Expression Builder, simply press the Enter key to have your expression displayed with the carriage-return-line-feed character sequence. This formatting is maintained even after you save the expression. To format output of the expression language, use the C-like escape character \n. Here's an example of using it with a simple expression:

```
"My Line breaks here\nAnd then here\n; )"
```

This returns the following string:

```
My Line breaks here
And then here
; )
```

Note that it is not necessary to show the expression in code form in one line. An expression can be written on multiple lines to clarify viewing of it at design time. The output would remain the same.

Literals

Literals are hard coded information that you must provide when building expressions. SSIS expressions have three types of literals: numeric, string, and Boolean.

Numeric Literals

A numeric literal is simply a fixed number. Typically, a number is assigned to a variable or used in an expression. Numeric literals in SSIS have the same behavior that they have in C# or Java — you can't just implicitly define numeric literals. Well, that's not completely true; SSIS does interpret numeric values with a few default rules, but the point is that the rules are probably not what you might expect. A value of 12 would be interpreted as the default data type of `DT_UI4`, or the 4-byte unsigned integer. This might be what you want, but if the value were changed to 3000000000 during the evaluation process, an error similar to this will be generated:

```
The literal "3000000000" is too large to fit into type DT_UI4. The magnitude of the
literal overflows the type.
```

SSIS operates on literals using logic similar to the underlying .NET CLR. Numeric literals are checked to see if they contain a decimal point. If they do not, the literal is cast using the unsigned integer `DT_UI4` data type. If there is a decimal point, the literal is cast as a `DT_NUMERIC`. To override these rules, you must append a suffix to the numeric literal. The suffix enables a declarative way to define the literal. The following are examples of suffixes that can be used on numeric literals:

SUFFIX	DESCRIPTION	EXAMPLE
`L` or `l`	Indicates that the numeric literal should be interpreted as the long version of either the `DT_I8` or `DT_R8` value types depending upon whether a decimal is present	3000000000L ⇨ `DT_I8` 3.14159265L ⇨ `DT_R8`

SUFFIX	DESCRIPTION	EXAMPLE
`U` or `u`	Indicates that the numeric literal should represent the unsigned data type	3000000000UL ⇨ `DT_UI8`
`F` or `f`	Indicates that the numeric literal represents a float value	100.55f ⇨ `DT_R4`
`E` or `e`	Indicates that the numeric literal represents scientific notation Note: Expects at least one digit scientific notation followed by float or long suffix	6.626 × 10 -34 J/s ⇨ 6.626E-34F ⇨ `DT_R8` 6.626E won't work. If you don't have a digit, then format as follows: 6.626E+0L or 6.626E+0f

Knowing these suffixes and rules, the previous example can be altered to 3000000000L, and the expression can be validated.

String Literals

When building strings, there are times when you need to supply special characters in them. For example, PostgreSQL database sources require the use of quoted column and table names. The key here is to understand the escape sequences that are understood by the expression syntax parser. The escape sequence for the double quote symbol is `\"`. A sample expression-generated SQL statement might look like this:

```
"Select \"myData\" from \"owner\".\"myTable\""
```

The preceding expression would generate the following string:

```
Select "myData" from "owner"."myTable"
```

Other common literals that you may need are listed in this table:

SUFFIX	DESCRIPTION	EXAMPLE

`\n`	New Line or
	Carriage
	Feed Line Return
		`"Print this on one line\nThis on another"`
		`Print this on one line`
		`This on another`

`\t`	Tab character	`"Print\twith\ttab\tseparation"` `Print    with    tab    separation`
`\"`	Double-quotation mark character	`"\"Hey! "\""` `"Hey! "`
`\\`	Backslash	`"c:\\myfile.txt"` `c:\myfile.txt`

A few other string escape sequences are supported, but the elements in this table list those most frequently used. The backslash escape sequences come in handy when building file and path strings. The double quote escape sequence is more often used to interact with data sources that require quoted identifiers. This escape sequence is also used in combination with the remaining new line and tab characters to format strings for logging or other reporting purposes.

Boolean Literals

The Boolean literals of `True` and `False` don't have to be capitalized, nor are they case sensitive. Boolean expressions are shortcut versions of the logical operators. To drive certain package functionality conditionally based on whether the package is running in an offline mode, you could write an expression in a variable using an artificial on or off type switch mechanism, as shown here:

```
@[System::OfflineMode]==True ? 1 : 0 (Not Recommended)
```

The idea is to use the results of this operation to determine whether a precedence constraint should operate. The precedence operator would retest the expression to determine whether the value was `1` or `0`. However, this is an awfully long way to do something. It's much easier to just create an expression that looks like this:

```
@[System::OfflineMode]==False
```

Then all you have to do is plug the expression into the Precedence Editor, as shown in Figure 5-10.

Note that using the literal is recommended over using any numeric values for evaluation. Programming any expression to evaluate numeric versions of Boolean values is dangerous and should not be a part of your SSIS techniques.

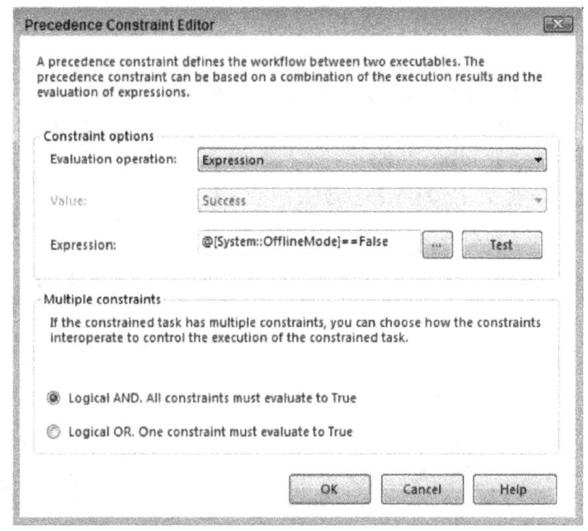

FIGURE 5-10

Referencing Variables

Referencing variables is easy using the Expression Builder. Drag and drop variables onto the Expression Builder to format the variable into the expression properly. As shown in the following example, notice that the format of the variable automatically dropped into the expression is preceded with an `@` symbol, followed by the namespace, a C++-like scope resolution operator, and then the variable name:

```
@[namespace::variablename]
```

Technically, if the variable is not repeated in multiple namespaces and there are no special characters (including spaces) in the variable name, you could get away with referring to the variable using a short identifier like `@variablename` or just the variable name. However, this type of lazy variable referencing can get you into trouble later. We recommend that you stick with the fully qualified way of referencing variables in all SSIS expressions.

Referencing Parameters

Referencing parameters is just as simple in the Expression Builder. When you drag and drop the parameter name, the value is automatically preceded with an @ symbol, followed by square brackets containing a dollar sign, the namespace of the package or project, the C++-like scope resolution operator, and the parameter name:

```
@[$namespace::parametername]
```

Typically, developers can run into trouble with variable and parameter references in the Precedence Constraint Editor (refer to Figure 5-10). That's probably because there is no Expression Builder to help build the expression, so it must be manually entered. This is where the tip of creating the dummy variable `MyExpressionTester` comes in handy. You can create an expression within this dummy variable Expression Builder and then simply cut and paste the value into the Precedence Constraint Editor.

Referencing Columns

Columns can be referenced in expressions, but only within components in a Data Flow task. This makes sense. Creating a global expression to reference a value in a Data Flow is the equivalent of trying to use a single variable to capture the value of a set-based processing operation. Even a variable expression defined at the same level or scope of a Data Flow task should not be able to reference a single column in the Data Flow under constant change. However, from within specific components like the Derived Column Transformation, the Expression Builder can reference a column because operations occur at the row level. Expressions within a data component can access column identifiers to allow point-and-click building of expressions. There are a couple things to remember when referencing columns in expressions:

- Data Flow column names must follow the SSIS standards for special characters.
- Column names must be uniquely named or qualified within a Data Flow.

A common issue with building expressions referencing columns in a Data Flow has less to do with the expression language than the names of the columns themselves. This is particularly true when dealing with Microsoft Excel or Access data, where columns can use nonstandard naming conventions. SSIS requires that the columns being used in an expression begin with either a valid Unicode letter or an underscore (_). With the exception of bracket characters, any other special characters require qualification of the column in order to be used within an expression.

Brackets (`[` and `]`) are the designators used by SSIS to qualify a column name. Qualification of column names is required if the name contains special characters — including spaces. Because bracket characters are column name qualifiers, any column with brackets in the name must be renamed to use an expression. This doesn't require changing the column name in the originating source. Column names also must be qualified when two or more columns in a Data Flow have the same name, in order to avoid ambiguous references. The following are examples of columns that need qualification:

COLUMN NAME	QUALIFIED COLUMN NAME	DESCRIPTION
`My Column`	`[My Column]`	Column names can't contain spaces.
`File#`	`[File#]`	Column names can't contain special characters.
`@DomainName`	`[@DomainName]`	
`Enrolled?`	`[Enrolled?]`	
`Source1 ID`	`[Source1].[ID]`	Column names can't have the same name within a Data Flow.
`Source2 ID`	`[Source2].[ID]`	

Another way to refer to columns, unique to SSIS, is by lineage number. A lineage number is something that SSIS assigns to each input and output as it is added to a transformation component in a package. The lineage number is quickly replaced by the real column name when the expression is syntax compiled. To find the lineage number for a column, look at any advanced editor dialog and find the column in the input column properties under LineageID. Keep in mind that as you add columns, the lineage numbers may change, so they should not be used for manipulation purposes, only for troubleshooting.

Boolean Expressions

Boolean expressions evaluate to either `True` or `False`. In their simplest implementation, precedence constraints use Booleans expressions as gatekeepers to determine whether or not an operation should occur. Within Data Flow operations, Boolean expressions are typically employed in the Conditional Split Transformation to determine whether a row in a Data Flow should be directed to another output.

For example, a Boolean expression to determine whether a Control Flow step would run only on Friday would require code to parse the day of the week from the current date and compare it to the sixth day, as shown here:

```
DATEPART( "dw", GETDATE() ) == 6
```

This is a useful Boolean expression for end of the week activities. To control tasks that run on the first day of the month, use an expression like this:

```
DATEPART ("dd", GETDATE() ) == 1
```

This expression validates as `True` only when the first day of the month occurs. Boolean expressions don't have to be singular. Compound expressions can be built to test a variety of conditions. Here is an example in which three conditions must all evaluate to `True` in order for the expression to return a `True` value:

```
BatchAmount == DepositAmount && @Not_Previously_Deposited == True &&
BatchAmount > 0.00
```

The @Not_Previously_Deposited argument in this expression is a variable; the other arguments represent columns in a Data Flow. Of course, an expression can just as easily evaluate alternate conditions, like this:

```
(BatchAmount > 0.00 || BatchAmount < 0.00) && @Not_Previously_Deposited == True
```

In this case, the BatchAmount must not be equal to 0.00. An alternative way to express the same thing is to use the inequality operator:

```
BatchAmount != 0.00 && @Not_Previously_Deposited == True
```

Don't be tripped up by these simple examples. They were defined for packages in which the data had known column data types, so there was no need to take extra precautions with casting conversions. If you are dealing with data from less reliable data sources, however, or you know that two columns have different data types, then take casting precautions with your expression formulas, such as in this expression:

```
(DT_CY)BatchAmount == (DT_CY)DepositAmount && @Not_Previously_Deposited ==
True && (DT_CY)BatchAmount > (DT_CY)0.00
```

The Boolean expression examples here are generally the style of expression that are used to enable dynamic SSIS package operations. We have not covered the conditional, date/time, and string-based Boolean expressions, which are in the following sections. String expression development requires a little more information about how to handle a NULL or missing value, which is covered next. You can see some examples of these Boolean expressions put to work at the end of this chapter.

Dealing with NULLs

In SSIS, variables can't be set to NULL. Instead, each variable data type maintains a default value in the absence of a value. For strings, the default value is an empty string, rather than the default of NULL that you might be used to in database development. However, Data Flow components can most certainly contain NULL values. This creates problems when variables are intermixed within Data Flow components. This mixture occurs either within a Script Task or within an expression.

However, if a value in the Data Flow needs to be set to NULL or even tested for a NULL value, this is another matter altogether and can be accomplished rather easily with the ISNULL() expression function and the NULL (type) casting functions. Just understand that variables are going to behave a little differently.

NULLs and Variables

The reason you can't set variables to NULL values is related to the COM object variant implementation of variables in the SSIS engine. Regardless of the technical issue, if you are testing a variable for the absence of a value, you have to decide ahead of time what value you are going to use to represent the equivalent of a NULL value, so that you can test for it accurately. For example, the DateTime variable data type defaults to 12/30/1899 12:00:00 a.m. if you purposely set it to NULL.

You can test this out yourself by creating a `DateTime` variable and setting it equal to an expression defined using the casting function `NULL(DT_DBTIMESTAMP)`.

It helps to get a handle on the default values for the SSIS variable data types. You can find them in this table:

VARIABLE DATA TYPE	DEFAULT VALUE
Boolean	False
Byte	0
Char	0
DateTime	12/30/1899
DBNull	(Can't test in an expression)
Double	0
Int16	0
Int32	0
Int64	0
Object	(Can't test in an expression)
SByte	0
Single	0
String	"" (empty string)
UInt32	0
UInt64	0

Using this table of default values, the following expression could be used in a precedence operation after testing for the absence of a value in a string variable `MyNullStringVar`:

```
@[User::MyNullStringVar]==""
```

If the value of the user variable is an empty string, the expression evaluates to a `True` value and the step is executed.

A frequent logic error that SSIS developers make is to use a variable to set a value from an expression that will be used within a multiple instance looping structure. If the value is not reset in a way that enables clean retesting, the value of the variable will remain the same for the life of the package. No error will be raised, but the package may not perform multiple iterations as expected. Make sure a variable is reset to enable retesting if the test will be performed multiple times. This may require additional variables to cache intermediate results.

NULLs in Data Flow

Using the NULL function in Data Flow Transformations is a different matter because values in a Data Flow can actually be NULL. Here you can use the expression function to test for NULL values in the data stream. Trouble usually stems from a misunderstanding of either how the ISNULL() function works or what to do after a NULL value is found. First, the ISNULL() expression function tests the expression in the parentheses for the value of NULL. It does not make a substitution if a NULL value is found, as the same-named function does in T-SQL. To emulate the T-SQL function ISNULL(), build an SSIS expression in a Data Flow, as shown here:

```
IsNull(DATA_COLUMN) ? YOUR_DEFAULT_VALUE : DATA_COLUMN
```

If instead you want to set a column to NULL based on some attribute of the data in the incoming data stream, the logical structure is similar. First, provide the testing expression followed by the actions to take if the test is True or False. Here is a function that sets a data column in a Data Flow to NULL if the first character starts with "A":

```
SUBSTRING([MyColumn], 1, 1)=="A" ? NULL(DT_WSTR, 255) : [MyColumn]
```

A typical issue that occurs when handling NULLs doesn't actually have anything to do with NULL values themselves but rather with string expressions. When creating data streams to punch back into RDBMS data destinations, you will often want to send back a column with NULL values when a test on the data can't be completed. The logic is to either send the column data back or replace the column data with a NULL value. For most data types, this works by sending the results of the NULL function for the data type desired. For some reason, this works differently when you want to save non-Unicode data with a NULL value. You'd expect the following expression to work, but it doesn't:

```
SUBSTRING([MyColumn] , 1, 1)=="A" ?
NULL(DT_STR, 255, 1252) : [MyColumn]     (This doesn't work in SSIS)
```

The preceding example won't work because of how SSIS handles NULL values for the non-Unicode string type as parameters. The only way to fix this is to cast the NULL function as follows:

```
SUBSTRING([MyColumn] , 1, 1)=="A" ?
(DT_STR, 255, 1252)NULL(DT_STR, 255, 1252) : [MyColumn]
```

This section should have clarified the common issues you are likely to encounter when dealing with NULL values, especially as they relate to strings. However, there are still some tricks to learn about dealing with strings, which we cover next.

String Functions

Handling strings in SSIS expressions is different from dealing with string data in SQL Server. The previous section discussed some of the differences with handling NULL values. You also have to pay attention to the Unicode and non-Unicode strings. If a package is moving data between multiple Unicode string sources, you have to pay attention to the code pages between the strings. If you are comparing strings, you also have to pay attention to string padding, trimming, and issues with data truncations. Handling strings is a little involved, but you really only need to remember a few things.

Expression functions return Unicode string results. If you are writing an expression to return the uppercase version of a `varchar`-type column of data, the result will be a Unicode column with all capital letters. The string function `Upper()` returns a Unicode string. In fact, SSIS sets all string operations to return a Unicode string. For example, note the date expression in the Derived Column Transformation in Figure 5-11.

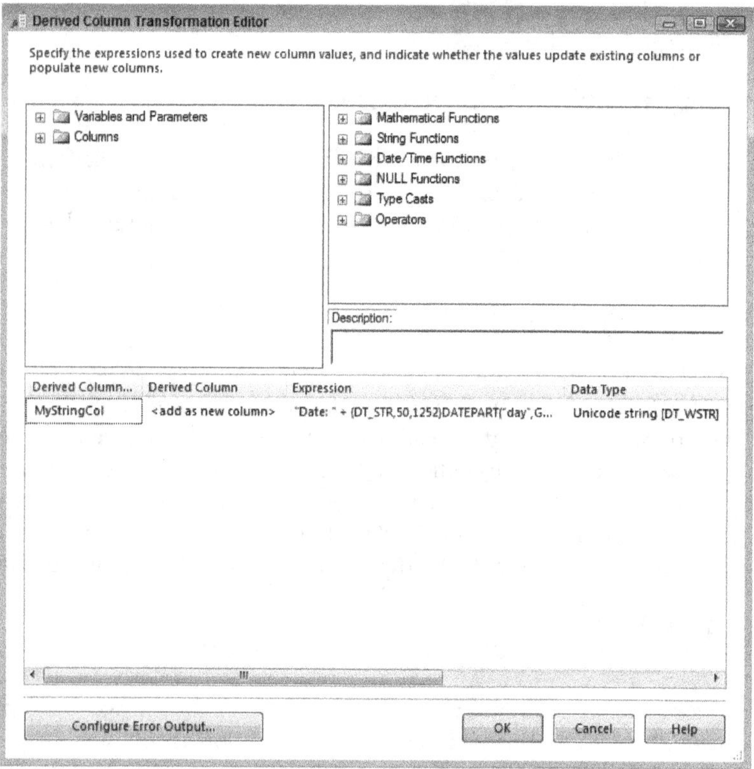

FIGURE 5-11

Here you are just adding a string column that includes the concatenation of a date value. The function is using a `DatePart()` function whose results are cast to a non-Unicode string, but the default data type chosen in the editor is a Unicode string data type. This can be overridden, of course, but it is something to watch for as you develop packages. On the one hand, if the data type is reverted to non-Unicode, then the string has to be converted for each further operation. On the other hand, if the value is left as a Unicode string and the result is persisted in a non-Unicode format, then at some point it has to be converted to a non-Unicode value. The rule of thumb that usually works out is to leave the strings converted as Unicode and then convert back to non-Unicode if required during persistence. Of course, this depends on whether there is a concern about using Unicode data.

Comparing strings requires that you have two strings of the same padding length and case. The comparison is case and padding sensitive. Expressions should use the concatenation operator (+) to get the strings into the same padding style. Typically, this is done when putting together date strings with an expected type of padding, like this:

```
RIGHT("0" + @Day, 2) + "/" + RIGHT("0" + @Month, 2) + "/" +
RIGHT("00" + @Year, 2)
```

This type of zero padding ensures that the values in both variables are in the same format for comparison purposes. By padding both sides of the comparison, you ensure the proper equality check:

```
RIGHT("0" + @Day, 2) + "/"
+ RIGHT("0" + @Month, 2) + "/"
+ RIGHT("00" + @Year, 2)
== RIGHT("0" + @FileDay, 2) + "/"
+ RIGHT("0" + @FileMonth, 2) + "/"
+ RIGHT("00" + @FileYear, 2)
```

A similar type of padding operation can be used to fill in spaces between two values:

```
SUBSTRING(@Val1 + " ", 1, 5) + SUBSTRING(@Val2 + " ", 1, 5) +
SUBSTRING(@Val3 + " ", 1, 5)
```

Typically, space padding is used for formatting output, but it could be used for comparisons. More often than not, spaces are removed from strings for comparison purposes. To remove spaces from strings in expressions, use the trim functions: `LTrim()`, `RTrim()`, and `Trim()`. These functions are self-explanatory, and they enable comparisons for strings that have leading and trailing spaces. For example, comparing the strings "Canterbury" and "Canterbury " return a `false` unless the expression is written like this:

```
Trim("Canterbury") == Trim("Canterbury  ")
```

This expression returns `true` because the significant spaces are declaratively removed. Be careful with these extra spaces in string expressions as well. Spaces are counted in all string functions, which can result in extra character counts for extra spaces when using the `LEN()` function and can affect carefully counted `SUBSTRING()` functions that do not expect leading and trailing spaces. If these issues are of importance, employ a Derived Column Transformation to trim these columns early in the Data Flow process.

Conditional Expressions

You use the conditional expression operator to build logical evaluation expressions in the format of an `IF..THEN` logical structure:

```
Boolean_expression ? expression_if_true : expression_if_false
```

The first part of the operator requires a Boolean expression that is tested for a `true` or `false` return value. If the Boolean expression returns `true`, then the first expression after the ternary operator

(?) will be evaluated and returned as the final result of the conditional expression. If the Boolean expression returns `false`, then the expression after the separation operator (:) will be evaluated and returned. Both expressions, as operands, must adhere to one of the following data type rules:

- Both operands must be numeric data types that can be implicitly converted.
- Both operands must be string data types of either Unicode or non-Unicode. Each operand can evaluate to separate types — except for the issue of setting explicit `NULL` values. In that case, the `NULL` value for `DT_STR` non-Unicode `NULL` values must be cast.
- Both operands must be date data types. If more than one data type is represented in the operands, the result is a `DT_DBTIMESTAMP` data type.
- Both operands for a text data type must have the same code pages.

If any of these rules are broken, or the compiler detects incompatible data types, you will have to supply explicit casting operators on one or both of the operands to cause the condition expression to evaluate. This is more of an issue as the conditional expression is compounded and nested. A typical troubleshooting issue is seeing an incompatible data type message resulting from a comparison deep in a compound conditional expression. This can be the result of a column that has changed to an incompatible data type, or a literal that has been provided without a suffix consistent with the rest of the expression. The best way to test the expression is to copy it into Notepad and test each piece of the expression until the offending portion is located.

Casting issues can also create false positives. You can see casting truncation in the following example of a Boolean expression comparing the `datetimestampoffset` and a date value:

```
(DT_DBDATE) "2014-01-31 20:34:52.123 -3:30" == (DT_DBDATE)"2014-01-31"
```

Casting converts the expression `(DT_DBDATE) "2014-01-31 20:34:52.123-3:30"` to `"2014-01-31"`, causing the entire expression to evaluate to `true`. Date and time conversions are one example of casting issues, but they can occur on any data type that allows forced conversion.

Date and Time Functions

Date and time functions tend to cause confusion for new SSIS developers. In most instances, the different syntax is causing the difficulty. As mentioned earlier, the `DatePart()` function is a perfect example of this. T-SQL programmers need to double quote the date part portion of the function, or they will see an error similar to this:

```
The expression contains unrecognized token "dd". If "dd" is a variable then it
should be expressed as "@dd". The specific token is not valid. If the token is
intended to be a variable name, it should be prefixed with the @ symbol.
```

The fix is simple: put double quotation marks around the date part. A properly formatted `DatePart()` expression should look like this:

```
DATEPART( "dd", GETDATE() )
```

Note that this expression returns the value of the day of the month — for example, 31 if the date is January 31, 2014. A common mistake is to expect this to be the day of the week. You can accomplish that task by changing the date part in the expression like this:

```
DATEPART( "dw", GETDATE() )
```

These are just minor adjustments to the SSIS expression language, but they can create some frustration. Another example can be found when attempting to reference the date values in an expression. If you're used to MS Access date literals, you may be tempted to use something like this:

```
"SELECT * FROM myTable WHERE myDate >= " + #01/31/2014# (DOESN'T WORK IN SSIS)
```

That won't work in SSIS; the # signs are used for a different purpose. If the string is going to be interpreted by SQL Server, just use the single quote around the date:

```
"SELECT * FROM MYTABLE WHERE MYDATE >= '" + "01/31/2014" + "'"
```

If the string is just going to be printed, the single quotes aren't needed. Alternatively, to plug in a date value from a variable, the expression would look like this:

```
"SELECT * FROM MYTABLE WHERE MYDATE >= '" +
(DT_WSTR, 255)@[System::ContainerStartTime] + "'"
```

Notice that the value of the date variable must be cast to match the default Unicode data type for all expression strings of `DT_WSTR`. The problem with simply casting a date to a string is the fact that you get the entire date, which doesn't translate into what you may want to use as a query parameter. This is clearer if the preceding expression is resolved:

```
SELECT * FROM MYTABLE WHERE MYDATE >= "02/22/2014 2:28:40 PM'
```

If your goal is truly to see results only from after 2:28:40 p.m., then this query will run as expected. If items from earlier in the day are also expected, then you need to do some work to parse out the values from the variable value. If the intent is just to return rows for the date that the package is running, it is much easier to create the expression like this (with your proper date style, of course):

```
"SELECT * FROM MYTABLE WHERE MYDATE >= CONVERT(nvarchar(10), getdate(), 101)"
```

This method allows SQL Server to do the work of substituting the current date from the server into the query predicate. However, if you need to parse a string from a date value in an expression, take apart one of the following formulas in this section to save you a bit of time:

DESCRIPTION	EXPRESSION
Convert filename with embedded date into the date-time type format: MM/dd/yyyy HH:mm:ss.	`SUBSTRING(@[User::FileName],5,2) + "/" +`

continues

(continued)

DESCRIPTION	EXPRESSION
	SUBSTRING(@[User::FileName],7,2) + "/" +
	SUBSTRING(@[User::FileName],1,4) + "" +
	SUBSTRING(@[User::FileName],9,2) + ":" +
	SUBSTRING(@[User::FileName],11,2) + ":" +
Filename format: yyyyMMddHHmmss	SUBSTRING(@[User::FileName],13,2)
Convert a date-time variable to a filename format of: yyyyMMddHHmmss	(DT_WSTR,4) YEAR(GETDATE()) + RIGHT("0" +
	(DT_WSTR,2) MONTH(GETDATE()), 2) + RIGHT("0" +
	(DT_WSTR,2) DAY(GETDATE()), 2) + RIGHT("0" +
	(DT_WSTR,2) DATEPART("hh", GETDATE()), 2) + RIGHT("0" +
	(DT_WSTR,2) DATEPART("mi", GETDATE()), 2) + RIGHT("0" +
	(DT_WSTR,2) DATEPART("ss", GETDATE()), 2)

This section covered most of the major syntactical issues that new users are likely to encounter with the expression language. The issues that have caused SSIS programmers the most trouble should not be a problem for you. Now you are ready to create some expressions and walk through the process of inserting them into SSIS packages to put them to work.

Using Expressions in SSIS Packages

Creating an expression requires understanding the syntax of the SSIS expression language. As discussed in the previous section, this expression language is part C#, part Visual Basic script, and sometimes some flavor of T-SQL mixed in. Once you can code in the expression language, you are ready to put the expressions to work. This section demonstrates how expressions can be used in SSIS package development, with some typical examples that you can use in your package development tasks.

You can download the packages used as examples in the following sections in their entirety by going to `www.wrox.com/go/prossis2014`.

Using Variables and Parameters as Expressions

Earlier in this chapter, you learned how to use expressions in variables. A good example of practical usage is to handle the task of processing files in a directory. This task should be familiar to everyone. A directory must be polled for files of a specific extension. If a file is found, it is processed and then copied into a final archival storage directory. An easy way to do this is to hardcode the source and destination paths along with the file extension into the Foreach Loop Container and File System Task. However, if you need to use a failover file server, you have to go through the package and change all these settings manually. It is much easier to use parameters that enable these properties to be set and then use expressions to create the destination directory and filenames. That way, when the server changes, only the parameter needs to change. The basic steps for such an SSIS package can be gleaned from Figure 5-12.

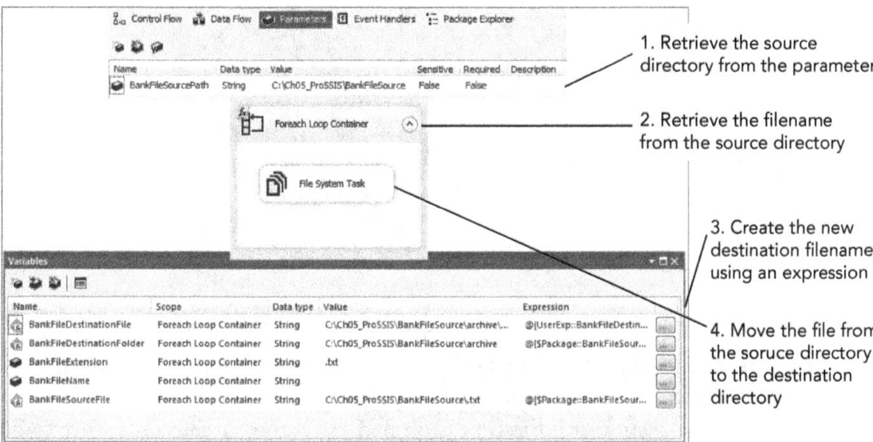

FIGURE 5-12

One of the things to notice in the expression of the `BankFileDestinationFile` is the namespace named `UserExp`. While there is an indicator on the variable icon to indicate whether it is an expression, it may behoove you to make the purpose of the variable even clearer using the Namespace column, which provides a nice way to separate variables. In this case, the namespace `UserExp` indicates that the variable is a user expression-based variable. The namespace `UserVar` indicates that the variable is defined by the user.

For this package, the Foreach Loop Container Collection tab is set by an expression to retrieve the folder (or directory) from the variable `BankFileSourcePath`. This variable is statically defined either from configuration processes or manually by an administrator. This tells the Foreach Loop where to start looking for files. To enumerate files of a specific extension, an expression sets the `FileSpec` property to the value of the variable `BankFileExtension`, which is also a static variable. Nothing very complicated here except that the properties of the Foreach Loop are set by expressions, rather than of hardcoded values. The container looks like what is shown in Figure 5-13.

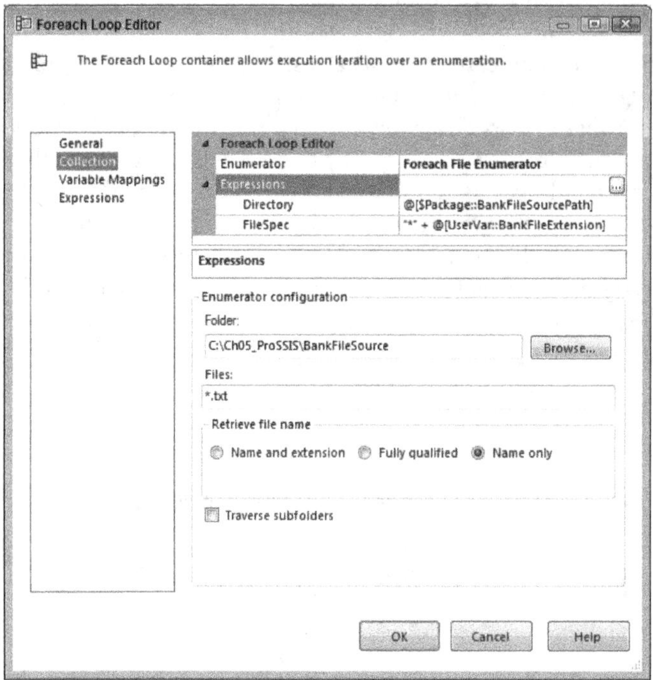

FIGURE 5-13

Notice that the Foreach Loop Container is retrieving the filename only. This value is stored in the variable `BankFileName`. This isn't shown in Figure 5-13, but it would be shown in the Variable Mappings tab. With the raw filename, no extension, and no path, some variables set up as expressions can be used to create a destination file that is named using the current date. First, you need a destination location. The source folder is known, so use this folder as a starting point to create a subfolder called "archive" by creating a variable named `BankFileDestinationFolder` that has the property `EvaluateAsExpression` set to `True` and defined by this expression:

```
@[UserVar::BankFileSourcePath] + "\\archive"
```

You need the escape sequence to properly build a string path. Now build a variable named `BankFileDestinationFile` that will use this `BankFileDestinationFolder` value along with a date-based expression to put together a unique destination filename. The expression would look like this:

```
@[UserExp::BankFileDestinationFolder] + "\\" + (DT_WSTR,4) YEAR(GETDATE())
+ RIGHT("0" + (DT_WSTR,2) MONTH(GETDATE()), 2)
+ RIGHT("0" + (DT_WSTR,2) DAY( GETDATE()), 2)
+ RIGHT("0" + (DT_WSTR,2) DATEPART("hh", GETDATE()), 2)
+ RIGHT("0" + (DT_WSTR,2) DATEPART("mi", GETDATE()), 2)
+ RIGHT("0" + (DT_WSTR,2) DATEPART("ss", GETDATE()), 2)
+ @[UserVar::BankFileExtension]
```

When evaluated, the expression results in a destination filename that looks like `c:\BankFileSource\Archive\20140101154006.txt` when the bank file destination folder is `c:\BankFileSource\Archive`. By using variables that evaluate to the value of an expression, combined with information set statically from administrator and environmental variables like the current date and time, you can create packages with dynamic capabilities.

Another best practice is to use expression-based variables to define common logic that you'll use throughout your SSIS package. If in the preceding example you wanted to use this date-based string in other places within your package, you could define the date portion of that expression in a separate variable called `DateTimeExpression`. Then the expression for the `BankFileDestinationFolder` variable could be simplified to look like this:

```
@[UserExp::BankFileDestinationFolder] + "\\" + @[UserExp::DateTimeExpression] +
  @[UserVar::BankFileExtension]
```

The power in separating logic like this is that an expression need not be buried in multiple places within an SSIS package. This makes maintenance for SSIS packages much easier and more manageable.

Using Expressions in Connection Manager Properties

Another simple example of using expressions is to dynamically change or set properties of an SSIS component. One of the common uses of this technique is to create a dynamic connection that enables packages to be altered by external or internal means. In this example, assume a scenario in which all logins are duplicated across environments. This means you need to change only the server name to make connections to other servers.

To start, create a variable named **SourceServerNamedInstance** that can be used to store the server name to which the package should connect for source data. Then create any connection manager in the Connection Managers section of the SSIS package and press F4, or right-click and select Properties to get to the Properties window for the connection object. The Properties window should look like Figure 5-14.

The secret here is the Expressions Collection property. If you click this property, an ellipsis will be displayed. Clicking that button will bring up the Property Expressions Editor shown in Figure 5-15, where you can see the properties that can be set to an expression, and ultimately do so in the Expression Builder.

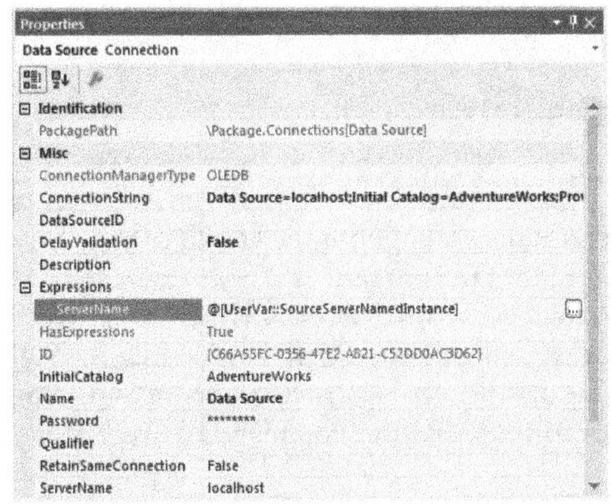

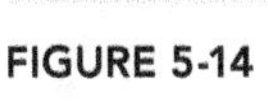
FIGURE 5-14

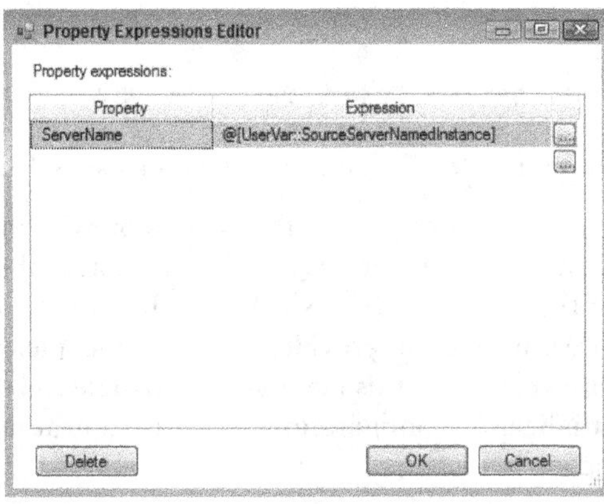

FIGURE 5-15

This example completes the demonstration by setting the property of the `ServerName` to the expression that is simply the value of the `SourceServerNamedInstance` variable. Here you affected only one property in the connection string, but this is not the only option. The entire connection string, as you may have noticed in the Property drop down, can be set by a string-based expression. This same technique can be used to set any connection property in the Data Flow components as well to dynamically alter the flat file and MS Excel-based connections. A common use is to set the connection source for a Data Flow component to a variable-based incoming filename.

Using Expressions in Control Flow Tasks

A common example of using expressions in Control Flow Tasks is to create SQL statements dynamically that are run by the Execute SQL Task. The Execute SQL Task has a property called `SQLStatement` that can be set to a file connection, a variable, or direct input. Instead of creating parameterized SQL statements that are subject to error and OLE provider interpretation, you can try building the SQL statement using an expression and putting the whole SQL statement into the `SQLStatement` property. This section walks through an example like this using a `DELETE` statement that should run at the start of a package to delete any data from a staging table that has the same `RunJobID` (a theoretical identifier for a unique SSIS data load).

To start, create one variable for the `DELETE` statement that doesn't include the dynamic portion of the SQL statement. A variable named `DeleteSQL` of type `String` would be set to a value of the string:

```
DELETE FROM tblStaging WHERE RunJobId =
```

Create another variable named `DeleteSQL_RunJobId` with the data type of `Int32` to hold the value of a variable `RunJobId`. This value could be set elsewhere in the SSIS package.

In the Execute SQL Task, bring up the editor and ensure that `SQLSourceType` is set to `DirectInput`. You could also set this value to use a variable if you built the SQL statement in its entirety within an expression-based variable. In this example, you'll build the expression in the Execute SQL Task. To get there, click the Expressions tab of the editor to view the Expressions collections property. Click the ellipses to access the Property Expressions Editor and build the SQL statement using the two variables that you defined. Make sure you use the casting operator to build the string like this:

```
@[UserVar::DeleteSQL] + (DT_WSTR, 8) @[UserVar::DeleteSQL_RunJobId]
```

The completed Execute SQL Task Property Expressions Editor will look like Figure 5-16.

When the package runs, the expression will combine the values from both the variables and construct a complete SQL statement that will be inserted into the property `SqlStatementSource` for the Execute SQL Task. This technique is more modular and works more consistently across the different OLE DB providers for dynamic query formation and execution than hardcoding the SQL statement. With this method it is possible to later define and then reconstruct your core SQL using initialization configurations. It is also a neat technique to show off your command of expressions and variables.

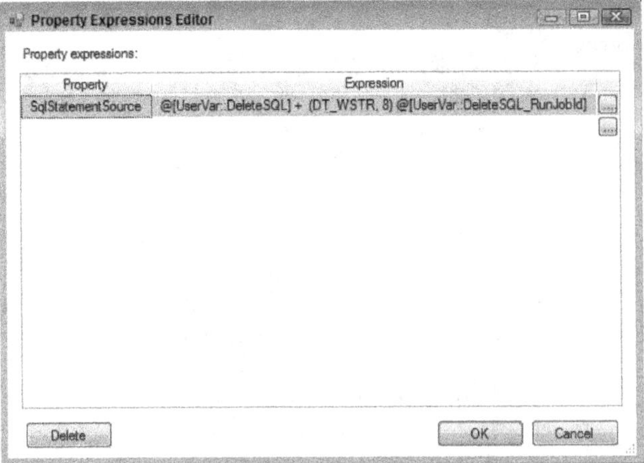

FIGURE 5-16

Using Expressions in Control Flow Precedence

Controlling the flow of SSIS packages is one of the key strengths of dynamic package development. Between each Control Flow Task is a precedence constraint that can have expressions attached to it for evaluation purposes. You can visually identify the precedence constraint as the arrow that connects two Control Flow Tasks. During runtime, as one Control Flow Task completes, the precedence constraint is evaluated to determine if the flow can continue to the next task. One common scenario is a single package that may have two separate sequence operations that need to occur based on some external factor. For example, on even days one set of tasks runs, and on odd days another separate set of tasks runs. A visual example of this type of package logic is shown in Figure 5-17.

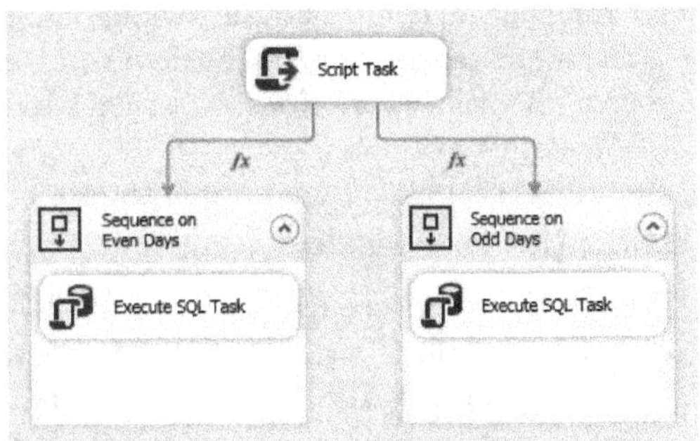

FIGURE 5-17

This is an easy task to perform by using an expression in a precedence constraint. To set this up, define a Boolean variable as an expression called `GateKeeperSequence`. Make sure the variable is in the namespace `UserExp` to indicate that this variable is an expression-based variable. Set the expression to this formula:

```
DATEPART( "dd", GetDate() ) % 2
```

This expression takes the current day of the month and uses the modulus operator to leave the remainder as a result. Use this value to test in the precedence constraint to determine which sequence to run in the package. The sequence on even days should be run if the `GateKeeperSequence` returns `0` as a result, indicating that the current day of the month is evenly divisible by two. Right-click the precedence constraint and select Edit to access the editor, and set it up to look like Figure 5-18.

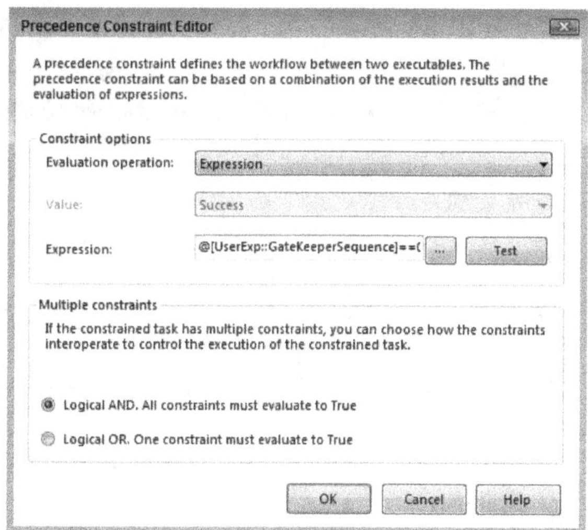

FIGURE 5-18

The expression `@[UserExp::GateKeeperSequence]==0` is a Boolean expression that tests the results of the first expression to determine whether the value is equal to zero. The second sequence should execute only if the current day is an odd day. The second precedence constraint needs an expression that looks like this:

```
@[UserExp::GateKeeperSequence]!=0
```

By factoring the first expression into a separate expression-based variable, you can reuse the same expression in both precedence constraints. This improves the readability and maintenance of your SSIS packages. With this example, you can see how a package can have sections that are conditionally executed. This same technique can also be employed to run Data Flow Tasks or other Control Flow Tasks conditionally using Boolean expressions. Refer back to the section "Boolean Expressions" if you need to review some other examples.

Using the Expression Task

Recently introduced in SQL Server 2012, the Expression Task enables you to set the value of variables in the Control Flow. If you are thinking, "But I could do that before!" you are absolutely correct. In previous editions of Integration Services, you could change a variable's value by using the `EvaluateAsExpression` property or by using a Script Task, as previously described in this chapter.

The beauty of the Expression Task is that it specifically calls out when in the package this change occurs. This means that you can make a similar change multiple times, if you placed an Expression Task in a Foreach Loop Container, or you can make it easier to see that the variable you are using is changed. The following example shows how to use an Expression Task to make an iterator variable that can count the number of times you loop through a section of the package.

Begin by using and editing an Expression Task from the SSIS Toolbox. The Expression Builder that appears limits you to variables and parameters because you are in the Control Flow designer. You assign a value to a variable by using the equals sign, so the final formula will look like this:

```
@[User::Iterator] = @[User::Iterator] + 1
```

A completed version of the property window is shown in Figure 5-19.

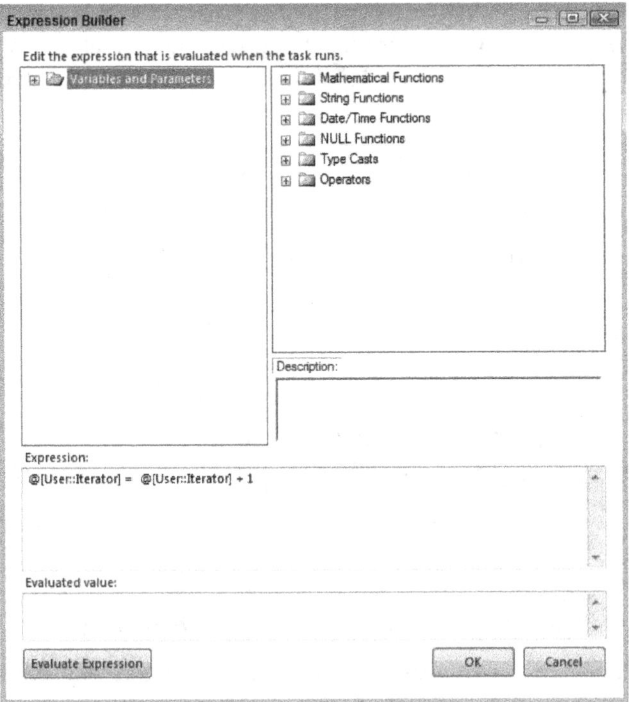

FIGURE 5-19

Using Expressions in the Data Flow

Although you can set properties on some of the Data Flow components, a typical use of an expression in a Data Flow is to alter a `WHERE` clause on a source component. In this example, you'll alter the SQL query in a source component using a supplied date as a variable to pull out address information from the AdventureWorks database. Then you'll use an expression to build a derived column that can be used for address labels.

First, set up these variables at the Data Flow scope level by selecting the Data Flow Task before creating the variable:

VARIABLE NAME	DATA TYPE	NAMESPACE	DESCRIPTION
`BaseSelect`	`String`	`UserVar`	Contains base `Select` statement
`SelectSQL_UserDateParm`	`DateTime`	`UserVar`	Contains supplied date parm
`SelectSQL`	`String`	`UserExp`	Derived SQL to execute
`SelectSQL_ExpDateParm`	`String`	`UserExp`	Safe Date Expression

Notice that the namespaces for the BaseSelect and SelectSQL_UserDateParm variables are using a namespace UserVar. As described previously, you use them because it makes it clear which variables are expression-based and which are not. Provide the following values for these variables:

VARIABLE NAME	VALUE
BaseSelect	SELECT AddressLine1, AddressLine2
	City, StateProvinceCode, PostalCode
	FROM Person.Address adr
	INNER JOIN Person.StateProvince stp
	ON adr.StateProvinceID = stp.StateProvinceID
	WHERE adr.ModifiedDate >=
SelectSQL_UserDateParm	1/12/2000

Note that you need to put the value from the BaseSelect variable into one continuous line to get it all into the variable. Make sure the entire string is in the variable value before continuing.

The remaining variables need to be set up as expression-based variables. At this point, you should be proficient at this. Set the EvaluateAsExpression property to True and prepare to add the expressions to each. Ultimately, you need a SQL string that contains the date from the SelectSQL_UserDateParm, but using dates in strings by just casting the date to a string can produce potentially unreliable results — especially if you are given the string in one culture and you are querying data stored in another collation. This is why the extra expression variable SelectSQL_ExpDateParm exists. This safe date expression looks like this:

```
(DT_WSTR, 4) DATEPART("yyyy", @[UserVar::SelectSQL_UserDateParm]) + "-" +
(DT_WSTR, 2) DATEPART("mm", @[UserVar::SelectSQL_UserDateParm]) + "-" +
(DT_WSTR, 2) DATEPART("dd", @[UserVar::SelectSQL_UserDateParm]) + " "+
(DT_WSTR, 2) DATEPART("hh", @[UserVar::SelectSQL_UserDateParm]) + ":" +
(DT_WSTR, 2) DATEPART("mi", @[UserVar::SelectSQL_UserDateParm]) + ":" +
(DT_WSTR, 2) DATEPART("ss", @[UserVar::SelectSQL_UserDateParm])
```

The expression parses out all the pieces of the date and creates an ISO-formatted date in a string format that can now be appended to the base SELECT SQL string. This is done in the last expression-based variable SelectSQL. The expression looks like this:

```
@[UserVar::BaseSelect] + "'" + @[UserExp::SelectSQL_ExpDateParm] + "'"
```

With all the pieces to create the SQL statement in place, all you need to do is apply the expression in a data source component. Drop an OLE DB Source component connected to the AdventureWorks database on the Data Flow surface, and set the Data access mode to retrieve the data as "SQL command from variable." Set the variable name to the SelectSQL variable. The OLE DB Source Editor should look like Figure 5-20.

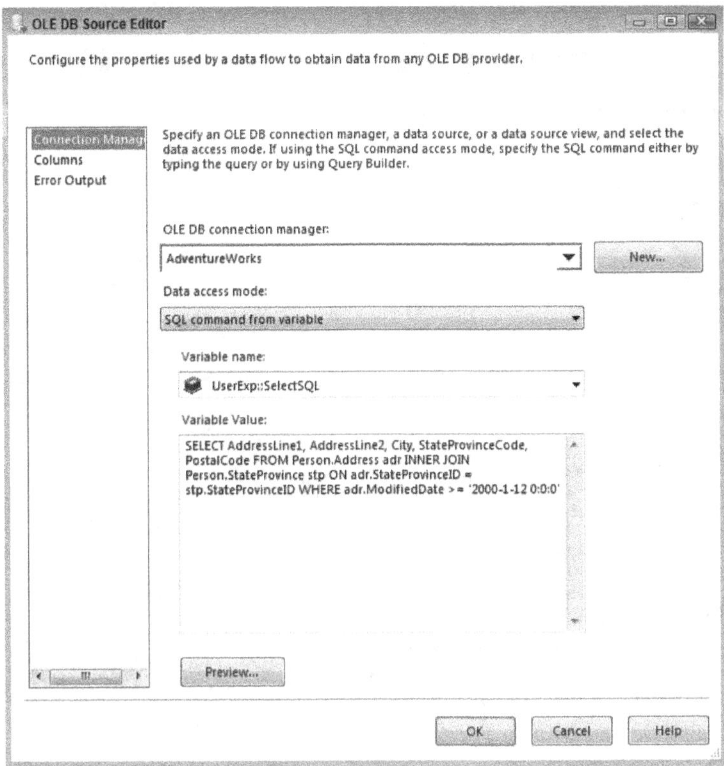

FIGURE 5-20

Click the Preview button to look at the data pulled with the current value of the variable `SelectSQL_UserDateParm`. Change the value and check whether the data changes as expected. Now the OLE DB source will contain the same columns, but the predicate can be easily and safely changed with a date parameter that is safe across cultures.

The final task is to create a one-column output that combines the address fields. Add a Derived Column Transformation to the Data Flow, and a new column of type `WSTR`, length of `2000`, named `FullAddress`. This column will need an expression that combines the columns of the address to build a one-column output. Remember that we are dealing with Data Flow data here, so it is possible to realize a `NULL` value in the data stream. If you simply concatenate every column and a `NULL` value exists anywhere, the entire string will evaluate to `NULL`. Furthermore, you don't want addresses that have blank lines in the body, so you only want to add a newline character conditionally after addresses that aren't `NULL`. Because the data tables involved can only contain `NULL` values in the two address fields, the final expression looks like this:

```
(ISNULL(AddressLine1) ? "" : AddressLine1 + "\n") +
(ISNULL(AddressLine2) ? "" : AddressLine2 + "\n") +
City + ", "+ StateProvinceCode + " " + PostalCode
```

The Derived Column Transformation should look similar to Figure 5-21.

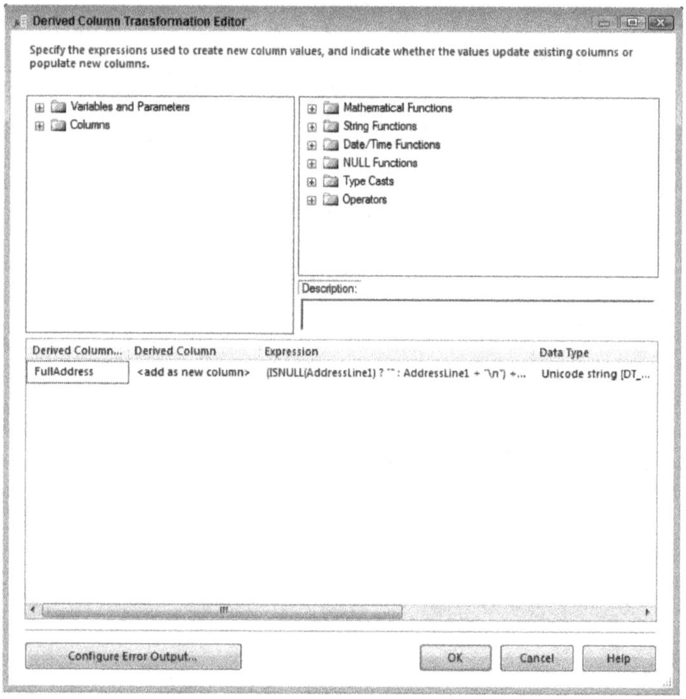

FIGURE 5-21

Running this example will create the one-output column of a combined address field that can be dynamically configured by a date parameter with a conditional `Address2` line, depending upon whether the data exists. Using expressions to solve problems like this makes SSIS development seem almost too easy.

SUMMARY

The aim of this chapter was to fill any gaps in your understanding of expressions. Clearly, this feature is powerful; it enables dynamic package development in an efficient way, getting you out of the code and into productive solutions. However, expressions can be frustrating if you don't pay attention to the data types and whether you are working with data in variables or in the Data Flow. This chapter has described the "gotchas" that typically plague SSIS developers, along with their solutions, so that you don't have to experience them. Along the way, we consolidated the common questions, answers, and best practices we've learned about using expressions, making them available to you in one chapter.

We discussed how you can set variables programmatically and use scripting tasks and components to further the SSIS dynamic package capabilities. We also covered how to use variables and parameters in expressions to create dynamic properties. There are still scenarios in which expressions don't fit the bill, and for these scripting tasks can be used to save the day. Stay tuned for Chapter 9, where you explore scripting tasks both in the control and Data Flow roles, and expand your SSIS capabilities. The next chapter will switch over to discuss the Control Flow, specifically containers.

Containers

WHAT'S IN THIS CHAPTER?

- Learning when to use containers
- Working with Sequence Containers
- Working with the For Loop Container
- Using a Foreach Loop Container to iterate through a list

WROX.COM DOWNLOADS FOR THIS CHAPTER

You can find the wrox.com code downloads for this chapter at `www.wrox.com/go/prossis2014` on the Download Code tab.

In Chapter 3, you read about tasks and how they interact in the Control Flow. Now we're going to cover one of the special types of items in the Control Flow: containers. *Containers* are objects that help SSIS provide structure to one or more tasks. They can help you loop through a set of tasks until a criterion has been met or group a set of tasks logically. Containers can also be nested, containing other containers. They are set in the Control Flow tab in the Package Designer. There are three types of containers in the Control Flow tab: Sequence, For Loop, and Foreach Loop Containers.

TASK HOST CONTAINERS

The Task Host Container is the default container under which single tasks fall and is used only behind the scenes for SSIS. You won't notice this type of container. You'll notice that this type of container is not in the Toolbox in Visual Studio and is implicitly assigned to each task. In fact, even if you don't specify a container for a task, it will be placed in a Task Host Container. The SSIS architecture extends variables and event handlers to the task through the Task Host Container.

SEQUENCE CONTAINERS

Sequence Containers handle the flow of a subset of a package and can help you divide a package into smaller, more manageable pieces. Some nice applications that you can use Sequence Containers for include the following:

- Grouping tasks so that you can disable a part of the package that's no longer needed
- Narrowing the scope of the variable to a container
- Managing the properties of multiple tasks in one step by setting the properties of the container
- Using one method to ensure that multiple tasks have to execute successfully before the next task executes
- Creating a transaction across a series of data-related tasks, but not on the entire package
- Creating event handlers on a single container, wherein you could send an e-mail if anything inside one container fails and perhaps page if anything else fails

Sequence Containers show up like any other task in your Control Flow tab. Once you drag and drop any container from your SSIS Toolbox onto the design pane, you just drag the tasks you want to use into the container. Figure 6-1 shows an example of a Sequence Container in which two tasks must execute successfully before the task called Run Script 3 will execute. If you click the up-pointing arrow at the top of the container, the tasks inside the container will minimize.

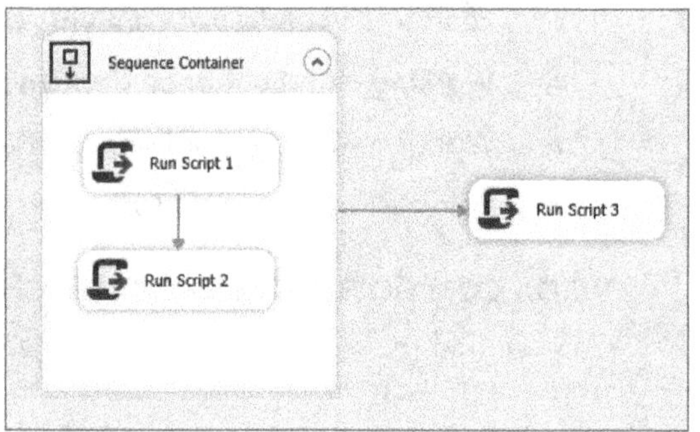

FIGURE 6-1

A container can be considered to be a miniature package. Inside the container, all task names must be unique, just as they must be within a package that has no containers. You cannot connect a task in one container to anything outside of the container. If you try to do this, you will receive the following error:

```
Cannot create connector.
Cannot connect executables from different containers.
```

Containers such as the Sequence Container can also be nested in each other. As a best practice, each of your SSIS packages should contain a series of containers to help organize the package and to make it easy to disable subject areas quickly. For example, each set of tables that you must load probably fits into a subject area, such as Accounting or HR. Each of these loads should be placed in its own Sequence Container. Additionally, you may want to create a Sequence Container for the preparation and cleanup stages of your package. This becomes especially handy if you want to execute all the tasks in the container at one time by right-clicking on the container and selecting Execute Container.

GROUPS

Groups are not actually containers but simply a way to group components together. A key difference between groups and containers is that properties cannot be delegated through a container. Because of this, groups don't have precedence constraints originating from them (only from the tasks). And you cannot disable the entire group, as you can with a Sequence Container. Groups are good for quick compartmentalization of tasks for aesthetics. Their only usefulness is to quickly group components in either a Control Flow or a Data Flow together.

To create a group, highlight the tasks that you wish to place in the group, right-click, and select Group. To ungroup the tasks, right-click the group and select Ungroup. To add additional tasks, simply drag the task into the group. This can be done in the Control Flow or Data Flow.

The same type of logic you saw in the Sequence Container in Figure 6-1 is also shown in Figure 6-2. In this case, the precedence constraint is originating from the task Run Script 2 to the task Run Script 3. You should always consider using Sequence Containers, instead of groups, because they provide a lot more functionality than groups.

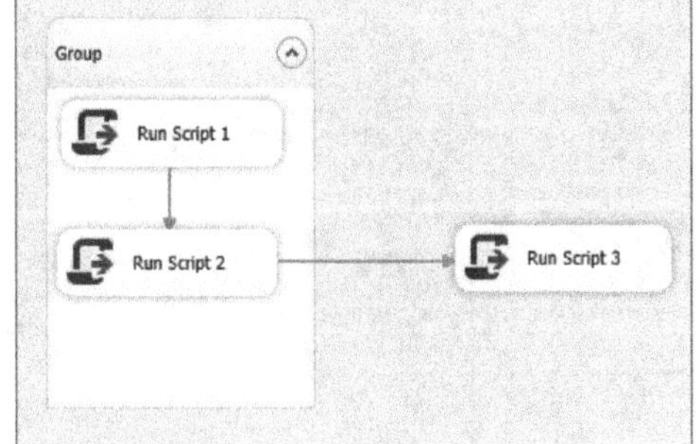

FIGURE 6-2

FOR LOOP CONTAINER

The For Loop Container enables you to create looping in your package similar to how you would loop in nearly any programming language. In this looping style, SSIS optionally initializes an expression and continues to evaluate it until the expression evaluates to false.

In the example in Figure 6-3, the Script Task called Wait for File to Arrive is continuously looped through until a condition is evaluated as false. Once the loop is broken, the Script Task is executed.

For another real-world example, use a Message Queue Task inside the loop to continuously loop until a message arrives in the queue. Such a configuration would allow for scaling out your SSIS environment.

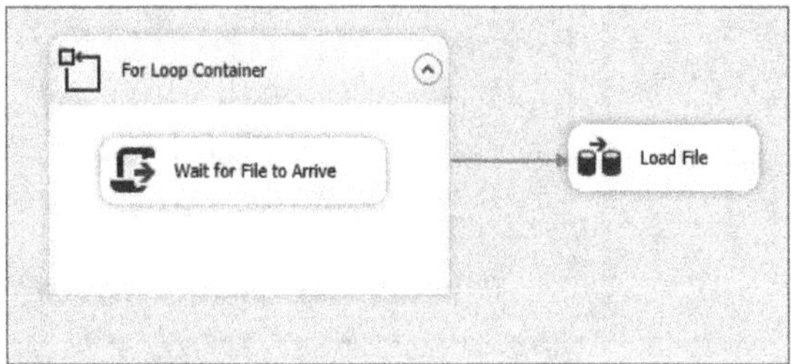

FIGURE 6-3

The following simple example demonstrates the functionality of the For Loop Container, whereby you'll use the container to loop over a series of tasks five times. Although this example is rudimentary, you can plug in whatever task you want in place of the Script Task.

1. Create a new SSIS project called **Chapter 6**, and change the name of the default package to ForLoopContainer.dtsx.

2. Open the ForLoopContainer.dtsx package, create a new variable, and call it **Counter**. You may have to open the Variables window if it isn't already open. To do this, right-click in the design pane and select Variables or click on the Variables icon on the top right of your package designer screen. Once the window is open, click the Add Variable button. Accept all the defaults for the variable (`int32`) and a default value of 0.

3. Drag the For Loop Container to the Control Flow and double-click it to open the editor. Set the InitExpression option to `@Counter = 0`. This will initialize the loop by setting the `Counter` variable to 0. Next, in the EvalExpression option, type **@Counter < 5** and **@Counter = @ Counter + 1** for the AssignExpression (shown in Figure 6-4). This means that the loop will iterate as long as the `Counter` variable is less than 5; each time it loops, 1 will be added to the variable. Click OK.

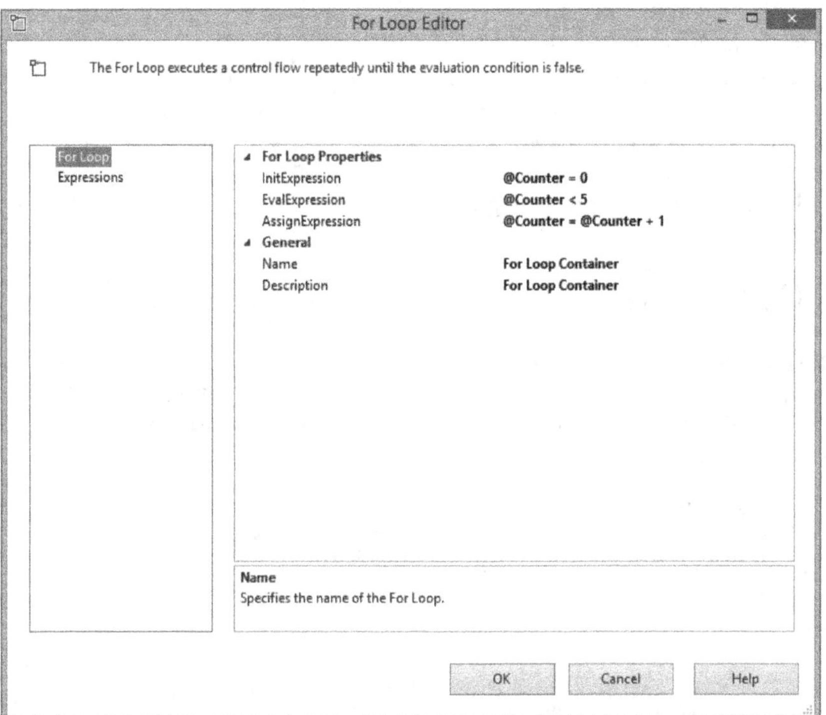

FIGURE 6-4

4. Drag a Script Task into the For Loop Container and double-click the task to edit it. In the General tab, name the task **Pop Up the Iteration**.

5. In the Script tab, set the ReadOnlyVariables (see Figure 6-5) to Counter and select Microsoft Visual Basic 2012. Finally, click Edit Script to open the Visual Studio designer. By typing **Counter** for that option, you're going to pass in the `Counter` parameter to be used by the Script Task.

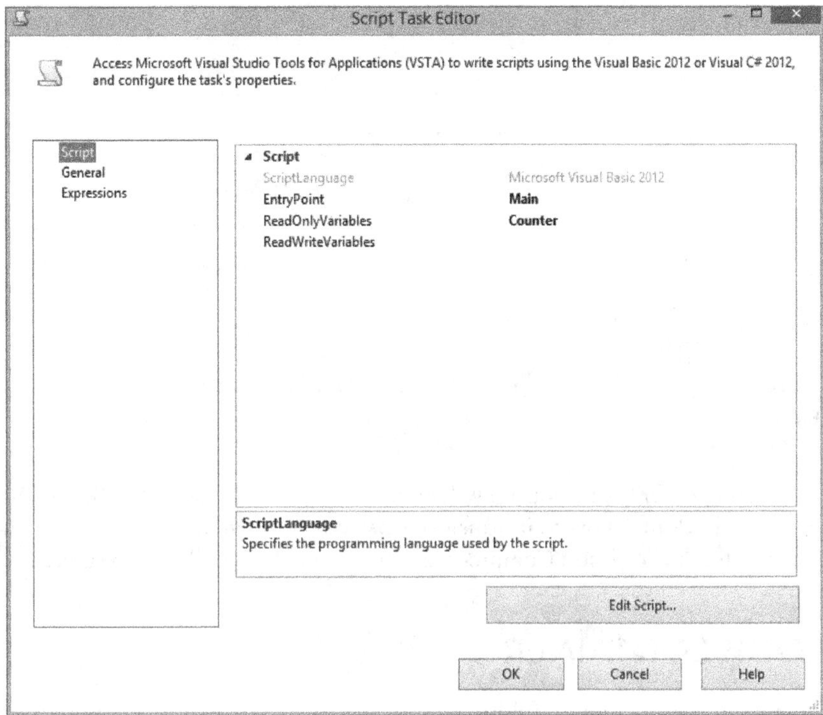

FIGURE 6-5

6. When you click Edit Script, the Visual Studio 2012 design environment will open. Replace the `Main()` subroutine with the following code. This code will read the variable and pop up a message box that displays the value of the `Counter` variable:

```
Public Sub Main()
'
' Add your code here
'
MessageBox.Show(Dts.Variables("Counter").Value)
Dts.TaskResult = ScriptResults.Success
End Sub
```

   Close the script editor and click OK to save the Script Task Editor.

7. Drag over a Data Flow task and name it Load File. Connect the success precedence constraint to the task from the For Loop Container. This task won't do anything, but it shows how the container can call another task.

8. Save and exit the Visual Studio design environment, then click OK to exit the Script Task. When you execute the package, you should see results similar to what is shown in Figure 6-6. That is, you should see five pop-up boxes one at a time, starting at iteration 0 and proceeding

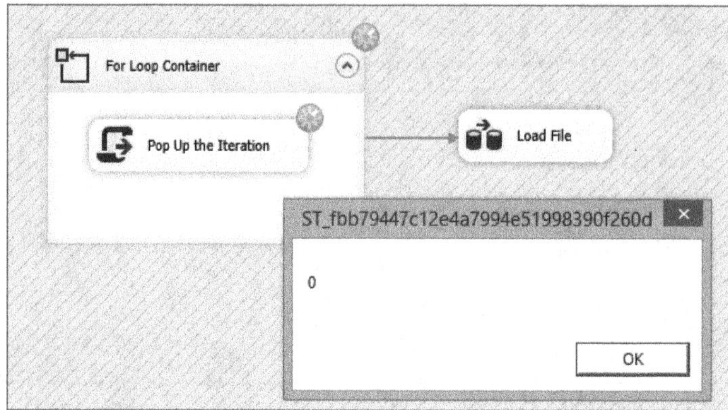

FIGURE 6-6

through iteration 4. Only one pop-up will appear at any given point. The Script Task will turn green and then back to yellow as it transitions between each iteration of the loop. After the loop is complete, the For Loop Container and the Script Task will both be green.

FOREACH LOOP CONTAINER

The Foreach Loop Container is a powerful looping mechanism that enables you to loop through a collection of objects. As you loop through the collection, the container assigns the value from the collection to a variable, which can later be used by tasks or connections inside or outside the container. You can also map the value to a variable. The types of objects that you will loop through vary based on the enumerator you set in the editor in the Collection page. The properties of the editor vary widely according to what you set for this option:

- **Foreach File Enumerator:** Performs an action for each file in a directory with a given file extension
- **Foreach Item Enumerator:** Loops through a list of items that are set manually in the container
- **Foreach ADO Enumerator:** Loops through a list of tables or rows in a table from an ADO recordset
- **Foreach ADO.NET Schema Rowset Enumerator:** Loops through an ADO.NET schema
- **Foreach From Variable Enumerator:** Loops through an SSIS variable
- **Foreach Nodelist Enumerator:** Loops through a node list in an XML document
- **Foreach SMO Enumerator:** Enumerates a list of SQL Management Objects (SMO)

The most important of the enumerators is the Foreach File enumerator since it's used more frequently. In this next example, you'll see how to loop over a number of files and perform an action on each file. The second most important enumerator is the Foreach ADO enumerator, which loops over records in a table.

Foreach File Enumerator Example

The following example uses the most common type of enumerator: the Foreach File enumerator. You'll loop through a list of files and simulate some type of action that has occurred inside the container. This example has been simplified in an effort to highlight the core functionality, but if you would like a more detailed example, turn to Chapter 8, which has an end-to-end example. For this example to work, you need a folder full of some dummy files and an archive folder to move them into, which SSIS will be enumerating through. The folder can contain any type of file.

1. To start, create a new package called ForEachFileEnumerator.dtsx. Then create a string variable called **sFileName** with a default value of the word **default**. This variable will hold the name of the file that SSIS is working on during each iteration of the loop.
2. Create the variable by right-clicking in the Package Designer area of the Control Flow tab and selecting Variables. Then, click the Add New Variable option, changing the data type to a String.
3. Next, drag a Foreach Loop Container onto the Control Flow and double-click on the container to configure it, as shown in Figure 6-7. Set the Enumerator option to Foreach File Enumerator.

Foreach Loop Editor

The Foreach Loop container allows execution iteration over an enumeration.

General
Collection
Variable Mappings
Expressions

Foreach Loop Editor
Enumerator: Foreach File Enumerator
Expressions

Enumerator
Specifies the enumerator type.

Enumerator configuration
Folder:
C:\ProSSIS\Containers\ForEachFile
Browse...
Files:
.
Retrieve file name
Name and extension
Fully qualified
Name only
Traverse subfolders

OK
Cancel
Help

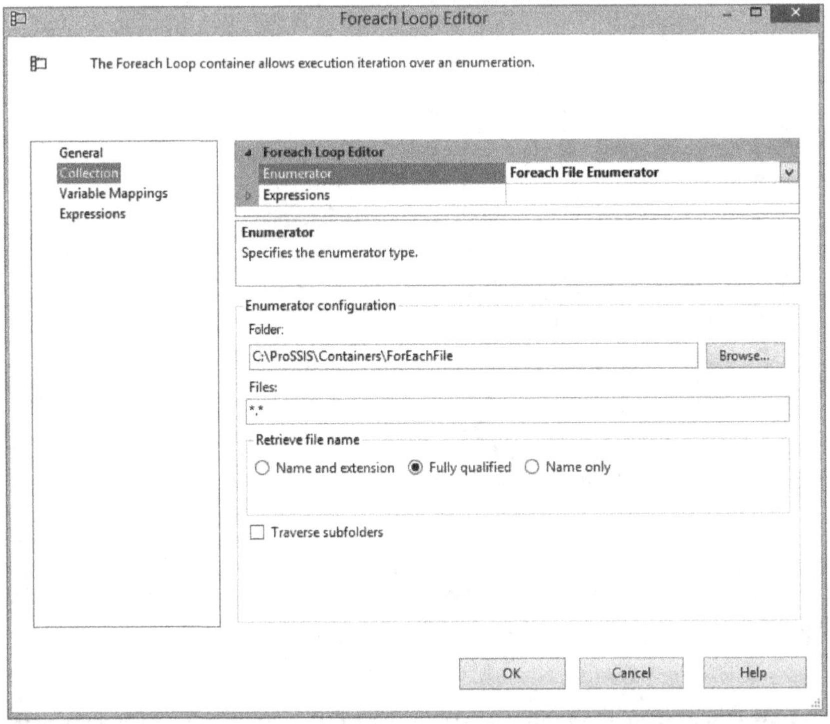

FIGURE 6-7

4. Then, set the Folder property to the folder that has the dummy files in it and leave the default Files property of *.*. In this tab, you can store the filename and extension (`Readme.txt`), the fully qualified filename (`c:\directoryname\readme.txt`), or just the filename without the extension (`readme`). You can also tell the container to loop through all the files in subfolders as well by checking Transverse Subfolders.

5. Click the Variable Mappings tab on the left, select the variable you created earlier from the Variable dropdown box, and then accept the default of 0 for the index, as shown in Figure 6-8. Click OK to save the settings and return to the Control Flow tab in the Package Designer.

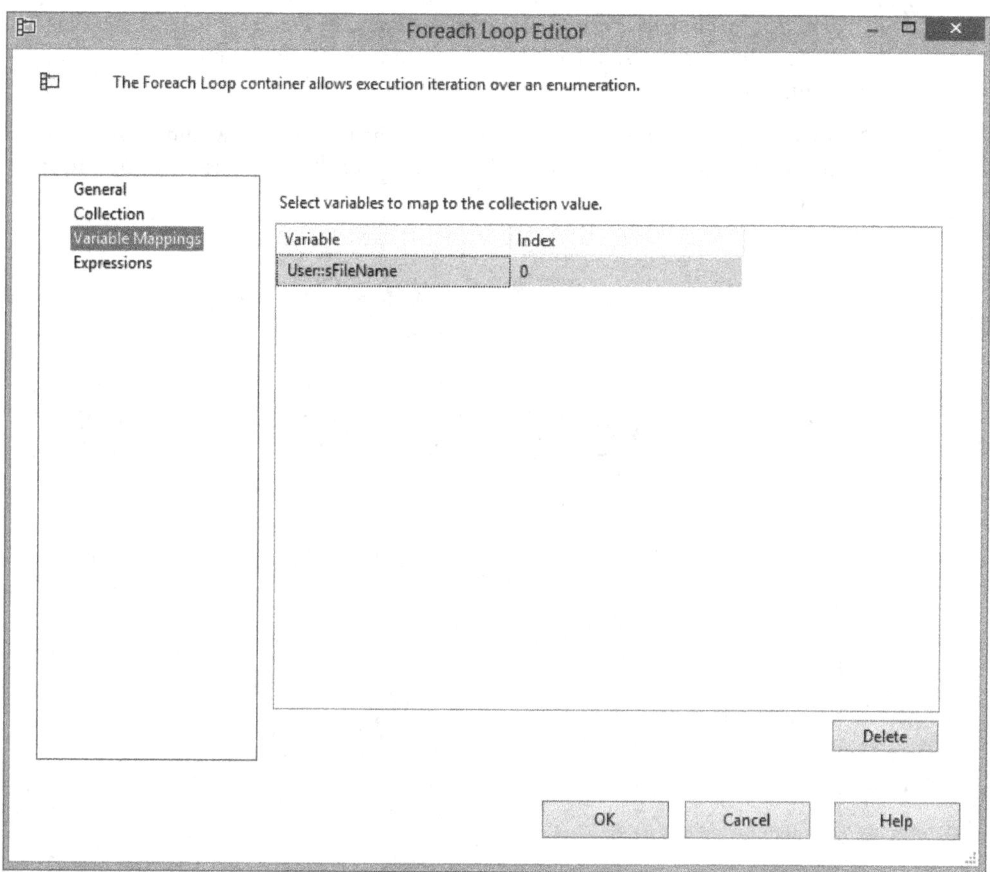

FIGURE 6-8

6. Drag a new File System Task into the container's box. Double-click the new task to configure it in the editor that appears. After setting the operation to Copy file, the screen's properties should look like what is shown in Figure 6-9. Select <New Connection> for the DestinationConnection property.

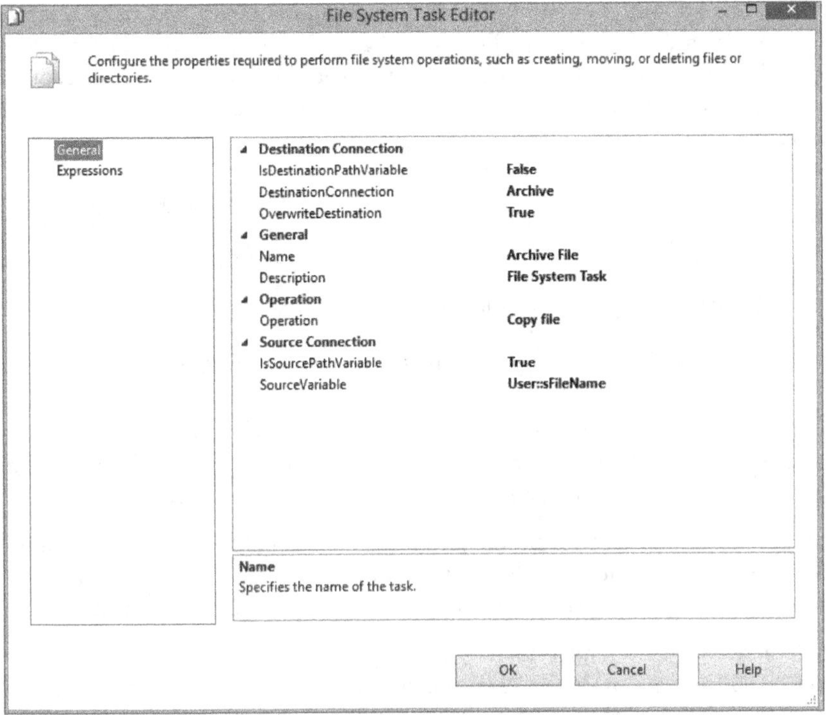

FIGURE 6-9

7. When the Connection Manager dialog opens, select Existing Folder and type the archive folder of your choosing, such as `C:\ProSSIS\Containers\ForEachFille\Archive`.
8. Lastly, set the IsSourcePathVariable property to True and set the SourceVariable to User::sFileName.
9. You're now ready to execute the package. Place any set of files you wish into the folder that you configured the enumerator to loop over, and then execute the package. During execution, you'll see each file picked up and moved in Windows Explorer, and in the package you'll see something resembling Figure 6-10. If you had set the OverwriteDestination property to True in the File System Task, the file would be overwritten if there was a conflict of duplicate filenames.

FIGURE 6-10

Foreach ADO Enumerator Example

The Foreach ADO Enumerator loops through a collection of records and will execute anything inside the container for each row that is found. For example, if you had a table such as the following that contained metadata about your environment, you could loop over that table and reconfigure the package for each iteration of the loop. This reconfiguration is done with SSIS expressions. We cover these in much more depth in Chapter 5. At a high level, the expression can reconfigure the connection to files, databases, or variables (to name just a few items) at runtime and during each loop of the container.

CLIENT	FTPLOCATION	SERVERNAME	DATABASENAME
Client1	C:\Client1\Pub	localhost	Client1DB
Client2	C:\Client2\Pub	localhost	Client2DB
Client3	C:\Client3\Pub	localhost	Client3DB

The first time through the loop, your Connection Managers would point to Client1, and retrieve their files from one directory. The next time, the Connection Managers would point to another client. This enables you to create a single package that will work for all your clients.

In this next example, you will create a simple package that simulates this type of scenario. The package will loop over a table and then change the value for a variable for each row that is found. Inside the container, you will create a Script Task that pops up the current variable's value.

1. Create a new OLE DB Connection. To start the example, create a new package called ForeachADOEnumerator.dtsx. Create a new Connection Manager called **MasterConnection** that points to the master database on your development machine. Create two variables: one called `sDBName`, which is a string with no default, and the other called `objResults`, which is an object data type.
2. Next, drag over an Execute SQL Task. You'll use the Execute SQL Task to populate the ADO recordset that is stored in a variable.
3. In the Execute SQL Task, point the Connection property to the MasterConnection Connection Manager. Change the ResultSet property to Full Result Set, which captures the results of the query run in this task to a result set in a variable. Type the following query for the SQLStatement property (as shown in Figure 6-11):

   ```
   Select database_id, name from sys.databases
   ```

4. Still in the Execute SQL Task, go to the Result Set page and type 0 for the Result Name, as shown in Figure 6-12.

   This is the zero-based ordinal position for the result that you want to capture into a variable. If your previously typed query created multiple recordsets, then you could capture each one here by providing its ordinal position. Map this recordset to a variable called `objResults` that is scoped to the package and an object data type. The object variable data type can store up to 2GB of data in memory. If you don't select that option, the package will fail upon execution because the object variable is the only way to store a recordset in memory in SSIS.

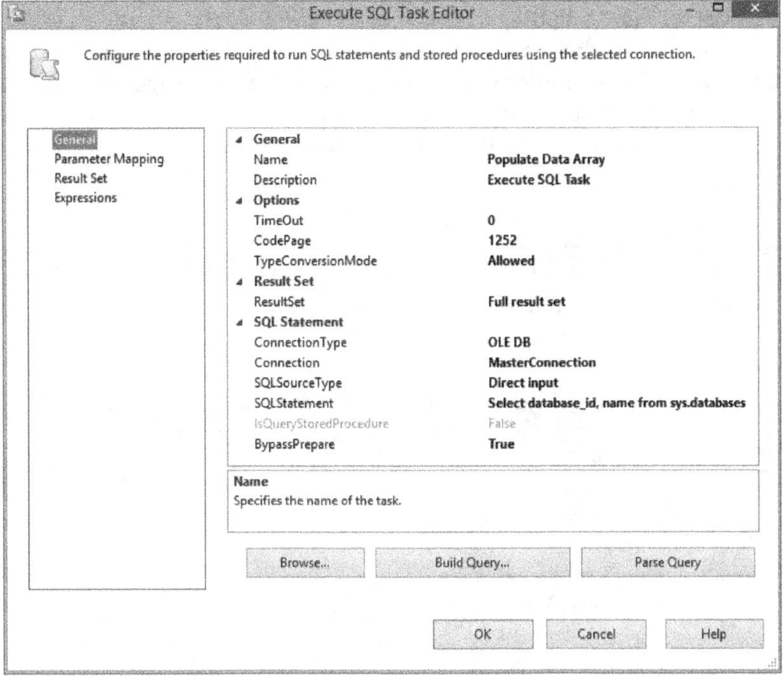

FIGURE 6-11

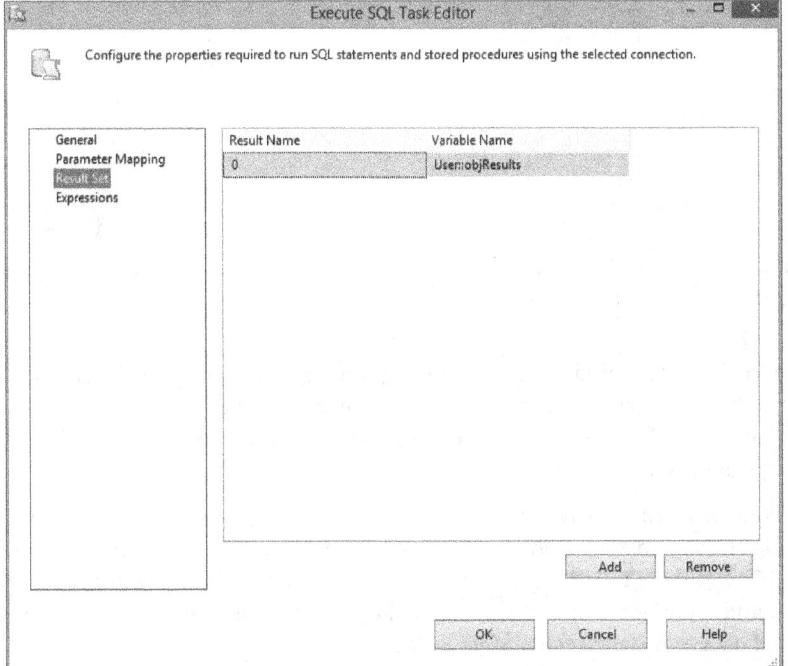

FIGURE 6-12

5. Back in the Control Flow tab, drag over a ForEach Loop Container and drag the green line from the Execute SQL Task to the Foreach Loop. Now open the Foreach Loop to configure the container. In the Collection page, select Foreach ADO Enumerator from the Enumerator dropdown box. Next, select the objResults variable from the ADO Object Source Variable dropdown, as seen in Figure 6-13. This tells the container that you wish to loop over the results stored in that variable.

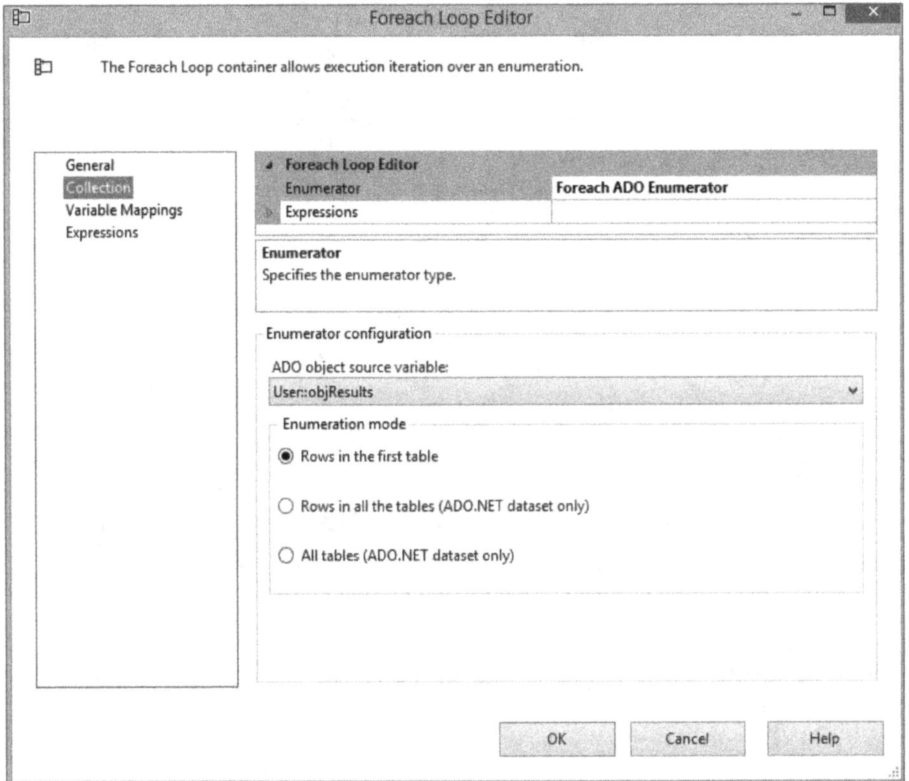

FIGURE 6-13

6. Go to the Variable Mappings page for the final configuration step of the container. Just like the Foreach File Enumerator, you must tell the container where you wish to map the value retrieved from the ADO result set. Your result set contains two columns: ID and Name, from the sys.databases table.

7. In this example, you are working with the second column, so select the sDBName variable by selecting the variable from the Variable dropdown and type 1 for the Index (shown in Figure 6-14). Entering 1 means you want the second column in the result set, as the index starts at 0 and increments by one for each column to the right. Because of this behavior, be careful if you change the Execute SQL Task's query.

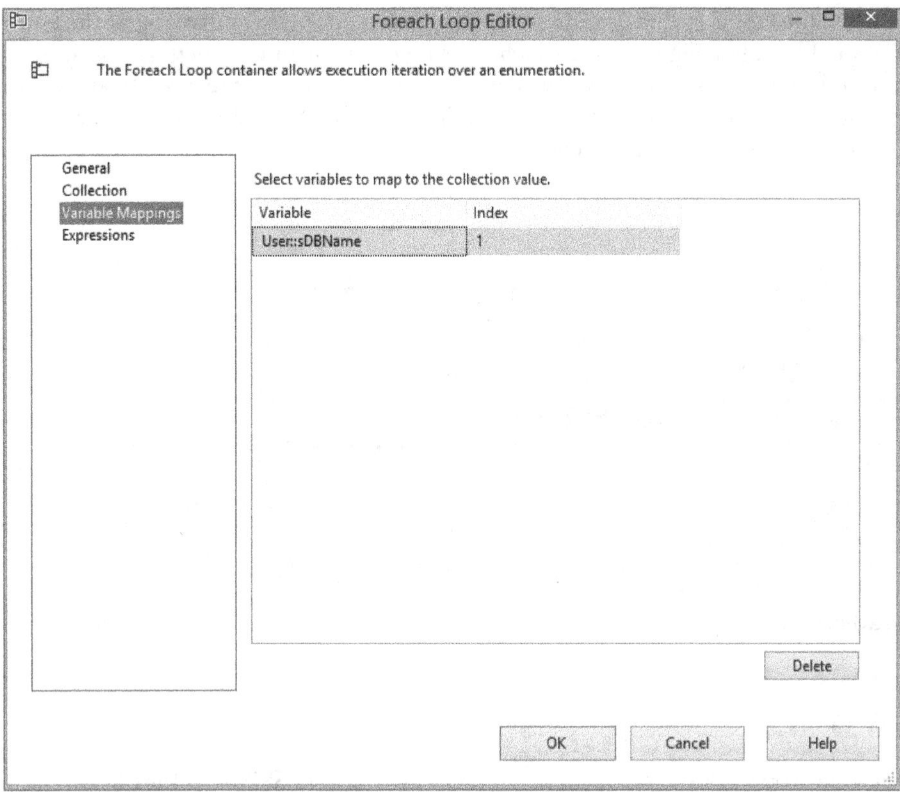

FIGURE 6-14

8. With the container now configured, drag a Script Task into the container's box. In the Script tab of the Script Task, set ReadOnlyVariables to sDBName and select Microsoft Visual Basic 2012.

9. Finally, click Edit Script to open the Visual Studio designer. By typing **sDBName** for the ReadOnlyVariables option in the Script tab, you're going to pass in the Counter parameter to be used by the Script Task.

10. When you click Edit Script, the Visual Studio 2012 design environment will open. Double-click `ScriptMain.vb` to open the script, and replace the `Main()` subroutine with the following code. This one line of code uses the `MessageBox` method to display the `sDBName` variable.

```
Public Sub Main()
'
' Add your code here
'
MessageBox.Show(Dts.Variables("sDBName").Value)
Dts.TaskResult = ScriptResults.Success
End Sub
```

11. Close the editor and task and execute the package. The final running of the package should look like Figure 6-15, which pops up the value of the `sDBName` variable, showing you the current database. As you click OK to each pop-up, the next database name will be displayed. In a less contrived example, this Script Task would obviously be replaced with a Data Flow Task to load the client's data.

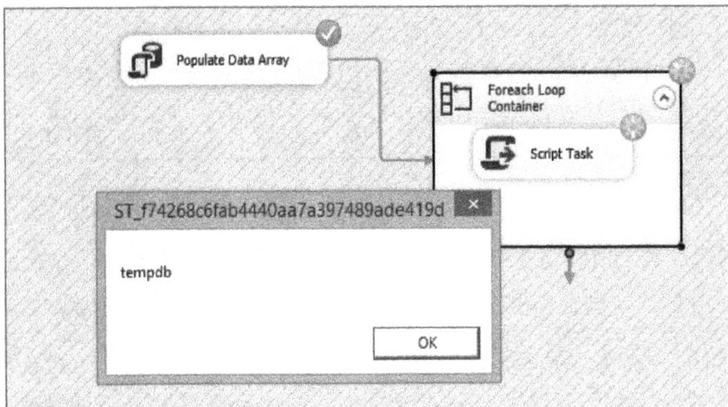

FIGURE 6-15

SUMMARY

In this chapter, you explored groups and the four containers in SSIS: the Task Host, the Sequence Container, the For Loop Container and the Foreach Loop Container.

- The Task Host Container is used behind the scenes on any task.
- A Sequence Container helps you compartmentalize your various tasks into logical groupings.
- The For Loop Container iterates through a loop until a requirement has been met.
- A Foreach Loop Container loops through a collection of objects such as files or records in a table.

This chapter covered one of the most common examples of a Foreach Loop Container, looping through all the records in a table and looping through files. Each of the looping containers will execute all the items in the container each time it iterates through the loop.

7

Joining Data

WHAT'S IN THIS CHAPTER?

- The Lookup Transformation
- Using the Merge Join Transformation
- Building a basic package
- Using the Lookup Transformation
- Loading Lookup cache with the Cache Connection Manager and Cache Transform

WROX.COM DOWNLOADS FOR THIS CHAPTER

You can find the wrox.com code downloads for this chapter at `www.wrox.com/go/prossis2014` on the Download Code tab.

In the simplest ETL scenarios, you use an SSIS Data Flow to extract data from a single source table and populate the corresponding destination table. In practice, though, you usually won't see such trivial scenarios: the more common ETL scenarios will require you to access two or more data sources simultaneously and merge their results together into a single destination structure. For instance, you may have a normalized source system that uses three or more tables to represent the product catalog, whereas the destination represents the same information using a single denormalized table (perhaps as part of a data warehouse schema). In this case you would need to join the multiple source tables together in order to present a unified structure to the destination table. This joining may take place in the source query in the SSIS package or when using a Lookup Transform in an SSIS Data Flow.

Another less obvious example of joining data is loading a dimension that would need to have new rows inserted and existing rows updated in a data warehouse. The source data is coming from an OLTP database and needs to be compared to the existing dimension to find the rows that need updating. Using the dimension as a second source, you can then join the data using a Merge Join Transformation in your Data Flow. The joined rows can then be compared to look for changes. This type of loading is discussed in Chapter 12.

In the relational world, such requirements can be met by employing a relational join operation if the data exists in an environment where these joins are possible. When you are creating ETL projects, the data is often not in the same physical database, the same brand of database, the same server, or, in the worst cases, even the same physical location (all of which typically render the relational join method useless). In fact, in one common scenario, data from a mainframe system needs to be joined with data from SQL Server to create a complete data warehouse in order to provide your users with one trusted point for reporting. The ETL solutions you build need to be able to join data in a similar way to relational systems, but they should not be constrained to having the source data in the same physical database. SQL Server Integration Services (SSIS) provides several methods for performing such joins, ranging from functionality implemented in Data Flow Transformations to custom methods implemented in T-SQL or managed code.

This chapter explores the various options for performing joins and provides guidelines to help you determine which method you should use for various circumstances and when to use it. After reading this chapter, you should be able to optimize the various join operations in your ETL solution and understand their various design, performance, and resource trade-offs.

THE LOOKUP TRANSFORMATION

The Lookup Transformation in SSIS enables you to perform the similar relational inner and outer hash-joins. The main difference is that the operations occur outside the realm of the database engine and in the SSIS Data Flow. Typically, you would use this component within the context of an integration process, such as the ETL layer that populates a data warehouse from source systems. For example, you may want to populate a table in a destination system by joining data from two separate source systems on different database platforms.

The component can join only two data sets at a time, so in order to join three or more data sets, you would need to chain multiple Lookup Transformations together, using an output from one Lookup Transformation as an input for another. Compare this to relational join semantics, whereby in a similar fashion you join two tables at a time and compose multiple such operations to join three or more tables.

The transformation is written to behave in a synchronous manner, meaning it does not block the pipeline while it is doing its work. While new rows are entering the Lookup Transformation, rows that have already been processed are leaving through one of four outputs. However, there is a catch here: in certain caching modes (discussed later in this chapter) the component will initially block the package's execution for a period of time while it loads its internal caches with the Lookup data.

The component provides several modes of operation that enable you to compare performance and resource usage. In full-cache mode, one of the tables you are joining is loaded in its entirety into memory, and then the rows from the other table are flowed through the pipeline one buffer at a time, and the selected join operation is performed. With no up-front caching, each incoming row in the pipeline is compared one at a time to a specified relational table. Between these two options is a third that combines their behavior. Each of these modes is explored later in this chapter (see the "Full-Cache Mode," "No-Cache Mode," and "Partial-Cache Mode" sections).

Of course, some rows will join successfully, and some rows will not be joined. For example, consider a customer who has made no purchases. His or her identifier in the Customer table would have no matches in the sales table. SSIS supports this scenario by having multiple outputs on the Lookup Transformation. In the simplest (default/legacy) configuration, you would have one output for matched rows and a separate output for nonmatched and error rows. This functionality enables you to build robust (error-tolerant) processes that, for instance, might direct nonmatched rows to a staging area for further review. Or the errors can be ignored, and a Derived Column Transformation can be used to check for null values. A conditional statement can then be used to add default data in the Derived Column. A more detailed example is given later in this chapter.

The Cache Connection Manager (CCM) is a separate component that is essential when creating advanced Lookup operations. The CCM enables you to populate the Lookup cache from an arbitrary source; for instance, you can load the cache from a relational query, an Excel file, a text file, or a Web service. You can also use the CCM to persist the Lookup cache across iterations of a looping operation. You can still use the Lookup Transformation without explicitly using the CCM, but you would then lose the resource and performance gains in doing so. CCM is described in more detail later in this chapter.

USING THE MERGE JOIN TRANSFORMATION

The Merge Join Transformation in SSIS enables you to perform an inner or outer join operation in a streaming fashion within the SSIS Data Flow. The Merge Join Transformation does not preload data like the Lookup Transformation does in its cached mode. Nor does it perform per-record database queries like the Lookup Transformation does in its noncached mode. Instead, the Merge Join Transformation accepts two inputs, which must be sorted, and produces a single output, which contains the selected columns from both inputs, and uses the join criteria defined by the package developer.

The component accepts two sorted input streams and outputs a single stream that combines the chosen columns into a single structure. It is not possible to configure a separate nonmatched output like the one supported by the Lookup Transformation. For situations in which unmatched records need to be processed separately, a Conditional Split Transformation can be used to find the null values on the nonmatched rows and send them down a different path in the Data Flow.

The Merge Join Transformation differs from the Lookup Transformation in that it accepts its reference data via a Data Flow path instead of through direct configuration of the transformation properties. Both input Data Flow paths must be sorted, but the data can come from any source supported by the SSIS Data Flow as long as they are sorted. The sorting has to occur using the same set of columns in exactly the same order, which can create some overhead upstream.

The Merge Join Transformation typically uses less memory than the Lookup Transformation because it maintains only the required few rows in memory to support joining the two streams. However, it does not support short-circuit execution, in that both pipelines need to stream their entire contents before the component considers its work done. For example, if the first input has five rows, and the second input has one million rows, and it so happens that the first five rows immediately join successfully, the component will still stream the other 999,995 rows from the second input even though they cannot possibly be joined anymore.

CONTRASTING SSIS AND THE RELATIONAL JOIN

Though the methods and syntax you employ in the relational and SSIS worlds may differ, joining multiple row sets together using congruent keys achieves the same desired result. In the relational database world, the equivalent of a Lookup is accomplished by joining two or more tables together using declarative syntax that executes in a set-based manner. The operation remains close to the data at all times; there is typically no need to move the data out-of-process with respect to the database engine as long as the databases are on the same SQL Server instance (except when joining across databases, though this is usually a nonoptimal operation). When joining tables within the same database, the engine can take advantage of multiple different internal algorithms, knowledge of table statistics, cardinality, temporary storage, cost-based plans, and the benefit of many years of ongoing research and code optimization. Operations can still complete in a resource-constrained environment because the platform has many intrinsic functions and operators that simplify multi-step operations, such as implicit parallelism, paging, sorting, and hashing.

In a cost-based optimization database system, the end-user experience is typically transparent; the declarative SQL syntax abstracts the underlying relational machinations such that the user may not in fact know how the problem was solved by the engine. In other words, the engine is capable of transforming a problem statement as defined by the user into an internal form that can be optimized into one of many solution sets — transparently. The end-user experience is usually synchronous and nonblocking; results are materialized in a streaming manner, with the engine effecting the highest degree of parallelism possible.

The operation is atomic in that once a join is specified, the operation either completes or fails in total — there are no substeps that can succeed or fail in a way the user would experience independently. Furthermore, it is not possible to receive two result sets from the query at the same time — for instance, if you specified a left join, then you could not direct the matches to go one direction and the nonmatches somewhere else.

Advanced algorithms allow efficient caching of multiple joins using the same tables — for instance, round-robin read-ahead enables separate T-SQL statements (using the same base tables) to utilize the same caches.

The following relational query joins two tables from the AdventureWorksDW database together. Notice how you join only two tables at a time, using declarative syntax, with particular attention being paid to specification of the join columns:

```
select sc.EnglishProductSubcategoryName, p.EnglishProductName
from dbo.DimProductSubcategory sc
inner join dbo.DimProduct p
on sc.ProductSubcategoryKey = p.ProductSubcategoryKey;
```

For reference purposes, Figure 7-1 shows the plan that SQL Server chooses to execute this join.

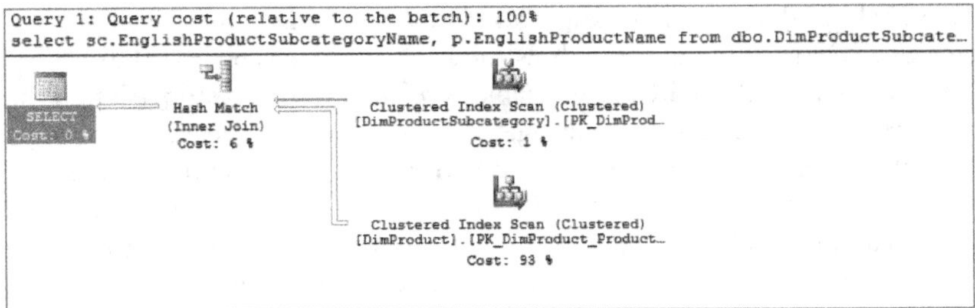

FIGURE 7-1

In SSIS, the data is usually joined using a Lookup Transformation on a buffered basis. The Merge Join Transformation can also be used, though it was designed to solve a different class of patterns. The calculus/algebra for these components is deterministic; the configuration that the user supplies is directly utilized by the engine — in other words, there is no opportunity for the platform to make any intelligent choices based on statistics, cost, cardinality, or count. Furthermore, the data is loaded into out-of-process buffers (with respect to the database engine) and is then treated on a row-by-row manner; therefore, because this moves the data away from the source, you can expect performance and scale to be affected.

Any data moving through an SSIS Data Flow is loaded into memory in data buffers. A batch process is performed on the data in synchronous transformations. The asynchronous transformations, such as the Sort or Aggregate, still perform in batch, but all rows must be loaded into memory before they complete, and therefore bring the pipeline process to a halt. Other transformations, like the OLE DB Command Transformation, perform their work using a row-by-row approach.

The end-user experience is synchronous, though in the case of some modes of the Lookup Transformation the process is blocked while the cache loads in its entirety. Execution is nonatomic in that one of multiple phases of the process can succeed or fail independently. Furthermore, you can direct successful matches to flow out the Lookup Transformation to one consumer, the nonmatches to flow to a separate consumer, and the errors to a third.

Resource usage and performance compete: in Lookup's full-cache mode — which is typically fastest with smaller data sets — the cache is acquired and then remains in memory until the process (package) terminates, and there are no implicit operators (sorting, hashing, and paging) to balance resource usage. In no-cache or partial-cache modes, the resource usage is initially lower because the cache is charged on the fly; however, overall performance will almost always be lower. The operation is explicitly parallel; individual packages scale out if and only if the developer intentionally created multiple pipelines and manually segmented the data. Even then, bringing the data back together with the Union All Transformation, which is partial blocking, can negate any performance enhancement. Benchmark testing your SSIS packages is necessary to determine the best approach.

There is no opportunity for the Lookup Transformation to implicitly perform in an SMP (or scale-out) manner. The same applies to the Merge Join Transformation — on suitable hardware it will run on a separate thread to other components, but it will not utilize multiple threads within itself.

Figure 7-2 shows an SSIS package that uses a Lookup Transformation to demonstrate the same functionality as the previous SQL statement. Notice how the Product table is pipelined directly into the Lookup Transformation, but the SubCategory table is referenced using properties on the component itself. It is interesting to compare this package with the query plan generated by SQL Server for the previous SQL query. Notice how in this case SQL Server chose to utilize a hash-join operation, which happens to coincide with the mechanics underlying the Lookup Transformation when used in full-cache mode. The explicit design chosen by the developer in SSIS corresponds almost exactly to the plan chosen by SQL Server to generate the same result set.

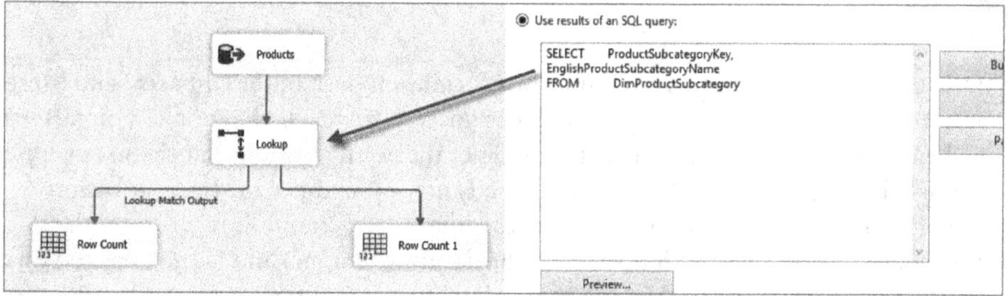

FIGURE 7-2

Figure 7-3 shows the same functionality, this time built using a Merge Join Transformation. Notice how similar this looks to the SQL Server plan (though in truth the execution semantics are quite different).

FIGURE 7-3

LOOKUP FEATURES

The Lookup Transformation allows you to populate the cache using a separate pipeline in either the same or a different package. You can use source data from any location that can be accessed by the SSIS Data Flow. This cache option makes it convenient to load a file or table into memory, and this data can be used by multiple Data Flows in multiple packages.

Prior to SQL Server 2008, you needed to reload the cache every time it was used. For example, if you had two Data Flow Tasks in the same package and each required the same reference data set, each Lookup Transformation would load its own copy of the cache separately. You can persist the cache to virtual memory or to permanent file storage. This means that within the same package, multiple Lookup Transformations can share the same cache. The cache does not need to be reloaded for multiple Data Flows or if the same Data Flow is executed multiple times during a package execution, such as when the Data Flow Task is executed within a Foreach Loop Container.

You can also persist the cache to a file and share it with other packages. The cache file format is optimized for speed; it can be much faster than reloading the reference data set from the original relational source.

Another enhancement in the Lookup Transformation in SQL Server 2008 SSIS is the miss-cache feature. In scenarios where the component is configured to perform the Lookups directly against the database, the miss-cache feature enables you to optimize performance by optionally loading into cache the rows without matching entries in the reference data set. For example, if the component receives the value `123` in the incoming pipeline, but there are no matching entries in the reference data set, the component will not try to find that value in the reference data set again. In other words, the component "remembers" which values it did not find before. You can also specify how much memory the miss-cache should use (expressed as a percentage of the total cache limit, by default 20%). This reduces a redundant and expensive trip to the database. The miss-cache feature alone can contribute to performance improvement especially when you have a very large data set.

In the 2005 version of the component, the Lookup Transformation had only two outputs — one for matched rows and another that combined nonmatches and errors. However, the latter output caused much dismay with SSIS users — it is often the case that a nonmatch is not an error and is in fact expected. In 2008 and later the component has one output for nonmatches and a separate output for true errors (such as truncations). Note that the old combined output is still available as an option for backward compatibility. This combined error and nonmatching output can be separated by placing a Conditional Split Transformation after the Lookup, but it is no longer necessary because of the separate outputs.

To troubleshoot issues you may have with SSIS, you can add Data Viewers into a Data Flow on the lines connecting the components. Data Viewers give you a peek at the rows in memory. They also pause the Data Flow at the point the data reaches the viewer.

BUILDING THE BASIC PACKAGE

To simplify the explanation of the Lookup Transformation's operation in the next few sections, this section presents a typical ETL problem that is used to demonstrate several solutions using the components configured in various modes.

The AdventureWorks database is a typical OLTP store for a bicycle retailer, and AdventureWorksDW is a database that contains the corresponding denormalized data warehouse structures. Both of these databases, as well as some secondary data, are used to represent a real-world ETL scenario. (If you do not have the databases, download them from `www.wrox.com`.)

The core operation focuses on extracting fact data from the source system (fact data is discussed in Chapter 12); in this scenario you will not yet be loading data into the warehouse itself. Obviously, you would not want to do one without the other in a real-world SSIS package, but it makes it easier to understand the solution if you tackle a smaller subset of the problem by itself.

You will first extract sales order (fact) data from the AdventureWorks, and later you will load it into the AdventureWorksDW database, performing multiple joins along the way. The order information in AdventureWorks is represented by two main tables: SalesOrderHeader and SalesOrderDetail. You need to join these two tables first.

The SalesOrderHeader table has many columns that in the real world would be interesting, but for this exercise you will scale down the columns to just the necessary few. Likewise, the SalesOrderDetail table has many useful columns, but you will use just a few of them. Here are the table structure and first five rows of data for these two tables:

SALESORDERID	ORDERDATE	CUSTOMERID
43659	2001-07-01	676
43660	2001-07-01	117
43661	2001-07-01	442
43662	2001-07-01	227
43663	2001-07-01	510

SALESORDERID	SALESORDERDETAILID	PRODUCTID	ORDERQTY	UNITPRICE	LINETOTAL
43659	1	776	1	2024.9940	2024.994000
43659	2	777	3	2024.9940	6074.982000
43659	3	778	1	2024.9940	2024.994000
43659	4	771	1	2039.9940	2039.994000
43659	5	772	1	2039.9940	2039.994000

As you can see, you need to join these two tables together because one table contains the order header information and the other contains the order details. Figure 7-4 shows a conceptual view of what the join would look like.

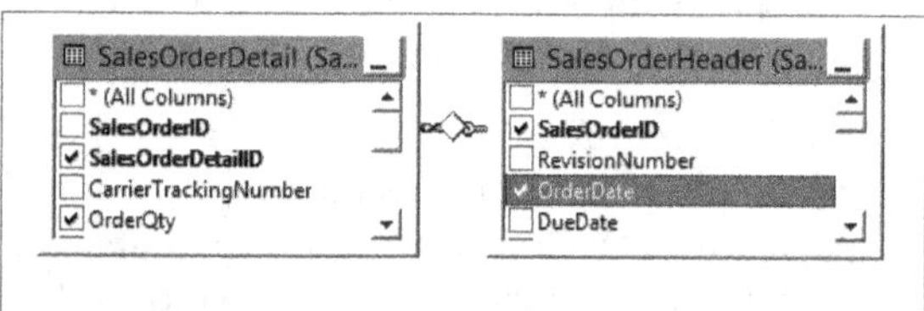

FIGURE 7-4

However, this does not get us all the way there. The CustomerID column is a surrogate key that is specific to the source system, and the very definition of surrogate keys dictates that no other system — including the data warehouse — should have any knowledge of them. Therefore, in order to populate the warehouse you need to get the original business (natural) key. Thus, you must join the SalesOrderHeader table (Sales.SalesOrderHeader) to the Customer table (Sales.Customer) in order to find the customer business key called AccountNumber. After doing that, your conceptual join now looks like Figure 7-5.

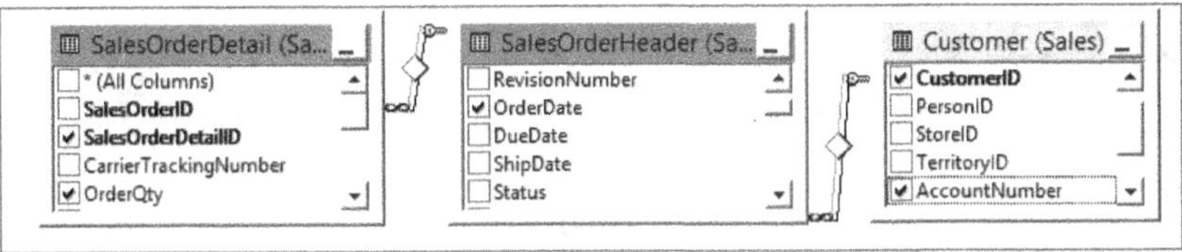

FIGURE 7-5

Similarly for Product, you need to add the Product table (Production.Product) to this join in order to derive the natural key called ProductNumber, as shown in Figure 7-6.

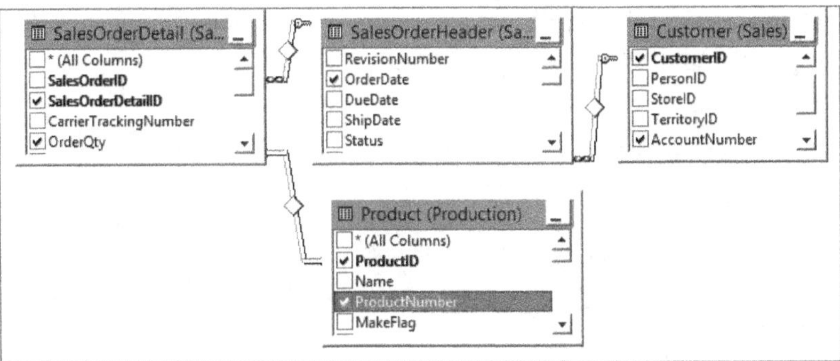

FIGURE 7-6

Referring to Figure 7-7, you can get started by creating a new SSIS package that contains an OLE DB Connection Manager called localhost.AdventureWorks that points to the AdventureWorks database and a single empty Data Flow Task.

Using a Relational Join in the Source

The easiest and most obvious solution in this particular scenario is to use a relational join to extract the data. In other words, you can build a package that has a single source (use an OLE DB Source Component) and set the query string in the source to utilize relational joins. This enables you to take advantage of the benefits of the relational source database to prepare the data before it enters the SSIS Data Flow.

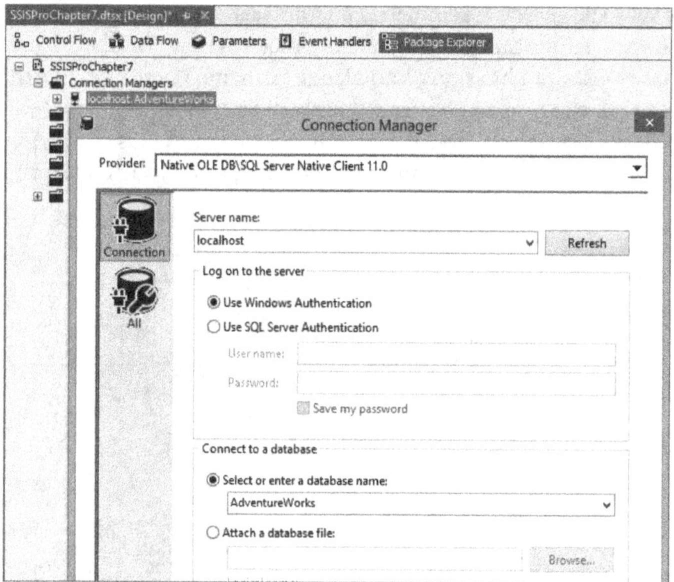

FIGURE 7-7

Drop an OLE DB Source Component on the Data Flow design surface, hook it up to the localhost .AdventureWorks Connection Manager, and set its query string as follows:

```
Select
--columns from Sales.SalesOrderHeader
oh.SalesOrderID, oh.OrderDate, oh.CustomerID,
--columns from Sales.Customer
c.AccountNumber,
--columns from Sales.SalesOrderDetail
od.SalesOrderDetailID, od.ProductID, od.OrderQty, od.UnitPrice, od.LineTotal,
--columns from Production.Product
p.ProductNumber
from Sales.SalesOrderHeader as oh
inner join Sales.Customer as c on (oh.CustomerID = c.CustomerID)
left join Sales.SalesOrderDetail as od on (oh.SalesOrderID = od.SalesOrderID)
inner join Production.Product as p on (od.ProductID = p.ProductID);
```

Note that you can either type this query in by hand or use the Build Query button in the user interface of the OLE DB Source Component to construct it visually. Click the Preview button and make sure that it executes correctly (see Figure 7-8).

For seasoned SQL developers, the query should be fairly intuitive — the only thing worth calling out is that a left join is used between the SalesOrderHeader and SalesOrderDetail tables because it is conceivable that an order header could exist without any corresponding details. If an inner join was used here, it would have lost all such rows exhibiting this behavior. Conversely, inner joins were used everywhere else because an order header cannot exist without an associated customer, and a details row cannot exist without an associated product. In business terms, a customer will buy one or (hopefully) more products.

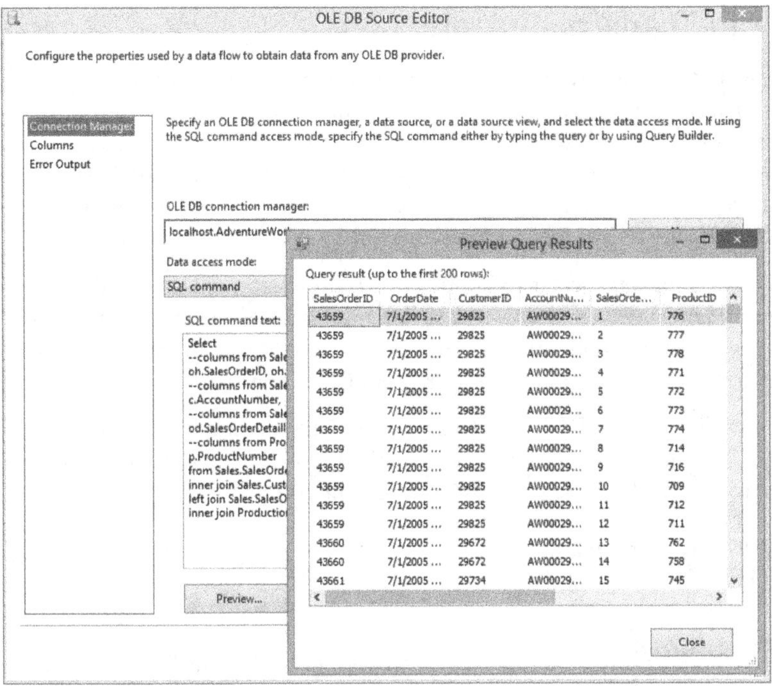

FIGURE 7-8

Close the preview dialog; click OK on the OLE DB Source Editor UI, and then hook up the Source Component to a Union All Transformation as shown in Figure 7-9, which serves as a temporary destination. Add a Data Viewer to the pipeline in order to watch the data travel through the system. Execute the package in debug mode and notice that the required results appear in the Data Viewer window.

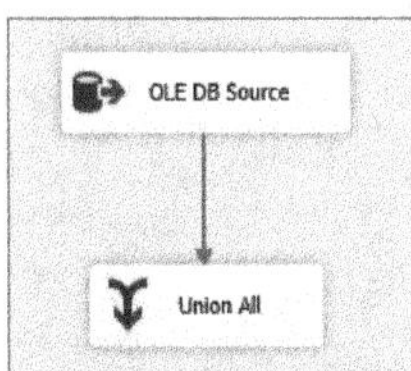

FIGURE 7-9

The Union All Transformation has nothing to do with this specific solution; it serves simply as a dead end in the Data Flow in order to get a temporary trash destination so that you don't have to physically land the data in a database or file. This is a great way to test your Data Flows during development; placing a Data Viewer just before the Union All gives you a quick peek at the data. After development you would need to replace the Union All with a real destination. Note that you could also use some other component such as the Conditional Split. Keep in mind that some components, like the Row Count, require extra setup (such as variables), which would make this approach more cumbersome. Third-party tools are also available (such as Task Factory by Pragmatic Works) that have trash destinations for testing purposes only.

Using the Merge Join Transformation

Another way you could perform the join is to use Merge Join Transformations. In this specific scenario it does not make much sense because the database will likely perform the most optimal joins, as all the data resides in one place. However, consider a system in which the four tables you are joining reside in different locations; perhaps the sales and customer data is in SQL Server, and the product data is in a flat file, which is dumped nightly from a mainframe. The following steps explain how you can build a package to emulate such a scenario:

1. Start again with the basic package (refer to Figure 7-7) and proceed as follows. Because you do not have any actual text files as sources, you will create them inside the same package and then utilize them as needed. Of course, a real solution would not require this step; you just need to do this so that you can emulate a more complex scenario.
2. Name the empty Data Flow Task "DFT Create Text Files." Inside this task create a pipeline that selects the required columns from the Product table in the AdventureWorks database and writes the data to a text file. Here is the SQL statement you will need:

```
select ProductID, ProductNumber
from Production.Product;
```

3. Connect the source to a Flat File destination and then configure the Flat File Destination Component to write to a location of your choice on your local hard drive, and make sure you select the delimited option and specify column headers when configuring the destination options, as shown in Figure 7-10. Name the flat file `Product.txt`.

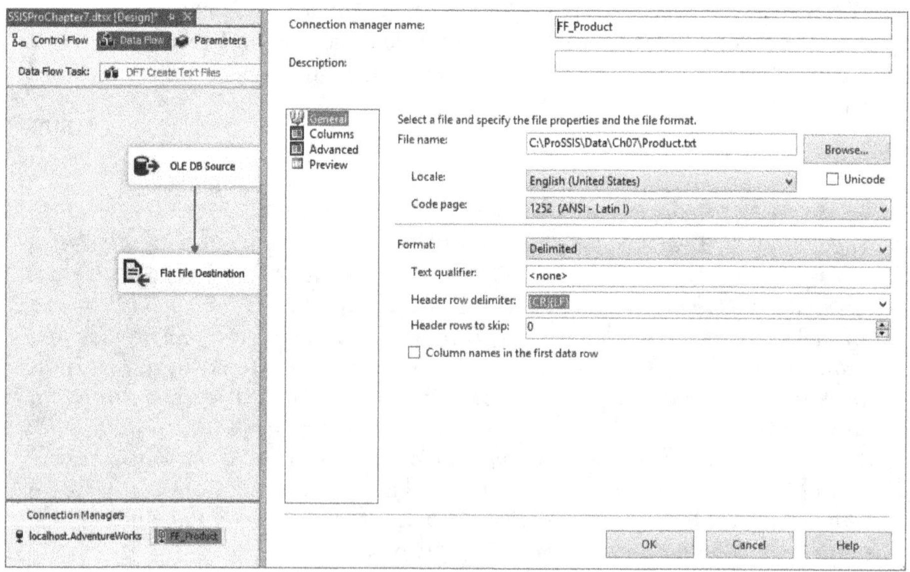

FIGURE 7-10

4. Execute the package to create a text file containing the Product data. Now create a second Data Flow Task and rename it "DFT Extract Source." Connect the first and second Data Flow Tasks with a precedence constraint so that they execute serially, as shown in Figure 7-11. Inside the second (new) Data Flow Task, you'll use the Lookup and Merge Join solutions to achieve the same result you did previously.

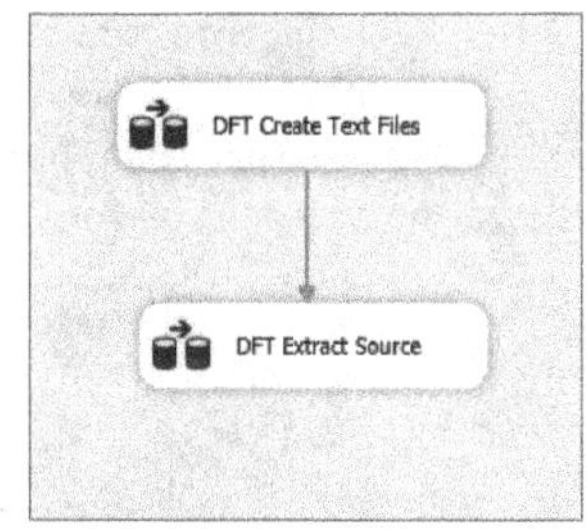

FIGURE 7-11

When using the Lookup Transformation, make sure that the largest table (usually a fact table) is streamed into the component, and the smallest table (usually a dimension table) is cached. That's because the table that is cached will block the flow while it is loaded into memory, so you want to make sure it is as small as possible. Data Flow execution cannot begin until all Lookup data is loaded into memory. Since all of the data is loaded into memory, it makes the 3GB process limit on 32-bit systems a real challenge. In this case, all the tables are small, but imagine that the order header and details data is the largest, so you don't want to incur the overhead of caching it. Thus, you can use a Merge Join Transformation instead of a Lookup to achieve the same result, without the overhead of caching a large amount of data. In some situations you can't control the table's server location, used in the Lookup, because the source data needs to run through multiple Lookups. A good example of this multiple Lookup Data Flow would be the loading of a fact table.

The simplest solution for retrieving the relational data would be to join the order header and order details tables directly in the Source Component (in a similar manner to that shown earlier). However, the following steps take a more complex route in order to illustrate some of the other options available:

1. Drop an OLE DB Source Component on the design surface of the second Data Flow Task and name it "SRC Order Header." Hook it up to the AdventureWorks Connection Manager and use the following statement as the query:

```
select SalesOrderID, OrderDate, CustomerID
from Sales.SalesOrderHeader;
```

Of course, you could just choose the Table or View option in the source UI, or use a `select*` *query, and perhaps even deselect specific columns in the Columns tab of the UI. However, these are all bad practices that will usually lead to degraded performance. It is imperative that, where possible, you specify the exact columns you require in the select clause. Furthermore, you should use a predicate (*`where` *clause) to limit the number of rows returned to just the ones you need.*

2. Confirm that the query executes successfully by using the Preview button, and then hook up a Sort Transformation downstream of the source you have just created. Open the editor for the Sort Transformation and choose to sort the data by the SalesOrderID column, as shown in Figure 7-12. The reason you do this is because you will use a Merge Join Transformation

later, and it requires sorted input streams. (Note that the Lookup Transformation does not require sorted inputs.) Also, an ORDER BY clause in the source would be better for performance, but this example is giving you experience with the Sort Transform.

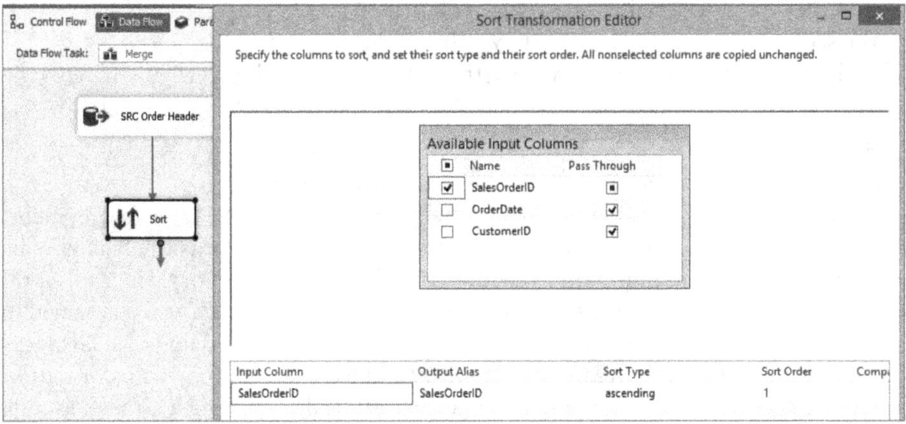

FIGURE 7-12

3. To retrieve the SalesOrderDetails data, drop another OLE DB Source Component on the design surface, name it SRC Details, and set its query as follows. Notice how in this case you have included an ORDER BY clause directly in the SQL select statement. This is more efficient than the way you sorted the order header data, because SQL Server can sort it for you before passing it out-of-process to SSIS. Again, you will see different methods to illustrate the various options available:

```
select SalesOrderID, SalesOrderDetailID, ProductID, OrderQty, UnitPrice,
LineTotal
from Sales.SalesOrderDetail
order by SalesOrderID, SalesOrderDetailID, ProductID;
```

4. Now drop a Merge Join Transformation on the surface and connect the outputs from the two Source Components to it. Specify the input coming from SRC Header (via the Sort Transformation) to be the left input, and the input coming from SRC Details to be the right input. You need to do this because, as discussed previously, you want to use a left join in order to keep rows from the header that do not have corresponding detail records.

After connecting both inputs, try to open the editor for the Merge Join Transformation; you should receive an error stating that "The IsSorted property must be set to True on both sources of this transformation." The reason you get this error is because the Merge Join Transformation requires inputs that are sorted exactly the same way. However, you did ensure this by using a Sort Transformation on one stream and an explicit T-SQL ORDER BY clause on the other stream, so what's going on? The simple answer is that the OLE DB Source Component works in a pass-through manner, so it doesn't know that the ORDER BY clause was specified in the second SQL query statement due to the fact that the metadata returned by SQL Server includes column names, positions, and data types but does not include the sort order. By using the Sort Transformation, you forced SSIS to perform the sort, so it is fully aware of the ordering.

In order to remedy this situation, you have to tell the Source Transformation that its input data is presorted. Be very careful when doing this — by specifying the sort order in the following way, you are asking the system to trust that you know what you are talking about and that the data is in fact sorted. If the data is not sorted, or it is sorted other than the way you specified, then your package can act unpredictably, which could lead to data integrity issues and data loss. Use the following steps to specify the sort order:

1. Right-click the SRC Details Component and choose Show Advanced Editor. Select the Input and Output Properties tab, shown in Figure 7-13, and click the Root Node for the default output (not the error output). In the property grid on the right-hand side is a property called IsSorted. Change this to True.

FIGURE 7-13

2. The preceding step tells the component that the data is presorted, but it does not indicate the order. Therefore, the next step is to select the columns that are being sorted on, and assign them values as follows:
   - If the column is not sorted, then the value should be zero.
   - If the column is sorted in ascending order, then the value should be positive.
   - If the column is sorted in descending order, then the value should be negative.

   The absolute value of the number should correspond to the column's position in the order list. For instance, if the query was sorted as follows, "SalesOrderID ascending, ProductID descending," then you would assign the value 1 to SalesOrderID and the value -2 to ProductID, with all other columns being 0.

3. Expand the Output Columns Node under the same default Output Node, and then select the SalesOrderID column. In the property grid, set the SortKeyPosition value to 1, as shown in Figure 7-14.

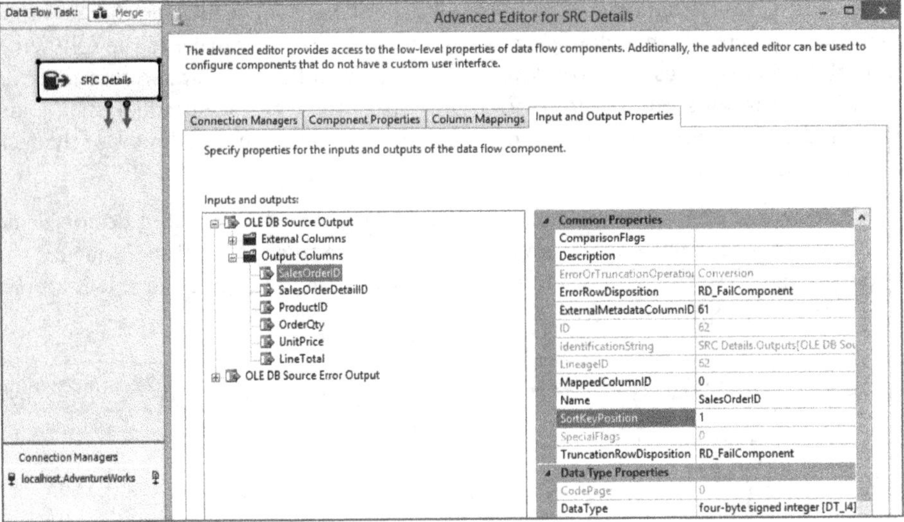

FIGURE 7-14

4. Close the dialog and try again to open the Merge Join UI; this time you should be successful. By default, the component works in inner join mode, but you can change that very easily by selecting (in this case) Left Outer Join from the Join type dropdown (see Figure 7-15). You can also choose a Full Outer Join, which would perform a Cartesian join of all the data, though depending on the size of the source data, this will have a high memory overhead.

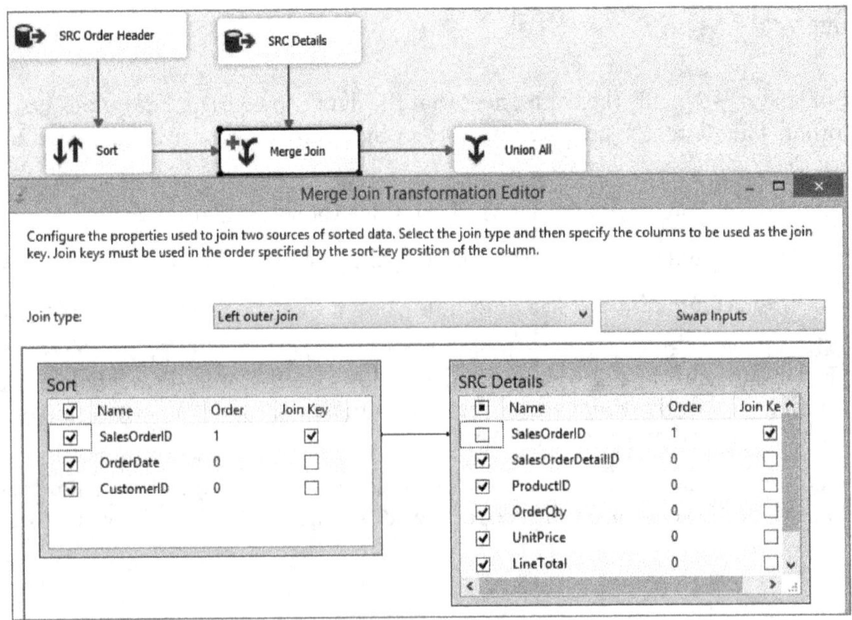

FIGURE 7-15

5. If you had made a mistake earlier while specifying which input was the left and which was the right, you can click the Swap Inputs button to switch their places. The component will automatically figure out which columns you are joining on based on their sort orders; if it gets it wrong, or there are more columns you need to join on, you can drag a column from the left to the right in order to specify more join criteria. However, the component will refuse any column combinations that are not part of the ordering criteria.
6. Finally, drop a Union All Transformation on the surface and connect the output of the Merge Join Transformation to it. Place a Data Viewer on the output path of the Merge Join Transformation and execute the package. Check the results in the Data Viewer; the data should be joined as required.

Merge Join is a useful component to use when memory limits or data size restricts you from using a Lookup Transformation. However, it requires the sorting of both input streams — which may be challenging to do with large data sets — and by design it does not provide any way of caching either data set. The next section examines the Lookup Transformation, which can help you solve join problems in a different way.

USING THE LOOKUP TRANSFORMATION

The Lookup Transformation solves join differently than the Merge Join Transformation. The Lookup Transformation typically caches one of the data sets in memory, and then compares each row arriving from the other data set in its input pipeline against the cache. The caching mechanism is highly configurable, providing a variety of different options in order to balance the performance and resource utilization of the process.

Full-Cache Mode

In full-cache mode, the Lookup Transformation stores all the rows resulting from a specified query in memory. The benefit of this mode is that Lookups against the in-memory cache are very fast — often an order of magnitude or more, relative to a no-cache mode Lookup. Full-cache mode is the default because in most scenarios it has the best performance of all of the techniques discussed in the chapter.

Continuing with the example package you built in the previous section ("Using the Merge Join Transformation"), you will in this section extend the existing package in order to join the other required tables. You already have the related values from the order header and order detail tables, but you still need to map the natural keys from the Product and Customer tables. You could use Merge Join Transformations again, but this example demonstrates how the Lookup Transformation can be of use here:

1. Open the package you created in the previous step. Remove the Union All Transformation. Drop a Lookup Transformation on the surface, name it **LKP Customer**, and connect the output of the Merge Join Transformation to it. Open the editor of the Lookup Transformation.

2. Select Full-Cache Mode, specifying an OLE DB Connection Manager. There is also an option to specify a Cache Connection Manager (CCM), but you won't use this just yet — later in this chapter you will learn how to use the CCM. (After you have learned about the CCM, you can return to this exercise and try to use it here instead of the OLE DB Connection Manager.)
3. Click the Connection tab and select the AdventureWorks connection, and then use the following SQL query:

```
select CustomerID, AccountNumber
from Sales.Customer;
```

4. Preview the results to ensure that everything is set up OK, then click the Columns tab. Drag the CustomerID column from the left-hand table over to the CustomerID column on the right; this creates a linkage between these two columns, which tells the component that this column is used to perform the join. Click the checkbox next to the AccountNumber column on the right, which tells the component that you want to retrieve the AccountNumber values from the Customer table for each row it compares. Note that it is not necessary to retrieve the CustomerID values from the right-hand side because you already have them from the input columns. The editor should now look like Figure 7-16.

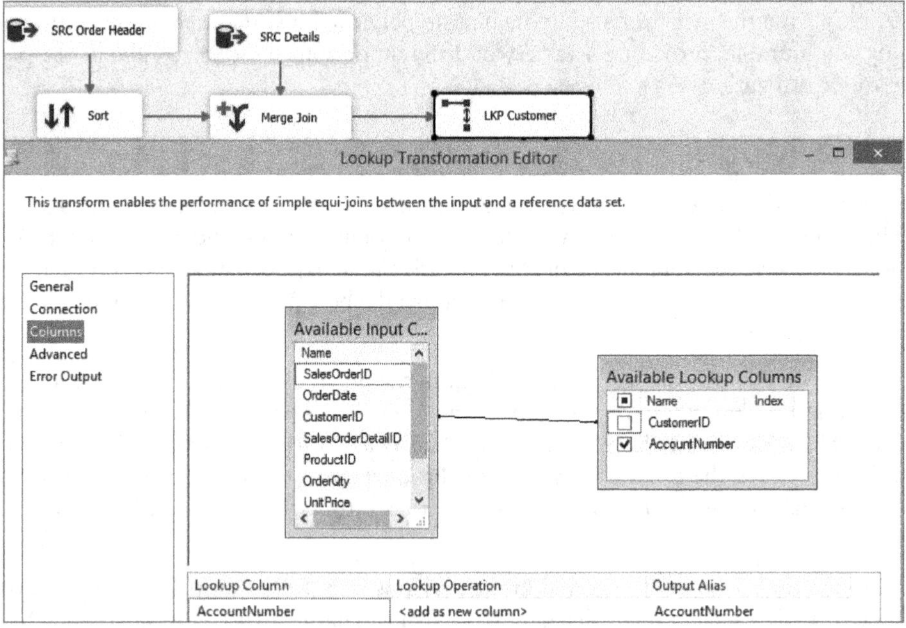

FIGURE 7-16

5. Click OK on the dialog, hook up a "trash" Union All Transformation (refer to Figure 7-9, choosing Lookup Match Output on the dialog that is invoked when you do this). Create a Data Viewer on the match output path of the Lookup Transformation and execute the package (you could also attach a Data Viewer on the no-match output and error output if needed). You should see results similar to Figure 7-17. Notice you have all the columns from the order and details data, as well as the selected column from the Customer table.

Lookup Match Output Data Viewer at DFT Extract Source

Detach | Copy Data

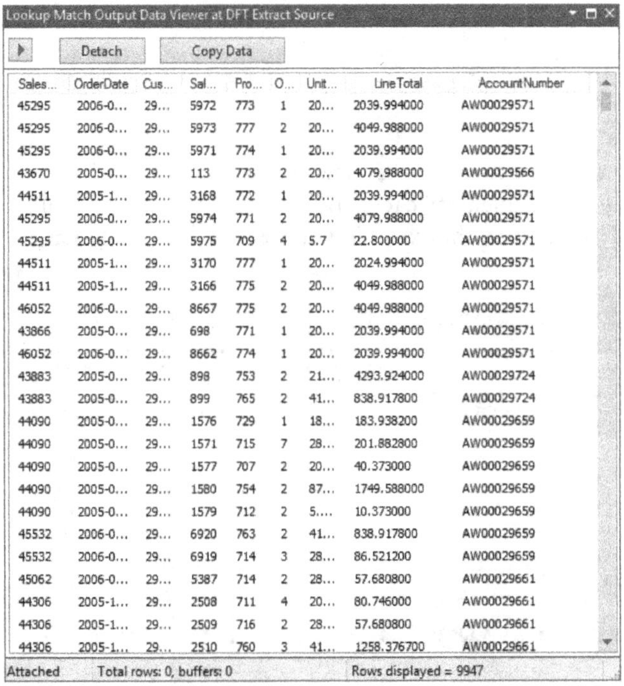

Sales...	OrderDate	Cus...	Sal...	Pro...	O...	Unit...	LineTotal	AccountNumber
45295	2006-0...	29...	5972	773	1	20...	2039.994000	AW00029571
45295	2006-0...	29...	5973	777	2	20...	4049.988000	AW00029571
45295	2006-0...	29...	5971	774	1	20...	2039.994000	AW00029571
43670	2005-0...	29...	113	773	2	20...	4079.988000	AW00029566
44511	2005-1...	29...	3168	772	1	20...	2039.994000	AW00029571
45295	2006-0...	29...	5974	771	2	20...	4079.988000	AW00029571
45295	2006-0...	29...	5975	709	4	5.7	22.800000	AW00029571
44511	2005-1...	29...	3170	777	1	20...	2024.994000	AW00029571
44511	2005-1...	29...	3166	775	2	20...	4049.988000	AW00029571
46052	2006-0...	29...	8667	775	2	20...	4049.988000	AW00029571
43866	2005-0...	29...	698	771	1	20...	2039.994000	AW00029571
46052	2006-0...	29...	8662	774	1	20...	2039.994000	AW00029571
43883	2005-0...	29...	898	753	2	21...	4293.924000	AW00029724
43883	2005-0...	29...	899	765	2	41...	838.917800	AW00029724
44090	2005-0...	29...	1576	729	1	18...	183.938200	AW00029659
44090	2005-0...	29...	1571	715	7	28...	201.882800	AW00029659
44090	2005-0...	29...	1577	707	2	20...	40.373000	AW00029659
44090	2005-0...	29...	1580	754	2	87...	1749.588000	AW00029659
44090	2005-0...	29...	1579	712	2	5....	10.373000	AW00029659
45532	2006-0...	29...	6920	763	2	41...	838.917800	AW00029659
45532	2006-0...	29...	6919	714	3	28...	86.521200	AW00029659
45062	2006-0...	29...	5387	714	2	28...	57.680800	AW00029661
44306	2005-1...	29...	2508	711	4	20...	80.746000	AW00029661
44306	2005-1...	29...	2509	716	2	28...	57.680800	AW00029661
44306	2005-1...	29...	2510	760	3	41...	1258.376700	AW00029661

Attached | Total rows: 0, buffers: 0 | Rows displayed = 9947

FIGURE 7-17

Because the Customer table is so small and the package runs so fast, you may not have noticed what happened here. As part of the pre-execution phase of the component, the Lookup Transformation fetched all the rows from the Customer table using the query specified (because the Lookup was configured to execute in full-cache mode). In this case there are only 20,000 or so rows, so this happens very quickly. Imagine that there were many more rows, perhaps two million. In this case you would likely experience a delay between executing the package and seeing any data actually traveling down the second pipeline.

Figure 7-18 shows a decision tree that demonstrates how the Lookup Transformation in full-cache mode operates at runtime. Note that the Lookup Transformation can be configured to send found and not-found rows to the same output, but the illustration assumes they are going to different outputs. In either case, the basic algorithm is the same.

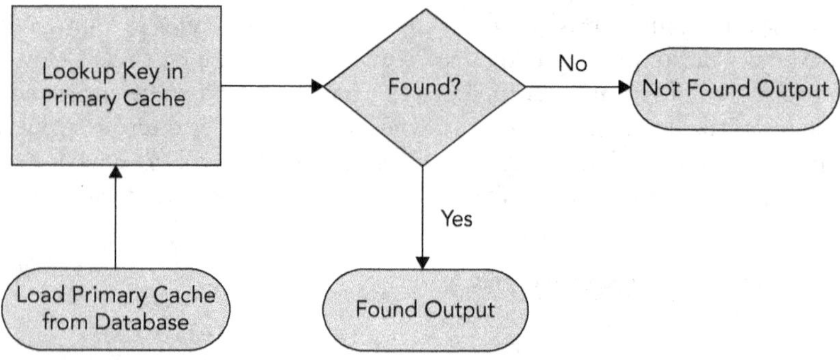

FIGURE 7-18

Check the Execution Results tab on the SSIS design surface (see Figure 7-19) and see how long it took for the data to be loaded into the in-memory cache. In larger data sets this number will be much larger and could even take longer than the execution of the primary functionality!

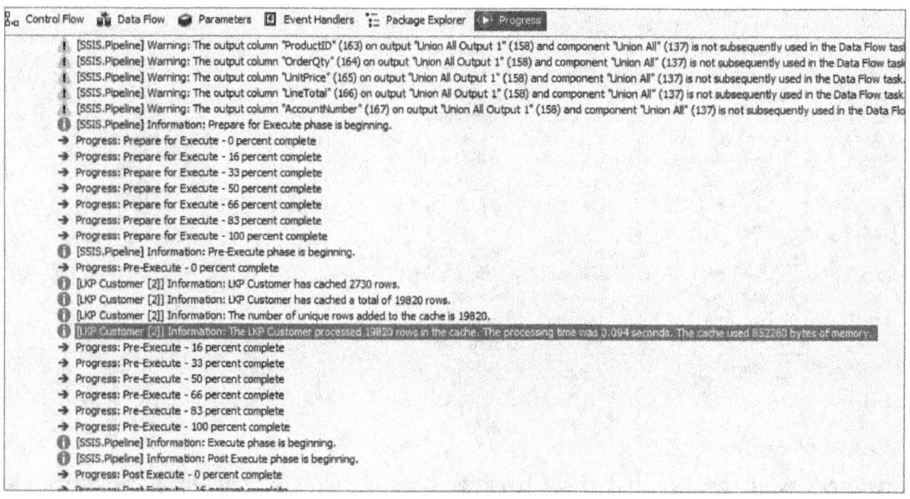

FIGURE 7-19

If during development and testing you want to emulate a long-running query, use the T-SQL `waitfor` *statement in the query in the following manner.*

```
waitfor delay '00:00:059'; --Wait 5 seconds before returning any
    rows
select CustomerID, AccountNumber
from Sales.Customer;
```

After fetching all the rows from the specified source, the Lookup Transformation caches them in memory in a special hash structure. The package then continues execution; as each input row enters the Lookup Transformation, the specified key values are compared to the in-memory hash values, and, if a match is found, the specified return values are added to the output stream.

No-Cache Mode

If the reference table (the Customer table in this case) is too large to cache all at once in the system's memory, you can choose to cache nothing or you can choose to cache only some of the data. This section explores the first option: no-cache mode.

In no-cache mode, the Lookup Transformation is configured almost exactly the same as in full-cache mode, but at execution time the reference table is not loaded into the hash structure. Instead, as each input row flows through the Lookup Transformation, the component sends a request to the reference table in the database server to ask for a match. As you would expect, this can have a high performance overhead on the system, so use this mode with care.

Depending on the size of the reference data, this mode is usually the slowest, though it scales to the largest number of reference rows. It is also useful for systems in which the reference data is highly volatile, such that any form of caching would render the results stale and erroneous.

Figure 7-20 illustrates the decision tree that the component uses during runtime. As before, the diagram assumes that separate outputs are configured for found and not-found rows, though the algorithm would be the same if all rows were sent to a single output.

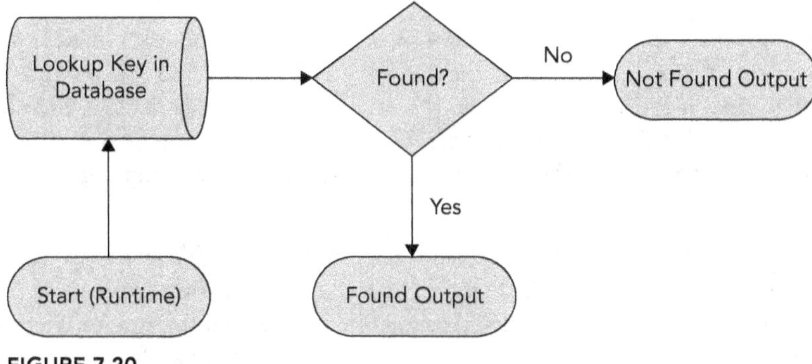

FIGURE 7-20

Here are the steps to build a package that uses no-cache mode:

1. Rather than build a brand-new package to try out no-cache mode, use the package you built in the previous section ("Full-Cache Mode"). Open the editor for the Lookup Transformation and on the first tab (General), choose the No-Cache option. This mode also enables you to customize (optimize) the query that SSIS will submit to the relational engine. To do this, click the Advanced tab and check the Modify the SQL Statement checkbox. In this case, the auto-generated statement is close enough to optimal, so you don't need to touch it. (If you have any problems reconfiguring the Lookup Transformation, then delete the component, drop a new Lookup on the design surface, and reconnect and configure it from scratch.)

2. Execute the package. It should take slightly longer to execute than before, but the results should be the same.

The trade-off you make between the caching modes is one of performance versus resource utilization. Full-cache mode can potentially use a lot of memory to hold the reference rows in memory, but it is usually the fastest because Lookup operations do not require a trip to the database. No-cache mode, on the other hand, requires next to no memory, but it's slower because it requires a database call for every Lookup. This is not a bad thing; if your reference table is volatile (i.e., the data changes often), you may want to use no-cache mode to ensure that you always have the latest version of each row.

Partial-Cache Mode

Partial-cache mode gives you a middle ground between the no-cache and full-cache options. In this mode, the component caches only the most recently used data within the memory boundaries specified under the Advanced tab in the Lookup Transform. As soon as the cache grows too big, the least-used cache data is thrown away.

When the package starts, much like in no-cache mode, no data is preloaded into the Lookup cache. As each input row enters the component, it uses the specified key(s) to attempt to find a matching record in the reference table using the specified query. If a match is found, then both the key and the Lookup values are added to the local cache on a just-in-time basis. If that same key enters the Lookup Transformation again, it can retrieve the matching value from the local cache instead of the reference table, thereby saving the expense and time incurred of requerying the database.

In the example scenario, for instance, suppose the input stream contains a CustomerID of 123. The first time the component sees this value, it goes to the database and tries to find it using the specified query. If it finds the value, it retrieves the AccountNumber and then adds the CustomerID/AccountNumber combination to its local cache. If CustomerCD 123 comes through again later, the component will retrieve the AccountNumber directly from the local cache instead of going to the database.

If, however, the key is not found in the local cache, the component will check the database to see if it exists there. Note that the key may not be in the local cache for several reasons: maybe it is the first time it was seen, maybe it was previously in the local cache but was evicted because of memory pressure, or finally, it could have been seen before but was also not found in the database.

For example, if CustomerID 456 enters the component, it will check the local cache for the value. Assuming it is not found, it will then check the database. If it finds it in the database, it will add 456 to its local cache. The next time CustomerID 456 enters the component, it can retrieve the value directly from its local cache without going to the database. However, it could also be the case that memory pressure caused this key/value to be dropped from the local cache, in which case the component will incur another database call.

If CustomerID 789 is not found in the local cache, and it is not subsequently found in the reference table, the component will treat the row as a nonmatch, and will send it down the output you have chosen for nonmatched rows (typically the no-match or error output). Every time that CustomerID

789 enters the component, it will go through these same set of operations. If you have a high degree of expected misses in your Lookup scenario, this latter behavior — though proper and expected — can be a cause of long execution times because database calls are expensive relative to a local cache check.

To avoid these repeated database calls while still getting the benefit of partial-cache mode, you can use another feature of the Lookup Transformation: the miss cache. Using the partial-cache and miss-cache options together, you can realize further performance gains. You can specify that the component remembers values that it did not previously find in the reference table, thereby avoiding the expense of looking for them again. This feature goes a long way toward solving the performance issues discussed in the previous paragraph, because ideally every key is looked for once — and only once — in the reference table.

To configure this mode, follow these steps (refer to Figure 7-21):

1. Open the Lookup editor, and in the General tab select the Partial Cache option. In the Advanced tab, specify the upper memory boundaries for the cache and edit the SQL statement as necessary. Note that both 32-bit and 64-bit boundaries are available because the package may be built and tested on a 32-bit platform but deployed to a 64-bit platform, which has more memory. Providing both options makes it simple to configure the component's behavior on both platforms.

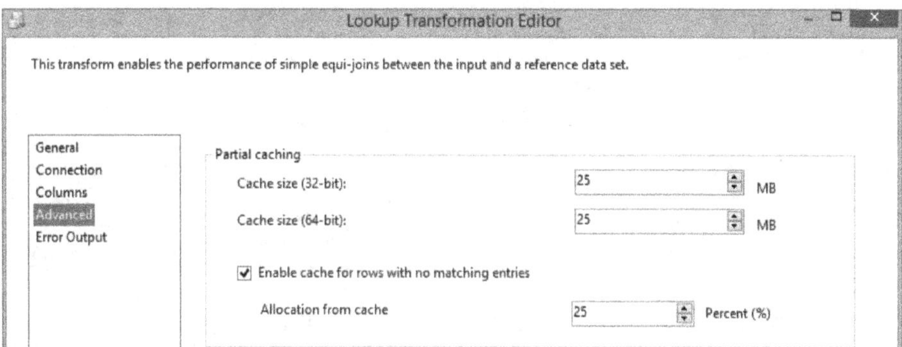

FIGURE 7-21

2. If you want to use the miss-cache feature, configure what percentage of the total cache memory you want to use for this secondary cache (say, 25%).

The decision tree shown in Figure 7-22 demonstrates how the Lookup Transformation operates at runtime when using the partial-cache and miss-cache options. Note that some of the steps are conceptual; in reality, they are implemented using a more optimal design. As per the decision trees shown for the other modes, this illustration assumes separate outputs are used for the found and not-found rows.

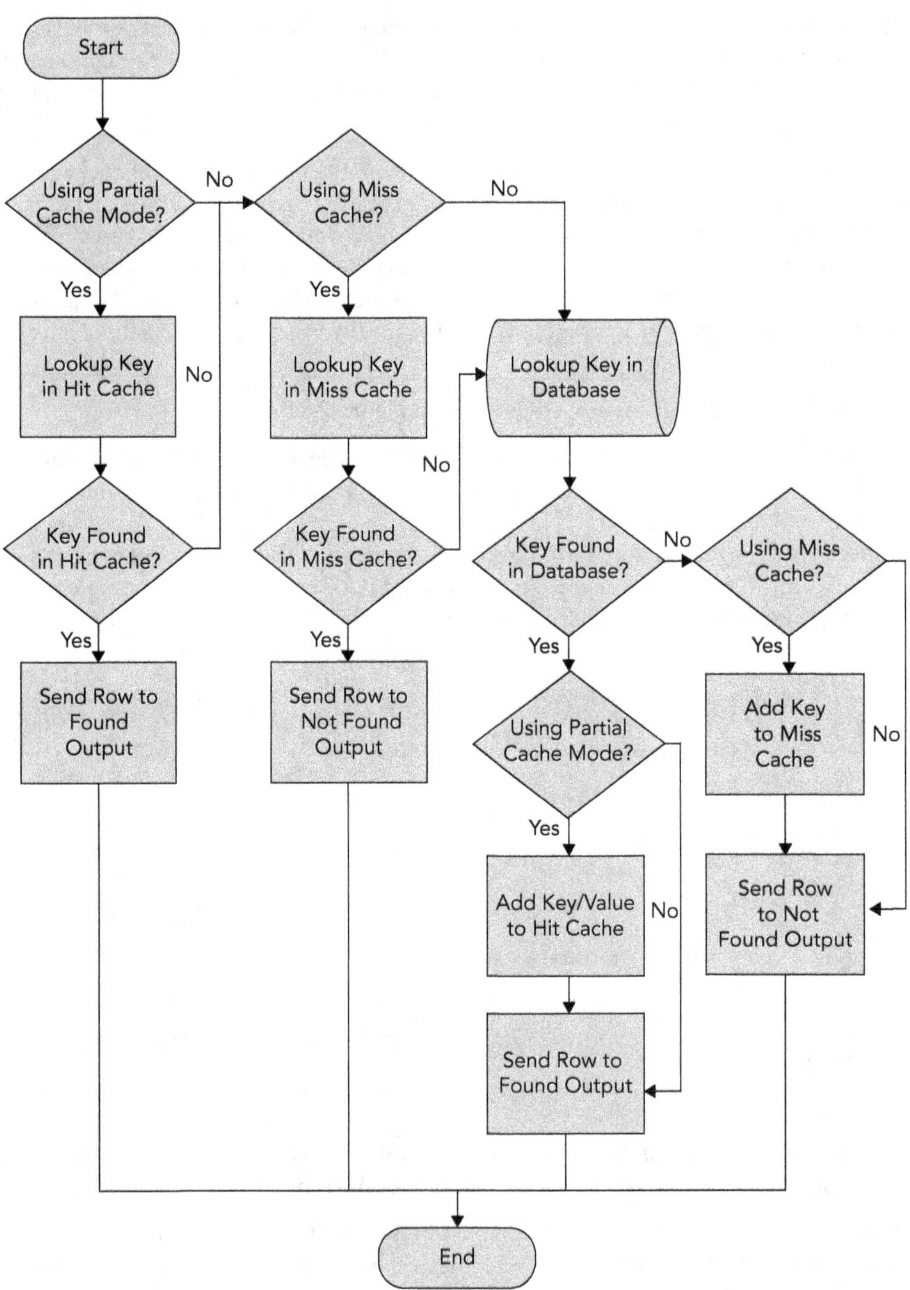
Start
Using Partial Cache Mode?
No
Yes
Using Miss Cache?
No
Yes
Lookup Key in Hit Cache
No
Lookup Key in Miss Cache
Lookup Key in Database
No
Key Found in Hit Cache?
Yes
Key Found in Miss Cache?
Yes
Key Found in Database?
No
Using Miss Cache?
Yes
Yes
Send Row to Found Output
Send Row to Not Found Output
Using Partial Cache Mode?
Add Key to Miss Cache
No
Yes
Add Key/Value to Hit Cache
No
Send Row to Not Found Output
Send Row to Found Output
End

FIGURE 7-22

Multiple Outputs

At this point, your Lookup Transformation is working, and you have learned different ways to optimize its performance using fewer or more resources. In this section, you'll learn how to utilize some of the other features in the component, such as the different outputs that are available.

Using the same package you built in the previous sections, follow these steps:

1. Reset the Lookup Transformation so that it works in full-cache mode. It so happens that, in this example, the data is clean and thus every row finds a match, but you can emulate rows not being found by playing quick and dirty with the Lookup query string. This is a useful trick to use at design time in order to test the robustness and behavior of your Lookup Transformations. Change the query statement in the Lookup Transformation as follows:

```
select CustomerID, AccountNumber
from Sales.Customer
where CustomerID % 7 <> 0; --Remove 1/7 of the rows
```

2. Run the package again. This time, it should fail to execute fully because the cache contains one-seventh fewer rows than before, so some of the incoming keys will not find a match, as shown in Figure 7-23. Because the default error behavior of the component is to fail on any nonmatch or error condition such as truncation, the Lookup halts as expected.

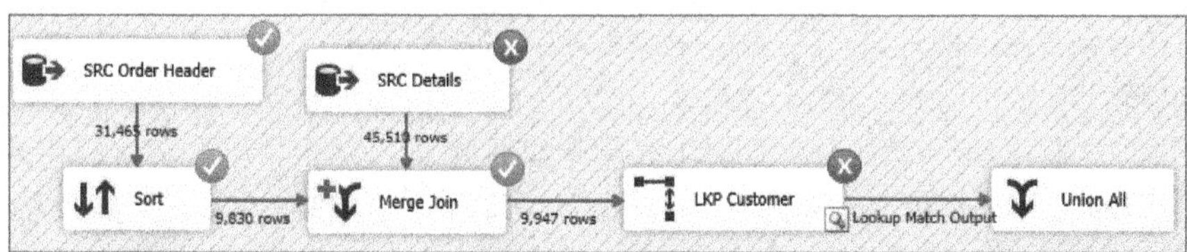

FIGURE 7-23

Try some of the other output options. Open the Lookup editor and on the dropdown listbox in the General tab, choose how you want the Lookup Transformation to behave when it does not manage to find a matching join entry:

- Fail Component should already be selected. This is the default behavior, which causes the component to raise an exception and halt execution if a nonmatching row is found or a row causes an error such as data truncation.
- Ignore Failure sends any nonmatched rows and rows that cause errors down the same output as the matched rows, but the Lookup values (in this case AccountNumber) will be set to null. If you add a Data Viewer to the flow, you should be able to see this; several of the AccountNumbers will have null values.
- Redirect Rows to Error Output is provided for backward compatibility with SQL Server 2005. It causes the component to send both nonmatched and error-causing rows down the same error (red) output.
- Redirect Rows to No Match Output causes errors to flow down the error (red) output, and no-match rows to flow down the no-match output.

3. Choose Ignore Failure and execute the package. The results should look like Figure 7-24. You can see that the number of incoming rows on the Lookup Transformation matches the number of rows coming out of its match output, even though one-seventh of the rows were not actually matched. This is because the rows failed to find a match, but because you configured the Ignore Failure option, the component did not stop execution.

Lookup Match Output Data Viewer at DFT Extract Source

Detach | Copy Data

Sal...	OrderDate	Cus...	Sal...	Pro...	O...	Unit...	LineTotal	AccountNu...
43...	2005-0...	29...	561	707	1	20...	20.186500	AW00029...
43...	2005-0...	29...	562	725	1	18...	183.938200	AW00029...
43...	2005-0...	29...	563	754	1	87...	874.794000	AW00029...
43...	2005-0...	29...	564	738	3	17...	535.742400	AW00029...
43...	2005-0...	29...	565	753	1	21...	2146.962000	AW00029...
43...	2005-0...	29...	566	765	1	41...	419.458900	AW00029...
43...	2005-0...	29...	567	712	1	5....	5.186500	AW00029...
43...	2005-0...	29...	568	708	3	20...	60.559500	AW00029...
43...	2005-0...	29...	569	776	1	20...	2024.994000	NULL
43...	2005-0...	29...	570	777	2	20...	4049.988000	NULL
43...	2005-0...	29...	571	773	1	20...	2039.994000	NULL
43...	2005-0...	29...	572	771	1	20...	2039.994000	NULL
43...	2005-0...	29...	573	776	4	20...	8099.976000	NULL
43...	2005-0...	29...	574	775	2	20...	4049.988000	NULL
43...	2005-0...	29...	575	778	3	20...	6074.982000	NULL
43...	2005-0...	29...	576	758	2	87...	1749.588000	NULL
43...	2005-0...	29...	577	765	2	41...	838.917800	NULL

Attached Total rows: 0, buffers: 0 Rows displayed = 9947

FIGURE 7-24

4. Open the Lookup Transformation and this time select "Redirect rows to error output." In order to make this option work, you need a second trash destination on the error output of the Lookup Transformation, as shown in Figure 7-25. When you execute the package using this mode, the found rows will be sent down the match output, and unlike the previous modes, not-found rows will not be ignored or cause the component to fail but will instead be sent down the error output.

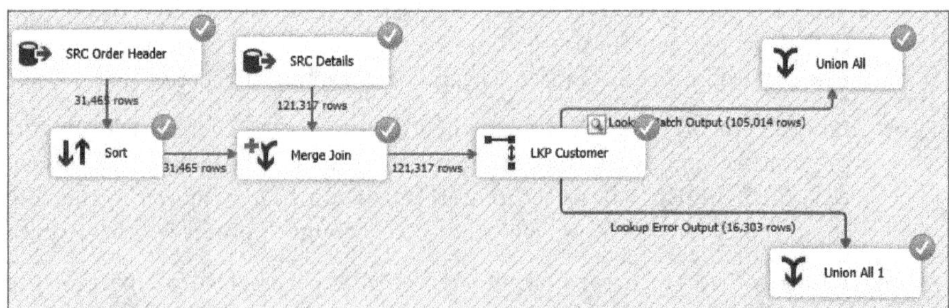

FIGURE 7-25

5. Finally, test the "Redirect rows to no match output" mode. You will need a total of three trash destinations for this to work, as shown in Figure 7-26.

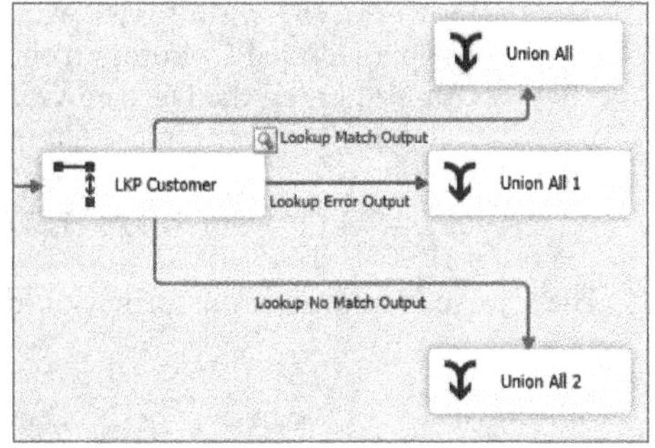

FIGURE 7-26

In all cases, add Data Viewers to each output, execute the package, and examine the results. The outputs should not contain any errors such as truncations, though there should be many nonmatched rows.

So how exactly are these outputs useful? What can you do with them to make your packages more robust? In most cases, the errors or nonmatched rows can be piped off to a different area of the package where the values can be logged or fixed as per the business requirements. For example, one common solution is for all missing rows to be tagged with an Unknown member value. In this scenario, all nonmatched rows might have their AccountNumber set to 0000. These fixed values are then joined back into the main Data Flow and from there treated the same as the rows that did find a match. Use the following steps to configure the package to do this:

1. Open the Lookup editor. On the General tab, choose the "Redirect rows to no match output" option. Click the Error Output tab (see Figure 7-27) and configure the AccountNumber column to have the value Fail Component under the Truncation column. This combination of settings means that you want a no-match output, but you don't want an error output; instead you want the component to fail on any errors. In a real-world scenario, you may want to have an error output that you can use to log values to an error table, but this example keeps it simple.

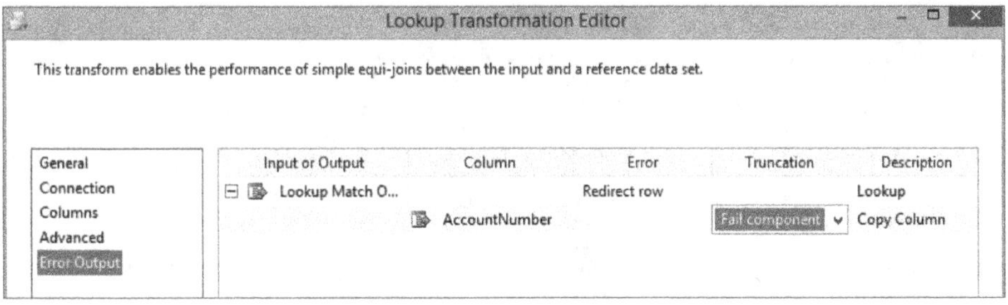

FIGURE 7-27

2. At this point, you could drop a Derived Column Transformation on the design surface and connect the no-match output to it. Then you would add the AccountNumber column in the derived column, and use a Union All to bring the data back together. This approach works, but the partially blocking Union All slows down performance.

However, there is a better way to design the Data Flow. Set the Lookup to Ignore Errors. Drop a Derived Column on the Data Flow. Connect the match output to the derived column. Open the Derived Column editor and replace the AccountNumber column with the following expression (see Chapter 5 for more details).

```
ISNULL(AccountNumber)?(DT_STR,10,1252)"0000":AccountNumber
```

The Derived Column Transformation dialog editor should now look something like Figure 7-28.

Derived Column Name	Derived Column	Expression	Data Type
AccountNumber	Replace 'AccountNumber'	ISNULL(AccountNumber) ? (DT_STR,10,1252)"0000" : Ac...	string [DT_STR]

FIGURE 7-28

Close the Derived Column editor, and drop a Union All Transformation on the surface. Connect the default output from the Derived Column to the Union All Transformation and then execute the package, as usual utilizing a Data Viewer on the final output. The package and results should look something like Figure 7-29.

The output should show AccountNumbers for most of the values, with 0000 shown for those keys that are not present in the reference query (in this case because you artificially removed them).

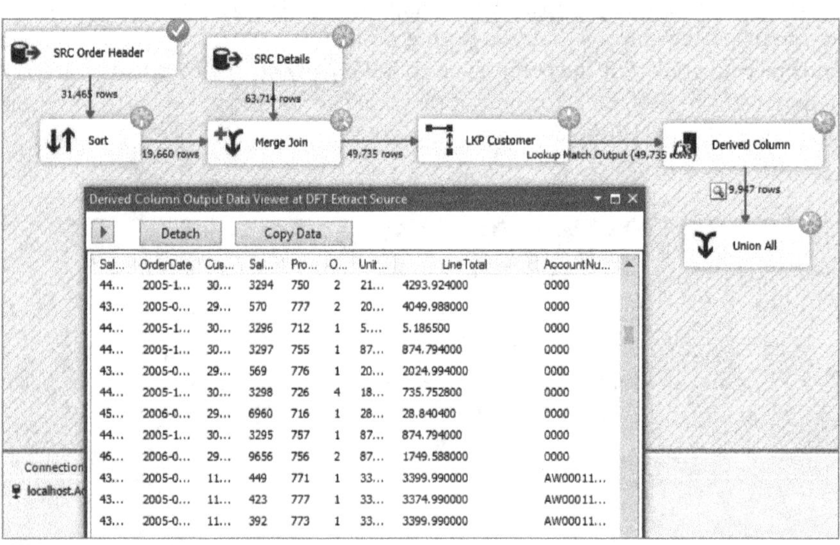

Sal...	OrderDate	Cus...	Sal...	Pro...	O...	Unit...	LineTotal	AccountNu...
44...	2005-1...	30...	3294	750	2	21...	4293.924000	0000
43...	2005-0...	29...	570	777	2	20...	4049.988000	0000
44...	2005-1...	30...	3296	712	1	5....	5.186500	0000
44...	2005-1...	30...	3297	755	1	87...	874.794000	0000
43...	2005-0...	29...	569	776	1	20...	2024.994000	0000
44...	2005-1...	30...	3298	726	4	18...	735.752800	0000
45...	2006-0...	29...	6960	716	1	28...	28.840400	0000
44...	2005-1...	30...	3295	757	1	87...	874.794000	0000
46...	2006-0...	29...	9656	756	2	87...	1749.588000	0000
43...	2005-0...	11...	449	771	1	33...	3399.990000	AW00011...
43...	2005-0...	11...	423	777	1	33...	3374.990000	AW00011...
43...	2005-0...	11...	392	773	1	33...	3399.990000	AW00011...

FIGURE 7-29

Expressionable Properties

If you need to build a package whose required reference table is not known at design time, this feature will be useful for you. Instead of using a static query in the Lookup Transformation, you can use an expression, which can dynamically construct the query string, or it could load the query string using the parameters feature. Parameters are discussed in Chapter 5 and Chapter 22.

Figure 7-30 shows an example of using an expression within a Lookup Transformation. Expressions on Data Flow Components can be accessed from the property page of the Data Flow Task itself. See Chapter 5 for more details.

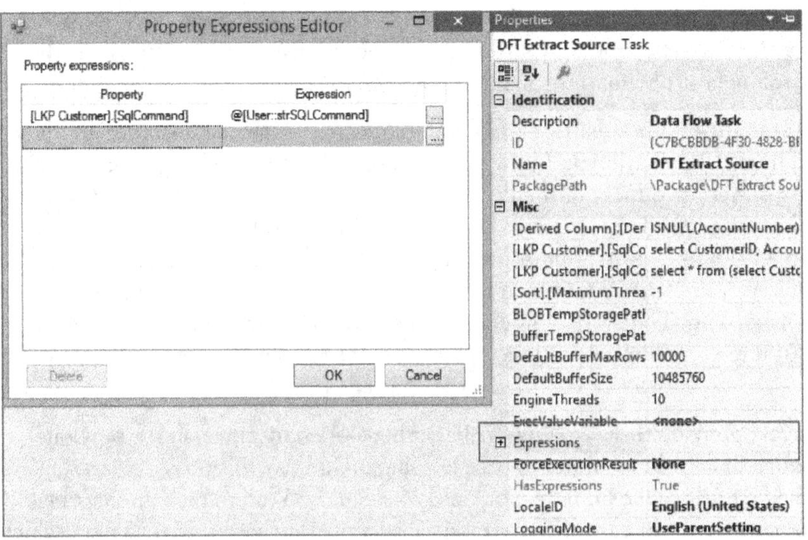

FIGURE 7-30

Cascaded Lookup Operations

Sometimes the requirements of a real-world Data Flow may require several Lookup Transformations to get the job done. By using multiple Lookup Transformations, you can sometimes achieve a higher degree of performance without incurring the associated memory costs and processing times of using a single Lookup.

Imagine you have a large list of products that ideally you would like to load into one Lookup. You consider using full-cache mode; however, because of the sheer number of rows, either you run out of memory when trying to load the cache or the cache-loading phase takes so long that it becomes impractical (for instance, the package takes 15 minutes to execute, but 6 minutes of that time is spent just loading the Lookup cache). Therefore, you consider no-cache mode, but the expense of all those database calls makes the solution too slow. Finally, you consider partial-cache mode, but again the expense of the initial database calls (before the internal cache is populated with enough data to be useful) is too high.

The solution to this problem is based on a critical assumption that there is a subset of reference rows (in this case product rows) that are statistically likely to be found in most, if not all, data loads. For instance, if the business is a consumer goods chain, then it's likely that a high proportion of sales transactions are from people who buy milk. Similarly, there will be many transactions for sales of bread, cheese, beer, and baby diapers. On the contrary, there will be a relatively low number of sales for expensive wines. Some of these trends may be seasonal — more suntan lotion sold in summer, and more heaters sold in winter. This same assumption applies to other dimensions besides products — for instance, a company specializing in direct sales may know historically which customers (or customer segments or loyalty members) have responded to specific campaigns. A bank might know which accounts (or account types) have the most activity at specific times of the month.

This statistical property does not hold true for all data sets, but if it does, you may derive great benefit from this pattern. If it doesn't, you may still find this section useful as you consider the different ways of approaching a problem and solving it with SSIS.

So how do you use this statistical approach to build your solution? Using the consumer goods example, if it is the middle of winter and you know you are not going to be selling much suntan lotion, then why load the suntan products in the Lookup Transformation? Rather, load just the high-frequency items like milk, bread, and cheese. Because you know you will see those items often, you want to put them in a Lookup Transformation configured in full-cache mode. If your Product table has, say, 1 million items, then you could load the top 20% of them (in terms of frequency/popularity) into this first Lookup. That way, you don't spend too much time loading the cache (because it is only 200,000 rows and not 1,000,000); by the same reasoning, you don't use as much memory.

Of course, in any statistical approach there will always be outliers — for instance, in the previous example suntan lotion will still be sold in winter to people going on holiday to sunnier places. Therefore, if any Lookups fail on the first full-cache Lookup, you need a second Lookup to pick up the strays. The second Lookup would be configured in partial-cache mode (as detailed earlier in this chapter), which means it would make database calls in the event that the item was not found in its dynamically growing internal cache. The first Lookup's not-found output would be connected to the second Lookup's input, and both of the Lookups would have their found outputs combined using a Union All Transformation in order to send all the matches downstream. Then a third Lookup is used in no-cache mode to look up any remaining rows not found already. This final Lookup output is combined with the others in another Union All. Figure 7-31 shows what such a package might look like.

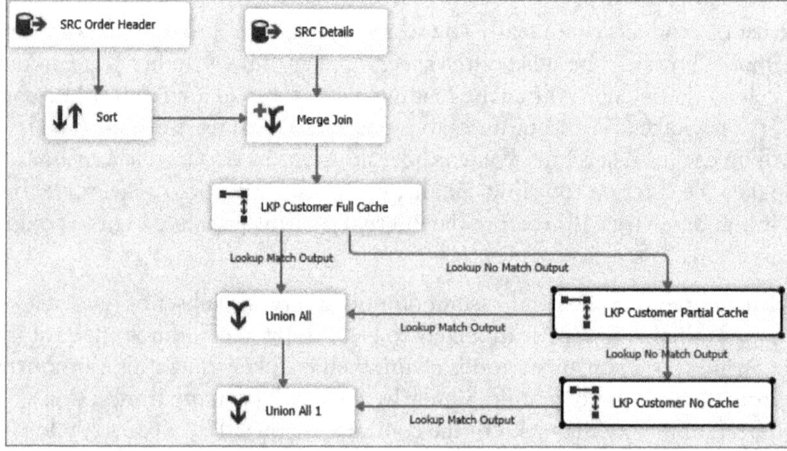

FIGURE 7-31

The benefit of this approach is that at the expense of a little more development time, you now have a system that performs efficiently for the most common Lookups and fails over to a slower mode for those items that are less common. That means that the Lookup operation will be extremely efficient for most of your data, which typically results in an overall decrease in processing time.

In other words, you have used the Pareto principle (80/20 rule) to improve the solution. The first (full-cache) Lookup stores 20% of the reference (in this case product) rows and hopefully succeeds in answering 80% of the Lookup requests. This is largely dependent on the user creating the right query to get the proper 20%. If the wrong data is queried then this can be a worst approach. For the 20% of Lookups that fail, they are redirected to — and serviced by — the partial-cache Lookup, which operates against the other 80% of data. Because you are constraining the size of the partial cache, you can ensure you don't run into any memory limitations — at the extreme, you could even use a no-cache Lookup instead of, or in addition to, the partial-cache Lookup.

The final piece to this puzzle is how you identify up front which items occur the most frequently in your domain. If the business does not already keep track of this information, you can derive it by collecting statistics within your packages and saving the results to a temporary location. For instance, each time you load your sales data, you could aggregate the number of sales for each item and write the results to a new table you have created for that purpose. The next time you load the product Lookup Transformation, you join the full Product table to the statistics table and return only those rows whose aggregate count is above a certain threshold. (You could also use the data-mining functionality in SQL Server to derive this information, though the details of that are beyond the scope of this chapter.)

CACHE CONNECTION MANAGER AND CACHE TRANSFORM

The Cache Connection Manager (CCM) and Cache Transform enable you to load the Lookup cache from any source. The Cache Connection Manager is the more critical of the two components — it holds a reference to the internal memory cache and can both read and write the cache to a disk-based file. In fact, the Lookup Transformation internally uses the CCM as its caching mechanism.

Like other Connection Managers in SSIS, the CCM is instantiated in the Connection Managers pane of the package design surface. You can also create new CCMs from the Cache Transformation Editor and Lookup Transformation Editor. At design time, the CCM contains no data, so at runtime you need to populate it. You can do this in one of two ways:

- You can create a separate Data Flow Task within the same package to extract data from any source and load the data into a Cache Transformation, as shown in Figure 7-32. You then configure the Cache Transformation to write the data to the CCM. Optionally, you can configure the same CCM to write the data to a cache file (usually with the extension `.caw`) on disk. When you execute the package, the Source Component will send the rows down the pipeline into the input of the Cache Transformation. The Cache Transformation will call the CCM, which loads the data into a local memory cache. If configured, the CCM will also save the cache to disk so you can use it again later. This method enables you to create persisted caches that you can share with other users, solutions, and packages.

- Alternatively, you can open up the CCM editor and directly specify the filename of an existing cache file (.caw file). This option requires that a cache file has previously been created for you to reuse. At execution time, the CCM loads the cache directly from disk and populates its internal memory structures.

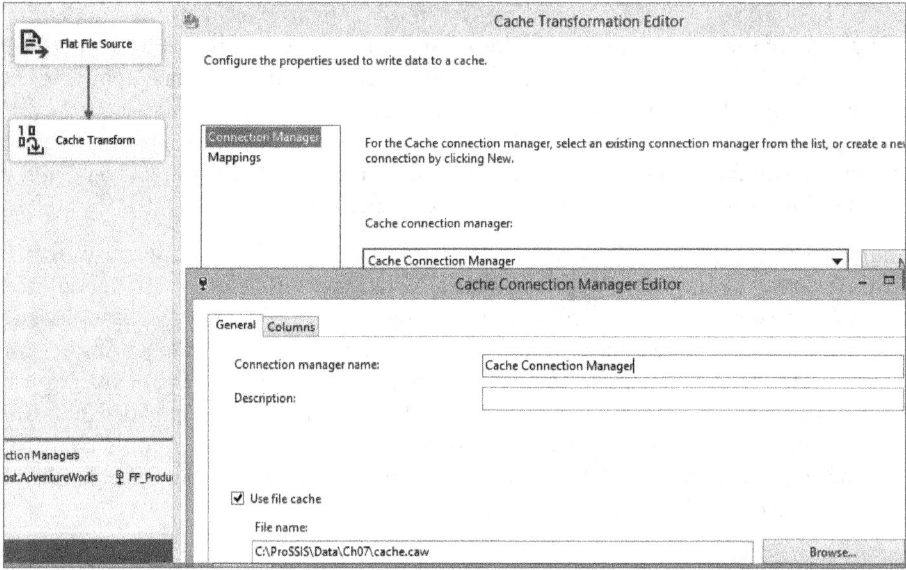

FIGURE 7-32

When you configure a CCM, you can specify which columns of the input data set should be used as index fields and which columns should be used as reference fields (see Figure 7-33). This is a necessary step — the CCM needs to know up front which columns you will be joining on, so that it can create internal index structures to optimize the process.

Cache Connection Manager Editor

General | Columns

Configure the properties of each column in the cache connection manager.

Column	Index Po...	Type	Length	Precision	Scale	Code Page
ProductID	1	four-byte signed int...	0	0	0	
ProductNum...	0	Unicode string [DT_...	25	0	0	

FIGURE 7-33

Whichever way you created the CCM, when you execute the package, the CCM will contain an in-memory representation of the data you specified. That means that the cache is now immediately available for use by the Lookup Transformation. Note that the Lookup Transformation is the only component that uses the caching aspects of the CCM; however, the Raw File Source can also read `.caw` files, which can be useful for debugging.

If you are using the Lookup Transformation in full-cache mode, you can load the cache using the CCM (instead of specifying a SQL query as described earlier in this chapter). To use the CCM option, open the Lookup Transformation and select Full Cache and Cache Connection Manager in the general pane of the editor, as shown in Figure 7-34. Then you can either select an existing CCM or create a new one. You can now continue configuring the Lookup Transformation in the same way you would if you had used a SQL query. The only difference is that in the Columns tab, you can only join on columns that you earlier specified as index columns in the CCM editor.

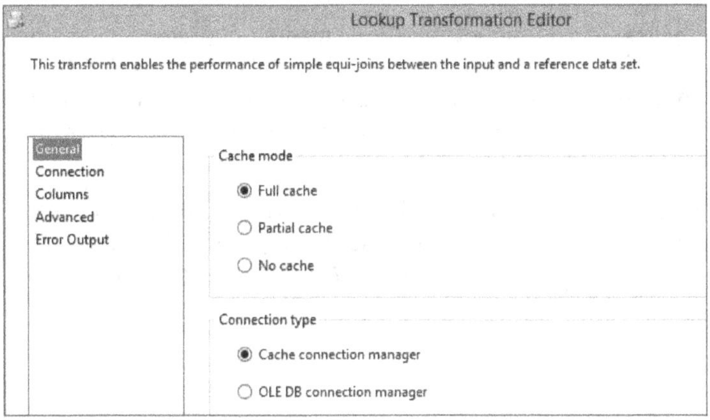

FIGURE 7-34

The CCM gives you several benefits. First of all, you can reuse caches that you previously saved to file (in the same or a different package). For instance, you can load a CCM using the Customer table and then save the cache to a `.caw` file on disk. Every other package that needs to do a Lookup against customers can then use a Lookup Transformation configured in full-cache/CCM mode, with the CCM pointing at the `.caw` file you created.

Second, reading data from a `.caw` file is generally faster than reading from OLE DB, so your packages should run faster. Of course, because the `.caw` file is an offline copy of your source data, it can become stale; therefore, it should be reloaded every so often. Note that you can use an expression for the CCM filename, which means that you can dynamically load specific files at runtime.

Third, the CCM enables you to reuse caches across loop iterations. If you use a Lookup Transformation in full-cache/OLE DB mode within an SSIS For Loop Container or Foreach Loop Container, the cache will be reloaded on every iteration of the loop. This may be your intended design, but if not, then it is difficult to mitigate the performance overhead. However, if you used a Lookup configured in full-cache/CCM mode, the CCM would be persistent across loop iterations, improving your overall package performance.

SUMMARY

This chapter explored different ways of joining data within an SSIS solution. Relational databases are highly efficient at joining data within their own stores; however, you may not be fortunate enough to have all your data living in the same database — for example, when loading a data warehouse. SSIS enables you to perform these joins outside the database and provides many different options for doing so, each with different performance and resource-usage characteristics.

The Merge Join Transformation can join large volumes of data without much memory impact; however, it has certain requirements, such as sorted input columns, that may be difficult to meet. Remember to use the source query to sort the input data, and avoid the Sort Transformation when possible, because of performance issues.

The Lookup Transformation is very flexible and supports multiple modes of operation. The Cache Connection Manager adds more flexibility to the Lookup by allowing caches to be explicitly shared across Data Flows and packages. With the CCM, the Lookup cache is also maintained across loop iterations. In large-scale deployments, many different patterns can be used to optimize performance, one of them being cascaded Lookups.

As with all SSIS solutions, there are no hard-and-fast rules that apply to all situations, so don't be afraid to experiment. If you run into any performance issues when trying to join data, try a few of the other options presented in this chapter. Hopefully, you will find one that makes a difference.

Creating an End-to-End Package

WHAT'S IN THIS CHAPTER?

- Walking through a basic transformation
- Performing mainframe ETL with data scrubbing
- Making packages dynamic

WROX.COM CODE DOWNLOADS FOR THIS CHAPTER

You can find the wrox.com code downloads for this chapter at `www.wrox.com/go/prossis2014` on the Download Code tab.

Now that you've learned about all the basic tasks and transformations in SSIS, you can jump into some practical applications for SSIS. You'll first start with a normal transformation of data from a series of flat files into SQL Server. Next you'll add some complexity to a process by archiving the files automatically. The last example demonstrates how to make a package that handles basic errors and makes the package more dynamic. As you run through the tutorials, remember to save your package and your project on a regular basis to avoid any loss of work.

BASIC TRANSFORMATION TUTORIAL

As you can imagine, the primary reason people use SSIS is to read the data from a source and write it to a destination after it's potentially transformed. This tutorial walks you through a common scenario: you want to copy data from a Flat File Source to a SQL Server table without altering the data. This may be a simple example, but the examples will get much more complex in later chapters.

Start the tutorial by going online to the website for this book and downloading the sample extract that contains zip code information about cities. The zip code extract was retrieved from public record data from the 1990 census and has been filtered to contain only Florida cities, in order to reduce download time. You'll use this in the next tutorial as well, so it's very important not to skip this first tutorial. You can download the sample extract file, called `ZipCodeExtract.csv`, from this book's web page at `www.wrox.com`. Place the file into a directory called `C:\ProSSIS\Data\Ch08`.

Open SQL Server Data Tools (SSDT) and select File ⇨ New ⇨ Project. Then select Integration Services Project as your project type. Type **ProSSISCh08** as the project name, and accept the rest of the defaults (as shown in Figure 8-1). You can place the project anywhere on your computer; the default location is under the `users\"Your User Name"\Documents\Visual Studio 2012\Projects` folder. In this example, the solution is created in `c:\ProSSIS\Data\Ch08`, but you may use the default location if you so desire.

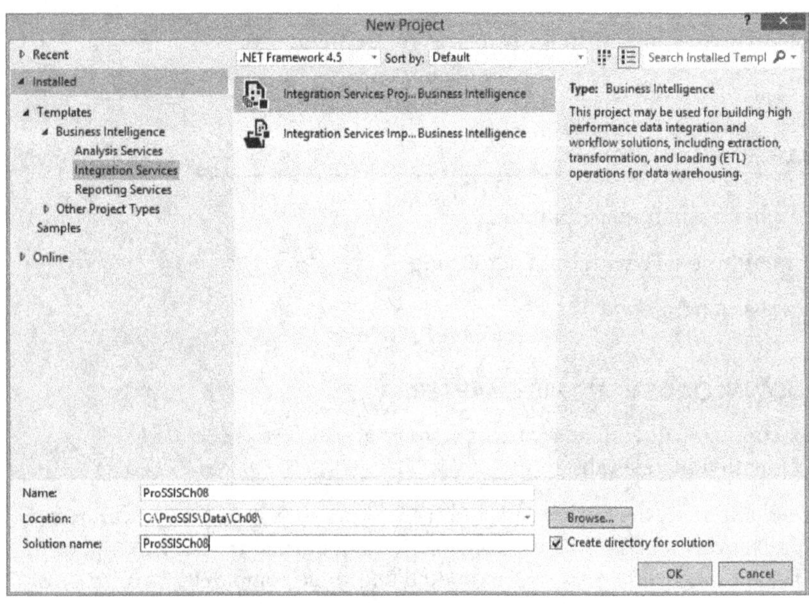

FIGURE 8-1

The project will be created, and you'll see a default `Package.dtsx` package file in the Solution Explorer. Right-click the file, select Rename, and rename the file `ZipLoad.dtsx`. If the package isn't open yet, double-click it to open it in the package designer.

Creating Connections

Now that you have the package created, you need to add a connection that can be used across multiple packages. In the Solution Explorer, right-click the Connection Managers folder and select New Connection Manager. This opens the Add SSIS Connection Manager window.

Select the OLEDB connection and click Add, which opens the Configure OLEDB Connection Manager window. If this is the first time you are creating a connection, then the Data Connection list in the left window will be empty.

> **NOTE** *There are many ways to create the connection. For example, you could create it as you're creating each source and destination. You can also use the new Source and Destination Assistants when building a Data Flow. Once you're more experienced with the tool, you'll find what works best for you.*

Click the New button at the bottom of the window. Your first Connection Manager for this example will be to SQL Server, so select Native OLE DB\SQL Native Client 11.0 as the Provider. For the Server Name option, type the name of your SQL Server and enter the authentication mode that is necessary for you to read and write to the database, as shown in Figure 8-2. If you are using a local instance of SQL Server, then you should be able to use Localhost as the server name and Windows authentication for the credentials. Lastly, select the AdventureWorks database. If you don't have the AdventureWorks database, select any other available database on the server. You can optionally test the connection. Now click OK. You will now have a Data Source in the Data Source box that should be selected. Click OK. You will now see a Data Source under the Connection Manager folder in the Solution Explorer, and the same Data Source in the Connection Manager window in the ZipLoad Package you first created.

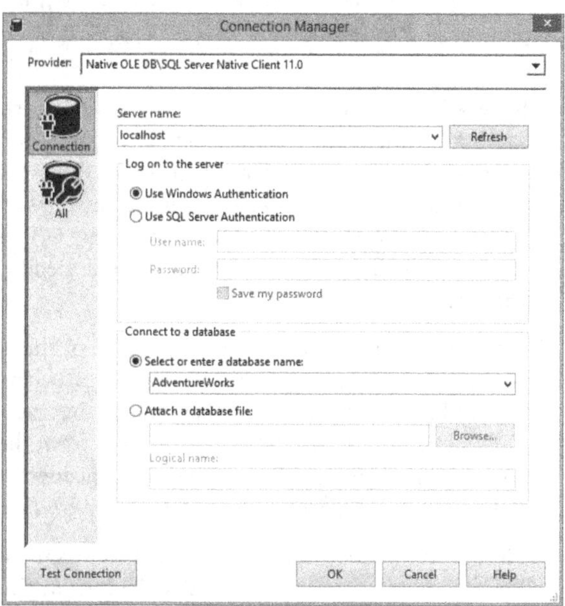

FIGURE 8-2

This new Data Source will start with "(project)". The name of the connection automatically contains the server name and the database name. This is not a good naming convention because packages are almost always moved from server to server — for example, development, QA, and production servers. Therefore, a better naming convention would be the connection type and the database name. Right-click on the Connection Manager you just created in the Solution Explorer and rename it to **OLEDB_AdventureWorks**. You can create connections in the package and convert them to project connections also. Any project-level connections automatically appear in the Connection Manager window in all packages in that project. If a connection is needed only in one package in the project, then it can be created at the package level. To create a connection at the package level, right-click in the Connection Manager window in a package and follow the same steps used to create the project-level connection described previously.

Next, create a Flat File connection and point it to the `ZipCodeextract.csv` file in your `C:\ProSSIS\Data\Ch08` directory. Right-click in the Connection Manager area of the package designer, and select New Flat File Connection. Name the connection **FF_ZipCode_CSV**, and add any description you like. Point the File Name option to `C:\ProSSIS\Data\Ch08\ZipCodeExtract.csv` or browse to the correct location by clicking Browse.

> **NOTE** *If you can't find the file, ensure that the file type filter is adjusted so you're not looking for just* `*.txt` *files, which is the default setting. Set the filter to All Files to ensure you can see the file.*

Set the Format dropdown box to Delimited, with <none> set for the Text Qualifier option; these are both the default options. The Text Qualifier option enables you to specify that character data is wrapped in quotes or some type of qualifier. This is helpful when you have a file that is delimited by commas and you also have commas inside some of the text data that you do not wish to separate by. Setting a Text Qualifier will ignore any commas inside the text data. Lastly, check the "Column names in the first data row" option. This specifies that your first row contains the column names for the file.

Select the Columns tab from the left side of the editor to see a preview of the file data and to set the row and column delimiters. The defaults are generally fine for this screen. The Row Delimiter option should be set to {CR}{LF}, which means that a carriage return and line feed separates each row. The Column Delimiter option is carried over from the first page and is therefore set to "Comma {,}". In some extracts that you may receive, the header record may be different from the data records, and the configurations won't be exactly the same as in the example.

Now select the Advanced tab from the left side of the editor. Here, you can specify the data types for each of the three columns. The default for this type of data is a 50-character string, which is excessive in this case. Click Suggest Types to comb through the data and find the best data type fit for it. This will open the Suggest Column Types dialog, where you should accept the default options and click OK.

At this point, the data types in the Advanced tab have changed for each column. One column in particular was incorrectly changed. When combing through the first 100 records, the Suggest Column Types dialog selected a "four-byte signed integer [DT_I4]" for the zip code column, but your Suggest Types button may select a smaller data type based on the data. While this would work for the data extract you currently have, it won't work for states that have zip codes that begin with a zero in the northeast United States. Change this column to a string by selecting "string [DT_STR]" from the DataType dropdown, and change the length of the column to 5 by changing the OutputColumnWidth option (see Figure 8-3). Finally, change the TextQualified option to False, and then click OK.

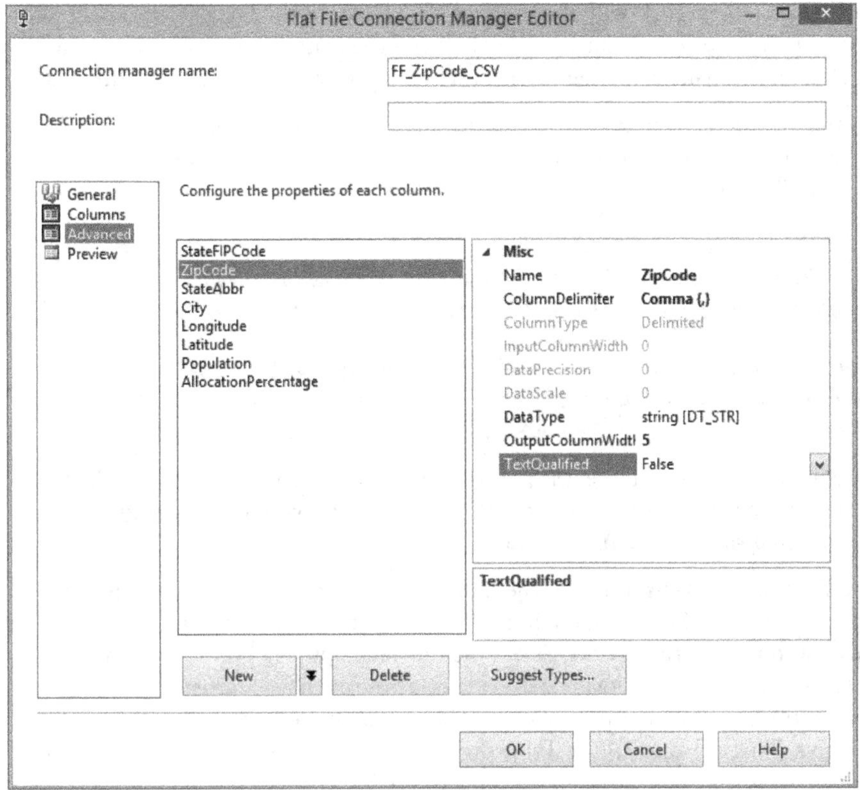

FIGURE 8-3

Creating the Control Flow

With the first two connections created, you can now define the package's Control Flow. In this tutorial, you have only a single task, the Data Flow Task. In the Toolbox, drag the Data Flow Task over to the design pane in the Control Flow tab. Next, right-click the task and select Rename to rename the task **Load ZipCode Data**.

Creating the Data Flow

This section reflects the most detailed portion of almost all of your packages. The Data Flow is where you will generally spend 70 percent of your time as an SSIS developer. To begin, double-click the Data Flow Task to drill into the Data Flow.

> **NOTE** *When opening a task for editing, always double-click the icon on the left side of the task. Otherwise, you may start renaming the task instead of opening it. You can also right-click on the task and select Edit.*

Double-clicking on the Data Flow Task will automatically take you to the Data Flow tab. Note that the name of the task — Load ZipCode Data — is displayed in the Data Flow Task dropdown. If you had more than one Data Flow Task, the names of each would appear as options in the dropdown.

Drag and drop a Source Assistant from the Toolbox onto the Data Flow design pane. Select Flat File in the left pane of the Source Assistant. Then select FF_ZipCode_CSV in the right pane and Click OK. Rename the source **Florida ZipCode File** in the Properties window.

> **NOTE** *All the rename instructions in these tutorials are optional, but they will keep you on the same page as the tutorials in this book. In a real-world situation, ensuring the package task names are descriptive will make your package self-documenting. This is due to the names of the tasks being logged by SSIS. Logging is discussed in Chapter 22.*

Double-click on the source, and you will see it is pointing to the Connection Manager called FF_ZipCode_CSV. Select the Columns tab and note the columns that you'll be outputting to the path. You've now configured the source, and you can click OK.

Next, drag and drop Destination Assistant onto the design pane. Select SQL Server in the left pane and OLEDB_AdventureWorks in the right pane in the Destination Assistant window and click OK. Rename the new destination **AdventureWorks.** Select the Florida ZipCode File Source and then connect the path (blue arrow) from the Florida ZipCode File Source to AdventureWorks. Double-click the destination, and AdventureWorks should already be selected in the Connection Manager dropdown box. For the Name of the Table or View option, click the New button next to the dropdown box. This is how you can create a table inside SSDT without having to go back to SQL Server Management Studio.

The default DDL for creating the table uses the destination's name (AdventureWorks), and the data types may not be exactly what you'd like. You can edit this DDL, as shown here:

```
CREATE TABLE [AdventureWorks] (
[StateFIPCode] smallint,
[ZipCode] varchar(5),
[StateAbbr] varchar(2),
[City] varchar(16),
[Longitude] real,
[Latitude] real,
[Population] int,
[AllocationPercentage] real
)
```

However, suppose this won't do for your picky DBA, who is concerned about performance. In this case, you should rename the table `ZipCode` (taking out the brackets) and change each column's data type to a more suitable size and type, as shown in the `ZipCode` and `StateAbbr` columns (Ch08SQL.txt):

```
CREATE TABLE [ZipCode] (
[StateFIPCode] smallint,
[ZipCode] char(5),
[StateAbbr] char(2),
```

```
[City] varchar(16),
[Longitude] real,
[Latitude] real,
[Population] int,
[AllocationPercentage] real
)
```

When you are done changing the DDL, click OK. The table name will be transposed into the Table dropdown box. Finally, select the Mapping tab to ensure that the inputs are mapped to the outputs correctly. SSIS attempts to map the columns based on name; in this case, because you just created the table with the same column names, it should be a direct match, as shown in Figure 8-4.

After confirming that the mappings look like Figure 8-4, click OK.

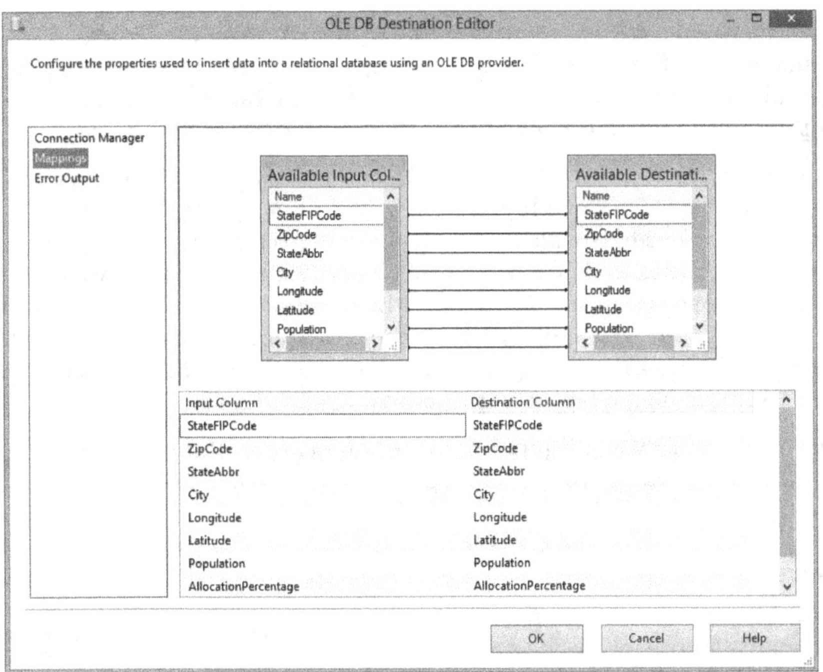

FIGURE 8-4

Completing the Package

With the basic framework of the package now constructed, you need to add one more task to the Control Flow tab to ensure that you can run this package multiple times. To do this, click the Control Flow tab and drag an Execute SQL task over to the design pane. Rename the task **Purge ZipCode Table.** Double-click the task and select OLEDB_AdventureWorks from the Connection dropdown. Finally, type the following query for the SQLStatement option (you can also click the ellipsis button and enter the query):

```
TRUNCATE TABLE ZipCode
```

Click OK to complete the task configuration. To connect the task as a parent to the Load ZipCode Info Task, click the Purge ZipCode Table Task and drag the green arrow onto the Load ZipCode Info Task.

Saving the Package

Your first package is now complete. To save the package, click the Save icon in the top menu or select File ➪ Save Selected Items. Note here that by clicking Save, you're saving the .DTSX file to the project, but you have not saved it to the server yet. To do that, you have to deploy the project. Also, SSIS does not version control your packages independently. To version control your packages, you need to integrate a solution like Subversion (SVN) into SSIS, as described in Chapter 17.

Executing the Package

With the package complete, you can attempt to execute it by right-clicking on the package name in the solution explorer and selecting Execute Package. This is a good habit to get into when executing, because other methods, like using the green debug arrow at the top, can cause more to execute than just the package. The package will take a few moments to validate, and then it will execute.

You can see the progress under the Progress tab or in the Output window. In the Control Flow tab, the two tasks display a small yellow circle that begins to spin (in the top right of the task). If all goes well, they will change to green circles with a check. If both get green checks, then the package execution was successful. If your package failed, you can check the Output window to see why. The Output window should be open by default, but in case it isn't, you can open it by clicking View ➪ Output. You can also see a graphical version of the Output window in the Progress tab (it is called the Execution Results tab if your package stops). The Execution Results tab will always show the results from the latest package run in the current SSDT session.

You can go to the Data Flow tab, shown in Figure 8-5, to see how many records were copied over. Notice the number of records displayed in the path as SSIS moves from source to destination.

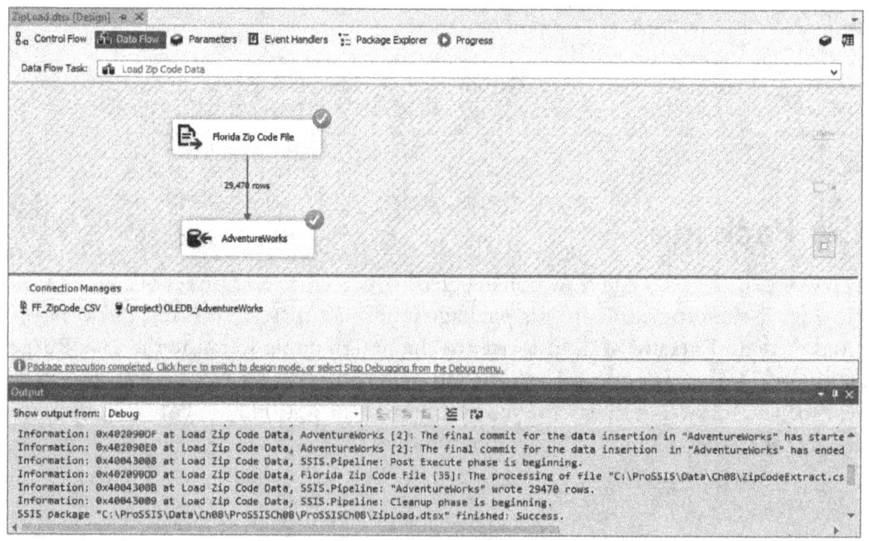

FIGURE 8-5

By default, when you execute a package, you are placed in debug mode. Changes you make in this mode are not made available until you run the package again, and you cannot add new tasks or enter some editors. To break out of this mode, click the square Stop icon or click Debug ➪ Stop Debugging.

TYPICAL MAINFRAME ETL WITH DATA SCRUBBING

With the basic ETL out of the way, you will now jump into a more complex SSIS package that attempts to scrub data. You can start this scenario by downloading the `010305c.dat` public data file from the website for this book into a directory called `C:\ProSSIS\Data\Ch08`. This file contains public record data from the Department of State of Florida.

In this scenario, you run a credit card company that's interested in marketing to newly formed domestic corporations in Florida. You want to prepare a data extract each day for the marketing department to perform a mail merge and perform a bulk mailing. Yes, your company is an old-fashioned, snail-mail spammer. Luckily, the Florida Department of State has an interesting extract you can use to empower your marketing department.

The business goals of this package are as follows:

- Create a package that finds the files in the `C:\ProSSIS\Data\Ch08` directory and loads the file into your relational database.
- Archive the file after you load it to prevent it from being loaded twice.
- The package must self-heal. If a column is missing data, the data should be added automatically.
- If the package encounters an error in its attempt to self-heal, output the row to an error queue.
- You must audit the fact that you loaded the file and how many rows you loaded.

Start a new package in your existing ProSSISCh08 SSDT project from the first tutorial. Right-click the SSIS Packages folder in the Solution Explorer and select New SSIS Package. This will create `Package1.dtsx`, or some numeric variation on that name. Rename the file **CorporationLoad.dtsx.** Double-click the package to open it if it is not already open.

Since the OLEDB_AdventureWorks connection you created earlier was a project-level connection, it should automatically appear in the Connection Manager window of the package. You now have two packages using the same project-level connection. If you were to change the database or server name in this connection, it would change for both packages.

Next, create a new Flat File Connection Manager just as you did in the last tutorial. When the configuration screen opens, call the connection **FF_Corporation_DAT** in the General tab.

> **NOTE** *Using naming conventions like this are a best practice in SSIS. The name tells you the type of file and the type of connection.*

Enter any description you like. For this Connection Manager, you're going to configure the file slightly differently. Click Browse and point to the `C:\ProSSIS\Data\Ch08\010305c.dat` file (keep in mind that the default file filter is `*.txt` so you will have to change the filter to All Files in order to see the file). You should also change the Text Qualifier option to a single double-quote ("). Check the "Column names in the first data row" option. The final configuration should resemble Figure 8-6. Go to the Columns tab to confirm that the column delimiter is Comma Delimited.

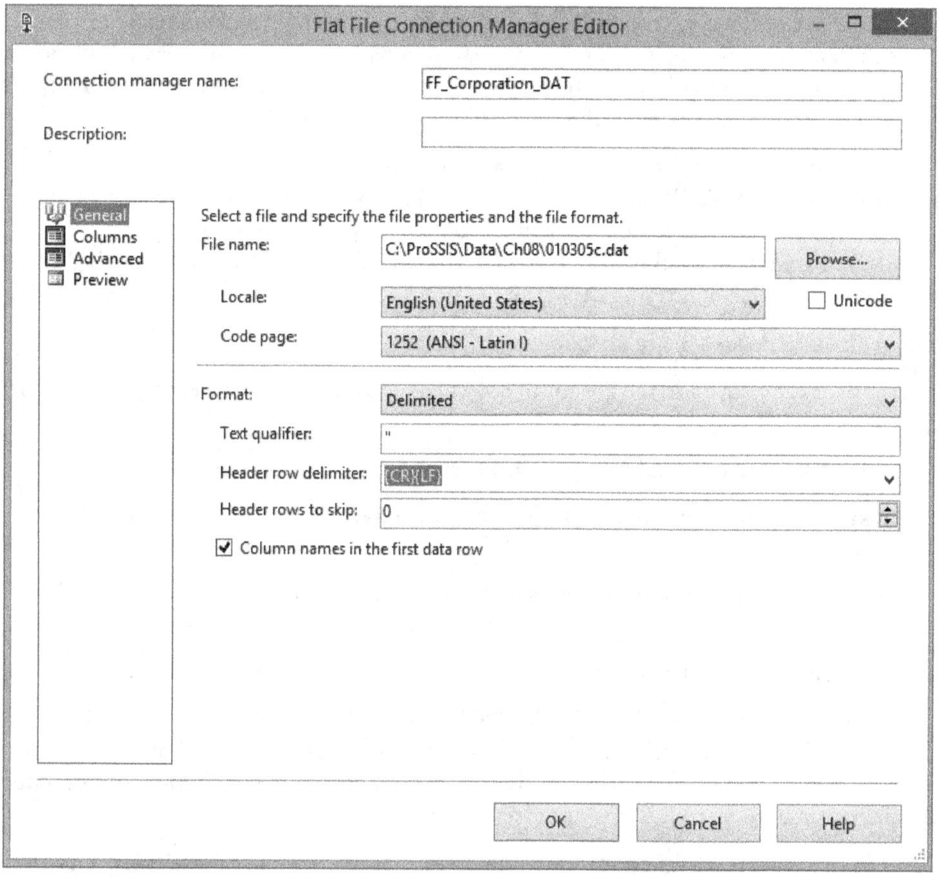

FIGURE 8-6

Next, go to the Advanced tab. By default, each of the columns is set to a 50-character [DT_STR] column. However, this will cause issues with this file, because several columns contain more than 100 characters of data, which would result in a truncation error. Therefore, change the AddressLine1 and AddressLine2 columns to String [DT_STR], which is 150 characters wide, as shown in Figure 8-7. After you've properly set these two columns, click OK to save the Connection Manager.

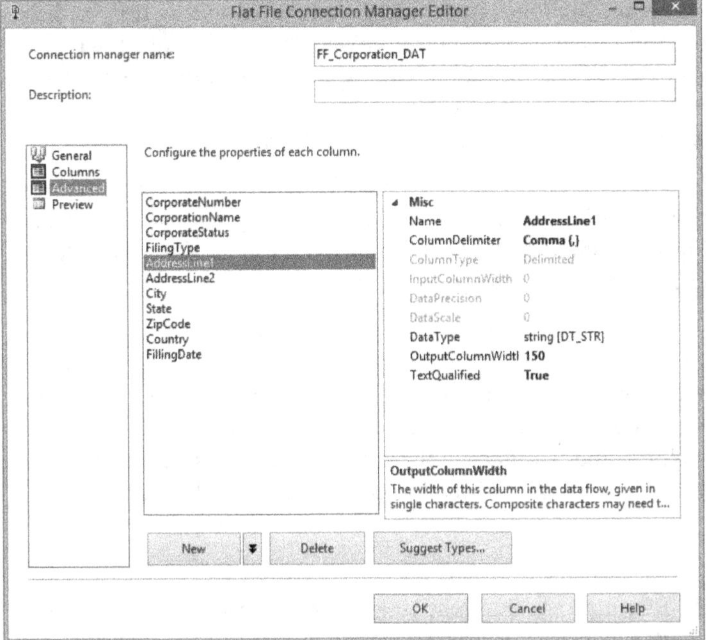

FIGURE 8-7

Creating the Data Flow

With the mundane work of creating the connections now out of the way, you can create the transformations. As you did in the last package, you must first create a Data Flow Task by dragging it from the Toolbox. Name this task **Load Corporate Data**. Double-click the task to go to the Data Flow tab.

Drag and drop a Flat File Source onto the design pane and rename it **Uncleansed Corporate Data**. (You could also use the Source Assistant as shown previously; you are being shown a different method here intentionally.) Double-click the source and select FF_Corporation_DAT as the Connection Manager you'll be using. Click OK to close the screen. You'll add the destination and transformation in a moment after the scenario is expanded a bit.

Handling Dirty Data

Before you go deeper into this scenario, take a moment to look more closely at this data. As you were creating the connection, if you are a very observant person (I did not notice this until it was too late), you may have noticed that some of the important data that you'll need is missing. For example, the city and state are missing from some of the records.

> **NOTE** *The Data Profiling Task can also help with this situation; it is covered in Chapter 12.*

To fix this for the marketing department, you'll use some of the transformations that were discussed in the last few chapters to send the good records down one path and the bad records down a different path. You will then attempt to cleanse the bad records and then send those back through the main path. There may be some records you can't cleanse (such as corporations with foreign postal codes), which you'll have to write to an error log and deal with another time.

First, standardize the postal code to a five-digit format. Currently, some have five digits and some have the full nine-digit zip code with a dash (five digits, a dash, and four more digits). Some are nine-digit zip codes without the dash. To standardize the zip code, you use the Derived Column Transformation. Drag it from the Toolbox and rename it **Standardize Zip Code.**

Connect the source to the transformation and double-click the Standardize Zip Code Transformation to configure it. Expand the Columns tree in the upper-left corner, find [ZipCode], and drag it onto the Expression column in the grid below. This will prefill some of the information for you in the derived column's grid area. You now need to create an expression that will take the various zip code formats in the [ZipCode] output column and output only the first five characters. An easy way to do this is with the `SUBSTRING` function. The `SUBSTRING` function code would look like this:

```
SUBSTRING ([ZipCode],1,5)
```

This code should be typed into the Expression column in the grid. Next, specify that the derived column will replace the existing ZipCode output by selecting that option from the Derived Column dropdown box. Figure 8-8 shows the completed options. When you are done with the transformation, click OK.

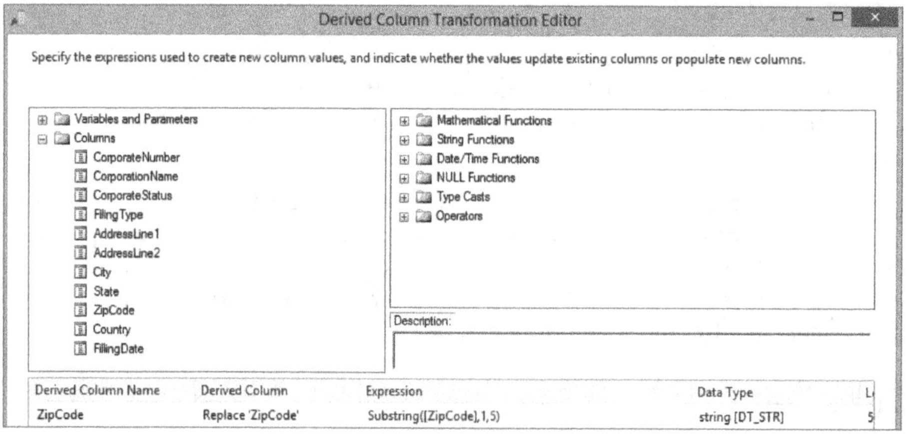

FIGURE 8-8

The Conditional Split Transformation

Now that you have standardized the data slightly, drag and drop the Conditional Split Transformation onto the design pane and connect the blue arrow from the Derived Column Transformation called Standardize Zip Code to the Conditional Split. Rename the Conditional Split Transformation **Find Bad Records.** The Conditional Split Transformation enables you to push bad records into a data-cleansing process.

To cleanse the data that lacks city or state, you'll write a condition specifying that any row missing a city or state should be moved to a cleansing path in the Data Flow. Double-click the Conditional Split Transformation after you have connected it from the Derived Column Transformation in order to edit it.

Create a condition called Missing State or City by typing its name in the Output Name column. You now need to write an expression that looks for empty records. One way to do this is to use the `LTRIM` function. The two vertical bars (| |) in the following code are the same as a logical `OR` in your code. Two `&` operators would represent a logical `AND` condition. (You can read much more about the expression language in Chapter 5.) The following code will check for a blank Column 6 or Column 7:

```
LTRIM([State]) == "" || LTRIM([City]) == ""
```

The last thing you need to do is give a name to the default output if the coded condition is not met. Call that output **Good Data,** as shown in Figure 8-9. The default output contains the data that did not meet your conditions. Click OK to close the editor.

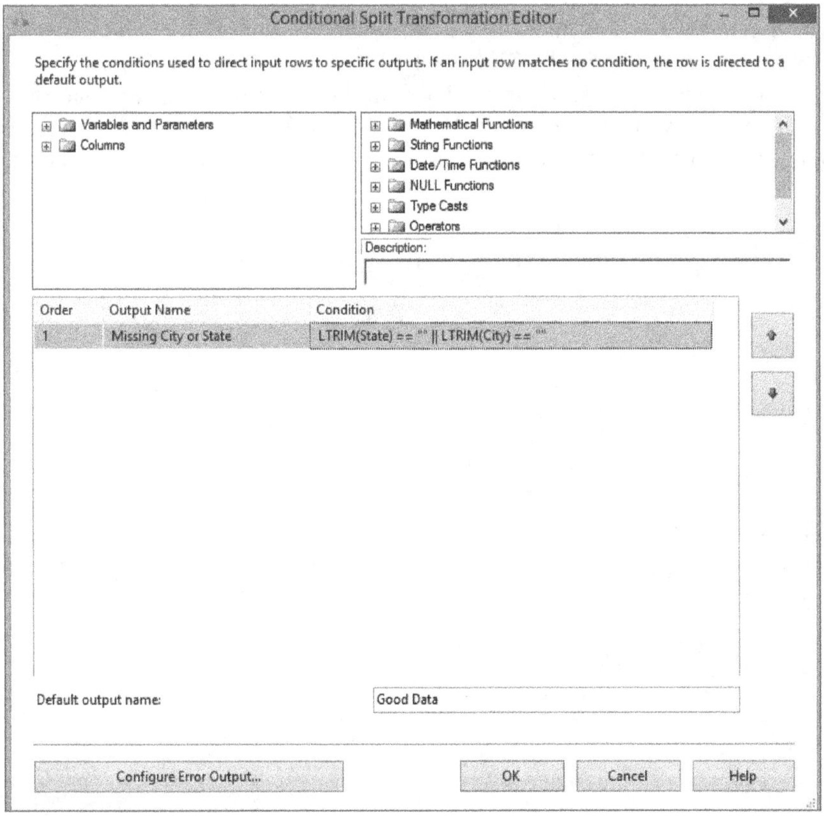

FIGURE 8-9

> **NOTE** *If you have multiple cases, always place the conditions that you think will capture most of the records at the top of the list, because at runtime the list is evaluated from top to bottom, and you don't want to evaluate records more times than needed.*

The Lookup Transformation

Next, drag and drop the Lookup Transformation onto the design pane. When you connect to it from the Conditional Split Transformation, you'll see the Input Output Selection dialog (shown in Figure 8-10). Select Missing State or City and click OK. This will send any bad records to the Lookup Transformation from the Conditional Split. Rename the Lookup Transformation **Fix Bad Records.**

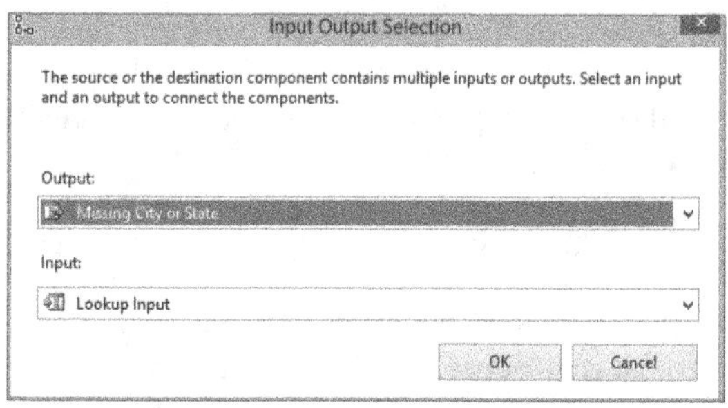

FIGURE 8-10

The Lookup Transformation enables you to map a city and state to the rows that are missing that information by looking the record up in the ZipCode table you loaded earlier. Open the transformation editor for the Lookup Transformation. Then, in the General tab, ensure that the Full Cache property is set and that you have the OLE DB Connection Manager property set for the Connection Type. Change the No Matching Entries dropdown box to "Redirect rows to no match output," as shown in Figure 8-11.

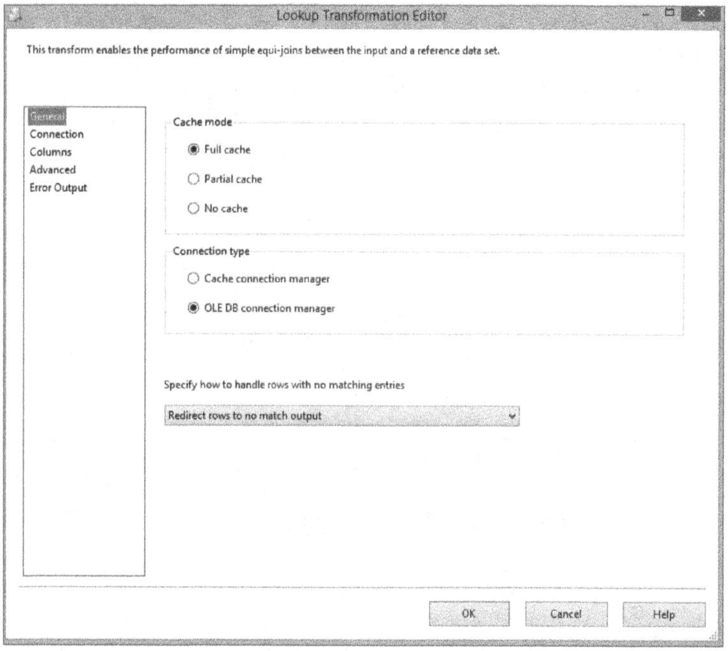

FIGURE 8-11

In the Connection tab, select OLEDB_AdventureWorks as the Connection Manager that contains your Lookup table. Select ZipCode from the "Use a Table or View" dropdown menu. For simplicity, you are just selecting the table, but the best practice is always to type in a SQL command and select only the needed columns.

Next, go to the Columns tab and drag ZipCode from the left Available Input Columns to the right ZipCode column in the Available Lookup Columns table. This will create an arrow between the two tables, as shown in Figure 8-12. Then, check the StateAbbr and City columns that you wish to output. This will transfer their information to the bottom grid. Change the Add as New Column option to Replace for the given column name as well. Specify that you want these columns to replace the existing City and State. Refer to Figure 8-12 to see the final configuration. Click OK to exit the transformation editor. There are many more options available here, but you should stick with the basics for the time being. With the configuration you just did, the potentially blank or bad city and state columns will be populated from the ZipCode table.

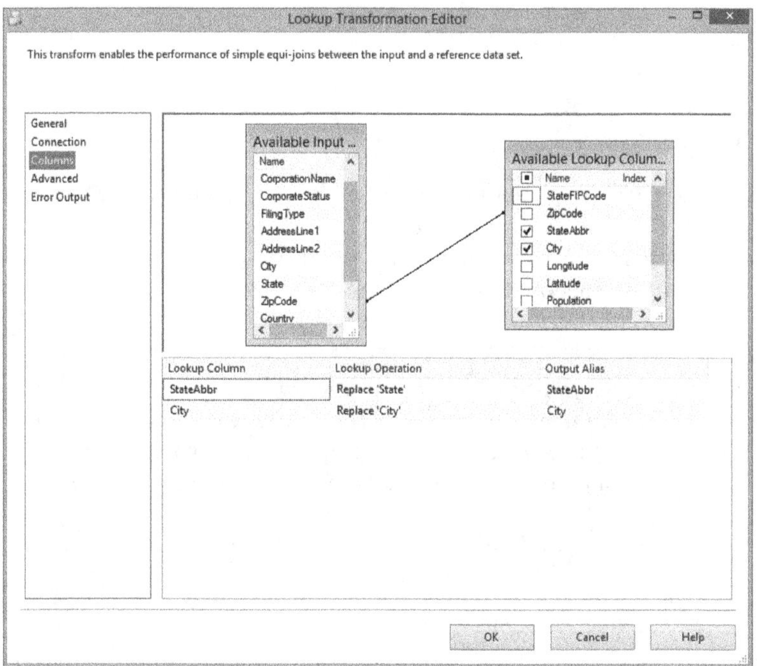

FIGURE 8-12

The Union All Transformation

Now that your dirty data is cleansed, send the sanitized data back into the main data path by using a Union All Transformation. Drag and drop the Union All Transformation onto the design pane and connect the Fix Bad Records Lookup Transformation and the Find Bad Records Conditional Split Transformation to the Union All Transformation. When you drag the blue line from the Lookup Transformation, you are prompted to define which output you want to send to the Union All Transformation. Select the Lookup Match Output. There is nothing more to configure with the Union All Transformation.

Finalizing

The last step in the Data Flow is to send the data to an OLE DB Destination. Drag the OLE DB Destination to the design pane and rename it **Mail Merge Table.** Connect the Union All Transformation to the destination. Double-click the destination and select OLEDB_AdventureWorks from the Connection Manager dropdown. For the Use a Table or View option, select the New button next to the dropdown. The default DDL for creating the table uses the destination's name (AdventureWorks), and the data types may not be exactly what you want, as shown here:

```
CREATE TABLE [Mail Merge Table] (
[CorporateNumber] varchar(50),
[CorporationName] varchar(50),
[CorporateStatus] varchar(50),
[FilingType] varchar(50),
[AddressLine1] varchar(150),
[AddressLine2] varchar(150),
[City] varchar(50),
[State] varchar(50),
[ZipCode] varchar(50),
[Country] varchar(50),
[FilingDate] varchar(50)
)
```

Go ahead and change the schema to something a bit more useful. Change the table name and each column to something more meaningful, as shown in the following example (Ch08SQL.txt). These changes may cause the destination to show warnings about truncation after you click OK. If so, these warnings can be ignored for the purpose of this example.

> **NOTE** *Warnings in a package do not indicate the package will fail. In this case the zip code is trimmed to 5 characters so you know the data is not going to be truncated as indicated by the warning. It is acceptable to run packages with warning, especially in cases where unnecessary tasks would need to be added to remove the warning.*

```
CREATE TABLE MarketingCorporation(
CorporateNumber varchar(12),
CorporationName varchar(48),
FilingStatus char(1),
FilingType char(4),
AddressLine1 varchar(150),
AddressLine2 varchar(50),
City varchar(28),
State char(2),
ZipCode varchar(10),
Country char(2),
FilingDate varchar(10) NULL
)
```

You may have to manually map some of the columns this time because the column names are different. Go to the Mappings tab and map each column to its new name. Click OK to close the editor.

Handling More Bad Data

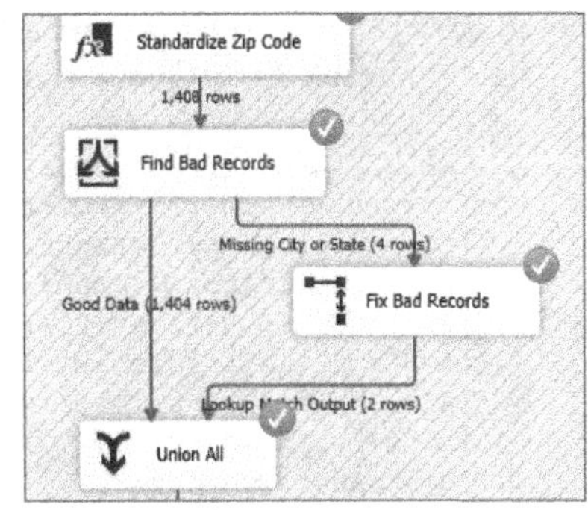

FIGURE 8-13

The unpolished package is essentially complete, but it has one fatal flaw that you're about to discover. Execute the package. As shown in Figure 8-13, when you do this, you can see, for example, that in the `010305c.dat` file, four records were sent to be cleansed by the Lookup Transformation. Of those, only two had the potential to be cleansed. The other two records were for companies outside the country, so they could not be located in the Lookup Transformation that contained only Florida zip codes. These two records were essentially lost because you specified in the Lookup Transformation to redirect the rows without a match to a "no match output" (refer to Figure 8-11), but you have not set up a destination for this output. Recall that the business requirement was to send marketing a list of domestic addresses for their mail merge product. They didn't care about the international addresses because they didn't have a business presence in other countries.

In this example, you want to send those two rows to an error queue for further investigation by a business analyst and to be cleaned manually. To do this properly, you need to audit each record that fails the match and create an ErrorQueue table on the SQL Server. Drag over the Audit Transformation found under the Other Transformations section of the SSIS Toolbox. Rename the Audit Transformation **Add Auditing Info** and connect the remaining blue arrow from the Fix Bad Records Transformation to the Audit Transformation.

With the Lookup problems now being handled, double-click the Audit Transformation to configure it. Add two additional columns to the output. Select Task Name and Package Name from the dropdown boxes in the Audit Type column. Remove the spaces in each default output column name, as shown in Figure 8-14, to make it easier to query later. You should output this auditing information because you may have multiple packages and tasks loading data into the corporation table, and you'll want to track from which package the error actually originated. Click OK when you are done.

Audit Transformation Editor

Configure the properties used to insert audit information into the data flow.

Output Column Name	Audit Type
PackageName	Package name
TaskName	Task name

FIGURE 8-14

The last thing you need to do to polish up the package is send the bad rows to the SQL Server ErrorQueue table. Drag another OLE DB Destination over to the design pane and connect the Audit Transformation to it. Rename the destination **Error Queue**. Double-click the destination and select

OLEDB_AdventureWorks as the Connection Manager, and click New to add the ErrorQueue table. Name the table **ErrorQueue** and follow a schema similar to the one shown here (Ch08SQL.txt):

```
CREATE TABLE [ErrorQueue] (
[CorporateNumber] varchar(50),
[CorporationName] varchar(50),
[CorporateStatus] varchar(50),
[FilingType] varchar(50),
[AddressLine1] varchar(150),
[AddressLine2] varchar(150),
[City] varchar(50),
[StateAbbr] varchar(50),
[ZipCode] varchar(50),
[Country] varchar(50),
[FilingDate] varchar(50),
[TaskName] nvarchar(19),
[PackageName] nvarchar(15)
)
```

> **NOTE** *In error queue tables like the one just illustrated, be very generous when defining the schema. In other words, you don't want to create another transformation error trying to write into the error queue table. Instead, consider defining everything as a* `varchar` *column, providing more space than actually needed.*

You may have to map some of the columns this time because of the column names being different. Go to the Mappings tab and map each column to its new name. Click OK to close the editor.

You are now ready to re-execute the package. This time, my data file contained four records that need to be fixed, and two of those were sent to the error queue. The final package would look something like the one shown in Figure 8-15 when executed.

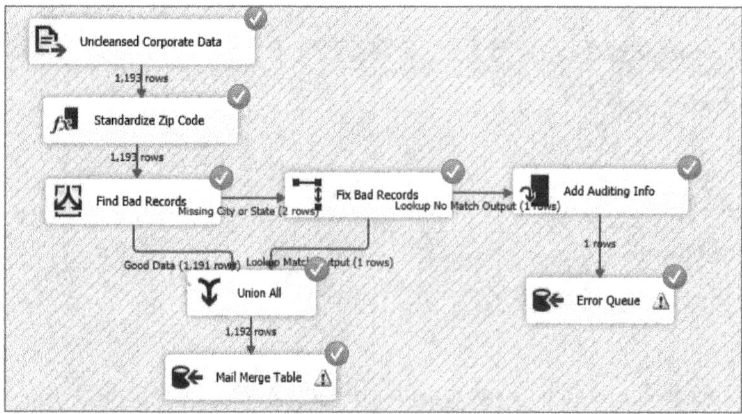

FIGURE 8-15

Looping and the Dynamic Tasks

You've gone a long way in this chapter toward creating a self-healing package, but it's not very reusable yet. Your next task in the business requirements is to configure the package so that it reads a directory for any `.DAT` file and performs the preceding tasks on that collection of files. To simulate this example, copy the rest of the `*.DAT` files from the Chapter 8 download content for this book available at `www.wrox.com` into `C:\ProSSIS\Data\Ch08`.

Looping

Your first task is to loop through any set of `.DAT` files in the `C:\ProSSIS\Data\Ch08` folder and load them into your database just as you did with the single file. To meet this business requirement, you need to use the Foreach Loop Container. Go to the Control Flow tab in the same package that you've been working in, and drag the container onto the design pane. Then, drag the "Load Corporate Data" Data Flow Task onto the container. Rename the container **Loop Through Files.**

Double-click the container to configure it. Go to the Collection tab and select Foreach File Enumerator from the Enumerator dropdown box. Next, specify that the folder will be `C:\ProSSIS\Data\Ch08` and that the files will have the `*.DAT` extension, as shown in Figure 8-16.

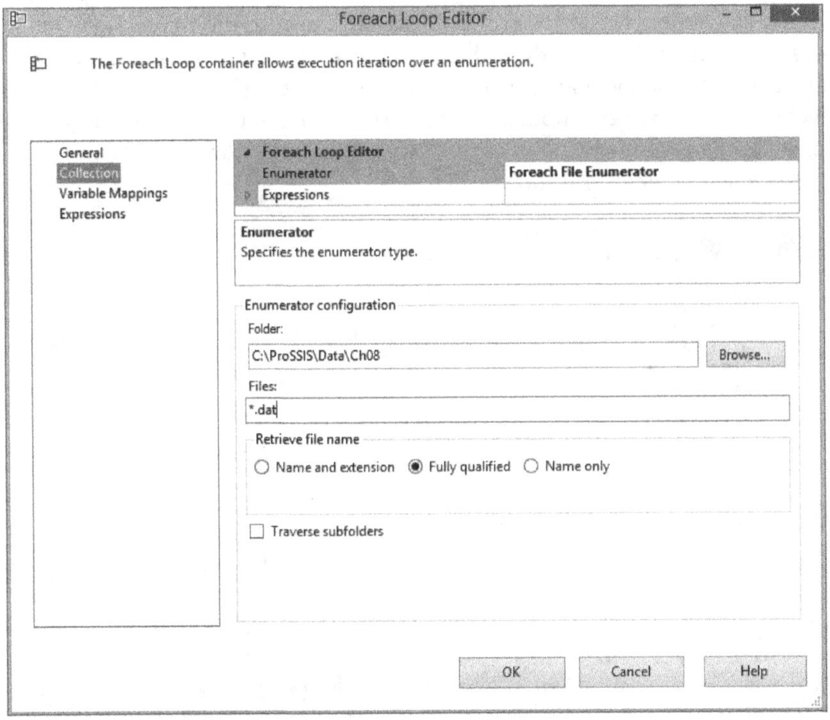

FIGURE 8-16

You need to now map the variables to the results of the Foreach File enumeration. Go to the Variable Mappings tab inside the Foreach Loop Editor and select <New Variable...> from the Variable column dropdown box. This will open the Add Variable dialog. For the container, you'll remain at the package level. You could assign the scope of the variable to the container, but keep things simple for this example. Name the variable **strExtractFileName** and click OK, leaving the rest of the options at their default settings.

You will then see the `User::strExtractFileName` variable in the Variable column and the number 0 in the Index option. Because the Foreach File Enumerator option has only one column, you'll see only an index of 0 for this column. If you used a different enumerator option, you could enter a number for each column that was returned from the enumerator. Click OK to leave the Foreach Loop editor.

Making the Package Dynamic

Now that the loop is created, you need to set the filename in the Corporation Extract Connection Manager to be equal to the filename that the enumerator retrieves dynamically. To meet this business requirement, right-click the Corporation Extract Connection Manager and select Properties (note that you're clicking Properties, not Edit as you've done previously). In the Properties pane for this Connection Manager, click the ellipsis button next to the Expressions option. By clicking the ellipsis button, you open the Property Expressions Editor. Select ConnectionString from the Property dropdown box and then click the ellipsis under the Expression column next to the connection string property you just selected, this will open the Expression Builder window, as shown in Figure 8-17. You can either type **@[User::strExtractFileName]** in the Expression column or click the ellipsis button, and then drag and drop the variable into the expression window. By entering **@[User::strExtractFileName]**, you are setting the filename in the Connection Manager to be equal to the current value of the `strExtractFileName` variable that you set in the Foreach Loop earlier. Click OK to exit the open windows. Note in the Property window that there is a single expression by clicking the plus sign next to Expressions.

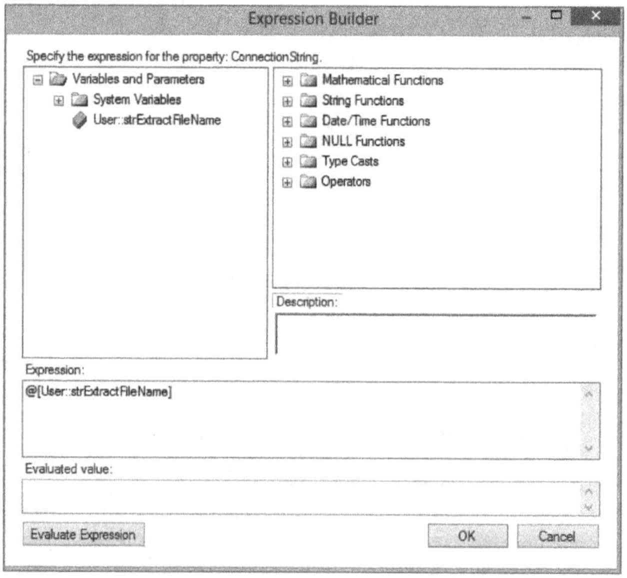

FIGURE 8-17

As it stands right now, each time the loop finds a `.DAT` file in the `C:\ProSSIS\Data\Ch08` directory, it will set the `strExtractFileName` variable to that path and filename. Then, the Connection Manager will use that variable as its filename and run the Data Flow Task one time for each file it finds. You now have a reusable package that can be run against any file in the format you designated earlier.

The only missing technical solution to complete is the archiving of the files after you load them. Before you begin solving that problem, manually create an archive directory under `C:\ProSSIS\Data\Ch08` called `C:\ProSSIS\Data\Ch08\Archive`. Right-click in the Connection Manager window and select New File Connection. Select Existing Folder for the Usage Type, and point the file to the `C:\ProSSIS\Data\Ch08\Archive` directory. Click OK and rename the newly created Connection Manager **Archive**.

Next, drag a File System Task into the Loop Through Files Container and connect the container to the "Load Corporate Data" Data Flow Task with an On Success constraint (the green arrow should be attached to the File System Task). Rename that task **Archive File**.

Double-click the "Archive File" File System Task to open the editor (shown in Figure 8-18). Set the Operation dropdown box to Move file. Next, change the Destination Connection from a variable to the archive Connection Manager that you just created. Also, select True for the OverwriteDestination option, which overwrites a file if it already exists in the archive folder. The SourceConnection dropdown box should be set to the FF_Corporation_DAT Connection Manager that you created earlier in this chapter. You have now configured the task to move the file currently in the Foreach Loop to the directory in the Archive File Connection Manager. Click OK to close the editor.

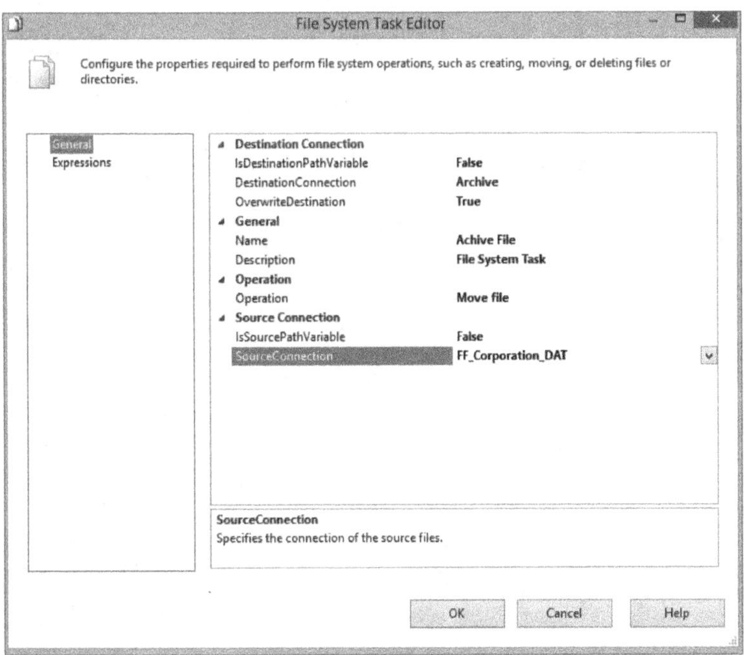

FIGURE 8-18

Your complete package should now be ready to execute. Save the package before you execute it. If you successfully implemented the solution, your Control Flow should look something like Figure 8-19 when executed. When you execute the package, you'll see the Control Flow items flash green once for each .DAT file in the directory. To run the package again, you must copy the files back into the working directory from the archive folder.

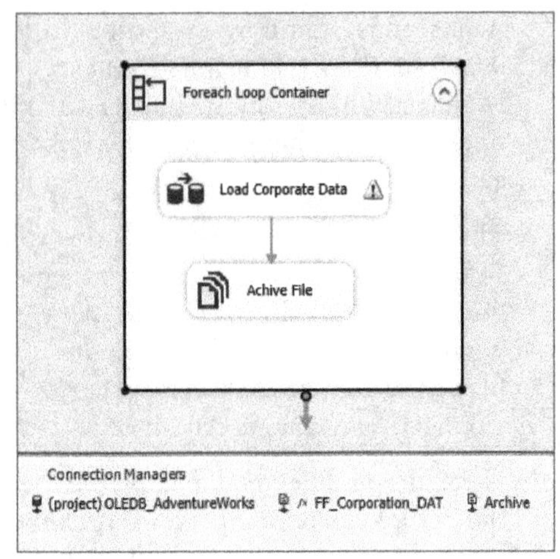

FIGURE 8-19

SUMMARY

This chapter focused on driving home the basic SSIS transformations, tasks, and containers. You performed a basic ETL procedure, and then expanded the ETL to self-heal when bad data arrived from your data supplier. You then set the package to loop through a directory, find each .DAT file, and load it into the database. The finale was archiving the file automatically after it was loaded. With this type of package now complete, you could use any .DAT file that matched the format you configured, and it will load with reasonable certainty. In the upcoming chapters, you'll dive deeply into Script Tasks and Components.

Scripting in SSIS

WHAT'S IN THIS CHAPTER?

- Selecting your scripting language and getting started
- Adding assemblies to SSIS Script objects
- Understanding Script Task usage
- Understanding Script Component usage
- Using external SSIS objects from within a script
- Using events and logging in debugging scripts

WROX.COM DOWNLOADS FOR THIS CHAPTER

You can find the wrox.com code downloads for this chapter at `www.wrox.com/go/prossis2014` on the Download Code tab.

Scripting is the Swiss Army knife of SSIS. As shown in previous chapters, many different SSIS features are available out-of-the-box. If you need to do something that you just can't find anywhere else, you will find additional functionality in three features: the Script Task, the Script Component, and expressions. Expressions, covered in Chapter 5, are small scripts that set properties. The other two scripting concepts provide access into a scripting development environment using Microsoft Visual Studio Tools for Applications (VSTA) that enables SSIS developers to script logic into packages using Microsoft Visual Basic 2012 or Microsoft Visual C# 2012 .NET code.

In this chapter, you will learn the differences between these script components and when you should use one over the other. You'll also learn all about the various scripting options available and how to use them in your package development tasks to control execution flow, perform custom transformations, manage variables, and provide runtime feedback.

INTRODUCING SSIS SCRIPTING

If you think of scripting as something that compiles at runtime and contains unstructured or unmanaged coding languages, then scripting in SSIS does not conform to your idea of scripting. Conversely, if you think of scripting as using small bits of code in specialized places to execute specific tasks, then SSIS scripting won't be an alien concept. It is helpful to understand why scripting is separated according to functional usage. In this chapter, you will examine the differences and look into the scripting IDE environment, walking through the mechanics of applying programmatic logic into these components — including how to add your own classes and compiled assemblies.

ETL developers have had creative ways of handling logic in their packages. Specifically, digging into what developers were doing, the functional activities can be divided into the following categories:

- Retrieving or setting the value of package variables
- Retrieving or setting properties within the package
- Applying business logic to validate or format data
- Controlling workflow in a package

Retrieving and setting the value of variables and package properties is so prevalent an activity that the SSIS team creates a completely separate feature that enabled this to be less of a programmatic task. Using the Expression Builder, you can easily alter package components by setting component properties to an expression or a variable that represents an expression.

> **NOTE** *Refer to Chapter 5 for detailed information about how to use expressions, parameters, and variables.*

To modify properties that connect to, manipulate, or define data, you can use the Data Flow Task to visually represent this activity. However, to achieve functionality not provided out of the box, you still need scripting, so the Script Component was added. The primary role of the Script Component is to extend the Data Flow capabilities and allow programmatic data manipulation within the context of the Data Flow. However, it can do more, as you'll learn later in this chapter.

To continue to enable the numerous miscellaneous tasks that are needed in ETL development, use the Script Task, which can be used only in the Control Flow design surface. In this task, you can perform various manipulations within the managed code framework of .NET.

The Script Task and Script Component use the Visual Studio Tools for Applications (VSTA) environment. VSTA is essentially a scaled-down version of Visual Studio that can be added to an application that allows coding extensions using managed code and .NET languages. Even though SSIS packages are built inside of Visual Studio, when you are in the context of a Script Task or Script Component, you are actually coding in the VSTA environment that is, in fact, a mini-project within the package. The VSTA IDE provides IntelliSense, full edit-and-continue capabilities, and the ability to code in either Visual Basic or C#. You can even access some of the .NET assemblies and use web references for advanced scripting.

> **NOTE** *To gain the most from this scripting chapter, you need a basic understanding of programming in either C# or Visual Basic. If you don't already have it, you can obtain this knowledge from either* Beginning Visual C# 2012 Programming *by Karli Watson and colleagues (Wrox; ISBN: 978-1-118-31441-8) or* Beginning Visual Basic 2012 *by Bryan Newsome (Wrox; ISBN: 978-1-118-31181-3).*

GETTING STARTED IN SSIS SCRIPTING

The Script Task and Script Component have greatly increased your possibilities when it comes to script-based ETL development in SSIS. However, it is important to know when to use which component and what things can be done in each.

The following matrix explains when to use each component:

COMPONENT	WHEN TO USE
Script Task	This task is used in the Control Flow. Use this task when you need to program logic that either controls package execution or performs a task of retrieving or setting variables within a package during runtime.
Script Component	This component is used in the Data Flow. Use this component when moving data using the Data Flow Task. Here you can apply programmatic logic to massage, create, or consume data in the pipeline.

To get a good look at the scripting model, the next example walks through a simple "Hello World" coding project in SSIS. Although this is not a typical example of ETL programming, it serves as a good introduction to the scripting paradigm in SSIS, followed by the specific applications of the Script Task and Script Component.

Selecting the Scripting Language

SSIS allows the developer to choose between two different scripting languages: C# or Visual Basic (VB). To see where you can make this choice, drop a Script Task onto the Control Flow design surface. Right-click the Script Task and click Edit from the context menu. The first thing you'll notice is the availability of two scripting languages: Microsoft Visual C# 2012 and Microsoft Visual Basic 2012 in the `ScriptLanguage` property of the task. Figure 9-1 shows these options in the Script Task Editor.

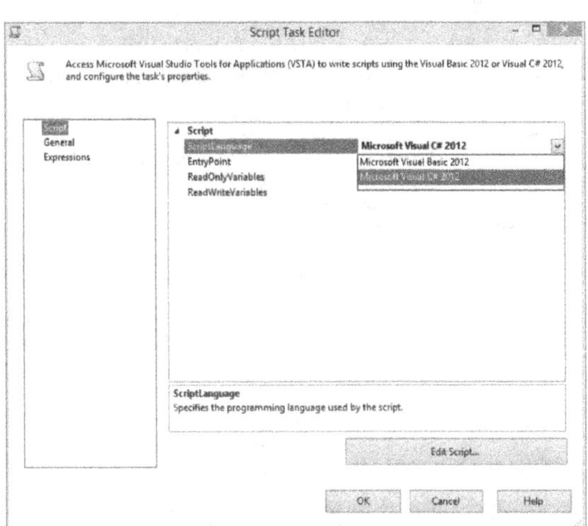

FIGURE 9-1

After clicking the Edit Script button, you'll be locked into the script language that you chose and you won't be able to change it without deleting and recreating the Script Task or Script Component.

This is because each Script item contains its own internal Visual Studio project in VB or C#. You can create separate Script items whereby each one uses a different language within a package. However, using Script items in both languages within the same package is not recommended, as it makes maintenance of the package more complex. Anyone maintaining the package would have to be competent in both languages.

Using the VSTA Scripting IDE

Clicking the Edit Script button on the editor allows you to add programmatic code to a Script Task or Script Component. Although the Script Task and Script Component editors look different, they both provide an Edit Script button to access the development IDE for scripting, as shown in Figure 9-2.

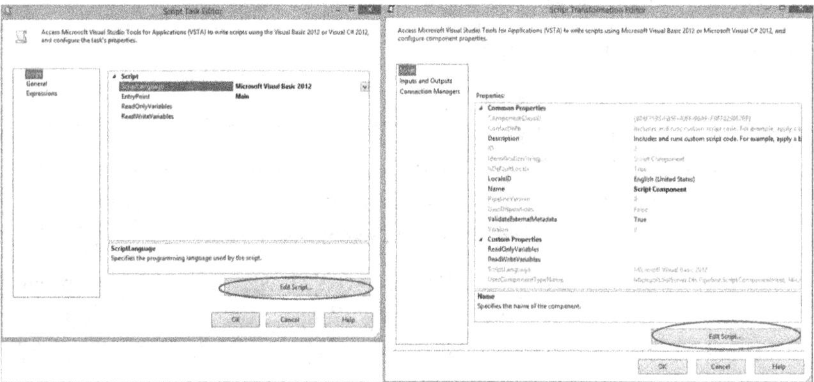

FIGURE 9-2

Once you are in the IDE, notice that it looks and feels just like Visual Studio. Figure 9-3 shows an example of how this IDE looks after opening the Script Task for the VB scripting language.

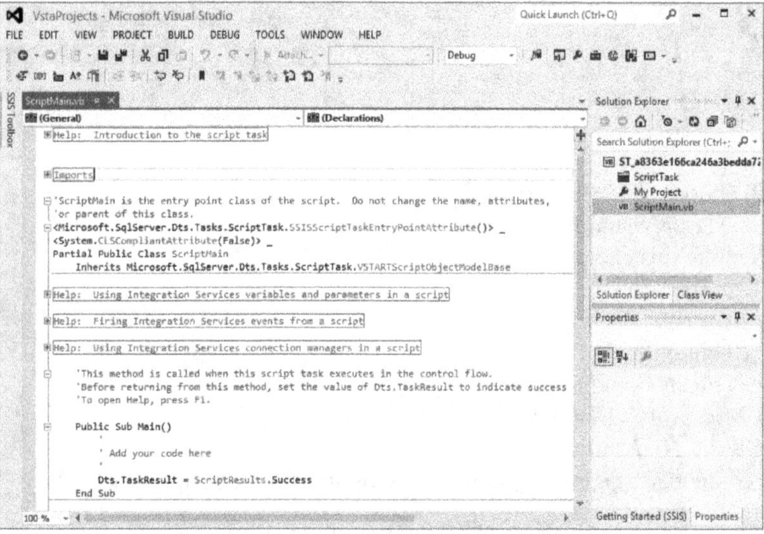

FIGURE 9-3

The code window on the left side of the IDE contains the code for the item selected in the Solution Explorer on the top-right window. The Solution Explorer shows the structure for the project that is being used within the Scripting Task. A complete .NET project is created for each Script Task or Component and is temporarily written to a project file on the local drive where it can be altered in the Visual Studio IDE. This persistence of the project is the reason why once you pick a scripting language, and generate code in the project, you are locked into that language for that Scripting item. Notice in Figure 9-3 that a project has been created with the namespace of `ST_a8363e166ca246a3bedda7`. However, you can't open this project directly, nor need you worry about the project during deployment. These project files are extracted from stored package metadata. With the project created and opened, it is ready for coding.

Example: Hello World

In the IDE, the Script Task contains only a class named `ScriptMain`. In the entry-point function, `Main()`, you'll put the code that you want executed. Part of that code can make calls to additional functions or classes. However, if you want to change the name of the entry-point function for some reason, type the new name in the property called `EntryPoint` on the Script page of the editor. (Alternatively, you could change the name of the entry point at runtime using an expression.)

In the VSTA co-generated class `ScriptMain`, you'll also see a set of assembly references already added to your project, and namespaces set up in the class. Depending upon whether you chose VB or C# as your scripting language, you'll see either:

C#

```
using System;
using System.Data;
using Microsoft.SqlServer.Dts.Runtime;
using System.Windows.Forms;
```

or

VB

```
Imports System
Imports System.Data
Imports System.Math
Imports Microsoft.SqlServer.Dts.Runtime
```

These assemblies are needed to provide base functionality as a jump-start to your coding. The remainder of the class includes VSTA co-generated methods for startup and shutdown operations, and finally the entry-point `Main()` function, shown here in both languages:

C#

```
public void Main()
{
// TODO: Add your code here
Dts.TaskResult = (int)ScriptResults.Success;
}
```

VB

```
Public Sub Main()
'
' Add your code here
'
Dts.TaskResult = ScriptResults.Success
End Sub
```

Note that the Script Task must return a result to notify the runtime of whether the script completed successfully or not. The result is passed using the `Dts.TaskResult` property. By your setting the result to `ScriptResults.Success`, the script informs the package that the task completed successfully.

> **NOTE** *The Script Component does not have to do this, since it runs in the context of a Data Flow with many rows. Other differences pertaining to each component are discussed separately later in the chapter.*

To get a message box to pop up with the phrase "Hello World!" you need access to a class called `MessageBox` in a namespace called `System.Windows.Forms`. This namespace can be called directly by its complete name, or it can be added after the `Microsoft.SqlServer.Dts.Runtime` namespace to shorten the coding required in the class. Both of these methods are shown in the following code (`ProSSIS\Code\Ch09_ProSSIS\02HelloWorld.dtsx`) to insert the `MessageBox` code into the `Main()` function:

C#

```
using System.Windows.Forms;
...
MessageBox.Show("Hello World!");
Or
System.Windows.Forms.MessageBox.Show("Hello World!");
```

VB

```
Imports System.Windows.Forms
...
MessageBox.Show("Hello World!")
Or
System.Windows.Forms.MessageBox.Show("Hello World!")
```

Get in the habit now of building the project after adding this code. The Build option is directly on the menu when you are coding. Previous versions of SSIS gave you the opportunity to run in precompile or compiled modes. SSIS now will automatically compile your code prior to executing the package at runtime. Compiling gives you an opportunity to find any errors before the package finds them. Once the build is successful, close the IDE and the editor, and right-click and execute the Script Task. A pop-up message box should appear with the words "Hello World!" (see Figure 9-4).

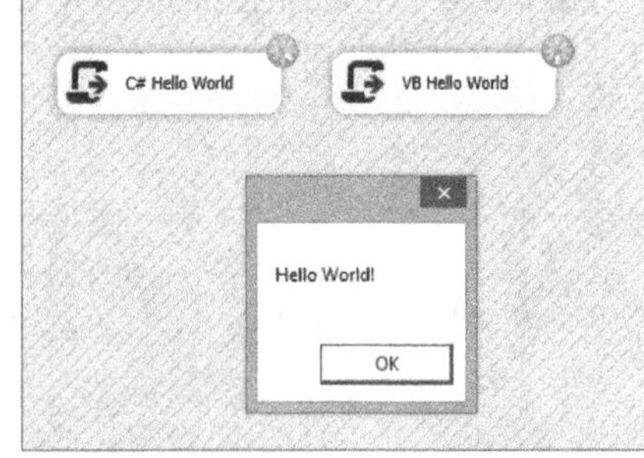

FIGURE 9-4

Adding Code and Classes

Using modal message boxes is obviously not the type of typical coding desired in production SSIS package development. Message boxes are synchronous and block until a click event is received, so they can stop a production job dead in its tracks. However, this is a basic debugging technique to demonstrate the capabilities in the scripting environments before getting into some of the details of passing values in and out using variables. You also don't want to always put the main blocks of code in the `Main()` function. With just a little more work, you can get some code reuse from previously written code using some cut-and-paste development techniques. At the very least, code can be structured in a less procedural way. As an example, consider the common task of generating a unique filename for a file you want to archive.

Typically, the filename might be generated by appending a prefix and an extension to a variable like a guid. These functions can be added within the `ScriptMain` class bodies to look like this (`ProSSIS\Code\Ch09_ProSSIS\03BasicScript.dtsx`):

C#

```
Public partial class ScriptMain
{
...
public void Main()
{
System.Windows.Forms.MessageBox.Show(GetFileName("bankfile", "txt"));
    Dts.TaskResult = (int)ScriptResults.Success;
}
public string GetFileName(string Prefix, string Extension)
{
return Prefix + "-" + Guid.NewGuid().ToString() + "." + Extension;
}
}
```

VB

```
Partial Class ScriptMain
...
Public Sub Main()
System.Windows.Forms.MessageBox.Show(GetFileName("bankfile", "txt"))
Dts.TaskResult = ScriptResults.Success
End Sub
Public Function GetFileName(ByVal Prefix As String, _
ByVal Extension As String) As String
GetFileName = Prefix + "-" + Guid.NewGuid.ToString + _
"." + Extension
End Function
End Class
```

Instead of all the code residing in the `Main()` function, structured programming techniques can separate and organize SSIS scripting. In this example, the `GetFileName` function builds the filename and then returns the value, which is shown in a message box, as shown in Figure 9-5.

FIGURE 9-5

Of course, copying and pasting the same code into multiple Script Tasks is pretty inefficient and produces solutions that are difficult to maintain. If you have preexisting compiled code, shouldn't you be able to reuse this code without finding the original source for the copy-and-paste operation? What a great question! You can, with some caveats.

Using Managed Assemblies

Reusing code, no matter what language it was written in, increases the maintainability and supportability of an application. While you can only write SSIS scripts using Visual Basic and C#, SSIS provides the capability to reuse code by reusing assemblies that are part of the .NET Framework or any assembly created using a .NET-compliant language, including C#, J#, and even Delphi, but there are some important qualifications:

- For a managed assembly to be used in an Integration Service, you must install the assembly in the global assembly cache (GAC).
- All dependent or referenced assemblies must also be registered in the GAC. This implies that the assemblies must be strongly named.
- For development purposes only, VSTA can use managed assemblies anywhere on the local machine.

If you think about this it makes sense, but within SSIS, it might seem confusing at first. On the one hand, a subproject is created for the Script Task, but it is deployed as part of the metadata of the package; there is no separate physical DLL file for the assembly. In this case, you don't have to worry about deployment of individual script projects. However, when you use an external assembly, it is not part of the package metadata, and here you *do* have to worry about deployment of the assembly. Where then do you deploy the assembly you want to use? Because SSIS packages are typically deployed within SQL Server, the most universal place to find the assembly would be in the GAC.

If you are using any of the standard .NET assemblies, they are already loaded and stored in the GAC and the .NET Framework folders. As long as you are using the same framework for your development and production locations, using standard .NET assemblies requires no additional work in your environment. To use a standard .NET assembly in your script, you must reference it. To add a reference in a scripting project, open the VSTA environment for editing your script code — not the SSIS package itself. Right-click the project name in the Solution Explorer or go to the Project menu and select the Add Reference option. The new Reference Manager dialog will appear, as in Figure 9-6.

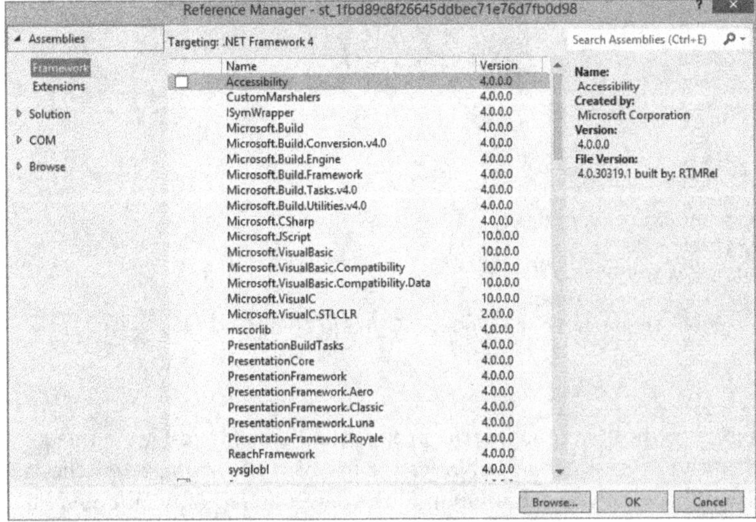

FIGURE 9-6

Select the assemblies from the list that you wish to reference and click the OK button to add the references to your project. Now you can use any objects located in the referenced assemblies either by directly referencing the full assembly or by adding the namespaces to your `ScriptMain` classes for shorter references, similar to the Windows Forms assembly used in the Hello World example. References can be removed from the project References screen. Find this screen by double-clicking the My Project node of the Solution Explorer. Select the References menu to see all references included in your project. To remove a reference, select the name and click the Delete key.

Example: Using Custom .NET Assemblies

Although using standard .NET assemblies is interesting, being able to use your own compiled .NET assemblies really extends the capabilities of your SSIS development. Using code already developed and compiled means not having to copy-and-paste code into each Script Task, enabling you to reuse code already developed and tested. To examine how this works, in this section you'll create an external custom .NET library that can validate a postal code and learn how to integrate this simple validator into a Script Task. (To do this, you need the standard class library project templates that are part of Visual Studio. If you installed only SQL Server Data Tools, these templates are not installed by default.) You can also download the precompiled versions of these classes, as well as any code from this chapter, at `www.wrox.com/go/prossis2014`.

To start, open a standard class library project in the language of your choice, and create a standard utility class in the project that looks something like this (`proSSIS\Code\Ch09_ProSSIS\SSISUtilityLib_VB\SSISUtilityLib_VB\DataUtilities.vb`):

C#

```
using System.Text.RegularExpressions;
namespace SSISUtilityLib_CSharp
{
public static class DataUtilities
{
```

```
public static bool isValidUSPostalCode(string PostalCode)
{
return Regex.IsMatch(PostalCode, "^[0-9]{5}(-[0-9]{4})?$");
}
}
}
```

VB

```
Imports System.Text.RegularExpressions
Public Class DataUtilities
Public Shared Function isValidUSPostalCode
(ByVal PostalCode As String) As Boolean
isValidUSPostalCode = Regex.IsMatch(PostalCode, "^[0-9]{5}(-[0-9]{4})?$")
End Function
End Class
```

Because you are creating projects for both languages, the projects (and assemblies) are named `SSISUtilityLib_VB` and `SSISUtilityLib_Csharp`. Notice the use of *static* or *shared* methods. This isn't required, but it's useful because you are simulating the development of what could later be a utility library loaded with many stateless data validation functions. A static or shared method allows the utility functions to be called without instantiating the class for each evaluation.

Now sign the assembly by right-clicking the project to access the Properties menu option. In the Signing tab, note the option to "Sign the assembly," as shown in Figure 9-7. Click New on the dropdown and name the assembly to have a strong name key added to it.

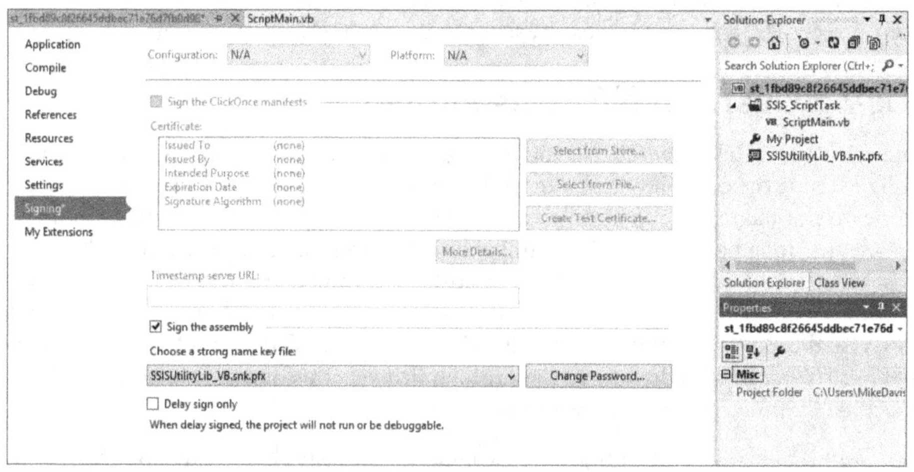

FIGURE 9-7

In this example, the VB version of the `SSISUtilityLib` project is being signed. Now you can compile the assembly by clicking the Build option in the Visual Studio menu. The in-process DLL will be built with a strong name, enabling it to be registered in the GAC.

On the target development machine, open a command-line prompt window to register your assembly with a command similar to this:

```
C:\Program Files (x86)\Microsoft SDKs\Windows\v7.0A\bin\NETFX 4.0 Tools>
Gacutil /i C:\ProSSIS\Code\SSISUtilityLib_CSharp\SSISUtilityLib_CSharp\
bin\Release\SSISUtilityLib_CSharp.dll
```

> **NOTE** *Note that you may have to run the command line as administrator or have the User Access Control feature turned off to register the assembly.*

If you are running on a development machine, you also need to copy the assembly into the appropriate .NET Framework directory so that you can use the assembly in the Visual Studio IDE. Using the Microsoft .NET Framework Configuration tool, select Manage the Assembly Cache. Then select Add an Assembly to the Assembly Cache to copy an assembly file into the global cache.

> **NOTE** *For a detailed step-by-step guide to the deployment, see the SSIS Developer's Guide on Custom Objects located at* `http://msdn.microsoft.com/en-us/library/ms403356(v=SQL.110).aspx`.

To use the compiled assembly in an SSIS package, open a new SSIS package and add a new Script Task to the Control Flow surface. Select the scripting language you wish and click Edit Script. You'll need to right-click the Solution Explorer node for references and find the reference for `SSISUtilityLib_VB.dll` or `SSISUtilityLib_CSharp.dll` depending on which one you built. If you have registered the assembly in the GAC, you can find it in the .NET tab. If you are in a development environment, you can simply browse to the `.dll` to select it.

Add the namespace into the `ScriptMain` class. Then add these namespaces to the `ScriptMain` class:

C#

```
using SSISUtilityLib_CSharp;
```

VB

```
Imports SSISUtilityLib_VB
```

Note that the SSIS C# Script Task in the sample packages you'll see if you download the chapter materials from `www.wrox.com/go/prossis2014` use both the C# and the VB versions of the utility library. However, this is not required. The compiled .NET class libraries may be intermixed within the SSIS Script Task or Components regardless of the scripting language you choose.

Now you just need to code a call to the utility function in the `Main()` function like this (`ProSSIS\Code\Ch09_ProSSIS\04SSISPackageUsingAssembly.dtsx`):

C#

```
public void Main()
{
string postalCode = "12345-1111";
string msg = string.Format(
"Validating PostalCode {0}\nResult..{1}", postalCode,
    DataUtilities.isValidUSPostalCode(postalCode));
MessageBox.Show(msg);
Dts.TaskResult = (int)ScriptResults.Success;
}
```

VB

```
Public Sub Main()
Dim postalCode As String = "12345-1111"
Dim msg As String = String.Format("Validating PostalCode {0}" + _
vbCrLf + "Result..{1}", postalCode, _
DataUtilities.isValidUSPostalCode(postalCode))
MessageBox.Show(msg)
Dts.TaskResult = ScriptResults.Success
End Sub
```

Compile the Script Task and execute it. The result should be a message box displaying a string to validate the postal code 12345-1111. The postal code format is validated by the `DataUtility` function `IsValidUSPostalCode`. There was no need to copy the function in the script project. The logic of validating the format of a U.S. postal code is stored in the shared `DataUtility` function and can easily be used in both Script Tasks and Components with minimal coding and maximum consistency. The only downside to this is that there is now an external dependency in the SSIS package upon this assembly. If the assembly changes version numbers, you'll need to open and recompile all the script projects for each SSIS package using this. Otherwise, you could get an error if you aren't following backward compatibility guidelines to ensure that existing interfaces are not broken. If you have a set of well-tested business functions that rarely change, using external assemblies may be a good idea for your SSIS development.

USING THE SCRIPT TASK

Now that you have a good overview of the scripting environment in SSIS, it's time to dig into the Script Task and give it a spin. The Script Task was used heavily to demonstrate how the SSIS scripting environment works with Visual Studio and during the execution of a package. Generally, anything that you can script in the .NET managed environment that should run once per package or code loop belongs in the Script Task. The Script Task is used in the Control Flow of a package. Script Tasks are extremely useful and end up being the general-purpose utility component if the desired functionality is not available in the out-of-the-box Control Flow tasks.

Configuring the Script Task Editor

An earlier look at the Script Task Editor pointed out that two selections are available for the scripting language, but there are other options as well. Drop a Script Task on the Control Flow surface to display the Script Task Editor shown in Figure 9-8.

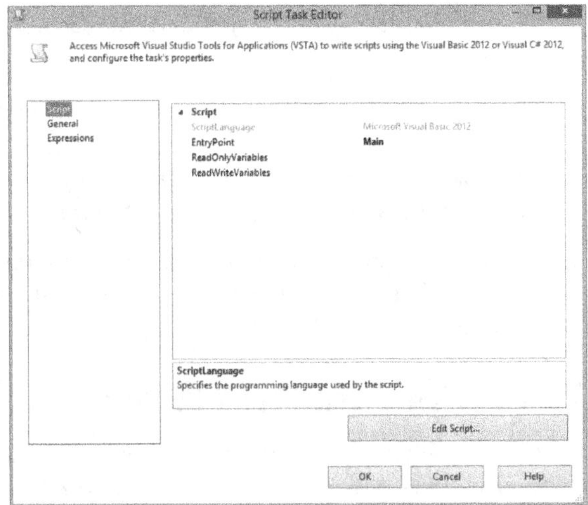

FIGURE 9-8

Here are the four properties on the Script tab to configure the Script Task:

- **ScriptLanguage:** This property defines the .NET language that will be used for the script. As demonstrated earlier, VB and C# are your two options.
- **EntryPoint:** This is the name of the method that will be called inside your script to begin execution.
- **ReadOnlyVariables:** This property enumerates a case-sensitive, comma-separated list of SSIS variables to which you allow explicit rights to be read by the Script Task.
- **ReadWriteVariables:** This property enumerates a case-sensitive, comma-separated list of SSIS variables to which you allow the script to read from and write to.

All scripts are precompiled by default, which improves performance and reduces the overhead of loading the language engine when running a package.

The second tab on the left, General, contains the task name and description properties.

The final page available on the left of this dialog is the Expressions tab. The Expressions tab provides access to the properties that can be set using an expression or expression-based variable. (See Chapter 5 for details about how to use expressions and variables.) Keep in mind that changing the `ScriptLanguage` property at runtime is neither possible nor desirable even though it is listed as a possibility in the Expression Editor.

Once the script language is set and the script accessed, a project file with a class named `ScriptMain` and a default entry point named `Main()` is created. As a reminder, an example of the `Main()` function is provided here (`ProSSIS\Code\Ch09_ProSSIS\01EmptyPackage.dtsx`), without the supporting class:

C#

```
public void Main()
{
Dts.TaskResult = (int)ScriptResults.Success;
}
```

VB

```
Public Sub Main()
Dts.TaskResult = ScriptResults.Success
End Try
```

The code provided includes the statement to set the `TaskResult` of the `Dts` object to the enumerated value for success. The Script Task itself is a task in the collection of tasks for the package. Setting the `TaskResult` property of the task sets the return value for the Script Task and tells the package whether the result was a success or a failure.

By now, you have probably noticed all the references to `Dts`. What is this object and what can you do with it? This question is answered in the next section, as you peel back the layers of the `Dts` object.

The Script Task Dts Object

The `Dts` object is actually a property on your package that is an instance of the `Microsoft.SqlServer.Dts.Tasks.ScriptTask.ScriptObjectModel` class. The `Dts` object provides a window into the package in which your script executes. Although you can't change properties of the package as it executes, the `Dts` object has seven properties and one method that allow you to interact with the package. The following is an explanation of these members:

- `Connections`: A collection of Connection Managers defined in the package. You can use these connections in your script to retrieve any extra data you may need.
- `Events`: A collection of events that are defined for the package. You can use this interface to fire off these predefined events and any custom events.
- `ExecutionValue`: A read-write property that enables you to specify additional information about your task's execution using a user-defined object. This can be any information you want.
- `TaskResult`: This property enables you to return the success or failure status of your Script Task to the package. This is the main way of communicating processing status or controlling flow in your package. This property must be set before exiting your script.
- `Transaction`: Obtains the transaction associated with the container in which your script is running.
- `VariableDispenser`: Gets the `VariableDispenser` object, which you can use to retrieve variables when using the Script Task.
- `Variables`: A collection of all the variables available to any script.
- `Log`: You can use this method to write to any log providers that have been enabled.

The next few sections describe some of the common things that the Script Task can be employed to accomplish.

Accessing Variables in the Script Task

Variables and expressions are an important feature of the SSIS road map. In the following scenario, "variables" describe objects that serve as intermediate communication mediums between your Script Task and the rest of your package. As discussed in Chapter 5, variables are used to drive the runtime changes within a package by allowing properties to infer their values at runtime from variables, which can be static or defined through the expression language.

The common method of using variables is to send them into a Script Task as decision-making elements or to drive downstream decisions by setting the value of the variable in the script based on some business rules. To use a variable in a script, the variable must be locked, accessed, and then unlocked. There are two ways of doing this: explicitly and implicitly.

The explicit method uses the `VariableDispenser` object, which provides methods for locking variables for read-only or read-write access and then retrieving them. At one time, this was the standard way of accessing variables in scripts. The explicit locking mechanism allows control in the Script Task to keep two processes from competing for accessing and changing a variable. This will also reduce the amount of time the variable is locked, but forces the developer to write code.

To retrieve a variable using the `VariableDispenser` object, you have to deal with the implementation details of locking semantics, and write code like the following (`ProSSIS\Code\Ch09_ProSSIS\13VarsScriptTask.dtsx`):

C#

```
Variables vars = null;
String myval = null;
Dts.VariableDispenser.LockForRead("User::SomeStringVariable");
Dts.VariableDispenser.GetVariables(ref vars);
myval = vars[0].Value.ToString;
vars.Unlock(); //Needed to unlock the variables
System.Windows.Forms.MessageBox.Show(myval);
```

VB

```
Dim vars As Variables
Dim myval As String
Dts.VariableDispenser.LockForRead("User::SomeStringVariable")
Dts.VariableDispenser.GetVariables(vars)
myval = vars(0).Value.ToString
vars.Unlock() 'Needed to unlock the variables
MsgBox(myval)
```

The implicit option of handling variables is the alternative to manually locking, using, and unlocking the variable. This option is best when you simply want the variables that you are using in a Script Task to be locked when you are reading and writing; you don't want to worry about the locking implementation details. The `Variables` collection on the `Dts` object and the `ReadOnlyVariables` and `ReadWriteVariables` properties for the Script Task allow you to set up the implicit variable locking. The only constraint is that you have to define up front which variables going into the Script Task can be read but not written to versus both readable and writable.

The `ReadOnlyVariables` and `ReadWriteVariables` properties tell the Script Task which variables to lock and how. The `Variables` collection in the `Dts` object is then populated with these variables. This simplifies the code to retrieve a variable, and the complexities of locking are abstracted, so you have to worry about only one line of code to read a variable (`ProSSIS\Code\Ch09_ProSSIS\13VarsScriptTask.dtsx`):

C#

```
Dts.Variables["User::SomeStringVariable"].Value = "MyValue";
```

VB

```
Dts.Variables("User::SomeStringVariable").Value = "MyValue"
```

It is safest to use the fully qualified variable name, such as `User::SomeStringVariable`. Attempting to read a variable from the `Variables` collection that hasn't been specified in one of the variable properties of the task will throw an exception. Likewise, attempting to write to a variable not included in the `ReadWriteVariables` property also throws an exception. The biggest frustration for new SSIS developers writing VB script is dealing with the following error message:

```
Error: 0xc0914054 at VB Script Task: Failed to lock variable "SomestringVariable"
for read access with error 0xc0910001 "The variable cannot be found. This occurs
when an attempt is made to retrieve a variable from the Variables collection on a
container during execution of the package, and the variable is not there. The
variable name may have changed or the variable is not being created."
```

The resolution is simple. Either the variable name listed in the Script Task Editor or the variable name in the script doesn't match, so one must be changed to match the other. It is more confusing for the VB developers because this language is not case sensitive. However, the SSIS variables are case sensitive, even within the VB script.

> **NOTE** *Although Visual Basic .NET is not case sensitive, SSIS variables are.*

Another issue that happens occasionally is that a developer can create more than one variable with the same name with different scopes. When this happens, you have to ensure that you explicitly refer to the variable by the fully qualified variable name. SSIS provides a Select Variables dialog, shown in Figure 9-9, that enables selection of the variables.

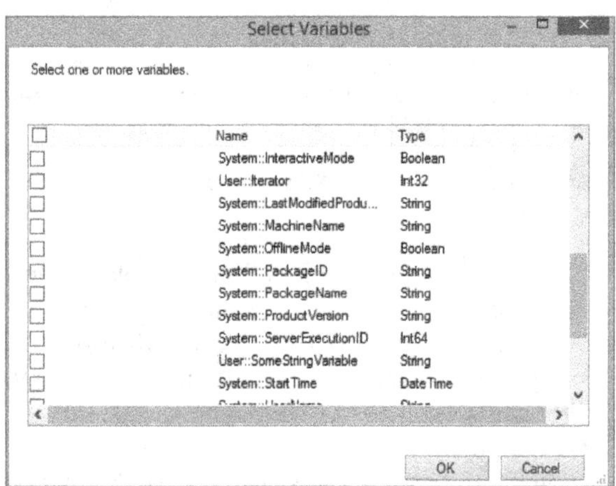

FIGURE 9-9

Fortunately, the Script Task property for the `ReadOnlyVariables` or `ReadWriteVariables` is auto-filled with the fully qualified names: `User::DecisionIntVar` and `User::DecisionStrVar`. This reduces most of the common issues that can occur when passing variables into the Script Task. All this information will now come in handy as you walk through an example using the Script Task and variables to control SSIS package flow.

Example: Using Script Task Variables to Control Package Flow

This example sets up a Script Task that uses two variables to determine which one of two branches of Control Flow logic should be taken when the package executes. First, create a new SSIS package and set up these three variables:

VARIABLE	TYPE	VALUE
DecisionIntVar	Int32	45
DecisionStrVar	String	txt
HappyPathEnum	Int32	0

Then drop three Script Tasks on the Control Flow design surface so that the package looks like Figure 9-10.

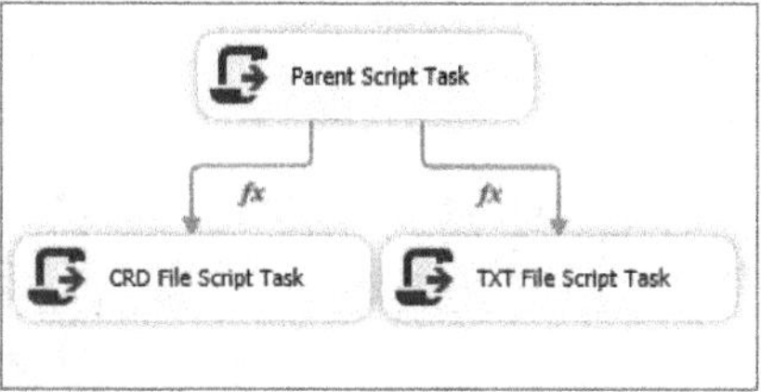

FIGURE 9-10

There are two variables, `DecisionIntVar` and `DecisionStrVar`, that represent the number of rows determined to be in a file and the file extension, respectively. These variables are fed into the Script Task. Assume that these values have been set by another process. Logic in the Script Task will determine whether the package should execute the CRD File Path Script Task or the TXT File Script Task. The control of the package is handled by the other external variable named `HappyPathEnum`. If the value of this variable is equal to 1, then the TXT File Script Task will be executed. If the value of the variable is equal to 2, then the CRD File Path Script Task will be executed. Open the Script Task Editor for the Parent Script Task to set up the properties (see Figure 9-11).

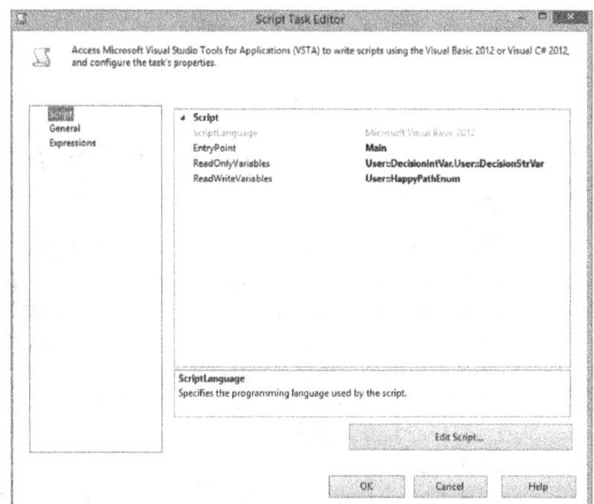

FIGURE 9-11

Set the Script Language and then use the ellipsis button to bring up the variable selection user interface (refer to Figure 9-9). Select the variables for `ReadOnlyVariables` and `ReadWriteVariables` separately if you are using this dialog. You can also type these variables in, but remember that the variable names are case sensitive. As shown in Figure 9-12, note the ordinal positions of the variables for this example.

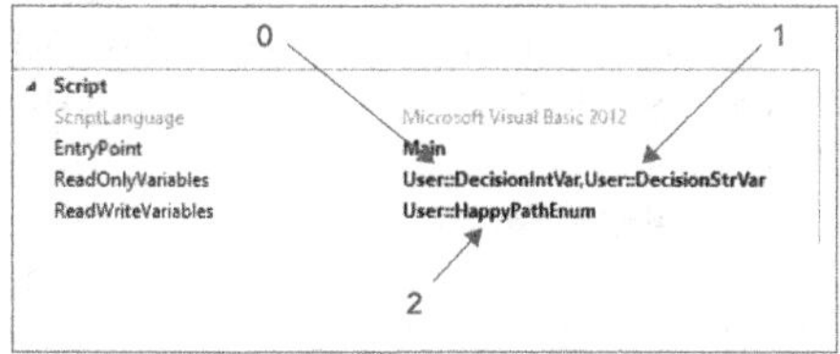

FIGURE 9-12

Keep this script simple for demonstration purposes. The most important parts are the retrieving and setting of the variables. This code uses the named references for the variables for the retrieval of the variable values:

C#

```
int rowCnt = (int)Dts.Variables["User::DecisionIntVar"].Value;
```

VB

```
Dim rowCnt As Integer = Dts.Variables("User::DecisionIntVar").Value
```

The setting of variables uses the same syntax but reverses the assignment. The code that should be pasted into the `Main()` function of the `ScriptMain` class will evaluate the two variables and set the `HappyPathEnum` variable (`ProSSIS\Code\Ch09_ProSSIS\05STVarControlFlow.dtsx`):

C#

```
//Retrieving the value of Variables
int rowCnt = (int)Dts.Variables["User::DecisionIntVar"].Value;
string fileExt = (string)Dts.Variables["User::DecisionStrVar"].Value;
if (fileExt.Equals("txt") && rowCnt > 0)
{
Dts.Variables["User::HappyPathEnum"].Value = 1;
}
else if (fileExt.Equals("crd") && rowCnt > 0)
{
Dts.Variables["User::HappyPathEnum"].Value = 2;
}
Dts.TaskResult = (int)ScriptResults.Success;
```

VB

```
'Retrieving the value of Variables
Dim rowCnt As Integer = Dts.Variables("User::DecisionIntVar").Value
Dim fileExt As String = Dts.Variables("User::DecisionStrVar").Value
If (fileExt.Equals("txt") And rowCnt > 0) Then
Dts.Variables("User::HappyPathEnum").Value = 1
ElseIf (fileExt.Equals("crd") And rowCnt > 0) Then
Dts.Variables("User::HappyPathEnum").Value = 2
End If
Dts.TaskResult = ScriptResults.Success
```

To alter the flow of the package, set the two precedence constraints in the package hierarchy to be based on a successful completion of the previous Script Task and an expression that tests the expected values of the `HappyPathEnum` variable. This precedence specifies that the Control Flow should go in a direction only if the value of an expression tests true. Set the precedence between each Script Task to one of these expressions going to the TXT and CRD tasks, respectively:

```
@HappyPathEnum == 1
```

Or

```
@HappyPathEnum == 2
```

A sample of the precedence between the Script Task and the TXT File Script Task should look like Figure 9-13.

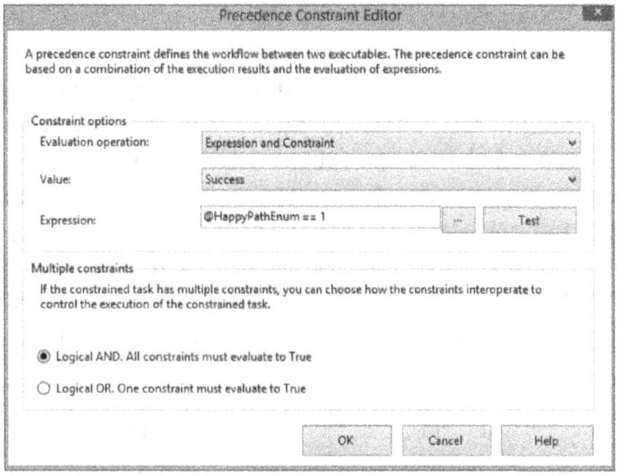

Now, to give the package something to do, simply retrieve the value of the set variable in each child Script Task to provide visual proof that the `HappyPathEnum` variable was properly set. Add this code into the `Main()` function of each child Script Task (make sure you set the message to display TXT or CRD for each associated Script Task) (`ProSSIS\Code\Ch09_ProSSIS\05STVarControlFlow.dtsx`):

FIGURE 9-13

C#

```
int ival = (int)Dts.Variables[0].
Value;
string msg = string.Format("TXT File
Found\nHappyPathEnum Value = {0}",
    Dts.Variables[0].Value.ToString());
System.Windows.Forms.MessageBox.Show(msg);
Dts.TaskResult = (int)ScriptResults.Success;
```

VB

```
Dim ival As Integer = Dts.Variables(0).Value
Dim msg As String = _
String.Format("TXT File Found" + vbCrLf + "HappyPathEnum Value = {0}", _
    Dts.Variables(0).Value.ToString())
System.Windows.Forms.MessageBox.Show(msg)
Dts.TaskResult = ScriptResults.Success
```

To see how this works, set the value of the `User::DecisionIntVar` variable to a positive integer number value, and the `User::DecisionStrVar` variable to either `txt` or `crd`, and watch the package switch from one Control Flow to the other. If you provide a value other than `txt` or `crd` (even `"txt"` with quotes will cause this), the package will not run either leg, as designed. This is a simple example that you can refer back to as your packages get more complicated and you want to update variables within a Script Task. Later in this chapter, you'll see how the Script Component accesses variables in a slightly different way.

Connecting to Data Sources in a Script Task

A common use of an ETL package is to grab a connection to retrieve decision-making data from various data sources, such as Excel files, INI files, flat files, or databases like Oracle or Access. This capability allows other data sources to configure the package or to retrieve data for objects that can't use a direct connection object. In SSIS, with the Script Task you can make connections using any of the .NET libraries directly, or you can use connections that are defined in a package. Connections in SSIS are abstractions for connection strings that can be copied, passed around, and easily configured.

The `Connections` collection is a property of the `Dts` object in the Script Task. To retrieve a connection, you call the `AcquireConnection` method on a specific named (or ordinal position) connection in the collection. The only thing you really should know ahead of time is what type of connection you are going to be retrieving, because you need to cast the returned connection to the proper connection type. In .NET, connections are not generic. Examples of concrete connections are `SqlConnection`, `OleDbConnection`, `OdbcConnection`, and the `OracleConnection` managers that connect using SqlClient, OLE DB, ODBC, and even Oracle data access libraries, respectively. There are some things you can do to query the Connection Manager to determine what is in the connection string or whether it supports transactions, but you shouldn't expect to use one connection in SSIS for everything, especially with the additional Connection Managers for FTP, HTTP, and WMI.

Assuming that you're up to speed on the different types of connections covered earlier in this book, it's time to look at how you can use them in everyday SSIS Script Tasks.

Example: Retrieving Data into Variables from a Database

Although SSIS provides configurable abilities to set package-level values, there are use cases that require you to retrieve actionable values from a database that can be used for package Control Flow or other functional purposes. While this example could be designed using other components, we'll use this to show how to access variables from a script.

For example, some variable aspect of the application may change, like an e-mail address for events to use for notification. In this example, you'll retrieve a log file path for a package at runtime using a connection within a Script Task. The database that contains the settings for the log file path stores this data using the package ID. You first need a table in the AdventureWorks database called SSIS_SETTING. Create the table with three fields, `PACKAGE_ID`, `SETTING`, and `VALUE`, or use this script (`ProSSIS\Scripts\Ch09_ProSSIS\Ch09_Table_Create_Script.sql`):

```
CREATE TABLE [dbo].[SSIS_SETTING](
[PACKAGE_ID] [uniqueidentifier] NOT NULL,
[SETTING] [nvarchar](2080) NOT NULL,
[VALUE] [nvarchar](2080) NOT NULL
) ON [PRIMARY]
GO
INSERT INTO SSIS_SETTING
SELECT '{INSERT YOUR PACKAGE ID HERE}', 'LOGFILEPATH', 'c:\myLogFile.txt'
```

You can find the package identifier in the properties of the package.

Then create an SSIS package with one ADO.NET Connection Manager to the AdventureWorks database called `AdventureWorks` and add a package-level variable named `LOGFILEPATH` of type `String`. Add a Script Task to the project and send in two variables: a read-only variable

System::PackageID and a read-write variable User::LOGFILEPATH. Click the Edit Script button to open the Script project and add the namespace System.Data.SqlClient in the top of the class. Then add the following code to the Main() method (ProSSIS\Code\Ch09_ProSSIS\06aScriptDataIntoVariable.dtsx):

C#

```
public void Main()
{
string myPackageId = Dts.Variables["System::PackageID"].Value.ToString();
string myValue = string.Empty;
string cmdString = "SELECT VALUE FROM SSIS_SETTING " +
"WHERE PACKAGE_ID= @PACKAGEID And SETTING= @SETTINGID";
try
{
SqlConnection mySqlConn =
    (SqlConnection)Dts.Connections[0].AcquireConnection(null);
mySqlConn = new SqlConnection(mySqlConn.ConnectionString);
mySqlConn.Open();
SqlCommand cmd = new SqlCommand();
cmd.CommandText = cmdString;
SqlParameter parm = new SqlParameter("@PACKAGEID", SqlDbType.UniqueIdentifier);
parm.Value = new Guid(myPackageId);
cmd.Parameters.Add(parm); parm = new SqlParameter("@SETTINGID",
    SqlDbType.NVarChar);
parm.Value = "LOGFILEPATH";
cmd.Parameters.Add(parm);
cmd.Connection = mySqlConn;
cmd.CommandText = cmdString;
SqlDataReader reader = cmd.ExecuteReader();
while (reader.Read())
{
myValue = reader["value"].ToString();
}
Dts.Variables["User::LOGFILEPATH"].Value = myValue;
reader.Close();
mySqlConn.Close();
mySqlConn.Dispose();
}
catch
{
Dts.TaskResult = (int)ScriptResults.Failure;
throw;
}
System.Windows.Forms.MessageBox.Show(myValue);
Dts.TaskResult = (int)ScriptResults.Success;
}
```

VB

```
Public Sub Main()
Dim myPackageId As String = _ Dts.Variables("System::PackageID").Value.ToString()
Dim myValue As String = String.Empty
Dim cmdString As String = "SELECT VALUE FROM SSIS_SETTING " + _ "WHERE PACKAGE_ID=
    @PACKAGEID And SETTING= @SETTINGID" Try
Dim mySqlConn As SqlClient.SqlConnection
mySqlConn = DirectCast(Dts.Connections(0).AcquireConnection(Nothing),
    SqlClient.SqlConnection)
```

```
mySqlConn = New SqlClient.SqlConnection(mySqlConn.ConnectionString)
mySqlConn.Open()
Dim cmd = New SqlClient.SqlCommand()
cmd.CommandText = cmdString
Dim parm As New SqlClient.SqlParameter("@PACKAGEID", _ SqlDbType.UniqueIdentifier)
parm.Value = New Guid(myPackageId)
cmd.Parameters.Add(parm)
parm = New SqlClient.SqlParameter("@SETTINGID", SqlDbType.NVarChar) parm.Value =
    "LOGFILEPATH"
cmd.Parameters.Add(parm)
cmd.Connection = mySqlConn
cmd.CommandText = cmdString
Dim reader As SqlClient.SqlDataReader = cmd.ExecuteReader()
Do While (reader.Read())
myValue = reader("value").ToString()
Loop
Dts.Variables("User::LOGFILEPATH").Value = myValue
reader.Close()
mySqlConn.Close()
mySqlConn.Dispose()
Catch ex As Exception
Dts.TaskResult = ScriptResults.Failure Throw
End Try
System.Windows.Forms.MessageBox.Show(myValue)
Dts.TaskResult = ScriptResults.Success
End Sub
```

In this code, the package ID is passed into the Script Task as a read-only variable and is used to build a T-SQL statement to retrieve the value of the `LOGFILEPATH` setting from the SSIS_SETTING table. The `AcquireConnection` method creates an instance of a connection to the AdventureWorks database managed by the Connection Manager and allows other `SqlClient` objects to access the data source. The retrieved setting from the SSIS_SETTING table is then stored in the writable variable `LOGFILEPATH`. This is a basic example, but you use this exact same technique to retrieve a recordset into an object variable that can be iterated within your package as well. Let's do that now.

Example: Retrieving Files from an FTP Server

A frequent source of data to use in a solution is files retrieved from an FTP server. SSIS provides an FTP Connection Manager and FTP Task to assist in this function. To use these objects, you need to know what file you want to retrieve from the FTP server. But what do you do if you don't know what the file name is, and you just want to pull everything from the server? This is a perfect use for a Script Task. The final package that we will create can be seen in Figure 9-14.

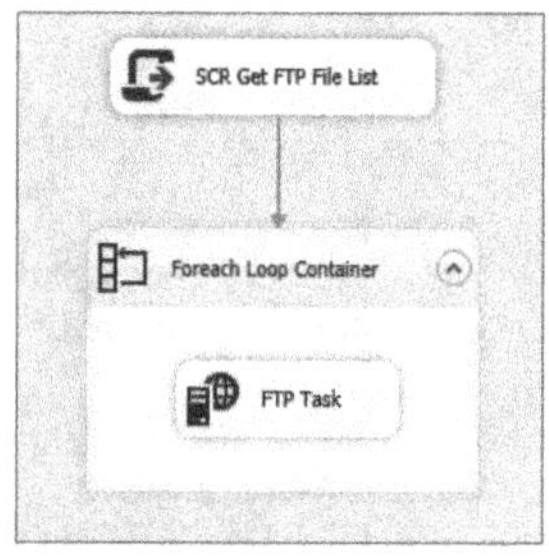

FIGURE 9-14

Begin by adding an FTP Connection Manager that points to your FTP server and a Script Task to your package. The Script Task will use one read/write variable, named `FileList`, to pass back the list of files to be transferred from the FTP server. We can then add the following code inside the script (`ProSSIS\Code\Ch09_ProSSIS\06bSTVariableForEachLoop.dtsx`):

VB

```
Dim conn As ConnectionManager
Dim ftp As FtpClientConnection
Dim folderNames As String()
Dim fileNames As String()
Dim fileArray As New ArrayList

conn = Dts.Connections("FTPServer")
ftp = New FtpClientConnection(conn.AcquireConnection(Nothing))
ftp.Connect()
ftp.GetListing(folderNames, fileNames)

For Each s As String In fileNames
    fileArray.Add(s)
Next
Dts.Variables("FileList").Value = fileArray
ftp.Close()
Dts.TaskResult = ScriptResults.Success
```

C#

```
ConnectionManager conn = default(ConnectionManager);
FtpClientConnection ftp = default(FtpClientConnection);
string[] folderNames = null;
string[] fileNames = null;
ArrayList fileArray = new ArrayList();

conn = Dts.Connections("FTPServer");
ftp = new FtpClientConnection(conn.AcquireConnection(null));
ftp.Connect();
ftp.GetListing(folderNames, fileNames);
foreach (string s in fileNames) {
    fileArray.Add(s);
}
Dts.Variables("FileList").Value = fileArray;
ftp.Close();
Dts.TaskResult = ScriptResults.Success;
```

This code connects to the FTP server and returns a list of the files available for download. To allow the information to be used in a Foreach Loop Container, the file names are put into an `ArrayList` and then into the `FileList` variable.

Our next step is to add the Foreach Loop Container, which will enumerate over the variable `FileList`. Each iteration will store the name of the file in the `FileName` variable. Finally, an FTP Task placed inside of the container will use the `FileName` variable as the source variable to retrieve the file.

With just a few steps, we were able to find out what files are available on the server and download all of them. Next we will look at saving information to an XML file.

Example: Saving Data to an XML File

Another common requirement is to generate data of a certain output format. When the output is a common format like Flat File, Excel, CSV, or other database format, you can simply pump the data stream into one of the Data Flow Destinations. If you want to save data to an XML file, the structure is not homogeneous and not as easy to transform from a column-based data stream into an XML structure without some logic or structure around it. This is where the Script Task comes in handy.

> **NOTE** *If you want to parse out the XML file and put the data into a destination, a Script Component could also be used here.*

The easiest way to get data into an XML file is to load and save the contents of a data set using the method `WriteXML` on the data set. With a new Script Task in a package with an ADO.NET connection to AdventureWorks, add a reference to `System.Xml.dll` and then add the namespaces for `System.Data.SqlClient`, `System.IO`, and `System.Xml`. Code the following (`ProSSIS\Code\Ch09_ProSSIS\07ScriptDataintoXMLFile.dtsx`) into the Script Task to open a connection and get all the SSIS_SETTING rows and store them as XML:

> **NOTE** *See the previous example for the DDL to create this table in the AdventureWorks database.*

C#

```
public void Main()
{
SqlConnection sqlConn;
string cmdString = "SELECT * FROM SSIS_SETTING ";
try
{
sqlConn = (SqlConnection)(Dts.Connections["AdventureWorks"])
    .AcquireConnection(Dts.Transaction
);
sqlConn = new SqlConnection(sqlConn.ConnectionString);
sqlConn.Open();
SqlCommand cmd = new SqlCommand(cmdString, sqlConn);
SqlDataAdapter da = new SqlDataAdapter(cmd);
DataSet ds = new DataSet();
da.Fill(ds);
ds.WriteXml(new System.IO.StreamWriter
    ("C:\\ProSSIS\\Files\\myPackageSettings.xml"));
sqlConn.Close();
}
```

```
catch
{
Dts.TaskResult = (int)ScriptResults.Failure;
throw;
}
Dts.TaskResult = (int)ScriptResults.Success;
}
```

VB

```
Public Sub Main()
Dim sqlConn As New SqlConnection
Dim cmdString As String = "SELECT * FROM SSIS_SETTING "
Try
sqlConn = DirectCast(Dts.Connections("AdventureWorks")
    .AcquireConnection(Dts.Transaction), SqlConnection)
sqlConn = New SqlConnection(sqlConn.ConnectionString)
sqlConn.Open()
Dim cmd = New SqlCommand(cmdString, sqlConn)
Dim da = New SqlDataAdapter(cmd)
Dim ds = New DataSet
da.Fill(ds)
ds.WriteXml(New StreamWriter("C:\\ProSSIS\\Files\\myPackageSettings.xml" ))
sqlConn.Close()
Catch
Dts.TaskResult = ScriptResults.Failure
Throw
End Try
Dts.TaskResult = ScriptResults.Success
End Sub
```

There is not much to note about these results, except that the file is in XML format:


```
<NewDataSet>
<Table>
<PACKAGE_ID>a5cf0c2f-8d85-42eb-91b9-cbd1fd47e5b1</PACKAGE_ID>
<SETTING>LOGFILEPATH</SETTING>
<VALUE>c:\myLogFile.txt</VALUE>
</Table>
</NewDataSet>
```


If you need more control of the data you are exporting, or you need to serialize data, you need to use the Script Task in a different way. The next example provides some tips on how to do this.

Example: Serializing Data to XML

In the last example, you looked at simply dumping database data into an XML format by loading data into a `DataSet` and using the `WriteToXML` method to push the XML out to a file stream. If you need more control over the format, or the data is hierarchical, using .NET XML object-based serialization can be helpful. Imagine implementations that pull data from flat-file mainframe feeds and fill fully hierarchical object models. Alternatively, imagine serializing data into an object structure to pop an entry into an MSMQ application queue. This is easy to do using some of the same concepts.

Create another package with a connection to the AdventureWorks database; add a Script Task with a reference to the `System.Data.SqlClient` namespace. Use the data from the previous example and create a class structure within your `ScriptMain` to hold the values for each row of settings that looks like this (`ProSSIS\Code\Ch09_ProSSIS\08ScriptDataintoSerializableObject.dtsx`):

C#

```
[Serializable()]
public class SSISSetting
{
public string PackageId { get; set; }
public string Setting { get; set; }
public string Value { get; set; }
}
```

VB

```
<Serializable()> Public Class SSISSetting
Private m_PackageId As String
Private m_Setting As String
Private m_Value As String
Public Property PackageId() As String
Get
PackageId = m_PackageId
End Get
Set(ByVal Value As String)
m_PackageId = Value
End Set
End Property
Public Property Setting() As String
Get
PackageId = m_Setting
End Get
Set(ByVal Value As String)
m_Setting = Value
End Set
End Property
Public Property Value() As String
Get
Value = m_Value
End Get
Set(ByVal Value As String)
m_Value = Value
End Set
End Property
End Class
```

This class will be filled based on the data set shown in the last example. It is still a flat model, but more complex class structures would have collections within the class. An example would be a student object with a collection of classes, or an invoice with a collection of line items. To persist this type of data, you need to traverse multiple paths to fill the model. Once the model is filled, the rest is easy.

First, add the namespaces `System.Xml.Serialization`, `System.Collections.Generic`, `System.IO`, and `System.Data.SqlClient` to your Script Task project. A simple example with the SSIS_SETTING table would look like this (`ProSSIS\Code\Ch09_ProSSIS\08ScriptDataintoSerializableObject.dtsx`):

C#

```
public void Main()
{
SqlConnection sqlConn;
string cmdString = "SELECT * FROM SSIS_SETTING ";
try
{
sqlConn = (SqlConnection)(Dts.Connections["AdventureWorks"])
    .AcquireConnection(Dts.Transaction);
sqlConn = new SqlConnection(sqlConn.ConnectionString);
sqlConn.Open();
SqlCommand cmd = new SqlCommand(cmdString, sqlConn);
SqlDataReader dR = cmd.ExecuteReader();
List<SSISSetting> arrayListSettings = new List<SSISSetting>();
while (dR.Read())
{
SSISSetting oSet = new SSISSetting();
oSet.PackageId = dR["PACKAGE_ID"].ToString();
oSet.Setting = dR["SETTING"].ToString();
oSet.Value = dR["VALUE"].ToString();
arrayListSettings.Add(oSet);
}
StreamWriter outfile = new StreamWriter
    ("C:\\ProSSIS\\Files\\myObjectXmlSettings.xml");
XmlSerializer ser = new XmlSerializer(typeof(List<SSISSetting>));
ser.Serialize(outfile, arrayListSettings);
outfile.Close();
outfile.Dispose();
sqlConn.Close();
}
catch
{
Dts.TaskResult = (int)ScriptResults.Failure;
throw;
}
Dts.TaskResult = (int)ScriptResults.Success;
}
```

VB

```
Public Sub Main()
Dim sqlConn As SqlConnection
Dim cmdString As String = "SELECT * FROM SSIS_SETTING "
Try
sqlConn = DirectCast(Dts.Connections("AdventureWorks")
    .AcquireConnection(Dts.Transaction), SqlConnection)
sqlConn = New SqlConnection(sqlConn.ConnectionString)
sqlConn.Open()
Dim cmd As SqlCommand = New SqlCommand(cmdString, sqlConn)
Dim dR As SqlDataReader = cmd.ExecuteReader()
Dim arrayListSettings As New List(Of SSISSetting)
Do While (dR.Read())
```

```
Dim oSet As New SSISSetting()
oSet.PackageId = dR("PACKAGE_ID").ToString()
oSet.Setting = dR("SETTING").ToString()
oSet.Value = dR("VALUE").ToString()
arrayListSettings.Add(oSet)
Loop
Dim outfile As New StreamWriter("C:\\ProSSIS\\Files\\myObjectXmlSettings.xml")
Dim ser As New XmlSerializer(GetType(List(Of SSISSetting)))
ser.Serialize(outfile, arrayListSettings)
outfile.Close()
outfile.Dispose()
sqlConn.Close()
Catch
Dts.TaskResult = ScriptResults.Failure
Throw
End Try
Dts.TaskResult = ScriptResults.Success
End Sub
```

> **NOTE** *Keep in mind that while this example uses a connection directly in the code, you can also use an SSIS Connection Manager, as shown in the FTP example. Using a connection manager will make your package more portable to a production environment if you use parameters or configurations.*

The `StreamWriter` here just gets an I/O stream from the file system to use for data output. The `XmlSerializer` does the heavy lifting and converts the data from the object format into an XML format.

The only trick here is understanding how to deal with the `Generic List` or the collection of `SSISSetting` objects. This is handled by using the override, whereby you can add the specific types to the serializer along with the `List`. The resulting XML payload will now look like this:


```
<?xml version="1.0" encoding="utf-8"?>
<ArrayOfSSISSetting xmlns:xsi="http://www.w3.org/2001/XMLSchema-instance"
    xmlns:xsd="http://www.w3.org/2001/XMLSchema">
<SSISSetting>
<PackageId>34050406-2e0f-423a-8af3-1ec95399a6c2</PackageId>
<Setting>LOGFILEPATH</Setting>
<Value>c:\myLogFile.txt</Value>
</SSISSetting>
</ArrayOfSSISSetting>
```


Although the XML content looks a little bit different from dumping the content of the recordset directly to XML as shown in the earlier example, it is optimized for object serialization. This is the type of content that you could push into application queues or share with external applications.

Raising an Event in a Script Task

All existing SSIS Tasks and Components raise events that can be captured and displayed by the Execution Results tab by default. Optionally, these events can also be captured and logged into SSIS logging or event handlers. Event handlers are Control Flows that you set up and define to respond to specific events. They are literally Control Flow workflows within a package, and they enable you to customize the diagnostic information that the packages can provide at runtime.

If you have done any Windows GUI programming, you are familiar with events. An *event* is simply a message sent from some object saying that something just happened or is about to happen. To raise or *fire* an event within a Script Task, you use the `Events` property of the `Dts` object. More information about events can be found in Chapter 18. The `Events` property on the `Dts` object is really an instance of the `IDTSComponentEvents` interface. This interface specifies seven methods for firing events:

- `FireBreakpointHit`: Supports the SQL Server infrastructure and is not intended to be used directly in code.
- `FireError`: Fires an event when an error occurs.
- `FireInformation`: Fires an event with information. You can fire this event when you want a set of information to be logged, possibly for auditing later.
- `FireProgress`: Fires an event when a certain progress level has been met.
- `FireQueryCancel`: Fires an event to determine if package execution should stop.
- `FireWarning`: Fires an event that is less serious than an error but more than just information.
- `FireCustomEvent`: Fires a custom-defined event.

In SSIS, any events you fire are written to all enabled log handlers that are set to log that event. Logging enables you to check what happened with your script when you're not there to watch it run. Using events is a best practice for troubleshooting and auditing purposes, as you'll see in the following example.

Example: Raising Some Events

The default way to view events while designing your package is to use the Execution Results tab at the top of your package in the SQL Server Data Tools design environment. To fire off some sample events and view them in this Execution Results tab, create a new package with a Script Task and add the System variable `System::TaskName` as a read-only variable. Then add the following code to the `Main()` function `(ProSSIS\Code\Ch09_ProSSIS\09RaisingEvents.dtsx)`:

C#

```
public void Main()
{
string taskName = Dts.Variables["System::TaskName"].Value.ToString();
```

```
bool retVal = false;
Dts.Events.FireInformation(0, taskName, String.Format
    ("Starting Loop Operation at {0} ",
DateTime.Now.ToString("MM/dd/yyyy hh:mm:ss")), "", 0,
ref retVal);
for(int i=0; i <= 10; i++)
{
Dts.Events.FireProgress(String.Format("Loop in iteration {0}", i),
i * 10, 0, 10, taskName, ref retVal);
}
Dts.Events.FireInformation(0, taskName, String.Format("Completion Loop Operation
    at {0} ", DateTime.Now.ToString("mm/dd/yyyy hh:mm:ss")), "", 0, ref retVal);
Dts.Events.FireWarning(1, taskName, "This is a warning we want to pay attention
    to...", "", 0);
Dts.Events.FireWarning(2, taskName, "This is a warning for debugging only...",
    "", 0);
Dts.Events.FireError(0, taskName, "If we had an error it would be here", "", 0);
}
```

VB

```
Public Sub Main()
Dim i As Integer = 0
Dim taskName As String = Dts.Variables("System::TaskName").Value.ToString()
Dim retVal As Boolean = False
Dts.Events.FireInformation(0, taskName, _
String.Format("Starting Loop Operation at {0} ", _ DateTime.Now.ToString
    ("MM/dd/yyyy hh:mm:ss")), "", 0, _
 True)
For i = 0 To 10
Dts.Events.FireProgress( _
 String.Format("Loop in iteration {0}", i), _
 i * 10, 0, 10, taskName, True)
Next
Dts.Events.FireInformation(0, taskName,
 _ String.Format("Completion Loop Operation at {0} ", _ DateTime.Now.ToString
    ("mm/dd/yyyy hh:mm:ss")), "", 0, False)
Dts.Events.FireWarning(1, taskName, _
 "This is a warning we want to pay attention to ...", _
 "", 0)
Dts.Events.FireWarning(2, taskName, _
 "This is a warning for debugging only ...", _
 "", 0)
Dts.Events.FireError(0, taskName, _
 "If we had an error it would be here", "", 0)
End Sub
```

This code will perform a simple loop operation that demonstrates firing the information, progress, warning, and error events. If you run the package, you can view the information embedded in these fire event statements in the final tab, either named Execution Results or Progress, depending on whether the designer is in Debug mode or not. These events are shown in Figure 9-15. Note that raising the error event results in the Script Task's failure. You can comment out the `FireError` event to see the task complete successfully.

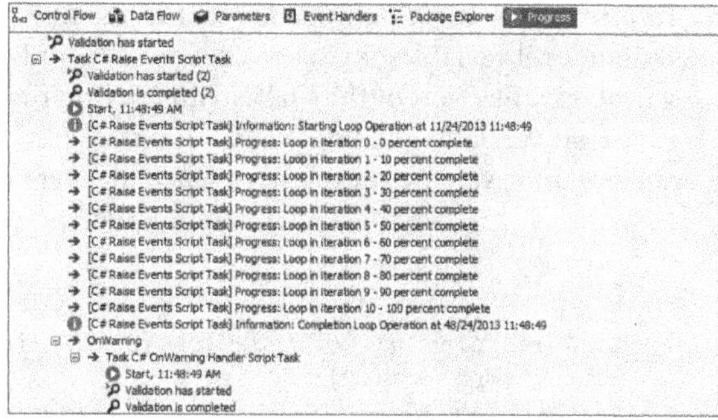

FIGURE 9-15

All the statements prefixed with the string `[Script Task]` were generated using these events fired from the Script Task. You can comment out the `Dts.Events.FireError` method calls to demonstrate to yourself that the task can complete successfully for warnings and informational events. Note that with the firing of an error, you can also force the task to generate a custom error with an error code and description. In fact, each of the events has a placeholder as the first parameter to store a custom information code. Continue to the next example to see how you can create an error handler to respond to the warning events that are fired from this Script Task.

Example: Responding to an Event

If you have already created a package for the preceding example, navigate to the Event Handlers tab. Event handlers are separate Control Flows that can be executed in response to an event. In the Raising Some Events example, you generated two warning events. One had an information code of one (1) and the other had the value of two (2). In this example, you are going to add an event handler to respond to those warning events and add some logic to respond to the event if the information code is equal to one (1). Select the Script Task executable and then select the `OnWarning` event handler. Click the hot link that states the following:

```
Click here to create an 'OnWarning' event handler for executable 'Script Task'
```

This will create a Control Flow surface onto which you can drop SSIS Control Tasks that will execute if an `OnWarning` event is thrown from the Script Task you added to the package earlier. Drop a new Script Task into the Event Handler Control Flow surface and name it **OnWarning Script Task**. Your designer should look like Figure 9-16.

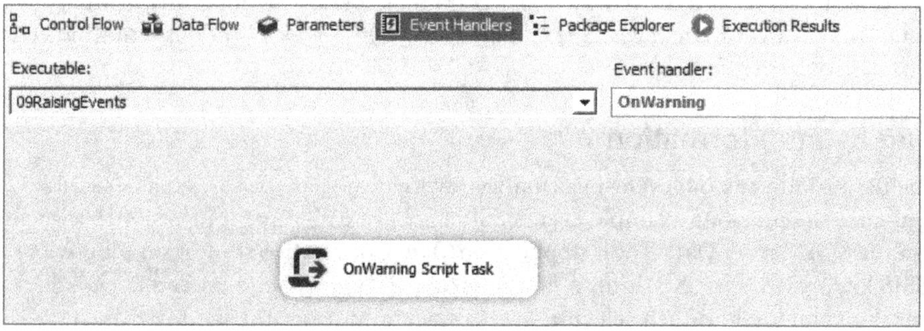

FIGURE 9-16

To retrieve the information code sent in the `Dts.Events.FireWarning` method call, add two system-level variables, `System::ErrorCode` and `System::ErrorDescription`, to the Read-Only Variables collection of the OnWarning Script Task. These variables will contain the values of the `InformationCode` and `Description` parameters in the `Dts.Events()` methods. You can then retrieve and evaluate these values when an event is raised by adding the following code (`ProSSIS\Code\Ch09_ProSSIS\09RaisingEvents.dtsx`):

C#

```
long lWarningCode = long.Parse(Dts.Variables[0].Value.ToString());
String sMsg = string.Empty;
if(lWarningCode == 1)
{
sMsg = String.Format(
"Would do something with this warning:\n{0}: {1}", lWarningCode.ToString(),
    Dts.Variables(1).ToString());
System.Windows.Forms.MessageBox.Show(sMsg);
}
Dts.TaskResult = (int)ScriptResults.Success;
```

VB

```
Dim lWarningCode As Long = _
 Long.Parse(Dts.Variables(0).Value.ToString())
Dim sMsg As String
If lWarningCode = 1 Then
sMsg = String.Format("Would do something with this warning: " _
 + vbCrLf + "{0}: {1}", _
lWarningCode.ToString(), Dts.Variables(1).ToString())
System.Windows.Forms.MessageBox.Show(sMsg)
End If
Dts.TaskResult = ScriptResults.Success
```

The code checks the value of the first parameter, which is the value of the `System::ErrorCode` and the value raised in the `Dts.Events.FireWarning` method. If the value is equivalent to one (1), an action is taken to show a message box. This action could just as well be logging an entry to a database or sending an e-mail. If you rerun the package now, you'll see that the first `FireWarning` event will be handled in your event handler and generate a message box warning. The second `FireWarning` event will also be captured by the event handler, but no response is made.

The event handler counter in the Progress or Execution Results tab is incremented to two (2). Raising events in the Script Tasks is a great way to get good diagnostic information without resorting to message boxes in your packages. See Chapter 18 for more details about handling errors and events in SSIS.

Example: Logging Event Information

Scripts can also be used to fire custom event information, which can then be logged as described previously. To configure the previous example events SSIS package to log event information, go to SSIS ➪ Logging in the SQL Server Data Tools application. The Configure SSIS Logs dialog will appear. Select "SSIS log provider for XML files" in the Provider Type dropdown and click Add. Click the Configuration column and then select <New Connection> from the list to create an XML

File Editor. For Usage type, select Create File and specify a path to a filename similar to `C:\ProSSIS\Files\myLogFile.xml`.

> **NOTE** *In a production package you would set this value using an expression or parameter during runtime.*

Click OK to close the File Connection Manager Editor dialog box. Your screen should look something like Figure 9-17.

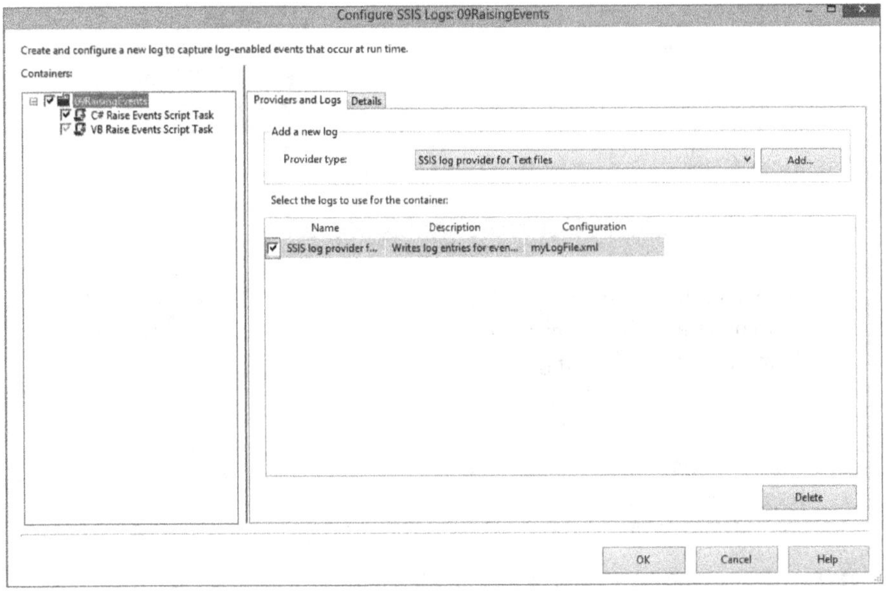

FIGURE 9-17

Now click the Package Node to start selecting what tasks in the package should log to the new provider, and check the box next to the provider name so that the log will be used. In the Details tab, select the specific `OnWarning` events to log. You can choose to log any of the available event types to the providers by also selecting them in the Details tab. Now your provider configuration should look like Figure 9-18.

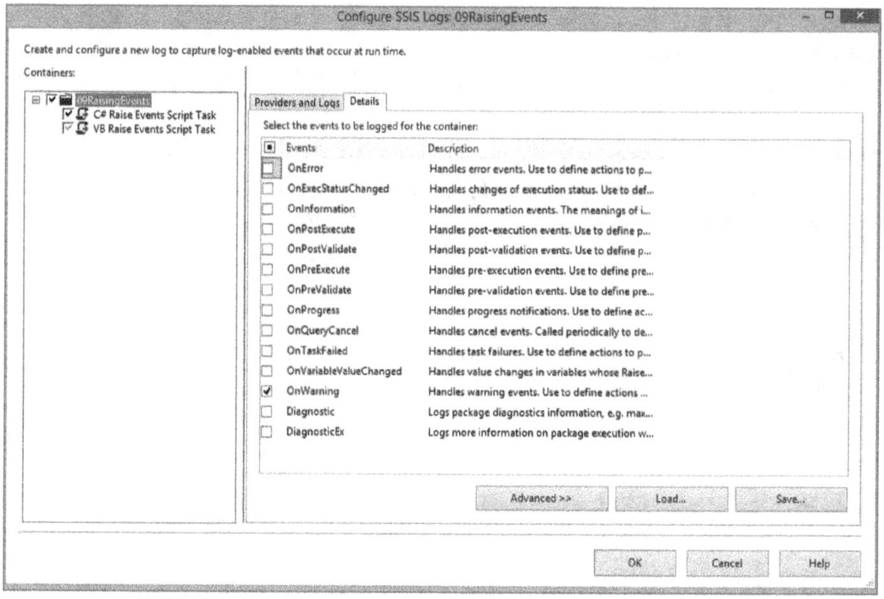

FIGURE 9-18

You can also use the Advanced tab for each selected event to control exactly what properties of the event are logged as well. If you run the package again, the file specified in the logging provider will be created with content similar to the following:

```
<record>
<event>OnWarning</event>
<message>This is a warning we want to pay attention to ...</message>
<computer>MYCOMPUTER</computer>
<operator>MYCOMPUTER\ADMIN</operator>
<source>Package</source>
<sourceid>{D86FF397-6C9B-4AD9-BACF-B4D41AC89ECB}</sourceid>
<executionid>{8B6F6392-1818-4EE5-87BF-EDCB5DC37ACB}</executionid>
<starttime>1/22/2012 9:30:08 PM</starttime>
<endtime>1/22/2012 9:30:08 PM</endtime>
<datacode>2</datacode>
<databytes>0x</databytes>
</record>
```

You'll have other events in the file too, such as Package Start and Package End, but the preceding code snippet focuses on the event that your code fired. This record contains basic information about the event, including the message, event execution time, and the computer and user that raised the event.

Using the Script Task to raise an event is just one way to get more diagnostic information into your SSIS log files. Read on to get a brief look at generating simple log entries.

Writing a Log Entry in a Script Task

Within a Script Task, the `Log` method of the `Dts` object writes a message to all enabled log providers. The `Log` method is simple and has three arguments:

- `messageText`: The message to log
- `dataCode`: A field for logging a message code
- `dataBytes`: A field for logging binary data

The `Log` method is similar to the `FireInformation` method of the `Events` property, but it is easier to use and more efficient — and you don't need to create a specialized event handler to respond to the method call. All you need to do is set up a log provider within the package. In the previous section, you learned how to add a log provider to a package. The code in the next section logs a simple message with some binary data to all available log providers. This is quite useful for troubleshooting and auditing purposes. You can write out information at important steps in your script and even print out variable values to help you track down a problem.

Example: Scripting a Log Entry

This example demonstrates how to script a log entry by adding a few lines of code to the package in the previous examples that you used to raise events. First, add the following lines to the appropriate Script Task that matches the language you chose in the previous example (`ProSSIS\Code\Ch09_ProSSIS\09RaisingEvents.dtsx`):

C#

```
Byte[] myByteArray[] = new byte[0];
Dts.Log("Called procedure: usp_Upsert with return code 4", 0, myByteArray);
```

VB

```
Dim myByteArray(0) As Byte
Dts.Log("Called procedure: usp_Upsert with return code 4", 0, myByteArray)
```

Next, select the events for the `ScriptTaskLogEntry` event in the Details tab of the logging configuration. This tells the SSIS package logger to handle any custom logging instructions such as the one you just coded. Then run the package. You'll see a set of additional logging instructions that look like this:

```
<record>
<event>User:ScriptTaskLogEntry</event>
<message>Called Procedure: usp_Upsert with return code 4</message>
<computer>MYCOMPUTER</computer>
<operator>MYCOMPUTER\ADMIN</operator>
<source>Raise Events C# Script Task</source>
<sourceid>{CE53C1BB-7757-47FF-B173-E6088DA0A2A3}</sourceid>
<executionid>{B7828A35-C236-451E-99DE-F679CF808D91}</executionid>
<starttime>4/27/2008 2:54:04 PM</starttime>
<endtime>4/27/2008 2:54:04 PM</endtime>
<datacode>0</datacode>
<databytes>0x</databytes>
</record>
```

As you can see, the Script Task is highly flexible with the inclusion of the .NET-based VSTA capabilities. As far as controlling package flow or one-off activities, the Script Task is clearly very important. However, the Script Task doesn't do all things well. If you want to apply programmatic logic to the Data Flow in an SSIS package, then you need to add to your knowledge of scripting in SSIS with the Script Component.

USING THE SCRIPT COMPONENT

The Script Component provides another area where programming logic can be applied in an SSIS package. This component, which can be used only in the Data Flow portion of an SSIS package, allows programmatic tasks to occur in the data stream. This component exists to provide, consume, or transform data using .NET code. To differentiate between the various uses of the Script Component, when you create one you have to choose one of the following three types:

- **Source Type Component:** The role of this Script Component is to provide data to your Data Flow Task. You can define outputs and their types and use script code to populate them. An example would be reading in a complex file format, possibly XML or something that requires custom coding to read, like HTTP or RSS Sources.
- **Destination Type Component:** This type of Script Component consumes data much like an Excel or Flat File Destination. This component is the end of the line for the data in your data stream. Here, you'll typically put the data into a `DataSet` variable to pass back to the Control Flow for further processing, or send the stream to custom output destinations not supported by built-in SSIS components. Examples of these output destinations can be web service calls, custom XML formats, and multi-record formats for mainframe systems. You can even programmatically connect and send a stream to a printer object.
- **Transformation Type Component:** This type of Script Component can perform custom transformations on data. It consumes input columns and produces output columns. You would use this component when one of the built-in transformations just isn't flexible enough.

In this section, you'll get up to speed on all the specifics of the Script Component, starting first with an explanation of the differences between the Script Task and the Script Component, and then looking at the coding differences in the two models. Finally, you'll see an example of each implementation type of the Script Component to put all of this information to use.

Differences from a Script Task

You might ask, "Why are there two controls, both the Script Task and the Script Component?" Well, underlying the SSIS architecture are two different implementations that define how the VSTA environment is used for performance. Each Script Task is called only once within a Control Flow, unless it is in a looping control. The Script Component has to be higher octane because it is going to be called *per row* of data in the data stream. You are also in the context of being able to access the data buffers directly, so you will be able to perform more tasks.

When you are working with these two controls, the bottom line is that there are slightly different ways of doing the same types of things in each. This section of the chapter cycles back through some of the things you did with the Script Task and points out the differences. First you'll look at the differences in configuring the editor. Then you'll see what changes when performing programmatic tasks such as accessing variables, using connections, raising events, and logging. Finally, you'll look at an example that ties everything together.

Configuring the Script Component Editor

You'll notice the differences starting with the item editor. Adding a Script Component to the Data Flow designer brings up the editor shown in Figure 9-19, requesting the component type.

> **NOTE** *In order to add the Script Component, you must first add a Data Flow Task to a package.*

Selecting one of these options changes how the editor is displayed to configure the control. Essentially, you are choosing whether the control has input buffers, output buffers, or both. Figure 9-20 shows an example of a Script Component Transformation that has both buffers.

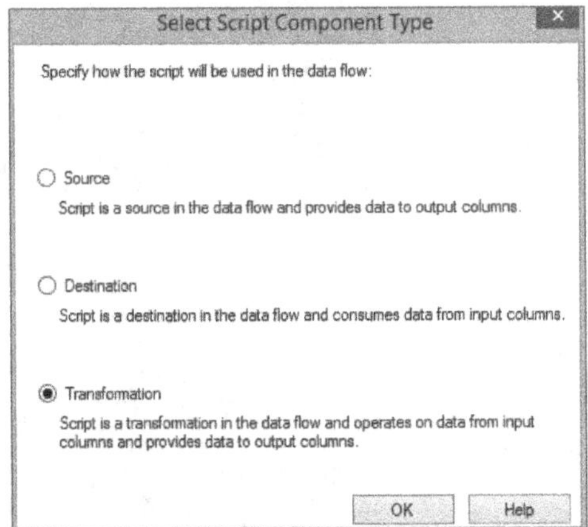

FIGURE 9-19

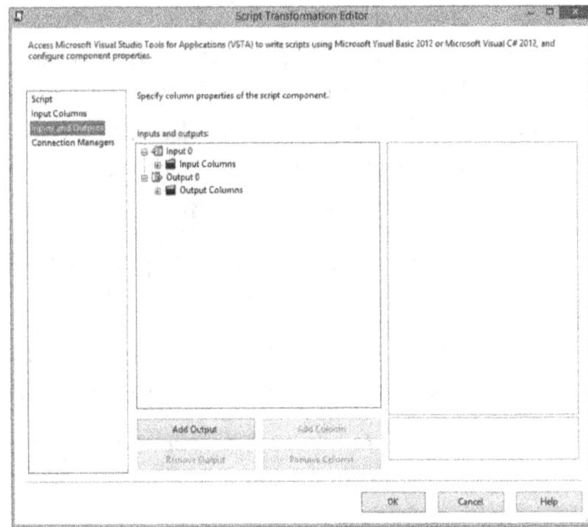

FIGURE 9-20

The Script Component Source has only output buffers available, and the Script Component Destination has only input buffers available. You are responsible for defining these buffers by providing the set of typed columns for either the input or outputs. If the data is being fed into the component, the editor can set these up for you. Otherwise, you have to define them yourself. You can do this programmatically in the code, or ahead of time using the editor. Just select the input or output columns collection on the user interface, and click the Add Column button to add a column, as shown in Figure 9-21.

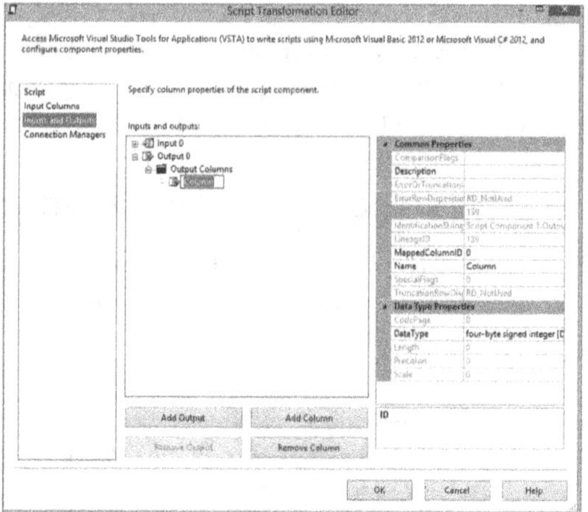

FIGURE 9-21

A helpful tip is to select the Output Columns node on the tree view, so that the new column is added to the bottom of the collection. Once you add a column, you can't move it up or down. After adding the column, you need to set the Data Type, Length, Precision, and Scale. For details about the SSIS data types, see Chapter 5.

When you access the scripting environment, you'll notice some additional differences between the Script Component and the Script Task. Namely, some new classes have been added to the Solution Explorer, as shown in Figure 9-22.

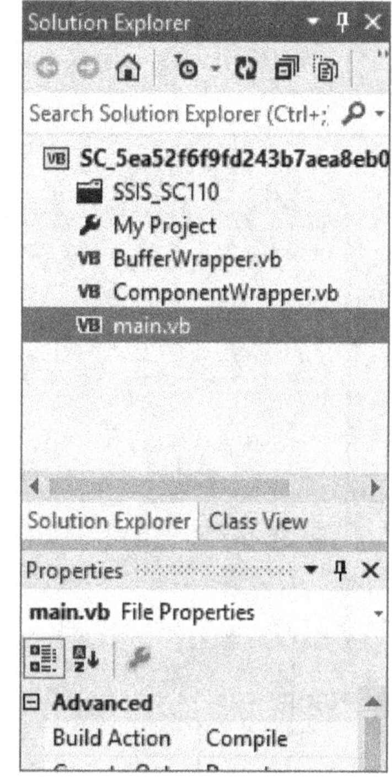

FIGURE 9-22

The name of the class that is used to host custom code is different from that used for the Script Task. Rather than `ScriptMain`, the class is called `main`. Internally there are also some differences. The primary difference is the existence of more than one entry point method. The methods you'll see in the `main` class depend upon the Script Component type. At least three of the following methods are typically coded and can be used as entry points in the Script Component:

- `PreExecute` is used for preprocessing tasks like creating expensive connections or file streams.
- `PostExecute` is used for cleanup tasks or setting variables at the completion of each processed row.
- `CreateNewOutputRows` is the method to manage the output buffers.
- `Input0_ProcessInputRow` is the method to manage anything coming from the input buffers. Note that the `Input0` part of the name will differ based on the name of the input set in the editor.

The remaining classes are generated automatically based on your input and output columns when you enter into the script environment, so don't make any changes to these; otherwise, they will be overwritten when you reenter the script environment.

One problem you might encounter in the Script Component Editor and the generation of the `BufferWrapper` class is that you can name columns in the editor that use keywords or are otherwise invalid when the `BufferWrapper` class is generated. An example would be an output column named `125K_AMOUNT`. If you create such a column, you'll get an error in the `BufferWrapper` class stating the following:

```
Invalid Token 125 in class, struct, or interface member declaration
```

Don't attempt to change the property in the buffer class to something like `_125K_AMOUNT`, because this property is rebuilt the next time you edit the script. Change the name of the output column to `_125K_AMOUNT`, and the buffer class will change automatically. The biggest difference that you need to pay attention to with the Script Component is that if you make *any* changes to this editor, you'll need to open the script environment so that all these base classes can be generated.

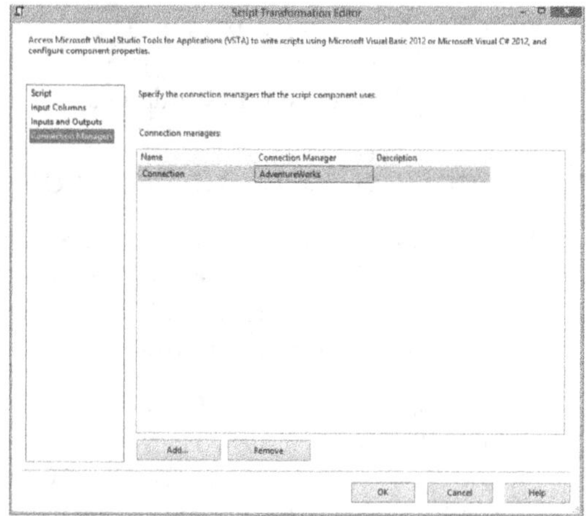

FIGURE 9-23

Last, but not least, you'll notice a Connection Managers tab that is not available in the Script Task Editor. This enables you to name specifically the connections that you want to be able to access within the Script Component. Although you are not required to name these connections up front, it is extremely helpful to do so. You'll see why later, when you connect to a data source. Figure 9-23 shows an example of the AdventureWorks connection added to a Script Component.

Now that you understand the differences between the Script Task and Script Component from a setup perspective, you can examine how the coding differs.

Accessing Variables in a Script Component

The same concepts behind accessing variables also apply to the Script Component. You can send the variables into the control by adding them to the `ReadOnlyVariables` or `ReadWriteVariables` properties of the editor. You can also choose not to specify them up front and just use the variable dispenser within your Script Component to access, lock, and manipulate variables. We recommend using the properties in the editor for this component because the variables provided in the editor are added to the auto-generated base class variables collection as strongly typed variables. In this control, adding variables to the editor not only removes the need to lock and unlock the variables but also means you don't have to remember the variable name within the component. Keep in mind that variables can't be modified in all aspects of the Script Component. Here's an example of setting the variable `ValidationErrors` within a Script Component:

C#

```
this.Variables.ValidationErrors = 1;
```

VB

```
me.Variables.ValidationErrors = 1
```

As you can see, using variables is easier and more maintainable than in the Script Task because the variable names are available in IntelliSense and checked at compile time. However, if you don't want to add a variable to each Script Component for some reason, you can still use the variable dispenser in this component. It is located on the base class and can be accessed using the base class, instead of the `Dts` object. Other than these differences, the variable examples in the Script Task section of this chapter are still applicable. The remaining tasks of connecting to data sources, raising events, and logging follow a similar pattern. The methods for performing the tasks are more strongly named, which makes sense because any late binding (or runtime type checking) within a high-performing Data Flow Task would slow it down.

Connecting to Data Sources in a Script Component

A typical use of a connection is in the Source type of the Script Component, because in these types of Data Flow Tasks, the mission is to create a data stream. The origination of that data is usually another external source. If you had a defined SSIS Source Component, then it would be used and you wouldn't need the Script Component to connect to it.

The coding to connect to a Connection Manager is very simple. You can instantiate a specific Connection Manager and assign the reference to a connection in the component's collection. Using the connections collection in the Script Component is very similar to using the variables collection. The collection of strongly typed Connection Managers is created every time the script editor is opened. Again, this is helpful because you don't have to remember the names, and you get compile-time verification and checking.

For example, if you had a package with an OLE DB Connection Manager named `myOracleServer` and added it to the Script Component with the name `OracleConnection`, you'd have access to the connection using this code:

C#

```
ConnectionManagerOleDb oracleConnection =
    (ConnectionManagerOleDb)base.Connections.OracleConnection;
```

VB

```
Dim oracleConnection as ConnectionManagerOleDb
oracleConnection = Connections.OracleConnection
```

Raising Events

For the Script Task, you've looked at SSIS's ability to raise events, and you walked through some examples that demonstrated its scripting capabilities for managing how the package can respond to these events. These same capabilities exist in Script Components, although you need to keep in mind that Script Components run in a data pipeline or stream, so the potential for repeated calls is highly likely. You should fire events sparingly within a Script Component that is generating or processing data in the pipeline to reduce overhead and increase performance. The methods are essentially the same, but without the static `Dts` object.

> **NOTE** *Event handling is covered in more detail in Chapter 18.*

Here is the code to raise an informational event in a Script Component (ProSSIS\Code\Ch09_ProSSIS\09RaisingEvents.dtsx):

C#

```
Boolean myBool=false;
this.ComponentMetaData.FireInformation(0, "myScriptComponent",
"Removed non-ASCII Character", "", 0, ref myBool);
```

VB

```
Dim myBool As Boolean
Me.ComponentMetaData.FireInformation(0, _
"myScriptComponent", "Removed non-ASCII Character", "", 0, myBool)
```

Either version of code will generate an event in the Progress Tab that looks like this:

```
[myScriptComponent] Information: Removed non-ASCII Character
```

Raising an event is preferred to logging because it enables you to develop a separate workflow for handling the event, but in some instances logging may be preferred.

Logging

Like the Script Task, logging in the Script Component writes a message to all enabled log providers. It has the same interface as the Script Task, but it is exposed on the base class. Remember that Script Components run in a data pipeline or stream, so the potential for repeated calls is highly likely. Follow the same rules as those for raising events, and log sparingly within a Script Component that is generating or processing data in the pipeline to reduce overhead and increase performance. If you need to log a message within a Data Flow, you can improve performance by logging only in the `PostExecute` method, so that the results are logged only once.

Example: Scripting a Log Entry

This example shows how to log one informational entry to the log file providers at the end of a Data Flow Task. To use this code, create a package with a Data Flow Task and add a Script Component as a source with one output column named NewOutputColumn. Create these integer variables as private variables to the `main.cs` class: `validationBadChars`, `validationLength`, and `validationInvalidFormat`. Then add the following code to the `CreateNewOutputRows()` method in the `main.cs` class (ProSSIS\Code\Ch09_ProSSIS\11aSCBasicLogging.dtsx):

C#

```
int validationLengthErrors = 0;
int validationCharErrors = 0;
int validationFormatErrors = 0;
//..in the CreateNewOutputRows() Method
string validationMsg = string.Format("Validation Errors:\nBad Chars {0}\nInvalid
    Length " + "{1}\nInvalid Format {2}", validationCharErrors,
    validationLengthErrors, validationFormatErrors);
this.Log(validationMsg, 0, new byte[0]);
//This is how to add rows to the outputrows Output0Buffer collection.
```

```
Output0Buffer.AddRow();
Output0Buffer.NewOutputColumn = 1;
```

VB

```
Dim validationLengthErrors As Integer = 0
Dim validationCharErrors As Integer = 0
Dim validationFormatErrors As Integer = 0
'..in the CreateNewOutputRows() Method
Dim validationMsg As String
validationMsg = String.Format("Validation Errors:" + _
vbCrLf + "Bad Chars {0}" + _
vbCrLf + "Invalid Length {1}" + _
vbCrLf + "Invalid Format {2}", _
validationCharErrors, validationLengthErrors, _ validationFormatErrors)
Dim myByteArray(0) As Byte
Me.Log(validationMsg, 0, myByteArray)
Output0Buffer.AddRow()
Output0Buffer.AddNewOutputColumn = 1
```

In order for this sample to produce a log entry, remember that you have to set up a logging provider (use the menu option SSIS ➪ Logging). Make sure you specifically select the Data Flow Task in which the Script Component is hosted within SSIS and the logging events specifically for the Script Component. Running the package will produce logging similar to this:

```
User:ScriptComponentLogEntry,MYPC,MYPC\ADMIN,"CSharp Basic Logging Script
    Component" (1),{00000001-0000-0000-0000-000000000000},
    {3651D743-D7F6-43F8- 8DE2-F7B40423CC28},
    4/27/2012 10:38:56 PM,4/27/2008 10:38:56 PM,0,0x, Validation Errors:
Bad Chars 0
Invalid Length 0
Invalid Format 0
OnPipelinePostPrimeOutput, MYPC,MYPC\ADMIN,Data Flow Task,
    {D2118DFD-DAEE-470B- 9AC3-9B01DFAA993E},
    {3651D743-D7F6-43F8-8DE2-F7B40423CC28},4/27/2008 10:38:55 PM,
    4/27/2008 10:38:55 PM,0,0x,A component has returned from its
    PrimeOutput call. : 1 : CSharp Basic Logging Script Component
```

Example: Data Validation

Compared to the Script Task, the Script Component has a steeper learning curve. The example presented in this section is more comprehensive and should enable you to get the bigger picture of how you can use this component in your everyday package development.

A typical use of the Script Component is to validate data within a Data Flow. In this example, contact information from a custom application did not validate its data entry, resulting in poor data quality. Because the destination database has a strict set of requirements for the data, your task is to validate the contact information from a Flat File Source and separate valid from invalid records into two streams: the good stream and the error stream. The good records can continue to another Data Flow; the error records will be sent to an error table for manual cleansing.

Create the contacts table with the following script (ProSSIS\Scripts\Ch09_ProSSIS\Ch09_Table_Create_Script.sql):

```
CREATE TABLE [dbo].[Contacts](
[ContactID] [int] IDENTITY(1,1) NOT NULL,
[FirstName] [varchar](50) NOT NULL,
[LastName] [varchar](50) NOT NULL,
[City] [varchar](25) NOT NULL,
[State] [varchar](15) NOT NULL,
[Zip] [char](11) NULL
) ON [PRIMARY]
```

The error queue table is virtually identical except it has no strict requirements and a column has been added to capture the rejection reason. All data fields are nullable and set to the maximum known size (ProSSIS\Scripts\Ch09_ProSSIS\Ch09_Table_Create_Script.sql):

```
CREATE TABLE dbo.ContactsErrorQueue
(
ContactErrorID int NOT NULL IDENTITY (1, 1),
FirstName varchar(50) NULL,
LastName varchar(50) NULL,
City varchar(50) NULL,
State varchar(50) NULL,
Zip varchar(50) NULL,
RejectReason varchar(50) NULL
) ON [PRIMARY]
```

Finally, the incoming data format is fixed-width and is defined as follows:

FIELD	STARTING POSITION	NEW FIELD NAME
First Name	1	FirstName
Last Name	11	LastName
City	26	City
State	44	State
Zip	52	Zip

The data file provided as a test sample looks like this (ProSSIS\Files\Ch09_ProSSIS\contacts.dat):

```
Jason  Gerard  Jacksonville  FL  32276-1911
Joseph  McClung  JACKSONVILLE  FLORIDA  322763939
Andrei  Ranga  Jax  fl  32276
Chad  Crisostomo  Orlando  FL  32746
Andrew  Ranger  Jax  fl
```

Create a sample of this data file or download a copy from `www.wrox.com/go/prossis2014`. Create a new package and add a Data Flow Task. Click on the Data Flow design surface and add a Connection Manager to the Connection Managers tab. Name the Connection Manager "Contacts Mainframe Extract," browse to the data file, and set the file format to Ragged Right. Flat files with spaces at the end of the specifications are typically difficult to process in some ETL platforms. The Ragged Right option in SSIS provides a way to handle these easily without having to run the file through a Script Task to put a character into a consistent spot or without having the origination system reformat its extract files. Use the Columns tab to visually define the columns. Flip to the Advanced tab to define each of the column names, types, and widths to match the desired values and the new database field name. (You may need to delete an unused column if this is added by the designer.) The designer at this point looks like Figure 9-24.

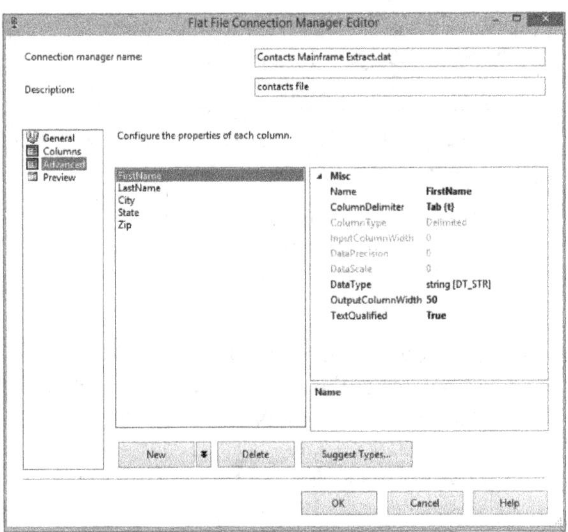

FIGURE 9-24

Typically, you may want to define some data with strong types. You can decide to do that here in the Connection Manager or you can do so later using a derived column depending on how confident you are in the source of the data. If the data source is completely unreliable, import data using Unicode strings and use your Data Flow Tasks to validate the data. Then move good data into a strong data type using the Derived Column Transformation.

On the Data Flow surface, drag a Flat File Source to the Data Flow editor pane. Edit the Flat File Source and set the Connection Manager to the Contract Mainframe Extract Connection Manager. This sets up the origination of the data to stream into the Data Flow Task. Check the box labeled "Retain null values from the source as null values in the Data Flow." This feature provides the consistent testing of null values later.

Now add a Script Component to the Data Flow. When you drop the Script Component, you will be prompted to pick the type of component to create. Select Transformation and click OK. Connect the output of the Flat File Source to the Script Component to pipe the data into this component, where you can program some validation on the data.

Open the Script Component and set the `ScriptLanguage` property to the language of your choice. On the Input Columns tab, you will notice that Input Name is a dropdown with the name Input 0. It is possible to have more than one source pointed to this Script Component. If so, this dropdown would allow you to individually configure the inputs and select the columns from each input. For this example, select all the input columns. Set the Usage Type for the State and Zip columns to ReadWrite. The reason will be clear later.

Select the Inputs and Outputs tab to see the collection of inputs and outputs and the input columns defined previously. Here you can create additional input and output buffers and columns within each. Expand all the nodes and add these two output columns:

COLUMN NAME	TYPE	SIZE
GoodFlag	DT_BOOL	N/A
RejectReason	DT_STR	50

You'll use the flag to separate the data from the data stream. The rejection reason will be useful to the person who has to perform any manual work on the data later. The designer with all nodes expanded should look like Figure 9-25.

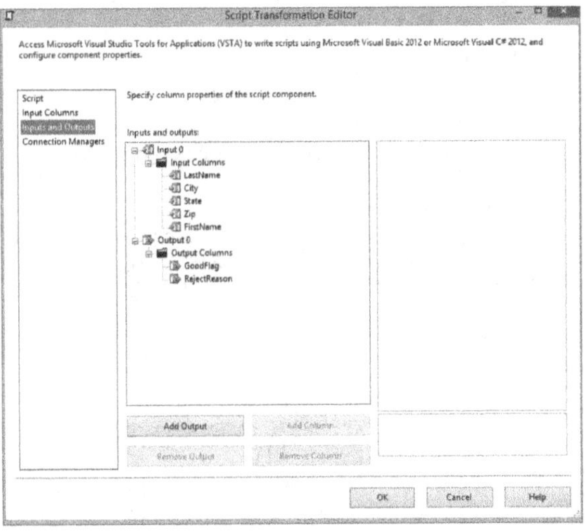

FIGURE 9-25

Back on the Script tab, click the Edit Script button to enter the VSTA scripting IDE. In the main class, the rules for validation need to be programmatically applied to each data row. In the `Input0_ProcessInputRow` method that was co-generated by SSIS using the Script Component designer, add the rules for data validation:

- All fields are required except for the zip code.
- The zip code must be in the format #####-#### or ##### and use numeric digits from 0 through 9. If the zip code is valid for the first five characters but the whole string is not, strip the trailing records and use the first five.
- The state must be two uppercase characters.

Here's the overall plan: the contents of the file will be sent into the Script Component. This is where programmatic control will be applied to each row processed. The incoming row has three data fields that need to be validated to determine whether all necessary data is present. The State and Zip columns need to be validated additionally by rule, and even cleaned up if possible. The need to fix the data in the stream is why the Zip and State column usage types had to be set to ReadWrite in the designer earlier.

To aid in accomplishing these rules, the data will be validated using regular expressions. Regular expressions are a powerful utility that should be in every developer's tool belt. They enable you to perform powerful string matching and replacement routines. You can find an excellent tutorial on regular expressions at `www.regular-expressions.info`. The regular expressions for matching the data are shown here:

REGULAR EXPRESSION	VALIDATION DESCRIPTION
^\d{5}([\-]\d{4})?$	Matches a five-digit or nine-digit zip code with dashes
\b([A-Z]{2})\b	Ensures that the state is only two capital characters

To use the regular expression library, add the .NET `System.Text.RegularExpressions` namespace to the top of the `main` class. For performance reasons, create the instances of the `RegEx` class to validate the `ZipCode` and the `State` in the `PreExecute()` method of the Script Component. This method and the private instances of the `Regex` classes should look like this (`ProSSIS\Code\Ch09_ProSSIS\10SCContactsExample.dtsx`):

C#

```
private Regex zipRegex;
private Regex stateRegex;
public override void PreExecute()
{
base.PreExecute();
zipRegex = new Regex("^\\d{5}([\\-]\\d{4})?$", RegexOptions.None);
stateRegex = new Regex("\\b([A-Z]{2})\\b", RegexOptions.None);
}
```

VB

```
Private zipRegex As Regex
Private stateRegex As Regex
Public Overrides Sub PreExecute()
MyBase.PreExecute()
zipRegex = New Regex("^\d{5}([\-]\d{4})?$", RegexOptions.None)
stateRegex = New Regex("\b([A-Z]{2})\b", RegexOptions.None)
End Sub
```

To break up the tasks, create two new private functions to validate the `ZipCode` and `State`. Using `byRef` arguments for the reason and the `ZipCode` enables the data to be cleaned and the encapsulated logic to return both a true or false and the reason. The `ZipCode` validation functions should look like this (`ProSSIS\Code\Ch09_ProSSIS\10SCContactsExample.dtsx`):

C#

```
private bool ZipIsValid(ref string zip, ref string reason)
{
zip = zip.Trim();
if (zipRegex.IsMatch(zip))
{
return true;
}
Else
{
if (zip.Length > 5)
{
zip = zip.Substring(0, 5);
if (zipRegex.IsMatch(zip))
```

```
{
return true;
}
Else
{
reason = "Zip larger than 5 Chars, " + "Retested at 5 Chars and Failed";
return false;
}
}
Else
{
reason = "Zip Failed Initial Format Rule";
return false;
}
}
}
```

VB

```
Private Function ZipIsValid(ByRef zip As String, _
 ByRef reason As String) As Boolean zip = zip.Trim()
If (zipRegex.IsMatch(zip)) Then
Return True
Else
If (zip.Length> 5) Then
zip = zip.Substring(0, 5)
If (zipRegex.IsMatch(zip)) Then
Return True
Else
reason = "Zip larger than 5 Chars, " + _
 "Retested at 5 Chars and Failed"
Return False
End If
Else
reason = "Zip Failed Initial Format Rule"
Return False
End If
End If
End Function
```

The state validation functions look like this (`ProSSIS\Code\Ch09_ProSSIS\10SCContactsExample.dtsx`):

C#

```
private bool StateIsValid(ref string state, ref string reason)
{
state = state.Trim().ToUpper();
if (stateRegex.IsMatch(state))
{
return true;
}
Else
{
reason = "Failed State Validation";
```

```
return false;
}
}
```

VB

```
Private Function StateIsValid(ByRef state As String, _
 ByRef reason As String) As Boolean state = state.Trim().ToUpper()
If (stateRegex.IsMatch(state)) Then Return True
Else
reason = "Failed State Validation"
Return False
End If
End Function
```

Now, to put it all together, add the driver method `Input0_ProcessInputRow()` that is fired upon each row of the flat file (`ProSSIS\Code\Ch09_ProSSIS\10SCContactsExample.dtsx`):

C#

```
public override void Input0_ProcessInputRow(Input0Buffer Row)
{
Row.GoodFlag = false;
string myZip = string.Empty;
string myState = string.Empty;
string reason = string.Empty;
if (!Row.FirstName_IsNull && !Row.LastName_IsNull && !Row.City_IsNull &&
    !Row.State_IsNull && !Row.Zip_IsNull)
{
myZip = Row.Zip;
myState = Row.State;
if (ZipIsValid(ref myZip, ref reason) && StateIsValid(ref myState, ref reason))
{
Row.Zip = myZip;
Row.State = myState;
Row.GoodFlag = true;
}
Else
{
Row.RejectReason = reason;
}
}
Else
{
Row.RejectReason = "All Required Fields not completed";
}
}
```

VB

```
Public Overrides Sub Input0_ProcessInputRow(ByVal Row As Input0Buffer)
Dim myZip As String = String.Empty
Dim myState As String = String.Empty
Dim reason As String = String.Empty
If (Row.FirstName_IsNull = False And _
Row.LastName_IsNull = False And _
Row.City_IsNull = False And _
Row.State_IsNull = False And _
```

```
Row.Zip_IsNull = False) Then
myZip = Row.Zip
myState = Row.State
If (ZipIsValid(myZip, reason) And _
 StateIsValid(myState, reason)) Then
Row.Zip = myZip
Row.State = myState
Row.GoodFlag = True
Else
Row.RejectReason = reason
End If
Else
Row.RejectReason = "All Required Fields not completed"
End If
End Sub
```

Notice that all fields are checked for null values using a property on the `Row` class that is the field name and an additional tag `_IsNull`. This is a property code generated by SSIS when you set up the input and output columns on the Script Component. Properties like `Zip_IsNull` explicitly allow the checking of a null value without encountering a null exception. This is handy as the property returns true if the particular column is `NULL`.

Next, if the Zip column is not `NULL`, its value is matched against the regular expression to determine whether it's in the correct format. If it is, the value is assigned back to the Zip column as a cleaned data element. If the value of the Zip column doesn't match the regular expression, the script checks whether it is at least five characters long. If true, then the first five characters are retested for a valid `ZipCode` pattern. Nonmatching values result in a `GoodFlag` in the output columns being set to `False`.

The state is trimmed of any leading or trailing white space, and then converted to uppercase and matched against the regular expression. The expression simply checks to see if it contains two uppercase letters between A and Z. If it does, the `GoodFlag` is set to `True` and the state value is updated; otherwise, the `GoodFlag` is set to `False`.

To send the data to the appropriate table based on the `GoodFlag`, you must use the Conditional Split Transformation. Add this task to the Data Flow designer and connect the output of the Script Component Task to the Conditional Split Transformation. Edit the Conditional Split Transformation, and add an output named Good with the condition `GoodFlag == TRUE` and name the default output `Bad`. This separates the data rows coming out of the Script Component Task into two separate streams. The Conditional Split Transformation Editor should look like Figure 9-26.

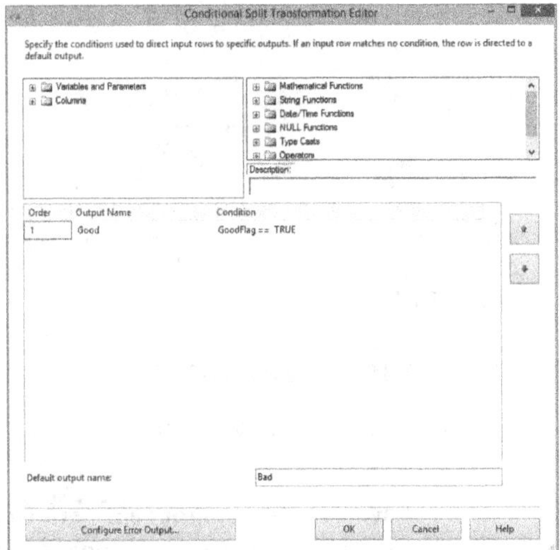

FIGURE 9-26

Add an OLE DB Connection Manager that uses the database you created for the Contacts and ContactsErrorQueue tables. Add two SQL Server Destinations to the Data Flow designer. One, named Validated Contacts SQL Server Destination, should point to the Contacts table; the other, named Error Contacts SQL Server Destination, should point to the ContactsErrorQueue table. Drag the output of the Conditional Split Transformation to the Validated Destination. Set the output stream named Good to the destination. Then open the Mappings tab in the Destination to map the input stream to the columns in the Contacts table. Repeat this for the other Bad output of the Conditional Split Transformation to the Error Destination.

Your final Data Flow should look something like Figure 9-27. If you run this package with the `Contacts.dat` file described at the top of the use case, three contacts will validate, and two will fail with these rejection reasons:

```
Failed State Validation
Joseph  McClung  JACKSONVILLE  FLORIDA  322763939
Zip Failed Initial Format Rule
Andrew  Ranger  Jax  fl
```

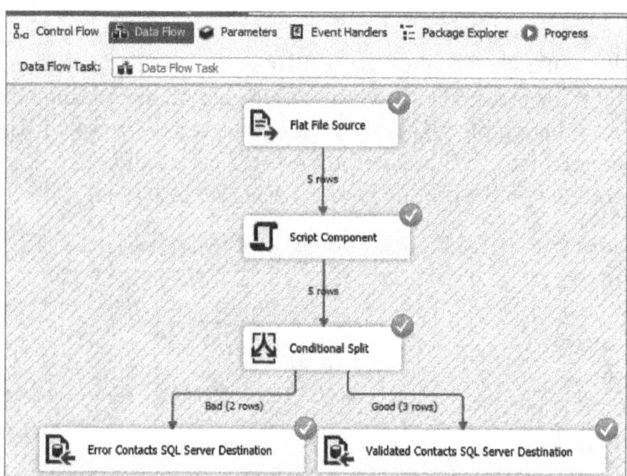

FIGURE 9-27

Synchronous versus Asynchronous

Data Flow transformations can handle data rows in one of two ways: synchronously or asynchronously.

- A **synchronous component** performs its stated operation for every row in the buffer of rows. It does not need to copy the buffer to a new memory space, and does not need to look at multiple rows to create its output. Examples of synchronous components include the Derived Column Transformation and the Row Count Transformation.
- The second type of transformation, an **asynchronous component**, creates another buffer for the output. It typically used multiple (or all) of the input rows to create a new output. The output usually looks quite different from the input, and the component tends to be

slower because of the copying of memory. Asynchronous component examples include the Aggregate Transformation and Sort Transformation.

Script Components can be written to act synchronously or asynchronously. The Data Validation example previously discussed is an example of a synchronous component. Let's create an asynchronous example for comparison. This example will show how to derive the median value from a set of source values.

Example: Creating a Median Value Asynchronously

As a starting point, use the AdventureWorks database to pull a set of values using an OLE DB Source, such as the `TotalDue` column from the `Sales.SalesOrderHeader` table. Similar to when you create a synchronous component, you can use a Script Component from the SSIS Toolbox as a transformation object and select the appropriate input columns, which in this case is the `TotalDue` column.

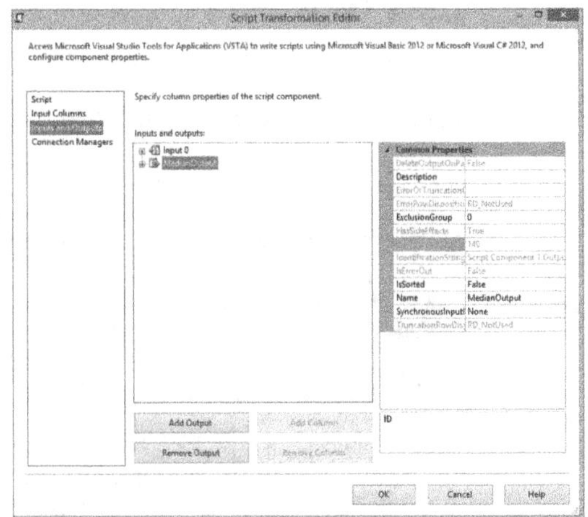

FIGURE 9-28

The Input and Outputs menu is where you veer off the same path that you would have followed with the synchronous component. The output property named `SynchronousInputID` needs to be set to None, which lets the component know that it should create a new buffer. The inputs and outputs created can be seen in Figure 9-28.

Once the inputs and outputs are prepared, it is time to write the script to perform the median calculation. The full script can be seen here in both languages (`ProSSIS\Code\Ch09_ProSSIS\11bSCAsync.dtsx`):

VB

```
Private valueArray As ArrayList
Public Overrides Sub PreExecute()
    MyBase.PreExecute()
    valueArray = New ArrayList
End Sub
Public Overrides Sub CreateNewOutputRows()
    MedianOutputBuffer.AddRow()
End Sub
Public Overrides Sub Input0_ProcessInputRow(ByVal Row As Input0Buffer)
    valueArray.Add(Row.TotalDue)
End Sub
Public Overrides Sub FinishOutputs()
    valueArray.Sort()
    If valueArray.Count Mod 2 = 0 Then
     MedianOutputBuffer.Value = (CDec(valueArray(valueArray.Count / 2 - 1)) + _
            CDec(valueArray(valueArray.Count / 2))) / 2
    Else
     MedianOutputBuffer.Value = CDec(valueArray(Floor(valueArray.Count / 2)))
    End If
```

```
End Sub
```

C#

```
private ArrayList valueArray;
public override void PreExecute()
{
    base.PreExecute();
    valueArray = new ArrayList();
}
public override void CreateNewOutputRows()
{
    MedianOutputBuffer.AddRow();
}
public override void Input0_ProcessInputRow(Input0Buffer Row)
{
    valueArray.Add(Row.TotalDue);
}
public override void FinishOutputs()
{
   base.FinishOutputs();
   valueArray.Sort();

    if (valueArray.Count % 2 == 0)
    {
        MedianOutputBuffer.Value =
                (Convert.ToDecimal(valueArray[valueArray.Count / 2 - 1]) +
                Convert.ToDecimal(valueArray[valueArray.Count / 2])) / 2;
    }
    else
    {
        MedianOutputBuffer.Value =
                Convert.ToDecimal(valueArray[Convert.ToInt32(
                    Math.Floor(valueArray.Count / 2.0))]);
    }
}
```

Note that there is an `ArrayList` that sits outside of the methods. This variable is accessed by multiple functions throughout the execution of the component, so it needs to be accessible by all. When then component runs its pre-execute phase, it will initialize the `ArrayList` and prepare it to be used. Then as each input row is processed, the value will be added to the `ArrayList`. Finally, in the `FinishOutputs` method, the median is calculated by sorting the values and pulling the middle value. This value is added to the output buffer and can be inserted into a file or database. The finished and executed package is shown in Figure 9-29.

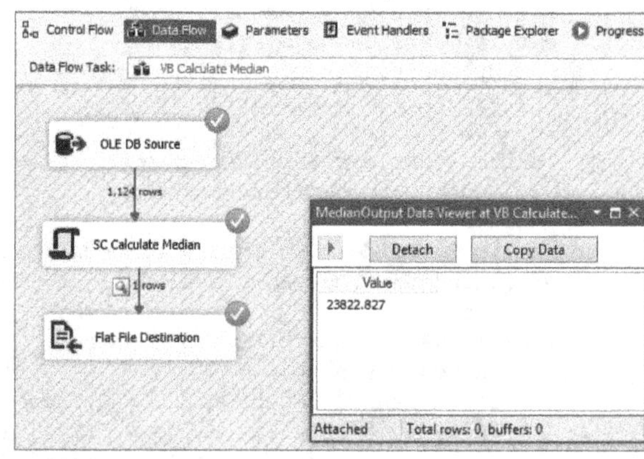

FIGURE 9-29

At this point, you have a good overview of how scripting works in SSIS and the difference between the Script Task and the Script Component, but as with any programming environment, you need to know how to troubleshoot and debug your code to ensure that everything works correctly. The next section describes some techniques you can use for more advanced SSIS scripting development.

ESSENTIAL CODING, DEBUGGING, AND TROUBLESHOOTING TECHNIQUES

You have now been all over the VSTA development environment and have been introduced to the different languages that move SSIS development into the managed code arena. Now, it is time to dig into some of the techniques for hardening your code for unexpected issues that may occur during runtime, and to look at some ways to troubleshoot SSIS packages. Any differences between the Script Task and the Script Component for some of these techniques are highlighted.

Structured Exception Handling

Structured exception handling (SEH) enables you to catch specific errors as they occur and perform any appropriate action needed. In many cases, you just want to log the error and stop execution, but in some cases you may want to try a different plan of action, depending on the error.

Here is an example of exception handling in SSIS scripting code in both languages (`ProSSIS\Code\Ch09_ProSSIS\12ScriptErrorSEH.dtsx`):

C#

```
public void Main()
{
Try
{
string fileText = string.Empty;
fileText = System.IO.File.ReadAllText("c:\\data.csv");
}
catch (System.IO.FileNotFoundException ex)
{
//Log Error Here
//MessageBox here for demo purposes only System.Windows.Forms.MessageBox.Show
    (ex.ToString());
Dts.TaskResult = (int)ScriptResults.Failure;
}
Dts.TaskResult = (int)ScriptResults.Success;
}
```

VB

```
Public Sub Main()
Try
Dim fileText As String fileText = FileIO.FileSystem.ReadAllText("C:\data.csv")
    Catch ex As System.IO.FileNotFoundException
'Log Error Here
'MessageBox here for demo purposes only System.Windows.Forms.MessageBox.Show
    (ex.ToString())
Dts.TaskResult = ScriptResults.Failure
```

```
Return
End Try
Dts.TaskResult = ScriptResults.Success
End Sub
```

This trivial example attempts to read the contents of the file at `C:\data.csv` into a string variable. The code makes some assumptions that might not be true. An obvious assumption is that the file exists. That is why this code was placed in a `Try` block. It is trying to perform an action that has the potential for failure. If the file isn't there, a `System.IO.FileNotFoundException` is thrown. A `Try` block marks a section of code that contains function calls with potentially known exceptions. In this case, the `FileSystem ReadAllText` function has the potentia l to throw a concrete exception.

The `Catch` block is the error handler for this specific exception. You would probably want to add some code to log the error inside the `Catch` block. For now, the exception is sent to the message box as a string so that it can be viewed. This code obviously originates from a Scripting Task, as it returns a result. The result is set to `Failure`, and the script is exited with the `Return` statement if the exception occurs. If the file is found, no exception is thrown, and the next line of code is executed. In this case, it would go to the line that sets the `TaskResult` to the value of the Success enumeration, right after the `End Try` statement.

If an exception is not caught, it propagates up the call stack until an appropriate handler is found. If none is found, the exception stops execution. You can have as many `Catch` blocks associated with a `Try` block as you wish. When an exception is raised, the `Catch` blocks are walked from top to bottom until an appropriate one is found that fits the context of the exception. Only the first block that matches is executed. Execution does not fall through to the next block, so it's important to place the most specific `Catch` block first and descend to the least specific. A `Catch` block specified with no filter will catch all exceptions. Typically, the coarsest `Catch` block is listed last. The previous code was written to anticipate the error of a file not being found, so not only does the developer have an opportunity to add some recovery code, but the framework assumes that you will handle the details of the error itself. If the same code contained only a generic `Catch` statement, the error would simply be written to the package output. To see what this looks like, replace the `Catch` statement in the preceding code snippet with these:

C#

```
Catch()
```

VB

```
Catch
```

In this case, the error would simply be written to the package output like this:

```
SSIS package "Package.dtsx" starting.
Error: 0x1 at VB Script Task: System.Reflection.TargetInvocationException, mscorlib
System.IO.FileNotFoundException, mscorlib
System.Reflection.TargetInvocationException: Exception has been thrown by the
    target of an invocation. ---> System.IO.FileNotFoundException: Could
    not find file 'C:\data.csv'.
File name: 'C:\data.csv'
```

```
at System.IO.__Error.WinIOError(Int32 errorCode, String maybeFullPath)
at System.IO.FileStream.Init(String path, FileMode mode, FileAccess access, Int32
    rights, Boolean useRights, FileShare share, Int32 bufferSize, FileOptions
    options, SECURITY_ATTRIBUTES secAttrs, String msgPath, Boolean bFromProxy)
...
Task failed: VB Script Task
SSIS package "Package.dtsx" finished: Success.
```

The full stack is omitted for brevity and to point out that the task status shows that it failed.

Another feature of structured error handling is the `Finally` block. The `Finally` block exists inside a `Try` block and executes after any code in the `Try` block and any `Catch` blocks that were entered. Code in the `Finally` block is always executed, regardless of what happens in the `Try` block and in any `Catch` blocks. You would put code to dispose of any resources, such as open files or database connections, in the `Finally` block. Following is an example of using the `Finally` block to free up a connection resource:

C#

```
public void OpenConnection(string myConStr)
{
SqlConnection con = new SqlConnection(myConStr);
Try
{
con.Open();
//do stuff with con
}
catch (SqlException ex)
{
//log error here
}
Finally
{
if (con != null)
{
con.Dispose();
}
}
}
```

VB

```
Public Sub OpenConnection(myConStr as String)
Dim con As SqlConnection = New SqlConnection(myConStr)
Try
con.Open()
'do stuff with con
Catch ex As SqlException
'Log Error Here
Dts.TaskResult = Dts.Results.Failure
Return
Finally
If Not con Is Nothing Then con.Dispose()
End Try
End Sub
```

In this example, the `Finally` block is hit regardless of whether the connection is open or not. A logical `If` statement checks whether the connection is open and closes it to conserve resources. Typically, you want to follow this pattern if you are doing anything resource intensive like using the `System.IO` or `System.Data` assemblies.

> **NOTE** *For a full explanation of the Try/Catch/Finally structure in Visual Basic or C#, see the language reference in MSDN or Books Online.*

Script Debugging and Troubleshooting

Debugging is an important feature of scripting in SSIS. You can still use the technique of popping up a message box function to see the value of variables, but there are more sophisticated techniques that will help you pinpoint the problem. Using the Visual Studio Tools for Applications environment, you now have the capability to set breakpoints, examine variables, and even evaluate expressions interactively.

Breakpoints

Breakpoints enable you to flag a line of code where execution pauses while debugging. Breakpoints are invaluable for determining what's going on inside your code, as they enable you to step into it to see what's happening as it executes.

> **NOTE** *A new feature since Integration Services 2012 is the ability to debug Script Components, which includes breakpoints and step abilities.*

You can set a breakpoint in several ways. One way is to click in the gray margin at the left of the text editor at the line where you wish to stop execution. Another way is to move the cursor to the line you wish to break on and press F9. Yet another way is to select Debug ➪ Toggle Breakpoint.

To continue execution from a breakpoint, press F10 to step to the next line, or F5 to run all the way through to the next breakpoint. When you have a breakpoint set on a line, the line has a red highlight like the one shown in Figure 9-30 (though you can't see the color in this figure).

When a Script Task has a breakpoint set somewhere in the code, it will have a red dot on it similar to the one in Figure 9-31.

```
Public Sub Main()
    Try
        Dim fileText As String
        fileText = FileIO.FileSystem.ReadAllText("C:\data.csv")
    Catch ex As System.IO.FileNotFoundException
        'Log Error Here
        'MessageBox here for demo purposes only
        System.Windows.Forms.MessageBox.Show(ex.ToString())
        Dts.TaskResult = ScriptResults.Failure
        Return
    End Try
    Dts.TaskResult = ScriptResults.Success
```

FIGURE 9-30

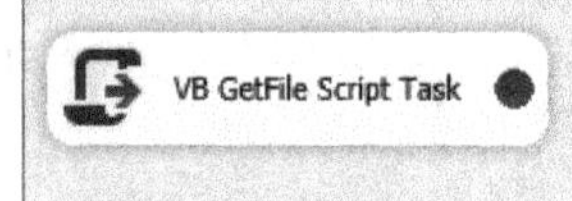

FIGURE 9-31

Row Count Component and Data Viewers

Previously, you looked at using the Visual Studio Tools for Applications environment to debug a Script Task or Script Component using breakpoints and other tools. Alternatively, you can inspect the data as it moves through the Data Flow using the Row Count Component or a Data Viewer.

The Row Count Component is very straightforward; it simply states how many rows passed through it. The Data Viewer contains additional information if desired. To add a Data Viewer, select the connector arrow that leaves the component for which you want to see data. In the previous example, this would be the connector from the Script Component to the Conditional Split Task. Right-click this connection, and select Enable Data Viewer. This automatically adds a Data Viewer that will show all columns on the stream. To remove any columns, double click the connector and select the Data Viewer menu. Figure 9-32 shows how to turn on the Data Viewer on the Data Flow Path.

Now when you run this package again, you will get a Data Viewer window after the Script Component has executed. This view will show the data output by the Script Component. Figure 9-33 shows an example. Click the play button to continue package execution, or simply close the window.

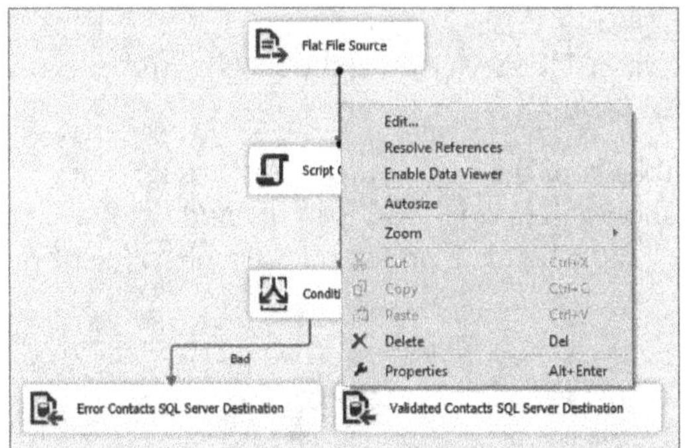

FIGURE 9-32

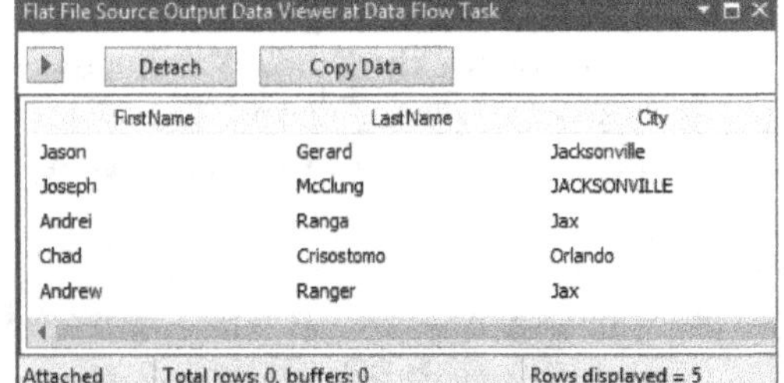

FIGURE 9-33

While using the Data Viewer certainly helps with debugging, it is no replacement for being able to step into the code. An alternative is to use the `FireInformation` event on the `ComponentMetaData` class in the Script Component. It is like the message box but without the modal effect.

Autos, Locals, and Watches

The SQL Server Data Tools environment provides you with some powerful views into what is happening with the execution of your code. These views consist of three windows: the Autos window, the Locals window, and the Watch window. These windows share a similar layout and display the value of expressions and variables, though each has a distinct method determining what data to display.

The Locals window displays variables that are local to the current statement, as well as three statements behind and in front of the current statement. For a running example, the Locals window would appear (see Figure 9-34).

FIGURE 9-34

Watches are another very important feature of debugging. Watches enable you to specify a variable to watch. You can set up a watch to break execution when a variable's value changes or some other condition is met. This enables you to see exactly when something is happening, such as a variable that has an unexpected value.

To add a watch, select the variable you want to watch inside the script, right-click it, and select Add Watch. This will add an entry to the Watch window.

You can also use the Quick Watch window, accessible from the Debug menu, or through the Ctrl+Alt+Q key combination. The Watch window shown in Figure 9-35 is in the middle of a breakpoint, and you can see the value of `Iterator` as it is being assigned the variable value of 2.

FIGURE 9-35

This window enables you to evaluate an expression at runtime and see the result in the window. You can then click the Add Watch button to move it to the Watch window.

The Immediate Window

The Immediate window enables you to evaluate expressions, execute procedures, and print out variable values. It is really a mode of the Command window, which enables you to issue commands to the IDE. Unfortunately, this too is useful only when you are within a breakpoint, and this can be done only within a Script Task.

> **NOTE** *If you can't find the Immediate window but see the Command window, just type the command* `immed` *and press Enter.*

The Immediate window is very useful while testing. You can see the outcome of several different scenarios. Suppose you have an object `obj` of type `MyType`, and `MyType` declares a method called `DoMyStuff()` that takes a single integer as an argument. Using the Immediate window, you could pass different values into the `DoMyStuff()` method and see the results. To evaluate an expression in the Immediate window and see its results, you must start the command with a question mark (?):

```
?obj.DoMyStuff(2)
"Hello"
```

Commands are terminated by pressing the Enter key. The results of the execution are printed on the next line. In this case, calling `DoMyStuff()` with a value of `2` returns the string "Hello."

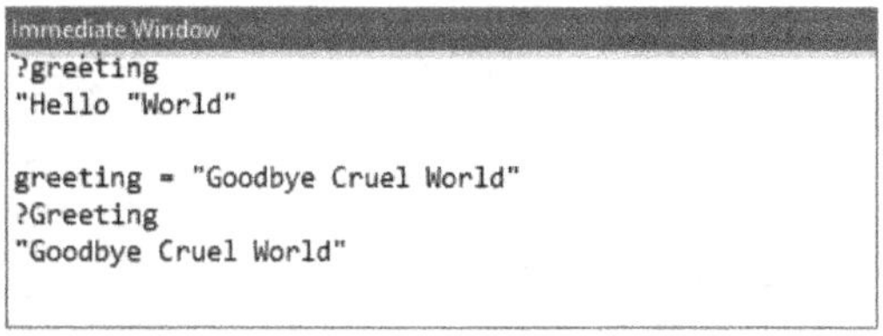

```
Immediate Window
?greeting
"Hello "World"

greeting = "Goodbye Cruel World"
?Greeting
"Goodbye Cruel World"
```

FIGURE 9-36

You can also use the Immediate window to change the value of variables. If you have a variable defined in your script and you want to change its value, perhaps for negative error testing, you can use this window, shown in Figure 9-36.

In this case, the value of the variable greeting is printed out on the line directly below the expression. After the value is printed, it is changed to "Goodbye Cruel World." The value is then queried again, and the new value is printed. If you are in a Script Task and need to get additional information, this is a useful way to do it.

SUMMARY

In this chapter, you learned about the available scripting options in SSIS, including those that support managed code development and a robust IDE development environment. You used the Visual Studio Tools for Applications IDE to develop some basic Script Tasks. Then, to see how all this fits together in SSIS, you dove right in to using the Script Task to retrieve data into variables and to save data into external XML files, and used some .NET serialization techniques that enable custom serialization into MSMQ queues or web services. To understand how to leverage existing code libraries, you even created a utility class, registered it into the GAC, and accessed it in an SSIS script to validate data.

SSIS scripting is powerful, but it has been difficult for some developers to differentiate between when to use a Script Task and when a Script Component is appropriate. You have now examined both of these in detail in this chapter and should be able to use them with confidence in your daily development.

Experiment with the scripting features of SSIS using the examples in this chapter, and you will find all kinds of uses for them. Don't forget to review Chapter 5, which covers expressions, to learn about the capabilities of controlling properties within the SSIS model at runtime. Now you are going to take what you have learned so far about SSIS's capabilities — from Control Flow and Data Flow Tasks to expressions and Scripting Tasks and Components — and put it to work. In the next chapter, you'll learn all about the techniques you have at your disposal to do a typical job of loading a data warehouse using SSIS.

10

Advanced Data Cleansing in SSIS

WHAT'S IN THIS CHAPTER?

- Using the Derived Column Transformation for advanced data cleansing
- Applying the Fuzzy Lookup and Fuzzy Grouping transformations and understanding how they work
- Introducing Data Quality Services
- Introducing Master Data Services

WROX.COM CODE DOWNLOADS FOR THIS CHAPTER

You can find the wrox.com code downloads for this chapter at `http://www.wrox.com/go/prossis2014` on the Download Code tab.

In this chapter, you will learn the ins and outs of data cleansing in SSIS, from the basics to the advanced. In a broad sense, one of SSIS's main purposes is to cleanse data — that is, transform data from a source to a destination and perform operations on it along the way. In that sense, someone could correctly say that every transformation in SSIS is about data cleansing. For example, consider the following transformations:

- The Data Conversion adjusts data types.
- The Sort removes duplicate data.
- The Merge Join correlates data from two sources.

- The Derived Column applies expression logic to data.
- The Data Mining predicts values and exceptions.
- The Script applies .NET logic to data.
- The Term Extraction and Term Lookup perform text mining.

In a stricter sense, data cleansing is about identifying incomplete, incorrect, or irrelevant data and then updating, modifying, or removing the "dirty" data. From this perspective, SSIS has four primary data cleansing transformations, which are reviewed in this chapter:

- **Derived Column Transformation:** This transformation can perform advanced expression-based data cleansing. If you have just basic data cleansing needs, like blanks or nulls or simple text parsing, this is the right place to start. The next section will walk through some examples.
- **Fuzzy Lookup Transformation:** Capable of joining to external data based on data similarity, the Fuzzy Lookup Transformation is a core data cleansing tool in SSIS. This transformation is perfect if you have dirty data input that you want to associate to data in a table in your database based on similar values. Later in the chapter, you'll take a look at the details of the Fuzzy Lookup Transformation and what happens behind the scenes.
- **Fuzzy Grouping Transformation:** The main purpose is de-duplication of similar data. The Fuzzy Grouping Transformation is ideal if you have data from a single source and you know you have duplicates that you need to find.
- **DQS Cleansing:** The Data Quality Services Cleansing Transformation leverages the DQS engine to perform predefined data quality rules and mapping. If you have any advanced cleansing where you would like to apply rules and manage cleansing logic, the DQS Transformation using the DQS engine is the right choice for you.

In addition to these data cleansing transformations, SSIS also has a Data Profiling Task that can help you identify any issues within your dirty data as you plan its necessary data cleansing. See Chapter 3 for an overview of the Data Profiling Task and Chapter 12 for a more detailed review of its functionality.

This chapter will also explore Master Data Services as a way of standardizing reference data. MDS give users the familiar interface of Excel to manage and correct data to truly have one version of the truth.

ADVANCED DERIVED COLUMN USE

If you've used the data flow in SSIS for any amount of data transformation logic, you will no doubt have used the Derived Column Transformation. It has many basic uses, from basic replacing of `NULL`s or blanks to text parsing and manipulation.

Using SSIS expressions, the Derived Column Transformation can be used for more advanced data cleansing operations than a simple single expression, such as the following:

- Advanced text code logic to identify and parse text values
- Checking for data ranges and returning a specified value
- Mathematical operations with advanced logic
- Date comparison and operations

Chapter 5 reviews the expression language in thorough detail. Figure 10-1 highlights the Derived Column Transformation expression toolbox within the Derived Column Transformation Editor.

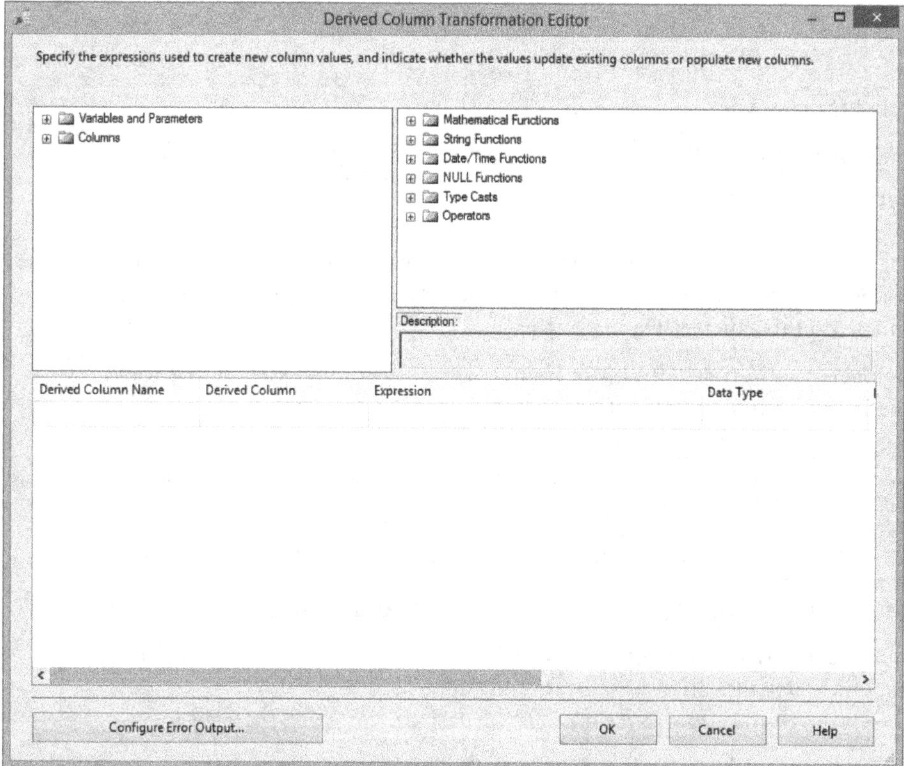

FIGURE 10-1

One challenge with the Derived Column Transformation is parsing more complicated text strings and effectively using expressions without duplicating expression logic. This next section walks you through an example of pulling out information from values.

Text Parsing Example

To see an example of text mining, consider the example source data from the following list. It contains oceanographic buoy locations off the coast of the United States. Some of them are near cities, while others are in locations farther off the coast. In addition to the location, the text values also contain some codes and switches irrelevant to what you need to parse.

6N26 /V S. HATTERAS, NC

3D13 /A EDISTO, SC

3D14 /A GRAYS REEF

6N46 /A CANAVERAL, FL

6N47 /A CANAVERAL EAST, FL

3D56 /A ST. AUGUSTINE, FL

3D55 /A FRYING PAN SHOALS

3D36 /D BILOXI, MS

3D35 /D LANEILLE, TX

3D44 /D EILEEN, TX

Can you use the Derived Column Transformation to pull out the locations embedded within the text? For locations that are near cities, can you also identify the appropriate state code? More important, can you do this efficiently and clearly?

Most ETL developers would try to do this in a single Derived Column step with one expression. They would end up with something like this:

```
SUBSTRING((ISNULL(Location) ? "Unknown" :
TRIM(Location)),FINDSTRING((ISNULL(Location) ? "Unknown" : TRIM(Location)),"/",1)
+ 3,(FINDSTRING((ISNULL(Location) ? "Unknown" : TRIM(Location)),",",1) == 0 ?
(LEN((ISNULL(Location) ? "Unknown" : TRIM(Location))) -
FINDSTRING((ISNULL(Location) ? "Unknown" : TRIM(Location)),"/",1) + 4) :
(FINDSTRING((ISNULL(Location) ? "Unknown" : TRIM(Location)),",",1) -
FINDSTRING((ISNULL(Location) ? "Unknown" : TRIM(Location)),"/",1) - 3)))
```

To be sure, this code will work. It identifies text values, where the location begins, and when a location has a state code appended to it. However, the clarity of the code leaves much to be desired.

One thing you can notice in the preceding code is the redundancy of some expressions. For example, it is replacing a `NULL` value in the Location column with `"Unknown"`. In addition, several `FINDSTRING` functions are used to locate the "/" in the code.

A better approach is to break the code into multiple steps. Figure 10-2 illustrates a Data Flow that contains two Derived Column Transformations.

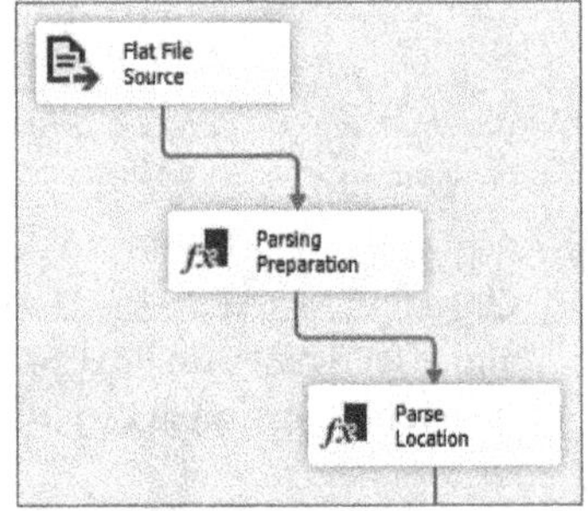

FIGURE 10-2

The first Derived Column Transformation performs a few preparation steps in the data that is then used in the second transformation. Figure 10-3 highlights the expressions used in the first "Parsing Preparation" transformation.

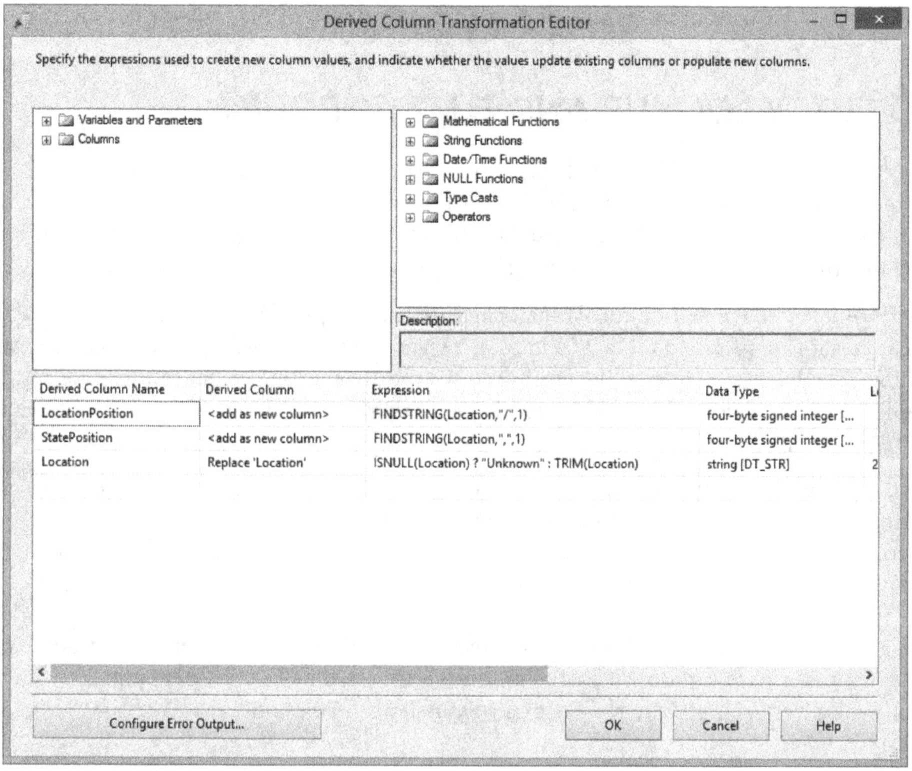

FIGURE 10-3

This transformation performs the three common expressions needed to handle the string logic that pulls out the location information from the data:

- **LocationPosition:** This new column simply identifies where the "/" is in the code, since that is immediately before the location is named.
- **StatePosition:** This expression looks for the existence of a comma (`,`), which would indicate that the location is a city with an accompanying state as part of the location description.
- **Location:** This column is replaced with "`Unknown`" if the Location value is missing.

With these preparation steps, the expression logic needed to perform the parsing of the text becomes a lot cleaner. The following code is part of the second Derived Column Transformation, which parses out the name of the location:

```
SUBSTRING(Location,LocationPosition + 3,(StatePosition == 0 ?
     (LEN(Location) - LocationPosition + 4) :
     (StatePosition - LocationPosition - 3)))
```

Now the expression is more readable and easier to follow. Note that to employ this approach, you need to break your Data Flow into two Derived Column Transformations because in order for expression logic to reference a Data Flow column, it must be available in the input of the transformation.

ADVANCED FUZZY LOOKUP AND FUZZY GROUPING

The two fuzzy transformations within SSIS, Fuzzy Lookup and Fuzzy Grouping, deal with associating data through data similarity, rather than exact data matching. The "fuzzy" part of the transformation name refers to data coupling based on selected data mapping using defined similarity and confidence measurements. Here is a brief description of each:

- **Fuzzy Lookup:** The Fuzzy Lookup Transformation takes input data from a Data Flow and matches it to a specified table within SQL Server joined across data similarity column matching. The Fuzzy Lookup is like the Lookup Transformation, except that the column mapping can be adjusted to evaluate data likeness and the output can be tuned to return one or more potential results.
- **Fuzzy Grouping:** This transformation takes a single input from the Data Flow and performs a comparison with itself to try to identify potential duplicates in the data. The grouping doesn't evaluate all the columns in the source input; it only searches for duplicates across the columns you select based on the similarity settings that you define.

This section begins with the Fuzzy Lookup Transformation by reviewing its general functionality. It then digs a little deeper to reveal how it works under the covers. The Fuzzy Grouping Transformation works very similarly to the Fuzzy Lookup Transformation.

Fuzzy Lookup

The very basic purpose of the Fuzzy Lookup is to match input data to a lookup table whose columns you are matching across that do not necessarily match exactly. The Fuzzy Lookup Transformation is therefore very similar to the Lookup Transformation, except you are not joining with identical values; you are joining with similar values. Figure 10-4 shows the (regular) Lookup Transformation, whereby several columns are mapped to a lookup table and a key column is returned.

The input data in Figure 10-4 is from Excel, a common source of dirty data due to issues with data conversion, missing data, or typographical errors. The simple Data Flow in Figure 10-5 shows that the Lookup has the error output configured to redirect missing rows; as you can see, seven rows do not match to the Lookup table when the Data Flow is executed.

To find the missing record matches for the seven rows, you can use the Fuzzy Lookup Transformation. The best way to use the Fuzzy Lookup is when you have a set of data rows that you have already tried matching with a Lookup, but there were no matches. The Fuzzy Lookup does not use cached data and requires SQL Server to help during the processing, so it is more efficient to take advantage of a cached Lookup to handle the large majority of records before using the Fuzzy Lookup.

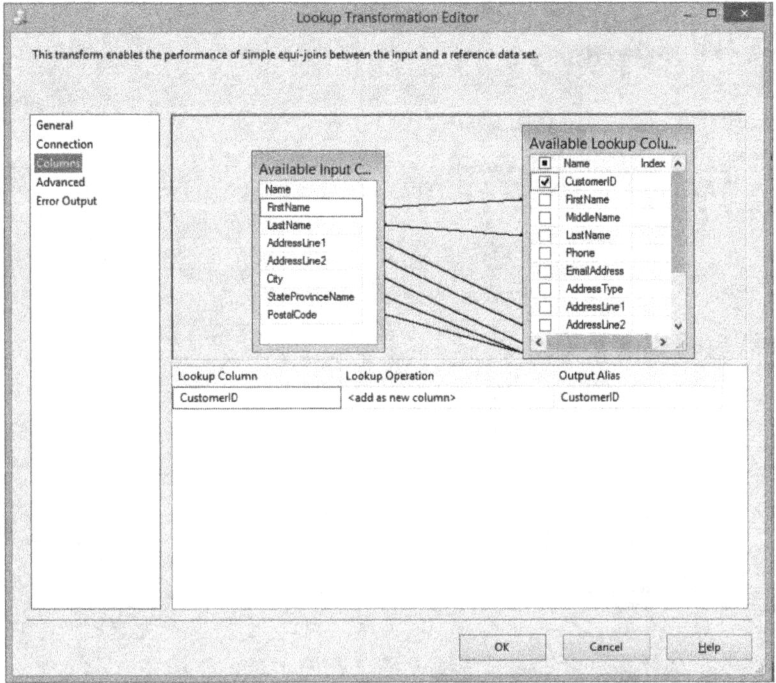

FIGURE 10-4

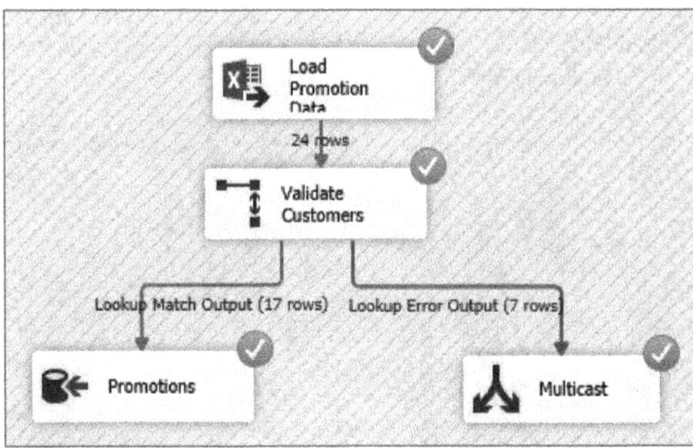

FIGURE 10-5

Figure 10-6 shows the Fuzzy Lookup Transformation Editor. The first tab, Reference Table, requires you to select the reference table that the Fuzzy Lookup needs to match, just like the Lookup Transformation. Later in this section, you will see the advanced settings.

On the Columns tab, you need to join the matching columns from the input to the Lookup reference table. Because the purpose is to find matches, you can then determine which columns in the lookup reference table need to be added to the Data Flow. The Fuzzy Lookup example in Figure 10-7 is identical to the Lookup mapping in Figure 10-4, where the primary key column, CustomerID, is returned to the Data Flow.

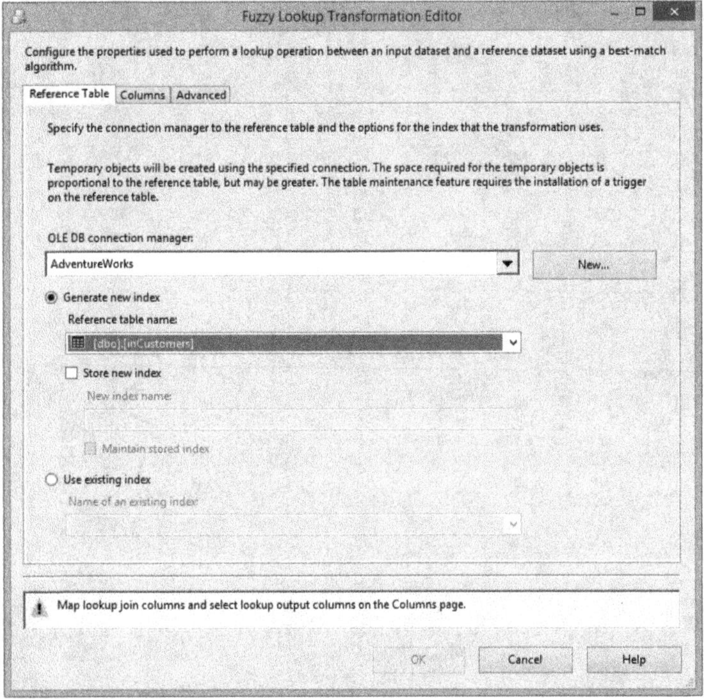

FIGURE 10-6

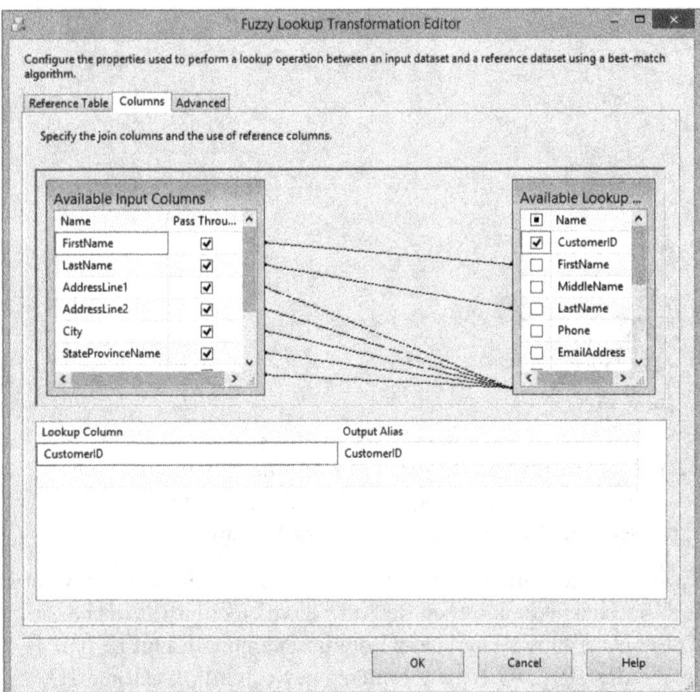

FIGURE 10-7

The Fuzzy Lookup Transformation has a few advanced features (see Figure 10-8) to help you determine what should be considered a match:

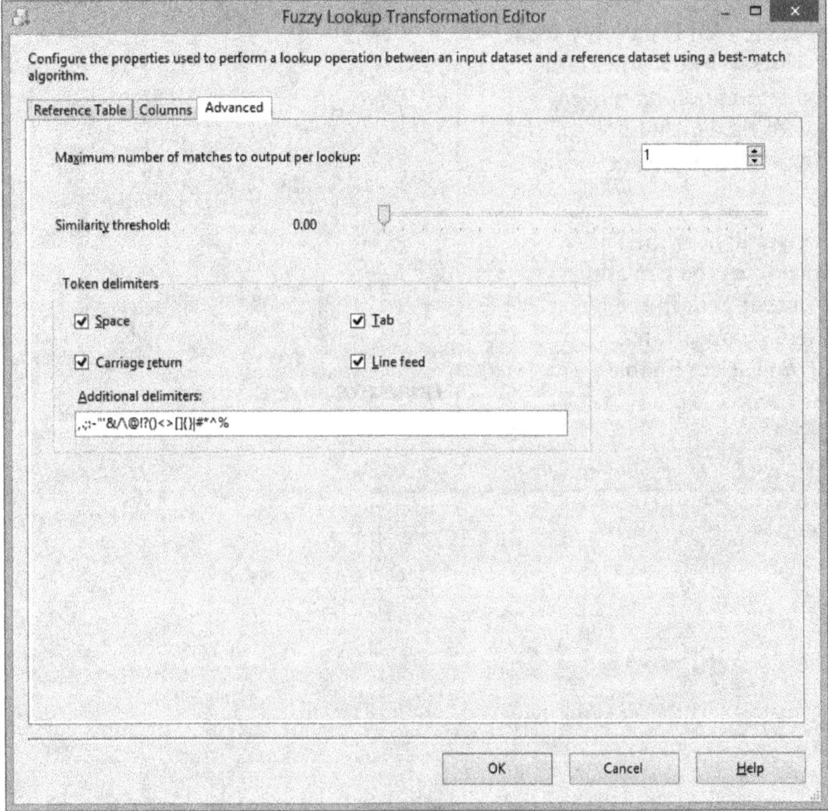

FIGURE 10-8

- For every input row, the "Maximum number of matches to output per lookup" option will limit the potential matches to the number that is set. The Fuzzy Lookup will always select the top matches ordered by similarity, highest to lowest.
- The "Similarity threshold" option defines whether you want to limit the matches to only values above a defined likeness (or similarity). If you set this to 0, you will always get the same number of lookup rows per input row as defined in the "Maximum number of matches to output per lookup" setting.
- Because the Fuzzy Lookup is matching on text, some custom features enable the Lookup to determine when to identify a separation in characters (like more than one word). These are the token delimiters.

In the example we are building, once the Fuzzy Lookup is configured a Union All is added to the Data Flow and the output of the Lookup and the Fuzzy Lookup are both connected to the Union All. The output of the Union All is then connected to the destination.

Figure 10-9 shows the completed Data Flow with the execution results. The seven rows that didn't match the Lookup Transformation have been successfully matched with the Fuzzy Lookup, and the data has been brought back together with the Union All.

In order to better understand how the Fuzzy Lookup is matching the data, you can add a Data Viewer to the output path in the Fuzzy Lookup. As Figure 10-10 demonstrates, right-click on the path and select Enable Data Viewer.

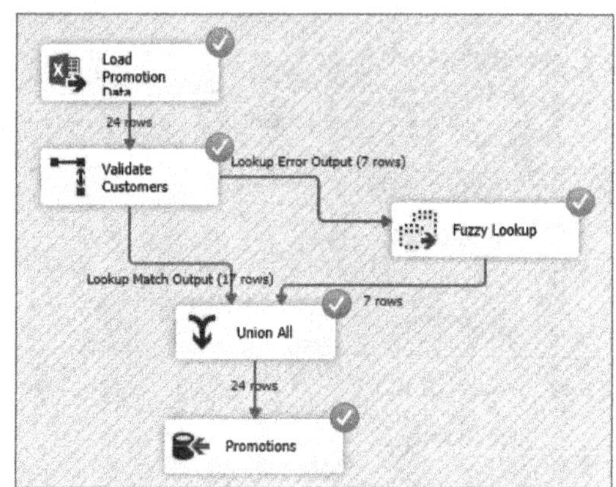

FIGURE 10-9

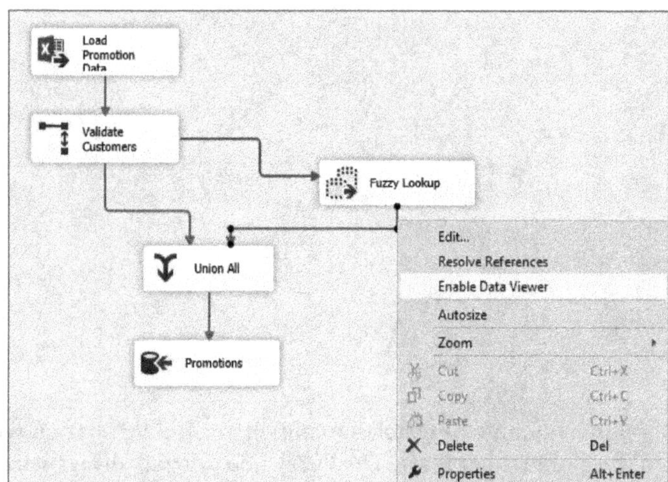

FIGURE 10-10

The Fuzzy Lookup has added more than just the reference table's lookup column, as shown in the Data Viewer output in Figure 10-11:

- **_Similarity:** This is the overall similarity of the source input row to the match row that the Fuzzy Lookup found.
- **_Confidence:** This is not about the current row but how many other rows are close in similarity. If other rows are identified as close in similarity, the confidence drops, because the Fuzzy Lookup is less confident about whether the match found is the right match.

- **_Similarity_[Column Name]:** For every column used in the match (refer to Figure 10-7), the Fuzzy Lookup includes the individual similarity of the input column to the match row in the reference table. These columns begin with "_Similarity_" and have the original column name as a suffix.

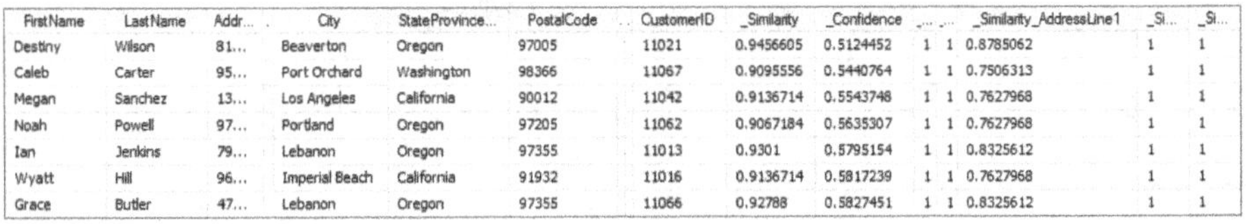

FirstName	LastName	Addr...	City	StateProvince...	PostalCode	..	CustomerID	_Similarity	_Confidence	_...	_...	_Similarity_AddressLine1	_Si...	_Si...
Destiny	Wilson	81...	Beaverton	Oregon	97005		11021	0.9456605	0.5124452	1	1	0.8785062	1	1
Caleb	Carter	95...	Port Orchard	Washington	98366		11067	0.9095556	0.5440764	1	1	0.7506313	1	1
Megan	Sanchez	13...	Los Angeles	California	90012		11042	0.9136714	0.5543748	1	1	0.7627968	1	1
Noah	Powell	97...	Portland	Oregon	97205		11062	0.9067184	0.5635307	1	1	0.7627968	1	1
Ian	Jenkins	79...	Lebanon	Oregon	97355		11013	0.9301	0.5795154	1	1	0.8325612	1	1
Wyatt	Hill	96...	Imperial Beach	California	91932		11016	0.9136714	0.5817239	1	1	0.7627968	1	1
Grace	Butler	47...	Lebanon	Oregon	97355		11066	0.92788	0.5827451	1	1	0.8325612	1	1

FIGURE 10-11

As you can see in the Data View output from Figure 10-11, the similarity of the matching rows varies between 91 and 96 percent. The columns on the right-hand side of Figure 10-11 indicate the degree of similarity between the matching columns. Notice that many of them have a value of 1, which indicates a perfect match. A value less than 1 indicates the percentage of similarity between the input and reference join.

Note that the confidence is in the 50 percent range. This is because most of the sample data is from matching cities and states, which increases the similarity of other rows and therefore reduces the confidence.

One final feature of the Fuzzy Lookup Transformation is the capability to define similarity thresholds for each column in the match. Referring back to Figure 10-7, if you double-click on one of the relationship lines, it will open the Create Relationships dialog, shown in Figure 10-12.

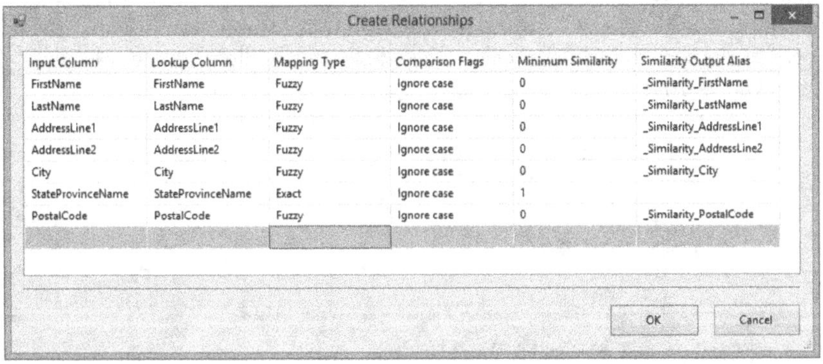

Create Relationships

Input Column	Lookup Column	Mapping Type	Comparison Flags	Minimum Similarity	Similarity Output Alias
FirstName	FirstName	Fuzzy	Ignore case	0	_Similarity_FirstName
LastName	LastName	Fuzzy	Ignore case	0	_Similarity_LastName
AddressLine1	AddressLine1	Fuzzy	Ignore case	0	_Similarity_AddressLine1
AddressLine2	AddressLine2	Fuzzy	Ignore case	0	_Similarity_AddressLine2
City	City	Fuzzy	Ignore case	0	_Similarity_City
StateProvinceName	StateProvinceName	Exact	Ignore case	1	
PostalCode	PostalCode	Fuzzy	Ignore case	0	_Similarity_PostalCode

OK Cancel

FIGURE 10-12

In this example, the StateProvinceName has been set to an Exact Match type, which is a minimum similarity of 1. Therefore, the Fuzzy Lookup will identify a potential match between rows only when the StateProvinceName is identical for both the input row and the reference table.

The easiest way to understand how the Fuzzy Lookup Transformation works (behind the scenes) is to open the Fuzzy Lookup Transformation Editor, edit the reference table, and then check the "Store new index" checkbox, as Figure 10-13 shows.

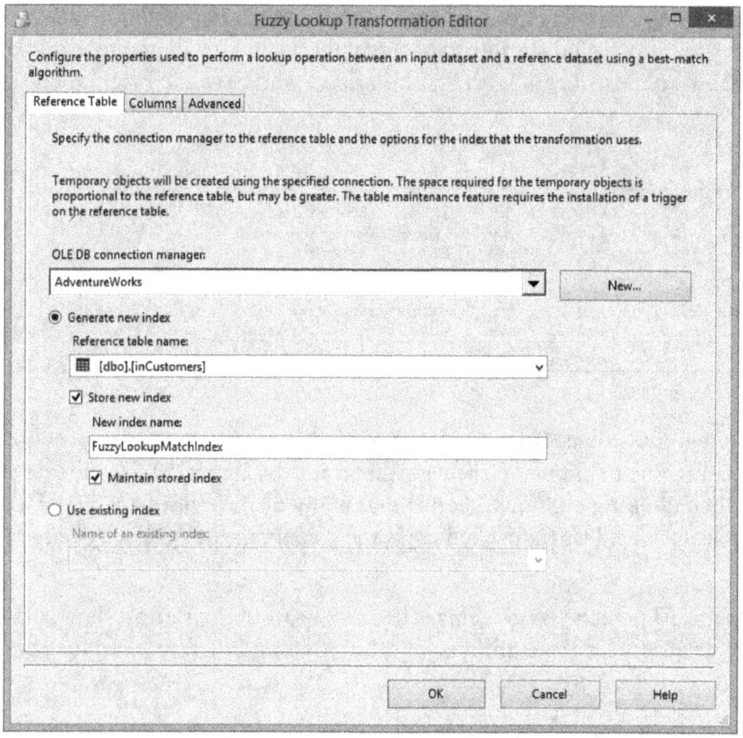

FIGURE 10-13

The Fuzzy Lookup requires a connection to a SQL Server database using the OLE DB provider because the transformation uses SQL Server to compute the similarity. To see how this works, begin by using SSMS to connect to the server and database where the lookup table is located. Expand the Tables folder, as shown in Figure 10-14.

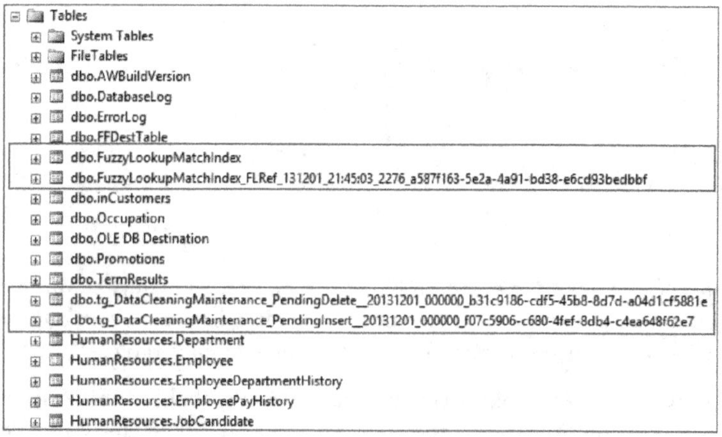

FIGURE 10-14

The Fuzzy Lookup has created a few tables. The FuzzyLookupMatchIndex tables contain the data in the reference table, tokenized for the Fuzzy Lookup operation. In addition, if you checked the "Maintain stored index" checkbox (refer to Figure 10-13), you will also get a couple of additional tables that contain data for inserts and deletes from the reference table. Not shown are the indexes on the reference table, which keep the data updated.

Figure 10-15 shows sample data from the FuzzyLookupMatchIndex table. The Token column contains partial data from the values for each row in the reference table. The ColumnNumber is the ordinal of the column from the input data set (basically, which column is being referenced in each row). The values in the Rids column look quite strange. This is because SSMS cannot display the binary data in text. However, this column contains the Row Identifiers (RIDs) for every row in the reference table that contains the same token. If you trace the Fuzzy Lookup during package execution, you will find that the input row is also tokenized and matched to the data in the Match Index table, which is how the engine determines the similarity.

	Token	ColumnNumber	TokenProp	BucketNumber	Freq	Rids
1	NULL	NULL	NULL	0x000000000000234F	NULL	Version=1.0.9 Delimiters=200009000d000a002c002e0...
2	0012	6	2	0x000000000000233E	1	
3	011t	2	2	0x000000000000226A	1	[illegible]
4	0241	6	2	0x000000000000233C	1	‖
5	040l	2	2	0x000000000000227D	1	[illegible]
6	064m	2	2	0x000000000000222E	1	[illegible]
7	0706	6	2	0x0000000000002332	1	[illegible]
8	1170	2	1	0x00000000000021F5	1	[illegible]
9	1170	2	2	0x0000000000002244	1	[illegible]
10	1203	6	2	0x000000000000234A	2	
11	1210	2	1	0x00000000000021FE	1	[illegible]
12	1210	2	2	0x0000000000002254	1	[illegible]

FIGURE 10-15

As you may have guessed from looking at how the Fuzzy Lookup Transformation works, it can consume a lot of server resources. This is why you may want to handle the exact matches first using a standard Lookup Transformation.

Fuzzy Grouping

The Fuzzy Grouping Transformation is similar to the Fuzzy Lookup in that it uses the same approach to find matches and it requires SQL Server. Rather than reference an external table, however, the Fuzzy Grouping matches the input data to itself in order to find duplicates. This process is commonly referred to as *de-duplication.*

Figure 10-16 shows an example Data Flow that performs several common transformations. Data is imported from Excel and transformed in a few steps. Right before the destination, a Fuzzy Grouping is added to the Data Flow.

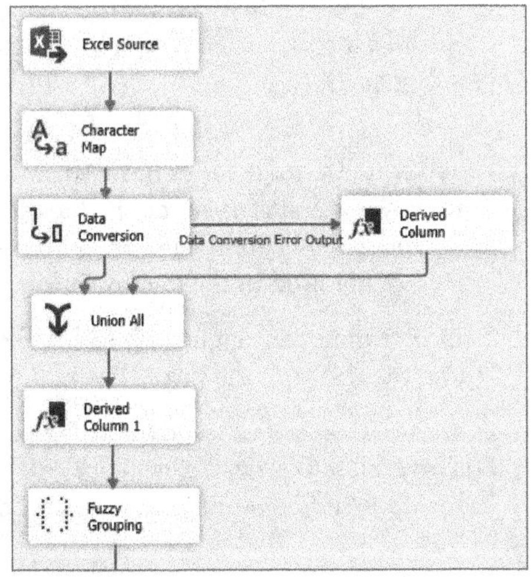

FIGURE 10-16

When you edit the Fuzzy Grouping, you will find some similar settings to the Fuzzy Lookup. Note that on the Connection Manager tab, shown in Figure 10-17, the only property is the connection to SQL Server. This is because there is no reference table that the Fuzzy Grouping needs to join. It just needs the connection where it can store its temporary data.

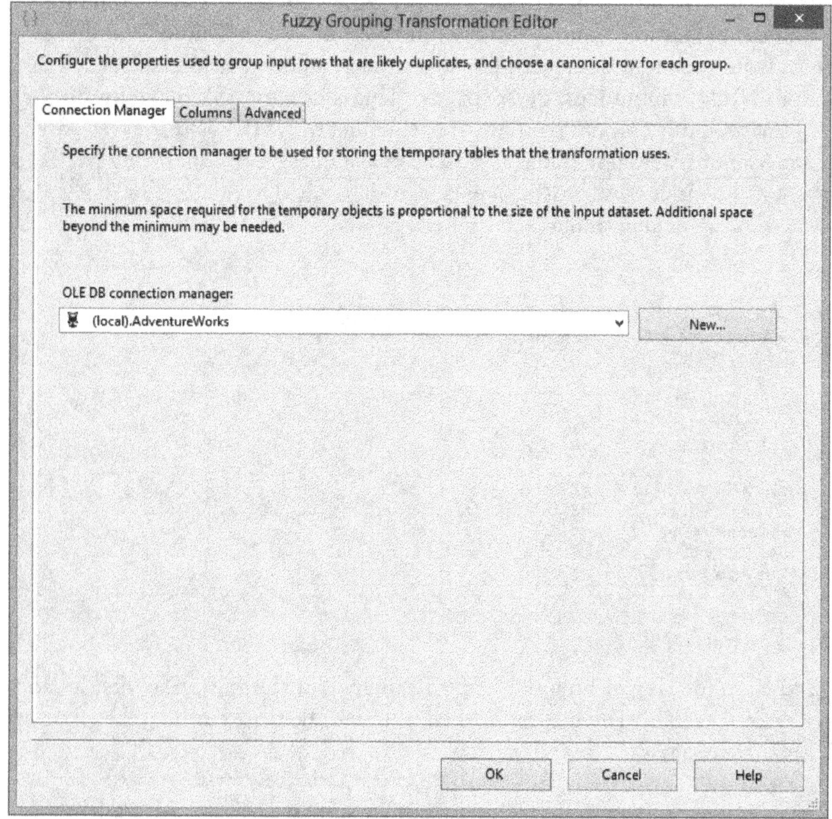

FIGURE 10-17

Each column in the input has two settings that you can set. The first is the checkbox (Figure 10-18 shows a few columns selected). This determines whether the Fuzzy Grouping will use this column to identify duplicates. The Pass Through column enables columns to appear downstream even when they are not used in the identification of duplicates.

Another thing that Figure 10-18 highlights is that the Fuzzy Grouping Transformation provides the same capability as the Fuzzy Lookup to set a minimum similarity on a column-by-column basis.

On the Advanced tab, shown in Figure 10-19, you can fine-tune the Fuzzy Grouping to specify the overall Similarity threshold. If a potential matching row does not meet this threshold, it is not considered in the de-duplication. You can also set the output columns.

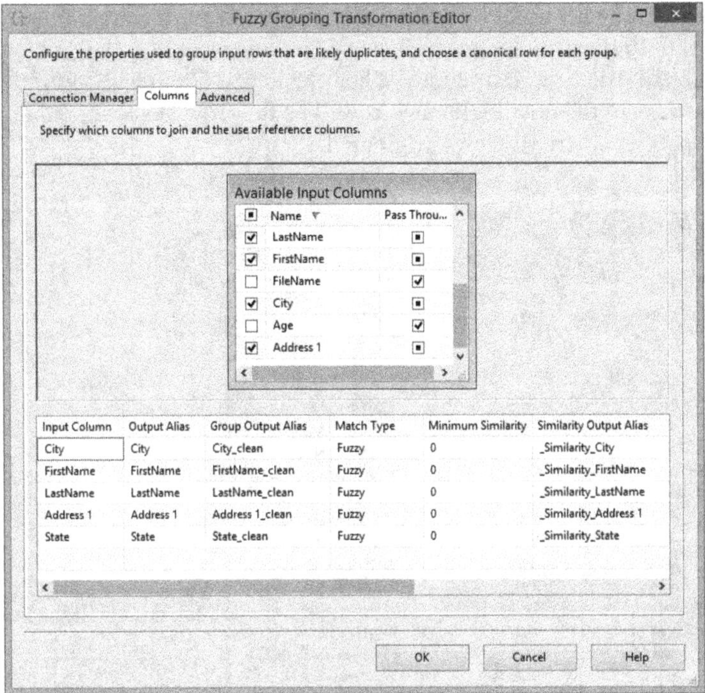

FIGURE 10-18

FIGURE 10-19

Just as in the Fuzzy Lookup, you can see the output by adding a Data Viewer to the output path from the Fuzzy Grouping. Figure 10-20 illustrates how the Fuzzy Grouping works. A _key_in column and a _key_out column are added to the Data Flow. When the Fuzzy Grouping identifies a potential match, it moves the row next to the potential match row. The first row key is shared in the _key_out column. The _key_in identifies where the rows originated.

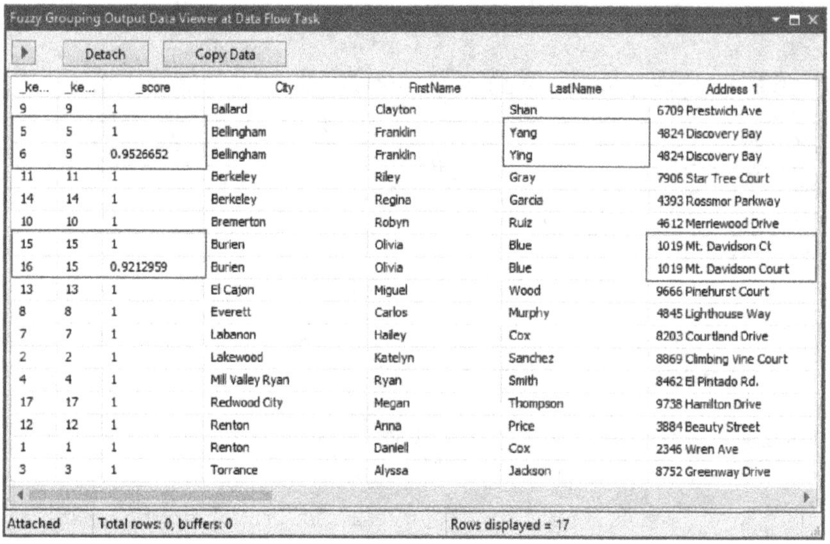

Fuzzy Grouping Output Data Viewer at Data Flow Task

Detach | Copy Data

_ke...	_ke...	_score	City	FirstName	LastName	Address 1
9	9	1	Ballard	Clayton	Shan	6709 Prestwich Ave
5	5	1	Bellingham	Franklin	Yang	4824 Discovery Bay
6	5	0.9526652	Bellingham	Franklin	Ying	4824 Discovery Bay
11	11	1	Berkeley	Riley	Gray	7906 Star Tree Court
14	14	1	Berkeley	Regina	Garcia	4393 Rossmor Parkway
10	10	1	Bremerton	Robyn	Ruiz	4612 Merriewood Drive
15	15	1	Burien	Olivia	Blue	1019 Mt. Davidson Ct
16	15	0.9212959	Burien	Olivia	Blue	1019 Mt. Davidson Court
13	13	1	El Cajon	Miguel	Wood	9666 Pinehurst Court
8	8	1	Everett	Carlos	Murphy	4845 Lighthouse Way
7	7	1	Labanon	Hailey	Cox	8203 Courtland Drive
2	2	1	Lakewood	Katelyn	Sanchez	8869 Climbing Vine Court
4	4	1	Mill Valley Ryan	Ryan	Smith	8462 El Pintado Rd.
17	17	1	Redwood City	Megan	Thompson	9738 Hamilton Drive
12	12	1	Renton	Anna	Price	3884 Beauty Street
1	1	1	Renton	Daniell	Cox	2346 Wren Ave
3	3	1	Torrance	Alyssa	Jackson	8752 Greenway Drive

Attached Total rows: 0, buffers: 0 Rows displayed = 17

FIGURE 10-20

As the example in Figure 10-20 shows, there are a couple of matches. LastName was misspelled in _key_in value of 6, but because the similarity _score is 95 percent, the engine determined it was a match (it was above the similarity threshold of 80 percent defined in Figure 10-19). In another couple of rows highlighted, the street address is slightly different.

The key to the Fuzzy Grouping is the _score column. If you wanted to just go with the Fuzzy Grouping results and de-duplicate your source, you would add a Conditional Split Transformation to the Data Flow and allow only rows through the Condition Split whose _score == 1 (the double equals is the expression language Boolean logic match check). Alternately, you could define custom expression logic to choose an alternate row.

As the preceding two sections have demonstrated, both the Fuzzy Lookup and the Fuzzy Grouping provide very powerful data cleansing features that can be used in a variety of data scenarios.

DQS CLEANSING

Introduced in SQL Server 2012 was a component called *Data Quality Services (DQS)*. This is not a feature of Integration Services, but it is very much connected to the data cleansing processes within SSIS. In fact, there is a data transformation called the DQS Cleansing Task. This task connects to DQS, enabling you to connect incoming Data Flow data and perform data cleansing operations.

Because this book focuses on SSIS, a full DQS tutorial is not included; however, this section provides a brief overview of DQS and highlights a few data quality examples. To gain more understanding, you can also watch the DQS one day course by the Microsoft DQS Team at `http://technet.microsoft.com/en-us/sqlserver/hh780961.aspx`.

Data Quality Services

The workflow to use DQS within SSIS requires a few preparatory steps. These need to be performed within the DQS client tool connected to a DQS service. The DQS client is available in the SQL Server 2014 Programs folder (from the Start button). There is a 32-bit version and a 64-bit version. In order to use Data Quality Services, you must have installed it during the SQL Server setup and run the configuration executable, called `DQSInstaller.exe`. The full setup instructions can be found on MSDN, `http://msdn.microsoft.com/en-us/library/gg492277(v=SQL.120).aspx`.

Once you pull up the client and connect to the server, you will be in the DQS main screen, shown in Figure 10-21.

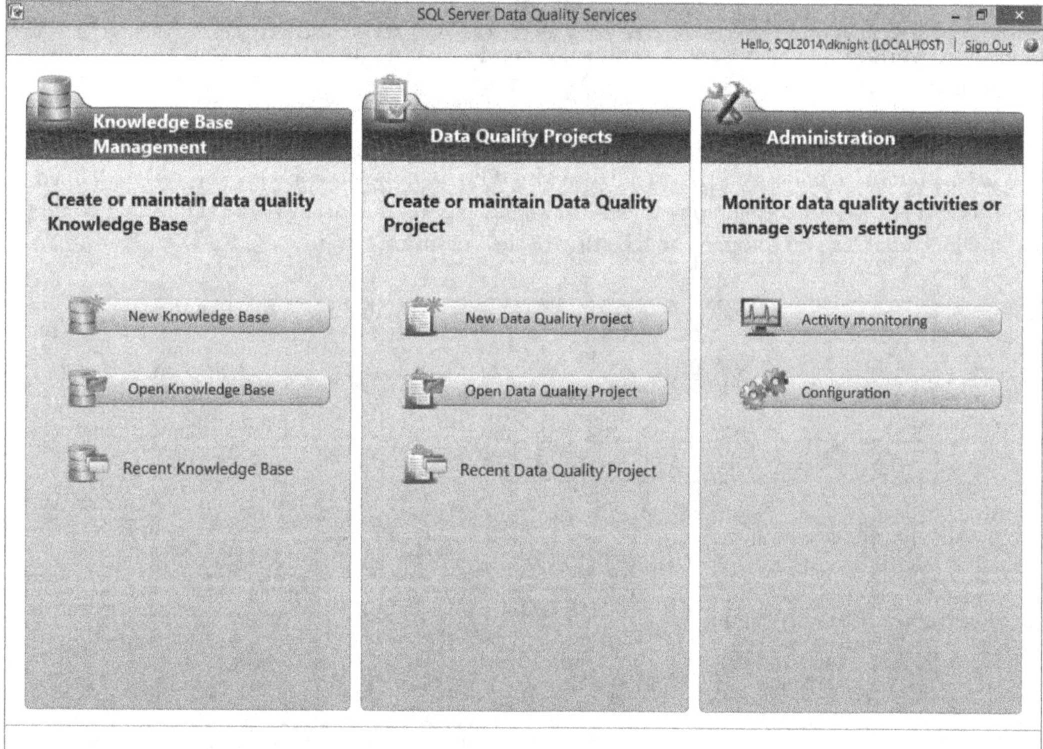

FIGURE 10-21

You can perform three primary tasks with DQS:

- **Knowledge Base Management** is how you define the data cleansing rules and policies.
- **Data Quality Projects** are for applying the data quality definitions (from the knowledge base) against real data. We will not be considering projects in this chapter; instead, you will see how to use the SSIS DQS Cleansing Task to apply the definitions.
- **Administration** is about configuring and monitoring the server and external connections.

To begin the process of cleansing data with DQS, you need to perform two primary steps within the Knowledge Base Management pane:

1. Create a DQS Knowledge Base (DQS KB). A DQS KB is a grouping of related data quality definitions and rules (called domains) that are defined up front. These definitions and rules are applied against data with various outcomes (such as corrections, exceptions, etc.). For example, a DQS KB could be a set of domains that relate to address cleansing, or a grouping of valid purchase order code rules and code relationships within your company.
2. Define DQS domains and composite domains. A DQS domain is a targeted definition of cleansing and validation properties for a given data point. For example, a domain could be "Country" and contain the logic on how to process values that relate to countries around the world. The value mapping and rules define what names are valid and how abbreviations map to which countries.

When you select the Open knowledge base option, you are presented with a list of KBs that you have worked with. The built-in KB included with DQS, DQS Data, contains several predefined domains and rules, and connections to external data. Figure 10-22 shows the right-click context menu, which enables you to open the KB and see the definition details.

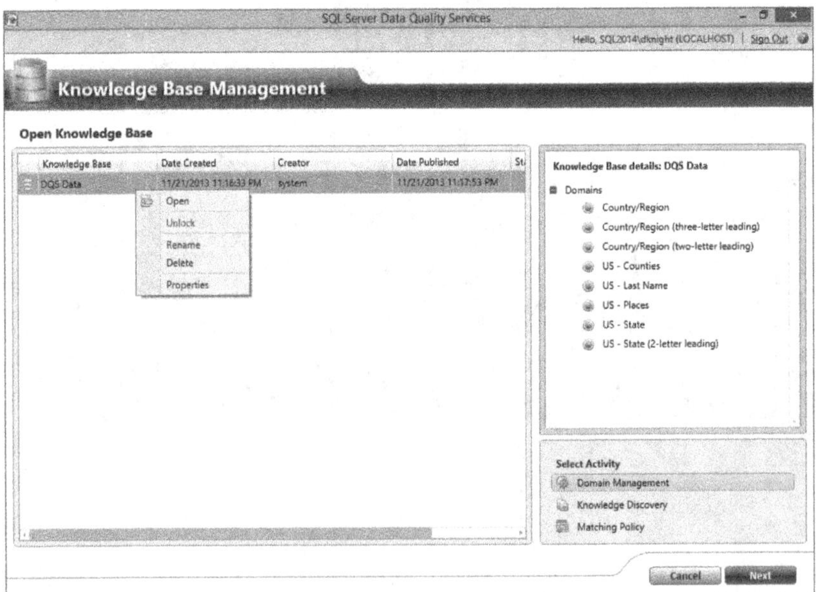

FIGURE 10-22

Knowledge bases are about domains, which are the building blocks of DQS. A domain defines what the DQS engine should do with data it receives: Is it valid? Does it need to be corrected? Should it look at external services to cleanse the data? For example, Figure 10-23 highlights the Domain Values tab of the State domain. It shows how values are cleansed and which values should be grouped. In this example, it lists state abbreviations and names and the Correct To value.

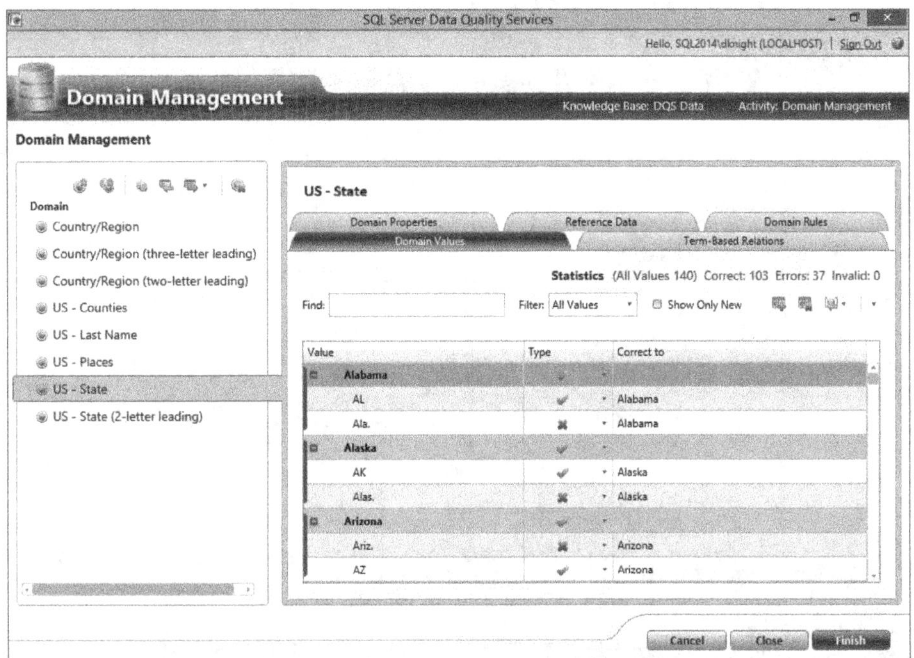

FIGURE 10-23

In the next example, a composite domain is selected. A composite domain is just what it sounds like: a group of domains. In this case, the domains involve companies, based on the business name, city, country, and state. Figure 10-24 shows the partial configuration of a composite domain. In this case, there is an external web service reference called "D&B - D&B Company Cleanse & Match" through which data will be processed. There are many sources you could connect to, such as Melissa Data for address cleansing (`www.melissadata.com`) or a host of data sources from the Windows Azure Data Marketplace (`https://datamarket.azure.com`). There are a variety of premium data sources available here. Some can be free on a trial basis, while others have a paid subscription–based fee.

Domains can also contain rules that validate the data as it is processed through DQS. In the example in Figure 10-25, the Zip (Address Check) field is validated so that the length is equal to `6`. You can also see some of the other options in the list. Multiple rules can be applied with logical `AND` or `OR` conditions. If a data element fails the rules, it is marked as bad data during the processing.

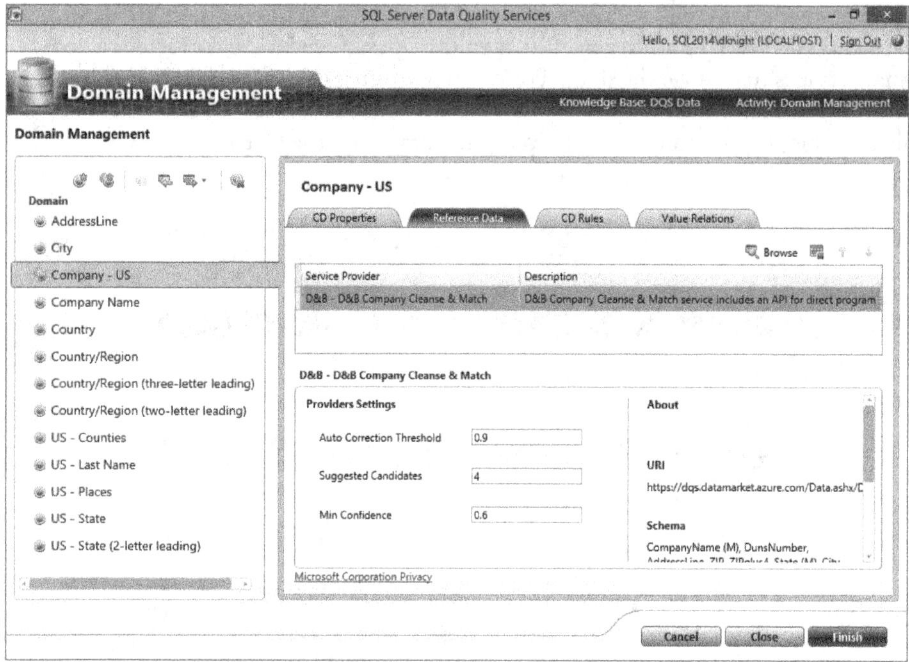

FIGURE 10-24

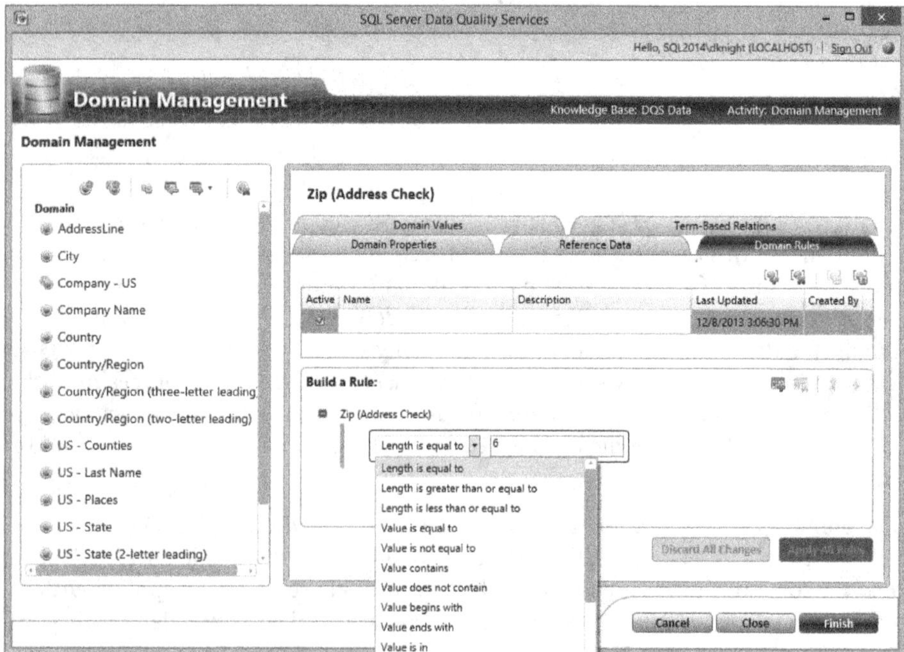

FIGURE 10-25

Other common rules include range rules to check that numeric data values fall within a given range and value lists to make sure that the data coming in meets specific requirements.

As shown in these few examples, DQS can serve as a powerful data quality engine for your organization. In addition to the common data validation and cleansing operations, you can apply a host of custom rules, matching criteria, and external links.

The next step, after your knowledge base is defined, is to process your data through SSIS.

DQS Cleansing Transformation

SSIS can connect to DQS using the DQS Cleansing Transformation. This is one of two ways that data can be applied against the knowledge bases within DQS. (A data quality project is the primary way to process data if you are not using SSIS for ETL. This is found in the DQS client tool, but it's not described in this book, which focuses on SSIS.)

In order to use the DQS Cleansing Transformation, you will first connect to a source within your Data Flow that contains the data you plan to associate with the knowledge base.

The next step is to connect the source (or other transformation) to a DQS Cleansing Transformation and edit the task.

Figure 10-26 shows the Connection Manager tab of the DQS Cleansing Transformation. You need to connect to the DQS server and choose the knowledge base that you will be using for your source input data within SSIS.

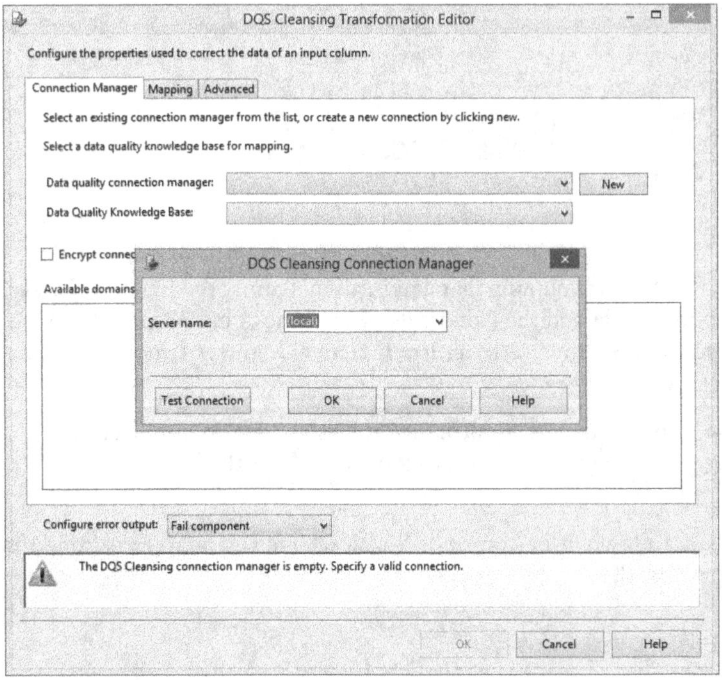

FIGURE 10-26

In this example, the source data contains states/provinces and countries, so you will use the built-in DQS Data KB to connect the states and countries. To see the list of domains, choose DQS Data from the Data Quality Knowledge Base dropdown, as shown in Figure 10-27.

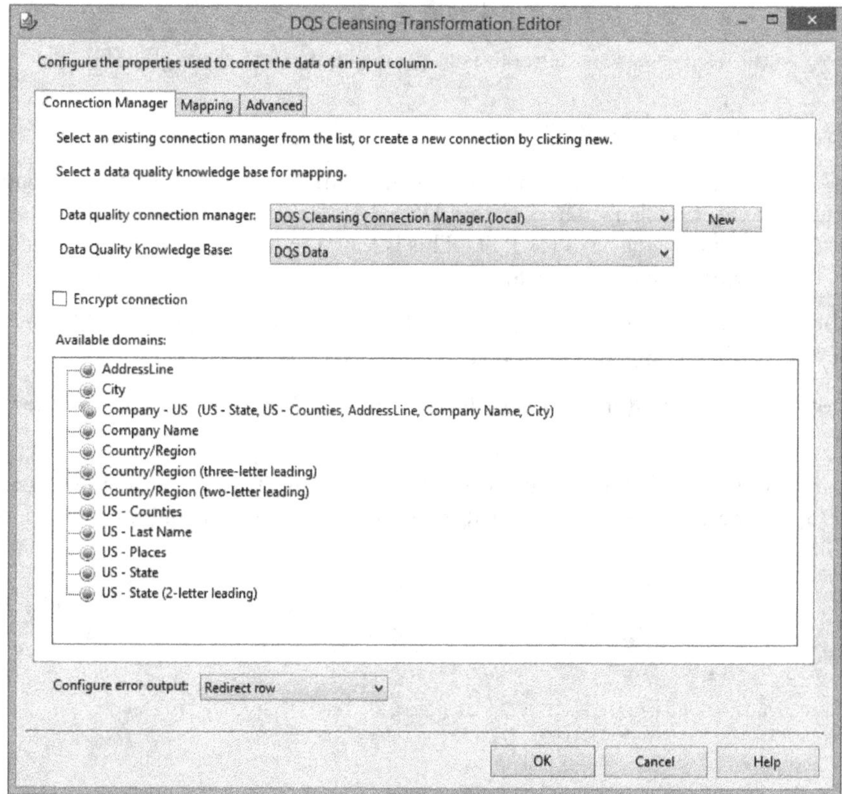

FIGURE 10-27

The Mapping tab contains the list of input columns that can be used against the KB domains. In Figure 10-28, both the StateProvinceCode and the CountryRegionName columns are selected in the input column list and matched to the US - State (2-letter leading) and Country/Region domains in the Domain dropdown.

You are also able to redirect the errors to the error output for the rows that do not meet the domain criteria and rules, using the Configure Error Output dropdown at the bottom of the DQS editor.

Figure 10-29 shows the simple Data Flow with a couple of Multicast Transformations so that the data can be viewed (for demo purposes).

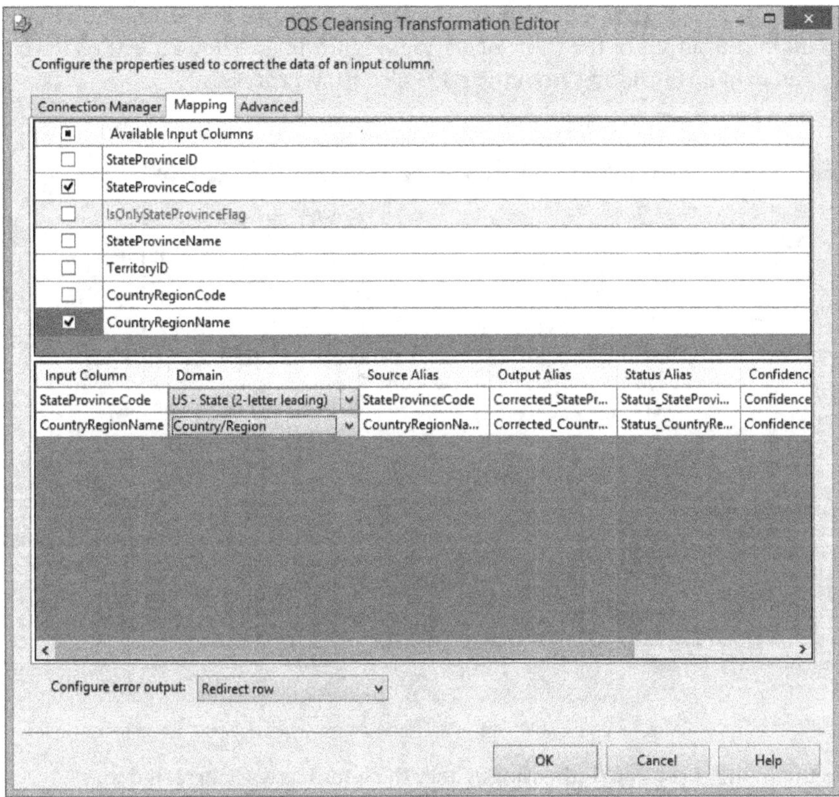

FIGURE 10-28

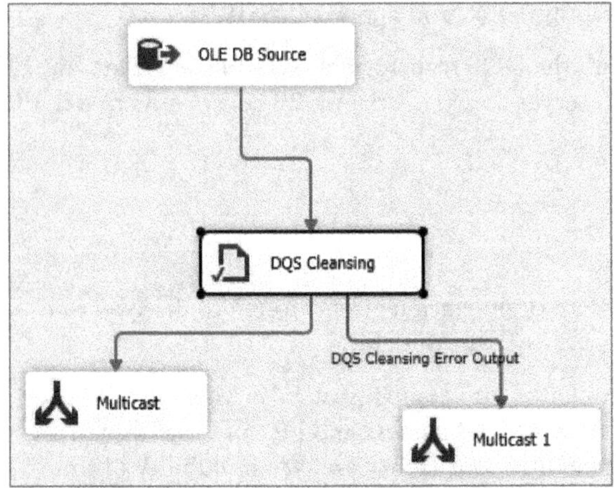

FIGURE 10-29

In addition to mapping the inputs to the DQS domain, the DQS Cleansing Transformation also provides additional data in the output of the transformation. Figure 10-30 shows a Data Viewer with the output rows and columns resulting from the DQS cleansing process.

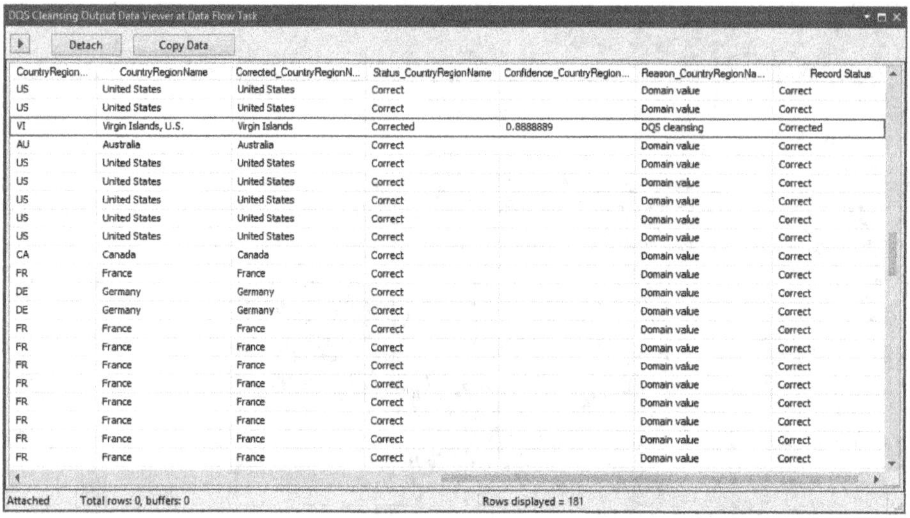

DQS Cleansing Output Data Viewer at Data Flow Task

Detach | Copy Data

CountryRegion...	CountryRegionName	Corrected_CountryRegionN...	Status_CountryRegionName	Confidence_CountryRegion...	Reason_CountryRegionNa...	Record Status
US	United States	United States	Correct		Domain value	Correct
US	United States	United States	Correct		Domain value	Correct
VI	Virgin Islands, U.S.	Virgin Islands	Corrected	0.8888889	DQS cleansing	Corrected
AU	Australia	Australia	Correct		Domain value	Correct
US	United States	United States	Correct		Domain value	Correct
US	United States	United States	Correct		Domain value	Correct
US	United States	United States	Correct		Domain value	Correct
US	United States	United States	Correct		Domain value	Correct
US	United States	United States	Correct		Domain value	Correct
CA	Canada	Canada	Correct		Domain value	Correct
FR	France	France	Correct		Domain value	Correct
DE	Germany	Germany	Correct		Domain value	Correct
DE	Germany	Germany	Correct		Domain value	Correct
FR	France	France	Correct		Domain value	Correct
FR	France	France	Correct		Domain value	Correct
FR	France	France	Correct		Domain value	Correct
FR	France	France	Correct		Domain value	Correct
FR	France	France	Correct		Domain value	Correct
FR	France	France	Correct		Domain value	Correct
FR	France	France	Correct		Domain value	Correct
FR	France	France	Correct		Domain value	Correct

Attached Total rows: 0, buffers: 0 Rows displayed = 181

FIGURE 10-30

In this example, note the highlighted row indicating where the country was corrected and standardized to the DQS domain definition. Besides the original and corrected value returned, you can also see a reason code, as well as a confidence level on the correction. These are similar to the Fuzzy Component outputs shown earlier, except you have much more control and flexibility in terms of how you define your data cleansing process within DQS and apply it in SSIS.

An alternate way to see the data flowing through the DQS transformation is to use a Data Tap. This is for when your package is deployed to an SSIS server catalog. Chapter 22 covers how to use a Data Tap in SSIS.

MASTER DATA MANAGEMENT

Master data management (MDM) is the process an organization goes through to discover and define data with the ultimate goal of compiling a master list of data.

Gartner, the well-known technology research and advisory company, defines Master data management as "a technology-enabled discipline in which business and IT work together to ensure the uniformity, accuracy, stewardship, semantic consistency and accountability of the enterprise's official shared master data assets" (`http://www.gartner.com/it-glossary/master-data-management-mdm`).

Along with choosing an MDM technology, any project will include an evaluation phase by the business to check and validate records. A successful MDM solution is reliable, centralized data that can be analyzed, resulting in better and more accurate business decisions.

Having a tool that can handle the management of a consistent data source can ease many common headaches that occur during data warehouse projects. For example, say your company recently acquired a former competitor. As the data integration expert your first task is to merge the newly acquired customer data into your data warehouse. As expected, your former competitor had many of the same customers you have listed in their transactional database. You clearly need a master customer list, which stores the most accurate data about customers from your database and also the most accurate data from the newly acquired data set. This is a very typical scenario where having an MDM solution can retain the data integrity of your data warehouse. Without such a solution the customer table in the data warehouse will start to have less accurate information and even duplicates of data.

Master Data Services

Master Data Services (MDS) was originally released in SQL Server 2008 R2 as Microsoft SQL Server's solution for master data management. Master Data Services includes the following components and tools to help configure, manage, and administrate each feature:

- **Master Data Services Configuration Manager** is the tool you use to create and configure the database and web applications that are required for MDS.
- **Master Data Manager** is the web application that users can access to update data and also where administrative tasks may be performed.
- **MDSModelDeploy.exe** is the deployment tool used to create packages of your model objects that can be sent to other environments.
- **Master Data Services web service** is an access point that .NET developers can use to create custom solutions for MDS.
- **Master Data Services Add-in for Excel** is used to manage data and create new entities and attributes.

Again, because this book focuses on SSIS, a full MDS tutorial is not included; however, this section provides a brief overview of MDS. To gain more understanding, you can also watch the MDS one day course by the Microsoft MDS Team at `http://msdn.microsoft.com/en-us/sqlserver/ff943581.aspx`.

To get started you must first run the Master Data Service Configuration Manger with the executable `MDSConfigTool.exe`. This requires the creation of a configuration database that stores the system settings that are enabled. Once the database is created, you can configure the web application called the Master Data Manager. You can find the full setup instructions on MSDN, `http://technet.microsoft.com/en-us/library/ee633884(SQL.120).aspx`.

The majority of the work in Master Data Services post-configuration is done by an information worker. They will use both the Master Data Manager web application and the Master Data Services Add-in for Excel. The Excel Add-in is a free download that is available here, `http://go.microsoft.com/fwlink/?LinkId=219530.`

The Master Data Manager allows the administrator to create new models and derived hierarchy, while the information worker uses the web interface to work with the model and hierarchy relationships. For example, if your company's data steward found that an entire subcategory of products were placed under the wrong category, then the data steward could use the Master Data Manger to quickly and easily correct that problem. Figure 10-31 shows the interface that the data steward would use to drag and drop hierarchy corrections.

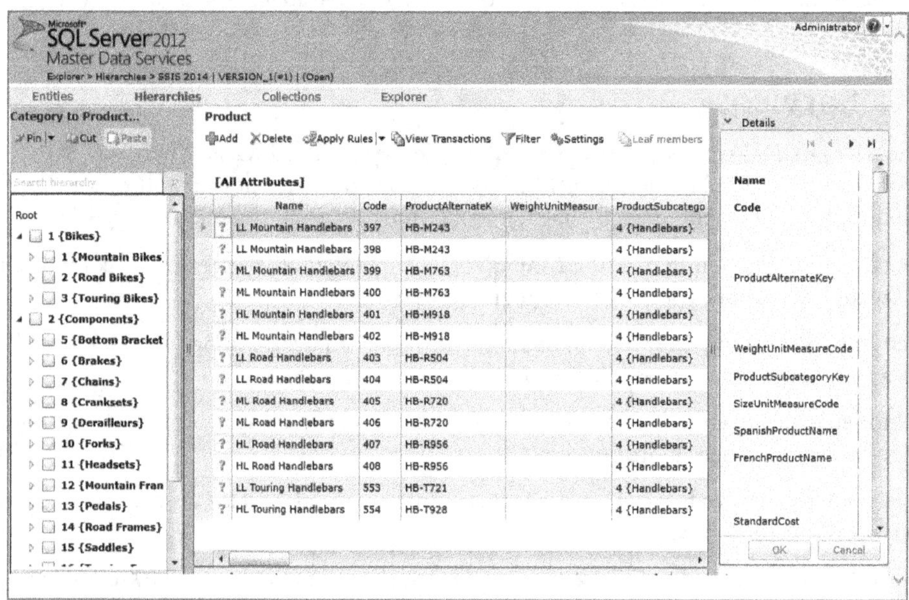

FIGURE 10-31

After installing the Master Data Services Add-in for Excel (Figure 10-32), the information worker has MDS in the environment they're most comfortable in. Using Excel a user can connect to the MDS server, shown in Figure 10-33, and then import appropriate data sets into MDS. To do this the user simply selects a table of data in Excel and then clicks Create Entity using the Excel Master Data Ribbon (Figure 10-34).

FILE HOME INSERT PAGE LAYOUT FORMULAS DATA REVIEW VIEW POWER QUERY Master Data INQUIR

Connect | Show Explorer | Refresh | Filter — Connect and Load
Save Query | Send Query — Save and Send
Publish | Delete | Combine Data | Apply Rules | Show Status — Publish and Validate
Match Data | Show Details — Data Quality
Create Entity | Attribute Properties — Build Model
Settings — Options
Help — Help

FIGURE 10-32

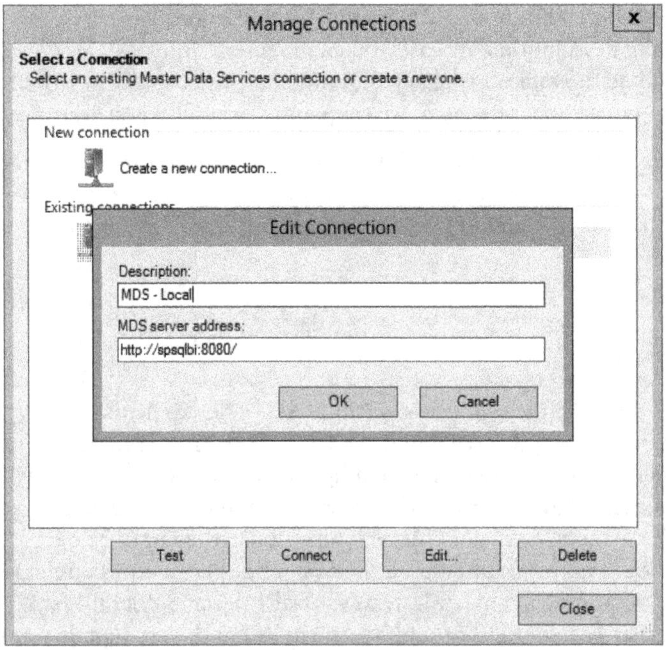

FIGURE 10-33

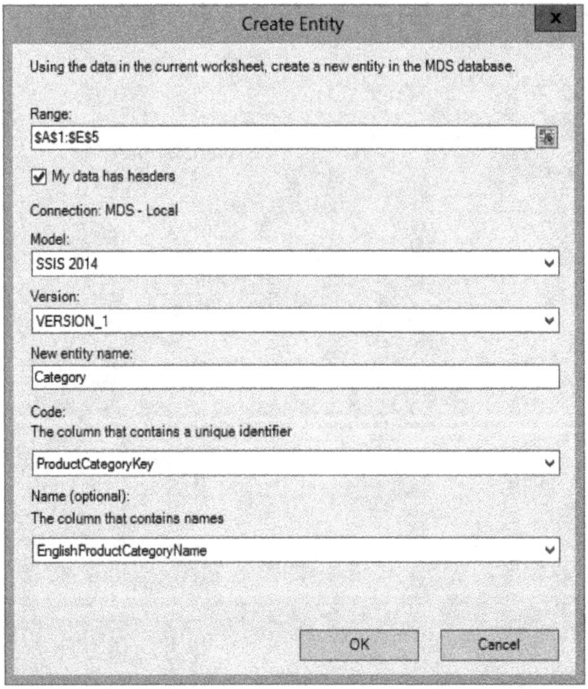

FIGURE 10-34

Any changes that are made through MDS remain in the MDS database. However, when you're ready to push these changes back to the destination database you can create a simple MDS view through the Master Data Manger to sync the tables using a T-SQL update statement. You would likely schedule these updates to occur once a day or even more frequently depending on your needs.

Because the heavy lifting with MDS is done by the information worker, there is no direct integration with SSIS. Tables that are updated from MDS views are used with traditional components like the Lookup Transformation to ensure incoming new data fits appropriately into the organization's master list.

SUMMARY

In this chapter, you looked at various data cleansing features within SSIS — in particular, the Derived Column, the Fuzzy Grouping and Fuzzy Lookup, and the DQS Cleansing Transformation. These can be categorized by basic data cleansing, dirty data matching, and advanced data rules. The Derived Column, as the basic feature, will allow you to do the most common data cleansing tasks — blanks and text parsing. When you go to the next level, you can use the Fuzzy Lookup and Fuzzy Grouping to find values that should match or should be the same, but because of bad data in the source, do not match. When your requirements necessitate advanced rules and domain-based cleansing, the DQS tool with SQL Server provides a thorough platform to handle data quality needs. Outside of SSIS you also explored tools like Master Data Services and Data Quality clients, which make the information worker now part of the data quality solution.

The bottom line: No two data cleansing solutions are exactly the same, but SSIS gives you the flexibility to customize your solution to whatever ETL needs you have.

11 Incremental Loads in SSIS

WHAT'S IN THIS CHAPTER?

- Using the Control Table pattern for incrementally loading data
- Working with Change Data Capture

WROX.COM CODE DOWNLOADS FOR THIS CHAPTER

You can find the wrox.com code downloads for this chapter at `http://www.wrox.com/go/prossis2014` on the Download Code tab.

So far, most of the data loading procedures that have been explained in this book have done a full load or a truncate and load. While this is fine for smaller amounts of rows, it would be unfeasible to do with millions of rows. In this chapter, you're going to learn how to take the knowledge you've gained and apply the practices to an incremental load of data.

The first pattern will be a control table pattern. In this pattern, you'll use a table to determine when the last load of the data was. Then the package will determine which rows to load based on the last load date. The other alternative used in this chapter is a Change Data Capture (CDC) pattern. This pattern will require that you have Enterprise Edition of SQL Server and will automatically identify the rows to be transferred based on a given date.

CONTROL TABLE PATTERN

The most conventional incremental load pattern is the control table pattern. The pattern uses a table that the developer creates to store operational data about the last load. A sample table looks like this:

```
CREATE TABLE [dbo].[ControlTable](
   [SourceTable] [varchar](50) NOT NULL,
   [LastLoadID] [int] NOT NULL,
```

```
    [LastLoadDate] [datetime] NOT NULL,
    [RowsInserted] [int] NOT NULL,
 CONSTRAINT [PK_ControlTable] PRIMARY KEY CLUSTERED
(
    [SourceTable] ASC
)
) ON [PRIMARY]
```

In this pattern, you would have a row in the control table for each table that you wish to create a load process for. This table is not only used by your SSIS package to determine how much data to load but it also becomes an audit table to see which tables have and have not been loaded. Each of the incremental load patterns in this chapter follow these steps:

1. An Execute SQL Task reads the last load data from the control table into a variable.
2. A Data Flow Task reads from the source table where they were modified or created after the date in the variable.
3. An Execute SQL Task sets the last load date in the control table to the time when the package began.

To start the example, run the Control Table Example Creation.sql file in the chapter's accompanying material (which you can download from `http://www.wrox.com/go/prossis2014`). This will create a table to read from called SourceTable and a table to load called DestTable. It will also create and load the control table. Notice the ControlTable table shows a LastLoadDate column of 1900-01-01, meaning the SourceTable has never been read from. The TableName column holds a record for each table you wish to read from. Optionally, there's a LastLoadID that could be used for identity columns.

Querying the Control Table

Querying the control table you created is simply done through an Execute SQL Task. Start by creating an OLE DB connection manager to whichever database you ran the setup script in. For the purpose of this example, we'll assume you created the tables in a variant of the AdventureWorks database.

To configure the Execute SQL Task, direct the task to use the previously created connection manager. Then, use a query similar to the one that follows for your SQLStatement property. This query will find out the last time you retrieved data from the table called SourceTable.

```
SELECT LastLoadDate from
ControlTable where SourceTable = 'SourceTable'
```

The answer to the query should be stored into a variable to be used later. To do this, set the ResultSet property (shown in Figure 11-1) to Single Row. Doing this will allow you to use the ResultSet tab. Go to that tab, and click the Add button to create a new resultset. Then change the ResultName property from NewResultName to 0. This stores the result from the first column into the variable of your choosing. You could have also typed the column name from the query as well (LastLoadDate) into the property.

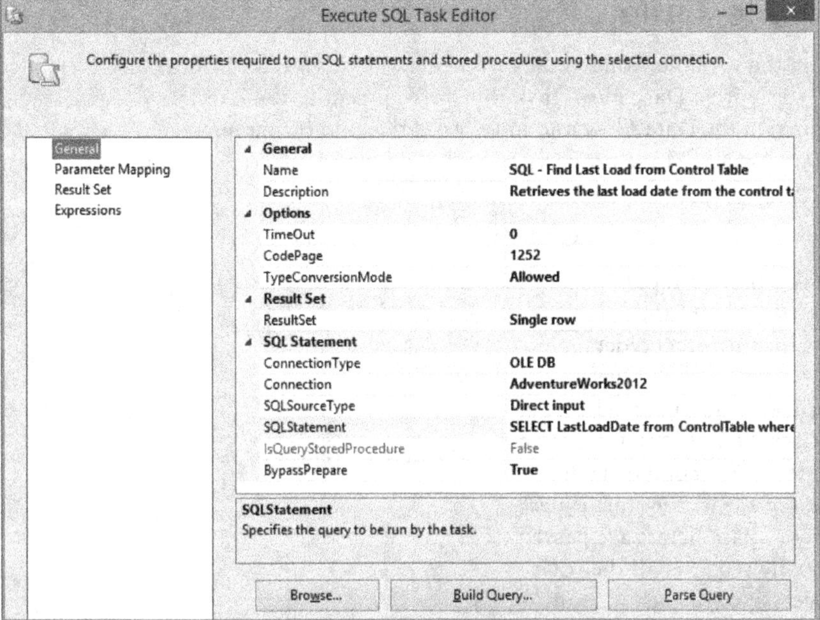

FIGURE 11-1

Next, select New Variable from the drop-down box in the ResultSet tab. This will open the Add Variable dialog box (shown in Figure 11-2). Ensure the variable is scoped to the package and call it **SourceTableLoadDate**. Define the data type of the variable as a DateTime and set the default value to 2099-01-01. This ensures that if someone were to run the package without running this Execute SQL Task, that no date will be retrieved.

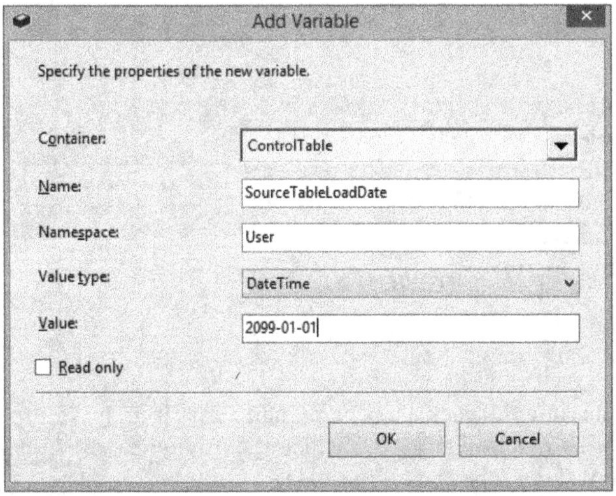

FIGURE 11-2

Querying the Source Table

With the date now set in the variable, you're ready to retrieve any new data from your table called SourceTable. You'll do this with a Data Flow Task that you connect to the Execute SQL Task. Create an OLE DB Source in the Data Flow and have it use the connection manager you created earlier. Then, set the Data Access Mode property to SQL Command and type the following query in the query window below:

```
SELECT * from SourceTable WHERE CreatedDate BETWEEN ? and ?
```

The two question marks represent input parameters that will be passed into the query. To set the values for the placeholders click Parameters, which opens the Set Query Parameters dialog box (shown in Figure 11-3). Set the first parameter to User::SourceTableLoadDate and the second parameter to System::StartTime. The StartTime variable represents the start time of the package. When both parameters are passed into the query, it essentially requests all the rows that have not been loaded since the last load until the time the package started.

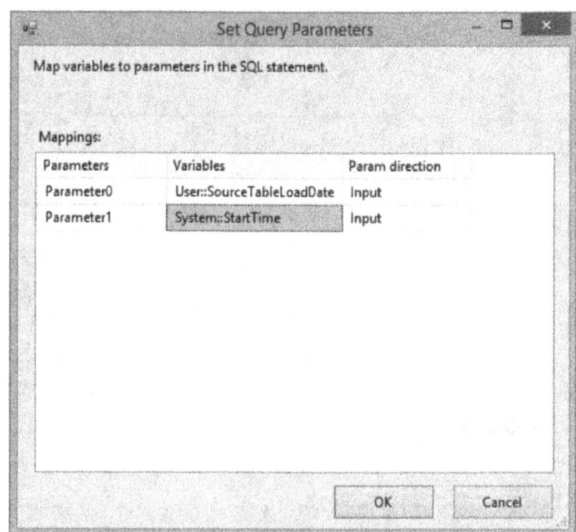

FIGURE 11-3

With the OLE DB Source now configured, drag an OLE DB Destination over to the Data Flow and connect it to the OLE DB Source. Configure the OLE DB Destination to use the same connection manager and load the table called `DestTable`. After configuring the mappings, the simple Data Flow is complete and the final Data Flow should resemble Figure 11-4.

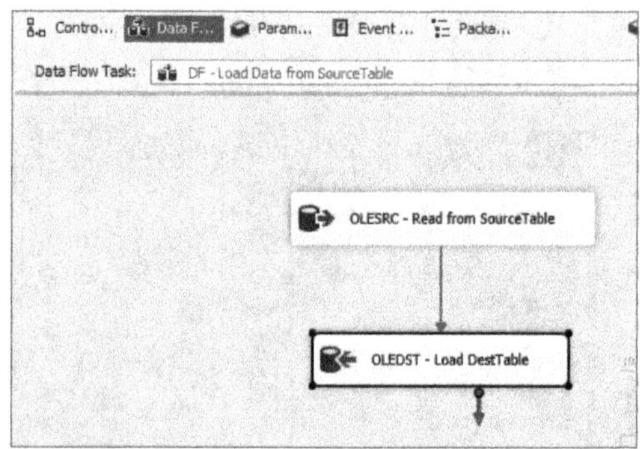

FIGURE 11-4

Updating the Control Table

Back in the Control Flow you need one more Execute SQL Task to update the control table. Connect it to the Data Flow Task. To configure the Execute SQL Task, connect it to the same connection manager you have been using and type the following query into the SQLStatement property.

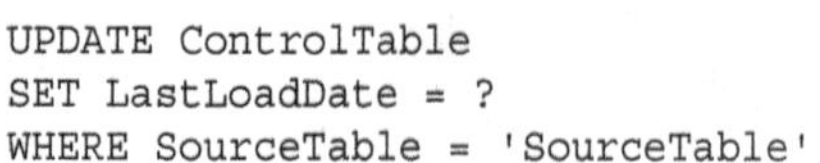

```
UPDATE ControlTable
SET LastLoadDate = ?
WHERE SourceTable = 'SourceTable'
```

The question mark in this case represents the time the package began, and to pass it in, go to the Parameter Mapping page and configure it as shown in Figure 11-5. Click the Add button and set the variable name being passed in as System::StartTime, the Data Type as Date, and the Parameter Name as 0.

Configure the properties required to run SQL statements and stored procedures using the selected connection.

General
Parameter Mapping
Result Set
Expressions

Variable Name	Direction	Data Type	Parameter Name	Parameter ...
System::StartTime	Input	DATE	0	-1

FIGURE 11-5

Once you're done configuring this, your package is ready to run (shown in Figure 11-6). This task is going to update the Control Table and set the last load date as the time the package started, so the next time the package runs it will only get current values. The first time you run the package, you should see three rows go through the data flow. Subsequent runs should show zero rows but try also adding a row to the SourceTable table and running the package over again. If configured correctly, only the single row will go through. You'll also see that the control table is constantly being updated with a new LastLoadDate column.

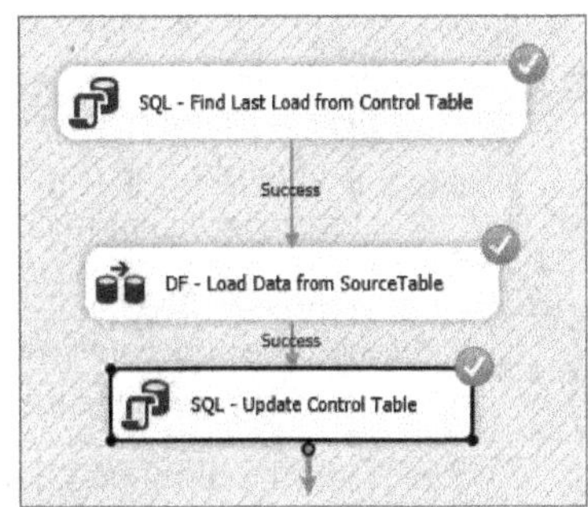

FIGURE 11-6

SQL SERVER CHANGE DATA CAPTURE

The advantage to the control table pattern you saw previously is it works across any database platform you may use. The negative is it requires a date or identity column to hook into it. It also doesn't handle deleted records. The alternative is using the Change Data Capture (CDC) feature built into SQL Server. This feature works only in the Enterprise Edition of SQL Server but handles deletes and is easier to configure than the previous control table example. This section is focused on how to configure CDC for SSIS but if you want more information on CDC, it is covered extensively in Books Online (by the actual developer of CDC) and demonstrated in more detail in the related CodePlex samples (`www.codeplex.com`).

In most nightly batches for your ETL, you want to ensure that you are processing only the most recent data — for instance, just the data from the preceding day's operations. Obviously, you don't want to process every transaction from the last five years during each night's batch. However, that's the ideal world, and sometimes the source system is not able to tell you which rows belong to the time window you need.

This problem space is typically called Change Data Capture, or CDC. The term refers to the fact that you want to capture just the changed data from the source system within a specified window of time.

The changes may include inserts, updates, and deletes, and the required window of time may vary, anything from "all the changes from the last few minutes" all the way through to "all the changes from the last day/week/year," and so on. The key requisite for a CDC solution is that it needs to identify the rows that were affected since a specific, granular point in time.

Following are some common techniques to handle this problem:

- **Adding new date/time columns to the source system:** This isn't usually feasible, either because it is a legacy system and no one knows how to add new functionality, or it is possible but the risk and change management cost is too high, or simply because the DBA or data steward won't let you! On some systems, such as ERP applications, this change is impossible because of the sheer number and size of tables and the prohibitive cost thereof.
- **Adding triggers to the source system:** Such triggers may watch for any data changes and then write an audit record to a separate logging table that the ETL then uses as a source. Though this is less invasive than the previous method, the same challenges apply. An issue here is that every database operation now incurs more I/O cost — when a row is inserted or updated, the original table is updated, and then the new log table is updated too in a synchronous manner. This can lead to decreased performance in the application.
- **Complex queries:** It is academically possible to write long complex queries that compare every source row/column to every destination row/column, but practically, this is usually not an alternative because the development and performance costs are too high.
- **Dump and reload:** Sometimes there is no way around the problem, and you are forced to delete and recopy the complete set of data every night. For small data sets, this may not be a problem, but once you start getting into the terabyte range you are in trouble. This is the worst possible situation and one of the biggest drivers for non-intrusive, low-impact CDC solutions.
- **Third-party solutions:** Some software vendors specialize in CDC solutions for many different databases and applications. This is a good option to look into, because the vendors have the experience and expertise to build robust and high-performance tools.
- **Other solutions:** Besides the preceding options, there are solutions such as using queues and application events, but some of these are nongeneric and tightly coupled.
- **Change Data Capture:** Last, but not least — and the subject of this section — is the functionality called Change Data Capture, which provides CDC right out of the box. This technology is delivered by the SQL Replication team, but it was designed in concert with the SSIS team. Note that there is another similarly named technology called Change Tracking, which is a synchronous technique that can also be used in some CDC scenarios.

Benefits of SQL Server CDC

Here are some of the benefits that SQL Server 2014 CDC (hereafter referred to as CDC) provides:

- **Low impact:** You do not need to change your source schema tables in order to support CDC. Other techniques for Change Data Capture, such as triggers and replication, require you to add new columns (such as timestamps and GUIDs) to the tables you want to track. With CDC, you can be up and running immediately without changing the schema. Obviously, your source system needs to be hosted on SQL Server 2008 or higher in order to take advantage of the CDC functionality.
- **Low overhead:** The CDC process is a job that runs asynchronously in the background and reads the changes off the SQL Server transaction log. What this means in plain English is

that, unlike triggers, any updates to the source data do not incur a synchronous write to a logging table. Rather, the writes are delayed until the server is idle, or the writes can be delayed until a time that you specify (for instance, 2:00 a.m. every day).

- **Granular configuration:** The CDC process allows you to configure the feature on a per-table basis, which means it is not an all-or-nothing proposition. You can try it out on one table, and once you iron out any issues, you can slowly start using it on more tables.
- **High fidelity capture:** The technology flags which rows were inserted, updated, and deleted. It can also tell you exactly which columns changed during updates. Other auditing details such as the event timestamp, as well as the specific transaction ID, are also provided.
- **High fidelity requests:** The CDC infrastructure allows you to make very granular requests to the CDC store, so that you can find out exactly when certain operations occurred. For instance, you can ask for changes within any batch window, ranging from a few minutes (near real time) to hours, days, weeks, or more. You can ask for the final aggregated image of the rows, and you can ask for the intermediate changes too.
- **Ease of use:** The APIs that you use to request the data are based on the same SQL semantics you are already used to — `SELECT` statements, user-defined functions, and stored procedures.
- **Resilient to change:** The replication team built the technology with change management in mind, meaning that if you set up CDC to work on a certain table, and someone adds or deletes a column in that table, the process is robust enough in most cases to continue running while you make the appropriate fixes. This means you don't lose data (or sleep!).
- **Transactional consistency:** The operations enable you to request changes in a transactionally consistent manner. For instance, if two tables in the source were updated within the context of the same source transaction, you have the means to establish that fact and retrieve the related changes together.
- **SSIS CDC components:** CDC and SSIS work hand in hand in the 2014 version of SQL Server because of the components added to the SSIS toolbox. These tools make it easier to query your CDC solution.

Preparing CDC

There are a few steps you need to take to get CDC working. CDC is intended for sources that reside on a SQL Server 2008 or later database. If your data resides on an earlier version of SQL Server or another vendor's solution, unless you migrate the data, this solution is probably not for you. However, you may still want to test the waters and see what benefits you can gain from the functionality — in which case find yourself a test server and follow these same steps.

First, the DBA or a member of the SQL sysadmin fixed server role needs to enable CDC on the SQL Server database. This is a very important point; there should be a clear separation of roles and duties, and open dialog between the DBA and the ETL developer. The ETL developer may be tempted to turn CDC on for every single table, but that is a bad idea. Although CDC has low overhead, it does not have zero overhead. DBAs, conversely, may be protective of their data store and not want anyone to touch it.

Whether the DBA and the ETL developer are different individuals or the same person, the respective parties should consider the pros and cons of the solution from all angles. Books Online has more details about these considerations, so this section will forge ahead with the understanding that much of this may be prototypical.

The rest of this discussion assumes that you are using a variant of the AdventureWorks on a SQL Server 2014 installation. In the below script, you will need Enterprise or Developer edition and you may have to change the AdventureWorks database to your own flavor or AdventureWorks. Here is how to enable the functionality at a database level:

```
USE AdventureWorks;
GO
EXEC sp_changedbowner 'sa'
GO

--Enable CDC on the database
EXEC sys.sp_cdc_enable_db;
GO
--Check CDC is enabled on the database
SELECT name, is_cdc_enabled
FROM sys.databases WHERE database_id = DB_ID();
```

When you flip this switch at the database level, SQL Server sets up some of the required infrastructure that you will need later. For instance, it creates a database schema called `cdc`, as well as the appropriate security, functions, and procedures.

The next step is to ensure that SQL Server Agent is running on the same server on which you just enabled CDC. Agent allows you to schedule when the CDC process will crawl the database logs and write entries to the capture instance tables (also known as *shadow tables*; the two terms are used interchangeably here). If these terms don't make sense to you right now, don't worry; they soon will. The important thing to do at this point is to use SQL Server 2014 Configuration Manager to ensure that Agent is running. Because this chapter is focused not on the deep technical details of CDC itself but rather on how to use its functionality within the context of ETL, you should visit Books Online if you are not sure how to get Agent running.

Next, you can enable CDC functionality on the tables of your choice. Run the following command in order to enable CDC on the HumanResources.Employee table:

```
USE AdventureWorks;
GO
--Enable CDC on a specific table
EXECUTE sys.sp_cdc_enable_table
@source_schema = N'HumanResources'
,@source_name = N'Employee'
,@role_name = N'cdc_Admin'
,@capture_instance = N'HumanResources_Employee'
,@supports_net_changes = 1;
```

The `supports_net_changes` option enables you to retrieve only the final image of a row, even if it was updated multiple times within the time window you specified. If there were no problems, then you should see the following message displayed in the output of the query editor:

```
Job 'cdc.AdventureWorks_capture' started successfully.
Job 'cdc.AdventureWorks_cleanup' started successfully.
```

If you want to verify that CDC is enabled for any particular table, you can issue a command of the following form:

```
--Check CDC is enabled on the table
SELECT [name], is_tracked_by_cdc FROM sys.tables
WHERE [object_id] = OBJECT_ID(N'HumanResources.Employee');
--Alternatively, use the built-in CDC help procedure
EXECUTE sys.sp_cdc_help_change_data_capture
@source_schema = N'HumanResources',
@source_name = N'Employee';
GO
```

If all has gone well, the CDC process is now alive and well and watching the source table for any changes.

You used the default configuration for setting up CDC on a table, but there are optional parameters that give you much more power. For instance, you can configure exactly which columns should and shouldn't be tracked, and the filegroup where the shadow table should live, and you can enable other modes. For now, simple is good, so the next step is to have a look at what SQL Server has done for you.

Capture Instance Tables

Capture instance tables — also known as *shadow tables* and *change tables* — are the tables that SQL Server creates behind the scenes to help the magic of CDC happen. Here is how the CDC process works:

1. The end user makes a data change in the source system table you are tracking. SQL Server writes the changes to the database log, and then writes the changes to the database. Note that SQL Server always does the log-write (and always has) regardless of whether or not CDC is enabled — in other words, the database log is not a new feature of CDC, but CDC makes good use of it.
2. CDC includes a process that runs on server idle time, or on a scheduled interval (controlled by SQL Server Agent) that reads the changes back out of the log and writes them to a separate change tracking (shadow) table with a special schema. In other words, the user wrote the change to the database; the change was implicitly written to the SQL log; the CDC process read it back out of the log and wrote it to a separate table. Why not write it to the second table in the first place? The reason is that synchronous writes impact the source system; users may experience slow application performance if their updates cause two separate writes to two separate tables. By using an asynchronous log reader, the DBA can amortize the writes to the shadow table over a longer period. Of course, you may decide to schedule the Agent job to run on a more frequent basis, in which case the experience may be almost synchronous, but that is an ETL implementation decision. Normally, the log reader runs during idle time or when users are not using the system, so there is little to no application performance overhead.
3. The ETL process then reads the data out of the change table and uses it to populate the destination. You will learn more about that later; for now let's continue our look at the SQL change tables.
4. There is a default schedule that prunes the data in the change tables to keep the contents down to three days' worth of data to prevent the amount of CDC data from becoming unwieldy. You should change this default configuration to suit your specific needs.

When you enabled CDC on the HumanResources.Employee table, SQL used a default naming convention to create a shadow table in the same database called cdc.HumanResources_Employee_CT. This table has the same schema as the source table, but it also has several extra metadata columns that CDC needs to do its magic. Issue the following command to see what the shadow table looks like. There should be no rows in the table right now, so you will get back an empty result set.

```
SELECT * FROM cdc.HumanResources_Employee_CT;
```

Here is a brief overview of the main metadata columns:

- The **__$start_lsn** and **__$seqval columns** identify the original transaction and order in which the operations occurred. These are important values — the API (which you will look at later) operates purely in terms of the LSNs (commit log sequence numbers), but you can easily map date/time values to and from LSNs to make things simpler.
- The **__$operation column** shows the source operation that caused the change (1 = delete, 2 = insert, 3 = update [before image], 4 = update [after image], and 5 = merge).
- The **__$update_mask column** contains a bit mask indicating which specific columns changed during an update. It specifies what columns changed on a row-by-row basis; however, the mask is just a bitmap, so you need to map the ordinal position of each bit to the column name that it represents. CDC provides functions such as `sys.fn_cdc_has_column_changed` to help you make sense of these masks.

Okay, now for the exciting part. Make a data change in the source table and then look at the shadow table again to see what happened. To keep it simple, update one specific field on the source table using the following command. Remember that the process runs asynchronously, so you may have to wait a few seconds before the changes appear in the shadow table. Therefore, after running the following statement, wait a few seconds and then run the preceding `SELECT` statement again.

```
--Make an update to the source table
UPDATE HumanResources.Employee
SET HireDate = DATEADD(day, 1, HireDate)
WHERE [BusinessEntityID] IN (1, 2, 3);
```

Rather than wait for the asynchronous log reader process to occur, you can also force the process to happen on demand by issuing this command:

```
--Force CDC log crawl
EXEC sys.sp_cdc_start_job;
```

The shadow table should contain two rows for every source row you updated. Why two rows, when you performed only one update per row? The reason is because for updates, the change table contains the before and after images of the affected rows. Now try inserting or deleting a row in the source and note what rows are added to the shadow table.

The CDC API

The previous section was just academic background on what is happening; you don't actually need all this knowledge in order to apply the solution to the problem at hand. CDC provides a set of functions and procedures that abstract away the details of the technology and make it very simple to use. When you enabled CDC on the table, SQL automatically generated several function wrappers for you so that you can query the shadow table with ease. Here is an example:

```
USE AdventureWorks;
GO
--Let's check for all changes since the same time yesterday
DECLARE @begin_time AS DATETIME = GETDATE() - 1;
--Let's check for changes up to right now
DECLARE @end_time AS DATETIME = GETDATE();
--Map the time intervals to a CDC query range (using LSNs)
DECLARE @from_lsn AS BINARY(10)
= sys.fn_cdc_map_time_to_lsn('smallest greater than or equal', @begin_time);
DECLARE @to_lsn AS BINARY(10)
= sys.fn_cdc_map_time_to_lsn('largest less than or equal', @end_time);
--Validate @from_lsn using the minimum LSN available in the capture instance
DECLARE @min_lsn AS BINARY(10)
= sys.fn_cdc_get_min_lsn('HumanResources_Employee');
IF @from_lsn < @min_lsn SET @from_lsn = @min_lsn;
--Return the NET changes that occurred within the specified time
SELECT * FROM
cdc.fn_cdc_get_net_changes_HumanResources_Employee(@from_lsn, @to_lsn,
N'all with mask');
```

The CDC functions understand only LSNs. Therefore, you first need to map the date/time values to LSN numbers, being careful to check the minimum and maximum extents. You then call a wrapper function for the table called cdc.fn_cdc_get_net_changes_<table name>(), which returns the rows that have changed. You specify all with mask, which means that the __$update_mask column is populated to tell you which columns changed. If you don't need the mask, just specify all, because calculating the mask is expensive. The all and all with mask options both populate the __$operation column accordingly.

If you had used the parameter value all with merge, the same results would come back, but the __$operation flag would contain only either 1 (delete) or 5 (merge). This is useful if you only need to know whether the row was deleted or changed, but you don't care what the specific change was. This option is computationally cheaper for SQL to execute.

The function you used in this example returns the net changes for the table — meaning if any specific row had multiple updates applied against it in the source system, the result returned would be the net combined result of those changes. For instance, if someone inserted a row and then later (within the same batch window) updated that same row twice, the function would return a row marked as Inserted (__$operation 5 2), but the data columns would reflect the latest values after the second update. Net changes are most likely what you will use for loading your warehouse, because they give you the final image of the row at the end of the specified window, and do not encumber you with any interim values the row might have had. Some near-real-time scenarios, and applications such as auditing and compliance tracking, may require the interim values too.

Instead of asking for only the net changes to the source table, you can also ask for the granular (interim) changes. To do this you use another function that CDC automatically generated for you, in this case called cdc.fn_cdc_get_all_changes_<table name>(). Here is an example that uses the update mask and the all-changes mode together (note that the BusinessEntityID column may be called EmployeeID in previous versions of AdventureWorks):

```
USE AdventureWorks;
GO
--First update another column besides the HireDate so you can
--test the difference in behavior
UPDATE HumanResources.Employee
SET VacationHours = VacationHours + 1
WHERE BusinessEntityID IN (3, 4, 5);
WAITFOR DELAY '00:00:10'; --Wait 10s to let the log reader catch up
--Map times to LSNs as you did previously
DECLARE @begin_time AS DATETIME = GETDATE() - 1;
DECLARE @end_time AS DATETIME = GETDATE();
DECLARE @from_lsn AS BINARY(10)
= sys.fn_cdc_map_time_to_lsn('smallest greater than or equal', @begin_time);
DECLARE @to_lsn AS BINARY(10)
= sys.fn_cdc_map_time_to_lsn('largest less than or equal', @end_time);
DECLARE @min_lsn AS BINARY(10)
= sys.fn_cdc_get_min_lsn('HumanResources_Employee');
IF @from_lsn <@min_lsn SET @from_lsn = @min_lsn;
--Get the ordinal position(s) of the column(s) you want to track
DECLARE @hiredate_ord INT
= sys.fn_cdc_get_column_ordinal(N'HumanResources_Employee', N'HireDate');
DECLARE @vac_hr_ord INT
= sys.fn_cdc_get_column_ordinal(N'HumanResources_Employee', N'VacationHours');
--Return ALL the changes and a flag to tell us if the HireDate changed
SELECT
BusinessEntityID,
--Boolean value to indicate whether hire date was changed
sys.fn_cdc_is_bit_set(@hiredate_ord, __$update_mask) AS [HireDateChg],
--Boolean value to indicate whether vacation hours was changed in the source
sys.fn_cdc_is_bit_set(@vac_hr_ord, __$update_mask) AS [VacHoursChg]
FROM cdc.fn_cdc_get_all_changes_HumanResources_Employee(@from_lsn, @to_lsn,
N'all');
```

This call should return every row from the shadow table without aggregating them into a net-changes view. This is useful if your destination system needs to track everything that happened to a source table, including interim values. It includes two BIT fields that indicate whether specific columns were changed. If you want to disable CDC on a table, use a command of the following form. Be careful, though; this command will drop the shadow table and any data it contains:

```
EXECUTE sys.sp_cdc_disable_table
@source_schema = N'HumanResources',
@source_name = N'Employee',
@capture_instance = N'HumanResources_Employee';
```

Using the SSIS CDC Tools

Now that you know how to set up CDC in your relational database engine, it is time to use SSIS to pull the data you need. Three tools in the SSIS toolbox work hand in hand with CDC.

- **CDC Control Task:** Used to control the CDC sequence of events in CDC packages. It controls the CDC package synchronization with the initial load package. It also governs the LSN ranges in a CDC package. It can also deal with errors and recovery.

- **CDC Source:** Used to query the CDC change tables.
- **CDC Splitter:** Sends data down different data paths for Inserts, Updates, and Deletions.

In the CDC Control Task there are several options for control operations:

- **Mark Initial Load Start:** Records the first load starting point
- **Mark Initial Load End:** Records the first load ending point
- **Mark CDC Start:** Records the beginning of the CDC range
- **Get Processing Range:** Retrieves the range for the CDC values
- **Mark Processed Range:** Records the range of values processed

These tools make it much easier for you to control CDC packages in SSIS. The CDC Control Task creates a new table in a database of your choosing that holds the CDC state. This state can then be retrieved using the same CDC Control Task. The CDC state is the place at which your CDC data is in at this time. This could mean the database needs to be queried back one hour, one week, or one year from now. The CDC state tells your SSIS package where to gather data. It also can tell if the data is already up-to-date.

After determining the CDC state, a Data Flow is then used to move the data. The CDC Source is used to query the data and push it down the Data Flow path. The CDC Splitter is then used to send the data down the appropriate paths for updating, deleting, or inserting. After the Data Flow is done loading the data, another CDC Control Task can update the CDC state.

The first steps to getting these CDC tools to work is to set up the CDC state table and create an ADO.NET connection to the database where the CDC state table is found. You can use the CDC Control Task itself to help with these steps. Open the CDC Control Task and you will see a screen like Figure 11-7.

Click on the New button next to the first Connection Manager option and create an ADO.NET connection to the AdventureWorks database. Then click the New button next to the Tables to use for storing state option. This will open a window as seen in Figure 11-8. The SQL command for creating the table and the index it automatically generated is shown in this window. Clicking the run button will create the table for the CDC state in the AdventureWorks database. You will also need a variable in the SSIS package to hold the CDC state. Click the New button next to the Variable containing the CDC state option to create this variable (shown in Figure 11-7). The default name of this variable is CDC_State.

Now that you have the CDC state table created with a connection to it and a variable to hold the state, you are ready to create a package to load the CDC data. In most situations you will have a CDC package that will do the initial load. This means you will have a package that runs one time to dump all of the data from the source into your data warehouse or any destination you are trying to keep updated. This initial load will consists of a package with a CDC Control Task to set the initial load start, then a Data Flow, and then a CDC Control Task to set to the initial load end. The following example is building the package that will be used on a schedule to update the data in your destination after the initial load has been done. To set the initial load end, just run a CDC Control Task set to "Mark Initial Load End." Afterward you can query the CDC table to ensure you have a value set.

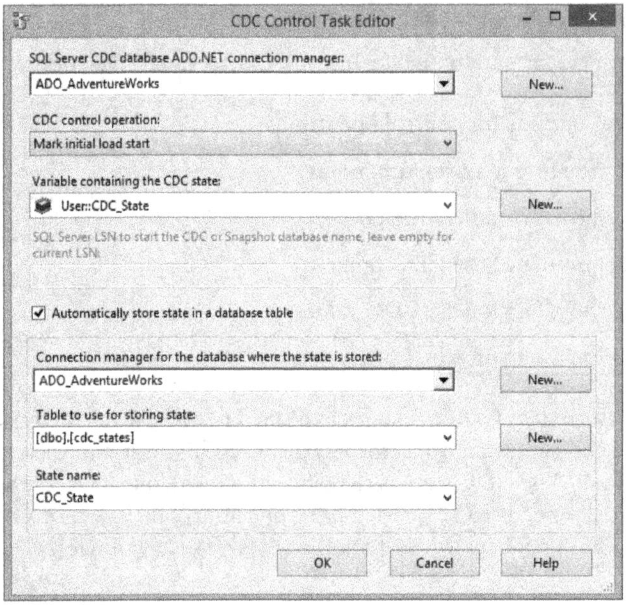

CDC Control Task Editor

SQL Server CDC database ADO.NET connection manager:
ADO_AdventureWorks
New...
CDC control operation:
Mark initial load start
Variable containing the CDC state:
User::CDC_State
New...
SQL Server LSN to start the CDC or Snapshot database name, leave empty for current LSN:
Automatically store state in a database table
Connection manager for the database where the state is stored:
ADO_AdventureWorks
New...
Table to use for storing state:
[dbo].[cdc_states]
New...
State name:
CDC_State
OK
Cancel
Help

FIGURE 11-7

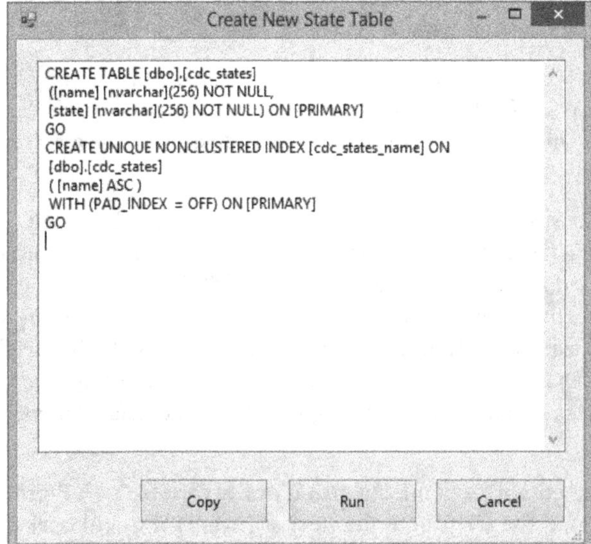

FIGURE 11-8

> **NOTE** *The State Name in the CDC Control Task must match the name in the initial load CDC package.*

The incremental package will start with a CDC Control Task that gets the processing range. A Data Flow is then used with the CDC Source and CDC Splitter. Then another CDC Control Task is used to mark the processed range. This ensures that the package is ready to run again and pick up the next batch of changes in the CDC.

In the following example we will not write the records to a destination, but you can use Data Viewers to see the CDC data.

1. Create a package named **CDC Demo**. Drag in a CDC Control Task and set up the options to match Figure 11-9. This will get the process range from the CDC state table and save it in the CDC_State variable in the SSIS package.

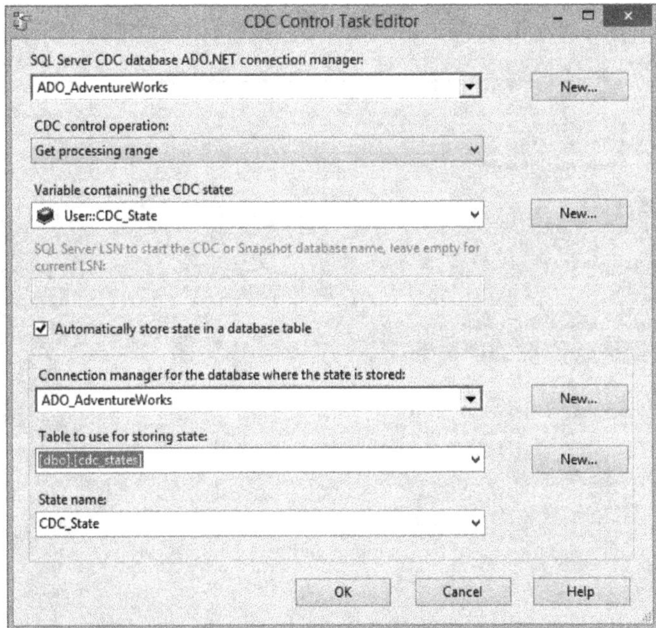

FIGURE 11-9

> **NOTE** *If you have been following along with the examples in the chapter then you have CDC enabled on the Employee table in the AdventureWorks database. If not then you will need to go back and run the code in this chapter to see the expected results in this package.*

2. Now drag in a Data Flow and connect the CDC Control Task to the Data Flow. The package should look like Figure 11-10.

3. Open the Data Flow and drag in the CDC Source and set the options in the source to match Figure 11-11. You are selecting the Employee table as the source and the All option to get all of the changes from the table. The CDC_State variable also needs to be set in the source.

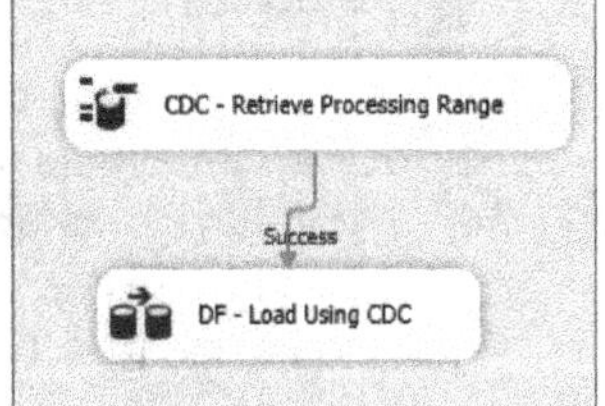

FIGURE 11-10

4. Once you have the source configured, drag in the CDC Splitter Transformation. Connect the CDC Source to the CDC Splitter. Drag in three Union All Transformations and connect each of the CDC Splitter outputs to the Union All Transformations. Once complete, your Data Flow should look like Figure 11-12.

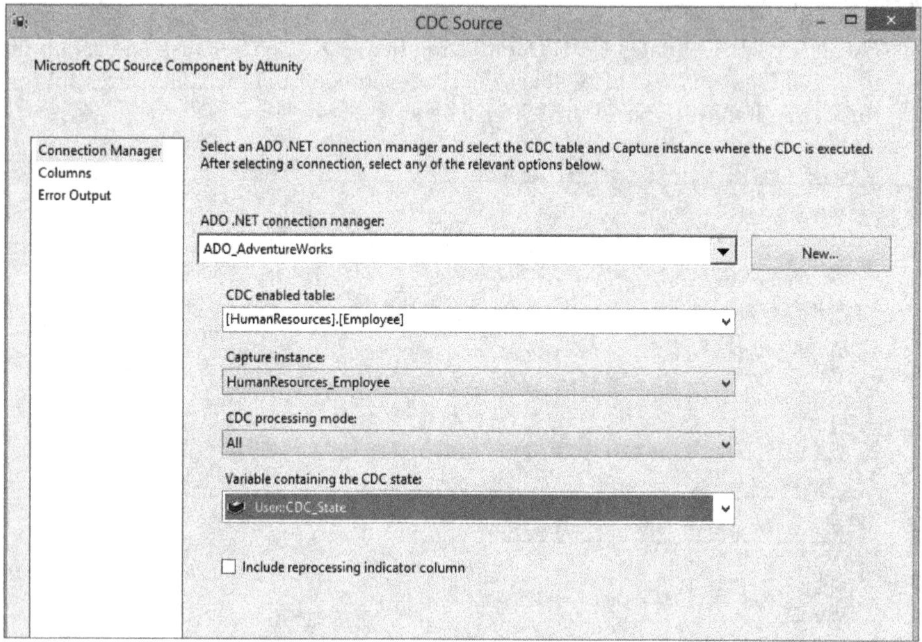

FIGURE 11-11

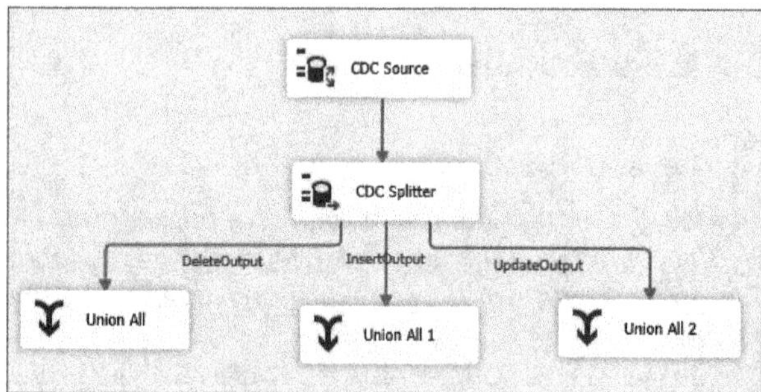

FIGURE 11-12

5. You can now place a Data Viewer on each on the CDC Splitter outputs and see the rows that have been updated, deleted, and inserted. If you want to test this further, go back to the Employee table and perform some SQL commands to add rows, delete rows, and perform some updates. These changes will show in the Data Viewers.

6. To complete this package you will need to add in three destinations in the Data Flow, one for each of the CDC Splitter outputs. You will also need to add another CDC Control Task after the Data Flow Tasks to mark the processed range. This ensures the package will not pick up the same rows twice.
7. Back in the Control Flow, add one more CDC Control Task. Configure it the same way you configured the first, but change the CDC Control Operation to Mark Processed Range. Attach this task to the Data Flow Task. This task writes back to the state table what transactions have already been transferred.

This example shows you the functionality of the CDC tools in SQL Server Integration Services. These tools should make CDC work much easier inside of SSIS. As you can see though, the steps that are done in this resemble the same steps with a control table.

> **NOTE** *There is also a SSIS Oracle CDC option now, too, though it is not specifically covered in this book.*

SUMMARY

As this chapter has shown, you can take advantage of many opportunities to use CDC in concert with SSIS in your ETL solution to incrementally load data into your database. You can also use the control table pattern to load data in a very similar pattern. While it requires more work to implement, it won't require Enterprise Edition of SQL Server.

12

Loading a Data Warehouse

WHAT'S IN THIS CHAPTER?

- Data profiling
- Dimension and fact table loading
- Analysis Services cube processing

WROX.COM DOWNLOADS FOR THIS CHAPTER

You can find the wrox.com code downloads for this chapter at `www.wrox.com/go/prossis2014` on the Download Code tab.

Among the various applications of SQL Server Integration Services (SSIS), one of the more common is loading a data warehouse or data mart. SSIS provides the extract, transform, and load (ETL) features and functionality to efficiently handle many of the tasks required when dealing with transactional source data that will be extracted and loaded into a data mart, a centralized data warehouse, or even a master data management repository, including the capabilities to process data from the relational data warehouse into SQL Server Analysis Services (SSAS) cubes.

SSIS provides all the essential elements of data processing — from your source, to staging, to your data mart, and onto your cubes (and beyond!). A few common architectures are prevalent in data warehouse solutions. Figure 12-1 highlights one common architecture of a data warehouse with an accompanying business intelligence (BI) solution.

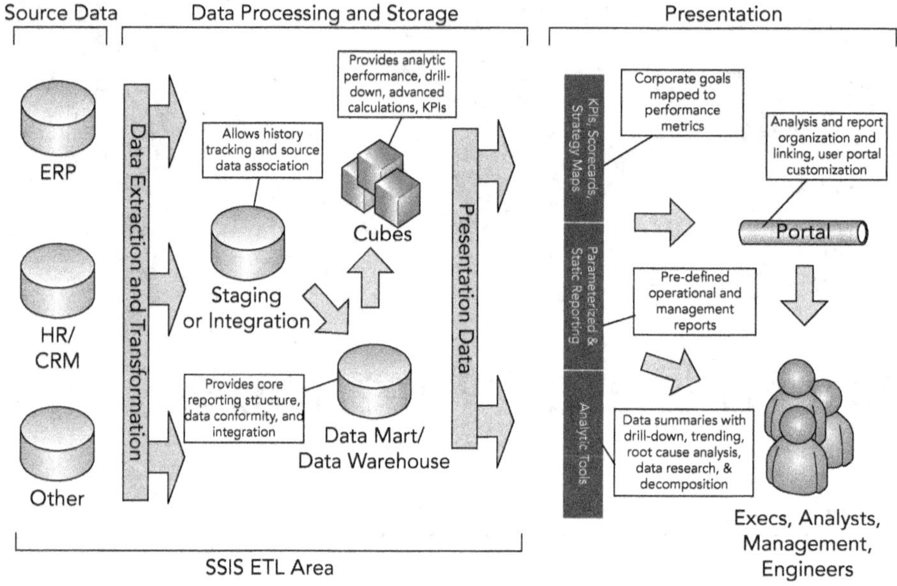

FIGURE 12-1

The presentation layer on the right side of Figure 12-1 shows the main purpose of the BI solution, which is to provide business users (from the top to the bottom of an organization) with meaningful data from which they can take actionable steps. Underlying the presentation data are the back-end structures and processes that make it possible for users to access the data and use it in a meaningful way.

Another common data warehouse architecture employs a central data warehouse with subject-oriented data marts loaded from the data warehouse. Figure 12-2 demonstrates this data warehouse architecture.

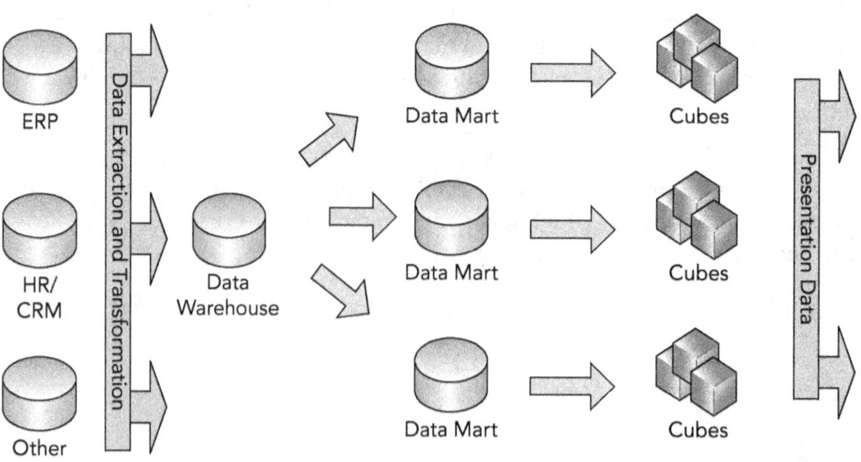

FIGURE 12-2

ETL is an important part of a data warehouse and data mart back-end process because it is responsible for moving and restructuring the data between the data tiers of the overall BI solution. This involves many steps, as you will see — including data profiling, data extraction, dimension table loading, fact table processing, and SSAS processing.

This chapter will set you on course to architecting and designing an ETL process for data warehouse and business intelligence ETL. In fact, SSIS contains several out-of-the-box tasks and transformations to get you well on your way to a stable and straightforward ETL process. Some of these components include the Data Profiling Task, the Slowly Changing Dimension Transformation, and the Analysis Services Execute DDL Task. The tutorials in this chapter, like other chapters, use the sample databases for SQL Server, called AdventureWorks and AdventureWorksDW. In addition to the databases, a sample SSAS cube database solution is also used. These databases represent a transactional database schema and a data warehouse schema. The tutorials in this chapter use the sample databases and demonstrate a coordinated process for the Sales Quota Fact table and the associated SSAS measure group, which includes the ETL required for the Employee dimension. You can go to `www.wrox.com/go/prossis2014` and download the code and package samples found in this chapter, including the version of the SSAS AdventureWorks database used.

DATA PROFILING

Ultimately, data warehousing and BI is about reporting and analytics, and the first step to reach that objective is understanding the source data, because that has immeasurable impact on how you design the structures and build the ETL.

Data profiling is the process of analyzing the source data to better understand its condition in terms of cleanliness, patterns, number of nulls, and so on. In fact, you probably have profiled data before with scripts and spreadsheets without even realizing that it was called data profiling.

A helpful way to data profile in SSIS, the Data Profiling Task, is reviewed in Chapter 3, but let's drill into some more details about how to leverage it for data warehouse ETL.

Initial Execution of the Data Profiling Task

The Data Profiling Task is unlike the other tasks in SSIS because it is not intended to be run repeatedly through a scheduled operation. Consider SSIS as the wrapper for this tool. You use SSIS to configure and run the Data Profiling Task, which outputs an XML file with information about the data you select. You then observe the results through the Data Profile Viewer, which is a standalone application. The output of the Data Profiling Task will be used to help you in your development and design of the ETL and dimensional structures in your solution. Periodically, you may want to rerun the Data Profiling task to see how the data has changed, but the task will not run in the recurring ETL process.

1. Open Visual Studio and create a new SSIS project called **ProSSIS_Ch12**. You will use this project throughout this chapter.
2. In the Solution Explorer, rename `Package.dtsx` to `Profile_EmployeeData.dtsx`.

3. The Data Profiling Task requires an ADO.NET connection to the source database (as opposed to an OLE DB connection). Therefore, create a new ADO.NET connection in the Connection Manager window by right-clicking and choosing "New ADO.NET Connection" and then click the New button. After you create a connection to the AdventureWorks database, return to the Solution Explorer window.
4. In the Solution Explorer, create a new project connection to your local machine or where the AdventureWorks sample database is installed, as shown in Figure 12-3.

FIGURE 12-3

5. Click OK to save the connection information and return to the SSIS package designer. (In the Solution Explorer, rename the project connection to **ADONETAdventureWorks.conmgr** so that you will be able to distinguish this ADO.NET connection from other connections.)
6. Drag a Data Profiling Task from the SSIS Toolbox onto the Control Flow and double-click the new task to open the Data Profiling Task Editor.
7. The Data Profiling Task includes a wizard that will create your profiling scenario quickly; click the Quick Profile Button on the General tab to launch the wizard.
8. In the Single Table Quick Profile Form dialog, choose the ADONETAdventureWorks connection; and in the Table or View dropdown, select the [Sales].[vSalesPerson] view from the list. Enable all the checkboxes in the Compute list and change the Functional Dependency Profile to use 2 columns as determinant columns, as shown in Figure 12-4. The next section reviews the results and describes the output of the data profiling steps.

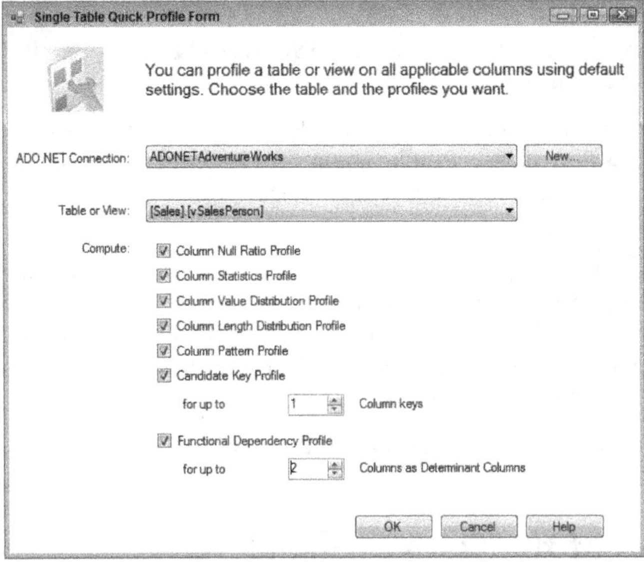

FIGURE 12-4

9. Click OK to save the changes, which will populate the Requests list in the Data Profiling Task Editor, as shown in Figure 12-5. Chapter 3 describes each of these different request types, and you will see the purpose and output of a few of these when we run the viewer.

Data Profiling Task Editor

Configure the properties used to profile data sources.

General
Profile Requests
Expressions

View All Requests

Profile Type	Request ID
Column Null Ratio Profile Request	NullRatioReq
Column Statistics Profile Request	StatisticsReq
Column Length Distribution Profile Request	LengthDistReq
Column Value Distribution Profile Request	ValueDistReq
Column Pattern Profile Request	PatternReq
Candidate Key Profile Request	KeyReq
Functional Dependency Profile Request	FDReq

Request Properties:

OK Cancel Help

FIGURE 12-5

10. Return to the General tab of the editor. In the Destination property box, choose New File Connection. This is where you will select the location of the XML file where the Data Profiling Task stores its profile output when it is run.

11. In the File Connection Manager Editor, change the Usage type dropdown to "Create file" and enter **C:\ProSSIS\Data\Employee_Profile.xml** in the File text box. Click OK to save your changes to the connection, and click OK again to save your changes in the Data Profiling Task Editor.

12. Now it is time to execute this simple package. Run the package in Visual Studio, which will initiate several queries against the source table or view (in this case, a view). Because this view returns only a few rows, the Data Profiling task will execute rather quickly, but with large tables it may take several minutes (or longer if your table has millions of rows and you are performing several profiling tests at once).

The results of the profile are stored in the `Employee_Profile.xml` file, which you will next review with the Data Profile Viewer tool.

Reviewing the Results of the Data Profiling Task

Despite common user expectations, data cannot be magically generated, no matter how creative you are with data cleansing. For example, suppose you are building a sales target analysis that uses employee data, and you are asked to build into the analysis a sales territory group, but the source column has only 50 percent of the data populated. In this case, the business user needs to rethink the value of the data or fix the source. This is a simple example for the purpose of the tutorials in this chapter, but consider a more complicated example or a larger table.

The point is that your source data is likely to be of varying quality. Some data is simply missing, other data has typos, sometimes a column has so many different discrete values that it is hard to analyze, and so on. The purpose of doing data profiling is to understand the source, for two reasons. First, it enables you to review the data with the business user, which can effect changes; second, it provides the insight you need when developing your ETL operations. In fact, even though we're bringing together business data that the project stakeholders use every day, we're going to be using that data in ways that it has never been used before. Because of this, we're going to learn things about it that no one knows — not even the people who are the domain experts. Data profiling is one of the up-front tasks that helps the project team avoid unpleasant (and costly) surprises later on.

Now that you have run the Data Profiling Task, your next objective is to evaluate the results:

1. Observing the output requires using the Data Profile Viewer. This utility is found in the Integration Services subdirectory for Microsoft SQL Server 2014 (Start Button ⇨ All Programs ⇨ Microsoft SQL Server 2014 ⇨ Integration Services) or in Windows 8, simply type **Data Profile Viewer** at the start screen.

2. Open the `Employee_Profile.xml` file created earlier by clicking the Open button and navigating to the `C:\ProSSIS\Data` folder (or the location where the file was saved), highlighting the file, and clicking Open again.

3. In the Profiles navigation tree, first click the table icon on the top left to put the tree viewer into Column View. Then drill down into the details by expanding Data Sources, server (local), Databases, AdventureWorks, and the [Sales].[vSalesPerson] table, as shown in Figure 12-6.

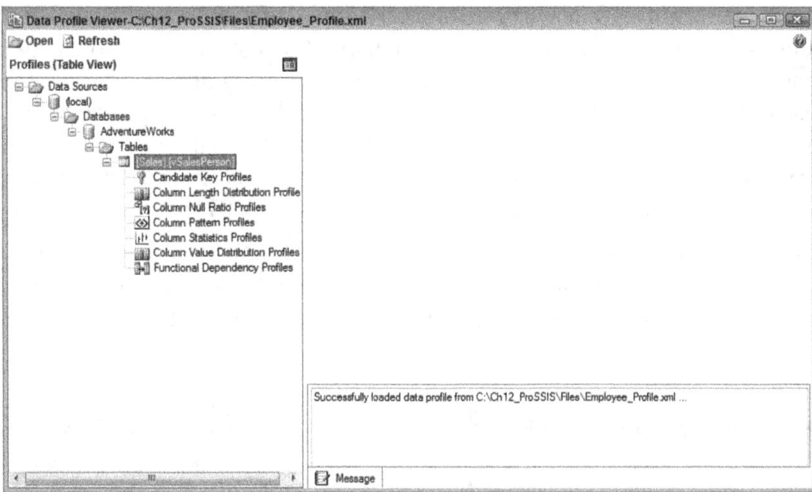

FIGURE 12-6

4. The first profiling output to observe is the Candidate Key Profiles, so click this item under the Columns list, which will open the results in the viewer on the right. Note that the Data Profiling Task has identified seven columns that are unique across the entire table (with 100 percent uniqueness), as shown in Figure 12-7.

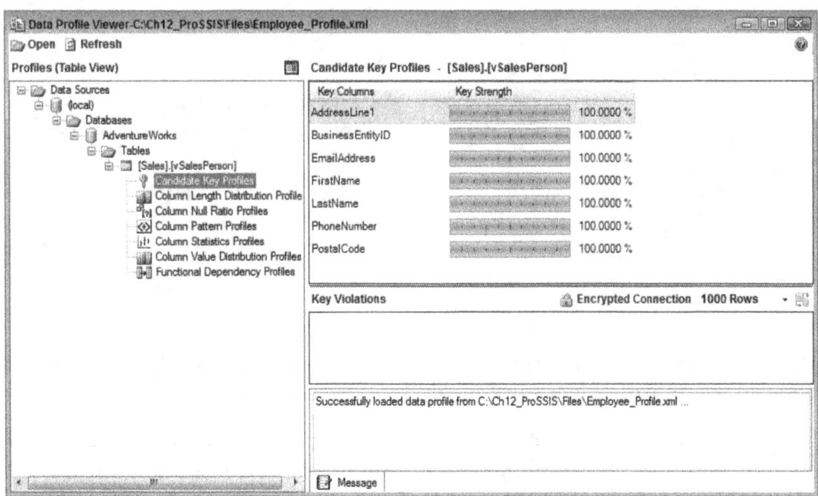

FIGURE 12-7

Given the small size of this table, all these columns are unique, but with larger tables, you will see fewer columns and less than 100 percent uniqueness, and any exceptions or key violations. The question is, which column looks to be the right candidate key for this table? In the next section you will see how this answer affects your ETL.

5. Click the Functional Dependency Profile object on the left and observe the results. This shows the relationship between values in multiple columns. Two columns are shown: Determinant Column(s) and Dependant Column. The question is, for every unique value (or combination) in the Determinant Column, is there only one unique value in the Dependant Column? Observe the output. What is the relationship between these combinations of columns: TerritoryGroup and TerritoryName, StateProvinceName, and CountryRegionName. Again, in the next section you will see how these results affect your ETL.

6. In the profile tree, click the "View Single Column by Profile" icon at the top right of the profile tree. Next, expand the TerritoryName column and highlight the Column Length Distribution. Then, in the distribution profile on the right, double-click the length distribution of 6, as shown in Figure 12-8.

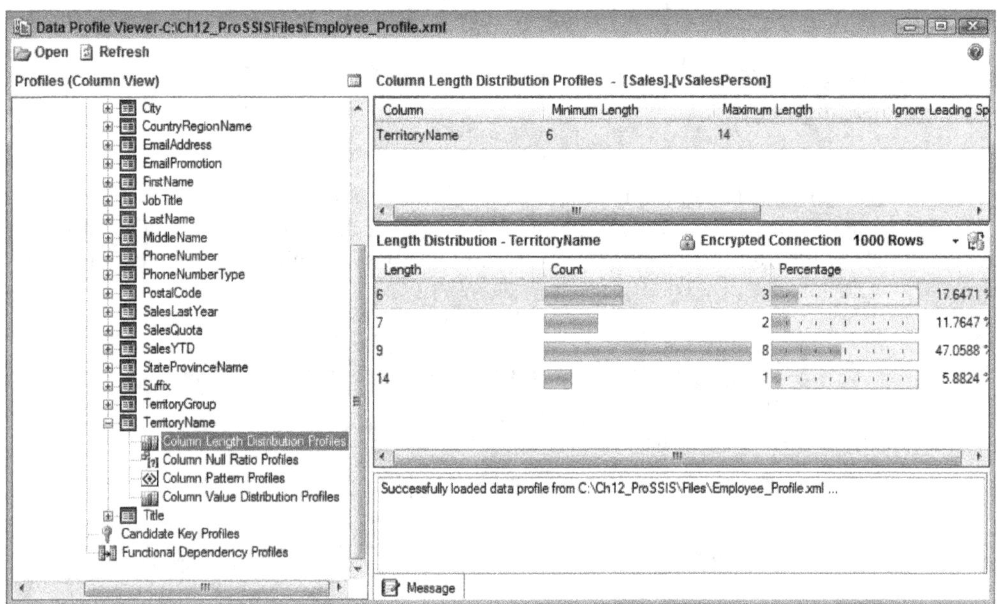

FIGURE 12-8

The column length distribution shows the number of rows by length. What are the maximum and minimum lengths of values for the column?

7. Under TerritoryName in the profile browser, select the Column Null Ratio Profile and then double-click the row in the profile viewer on the right to view the detail rows.

   The Column Null Ratio shows what percentage of rows in the entire table have `NULL` values. This is valuable for ETL considerations because it spells out when `NULL` handling is required for the ETL process, which is one of the most common transformation processes.

8. Select the Column Value Distribution Profile on the left under the TerritoryName and observe the output in the results viewer. How many unique values are there in the entire table? How many values are used only one time in the table?

9. In the left navigation pane, expand the PhoneNumber column and then click the Column Pattern Profile. Double-click the first pattern, number 1, in the list on the right, as shown in Figure 12-9. As you can see, the bottom right of the window shows the actual data values for the phone numbers matching the selected pattern. This data browser is helpful in seeing the actual values so that you can analyze the effectiveness of the Data Profile Task.

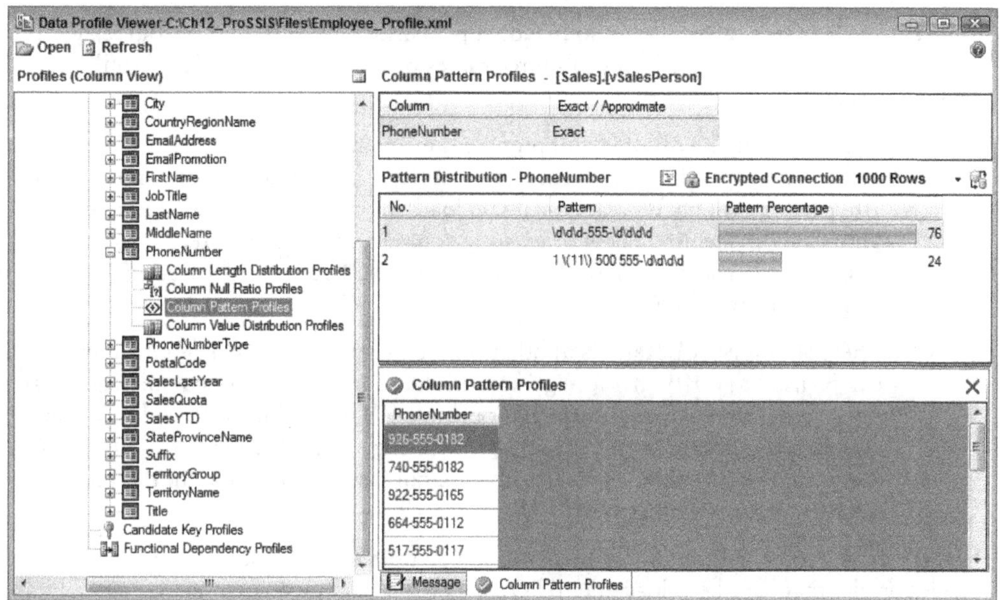

FIGURE 12-9

The Column Pattern Profile uses regular expression syntax to display what pattern or range of patterns the data in the column contains. Notice that for the PhoneNumber column, two patterns emerge. The first is for phone numbers that are in the syntax ###-555-####, which is translated to \d\d\d-555-\d\d\d\d in regular expression syntax. The other pattern begins with 1 \(11\) 500 555- and ends with four variable numbers.

10. The final data profiling type to review is the Column Statistics Profile. This is applicable only to data types related to numbers (integer, float, decimal, numeric) and dates (dates allow only minimum and maximum calculations). In the Profiles tree view on the left of the Data Profile Viewer, expand the SalesYTD column and then click the Column Statistics Profile. Four results are calculated across the spread of values in the numeric column:

   a. **Minimum:** The lowest number value in the set of column values

   b. **Maximum:** The highest number value in the set of column values

   c. **Mean:** The average of values in the set of column values

   d. **Standard Deviation:** The average variance between the values and the mean

The Column Statistics Profile is very valuable for fact table source evaluation, as the measures in a fact table are almost always numeric based, with a few exceptions.

Overall, the output of the Data Profiling Task has helped to identify the quality and range of values in the source. This naturally leads to using the output results to formulate the ETL design.

Turning Data Profile Results into Actionable ETL Steps

The typical first step in evaluating source data is to check the existence of source key columns and referential completeness between source tables or files. Two of the data profiling outputs can help in this effort:

- The Candidate Key Profile will provide the columns (or combination of columns) with the highest uniqueness. It is crucial to identify a candidate key (or composite key) that is 100 percent unique, because when you load your dimension and fact tables, you need to know how to identify a new or existing source record. In the preceding example, shown in Figure 12-7, several columns meet the criteria. The natural selection from this list is the BusinessEntityID column.
- The Column NULL Ratio is another important output of the Data Profiling Task. This can be used to verify that foreign keys in the source table have completeness, especially if the primary key to foreign key relationships will be used to relate a dimension table to a fact, or a dimension table to another dimension table. Of course, this doesn't verify that the primary-to-foreign key values line up, but it will give you an initial understanding of referential data completeness.

As just mentioned, the Column NULL Ratio can be used for an initial review of foreign keys in source tables or files that have been loaded into SQL Server for data profiling review. The Column NULL Ratio is an excellent output, because it can be used for almost every destination column type, such as dimension attributes, keys, and measures. Anytime you have a column that has NULLs, you will most likely have to replace them with unknowns or perform some data cleansing to handle them.

In Step 7 of the previous section, the Territory Name has approximately a 17 percent NULL ratio. In your dimension model destination this is a problem, because the Employee dimension has a foreign surrogate key to the Sales Territory dimension. Because there isn't completeness in the SalesTerritory, you don't have a reference to the dimension. This is an actionable item that you will need to address in the dimension ETL section later.

Other useful output of the Data Profiling Task includes the column length and statistics presented. Data type optimization is important to define; when you have a large inefficient source column where most of the space is not used (such as a `char(1000)`), you will want to scale back the data type to a reasonable length. To do so, use the Column Length Distribution (refer to Figure 12-8).

The column statistics can be helpful in defining the data type of your measures. Optimization of data types in fact tables is more important than dimensions, so consider the source column's max and min values to determine what data type to use for your measure. The wider a fact table, the slower it will perform, because fewer rows will fit in the server's memory for query execution, and the more disk space it will occupy on the server.

Once you have evaluated your source data, the next step is to develop your data extraction, the "E" of ETL.

DATA EXTRACTION AND CLEANSING

Data extraction and cleansing applies to many types of ETL, beyond just data warehouse and BI data processing. In fact, several chapters in this book deal with data extraction for various needs, such as incremental extraction, change data capture, and dealing with various sources. Refer to the following chapters to plan your SSIS data extraction components:

- Chapter 4 takes an initial look at the Source components in the Data Flow that will be used for your extraction.
- Chapter 10 considers data cleansing, which is a common task for any data warehouse solution.
- Chapter 13 deals with using the SQL Server relational engine to perform change data capture.
- Chapter 14 is a look at heterogeneous, or non-SQL Server, sources for data extraction.

The balance of this chapter deals with the core of data warehouse ETL, which is dimension and fact table loading, SSAS object processing, and ETL coordination.

DIMENSION TABLE LOADING

Dimension transformation and loading is about tracking the current and sometime history of associated attributes in a dimension table. Figure 12-10 shows the dimensions related to the Sales Quota Fact table in the AdventureWorksDW database (named FactSalesQuota). The objective of this section is to process data from the source tables into the dimension tables.

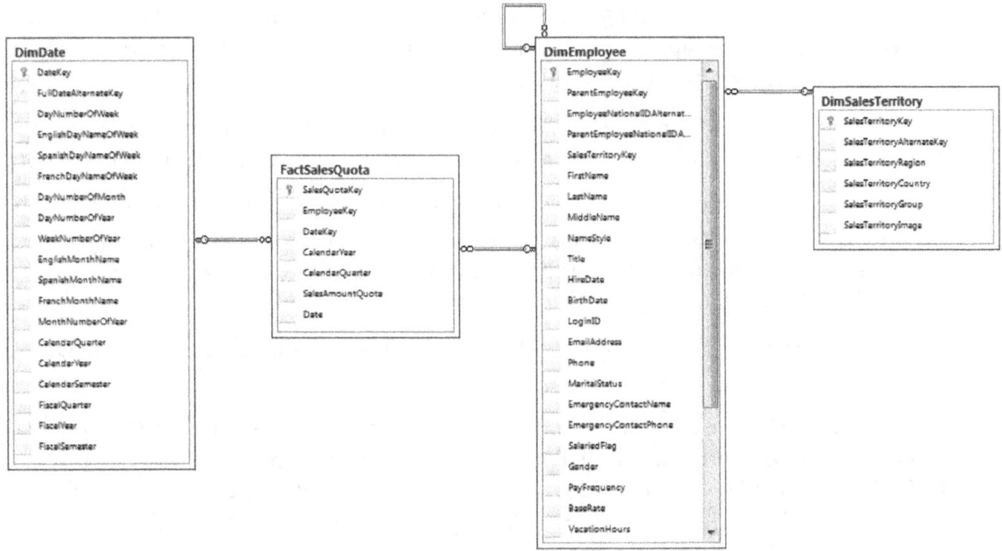

FIGURE 12-10

In this example, notice that each dimension (DimEmployee, DimSalesTerritory, and DimDate) has a surrogate key named *Dimension Key*, as well as a candidate key named *Dimension AlternateKey*. The surrogate key is the most important concept in data warehousing because it enables the tracking of change history and optimizes the structures for performance. See *The Data Warehouse Toolkit*, Third Edition, by Ralph Kimball and Margy Ross (Wiley, 2013), for a detailed review of the use and purpose of surrogate keys. Surrogate keys are often auto-incrementing identity columns that are contained in the dimension table.

Dimension ETL has several objectives, each of which is reviewed in the tutorial steps to load the DimSalesTerritory and DimEmployee tables, including the following:

- Identifying the source keys that uniquely identify a source record and that will map to the alternate key
- Performing any Data Transformations to align the source data to the dimension structures
- Handling the different change types for each source column and adding or updating dimension records

SSIS includes a built-in transformation called the Slowly Changing Dimension (SCD) Transformation to assist in the process. This is not the only transformation that you can use to load a dimension table, but you will use it in these tutorial steps to accomplish dimension loading. The SCD Transformation also has some drawbacks, which are reviewed at the end of this section.

Loading a Simple Dimension Table

Many dimension tables are like the Sales Territory dimension in that they contain only a few columns, and history tracking is not required for any of the attributes. In this example, the DimSalesTerritory table is sourced from the [Sales].[SalesTerritory] table, and any source changes to any of the three columns will be updated in the dimension table. These columns are referred to as *changing dimension attributes*, because the values can change.

1. To begin creating the ETL for the DimSalesTerritory table, return to your SSIS project created in the first tutorial and create a new package named **ETL_DimSalesTerritory.dtsx**.
2. Because you will be extracting data from the AdventureWorks database and loading data into the AdventureWorksDW database, create two OLE DB project connections to these databases named **AdventureWorks** and **AdventureWorksDW**, respectively. Refer to Chapter 2 for help about defining the project connections.
3. Drag a new Data Flow Task from the SSIS Toolbox onto the Control Flow and navigate to the Data Flow designer.
4. Drag an OLE DB Source component into the Data Flow and double-click the new source to open the editor. Configure the OLE DB Connection Manager dropdown to use the Adventure Works database and leave the data access mode selection as "Table or view." In the "Name of the table or the view" dropdown, choose [Sales].[SalesTerritory], as shown in Figure 12-11.
5. On the Columns property page (see Figure 12-12), change the Output Column value for the TerritoryID column to SalesTerritoryAlternateKey, change the Name column to SalesTerritoryRegion, and change the Output Column for the Group column to SalesTerritoryGroup. Also, uncheck all the columns under SalesTerritoryGroup because they are not needed for the DimSalesTerritory table.

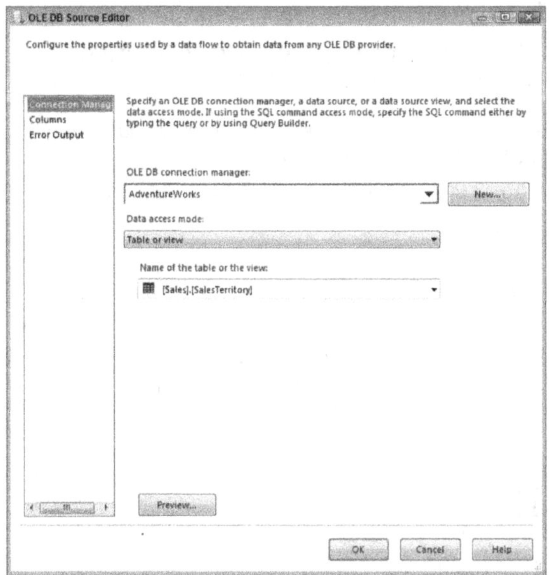

FIGURE 12-11

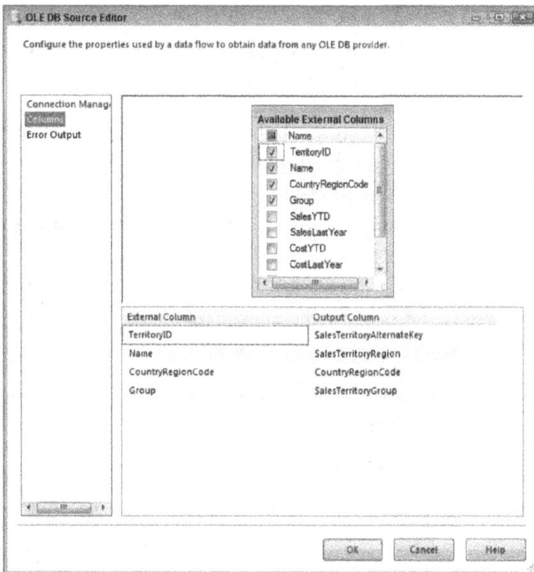

FIGURE 12-12

6. Click OK to save your changes and then drag a Lookup Transformation onto the Data Flow and connect the blue data path from the OLE DB Source onto the Lookup.
7. On the General property page, shown in Figure 12-13, edit the Lookup Transformation as follows: leave the Cache mode setting at Full cache, and leave the Connection type setting at OLE DB Connection Manager.

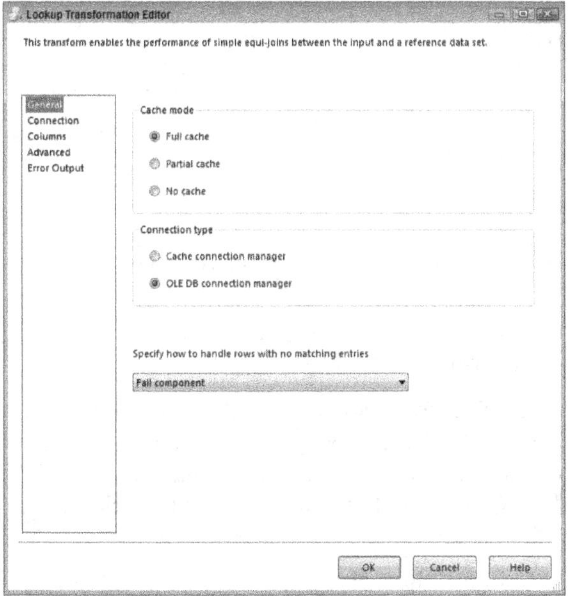

FIGURE 12-13

8. On the Connection property page, set the OLE DB Connection Manager dropdown to the AdventureWorks connection. Change the "Use a table or a view" dropdown to [Person].[CountryRegion].

9. On the Columns property page, drag the CountryRegionCode from the available Input Columns list to the matching column in the Available Lookup Columns list, then select the checkbox next to the Name column in the same column list. Rename the Output Alias of the Name column to **SalesTerritoryCountry**, as shown in Figure 12-14.

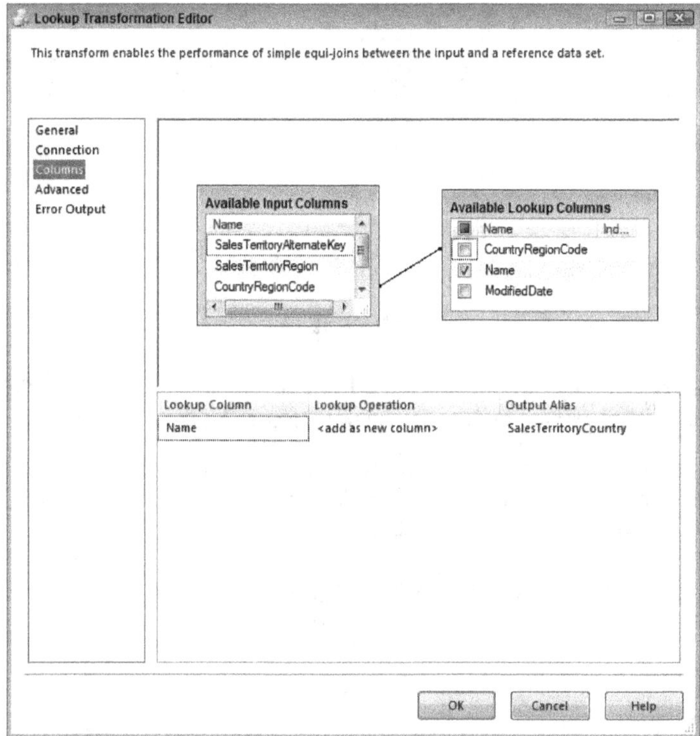

FIGURE 12-14

10. Select OK in the Lookup Transformation Editor to save your changes.

At this point in the process, you have performed some simple initial steps to align the source data up with the destination dimension table. The next steps are the core of the dimension processing and use the SCD Transformation.

11. Drag a Slowly Changing Dimension Transformation from the SSIS Toolbox onto the Data Flow and connect the blue data path output from the Lookup onto the Slowly Changing Dimension Transformation. When you drop the path onto the SCD Transformation, you will be prompted to select the output of the Lookup. Choose Lookup Match Output from the dropdown and then click OK.

12. To invoke the SCD wizard, double-click the transformation, which will open up a splash screen for the wizard. Proceed to the second screen by clicking Next.

13. The first input of the wizard requires identifying the dimension table to which the source data relates. Therefore, choose AdventureWorksDW as the Connection Manager and then choose [dbo].[DimSalesTerritory] as the table or view, which will automatically display the dimension table's columns in the list, as shown in Figure 12-15. For the SalesTerritoryAlternateKey, change the Key Type to Business key. Two purposes are served here:

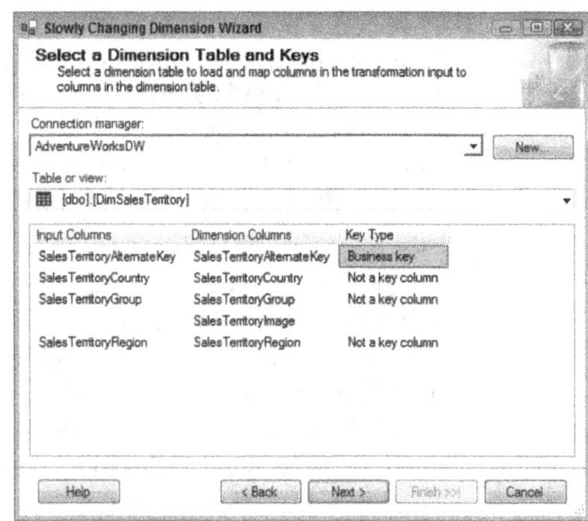

FIGURE 12-15

- ➤ One, you identify the candidate key (or business key) from the dimension table and which input column it matches. This will be used to identify row matches between the source and the destination.
- ➤ Two, columns are matched from the source to attributes in the dimension table, which will be used on the next screen of the wizard to identify the change tracking type. Notice that the columns are automatically matched between the source input and the destination dimension because they have the same name and data type. In other scenarios, you may have to manually perform the match.

14. On the next screen of the SCD wizard, you need to identify what type of change each matching column is identified as. It has already been mentioned that all the columns are changing attributes for the DimSalesTerritory dimension; therefore, select all the columns and choose the "Changing attribute" Change Type from the dropdown lists, as shown in Figure 12-16.

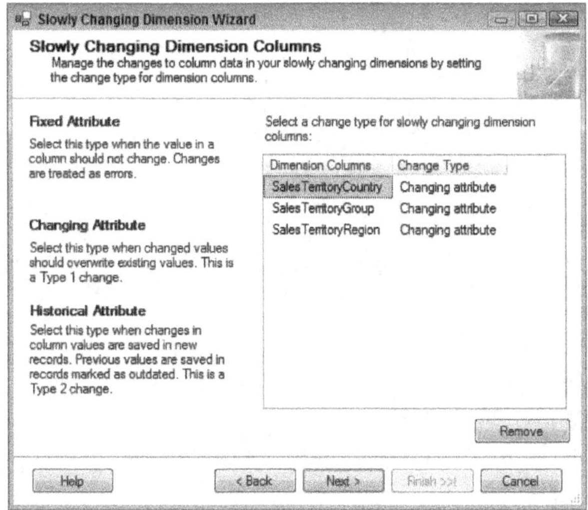

FIGURE 12-16

Three options exist for the Change Type: Changing attribute, Historical attribute, and Fixed attribute. As mentioned earlier, a Changing attribute is updated if the source value changes. For the Historical attribute, when a change occurs, a new record is generated, and the old record preserves the history of the change. You'll learn more about this when you walk through the DimEmployee dimension ETL in the next section of this chapter. Finally, a Fixed attribute means no changes should happen, and the ETL should either ignore the change or break.

15. The next screen, titled "Fixed and Changing Attribute Options," prompts you to choose which records you want to update when a source value changes. The "Fixed attributes" option is grayed out because no Fixed attributes were selected on the prior screen. Under the "Changing attributes" option, you can choose to update the changing attribute column for all the records that match the same candidate key, or you can choose to update only the most recent one. It doesn't matter in this case because there will be only one record per candidate key value, as there are no Historical attributes that would cause a new record. Leave this box unchecked and proceed to the next screen.

16. The "Inferred Dimension Members" screen is about handling placeholder records that were added during the fact table load, because a dimension member didn't exist when the fact load was run. Inferred members are covered in the DimEmployee dimension ETL, later in this chapter.

17. Given the simplicity of the Sales Territory dimension, this concludes the wizard, and on the last screen you merely confirm the settings that you configured. Select Finish to complete the wizard.

The net result of the SCD wizard is that it will automatically generate several downstream transformations, preconfigured to handle the change types based on the candidate keys you selected. Figure 12-17 shows the completed Data Flow with the SCD Transformation.

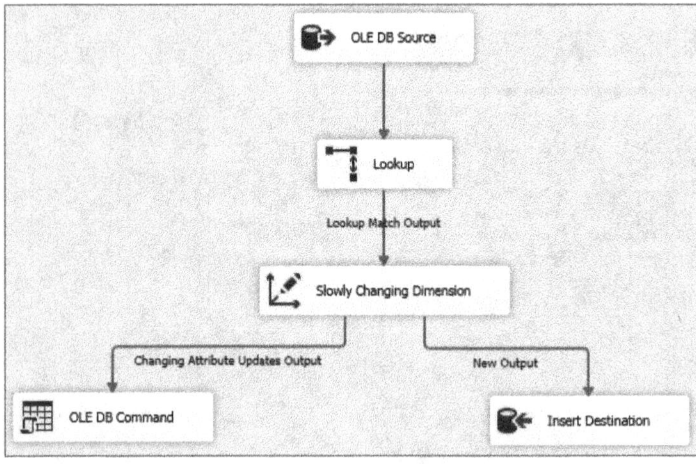

FIGURE 12-17

Since this dimension is simple, there are only two outputs. One output is called New Output, which will insert new dimension records if the candidate key identified from the source does not have a match in the dimension. The second output, called Changing Attribute Updates Output, is used when you have a match across the candidate keys and one or more of the changing attributes does not match between the source input and the dimension table. This OLE DB command uses an `UPDATE` statement to perform the operation.

Loading a Complex Dimension Table

Dimension ETL often requires complicated logic that causes the dimension project tasks to take the longest amount of time for design, development, and testing. This is due to change requirements for various attributes within a dimension such as tracking history, updating inferred member records, and so on. Furthermore, with larger or more complicated dimensions, the data preparation tasks often require more logic and transformations before the history is even handled in the dimension table itself.

Preparing the Data

To exemplify a more complicated dimension ETL process, in this section you will create a package for the DimEmployee table. This package will deal with some missing data, as identified earlier in your data profiling research:

1. In the SSIS project, create a new package called **ETL_DimEmployee.dtsx**. Since you've already created project connections for AdventureWorks and AdventureWorksDW, you do not need to add these to the new DimEmployee SSIS package.
2. Create a Data Flow Task and add an OLE DB Source component to the Data Flow.
3. Configure the OLE DB Source component to connect to the AdventureWorks connection and change the data access mode to SQL command. Then enter the following SQL code in the SQL command text window (see Figure 12-18):

```
SELECT
e.NationalIDNumber as EmployeeNationalIDAlternateKey
, manager.NationalIDNumber as ParentEmployeeNationalIDAlternateKey
, s.FirstName, s.LastName, s.MiddleName, e.JobTitle as Title
, e.HireDate, e.BirthDate, e.LoginID, s.EmailAddress
, s.PhoneNumber as Phone, e.MaritalStatus, e.SalariedFlag
, e.Gender, e.VacationHours, e.SickLeaveHours, e.CurrentFlag
, s.CountryRegionName as SalesTerritoryCountry
, s.TerritoryGroup as SalesTerritoryGroup
, s.TerritoryName as SalesTerritoryRegion
, s.StateProvinceName
FROM [Sales].[vSalesPerson] s
INNER JOIN [HumanResources].[Employee] e
ON e.[BusinessEntityID] = s.[BusinessEntityID]
LEFT OUTER JOIN HumanResources.Employee manager
ON (e.OrganizationNode.GetAncestor(1)) = manager.[OrganizationNode]
```

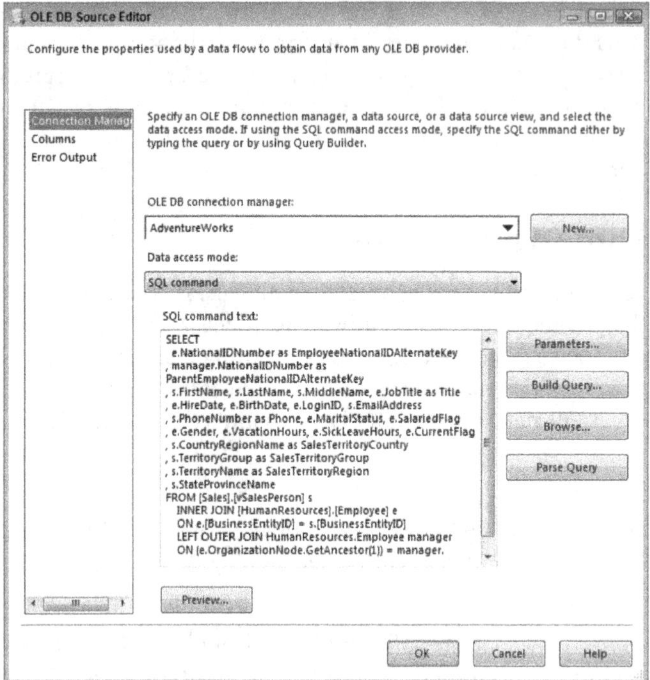

FIGURE 12-18

4. Click OK to save the changes to the OLE DB Source component.
5. Drag a Lookup Transformation to the Data Flow and connect the blue data path output from the OLE DB Source to the Lookup. Name the Lookup **Sales Territory**.
6. Double-click the Lookup Transformation to bring up the Lookup editor. On the General page, change the dropdown named "Specify how to handle rows with no matching entries" to "Redirect rows to no match output." Leave the Cache mode as Full cache and the Connection type as OLE DB Connection Manager.
7. On the Connection property page, change the OLE DB connection to AdventureWorksDW and then select [dbo].[DimSalesTerritory] in the dropdown below called "Use a table or a view."
8. On the Columns property page, join the SalesTerritoryCountry, SalesTerritoryGroup, and SalesTerritoryRegion columns between the input columns and lookup columns, as shown in Figure 12-19. In addition, select the checkbox next to SalesTerritoryKey in the lookup columns to return this column to the Data Flow.

   At this point, recall from your data profiling that some of the sales territory columns in the source have NULL values. Also recall that TerritoryGroup and TerritoryName have a one-to-many functional relationship. In fact, assume that you have conferred with the business users, and they confirmed that you can look at the StateProvinceName and CountryRegionName, and if another salesperson has the same combination of values, you can use their SalesTerritory information.

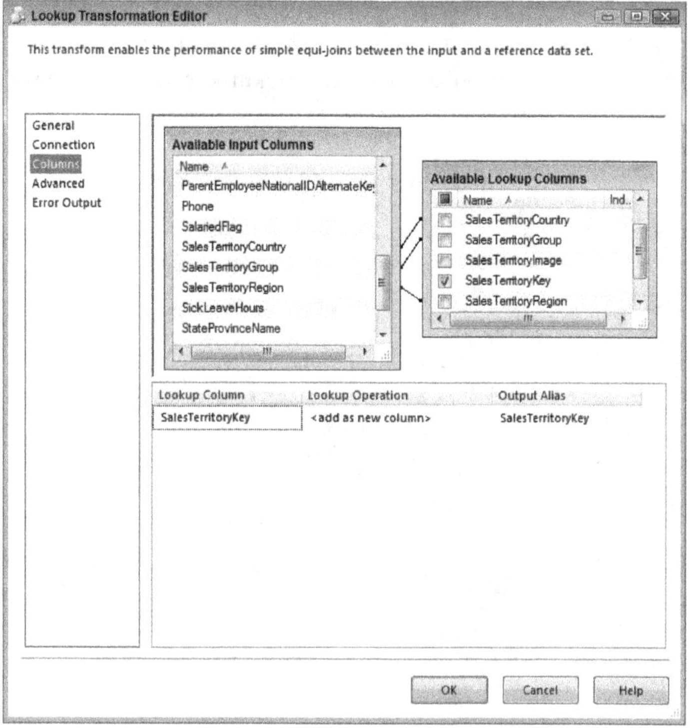

FIGURE 12-19

9. To handle the missing SalesTerritories with the preceding requirements, add a second Lookup Transformation to the Data Flow, and name it **Get Missing Territories.** Then connect the blue path output of the Sales Territory Lookup to this new Lookup. You will be prompted to choose the Output; select Lookup No Match Output from the dropdown list, as shown in Figure 12-20.

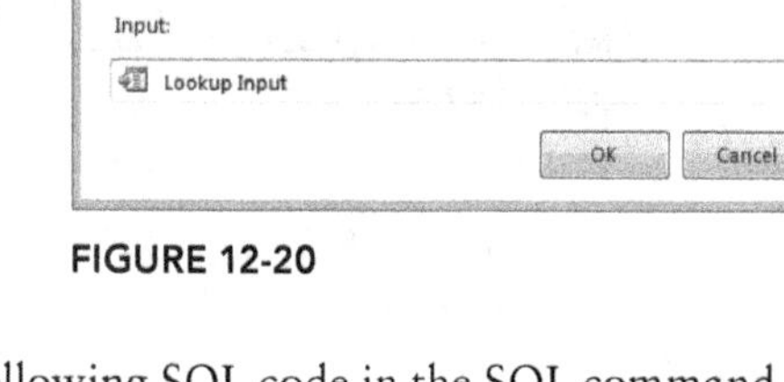

FIGURE 12-20

10. Edit the new Lookup and configure the OLE DB Source component to connect to the AdventureWorks connection. Then change the data access mode to SQL command. Enter the following SQL code in the SQL command text window:

```
SELECT DISTINCT
CountryRegionName as SalesTerritoryCountry
, TerritoryGroup as SalesTerritoryGroup
, TerritoryName as SalesTerritoryRegion
, StateProvinceName
FROM [Sales].[vSalesPerson]
WHERE TerritoryName IS NOT NULL
```

11. On the Columns property page, join the SalesTerritoryCountry and StateProvinceName between the input and lookup columns list and then enable the checkboxes next to SalesTerritoryGroup and SalesTerritoryRegion on the lookup list. Append the word "New" to the OutputAlias, as shown in Figure 12-21.

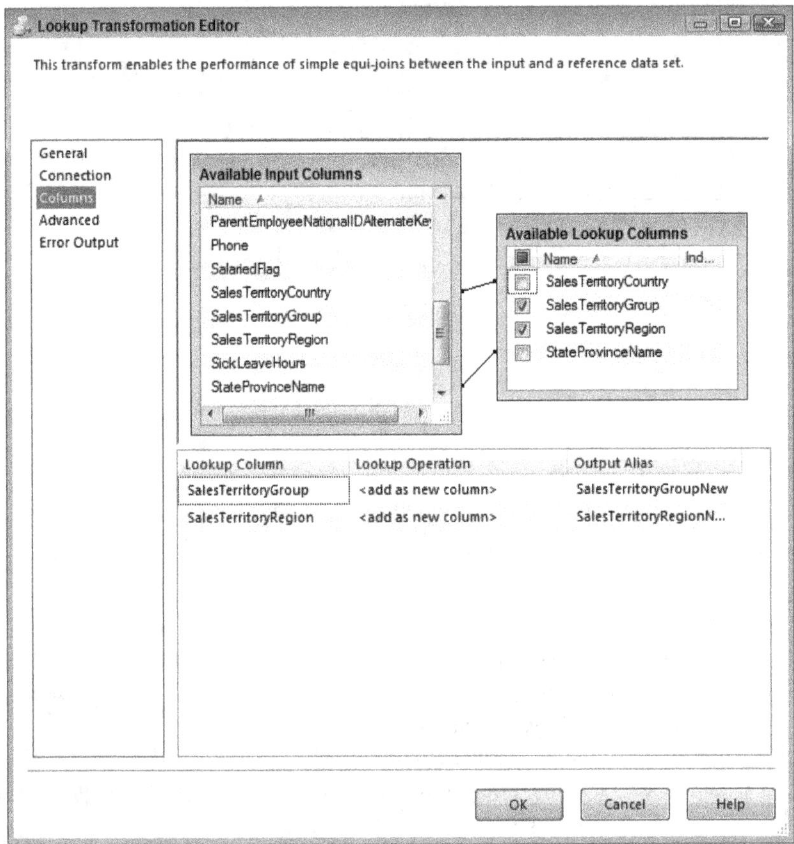

FIGURE 12-21

Next, you will recreate the SalesTerritory Lookup from the prior steps to get the Sales TerritoryKey for the records that originally had missing data.

12. Add a new Lookup to the Data Flow named **Reacquire SalesTerritory** and connect the output of the Get Missing Territories Lookup (use the Lookup Match Output when prompted). On the General tab, edit the Lookup as follows: leave the Cache mode as Full cache and the Connection type as OLE DB Connection Manager.

13. On the Connections page, specify the AdventureWorksDW Connection Manager and change the "Use a table or a view" option to [dbo].[DimSalesTerritory].

14. On the Columns property page (shown in Figure 12-22), match the columns between the input and lookup table, ensuring that you use the “New” Region and Group column. Match across SalesTerritoryCountry, SalesTerritoryGroupNew, and SalesTerritoryRegionNew. Also return the SalesTerritory Key and name its Output Alias **SalesTerritoryKeyNew.**

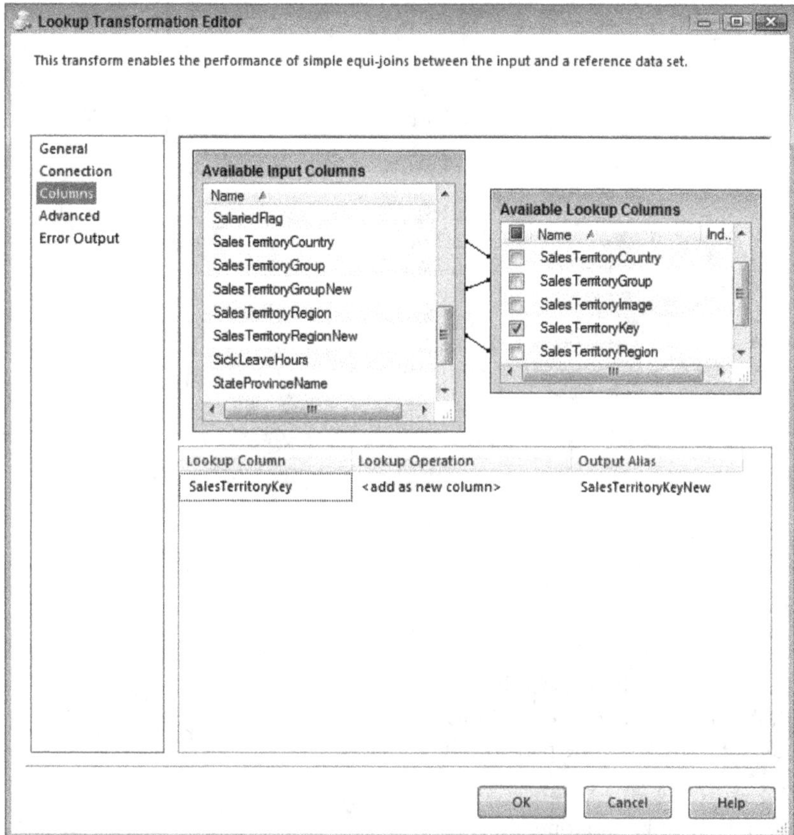

FIGURE 12-22

15. Click OK to save your Lookup changes and then drag a Union All Transformation onto the Data Flow. Connect two inputs into the Union All Transformation:

- The Lookup Match Output from the original Sales Territory Lookup
- The Lookup Match Output from the Reacquire SalesTerritory Lookup (from steps 12–14)

16. Edit the Union All Transformation as follows: locate the SalesTerritoryKey column and change the <ignore> value in the dropdown for the input coming from second lookup to use the SalesTerritoryKeyNew column. This is shown in Figure 12-23.

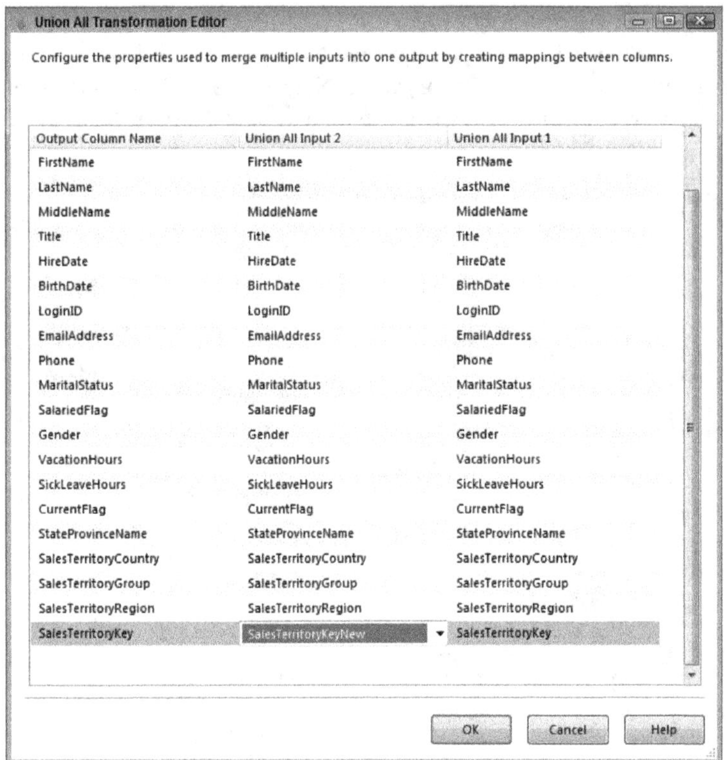

FIGURE 12-23

17. Click OK to save your changes to the Union All. At this point, your Data Flow should look similar to the one pictured in Figure 12-24.

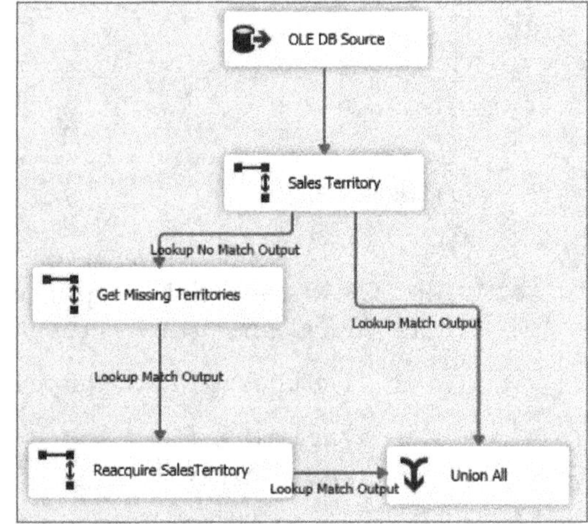

FIGURE 12-24

These steps described how to handle one data preparation task. When you begin to prepare data for your dimension, chances are good you will need to perform several steps to get it ready for the dimension data changes.

You can use many of the other SSIS transformations for this purpose, described in the rest of the book. A couple of examples include using the Derived Column to convert NULLs to Unknowns and the Fuzzy Lookup and Fuzzy Grouping to cleanse dirty data. You can also use the Data Quality Services of SQL Server 2014 to help clean data. A brief overview of DQS is included in Chapter 10.

Handling Complicated Dimension Changes with the SCD Transformation

Now you are ready to use the SCD Wizard again, but for the DimEmployee table, you need to handle different change types and inferred members:

1. Continue development by adding a Slowly Changing Dimension Transformation to the Data Flow and connecting the data path output of the Union All to the SCD Transformation. Then double-click the SCD Transformation to launch the SCD Wizard.
2. On the Select a Dimension Table and Keys page, choose the AdventureWorksDW Connection Manager and the [dbo].[DimEmployee] table.
   a. In this example, not all the columns have been extracted from the source, and other destination columns are related to the dimension change management, which are identified in Step 3. Therefore, not all the columns will automatically be matched between the input columns and the dimension columns.
   b. Find the EmployeeNationalIDAlternateKey and change the Key Type to Business Key.
   c. Select Next.
3. On the Slowly Changing Dimension Columns page, make the following Change Type designations, as shown in Figure 12-25:

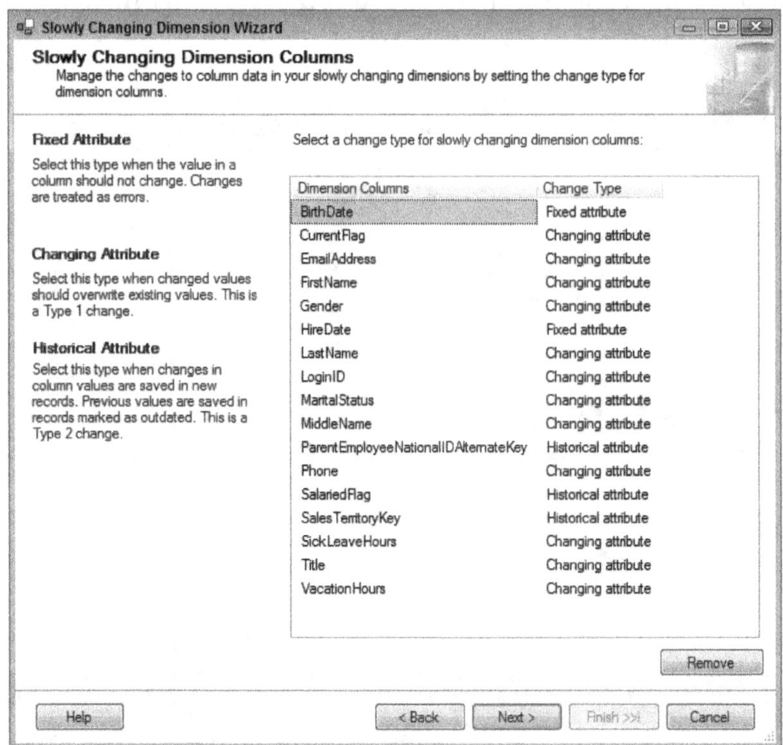

FIGURE 12-25

   a. Fixed Attributes: BirthDate, HireDate
   b. Changing Attributes: CurrentFlag, EmailAddress, FirstName, Gender, LastName, LoginID, MaritalStatus, MiddleName, Phone, SickLeaveHours, Title, VacationHours
   c. Historical Attributes: ParentEmployeeNationalIDAlternateKey, SalariedFlag, SalesTerritoryKey

4. On the Fixed and Changing Attribute Options page, uncheck the checkbox under the Fixed attributes label. The result of this is that when a value changes for a column identified as a fixed attribute, the change will be ignored, and the old value in the dimension will not be updated. If you had checked this box, the package would fail.
5. On the same page, check the box for Changing attributes. As described earlier, this ensures that all the records (current and historical) will be updated when a change happens to a changing attribute.
6. You will now be prompted to configure the Historical Attribute Options, as shown in Figure 12-26. The SCD Transformation needs to know how to identify the current record when a single business key has multiple values (recall that when a historical attribute changes, a new copy of the record is created). Two options are available. One, a single column is used to identify the record. The better option is to use a start and end date. The DimEmployee table has a StartDate and EndDate column; therefore, use the second configuration option button and set the "Start date column" to StartDate, and the "End date column" to EndDate. Finally, set the "Variable to set date values" dropdown to System::StartTime.

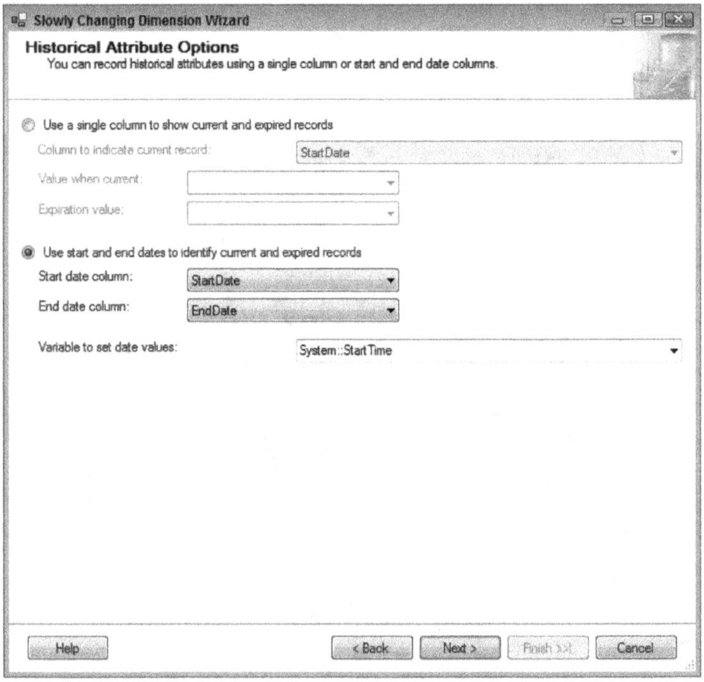

FIGURE 12-26

7. Assume for this example that you may have missing dimension records when processing the fact table. In this case, a new inferred member is added to the dimension. Therefore, on the Inferred Dimension Members page, leave the "Enable inferred member support" option checked. The SCD Transformation needs to know when a dimension member is an inferred member. The best option is to have a column that identifies the record as inferred; however, the DimEmployee table does not have a column for this purpose. Therefore, leave the "All columns with a change type are null" option selected.
8. This concludes the wizard settings. Click Finish so that the SCD Transformation can build the downstream transformations needed based on the configurations. Your Data Flow will now look similar to the one shown in Figure 12-27.

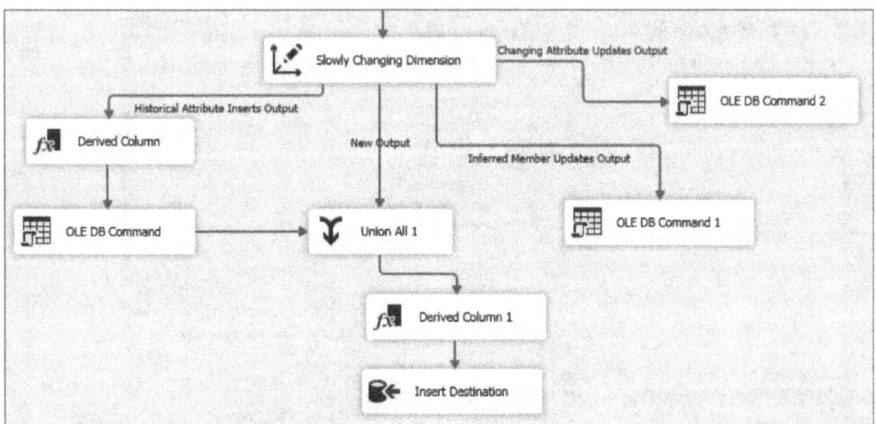

FIGURE 12-27

As you have seen, when dealing with historical attribute changes and inferred members, the output of the SCD Transformation is more complicated with updates, unions, and derived calculations. One of the benefits of the SCD Wizard is rapid development of dimension ETL. Handling changing attributes, new members, historical attributes, inferred members, and fixed attributes is a complicated process that usually takes hours to code, but with the SCD Wizard, you can accomplish this in minutes. Before looking at some drawbacks and alternatives to the SCD Transformation, consider the outputs (refer to Figure 12-27) and how they work:

- **Changing Attribute Updates Output:** The changing attribute output records are records for which at least one of the attributes that was identified as a changing attribute goes through a change. This update statement is handled by an OLE DB Command Transformation with the code shown here:

```
UPDATE [dbo].[DimEmployee]
 SET [CurrentFlag] = ?,[EmailAddress] = ?,[FirstName] = ?,[Gender] =
?,[LastName] = ?,[LoginID] = ?,[MaritalStatus] = ?,[MiddleName] = ?,
[Phone] = ?,[SickLeaveHours] = ?,[Title] = ?,[VacationHours] = ?
WHERE [EmployeeNationalIDAlternateKey] = ?
```

The question marks (?) in the code are mapped to input columns sent down from the SCD Transformation. Note that the last question mark is mapped to the business key, which ensures that all the records are updated. If you had unchecked the changing attribute checkbox in Step 4 of the preceding list, then the current identifier would have been included and only the latest record would have changed.

- **New Output:** New output records are simply new members that are added to the dimension. If the business key doesn't exist in the dimension table, then the SCD Transformation will send the row out this output. Eventually these rows are inserted with the Insert Destination (refer to Figure 12-27), which is an OLE DB Destination. The Derived Column 1 Transformation shown in Figure 12-28 is to add the new StartDate of the record, which is required for the metadata management.

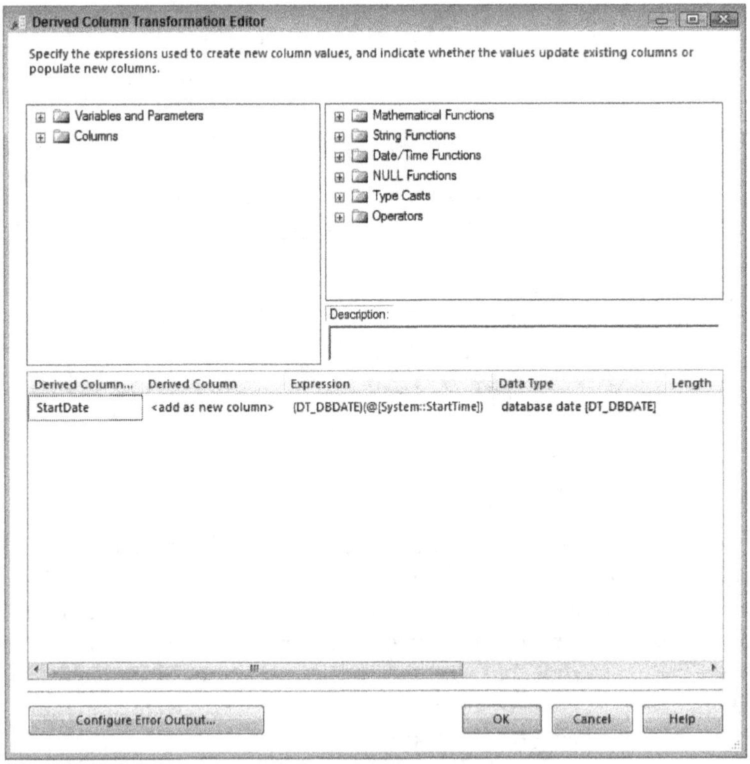

FIGURE 12-28

This dimension is unique, because it has both a StartDate column and a Status column (most dimension tables that track history have either a Status column that indicates whether the record is current or datetime columns that indicate the start and end of the record's current status, but usually not both). The values for the Status column are Current and <NULL>, so you should add a second Derived Column to this transformation called Status and force a "Current" value in it. You also need to include it in the destination mapping.

- **Historical Attribute Inserts Output:** The historical output is for any attributes that you marked as historical and underwent a change. Therefore, you need to add a new row to the dimension table. Handling historical changes requires two general steps:

  - Update the old record with the EndDate (and NULL Status). This is done through a Derived Column Transformation that defines the EndDate as the `System::StartTime` variable and an OLE DB command that runs an update statement with the following code:

  ```
  UPDATE [dbo].[DimEmployee]
   SET [EndDate] = ?
   , [Status] = NULL
   WHERE [EmployeeNationalIDAlternateKey] = ?
   AND [EndDate] IS NULL
  ```

  This update statement was altered to also set the Status column to NULL because of the requirement mentioned in the new output. Also, note that `[EndDate] IS NULL` is included in the `WHERE` clause because this identifies that the record is the latest record.

  - Insert the new version of the dimension record. This is handled by a Union All Transformation to the new outputs. Because both require inserts, this can be handled in one destination. Also note that the Derived Column shown earlier in Figure 12-28 is applicable to the historical output.

- **Inferred Member Updates Output:** Handling inferred members is done through two parts of the ETL. First, during the fact load when the dimension member is missing, an inferred member is inserted. Second, during the dimension load, if one of the missing inferred members shows up in the dimension source, then the attributes need to be updated in the dimension table. The following update statement is used in the OLE DB Command 1 Transformation:

  ```
  UPDATE [dbo].[DimEmployee]
   SET [BirthDate] = ?,[CurrentFlag] = ?,[EmailAddress] = ?,[FirstName] =
  ?,[Gender] = ?,[HireDate] = ?,[LastName] = ?,[LoginID] = ?,[MaritalStatus]
  = ?,[MiddleName] = ?,[ParentEmployeeNationalIDAlternateKey] = ?,[Phone] =
  ?,[SalariedFlag] = ?,[SalesTerritoryKey] = ?,[SickLeaveHours] = ?, [Title]
  = ?,[VacationHours] = ?
  WHERE [EmployeeNationalIDAlternateKey] = ?
  ```

  What is the difference between this update statement and the update statement used for the changing attribute output? This one includes updates of the changing attributes, the historical attributes, and the fixed attributes. In other words, because you are updating this as an inferred member, all the attributes are updated, not just the changing attributes.

- **Fixed Attribute Output (not used by default):** Although this is not used by default by the SCD Wizard, it is an additional output that can be used in your Data Flow. For example, you may want to audit records whose fixed attribute has changed. To use it, you can simply take the blue output path from the SCD Transformation and drag it to a Destination component where your fixed attribute records are stored for review. You need to choose the Fixed Attribute Output when prompted by adding the new path.

- **Unchanged Output (not used by default):** This is another output not used by the SCD Transformation by default. As your dimensions are being processed, chances are good that most of your dimension records will not undergo any changes. Therefore, the records do not need to be sent out for any of the prior outputs. However, you may wish to audit the number of records that are unchanged. You can do this by adding a Row Count Transformation and then dragging a new blue data path from the SCD Transformation onto the Row Count Transformation and choosing the Unchanged Output when prompted by adding the new path. With SSIS in SQL Server 2014, you can also report on the Data Flow performance and statistics when a package is deployed to the SSIS server. Chapter 16 and Chapter 22 review the Data Flow reporting.

Considerations and Alternatives to the SCD Transformation

As you have seen, the SCD Transformation boasts powerful, rapid development, and it is a great tool to understand SCD and ETL concepts. It also helps to simplify and standardize your dimension ETL processing. However, the SCD Transformation is not always the right choice for handling your dimension ETL.

Some of the drawbacks include the following:

- For each row in the input, a new lookup is sent to the relational engine to determine whether changes have occurred. In other words, the dimension table is not cached in memory. That is expensive! If you have tens of thousands of dimension source records or more, the performance of this approach can be a limiting feature of the SCD Transformation.
- For each row in the source that needs to be updated, a new update statement is sent to the dimension table (and updates are used by the changing output, historical output, and inferred member output). If a lot of updates are happening every time your dimension package runs, this will also cause your package to run slowly.
- The Insert Destination is not set to fast load. This is because deadlocks can occur between the updates and the inserts. When the insert runs, each row is added one at a time, which can be very expensive.
- The SCD Transformation works well for historical, changing, and fixed dimension attributes, and, as you saw, changes can be made to the downstream transformations. However, if you open the SCD Wizard again and make a change to any part of it, you will automatically lose your customizations.

Consider some of these approaches to optimize your package that contains the output from the SCD wizard:

- Create an index on your dimension table for the business key, followed by the current row identifier (such as the EndDate). If a clustered index does not already exist, create this index as a clustered index, which will prevent a query plan lookup from getting the underlying row. This will help the lookup that happens in the SCD Transformation, as well as all of the updates.

- The row-by-row updates can be changed to set-based updates. To do this, you need to remove the OLE DB Command Transformation and add a Destination component in its place to stage the records to a temporary table. Then, in the Control Flow, add an Execute SQL Task to perform the set-based update after the Data Flow is completed.
- If you remove all the OLE DB Command Transformations, then you can also change the Insert Destination to use fast load and essentially bulk insert the data, rather than perform per-row inserts.

Overall, these alterations may provide you with enough performance improvements that you can continue to use the SCD Transformation effectively for higher data volumes. However, if you still need an alternate approach, try building the same SCD process through the use of other built-in SSIS transformations such as these:

- The Lookup Transformation and the Merge Join Transformation can be used to cache the dimension table data. This will greatly improve performance because only a single select statement will run against the dimension table, rather than potentially thousands.
- The Derived Column Transformation and the Script component can be used to evaluate which columns have changed, and then the rows can be sent out to multiple outputs. Essentially, this would mimic the change evaluation engine inside of the SCD Transformation.
- After the data is cached and evaluated, you can use the same SCD output structure to handle the changes and inserts, and then you can use set-based updates for better performance.

FACT TABLE LOADING

Fact table loading is often simpler than dimension ETL, because a fact table usually involves just inserts and, occasionally, updates. When dealing with large volumes, you may need to handle partition inserts and deal with updates in a different way.

In general, fact table loading involves a few common tasks:

- Preparing your source data to be at the same granularity as your fact table, including having the dimension business keys and measures in the source data
- Acquiring the dimension surrogate keys for any related dimension
- Identifying new records for the fact table (and potentially updates)

The Sales Quota fact table is relatively straightforward and will give you a good start toward developing your fact table ETL:

1. In your SSIS project for this chapter, create a new package and rename it **ETL_FactSalesQuota.dtsx**.
2. Just like the other packages you developed in this chapter, you will use two Connection Managers, one for AdventureWorks, and the other for AdventureWorksDW. If you haven't already created project-level Connection Managers for these in Solution Explorer, add them before continuing.

3. Create a new Data Flow Task and add an OLE DB Source component. Name it **Sales Quota Source.** Configure the OLE DB Source component to connect to the AdventureWorks Connection Manager, and change the data access mode to SQL command, as shown in Figure 12-29. Add the following code to the SQL command text window:

```
SELECT QuotaDate, SalesQuota, NationalIDNumber as
EmployeeNationalIDAlternateKey FROM Sales.SalesPersonQuotaHistory
INNER JOIN HumanResources.Employee
 ON SalesPersonQuotaHistory.BusinessEntityID = Employee.BusinessEntityID
```

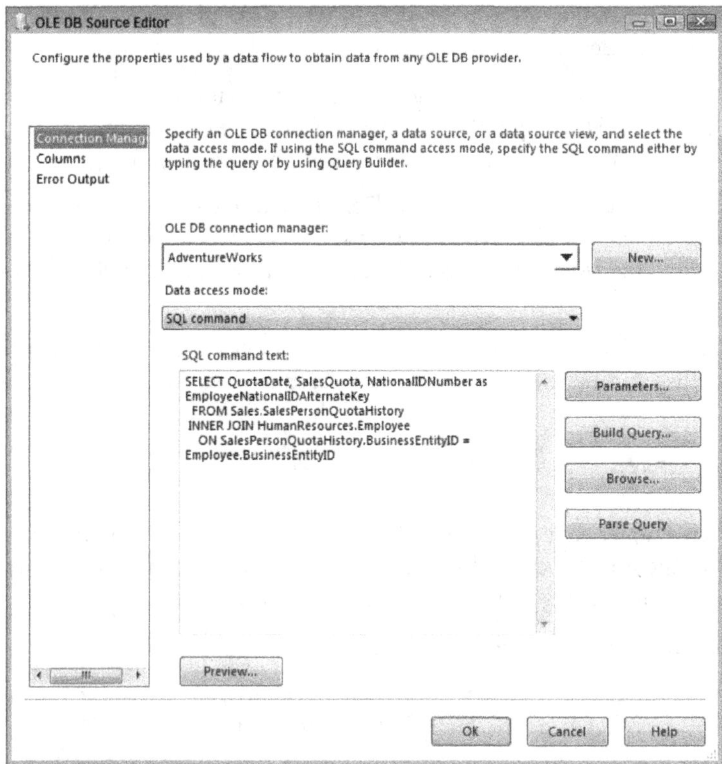

FIGURE 12-29

4. To acquire the surrogate keys from the dimension tables, you will use a Lookup Transformation. Drag a Lookup Transformation onto the Data Flow and connect the blue data path output of the OLE DB Source component onto the Lookup Transformation. Rename the Lookup **Employee Key**.

5. Double-click the Employee Key Transformation to bring up the Lookup Editor. On the General property page, leave the Cache mode set to Full cache and the Connection type set to OLE DB Connection Manager.

6. On the Connection property page, change the OLE DB Connection Manager dropdown to AdventureWorksDW and enter the following code:

```
SELECT EmployeeKey, EmployeeNationalIDAlternateKey
 FROM DimEmployee
 WHERE EndDate IS NULL
```

Including the `EndDate IS NULL` filter ensures that the most current dimension record surrogate key is acquired in the Lookup.

7. Change to the Columns property page and map the EmployeeNationalIDAlternateKey from the input columns to the lookup columns. Then select the checkbox next to the EmployeeKey of the Lookup, as shown in Figure 12-30.

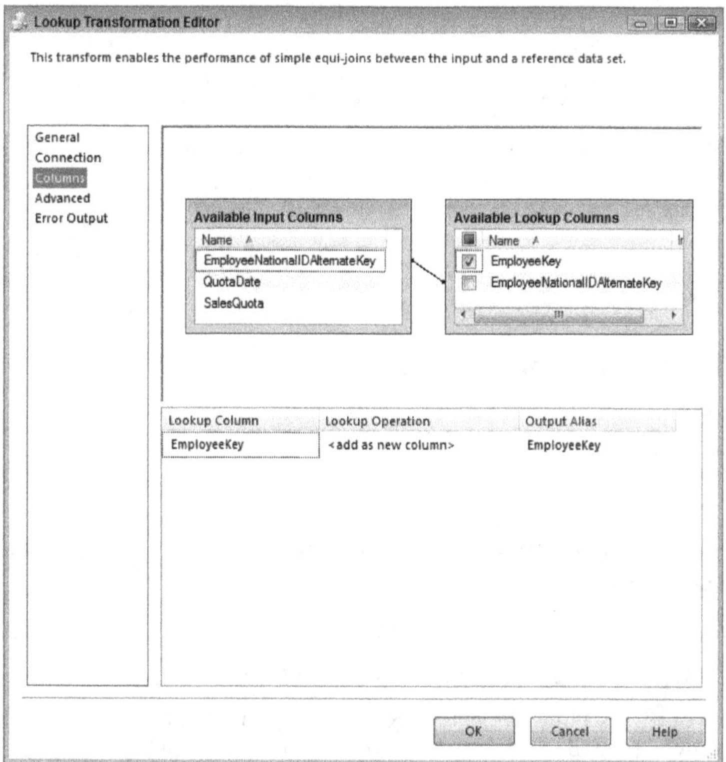

FIGURE 12-30

8. Click OK to save your changes to the Lookup Transformation.

9. For the DateKey, a Lookup is not needed because the DateKey is a "smart key," meaning the key is an integer value based on the date itself in YYYYMMDD format. Therefore, you will use a Derived column to calculate the DateKey for the fact table. Add a Derived Column Transformation to the Data Flow and connect the blue data path output of the Employee Lookup to the Derived Column Transformation. When prompted, choose the Lookup Match Output from the Lookup Transformation. Name the Derived Column **Date Keys**.

10. Double-click the Derived Column Transformation and add the following three new Derived Column columns and their associated expressions, as shown in Figure 12-31:

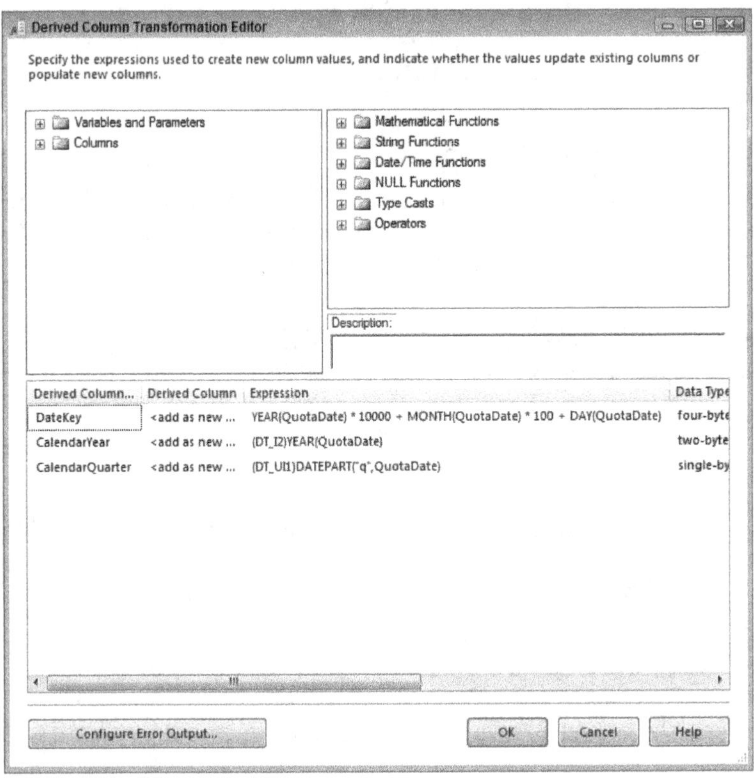

FIGURE 12-31

- DateKey: `YEAR([QuotaDate]) *10000 + MONTH([QuotaDate]) *100 + DAY([QuotaDate])`
- CalendarYear: `(DT_I2) YEAR([QuotaDate])`
- CalendarQuarter: `(DT_UI1) DATEPART("q", [QuotaDate])`

At this point in your Data Flow, the data is ready for the fact table. If your data has already been incrementally extracted, so that you are getting only new rows, you can use an OLE DB Destination to insert it right into the fact table. Assume for this tutorial that you need to identify which records are new and which records are updates, and handle them appropriately. The rest of the steps accomplish fact updates and inserts.

A Merge Join will be used to match source input records to the actual fact table records, but before you add the Merge Join, you need to add a Sort Transformation to the source records (a requirement of the Merge Join) and extract the fact data into the Data Flow.

11. Add a Sort Transformation to the Data Flow and connect the blue data path output from the Derived Column Transformation to the Sort Transformation. Double-click the Sort Transformation to bring up the Sort Transformation Editor and sort the input data by the following columns: EmployeeKey, CalendarYear, and CalendarQuarter, as shown in Figure 12-32. The CalendarYear and CalendarQuarter are important columns for this fact table because they identify the *date grain*, the level of detail at which the fact table

is associated with the date dimension. As a general rule, the Sort Transformation is a very powerful transformation as long as it is working with manageable data sizes, in the thousands and millions, but not the tens or hundreds of millions (if you have a lot of memory, you can scale up as well). An alternate to the Sort is described in steps 12–14, as well as in Chapters 7 and 16.

Figure 12-33 shows what your Data Flow should look like at this point.

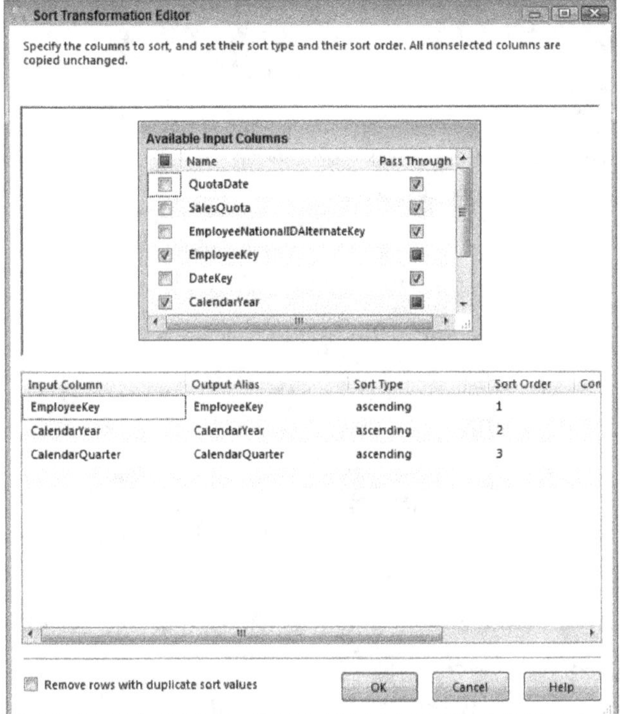

FIGURE 12-32

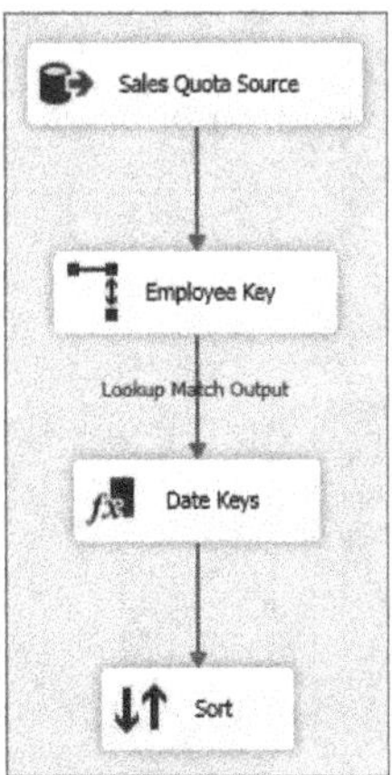

FIGURE 12-33

12. Add a new OLE DB Source component to the Data Flow and name it **Sales Quota Fact**. Configure the OLE DB Source to use the AdventureWorksDW Connection Manager and use the following SQL command:

```
SELECT EmployeeKey, CalendarYear
 , CalendarQuarter, SalesAmountQuota
 FROM dbo.FactSalesQuota
 ORDER BY 1,2,3
```

13. Because you are using an `ORDER BY` statement in the query (sorting by the first three columns in order), you need to configure the OLE DB Source component to know that the data is entering the Data Flow sorted. First, click OK to save the changes to the OLE DB Source and then right-click the Sales Quota Fact component and choose Show Advanced Editor.

14. On the Input and Output Properties tab, click the OLE DB Source Output object in the left window; in the right window, change the IsSorted property to True, as shown in Figure 12-34.

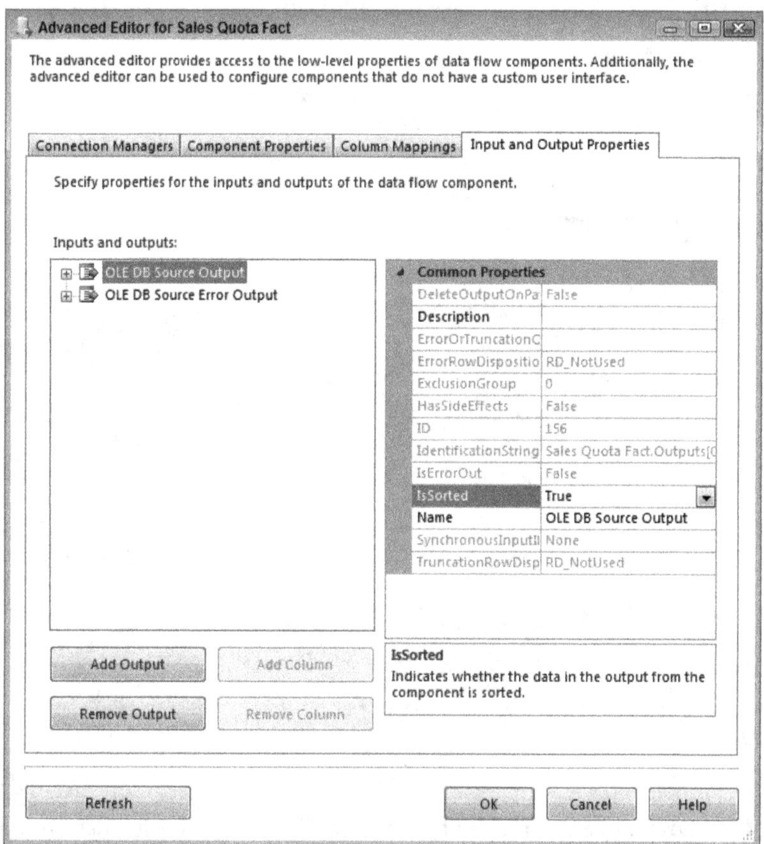

FIGURE 12-34

15. Expand the OLE DB Source Output on the left and then expand the Output Columns folder. Make the following changes to the Output Column properties:

    a. Select the EmployeeKey column and change its SortKeyPosition to 1, as shown in Figure 12-35. (If the sort order were descending, you would enter a -1 into the SortKeyPosition.)

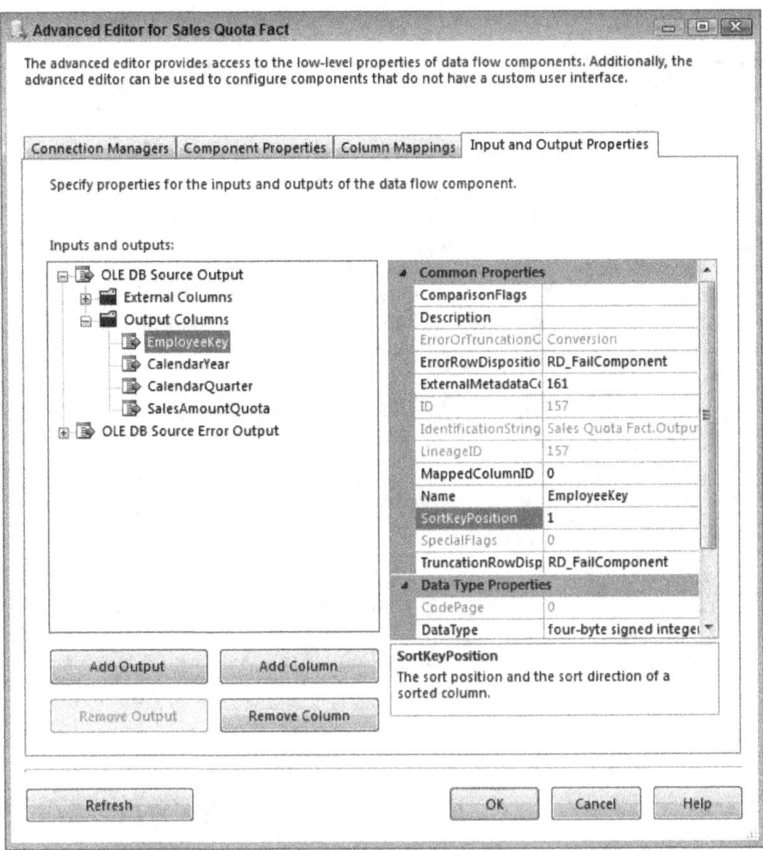

FIGURE 12-35

b. Select the CalendarYear column and change its SortKeyPosition to 2.

c. Select the CalendarQuarter column and change its SortKeyPosition to 3.

d. Click OK to save the changes to the advanced properties.

16. Add a Merge Join Transformation to the Data Flow. First, connect the blue data path output from the Sort Transformation onto the Merge Join. When prompted, choose the input option named Merge Join Left Input. Then connect the blue data path output from the Sales Quota Fact Source to the Merge Join.

17. Double-click the Merge Join Transformation to open its editor. You will see that the EmployeeKey, CalendarYear, and CalendarQuarter columns are already joined between inputs. Make the following changes, as shown in Figure 12-36:

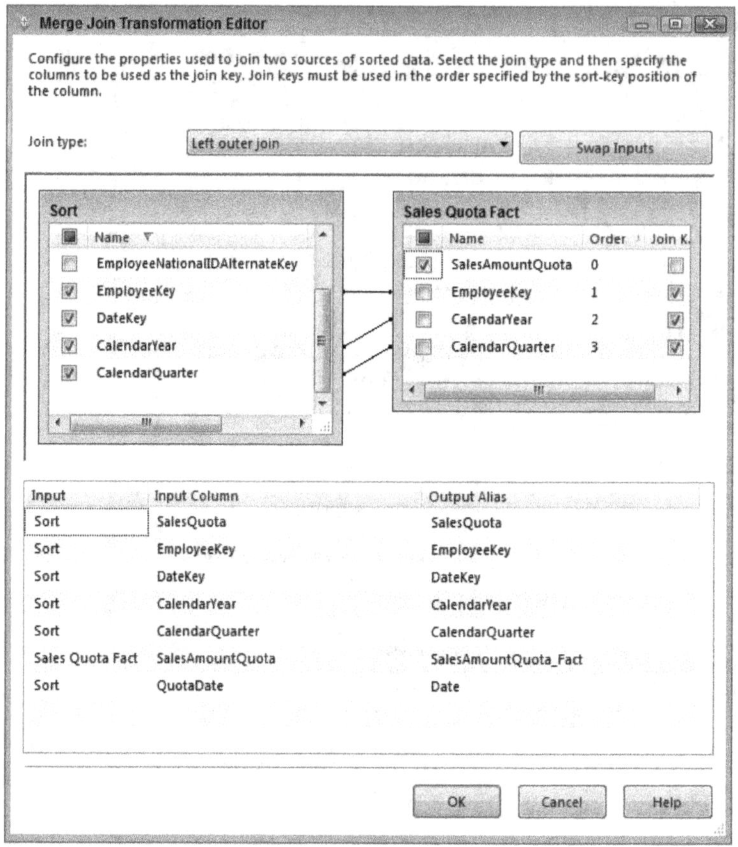

FIGURE 12-36

a. Change the Join type dropdown to a Left outer join.

b. Check the SalesQuota, EmployeeKey, DateKey, CalendarYear, CalendarQuarter, and QuotaDate columns from the Sort input list and then change the Output Alias for QuotaDate to Date.

c. Check the SalesAmountQuota from the Sales Quota Fact column list and then change the Output Alias for this column to SalesAmountQuota_Fact.

18. Click OK to save your Merge Join configuration.

19. Your next objective is to identify which records are new quotas and which are changed sales quotas. A conditional split will be used to accomplish this task; therefore, drag a Conditional Split Transformation onto the Data Flow and connect the blue data path output from the Merge Join Transformation to the Conditional Split. Rename the Conditional Split to **Identify Inserts and Updates**.

20. Double-click the Conditional Split to open the editor and make the following changes, as shown in Figure 12-37:

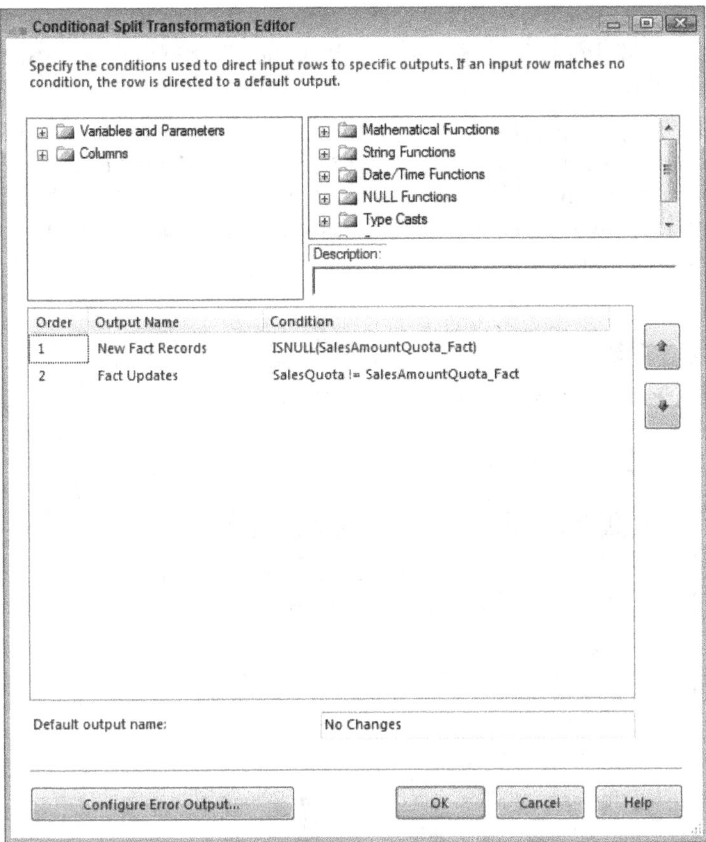

FIGURE 12-37

a. Add a new condition named **New Fact Records** with the following condition: `ISNULL([SalesAmountQuota_Fact])`. If the measure from the fact is null, it indicates that the fact record does not exist for the employee and date combination.

b. Add a second condition named **Fact Updates** with the following condition: `[SalesQuota] != [SalesAmountQuota_Fact]`.

c. Change the default output name to No Changes.

21. Click OK to save the changes to the Conditional Split.

22. Add an OLE DB Destination component to the Data Flow and name it **Fact Inserts.** Drag the blue data path output from the Conditional Split Transformation to the OLE DB Destination. When prompted to choose an output from the Conditional Split, choose the New Fact Records output.

23. Double-click the Fact Inserts Destination and change the OLE DB Connection Manager to AdventureWorksDW. In the "Name of the table or view" dropdown, choose the [dbo].[FactSalesQuota] table.

24. Switch to the Mappings property page and match up the SalesQuota column from the Available Input Columns list to the SalesAmountQuota in the Available Destinations column list, as shown in Figure 12-38. The other columns (EmployeeKey, DateKey, CalendarYear, and CalendarQuarter) should already match. Click OK to save your changes to the OLE DB Destination.

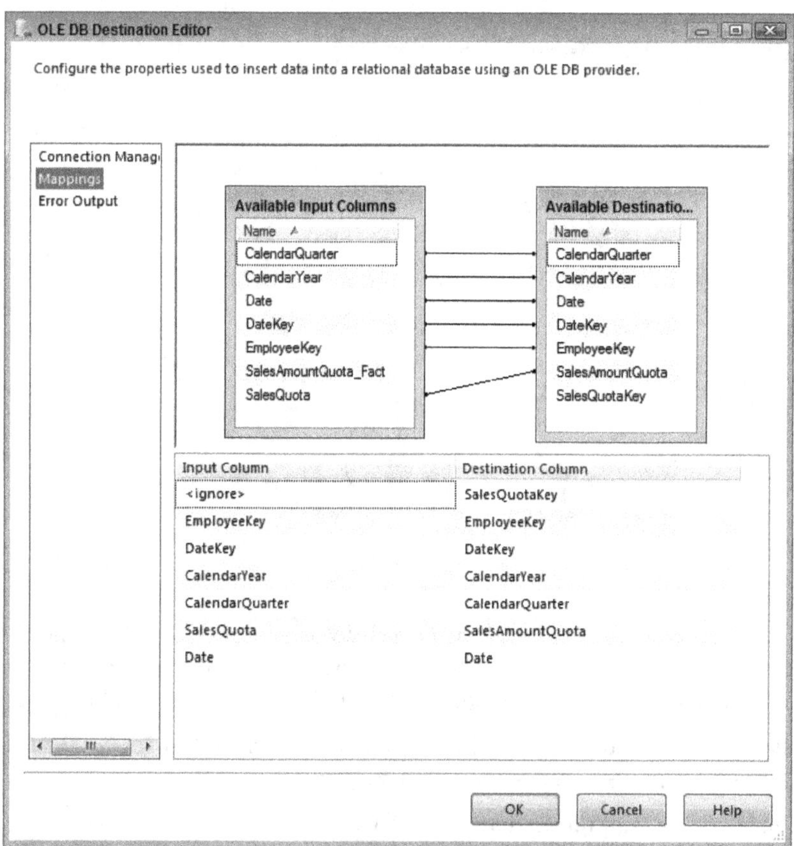

FIGURE 12-38

25. To handle the fact table updates, drag an OLE DB Command Transformation to the Data Flow and rename it **Fact Updates**. Drag the blue data path output from the Conditional Split onto the Fact Updates Transformation, and when prompted, choose the Fact Update output from the Conditional Split.

26. Double-click the OLE DB Command Transformation and change the Connection Manager dropdown to AdventureWorksDW. On the Component Properties tab, add the following code to the SQLCommand property (make sure you click the ellipsis button to open an editor window):

```
UPDATE dbo.FactSalesQuota
SET SalesAmountQuota = ?
WHERE EmployeeKey = ?
AND CalendarYear = ?
AND CalendarQuarter = ?
```

27. Switch to the Column Mappings tab and map the SalesQuota to Param_0, Employee_Key to Param_1, CalendarYear to Param_2, and CalendarQuarter to Param_3, as shown in Figure 12-39.

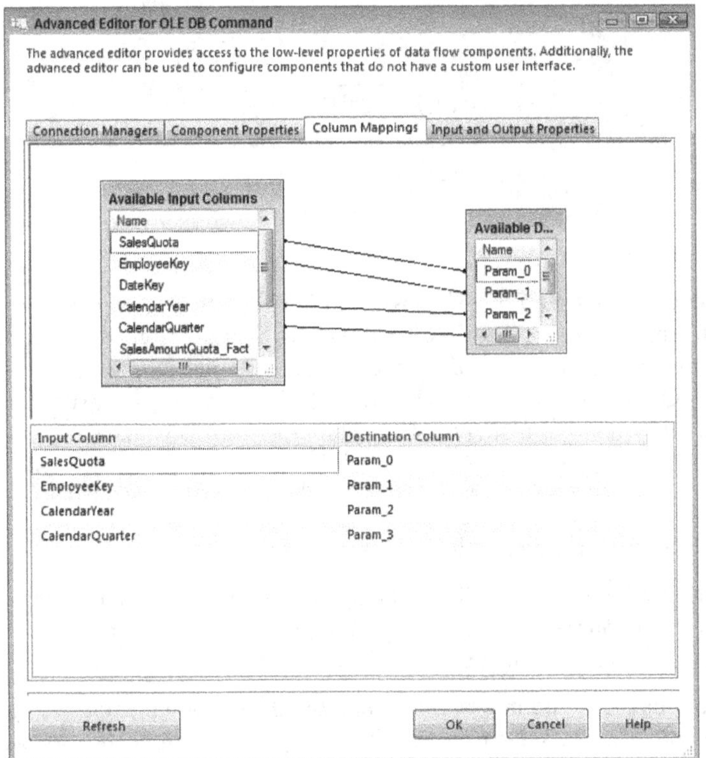

FIGURE 12-39

28. Click OK to save your changes to the OLE DB Command update. Your fact table ETL for the FactSalesQuota is complete and should look similar to Figure 12-40.

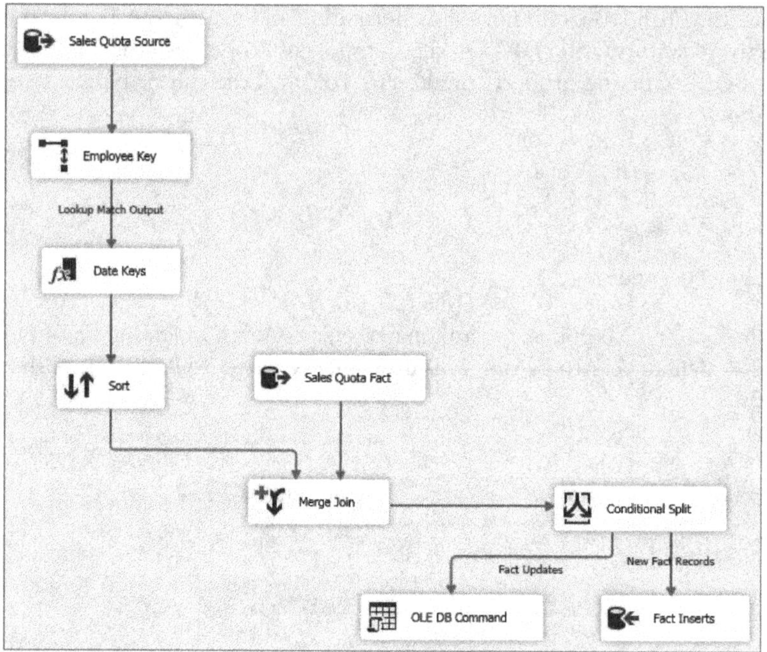

FIGURE 12-40

If you test this package out, you will find that the inserts fail. This is because the date dimension is populated through 2006, but several 2007 and 2008 dates exist that are needed for the fact table. For the purposes of this exercise, you can just drop the foreign key constraint on the table, which will enable your FactSalesQuota package to execute successfully. In reality, as part of your ETL, you would create a recurring script that populated the DateDim table with new dates:

```
ALTER TABLE [dbo].[FactSalesQuota] DROP CONSTRAINT [FK_FactSalesQuota_DimDate]
```

Here are some final considerations for fact table ETL:

- A Merge Join was used in this case to help identify which records were updates or inserts, based on matching the source to the fact table. Refer to the Chapter 7 to see other alternatives to associating the source to fact table.
- For the inserts and updates, you may want to leverage the relational engine to handle either the insert or the update at the same time. T-SQL in SQL Server supports a `MERGE` statement that will perform either an insert or an update depending on whether the record exists. See Chapter 13 for more about how to use this feature.
- Another alternative to the OLE DB Command fact table updates is to use a set-based update. The OLE DB command works well and is easy for small data volumes; however, your situation may not allow per-row updates. Consider staging the updates to a table and then performing a set-based update (through a multirow SQL `UPDATE` statement) by joining the staging table to the fact table and updating the sales quota that way.

- Inserts are another area of improvement considerations. Fact tables often contain millions of rows, so you should look for ways to optimize the inserts. Consider dropping the indexes, loading the fact table, and then recreating the indexes. This could be much faster. See Chapter 16 for ideas on how to tune the inserts.
- If you have partitions in place, you can insert the data right into the partitioned fact table; however, when you are dealing with high volumes, the relational engine overhead may inhibit performance. In these situations, consider switching the current partition out in order to load it separately, then you can switch it back into the partitioned table.

Inferred members are another challenge for fact table ETL. How do you handle a missing dimension key? One approach includes scanning the fact table source for missing keys and adding the inferred member dimension records before the fact table ETL runs. An alternative is to redirect the missing row when the lookup doesn't have a match, then add the dimension key during the ETL, followed by bringing the row back into the ETL through a Union All. One final approach is to handle the inferred members after the fact table ETL finishes. You would need to stage the records that have missing keys, add the inferred members, and then reprocess the staged records into the fact table.

As you can see, fact tables have some unique challenges, but overall they can be handled effectively with SSIS. Now that you have loaded both your dimensions and fact tables, the next step is to process your SSAS cubes, if SSAS is part of your data warehouse or business intelligence project.

SSAS PROCESSING

Processing SSAS objects in SSIS can be as easy as using the Analysis Services Processing Task. However, if your SSAS cubes require adding or processing specific partitions or changing the names of cubes or servers, then you will need to consider other approaches. In fact, many, if not most, solutions require using other processing methods.

SSAS in SQL Server 2014 has two types of models, multidimensional and tabular. Both of these models require processing. For multidimensional models, you are processing dimensions and cube partitions. For tabular models, you are processing tables and partitions. However, both models have similar processing options.

The primary ways to process SSAS models through SSIS include the following:

- **Analysis Services Processing Task:** Can be defined with a unique list of dimensions, tables, and partitions to process. However, this task does not allow modifications of the objects through expressions or configurations.
- **Analysis Services Execute DDL Task:** Can process objects through XMLA scripts. The advantage of this task is the capability to make the script dynamic by changing the script contents before it is executed.
- **Script Task:** Can use the API for SSAS, which is called AMO (or Analysis Management Objects). With AMO, you can create objects, copy objects, process objects, and so on.
- **Execute Process Task:** Can run `ascmd.exe`, which is the SSAS command-line tool that can run XMLA, MDX, and DMX queries. The advantage of the `ascmd.exe` tool is the capability to pass in parameters to a script that is run.

To demonstrate the use of some of these approaches, this next tutorial demonstrates processing a multidimensional model using the Analysis Services Processing Task to process the dimensions related to the sales quotas, and then the Analysis Services Execute DDL Task to handle processing of the partitions.

Before beginning these steps, create a new partition in SSAS for the Sales Targets Measure called **Sales_Quotas_2014**. This is for demonstration purposes. An XMLA script has been created and included in the downloadable content at `www.wrox.com/go/prossis2014` for this chapter called `Sales_Quotas_2014.xmla`.

1. In your SSIS project for this chapter, create a new package and rename it **SSAS_SalesTargets.dtsx**.
2. Since this is the only package that will be using the SSAS connection, you will create a package connection, rather than a project connection. Right-click in the Connection Managers window and choose New Analysis Services Connection. In the Add Analysis Services Connection Manager window, click the Edit button to bring up the connection properties, as shown in Figure 12-41.

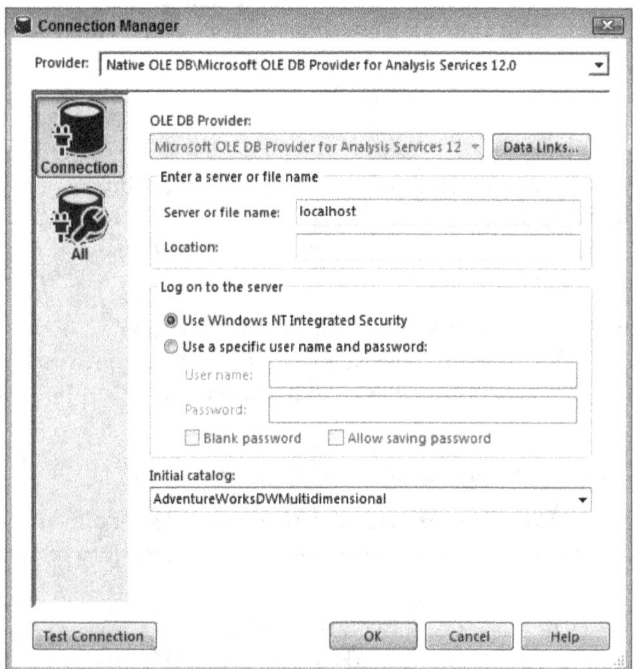

FIGURE 12-41

   a. Specify your server in the "Server or file name" text box (such as localhost if you are running SSAS on the same machine).
   b. Change the "Log on to the server" option to Use Windows NT Integrated Security.

c. In the Initial catalog dropdown box, choose the Adventure Works SSAS database, which by default is named Adventure Works DW Multidimensional. Please remember that you will need to download and install the sample SSAS cube database, which is available from `www.wrox.com/go/prossis2014`.

d. Click OK to save your changes to the Connection Manager and then click OK in the Add Analysis Services Connection Manager window.

e. Finally, rename the connection in the SSIS Connection Managers window to **AdventureWorksAS**.

3. To create the dimension processing, drag an Analysis Services Processing Task from the SSIS Toolbox onto the Control Flow and rename the task **Process Dimensions**.

4. Double-click the Process Dimensions Task to bring up the editor and navigate to the Processing Settings property page.

   a. Confirm that the Analysis Services Connection Manager dropdown is set to AdventureWorksAS.

   b. Click the Add button to open the Add Analysis Services Object window. As shown in Figure 12-42, check the Date, Employee, and Sales Territory dimensions and then click OK to save your changes.

   c. For each dimension, change the Process Options dropdown to Process Default, which will either perform a dimension update or, if the dimension has never been processed, fully process the dimension.

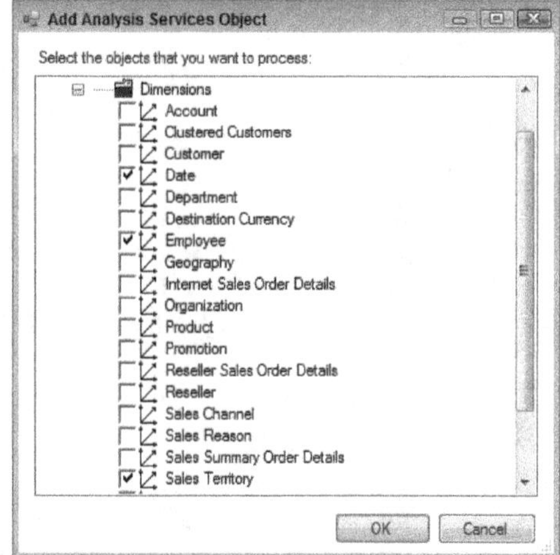

FIGURE 12-42

   d. Click the Change Settings button, and in the Change Settings editor, click the Parallel selection option under the Processing Order properties. Click OK to save your settings.

   e. Click OK to save your changes to the Analysis Services Processing Task.

5. Before continuing, you will create an SSIS package variable that designates the XMLA partition for processing. Name the SSIS variable **Sales_Quota_Partition** and define the variable with a String data type and a value of "Fact Sales Quota."

6. Drag an Analysis Services Execute DDL Task onto the Data Flow and drag the green precedence constraint from the Process Dimensions Task onto the Analysis Services Execute DDL Task. Rename the Analysis Services Execute DDL Task **Process Partition**.

   a. Edit the Process Partition Task and navigate to the DDL property page.

   b. Change the Connection property to AdventureWorksAS and leave the SourceType as Direct Input, as shown in Figure 12-43.

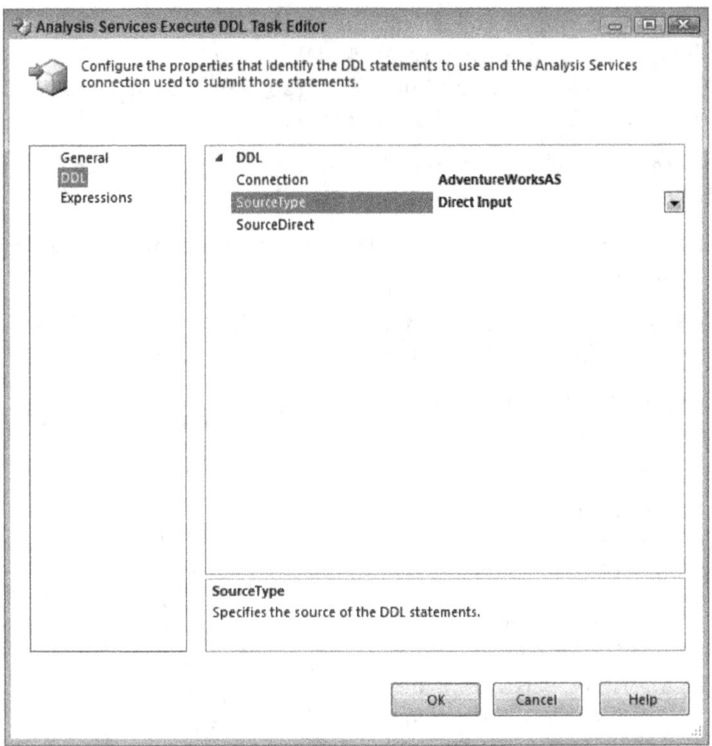

FIGURE 12-43

c. Change to the Expressions property page of the editor and click the Expressions property in the right window. Click the ellipsis on the right side of the text box, which will open the Property Expressions Editor. Choose Source from the dropdown, as shown in Figure 12-44.

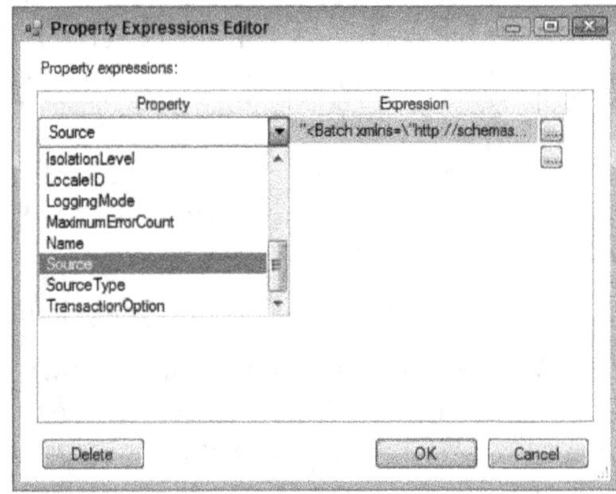

FIGURE 12-44

d. Now you need to add the XMLA code that will execute when the package is run. The expressions will dynamically update the code when this task executes. Click the ellipsis on the right side of the Source property (refer to Figure 12-44) to open Expression Builder.

e. Enter the following code in the Expression text box, which is also shown in Figure 12-45:

```
"<Batch xmlns=\"http://schemas.microsoft.com/analysisservices/2003/engine\">
  <Parallel>
    <Process>
      <Object>
        <DatabaseID>Adventure Works DW</DatabaseID>
        <CubeID>Adventure Works DW</CubeID>
        <MeasureGroupID>Fact Sales Quota</MeasureGroupID>
        <PartitionID>"
+ @[User::Sales_Quota_Partition]
+ "</PartitionID>
      </Object>
      <Type>ProcessFull</Type>

<WriteBackTableCreation>UseExisting</WriteBackTableCreation>
    </Process>
  </Parallel>
</Batch>"
"
```

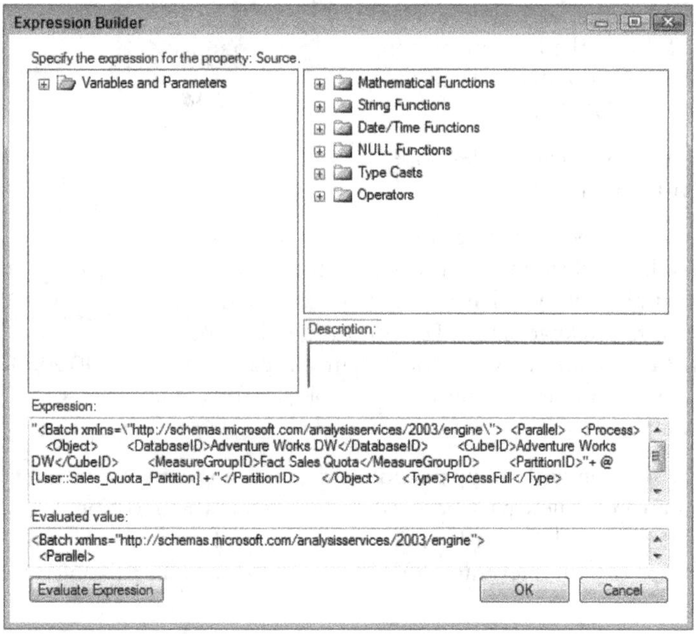

FIGURE 12-45

f. This code generates the XMLA and includes the `Sales_Quota_Partition` variable. The good news is that you don't need to know XMLA; you can use SSMS to generate it for you.

To automatically generate the XMLA code that will process a Sales Quota partition, open SSMS and connect to SSAS. Expand the Databases folder, then the Adventure Works SSAS database, then the Cubes folder; then expand the Adventure Works cube; and finally expand the Sales Targets measure group. Right-click the Sales Quota 2014 partition and choose Process, as shown in Figure 12-46.

The processing tool in SSMS looks very similar to the SSAS processing task in SSIS except that the SSMS processing tool has a Script button near the title bar. Click the Script button.

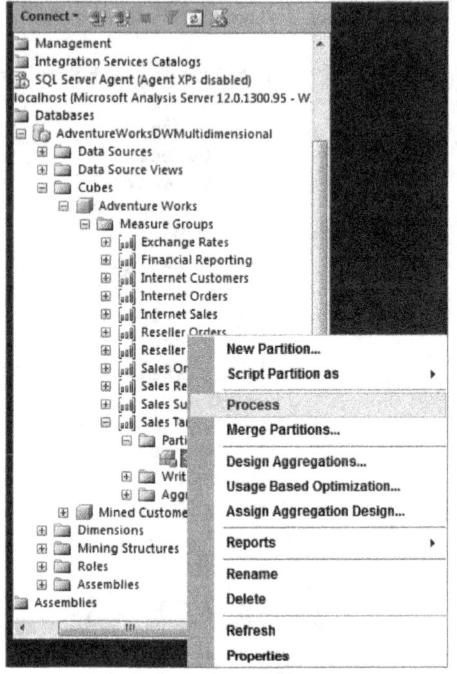

FIGURE 12-46

g. Click OK in the open windows to save your changes. The purpose of creating the script and saving the file is to illustrate that you can build your own processing with XMLA and either execute the code in SSMS (clicking on the Execute button) or execute the file through the Analysis Services Execute DDL Task.

7. The SSIS package that you have just developed should look similar to Figure 12-47.

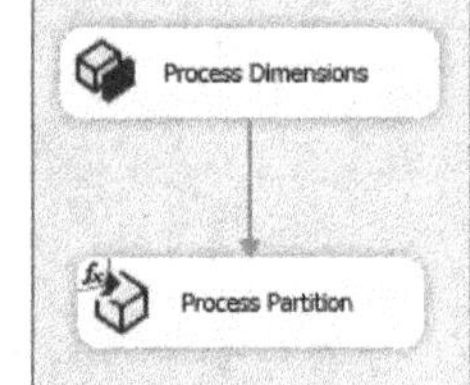

FIGURE 12-47

If you were to fully work out the development of this package, you would likely have a couple more tasks involved in the process. First, the current partition is entered in the variable, but you haven't yet put the code in place to update this variable when the package is run. For this task, either you could use an Execute SQL Task to pull the value for the current partition from a configuration table or the system date into the variable, or you could use a Script Task to populate the variable.

Second, if you have a larger solution with many partitions that are at the weekly or monthly grain, you would need a task that created a new partition, as needed, before the partition was run. This could be an Analysis Services Execute DDL Task similar to the one you just created for the processing Task, or you could use a Script Task and leverage AMO to create or copy an existing partition to a new partition.

As you have seen, processing SSAS objects in SSIS can require a few simple steps or several more complex steps depending on the processing needs of your SSAS solution.

USING A MASTER ETL PACKAGE

Putting it all together is perhaps the easiest part of the ETL process because it involves simply using SSIS to coordinate the execution of the packages in the required order.

The best practice to do this is to use a master package that executes the child packages, leveraging the Execute Package Task. The determination of precedence is a matter of understanding the overall ETL and the primary-to-foreign key relationships in the tables.

The following steps assume that you are building your solution using the project deployment model. With the project deployment model, you do not need to create connections to the other packages in the project. If you are instead deploying your packages to the file system, you need to create and configure File Connection Managers for each child package, as documented in SQL Server Books Online.

1. Create a new package in your project called **Master_ETL.dtsx.**
2. Drag an Execute Package Task from the SSIS Toolbox into the Control Flow.
3. Double-click the Execute Package Task to open the task editor.
4. On the Package property page, leave the ReferenceType property set to Project Reference. For the PackageNameFromProjectReference property, choose the ETL_DimSalesTerritory.dtsx package.

Your Execute Package Task will look like the one pictured in Figure 12-48.

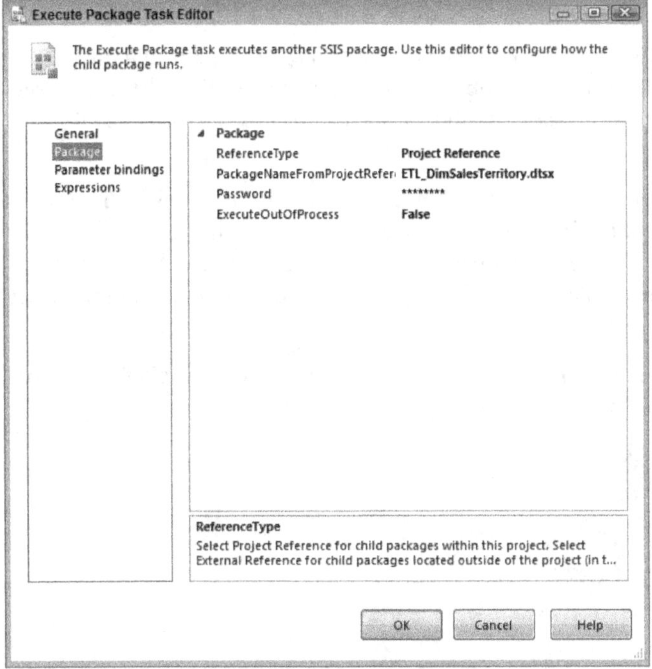

FIGURE 12-48

The ETL packages for the dimension tables are executed, followed by the fact table ETL and concluding with the cube processing. The master package for the examples in this chapter is shown in Figure 12-49.

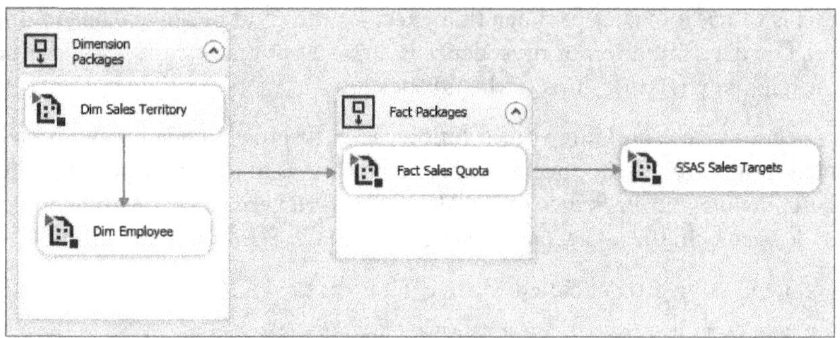

FIGURE 12-49

The related packages are grouped with Sequence containers to help visualize the processing order. In this case, the Dim Sales Territory package needs to be run before the Dim Employee package because of the foreign key reference in the DimEmployee table. Larger solutions will have multiple dimension and fact packages.

SUMMARY

Moving from start to finish in a data warehouse ETL effort requires a lot of planning and research. This research should include both data profiling and interviews with the business users to understand how they will be using the dimension attributes, so that you can identify the different attribute change types.

As you develop your dimension and fact packages, you will need to carefully consider how to most efficiently perform inserts and updates, paying particular attention to data changes and missing members. Finally, don't leave your SSAS processing packages for the last minute. You may be surprised at the time it can take to develop a flexible package that can dynamically handle selective partition processing and creation.

In the next chapter, you will learn about the pros and cons of using the relational engine instead of SSIS.

13

Using the Relational Engine

WHAT'S IN THIS CHAPTER?

- Using the relational engine to facilitate SSIS data extraction
- Loading data with SSIS and the relational engine
- Understanding when to use the relational engine versus SSIS

WROX.COM CODE DOWNLOADS FOR THIS CHAPTER

You can find the wrox.com code downloads for this chapter at `http://www.wrox.com/go/prossis2014` on the Download Code tab.

An old adage says that when you're holding a hammer, everything looks like a nail. When you use SSIS to build a solution, make sure that you use the right tool for each problem you tackle. SSIS will be excellent for some jobs, and SQL Server will shine at other tasks. When used in concert, the combination of the two can be powerful.

This chapter discusses other features in the SQL Server arsenal that can help you build robust and high-performance ETL solutions. The SQL Server relational database engine has many features that were designed with data loading in mind, and as such the engine and SSIS form a perfect marriage to extract, load, and transform your data.

This chapter assumes you are using SQL Server 2014 as the source system, though many of the same principles will apply to earlier versions of SQL Server and to other relational database systems too. You should also have the SQL Server 2014 versions of AdventureWorks and AdventureWorksDW installed; these are available from `www.wrox.com`.

The easiest way to understand how the relational database engine can help you design ETL solutions is to segment the topic into the three basic stages of ETL: extraction, transformation, and loading. Because the domain of transformation is mostly within SSIS itself, there is not much to say there about the relational database engine, so our scope of interest here is narrowed down to extraction and loading.

DATA EXTRACTION

Even if a data warehouse solution starts off simple — using one or two sources — it can rapidly become more complex when the users begin to realize the value of the solution and request that data from additional business applications be included in the process. More data increases the complexity of the solution, but it also increases the execution time of the ETL. Storage is certainly cheap today, but the size and amount of data are growing exponentially. If you have a fixed batch window of time in which you can load the data, it is essential to minimize the expense of all the operations. This section looks at ways of lowering the cost of extraction and how you can use those methods within SSIS.

SELECT * Is Bad

In an SSIS Data Flow, the OLE DB Source and ADO.NET Source Components allow you to select a table name that you want to load, which makes for a simple development experience but terrible runtime performance. At runtime the component issues a `SELECT * FROM «table»` command to SQL Server, which obediently returns every single column and row from the table.

This is a problem for several reasons:

- **CPU and I/O cost:** You typically need only a subset of the columns from the source table, so every extra column you ask for incurs processing overhead in all the subsystems it has to travel through in order to get to the destination. If the database is on a different server, then the layers include NTFS (the file system), the SQL Server storage engine, the query processor, TDS (tabular data stream, SQL Server's data protocol), TCP/IP, OLE DB, the SSIS Source component, and finally the SSIS pipeline (and probably a few other layers). Therefore, even if you are extracting only one redundant integer column of data from the source, once you multiply that cost by the number of rows and processing overhead, it quickly adds up. Saving just 5 percent on processing time can still help you reach your batch window target.
- **Robustness:** If the source table has ten columns today and your package requests all the data in a `SELECT *` manner, then if tomorrow the DBA adds another column to the source table, your package could break. Suddenly the package has an extra column that it doesn't know what to do with, things could go awry, and your Data Flows will need to be rebuilt.
- **Intentional design:** For maintenance, security, and self-documentation reasons, the required columns should be explicitly specified.
- **DBA 101:** If you are still not convinced, find any seasoned DBA, and he or she is likely to launch into a tirade of why `SELECT *` is the root of all evil.

As Figure 13-1 shows, the Source components also give you the option of using checkboxes to select or deselect the columns that you require, but the problem with this approach is that the filtering occurs on the client-side. In other words, all the columns are brought across (incurring all that I/O overhead), and then the deselected columns are deleted once they get to SSIS.

So what is the preferred way to extract data using these components? The simple answer is to forget that the table option exists and instead use only the query option. In addition, forget that the column checkboxes exist. For rapid development and prototyping these options may be useful, but for deployed solutions you should type in a query to only return the necessary columns. SSIS makes it simple to do this by providing a query builder in both the OLE DB and ADO.NET Source Components, which enables you to construct a query in a visual manner, as shown in Figure 13-2.

FIGURE 13-1

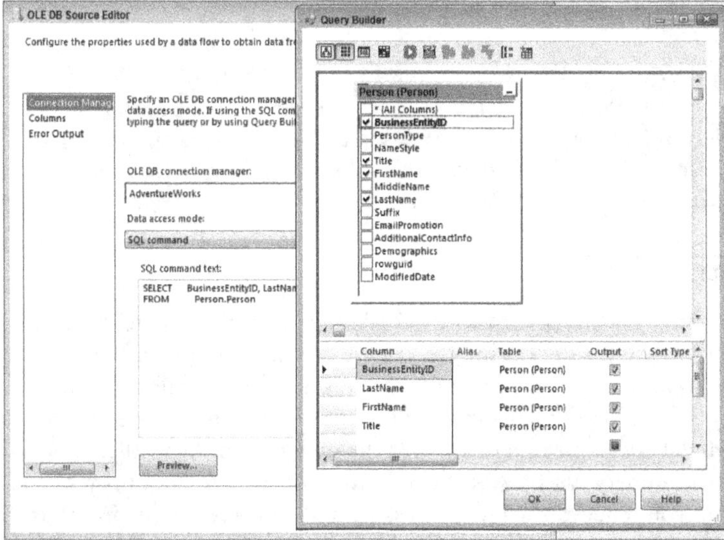

FIGURE 13-2

If you forget to use the query option or you use a `SELECT *` while using the query option and do not need the extraneous columns, SSIS will gently remind you during the execution of the package. The Data Flow Task's pipeline recognizes the unused columns and throws warning events when the package runs. These messages provide an easy way to verify your column listing and performance tune your package. When running the package in debug mode, you can see the messages on the Progress tab, as shown in Figure 13-3. An example full message states: "`[SSIS.Pipeline] Warning: The output column "PersonType" (31) on output "OLE DB Source Output" (29) and component "Table Option Source - Bad Practice" (18) is not subsequently used in the Data Flow task. Removing this unused output column can increase Data Flow task performance.`" This reminds you to remove the column `PersonType` from the source query to prevent the warning from reoccurring and affecting your future package executions.

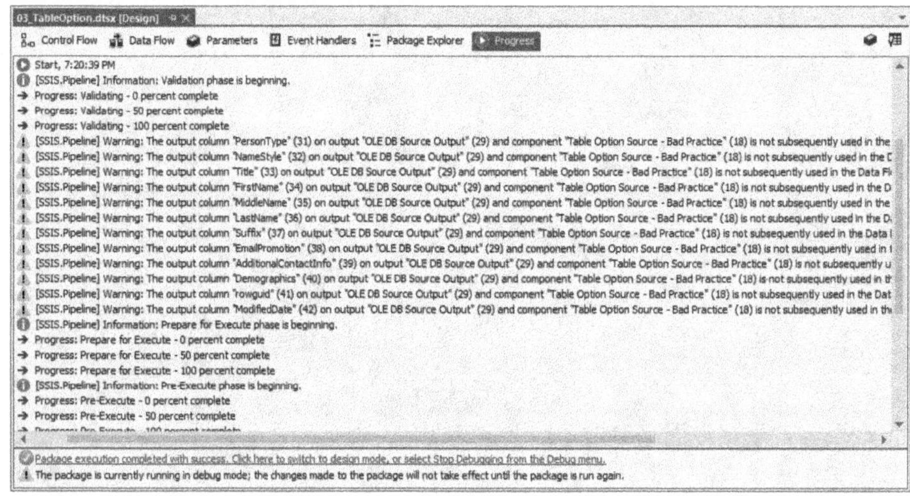

FIGURE 13-3

> **NOTE** *When using other SSIS sources, such as the Flat File Source, you do not have the option of selecting specific columns or rows with a query. Therefore, you will need to use the method of unchecking the columns to filter these sources.*

WHERE Is Your Friend

As an ancillary to the previous tenet, the `WHERE` clause (also called the query predicate) is one of the most useful tools you can use to increase performance. Again, the table option in the Source components does not allow you to narrow down the set of columns, nor does it allow you to limit the number of rows. If all you really need are the rows from the source system that are tagged with yesterday's date, then why stream every single other row over the wire just to throw them away once they get to SSIS? Instead, use a query with a `WHERE` clause to limit the number of rows being returned. As before, the less data you request, the less processing and I/O is required, and thus the faster your solution will be.

```
--BAD programming practice (returns 11 columns, 121,317 rows)
SELECT * FROM Sales.SalesOrderDetail;

--BETTER programming practice (returns 6 columns, 121,317 rows)
SELECT SalesOrderID, SalesOrderDetailID, OrderQty,
ProductID, UnitPrice, UnitPriceDiscount
FROM Sales.SalesOrderDetail;

--BEST programming practice (returns 6 columns, 79 rows)
SELECT SalesOrderID, SalesOrderDetailID, OrderQty,
ProductID, UnitPrice, UnitPriceDiscount
FROM Sales.SalesOrderDetail
WHERE ModifiedDate = '2008-07-01';
```

> **NOTE** *All code samples in this chapter are available as part of the Chapter 13 code download for the book at* `http://www.wrox.com/go/prossis2014.`

In case it is not clear, Figure 13-4 shows how you would use this `SELECT` statement (and the other queries discussed next) in the context of SSIS. Drop an OLE DB or ADO.NET Source Component onto the Data Flow design surface, point it at the source database (which is AdventureWorks in this case), select the SQL command option, and plug in the preceding query.

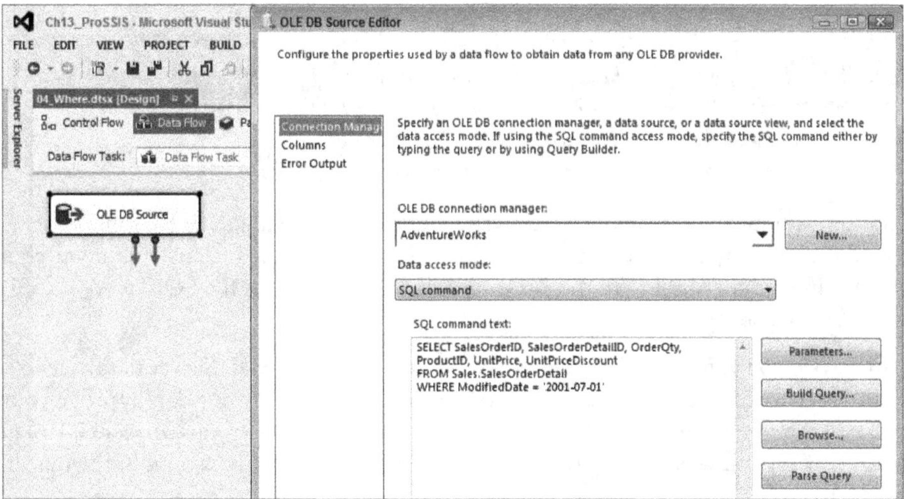

FIGURE 13-4

Transform during Extract

The basic message here is to do some of your transformations while you are extracting. This is not a viable approach for every single transformation you intend to do — especially if your ETL solution is used for compliance reasons, and you want to specifically log any errors in the data — but it does make sense for primitive operations, such as trimming whitespace, converting magic numbers to `NULL`s, sharpening data types, and even something as simple as providing a friendlier column name.

> **NOTE** *A magic number is a value used to represent the "unknown" or* `NULL` *value in some systems. This is generally considered bad database design practice; however, it is necessary in some systems that don't have the concept of a* `NULL` *state. For instance, you may be using a source database for which the data steward could not assign the value "Unknown" or* `NULL` *to, for example, a date column, so instead the operators plugged in* `1999/12/31`*, not expecting that one day the "magic number" would suddenly gain meaning!*
>
> *The practice of converting data values to the smallest type that can adequately represent them is called* data sharpening. *In one of the following examples, you convert a* `DECIMAL(37,0)` *value to* `BIT` *because the column only ever contains the values* `0` *or* `1`*, as it is more efficient to store and process the data in its smallest (sharpest) representation.*

Many data issues can be cleaned up as you're extracting the data, before it even gets to SSIS. This does not mean you physically fix the data in the source system (though that would be an ideal solution).

> **NOTE** *The best way to stop bad data from reaching your source system is to restrict the entry of the data in operational applications by adding validation checks, but that is a topic beyond the scope of this book.*

To fix the extraction data means you will need to write a query smart enough to fix some basic problems and send the clean data to the end user or the intended location, such as a data warehouse. If you know you are immediately going to fix dirty data in SSIS, fix it with the SQL query so SSIS receives it clean from the source.

By following this advice you can offload the simple cleanup work to the SQL Server database engine, and because it is very efficient at doing this type of set-based work, this can improve your ETL performance, as well as lower the package's complexity. A drawback of this approach is that data quality issues in your source systems are further hidden from the business, and hidden problems tend to not be fixed!

To demonstrate this concept, imagine you are pulling data from the following source schema. The problems demonstrated in this example are not merely illustrative; they reflect some real-world issues that the authors have seen.

COLUMN NAME	DATA TYPE	EXAMPLES	NOTES
CUSTOMER_ID	Decimal(8,0)	1, 2, 3	The values in this column are integers (4 bytes), but the source is declared as a decimal, which takes 5 bytes of storage per value.
CUSTOMER_NAME	Varchar(100)	"Contoso Traders__", "_XXX", "_Adventure Works", "_", "Acme Apples", "___", ""	The problem with this column is that where the customer name has not been provided, a blank string "" or "XXX" is used instead of NULL. There are also many leading and trailing blanks in the values (represented by "_" in the examples).
ACTIVE_IND	Decimal(38,0)	1, 0, 1, 1, 0	Whether by intention or mistake, this simple True/False value is represented by a 17-byte decimal!
LOAD_DATE	DateTime	"2000/1/1", "1972/05/27", "9999/12/31"	The only problem in this column is that unknown dates are represented using a magic number — in this case, "9999/12/31". In some systems dates are represented using text fields, which means the dates can be invalid or ambiguous.

If you retrieve the native data into SSIS from the source just described, it will obediently generate the corresponding pipeline structures to represent this data, including the multi-byte decimal `ACTIVE_IND` column that will only ever contain the values 1 or 0. Depending on the number of rows in the source, allowing this default behavior incurs a large amount of processing and storage overhead. All the data issues described previously will be brought through to SSIS, and you will have to fix them there. Of course, that may be your intention, but you could make your life easier by dealing with them as early as possible.

Here is the default query that you might design:

```
--Old Query
SELECT [BusinessEntityID]
      ,[FirstName]
      ,[EmailPromotion]
FROM [AdventureWorks].[Person].[Person]
```

You can improve the robustness, performance, and intention of the preceding query. In the spirit of the "right tool for the right job," you clean the data right inside the query so that SSIS receives it in a cleaner state. Again, you can use this query in a Source component, rather than use the table method or plug in a default `SELECT *` query:

```
--New Query
SELECT
  --Cast the ID to an Int and use a friendly name
  cast([BusinessEntityID] as int) as BusinessID
  --Trim whitespaces, convert empty strings to Null
  ,NULLIF(LTRIM(RTRIM(FirstName)), '') AS FirstName
  --Cast the Email Promotion to a bit
  ,cast((Case EmailPromotion When 0 Then 0 Else 1 End) as bit) as EmailPromoFlag
FROM [AdventureWorks].[Person].[Person]
--Only load the dates you need
Where [ModifiedDate] > '2008-12-31'
```

Let's look at what you have done here:

- First, you have cast the `BusinessEntityID` column to a 4-byte integer. You didn't do this conversion in the source database itself; you just converted its external projection. You also gave the column a friendlier name that your ETL developers many find easier to read and remember.
- Next, you trimmed all the leading and trailing whitespace from the `FirstName` column. If the column value were originally an empty string (or if after trimming it ended up being an empty string), then you convert it to NULL.
- You sharpened the `EmailPromotion` column to a Boolean (BIT) column and gave it a name that is simpler to understand.
- Finally, you added a `WHERE` clause in order to limit the number of rows.

What benefit did you gain? Well, because you did this conversion in the source extraction query, SSIS receives the data in a cleaner state than it was originally. Of course, there are bound to be other data quality issues that SSIS will need to deal with, but at least you can get the trivial ones out of the way while also improving basic performance. As far as SSIS is concerned, when it sets up the pipeline column structure, it will use the names and types represented by the query. For instance, it will believe the `IsActive` column is (and always has been) a `BIT` — it doesn't waste any time or space treating it as a 17-byte `DECIMAL`. When you execute the package, the data is transformed inside the SQL engine, and SSIS consumes it in the normal manner (albeit more efficiently because it is cleaner and sharper).

You also gave the columns friendlier names that your ETL developers may find more intuitive. This doesn't add to the performance, but it costs little and makes your packages easier to understand and maintain. If you are planning to use the data in a data warehouse and eventually in an Analysis Services cube, these friendly names will make your life much easier in your cube development.

The results of these queries running in a Data Flow in SSIS are very telling. The old query returns over 19,000 rows, and it took about 0.3 seconds on the test machine. The new query returned only a few dozen rows and took less than half the time of the old query. Imagine this was millions of rows or even billions of rows; the time savings would be quite significant. So query tuning should always be performed when developing SSIS Data Flows.

Many ANDs Make Light Work

OK, that is a bad pun, but it's also relevant. What this tenet means is that you should let the SQL engine combine different data sets for you where it makes sense. In technical terms, this means do any relevant `JOIN`s, `UNION`s, subqueries, and so on directly in the extraction query.

That does not mean you should use relational semantics to join rows from the source system to the destination system or across heterogeneous systems (even though that might be possible) because that will lead to tightly coupled and fragile ETL design. Instead, this means that if you have two or more tables in the same source database that you are intending to join using SSIS, then `JOIN` or `UNION` those tables together as part of the `SELECT` statement.

For example, you may want to extract data from two tables — SalesQ1 and SalesQ2 — in the same database. You could use two separate SSIS Source components, extract each table separately, then combine the two data streams in SSIS using a Union All Component, but a simpler way would be to use a single Source component that uses a relational `UNION ALL` operator to combine the two tables directly:

```
--Extraction query using UNION ALL
SELECT --Get data from Sales Q1
SalesOrderID,
SubTotal
FROM Sales.SalesQ1
UNION ALL --Combine Sales Q1 and Sales Q2
SELECT --Get data from Sales Q2
SalesOrderID,
SubTotal
FROM Sales.SalesQ2
```

Here is another example. In this case, you need information from both the Product and the Subcategory table. Instead of retrieving both tables separately into SSIS and joining them there, you issue a single query to SQL and ask it to `JOIN` the two tables for you (see Chapter 7 for more information):

```
--Extraction query using a JOIN
SELECT
p.ProductID,
p.[Name] AS ProductName,
p.Color AS ProductColor,
sc.ProductSubcategoryID,
sc.[Name] AS SubcategoryName
FROM Production.Product AS p
INNER JOIN --Join two tables together
Production.ProductSubcategory AS sc
ON p.ProductSubcategoryID = sc.ProductSubcategoryID;
```

SORT in the Database

SQL Server has intimate knowledge of the data stored in its tables, and as such it is highly efficient at operations such as sorting — especially when it has indexes to help it do the job. While SSIS allows you to sort data in the pipeline, you will find that for large data sets SQL Server is more proficient. As an example, you may need to retrieve data from a table, then immediately sort it so that a Merge Join Transformation can use it (the Merge Join Transformation requires pre-sorted inputs).

You could sort the data in SSIS by using the Sort Transformation, but if your data source is a relational database, you should try to sort the data directly during extraction in the SELECT clause. Here is an example:

```
--Extraction query using a JOIN and an ORDER BY
SELECT
p.ProductID,
p.[Name] AS ProductName,
p.Color AS ProductColor,
sc.ProductSubcategoryID,
sc.[Name] AS SubcategoryName
FROM
Production.Product AS p
INNER JOIN --Join two tables together
Production.ProductSubcategory AS sc
ON p.ProductSubcategoryID = sc.ProductSubcategoryID
ORDER BY --Sorting clause
p.ProductID,
sc.ProductSubcategoryID;
```

In this case, you are asking SQL Server to pre-sort the data so that it arrives in SSIS already sorted. Because SQL Server is more efficient at sorting large data sets than SSIS, this may give you a good performance boost. The Sort Transformation in SSIS must load all of the data in memory; therefore, it is a fully blocking asynchronous transform that should be avoided whenever possible. See Chapter 7 for more information on this.

Note that the OLE DB and ADO.NET Source Components submit queries to SQL Server in a pass-through manner — meaning they do not parse the query in any useful way themselves. The ramification is that the Source components will not know that the data is coming back sorted. To work around this problem, you need to tell the Source components that the data is ordered, by following these steps:

1. Right-click the Source component and choose Show Advanced Editor.
2. Select the Input and Output Properties tab and click the root node for the default output (not the error output). In the property grid on the right is a property called IsSorted. Change this to True. Setting the IsSorted property to true just tells the component that the data is pre-sorted, but it does not tell it in what order.
3. Next, select the columns that are being sorted on, and assign them values as follows: If the column is not sorted, the value should be zero. If the column is sorted in ascending order, the value should be positive. If the column is sorted in descending order, the value should be negative. The absolute value of the number should correspond to the column's position in the order list. For instance, if the query was sorted with ColumnA ascending, ColumnB descending, then you would assign the value 1 to ColumnA and the value -2 to ColumnB, with all other columns set to 0.
4. In Figure 13-5, the data is sorted by the ProductID column. Expand the Output Columns node under the default output node, and then select the ProductID column. In the property grid, set the SortKeyPosition value to 1. Now the Source component is aware that the query is returning a sorted data set; furthermore, it knows exactly which columns are used for the sorting. This sorting information will be passed downstream to the next tasks. The passing down of information allows you to use components like the Merge Join Transformation, which requires sorted inputs, without using an SSIS Sort Transformation in the Data Flow.

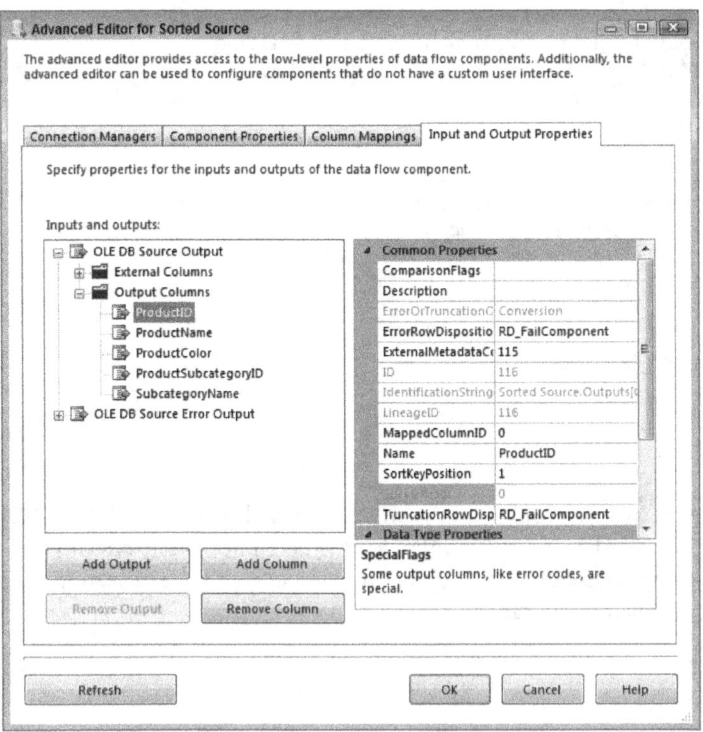

FIGURE 13-5

Be very careful when specifying the sort order — you are by contract telling the system to trust that you know what you are talking about, and that the data is in fact sorted. If the data is not sorted, or it is sorted in a manner other than you specified, then your package can act unpredictably, which could lead to data and integrity loss.

Modularize

If you find you have common queries that you keep using, then try to encapsulate those queries in the source system. This statement is based on ideal situations; in the real world you may not be allowed to touch the source system, but if you can, then there is a benefit. Encapsulating the queries in the source system entails creating views, procedures, and functions that read the data — you are not writing any data changes into the source. Once the (perhaps complex) queries are encapsulated in the source, your queries can be used in multiple packages by multiple ETL developers. Here is an example:

```
USE SourceSystemDatabase;
GO
CREATE PROCEDURE dbo.up_DimCustomerExtract(@date DATETIME)
-- Test harness (also the query statement you'd use in the SSIS source component):
-- Sample execution: EXEC dbo.up_DimCustomerExtract '2004-12-20';
AS BEGIN
  SET NOCOUNT ON;
  SELECT
    --Convert to INT and alias using a friendlier name
```

```
        Cast(CUSTOMER_ID as int) AS CustomerID
        --Trim whitespace, convert empty strings to NULL and alias
        ,NULLIF(LTRIM(RTRIM(CUSTOMER_NAME)), '') AS CustomerName
        --Convert to BIT and use friendly alias
        ,Cast(ACTIVE_IND as bit) AS IsActive
        ,CASE
          --Convert magic dates to NULL
          WHEN LOAD_DATE = '9999-12-31' THEN NULL
          --Convert date to smart surrogate number of form YYYYMMDD
          ELSE CONVERT(INT, (CONVERT(NVARCHAR(8), LOAD_DATE, 112)))
          --Alias using friendly name
        END AS LoadDateID
      FROM dbo.Customers
      --Filter rows using input parameter
      WHERE LOAD_DATE = @date;
      SET NOCOUNT OFF;
    END;
    GO
```

To use this stored procedure from SSIS, you would simply call it from within an OLE DB or ADO .NET Source Component. The example shows a static value for the date parameter, but in your solution you would use a variable or expression instead, so that you could call the procedure using different date values (see Chapter 5 for more details):

```
EXEC dbo.up_DimCustomerExtract '2013-12-20';
```

Here are some notes on the benefits you have gained here:

- In this case you have encapsulated the query in a stored procedure, though you could have encased it in a user-defined function or view just as easily. A side benefit is that this complex query definition is not hidden away in the depths of the SSIS package — you can easily access it using SQL Server.
- The benefit of a function or procedure is that you can simply pass a parameter to the module (in this case `@date`) in order to filter the data (study the `WHERE` clause in the preceding code). Note, however, that SSIS Source components have difficulty parsing parameters in functions, so you may need to use a procedure instead (which SSIS has no problems with), or you can build a dynamic query in SSIS to call the function (see Chapter 5 for more information).
- If the logic of this query changes — perhaps because you need to filter in a different way, or you need to point the query at an alternative set of tables — then you can simply change the definition in one place, and all the callers of the function will get the benefit. However, there is a risk here too: If you change the query by, for example, removing a column, then the packages consuming the function might break, because they are suddenly missing a column they previously expected. Make sure any such query updates go through a formal change management process in order to mitigate this risk.

SQL Server Does Text Files Too

It is a common pattern for source systems to export nightly batches of data into text files and for the ETL solution to pick up those batches and process them. This is typically done using a Flat File Source Component in SSIS, and in general you will find SSIS is the best tool for the job. However, in some cases you may want to treat the text file as a relational source and sort it, join it, or perform calculations on it in the manner described previously. Because the text file lives on disk, and it is a file not a database, this is not possible — or is it?

Actually, it is possible! SQL Server includes a table-valued function called `OPENROWSET` that is an ad hoc method of connecting and accessing remote data using OLE DB from within the SQL engine. In this context, you can use it to access text data, using the `OPENROWSET(BULK ...)` variation of the function.

> **NOTE** *Using the* `OPENROWSET` *and* `OPENQUERY` *statements has security ramifications, so they should be used with care in a controlled environment. If you want to test this functionality, you may need to enable the functions in the SQL Server Surface Area Configuration Tool. Alternatively, use the T-SQL configuration function as shown in the following code. Remember to turn this functionality off again after testing it (unless you have adequately mitigated any security risks). See Books Online for more information.*

```
sp_configure 'show advanced options', 1; --Show advanced configuration options
GO
RECONFIGURE;
GO
sp_configure 'Ad Hoc Distributed Queries', 1; --Switch on OPENROWSET functionality
GO
RECONFIGURE;
GO
sp_configure 'show advanced options', 0; --Remember to hide advanced options
GO
RECONFIGURE;
GO
```

The SQL Server documentation has loads of information about how to use these two functions, but the following basic example demonstrates the concepts. First create a text file with the following data in it. Use a comma to separate each column value. Save the text file using the name `BulkImport.txt` in a folder of your choice.

```
1,AdventureWorks
2,Acme Apples Inc
3,Contoso Traders
```

Next create a format file that will help SQL Server understand how your custom flat file is laid out. You can create the format file manually or you can have SQL Server generate it for you: Create a table in the database where you want to use the format file (you can delete the table later; it is just a shortcut to build the format file). Execute the following statement in SQL Server Management Studio — for this example, you are using the AdventureWorks database to create the table, but you can use any database because you will delete the table afterward. The table schema should match the layout of the file.

```
--Create temporary table to define the flat file schema
USE AdventureWorks
GO
CREATE TABLE BulkImport(ID INT, CustomerName NVARCHAR(50));
```

Now open a command prompt, navigate to the folder where you saved the `BulkImport.txt` file, and type the following command, replacing "AdventureWorks" with the database where you created the BulkImport table:

```
bcp AdventureWorks..BulkImport format nul -c -t , -x -f BulkImport.fmt -T
```

If you look in the folder where you created the data file, you should now have another file called `BulkImport.fmt`. This is an XML file that describes the column schema of your flat file — well, actually it describes the column schema of the table you created, but hopefully you created the table schema to match the file. Here is what the format file should look like:

```
<?xml version="1.0"?>
<BCPFORMAT xmlns="http://schemas.microsoft.com/sqlserver/2004/bulkload/format"
xmlns:xsi=http://www.w3.org/2001/XMLSchema-instance>
<RECORD>
<FIELD ID="1" xsi:type="CharTerm" TERMINATOR="," MAX_LENGTH="12"/>
<FIELD ID="2" xsi:type="CharTerm" TERMINATOR="\r\n" MAX_LENGTH="100"
COLLATION="SQL_Latin1_General_CP1_CI_AS"/>
</RECORD>
<ROW>
<COLUMN SOURCE="1" NAME="ID" xsi:type="SQLINT"/>
<COLUMN SOURCE="2" NAME="CustomerName" xsi:type="SQLNVARCHAR"/>
</ROW>
</BCPFORMAT>
```

Remember to delete the table (BulkImport) you created, because you don't need it anymore. If you have done everything right, you should now be able to use the text file in the context of a relational query. Type the following query into SQL Server Management Studio, replacing the file paths with the exact folder path and names of the two files you created:

```
--Select data from a text file as if it was a table
SELECT
T.* --SELECT * used for illustration purposes only
FROM OPENROWSET(--This is the magic function
BULK 'c:\ProSSIS\Data\Ch13\BulkImport.txt', --Path to data file
FORMATFILE = 'c:\ProSSIS\Data\Ch13\BulkImport.fmt' --Path to format file
) AS T; --Command requires a table alias
```

After executing this command, you should get back rows in the same format they would be if they had come from a relational table. To prove that SQL Server is treating this result set in the same manner it would treat any relational data, try using the results in the context of more complex operations such as sorting:

```
--Selecting from a text file and sorting the results
SELECT
T.OrgID, --Not using SELECT * anymore
T.OrgName
FROM OPENROWSET(
BULK 'c:\ProSSIS\Data\Ch13\BulkImport.txt',
FORMATFILE = 'c:\ProSSIS\Data\Ch13\BulkImport.fmt'
) AS T(OrgID, OrgName) --For fun, give the columns different aliases
ORDER BY T.OrgName DESC; --Sort the results in descending order
```

You can declare if and how the text file is pre-sorted. If the system that produced the text file did so in a sorted manner, then you can inform SQL Server of that fact. Note that this is a contract from you, the developer, to SQL Server. SQL Server uses something called a *streaming assertion* when reading the text file to double-check your claims, but in some cases this can greatly improve performance. Later you will see how this ordering contract helps with the MERGE operator, but here's a simple example to demonstrate the savings.

Run the following query. Note how you are asking for the data to be sorted by OrgID this time. Also note that you have asked SQL Server to show you the query plan that it uses to run the query:

```
SET STATISTICS PROFILE ON; --Show query plan
SELECT
T.OrgID,
T.OrgName
FROM OPENROWSET(
BULK 'c:\ProSSIS\Data\Ch13\BulkImport.txt',
FORMATFILE = 'c:\ProSSIS\Data\Ch13\BulkImport.fmt'
) AS T(OrgID, OrgName)
ORDER BY T.OrgID ASC; --Sort the results by OrgID
SET STATISTICS PROFILE OFF; --Hide query plan
```

Have a look at the following query plan that SQL Server generates. The query plan shows the internal operations SQL Server has to perform to generate the results. In particular, note the second operation, which is a SORT:

```
SELECT <...snipped...>
  |--Sort(ORDER BY:([BULK].[OrgID] ASC))
    |--Remote Scan(OBJECT:(STREAM))
```

This is obvious and expected; you asked SQL Server to sort the data, and it does so as requested. Here's the trick: In this case, the text file happened to be pre-sorted by OrgID anyway, so the sort you requested was actually redundant. (Note the text data file; the ID values increase monotonically from 1 to 3.)

To prove this, type the same query into SQL again, but this time use the OPENROWSET(... ORDER) clause:

```
SET STATISTICS PROFILE ON; --Show query plan
SELECT
T.OrgID,
T.OrgName
FROM OPENROWSET(
BULK 'c:\ProSSIS\Data\Ch13\BulkImport.txt',
FORMATFILE = 'c:\ProSSIS\Data\Ch13\BulkImport.fmt',
ORDER (OrgID ASC) --Declare the text file is already sorted by OrgID
)AS T(OrgID, OrgName)
ORDER BY T.OrgID ASC; --Sort the results by OrgID
SET STATISTICS PROFILE OFF; --Hide query plan
```

Once again you have asked for the data to be sorted, but you have also contractually declared that the source file is already pre-sorted. Have a look at the new query plan. Here's the interesting result: Even though you asked SQL Server to sort the result in the final ORDER BY clause, it didn't bother doing so because you indicated (and it confirmed) that the file was already ordered as such:

```
SELECT <...snipped...>
  |--Assert <...snipped...>
    |--Sequence Project(<...snipped...>)
      |--Segment
        |--Remote Scan(OBJECT:(STREAM))
```

As you can see, there is no SORT operation in the plan. There are other operators, but they are just inexpensive assertions that confirm the contract you specified is true. For instance, if a row arrived that was not ordered in the fashion you declared, the statement would fail. The streaming assertion check is cheaper than a redundant sort operation, and it is good logic to have in place in case you got the ordering wrong, or the source system one day starts outputting data in a different order than you expected.

So after all that, why is this useful to SSIS? Here are a few examples:

- You may intend to load a text file in SSIS and then immediately join it to a relational table. Now you could do all that within one `SELECT` statement, using a single OLE DB or ADO .NET Source Component.
- Some of the SSIS components expect sorted inputs (the Merge Join Component, for example). Assuming the source is a text file, rather than sort the data in SSIS you can sort it in SQL Server. If the text file happens to be pre-sorted, you can declare it as such and save even more time and expense.
- The Lookup Transformation can populate data from almost anywhere (see Chapter 7). This may still prove a useful technique in some scenarios.

> **WARNING** *Using* `OPENROWSET` *to select from a text file should be used only as a temporary solution, as it has many downfalls. First, there are no indexes on the file, so performance is going to be degraded severely. Second, if the sourcetype="warning" data file changes in structure (for instance, a column is dropped), and you don't keep the format file in sync, then the query will fail. Third, if the format file is deleted or corrupted, the query will also fail. This technique can be used when SSIS is not available or does not meet your needs. In most cases, loading the file into a table with SSIS and then querying that table will be your best option.*

Using Set-Based Logic

Cursors are infamous for being very slow. They usually perform row-by-row operations that are time-consuming. The SQL Server relational database engine, along with SSIS, performs much faster in set-based logic. The premise here is simple: Avoid any use of cursors like the plague. Cursors are nearly always avoidable, and they should be used only as a final resort. Try out the following features and see if they can help you build efficient T-SQL operations:

- Common table expressions (CTEs) enable you to modularize subsections of your queries, and they also support recursive constructs, so you can, for instance, retrieve a self-linked (parent-child) organizational hierarchy using a single SQL statement.
- Table-valued parameters enable you to pass arrays into stored procedures as variables. This means that you can program your stored procedure logic using the equivalent of dynamic arrays.
- `UNION` is now joined by its close cousins, `INTERSECT` and `EXCEPT`, which completes the primitive set of operations you need to perform set arithmetic. `UNION` joins two rowsets together, `INTERSECT` finds their common members, and `EXCEPT` finds the members that are present in one rowset but not the other.

The following example brings all these ideas together. In this example scenario, suppose you have two tables of data, both representing customers. The challenge is to group the data into three subsets: one set containing the customers who exist in the first table only, the second set containing customers who exist in the second table only, and the third set containing the customers who exist in both tables. The specific example illustrates the power and elegance of common table expressions (CTEs) and set-arithmetic statements. If you remember Venn diagrams from school, what you are trying to achieve is the relational equivalent of the diagram shown in Figure 13-6.

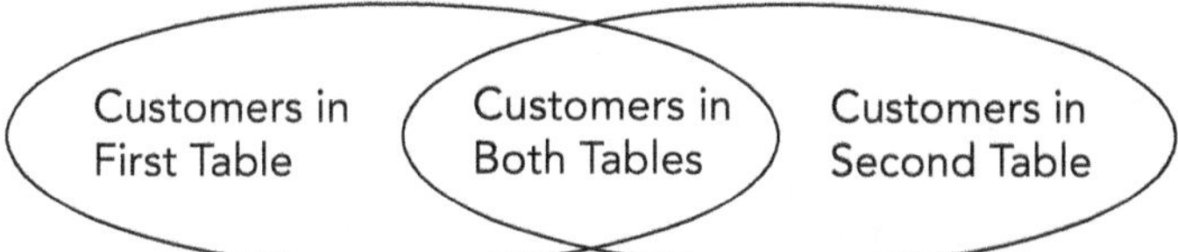

FIGURE 13-6

Following is a single statement that will partition the data as required. This statement is not meant to convey good programming practice, because it is not the most optimal or concise query you could write to derive these results. It is simply meant to demonstrate the manner in which these constructs can be used. By studying the verbose form, you can appreciate the elegance, composability, and self-documenting nature of the syntax.

For convenience you will use related tables from AdventureWorks and AdventureWorksDW. Note the use of multiple CTE structures to generate intermediate results (though the query optimizer is smart enough to not execute the statements separately). Also notice the use of `UNION`, `EXCEPT`, and `INTERSECT` to derive specific results:

```
WITH SourceRows AS ( --CTE containing all source rows
SELECT TOP 1000 AccountNumber
FROM AdventureWorks.Sales.Customer
ORDER BY AccountNumber
),
DestinationRows(AccountNumber) AS ( --CTE containing all destination rows
SELECT CustomerAlternateKey
FROM AdventureWorksDW.dbo.DimCustomer
),
RowsInSourceOnly AS ( --CTE: rows where AccountNumber is in source only
SELECT AccountNumber FROM SourceRows --select from previous CTE
EXCEPT --EXCEPT means 'subtract'
SELECT AccountNumber FROM DestinationRows --select from previous CTE
),
RowsInSourceAndDestination AS( --CTE: AccountNumber in both source & destination
SELECT AccountNumber FROM SourceRows
INTERSECT --INTERSECT means 'find the overlap'
SELECT AccountNumber FROM DestinationRows
),
RowsInDestinationOnly AS ( --CTE: AccountNumber in destination only
SELECT AccountNumber FROM DestinationRows
EXCEPT --Simply doing the EXCEPT the other way around
SELECT AccountNumber FROM SourceRows
),
```

```
RowLocation(AccountNumber, Location) AS ( --Final CTE
SELECT AccountNumber, 'Source Only' FROM RowsInSourceOnly
UNION ALL --UNION means 'add'
SELECT AccountNumber, 'Both' FROM RowsInSourceAndDestination
UNION ALL
SELECT AccountNumber, 'Destination Only' FROM RowsInDestinationOnly
)
SELECT * FROM RowLocation --Generate final result
ORDER BY AccountNumber;
```

Here is a sample of the results:

```
AccountNumber    Location
-----------    -----------
AW00000700     Source Only
AW00000701     Source Only
AW00011000     Both
. . .
AW00011298     Both
AW00011299     Destination Only
AW00011300     Destination Only
```

SQL Server provides many powerful tools for use in your data extraction arsenal. Learn about them and then start using the SQL Server relational database engine and SSIS in concert to deliver optimal extraction routines. The list presented previously is not exhaustive; you can use many other similar techniques to improve the value of the solutions you deliver.

DATA LOADING

This section focuses on data loading. Many of the same techniques presented in the data extraction section apply here too, so the focus is on areas that have not been covered before.

Database Snapshots

Database snapshots were introduced as a way to persist the state of a database at a specific point in time. The underlying technology is referred to as *copy-on-first-write*, which is a fancy way of saying that once you create the database snapshot, it is relatively cheap to maintain because it only tracks things that have changed since the database snapshot was created. Once you have created a database snapshot, you can change the primary database in any way — for instance, changing rows, creating indexes, and dropping tables. If at any stage you want to revert all your changes back to when you created the database snapshot, you can do that very easily by doing a database restore using the database snapshot as the media source.

In concept, the technology sounds very similar to backup and restore, the key difference being that this is a completely online operation, and depending on your data loads, the operations can be near instantaneous. This is because when you create the snapshot, it is a metadata operation only — you do not physically “back up” any data. When you “restore” the database from the snapshot, you do not restore all the data; rather, you restore only what has changed in the interim period.

This technique proves very useful in ETL when you want to prototype any data changes. You can create a package that makes any data changes you like, confident in the knowledge that you can easily roll back the database to a clean state in a short amount of time. Of course, you could achieve the same goals using backup and restore (or transactional semantics), but those methods typically have more overhead and/or take more time. Snapshots may also be a useful tool in operational ETL; you can imagine a scenario whereby a snapshot is taken before an ETL load and then if there are any problems, the data changes can be easily rolled back.

There is a performance overhead to using snapshots, because you can think of them as a "live" backup. Any activity on the source database incurs activity on the snapshot database, because the first change to any database page causes that page to be copied to the database snapshot. Any subsequent changes to the same page do not cause further copy operations but still have some overhead due to the writing to both source and snapshot. You need to test the performance overhead in the solutions you create, though you should expect to see an overhead of anywhere from 5 percent to 20 percent.

Because you are writing data to the destination database in this section, it is useful to create a database snapshot so you can roll back your changes very easily. Run this complete script:

```
--Use a snapshot to make it simple to rollback the DML
USE master;
GO
--To create a snapshot you need to close all other connections on the DB
ALTER DATABASE [AdventureWorksDW] SET SINGLE_USER WITH ROLLBACK IMMEDIATE;
ALTER DATABASE [AdventureWorksDW] SET MULTI_USER;
--Check if there is already a snapshot on this DB
IF EXISTS (SELECT [name] FROM sys.databases
WHERE [name] = N'AdventureWorksDW_Snapshot') BEGIN
--If so RESTORE the database from the snapshot
RESTORE DATABASE AdventureWorksDW
FROM DATABASE_SNAPSHOT = N'AdventureWorksDW_Snapshot';
--If there were no errors, drop the snapshot
IF @@error = 0 DROP DATABASE [AdventureWorksDW_Snapshot];
END; --if
--OK, let's create a new snapshot on the DB
CREATE DATABASE [AdventureWorksDW_Snapshot] ON (
NAME = N'AdventureWorksDW_Data',
--Make sure you specify a valid location for the snapshot file here
FILENAME = N'c:\ProSSIS\Data\Ch13\AdventureWorksDW_Data.ss')
AS SNAPSHOT OF [AdventureWorksDW];
GO
```

The script should take only a couple of seconds to run. It creates a database file in the specified folder that it tagged as being a snapshot of the AdventureWorksDW database. You can run the following command to list all the database snapshots on the server:

```
--List database snapshots
SELECT
d.[name] AS DatabaseName,
s.[name] AS SnapshotName
FROM sys.databases AS s
INNER JOIN sys.databases AS d
ON (s.source_database_id = d.database_id);
```

You should now have a snapshot called "AdventureWorksDW_Snapshot." This snapshot is your "live backup" of AdventureWorksDW. Once you have ensured that the database snapshot is in place, test its functionality by changing some data or metadata in AdventureWorksDW. For instance, you can create a new table in the database and insert a few rows:

```
--Create a new table and add some rows
USE AdventureWorksDW;
GO
CREATE TABLE dbo.TableToTestSnapshot(ID INT);
GO
INSERT INTO dbo.TableToTestSnapshot(ID) SELECT 1 UNION SELECT 2 UNION SELECT 3;
```

You can confirm the table is present in the database by running this statement. You should get back three rows:

```
--Confirm the table exists and has rows
SELECT * FROM dbo.TableToTestSnapshot;
```

Now you can test the snapshot rollback functionality. Imagine that the change you made to the database had much more impact than just creating a new table (perhaps you dropped the complete sales transaction table, for instance) and you now want to roll the changes back. Execute the same script that you used to originally create the snapshot; you will notice that the script includes a check to ensure that the snapshot exists; then, if so, it issues a `RESTORE ... FROM DATABASE_SNAPSHOT` command.

After running the script, try running the `SELECT` command again that returned the three rows. You should get an error saying the table "TableToTestSnapshot" does not exist. This is good news; the database has been restored to its previous state! Of course, this same logic applies whether you created a table or dropped one, added or deleted rows, or performed just about any other operation. The really cool benefit is that it should have taken only a couple of seconds to run this "live restore."

As part of the original snapshot script, the database was rolled back, but the script should also have created a new snapshot in the old one's place. Make sure the snapshot is present before continuing with the next sections, because you want to make it simple to roll back any changes you make.

Not only can you use database snapshots for prototyping, you can add tasks to your regularly occurring ETL jobs to create the snapshots — and even restore them if needed! A solution that uses this methodology is robust enough to correct its own mistakes and can be part of an enterprise data warehouse solution.

The MERGE Operator

If your source data table is conveniently partitioned into data you want to insert, data you want to delete, and data you want to update, then it is simple to use the `INSERT`, `UPDATE`, and `DELETE` statements to perform the respective operations. However, it is often the case that the data is not presented to you in this format. More often than not you have a source system with a range of data that needs to be loaded, but you have no way of distinguishing which rows should be applied in which way. The source contains a mix of new, updated, and unchanged rows.

One way you can solve this problem is to build logic that compares each incoming row with the destination table, using a Lookup Transformation (see Chapter 7 for more information). Another way to do this would be to use Change Data Capture (see Chapter 11 for more information) to tell you explicitly which rows and columns were changed, and in what way.

There are many other ways of doing this too, but if none of these methods are suitable, you have an alternative, which comes in the form of the T-SQL operator called MERGE (also known in some circles as "upsert" because of its mixed Update/Insert behavior).

The MERGE statement is similar in usage to the INSERT, UPDATE, and DELETE statements; however, it is more useful in that it can perform all three of their duties within the same operation. Here is pseudocode to represent how it works; after this you will delve into the real syntax and try some examples:

```
MERGE INTO Destination
Using these semantics:
{
<all actions optional>
If a row in the Destination matches a row in the Source then: UPDATE
If a row exists in the Source but not in the Destination then: INSERT
If a row exists in the Destination but not in the Source then: DELETE
}
FROM Source;
```

As you can see, you can issue a single statement to SQL Server, and it is able to figure out on a row-by-row basis which rows should be INSERT-ed, UPDATE-ed, and DELETE-ed in the destination. This can provide a huge time savings compared to doing it the old way: issuing two or three separate statements to achieve the same goal. Note that SQL Server is not just cleverly rewriting the MERGE query back into INSERT and UPDATE statements behind the scenes; this functionality is a DML primitive deep within the SQL core engine, and as such it is highly efficient.

Now you are going to apply this knowledge to a real set of tables. In the extraction section of this chapter you used customer data from AdventureWorks and compared it to data in AdventureWorksDW. There were some rows that occurred in both tables, some rows that were only in the source, and some rows that were only in the destination. You will now use MERGE to synchronize the rows from AdventureWorks to AdventureWorksDW so that both tables contain the same data.

This is not a real-world scenario because you would not typically write rows directly from the source to the destination without cleaning and shaping the data in an ETL tool like SSIS, but for the sake of convenience the example demonstrates the concepts.

First, you need to add a new column to the destination table so you can see what happens after you run the statement. This is not something you would need to do in the real solution.

```
USE AdventureWorksDW;
GO
--Add a column to the destination table to help us track what happened
--You would not do this in a real solution, this just helps the example
ALTER TABLE dbo.DimCustomer ADD Operation NVARCHAR(10);
GO
```

Now you can run the MERGE statement. The code is commented to explain what it does. The destination data is updated from the source in the manner specified by the various options. There are blank lines between each main section of the command to improve readability, but keep in mind that this is a single statement:

```
USE AdventureWorksDW;
GO
--Merge rows from source into the destination
MERGE
--Define the destination table
INTO AdventureWorksDW.dbo.DimCustomer AS [Dest] --Friendly alias
--Define the source query
USING (
SELECT AccountNumber AS CustomerAlternateKey,
--Keep example simple by using just a few data columns
p.FirstName,
p.LastName
FROM AdventureWorks.Sales.Customer c
INNER JOIN AdventureWorks.Person.Person p on c.PersonID=p.BusinessEntityID
) AS [Source] --Friendly alias
--Define the join criteria (how SQL matches source/destination rows)
ON [Dest].CustomerAlternateKey = [Source].CustomerAlternateKey

--If the same key is found in both the source & destination
WHEN MATCHED
--For *illustration* purposes, only update every second row
--AND CustomerAlternateKey % 2 = 0
--Then update data values in the destination
THEN UPDATE SET
[Dest].FirstName  = [Source].FirstName ,
[Dest].LastName = [Source].LastName,
[Dest].Operation = N'Updated'
--Note: <WHERE CustomerAlternateKey =…> clause is implicit

--If a key is in the source but not in the destination
WHEN NOT MATCHED BY TARGET
--Then insert row into the destination
THEN INSERT
(
GeographyKey, CustomerAlternateKey, FirstName,
LastName, DateFirstPurchase, Operation
)
VALUES
(
1, [Source].CustomerAlternateKey, [Source].FirstName,
[Source].LastName, GETDATE(), N'Inserted'
)

--If a key is in the destination but not in the source…
WHEN NOT MATCHED BY SOURCE
--Then do something relevant, say, flagging a status field
THEN UPDATE SET
[Dest].Operation = N'Deleted';
--Note: <WHERE ContactID =…> clause is implicit
--Alternatively you could have deleted the destination row
--but in AdventureWorksDW that would fail due to FK constraints
--WHEN NOT MATCHED BY SOURCE THEN DELETE;
GO
```

After running the statement, you should get a message in the query output pane telling you how many rows were affected:

```
(19119 row(s) affected)
```

You can now check the results of the operation by looking at the data in the destination table. If you scroll through the results you should see each row's `Operation` column populated with the operation that was applied to it:

```
--Have a look at the results
SELECT CustomerAlternateKey, DateFirstPurchase, Operation
FROM AdventureWorksDW.dbo.DimCustomer;
```

Here is a subset of the results. For clarity, the different groups of rows have been separated in this book by blank lines:

```
CustomerAlternateKey DateFirstPurchase       Operation
-------------------- ----------------------- -----------
AW00019975           2002-04-11 00:00:00.000 NULL
AW00019976           2003-11-27 00:00:00.000 Updated
AW00019977           2002-04-26 00:00:00.000 NULL

AW00019978           2002-04-20 00:00:00.000 Deleted
AW00019979           2002-04-22 00:00:00.000 Deleted

AW00008000           2008-02-24 20:48:12.010 Inserted
AW00005229           2008-02-24 20:48:12.010 Inserted
AW00001809           2008-02-24 20:48:12.010 Inserted
```

As you can see, a single `MERGE` statement has inserted, updated, and deleted rows in the destination in the context of just one operation. The reason why some of the updates could show a `NULL` operation is if a predicate was used in the `WHEN MATCHED` section to only `UPDATE` every second row.

Note that the source query can retrieve data from a different database (as per the example); furthermore, it can even retrieve data using the `OPENROWSET()` function you read about earlier. However, `MERGE` requires sorting the source data stream on the join key; SQL Server will automatically sort the source data for you if required, so ensure that the appropriate indexes are in place for a more optimal experience. These indexes should be on the join key columns. Do not confuse this operator with the Merge Join Transformation in SSIS.

If the source query happens to be of the form `OPENROWSET(BULK...)` — in other words, you are reading from a text file — then make sure you have specified any intrinsic sort order that the text file may already have. If the text file is already sorted in the same manner as the order required for `MERGE` (or you can ask the source extract system to do so), then SQL is smart enough to not incur a redundant sort operation.

The `MERGE` operator is a very powerful technique for improving mixed-operation data loads, but how do you use it in the context of SSIS?

If you do not have the benefit of Change Data Capture (discussed in Chapter 11) and the data sizes are too large to use the Lookup Transformation in an efficient manner (see Chapter 7), then you may have to extract your data from the source, clean and shape it in SSIS, and then dump the results to a staging table in SQL Server. From the staging table, you now need to apply the rows against the true destination table. You could certainly do this using two or three separate `INSERT`, `UPDATE`, and `DELETE` statements — with each statement `JOIN`-ing the staging table and the destination table together in order to compare the respective row and column values. However, you can now use a `MERGE` statement instead. The `MERGE` operation is more efficient than running the separate statements, and it is more intentional and elegant to develop and maintain. This is also more efficient with larger data sets than the SCD wizard and its OLE DB Command Transformation approach.

Make sure you execute the original snapshot script again in order to undo the changes you made in the destination database.

SUMMARY

As this chapter has shown, you can take advantage of many opportunities to use SQL in concert with SSIS in your ETL solution. The ideas presented in this chapter are not exhaustive; many other ways exist to increase your return on investment using the Microsoft data platform. Every time you find a way to use a tool optimized for the task at hand, you can lower your costs and improve your efficiencies. There are tasks that SSIS is much better at doing than the SQL Server relational database engine, but the opposite statement applies too. Make sure you think about which tool will provide the best solution when building ETL solutions; the best solutions often utilize a combination of the complete SQL Server business intelligence stack.

14

Accessing Heterogeneous Data

WHAT'S IN THIS CHAPTER?

- Dealing with Excel and Access data
- Integrating with Oracle
- Working with XML files and web services
- Extracting from flat files
- Integrating with ODBC

WROX.COM CODE DOWNLOADS FOR THIS CHAPTER

You can find the wrox.com code downloads for this chapter at `http://www.wrox.com/go/prossis2014` on the Download Code tab.

In this chapter, you will learn about importing and working with data from heterogeneous, or various non–SQL Server, sources. In today's enterprise environments, data may exist in many diverse systems, such as Oracle, DB2, Teradata, SQL Azure, SQL Parallel Data Warehouse (PDW), Office documents, XML, or flat files, to name just a few. The data may be generated within the company, or it may be delivered through the Internet from a trading partner. Whether you need to import data from a spreadsheet to initially populate a table in a new database application or pull data from other sources for your data warehouse, accessing heterogeneous data is probably a big part of your job.

You can load data into SQL Server using SSIS through any ODBC-compliant, OLE DB–compliant, or ADO.NET managed source. Many ODBC, OLE DB, and .NET providers are supplied by Microsoft for sources like Excel, Access, DB2, FoxPro, Sybase, Oracle, Teradata, and dBase. Others are available from database vendors. A variety of Data Source Components are found in SSIS. These include Excel, Flat File, XML, ADO.NET (which is used to connect to .NET Sources), OLE DB (which allows connections to many different types of data), and Raw File (a special source used to read data that has been previously exported to a Raw File Destination). If the supplied Data Sources do not meet your needs, you can also create custom Data Sources.

SSIS can consume many of these sources from out-of-the-box features. In addition, Microsoft has also provided a set of free downloads in the SQL Server feature pack for advanced data source extraction. They include a set of source components from Attunity, third-party components that Microsoft has licensed for use with SSIS. The Attunity connectors allow advanced sourcing from Oracle (with bulk load capabilities), Teradata, and ODBC sources.

Figure 14-1 highlights the Source Assistant within the Data Flow Toolbox. It shows the various source options within SSIS. Many of them require the installation of a client tool; the gray information window at the bottom of the figure describes where to find the additional application if required.

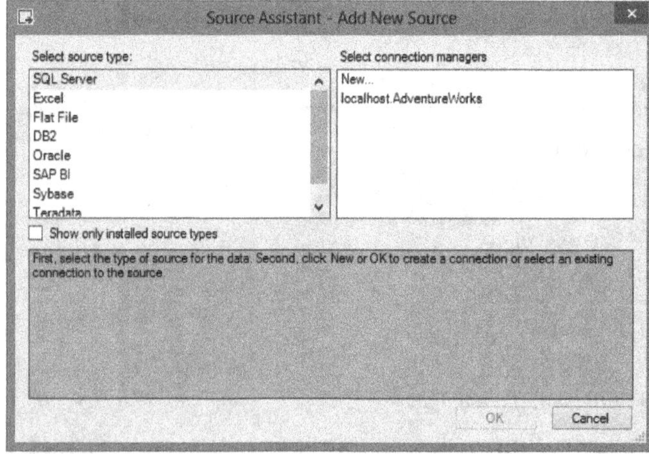

FIGURE 14-1

This chapter begins with the built-in features and walks you through accessing data from several of the most common sources. In addition to working in SSIS, you will become familiar with the differences between 32-bit and 64-bit drivers, as well as the client tools you need to install for the provider for DB2, Oracle, SAP BI, and Teradata, as available from those websites. This chapter targets the following sources:

- **Excel and MS Access (versions 2013 and earlier):** Excel is often used as a quick way to store data because spreadsheets are easy to set up and use. Access applications are frequently upsized to SQL Server as the size of the database and number of users increase.
- **Oracle:** Even companies running their business on Oracle or another of SQL Server's competitors sometimes make use of SQL Server because of its cost-effective reporting and business intelligence solutions.

- **XML and Web Services:** XML and web services (which is XML delivered through HTTP) are standards that enable very diverse systems to share data. The XML Data Source enables you to work with XML as you would with almost any other source of data.
- **Flat Files:** Beyond just standard delimited files, SSIS can parse flat files of various types and code page encoding, which allows files to be received from and exported to different operating systems and non-Windows-based systems. This reduces the need to convert flat files before or after working with them in SSIS.
- **ODBC:** Many organizations maintain older systems that use legacy ODBC providers for data access. Because of the complexities and cost of migrating systems to newer versions, ODBC is still a common source.
- **Teradata:** Teradata is a data warehouse database engine that scales out on multiple nodes. Large organizations that can afford Teradata's licensing and ongoing support fees often use it for centralized warehouse solutions.
- **Other Heterogeneous Sources:** The sources listed previously are the most common; however, this only touches on the extent of Data Sources that SSIS can access. The last section of this chapter provides third-party resources for when you are trying to access other sources such as SAP or Sybase.

EXCEL AND ACCESS

SSIS deals with Excel and Access data in a similar fashion because they use the same underlying provider technology for data access. For Microsoft Office 2003 and earlier, the data storage technology is called the JET Engine, which stands for Join Engine Technology; therefore, when you access these legacy releases of Excel or Access, you will be using the JET OLE DB Provider (32-bit only).

Office 2007 introduced a new engine called ACE that is essentially a newer version of the JET but supports the new file formats of Excel and Access. ACE stands for Access Engine and is used for Office 2007 and later. In addition, with the release of Office 2010, Microsoft provided a 64-bit version of the ACE provider. You will find both the 32-bit and 64-bit drivers under the name "Microsoft Office 12.0 Access Database Engine OLE DB Provider" in the OLE DB provider list. Therefore, when connecting to Access or Excel in these versions, you will use the ACE OLE DB Provider. If you have the 64-bit version of Office 2010 or 2013 installed, the next section will also review working with the 32-bit provider, because it can be confusing.

Later in this section you will learn how to connect to both Access and Excel for both the JET and ACE engines.

64-Bit Support

In older versions of Office (Office 2007 and earlier), only a 32-bit driver was available. That meant if you wanted to extract data from Excel or Access, you had to run SSIS in 32-bit mode. Beginning with Office 2010, however, a 64-bit version of the Office documents became available that enables you to extract data from Excel and Access using SSIS on a 64-bit server in native mode. In order to use the 64-bit versions of the ACE engine, you need to install the 64-bit access provider either by installing the 64-bit version of Microsoft Office 2010 or later or by installing the 64-bit driver from Microsoft's download site: `http://www.microsoft.com/en-us/download/details.aspx?id=39358`.

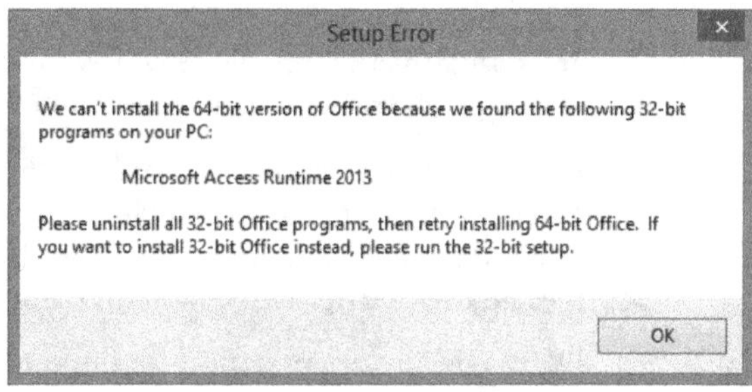

FIGURE 14-2

However, even though a 64-bit version of the ACE provider is available, you cannot develop packages with the 64-bit driver. This is because Visual Studio is a 32-bit application and is unable to see a 64-bit driver. With ACE, if you try to install both 32-bit and 64-bit, you will receive the error shown in Figure 14-2.

Therefore, the 64-bit driver can be used for a test or production server where packages are not executed through the design-time environment. The approach to using the 64-bit driver is to design your package with the 32-bit driver and then deploy your package to a server that has the 64-bit ACE driver installed.

To be sure, SSIS can run natively on a 64-bit machine (just like it can on a 32-bit machine). This means that when the operating system is running the X64 version of Windows Server 2003, Windows 7, Windows 8, Windows Server 2008, or a future version of Windows Server, you can natively install and run SQL Server in the X64 architecture (an IA64 Itanium build is also available from Microsoft support). When you execute a package in either 64-bit or 32-bit mode, the driver needs to either work in both execution environments or, like the ACE provider, have the right version for either the 32-bit or 64-bit execution mode.

When you install SSIS with the native X64 installation bits, you also get the 32-bit runtime executables that you can use to run packages that need access to 32-bit drivers not supported in the 64-bit environment. When working on a 64-bit machine, you can run packages in 32-bit emulation mode through the SSDT design environment and through the 32-bit version of DTExec. In addition, when using the SSIS Server Catalog in SQL 2014, you are also able to run packages in 32-bit or 64-bit mode.

Here are the details:

- **Visual Studio 2012:** By default, when you are in a native 64-bit environment and you run a package, you are running the package in 64-bit mode. However, you can change this behavior by modifying the properties of your SSIS project. Figure 14-3 shows the Run64bitRuntime property on the Debugging property page. When you set this to False, the package runs in 32-bit emulation mode even though the machine is 64-bit.
- **32-bit version of DTExec:** By default, a 64-bit installation of SSIS references the 64-bit version of DTExec, usually found in the `C:\Program Files\Microsoft SQL Server\120\DTS\Binn` folder. However, a 32-bit version is also included in `C:\Program Files (X86)\Microsoft SQL Server\120\DTS\Binn`, and you can reference that directly if you want a package to run in 32-bit emulation mode in order to access the ACE and JET providers.

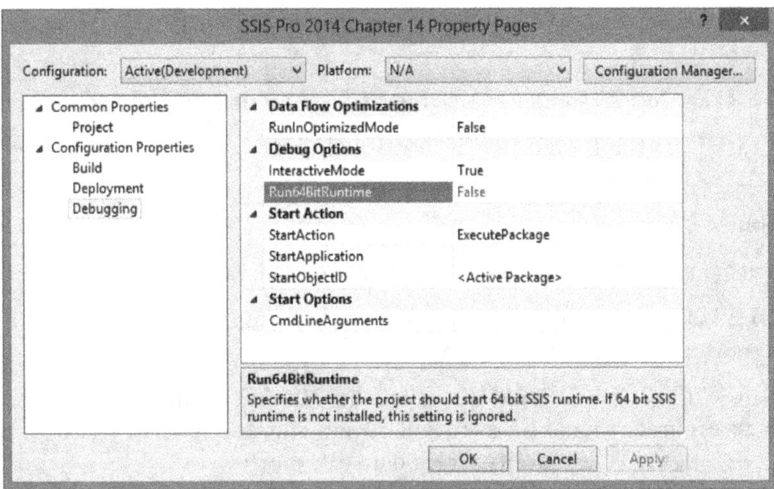

FIGURE 14-3

- **32-bit version for packages deployed to SSIS catalog:** When running a package that has been deployed to the SSIS 2014 catalog, an advanced configuration option, "32-bit runtime," will allow your package to be executed in legacy 32-bit execution mode. This option is available both in SQL Agent and in the package execution UI in the SSIS 2014 catalog. The default is to have this option unchecked so that packages run in 64-bit mode.

Be careful not to run all your packages in 32-bit emulation mode when running on a 64-bit machine, just the ones that need 32-bit support. The 32-bit emulation mode limits the memory accessibility and the performance. The best approach is to modularize your packages by developing more packages with less logic in them. One benefit to this is the packages that need 32-bit execution can be separated and run separately.

Working with Excel Files

Excel is a common source and destination because it is often the favorite "database" software of many people without database expertise (especially in your accounting department!). SSIS has Data Flow Source and Destination Components made just for Excel that ease the connection setup, whether connecting to Excel 2003 or earlier or to Excel 2007 or later (the JET and ACE providers).

You can be sure that these components will be used in many SSIS packages, because data is often imported from Excel files into a SQL Server database or exported into Excel for many high-level tasks such as sales forecasting. Because Excel is so easy to work with, it is common to find inconsistencies in the data. For example, while lookup lists or data type enforcement is possible to implement, it is less likely for an Excel workbook to have it in place. It's often possible for the person entering data to type a note in a cell where a date should go. Of course, cleansing the data is part of the ETL process, but it may be even more of a challenge when importing from Excel.

Exporting to All Versions of Excel

In this section, you will use SSDT to create SSIS packages to export data to Excel files. The first example shows how to create a package that exports a worksheet that the AdventureWorks inventory staff will use to record the physical inventory counts. Follow these steps to learn how to export data to Excel:

1. Create a new SSIS package in SSDT and Rename the package **Export Excel.dtsx**.
2. Drag a Data Flow Task from the Toolbox to the Control Flow design area and then switch to the Data Flow tab.
3. Add an OLE DB Source Component.
4. Create a Connection Manager pointing to the AdventureWorks database.
5. Double-click the OLE DB Source Component to bring up the OLE DB Source Editor. Make sure that Connection Manager is selected on the left.
6. Choose the AdventureWorks Connection Manager for the OLE DB Connection Manager property. The data access mode should be set to SQL Command. In this case, you will write a query (`Excel_Export_SQL.txt`) to specify which data to export:

```
SELECT ProductID, LocationID, Shelf, Bin,
  Null as PhysicalCount
FROM Production.ProductInventory
ORDER by LocationID, Shelf, Bin
```

7. If you select Columns in the left pane, you have the opportunity to deselect some of the columns or change the name of the output columns. Click OK to accept the configuration.
8. Drag an Excel Destination Component from the SSIS Toolbox, found under the Other Destinations grouping and drag the Data Flow Path (blue arrow on your screen) from the OLE DB Source to the Excel Destination. Double-click the Excel Destination.
9. Click the New button for the Connection Manager, and in the Excel Connection Manager window, choose Microsoft Excel 2007 from the Excel Version dropdown, and then enter the path to your destination (`C:\ProSSIS\Data\Inventory_Worksheet.xlsx`).
10. Select OK in the Excel Connection Manager window, and then click New on the Name of Excel sheet dropdown to create a new worksheet.
11. In the Create Table window, you can leave the name of the worksheet or change it and modify the columns as Figure 14-4 shows. Click OK to create the new worksheet.
12. The data access mode should be set to Table or View (more about this later). Click OK to create a new worksheet with the appropriate column headings in the Excel file. Make sure that Name of the Excel sheet is set to Inventory Worksheet.
13. You must click Mappings on the left to set the mappings between the source and

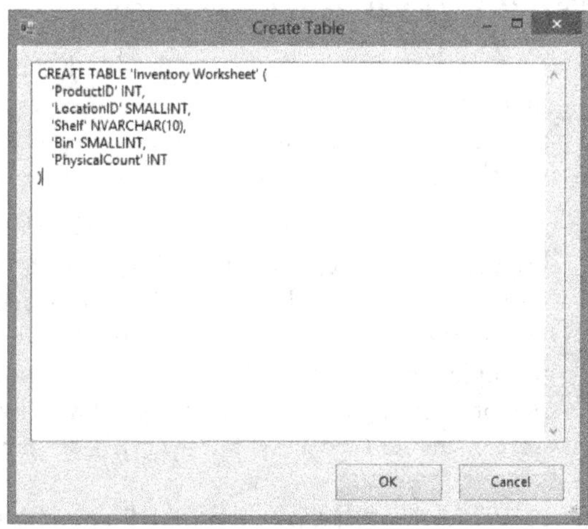

FIGURE 14-4

the destination. Each one of the Available Input Columns should match up exactly with an Available Output Column. Click OK to accept the Inventory Worksheet settings.

Run the package to export the product list. The fields selected in the Production.Inventory table will export to the Excel file, and your inventory crew members can each use a copy of this file to record their counts.

Importing from Excel 2003 and Earlier

For this example of importing Excel data, assume that you work for AdventureWorks and the AdventureWorks inventory crew divided up the assignments according to product location. As each assignment is completed, a partially filled-out worksheet file is returned to you. In this example, you create a package to import the data from each worksheet that is received:

1. Open SQL Server Data Tools (SSDT) and create a new SSIS package.
2. Drag a Data Flow Task to the Control Flow design pane.
3. Click the Data Flow and add an Excel Source and an OLE DB Destination Component. Rename the Excel Source to Inventory Worksheet and rename the OLE DB Destination to Inventory Import.
4. Drag the blue Data Flow Path from the Inventory Worksheet Component to the Inventory Import Component.

> **NOTE** *The OLE DB Destination sometimes works better than the SQL Server Destination Component for importing data from non-SQL Server sources! When using the SQL Server Destination Component, you cannot import into integer columns or varchar columns from an Excel spreadsheet, and must import into double precision and nvarchar columns. The SQL Server Destination Component does not support implicit data type conversions and works as expected when moving data from SQL Server as a source to SQL Server as a destination.*

5. Create a Connection Manager for the Excel file you have been working with by following the instructions in the previous section (select Microsoft Excel 97-2003 in the Excel version dropdown).
6. Rename the Excel Connection Manager in the Properties window to **Inventory Source**.
7. Create a Connection Manager pointing to the AdventureWorks database.
8. Double-click the Inventory Worksheet Component to bring up the Excel Source Editor (see Figure 14-5).
9. For this example the data access mode should be set to SQL Command because you only want to import rows with the physical count filled in. Type the following query (`Excel_Import_SQL.txt`) into the SQL command text box (see Figure 14-6):

```
SELECT ProductID, PhysicalCount, LocationID, Shelf, Bin
FROM Inventory_Worksheet
WHERE PhysicalCount IS NOT NULL
```

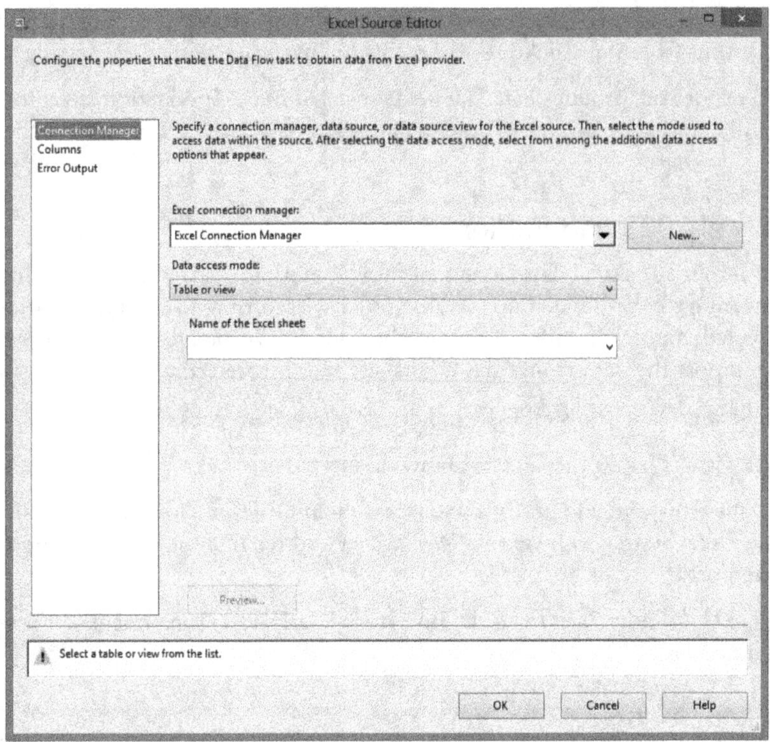

FIGURE 14-5

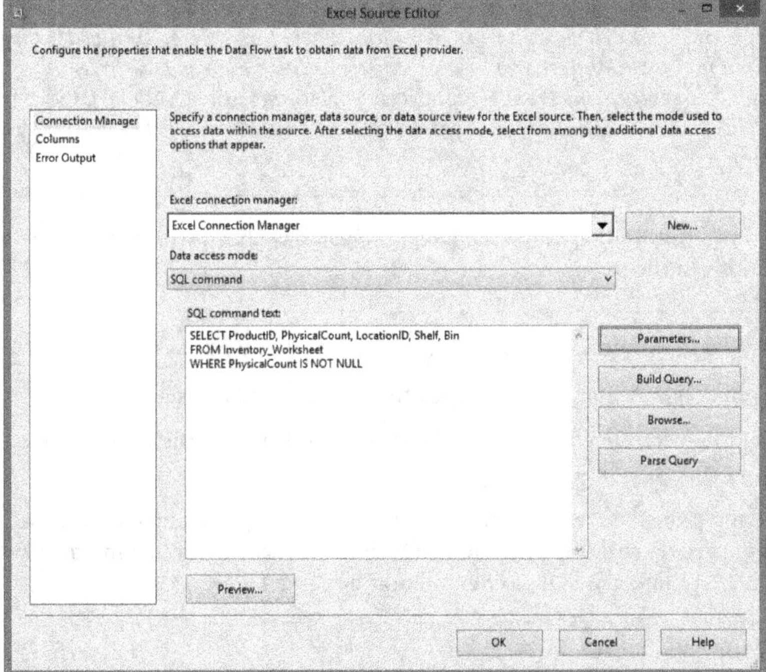

FIGURE 14-6

10. Double-click the Inventory Import Component to bring up the OLE DB Destination Editor. Make sure the AdventureWorks connection is chosen. Under Data access mode, choose Table or View.
11. Click the New button next to Name of the table or the view to open the Create Table dialog.
12. Change the name of the table to **InventoryImport** and click OK to create the table. Select Mappings. Each field from the worksheet should match up to a field in the new table.
13. Click OK to accept the configuration.

While this is a simple example, it illustrates just how easy it is to import from and export to Excel files.

Importing from Excel 2007 and Later

Setting up an SSIS package to import from Excel 2007 and later is very similar to setting up the connection when exporting to Excel 2007.

When you set up the connection, choose Excel 2007 from the Excel version dropdown (step 5 above). Once you have set up the connection as already shown in Figures 14-5 and 14-6, you need to create an OLE DB Source adapter in the Data Flow. You can either reference the worksheet directly or specify a query that extracts data from specific Excel columns. Figure 14-7 shows a worksheet directly referenced, called "Inventory_Worksheet$."

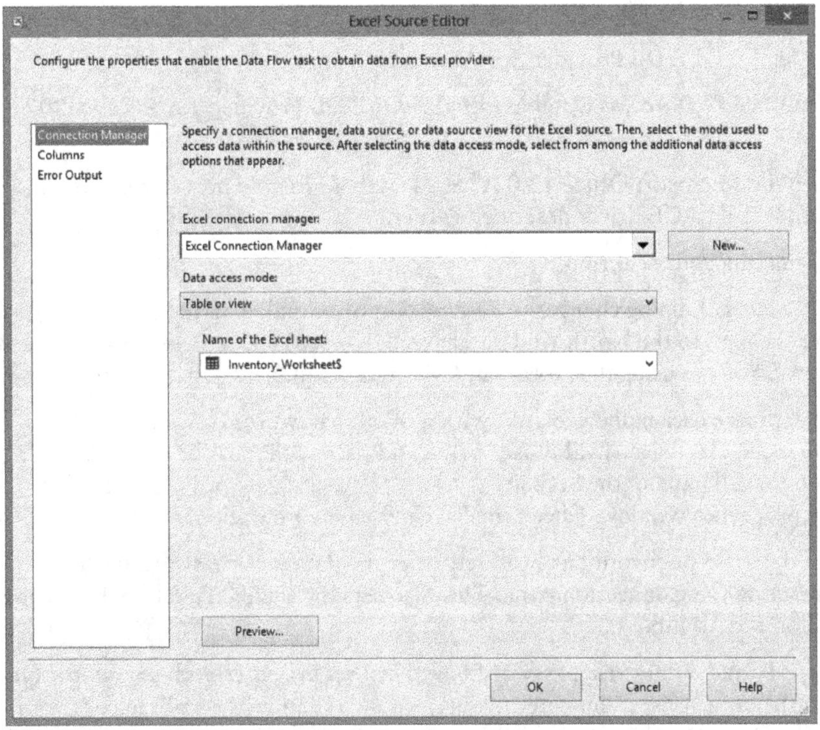

FIGURE 14-7

Working with Access

MS Access is the departmental database of choice for countless individual users and small workgroups. It has many great features and wizards that enable a small application or prototype to be quickly developed. Often, when an application has outgrown its humble Access origins, discussions about moving the data to SQL Server emerge. Many times, the client will be rewritten as a web or desktop application using VB.NET or another language. Sometimes the plan is to link to the SQL Server tables, utilizing the existing Access front end. Unfortunately, if the original application was poorly designed, moving the data to SQL Server will not improve performance. This section demonstrates how you can use SSIS to integrate with Microsoft Access. Access 2007 and later use the same ACE provider as Excel does, so as you work with Access in a 32-bit or 64-bit mode, please refer to the 64-bit discussion of Excel in the previous section.

Configuring an Access Connection Manager

Once the Connection Manager is configured properly, importing from Access is simple. First, look at the steps required to set up the Connection Manager:

1. Create a new SSIS package and create a new Connection Manager by right-clicking in the Connection Managers section of the design surface.
2. Select New OLE DB Connection to bring up the Configure OLE DB Connection Manager dialog.
3. Click New to open the Connection Manager. In the Provider dropdown list, choose one of the following access provider types:
   - Microsoft Jet 4.0 OLE DB Provider (for Access 2003 and earlier)
   - Microsoft Office 12.0 Access Database Engine OLE DB Provider (for Access 2007 and later)

   If you do not see the Microsoft Office 12.0 Access Database Engine provider in the list, you need to install the 32-bit ACE driver described earlier.
4. Click OK after making your selection.
5. The Connection Manager dialog changes to an Access-specific dialog. In the server or file name box, enter the path to the Northwind database, `C:\ProSSIS\Data\Northwind.mdb`, as Figure 14-8 shows. You are using the Northwind MS Access sample database for this example.
6. By default, the database user name is blank, with a blank password. If security has been enabled for the Access database, a valid user name and password must be entered. Enter the password on the All pane in the Security section. The user Password property is also available in the properties window. Check the Save my password option.
7. If, conversely, a database password has been set, enter the database password in the Password property on the Connection pane. This also sets the ODBC:Database Password property found on the All tab.
8. If both user security and a database password have been set up, enter both passwords on the All pane. In the Security section, enter the user password and the database password for the Jet OLEDB:New Database Password property. Check the Save my password option. Be sure to test the connection and click OK to save the properties.

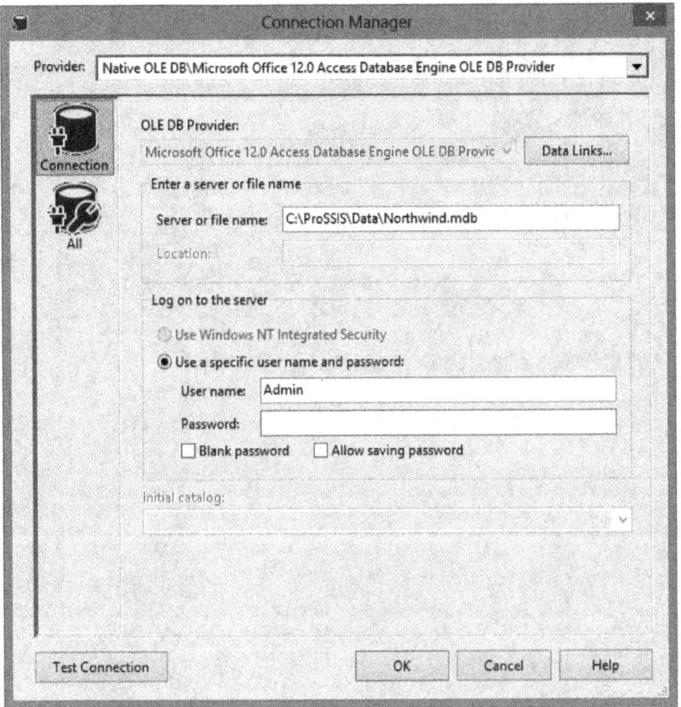

FIGURE 14-8

Importing from Access

Once you have the Connection Manager created, follow these steps to import from Access:

1. Using the project you created in the last section with the Access Connection Manager already configured, add a Data Flow Task to the Control Flow design area.
2. Click the Data Flow tab to view the Data Flow design area. Add an OLE DB Source Component and name it **Customers**.
3. Double-click the Customers icon to open the OLE DB Source Editor. Set the OLE DB Connection Manager property to the Connection Manager that you created in the last section.
4. Select Table or View from the Data access mode dropdown list. Choose the Customers table from the list under Name of the table or the view (see Figure 14-9).
5. Click Columns on the left of the Source Editor to choose which columns to import and change the output names if needed.
6. Click OK to accept the configuration.
7. Create a Connection Manager pointing to AdventureWorks.
8. Create an OLE DB Destination Component and name it **NW_Customers**. Drag the connection (blue arrow on your screen) from the Customers Source Component to the NW_Customers Destination Component.

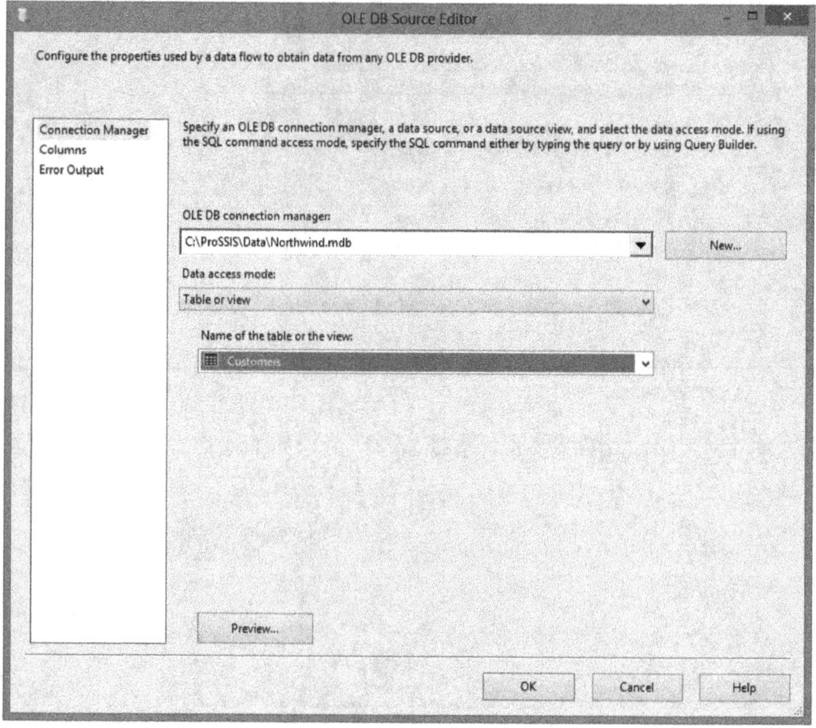

FIGURE 14-9

9. Double-click the Destination Component to bring up the OLE DB Destination Editor and configure it to use the AdventureWorks Connection Manager.

10. You can choose an existing table or you can click New to create a new table as the Data Destination. If you click New, notice that the Create Table designer does not script any keys, constraints, defaults, or indexes from Access. It makes its best guess as to the data types, which may not be the right ones for your solution. When building a package for use in a production system, you will probably want to design and create the SQL Server tables in advance.

11. For now, click New to bring up the table definition (see Figure 14-10). Notice that the table name is the same as the Destination Component, so change the name to **NW_Customers** if you did not name the OLE DB Destination as instructed previously.

12. Click OK to create the new table.

13. Click Mappings on the left to map the source and destination columns.

14. Click OK to accept the configuration.

15. Run the package. All the Northwind customers should now be listed in the SQL Server table. Check this by clicking New Query in Microsoft SQL Server Management Studio. Run the following query (`Access_Import.txt`) to see the results:

```
USE AdventureWorks
GO
SELECT * FROM NW_Customers
```

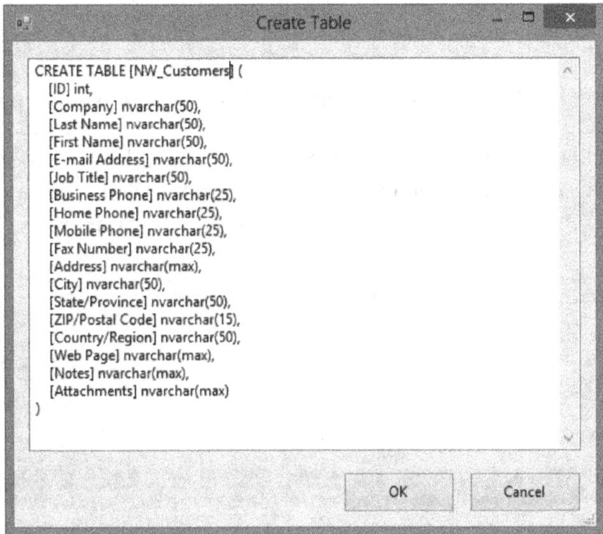

FIGURE 14-10

16. Empty the table to prepare for the next example by running this query:

```
TRUNCATE TABLE NW_CUSTOMERS
```

Using a Parameter

Another interesting feature is the capability to pass a parameter from a package variable to a SQL command. The following steps demonstrate how:

> **NOTE** *In Access, you can create a query that prompts the user for parameters at runtime. You can import most Access select queries as tables, but data from an Access parameter query cannot be imported using SSIS.*

1. Select the package you started in the last section.
2. Navigate back to the Control Flow tab and right-click the design area.
3. Choose Variables and add a variable by clicking the Add Variable icon. Name it **CustomerID**. Change the Data Type to String, and give it a value of ANTON (see Figure 14-11). Close the Variables window and navigate back to the Data Flow tab.

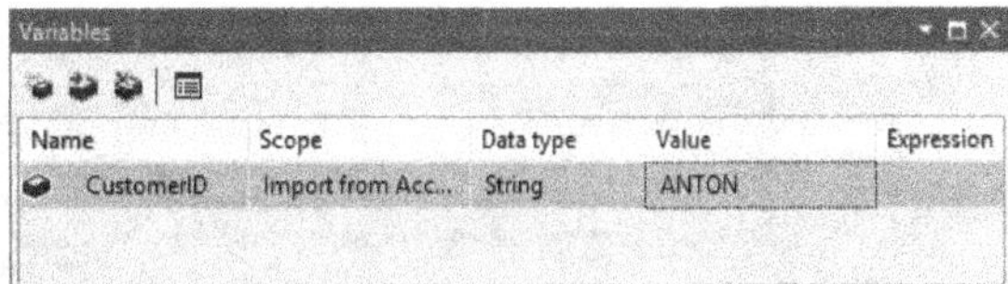

FIGURE 14-11

> **NOTE** *The design area or component that is selected determines the scope of the variable when it is created. The scope can be set to the package if it is created right after clicking the Control Flow design area. You can also set the scope to a Control Flow Task, Data Flow Component, or Event Handler Task.*

4. Double-click the Customers Component to bring up the OLE DB Source Editor and change the data access mode to SQL Command. A SQL Command text box and some buttons appear. You can click the Build Query button to bring up a designer to help build the command or click Browse to open a file with the command you want to use. For this example, type in the following SQL statement (`Access_Import_Parameter.txt`) (see Figure 14-12):

```
SELECT CustomerID, CompanyName, ContactName, ContactTitle,
Address, City, Region, PostalCode, Country, Phone, Fax
FROM Customers
WHERE (CustomerID = ?)
```

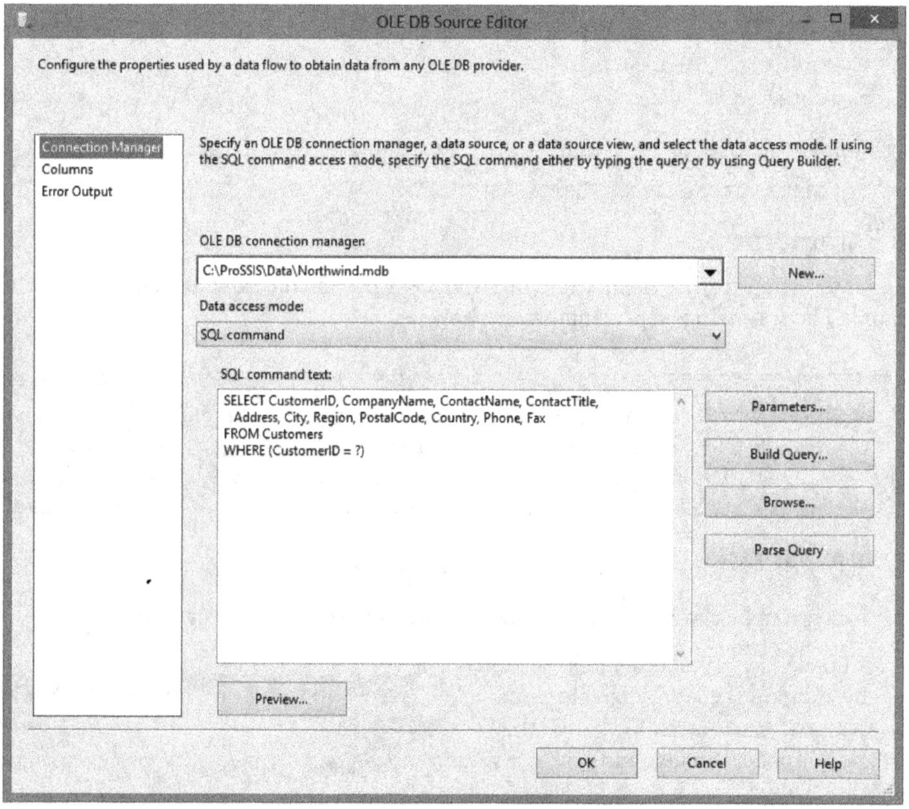

FIGURE 14-12

5. The `?` symbol is used as the placeholder for the parameter in the query. Map the parameters to variables in the package by clicking the Parameters button. Choose User::CustomerID from the Variables list and click OK (see Figure 14-13).

   Note that you cannot preview the data after setting up the parameter because the package must be running to load the value into the parameter.

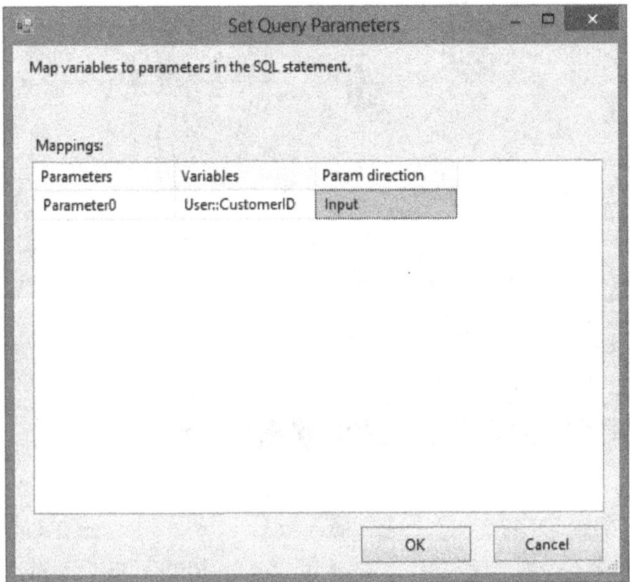

FIGURE 14-13

> **NOTE** *Variables in SSIS belong to namespaces. By default, there are two namespaces, User and System. Variables that you create belong to the User namespace. You can also create additional namespaces.*

6. Click OK to accept the new configuration and run the package. This time, only one record is imported (see Figure 14-14).

   You can also return to SQL Server Management Studio to view the results:

```
USE AdventureWorks
GO
SELECT * FROM NW_Customers
```

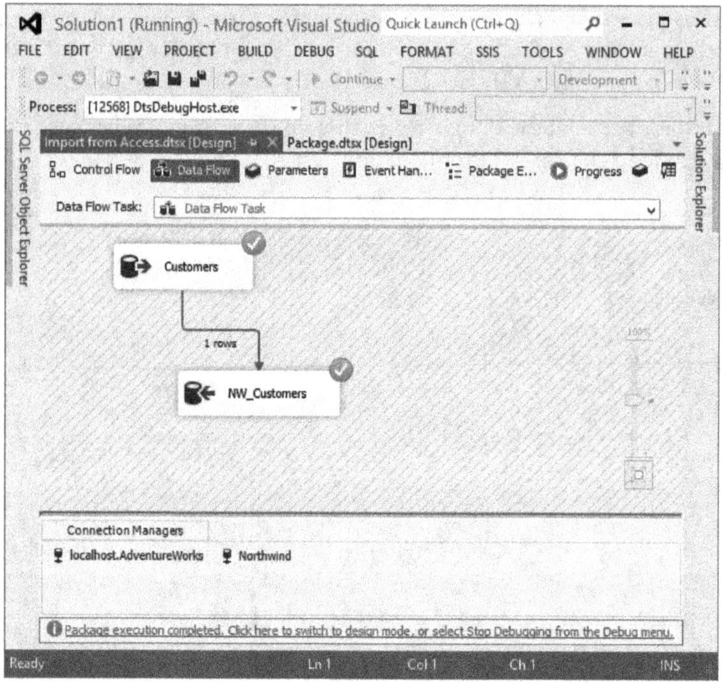

FIGURE 14-14

If you wish to use multiple parameters in your SQL command, use multiple question marks (?) in the query and map them in order to the parameters in the parameter mapping. To do this, you set up a second package-level variable for CompanyName and set the value to Island Trading. Change the query in the Customers Component to the following (`Access_Import_Parameter2.txt`):

```
SELECT CustomerID, CompanyName,
ContactName, ContactTitle, Address, City, Region,
PostalCode, Country, Phone, Fax
FROM Customers
WHERE (CustomerID = ?) OR
(CompanyName = ?)
```

Now the Parameters dialog will show the two parameters. Associate each parameter with the appropriate variable (see Figure 14-15).

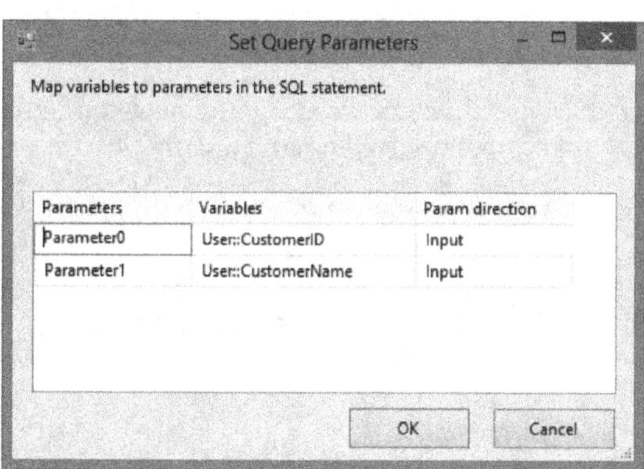

FIGURE 14-15

Importing data from Access is a simple process as long as Access security has not been enabled. Often, porting an Access application to SQL Server is the desired result. Make sure you have a good book or other resource to help ensure success.

IMPORTING FROM ORACLE

Because of SQL Server's world-class reporting and business intelligence tools, more and more shops running Oracle rely on SQL Server for their reporting needs.

Luckily, importing data from Oracle is much like importing from other sources, such as a text file or another SQL Server instance. In this section, you learn how to access data from an Oracle database with the built-in OLE DB provider and the Oracle client.

Oracle Client Setup

Connecting to Oracle in SSIS is a two-step process. First you install the Oracle client software, and then you use the OLE DB provider in SSIS to connect to Oracle.

To be sure, the Microsoft Data Access Components (MDAC) that comes with the operating system include an OLE DB provider for Oracle. This is the 32-bit Microsoft-written OLE DB provider to access an Oracle source system. However, even though the OLE DB provider is installed, you cannot use it until you install a second component, the Oracle client software. In fact, when you install the Oracle client software, Oracle includes an OLE DB provider that can be used to access an Oracle source. The OLE DB providers have subtle differences, which are referenced later in this section.

Installing the Oracle Client Software

To install the Oracle client software, you first need to locate the right download from the Oracle website at `www.oracle.com`. Click Downloads and then click the button to download 12c. Accept the licensing agreement and select your operating system. As you are well aware, there are several versions of Oracle (currently Oracle 11g, 11g Release 2, 12c), and each has a different version of the Oracle client. Some of them are backward compatible, but it is always best to go with the version that you are connecting to.

It is best to install the full client software in order to ensure that you have the right components needed for the OLE DB providers.

Configuring the Oracle Client Software

Once you download and install the right client for the version of Oracle you will be connecting to and the right platform of Windows you are running, the final step is configuring it to reference the Oracle servers. You will probably need help from your Oracle DBA or the support team of the Oracle application to configure this.

There are two options: an Oracle name server or manually configuring a TNS file. The TNS file is more common and is found in the Oracle install directory under the network\ADMIN folder. This is called the Oracle Home directory. The Oracle client uses the Windows environment variables `%Path%` and `%ORACLE_HOME%` to find the location to the client files. Either replace the default TNS file with one provided by an Oracle admin or create a new entry in it to connect to the Oracle server.

A typical TNS entry looks like this:

```
[Reference name] =
(DESCRIPTION =
(ADDRESS_LIST = (ADDRESS = (PROTOCOL = TCP)
(HOST = [Server])(PORT = [Port Number])) )
(CONNECT_DATA =
(SID = [Oracle SID Name])
)
)
```

Replace the brackets with valid entries. The `[Reference Name]` will be used in SSIS to connect to the Oracle server through the provider.

64-Bit Considerations

As mentioned earlier, after you install the Oracle client software, you can then use the OLE DB provider for Oracle in SSIS to extract data from an Oracle source or to send data to an Oracle Destination. These procedures are described next. However, if you are working on a 64-bit server, you may need to make some additional configurations.

First, if you want to connect to Oracle with a native 64-bit connection, you have to use the Oracle-written OLE DB provider for Oracle because the Microsoft-written OLE DB driver for Oracle is `available` only in a 32-bit mode. Be sure you also install the right 64-bit Oracle client (Itanium IA64 or X64) if you want to connect to Oracle in native 64-bit mode. Although it is probably obvious to you, it bears mentioning that even though you may have X64 hardware, in order to leverage it in 64-bit mode, the operating system must be installed with the X64 version.

Furthermore, even though you may be working on a 64-bit server, you can still use the 32-bit provider through the 32-bit Windows emulation mode. Review the 64-bit details in the "Excel and Access" section earlier in this chapter for details about how to work with packages in 32-bit mode when you are on a 64-bit machine. You need to use the 32-bit version of DTExec for package execution, and when working in SSDT, you need to change the Run64bitRuntime property of the project to False.

Importing Oracle Data

In this example, the alias ORCL is used to connect to an Oracle database named orcl. Your Oracle administrator can provide more information about how to set up your `tnsnames.ora` file to point to a test or production database in your environment. The following `tnsnames` file entry is being used for the subsequent steps:

```
ORCL =
(DESCRIPTION =
(ADDRESS = (PROTOCOL = TCP)(HOST = VPC-XP)(PORT = 1521))
(CONNECT_DATA =
(SERVER = DEDICATED) (SERVICE_NAME = orcl)
)
)
```

To extract data from an Oracle server, perform the following steps. These assume that you have installed the Oracle client and configured a `tnsnames` file or an Oracle names server.

1. Create a new Integration Services project using SSDT.
2. Add a Data Flow Task to the design area. On the Data Flow tab, add an OLE DB source. Name the OLE DB source **Oracle**.
3. In the Connection Managers area, right-click and choose New OLE DB Connection to open the Configure OLE DB Connection Manager dialog.
4. Click New to open the Connection Manager dialog. Select Microsoft OLE DB Provider for Oracle from the list of providers and click OK.
5. Type the alias from your `tnsnames.ora` file for the Server Name.
6. Type in the user name and password and check Save my password (see Figure 14-16). This example illustrates connecting to the widely available scott sample database schema. The user name is scott; the password is tiger. Verify the credentials with your Oracle administrator. Test the connection to ensure that everything is configured properly. Click OK to accept the configuration.

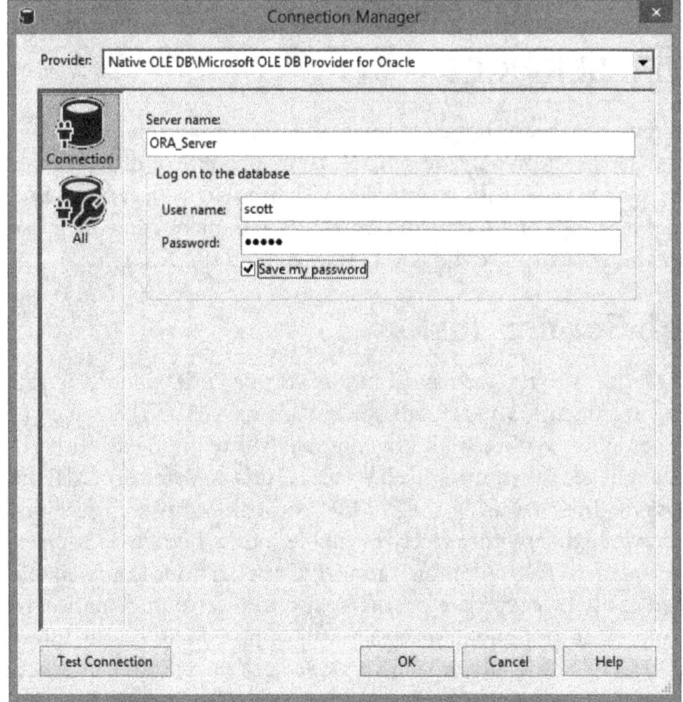

FIGURE 14-16

7. In the custom properties section of the Oracle Component's property dialog, change the AlwaysUseDefaultCodePage property to True.
8. Open the OLE DB Source Editor by double-clicking the Oracle Source Component. With the Connection Manager tab selected, choose the Connection Manager pointing to the Oracle database.

9. Select Table or view from the Data access mode dropdown. Click the dropdown list under Name of the table or the view to see a list of the available tables. Choose the "Scott"."Dept" table from the list.
10. Select the Columns tab to see a list of the columns in the table.
11. Click Preview to see sample data from the Oracle table. At this point, you can add a Data Destination Component to import the data into SQL Server or another OLE DB Destination. This is demonstrated several times elsewhere in the chapter, so it isn't covered again here.

Importing Oracle data is very straightforward, but there are a few things to watch out for. The current Microsoft ODBC driver and Microsoft-written OLE DB provider for Oracle were designed for Oracle 7. At the time of this writing, Oracle 11*g* is the latest version available. Specific functionality and data types that were implemented after the 7 release will probably not work as expected. See Microsoft's Knowledge Base article 244661 for more information. If you want to take advantage of newer Oracle features, you should consider using the Oracle-written OLE DB provider for Oracle, which is installed with the Oracle client software.

USING XML AND WEB SERVICES

Although XML is not a common source for large volumes of data, it is an integral technology standard in the realm of data. This section considers XML from a couple of different perspectives. First, you will work with the Web Service Task to interact with a public web service. Second, you will use the XML Source adapter to extract data from an XML document embedded in a file. In one of the web service examples, you will also use the XML Task to read the XML file.

Configuring the Web Service Task

In very simple terms, a web service is to the web as a function is to a code module. It accepts a message in XML, including arguments, and returns the answer in XML. The value of XML technology is that it enables computer systems that are completely foreign to each other to communicate in a common language. When using web services, this transfer of XML data occurs across the enterprise or across the Internet using the HTTP protocol. Many web services — for example, stock-tickers and movie listings — are freely available for anyone's use. Some web services, of course, are private or require a fee. Two common and useful applications are to enable orders or other data to be exchanged easily by corporate partners, and to receive information from a service — either one that you pay for or a public service that is exposed free on the Internet. In the following examples, you'll learn how to use a web service to get the weather forecast of a U.S. zip code by subscribing to a public web service, and how to use the Web Service Task to perform currency conversion. Keep in mind that the web service task depends on the availability of a server. The Web Service Task could return errors if the server is unreachable or if the server is experiencing any internal errors.

Weather by Zip Code Example

This example demonstrates how to use a web service to retrieve data:

1. Create a new package and create an HTTP Connection by right-clicking in the Connection Managers pane and choosing New Connection.
2. Choose HTTP and click Add to bring up the HTTP Connection Manager Editor. Type `http://www.webservicex.net/WeatherForecast.asmx?wsdl` as the Server URL (see Figure 14-17). In this case, you'll use a publicly available web service, so you won't have to worry about any credentials or certificates. If you must supply proxy information to browse the web, fill that in on the Proxy tab.
3. Before continuing, click the Test Connection button, and then click OK to accept the Connection Manager.

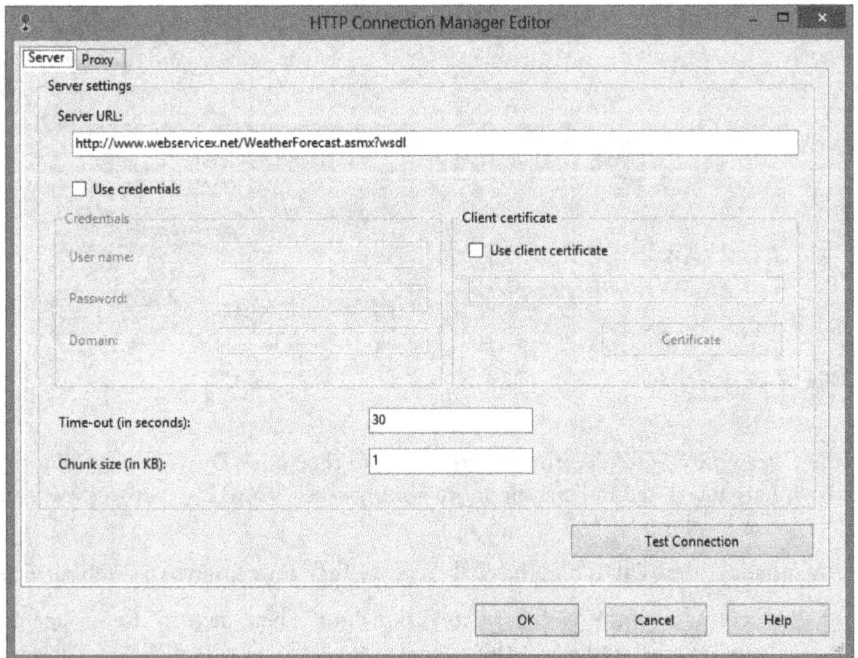

FIGURE 14-17

4. Add a Web Service Task from the Toolbox to the Control Flow workspace.
5. Double-click the Web Service Task to bring up the Web Service Task Editor. Select the General pane. Make sure that the HttpConnection property is set to the HTTP connection you created in step number 2.
6. In order for a web service to be accessed by a client, a Web Service Definition Language (WSDL) file must be available that describes how the web service works — that is, the methods available and the parameters that the web service expects. The Web Service Task provides a way to automatically download this file.
7. In the WSDLFile property, enter the fully qualified path `c:\ProSSIS\Data\weather.wsdl` where you want the WSDL file to be created (see Figure 14-18).

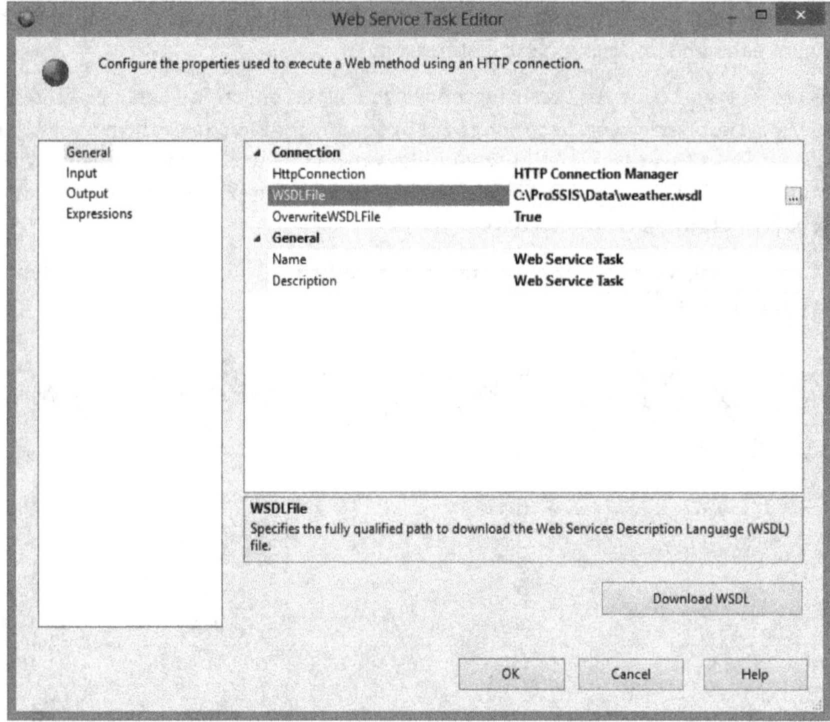

FIGURE 14-18

8. Set the OverwriteWSDLFile property to True and then click Download WSDL to create the file. If you are interested in learning more about the file's XML structure, you can open it with Internet Explorer.

   By downloading the WSDL file, the Web Service Task now knows the web service definition.

9. Select the Input pane of the Web Service Task Editor. Then, next to the Service property, open the dropdown list and select the one service provided, called WeatherForecast.

10. After selecting the WeatherForecast service, click in the Method property and choose the GetWeatherByZipCode option.

11. Web services are not limited to providing just one method. If multiple methods are provided, you'll see all of them listed. Notice another option called GetWeatherByPlaceName. You would use this if you wanted to enter a city instead of a zip code. Once the GetWeatherByZipCode method is selected, a list of arguments appears. In this case, a ZipCode property is presented. Enter a zip code location of a U.S. city (such as 30303 for Atlanta, or, if you live in the U.S., your own zip code). See Figure 14-19.

12. Now that everything is set up to invoke the web service, you need to tell the Web Service Task what to do with the result. Switch to the Output property page of the Web Service Task Editor. Choose File Connection in the dropdown of the OutputType property. You can also store the output in a variable to be referenced later in the package.

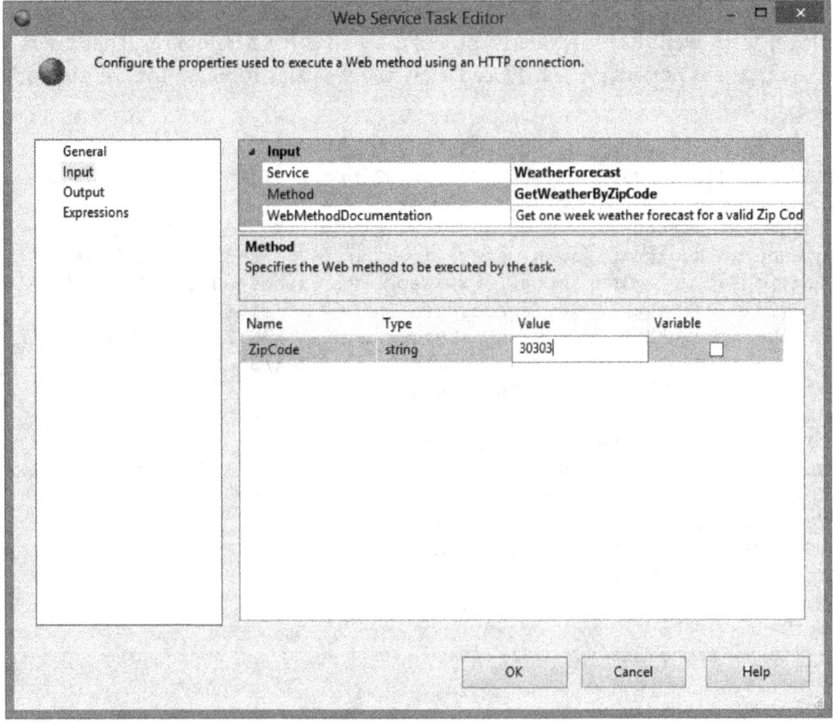

FIGURE 14-19

13. In the File property, open the dropdown list and choose <new connection>.
14. When you are presented with the File Connection Manager Editor, change the Usage type property to Create file and change the File property to `C:\ProSSIS\Data\weatheroutput.xml`, as shown in Figure 14-20.

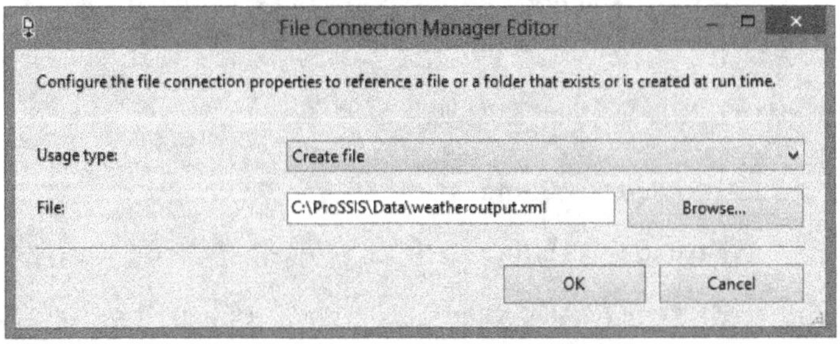

FIGURE 14-20

15. Select OK in the File Connection Manager Editor, and OK in the Web Service Task Editor to finish configuring the SSIS package.

Now you're ready to run the package. After executing it, wait for the Web Service Task to complete successfully. If all went well, use Internet Explorer to open the XML file returned by the web service (`c:\ProSSIS\data\weatheroutput.xml`) and view the weather forecast for the zip code. It will look something like this:


```
<?xml version="1.0" encoding="utf-16" ?>
  <WeatherForecasts xmlns:xsi=http://www.w3.org/2001/XMLSchema-instance
xmlns:xsd="http://www.w3.org/2001/XMLSchema">
  <Latitude xmlns="http://www.webservicex.net">33.7525024</Latitude>
  <Longitude xmlns="http://www.webservicex.net">84.38885</Longitude>
  <AllocationFactor xmlns="http://www.webservicex.net">0.000285</AllocationFactor>
  <FipsCode xmlns="http://www.webservicex.net">13</FipsCode>
  <PlaceName xmlns="http://www.webservicex.net">ATLANTA</PlaceName>
  <StateCode xmlns="http://www.webservicex.net">GA</StateCode>
  <Details xmlns="http://www.webservicex.net">
  <WeatherData>
  <Day>Thursday, September 01, 2011</Day>
  <WeatherImage>http://forecast.weather.gov/images/wtf/nfew.jpg</WeatherImage>
  <MaxTemperatureF>93</MaxTemperatureF>
  <MinTemperatureF>72</MinTemperatureF>
  <MaxTemperatureC>34</MaxTemperatureC>
  <MinTemperatureC>22</MinTemperatureC>
  </WeatherData>
 <WeatherData>
  <Day>Friday, September 02, 2011</Day>
    </Details>
  </WeatherForecasts>
```


The Currency Conversion Example

In this second example, you learn how to use a web service to get a value that can be used in the package to perform a calculation. To convert a price list to another currency, you'll use the value with the Derived Column Transformation:

1. Begin by creating a new SSIS package. This example requires three variables. To set them up, ensure that the Control Flow tab is selected. If the Variables window is not visible, right-click in the design area and select Variables. Set up the three variables as shown in the following table. At this time, you don't need initial values. (You can also use package parameters instead of variables for this example.)

NAME	SCOPE	DATA TYPE
XMLAnswer	Package	String
Answer	Package	String
ConversionRate	Package	Double

2. Add a Connection Manager pointing to the AdventureWorks database.
3. Add a second connection. This time, create an HTTP Connection Manager and set the Server URL to `http://www.webservicex.net/CurrencyConvertor.asmx?wsdl`.

> **NOTE** *Note that this web service was valid at the time of publication, but the authors cannot guarantee its future availability.*

4. Drag a Web Service Task to the design area and double-click the task to open the Web Service Task Editor. Set the HTTPConnection property to the Connection Manager you just created.
5. Type in a location to store the WSDLFile, such as **c:\ProSSIS\data\CurrencyConversion .wsdl**, and then click the Download WSDL button as you did in the last example to download the WSDL file.
6. Click Input to see the web service properties. Select CurrencyConvertor as the Service property and ConversionRate as the Method.
7. Two parameters will be displayed: FromCurrency and ToCurrency. Set FromCurrency equal to USD, and ToCurrency equal to EUR (see Figure 14-21).

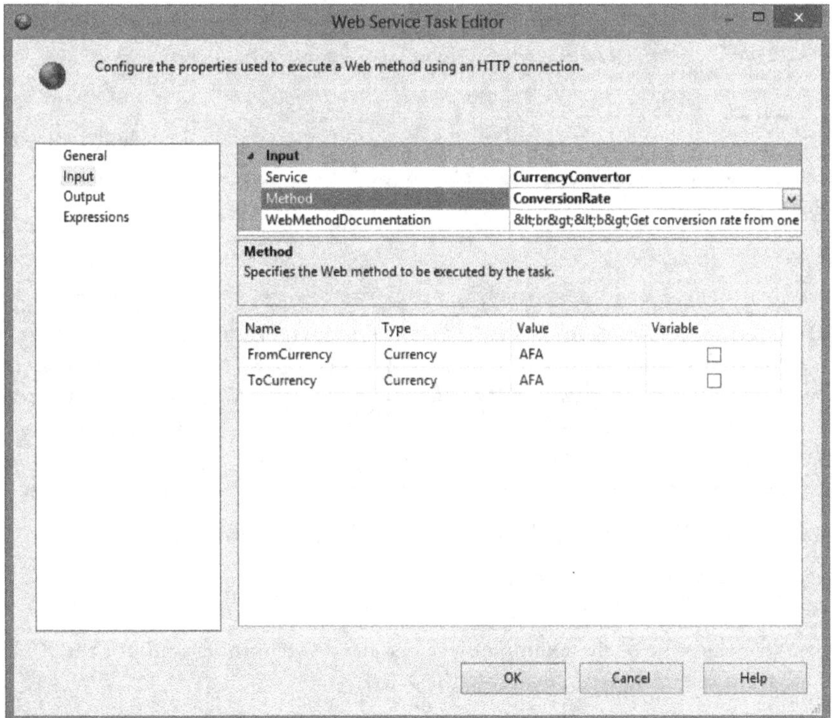

FIGURE 14-21

8. Click Output and set the OutputType to Variable.
9. The variable name to use is User::XMLAnswer (see Figure 14-22). Click OK to accept the configuration.

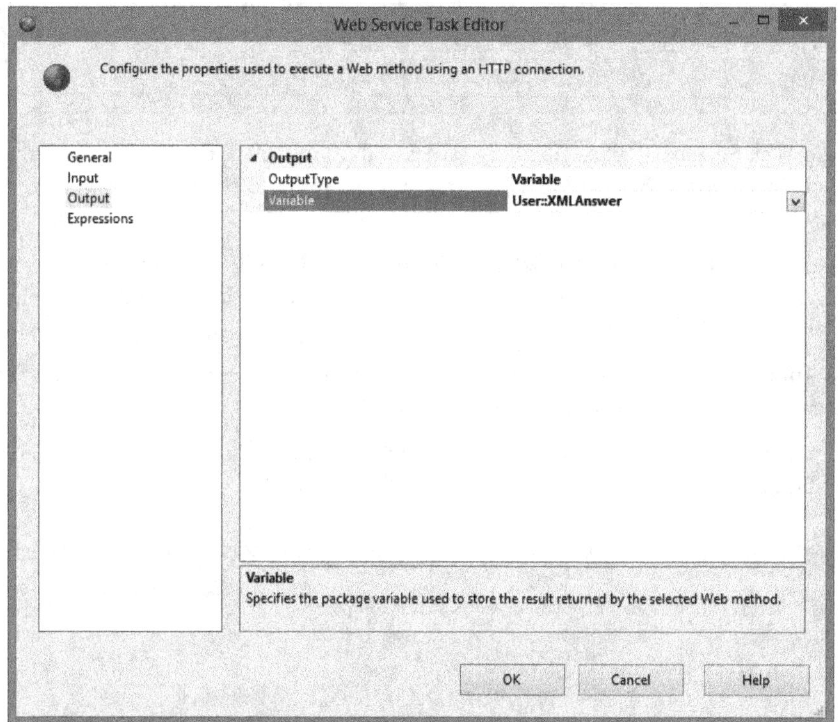

FIGURE 14-22

> **NOTE** *At this point, you may be interested in viewing the XML that it returned from the web service. You can save the XML in a file instead of a variable. Then, after running the task, examine the file. Alternately, you can set a breakpoint on the task and view the variable at runtime. See Chapter 18 to learn more about breakpoints and debugging.*

The value of the XML returned will look something like this:

```
<?xml version="1.0" encoding="utf-8">
<double>0.836</double>
```

10. Because (for the sake of the example) you just need the number and not the XML, add an XML Task to the designer to evaluate the XML.
11. Drag the precedence constraint from the Web Service Task to the XML Task, and then open the XML Task Editor by double-clicking the XML Task.
12. Change the OperationType to XPATH. The properties available will change to include those specific for the XPATH operation. Set the properties to match those in the following table:

SECTION	PROPERTY	VALUE
Input	OperationType	XPATH
	SourceType	Variable
	Source	User:XMLAnswer
Output	SaveOperationResult	True
Operation Result	OverwriteDestination	True
	Destination	User::Answer
	DestinationType	Variable
Second Operand	SecondOperandType	Direct Input
	SecondOperand	/
Xpath Options	PutResultInOneNode	False
	XpathOperation	Values

A discussion about the XPATH query language is beyond the scope of this book, but this XML is very simple with only a root element that can be accessed by using the slash character (/). Values are returned from the query as a list with a one-character unprintable row delimiter. In this case, only one value is returned, but it still has the row delimiter that you can't use.

You have a couple of options here. You could save the value to a file, then import using a File Source Component into a SQL Server table, and finally use the Execute SQL Task to assign the value to a variable; but in this example, you will get a chance to use the Script Task to eliminate the extra character:

1. Add a Script Task to the design area and drag the precedence constraint from the XML Task to the Script Task.
2. Open the Script Task Editor and select the Script pane.
3. In order for the Script Task to access the package variables, they must be listed in the ReadOnlyVariables or ReadWriteVariables properties (as appropriate considering whether you will be updating the variable value in the script) in a semicolon-delimited list. Enter **User::Answer** in the ReadOnlyVariables property and **User::ConversionRate** in the ReadWriteVariables property (see Figure 14-23).
4. Click Design Script to open the code window. A Microsoft Visual Studio Tools for Applications environment opens. The script will save the value returned from the web service call to a variable. One character will be removed from the end of the value, leaving only the conversion factor. This is then converted to a double and saved in the ConversionRate variable for use in a later step.

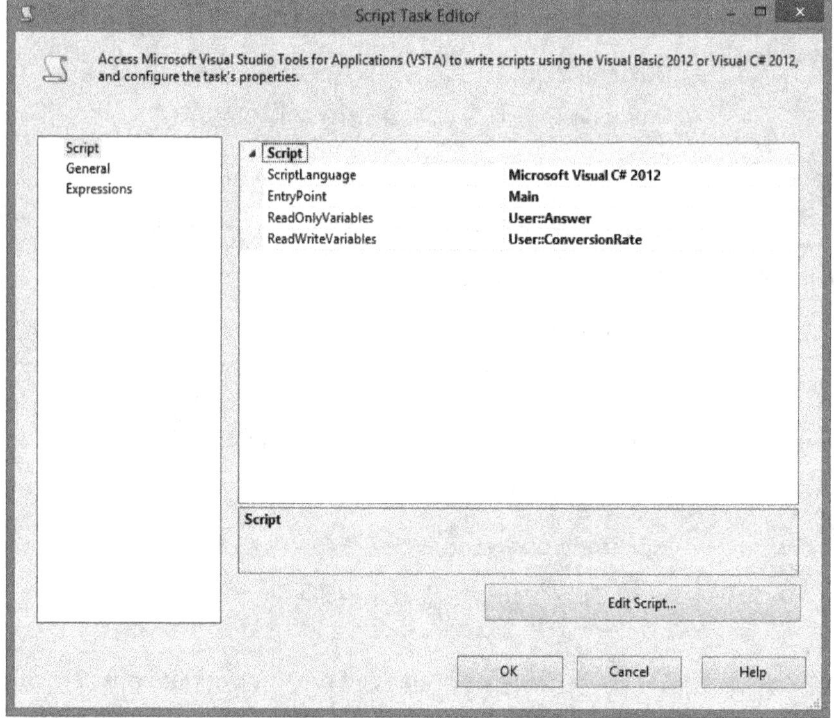

FIGURE 14-23

5. Replace `Sub Main` with the following code (`Currency_Script.txt`):

```
Public Sub Main()
Dim strConversion As String
strConversion = Dts.Variables("User::Answer").Value.ToString
strConversion = strConversion.Remove(strConversion.Length -1,1)
Dts.Variables("User::ConversionRate").Value = CType(strConversion,Double)
Dts.TaskResult = Dts.Results.Success
End Sub
```

6. Close the scripting environment, and then click OK to accept the Script Task configuration.
7. Add a Data Flow Task to the design area and connect the Script Task to the Data Flow Task. The Control Flow area should resemble what is shown in Figure 14-24.
8. Move to the Data Flow tab and add a Connection Manager pointing to the AdventureWorks database, if you did not do so when getting started with this example.
9. Drag an OLE DB Source Component to the design area.
10. Open the OLE DB Source Editor and set the OLE DB Connection Manager property to the AdventureWorks connection. Change the data access mode property to SQL Command. Type the following query (`Currency_Select.txt`) in the command window:

```
SELECT ProductID, ListPrice
FROM Production.Product
WHERE ListPrice> 0
```

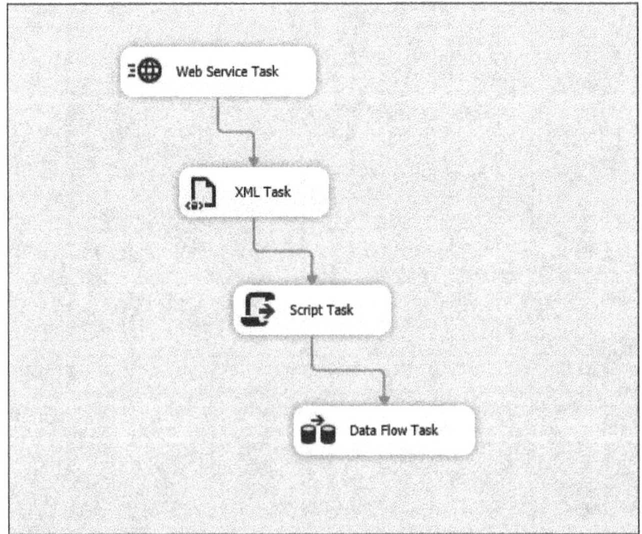

FIGURE 14-24

11. Click OK to accept the properties.
12. Add a Derived Column Transformation to the design area.
13. Drag the Data Flow Path from the OLE DB Source to the Derived Column Component.
14. Double-click to open the Derived Column Transformation Editor dialog. Variables, columns, and functions are available for easily building an expression. Add a derived column called EuroListPrice. In the Expression field, type the following (`Currency_Expression.txt`):

    ```
    ListPrice * @[User::ConversionRate]
    ```

15. The Data Type should be a decimal with a scale of 2. Click OK to accept the properties (see Figure 14-25).
16. Add a Flat File Destination Component to the Data Flow design area. Drag the Data Flow Path from the Derived Column Component to the Flat File Destination Component.
17. Bring up the Flat File Destination Editor and click New to open the Flat File Format dialog.
18. Choose Delimited and click OK. The Flat File Connection Manager Editor will open.
19. Browse to or type in the path to a file, `C:\ProSSIS\data\USD_EUR.txt`. Here you can modify the file format and other properties if required (see Figure 14-26). Check Column names in the first data row.
20. Click OK to dismiss the Flat File Connection Manager Editor dialog and return to the Flat File Destination Editor.
21. Click Mappings and then click OK.

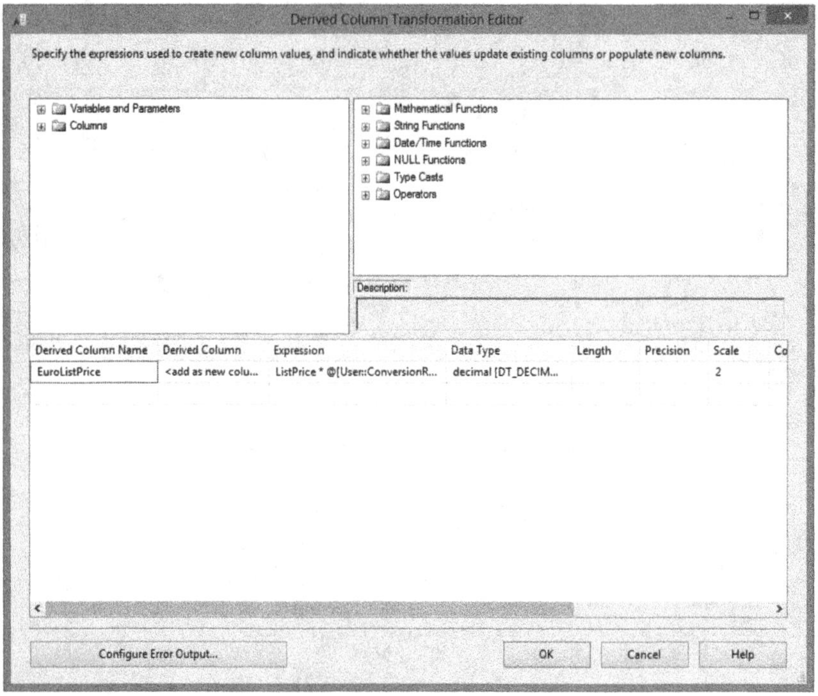

FIGURE 14-25

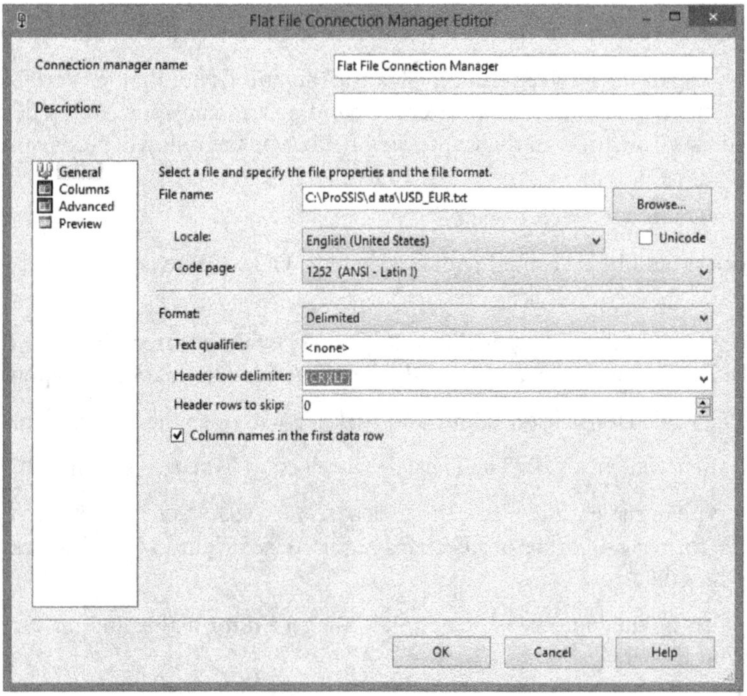

FIGURE 14-26

22. Run the package and then open the file that was created by the destination adapter, `C:\ProSSIS\data\USD_EUR.txt`. You should see a list of products along with the list price and the list price converted to euros.

Many web services are available for you to try. See `www.xmethods.net` for a list of services, some of which are free. In the next section, you learn how to import an XML file into relational tables.

Working with XML Data as a Source

SQL Server provides many ways to work with XML. The XML Source adapter is yet another jewel in the SSIS treasure chest. It enables you to import an XML file directly into relational tables if that is what you need. In this example, you import an RSS (Really Simple Syndication) file from the web.

To use the XML Source adapter in SSIS, you first connect to an XML file, and then you need to provide the XSD definition of the XML structure, so that SSIS can read the file and correctly interpret the XML elements and attribute structure. Don't have an XSD? No problem; SSIS can self-generate the XSD from within the XML Source adapter. There is no guarantee that the generated XSD will work with another XML file coming from the same source, which is why it is better to have an XSD definition that is provided by the XML Source that will universally apply to the related files used by SSIS.

1. Create a new Integration Services package to get started.
2. Add a Data Flow Task to the Control Flow design area and then click the Data Flow tab to view the Data Flow design area.
3. Add an XML Source and name it **CD Collection**.
4. Double-click the CD Collection Component to open the XML Source Editor.
5. Make sure that the Connections Manager property page is selected on the left.
6. Select XML File Location for the data access mode. For the XML location property, type in the following address:

   ```
   C:\ProSSIS\Data\cd_catalog.xml
   ```

   If you click the Browse button, a regular File Open dialog opens. It isn't obvious at first that you can use a URL instead of a file on disk.

   The XML file must be defined with an XML Schema Definition (XSD), which describes the elements in the XML file. Some XML files have an in-line XSD, which you can determine by opening the file and looking for `xsd` tags. There are many resources and tutorials available on the web if you want to learn more about XML schemas. If the file you are importing has an in-line schema, make sure that Use inline schema is checked. If an XSD file is available, you can enter the path in the XSD location property (see Figure 14-27). In this case, you will create the XSD file right in the Source adapter.

7. Click Generate XSD and put the file in a directory on your machine (such as `c:\ProSSIS\data\cd_catalog.xsd`). Once the file is generated, you can open it with Internet Explorer to view it if you are interested in learning more.

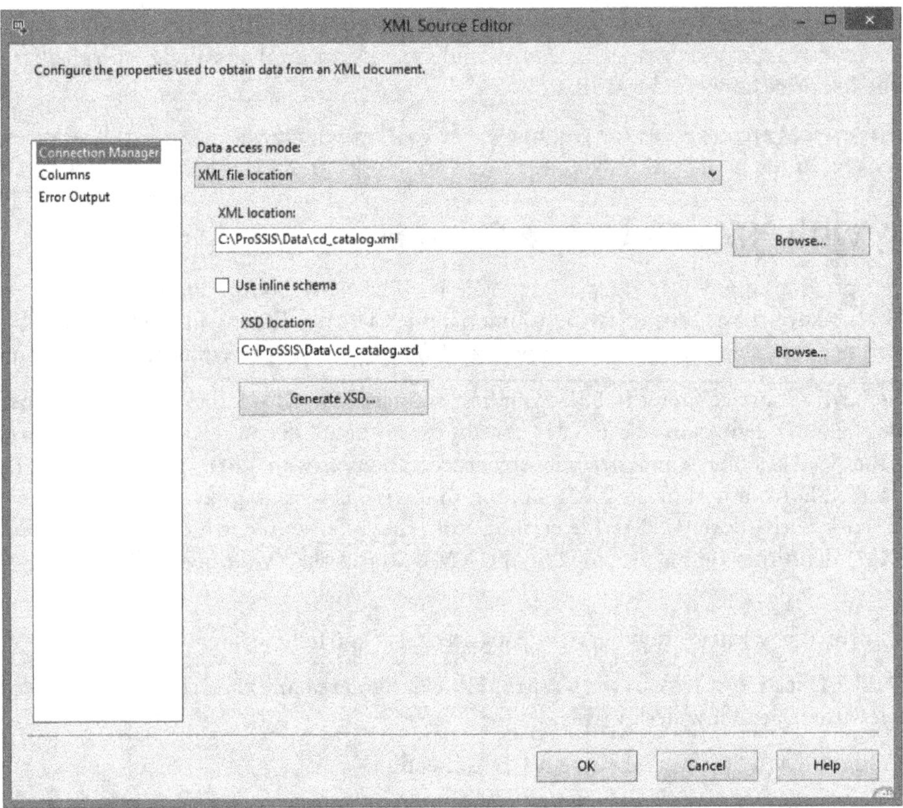

FIGURE 14-27

8. Now that the CD Collection Component understands the XML file, click Columns. You will see all the columns defined in the XML file, as Figure 14-28 shows.

Even though the XML document is one file, it represents two tables with a one-to-many relationship. If you browse to `C:\ProSSIS\Data\cd_catalog.xml`, you'll see a channel, which describes the source of the information, usually news, and several items, or articles, defined. One note of caution here: if you are importing into tables with primary/foreign key constraints, there is no guarantee that the parent rows will be inserted before the child rows. Be sure to keep that in mind as you design your XML solution.

The properties of the channel and item tags match the columns displayed in the XML Source Editor. At this point, you can choose which fields you are interested in importing and change the output names if required. When you use the XML Source adapter, all the output name selections will be available as downstream paths. When you use an output path from the XML Source adapter, you will be able to choose which output you want to use.

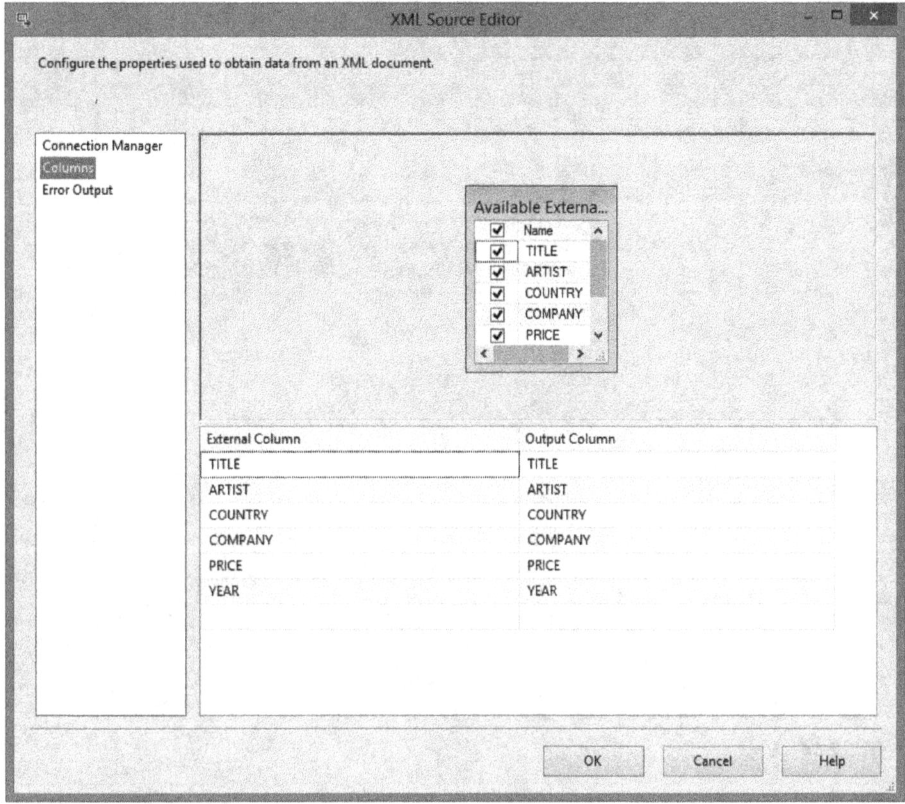

FIGURE 14-28

1. Create a new Connection Manager pointing to the AdventureWorks database or another test database.
2. Add an OLE DB Destination Component to the design area and name it **CD Collection _Table.**
3. Drag the Data Flow Path (blue arrow on the screen) from the XML Source to CD Collection Table.
4. Double-click the CD Collection Table icon to bring up the OLE DB Destination Editor. Make sure that the OLE DB Connection Manager property is set to point to your sample database.
5. Next to Use Table or View, click New. A window with a table definition will pop up. Click OK to create the table. Click Mappings and then click OK to accept the configuration.
6. Add another OLE DB Destination Component and name it **Errors.** Drag a red Data Flow Path from the XML Source to the Errors Component. Click OK. The Configure Error Output dialog will open.
7. In the Truncation property of the Description row, change the value to Redirect row (see Figure 14-29) and click OK.

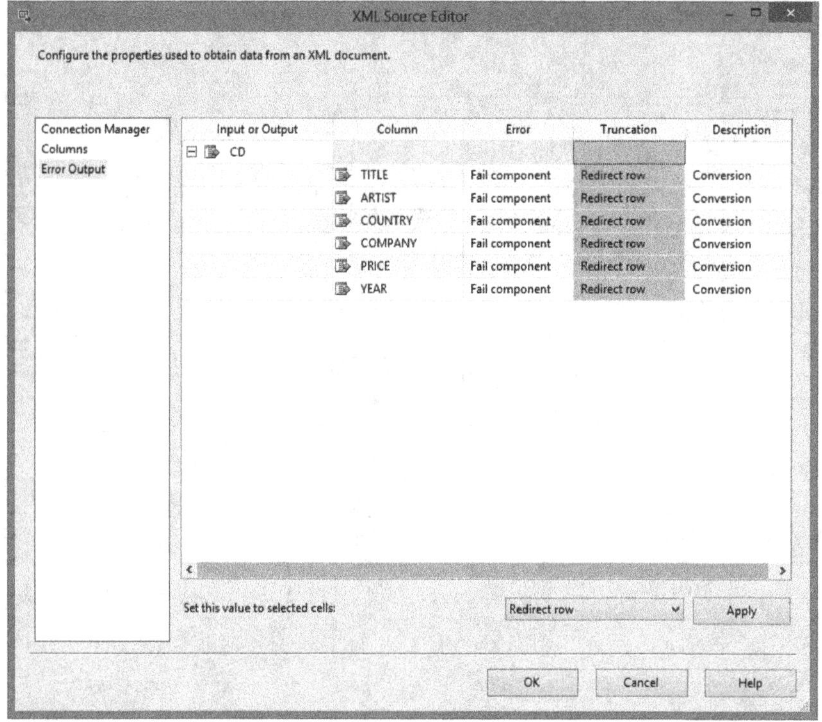

FIGURE 14-29

8. Double-click the OLE DB Destination that you named Errors and make sure it is pointing to the test database. Click New next to "Name of the table or the view," and then click OK to create an Errors table. Click Mappings to accept the mappings, and then click OK to save the configuration. The Data Flow design area should now resemble Figure 14-30.

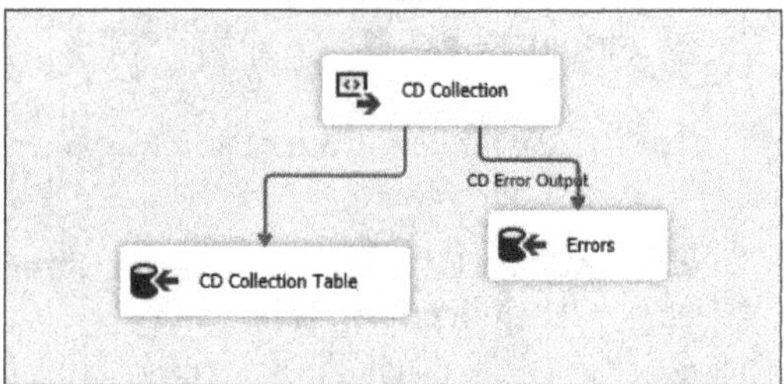

FIGURE 14-30

Run the package. If it completed successfully, some of the rows will be added to the NewsItem table. Any row with a description that exceeds 2,000 characters will end up in the Errors table.

FLAT FILES

Flat files are one of the more common sources to work with because data in the flat files is easy to read and create by most RDBMS systems and ETL tools. The challenges in working with flat files deal with handling data in a format in which data types are not enforced, and data that is structured in challenging ways. You may also run into files that are encoded into a different code page than ASCII, such as a UNIX encoding.

SSIS can handle various formats of flat files with varying code pages. The only challenging data is unstructured data, but this can also be handled in SSIS — not with the Flat File Source adapter but rather through a Script Component that is acting as a source. Refer to Chapter 9 for a primer on using the Script Component.

Loading Flat Files

Loading flat files from SSIS is a lot more straightforward than extracting data from a flat file. That's because when you are loading data into a flat file from an SSIS Data Flow, SSIS already knows the specific data types and column lengths. Extracting data is harder because flat files do not contain information about the data types of the column or the structure of the file. This first example demonstrates how to use SSIS to create and load a flat file:

1. Create a new SSIS package with a Data Flow Task.
2. From the Toolbox, drag an OLE DB Source adapter onto the Data Flow and configure it to connect to the AdventureWorks database.
3. Change the data access mode to SQL Command and type the following SQL statement (Flat_File_Select.txt) in the text window:

    ```
    SELECT Name, ProductNumber, ListPrice
    FROM [Production].[Product]
    ```

4. Switch to the Columns property page of the OLE DB Source Editor and change the column selection to include only ProductID, Name, ProductNumber, ListPrice, and Size (these should be the only columns that are checked).
5. Select OK to save your changes to the OLE DB Source adapter.
6. Add a Flat File Destination adapter to the Data Flow (be sure to use the Flat File Destination and not the Source!) and connect the blue data path from the OLE DB Source to the Flat File Destination.
7. Double-click the Flat File Destination to open the editor.
8. Select New next to the Flat File Connection Manager dropdown, which opens a new window named Flat File Format (see Figure 14-31). Choose Fixed Width and select OK, which opens the Flat File Connection Manager Editor.

    Creating and configuring a Flat File Connection Manager is easier to create from within a Destination adapter that already understands the data than by adding a Flat File Connection Manager directly in the Connection Manager window.

    As Figure 14-31 shows, there are several options for the format of the flat file. The options for the flat file are described right in the selection window.

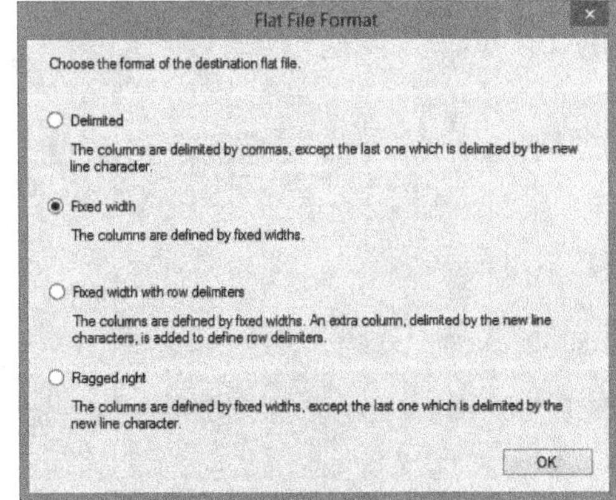

FIGURE 14-31

9. At this point, in the Flat File Connection Manager Editor, name your connection **Products Flat File Destination**, and pick a location and name for your file and enter it in the Filename window, such as **c:\ProSSIS\data\products.txt**.

10. Open the Code Page dropdown list and observe the dozens of supported code pages — from ANSI 1252 to IBM EBCDIC to UTF to MAC. Any of these can be selected if you intend to send the file to another machine that will consume the data in a different format. Change the Code page to 65001 (UTF-8), which should be the last one on the list.

11. Switch to the Advanced property page on the left, which displays a list of the columns that the Flat File Destination adapter received from the upstream transformation (in this case the Source adapter). Select OK to save the Flat File Connection Manager properties.

12. Finally, in the Flat File Destination Editor, click the Mappings property page on the left, which by default maps the input columns to the columns created in the destination file.

    Note that in the Flat File Destination Editor, on the Connection Manager tab, there is a checkbox called "Overwrite data in the file" as Figure 14-32 shows. When this is checked, the file will be cleared before data is loaded in the Data Flow. If this is unchecked, then data will be appended to the file.

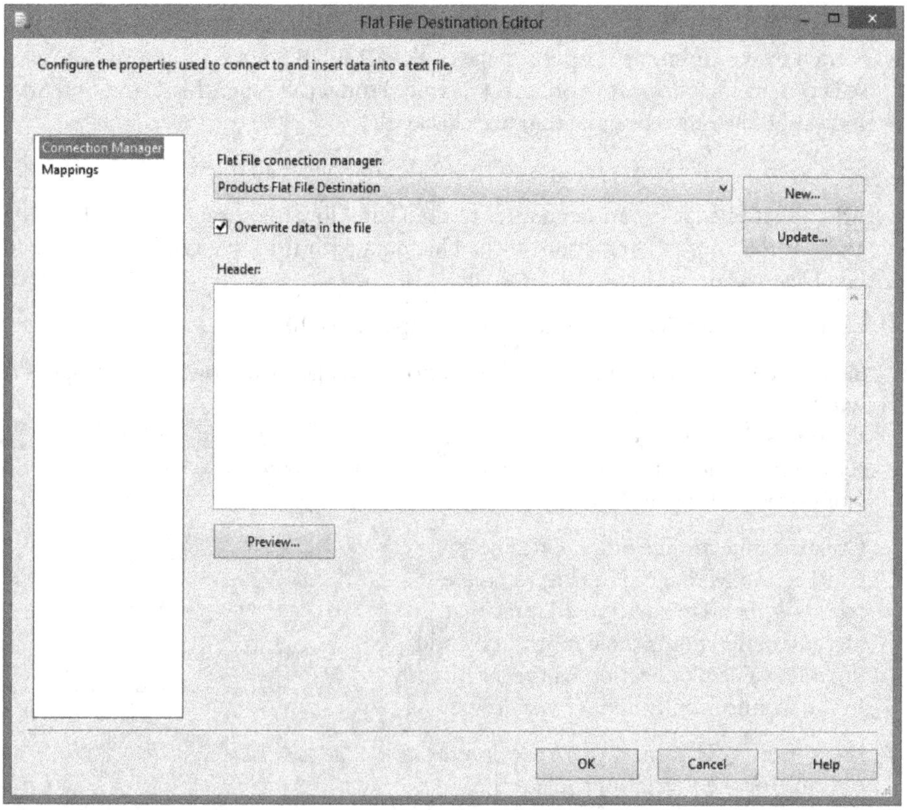

FIGURE 14-32

13. Leave "Overwrite data in the file" checked and select OK to save the Flat File Destination properties.
14. Run this simple package, which will create the flat file and overwrite any data that previously existed.

Extracting Data from Flat Files

Now that you have created and loaded a flat file, the next task is to understand how to extract data from a flat file. Of course, when you are working in your work environment, the first step in extracting data from a flat file is to make sure you have access to the file and you somewhat understand how the data is structured.

In this example, you will be working with a fixed-width file created in the prior example, encoded in UTF-8 code page format. The file contains a list of AdventureWorks products.

1. Create a new SSIS package and a new Data Flow Task within the package.
2. Drag the Flat File Source adapter from the Toolbox onto the Data Flow workspace and then double-click the Flat File Source to open the Flat File Source Editor.
3. Connecting to a flat file requires using a package connection. Therefore, in the Flat File Source Editor, click the New button next to the Flat File Connection Manager dropdown, which opens the Flat File Connection Manager Editor.
4. Name the connection **Products File Source** in the Connection manager name text box.
5. Click the Browse button and find the `products.txt` file that you created in the last exercise (such as `c:\ProSSIS\data\products.txt`).
6. Change the Code page to 65001 (UTF-8).
7. Change the Format dropdown to the Fixed-width selection option, and be sure to uncheck the option Column names in the first data row.
8. Switch to the Columns property page and note that because this file is a fixed-width file, you need to set the column widths. Click on the red vertical line and drag it to the right until the fields line up based on rows and columns, as Figure 14-33 shows (it is easier if your window is maximized, and alternately, you can just change the Row width property to 97).
9. Now you need to identify the fixed-width columns by clicking in the text space right before each column starts. You need to do this for every column.
10. Click the Advanced property page tab and then click the Suggest Types button, which opens the Suggest Column Types window. Click OK to have SSIS scan the file and then suggest data types for the file.
11. While you are still in the Advanced Editor, you should see Column 0 through Column 2. Click Column 0, and in the properties in the right window, change the Name property to **ProductName**.
12. Click Column 2 and change its Name to **ProductNumber**.
13. For Column 2, change the Name property to **ListPrice** and change the DataType dropdown to **[DT_CY]**, as Figure 14-34 shows.

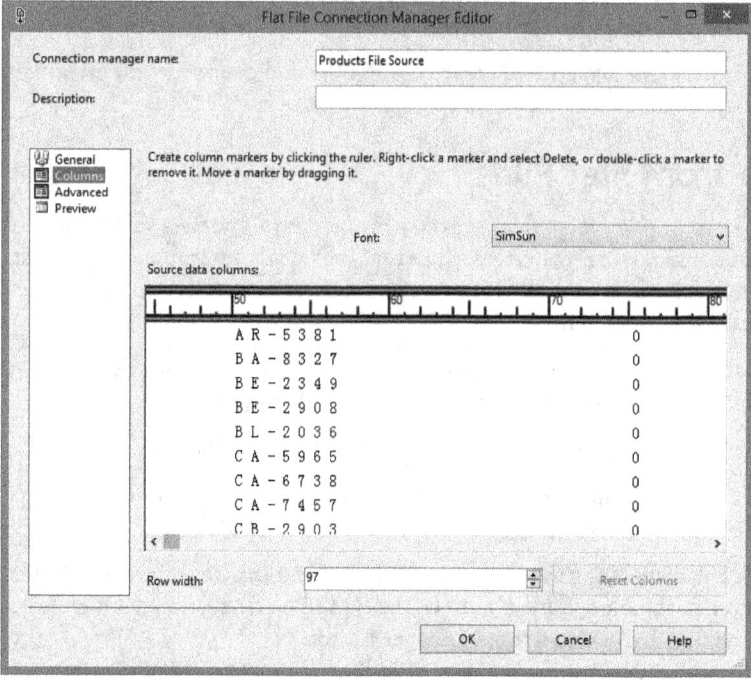

FIGURE 14-33

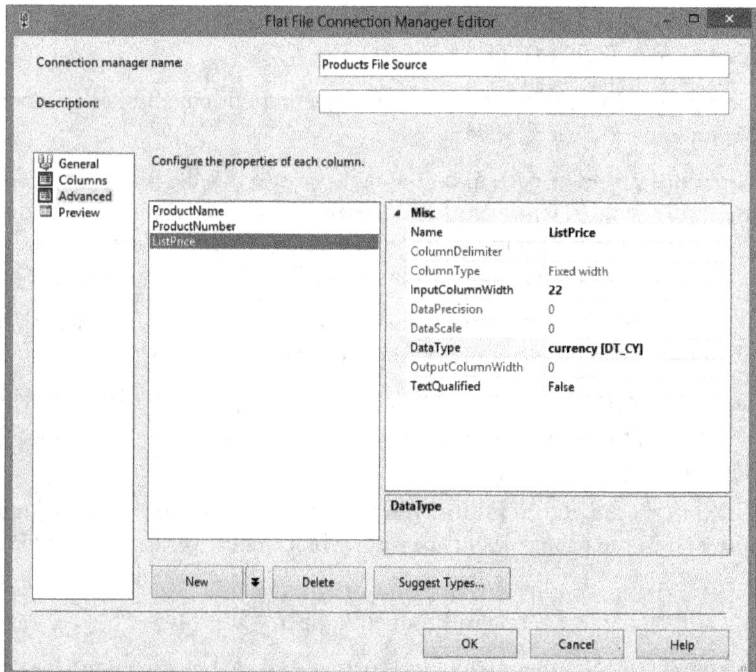

FIGURE 14-34

14. Select OK to save the Flat File Connection Manager properties.
15. While still in the Flat File Source Editor, select the Columns tab, and verify that all the columns are checked in the Available External Columns list.
16. Select OK to save the properties.
17. From the Data Flow Toolbox, drag a Multicast Transformation to the Data Flow workspace and connect the blue data path from the Flat File Source adapter to the Multicast.

At this point, you would usually create downstream transformations or a destination. For the purpose of this example, run the package and observe how the flat file data is extracted into the Data Flow. Nothing is done with it, but it demonstrates how to extract data from a flat file.

ODBC

ODBC stands for *Open Database Connectivity* and is a technology connection standard for passing data between systems that is widely used today for access to RDBMS systems that do not have an OLE DB or ADO.NET provider.

Just like the standard OLE DB providers, ODBC is part of the Windows operating system, included in the MDAC (Microsoft Data Access Components) when the operating system is installed. However, ODBC works differently than the OLE DB providers in that you need to set up the connection information through an applet in the Administrative Tools called Data Sources (ODBC). The OLE DB connections, conversely, are managed directly by the applications and not by the OS. There are some similarities in connecting to Oracle because for Oracle connections, you need to have the configuration managed external to SSIS as well.

For SSIS in SQL 2014, ODBC connectivity is handled by source and destination adapters in the Data Flow. Therefore, the process to get access to an ODBC Source or Destination is to first configure the connection in the Data Sources (ODBC) applet and then reference the ODBC connection through the ODBC adapters in SSIS.

The following example uses public domain data from a DBF Source file, which can be accessed through an ODBC connection. The file is a set of records containing a list of U.S. cities and their properties and is available for download with this book's examples in a file called `tl_2013_13_concity.dbf`. Use the following steps to connect to an ODBC-based source:

1. The first step varies according to the machine on which you are working:
   - For machines with an X64 version of Windows installed, go to a run command and enter the following to bring up the 32-bit version of the ODBC administrator program: `%systemdrive%\Windows\SysWoW64\odbcad32.exe`. Because you are developing a package in SSDT, which is a 32-bit program, you need to make an entry in the 32-bit version of the ODBC administrator tool.
   - If you are on a 32-bit machine, go to the Administrative Tools folder found in the Control Panel list. Then open the Data Sources (ODBC) application from this list of administrative programs. Figure 14-35 shows the ODBC Data Source Administrator tool.

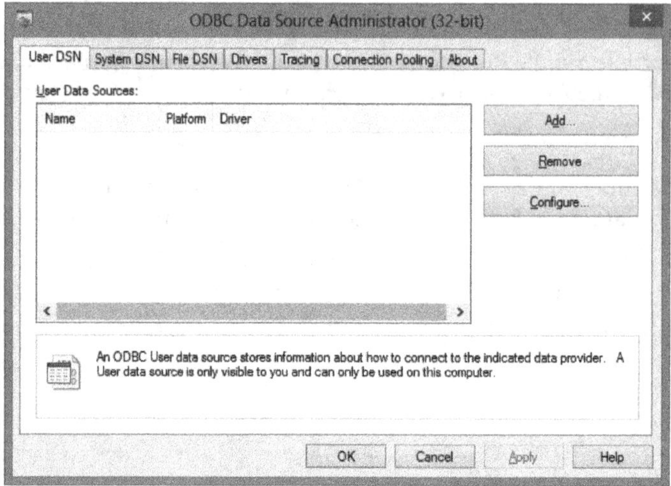

FIGURE 14-35

2. Switch to the System DSN tab, where you will create the ODBC reference (so it is accessible to all users) and click Add.
3. In the Create New Data Source window, scroll down and choose the Microsoft dBase Driver (not the Microsoft Access dBase Driver) and select Finish.
4. In the ODBC dBase Setup window, change the Data Source Name to **US_Cities** and uncheck the Use Current Directory checkbox.
5. Click the Select Directory button and navigate to the folder where the `tl_2013_13_concity.dbf` file is located (provided with the book's online files). Select OK to save the directory path. Figure 14-36 shows the ODBC dBASE Setup dialog (in this case, the `.dbf` file is located at the root of the `c:\ProSSIS\data` drive).

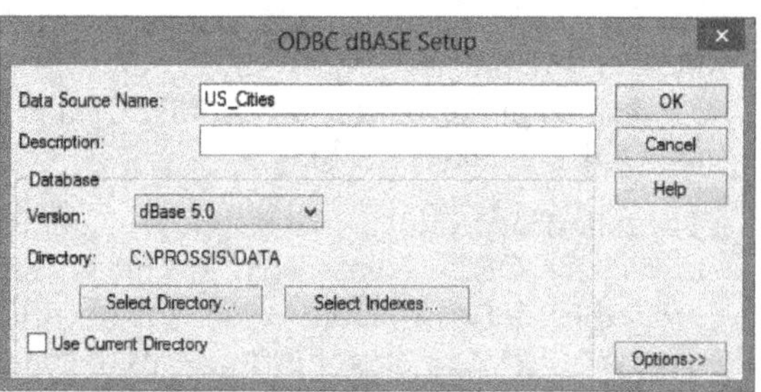

FIGURE 14-36

6. Select OK in the ODBC dBASE Setup dialog and OK in the ODBC Data Sources Administrator to save the US Cities DBF reference.
7. Create a new package in SSIS and a new Data Flow.
8. Drag an ODBC Source adapter from the Toolbox into the Data Flow workspace and double-click the ODBC Source to open its editor.
9. In the ODBC Source Editor, click the New button next to the ODBC Connection Manager window.
10. Select the New button again when the Configure ODBC Connection Manager dialog opens.

11. The Connection Manager dialog enables you to reference the DBF file through an ODBC connection. Select US_Cities from the list, as shown in Figure 14-37.

FIGURE 14-37

12. Select OK in the Connection Manager dialog, and OK in the Configure ODBC Connection Manager dialog, which will return you to the ODBC Source Editor with the US_Cities connection selected.

13. In the "Name of the table or the view" dropdown list, choose the tl_2013_13_concity table in the list. Figure 14-38 shows the ODBC Source Editor dialog.

14. Click the Columns property page tab to bring up a list of the columns available in this file.

15. Select OK to save the changes of the ODBC Source adapter.

16. To demonstrate loading this ODBC Source to a destination table, drag an OLE DB Destination adapter and connect the blue data path from the ODBC Source adapter to the OLE DB Destination adapter.

17. Configure the OLE DB Destination to load the data to a new table in one of the sample databases.

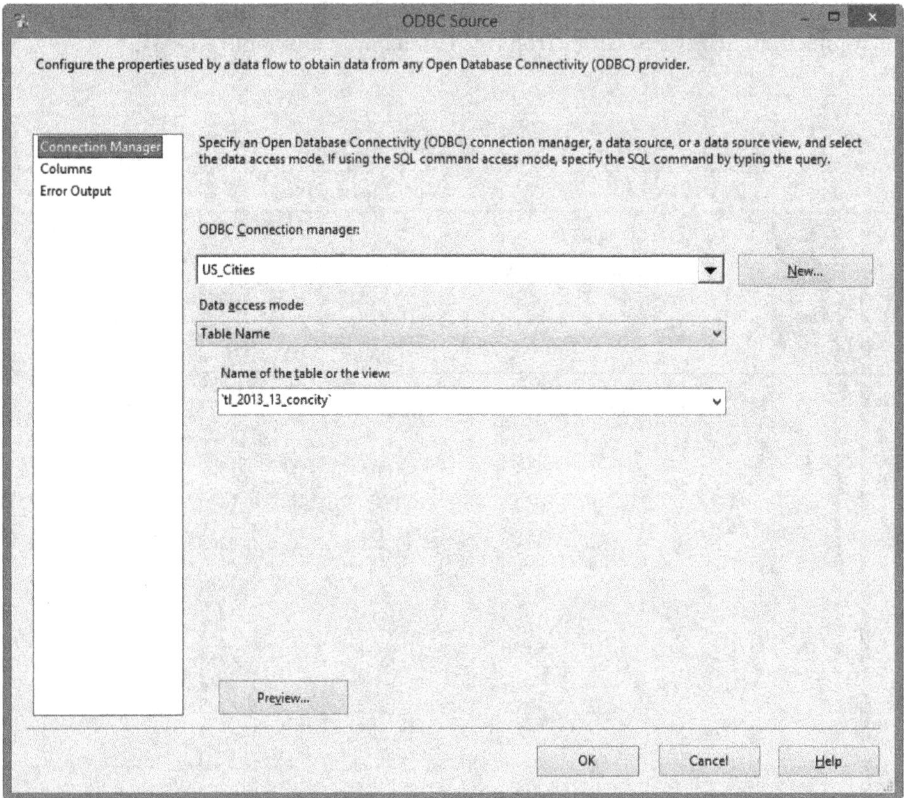

FIGURE 14-38

After you run this new package, use SSMS to open the table you just loaded and observe the loaded results.

If you have a need to load data to an ODBC Destination, the process is very similar, but you use the ODBC Destination adapter to perform this operation.

OTHER HETEROGENEOUS SOURCES

Beyond the heterogeneous data already discussed, you may come across other non-SQL Server systems to which you need access. Examples of this include DB2 or Teradata or applications like SalesForce, SAP, or PeopleSoft or even decision support systems (DSS). A general approach in connecting to these is to first search for an OLE DB provider, so that you can then use the OLE DB adapters in the Data Flow to extract and load data to the system.

The Codeplex SSIS Community Tasks and Components list gives several of the available third-party connection managers (free and paid) that you can use with SSIS at `http://ssisctc.codeplex.com/`.

Also, if you need to connect to an IBM DB2 system, an OLE DB provider is available from Microsoft at `http://msdn2.microsoft.com/en-us/library/Aa213281.aspx`. This provider was originally used in the Host Integration Server but has been made available for broad use.

For SAP connectors, Microsoft has historically provided them with the SQL Server feature pack, which can be found on the Microsoft download site (`www.microsoft.com/download`). At the time of writing, the feature pack has not been released for SQL Server 2014, but these will be available when released.

If an OLE DB provider is not available from Microsoft, you can always check the company that owns the system to see if they provide a free OLE DB or ODBC driver. Be aware that sometimes it is not in their interest to make it easy to connect to their systems, so even if they do have a provider, it may be slow. Alternatively, some software companies sell providers. The following is a list of companies to research that can assist in expanding your connectivity options:

- Attunity (`www.attunity.com`) has several SSIS connectors including Teradata, BizTalk, and SharePoint. In SQL Server 2008, Microsoft licensed the use of the Oracle and Teradata Attunity connectors for SSIS and provided a free download from the Microsoft download site. As of this writing, the SSIS 2014 components have not yet been released, but check the Microsoft download site (`www.microsoft.com/download`) for latest updates.
- CozyRoc (`www.cozyroc.com`) has dozens of SSIS connectors, tasks, and transformations that you can use with SSIS, including connectors to Amazon S3 cloud, Microsoft Dynamics, and SharePoint to name a few.
- Data Direct (`www.datadirect.com`) sells data connection providers (ODBC and OLE DB) that can be installed on Windows operating systems. Some of the connections include Sybase, IBM DB2, Teradata, Informix, and Lotus Notes.
- Pragmatic Works (`www.pragmaticworks.com`) sells a product called Task Factory that is a collection of custom SSIS components including a destination for Oracle.

> **NOTE** *Some systems offer only APIs that enable you to connect to the data programmatically. In these cases, you can also use the Script Component as a source and leverage the system API. See Chapter 9 for more information about leveraging the Script Component.*

SUMMARY

SSIS is capable of connecting to a variety of Data Sources for extraction and loading, but getting there may take a little bit of configuring. Data connects can sometimes be tricky, as they require the coordination of third-party software and SSIS adapters. The good news is that most sources are accessible in SSIS — whether through the standard built-in providers or through external providers that can be installed on your SSIS server.

So far this book has covered the basic techniques of building SSIS packages. You now have enough knowledge to put all the pieces together and build a more complex package. The next chapter focuses on how to guarantee that your SSIS packages will scale and work reliably.

15

Reliability and Scalability

WHAT'S IN THIS CHAPTER?

- Restarting packages
- Using package transactions for data consistency
- Using error outputs for reliability and scalability
- Scaling out efficiently and reliably

WROX.COM CODE DOWNLOADS FOR THIS CHAPTER

You can find the wrox.com code downloads for this chapter at `http://www.wrox.com/go/prossis2014` on the Download Code tab.

Reliability and scalability are goals for all your systems, and although it may seem strange to combine them in one chapter, they are often directly linked, as you will see. Errors and the unexpected conditions that precipitate them are the most obvious threats to a reliable process. Several features of SQL Server 2014 Integration Services enable you to handle these situations with grace and integrity, keeping the data moving and the systems running.

Error outputs and checkpoints are the two features you will focus on in this chapter, and you will see how they can be used in the context of reliability. Implementation of these methods can also have a direct effect on package performance, and therefore scalability, and you will learn how to take into account these considerations for your package and process design. The capability to provide checkpoints does not natively extend inside the Data Flow Task, but there are methods you can apply to achieve this. The methods can then be transferred almost directly into the context of scalability, enabling you to partition packages and improve both reliability and scalability at the same time. All of these methods can be combined, and while there is no one-size-fits-all solution, this chapter describes all your options so you have the necessary information to make informed choices for your own SSIS implementations.

RESTARTING PACKAGES

Everyone has been there — one of your Data Transformation Services (DTS) packages failed overnight, and you now have to completely rerun the package. This is particularly painful if some of the processes inside the package are expensive in terms of resources or time. In DTS, it wasn't possible to restart a package from where it left off, and picking apart a package to run just those tasks that failed was tedious and error prone. A variety of exotic solutions have been used, such as a post-execution process that goes into the package and recreates the package from the failed step forward. Although this worked, it required someone with a detailed knowledge of the DTS object model, which most production DBAs did not have. If your process takes data from a production SQL Server that has a very small window of ETL opportunity, you can be sure that most DBAs are not going to be pleased when you tell them you need to run the extract again, and that it may impact the users.

For this reason, "package restartability" or checkpoints in SQL Server Integration Services was a huge relief. In this chapter, you are going to learn everything you need to know to enable restartability in your SSIS packages.

Checkpoints are the foundation for restarting packages in SSIS, and they work by writing state information to a file after each task completes. This file can then be used to determine which tasks have run and which have failed. More detail about these files is provided in the "Inside the Checkpoint File" section. To ensure that the checkpoint file is created correctly, you must set three package properties and one task property, which can be found on the property pages of the package and task. The package properties are as follows:

- **CheckpointFilename:** This is the filename of the checkpoint file, which must be provided. There are no specific conventions or requirements for the filename.
- **CheckpointUsage:** There are three values, which describe how a checkpoint file is used during package execution:
  - **Never:** The package will not use a checkpoint file and therefore will never restart.
  - **If Exists:** If a checkpoint file exists in the place you specified for the CheckpointFilename property, then it will be used, and the package will restart according to the checkpoints written.
  - **Always:** The package will always use a checkpoint file to restart; if one does not exist, the package will fail.
- **SaveCheckpoints:** This is a simple Boolean to indicate whether checkpoints are to be written. Obviously, this must be set to true for this scenario.

The one property you have to set on the task is FailPackageOnFailure. This must be set for each task or container that you want to be the point for a checkpoint and restart. If you do not set this property to true and the task fails, no file will be written, and the next time you invoke the package, it will start from the beginning again. You'll see an example of this happening later.

> **NOTE** *As you know, SSIS packages are broken down into the Control Flow and Data Flow Tasks. Checkpoints occur only at the Control Flow; it is not possible to checkpoint transformations or restart inside a Data Flow Task. The Data Flow Task can be a checkpoint, but it is treated like any other task. This ensures Data Flow Tasks write all or none of their data, like a SQL transaction with commits and rollbacks. Implementing your own checkpoint and restart feature for data is described later in the chapter.*

Keep in mind that if nothing fails in your package, no file will be generated. You'll have a look later at the generated file itself and try to make some sense out of it, but for now you only need to know that the file contains all the information needed by the package when it is restarted, enabling it to behave like nothing untoward had interrupted it. That's enough information to be able to start using checkpoints in your packages, so now you can proceed with some examples.

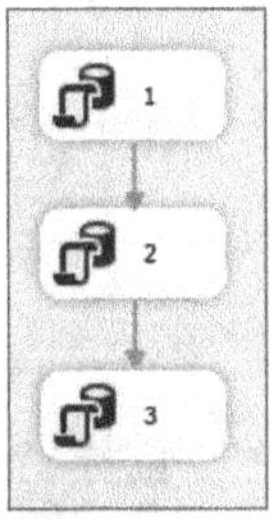

FIGURE 15-1

Simple Control Flow

The first example package you will create contains a simple Control Flow with a series of tasks meant to highlight the power of checkpoints. Create a package named **Checkpoint.dtsx** that contains three Execute SQL Tasks, as shown in Figure 15-1.

In the new package, add a connection manager to the AdventureWorksDW database. Then, add a simple select statement, such as "select 1" to the first and third tasks. The second of these tasks, aptly named "2," is set to fail with a divide-by-zero error, as shown in the Task Editor in Figure 15-2.

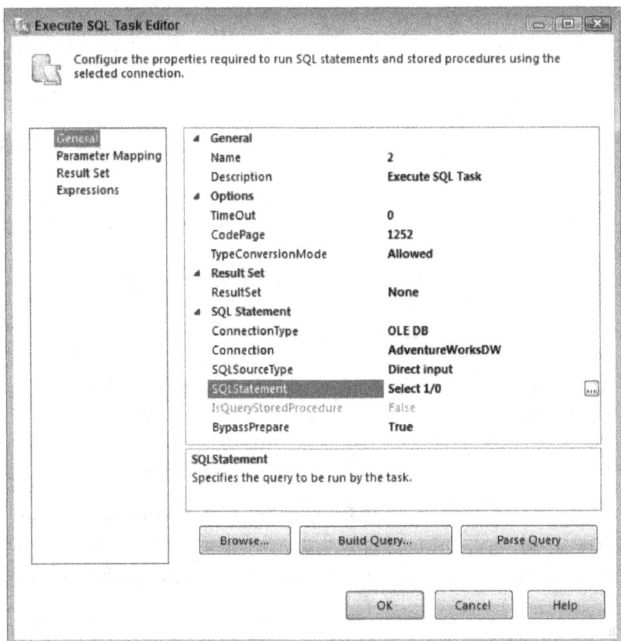

FIGURE 15-2

Assume that the task labeled "1" is expensive, and you want to ensure that you don't need to execute it twice if it finishes and something else in the package fails. You now need to set up the package to use checkpoints and the task itself. First, set the properties of the package described earlier, as shown in Figure 15-3.

Next, set the properties of the task labeled "2" to use checkpoints (see Figure 15-4). Change the `FailPackageOnFailure` property to True.

Now you can execute the package. The expected outcome is shown in Figure 15-5 — the first task completes successfully with a check mark in a green circle, but the second task fails with an X in a red circle. The third task did not execute. Because the screenshots for this book are in black and white, you won't be able to see the colors here, but you can see that the tasks contain different symbols in the top-right corner.

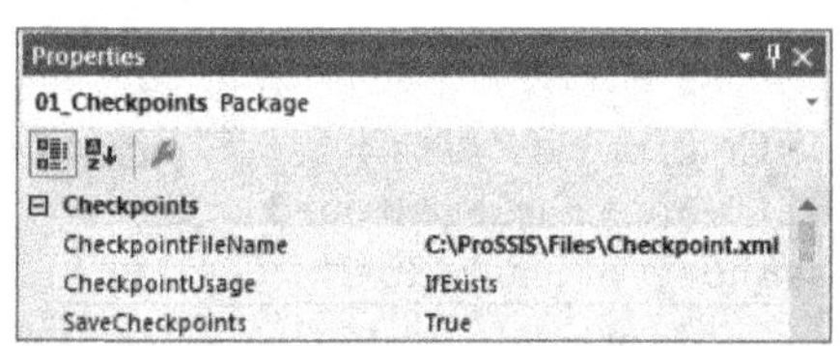

FIGURE 15-3

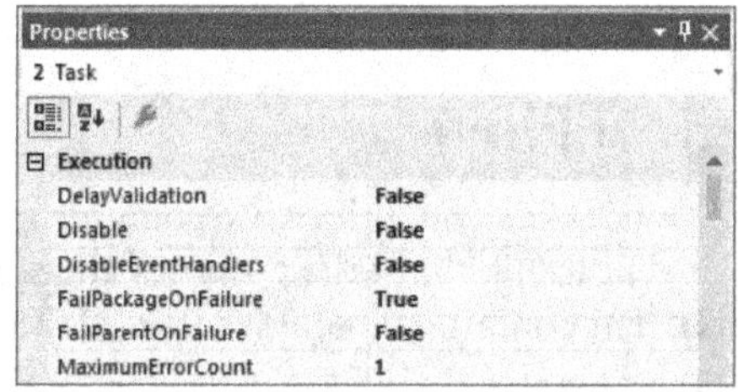

FIGURE 15-4

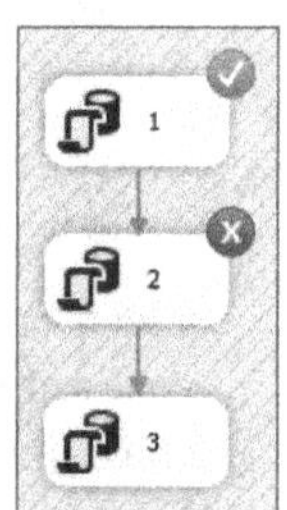

FIGURE 15-5

If you had created this package in DTS, you would have had to write some logic to cope with the failure in order to not have to execute task 1 again. Because you are working in SSIS and have set the package up properly, you can rely on checkpoints. When the package failed, the error output window said something like this:

```
SSIS package "C:\ProSSIS\Code\Ch15\01_Checkpoints.dtsx" starting.
Information: 0x40016045 at 01_Checkpoints: The package will be saving checkpoints
to file "C:\ProSSIS\Files\Checkpoint.xml" during execution. The package is
configured to save checkpoints.
Information: 0x40016049 at 01_Checkpoints: Checkpoint file "C:\ProSSIS\Files\
Checkpoint.xml" update starting.
Information: 0x40016047 at 1: Checkpoint file "C:\ProSSIS\Files\Checkpoint.xml" was
updated to record completion of this container.
Error: 0xC002F210 at 2, Execute SQL Task: Executing the query "Select 1/0"
failed with the following error: "Divide by zero error encountered.". Possible
failure reasons: Problems with the query, "ResultSet" property not set correctly,
parameters not set correctly, or connection not established correctly.
Task failed: 2
SSIS package "C:\ProSSIS\Code\Ch15\01_Checkpoints.dtsx" finished: Failure.
```

As you can see, the output window says that a checkpoint file was written. If you look at the file system, you can see that this is true, as shown in Figure 15-6. You'll look inside the file later when you have a few more things of interest in there, but for the moment just understand that the package now knows what happened and where.

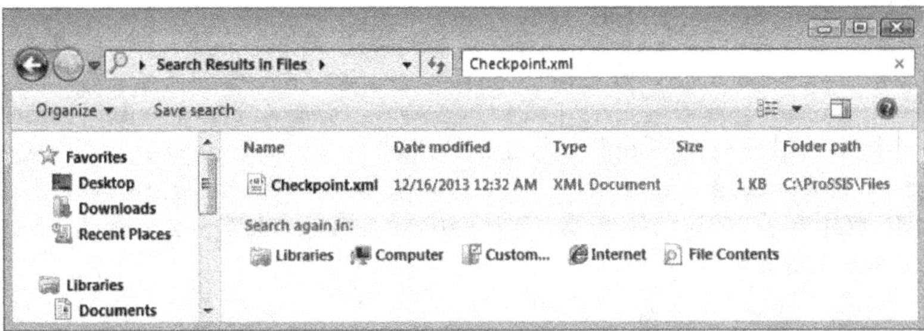

FIGURE 15-6

Now you need to fix the problem by removing the divide-by-zero issue in the second task (change the SQL Statement to Select 1 instead of Select 1/0) and run the package again. Figure 15-7 shows what happens after you do that.

Task 2 was executed again and then task 3. Task 1 was oblivious to the package running again.

Recall from earlier that the task you want to be the site for a checkpoint must have the FailPackageOnFailure property set to true. Otherwise, no file will be written; and when the package executes again it will start from the beginning. Here is how that works. Set task 2 to not use checkpoints by setting this property to false, as shown in Figure 15-8.

Change the SQL Statement in task 2 back to Select 1/0 and then execute the package again. No checkpoint file is written, as expected. This means that after you fix the error in the task again and rerun the package one more time, the results look like Figure 15-9; all tasks have a green check mark in the top right corner, which may or may not be what you want.

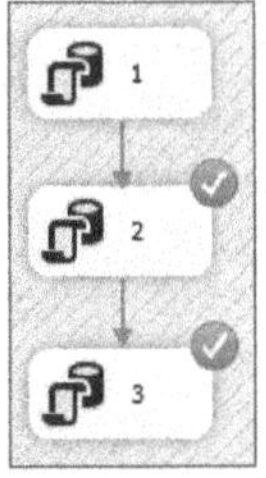

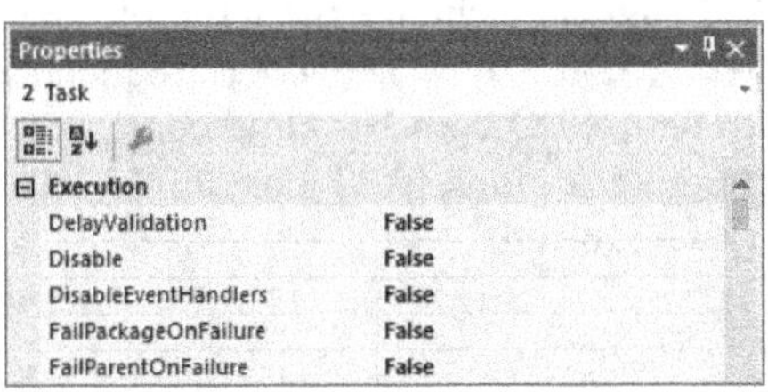

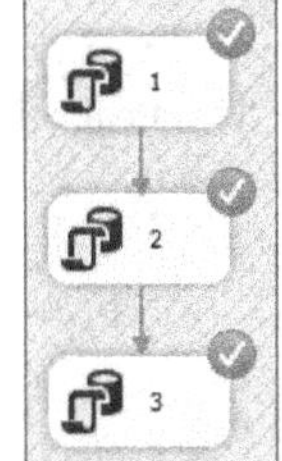

FIGURE 15-7 FIGURE 15-8 FIGURE 15-9

This example is a very simple one that involves only three tasks joined by a workflow, but hopefully it has given you an idea about restartability in SSIS packages; the examples that follow are more complicated.

Containers within Containers and Checkpoints

Containers and transactions have an effect on checkpoints. You will see these effects in this example, and change some properties and settings while you're at it. First, you will create a new package named ContainerCheckpoints.dtsx using Sequence Containers and checkpoints. In this package you have two Sequence Containers, which themselves contain Execute SQL Tasks, as shown in Figure 15-10.

Make sure the package has all the settings necessary to use checkpoints, as in the previous example. On the initial run-through of this package, the only container that you want to be the site for a checkpoint is task 3, so set the FailPackageOnFailure property of task 3 to true. Figure 15-11 shows what happens when you deliberately set this task to fail, perhaps with a divide-by-zero error (refer to the previous example to see how to do that).

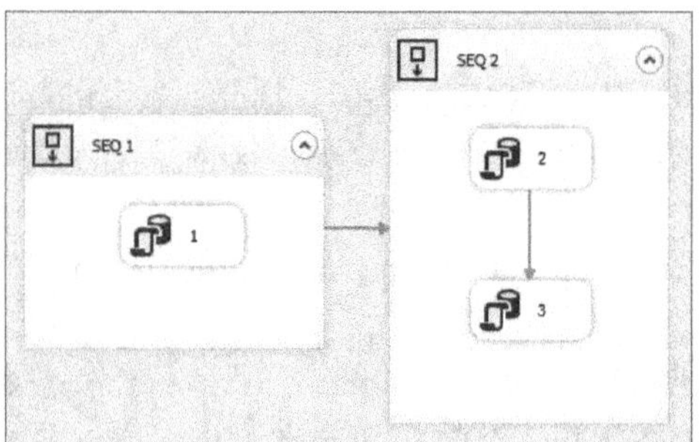

FIGURE 15-10

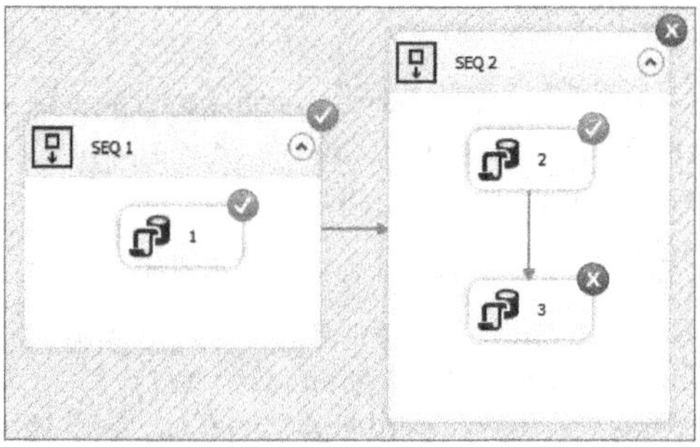

FIGURE 15-11

As expected, task 3 has failed, and the Sequence Container, SEQ 2, has also failed because of this. If you now fix the problem with task 3 and re-execute the package, you will see results matching those shown in Figure 15-12.

Therefore, there's no real difference here from the earlier example except that the Sequence Container "SEQ 2" has a green check. Now you'll change the setup of the package to see the behavior change dramatically. What you're going to do is make the Sequence Container SEQ 2 *transacted*. That means you're going to wrap SEQ 2 and its child containers in a transaction. Change the properties of the SEQ 2 container to look like Figure 15-13 so that the TransactionOption property is set to Required.

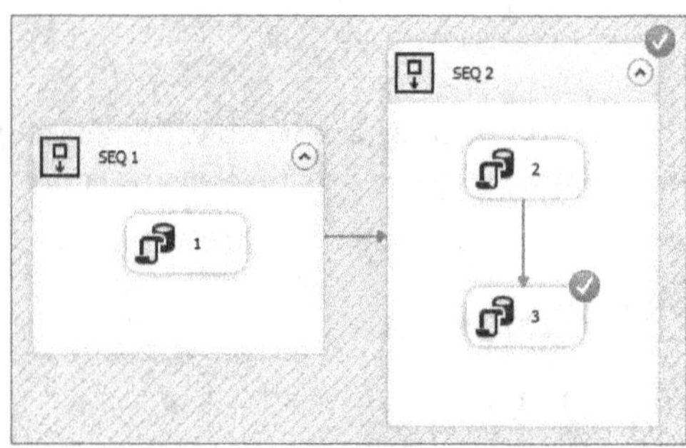

FIGURE 15-12

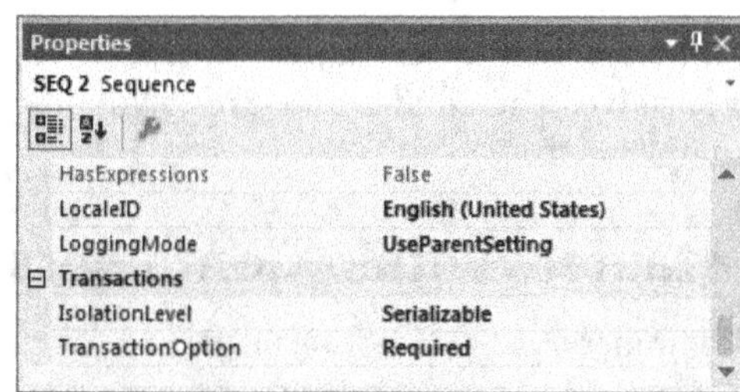

FIGURE 15-13

Setting the TransactionOption property of the SEQ 2 container to Required means that it will start its own transaction. Now open the properties window of the two child Execute SQL Tasks and set their TransactionOption properties to Supported, as shown in Figure 15-14, so that they will join a transaction if one exists.

> **WARNING** *SSIS uses the Microsoft Distributed Coordinator to manage its transactions. Before setting the TransactionOption property to Required, be sure to start Microsoft Distributed Transaction Coordinator (MSDTC) service.*

Now execute the package again. On the first run-through, the package fails as before at task 3. The difference occurs when you fix the problem with task 3 and re-execute the package. The result looks like Figure 15-15.

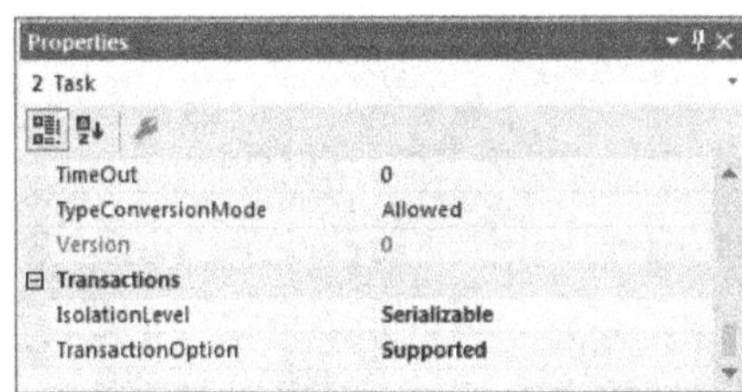

FIGURE 15-14

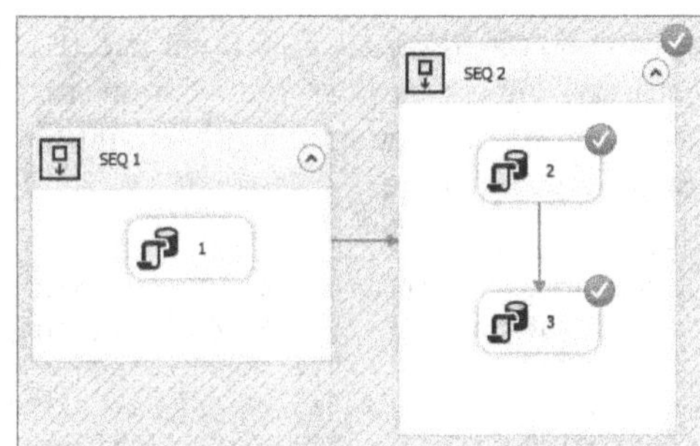

FIGURE 15-15

Because the container was transacted, the fact that task 3 failed is not recorded in the checkpoint file. Instead, the fact that the Sequence Container failed is recorded; hence, the Sequence Container is re-executed in its entirety when the package is rerun. Therefore, tasks 2 and 3 execute on the second run. Note that the transaction was on the Sequence Container and not the individual tasks. If you have a set of tasks that need to be run in a transaction, the Sequence Container will handle this for you.

Variations on a Theme

You may have noticed another property in the task property pages next to the FailPackageOnFailure property — the FailParentOnFailure property. In the previous example, the SEQ 2 container is the parent to the two Execute SQL Tasks 2 and 3. You'll run through a few variations of the parent/child relationship here so that you can see the differences. In each example, you will force a failure on the first run-through; then you will correct the problem and run the package a second time.

Failing the Parent, Not the Package

What happens if instead of setting the FailPackageOnFailure property of task 3 to true, you set the FailParentOnFailure property to true? After a failed execution and then issue resolution, the whole package will be run again on re-execution of the package. Why? Because no checkpoint file has been written.

> **NOTE** *Remember that if you want a checkpoint file to be written, the task that fails must have the FailPackageOnFailure property set to true; otherwise, no file is written.*

Failing the Parent and the Package

In this variation, you still have a transacted Sequence Container, and you still have task 3's FailParentOnFailure property set to true. In addition, set the SEQ 2 Sequence Container's FailPackageOnFailure property to true. Figure 15-16 shows what happens on the rerun of the package after a failure.

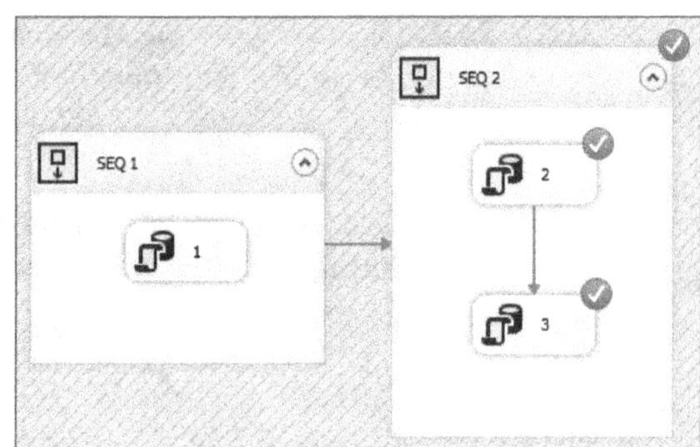

FIGURE 15-16

As you can see, the Sequence Container executes in its entirety, and the output window from the package confirms that you used a checkpoint file and started a transaction:

```
SSIS package "C:\ProSSIS\Code\Ch15\02_ContainerCheckpoints.dtsx" starting.
Information: 0x40016046 at 02_ContainerCheckpoints: The package restarted from
checkpoint file "C:\ProSSIS\Files\ContainerCheckpoint.xml". The package was
configured to restart from checkpoint.
Information: 0x40016045 at 02_ContainerCheckpoints: The package will be saving
checkpoints to file "C:\ProSSIS\Files\ContainerCheckpoint.xml" during execution.
The package is configured to save checkpoints.
Information: 0x4001100A at SEQ 2: Starting distributed transaction for this
container.
Information: 0x4001100B at SEQ 2: Committing distributed transaction started by
this container.
SSIS package "C:\ProSSIS\Code\Ch15\02_ContainerCheckpoints.dtsx" finished: Success.
```

Failing the Task with No Transaction

The next variation will show what happens if you set some of the checkpoint properties without having a transaction in place. Start by removing the transactions from your package by setting the SEQ 2's TransactionOption property to Supported. Force an error in task 3, and run the package again to see it fail at task 3. Then, fix the problem, and re-execute the package. Remember that task 3 has its FailParentOnFailure property set to true, and the SEQ 2 Sequence Container has its FailPackageOnFailure set to true. The outcome, shown in Figure 15-17, is not exactly what you likely expected. As you can imagine, this is not very useful. The Sequence Container shows success, yet none of the tasks in the container executed. It's important to ensure that you have the properties of the tasks and the containers set properly in order to ensure that the desired tasks execute after the checkpoint is created.

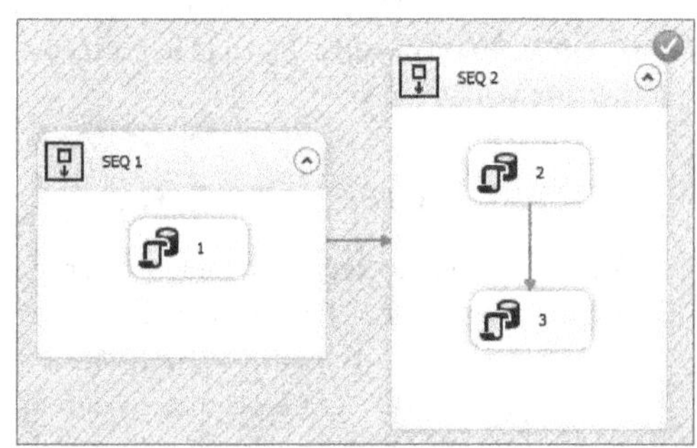

FIGURE 15-17

Failing the Package, Not the Sequence

You might assume that if tasks 2 and 3 have the Sequence Container as a parent, then the package itself must be the parent of the Sequence Container. If this is the case, wouldn't setting FailParentOnFailure on the Sequence Container be the same as setting FailPackageOnFailure on the same container? The quick answer is no. If you try this, you will see that no checkpoint file is written, and by now you know what that means. The message here is that if you want a checkpoint file to be written, then make sure that the restart point has FailPackageOnFailure set to true.

Inside the Checkpoint File

As promised earlier, it's time to look inside the checkpoint file to see what it contains now that you have more things to put in there. In the CheckpointScripts.dtsx package shown in Figure 15-18, although you have only three tasks, you also have a variable value being changed. The purpose of this package is to show you what kind of information is stored in a checkpoint file. To add a variable, simply click the designer while in the Control Flow and choose Variables from the SSIS menu or right-click on the Control Flow background and select Variables. Create a Variable named **intVar** and make the variable type integer. Leave the default value of zero.

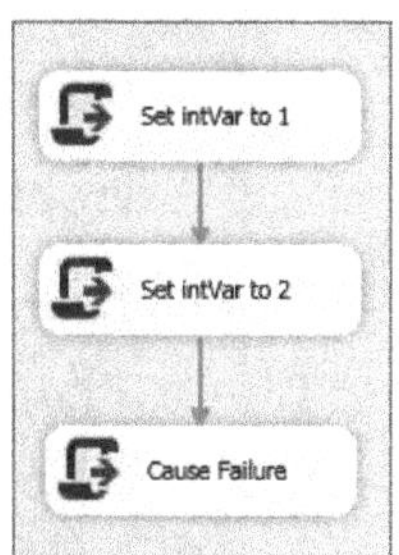

FIGURE 15-18

The Script Tasks will change the value of the intVar variable to 1 and then to 2, and the last Script Task will try to set the variable to the letter "x". This will cause the last Script Task to fail because of nonmatching data types. To alter the value of a variable in all Script Tasks, you add the variable name to the ReadWriteVariables section on the Script Task's editor. You then need to add some script to change the value. The following is the Visual Basic script in the first Script Task:

```
Public Sub Main()
    Dts.Variables("intVar").Value = 1
    Dts.TaskResult = ScriptResults.Success
End Sub
```

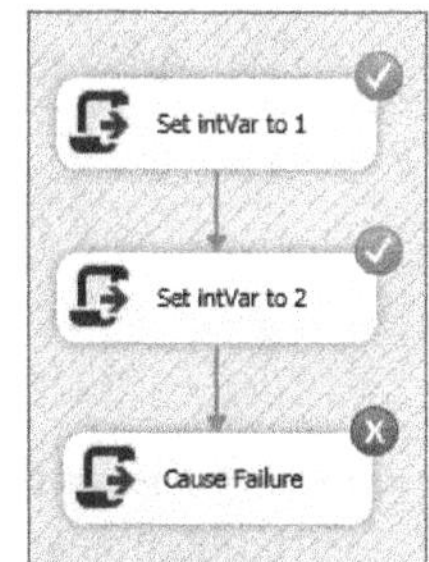

FIGURE 15-19

> **NOTE** *Code samples for this chapter can be found as part of the code download for this book available at* `http://www.wrox.com/go/prossis2014`.

Now run the package. It will fail, as shown in Figure 15-19. A Script Task Error Window may appear. If so, just click Close.

> **NOTE** *Instead of altering the Script Task code to make your task fail, you can simply set the ForceExecutionResult on the task to Failure. You can also do this on any Containers too.*

Inside the generated checkpoint file, you should find something like this:

```
<DTS:Checkpoint xmlns:DTS="www.microsoft.com/SqlServer/Dts"
  DTS:PackageID="{16EDDCF1-5141-44B6-8997-0A42EB82A767}">
  <DTS:Variables DTS:ContID="{16EDDCF1-5141-44B6-8997-0A42EB82A767}">
    <DTS:Variable DTS:Namespace="User" DTS:IncludeInDebugDump="6789"
        DTS:ObjectName="intVar" DTS:DTSID="{4DA0C488-4CCA-4F33-B2FE-DAE1219A5A77}"
        DTS:CreationName="">
      <DTS:VariableValue DTS:DataType="3">2</DTS:VariableValue>
    </DTS:Variable>
  </DTS:Variables>
  <DTS:Container DTS:ContID="{D0B7A051-AAD4-44C5-A9CB-1854DB7E2FC7}"
    DTS:Result="0" DTS:PrecedenceMap=""/>
  <DTS:Container DTS:ContID="{A55EB798-6144-4DC2-820B-571DAE6ED606}"
    DTS:Result="0" DTS:PrecedenceMap="Y"/>
</DTS:Checkpoint>
```

The file is easier to understand broken down into its constituent parts. The first part tells you about the package to which this file applies:

```
<DTS:Checkpoint xmlns:DTS="www.microsoft.com/SqlServer/Dts"
  DTS:PackageID="{16EDDCF1-5141-44B6-8997-0A42EB82A767}">
```

The next section of the file, the longest part, details the package variable that you were manipulating:

```
  <DTS:Variables DTS:ContID="{16EDDCF1-5141-44B6-8997-0A42EB82A767}">
    <DTS:Variable DTS:Namespace="User" DTS:IncludeInDebugDump="6789"
        DTS:ObjectName="intVar" DTS:DTSID="{4DA0C488-4CCA-4F33-B2FE-DAE1219A5A77}"
        DTS:CreationName="">
      <DTS:VariableValue DTS:DataType="3">2</DTS:VariableValue>
    </DTS:Variable>
  </DTS:Variables>
```

One of the most important things this part of the file tells you is that the last value assigned to the variable, intVar, was 2. When the package re-executes, it is this value that will be used.

The final part of the file tells you about the tasks in the package and what their outcomes were. It tells you only about the two tasks that succeeded, not the one that failed:

```
  <DTS:Container DTS:ContID="{D0B7A051-AAD4-44C5-A9CB-1854DB7E2FC7}"
    DTS:Result="0" DTS:PrecedenceMap=""/>
  <DTS:Container DTS:ContID="{A55EB798-6144-4DC2-820B-571DAE6ED606}"
    DTS:Result="0" DTS:PrecedenceMap="Y"/>
</DTS:Checkpoint>
```

The first container mentioned is the "Set intVar value to 2" Task:

```
  <DTS:Container DTS:ContID="{D0B7A051-AAD4-44C5-A9CB-1854DB7E2FC7}"
    DTS:Result="0" DTS:PrecedenceMap=""/>
```

The next, and final, task to be mentioned is the "Set intVar value to 1" Task:

```
  <DTS:Container DTS:ContID="{A55EB798-6144-4DC2-820B-571DAE6ED606}"
    DTS:Result="0" DTS:PrecedenceMap="Y"/>
```

Checkpoints are a great help in controlling the start location in SSIS. This restartability can result in a huge time savings. In packages with dozens or even hundreds of tasks, you can imagine the time saved by skipping tasks that do not need to be executed again. Keep in mind that if two tasks are required to run together during one package run, place these tasks in a Sequence Container, set the container to fail the package, and set the tasks to fail the parent.

PACKAGE TRANSACTIONS

This part of the chapter describes how you can use transactions within your packages to handle data consistency. Two types of transactions are available in an SSIS package:

- **Distributed Transaction Coordinator (DTC) Transactions:** One or more transactions that require a DTC and can span connections, tasks, and packages
- **Native Transaction:** A transaction at a SQL Server engine level, using a single connection managed through use of T-SQL transaction commands

> **NOTE** *Here is how Books Online defines the Microsoft DTC: "The Microsoft Distributed Transaction Coordinator (MS DTC) allows applications to extend transactions across two or more instances of SQL Server. It also allows applications to participate in transactions managed by transaction managers that comply with the X/Open DTP XA standard."*

You will learn how to use them by going through four examples in detail. Each example builds on the previous example, except for the last one:

- **Single Package:** Single transaction using DTC
- **Single Package:** Multiple transactions using DTC
- **Two Packages:** One transaction using DTC
- **Single Package:** One transaction using a native transaction in SQL Server

For transactions to happen in a package and for tasks to join them, you need to set a few properties at both the package and the task level. As you go through the examples, you will see the finer details behind these transactions, but the following table will get you started by describing the possible settings for the TransactionOption property.

PROPERTY VALUE	DESCRIPTION
Supported	If a transaction already exists at the parent, the container will join the transaction.
Not Supported	The container will not join a transaction, if one is present.
Required	The container will start a transaction if the parent has not; otherwise, it will join the parent transaction.

Armed with these facts, you can get right into the thick of things and look at the first example.

Single Package, Single Transaction

To start the first example, create the simple package shown in Figure 15-20.

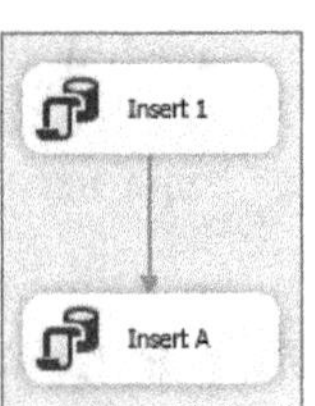

FIGURE 15-20

This package is quite basic in that all it does is insert some data into the table and then the last task will deliberately fail. Open SSMS and run the following code on the AdventureWorksDW database:

```
CREATE TABLE dbo.T1(col1 int)
```

In the Execute SQL Task named "Insert 1", use the following code in the SQLStatement property to insert data into the table you just created:

```
INSERT dbo.T1(col1) VALUES(1)
```

To make the final task fail at runtime, use the following code in the SQLStatement property of the Execute SQL Task names "Insert A":

```
INSERT dbo.T1(col1) VALUES("A")
```

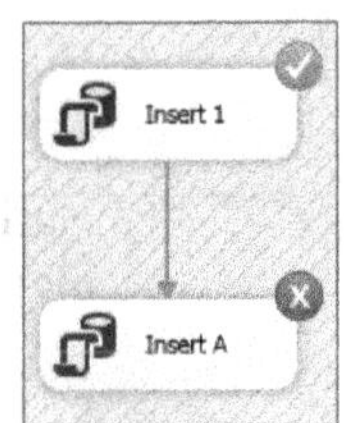

FIGURE 15-21

Run the package with no transactions in place and see what happens. The results should look like Figure 15-21: The first task succeeds, and the second fails.

If you go to your database, you should see data inserted, as shown in Figure 15-22.

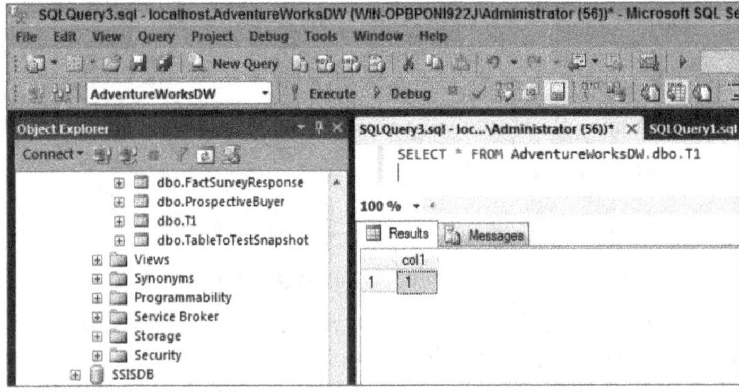

FIGURE 15-22

Now run the following code in SSMS to delete the data from the table:

```
TRUNCATE TABLE dbo.T1
```

Next, you want to set up the package to start a transaction that the tasks can join. You do that by setting the properties of the package, as shown in Figure 15-23. Set the TransactionOption property to Required.

You now need to tell the tasks in the package to join this transaction, by setting their TransactionOption properties to Supported, as shown in Figure 15-24.

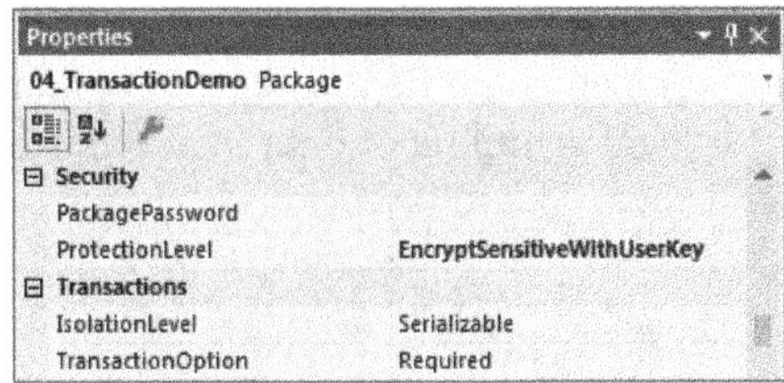

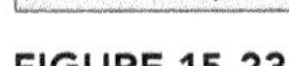
FIGURE 15-23

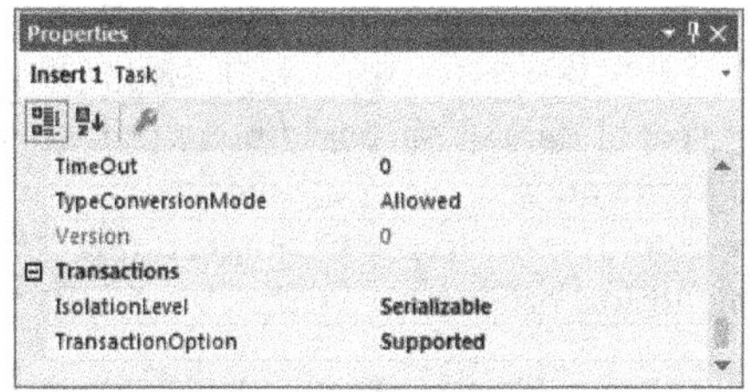

FIGURE 15-24

> **NOTE** *To quickly set the properties for all these tasks at once, select them by holding down the Ctrl key and clicking on each task, and set the TransactionOption property to the desired value.*

Now when you re-execute the package, a DTC transaction will be started by the package, all the tasks will join, and because of the failure in the last task, the work in the package will be undone. Go back to SSMS and query the table. You should see no data in it. A good way to see the DTC transaction that was started is to look at the output window in SSIS:

```
SSIS package "C:\ProSSIS\Code\Ch15\04_TransactionDemo.dtsx" starting.
Information: 0x4001100A at 04_TransactionDemo: Starting distributed transaction for
this container.
Error: 0xC002F210 at Insert A, Execute SQL Task: Executing the query "INSERT dbo.
T1(col1) VALUES("A")" failed with the following error: "Invalid column name 'A'.".
Possible failure reasons: Problems with the query, "ResultSet" property not set
correctly, parameters not set correctly, or connection not established correctly.
Task failed: Insert A
Information: 0x4001100C at Insert A: Aborting the current distributed transaction.
Warning: 0x80019002 at 04_TransactionDemo: SSIS Warning Code
DTS_W_MAXIMUMERRORCOUNTREACHED. The Execution method succeeded, but the number
of errors raised (1) reached the maximum allowed (1); resulting in failure. This
occurs when the number of errors reaches the number specified in MaximumErrorCount.
Change the MaximumErrorCount or fix the errors.
Information: 0x4001100C at 04_TransactionDemo: Aborting the current distributed
transaction.
SSIS package "C:\ProSSIS\Code\Ch15\04_TransactionDemo.dtsx" finished: Failure.
```

Single Package, Multiple Transactions

The goal of this second package is to have two transactions running in the same package at the same time. Create the package as shown in Figure 15-25. If you're not feeling creative, you can use the same statements in the tasks that you used in the previous example.

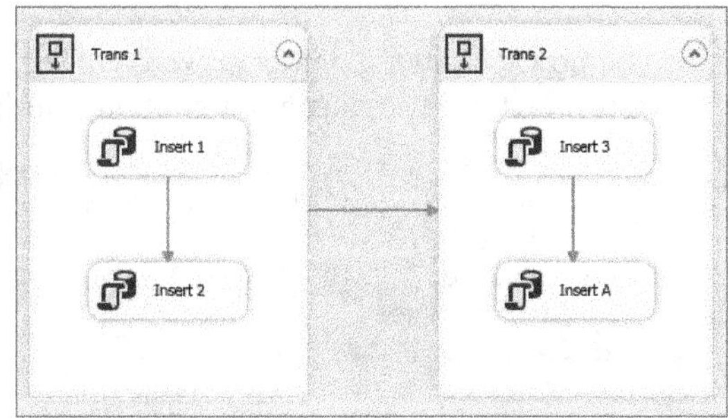

FIGURE 15-25

The package contains two Sequence Containers, each containing its own child tasks. The Trans 1 Container begins a transaction, and the child tasks join the transaction. The Trans 2 Container also starts a transaction of its own, and its child task joins that transaction. As you can see, the task in Trans 2 will deliberately fail. A real-world purpose of this scenario could be the logical loading of different sets of data. This could be useful when you have logical grouping of data manipulation routines to perform, and either all succeed or none of them succeed. The following table shows the tasks and containers in the package, along with the package itself and the setting of their TransactionOption property.

TASK/CONTAINER	TRANSACTIONOPTION PROPERTY VALUE
Package	Supported
Trans 1	Required
Insert 1	Supported
Insert 2	Supported
Trans 2	Required
Insert 3	Supported
Insert 4	Supported

After you execute the package, the results should look like Figure 15-26. The first container succeeded, but the second one failed because its child task failed.

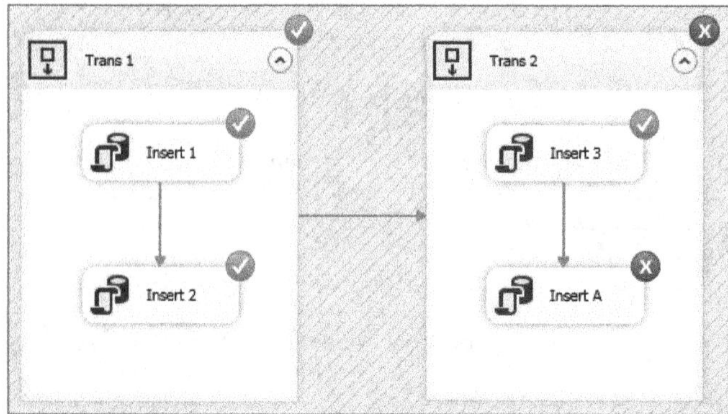

FIGURE 15-26

If you now look in the database, you will see that the numbers 1 and 2 were inserted. To prove that two transactions were instantiated, take another look at the output window:

```
SSIS package "C:\ProSSIS\Code\Ch15\05_MultipleTransactionDemo.dtsx" starting.
Information: 0x4001100A at Trans 1: Starting distributed transaction for this
container.
Information: 0x4001100B at Trans 1: Committing distributed transaction started by
this container.
Information: 0x4001100A at Trans 2: Starting distributed transaction for this
container.
Error: 0xC002F210 at Insert A, Execute SQL Task: Executing the query "INSERT
dbo.T1(col1) VALUES("A") " failed with the following error: "Invalid column name 'A'.".
```

```
Possible failure reasons: Problems with the query, "ResultSet" property not set
correctly, parameters not set correctly, or connection not established correctly.
Task failed: Insert A
Information: 0x4001100C at Insert A: Aborting the current distributed transaction.
Warning: 0x80019002 at Trans 2: SSIS Warning Code DTS_W_MAXIMUMERRORCOUNTREACHED.
The Execution method succeeded, but the number of errors raised (1) reached the
maximum allowed (1); resulting in failure. This occurs when the number of errors
reaches the number specified in MaximumErrorCount. Change the MaximumErrorCount or
fix the errors.
Information: 0x4001100C at Trans 2: Aborting the current distributed transaction.
Warning: 0x80019002 at 05_MultipleTransactionDemo: SSIS Warning Code
DTS_W_MAXIMUMERRORCOUNTREACHED.  The Execution method succeeded, but the number
of errors raised (1) reached the maximum allowed (1); resulting in failure. This
occurs when the number of errors reaches the number specified in MaximumErrorCount.
Change the MaximumErrorCount or fix the errors.
SSIS package "C:\ProSSIS\Code\Ch15\05_MultipleTransactionDemo.dtsx" finished:
Failure.
```

Two Packages, One Transaction

The third package in this series will highlight a transaction that spans multiple packages. Specifically, there will be two packages: "TransactionParent" and "TransactionChild." The TransactionParent package will insert two rows into a table and then call the TransactionChild package using an Execute Package Task, which itself will insert two rows into the same table. You will then introduce an error in the TransactionParent package that causes it to fail. As a result, the work done in both packages is undone. Figure 15-27 shows the TransactionParent package, and Figure 15-28 shows the TransactionChild package.

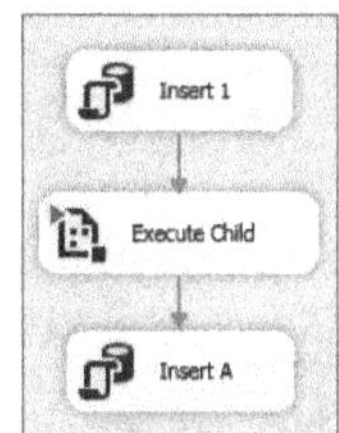

FIGURE 15-27

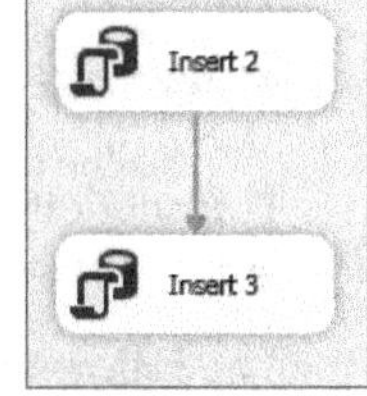

FIGURE 15-28

As in the previous example, you need to set the TransactionOption property on the tasks and containers. Use the values in the following table:

PACKAGE	TASK/CONTAINER	TRANSACTIONOPTION PROPERTY VALUE
TransactionParent	TransactionParent	Required
TransactionParent	Insert 1	Supported
TransactionParent	Execute Child	Supported
TransactionParent	Insert A	Supported
TransactionChild	TransactionChild	Supported
TransactionChild	Insert 2	Supported
TransactionChild	Insert 3	Supported

The point to note here is that the TransactionChild package becomes nothing more than another task. The parent of the TransactionChild package is the Execute Package Task in the TransactionParent package. Because the Execute Package Task is in a transaction, and the TransactionChild package also has its TransactionOption set to Supported, it will join the transaction in the TransactionParent package.

If you change the TransactionOption property on the Execute Package Task in the TransactionParent package to Not Supported (refer to Figure 15-24), when the final task in the TransactionParent package fails, the work in the TransactionChild package will not be undone.

Single Package Using a Native Transaction in SQL Server

This example differs from the others in that you are going to use the transaction-handling abilities of SQL Server and not those of MS DTC. Although the example is short, it does demonstrate that transactions can be used in packages that are not MS DTC transactions. Native SQL transactions provide you with a finer level of granularity when deciding what data is rolled back and committed, but they are possible only with SQL Server. The package for this example is shown in Figure 15-29.

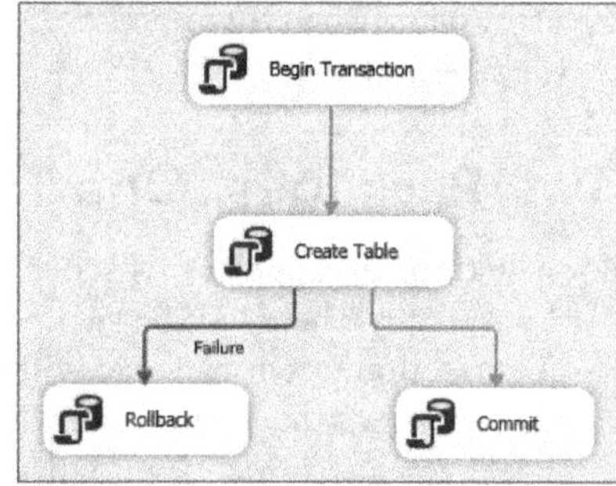

FIGURE 15-29

Although you cannot see it because the screenshot is black and white, the workflow line from the Create Table Transactions Task to the Rollback Task is red, indicating failure; however, you can see the word *failure* next to the precedence constraint line.

The following table lists the contents of the SQLStatement property for each of the Execute SQL Tasks:

TASK	SQLSTATEMENT PROPERTY VALUE
Begin Transaction	BEGIN TRANSACTION
Create Table	CREATE TABLE dbo.Transactions(col1 int)
Rollback	ROLLBACK TRANSACTION
Commit	COMMIT TRANSACTION

The key to making the package use the native transaction capabilities in SQL Server is to have all the tasks use the same Connection Manager. In addition, you must ensure that the RetainSameConnection property on the Connection Manager is set to True, as shown in Figure 15-30.

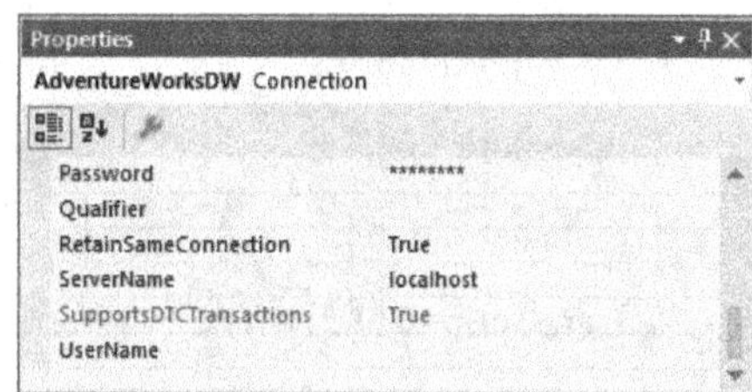

FIGURE 15-30

When the package is executed, SQL Server will fire up a transaction and either commit or rollback that transaction at the end of the package.

Now have a look at that happening on SQL Server by using Profiler, as shown in Figure 15-31. Profiler is very useful in situations like this. Here you simply want to confirm that a transaction was started and that it either finished successfully or failed. You can also use Profiler when firing SSIS packages to ensure that what you assume you are executing is what you are actually executing. Explaining how to use SQL Server Profiler is beyond the scope of this book, and more information can be found in SQL Server Books Online.

EventClass	TextData	ApplicationName	NTUserName	LoginName	CPU	Reads	Writes	Duration
ExistingConnection	-- network protocol: LPC set quote...	DQ Services ...	Adminis...	WIN-OP...				
Audit Login	-- network protocol: LPC set quote...	Microsoft SQ...	Adminis...	WIN-OP...				
SQL:BatchStarting	BEGIN TRANSACTION	Microsoft SQ...	Adminis...	WIN-OP...				
SQL:BatchCompleted	BEGIN TRANSACTION	Microsoft SQ...	Adminis...	WIN-OP...	0	0	0	0
SQL:BatchStarting	CREATE TABLE dbo.Transactions(col1 ...	Microsoft SQ...	Adminis...	WIN-OP...				
SQL:BatchCompleted	CREATE TABLE dbo.Transactions(col1 ...	Microsoft SQ...	Adminis...	WIN-OP...	0	7	0	50
SQL:BatchStarting	ROLLBACK TRANSACTION	Microsoft SQ...	Adminis...	WIN-OP...				
SQL:BatchCompleted	ROLLBACK TRANSACTION	Microsoft SQ...	Adminis...	WIN-OP...	0	0	0	6
Audit Logout		Microsoft SQ...	Adminis...	WIN-OP...	0	7	0	820
Trace Stop								

FIGURE 15-31

That ends your whistle-stop look at transactions within SSIS packages. Next, it's time to look at error outputs and how they can help with scalability.

ERROR OUTPUTS

Error outputs can obviously be used to improve reliability, but they also have an important part to play in terms of scalability as well. From a reliability perspective, they are a critical feature for coping with bad data. An appropriately configured component will direct failing rows down the error output, rather than the main output. After being removed from the main Data Flow path, these rows may receive additional treatment and cleansing to enable them to be recovered and merged back into the main flow. They can be merged explicitly, such as with a Union All Transformation, or implicitly through a second adapter directed at the final destination. Alternatively, they could be discarded. Be careful of discarding rows entirely; you may find out you need them later! More often, rows on the error output are logged and dealt with later.

> **WARNING** *The error outputs are not always accurate in removing just the bad rows. In the scenario of using delimited flat files as a source, you may have rows missing delimiters. This can cause havoc with the data written to the error output and the expected good data.*

The capability to recover rows is perhaps the most useful course of action. If a data item is missing in the source extract but required in the final destination, the error flow path can be used to fix this. If the data item is available from a secondary system, then a lookup could be used. If the data item is not available elsewhere, then perhaps a default value could be used instead.

In other situations, the data may be out of range for the process or destination. If the data causes an integrity violation, then the failed data could be used to populate the constraining reference with new values, and then the data itself could be successfully processed. If a data type conflict occurs, then maybe a simple truncation would suffice, or an additional set of logic could be applied to try to detect the real value, such as with data time values held in strings. The data could then be converted into the required format.

When assumptions or fixes have been made to data in this way, it is best practice to always mark rows as having been manipulated; that way, if additional information becomes available later, they can be targeted directly. In addition, whenever an assumption is made, it should be clearly identified as such to the end user.

All the scenarios described here revolve around trying to recover from poor data, within the pipeline and the current session, allowing processing to continue, and ideally fixing the problem such that data is recovered. This is a new concept compared with DTS and several other products, but the ability to fix errors in real time is a very valuable option that you should always consider when building solutions.

The obvious question that then occurs is this: Why not include the additional transformations used to correct and cleanse the data in the main Data Flow path, so that any problems are dealt with before they cause an error? This would mean that all data flows down a single path, and the overall Data Flow design may be simpler, with no branching and merging flows. This is where the scalability factor should enter into your solution design. Ideally, you want to build the simplest Data Flow Task possible, using as few transformations as possible. The less work you perform, the greater the performance and therefore scalability.

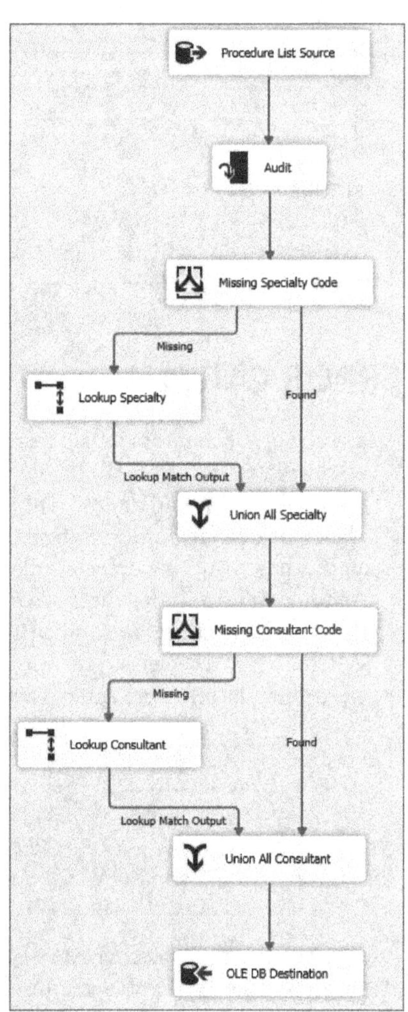

FIGURE 15-32

Figure 15-32 illustrates a Data Flow Task used to load some data. In this contrived scenario, some of the rows will be missing values for SpecialtyCode and ConsultantCode. The source data contains text descriptions as well, so these are being used to perform a lookup to retrieve the missing values. The initial design logic specifies evaluating the column for NULL values in a Conditional Split Transformation. Bad rows are directed to an alternate output that connects to the Lookup Transformation. Once the lookup has populated the missing value, the rows are then fed back into the main pipeline through the Union All Transformation. The same pattern is followed for the SpecialtyCode and ConsultantCode columns, ensuring that the final insert through the OLE DB Destination has all good data. This is the base design for solving your problem, and it follows the procedural logic quite closely.

Figure 15-33 shows two alternative Data Flow Task designs, presented side by side for easy comparison. In the first design, you disregard any existing data in the SpecialtyCode and ConsultantCode columns and populate them entirely through the lookup. Although this may seem like wasted effort, the overall design is simpler, and in testing it was slightly faster compared to the more complicated design in Figure 15-32. This example used a test data set that had a bad row ratio of 1 in 3 — that is, one row in three had missing values. If the ratio dropped to 1 in 6 for the bad rows, then the two methods performed the same.

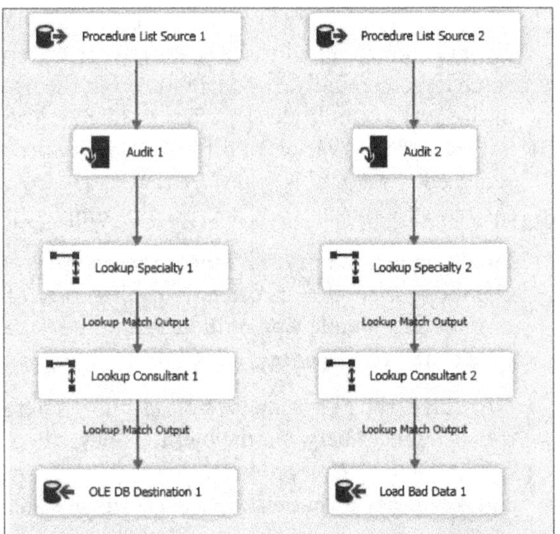

FIGURE 15-33

The second design assumes that all data is good until proven otherwise, so you insert directly into the destination. Rows that fail because of the missing values pass down the error output, "OLE DB Destination Error Output," and are then processed through the two lookups. The choice between the two designs is whether you fix all rows or only those that fail. Using the 1 in 3 bad rows test data, fixing only the failed rows was 20 percent faster than fixing all rows. When the bad row ratio dropped to 1 in 6, the performance gain also dropped, to only 10 percent.

As demonstrated by the preceding examples, the decision regarding where to include the corrective transformations is based on the ratio of good rows to bad rows, as compared to how much work is required to validate the quality of the data. The cost of fixing the data should be excluded if possible, as that is required regardless of the design, but often the two are inseparable.

The performance characteristics of the corrective transformations should also be considered. In the preceding examples, you used lookups, which are inherently expensive transformations. The test data and lookup reference data included only six distinct values to minimize the impact on overall testing. Lookups with more distinct values, and higher cardinality, will be more expensive, as the caching becomes less effective and itself consumes more resources. The cache modes are discussed in Chapter 7 of this book.

In summary, the more expensive the verification, the more bad rows you require to justify adding the validation and fix to the main flow. For fewer bad rows, or a more expensive validation procedure, you have increased justification for keeping the main flow simple and for using the error flow to perform the corrective work.

The overall number of rows should also influence your design, because any advantages or disadvantages are amplified with a greater number of rows, regardless of the ratio. For a smaller number of rows, the fixed costs may outweigh the implied benefits, as any component has a cost to manage at runtime, so a more complicated Data Flow Task may not be worthwhile with fewer overall rows.

This concept of using error flows versus the main flow to correct data quality issues and related errors is not confined to those outputs that implement the error output explicitly. You can apply the same logic manually, primarily through the use of the Conditional Split Transformation, as shown in the first example (refer to Figure 15-32). You can perform a simple test to detect any potential issues, and direct rows of differing quality down different outputs. Where expensive operations are required, your goal is to ensure that as few rows as possible follow this path and that the majority of the rows follow cheaper, and usually simpler, routes to their destination.

Finally, don't be put off by the term *error output*; it isn't something to be avoided at all costs. Component developers often take advantage of the rich underlying pipeline architecture, using error outputs as a simple way of indicating the result of a transformation for a given row. They don't affect the overall success or failure state of a package, so don't be put off from using them.

Of course, the performance figures quoted here are for demonstration purposes only. They illustrate the differences between the methods described, but they should not be taken as literal values that you can expect to reproduce, unless you're using exactly the same design, data, and environment. The key point is that testing such scenarios should be a routine part of your development practice.

SCALING OUT

You are no doubt already familiar with the term *scaling out*, and of course the concept can be applied to SSIS systems. Although there are no magical switches here, SSIS offers several interesting features, and in this section you will see how they can be applied and how they can benefit reliability as well.

Architectural Features

There are two important architectural features in Integration Services that give the tool great capabilities. The first feature is the Lookup Transformation. The second feature is the data pipeline itself. These features give SSIS the abilities to move and compare data in a very fast and efficient manner.

Lookup Transformation

The Lookup Transformation has the ability to cache data, and it has several options available to optimize that configuration. The Cache Data Sources available to this transformation include pure in-memory cache and persistent file storage (also called *persisted cache*). Both of these options require the transformation to be configured to use the full-cache option, however. A Connection Manager called the Cache Connection Manager governs these two types of caching options.

Caching operations in the Lookup Transformation provide three modes to choose from: full, partial, or none. Using the full-cache mode, the lookup set will be stored in its entirety and will load before the lookup operation actually runs, but it will not repopulate on every subsequent lookup operation. A partial cache stores only matched lookups, and no-cache will repopulate the cache every time. Of course, you can also manually configure the size of the cache to store, measured in megabytes.

Persistent file storage is another very exciting caching feature, as it will store your cache in a file that can be reused across other packages. Talk about reusability! To add to the benefit, the cache can be loaded from a variety of sources, including text files, XML files, or even web services. Lastly, partial-cache mode has a cache option called miss-cache, in which items being processed for lookup that do not have a match will be cached, so they will not be retried in future lookup operations. All these features translate into scalability and performance gains.

Data Pipeline

The data pipeline is the workhorse of the data processing engine. The data pipeline architecture is able to provide a fully multi-threaded engine for true parallelism. This allows most pipelines to scale out well without a lot of manual tweaking.

Scaling Out Memory Pressures

By design, pipeline processing takes place almost exclusively in memory. This enable faster data movement and transformations, and a design goal should always include making a single pass over your data. This eliminates time-consuming staging and the costs of reading and writing the same data several times. The potential disadvantage of this is that for large amounts of data and complicated sets of transformations, you need a large amount of memory, and it needs to be the right type of memory for optimum performance.

The virtual memory space for 32-bit Windows operating systems is limited to 2GB by default. Although you can increase this amount through the use of the `/3GB` switch applied in the `boot.ini` file, this often falls short of the total memory currently available. This limit is applied per process, which for your purposes means a single package during execution. Therefore, by partitioning a process across multiple packages, you can ensure that each of the smaller packages is its own process, thereby taking advantage of the full 2–3GB virtual space independently. The most common method of chaining packages together to form a consolidated process is through the Execute Package Task, in which case it is imperative that you set the Child package to execute out of process. To enable this behavior, you must set the ExecuteOutOfProcess property to true.

Note that unlike the SQL Server database engine, SSIS does not support Advanced Windowing Extensions (AWE), so scaling out to multiple packages across processes is the only way to take advantage of larger amounts of memory. If you have a very large memory requirement, then you should consider a 64-bit system for hosting these processes. Whereas just a few years ago it would have been very expensive and hard to find software and drivers for all your needs, 64-bit systems are now common for enterprise hardware and should be considered for any business database.

For a more detailed explanation of how SSIS uses memory, and the in-memory buffer structure used to move data through the pipeline, see Chapter 16.

Scaling Out by Staging Data

The staging of data is very much on the decline; after all, why incur the cost of writing to and reading from a staging area when you can perform all the processing in memory with a single pass of data? With the inclusion of the Dimension and Partition Processing Destinations, you no longer need a physical Data Source to populate your SQL Server Analysis Services (SSAS) cubes — yet another reason for the decline of staging or even the traditional data warehouse. Although this is still a contentious debate, the issue here is this: Should you use staging during the SSIS processing flow? Although it may not be technically required to achieve the overall goal, there are still certain scenarios when you may want to, for both scalability and reliability reasons.

For this discussion, staging could also be described as partitioning. Although the process can be implemented within a single Data Flow Task, for one or more of the reasons described next, it may be subdivided into multiple Data Flow Tasks. These smaller units could be within a single package, or they might be distributed through several, as discussed next. The staged data will be used only by another Data Flow Task and does not need to be accessed directly through regular interfaces. For this reason, the ideal choices for the source and destinations are the raw file adapters. This could be described as vertical partitioning, but you could also overlay a level of horizontal partitioning, by executing multiple instances of a package in parallel.

Raw file adapters enable you to persist the native buffer structures to disk. The in-memory buffer structure is simply dumped to and from the file, without any translation or processing as found in all other adapters, making these the fastest adapters for staging data. You can take advantage of this to artificially force a memory checkpoint to be written to disk, thereby enabling you to span multiple Data Flow Tasks and packages. Staging environments and raw files are also discussed in Chapter 16, but some specific examples are illustrated here.

The key use for raw files is that by splitting one Data Flow Task into at least two individual Data Flow Tasks, the primary task can end with a raw file destination and the secondary task can begin with a raw file source. The buffer structure is exactly the same between the two tasks, so the split is basically irrelevant from an overall flow perspective, but it provides perfect preservation of the two tasks.

Data Flow Restart

As covered previously in this chapter, the checkpoint feature provides the capability to restart a package from the point of failure, but it does not extend inside a Data Flow Task. However, if you divide a Data Flow Task into one or more individual tasks, each linked together by raw files, you immediately gain the capability to restart the combined flow. Through the correct use of native checkpoints at the (Data Flow) task level, this process becomes very simple to manage.

Deciding where to divide a flow is subjective, but two common choices are immediately after extraction and immediately after transformation, prior to load. The post-extraction point offers several key benefits, including performance, meeting source system service level agreements (SLAs), and consistency. Many source systems are remote, so extraction might take place over suboptimal network links, and it can be the slowest part of the process. By staging immediately after the extraction, you don't have to repeat this slow step in the event of a failure and restart. There may also be an impact on the source system during the extraction, which often takes place during a specified time window when utilization is low. In this case, it may be unacceptable to repeat the extract in the event of a failure until the next time window, usually the following night. Finally, the initial extraction will take place at a more consistent time each night, which could provide a better base for tracking history. Staging post-transformation simply ensures that the transformation is not wasted if the destination system is unavailable. If the transformations are time intensive, this cost-savings can really add up!

You may wish to include additional staging points mid-transformation. These would usually be located after particularly expensive operations and before those that you suspect are at risk to fail. Although you can plan for problems, and the use of error outputs described previously should enable you to handle many situations, you can still expect the unexpected and plan a staging point with this in mind. The goal remains the same — the ability to restart as close to the failure point as possible and to reduce the cost of any reprocessing required.

Figure 15-34 shows an example data load process that you may wish to partition into multiple tasks to take advantage of Data Flow restart.

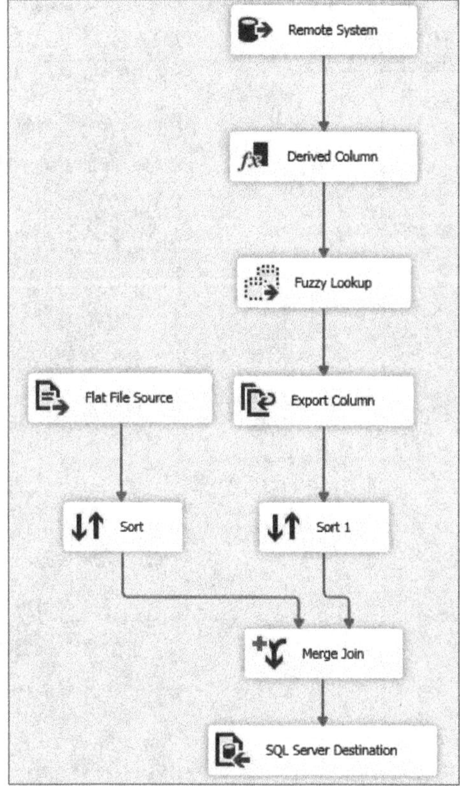

FIGURE 15-34

For this scenario, the OLE DB Source Component connects to a remote SQL Server over a slow network link. Because of the time taken for this data extraction and the impact on the source system, it is not acceptable to repeat the extract if the subsequent processing fails for any reason. Therefore, you choose to stage data through a raw file immediately after the Source Component. The resulting Data Flow Task layout is shown in Figure 15-35.

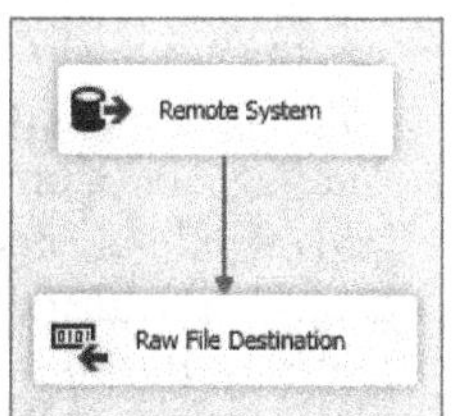

FIGURE 15-35

The Flat File Source data is accessed across the LAN, and it needs to be captured before it is overwritten. The sort operation is also particularly expensive because of the volume of data. For this reason, you choose to stage the data after the sort is complete. The resulting Data Flow Task is shown in Figure 15-36.

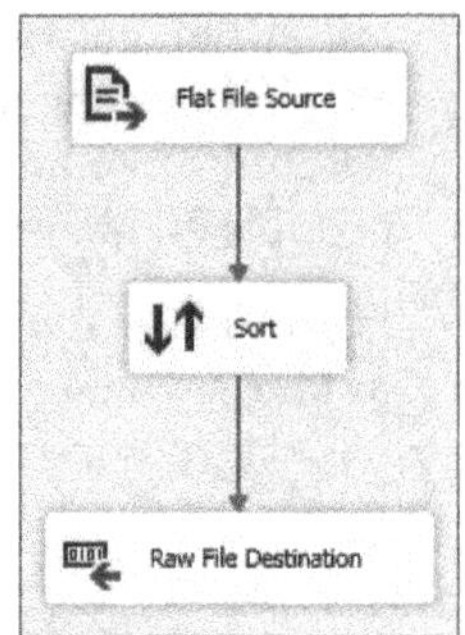

FIGURE 15-36

Finally, you use a third Data Flow Task to consume the two staging raw files and complete the process, as shown in Figure 15-37.

Following this example, a single Data Flow Task has been divided into three separate tasks. For the purpose of restarting a failed process, you would use a single package and implement checkpoints on each of the three Data Flow Tasks.

Scaling across Machines

In a similar manner to the Data Flow restart just discussed, you can also use raw file adapters to partition the Data Flow Task. By separating tasks into different packages, you can run packages across machines. This may be advantageous if a specific machine has properties not shared with others. Perhaps the machine capable of performing the extract is situated in a different network segment from the machine best suited for processing the data, and direct access is unavailable between the main processing machine and the source. The extract could be performed, and the main processing machine would then retrieve the raw data to continue the process. These situations are organizational restrictions, rather than decisions driven by the design architecture.

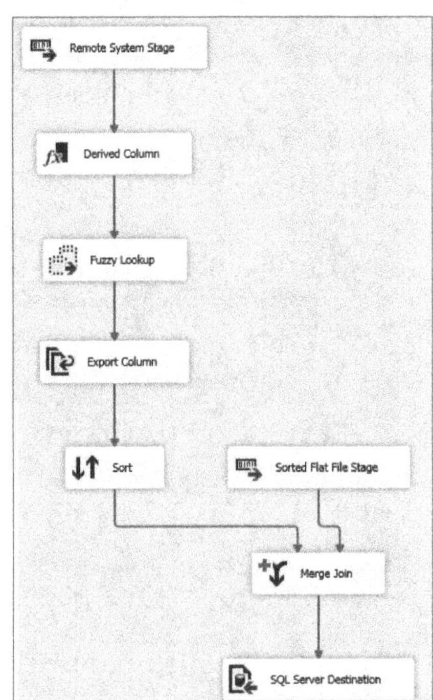

FIGURE 15-37

Another method for scaling across machines is to use horizontal partitioning. A simple scenario would utilize two packages. The first package would extract data from the source system, and through the Conditional Split you produce two or more exclusive subsets of the data and write this to individual raw files. Each raw file would contain some of the rows from the extract, as determined by the expression used in the Conditional Split. The most common horizontal partition scheme is time-based, but any method could be used here. The goal is to subdivide the total extract into manageable chunks; so, for example, if a sequential row number is already available in the source, this would be ideal, or one could be applied (see the T-SQL `ROW_NUMBER` function). Similarly a Row Number Transformation could be used to apply the numbering, which could then be used by the split, or the numbering and splitting could be delivered through a Script Component.

With a sorted data set, each raw file may be written in sequence, completing in order, before moving on to the next one. While this may seem uneven and inefficient, it is assumed that the time delay between completion of the first and final destinations is inconsequential compared to the savings achieved by the subsequent parallel processing.

Once the partitioned raw files are complete, they are consumed by the second package, which performs the transformation and load aspects of the processing. Each file is processed by an instance of the package running on a separate machine. This way, you can scale across machines and perform expensive transformations in parallel. For a smaller-scale implementation, where the previously described 32-bit virtual memory constraints apply, you could parallel process on a single machine, such that each package instance would be a separate thread, with its own allocation of virtual memory space.

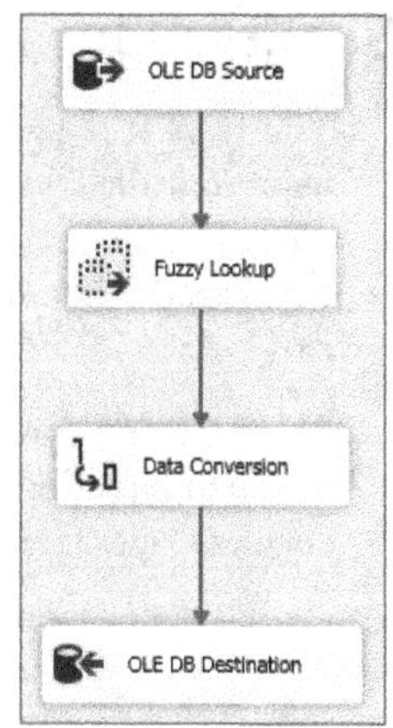

FIGURE 15-38

For destinations that are partitioned themselves, such as a SQL Server data warehouse with table partitions or a partitioned view model, or Analysis Services partitions, it may also make sense to match the partition schema to that of the destination, such that each package addresses a single table or partition.

Figure 15-38 shows a sample package that for the purposes of this example you will partition horizontally.

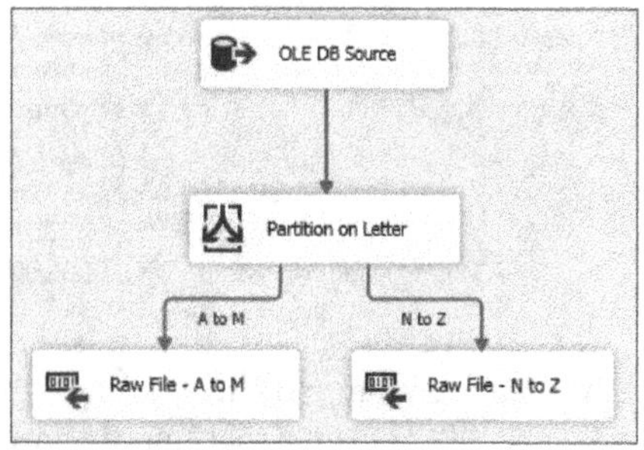

FIGURE 15-39

In this scenario, the Fuzzy Lookup is processing names against a very large reference set, and this is taking too long. To introduce some parallel processing, you decide to partition on the first letter of a name field. It is deemed stable enough for matches to be within the same letter, although in a real-world scenario this may not always be true. You use a Conditional Split Transformation to produce the two raw files partitioned from A to M and from N to Z. This primer package is illustrated in Figure 15-39.

Ideally, you would then have two instances of the second package (Figure 15-40) running in parallel on two separate machines. However, you need to ensure that the lookup data is filtered on name to match the raw file. Not all pipeline component properties are exposed as expressions, allowing you to dynamically control them, so you would need two versions of the package, identical except for a different Reference table name property in the Fuzzy Lookup, also shown in Figure 15-40. In preparation, you would create two views, one for names A to M and the other for names N to Z, to match the two raw files. The two package versions would each use the view to match the raw file they will process.

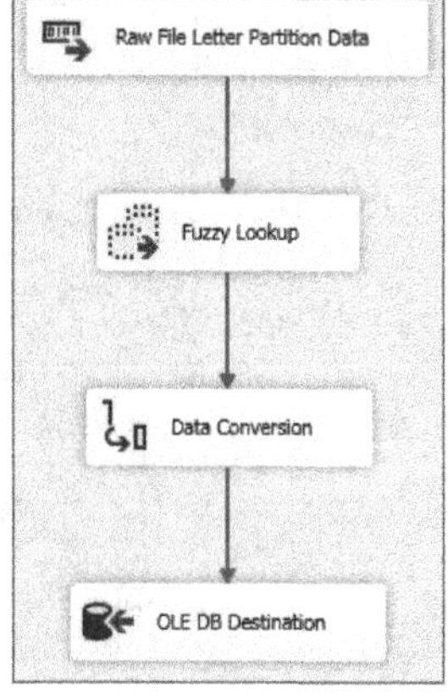

FIGURE 15-40

For any design that uses raw files, the additional I/O cost must be evaluated against the processing performance gains, but for large-scale implementations it offers a convenient way of ensuring consistency within the overall flow and doesn't incur the translation penalty associated with other storage formats.

Scaling Out with Parallel Loading

You have seen several ways to scale out SSIS in this chapter. Now you will learn how to scale out using parallelization with the data loads. You can accomplish faster load times by loading multiple partitions at once using SSIS from either a staging environment or multiple files of sorted data. If the data resides in a flat file, you may want to consider loading those files into a staging table so the data can be pre-sorted.

The first item you will need is a control table. This will tell the SSIS packages which data to pull for each partition in the destination. The control table will contain a list of data that needs to be checked out. The following code will create this table:

```
USE [AdventureWorksDW]
GO
CREATE TABLE [dbo].[ctlTaskQueue](
     [TaskQueueID] [smallint] IDENTITY(1,1) NOT NULL,
     [PartitionWhere] [varchar](20) NOT NULL,
     [Priority] [tinyint] NOT NULL,
     [StartDate] [datetime] NULL,
     [CompleteDate] [datetime] NULL,
 CONSTRAINT [PK_ctlTaskQueue] PRIMARY KEY CLUSTERED
(
     [TaskQueueID] ASC
)WITH (PAD_INDEX = OFF, STATISTICS_NORECOMPUTE = OFF, IGNORE_DUP_KEY = OFF,
ALLOW_ROW_LOCKS = ON, ALLOW_PAGE_LOCKS = ON) ON [PRIMARY])
```

The `PartitionWhere` column is the data used to divide the data up into parallel loading. This will be a part of the `WHERE` clause that queries from the source of the staging table conditionally. For example, Figure 15-41 shows you a table that's ready to be used. Each `WHERE` clause should ideally align with a partition on your destination table. The `StartDate` and `CompleteDate` columns show you when the work was checked out and completed.

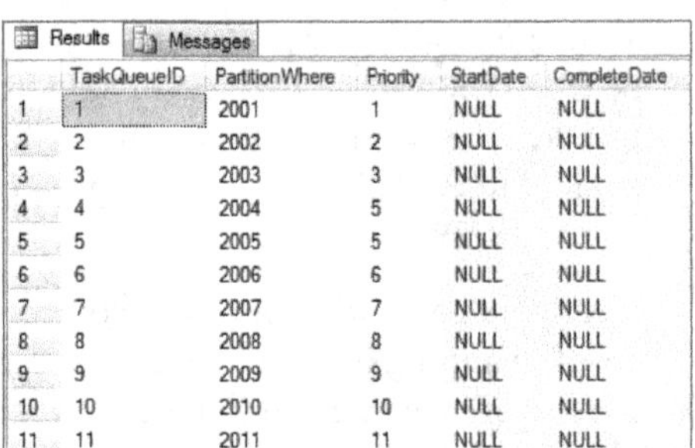

Results | Messages

	TaskQueueID	PartitionWhere	Priority	StartDate	CompleteDate
1	1	2001	1	NULL	NULL
2	2	2002	2	NULL	NULL
3	3	2003	3	NULL	NULL
4	4	2004	5	NULL	NULL
5	5	2005	5	NULL	NULL
6	6	2006	6	NULL	NULL
7	7	2007	7	NULL	NULL
8	8	2008	8	NULL	NULL
9	9	2009	9	NULL	NULL
10	10	2010	10	NULL	NULL
11	11	2011	11	NULL	NULL

FIGURE 15-41

Run the following code to populate these values:

```
USE [AdventureWorksDW]
GO
INSERT INTO [dbo].[ctlTaskQueue]
           ([PartitionWhere]
           ,[Priority]
           ,[StartDate]
           ,[CompleteDate])
     VALUES
      (2001,1, null, null),
      (2002,2, null, null),
      (2003,3, null, null),
      (2004,4, null, null),
      (2005,5, null, null),
      (2006,6, null, null),
      (2007,7, null, null),
```

```
        (2008,8, null, null),
        (2009,9, null, null),
        (2010,10, null, null),
        (2011,11, null, null)
GO
```

Now create an SSIS package named **ParallelDemo.dtsx** that will perform the parallel load. This section will show you the basics for creating a package to perform a parallel load. You will still need to apply best practices to this package afterward, for example, additional elements like package checkpoints, parameters, and a master package to run all of your parallel loads. Create three SSIS variables in the package, as shown in Figure 15-42. Don't worry about the value of the strSQLStatement variable, as you will modify it later to use an expression.

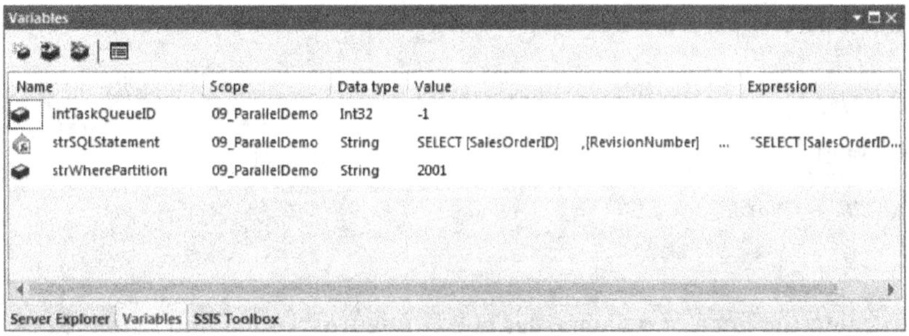

Name	Scope	Data type	Value	Expression
intTaskQueueID	09_ParallelDemo	Int32	-1	
strSQLStatement	09_ParallelDemo	String	SELECT [SalesOrderID] ,[RevisionNumber] ...	"SELECT [SalesOrderID...
strWherePartition	09_ParallelDemo	String	2001	

FIGURE 15-42

Next drag in a For Loop Container, which will be used to look for new work in the control table you just created. Configure the container to use the `intTaskQueueID` variable, as shown in Figure 15-43. The loop will repeat while `intTaskQueueID` is not 0. The tasks inside the loop will be responsible for setting the variable to 0 once the work is complete.

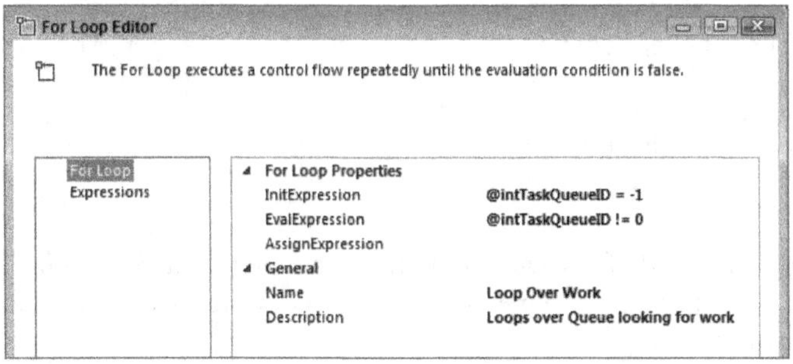

For Loop Editor

The For Loop executes a control flow repeatedly until the evaluation condition is false.

For Loop Properties	
InitExpression	@intTaskQueueID = -1
EvalExpression	@intTaskQueueID != 0
AssignExpression	
General	
Name	Loop Over Work
Description	Loops over Queue looking for work

FIGURE 15-43

Next you will run the following code to create a stored procedure that will check out the work to be done. The stored procedure is going to output two variables: one for the task that needs to be worked on (`@TaskQueueID`) and the filter that will be applied on the source table (`@PartitionWhere`). After the task is read, it also checks the work out by updating the `StartDate` column.

```
USE [AdventureWorksDW]
GO
CREATE PROCEDURE [dbo].[ctl_UseTask]
  @TaskQueueID int OUTPUT,
  @PartitionWhere varchar(50) OUTPUT
AS
SELECT TOP 1
@TaskQueueID = TaskQueueID,
@PartitionWhere = PartitionWhere
from ctlTaskQueue
WHERE StartDate is NULL
AND CompleteDate is NULL
ORDER BY Priority asc
IF @TaskQueueID IS NULL
BEGIN
  SET @TaskQueueID = 0
END
ELSE
BEGIN
  UPDATE ctlTaskQueue
  SET StartDate = GETDATE()
  WHERE TaskQueueID = @TaskQueueID
END
GO
```

Drag an Execute SQL Task into the For Loop Container and configure it to match Figure 15-44, using the following code in the SQLStatement. This will execute the stored procedure and get the task queue and the `WHERE` clause values from the table. You could also have altered the stored procedure to have an input variable of what queue you'd like to read from.

```
DECLARE @return_value int,
    @TaskQueueID int,
    @PartitionWhere varchar(50)

EXEC @return_value = [dbo].[ctl_UseTask]
    @TaskQueueID = @TaskQueueID OUTPUT,
    @PartitionWhere = @PartitionWhere OUTPUT

SELECT convert(int,@TaskQueueID) as N'@TaskQueueID',
    @PartitionWhere as N'@PartitionWhere'

GO
```

Open the Result Set window in the Execute SQL Task and configure it to match Figure 15-45. Each value maps to a variable in SSIS. The Result Name of 0 means the first column returned, and the columns are sequentially numbered from there.

Now you will set the variable `strSQLStatement` to be dynamic by adding the following code to the Expression property in the `strSQLStatement` variable. This `strSQLStatement` variable will be used as your OLE DB Source Component in the Data Flow Task you will create in a moment. This query could be whatever you'd like. In this example, you are gathering data out of a Transactions table between a given date range. The `strWherePartition` is populated from the previous Execute SQL Task, and the date range should match your target table's partition layout. The `ORDER BY` clause is going to pre-sort the data on the way out. Ideally this column would have a clustered index on it to make the sort more efficient.

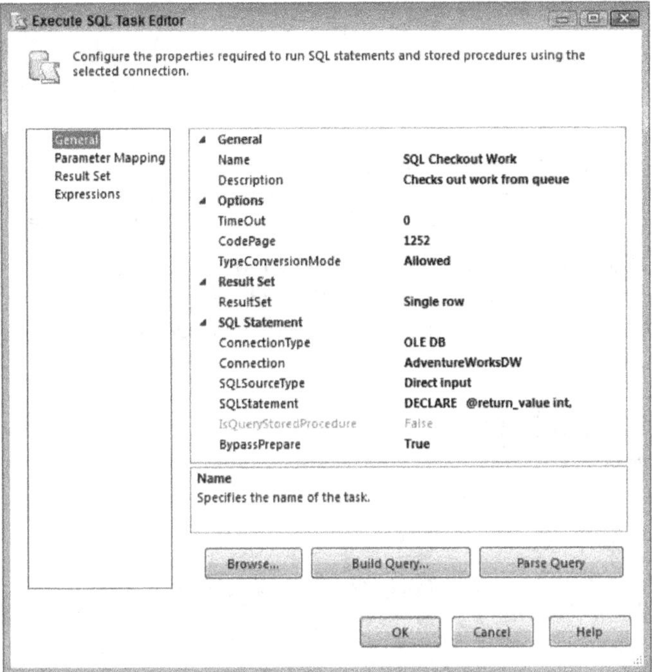

FIGURE 15-44

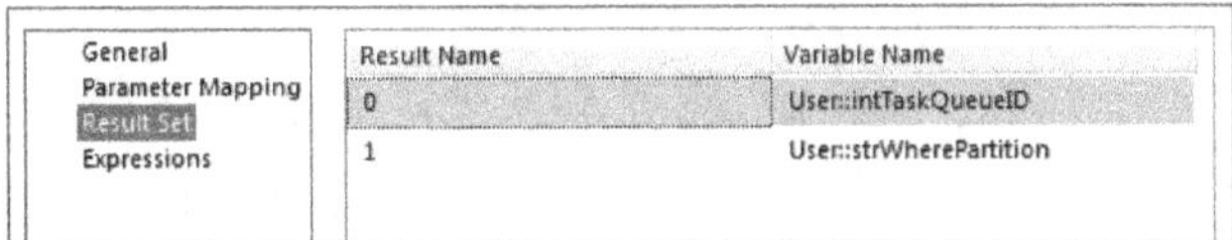

FIGURE 15-45

```
"SELECT [SalesOrderID]
      ,[RevisionNumber]
      ,[OrderDate]
      ,[DueDate]
      ,[ShipDate]
      ,[Status]
      ,[OnlineOrderFlag]
      ,[SalesOrderNumber]
      ,[PurchaseOrderNumber]
      ,[AccountNumber]
      ,[CustomerID]
      ,[SalesPersonID]
      ,[TerritoryID]
      ,[BillToAddressID]
      ,[ShipToAddressID]
      ,[ShipMethodID]
      ,[CreditCardID]
      ,[CreditCardApprovalCode]
      ,[CurrencyRateID]
      ,[SubTotal]
```

```
        , [TaxAmt]
        , [Freight]
        , [TotalDue]
        , [Comment]
        , [rowguid]
        , [ModifiedDate]
   FROM [AdventureWorks].[Sales].[SalesOrderHeader]
 WHERE [ShipDate] > '"+ @[User::strWherePartition]  + "-01-01' and
 [ShipDate] <= '" + @[User::strWherePartition]  + "-12-31' ORDER BY [ShipDate] "
```

Now you are ready to create the Data Flow Task. Drag a Data Flow Task over and connect it to the Execute SQL Task inside the loop. In the Data Flow tab, drag an OLE DB Source Component over and connect it to your source connection manager and use the `strSQLStatement` variable as your source query, as seen in Figure 15-46.

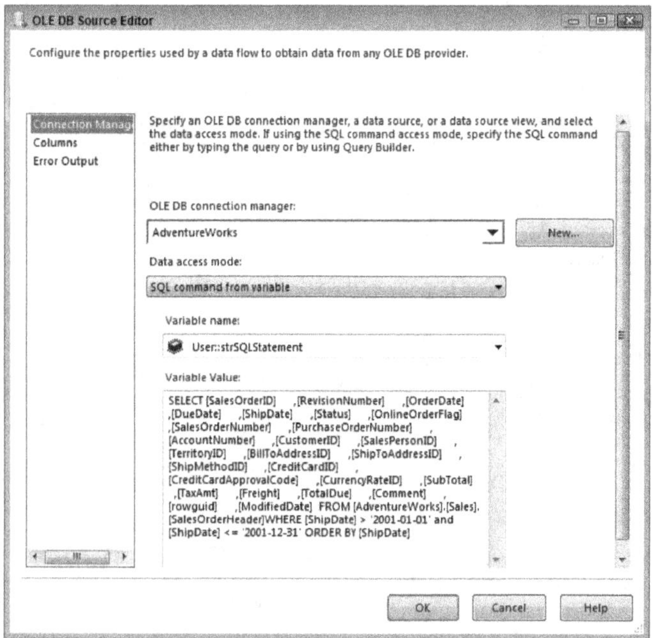

FIGURE 15-46

You can connect the OLE DB Source Component to any other component you'd like for this example, such as a Union All Transformation. You are using a Union All Transformation as a temporary dead-end destination so you can see the number of rows that flow down that part of the Data Flow path. You can also use a Data Viewer before the Union All Transformation to see the data in those rows. Ideally though, you should connect the source to any business logic that you may have and then finally into a destination. Your ultimate destination should ensure that the data is committed into a single batch. Otherwise, fragmentation may occur. You can do this by ensuring that the destination's "Max Insert Commit Size" is a high number, well above the number of rows that you expect (though in some cases you may not know this number). Keep in mind that the source query partition should have already sorted the data and be a small enough chunk of data to not cause major impact to the transaction log in SQL Server.

Back in the Control Flow, you'll want to add conditional logic between the Execute SQL Task and the Data Flow Task to execute the Data Flow Task only if more work is pending. To do this, double-click on the green precedence constraint connecting the two tasks and change the Evaluation operation property to be Expression and Constraint. Then, set the expression to @intTaskQueueID > 0, as seen in Figure 15-47.

FIGURE 15-47

The final step is to update the queue table to say the work is complete. You can do this by connecting an Execute SQL Task to the Data Flow Task. This task should update the `ctlTaskQueue` table in the AdventureWorksDW database to show the `CompleteDate` to the current time. This can be done in the following query or stored procedure:

```
UPDATE ctlTaskQueue
SET CompleteDate = GETDATE()
WHERE TaskQueueID = ?
```

The question mark in the previous code will be mapped to the `intTaskQueueID` variable in the Parameter Mapping tab in the Execute SQL Task. The final Control Flow of the package should look like Figure 15-48.

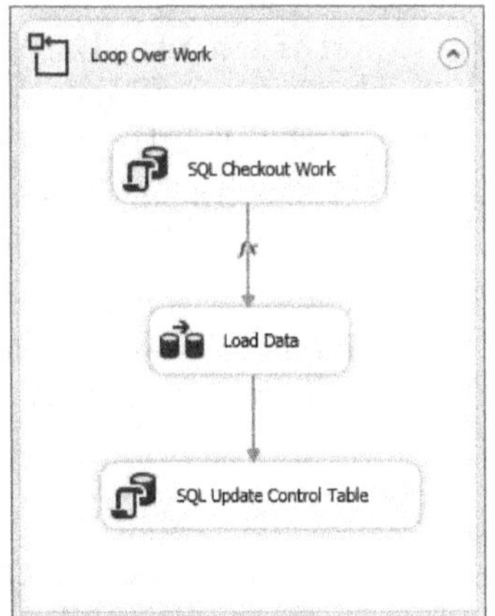

FIGURE 15-48

With the plumbing done, you're now ready to create parallelism in your package. One way of accomplishing this is through a batch file. The following batch file will perform this with the `START` command. Optionally, you can reset your tables through the SQLCMD executable, as shown here as well. The batch file will execute DTEXEC.exe *N* number of times in parallel and work on independent workloads. Where you see the SQLCMD command, you may also want to ensure that the trace flags are on if they're not on already.

```
@Echo off
sqlcmd -E -S localhost -d AdventureWorksDW -Q "update dbo.ctlTaskQueue set
StartDate = NULL, CompleteDate = NULL"
FOR /L %%i IN (1, 1, %1) DO (
ECHO Spawning thread %%i
START "Worker%%i" /Min "C:\Program Files\Microsoft SQL Server\120\DTS\Binn\
DTEXEC.exe" /FILE "C:\ProSSIS\Code\Ch15\09_ParallelDemo.dtsx" /CHECKPOINTING
OFF /REPORTING E
)
```

The `%1` in the preceding code represents the `N` variable that is passed in. To use the batch file, use the following command, where `5` represents the number of DTEXEC.exe commands that you wish to run in parallel. Save this file as ParallelBatch.cmd. You can do this from Notepad. Then, run the batch file with the following code in a command window.

```
ParallelBatch.cmd 5
```

As each worker thread spins up, it will log its number. The results will look like Figure 15-49.

> **WARNING** *Beware of executing packages from the command line. Even though executing packages from the command line can seem like an easy way to achieve parallelism and scalability, the execution functionality is limited. Using the DTEXEC.exe command will only work with Legacy Package Model features. If you want to take advantage of the latest Project Model features, you will need to utilize an alternative method.*

One final note about parallelism is that if you load data using multiple cores into a target table, it will cause fragmentation in the target table. Each core would handle sorting its individual chunk of data that it's responsible for; then when each chunk of data is pieced together, data may be inserted into different pages. One way to prevent that is to ensure that each thread of DTEXEC.exe connects to a different TCP/IP port and in soft NUMA node. With soft NUMA, you can bind any port or IP address to a given CPU core. By doing this, each SQL Server Destination in the Data Flow Task would always use only one CPU in SQL Server. It essentially allows SSIS and the SQL Server Destination to mimic MAXDOP 1 in T-SQL.

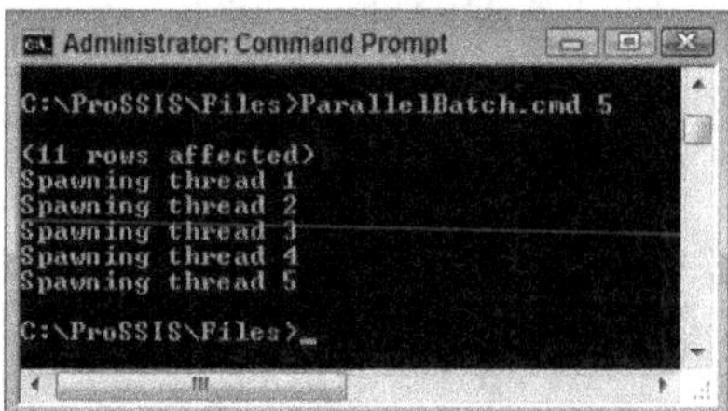

FIGURE 15-49

There is more setup needed to create the soft NUMA node. A complete soft NUMA explanation is beyond the scope of this book, and you can learn more on SQL Server Books Online. The following steps will point you in the right direction to getting soft NUMA working:

1. Create the soft NUMA node in the registry of the SQL Server instance, which isolates each node to a CPU core.
2. Bind the soft NUMA nodes to a given port in SQL Server Configuration Manager under Network Configuration.
3. Restart the SQL Server instance.
4. Change the package to bind the connection manager in the worker package to a different port by changing the ServerName property and adding the port following the server name (InstanceName, 1433, for example). You'll want this port to be dynamically set through an expression and variable so the variable can be passed in through the calling batch file.

SUMMARY

In this chapter, you looked at some of the obvious SSIS features provided to help you build reliable and scalable solutions, such as checkpoints and transactions. You also learned some practices you can employ, such as Data Flow Task restarts and scaling across machines; although these may not be explicit features, they are nonetheless very powerful techniques that can be implemented in your package designs.

16

Understanding and Tuning the Data Flow Engine

WHAT'S IN THIS CHAPTER?

- Understanding the Control Flow and Data Flow
- Learning the Data Flow architecture and transformation types
- Designing and tuning the Data Flow
- Troubleshooting Data Flow performance

WROX.COM DOWNLOADS FOR THIS CHAPTER

You can find the wrox.com code downloads for this chapter at `www.wrox.com/go/prossis2014` on the Download Code tab.

This chapter focuses on how the Data Flow engine works, because as you seek to expand your knowledge and skills with SSIS, you will need to understand how to best leverage and tune your packages and Data Flows. The chapter begins with a consideration of the architecture of the engine and its components, and then describes best practices for design and optimization, including the following concepts:

- Control Flow and Data Flow comparison
- Data Flow Transformation types
- Data Flow buffer architecture and execution trees
- Data Flow execution monitoring
- Data Flow design practices
- Data Flow engine tuning
- Performance monitoring

The initial part of this chapter is more abstract and theoretical, but we'll then move into the practical and tangible. In the concluding sections, you will apply the knowledge you have developed here, considering a methodology for optimization and looking at a few real-world scenarios.

Some of you will have worked with a previous edition of SSIS; for others, this will be your first time working with the tool. In many ways, each new version of SSIS has made improvements to the Data Flow architecture, adding more scalability and performance and fine-tuning the performance of the Data Flow engine.

For those of you with some knowledge of the SSIS pipeline architecture, two important features for the Data Flow engine are backpressure management and active component logging in the SSIS Server. These features provide scalability and advanced insight into the Data Flow. But let's begin with the basics of the SSIS engine.

THE SSIS ENGINE

Before learning about buffers, asynchronous components, and execution trees, you might find it useful to consider this analogy — traffic management. While driving in a big city, have you ever wondered how the traffic system works? It's remarkable how well coordinated the traffic lights are. In Manhattan, for example, a taxi ride can take you from midtown to downtown in minutes — in part because the lights are timed in a rolling fashion to maintain efficiency. The heavy fine assessed to anyone who "locks the box" (remains in the intersection after the light turns red) demonstrates how detrimental it is to interfere with the synchronization of such a complex traffic grid.

Contrast the efficiency of Manhattan with the gridlock and delays that result from a poorly designed traffic system. We have all been there before — sitting at a red light for minutes despite the absence of traffic on the intersecting streets, and then after the light changes, you find yourself in the same scenario at the next intersection! Even in a light-traffic environment, progress is impeded by poor coordination and inefficient design.

In the case of optimizing traffic patterns in a big city, good traffic management design focuses on easing congestion by keeping traffic moving or redirecting more highly congested areas to less utilized streets. A traffic jam occurs when something slows or blocks the flow of traffic. This causes *backpressure* behind the cause of the jam as cars queue up waiting to pass.

Bringing this back around to SSIS, in some ways the engine is similar to the grid management of a big city because the SSIS engine coordinates server resources and Data Flow for efficient information processing and management of data backpressure. Part of the process of making package execution efficient requires your involvement. In turn, this requires knowing how the SSIS engine works and some important particulars of components and properties that affect the data processing. That is the purpose of this chapter: to provide the groundwork for understanding SSIS, which will lead to better — that is, more efficient — design.

Understanding the SSIS Data Flow and Control Flow

From an architectural perspective, the difference between the Data Flow and Control Flow is important. One aspect that will help illustrate the distinction is to look at them from the perspective of how the components are handled. In the Control Flow, the *task* is the smallest unit of work, and a task requires completion (success, failure, or just completion) before subsequent tasks are handled. In the Data Flow, the *transformation*, *source*, and *destination* are the basic components; however, the Data Flow Components function very differently from a task. For example, instead of one transformation necessarily waiting for another transformation to complete before it can proceed with the next set of transformation logic, the components work together to process and manage data.

Comparing Data Flow and Control Flow

Although the Control Flow looks very similar to the Data Flow, with processing objects (tasks and transformations) and connectors that bridge them, there is a world of difference between them. The Control Flow, for example, does not manage or pass data between components; rather, it functions as a task coordinator with isolated units of work. Here are some of the Control Flow concepts:

- Workflow orchestration
- Process-oriented
- Serial or parallel tasks execution
- Synchronous processing

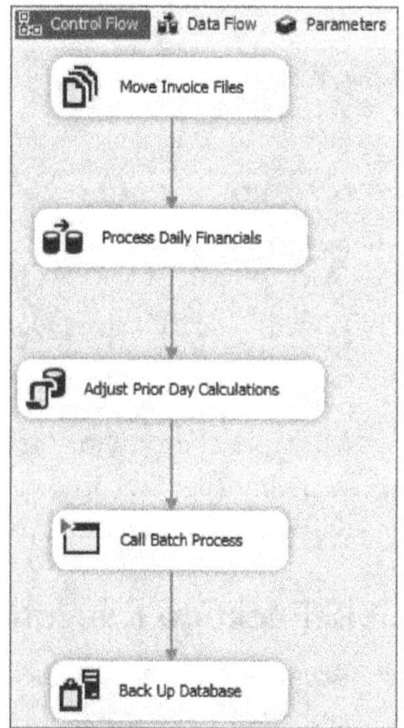

FIGURE 16-1

As highlighted, the Control Flow Tasks can be designed to execute both serially and in parallel — in fact, more often than not there will be aspects of both. A Control Flow Task can branch off into multiple tasks that are performed in parallel or as a single next step that is performed essentially in serial from the first. To show this, Figure 16-1 illustrates a very simple Control Flow process whose tasks are connected in a linear fashion. The execution of this package shows that the components are serialized — only a single task is executing at a time.

The Data Flow, conversely, can branch, split, and merge, providing parallel processing, but this concept is different from the Control Flow. Even though there may be a set of connected linear transformations, you cannot necessarily call the process a serial process, because the transformations in most cases will run at the same time, handling subsets of the data in parallel and passing groups of data downstream. Here are some of the unique aspects of the Data Flow:

- Information-oriented
- Data correlation and transformation
- Coordinated processing
- Streaming in nature
- Source extraction and destination loading

Similar to the Control Flow shown in Figure 16-2, Figure 16-2 also models a simple Data Flow whose components are connected one after the other. The difference between the Data Flow in Figure 16-2 and the Control Flow in Figure 16-2 is that only a single task is executing in the linear flow. In the Data Flow, however, all the transformations are doing work at the same time.

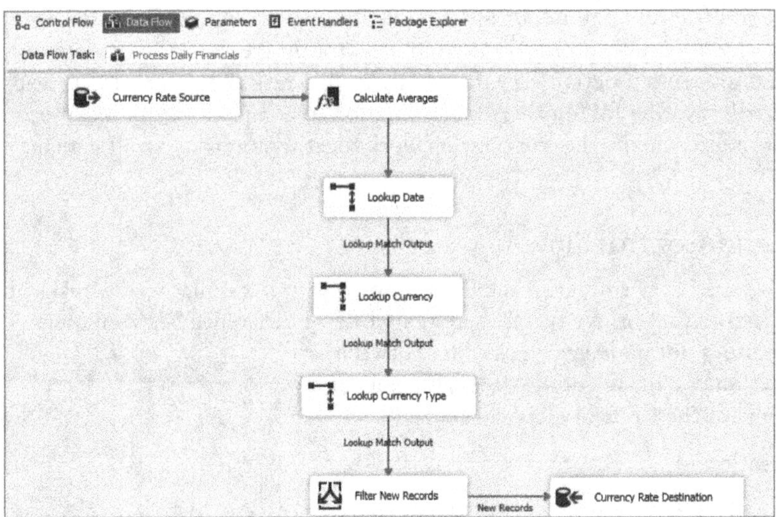

FIGURE 16-2

In other words, the first batch of data flowing in from the source may be in the final destination step (Currency Rate Destination), while at the same time data is still flowing in from the source.

Multiple components are running at the same time because the Data Flow Transformations are working together in a coordinated streaming fashion, and the data is being transformed in groups (called buffers) as it is passed down from the source to the subsequent transformations.

SSIS Package Execution Time from Package Start to Package Finish

Because a Data Flow is merely a type of Control Flow Task, and more than one Data Flow can be embedded in a package (or none!), the total time it takes to execute a package is measured from the execution of the first Control Flow Task or Tasks through the completion of the last task being executed, regardless of whether the components executing are Data Flow Transformations or Control Flow Tasks. This may sound obvious, but it is worth mentioning because when you are designing a package, maximizing the parallel processing where appropriate (with due regard to your server resources) helps optimize the flow and reduce the overall processing time.

The package shown in Figure 16-3 has several tasks executing a variety of processes and using precedence constraints in a way that demonstrates parallel execution of tasks. The last task, Back Up Database, is the only task that does not execute in parallel because it has to wait for the execution of all the other tasks. Because the Control Flow has been designed with parallelization, the overlap in tasks enables faster package execution than it would if the steps were executed in a serial manner as earlier shown (refer to Figure 16-1).

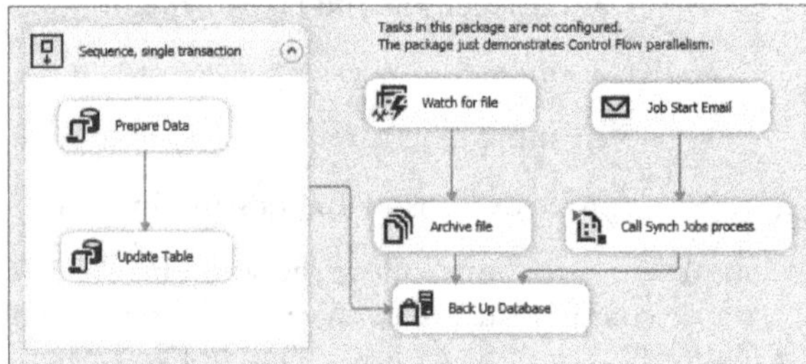

FIGURE 16-3

Handling Workflows with the Control Flow

Both of the components of the Control Flow have been discussed in Chapter 3, as well as the different types of precedence constraints. Because the Control Flow contains standard workflow concepts that are common to most scheduling and ETL tools, the rest of this chapter focuses on the Data Flow; however, a brief look at Control Flow parallelization and processing is warranted.

The Control Flow, as already mentioned, can be designed to execute tasks in parallel or serially, or a combination of the two. Tasks are also *synchronous* in nature, meaning a task requires completion before handing off an operation to another process. While it is possible to design a Control Flow containing tasks that are not connected with constraints to other tasks, the tasks are still synchronously tied to the execution of the package. Said in another way, a package cannot kick off the execution of a task and then complete execution while the task is still executing. Rather, the SSIS execution thread for the task is synchronously tied to the task's execution and will not release until the task completes successfully or fails.

> **NOTE** *The synchronous nature of tasks should not be confused with the synchronous and asynchronous nature of transformations in the Data Flow. The concepts are slightly different. In the Data Flow, a transformation's synchronicity is a matter of communication (how data is passed between transformations), rather than the process orientation of the Control Flow.*

Data Processing in the Data Flow

The Data Flow is the core data processing factory of SSIS packages, where the primary data is handled, managed, transformed, integrated, and cleansed. Think of the Data Flow as a pipeline for data. A house, for example, has a primary water source, which is branched to all the different outlets in the house.

When a faucet is turned on, water flows out of it, while at the same time water is coming in from the source. If all the water outlets in a house are turned off, then the pressure backs up to the source to the point where water will no longer flow into the house until the pressure is relieved. Conversely, if all the water outlets in the house are opened at once, then the source pressure may not be able to keep up with the flow of water, and the pressure coming out of the faucets will be weaker. (Of course, don't try this at home; it may produce other problems!)

The Data Flow is appropriately named because the data equates to the water in the plumbing analogy. The data flows from the Data Sources through the transformations to the Data Destinations. In addition to the flowing concept, there are similarities to the Data Flow pressure within the pipeline. For example, while a Data Source may be able to stream 10,000 rows per second, if a downstream transformation consumes too much server resources, it could apply backward pressure on the source and reduce the number of rows coming from the source. Essentially, this creates a bottleneck that may need to be addressed to optimize the flow. In order to understand and apply design principles in a Data Flow, an in-depth discussion of the Data Flow architecture is merited. Understanding several Data Flow concepts will give you a fuller perspective regarding what is going on under the hood of an executing package. Each of these concepts is addressed over the next few pages:

- Data buffer architecture
- Transformation types
- Transformation communication
- Execution trees

After reviewing the architecture, you can shift to monitoring packages in order to determine how the Data Flow engine handles data processing.

Memory Buffer Architecture

The Data Flow manages data in groups of data called *buffers*. A buffer is merely memory that is allocated for the use of storing rows and columns of data where transformations are applied. This means that as data is being extracted from sources into the engine, it is put into these preallocated memory buffers. Buffers are dynamically sized based on row width (the cumulative number of bytes in a row) and other package and server criteria. A buffer, for example, may include 9,000 rows of data with a few columns of data. Figure 16-4 shows a few groupings of buffers.

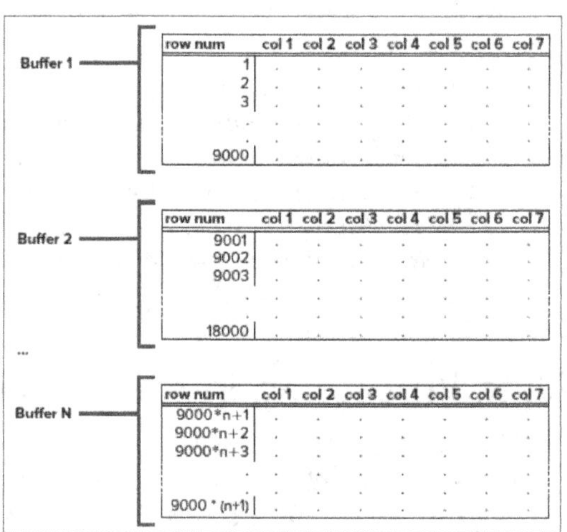

FIGURE 16-4

Although it is easy to imagine data being passed down from transformation to transformation in the Data Flow, like the flow of water in the pipeline analogy, this is not a complete picture of what is going on behind the scenes. Instead of data being passed down through the transformations, groups of transformations pass over the buffers of data and make in-place changes as defined by the transformations. Think of how much more efficient this process is than copying the data from one transformation to the next every time a transformation specified a change in the data! To be sure, there are times when the buffers are copied and other times when the buffers are held up in cache by transformations. Understanding how and when this happens will enable you to determine the best design to optimize your Data Flow.

This understanding of how memory buffers are managed requires knowing something about the different types of Data Flow Components — transformations, sources, and destinations.

Types of Transformations

The transformations in the Data Flow have certain characteristics that group each into different categories. The base-level differences between them are the way they communicate with each other, and how and when data is handed off from one transformation to another. Evaluating transformations on two fronts provides the background you need to understand how the buffers are managed:

- **Blocking nature:** Non-blocking (sometimes called streaming), semi-blocking, blocking
- **Communication mechanism:** Synchronous and asynchronous

In reality, these classifications are related, but from a practical standpoint, discussing them separately provides some context for data management in the Data Flow.

Non-Blocking, Semi-Blocking, and Blocking Transformations

The most obvious distinction between transformations is their blocking nature. All transformations fall into one of three categories: non-blocking, semi-blocking, or blocking. These terms describe whether data in a transformation is passed downstream in the pipeline immediately, in increments, or after all the data is fully received.

The blocking nature of a transformation is related to what a transformation is designed to accomplish. Because the Data Flow engine just invokes the transformations without knowing what they internally do, there are no properties of the transformation that discretely identify this nature. However, when we look at the communication between transformations in the next section (the synchronous and asynchronous communication), we can identify how the engine will manage transformations one to another.

Non-Blocking, Streaming, and Row-Based Transformations

Most of the SSIS transformations are non-blocking. This means that the transformation logic applied in the transformation does not impede the data from moving on to the next transformation after the transformation logic is applied to the row. Two categories of non-blocking transformations exist: *streaming* and *row-based*. The difference is whether the SSIS transformation can use internal information and processes to handle its work or whether the transformation has to call an external process to retrieve information it needs for the work. Some transformations can be categorized as streaming or row-based depending on their configuration, which are indicated in the list below.

Streaming transformations are usually able to apply transformation logic quickly, using precached data and processing calculations within the row being worked on. In these transformations, it is usually the case that a transformation will not slip behind the rate of the data being fed to it. These transformations focus their resources on the CPUs, which in most cases are not the bottleneck of an ETL system. Therefore, they are classified as streaming. The following transformations stream the data from transformation to transformation in the Data Flow:

- Audit
- Cache Transform
- Character Map
- Conditional Split
- Copy Column
- Data Conversion

- Derived Column
- Lookup (with a full-cache setting)
- Multicast
- Percent Sampling
- Row Count
- Script Component (provided the script is not configured with an asynchronous output, which is discussed in the "Advanced Data Flow Execution Concepts" section)
- Union All (the Union All acts like a streaming transformation but is actually a semi-blocking transformation because it communicates asynchronously, which is covered in the next section)

The second grouping of non-blocking transformations is identified as *row-based*. These transformations are still non-blocking in the sense that the data can flow immediately to the next transformation after the transformation logic is applied to the buffer. The row-based description indicates that the rows flowing through the transformation are acted on one by one with a requirement to interact with an outside process such as a database, file, or component. Given their row-based processes, in most cases these transformations may not be able to keep up with the rate at which the data is fed to them, and the buffers are held up until each row is processed. The following transformations are classified as row-based:

- DQS Cleansing
- Export Column
- Import Column
- Lookup (with a no-cache or partial-cache setting)
- OLE DB Command
- Script Component (where the script interacts with an external component)
- Slowly Changing Dimension (each row is looked up against the dimension in the database)

Figure 16-5 shows a Data Flow composed of only streaming transformations. If you look at the row counts in the design UI, you will notice that the transformations are passing rows downstream in the pipeline as soon as the transformation logic is completed. Streaming transformations do not have to wait for other operations in order for the rows being processed to be passed downstream.

Also, notice in Figure 16-5 that data is inserted into the destination even while transformation logic is still being applied to some of the earlier transformations. This very simple Data Flow is handling a high volume of data with minimal resources, such as memory usage, because of the streaming nature of the Transformation Components used.

Semi-Blocking Transformations

The next category of Transformation Components are the ones that hold up records in the Data Flow for a period of time before allowing the memory buffers to be passed downstream. These are typically called semi-blocking transformations, given their nature. Only a few out-of-the-box transformations are semi-blocking in nature:

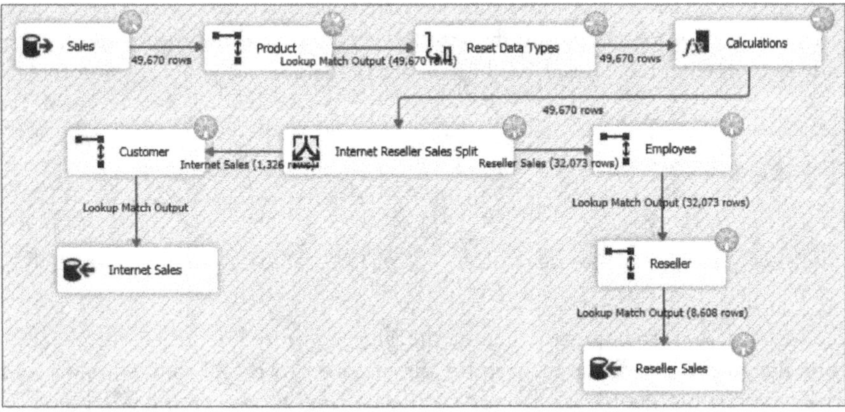

FIGURE 16-5

- Data Mining Query
- Merge
- Merge Join
- Pivot
- Term Lookup
- Unpivot
- Union All (also included in the streaming transformations list, but under the covers, the Union All is semi-blocking)

The Merge and Merge Join Transformations are described in detail in Chapter 4 and Chapter 7, but in relation to the semi-blocking nature of these components, note that they require the sources to be sorted on the matching keys of the merge. Both of these transformations function by waiting for key matches from both sides of the merge (or join), and when the matching sorted keys from both sides pass through the transformations, the records can then be sent downstream while the next set of keys is handled. Figure 16-6 shows how a Merge Join within a Data Flow will partially hold up the processing of the rows until the matches are made.

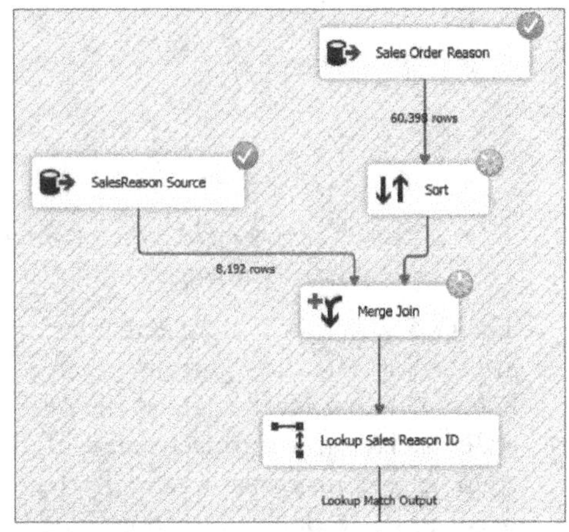

FIGURE 16-6

Typically, the row count upstream of the Merge Join is much higher than the row count just below the Merge Join, because the Merge Join waits for the sorted key matches as they flow in from both sides of the merge. Buffers are being released downstream, just not in a streaming fashion as in the non-blocking Transformation Components. You may also be wondering why there is no Sort Transformation on the right-side source of the Merge Join despite the fact that the transformations require the sources to be sorted. This is because the source data was presorted, and the Source component was configured to recognize that data flowing into the Data Flow was already sorted. Chapter 7 describes how to set the `IsSorted` property of a source.

> **NOTE** *Semi-blocking transformations require a little more server resources than non-blocking transformations because the buffers need to stay in memory until the right data is received.*

In a large data processing situation, the question is how the Merge Join will handle a large data set coming in from one side of the join while waiting for the other set or if one source is slow and the other fast. The risk is exceeding the buffer memory while waiting. However, SSIS 2014 can throttle the sources by limiting the requests from the upstream transformations and sources, thereby preventing SSIS from getting into an out-of-memory situation. This very valuable engine feature of SSIS 2014 resolves the memory tension, enabling a Data Flow to continue without introducing a lot of data paging to disk in the process.

Blocking Transformations

The final category of transformation types is the actual blocking transformation. These components require a complete review of the upstream data before releasing any row downstream to the connected transformations and destinations. The list is also smaller than the list of non-blocking transformations because there are only a few transformations that require "blocking" all the data to complete an operation. Here is the list of the blocking transformations:

- Aggregate
- Fuzzy Grouping
- Fuzzy Lookup
- Row Sampling
- Sort
- Term Extraction
- Script Component (when configured to receive all rows before sending any downstream)

The two most widely used examples of the blocking transformations are the Sort and the Aggregate; each of these requires the entire data set before handing off the data to the next transformation. For example, in order to have an accurate average, all the records need to be held up by the Aggregate Transformation. Similarly, to sort data in a flow, all the data needs to be available to the Sort Transformation before the component knows the order in which to release records downstream. Figure 16-7 shows a Data Flow that contains an Aggregate Transformation. The screen capture of this process shows that the entire source has already been brought into the Data Flow, but no rows have been released downstream while the transformation is determining the order.

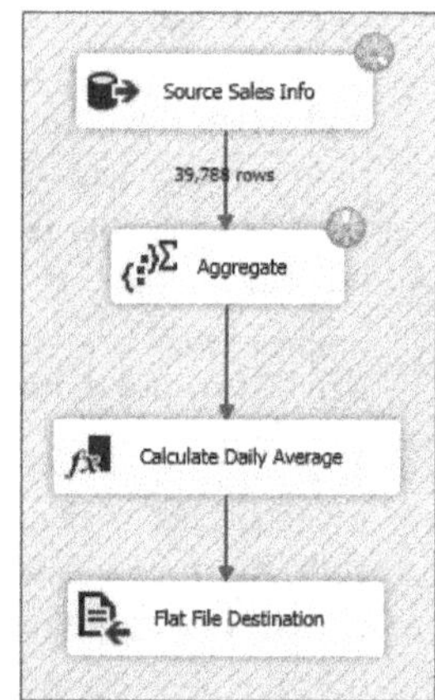

FIGURE 16-7

With a Blocking Component in the Data Flow (refer to Figure 16-7), the data is no longer streaming through the Data Flow. Instead, data is held up so that all the rows remain in the blocking transformation until the last row flows through the transformation.

> **NOTE** *Blocking transformations are usually more resource intensive than other types of transformations for two main reasons. First, because all the data is being held up, either the server must use a lot of memory to store the data or, if the server does not have enough memory, a process of file staging happens, which requires the I/O overhead of staging the data to disk temporarily. Second, these transformations usually put a heavy burden on the processor to perform the work of data aggregation, sorting, or fuzzy matching.*

Synchronous and Asynchronous Transformation Outputs

Another important differentiation between transformations is related to how transformations that are connected to one another by a path communicate. While closely related to the discussion on the blocking nature of transformations, *synchronous* and *asynchronous* refer more to the relationship between the Input and Output Component connections and buffers.

Some transformations have an Advanced Editor window, which, among other things, drills into specific column-level properties of the transformations' input and output columns, which is useful in understanding the difference between synchronous and asynchronous outputs. Figure 16-8 shows the Advanced Editor of the Sort Transformation, highlighting the Input and Output Properties tab. This particular transformation has a Sort Input and Sort Output group with a set of columns associated with each.

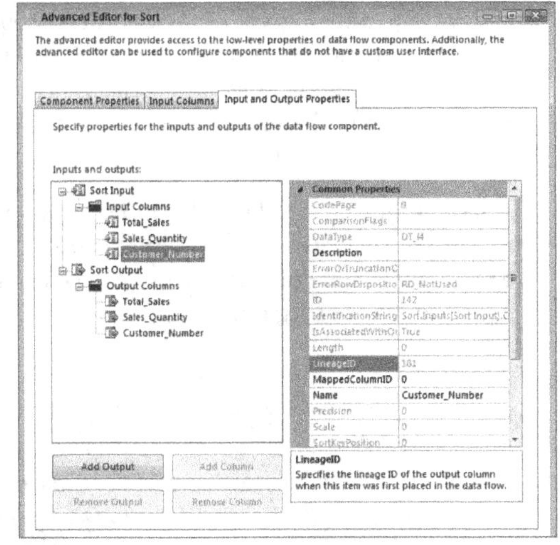

FIGURE 16-8

When a column is highlighted, the advanced properties of that column are displayed on the right, as shown in the figure. The advanced properties include such things as the data type of the column, the description, and so on. One important property to note is the `LineageID`. This is the integer pointer to the column within the buffers. Every column used in the Data Flow has at least one `LineageID` in the Data Flow. A column can have more than one `LineageID` as it passes through the Data Flow based on the types of transformation outputs (synchronous or asynchronous) that a column goes through in the Data Flow.

Asynchronous Transformation Outputs

It is easier to begin with the *asynchronous* definition because it leads into a comparison of the two kinds of transformation outputs, *synchronous* and asynchronous. A transformation output is asynchronous if the buffers used in the input are different from the buffers used in the output. In other words, many of the transformations cannot both perform the specified operation and preserve the buffers (the number of rows or the order of the rows), so a copy of the data must be made to accomplish the desired effect.

The Aggregate Transformation, for example, may output only a fraction of the number of rows coming into it; or when the Merge Join Transformation has to join two data sets together, the resulting number of rows may not be equivalent to the number of input rows. In both cases, the buffers are received, the processing is handled, and new buffers are created.

For example, returning to the Advanced Editor of the Sort dialog shown in Figure 16-8, note the `LineageID` property of the input column. In this transformation, all the input columns are duplicated in the output columns list. In fact, as Figure 16-9 shows, the output column highlighted for the same input has a different `LineageID`.

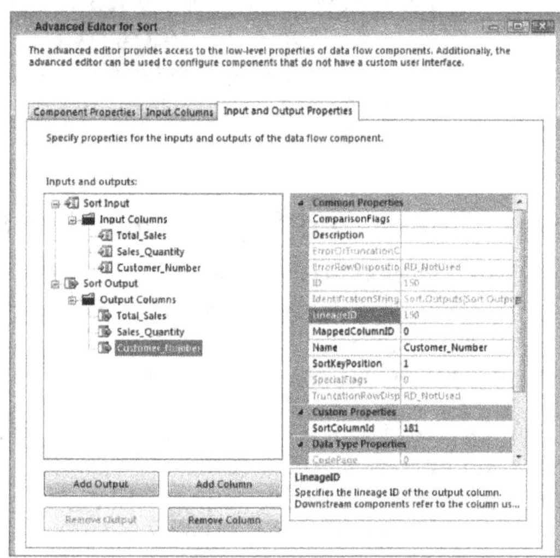

FIGURE 16-9

The `LineageIDs` are different for the same column because the Sort Transformation output is asynchronous, and the data buffers in the input are not the same buffers in the output; therefore, a new column identifier is needed for the output. In the preceding example, the input `LineageID` is 181, whereas in the output column the `LineageID` is 150.

A list doesn't need to be included here, because all the semi-blocking and blocking transformations already listed have asynchronous outputs by definition — none of them can pass input buffers on downstream because the data is held up for processing and reorganized.

> **NOTE** *One of the SSIS engine components is called the* buffer manager. *For asynchronous component outputs, the buffer manager is busy at work, decommissioning buffers for use elsewhere (in sources or other asynchronous outputs) and reassigning new buffers to the data coming out of the transformation. The buffer manager also schedules processor threads to components as threads are needed.*

Synchronous Transformation Outputs

A synchronous transformation is one in which the buffers are immediately handed off to the next downstream transformation at the completion of the transformation logic. If this sounds like the definition for streaming transformations, that's because there is almost complete overlap between streaming transformations and synchronous transformations. The word *buffers* was intentionally used in the definition of synchronous outputs, because the important point is that the same buffers received by the transformation input are passed out the output.

The `LineageIDs` of the columns remain the same as the data is passed through the synchronous output, without a need to copy the buffer data and assign a new `LineageID` (as discussed previously for asynchronous transformation output).

To illustrate this point, refer back to Figure 16-5. In this example, each transformation, including the Conditional Split, has asynchronous outputs. This means that there are no buffer copies while this Data Flow runs. For the Source component called Sales, several of the columns are used in both the destinations. Now consider Figure 16-10, which shows the Advanced Editor of the source and highlights the `TaxAmt` column, which has a `LineageID` of 318.

This `LineageID` for `TaxAmt` (as well as the other columns) is preserved throughout the Data Flow all the way to the destination. Figure 16-11 shows the Advanced Editor for one of the destination components, Reseller Sales, and indicates that the `LineageID` of 318 has been preserved through the entire Data Flow.

FIGURE 16-10

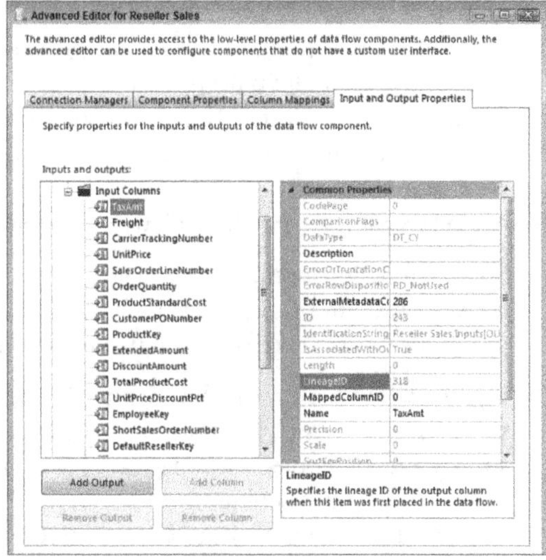

FIGURE 16-11

In fact, if you look at the `LineageID` of `TaxAmt` in the Internet Sales destination, you would also find that it is 299. Even for the Conditional Split (because it has asynchronous outputs), the data is not copied to new buffers; rather, the Data Flow engine maintains pointers to the right rows in the buffers, so if there is more than one destination, the data can be inserted into each destination without requiring data to be copied. This explains why the execution of the Data Flow shown earlier in Figure 16-5 allows the data to flow in a streaming way through the Data Flow.

> **NOTE** *A transformation is not limited to a single synchronous output. Both the Multicast and the Conditional Split can have multiple outputs, but all the outputs are synchronous.*

With the exception of the Union All, all the non-blocking transformations listed in the previous section also have synchronous outputs. The Union All, while it functions like a streaming transformation, is really an asynchronous transformation. Given the complexity of unioning multiple sources together and keeping track of all the pointers to the right data from the different source inputs, the Union All instead copies the upstream data to new buffers as it receives them and passes the new buffers off to the downstream transformations.

> **NOTE** *Synchronous transformation outputs preserve the sort order of incoming data, whereas some of the asynchronous transformations do not. The Sort, Merge, and Merge Join asynchronous components, of course, have sorted outputs because of their nature, but the Union All, for example, does not.*

A definitive way to identify synchronous versus asynchronous components is to look at the `SynchronousInputID` property of the Column Output properties. If this value is 0, the component output is asynchronous, but if this property is set to a value greater than 0, the transformation output is synchronous to the input whose ID matches the `SynchronousInputID` value.

Source and Destination Components

Source and Destination components are integral to the Data Flow and therefore merit brief consideration in this chapter. In fact, because of their differences in functionality, sources and destinations are therefore classified differently.

First of all, in looking at the advanced properties of a Source component, the source will have the same list of external columns and output columns. The external columns come directly from the source and are copied into the Data Flow buffers and subsequently assigned `LineageIDs`. While the external source columns do not have `LineageIDs`, the process is effectively the same as an asynchronous component output. Source components require the allocation of buffers, where the incoming data can be grouped and managed for the downstream transformations to perform work against.

Destination components, conversely, de-allocate the buffer data when it is loaded into the destinations. The advanced properties of the Destination component include an External Column list, which represents the destination columns used in the load. The input columns are mapped to this External Column list on the Mapping page of the Destination component editor. In the advanced properties, you should note that there is no primary Output Container (besides the Error Output) for the Destination component, as the buffers do not flow through the component but rather are committed to a Destination component as a final step in the Data Flow.

Advanced Data Flow Execution Concepts

The preceding discussion of transformation types and how outputs handle buffers leads into a more advanced discussion of how SSIS coordinates and manages Data Flow processing overall. This section ties together the discussion of synchronous and asynchronous transformations to provide the bigger picture of a package's execution.

Relevant to this discussion is a more detailed understanding of buffer management within an executing package based on how the package is designed.

Execution Trees

In one sense, you have already looked at execution trees, although they weren't explicitly referred to by this name. An *execution tree* is a logical grouping of Data Flow Components (transformations, sources, and destinations) based on their synchronous relationship to one another. Groupings are delineated by asynchronous component outputs that indicate the completion of one execution tree and the start of the next.

Figure 16-12 shows the execution trees of a moderately complex Data Flow that uses multiple components with asynchronous outputs. The "paths" indicated are numbered based on the SSIS Data Flow logging, not the order in which the data flows. See the PipelineExecutionTrees log example in the "Monitoring Data Flow Execution" section of this chapter.

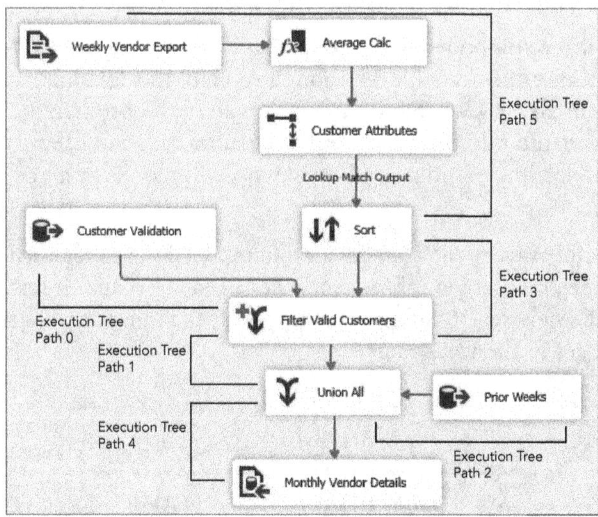

FIGURE 16-12

Recall that components with asynchronous outputs use different input buffers. The input participates in the upstream execution tree, while the asynchronous output begins the next execution tree. In light of this, the execution trees for Figure 16-12 start at the Source components and are then completed, and a new execution tree begins at every asynchronous transformation.

Execution trees are base 0, meaning you count them starting with a 0. In the next section, you will see how the pipeline logging identifies them. Although the execution trees seem out of order, you have used the explicit order given by the pipeline logging.

In the next section, you will look at ways to log and track the execution trees within a Data Flow, but for now the discussion focuses on a few principles that clarify what happens in an execution tree.

When SSIS executes a package, the buffer manager defines different buffer profiles based on the execution trees within a package. All the buffers used for a particular execution tree are identical in definition. When defining the buffer profile for each execution tree, the SSIS buffer manager looks at all the transformations used in the execution tree and includes every column in the buffer that is needed at any point within the execution tree. Note that execution tree path #5 in Figure 16-12 contains a Source component, a Derived Column Transformation, and a Lookup. Without looking at the source properties, the following list defines the four columns that the Source component is using from the source:

- CurrencyCode
- CurrencyRate
- AverageRate
- EndofDayRate

The Derived Column Transformation adds two more columns to the Data Flow: Average_Sale and Audit_Date. Finally, the Lookup Transformation adds another three columns to the Data Flow.

Added together, the columns used in these three components total nine. This means that the buffers used in this execution tree will have nine columns allocated, even though some of the columns are not used in the initial components. Optimizing a Data Flow can be compared to optimizing a relational table, where the smaller the width and number of columns, the more that can fit into a Data Flow buffer. This has some performance implications, and the next section looks in more detail at optimizing buffers.

When a buffer is used in an execution tree and reaches the transformation input of the asynchronous component (the last step in the execution tree), the data is subsequently not needed because it has been passed off to a new execution tree and a new set of buffers. At this point, the buffer manager can use the allocated buffer for other purposes in the Data Flow.

> **NOTE** *One final note about execution trees — the process thread scheduler can assign more than one thread to a single execution tree if threads are available and the execution tree requires intense processor utilization. Each transformation can receive a single thread, so if an execution tree has only two components that participate, then the execution tree can have a maximum of two threads. In addition, each source component receives a separate thread.*

One advanced property of the Data Flow is the `EngineThreads` property. In the Control Flow, when a Data Flow Task is highlighted, this property appears in the Properties window list (see Figure 16-13).

It is important to modify the `EngineThreads` property of the Data Flow so that the execution trees are not sharing process threads, and extra threads are available for large or complex execution trees. Furthermore, all the execution trees in a package share the number of processor threads allocated in the `EngineThreads` property of the Data Flow. A single thread or multiple threads are assigned to an execution tree based on availability of threads and complexity of the execution tree.

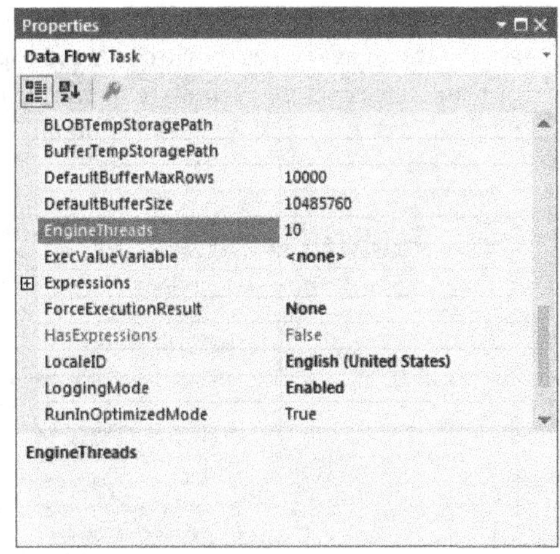

FIGURE 16-13

In the last section of this chapter, you will see how the threads available in a Data Flow are allocated to the execution trees. The value for `EngineThreads` does not include the threads allocated for the number of sources in a Data Flow, which are automatically allocated separate threads.

Monitoring Data Flow Execution

Built into SSIS 2014 is the capability to report on Data Flow performance and identify execution trees and threads. The reports and log events can be very useful in understanding your Data Flow and how the engine is managing buffers and execution.

First of all, pipeline logging events are available in the Logging features of SSIS. As shown in the following list, several logging events provide details about what is happening in the Data Flow. Books Online describes each of these in detail, with examples, at `http://msdn.microsoft.com/en-us/library/ms141122(v=SQL.120).aspx`.

- OnPipelinePostEndOfRowset
- OnPipelinePostPrimeOutput
- OnPipelinePreEndOfRowset
- OnPipelinePrePrimeOutput
- OnPipelineRowsSent
- PipelineBufferLeak
- PipelineComponentTime
- PipelineExecutionPlan
- PipelineExecutionTrees
- PipelineInitialization

> **NOTE** *When executing a package on the SSIS server, you can turn on the Verbose logging to capture all the events. This is found on the Advanced tab of the Execute Package dialog under Logging level.*

To better understand execution trees, you can capture the PipelineExecutionTrees log event. To do so, create a new log entry through the logging designer window under the SSIS menu's Logging option. The pipeline events are available only when a Data Flow is selected in the tree menu navigator of the package executable navigator, as shown in Figure 16-14.

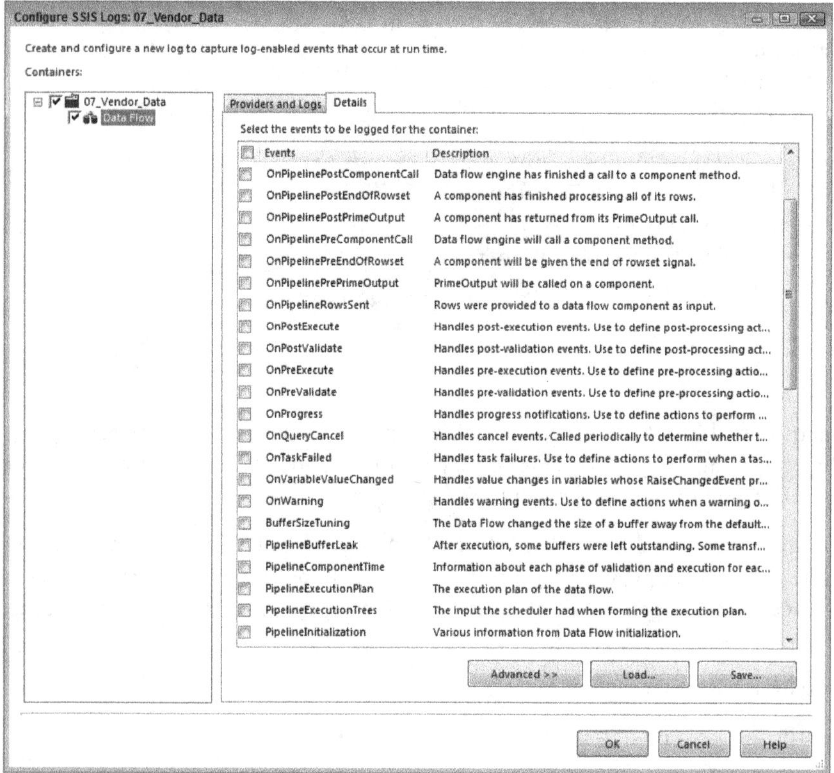

FIGURE 16-14

On the Details tab of this Configure SSIS Logs dialog, the two execution information log events just listed are available to capture. When the package is run, these events can be tracked to the selected log provider as defined. However, during development, it is useful to see these events when testing and designing a package. SSIS includes a way to see these events in the SQL Server Data Tools as a separate window. The Log Events window can be pulled up either from the SSIS menu by selecting Log Events or through the View menu, listed under the Other Windows submenu.

When the package is executed in design time through the interface, the log events selected are displayed in the Log Events window. For each Data Flow, there is one event returned for the PipelineExecutionPlan event and one for the PipelineExecutionTrees event, as shown in Figure 16-15. These log details have been captured from the sample Data Flow used in Figure 16-12.

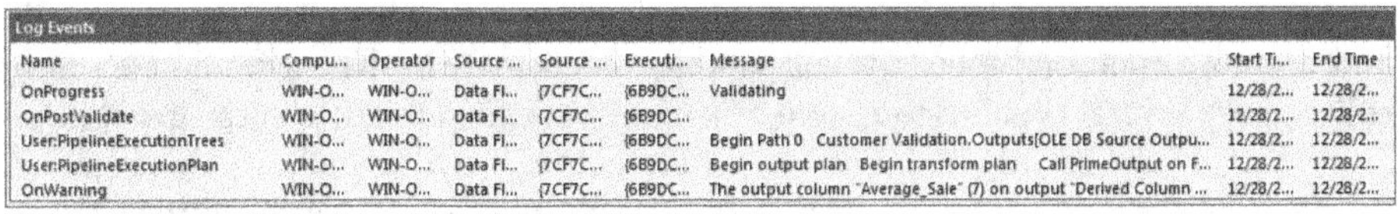

Log Events

Name	Compu...	Operator	Source ...	Source ...	Executi...	Message	Start Ti...	End Time
OnProgress	WIN-O...	WIN-O...	Data Fl...	{7CF7C...	{6B9DC...	Validating	12/28/2...	12/28/2...
OnPostValidate	WIN-O...	WIN-O...	Data Fl...	{7CF7C...	{6B9DC...		12/28/2...	12/28/2...
User:PipelineExecutionTrees	WIN-O...	WIN-O...	Data Fl...	{7CF7C...	{6B9DC...	Begin Path 0 Customer Validation.Outputs[OLE DB Source Outpu...	12/28/2...	12/28/2...
User:PipelineExecutionPlan	WIN-O...	WIN-O...	Data Fl...	{7CF7C...	{6B9DC...	Begin output plan Begin transform plan Call PrimeOutput on F...	12/28/2...	12/28/2...
OnWarning	WIN-O...	WIN-O...	Data Fl...	{7CF7C...	{6B9DC...	The output column "Average_Sale" (7) on output "Derived Column ...	12/28/2...	12/28/2...

FIGURE 16-15

Note that all pipeline events selected in the Logging configuration are included in the Log window. To capture the details for a more readable view of the Message column, simply right-click the log entry and copy, which puts the event message onto the clipboard.

Pipeline Execution Trees Log Details

The PipelineExecutionTrees log event describes the grouping of transformation inputs and outputs that participate in each execution tree. Each execution tree is numbered for readability. The following text comes from the message column of the PipelineExecutionTrees log entry from the execution of the Data Flow shown in Figure 16-12:

```
Begin Path 0
   Customer Validation.Outputs[OLE DB Source Output]; Customer Validation
   Filter Valid Customers.Inputs[Merge Join Right Input]; Filter Valid Customers
End Path 0

Begin Path 1
   Filter Valid Customers.Outputs[Merge Join Output]; Filter Valid Customers
   Union All.Inputs[Union All Input 1]; Union All
End Path 1

Begin Path 2
   Prior Weeks.Outputs[OLE DB Source Output]; Prior Weeks
   Union All.Inputs[Union All Input 2]; Union All
End Path 2

Begin Path 3
   Sort.Outputs[Sort Output]; Sort
   Filter Valid Customers.Inputs[Merge Join Left Input]; Filter Valid Customers
End Path 3

Begin Path 4
   Union All.Outputs[Union All Output 1]; Union All
   Monthly Vendor Details.Inputs[SQL Server Destination Input]; Monthly Vendor
      Details
End Path 4

Begin Path 5
   Weekly Vendor Export.Outputs[Flat File Source Output]; Weekly Vendor Export
   Average Calc.Inputs[Derived Column Input]; Average Calc
   Average Calc.Outputs[Derived Column Output]; Average Calc
   Customer Attributes.Inputs[Lookup Input]; Customer Attributes
   Customer Attributes.Outputs[Lookup Match Output]; Customer Attributes
   Sort.Inputs[Sort Input]; Sort
End Path 5
```

In the log output, each execution tree evaluated by the engine is listed with a `begin path` and an `end path`, with the transformation inputs and outputs that participate in the execution tree. Some execution trees may have several synchronous component outputs participating in the grouping, while others may be composed of only an input and output between two asynchronous components. As mentioned earlier, the execution trees use base 0, so the total number of execution trees for your Data Flow will be the numeral of the last execution tree plus one. In this example, there are six execution trees. A quick way to identify synchronous and asynchronous transformation outputs in your Data Flow is to review this log. Any transformation for which both the inputs and the outputs are contained within one execution tree is synchronous. Conversely, any transformation for which one or more inputs are separated from the outputs in different execution trees has asynchronous outputs.

Pipeline Execution Reporting

SSIS 2014 comes with a set of execution and status reports that highlight the current executions, history, and errors of package execution. Chapter 22 covers the reports in general. These reports are available only if you have your packages in the project deployment model, have deployed them to an SSIS server, and run the package on the server. In addition to the report highlighted later, you can also query the execution data in the SSISDB database on the server. The log information named in SSIS 2014 is available in the catalog. In addition, there is a table-value function catalog.dm_execution_performance_counters that can provide execution instance-specific information such as the number of buffers used.

One very valuable data collection point for Data Flow execution is the "Active Time" (in seconds) of each Data Flow Component. If you want to know how long a transformation is being used during a Data Flow execution, you can compare the active time to the total time of the Data Flow. In order to capture these details, you need to enable the performance logging level when the package is executed. Figure 16-16 shows the Advanced tab of the Execute Package window when executing a package on the SSIS server.

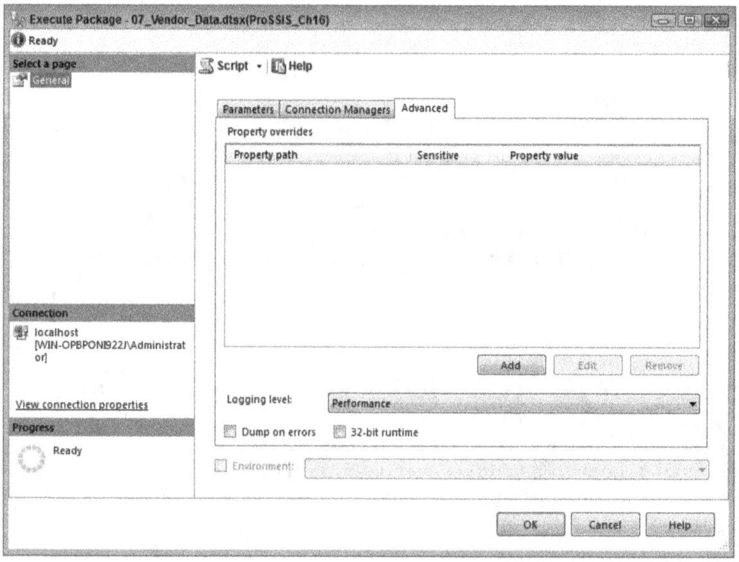

FIGURE 16-16

This logging level is also available in SQL Server Agent when you schedule a package to be run through the SQL Server Integration Services Package job step.

The benefit of logging this level of detail for a package is that it retains the performance details of the Data Flow. If you run the Execution Performance report (right-click the package in the SSIS Catalog project and run the All Executions report, then drill down to Execution Performance), you can see the history of the package, as well as the Data Flow Components and how long each were active. Figure 16-17 shows a sample Execution Performance report.

Package Name	Task Name	Subcomponent Name	Execution Path	Active Time (sec)
07_Vendor_Data.dtsx	Data Flow	Customer Attributes	\07_Vendor_Data\Data Flow	0.516
07_Vendor_Data.dtsx	Data Flow	Weekly Vendor Export	\07_Vendor_Data\Data Flow	0.348
07_Vendor_Data.dtsx	Data Flow	Customer Validation	\07_Vendor_Data\Data Flow	0.242
07_Vendor_Data.dtsx	Data Flow	Monthly Vendor Details	\07_Vendor_Data\Data Flow	0.213
07_Vendor_Data.dtsx	Data Flow	Prior Weeks	\07_Vendor_Data\Data Flow	0.212
07_Vendor_Data.dtsx	Data Flow	Average Calc	\07_Vendor_Data\Data Flow	0.03
07_Vendor_Data.dtsx	Data Flow	Filter Valid Customers	\07_Vendor_Data\Data Flow	0
07_Vendor_Data.dtsx	Data Flow	Sort	\07_Vendor_Data\Data Flow	0
07_Vendor_Data.dtsx	Data Flow	Union All	\07_Vendor_Data\Data Flow	0

FIGURE 16-17

As you can imagine, if you are having performance problems with your Data Flows, you can run this report and quickly identify the trouble spots that you need to work on. The next section describes ways to efficiently design, optimize, and tune your Data Flow.

SSIS DATA FLOW DESIGN AND TUNING

Now that you know how the Data Flow engine works, it will be easier to understand Data Flow design principles and tuning practices.

Designing a data-processing solution requires more than just sending the source data into a black-box transformation engine with outputs that push the data into the destination. Of course, system requirements will dictate the final design of the process, including but not limited to the following:

- Source and destination system impact
- Processing time windows and performance
- Destination system state consistency
- Hard and soft exception handling and restartability needs
- Environment architecture model, distributed hardware, or scaled-up servers
- Solution architecture requirements, such as flexibility of change or OEM targeted solutions
- Modular and configurable solution needs
- Manageability and administration requirements

Looking at this list, you can quickly map several of these items to what you have learned about SSIS already. In most cases, a good architecture leverages the built-in functionality of the tool, which reduces administrative and support requirements. The tool selection process, if it is not completed before a solution is developed, should include a consideration of the system requirements and the functionality of available products.

Data Flow Design Practices

Keep the following four design practices in mind when creating new packages:

- Limit synchronous processes
- Monitor the memory use of blocking and semi-blocking transformations
- Reduce staging and disk I/O
- Reduce reliance on an RDBMS

To limit synchronous processes, you should be conscious of processes that need to complete before the next process begins. For example, if you run a long `INSERT` T-SQL statement that takes one-half hour to complete, and then run an `UPDATE` statement that updates the same table, the `UPDATE` statement cannot run until the `INSERT` script finishes. These processes are synchronous. In this case, it would be better to design a Data Flow that handles the same logic as the `INSERT` statement and combines the `UPDATE` logic at the same time (also using a SQL `UPDATE`); that way, you are not only taking advantage of the Data Flow but making the logic asynchronous. You can seriously reduce overall process times by taking this approach.

As mentioned earlier, blocking and semi-blocking transformations require buffers to be pooled in memory until either the last row is available or a match is received (in the case of a Merge Join). These transformations can be very useful, but you need to ensure that you have sufficient memory on your server in order for them to perform well. If you have a large aggregate operation across 100 million rows, you are likely better off handling this through the SQL Server relational engine.

Reducing disk I/O is about minimizing the staging requirements in your ETL process. Disk I/O is often the biggest bottleneck in an ETL job because the bulk operations involve moving a lot of data, and when you add staging data to a database, that data ultimately needs to be saved to the disk drives. Instead, reduce your need on staging tables and leverage the Data Flow for those same operations; that way, you decrease the disk overhead of the process and achieve better scalability. The Data Flow primarily uses memory, and memory is a lot faster to access than disks, so you will gain significant improvements in terms of speed. In addition, when you stage data to a table, you are doubling the disk I/O of the data, because you are both inserting and retrieving table data.

Keep in mind that solution requirements often drive design decisions, and there are situations where staging or the RDBMS are useful in data processing. Some of these are discussed in this section. Your goal, though, is to rethink your design paradigms with SSIS.

Reducing the RDBMS reliance is similar to reducing staging environments, but it also means reducing the logic you place on the DBMS to perform operations like grouping and data cleansing. This not only reduces the impact on your RDBMS, but when using production databases, it alleviates the load and makes room for more critical RDBMS operations.

These four principles are worked out further in the next section, which discusses ways to leverage the Data Flow for your ETL operations.

Leveraging the Data Flow

The biggest value that SSIS brings is the power of the Data Flow. Not to minimize the out-of-the-box functionality of restartability, configurations, logging, event handlers, or other Control Flow Tasks, the primary goal of the engine is to "integrate," and the Data Flow is the key to realizing that goal. Accomplishing data-processing logic through Data Flow Transformations provides enhanced performance and greater flexibility.

Many data architects come from DBA backgrounds, so when they are trying to solve a data integration, processing, or cleansing scenario, their first impulse is to use an RDBMS, such as SQL Server, for ETL operations.

In some ways, moving to SSIS requires thinking in different terms — Data Flow terms. In previous chapters, you looked at the different Data Flow Transformations, so the focus in this section is on applying some of those components to design decisions and translating the SQL-based designs into Data Flow processes.

In summary, the four architecture best practices described in the preceding section relate directly to the value that the Data Flow provides:

- **Limit synchronous processes:** By bringing more of the processing logic into the Data Flow, the natural result is fewer process-oriented steps that require completion before proceeding. In the previous chapter, you looked at the general streaming nature of the Data Flow. This translates to reduced overall processing times.
- **Monitor the memory use of blocking and semi-blocking transformations:** When memory becomes scarce on your server, SSIS begins to copy buffers to disk or spool them to disk. Once this happens, your package slows down dramatically. The most intensive memory transformations are blocking and semi-blocking transformations. However, other transformations, like the cached Lookup, also can require a lot of memory if the Lookup table contains millions of items. All these transformations perform very well until they near the threshold of memory on your server. It is best to monitor the memory to ensure that you avoid a low-memory situation. In particular, throttle the memory of SQL Server if it is on the same server where your SSIS packages are running.
- **Reduce staging and expensive IO operations:** The Data Flow performs most operations in memory (with occasional use of temp folders and some interaction with external systems). Whenever processing happens on data that resides in RAM, processing is more efficient. Disk I/O operations rely on the performance of the drives, the throughput of the I/O channels, and the overhead of the operating system to write and read information to and from the disk. With high volumes or bursting scenarios typical with data processing and ETL, disk I/O is often a bottleneck.
- **Reduce reliance on RDBMS:** Relational engines are powerful tools, and the point here is not to detract from their appropriate uses to store and manage data. By using the Data Flow to cleanse and join data rather than the RDBMS, the result is reduced impact on the relational system, which frees it up for other functions that may be higher priority. Reading data from

a database is generally less expensive than performing complex joins or complicated queries. In addition, related to the first bullet, all RDBMS operations are synchronous. Set-based operations, while they are very useful and optimized in a relational database system, still require that the operation be complete before the data is available for other purposes. The Data Flow, conversely, can process joins and Lookups and other cleansing steps in parallel while the data is flowing through the pipeline. However, note that an RDBMS engine can be leveraged in certain ways; for example, if a table has the right indexes, you can use an `ORDER BY`, which may be faster than an SSIS Sort Transformation.

Data Integration and Correlation

As discussed in Chapter 7, the Data Flow provides the means to combine data from different source objects completely independent of the connection source where the data originates. The most obvious benefit of this is the ability to perform in-memory correlation operations against heterogeneous data without having to stage the data. Said in another way, with SSIS, you can extract data from a flat file and join it to data from a database table inside the Data Flow, without first having to stage the flat file to a table and then perform a SQL Join operation. This can be valuable even when the data is coming from the same source, such as a relational database engine; source data extractions are more efficient without complex or expensive joins, and data can usually begin to flow into the Data Flow immediately.

In addition, single-table `SELECT` statements provide less impact on the source systems than do pulls where join logic is applied. Certainly there are situations where joining data in the source system may be useful and efficient; in many cases, however, focusing on data integration within the Data Flow will yield better performance. When different source systems are involved, the need to stage the data is reduced.

Several of the built-in transformations can perform data correlation similar to how a database would handle joins and other more complex data relationship logic. The following transformations provide data association for more than one Data Source:

- Lookup
- Merge Join
- Merge
- Union All
- Fuzzy Lookup
- Term Lookup
- Term Extract

Chapter 7 describes how to leverage the joining capabilities of SSIS, a great reference for designing your SSIS Data Flows.

Furthermore, beyond the built-in capabilities of SSIS, custom components allow more complex or unique scenarios to be handled. This is discussed in Chapter 19.

Data Cleansing and Transformation

The second major area to which you can apply the Data Flow is data cleansing. As discussed in Chapter 10, cleansing data involves managing missing values; correcting out-of-date, incomplete, or miskeyed data; converting values to standard data types; changing data grain or filtering data subsets; and de-duplicating redundant data. Consistency is the goal of data cleansing, whether the Data Source is a single system or multiple disparate sources.

Many of the Data Flow Components provide data-cleansing capabilities or can participate in a data-cleansing process. Some of the more explicit transformations usable for this process include the following:

- Aggregate
- Character Map
- Conditional Split
- Data Conversion
- Derived Column
- DQS Cleansing
- Fuzzy Grouping
- Fuzzy Lookup
- Pivot
- Script Component
- Sort (with de-duplicating capabilities)
- Unpivot

Each of these transformations, or a combination of them, can handle many data-cleansing scenarios. A few of the transformations provide compelling data-cleansing features that even go beyond the capabilities of many relational engines by using the Data Flow. For example, the Fuzzy Lookup and Fuzzy Grouping (de-duplication) provide cleansing of dirty data by comparing data similarity within certain defined ranges. Pivot and Unpivot have the ability to transform data coming in by pivoting rows to columns or vice versa.

Also, the Script Transformation offers very powerful data-cleansing capabilities with the full features of VB.NET embedded; it is highlighted in detail in Chapter 9. Because the goal of this chapter is to discuss the application of SSIS, the example focuses on a couple of common examples of data cleansing using the Derived Column Transformation and the Aggregate Transformation. These two transformations are particularly relevant to how data cleansing can be accomplished in the Data Flow in comparison with common query logic.

Staging Environments

So far in this chapter, the emphasis has been on thinking in Data Flow terms by moving core data process logic into the Data Flow. In most cases, this will yield high-performance results, especially when the timeliness of moving the data from point A to point B is the highest priority, such as in near real-time or tight-processing-window scenarios. Doing this also mitigates some management overhead, limiting interim database usage.

A few situations merit staging environments and are worth mentioning for consideration:

- **Restartability:** The built-in checkpoint logic of SSIS revolves around the Control Flow. This means that a failure in the Data Flow will not persist the data state. Rather, when the package is restarted, the Data Flow will restart from the beginning. The implications affect design if the source system is in flux and an error in the Data Flow causes a processing window to be missed. By landing the raw data first, the chance for data errors is minimized, and in the event of a failure during the load process, the package can be restarted from the staged data.
- **Processing windows and precedence:** Certain requirements may dictate that the various source extraction windows do not line up with each other or with the data load window for the destination. In these scenarios, it would be necessary to stage the data for a period of time until the full data set is available or the destination database load window has been reached.
- **Source backpressure:** At times, the Data Flow Transformations may apply backpressure on the source extractions. This would happen when the flow of incoming data is faster than the ability of the transformations to handle the data processing in the pipeline. The backpressure created slows down the extraction on the source system, and if the requirement is to extract the data in the fastest time with the least impact, then staging the raw data extract may help eliminate the backpressure.
- **Data Flow optimization:** Staging certain elements, such as business keys, can actually provide valuable data to optimize the primary Data Flow. For example, if the Lookup Source query can be filtered based on a set of keys that was prestaged, this may allow overall gains in processing times by reducing the time it takes to load the Lookup plus the amount of memory needed for the operation. A second example is the use of staging to perform set-based table updates. Updates in a large system are often the source of system bottlenecks, and because SSIS cannot perform set-based updates in the Data Flow, one solution is to stage tables that can be used in a later Execute SQL Task for a set-based update, which may provide a more efficient process.

Staged data can also prove useful in data validation and error handling. Given some of the uses of staging, is there a way to accomplish data staging but still retain the performance gain by leveraging the Data Flow? Yes. One suggestion is the reduction of synchronous processing in the Control Flow. When you want to introduce a data-staging environment, it's natural to first pick up the data from the source and land it to a staging environment, and then pick the data back up from the staging environment and apply the transformation logic to it; but what about landing the raw data to a staging environment at the same time that the transformations are applied? Figure 16-18 shows a Data Flow designed

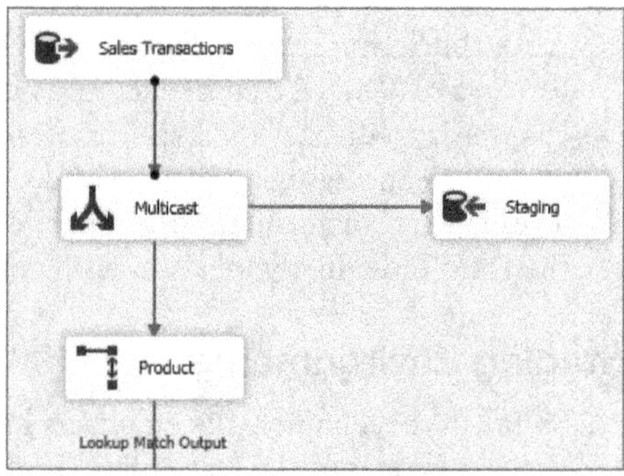

FIGURE 16-18

with a staging table that does not require the data to reside in the table before the transformation logic is applied.

The Multicast Transformation in this example is taking the raw source data and allowing it to stream down to the core Data Flow, while at the same time the raw source data is being staged to a table. The data within the table is now available to query for data validation and checking purposes; in addition, it provides a snapshot of the source system that can then be used for reprocessing when needed. Although the data is landed to staging, two differences distinguish this example from a model that first stages data and then uses the staged data as a source.

First, as already mentioned, the process is no longer synchronous; in many cases, data can move from point A to point B in the time it takes to simply extract the data from A. Second, the staging process requires only a single pass on the staging table (for the writes), rather than the I/O overhead of a second pass that reads the data from the staging. If your restartability requirements and source systems allow, this approach may provide the best of both worlds — leveraging the Data Flow but providing the value of a staging environment.

Optimizing Package Processing

There are a few techniques you can apply when you're streamlining packages for performance. This section covers how to apply certain optimization techniques to achieve better throughput.

Optimizing Buffers, Execution Trees, and Engine Threads

Recall from earlier in this chapter that for each execution tree in a Data Flow, a different buffer profile is used. This means that downstream execution trees may require different columns based on what is added or subtracted in the Data Flow. You also saw that the performance of a buffer within a Data Flow is directly related to the row width of the buffer. Narrow buffers can hold more rows, enabling higher throughput.

Some columns that are used in an execution tree may not be needed downstream. For example, if an input column to a Lookup Transformation is used as the key match to the reference table, this column may not be needed after the Lookup and therefore should be removed before the next execution tree. SSIS does a good job of providing warnings when columns exist in an execution tree but are not used in any downstream transformation or destination component. Figure 16-19 shows

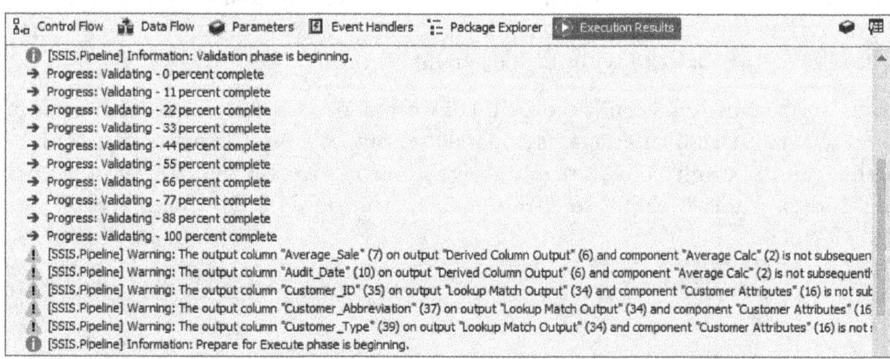

FIGURE 16-19

the Execution Results tab (also called the Progress tab when in runtime mode) within a package for which column usage has not been optimized in the Data Flow. Each warning, highlighted with a yellow exclamation point, indicates the existence of a column not used later in downstream components and which therefore should be removed from the pipeline after initial use.

The warning text describes the optimization technique well:

```
[SSIS.Pipeline] Warning: The output column "Average_Sale" (7) on output "Derived
Column Output" (6) and component "Average Calc" (2) is not subsequently used in
the Data Flow task. Removing this unused output column can increase Data Flow task
performance.
```

Any component with asynchronous outputs whose input closes out an execution tree has the option of removing columns in the output. You would normally do this through the edit dialog of the transformation, but you can also do it in the Advanced Editor if the component provides an advanced properties window. For example, in the Union All Transformation, you can highlight a row in the editor and delete it with the Delete keyboard key. This ensures that the column is not used in the next execution tree.

A second optimization technique involves increasing processor utilization by adding the more execution threads for the Data Flow. Increasing the `EngineThreads` Data Flow property to a value greater than the number of execution trees plus the number of Source Components ensures that SSIS has enough threads to use.

Careful Use of Row-Based Transformations

Row-based transformations, as described earlier in this chapter, are non-blocking transformations, but they exhibit the functionality of interacting with an outside system (for example, a database or file system) on a row-by-row basis. Compared with other non-blocking transformations, these transformations are slower because of this behavior. The other type of non-blocking transformation, streaming, can use internal cache or provide calculations using other columns or variables readily available to the Data Flow, making them perform very fast. Given the nature of row-based transformations, their usage should be cautious and calculated.

Of course, some row-based transformations have critical functionality, so this caution needs to be balanced with data-processing requirements. For example, the Export and Import Column Transformation can read and write from files to columns, which is a very valuable tool, but it has the obvious overhead of the I/O activity with the file system.

Another useful row-based transformation is the OLE DB Command, which can use input column values and execute parameterized queries against a database, row by row. The interaction with the database, although it can be optimized, still requires overhead to process. Figure 16-20 shows a SQL Server Trace run against a database that is receiving updates from an OLE DB Command.

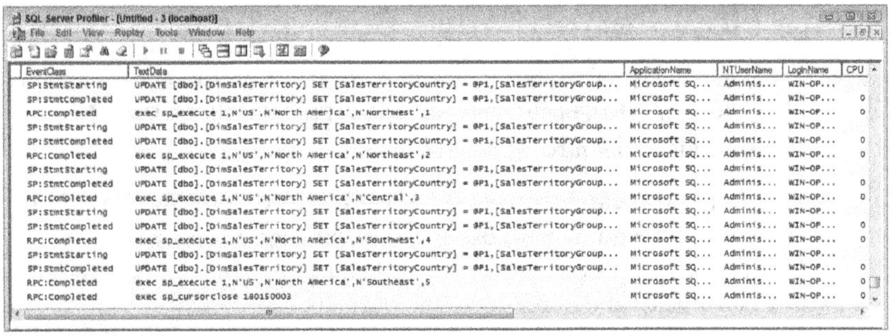

FIGURE 16-20

This is only a simple example, but for each row that goes through the OLE DB Command, a separate UPDATE statement is issued against the database. Taking into consideration the duration, reads, and writes, the aggregated impact of thousands of rows will cause Data Flow latency at the transformation.

For this scenario, one alternative is to leverage set-based processes within databases. In order to do this, the data needs to be staged during the Data Flow, and you need to add a secondary Execute SQL Task to the Control Flow that runs the set-based update statement. The result may actually reduce the overall processing time when compared with the original OLE DB Command approach. This alternative approach is not meant to diminish the usefulness of the OLE DB Command but rather meant to provide an example of optimizing the Data Flow for higher-volume scenarios that may require optimization.

Understanding Blocking Transformation Effects

A blocking transformation requires the complete set of records cached from the input before it can release records downstream. Earlier in the chapter, you saw a list of nearly a dozen transformations that meet this criterion. The most common examples are the Sort and Aggregate Transformations.

Blocking transformations are intensive because they require caching all the upstream input data, and they also may require more intensive processor usage based on their functionality. When not enough RAM is available in the system, the blocking transformations may also require temporary disk storage. You need to be aware of these limitations when you try to optimize a Data Flow. Mentioning the limitations of blocking transformations is not meant to minimize their usefulness. Rather it's to emphasize how important it is to understand when to use these transformations as opposed to alternative approaches and to know the resource impact they may have.

Because sorting data is a common requirement, one optimization technique is valuable to mention. Source data that can be sorted in the component through an ORDER BY statement (if the right indexes are in the source table) or presorted in a flat file does not require the use of a Sort Transformation. As long as the data is physically sorted in the right order when entering the Data Flow, the Source component can be configured to indicate that the data is sorted and which columns are sorted in what order. As mentioned earlier, the IsSorted advanced property of the Source component is documented in Chapter 7.

Troubleshooting Data Flow Performance Bottlenecks

The pipeline execution reports (reviewed earlier in the chapter) are a great way to identify which component in your Data Flow is causing a bottleneck. Another way to troubleshoot Data Flow performance is to isolate transformations and sources by themselves.

While you are developing your package, you can identify bottlenecks within a specific Data Flow by making a copy of your Data Flow and begin decomposing it by replacing components with placeholder transformations. In other words, take a copy of your Data Flow and run it without any changes. This will give you a baseline of the execution time of the package.

Next, remove all the Destination components, and replace them with Multicast Transformations (the Multicast is a great placeholder transformation because it can act as a destination without any outputs and has no overhead). Figure 16-21 represents a modified package in which the Destination components have been replaced with Multicast Transformations.

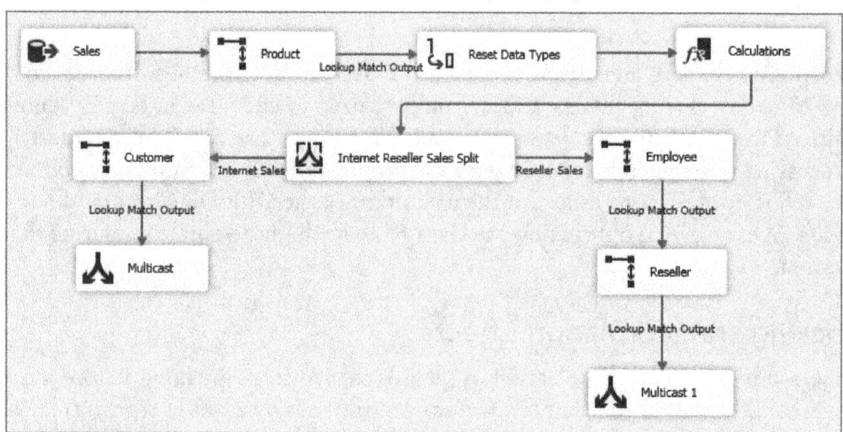

FIGURE 16-21

Run this modified Data Flow and evaluate your execution time. Is it a lot faster? If so, you have identified your problem — it's one or more of your destinations.

If your package without the destinations still runs the same, then your performance bottleneck is a source or one of the transformations. The next most common issue is the source, so this time, delete all your transformations and replace them with Multicast Transformations, as Figure 16-22 shows.

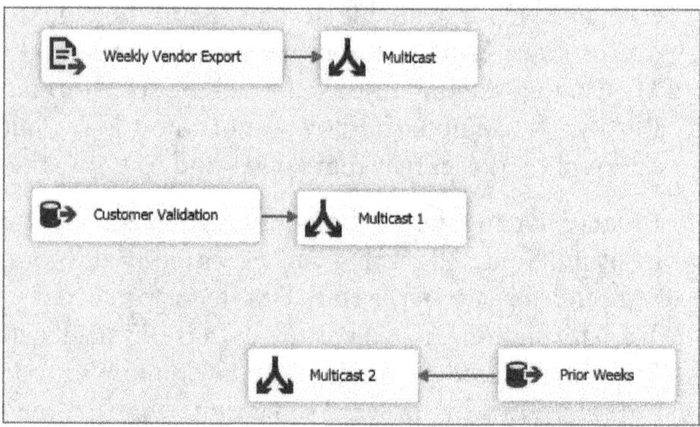

FIGURE 16-22

Run your package. If the execution time is just as slow as the first run, then you can be sure that the performance issue is one or more of the sources. If the performance is a lot faster, then you have a performance issue with one of the transformations. Even the Active Time report shown in Figure 16-17 can give deceptive results if the source is the bottleneck. The source and all transformations in the first execution tree will show high active time. In fact, all your Data Flow components may have a high active time if you don't have any blocking transformations. Therefore, checking the sources will assist in identifying whether the Source component is the hidden bottleneck.

In fact, the Multicast approach can be applied repeatedly until you figure out where the issue lies. In other words, go back to your original copy of the Data Flow and replace transformations until you have identified the transformation that causes the biggest slowdown. It may be the case that you have more than one component that is the culprit, but with this approach you will know where to focus your redesign or reconfiguration efforts.

PIPELINE PERFORMANCE MONITORING

Earlier in this chapter, you looked at the built-in pipeline logging functionality and the active time reports and how they can help you understand what SSIS is doing behind the scenes when running a package with one or more Data Flows. Another tool available to SSIS is the Windows operating system tool called *Performance Monitor* (*PerfMon* for short), which is available to local administrators in the machine's Administrative Tools. When SSIS is installed on a machine, a set of counters is added that enables tracking of the Data Flow's performance.

As Figure 16-23 shows, the Pipeline counters can be used when selecting the SQLServer:SSIS Pipeline 12.0 object.

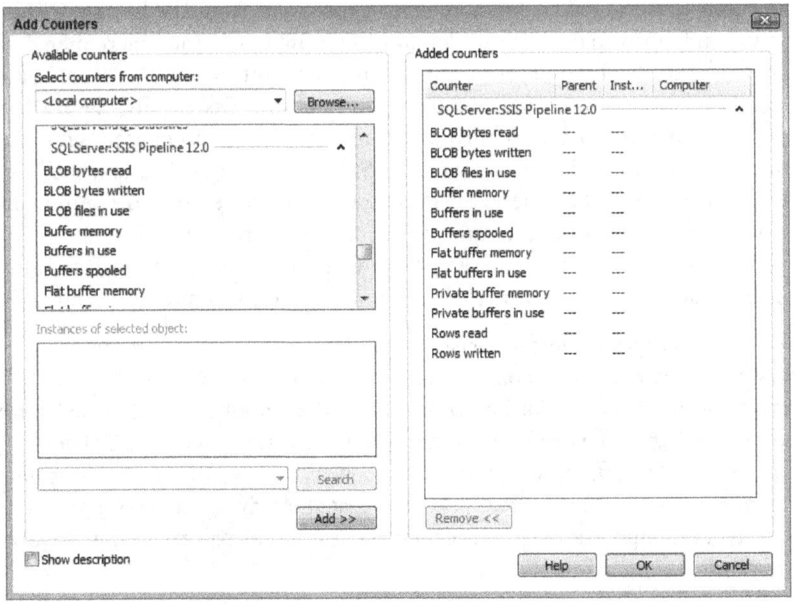

FIGURE 16-23

The following counters are available in the SQLServer:SSIS Pipeline object within PerfMon. Descriptions of these counters are provided next:

- BLOB bytes read
- BLOB bytes written
- BLOB files in use
- Buffer memory
- Buffers in use
- Buffers spooled
- Flat buffer memory
- Flat buffers in use
- Private buffer memory
- Private buffers in use
- Rows read
- Rows written

The BLOB counters (Binary Large Objects, such as images) help identify the volume of the BLOB data types flowing through the Data Flow. Because handling large binary columns can be a huge drain on the available memory, understanding how your Data Flow is handling BLOB data types is important. Remember that BLOB data can be introduced to the Data Flow not only by Source components but also by the Import (and Export) Column Transformations.

Because buffers are the mechanism that the Data Flow uses to process all data, the buffer-related counters provide the most valuable information for understanding how much and where memory is being used in the Data Flow. The Buffer Memory and Buffers in Use counters are high-level counters that provide totals for the server, both memory use and total buffer count. Essentially, the Buffer Memory counter shows the total memory being used by SSIS, and this can be compared with the amount of available system memory to determine whether SSIS processing is bottlenecked by the available physical memory. Furthermore, the Buffers Spooled counter provides even more indication of resource limitations on your server. It shows the number of buffers temporarily written to disk if enough system memory is not available. Anything greater than zero indicates that your Data Flow is using temporary disk storage to accomplish its work, which incurs I/O impact and overhead.

In regard to the buffer details, two types of buffers exist, flat and private. Flat buffers are the primary Data Flow buffers used when a Source component sends data into the Data Flow. Synchronous transformation outputs pass the flat buffers to the next component, and asynchronous outputs use reprovisioned or new flat buffers to be passed to the next transformation. Conversely, some transformations require *private buffers*, which are not received from upstream transformations or passed on to downstream transformations. Instead, they represent a private cache of data that a transformation uses to perform its operation. Three primary examples of private buffer use are found in the Aggregate, Sort, and Lookup Transformations, which use private buffers to cache data that is used for calculations and matching. These transformations still use flat buffers for data being received and passed, but they also use private buffers to manage and cache supplemental data used in the transformation. The flat and private buffer counters show the breakdown of these usages and help identify where buffers are being used and to what extent.

The last counters in the Pipeline counters list simply show the number of rows handled in the Data Flow, whether Rows Read or Rows Written. These numbers are aggregates of the rows processed since the counters were started.

When reviewing these counters, remember that they are an aggregate of all the SSIS packages and embedded Data Flows running on your server. If you are attempting to isolate the performance impact of specific Data Flows or packages, consider querying the catalog.dm_execution_performance_counters in the SSISDB database.

The Pipeline counters can be tracked in the UI of Performance Monitor in real time or captured at a recurring interval for later evaluation. Figure 16-24 shows the Pipeline counters tracked during the execution of a package.

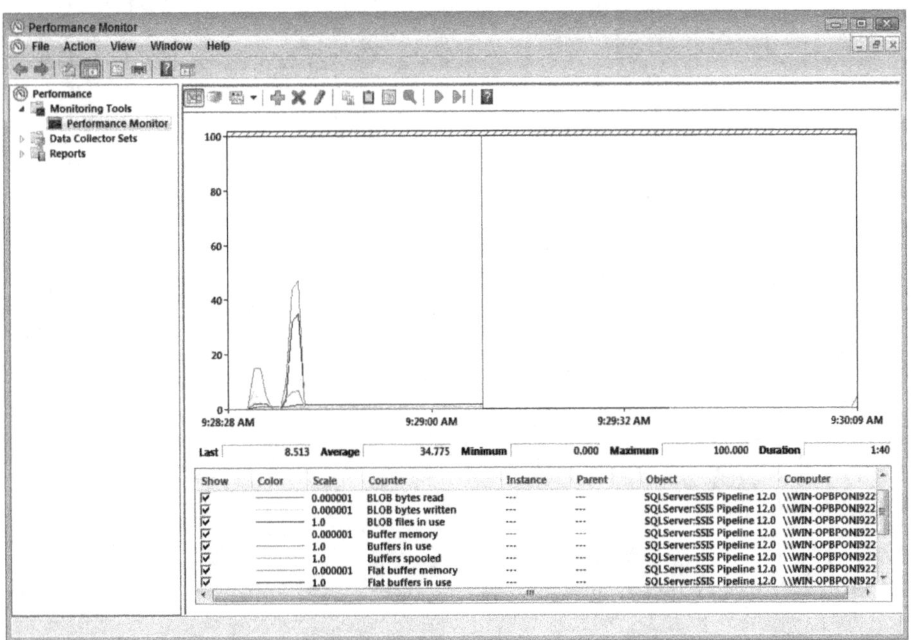

FIGURE 16-24

Notice that the buffer usage scales up and then drops and that the plateau lines occur during the database commit process, when SSIS has completed its processes and is waiting on the database to commit the insert transaction. When the package is complete, the buffers are released and the buffer counters drop to zero, while the row count buffers remain stable, as they represent the aggregate rows processed since PerfMon was started.

SUMMARY

The flexibility of SSIS provides more design options and in turn requires you to pay more attention to establishing your architecture. As you've seen in this chapter, understanding and leveraging the Data Flow in SSIS reduces processing time, eases management, and opens the door to scalability. Therefore, choosing the right architecture up front will ease the design burden and provide overall gains to your solution.

Once you have established a model for scalability, the reduced development time of SSIS enables you to give more attention to optimization, where fine-tuning the pipeline and process makes every second count. In the next chapter, you will learn about the process of building packages using the software development life cycle.

17

SSIS Software Development Life Cycle

WHAT'S IN THIS CHAPTER?

- Understanding the different types of SDLCs
- Versioning and source control overview
- Working with Subversion (SVN)
- Working with Visual Studio Team System

The software development life cycle (SDLC) plays an important role in any type of application development. Many SQL Server database administrators and ETL developers have little experience with source control tools because the tools themselves have been less than "database project-friendly."

In addition, many SQL Server DBAs have not been involved with SDLCs beyond executing scripts attached to change control documentation. Legislation around the world has changed the role of the SQL Server DBA in the enterprise because of new requirements for tracking changes. Regarding software development life cycles, DBAs now must participate in ever-earlier phases of the project's development.

In addition, SQL Server DBAs — especially SSIS developers — will realize greater productivity and development cycle fault tolerance as they employ source-controlled development practices. These practices produce code that is auditable, an added benefit in the current corporate climate.

This chapter provides an overview of some of the available features in the source control offerings you have to choose from. It includes a brief description of how to store a project in Subversion (SVN), a common open-source tool, and a detailed walkthrough describing how to create a Team Project using Visual Studio 2013 Team System. In practice, Team Projects will most likely be created by someone else in the software development enterprise.

> **NOTE** *Chapter 22 on SSIS administration reviews how to deploy projects to the SSIS Server.*

Because the line between database administrator and software developer has blurred and blended over the years, the Team Project walkthrough is built in Visual Studio 2013. In order to demonstrate working with the tool and complying with your SDLC process, in the Team Project walkthrough you will put together a project that uses the source control and collaboration functionality provided by Visual Studio Team System.

> **NOTE** *A detailed examination of Team System is beyond the scope of this book but can be found in* Professional Team Foundation Server 2012 *by Ed Blankenship, Martin Woodward, Grant Holliday, and Brian Keller (Wrox, 2013).*

Included is a discussion regarding development and testing, with an emphasis on the agile development methodology, which is very well suited for SSIS development because of the methodology's ability to adapt to changes — a common occurrence in ETL development.

ETL TEAM PREPARATION

ETL planning is critical in any project. For smaller projects, this may just be a simple mapping document that identifies the sources and destinations and describes how the data needs to be transformed.

Projects with more than one ETL developer need more structured planning. Besides the mapping and lineage, the work breakout needs to be mapped. This, of course, means that you need to have the logical grouping of ETL processes defined. This logical grouping needs to be at the package level because ETL developers need to have exclusive access to a package.

Here are a few more considerations as you are planning the ETL portion of your project:

- In order to dive right into ETL development, the data architect needs to have the destination schema defined and implemented on the destination relational database. In addition, it needs to be stable. Nothing is more difficult for an ETL developer than to find the destination schema changing while he or she is working! Table schemas will need to change, but once the ETL effort is underway, a change process needs to be in place so all affected developers are notified.

- The second most important aspect that needs to be in place is the source data access. ETL cannot be developed without source data. This means that ETL developers can run extractions from a test source system or have source files to work with. It is not acceptable to have dummy data from the source — this approach never works and results in major rework once the data is available. When source data is not available, flag this as a major risk in the project and you will need to put the ETL portion of the project on hold. It's that serious.
- Effective coordinated SSIS package design, especially with a team of developers, involves having modular packages. This means you need to define your SSIS packages with smaller increments of work that each package handles. Packages with too much logic in them are hard to troubleshoot, are more difficult to develop, and don't work well in a team when more than one person needs to be working on the same package at the same time — it doesn't work. A good rule of thumb is to limit packages to no more than two to three Data Flows and to try to have all the Control Flow Tasks visible at one time on your monitor.
- Another important step in planning your ETL is to make sure you have designed a configuration and logging framework for your SSIS packages. ETL developers need to have template SSIS packages to start with that have all the logging in place. If you are deploying your packages to the SSIS Server in SSIS 2014, the server will handle your logging, but you still need to plan out your project parameters and shared connections beforehand. (See Chapter 22 for more on deployment and the SSIS server.) If you don't have these basics defined, you will have a lot of retrofitting later on, which will slow down your ETL development, introduce risk, and probably affect your project at a critical time of testing. Not to mention, having all of this in place during development will give you more insight into your ETL processes while you are developing them!
- Finally, be sure to set up your source control environment. This is a great lead-in to this chapter since you will learn how to use two source control tools, Subversion (SVN) and Visual Studio Team System.

INTRODUCTION TO SOFTWARE DEVELOPMENT LIFE CYCLES

Software Development Life Cycles (SDLCs) represent a systematic approach to each component of application development — from the initial idea to a functioning production application. A *step* (or *phase*) is a unit of related work in an SDLC. A *methodology* is a collection of SDLC steps in action, applied to a project. *Artifacts* are the recorded output from steps.

For example, the first step of an SDLC is analysis. The methodology requires a requirements document as an analysis artifact.

SDLCs: A Brief History

Software development life cycles have existed in some form or other since the first software applications were developed. The true beginning of what is now termed "software" is debatable. For our purposes, the topic is confined to binary operations based on boolean algebra.

In 1854, mathematician George Boole published *An Investigation of the Laws of Thought, on which Are Founded the Mathematical Theories of Logic and Probabilities.* This work became the foundation of what is now called boolean algebra. Some 80 years later, Claude Shannon applied Boole's theories to the computing machines of Shannon's era. Shannon later went to work for Bell Labs.

Another Bell Labs employee, Dr. Walter Shewhart, was tasked with quality control. Perhaps the pinnacle of Dr. Shewhart's work is *statistical process control* (SPC). Most quality control and continuous improvement philosophies in practice today utilize SPC. Dr. Shewhart's work produced a precursor to software development life cycles, a methodology defined by four principles: Plan, Do, Study, and Act (PDSA).

Dr. Shewhart's ideas influenced many people at Bell Labs, making an accurate and formal trace of the history difficult. Suffice it to say that Dr. Shewhart's ideas regarding quality spread throughout many industries; one industry influenced was the software industry.

Types of Software Development Life Cycles

SQL Server Integration Services provides integrated support for many SDLC methodologies. This chapter touches on a few of them. In general, SDLCs can be placed into one of two categories: *waterfall* and *iterative.*

Waterfall SDLCs

The first type of formal software development life cycles is sequential, or linear. That is, it begins with one step and proceeds through subsequent steps until reaching a final step. A typical example of linear methodology steps is the following:

1. **Analysis:** Review the business needs and develop requirements.
2. **Design:** Develop a plan to meet the business requirements with a software solution.
3. **Development:** Build the software solution.
4. **Implementation:** Install and configure the software solution.
5. **Maintenance:** Address software issues identified after implementation.

This type of methodology is referred to as a *waterfall* methodology because information and software "fall" one way from plateau to plateau (step to step).

The waterfall methodology has a lot of appeal for project managers. It is easier to determine the status and completeness of a linear project: It's either in analysis, in development, in implementation, or in maintenance.

A potential downside to the waterfall methodology is that the analysis and design steps are traditionally completed in a single pass at the beginning of the project. This does not allow much flexibility should business needs change after the project starts. In addition, the development and implementation steps are expected to be defined prior to any coding.

Iterative SDLCs

An *iterative* methodology begins with the premise that it's impossible to know all requirements for a successful application before development starts. Conversely, iterative development holds that software is best developed within the context of knowledge gained during earlier development of the project. Development therefore consists of several small, limited-scope, feature-based iterations that deliver a product ever closer to the customer's vision.

The following are examples of iterative SDLCs:

- **Spiral:** Typified by ever-expanding scope in hopes of identifying large design flaws as soon as possible
- **Agile:** A collection of methodologies fall into this category, including Scrum, Feature-Driven Development, Extreme Programming, Test-Driven Design, and others.
- **Microsoft Solutions Framework:** Microsoft's own practice gleaned from a sampling of best practices from different methodologies

What happens if, hypothetically, an iteration fails to produce the desired functionality? The developer or DBA must remove the changes of the last iteration from the code and begin again. This is much easier to accomplish if the developer or DBA has stored a copy of the previous version someplace safe — hence, the need for *source control.*

Source control is defined as preserving the software source code in a format that enables recovery to a previous state of development or version, and it is a basic tenet of all iterative software development life cycles.

SSIS and SDLCs

As mentioned, SSIS is very suitable for applying different SDLCs. This is because SSIS is broken down to units of work that can be planned out for longer waterfall projects or designed in a more iterative agile project. While an agile project approach is most appropriate for business intelligence solutions, if you are working on a big system migration, this is usually a waterfall type project effort, and your ETL most commonly is for data migration to the new system.

A few of the common ways that SSIS integrates into SDLCs includes:

- ETL tasks can be included as part of a product backlog
- Packages can be assigned to developers
- Packages can be checked into source control through the file system or through Visual Studio
- Packages can be grouped together and deployed as a set

VERSIONING AND SOURCE CODE CONTROL

SQL Server 2014 and SQL Server Integration Services (SSIS) integrate with source control products such as Subversion (SVN) and Visual Studio Team System. SVN is an open-source control product commonly used on many types of development platforms. Given the open-source nature of the product, several people have written extensions and integration points into different tools, such as

Visual Studio. Visual Studio Team System is part of Microsoft's Team Foundation Server, a suite of SDLC management tools — which includes a source control engine.

Subversion (SVN)

SVN is an open-source product that you can download and install. The easiest version to work with on the Windows platform is from `www.visualsvn.com` because it includes a SVN server management UI. You can download and install the server repository VisualSVNServer from the site just mentioned. This section also uses a Visual Studio plug-in for SVN called AhnkSVN, which is available from `http://ankhsvn.open.collab.net`. This integrates Visual Studio with the SVN repository. In this section, you'll create a project in SQL Server Data Tools (SSDT) that demonstrates integrated source control with SVN.

To begin, install VisualSVNServer and AhnkSVN from the sites just mentioned.

To configure SSIS source control integration with SVN, open the SQL Server Business Intelligence Development Studio. You don't need to connect to an instance of SQL Server to configure integrated source control.

To configure SVN as your SSIS source control, click Tools ➪ Options. Click Source Control and select Plug-in Selection. Select "Ankh - Subversion Support for Visual Studio" for the Current source control plug-in, as shown in Figure 17-1.

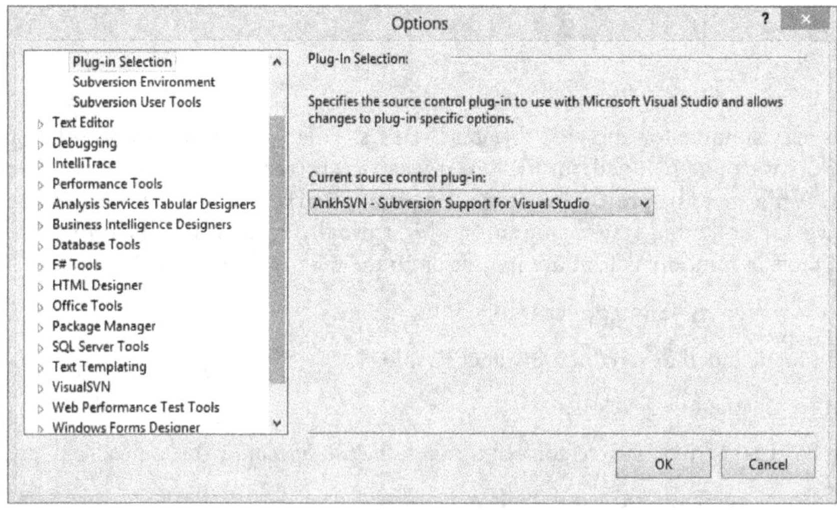

FIGURE 17-1

For the purposes of this example, use "AnkhSVN – Subversion Support for Visual Studio" from the Source Control Environment Settings dropdown list and use the source control default options (refer to Figure 17-1). This SVN walkthrough assumes that you have installed SVN server and AnkhSVN on your local machine.

1. Open SQL Server Business Intelligence Development Studio. Because SSDT uses the Visual Studio Integrated Development Environment (IDE), opening SQL Server Business Intelligence Development Studio will open Visual Studio 2013.
2. When the SSDT IDE opens, click File ➪ New ➪ Project to start a new project. Enter a project name in the New Project dialog. For now, do *not* check the Add to source control checkbox, as shown in Figure 17-2.

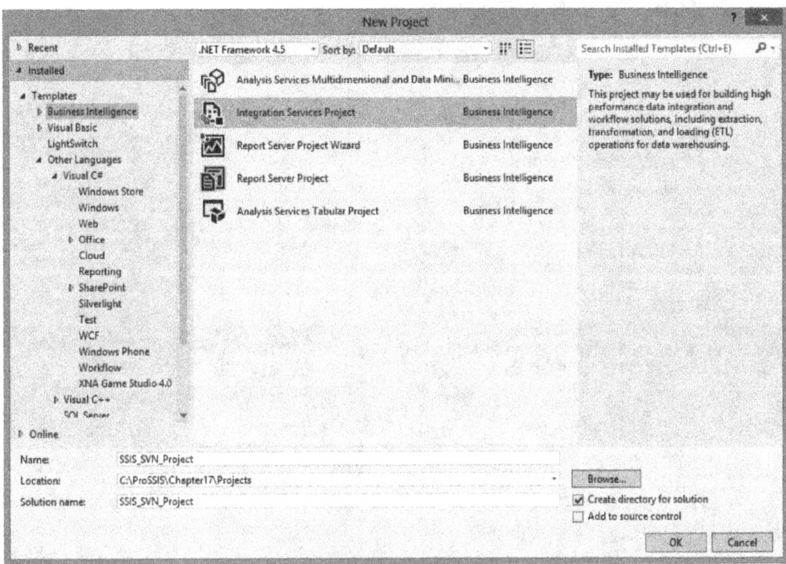

FIGURE 17-2

3. Click OK to proceed, and a new project is created in the SSDT IDE.
4. Add the project to SVN by right-clicking the project name in Solution Explorer and selecting Add Selected Projects to Subversion.
5. You will be prompted to choose the Subversion repository and folders.
    a. The Project Name is what will be named within the SVN repository.
    b. The Repository Url is the location of the Project within your SVN repository. Figure 17-3 shows a new folder created in the ProSSIS repository within SVN.

> **NOTE** *You will have to have a repository created to go through this exercise. This is done through the Visual SVN Server application.*

6. Select OK to add your project to the SVN repository.
7. In the next screen, specify a log message, which is created as part of any operation with SVN so that changes can be documented, as shown in Figure 17-4. Click OK.
8. The final dialog asks if you would like to mark the project as managed by Subversion. Click Yes.

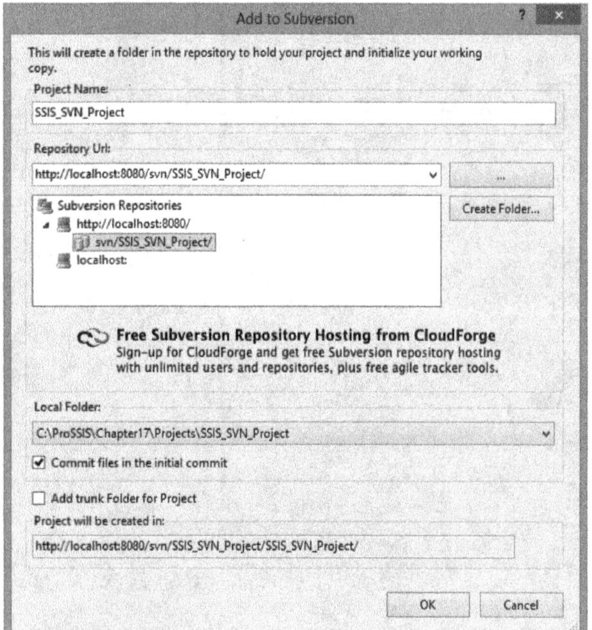

FIGURE 17-3

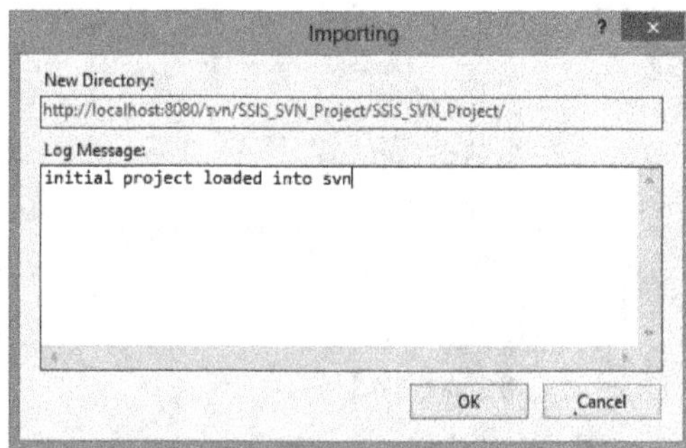

FIGURE 17-4

After successfully connecting the project to SVN, you will notice a few new indicators in Visual Studio that demonstrate the integration. Figure 17-5 shows the Solution Explorer on the right with a few indicators next to the files. The blue plus symbol indicates that a file is pending initial addition to the Subversion project. The Pending Changes window at the bottom shows all the operations that need to be committed to SVN. SVN uses a commit process to save all changes.

The project shown here has a few packages added for demonstration purposes. You can add any existing packages to your project to test the source control integration.

To complete the connection of the project with SVN, click the Commit button within the Pending Changes window. This will add all the files to the SVN repository. To confirm this, open the VisualSVN Server component from the Start ➪ All Programs menu. Drill into the local server repository and the folder you created for the project. You should now see all the files from the project listed in the details window (see Figure 17-6). You may need to right-click on the Repository in Visual SVN Server and click "Refresh" to see the files.

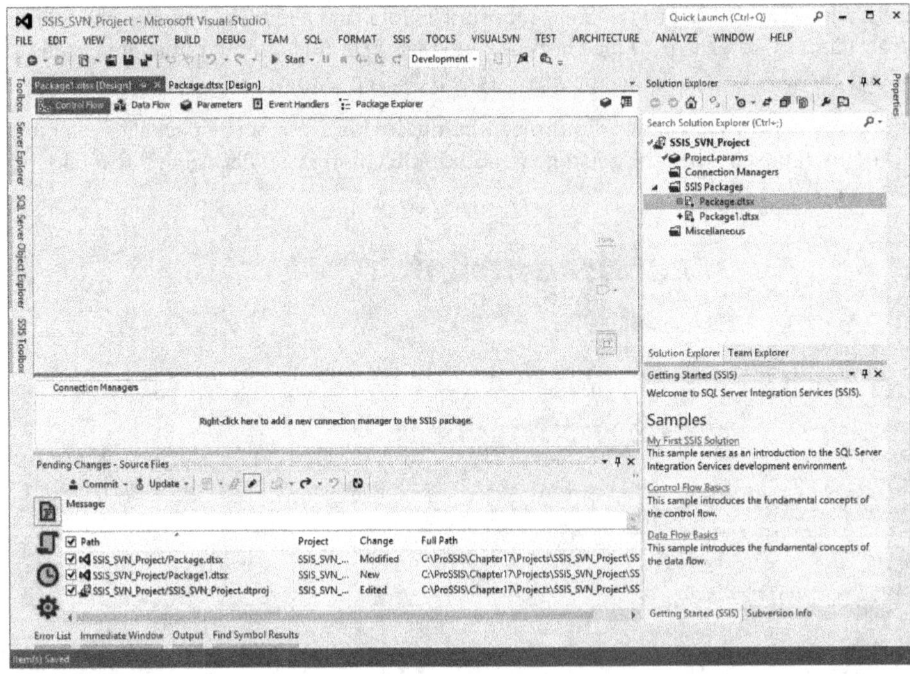

FIGURE 17-5

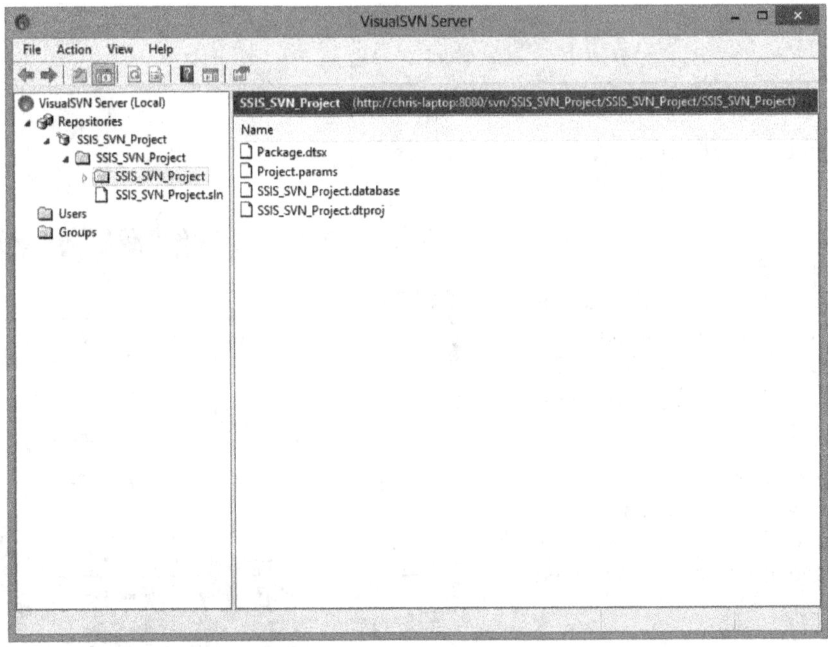

FIGURE 17-6

In addition to the files being added to the SVN repository, note that the files shown in the Solution Explorer in Visual Studio now have a blue checkbox next to them (instead of a blue plus symbol). This indicates that the files have now been added to the SVN repository.

To test SVN integration with your new SSIS project, manually lock one of the packages in your project for editing by right-clicking the package in Solution Explorer and choosing Subversion ➪ Lock, as shown in Figure 17-7.

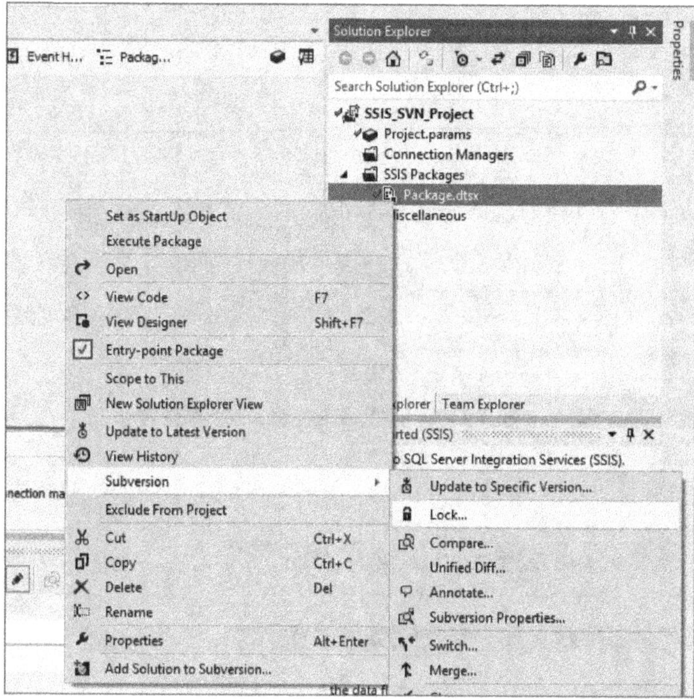

FIGURE 17-7

When you lock a file for editing, you prevent other people from checking in any edits of the file until you have completed your edits. The Select Files to Lock dialog appears, as shown in Figure 17-8. You can enter a comment to identify why you are locking the package.

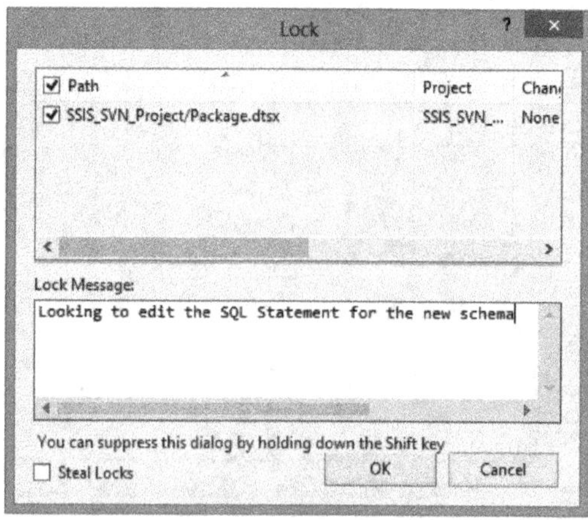

FIGURE 17-8

After you edit and save the package, the file is displayed in the Pending Changes list, and it has updated icons in Solution Explorer to indicate both that it has been changed and that it is locked (see Figure 17-9).

> **NOTE** *This is a good location for change control documentation references or meaningful notes. Although it may seem obvious what change you have made in the code, documenting the change will help you in the future if you need to roll back a change or remember what changes were made!*

You can now commit your changes by clicking the Commit button in the Pending Changes window, and the packages will be checked in and unlocked for the next operation.

Like many source control tools, SVN comes with several valuable features for working in a team situation and for code and process management. One of those features is versioning.

Every check-in operation preserves the previous version, so the entire version history can be acted upon. Figure 17-10 shows the version history of a file with the right-click context menu displayed. Older versions can be restored and compared with current versions, logs can be updated, and changes can be highlighted.

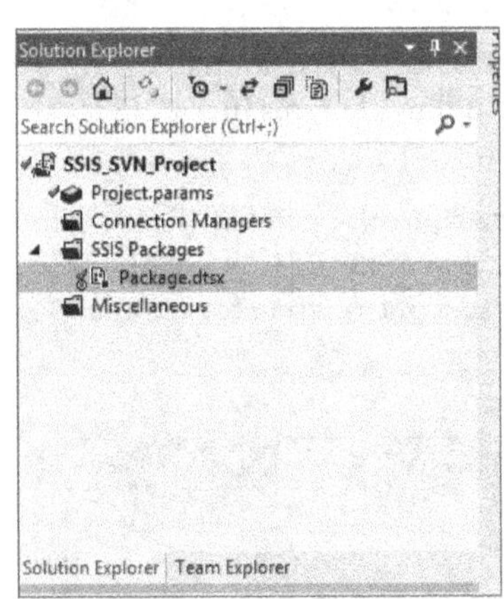

FIGURE 17-9

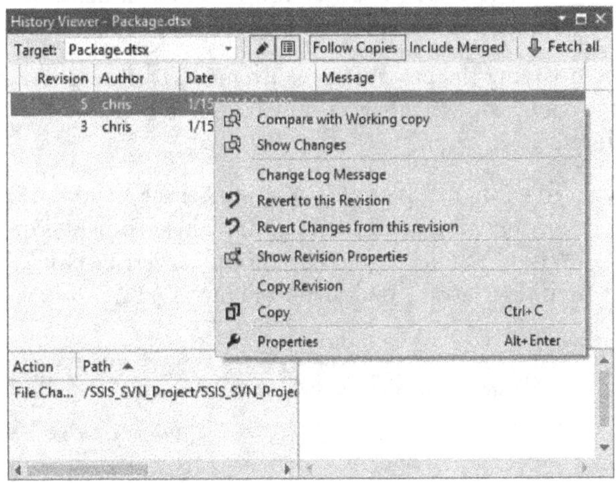

FIGURE 17-10

Now that you've taken a look at what a common open-source tool (SVN) can do in terms of source code management and team coordination, it's time to look at an enterprise tool in the Microsoft technology stack. The next section provides a brief introduction to Microsoft's source control server and client tools known collectively as Visual Studio Team System.

Team Foundation Server, Team System, and SSIS

When Visual Studio 2010 was released, Microsoft updated Team System and Team Foundation Server — a powerful enterprise software development life cycle suite and project management repository consisting of collaborative services, integrated functionality, and an extensible application programming interface (API). Team System seamlessly integrates software development, project management, testing, and source control into the IDE for Visual Studio 2013.

Using Team System with SSDT and SSIS requires that you have at least Visual Studio Team System 2010 on your network and have installed at least Team Explorer 2010 on your development machine. For the purposes of this chapter we've installed TFS 2013 and Visual Studio 2013. Also keep in mind that in order to create Projects and Team Collections the version of TFS must match the version of Visual Studio that is being used. For instance, Visual Studio 2013 cannot create Projects and Team Collections in TFS 2010, but Visual Studio 2010 can.

- Visual Studio Team System 2013 (VSTS) can be purchased for use, but if you would like to evaluate the software, Microsoft provides a virtual machine that you can download and used for a period of time. Trial versions are available for both virtual PC and Hyper-V images and can be found at `http://download.microsoft.com`. Search for VSTS 2013 Trial on the Microsoft download page, and the results will include both virtual machines that can be used for testing. The examples in this section use the same trial version of VSTS.
- Visual Studio Team Explorer 2013 is the client tool that integrates with Visual Studio and allows you to connect to the Team System server and explore the development items and work with the source control environment built into VSTS. The source control used by VSTS is a robust source control environment. You can search for and download Visual Studio Team Explorer from `http://download.microsoft.com`.

After satisfying the preceding requirements, follow these steps to use the VSTS source control. In the next section, you will also see how to create bug tracking tickets and work items in the VSTS Team Explorer.

1. To configure Team Foundation Server as your SSIS source control, open SSDT (or close any existing open projects) and click Tools ➪ Options. Choose Source Control and select Visual Studio Team Foundation Server. Expand the Source Control node for detailed configuration, as shown in Figure 17-11.

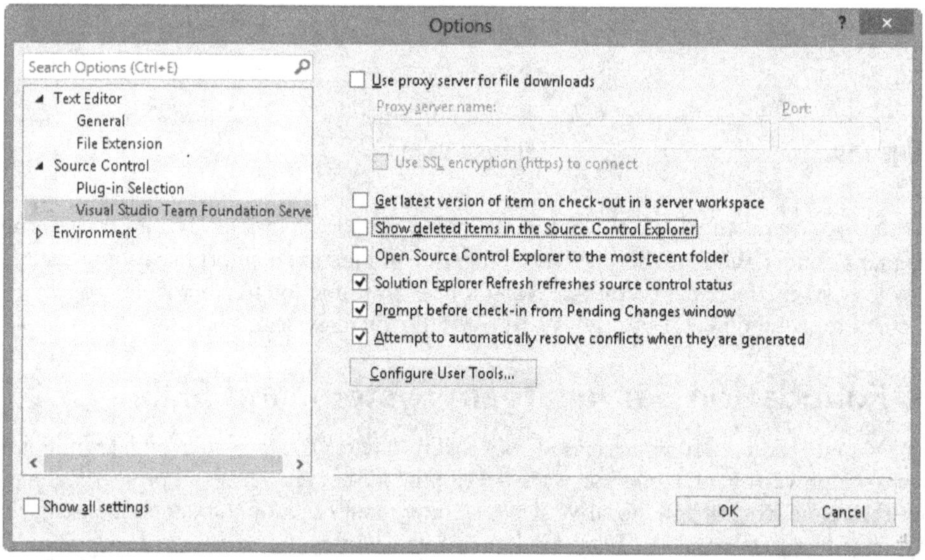

FIGURE 17-11

This section discusses the relationship between Team System and SQL Server Integration Services. The walkthrough is shown using SQL Server Data Tools (SSDT). If the SQL Server 2014 client tools are installed or Visual Studio 2013 is installed, opening SSDT will open Visual Studio 2013. If Team System is specified as the source controller for either environment, the environment, upon opening, will attempt to connect to a Team Foundation Server.

2. Once Visual Studio 2013 is configured to use Visual Studio Team Foundation Server as the source control, press Ctrl+\, Ctrl+M, or click the Team Explorer tab to view the Team System properties (or choose Team Explorer under the View menu).
3. In the Team Explorer window, click the "Select Team Projects..." link to connect to the Team System server.
4. Click the "Servers..." button as shown in Figure 17-12 to browse for a Team Foundation Server. Alternatively, any Team Foundation Server that has already been added will be available to select from the dropdown list. In the Add/Remove Team Foundation Server dialog, click the "Add" button to add a new server. Figure 17-13 shows the name of the trial version server to be added to the list.

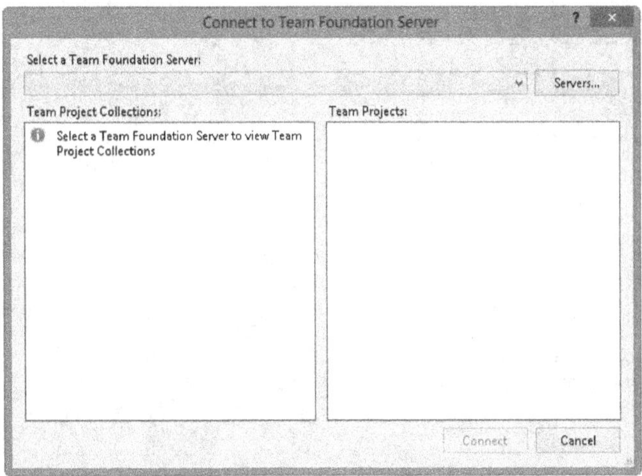

FIGURE 17-12

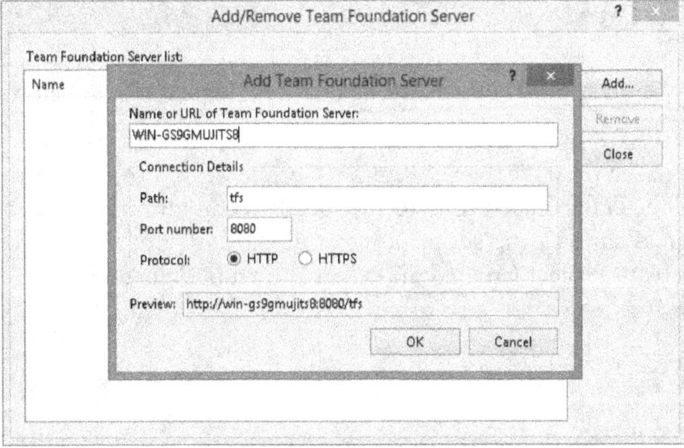

FIGURE 17-13

5. After adding the server (you will be prompted to log in using the credentials provided with the VSTS trial), close the server list dialog and choose the new server from the dropdown list. Click OK to save your server selection changes.
6. Once you have connected to the Team Foundation Server, open the Team Explorer panel, click the "Connect" icon and then click the "Create Team Project..." link to launch the New Team Project Wizard. Enter a name (such as SSIS VSTS Project) and an optional description for the new Team Project, and then click the "Next" button to continue.
7. Select a Process Template on the next step as shown in Figure 17-14, and then click the "Next" button to continue.

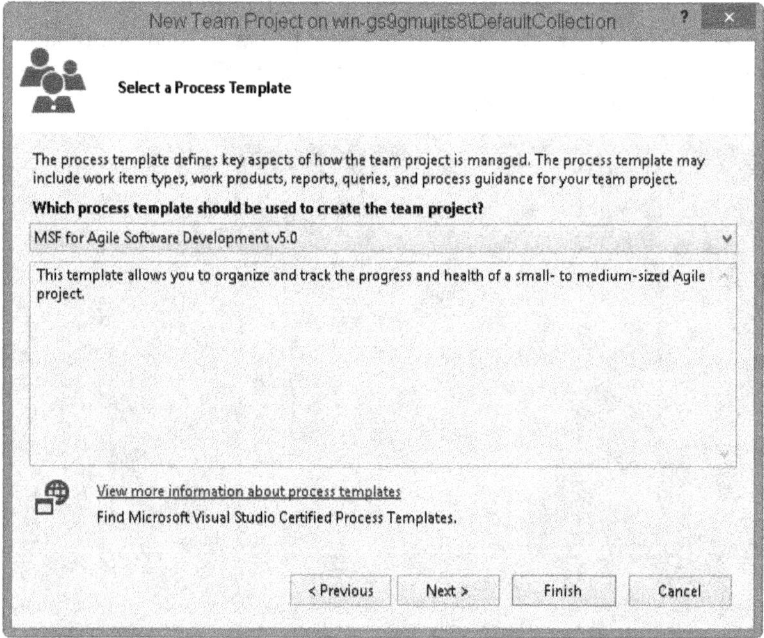

FIGURE 17-14

8. Select a version control system on the next step, as shown in Figure 17-15, and then click the "Next" button to continue.
9. The final step of the wizard presents a brief summary of the Team Project's settings, and a new Team Project will be defined according to the specified configurations. Creation status is indicated by a progress bar as setup scripts are executed. If all goes as expected, the wizard will display a Team Project Created dialog, as shown in Figure 17-16.

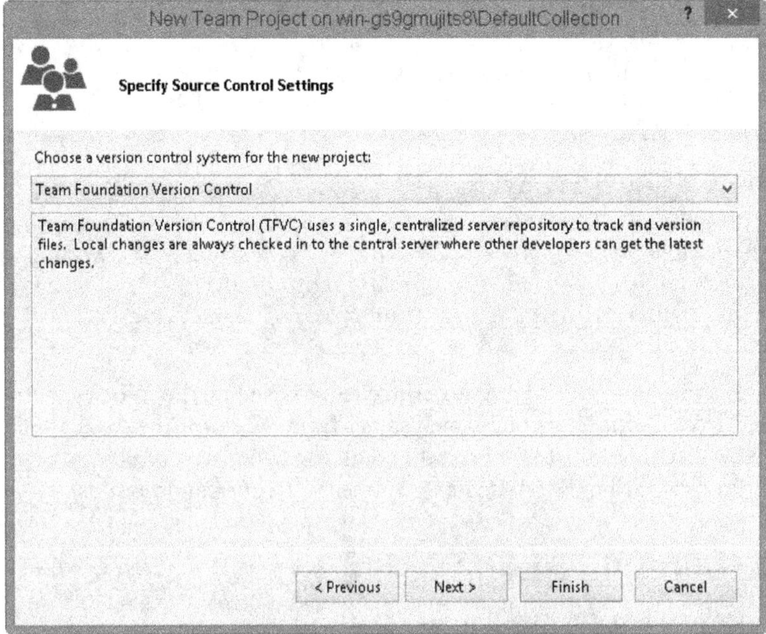

FIGURE 17-15

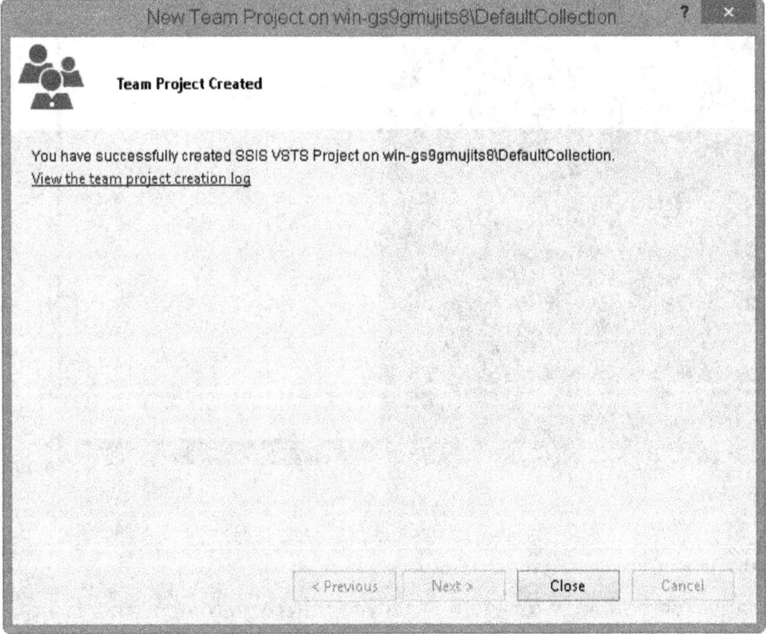

FIGURE 17-16

> **NOTE** *At this point, you have created a Team Project container for your SSIS projects. A Team Project is similar to a Visual Studio solution in that you can add several SSIS projects (or any other type of project) to it.*

> **NOTE** *"Why create a Team Project?" you ask. The short answer is because the practice of database development is changing. Team development is becoming practical, even required, for DBAs in software shops of all sizes. It is no longer confined to the enterprise with dozens or hundreds of developers.*

Team System provides a mechanism for DBAs to utilize team-based methodologies, perhaps for the first time. The Team Project is the heart of Team System's framework for the database developer. Figure 17-17 shows the Visual Studio Team Project and all the containers of objects that can be created in the Team Project (such as Work Items, Documents, Reports, and Builds).

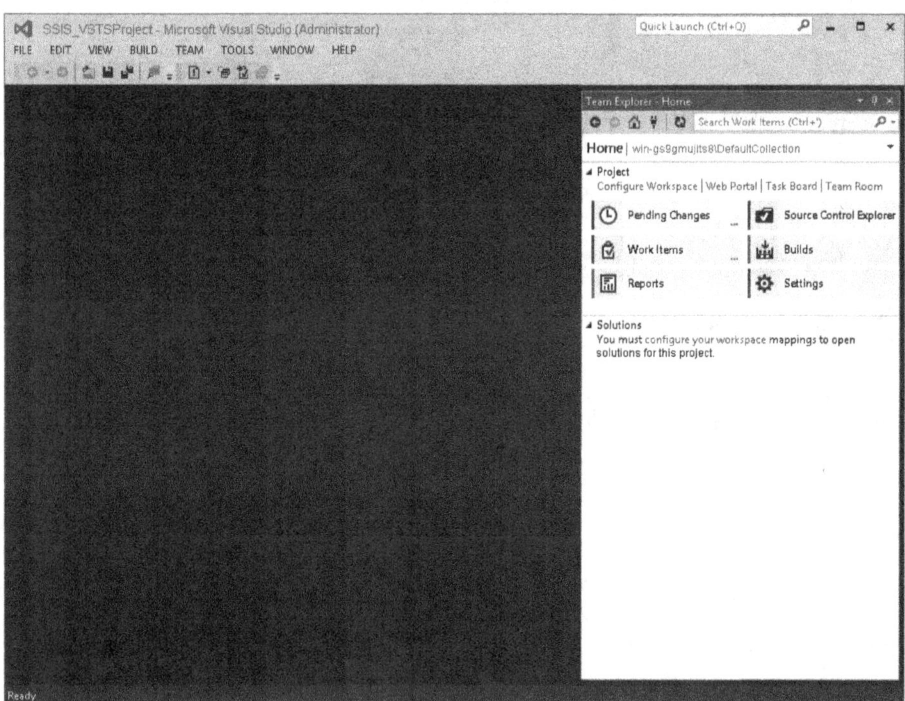

FIGURE 17-17

MSF Agile and SSIS

MSF Agile is an iterative methodology template included with Team System. In a typical agile software project, a time- and scope-limited project — called an *iteration* — is defined by collaboration with the customer. Deliverables are established, but they may be de-scoped in the interests of delivering a completed feature-set at the end of the iteration. An important aspect of agile iterations is that features slip, but timelines do not. In other words, if the team realizes that all features cannot be developed to completion during the time allotted, the time is not extended, and features that *cannot* be developed to completion are removed from the feature-set.

> **NOTE** *Agile methodologies are very suitable to SSIS and BI development projects because they allow more flexibility; changes can be readily adopted to provide an end solution that is suited to the user's needs.*

No one uses a single methodology alone. There are facets of waterfall thinking in any iterative project. In practice, your methodology is a function of the constraints of the development environment imposed by regulatory concerns, personal style, and results.

Once an MSF Agile Team Project hierarchy has been successfully created, the following subitems are available under the project in Team Explorer (refer to Figure 17-17):

- Work Items
- Documents
- Reports
- Team Builds
- Source Control

The next sections cover what's available to you in each of these subitems.

Work Items

In MSF Agile projects, work items consist of tasks, bugs, scenarios, and Quality of Service (QoS) requirements.

- **Bugs** are self-explanatory — they are deficiencies or defects in the code or performance of the application.
- **Scenarios** map to requirements and are akin to use cases in practice.
- **Quality of Service (QoS) requirements** include acceptable performance under attack or stress. QoS includes scalability and security.
- **Tasks** are a catchall category for work items that includes features yet to be developed.

To create a work item, right-click the Work Item folder, select Add Work Item, and choose one of the work item types. Figure 17-18 shows the work item Bug template, which enables bugs to be tracked and handled for your SSIS project.

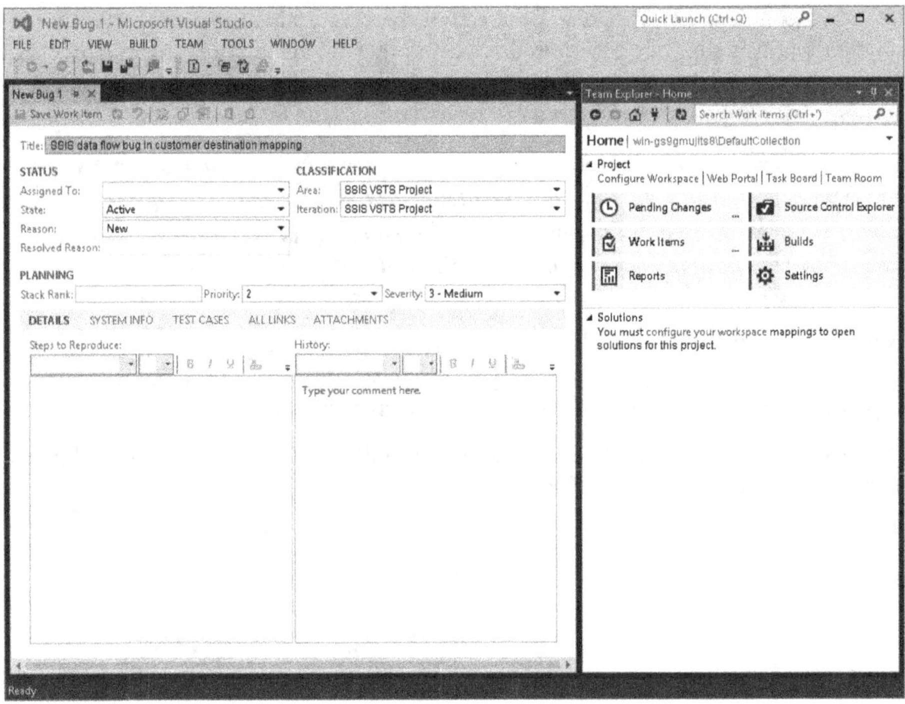

FIGURE 17-18

Documents

The MSF Agile template includes several document templates to get you started with project documentation. Included are the following:

- **Development:** Microsoft Project templates for development and testing efforts
- **Process Guidance:** An HTML document that describes the MSF Agile process
- **Project Management:** An Excel template containing a project "to do" list and an issues and triage spreadsheet
- **Requirements:** Listing requirements for validation scenarios and a Quality of Service (QoS) Requirements list
- **Security:** Document sample defining the security plan for functional areas in the solution
- **Shared Documents:** A repository for miscellaneous project documents
- **Test:** Test plans for unit and integration testing

Reports

The MSF Agile template contains several built-in Reporting Services project status reports. These reports are accessible directly from Reporting Services or from the Project Portal (SharePoint Portal Services) website.

The Reporting Services home page contains links to several reports grouped by report type, as shown in Figure 17-19.

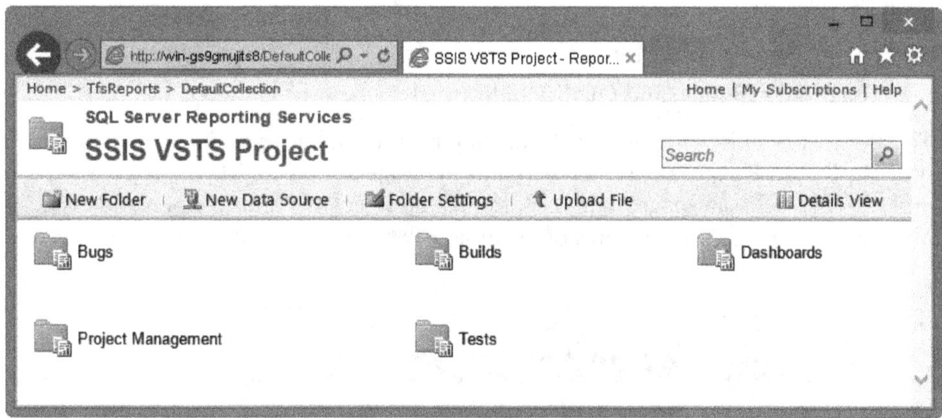

FIGURE 17-19

A few examples of valuable reports include:

- **Capacity Chart with Work Assigned** gives a snapshot of the capacity of the amount of work that can be performed given the current team and the development velocity.
- **Burn Rate Chart** shows the amount of work that can't be performed given the number of hours left and the current trend of work velocity. This report shows hours completed, hours remaining, ideal trend, and actual trend.
- **Remaining Work** report shows the teams progress on a current iteration by highlighting the work completed versus the work remaining trended over time. The Remaining Work report is part of the larger reporting solution provided by the Project Portal (discussed later in this chapter).

Team Builds

A Team Build is the compilation of the code together to be used for deployment. For SSIS, this would be packages in your project that are deployed to the server. If you will be using the SSIS 2014 and deploying your packages to the SSIS Server, then you will be using the deployment functionality in Project Deployment Model in SSIS. This is covered in Chapter 22.

Source Control

Source control within Visual Studio Team System is very similar to the SVN functionality walked through earlier in the chapter. You are able to check items into the source control, revert to a prior version of a package, keep notes as to what was changed, and so on. The section "Version and Source Control with Team System" later in the chapter covers the VSTS source control features.

The Project Portal

The Project Portal is implemented in SharePoint Portal Services and contains several helpful portals, including the following:

- Announcements
- Shared documents and Wiki sites
- Reports (Bug Rates, Builds, and Quality Indicators)

The Project Portal provides a nice interface for the development team, but project managers are the target audience. The Project Portal can also serve to inform business stakeholders of project status. To navigate to the Project Portal home page, right-click the Team Project in Team Explorer and click Show Project Portal. Figure 17-20 shows an example of the Project Portal with one of the reports viewed.

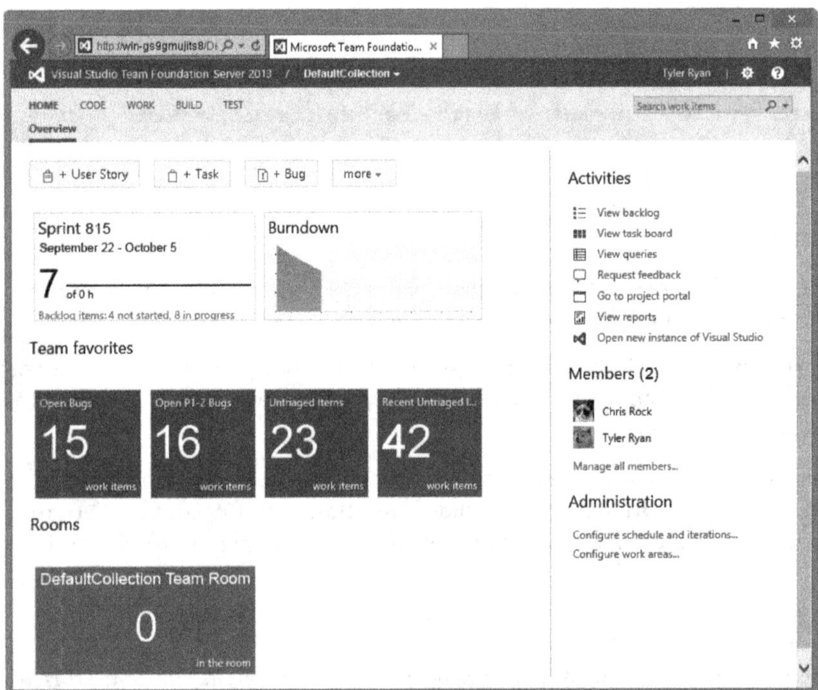

FIGURE 17-20

Putting Team System to Work

In this section, you'll create a small SSIS package to demonstrate some fundamental Team System features.

1. Create a new SSIS project in SSDT by clicking File ➪ New ➪ Project. From the Project Types tree view, select Business Intelligence Projects. From the Templates list view, select Integration Services Project. Do not check the Add to Source Control checkbox. Enter **SSIS VSTS Integration Example** as the project name in the Name text box, as shown in Figure 17-21.

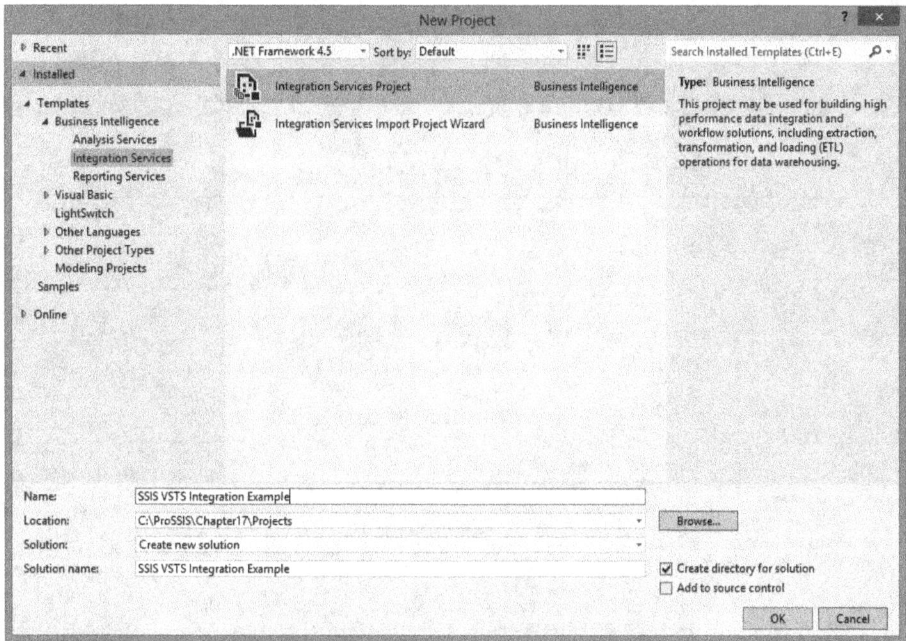

FIGURE 17-21

2. Click OK to create the new project. Drag a Data Flow Task onto the Control Flow workspace.
3. Right-click in the Connection Managers tab and select New OLE DB Connection to add a database connection. Click the New button to create a new OLE DB Connection.
4. Select your local server from the Server Name dropdown list. Configure the connection for Windows or SQL Server authentication. Select AdventureWorks as the database name. You can click the Test Connection button to test the connectivity configuration. Click OK to close the Connection Manager dialog, and OK again to continue.
5. Double-click the Data Flow Task to edit it. Drag an OLE DB source onto the Data Flow workspace. Double-click the OLE DB source to edit it.
6. In the OLE DB Source Editor window, select the AdventureWorks connection in the OLE DB Connection Manager dropdown list. Select Table or View in the Data Access Mode dropdown list. Select [Sales].[SalesOrderHeader] in the "Name of the table or the view" dropdown list. Click OK to continue.
7. Drag an Aggregate Transformation onto the Data Flow workspace. Connect the output of the OLE DB source to the Aggregate Transformation by dragging the blue arrow from the source to the transformation. From the Available Input Columns table, select OrderDate and SubTotal. In the grid below, ensure that the operation for OrderDate is Group by, and the operation for SubTotal is Sum, as shown in Figure 17-22.

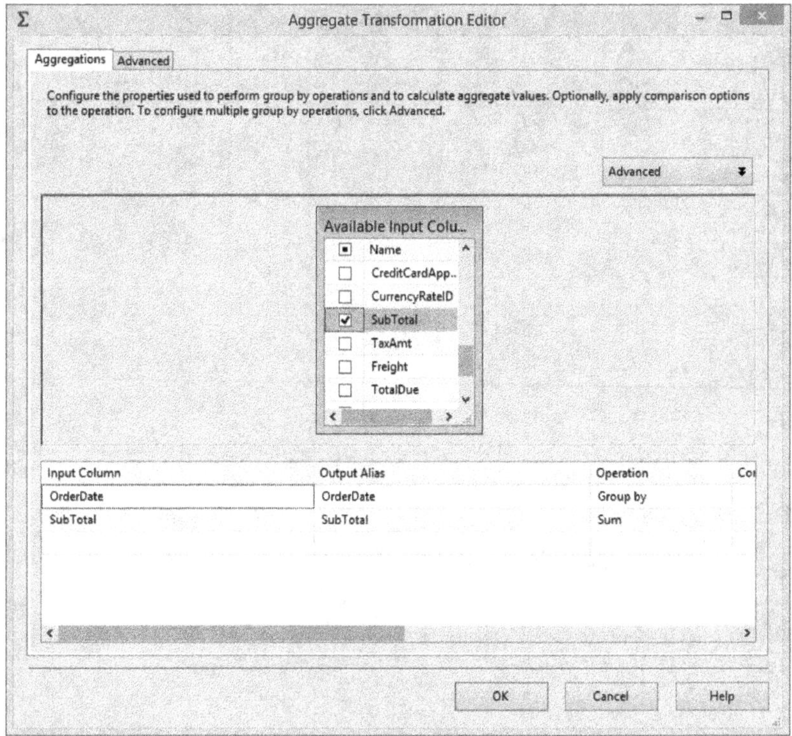

FIGURE 17-22

8. Click OK to close the Aggregate Transformation Editor.

9. Drag an Excel Destination onto the Data Flow workspace and connect the Aggregate output to it. Double-click the Excel Destination to open the Excel Destination Editor. Click the New button beside the OLE DB Connection Manager dropdown list to create a new Excel connection object. Enter **c:\SSIS_output.xlsx** in the Excel file path text box. Click OK to continue.

10. You can create an Excel spreadsheet in this step. If you enter the desired name of a spreadsheet that does not yet exist, the Excel Destination Editor will not be able to locate a worksheet name. In this case, the "No tables or views could be loaded" message will appear in the Name of Excel Worksheet dropdown list.

11. To create a worksheet, click the New button beside the Name of the Excel Sheet dropdown list. A Create Table dialog will appear. Click OK to accept the defaults and create the worksheet and Excel workbook.

12. Click Mappings in the Excel Destination Editor to configure column-to-data mappings. Accept the defaults by clicking OK.

13. Click File ➪ Save All to save your work.

Now that you have created a simple SSIS package, you will use this package to test the Team System functionality with SSIS.

Version and Source Control with Team System

The objective in this section is to walk you through integrating your SSIS project and package with Team System source control and versioning functionality.

1. To add your SSIS project to the Team Project, open Solution Explorer, right-click the project, and click Add Project to Source Control.
2. The Add Solution SSIS VSTS Integration Example to Source Control dialog appears, containing a list of Team Projects. Select the SSIS VSTS Project you created earlier, as shown in Figure 17-23.
3. Click OK to continue. You have successfully created a Team Project and an SSIS project. The Team Project contains version control information — even now.
4. Click View ➪ Other Windows ➪ Pending Changes to view the current source control status for the SSIS project, as shown in Figure 17-24.

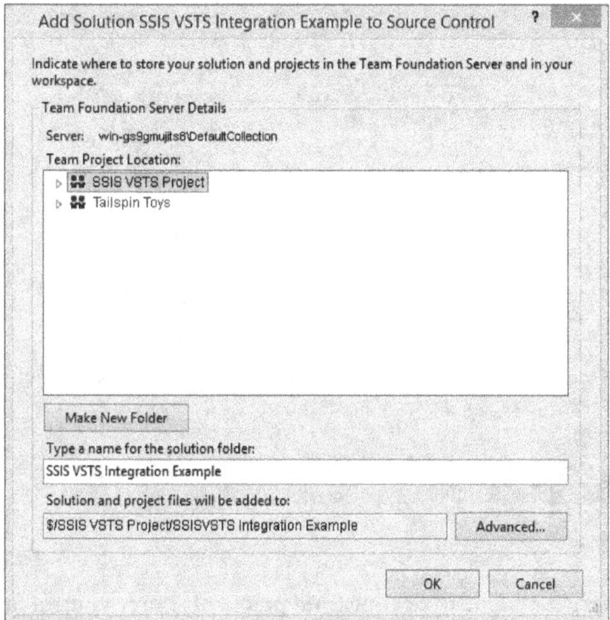

FIGURE 17-23

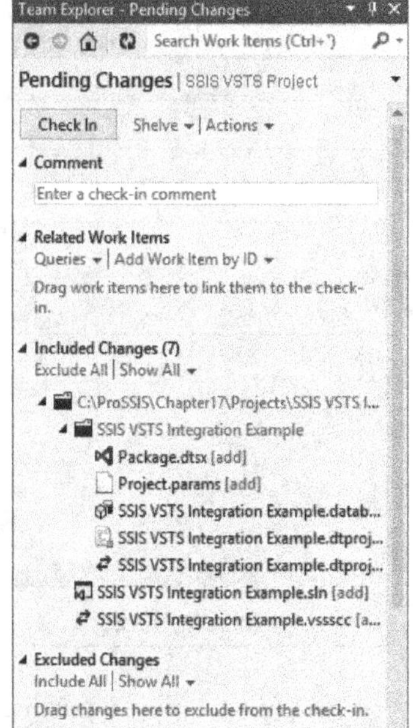

FIGURE 17-24

The Change column indicates that the files are currently in an Add status. This means the files are not yet source-controlled but are ready to be added to source control.

5. Click the Check In button to add the current SSIS VSTS Integration Example project to the SSIS VSTS Project's source control. This clears the Pending Checkin list. Editing the SSIS VSTS Integration Example project will cause the affected files to reappear in the Pending Checkin list.

> **NOTE** *Any change made to the SSIS VSTS Integration Example project is now tracked against the source-controlled version maintained by the SSIS VSTS Project. Seemingly insignificant changes count: For instance, moving any item in the Data Flow workspace is considered an edit to the package item and is tracked.*

The default behavior for source control in Visual Studio is that checked-in items are automatically checked out when edited.

6. You can view the current status of all Team Projects on your Team Foundation Server in the Source Control Explorer, as shown in Figure 17-25. To access the Source Control Explorer, double-click Source Control in the Team Explorer or click View ➪ Other Windows ➪ Source Control Explorer.

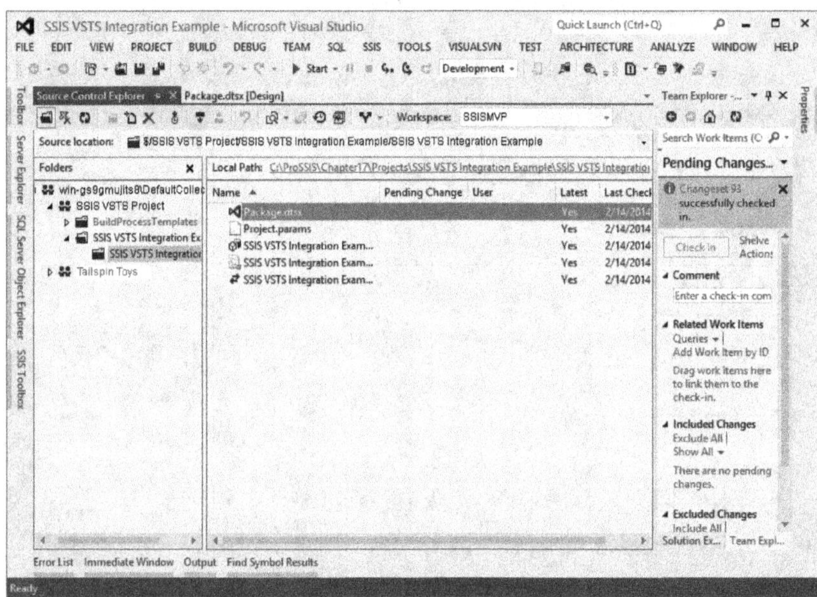

FIGURE 17-25

This next example implements a larger change to demonstrate practical source control management, before moving into some advanced source control functionality.

1. In your SSIS project, add an Execute SQL Task to the Control Flow workspace. Configure the task by setting the Connection Type to OLE DB, the Connection to your AdventureWorks connection, and the SQLSourceType to Direct input. Set the SQL Statement to the following:

```
1. if not exists(select * from sysobjects where id = object_id('Log') and
ObjectProperty(id, 'IsUserTable') = 1)
 begin
 CREATE TABLE Log (
```

```
    LogDateTime datetime NOT NULL,
    LogLocation VarChar(50) NOT NULL,
    LogEvent VarChar(50) NOT NULL,
    LogDetails VarChar(1000) NULL,
    LogCount Int NULL
    ) ON [Primary]
    ALTER TABLE Log ADD CONSTRAINT DF_Log_LogDateTime DEFAULT (getdate()) FOR
   LogDateTime
    end
    INSERT INTO Log
    (LogLocation, LogEvent, LogDetails, LogCount)
    VALUES('SSISDemo', 'DataFlow', 'Completed','1st Run')
```

2. It is always a good practice to check your SQL before execution. Do so by clicking the Parse Query button, and correct the SQL if necessary. Then click OK to continue.
3. Connect the Data Flow Task to the Execute SQL Task by dragging the output (green arrow) of the Data Flow Task over to the Execute SQL Task.
4. Save your changes by clicking the Save button on the toolbar. You now have updated your SSIS project and saved the changes to disk, but you have not committed the changes to source control. You can verify this in the Pending Changes window by clicking View ➪ Other Windows ➪ Pending Changes.
5. The Change column indicates that `Package.dtsx` is in an Edit status. This means that changes to the existing source-controlled `Package.dtsx` file have been detected. Click the Check In button to publish your changes to source control.

Shelving and Unshelving

Shelving is a concept used in Microsoft source control technology since the release of VSTS. It enables you to preserve a snapshot of the current source state on the server for later retrieval and resumed development. You can also shelve code and pass it to another developer as part of a workload reassignment. In automated nightly build environments, shelving provides a means to preserve semi-complete code in a source control system without fully checking it into the build.

1. Shelving a package requires that you have a pending check-in. If no packages are pending a check-in, first make a change to the package such as moving the Data Flow Task. To shelve code, click the Shelve link at the top of the Pending Change panel. The Shelve dialog appears, as shown in Figure 17-26.

   The "Preserve pending changes locally" checkbox enables you to choose between rolling back or keeping the edits since the last source code check-in. Checking the checkbox will keep the changes. Unchecking the checkbox will roll changes back to the last source-controlled version.

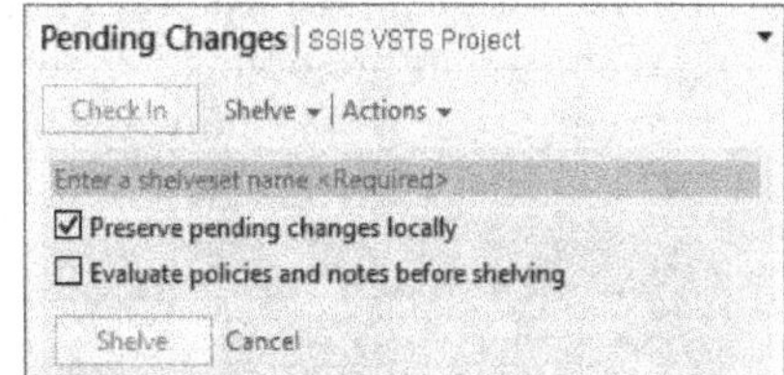

FIGURE 17-26

> **NOTE** *The rollback will effectively "undo" all changes — even changes saved to disk.*

2. Leave the "Preserve pending changes locally" checkbox checked, provide a Shelveset name, and click Shelve to proceed.

The shelving process stores the code changes for later use, and you or other developers on your team can resume the development process from the point of the original code check-in before the modified version was shelved. At some point you may need to go back and unshelve the code. This can be handled with the following steps, but before unshelving, you need to have all pending code checked in.

1. To unshelve code, click the Actions link at the top of the Pending Changes dialog. Click the Find Shelvesets action. You should see the Shelveset you just created in the previous step.
2. Right-click on the shelveset and select Unshelve. This will unshelve the changes.

Note that an administrator or the user who created the shelving can now delete the shelved files after the code is checked back in.

Unshelving code with conflicts will roll the project back to its state at the time of shelving. For this reason, you may wish to consider shelving your current version of the code prior to unshelving a previous version.

If you are prompted to reload objects in your Visual Studio project, respond by clicking Yes or Yes to All. Your current version will be rolled back to the shelve set version.

Branching

The capability to *branch* code provides a mechanism to preserve the current state of a SSIS project *and* modify it in some fashion. Think of it as driving a stake in the ground of a project by marking the status of the current change set as "good." In other words, you've come to a point where all the SSIS packages are working together and checked in and you want to be able to identify this point for stability and have the opportunity to branch the code for some new development or to test some new approaches without affecting the main code.

To branch, open Source Control Explorer by clicking View ➪ Other Windows ➪ Source Control Explorer. Right-click the project name you wish to branch and click Branching and Merging ➪ Branch from the context menu, which brings up the Branch dialog shown in Figure 17-27. Select a name for the branched project and enter it into the To text box. Note the option to lock the new branch — thus preserving it indefinitely from accidental modification. You can further secure the branched code by including the option to not create local working copies for the new branch.

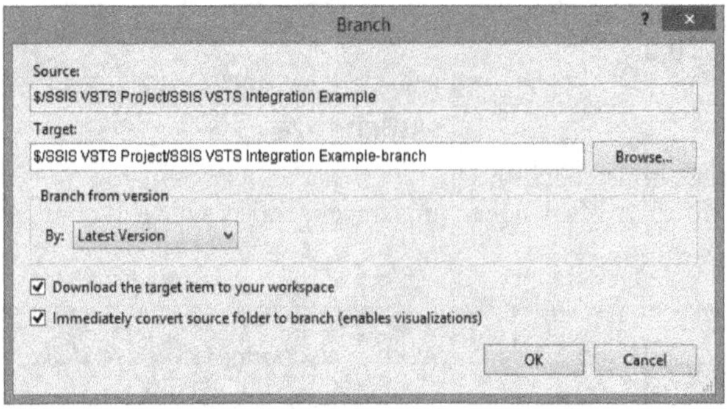

FIGURE 17-27

Merging

Merging is the inverse operation for branching. It involves recombining code that has been modified with a branch that has not been modified. A merge operation requires that the code has first been changed and checked-in. Follow these steps to merge two branches:

1. To merge projects, open Source Control Explorer. Right-click the name of the branched project containing the changes and click Branching and Merging ➪ Merge.
2. The project you right-clicked in the previous step should appear in the Source Branch text box of the Version Control Merge Wizard. Select the Target branch (the branch containing no changes) from the Target Branch dropdown. Note the options to merge all or selected changes from the Source branch into the Target branch. Click Next to proceed.
3. The Source Control Merge Wizard enables users to select the version criteria during merge. The options are Latest Version (default), Workspace, Label, Date, and Change Set. Click Finish to proceed.

If the Version Control Merge Wizard encounters errors while attempting the merge, the Resolve Conflicts dialog is displayed. Click Auto-Merge All to attempt an automatic merge. Click Resolve to manually merge branches. When all conflicts have been resolved, the Resolve Conflicts dialog will reflect that.

> **NOTE** *Never merge the XML code within a package file from different versions. This could corrupt the file. Therefore, when merging projects, always merge the list of objects, not the files themselves.*

Labeling (Striping) Source Versions

Labeling provides a means to mark (or "stripe") a version of the code. Generally, labeling is the last step performed in a source-controlled version of code — marking the version as complete. Additional changes require a branch.

1. To label a version, open Source Control Explorer. Right-click the project and click Advanced ➪ Apply Label. Enter a name for the Label and an optional comment. Click the Add button to select files or project(s) to be labeled. This will invoke the New Label dialog, as shown in Figure 17-28.
2. Click OK to complete labeling.

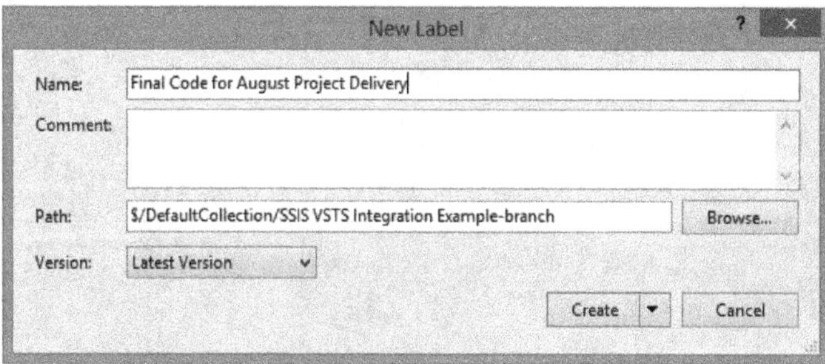

FIGURE 17-28

There has been much debate about when to shelve, branch, or label. To standardize your SSIS development process, use the following recommended advice:

- **Shelve:** Use when your code is not code complete. In other words, if your code isn't ready for the nightly or weekly build, shelve it for now.
- **Branch:** Use when you need to add functionality and features to an application that can be considered complete in some form. Some shops will have you branch if the code can be successfully built; others insist on no branching unless the code can be labeled.
- **Label:** Use when you wish to mark a version of the application as "complete." In practice, labels *are* the version, for instance, "1.2.0.2406."

SUMMARY

Having worked through the several examples in this chapter, you should now have a clearer picture of software development life cycles and planning your ETL team development with SSIS. In addition to learning how to use Visual Studio to add SSIS projects to Subversion (SVN), you also learned how to do the following in Visual Studio Team System (VSTS):

- Create a Team Project in Team System
- Add an SSIS project to the Team Project
- Manage and report project status
- Manage SSIS packages with the VSTS source control functionality

You also looked at some common software development methodologies and saw how Team Foundation Server enables you to customize Team System to clearly reflect your methodology of choice.

Armed with these tools, you are now ready to begin down the path of code development. Whether you come from a DBA background and SDLCs are a new world or you come from a development background and you need to apply your SDLC experience to SSIS, this chapter should have helped you move forward to your next level of skill.

18

Error and Event Handling

WHAT'S IN THIS CHAPTER?

- Working with precedence constraints
- Creating failure flows with expressions
- Defining SSIS events
- Handling events in a package
- Troubleshooting with breakpoints and logging

WROX.COM CODE DOWNLOADS FOR THIS CHAPTER

You can find the wrox.com code downloads for this chapter at `www.wrox.com/go/prossis2014` on the Download Code tab.

SQL Server Integration Services provides some valuable features that enable you to control the workflow of your SSIS packages at a very granular level. Functionality that you might expect to be available only by scripting can often be accomplished by setting a few properties of a component. In addition, SSIS comes with powerful error-handling capabilities, the capability to log detailed information as the package runs, and debugging functionality that speeds up troubleshooting and design.

This chapter walks you through controlling the package workflow, beginning at the highest level using precedence constraints and then drilling down to event handling. You'll see how trappable events play a role in breakpoints, and how to perform exception handling for incorrect data in the Data Flow. Finally, you learn how these features can be used for troubleshooting, debugging, and building robust SSIS packages.

USING PRECEDENCE CONSTRAINTS

Precedence constraints are the green, red, and grey connectors in the Control Flow that link the tasks together and can be used to manage the workflow of a package and handle error conditions.

> **NOTE** *Be aware that grey precedence constraints look a lot like data paths in the Data Flow, but they are much different. On the one hand, precedence constraints define what tasks should be executed in which order; on the other hand, Data Flow paths define to which transformations and destinations data should be routed. Data Flow paths deal with moving data; precedence constraints deal with workflow handling.*

Precedence Constraint Basics

The main purpose of precedence constraints is to control when tasks and containers should run in relation to one another. This revolves around whether tasks succeed (green), fail (red), or just complete with either a success or a failure (grey). Precedence constraints can also be more granularly controlled through advanced properties, which are addressed in the next section.

Figure 18-1 shows a typical example. If the Initial Data Flow Task completes successfully, the Success Data Flow Task will execute. A green arrow (on the left) points to the Success Data Flow Task. If the Initial Data Flow Task fails, the Failure Send Mail Task executes, sending notification of the failure. A red arrow (in the middle) points to the Failure Send Mail Task. No matter what happens, the Completion Script Task will always execute. A grey arrow (on the right) points to the Completion Script Task.

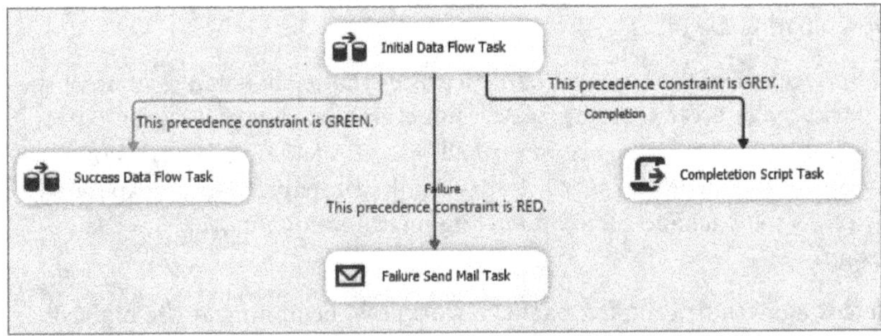

FIGURE 18-1

When you are initially connecting two tasks, you'll see that the default precedence constraint is a green arrow designating success. To change how the precedence constraint is evaluated, you can right-click the arrow and choose a different outcome from the pop-up menu, as shown in Figure 18-2.

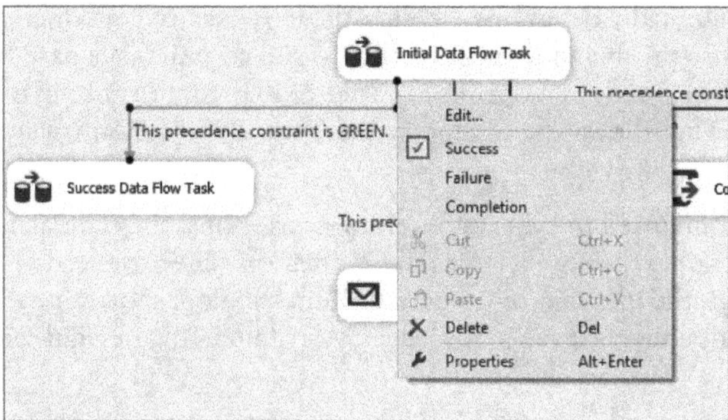

FIGURE 18-2

You can also combine tasks into groups by using containers, in which case the workflow can be controlled by the success or failure of the container. For example, a package may have several Data Flow Tasks that run in parallel, each loading data from a different source. All tasks must complete successfully for the container to determine success and allow the flow to continue to the next step. A Sequence Container contains the tasks, and the precedence constraint is drawn from the container to the next step. The example shown in Figure 18-3 illustrates how a Sequence Container might be used. After the Initialization Script runs, the Import Data Container executes. Within it, three Data Flow processes run in parallel. A failure of any of the Data Flow Tasks will cause the Import Data Container to fail, and the failure message will be sent. If all three complete successfully, the Clean Up Script will run.

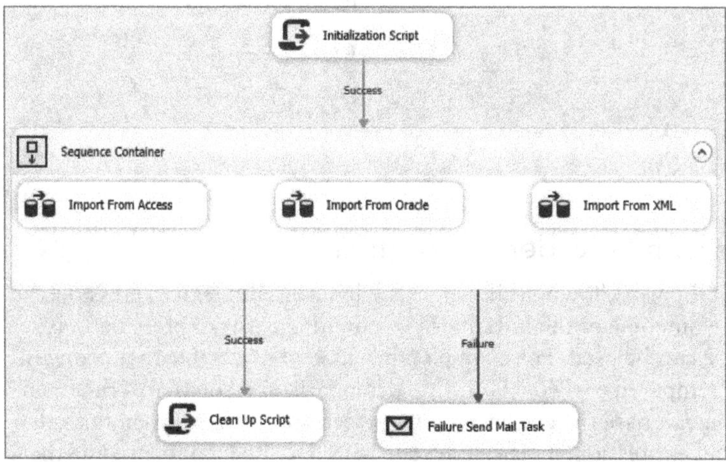

FIGURE 18-3

Advanced Precedence Constraints and Expressions

While using a standard constraint evaluation in a precedence constraint provides an impressive way of managing the execution of certain tasks, the precedence constraint provides even more flexibility to manage the flow of the package. Using the advanced functionality of SSIS expressions inside of the precedence constraint, you can dynamically determine whether the next task or container should run at package runtime. You can use the dynamic functionality to run certain tasks based on different criteria, such as running only on Sundays, not running after 2:00 a.m., or running if an external parameter flag is set to True. This allows you to modify the Control Flow in any way required.

Not only can precedence constraints be configured to evaluate Boolean expressions, they can also be combined with other precedence constraints through a logical OR evaluation. The advanced precedence constraints are defined through the Precedence Constraint Editor dialog, shown in Figure 18-4. To pull up the editor, either double-click the precedence constraint arrow or right-click the arrow and choose Edit.

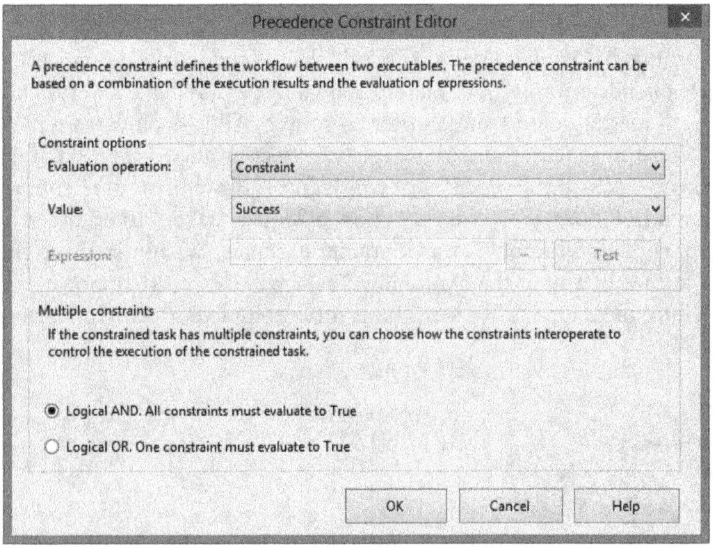

FIGURE 18-4

Using Boolean Expressions with Precedence Constraints

With the editor, you can control the workflow within a package by using Boolean expressions in place of, or in addition to, the outcome of the initial task or container. Any expression that can be evaluated to True or False can be used. For example, the value of a variable that changes as the package executes can be compared to a constant. If the comparison resolves to True, then the connected task executes. You can base the evaluation of a precedence constraint on both the outcome of the initial task and an expression. This enables the SSIS developer to finely tune the workflow of a package. The following table shows the four Evaluation Operation options contained in the dropdown menu for configuring a precedence constraint:

EVALUATION OPERATION	DEFINITION
Constraint	The execution result is applied to the constraint (success, failure, or completion) without the use of an expression.
Expression	Any expression that evaluates to True or False is used to evaluate the constraint without the consideration of the execution result.
Expression and Constraint	*Both* the specified execution result *and* an expression condition must be satisfied for the constraint to allow the next task to run.
Expression or Constraint	*Either* the specified execution result *or* an expression condition must be satisfied for the constraint to allow the next task to run.

In the precedence constraint configuration, you can choose which type of Evaluation Operation to use and set the value of the constraint and/or supply the expression.

In the following example, you will simulate flipping a coin to learn more about using expressions with precedence constraints. The Coin Toss example uses Execute SQL Tasks, Script Tasks, and For Loop Containers, as well as advanced precedence constraint logic, to create the replica. The final package you will create is shown in Figure 18-5.

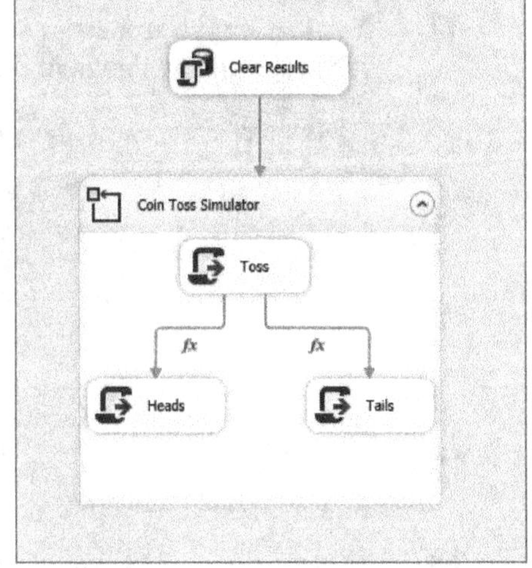

FIGURE 18-5

1. To start the process, create a new table to hold the results using this script (`ProSSIS\Scripts\Ch18_ProSSIS\Scripts.sql`) in the AdventureWorks database:

```
CREATE TABLE CoinToss (
 Heads INT NULL,
 Tails INT NULL )
GO
INSERT INTO CoinToss SELECT 0,0
```

2. Create a new SSIS project in SQL Server Data Tools and create a new package.
3. Create an OLE DB Connection Manager pointing to the AdventureWorks database where the CoinToss table was created. The steps for creating a Connection Manager are covered in Chapter 3.
4. To reset the value of the coin toss each time you run the package, add an Execute SQL Task named **Clear Results** to the Control Flow design area.
5. Double-click the Clear Results Task to open the Execute SQL Task Editor.
6. Set the `Connection` property to point to the AdventureWorks Connection Manager and type the following code in the SQLStatement field:

```
UPDATE CoinToss
SET Tails = 0, Heads = 0
```

Now that the package is prepared, it is time to set up the simulator.

7. Right-click the Control Flow design area and select Variables from the pop-up menu to open the Variables window.
8. Create a new package level variable called `Result` with a data type of Int32 to hold the "result" of the coin toss.
9. To toss the coin multiple times, you will use a For Loop Container. Add the container to the design area, and name it **Coin Toss Simulator**. Connect the precedence constraint from the Clear Results Task to the Coin Toss Simulator.
10. With the Coin Toss Simulator selected, open the Variables window to add a variable called **Count** with a data type of Int32. In this case, the variable will be used only by the For Loop Container, so the scope can be the Coin Toss Simulator.
11. You can set the properties of the Coin Toss Simulator Container by opening the editor. Set the properties as shown in the following table and click OK:

PROPERTY	VALUE
`InitExpression`	`@Count = 0`
`EvalExpression`	`@Count <100`
`AssignExpression`	`@Count = @Count + 1`

This should look familiar to you if you have programmed in almost any language: The For Loop Container will execute whatever is inside of it 100 times.

12. In this case, drag a Script Task named **Toss** into the Coin Toss Simulator to perform the coin toss.
13. To set up the code to simulate the coin toss, double-click the Toss Script Task to open the Script Task Editor.
14. In the Script pane, select the ScriptLanguage of Microsoft Visual Basic 2012 and select the variable `User::Result` in the `ReadWriteVariables` property. The script will have access only to variables set up in this way.
15. Click Edit Script to open the Visual Studio Tools for Applications design environment. Each time this script runs, it will randomly pick a value of one or two and store the value in the `Result` variable. Replace `Public Sub Main` with this code:

```
Public Sub Main()
 Randomize()
 Dts.Variables("User::Result").Value = CInt(Int((2 * Rnd()) + 1))
 Dts.TaskResult = ScriptResults.Success
End Sub
```

Close out of the script editor and then click OK in the Script Task editor to close it and return to SSDT.

16. Set up the outcome tasks for the coin toss. Drag two Execute SQL Tasks into the Coin Toss Simulator Container, with one named Heads and the other Tails. Connect the Toss Script Task to each of the Execute SQL Tasks.

17. Now you need to change the precedence constraints so that the control will pass to the appropriate tasks.

18. Double-click the precedence constraint pointing to Heads to bring up the Precedence Constraint Editor. Change the Evaluation Operation from Constraint to Expression. As shown in Figure 18-6, the Expression text box will become available, enabling you to type the following into the `Expression` property:

```
@Result == 1
```

The precedence constraint will have an *fx* symbol next to it specifying that it uses an expression.

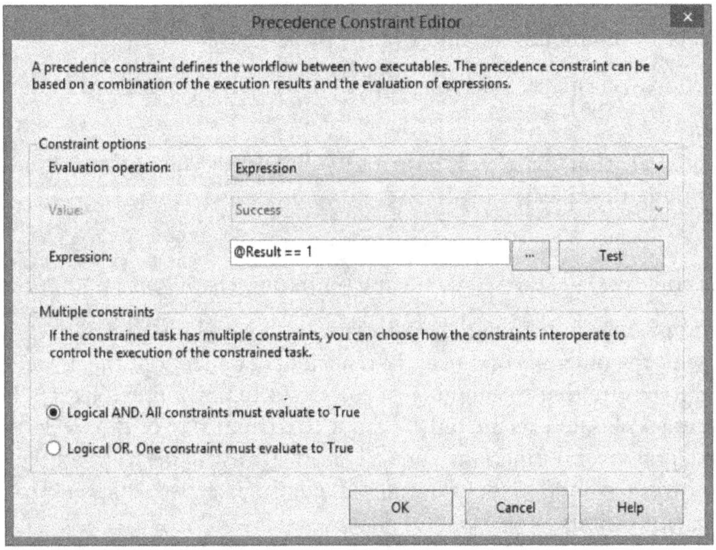

FIGURE 18-6

NOTE *When evaluating two values in an SSIS Boolean expression, you need to use two equals signs (==). This indicates that the expression returns* `TRUE` *or* `FALSE` *depending on whether the values are equal.* `NULL` *values do not evaluate, so be sure to ensure that both sides of the == return an actual value. The only time you use a single equals sign is when you are using an SSIS expression or the Expression Task to set the value of a variable, such as inside of a For Loop Container.*

19. To continue with the example, open the properties of the precedence constraint that is connected to Tails. Change the Evaluation Operation from Constraint to Expression, and type this in the `Expression` property:

```
@Result == 2
```

20. Click OK to accept the properties. Just a couple more details and you'll be ready to run the package!

21. Double-click Heads to open the Execute SQL Task Editor. In the `Connection` property, set the value to the AdventureWorks Connection Manager. Type the following code in the `SQLStatement` property to increment the count in the CoinToss table:

    ```
    UPDATE CoinToss SET Heads = Heads + 1
    ```

22. Click OK to accept the changes.

23. Bring up the Execute SQL Task Editor for the Tails object. Set the `Connection` property to the AdventureWorks Connection Manager. Type this code in the `SQLStatement` property:

    ```
    UPDATE CoinToss SET Tails = Tails + 1
    ```

24. Click OK to accept the configuration and run the package.

    As the package runs, you can see that sometimes `Heads` will execute, and sometimes `Tails` will execute.

25. Once the package execution completes, return to SQL Server Management Studio to view the results by running this query:

    ```
    SELECT * FROM CoinToss
    ```

    Similar to a real coin toss, `Heads` will come up approximately 50 out of 100 times.

This simple example demonstrates how to use an expression to control the package workflow, instead of or combined with the outcome of a task. In a business application, the precedence constraint might be used to ensure that the number of rows affected by a previous step is less than a certain value, or maybe a task should execute only if it is a particular day of the week. Any variable within scope can be used, and several functions and operators are available to build the expression. Any valid expression will work as long as it evaluates to True or False. See Chapter 5 to learn more about building and using expressions.

Working with Multiple Precedence Constraints

In your package workflow, you can have multiple precedence constraints pointing to the same task. By default, the conditions of *both must be True* to enable execution of the constrained task. You also have the option of running a task if at *least one of the conditions is True* by setting the Multiple constraints option to "Logical OR. One constraint must evaluate to True," as shown in Figure 18-7.

The solid precedence constraints change to dashed precedence constraints when the Logical OR option is chosen. You only need to select Logical OR for one constraint, as all other constraints that point to the same task or container will also change to Logical OR. Figure 18-8 shows how the Send Mail Task named Error Message will execute if either of the Import Data Flow Tasks fails. In this example, both precedence constraints are configured to fail but the Logical OR has been set instead of the Logical AND. Because the Logical OR has been enabled, the precedence constraints are dashed lines. Figure 18-8 shows the Import Customers Data Flow is successful (the circle with a check mark), but the Import Orders Data Flow failed (the circle with an X). Although not shown in the picture, the successful circle will be green and the failure circle will be red. Because one of the Data Flows failed, the Error Message Send Mail Task is executing. If both Data Flows had been successful, the Error Message Task would not have run.

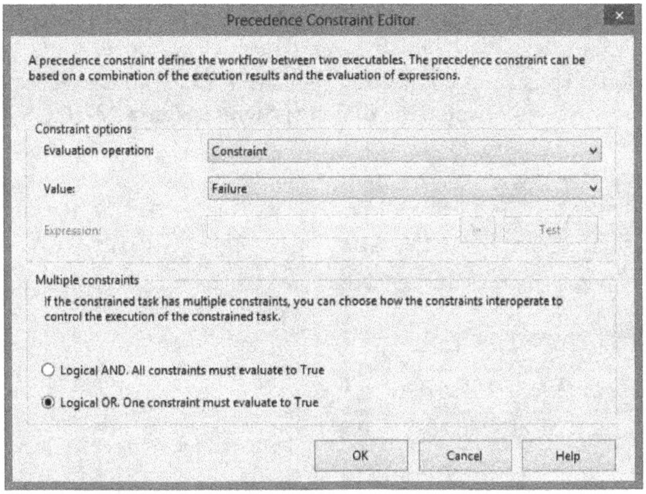

Precedence Constraint Editor

A precedence constraint defines the workflow between two executables. The precedence constraint can be based on a combination of the execution results and the evaluation of expressions.

Constraint options

Evaluation operation: Constraint

Value: Failure

Expression: Test

Multiple constraints

If the constrained task has multiple constraints, you can choose how the constraints interoperate to control the execution of the constrained task.

Logical AND. All constraints must evaluate to True

Logical OR. One constraint must evaluate to True

OK Cancel Help

FIGURE 18-7

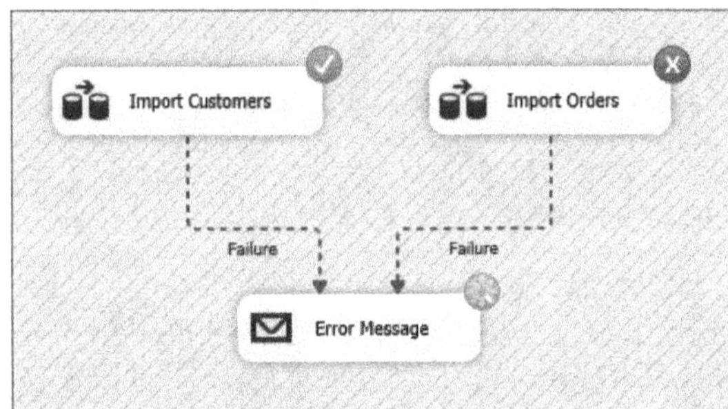

FIGURE 18-8

Combining Expressions and Multiple Precedence Constraints

In the next example, an expression is evaluated in addition to using multiple constraints. This workflow loads data from a series of files into a SQL database. The business rules require that no file can be loaded into the database more than once, and the files must be archived, whether they have been loaded previously or not. Figure 18-9 shows the workflow with the required business rules implemented.

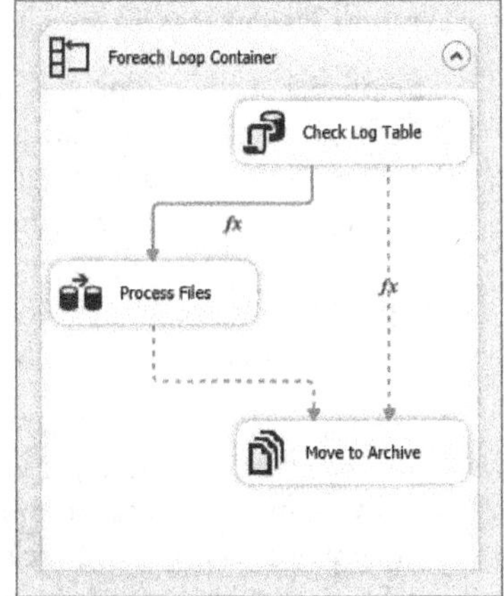

FIGURE 18-9

In this workflow, a Foreach Loop Container is used to loop through the files you want to load into the database. With each iteration of the loop, the filename is assigned to a variable, which is then used in the first task (the Execute SQL Task) to determine whether it has been previously loaded. The Execute SQL Task called Check Log Table will use the variable that holds the current filename as an input parameter to a SQL statement to determine whether it does in fact exist in the table. The result of the query will return either true or false, to be stored in a variable that is called `User::blnFlag`. This task is pivotal in that it is the basis for the evaluation within the precedence constraints. Double-clicking the precedence constraint connecting the Check Log Table Execute SQL Task to the Process Files Data Flow Task will display the dialog shown in Figure 18-10.

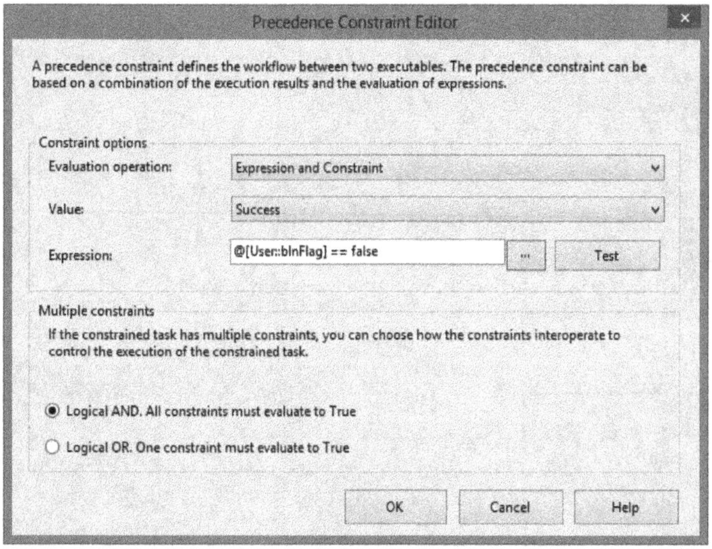

FIGURE 18-10

The properties of the precedence constraint in Figure 18-10 are set to allow the workflow to pass through to the next task (the Process Files Data Flow Task) if the previous step succeeded and the expression has evaluated to false. This constraint is essentially asking, "Was the previous step successful and is this a new file that has not been previously loaded?"

Now that you have determined the business rule behind that constraint, double-click the dashed precedence constraint that connects the Check Log Table Execute SQL Task and the Move to Archive File System Task. The dialog presented for this constraint is shown in Figure 18-11.

The properties of the precedence constraint in Figure 18-11 represent a couple of pieces of business rule logic. First, the evaluation operation is set to Expression and Constraint. Second, the expression is testing whether your variable `@[User::blnFlag]` is true. The interpretation of this expression is asking, "Has the current file been previously loaded?" Lastly, the Logical OR radio button is selected to facilitate an OR condition between your two precedence constraints. In plain English, the properties that are defined for the two precedence constraints will allow the file to be processed and archived if it has or has not been previously loaded.

By using precedence constraints, you control the order of events within a package. After a task or container executes, and depending on how the precedence constraint between the two components was evaluated, the second task or container runs. With all of these options, you can control the workflow of your package at a very granular level. The great thing about precedence constraints in SSIS is that they give you the flexibility to implement complex business rules like the scenario previously demonstrated. Drilling down a bit more, you will next learn another way to control package execution: event handling.

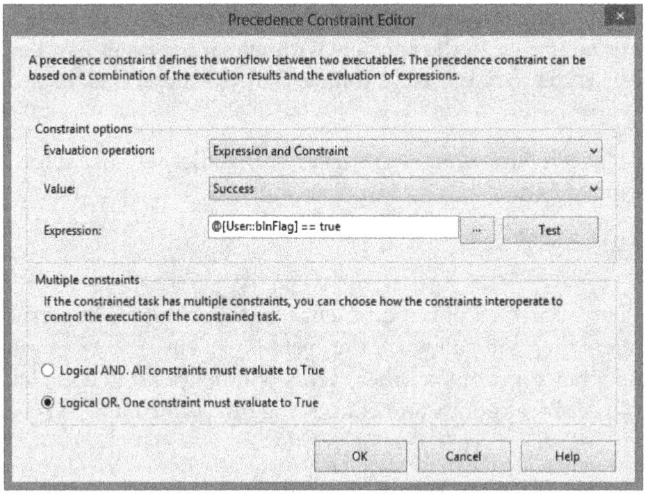

FIGURE 18-11

EVENT HANDLING

Each task and container raises events as it runs, such as an `OnError` event, among several others that are discussed shortly. SSIS enables you to trap and handle these events by setting up workflows that will run when particular events fire. This functionality in SSIS is called *event handlers*.

You can set up event handlers by navigating to the Event Handlers tab in the SSIS package design environment (see Figure 18-12). The Event Handler design area is just like the Control Flow area — you can use the same component types and do anything that is possible at the Control Flow level.

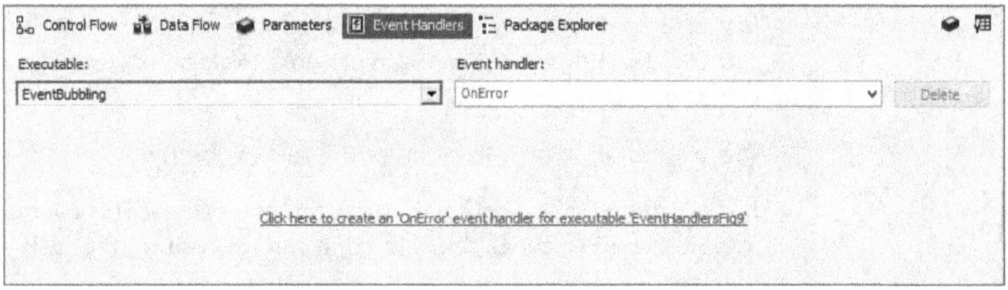

FIGURE 18-12

After adding several event handlers to a package, the workflow can become very complicated, which could be difficult to understand if you had to view it all at once, so separating event handlers from the Control Flow makes sense.

> **NOTE** *Make sure your packages are well designed and documented because an event handler that was set up and then forgotten can be the source of a hard-to-troubleshoot problem within the package.*

As shown in Figure 18-12, the event handler functionality is driven by two dropdown menus. The first, Executable, is used to set the task or container in the package with which the event handler is associated. The highest-level executable is the package itself, followed by the hierarchical list of tasks and containers contained in the Control Flow.

The second dropdown, called Event handler, defines what event the event handler will listen for in the defined executable. Events are described next.

Events

As the package and each task or container executes, a dozen different events are raised. You can capture the events by adding event handlers that will run when the event fires. The `OnError` event may be the event most frequently handled, but some of the other events will be useful in complex ETL packages. Events can also be used to set breakpoints and control logging, which are all covered later in the chapter.

The following table describes the events available in SSIS at the package level:

EVENT	DESCRIPTION
`OnError`	This event is raised whenever an error occurs. You can use this event to capture errors instead of using the failure precedence constraint to redirect the workflow.
`OnExecStatusChanged`	Each time the execution status changes on a task or container, this event fires.
`OnInformation`	During the validation and execution events of the tasks and containers, this event reports information. This is the information displayed in the Progress tab.
`OnPostExecute`	Just after task or container execution completes, this event fires. You could use this event to clean up work tables or delete files no longer needed.
`OnPostValidate`	This event fires after validation of the task is complete.
`OnPreExecute`	Just before a task or container runs, this event fires. This event could be used to check the value of a variable before the task executes.
`OnPreValidate`	Before validation of a task begins, this event fires.
`OnProgress`	As measurable progress is made, this event fires. Information about the progress of an event can be viewed in the Progress tab.
`OnQueryCancel`	This event is raised when an executable checks to see if it should stop or continue running.

`OnTaskFailed`	It's possible for a task or container to fail without actual errors. You can trap that condition with this event.
`OnVariableValueChanged`	Anytime a variable value changes, this event fires. Setting the `RaiseChangeEvent` property to False prevents this event from firing. This event is very useful when debugging a package.
`OnWarning`	Warnings are less critical than errors. This event fires when a warning occurs. Warnings are displayed in the Progress tab.
`Diagnostic`	This event is included only if the logging level is set to Verbose mode. This event fires on the package level if there is specific information that could be helpful to debug the package, such as the number of maximum concurrent executables.
`DiagnosticEx`	This event is included only if the logging level is set to Verbose mode. This event fires at the package level to share information about the execution of the package, such as how much memory is used during processing.

In addition to the events fired at the package level, some tasks fire events as well. The following table lists the tasks that have custom events.

Bulk Insert Task	Transfer Error Messages Task
Data Flow Task	Transfer Jobs Task
Execute Process Task	Transfer Logins Task
Execute SQL Task	Transfer Master Stored Procedures Task
File System Task	Transfer SQL Server Objects Task
FTP Task	Web Services Task
Message Queue Task	WMI Data Reader Task
Script Task	WMI Event Watcher Task
Send Mail Task	XML Task
Transfer Database Task	

Using Event Handlers

Now that you know what each event is and when you may be interested in each event, you need to know how to work with them. As you learned earlier, event handlers provide the means to interact with events. This interaction can be used to log information, perform additional steps, or even pass information to other package items.

The following example demonstrates how to use event handlers by simulating a scenario of checking the inventory status of some random products from AdventureWorks. For this example, you set up a new SSIS package that performs several steps, you define an `OnError` event handler event to fire when an error occurs, and then you use the `OnPreExecute` event to capture execution details of the package.

1. Begin by running the following script (`ProSSIS\Scripts\Ch18_ProSSIS\Scripts.sql`) against the AdventureWorks database to create the tables and stored procedure used:

```
CREATE TABLE InventoryCheck (
 ProductID INT )
 GO
CREATE TABLE InventoryWarning (
 ProductID INT, ReorderQuantity INT )
 GO
CREATE TABLE MissingProductID (
 ProductID INT )
 GO
CREATE PROC usp_GetReorderQuantity @ProductID INT,
 @ReorderQuantity INT OUTPUT AS
 IF NOT EXISTS(SELECT ProductID FROM Production.ProductInventory
 WHERE ProductID = @ProductID) BEGIN
 RAISERROR('InvalidID',16,1)
 RETURN 1
 END
SELECT @ReorderQuantity = SafetyStockLevel - SUM(Quantity)
 FROM Production.Product AS p
INNER JOIN Production.ProductInventory AS i
 ON p.ProductID = i.ProductID
 WHERE p.ProductID = @ProductID
 GROUP BY p.ProductID, SafetyStockLevel
 RETURN 0
GO
```

2. Next, you can put the SSIS package together. In a new package, add an OLE DB Connection Manager pointing to the AdventureWorks database. Because this example uses an Execute SQL Task with parameters, you need to be particular about which provider you use. The parameters work differently depending on which provider is being used. For example, parameters used with the OLE DB provider are numerically named starting with zero. Parameters used with ADO.NET providers use names beginning with the @ symbol.

3. Set up the variables in the following table. (Click the Control Flow area right before opening the Variables window so that the scope of the variables will be at the Package level.)

NAME	SCOPE	DATA TYPE	VALUE
`Count`	Package	Int32	0
`ProductID`	Package	Int32	0
`ReorderQuantity`	Package	Int32	0

4. Drag a Sequence Container to the Control Flow design area and name it **Inventory Check**. You can use a Sequence Container to group tasks, treating the tasks as a unit in the package's workflow. In this case, you use it to experiment with the event handlers.

5. Set the `MaximumErrorCount` property of Inventory Check to 9999 in the Property window. This example raises errors by design, and setting the `MaximumErrorCount` property will allow the simulation to continue running after the errors fire.

6. Drag an Execute SQL Task into the Inventory Check Container, and name it **Empty Tables**.

7. Double-click the task to open the Execute SQL Task Editor. Ensure that the `ConnectionType` property is set to OLE DB, and set the `Connection` property to the AdventureWorks Connection Manager.

8. Click the ellipsis button next to the `SQLStatement` property and type the following into the Enter SQL Query window to complete the Execute SQL Task configuration:

```
DELETE FROM MissingProductID
DELETE FROM InventoryWarning
DELETE FROM InventoryCheck
```

9. Drag a For Loop Container into the Inventory Check Container and name it **Inventory Query Simulator**.

10. Double-click the Inventory Query Simulator and fill in the properties as shown in the following table:

PROPERTY	VALUE
`InitExpression`	`@Count =1`
`EvalExpression`	`@Count <= 50`
`AssignExpression`	`@Count = @Count + 1`

11. Click OK to accept the configuration, and complete the container's setup by changing the `MaximumErrorCount` property of the Inventory Query Simulator to 9999 in the Properties window.

12. Drag a precedence constraint from the Empty Tables Task to the Inventory Query Simulator, and add a Script Task to the Inventory Query Simulator Container named **Generate ProductID**.

13. Double-click the Script Task to open the Script Task Editor.

14. Select the Script pane, setting the `ReadWriteVariables` property to `User::ProductID`, as shown in Figure 18-13.

15. Check the `ScriptLanguage` property. If this property is set to Microsoft Visual C# 2012 or 2013, change the dropdown to Microsoft Visual Basic 2012 or 2013, based on what version of Visual Studio you're using the edit packages.

16. Click Edit Script to open the Visual Studio Tools for Applications design environment. You will use this Script Task to generate a random product identifier.

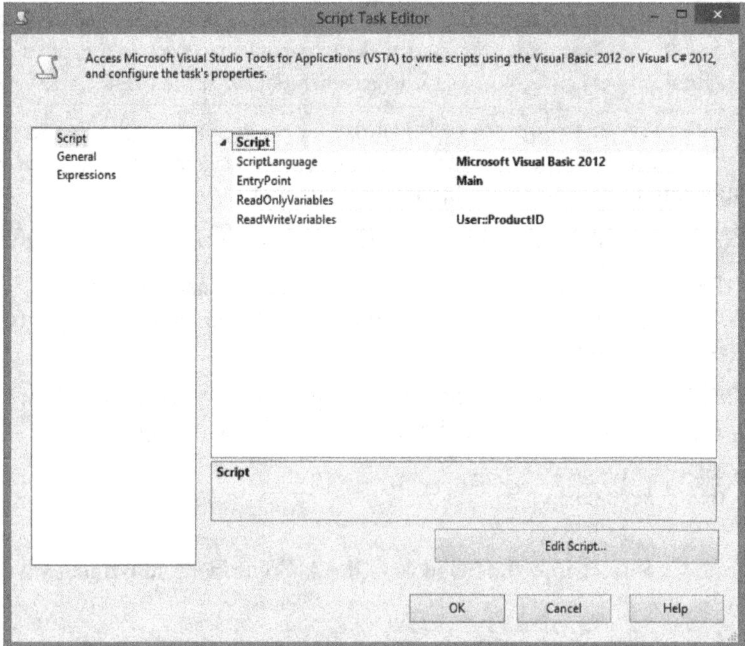

FIGURE 18-13

17. Replace `Public Sub Main` with the following code:

```
Public Sub Main()
 Randomize()
 Dts.Variables("User::ProductID").Value = _
   CInt(Int((900 * Rnd()) + 1))
 Dts.TaskResult = ScriptResults.Success
End Sub
```

18. Close the Visual Studio script design environment and then click OK to accept the changes to the Script Task.

19. After setting up the script to get the inventory level, you need to check that value. Do this by adding an Execute SQL Task named Check Inventory Level to the Inventory Query Simulator.

20. Drag a Precedence Constraint from Generate ProductID to Check Inventory Level.

21. Double-click the Check Inventory Level Task to open the Execute SQL Task Editor.

22. Find the Connection Manager for the AdventureWorks database in the list of connections and change the `SQLStatement` property to `usp_GetReorderQuantity`. This task will call the `usp_GetReorderQuantity` with two parameters, set on the Parameter Mapping window: `ProductID` and `ReorderQuantity` as described in the following table. The `ResultSet` property should be set to `None` because you are using an output parameter to get the `ReorderQuantity` value from the stored procedure. The General pane of the Execute SQL Task Editor should now look like Figure 18-14.

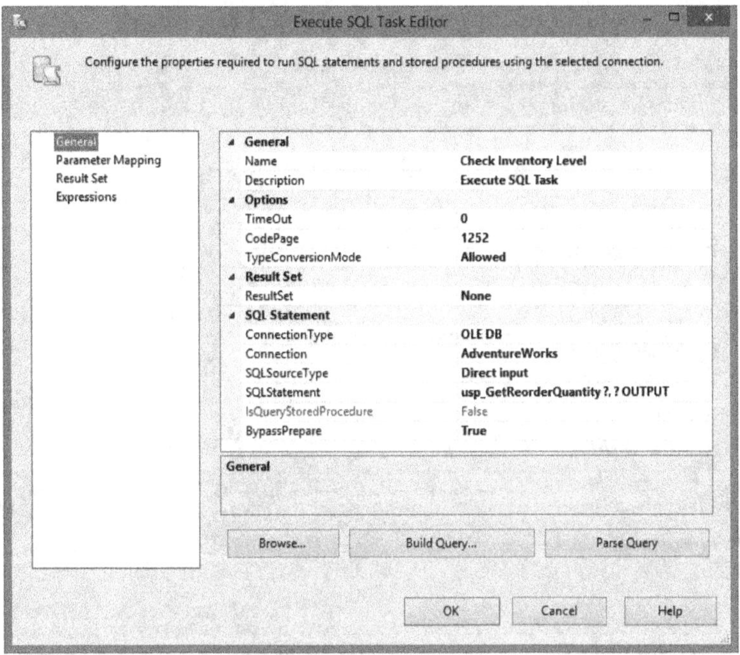

FIGURE 18-14

23. On the Parameter Mapping pane, set up the parameters, as shown in the following table:

VARIABLE NAME	DIRECTION	DATA TYPE	PARAMETER NAME
`User::ProductID`	Input	LONG	0
`User::ReorderQuantity`	Output	LONG	1

24. Click OK to accept the configuration. As described earlier, set the `MaximumErrorCount` property of the Check Inventory Level Task to 9999 using the Properties window.

25. Add another Execute SQL Task and name it **Insert Warning**. This task will be used to insert a row into the InventoryWarning table whenever the current inventory is less than the established reorder point for a particular product. Connect Check Inventory Level to Insert Warning.

26. Double-click the precedence constraint and set the `Evaluation operation` property to Expression and Constraint. The `Expression` property should be `@ReorderQuantity > 0` and the `Value` property should be left at Success, as shown in see Figure 18-15.

27. Once configured, click OK to accept the changes to the precedence constraint.

28. Next, you will set up the Warning task. Double-click the Insert Warning Task and set the ConnectionType to OLE DB. Choose the AdventureWorks Connection Manager from the Connection list, and click the ellipsis next to SQLStatement to add the following query to the Enter SQL Query dialog:

```
INSERT INTO InventoryWarning (ProductID, ReorderQuantity)
SELECT ?, ? OUTPUT
```

Precedence Constraint Editor

A precedence constraint defines the workflow between two executables. The precedence constraint can be based on a combination of the execution results and the evaluation of expressions.

Constraint options

Evaluation operation: Expression and Constraint

Value: Success

Expression: @ReorderQunatity > 0 ... Test

Multiple constraints

If the constrained task has multiple constraints, you can choose how the constraints interoperate to control the execution of the constrained task.

(•) Logical AND. All constraints must evaluate to True

( ) Logical OR. One constraint must evaluate to True

OK Cancel Help

FIGURE 18-15

29. Click OK to accept the command. On the Parameter Mapping pane, set up two parameters, as shown in the following table. In this case they will both be input parameters.

VARIABLE NAME	DIRECTION	DATA TYPE	PARAMETER NAME
`User::ProductID`	Input	LONG	0
`User::ReorderQuantity`	Input	LONG	1

30. Click OK to accept the configuration. The package should now resemble Figure 18-16.

When you run the package, sometimes the Check Inventory Level Task will fail. The Generate ProductID script will not always result in a valid ProductID. When that happens, the stored procedure will raise an error and cause the Check Inventory Level Task to fail. Because the `FailParentOnFailure` and `FailPackageOnFailure` properties are set to False by default and the `MaximumErrorCount` property is set to 9999 on the task and parent containers, the package will continue to run through the simulation even after a failure of this task.

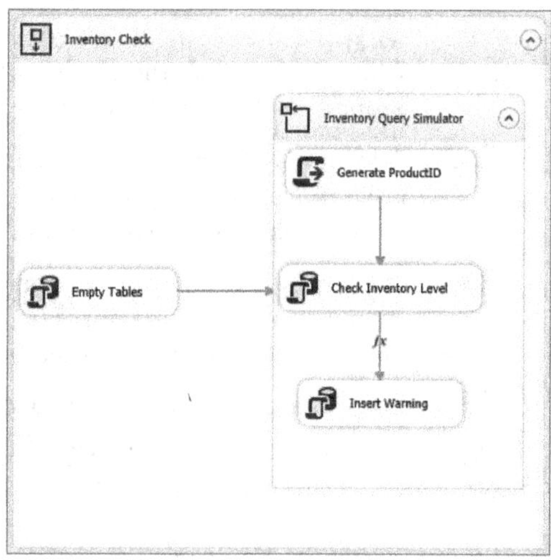

FIGURE 18-16

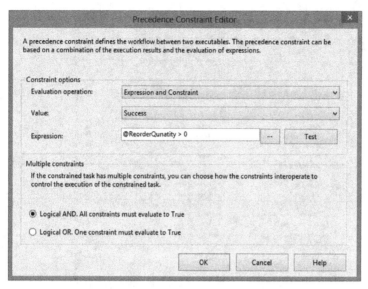

Notice that when the Check Inventory Level Task fails, it will be marked with a red circle with an "X"; but the simulation will continue running and the loop will cause the icon to change between the red circle and a green circle with a check mark. To view what is going on as the package runs, click the Progress tab. This is also a fantastic troubleshooting tool, providing detailed information about each step. Once the package completes and debugging is stopped, you can continue to view the information on the Execution Results tab.

After running the package, you can view the results by querying the InventoryWarning table to see the rows that were inserted when the `User::ReorderQuantity` variable was greater than 0. Run the following query in SQL Server Management Studio:

```
SELECT * FROM InventoryWarning
```

Using the OnError Event Handler Event

The package you just created is almost guaranteed to generate some errors at the Check Inventory Level Task every time it runs. You could add a task connected to the Check Inventory Level Task with the precedence constraint set to Failure, but in this case you will create an event handler to add a row to the MissingProductID table each time the Check Inventory Level Task fails.

1. Click the Event Handlers tab. Because you can have a large number of event handlers in a package, you must select the object and the event from the dropdown lists. Clicking the Executable dropdown enables you to see the package objects in a hierarchy. An example is shown in Figure 18-17, where the package has a child, Inventory Check, which has children Empty Tables, Inventory Query Simulator, and so on.

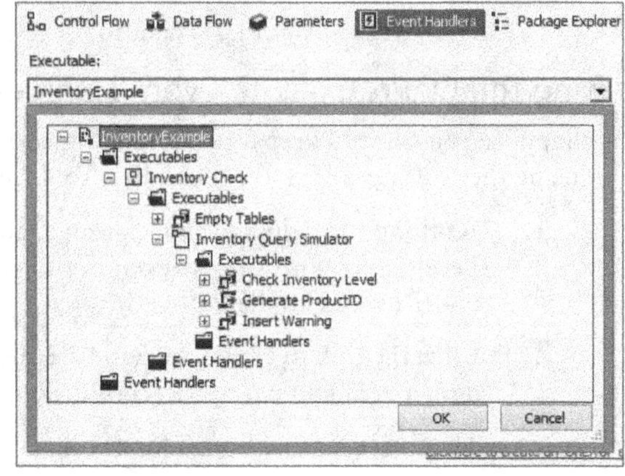

FIGURE 18-17

2. Select Check Inventory Level and click OK to close the list.
3. Choose OnError in the Event Handler list if it isn't there by default. You must click the link "Click here to create an 'OnError' event handler for executable 'Check Inventory Level'" to create the new event handler. The screen will change to a design area very much like the Control Flow tab. You can now drag any Control Flow Level Task or Container to the design area. In this case, you will add an Execute SQL Task that adds a row to the MissingProductID table whenever the Check Inventory Level Task fails.

   Event handlers can be as simple or as complex as needed. All functionality available at the Control Flow level is available at the Event Handler level, including the capability to add an event handler to an event handler.

4. Drag an Execute SQL Task to the Event Handler design area and name it **Insert Missing ProductID**.

5. In the properties of the task, set the Connection Type to OLE DB and select the AdventureWorks Connection Manager.
6. Enter the following statement into the Enter SQL Query window under the `SQLStatement` property:

```
INSERT INTO MissingProductID (ProductID) SELECT ?
```

7. Click OK to accept the query and then switch to the Parameter Mapping pane.
8. Add one parameter with the properties shown in the following table:

VARIABLE NAME	DIRECTION	DATA TYPE	PARAMETER NAME
`User::ProductID`	Input	Long	0

9. Click OK to accept the configuration.

Now, when you run the package, the new event handler will fire whenever the Check Inventory Level Task raises an error. You can query the MissingProductID table to see the results by running the following query in SQL Server Management Studio:

```
SELECT * from MissingProductID
```

Using the OnPreExecute Event Handler Event

Suppose you want to keep a record of all the ProductID numbers that were tested. You can do this using the `OnPreExecute` event handler. To do so, follow these steps:

1. Working from the previous package, add another event handler to the Check Inventory Level Task. With Check Inventory Level selected in the Executable list, select `OnPreExecute` under Event Handler.
2. Click the link to create the handler, and add an Execute SQL Task to the Event Handler design area and name it **Record ProductID**.

   The Execute SQL Task Editor will store the ProductID numbers.
3. Double-click the Execute SQL Task to open the Execute SQL Task Editor. Use the OLE DB AdventureWorks Connection Manager, and add this statement to the `SQLStatement` property by typing in the property text box or using the Enter SQL Query dialog:

```
INSERT INTO InventoryCheck (ProductID) SELECT ?
```

4. Add one parameter on the Parameter Mapping pane with exactly the same properties as the one added to the `OnError` event task, as the following table shows.

VARIABLE NAME	DIRECTION	DATA TYPE	PARAMETER NAME
`User::ProductID`	Input	LONG	0

5. Click OK to accept the configuration and run the package.

6. Once execution of the package has completed, go back to SQL Server Management Studio to see the results by running the following queries:

```
SELECT * FROM InventoryCheck
SELECT * FROM MissingProductID
SELECT * FROM InventoryWarning
```

The InventoryCheck table should have one row for each ProductID that was generated. This row was entered at the Check Inventory Level `OnPreExecute` event — in other words, before the task actually executed. The MissingProductID table should have several rows, one for each ProductID that caused the `usp_GetReorderQuantity` stored procedure to raise an error. These rows were added at the Check Inventory Level `OnError` event. Finally, the InventoryWarning table will have some rows if the inventory level of any of the products was low. These rows were added at the Control Flow level.

Event Handler Inheritance

Events handlers will inherit the events of their children. This means that if you have a container, and the container has an event handler `OnError` event defined on it, then if a child task that exists in the container errors, the event handler of the container will fire. This is sometimes referred to as the event "bubbling" or traveling up from child task to parent container. As mentioned already, the highest level executable is the package itself. Therefore, if you define an event handler event at the package level, then whenever that event occurs in the package, the event handler will fire.

The same inheritance occurs if a parent package executes a child package using the Execute Package Task. It will appear as though duplicated events are fired, but it is simply the event handler for both the child package and the parent package handling the event. You can prevent this phenomenon by setting the `Propagate` variable to false in the child package.

To demonstrate this with the example inventory package, you'll move the `OnError` event handler from the task to a parent container:

1. Using the package created in the previous section, navigate to the Check Inventory Level `OnError` event handler.
2. Copy the Insert Missing ProductID Task, and paste it into a new `OnError` event handler for the Inventory Check Container.
3. You can delete the original event handler and run your package again. You can see that the errors are now trapped at the Inventory Check Container level by viewing the error handler as the package runs. The `OnError` event bubbled up from the task to the For Loop Container to the Inventory Check Container.

What would happen if you had an `OnError` event handler on both the Check Inventory Level Task and the Sequence Container? Surprisingly, both will fire when an error is raised at the Check Inventory Level Task. This could cause some unexpected results. For example, suppose you had an error handler at the parent container to perform a particular task, such as sending an e-mail message. An error in a child container that you expected to be handled at that level would also cause the parent's `OnError` handler to execute. To prevent this from happening, you can set a system variable, `Propagate`, to False at the child task's Error Handler level. To demonstrate this, follow the steps:

1. Add the `OnError` event handler back to the Check Inventory Level Task.
2. Once again, create an event handler for the Check Inventory Level `OnError` event. You can copy and paste the Insert Missing ProductID Task from the Inventory Check `OnError` event handler.
3. While still working in the Check Inventory Level `OnError` Event design area, click the design area and open the Variables window.
4. If the system variables are not visible, click the Grid Options icon and check the `Show system variables` property. As shown in Figure 18-18, make sure that the `Propagate` property is set to True, the default.

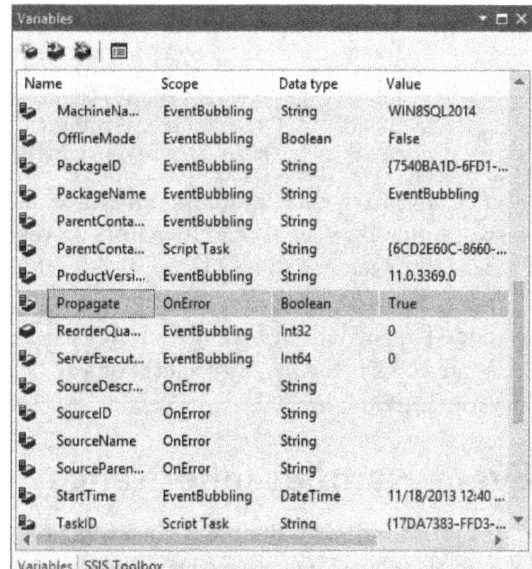

FIGURE 18-18

5. Run the package. While it is running, navigate to each of the error handlers to watch as they execute. Notice that both `OnError` events will fire and the MissingProductID table ends up with two rows for every invalid ProductID.
6. After execution of the package is complete, change the `Propagate` property to False (use the Variables window). Now only the Check Inventory Level `OnError` event handler will execute. The `OnError` event will no longer bubble to the parent containers.
7. Run the package again. This time, you should find the expected behavior; the error is handled only at the Check Inventory Level Task.

> **NOTE** *When the* `Propagate` *property is set to False on an* `OnEvent` *handler, you no longer need to modify the* `MaximumErrorCount` *property of the parent containers from the default setting of 1 to keep the package running after the error.*

BREAKPOINTS

Many programmers use breakpoints to debug programs, viewing the value of variables and following the flow of the logic as they step through the source code. SSIS enables you to set breakpoints on the package or any Control Flow Task or Container. You can also set breakpoints in Script Task code just like most programming environments.

Using the Inventory Example package created in the previous section, follow these steps to enable and use breakpoints.

1. Right-click the Inventory Query Simulator For Loop Container, and choose Edit Breakpoints from the pop-up menu. The Set Breakpoints dialog opens, displaying a list of possible events at which you can set a breakpoint, as shown in Figure 18-19.

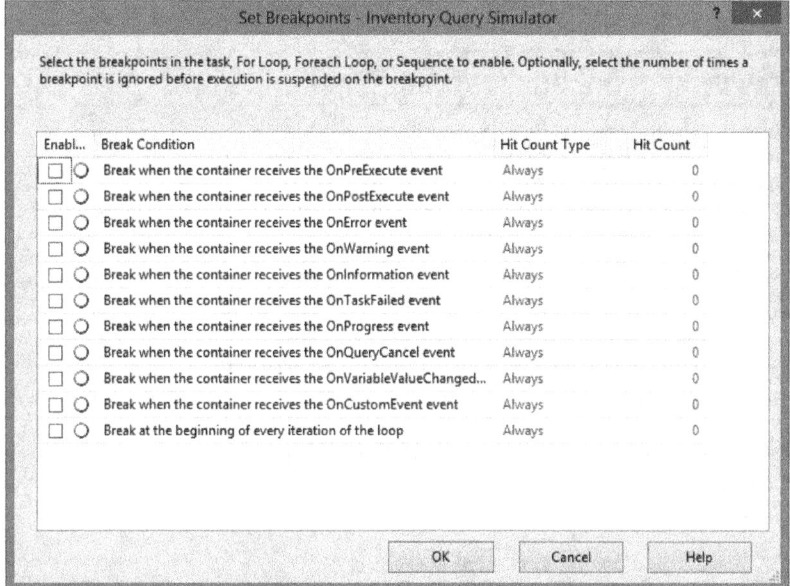

FIGURE 18-19

2. Enable the last item, "Break at the beginning of every iteration of the loop," which is available only for looping containers. Hit Count Type has the following options:

   - Always
   - Hit Count Equals
   - Hit Count Greater Than or Equal To
   - Hit Count Multiple.

   The last item will suspend execution when the hit count is equal to a multiple of the value set for Hit Count. For example, setting the Hit Count Type to Hit Count Multiple and the Hit Count to 5 will cause the execution to be suspended every fifth time through the loop.

3. Go ahead and set the type to Hit Count Multiple and the Hit Count to 5, as in Figure 18-20.

4. Click OK. The container will now have a red circle in its top-right corner specifying that a breakpoint has been set (see Figure 18-21, though you can't see the color of the circle in the figure here).

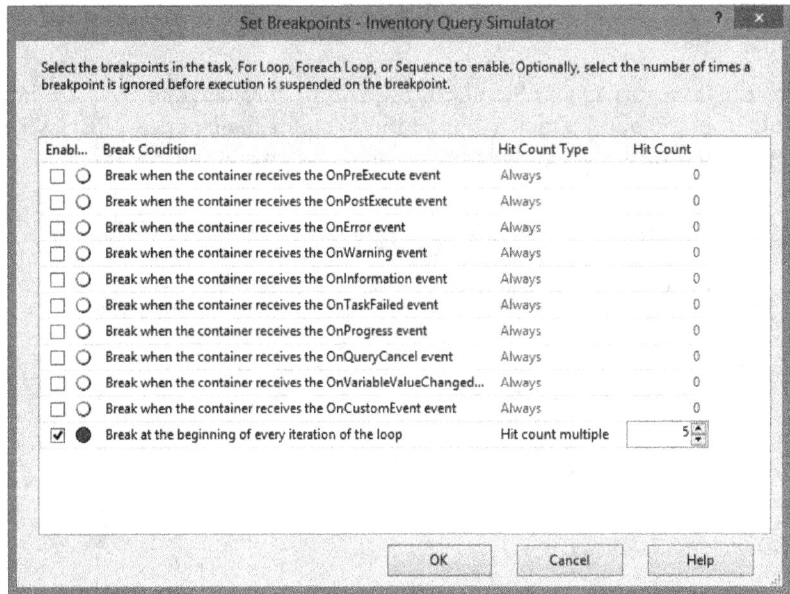

FIGURE 18-20

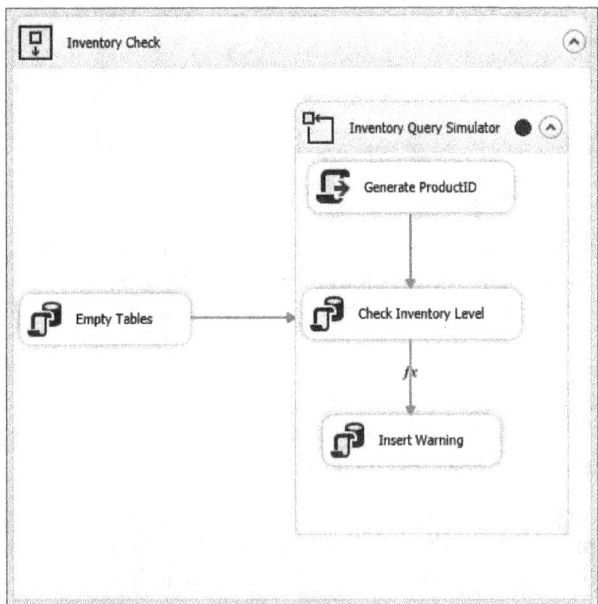

FIGURE 18-21

5. Run the package. When the Hit Count reaches 5, the execution will stop and the red dot will change to a red circle with an arrow. You can now view the values of the variables in the Locals window. If the Locals window is not visible, select it by choosing Debug ➪ Windows ➪ Locals. Expand Variables, and look for the `User` variables that were set up

for the package (see Figure 18-22). `User::Count` should have a value of `5`. If the value of a variable cannot be completely viewed in the window, such as a long string, you can mouse over it to see the entire value in a tooltip.

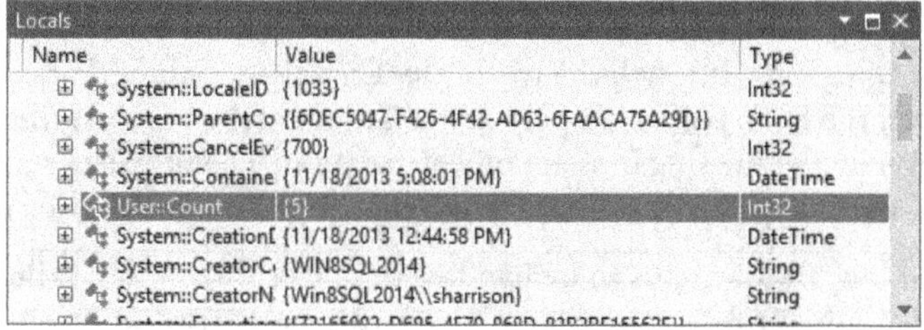

FIGURE 18-22

6. Restart the package, and it will run until the Hit Count reaches 10.

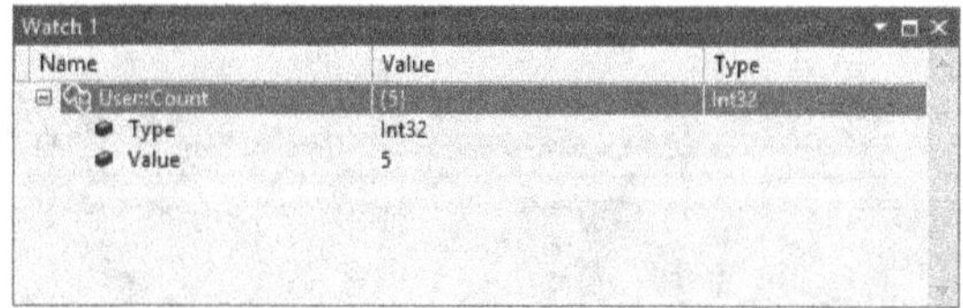

FIGURE 18-23

There are also watch windows to make it easier to view the variables you are interested in viewing. Open the Locals watch window by selecting Debug ➪ Windows ➪ Watch ➪ WatchLocals. In the first row of the Watch 1 window, type **`User::Count`** in the Name field, as shown in Figure 18-23. You can view the values of all system and user variables from the Locals window. You can also add variables to the watch windows by right-clicking the variables you want to add in the Locals window and choosing Add Watch.

Another very helpful feature is the capability to change the value of variables on the fly. In the watch window, expand `User::Count`. Right-click and choose Edit Value. Change the value to 40 and restart the package. The next time the execution is suspended, the value should be at 45.

The value of some system variables may also be interesting to view and change. For example, you might modify the value of a task property as the package executes. You can use breakpoints and the watch windows to view the value to confirm it is what you expected or to change the value manually to correct it.

An additional debugging window known as the Call Stack window may also help troubleshoot packages. This window shows a list of the tasks that have executed up to the breakpoint. This can be very useful when trying to figure out a very complex workflow.

The capability to set breakpoints on the tasks and containers will save you a lot of time while troubleshooting your packages.

> **NOTE** *Data Viewers are similar to breakpoints, but they are used to view data as the package executes. See Chapter 4 for more information on how you can use Data Viewers in your packages.*

ERROR ROWS

Error rows have been briefly touched upon in several chapters, including Chapter 4, Chapter 14, and Chapter 16. However, a chapter on SSIS error and event handling would be only partially complete without a further discussion on handling errors.

Error rows are handled in the Data Flow through the use of the Error Row Configuration properties. These properties tell the Data Flow Components what to do when a row fails an operation, such as a data conversion, a missing lookup, or a truncation. The properties are found in sources, transformations, and destinations, depending on whether an error can occur or not.

The basic error properties window allows errors to be handled in one of three ways: failure of the Data Flow Task, ignoring the failure, or redirecting the row. Furthermore, truncation errors can be handled separately from conversion errors. Figure 18-24 shows the Error Output property page of an OLE DB Source.

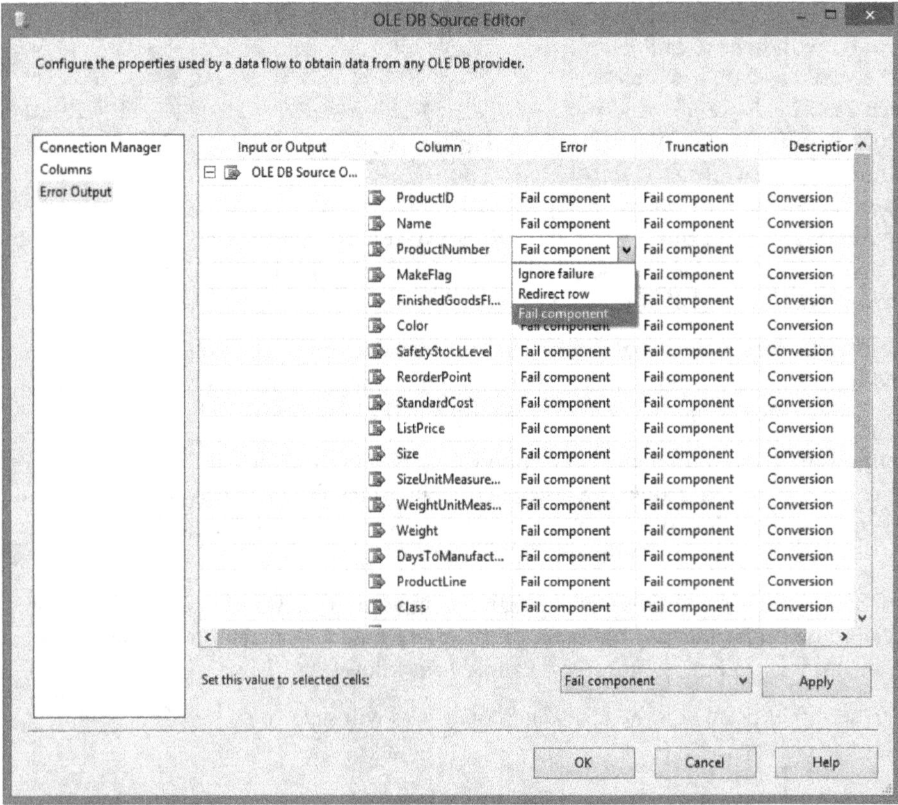

FIGURE 18-24

Figure 18-24 also shows the dropdown selection of the ProductNumber column that defines how the SSIS Data Flow engine should handle an error row for the selected column. The following table clarifies the implications of the error handling section.

ERROR HANDLER	DESCRIPTION
Fail Component	When Fail Component is chosen for a column or the component and an error occurs (such as a conversion from a source to the Data Flow pipeline), the Data Flow will stop and fail, and any `OnError` events will fire for the Data Flow Task.
Redirect Row	Redirect Row means that when a row reaches an error for any column marked to be redirected, the entire row is sent out the red error path output and the Data Flow will not fail. If the red error path output is not used, then the row will be tossed out of the Data Flow. When Redirect Row is selected for any column (error or truncation), be aware that when the condition is met, the entire row will be redirected out the red error path output.
Ignore Failure	Ignore Failure simply means that the error will be ignored. If the error is in a source or transformation such as a conversion or a missing lookup record, then the error column values will be set to `NULL`. If the error is a truncation, then the value will be sent downstream with just the partially truncated value. Be aware that when you are dealing with destinations, an ignore failure for a truncation or other error will ignore the entire row, not just the error column.

To demonstrate how to use the error row handling, create a new package in SQL Server Data Tools (SSDT) with an OLE DB connection to the AdventureWorks database. In a new Data Flow Task, follow these steps:

1. Begin by running the following script (`ProSSIS\Scripts\Ch18_ProSSIS\Scripts.sql`) against the AdventureWorks database to create the tables used later by this package:

```
CREATE TABLE [UpdatedProducts] (
   [ProductID] int,
   [Name] nvarchar(50),
   [ProductNumber] nvarchar(25),
   [MakeFlag] bit,
   [FinishedGoodsFlag] bit,
   [Color] nvarchar(15),
   [SafetyStockLevel] smallint,
   [ReorderPoint] smallint,
   [StandardCost] money,
   [ListPrice] money,
   [Size] nvarchar(5),
   [SizeUnitMeasureCode] nvarchar(3),
   [WeightUnitMeasureCode] nvarchar(3),
   [Weight] numeric(8,2),
   [DaysToManufacture] int,
   [ProductLine] nvarchar(2),
   [Class] nvarchar(2),
   [Style] nvarchar(2),
   [ProductSubcategoryID] int,
   [ProductModelID] int,
```

```
    [SellStartDate] datetime,
    [SellEndDate] datetime,
    [DiscontinuedDate] datetime,
    [rowguid] uniqueidentifier,
    [ModifiedDate] datetime,
    [Size_Numeric] numeric(18,0)
)
GO
```

2. Drag an OLE DB Source to the Data Flow and configure it to use the AdventureWorks connection for the OLE DB Connection Manager. Keep the default Data access mode option of "Table or view"; in the "Name of the table or the view" dropdown, choose the [Production].[Product] table from the list.

3. Drag a Data Conversion Component onto the Data Flow region, and then connect the OLE DB Source to the Data Conversion.

4. Edit the Data Conversion Component and add a new row based on the input column Size. Name the output alias **Size_Numeric** and configure the new data type to be `numeric [DT_NUMERIC]`, as shown in Figure 18-25.

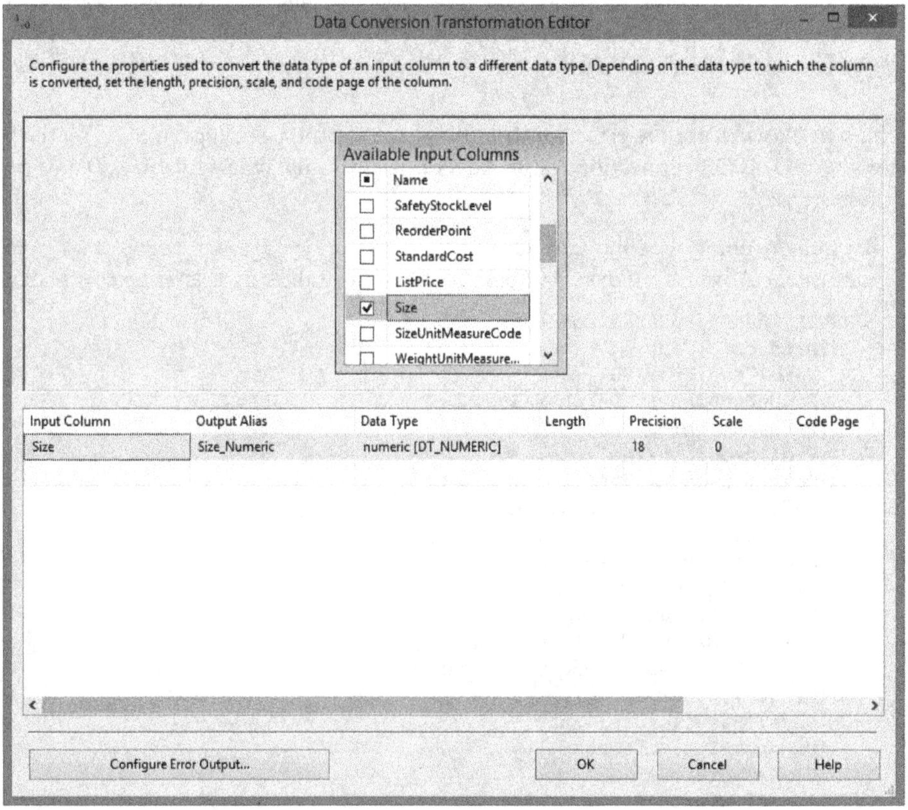

FIGURE 18-25

The Data Conversion Component will create a new column in the Data Flow called Size_Numeric with a numeric data type, but the original Size column will remain, with the Unicode String data type with a length of 5.

5. Within the Data Conversion Component, click the Configure Error Output button in the bottom-left corner of the transformation, which will bring up the Configure Error Output window. Because only one column is defined in the Data Conversion Transformation, only one column is displayed for changing the error settings.

6. Change the Error value to Redirect Row for the Size_Numeric column, as Figure 18-26 demonstrates.

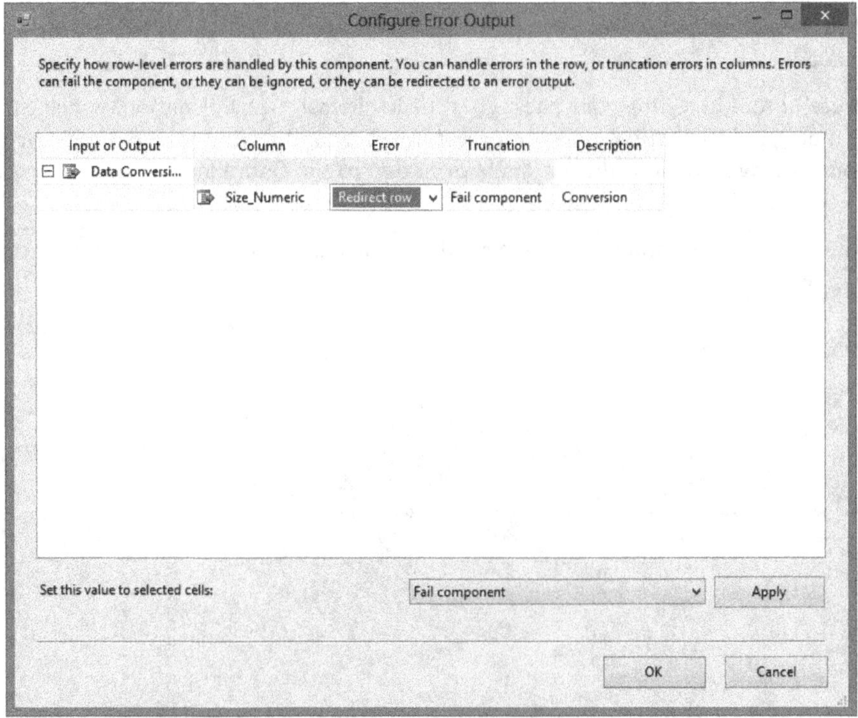

FIGURE 18-26

7. Return to the Data Flow by selecting OK in both the Configure Error Output and the Data Conversion Transformation Editor.

   The Data Conversion Component now has a yellow exclamation mark on it, indicating that an error row was configured to be redirected, but the red error path has not yet been used.

8. To fix this warning, you will set up an alternative path to direct those rows. Drag a Derived Column Transformation to the Data Flow and then connect the red error path from the Data Conversion to the new Derived Column Transformation. When you do this, the Configure Error Output window will automatically pop up for the Data Conversion Transformation. This is an alternate method to set the error handling for a failure. Click OK to return to the Data Flow.

9. Edit the Derived Column Transformation and add a new column named **Size_Numeric**. For the Expression field, type in the following code to add a 0 value to the records that failed the conversion in the prior transformation:

```
(DT_NUMERIC,18,0) 0
```

10. After saving the Derived Column Transformation, drag a Union All Transformation to the Data Flow and then connect both the blue data path output from the Data Conversion Transformation and the blue data path output from the Derived Column Transformation to the Union All Transformation.

11. Double-click the Union All Transformation to bring up its editor, and scroll down to the bottom of the column list. Multi-select both the ErrorCode and the ErrorColumn columns if they exist in the list, and then press Delete on your keyboard. Click OK to save the changes.

12. A useful tool in testing your package is the Multicast Transformation, which can be used as a placeholder destination as you are developing and testing your package. Before testing your package, add a Multicast Transformation to the Data Flow connected to the output of the Union All.

13. Run your package and observe the results. Your Data Flow execution will look similar to Figure 18-27.

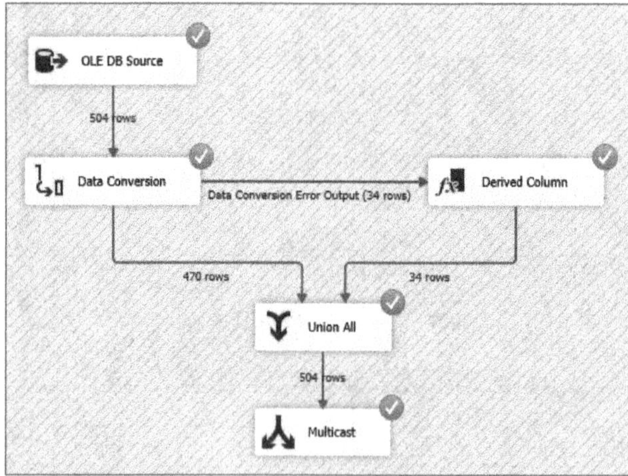

FIGURE 18-27

Note that some of the rows are sent to the Derived Column Transformation but are brought back together with the main Data Flow rows through the Union All Transformation. At this point you have not added a destination, so the next step in this example is to land the data to a new destination table, where you can also handle errors.

14. Stop the package execution and replace the Multicast Transformation with an OLE DB Destination. In the editor, confirm that the AdventureWorks connection is listed in the OLE DB Connection Manager dropdown and change the data access mode to "Table or view."

Assign the data to load into the table UpdatedProducts that you created at the beginning of this exercise. On the Mappings property page, ensure that the default map of all the input columns from the Data Flow to the destination table columns based on name and data type looks accurate. Click OK to save the changes.

In the Data Flow designer, notice that the OLE DB Destination has a yellow exclamation point on it, and when you hover the mouse over it (or display the error window), it indicates that there may be a truncation error for the Name column going from a length of 50 to a length of 21. To finish this example, you will now redirect the error rows to a flat file.

15. Drag a Flat File Destination onto the Data Flow and connect the red error path output from the OLE DB Destination onto the Flat File Destination. When the Configure Error Output window pops up, change the Error handling dropdown to Redirect Row and click OK to save your changes.
16. Edit the Flat File Destination and click the New button next to the Flat File Connection Manager dropdown. When prompted, leave the Flat File Format selected on Delimited and click OK, which will bring up the Flat File Connection Manager Editor.
17. Type **C:\ProSSIS\Files\Truncated_Names.txt** in the File name text box and then click OK to save the connection properties. You will be returned to the Flat File Destination Editor.
18. To finish, click the Mappings page in the Flat File Destination Editor, which will automatically map the columns from the error path to the flat file. Click OK to close the Destination Editor.

When you run your package, your results should look like what is shown in Figure 18-28.

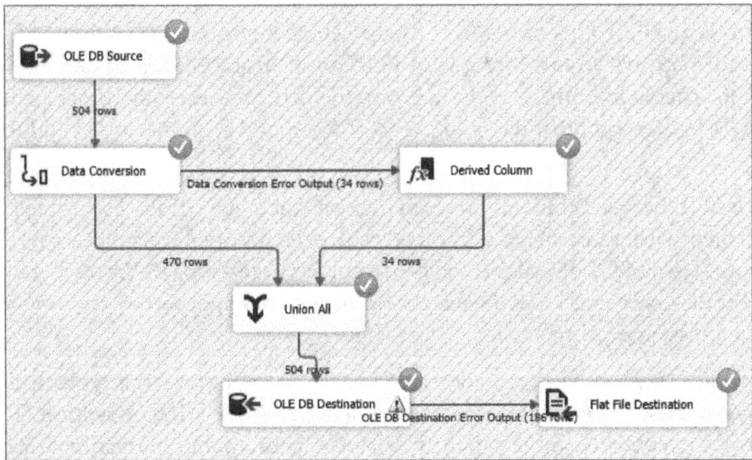

FIGURE 18-28

The rows with the Name column truncation were sent to the flat file. You can check your results by opening the flat file in your `C:\ProSSIS\Files` folder, which will show that the full names were added to the flat file. As noted earlier, if you had set the OLE DB Destination error to Ignore Failure, the entire error row would be ignored, not just the column value.

LOGGING

Logging is an important part of any data process, because it gives administrators and developers insight into what transpired during a process, with the following benefits:

- Error triage to help identify as quickly as possible what was the point and cause of the failure, such as the failure of a Lookup Component to match a record
- Root cause analysis so that a solution can be put in place to prevent a failure situation in the future
- Performance metrics such as package and execution times so that negative performance trends can be observed and addressed before the performance impact causes an ETL failure

SSIS contains built-in logging features that capture execution details about your packages. Logging enables you to record information about events you are interested in as the package runs. The logging information can be stored in a text or XML file, to a SQL Server table, to the Windows event log, or to a file suitable for Profiler.

Logging can be enabled for all or some tasks and containers and for all or any events. Tasks and containers can inherit the settings from parent containers. Multiple logs can be set up, and a task or event can log to any or all logs configured. You can also control which pieces of information are recorded for any event.

Logging Providers

SSIS includes several default log providers. These providers are selected in the Provider type combo box and are defined as follows:

- **SSIS Log Provider for Text Files:** This provider is used to store log information to a CSV file on the file system. It requires you to configure a File Connection object that defines the location of the file. Storing log information in a text file is the easiest way to persist a package's execution. Text files are portable, and the CSV format is a simple-to-use industry-wide standard.
- **SSIS Log Provider for SQL Server Profiler:** This provider produces a SQL Profiler trace file. The file must be specified with a `trc` file extension so that you can open it using the SQL Profiler diagnostic tool. Using SQL Profiler trace files is an easy way for DBAs to view log information. Using Profiler, you can view the execution of the package step by step, even replaying the steps in a test environment.
- **SSIS Log Provider for SQL Server:** This provider sends package log events to a table in the specified SQL Server database. The database is defined using an OLE DB Connection. The first time this package is executed, a table called sysssislog is created automatically. Storing log information in a SQL Server database inherits the benefits of persisting information in a relational database system. You can easily retrieve log information for analysis across multiple package executions.
- **SSIS Log Provider for Windows Event Log:** This provider sends log information to the Application event store. The entries created are under the Source name SQLISPackage110. No additional configuration is required for this provider. Logging package execution to the

Windows event log is possibly the easiest way to store log events. The Windows event log is easy to view and can be viewed remotely if required.

- **SSIS Log Provider for XML files:** This provider stores log information in a specified XML file on the file system. The file is specified through a File Connection object. Make sure you save the file with an `xml` file extension. Logging events to XML inherits the advantages of the XML specification. XML files are very portable across systems and can be validated against a schema definition.

Log Events

Once you have configured the log providers you wish to employ, you must define what events in the package to log. This is done in the Details tab of the Configure SSIS Logs dialog, shown in Figure 18-29. To enable an event to be logged, check the box next to its name. For instance, in Figure 18-29, the `OnError` event for the package has been selected for logging. By selecting other containers on the left side of the dialog, you can select additional events down to an individual task or Data Flow event level. To select all events at once, check the box in the header row of the table. By selecting individual containers in the tree view on the left, you can configure the logging of events on an individual task level. When you configure logging at the task level, the special events exposed by a task can additionally be included in the log.

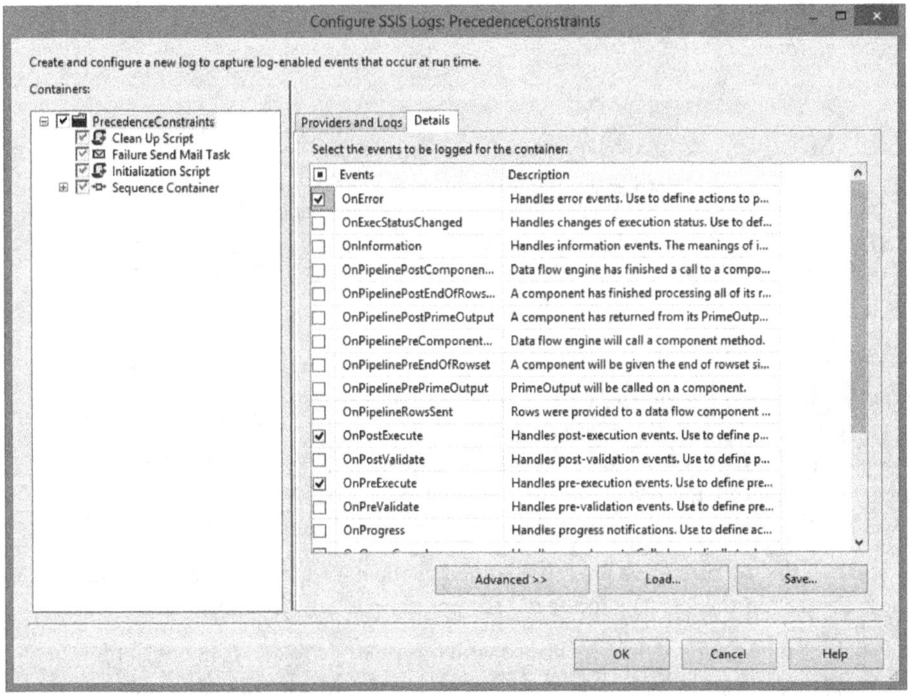

FIGURE 18-29

You can see how SSIS logging works by working with a previously created package.

1. Open one of the packages you created earlier in this chapter or any package with several Control Flow Tasks.
2. From the menu, navigate to SSIS ➪ Logging to open the Configure SSIS Logs dialog. To enable logging, you must first check the box next to the package name in the left pane (see Figure 18-30); in this case, the package is named "10Logging."

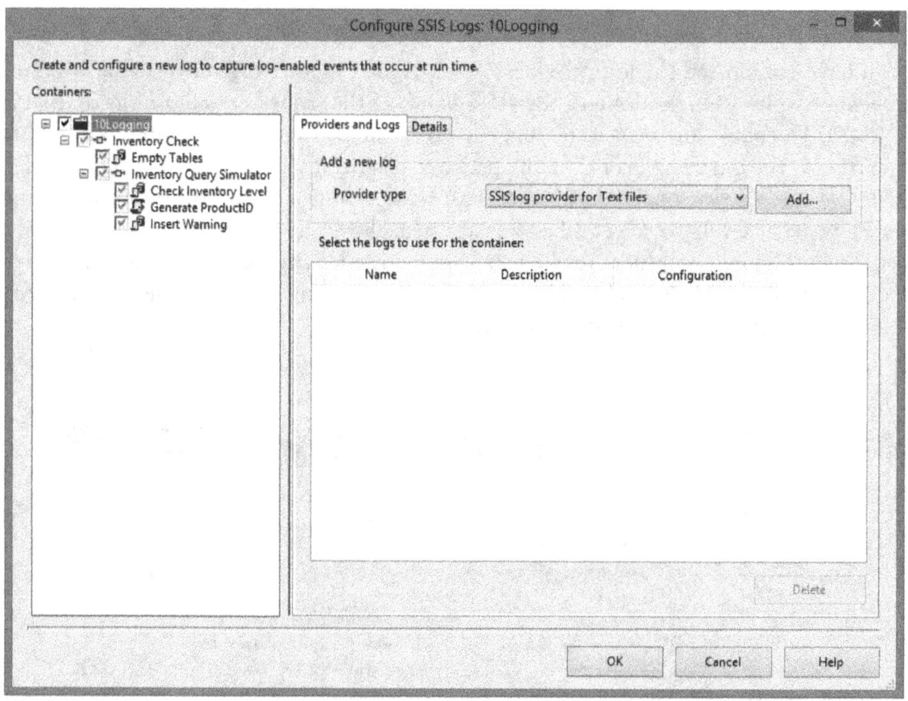

FIGURE 18-30

> **NOTE** *Notice that the checkboxes for the child objects in the package are greyed out. This means that they will inherit the logging properties of the package. You can click in any checkbox to uncheck an object. Clicking again to check the box enables you to set up logging properties specific to that task or container.*

3. To get started, the log providers must be defined at the package level. Select package in the TreeView control on the left (the top level) so that the package is highlighted.
4. In the Provider type dropdown list, choose which type of provider you would like to configure; as an example, choose SSIS Log Provider for XML files. Click Add to add the provider to the list. Click the dropdown under Configuration and choose <New Connection>.

5. Once the File Connection Manager Editor opens, set the `Usage Type` property to Create File. Type **`C:\ProSSIS\Files\Log.xml`** as the path for the XML file or click Browse to find the path for the XML file location (see Figure 18-31).

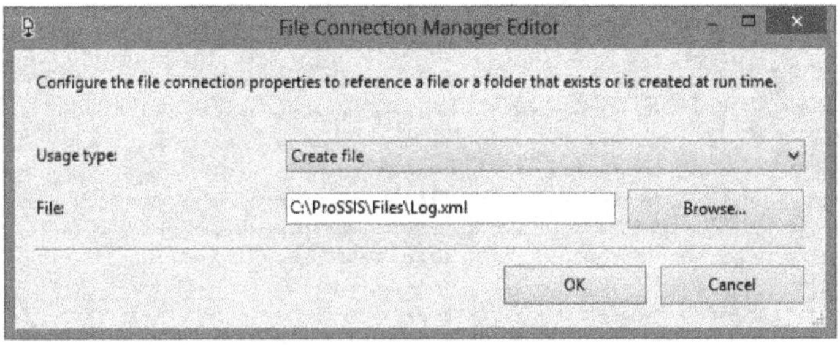

File Connection Manager Editor

Configure the file connection properties to reference a file or a folder that exists or is created at run time.

Usage type: Create file

File: C:\ProSSIS\Files\Log.xml Browse...

OK Cancel

FIGURE 18-31

6. Click OK to accept the configuration and dismiss the dialog. In the Configure SSIS Logs dialog, you should now see the new log provider and its properties. Check the box next to the new logging provider to enable it at the package level. At this point, you can give the log provider a descriptive name if you want, as shown in Figure 18-32.

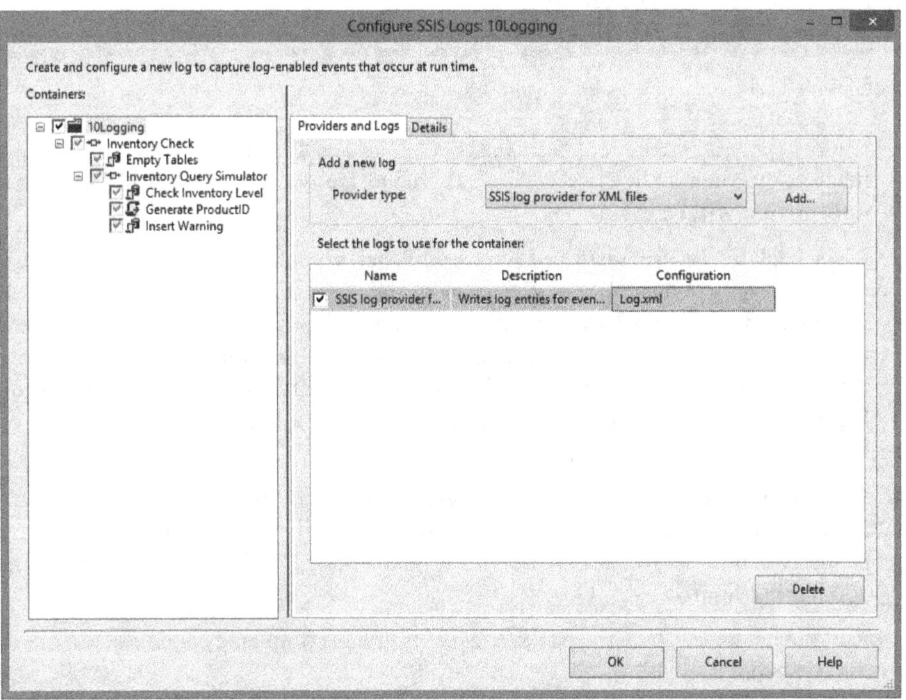

FIGURE 18-32

7. Click the Details tab to view a list of events you can log. If you click Advanced, you will also see a list of possible fields (see Figure 18-33).

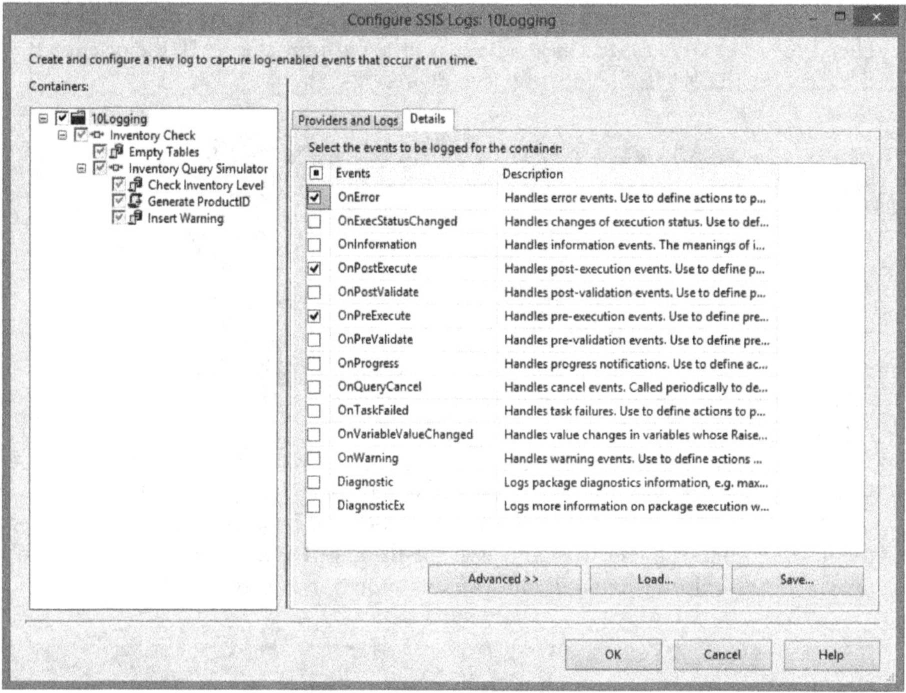

FIGURE 18-33

8. Choose the `OnPreExecute`, `OnPostExecute`, and `OnError` events. Notice that all of the fields are automatically chosen. You can uncheck any fields for which you don't think the information will be useful.

9. Move back to the Providers and Logs tab. When you checked the log provider at the package level (by checking the checkbox at the highest level in the tree view of the left pane), you enabled that log for all components in the package that are set to inherit settings from their parent container. Even if that log provider is chosen for an object that does not inherit the log settings, you can use it to select different events and fields. Once you modify the logging on a parent container, such as a For Loop Container, the child objects will inherit from the container, not the package.

10. When you are satisfied with the logging settings, click OK to close the dialog. If you view the Properties window of a task or container, you will find the `LoggingMode` property. This property can be set to UseParentSetting, Enabled, or Disabled and will match the settings you just configured.

11. Run the package. Once the package execution has completed, open the log file to view the XML (see Figure 18-34).

Setting up logging for a package can be as complicated or as simple as required. It's possible that you may want to log similar information, such as the `OnError` event, for all packages. If so, you can save the settings as a template by clicking Save on the Details tab of the Configure SSIS Logs dialog. Alternatively, you can load a previously saved template by clicking the Load button.

```
<?xml version="1.0"?>
- <dtslogs>
    <dtslog> </dtslog>
    <dtslog> </dtslog>
  - <dtslog>
    - <record>
        <event>PackageStart</event>
        <message>Beginning of package execution. </message>
        <computer>WIN8SQL2014</computer>
        <operator>Win8SQL2014\sharrison</operator>
        <source>10Logging</source>
        <sourceid>{7D44718F-4A02-456C-A20E-75F21FA88DC2}</sourceid>
        <executionid>{018F1BD5-72ED-4C3F-A3AD-6AD9DDD782C2}</executionid>
        <starttime>11/18/2013 6:48:16 PM</starttime>
        <endtime>11/18/2013 6:48:16 PM</endtime>
        <datacode>0</datacode>
        <databytes>0x</databytes>
      </record>
    - <record>
        <event>OnPreExecute</event>
        <message/>
        <computer>WIN8SQL2014</computer>
        <operator>Win8SQL2014\sharrison</operator>
        <source>10Logging</source>
        <sourceid>{7D44718F-4A02-456C-A20E-75F21FA88DC2}</sourceid>
        <executionid>{018F1BD5-72ED-4C3F-A3AD-6AD9DDD782C2}</executionid>
        <starttime>11/18/2013 6:48:16 PM</starttime>
        <endtime>11/18/2013 6:48:16 PM</endtime>
        <datacode>0</datacode>
        <databytes>0x</databytes>
      </record>
    - <record>
```


FIGURE 18-34

Catalog Logging

In addition to logging that can be turned on at a package level, SSIS 2014 introduces another layer of logging as part of the Integration Services catalog. If your SSIS project is set to Project Deployment Model, your deployed packages can utilize the SSIS service. This is especially handy when the package encounters a problem while running in production, rather than during development. In comparison to traditional logging, you do not need to add a logging provider to the package and can apply the catalog logging after the fact. Catalog logging also provides additional information for the administrator after the package has been deployed.

Once your project has been deployed to the server, it will automatically participate in the catalog logging. You can modify the amount of logging that occurs by changing the logging level at execution time. The logging can be set to four levels, as described in the following table.

LOGGING LEVEL	DESCRIPTION
None	Includes minimal logging of executions, tasks, and parameters
Basic	Includes standard logging, as well as execution statistics and messages for specific events, including pre- and post-executions and pre- and post-validations
Performance	Includes standard logging and error and warning events and event contexts for performance tuning purposes
Verbose	Includes all prior logging categories, as well as additional performance tuning and custom task entries

A variety of tables, views, stored procedures, and built-in reports are set up as part of the SSISDB database on whichever database server your Integration Services catalog is created. If you open

Management Studio and go to the Integration Services Catalogs node, you can view the available reports by following these steps:

1. Under the Integration Services Catalogs node, right-click the SSISDB node. If you named your catalog differently, that name will appear here instead.
2. Select Reports ➪ Standard Reports to see the reports that are available to you, as shown in Figure 18-35.

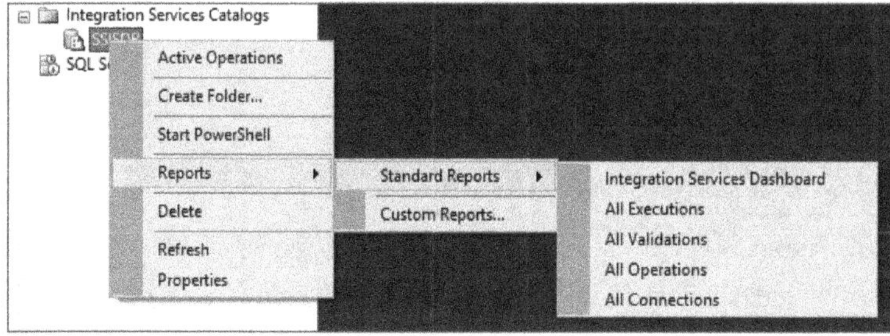

FIGURE 18-35

These reports enable you to see which packages have succeeded or failed or are still running. They break a package down to a more granular level and even show the task or component that could have a problem. For more detailed information on additional reports, please read Chapter 22.

3. If you select the All Execution report, and then click the Overview link on a package you've just run, you will see this granular detail.

By running the last package you created and following these steps, you can see the successes and failures of the package, as shown in Figure 18-36.

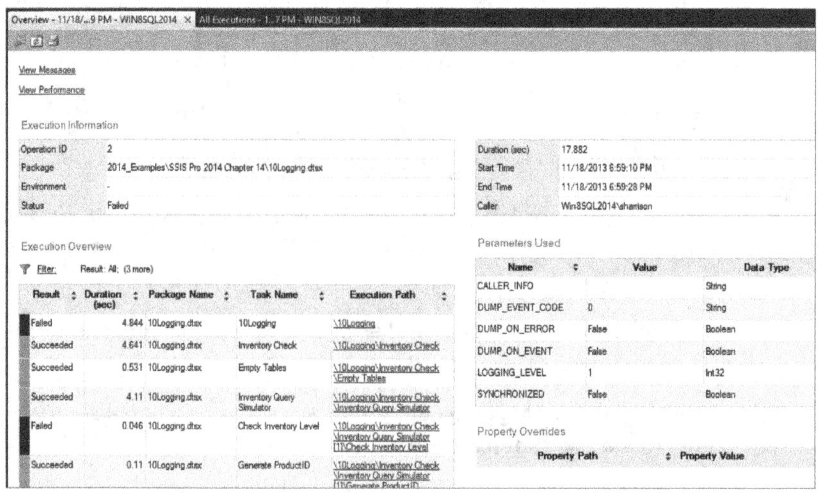

FIGURE 18-36

If you need to see information that is not readily available on the provided reports, you can create your own reports or write your own queries by using the SSISDB database. Figure 18-37 shows a sample of the views that can be used. By utilizing these views, you can investigate the executions of the packages. For example, the `catalog.executions` view provides information on the server's memory information at the start of execution.

4. To create a query that will show you the longest-running objects in your package, you can use the `catalog.executable_statistics` and `catalog.executables` views. Always be sure to filter the query on an execution identifier to limit the amount of information returned. Figure 18-38 shows the final query that returns the top five longest-running objects in the package.

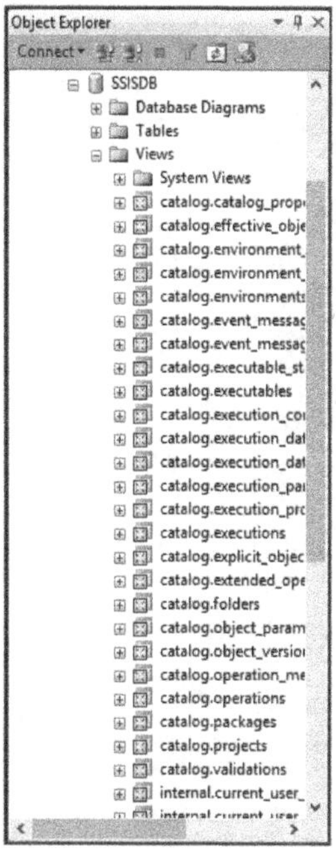

FIGURE 18-37

The addition of catalog logging combined with the package logging previously discussed makes knowing what happened in your package a breeze. You can pull out any set of information you require to help you make your existing or future packages perform better and succeed more often.

SUMMARY

SSIS provides strong support for handling errors during execution and while troubleshooting:

```
select top 5 e.executable_name, es.execution_duration
from catalog.executable_statistics es
left join catalog.executables e on es.executable_id=e.executable_id
where es.execution_id = 2/*put your id here*/
order by execution_duration desc
```

	executable_name	execution_duration
1	10Logging	4844
2	Inventory Check	4641
3	Inventory Query Simulator	4110
4	Empty Tables	531
5	Check Inventory Level	453

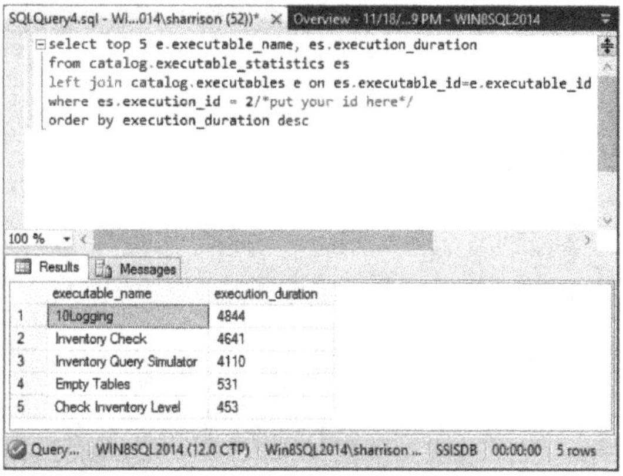

FIGURE 18-38

- During execution you can handle errors gracefully by using the precedence constraints to control what tasks execute when errors occur, by using the event handlers to trap specific events in the package at different levels and run code to perform cleanup and alerting, and by configuring the Data Flow error paths to handle data exceptions gracefully without failing the package.
- While troubleshooting and developing, you can use the breakpoint functionality to pause execution and monitor variable values and package state information, and you can turn on SSIS package logging to capture execution information that provides insight about details such as errors, warnings, and execution times.
- You can determine performance issues or error causes after deploying a package in Project Deployment mode without setting up a logging provider within the package itself. The information logged in the SSIS catalog provides even more information than in prior releases.

Now that the core features of SSIS have been covered, the final chapters focus on advanced topics, including building custom components, integrating SSIS with applications, and managing SSIS externally.

19

Programming and Extending SSIS

WHAT'S IN THIS CHAPTER?

- Examining methods used to create custom components
- Creating custom SSIS Source adapters
- Creating custom SSIS transforms
- Creating custom SSIS Destination adapters

WROX.COM DOWNLOADS FOR THIS CHAPTER

You can find the wrox.com code downloads for this chapter at `www.wrox.com/go/prossis2014` on the Download Code tab.

Once you start implementing a real-world integration solution, you may have requirements that the built-in functionality in SSIS does not meet. For instance, you may have a legacy system that has a proprietary export file format, and you need to import that data into your warehouse. You have a robust SSIS infrastructure that you have put in place that enables you to efficiently develop and manage complex ETL solutions, but how do you meld that base infrastructure with the need for customization? That's where custom component development comes into play. Out of the box, Microsoft provides a huge list of components for you in SSIS; however, you can augment those base components with your own more specialized tasks.

The benefit here is not only to businesses but also to software vendors. You may decide to build components and sell them on the Web, or maybe start a community-driven effort on a site such as `codeplex.com`. Either way, the benefit you get is that your components will be built in exactly the same way that the ones that ship with SSIS are built; there is no secret sauce (besides expertise) that Microsoft adds to its components to make them behave any differently from your own. This gives you the opportunity to truly "build a better mousetrap" — if you don't like the way that one of the built-in components behaves, you can simply build your own instead.

Building your first component may be a little challenging, but with the help of this chapter it is hoped that you will be able to overcome this. This chapter focuses on the pipeline — not because it is better than any other area of programmability within SSIS but because it will probably be the area in which you have the most benefit to gain, and it does require a slightly greater level of understanding of basic programming concepts than most SSIS developers need to create script tasks. The pipeline also gives you a glimpse of the really interesting things that Microsoft has done in SSIS. All forms of extensibility are well covered in the SQL Server documentation and samples, so don't forget to leverage those resources as well.

THE SAMPLE COMPONENTS

Three sample components are defined in this section to demonstrate the main component types. The Transform Component is expanded in Chapter 20 to include a user interface. All code samples are available on the website for this book, which you can find at `www.wrox.com/go/prossis2014`.

The *pipeline*, for all intents and purposes, is the way your data moves from A to B and how it is manipulated, if at all. You can find it on the Data Flow tab of your packages after you have dropped a Data Flow Task into the Control Flow. There's no need to go into any more detail about where to find the pipeline in your package, because this has been covered elsewhere in this book.

As discussed in other chapters, Integration Services enables you to use three basic component types in the pipeline. The first component type is a Source, which retrieves data from an external location (for instance, a SQL Server query, a text file, or a Web service) and transforms the input into the internal buffer format that the pipeline expects.

The Transformation-Type Component accepts buffers of data from the pipeline on one side, does something useful with the data (for instance, sorting it, calculating totals, or multicasting the rows), and then pushes the rows downstream for the next component to consume.

The Destination-Type Component also accepts buffers of data from the pipeline on its input, but rather than write the output rows to the pipeline again, it writes them to a specific external source, such as a text file or SQL Server table.

This chapter walks you through the process of building three components — one example for each of the component types just mentioned. Note that there are further classifications of components, such as synchronous and asynchronous components, but this chapter will help you get the basics right. Following is a high-level description of what each sample component will do.

Component 1: Source Adapter

The Source adapter needs to be able to do quite a few things in order to present the data to the downstream components in the pipeline in a format that the next component understands and expects. Here is a list of what the component needs to do:

- Accept a Connection Manager. A Connection Manager is an optional component for Source adapters, since it is possible to write a Source adapter that does not require a Connection Manager. However, a Connection Manager helps to isolate the connectivity logic (such as the credentials) from the user-specific functionality (such as the query) defined in the Source adaptor. As such, a Connection Manager is highly recommended.

- Validate a Connection Manager.
- Add output columns to the component for the downstream processes.
- Connect to the Data Source.
- Get the data from the Data Source.
- Assign the correct parts of the data to the correct output columns.
- Handle any data errors.

As previously indicated, this component needs to do some work in order to present its data to the outside world. However, stick with it and you'll see how easy this can be. Your aim in the Source adapter is to be able to take a file with a custom format, read it, and present its data to the downstream components.

The real-world sample scenario that we will cover is that there are many systems that export data in a proprietary format, which is hard to then import into another system. Assume that the legacy system exports customer data in the following format:

```
<START>
Name:
Age:
Married:
Salary:
<END>
```

As you can see, this is a nonstandard format that none of the out-of-the-box Source adapters could deal with adequately. Of course, you could use a Script Component to read and parse the file using VB or C#, but then you would need to duplicate the code in every package that needed to read this type of file. Writing a custom Source Component means that you can reuse the component in many different packages, which saves you time and simplifies maintenance compared to the scripting route.

Component 2: Transform

A transform component enables you to take data from a source, manipulate it, and then present the newly arranged data to the downstream components. This component performs the following tasks:

- Creates input columns to accept the data from upstream
- Validates the data to ensure that it conforms to the component's expectations
- Checks the column properties because this transform will be changing them in place
- Handles the case of somebody trying to change the metadata of the transform by adding or removing inputs and/or outputs

In the scenario we will use for this component, we want to create a simple data obfuscation device that will take data from the source and reverse the contents. The catch, though, is that the column properties must be set correctly, and you can perform this operation only on certain data types.

Component 3: Destination Adapter

The Destination adapter will take the data received from the upstream component and write it to the destination. This component needs to do the following:

- Create an input that accepts the data
- Validate that the data is correct
- Accept a Connection Manager
- Validate the Connection Manager (did you get the right type of Connection Manager?)
- Connect to the Data Source
- Write data from the Data Source

For this component, we will use the opposite scenario to the one used earlier in the chapter for the Source adapter. Instead of retrieving data from source to be used in the SSIS package, in this case, we will imagine that the pipeline retrieved data from some standard source (such as SQL Server) but we now want to write the data out to a custom flat file format, perhaps as the input file for a legacy system.

The Destination adapter will basically be a reverse of the Source adapter. When it receives the input rows, it needs to create a new file with a data layout resembling that of the source file.

The components you'll build are actually quite simple, but the point is not complexity but how you use the methods in Microsoft's SSIS object model. You can use the methods presented for tackling these tasks as the basis for more complex operations.

THE PIPELINE COMPONENT METHODS

Components are normally described as having two distinct phases: design time and runtime. The design-time phase refers to the methods and interfaces that are called when the component is being used in a development environment — in other words, the code that is being run when the component is dragged onto the SSIS design surface, and when it is being configured. The runtime functionality refers to the calls and interfaces that are used when the component is actually being executed — in other words, when the package is being run.

When you implement a component, you *inherit* from the base class, `Microsoft.SqlServer.Dts.Pipeline.PipelineComponent`, and provide your own functionality by *overriding* the base methods, some of which are primarily design time, others runtime. If you are using native code to write SSIS components, then the divide between the runtime and the design time is clearer because the functionality is implemented on different interfaces. Commentary on the methods has been divided into these two sections, but there are some exceptions, notably the connection-related methods; a section on connection time–related methods is included later in this chapter.

> **NOTE** *In programming terms, a class can inherit functionality from another class, termed the base class. If the base class provides a method, and the inheriting class needs to change the functionality within this method, it can override the method. In effect, you replace the base method with your own. From within the overriding method, you can still access the base method, and call it explicitly if required, but any consumer of the new class will see only the overriding method.*

Design-Time Functionality

The following methods are explicitly implemented for design time, overriding the `PipelineComponent` methods, although they will usually be called from within your overriding method. Not all of the methods are listed, because for some there is little more to say, and others have been grouped together according to their area of function. Refer to the SQL Server documentation for a complete list.

Some methods are described as *verification methods*, and these are a particularly interesting group. They provide minor functions, such as adding a column or setting a property value, and you might quite rightly assume that there is little point in ever overriding them, because there isn't much value to add to the base implementation. These verification methods have code added to verify that the operation about to take place within the base class is allowed. The following sections expand on the types of checks you can do; if you want to build a robust component, these are well worth looking into.

Another very good reason to implement these methods as described is to reduce code. These methods will be used by both a custom user interface (UI) and the built-in component editor, or Advanced Editor. If you raise an error saying that a change is not allowed, then both user interfaces can capture this and provide feedback to the user. Although a custom UI would be expected to prevent blatantly inappropriate actions, the Advanced Editor is designed to offer all functionality, so you are protecting the integrity of your component regardless of the method used.

ProvideComponentProperties

This method is provided so you can set up your component. It is called when a component is first added to the Data Flow, and it initializes the component. It does not perform any column-level activity, because this is left to `ReinitializeMetadata`; when this method is invoked, there are generally no inputs or outputs to be manipulated anyway. Following are the sorts of procedures you may want to set in here:

- Remove existing settings, such as inputs and outputs. This allows the component to be rebuilt and can be useful when things go wrong.
- Add inputs and outputs, ready for column work later in the component's lifetime. You may also define custom properties on them and specify related properties, such as linking them together for synchronous behavior.
- Define the connection requirements. By adding an item to the `RuntimeConnectionCollection`, you have a placeholder prepared for the Connection Manager at runtime, and inform the designer of this requirement.

- The component may have custom properties that are configurable by a user in addition to those you get free from Microsoft. These will hold settings other than the column-related one that affect the overall operation or behavior of the component.

Validate

`Validate` is called numerous times during the lifetime of the component, both at design time and at runtime, but the most interesting work is usually the result of a design-time call. As the name suggests, it validates that the content of the component is correct and will enable you to at least run the package. If the validation encounters a problem, then the return code used is important to determine any further actions, such as calling `ReinitializeMetaData`. The base class version of `Validate` performs its own checks in the component, and you will need to extend it further in order to cover your specific needs. `Validate` should *not* be used to change the component at all; it should *only report* the problems it finds.

ReinitializeMetaData

The `ReinitializeMetaData` method is where all the building work for your component is done. You add new columns, remove invalid columns, and generally build up the columns. It is called when the `Validate` method returns `VS_NEEDSNEWMETADATA`. It is also your opportunity to do any component repairs that need to be done, particularly regarding invalid columns, as mentioned previously.

MapInputColumn and MapOutputColumn

These methods are used to create a relationship between an input/output column and an external metadata column. An external metadata column is an offline representation of an output or input column and can be used by downstream components to create an input. For instance, you may connect your Source Component to a database table to retrieve the list of columns. However, once you disconnect from the database and edit the package in an offline manner, it may be useful for the source to "remember" the external database columns.

This functionality enables you to validate and maintain columns even when the Data Source is not available. It is not required, but it makes the user experience better. If the component declares that it will be using External Metadata (`IDTSComponentMetaData100.ValidateExternalMetadata`), then the user in the advanced UI will see upstream columns on the left and the external columns on the right; if you are validating your component against an output, you will see the checked list box of columns.

Input and Output Verification Methods

There are several methods you can use to deal with inputs and outputs. The three functions you may need to perform are adding, deleting, and setting a custom property. The method names clearly indicate their function:

- `InsertInput`
- `DeleteInput`
- `SetInputProperty`
- `InsertOutput`

- `DeleteOutput`
- `SetOutputProperty`

For most components, the inputs and outputs will have been configured during `ProvideComponentProperties`, so unless you expect a user to add additional inputs and outputs and fully support this, you should override these methods and fire an error to prevent this. Similarly, unless you support additions, you would also want to deny deletions by overriding the corresponding methods. Properties can be checked for validity during the Set methods as well.

Set Column Data Types

Two methods are used to set column data types: one for output columns and the other for external metadata columns. There is no input column equivalent, because the data types of input columns are determined by the upstream component.

- `SetOutputColumnDataTypeProperties`
- `SetExternalMetadataColumnDataTypeProperties`

These are verification methods that can be used to validate or prevent changes to a column. For example, in a Source Component, you would normally define the columns and their data types within `ReinitializeMetaData`. You could then override `SetOutputColumnDataTypeProperties`, and by comparing the method's supplied data types to the existing column, you could prevent data type changes but allow length changes.

There is quite a complex relationship between all the parameters for these methods; please refer to SQL Server documentation for reference when using this method yourself.

PerformUpgrade

This method enables you to update an existing version of the component with a new version in a transparent manner on the destination machine.

RegisterEvents

This method enables you to register custom events in a Pipeline Component. You can therefore have an event fire on something happening at runtime in the package. This is then eligible to be logged in the package log.

RegisterLogEntries

This method decides which of the new custom events are going to be registered and selectable in the package log.

SetComponentProperty

In the `ProvideComponentProperties` method, you tell the component about any custom properties that you would like to expose to the users of the component and perhaps allow them to set. Using the `SetComponentProperty` verification method, you can check what the user has entered for which custom property on the component and ensure that the values are valid.

Setting Column Properties

There are three column property methods, each of which enables you to set a property for the relevant column type:

- `SetInputColumnProperty`
- `SetOutputColumnProperty`
- `SetExternalMetadataColumnProperty`

These are all verification methods and should be used accordingly. For example, if you set a column property during `ReinitializeMetaData` and want to prevent users from interfering with this, you could examine the property name (or index) and throw an exception if it is a restricted property, in effect making it read-only.

Similarly, if several properties are used in conjunction with each other at runtime to provide direction on the operation to be performed, you could enumerate all column properties to ensure that those related properties exist and have suitable values. You could assign a default value if a value is not present or raise an exception depending on the exact situation.

For an external metadata column, which will be mapped to an input or output column, any property set directly on this external metadata column can be cascaded down onto the corresponding input or output column through this overridden function.

SetUsageType

This method deals with the columns on inputs into the component. In a nutshell, you use it to select a column and to tell the component how you will treat each column. What you see coming into this method is the virtual input. This means that it is a representation of what is available for selection to be used by your component. These are the three possible usage types for a column:

- `DTSUsageType.UT_IGNORED`: The column will not be used by the component. You are removing this `InputColumn` from the `InputColumnCollection`. This differs from the other two usage types, which add a reference to the `InputColumn` to the `InputColumnCollection` if it does not exist already or you may be changing its Read/Write property.
- `DTSUsageType.UT_READONLY`: The column is read-only. The column is selected, and data can be read and used within the component but cannot be modified.
- `DTSUsageType.UT_READWRITE`: The column is selected, and you can read and write or change the data within your component.

This is another of the verification methods, and you should use it to ensure that the columns selected are valid. For example, the Reverse String sample shown later in the chapter can operate only on string columns, so you must check that the data type of the input column is `DT_STR` for string or `DT_WSTR` for Unicode strings. Similarly, the component performs an in-place change, so the usage type must be read/write. Setting it to read-only would cause problems during execution when you try to write the changed data back to the pipeline buffer. The Data Flow makes important decisions on column handling based on the read/write flag, and if the component writes to a read-only column, it will likely corrupt the data and the user will get incorrect results. Therefore, you should validate the columns as they are selected to ensure that they meet the design requirements for your component.

On Path Attachment

There are three closely related path attachment methods, called when the named events occur, and the first two in particular can be used to improve the user experience:

- `OnInputPathAttached`
- `OnOutputPathAttached`
- `OnInputPathDetached`

These methods handle situations in which, for instance, the inputs or outputs are all identical and interchangeable. Using the multicast as an example, you attach to the dangling output and another dangling output is automatically created. You detach, and the extra output is deleted.

Runtime

Runtime, also known as execution time, is when you actually work with the data, through the pipeline buffer, with columns and rows of data. The following methods are used for preparing the component, doing the job it was designed for, and then cleaning up afterward.

PrepareForExecute

This method, which is similar to the `PreExecute` method described next, can be used for setting up anything in the component that you will need at runtime. The difference between them is that you do not have access to the Buffer Manager, so you cannot get your hands on the columns in either the output or the input at this stage. Otherwise, the distinction between the two is very fine, so usually you will end up using `PreExecute` exclusively, because you will need access to the Buffer Manager anyway.

PreExecute

`PreExecute` is called once and once only each time the component is run, and Microsoft recommends that you do as much preparation as possible for the execution of your component in this method. In this case, you'll use it to enumerate the columns, reading off values and properties, calling methods to get more information, and generally preparing by gathering all the information you require in advance. For instance, you may want to save references to common properties, column indexes, and state information to a variable so that you access it efficiently once you start pumping rows through the component.

This is the earliest point in the component that you will access the component's Buffer Manager, so you have the live context of columns, as opposed to the design-time representation. As mentioned, you do the column preparation for your component in this method, because it is called only once per component execution, unlike some of the other runtime methods, which are called multiple times.

The live and design-time representations of the columns may not match. An example of this is that typically data in the buffer is not in the same order as it is in the design time. This means that just because Column1 has an index of 0 in the design time, the buffer may not have the same index for Column1. To solve this mismatch there is a function named `FindColumnByLineageID` that will be used to locate the columns in the buffer. An example of `FindColumnByLineageID` can be found later in the chapter in the "Building the Source Component" section in the `ParseTheFileAndAddToBuffer` function.

PrimeOutput and ProcessInput

These two methods are covered together because they are so closely linked. Essentially, these two methods reflect how the data flows through components. Sometimes you use only one of them, and sometimes you use both. There are some rules you can follow.

In a Source adapter, the `ProcessInput` method is never called, and all of the work is done through `PrimeOutput`. In a Destination adapter, the reverse is true; the `PrimeOutput` method is never called, and the whole of the work is done through the `ProcessInput` method.

Things are not quite that simple with a transformation. There are two types of transformations, and the type of transformation you are writing will dictate which method, or indeed methods, your component should call. For a discussion on synchronous versus asynchronous transformations, see Chapter 4.

- **Synchronous:** `PrimeOutput` is not called; therefore, all the work is done in the `ProcessInput` method. The buffer `LineageIDs` remain the same. For a detailed explanation of buffers and `LineageIDs`, please refer to Chapter 16.
- **Asynchronous:** Both methods are called here. The key difference between a synchronous component and an asynchronous component is that the latter does not reuse the input buffer. The `PrimeOutput` method hands the `ProcessInput` method a buffer to fill with its data.

PostExecute

You can use this method to clean up anything that you started in `PreExecute`. However, this is not its only function. After reading the description of the `Cleanup` method, covered next, you may wonder what the difference is between them. The answer is, for this release, nothing. It might be easiest to think of `PostExecute` as the counterpart to `PreExecute`.

Cleanup

As the method name suggests, this is called as the very last thing your component will do, and it is your chance to clean up whatever resources may be left. However, it is rarely used. Like `PreExecute` and `PostExecute`, you can consider `Cleanup` to be the opposite of `PrepareForExecute`.

DescribeRedirectedErrorCode

If you are using an error output and directing rows there in case of errors, then you should expose this method to provide more information about the error. When you direct a row to the error output, you specify an error code. This method will be called by the pipeline engine, passing in that error code, and it is expected to return a full error description string for the code specified. These two values are then included in the columns of the error output.

Connection Time

The following two methods are called several times throughout the life cycle of a component, both at design time and at runtime, and are used to manage connections within the component.

AcquireConnections

This method is called both at design time and when the component executes. There is no explicit result, but the connection is normally validated and then cached in a member variable within the component for later use. At this stage, a connection should be open and ready to use.

There is a single parameter used by the `AcquireConnections`, which is named `transaction`. The `transaction` parameter is set to the transaction that the connection being retrieved in `AcquireConnections` is participating in. The `transaction` parameter is set to `null` unless a transaction has been started by the SSIS execution engine. An example of where the transaction object would not be null would be to set the SSIS package setting of `TransactionOption` to `Required`.

ReleaseConnections

If you have any open connections, as set in the `AcquireConnections` method, then this is where they should be closed and released. If the connection was cached in a member variable, use that reference to issue any appropriate `Close` or `Dispose` methods. For some connections, such as a File Connection Manager, this may not be relevant because only a file path string was returned, but if you took this a stage further and opened a text stream or similar on the file, it should now be closed.

Here is a list of common Connection Managers and the values that are returned.

CONNECTION MANAGER TYPE	CONNECTION MANAGER NAME	TYPE OF RETURN VALUE	ADDITIONAL INFO
ADO.NET	ADO.NET Connection Manager	`System.Data .SqlClient .SqlConnection`	ADO.NET
FILE	File Connection Manager	`System.String`	Path to the file
FLATFILE	Flat File Connection Manager	`System.String`	Path to the file
SMTP	SMTP Connection Manager	`System.String`	For example: `SmtpServer=<server name>; UseWindowsAuthentication=True; EnableSsl=False;`
WMI	WMI Connection Manager	`System.Management .ManagementScope`	WMI

BUILDING THE COMPONENTS

Now you can move on to actually building the components. These components are simple and demonstrate the most commonly used methods when building your own components. They also help give you an idea of the composition of a component, the order in which things happen, and which method does what. While they will not implement all the available methods, these components have been built and can be extended, so why not download them and give them a go? If you happen to break them, simply revert back to a previous good copy. No programmer gets things right the first time, so breaking the component is part of the experience. (At least, that's what programmers tell themselves at 2:00 a.m. when they are still trying to figure out why the thing isn't doing what they wanted.)

The component classes are covered in the next sections. You will then be shown how to ensure that your component appears in the correct folder, what to put in the `AssemblyInfo` file, how it is registered in the global assembly cache (GAC), and how to sign the assembly. This is common to all three components, so it is covered as one topic.

Preparation

In this section of the chapter, you'll go through the steps that are common to all the Pipeline Components. These are the basic sets of tasks you need to do before you fly into coding.

Start by opening Visual Studio 2013, and create a new project, a Class Library project, as shown in Figure 19-1.

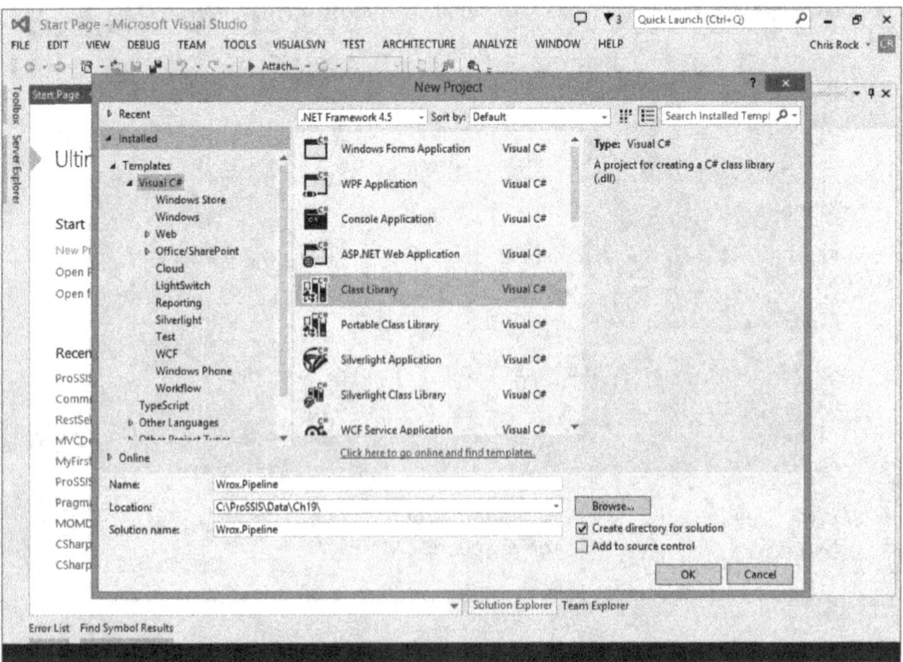

FIGURE 19-1

Now select the Add Reference option from the Project menu, and select the following assemblies, which are shown in Figure 19-2:

- `Microsoft.SqlServer.DTSPipelineWrap`
- `Microsoft.SqlServer.DTSRuntimeWrap`
- `Microsoft.SqlServer.ManagedDTS`
- `Microsoft.SqlServer.PipelineHost`

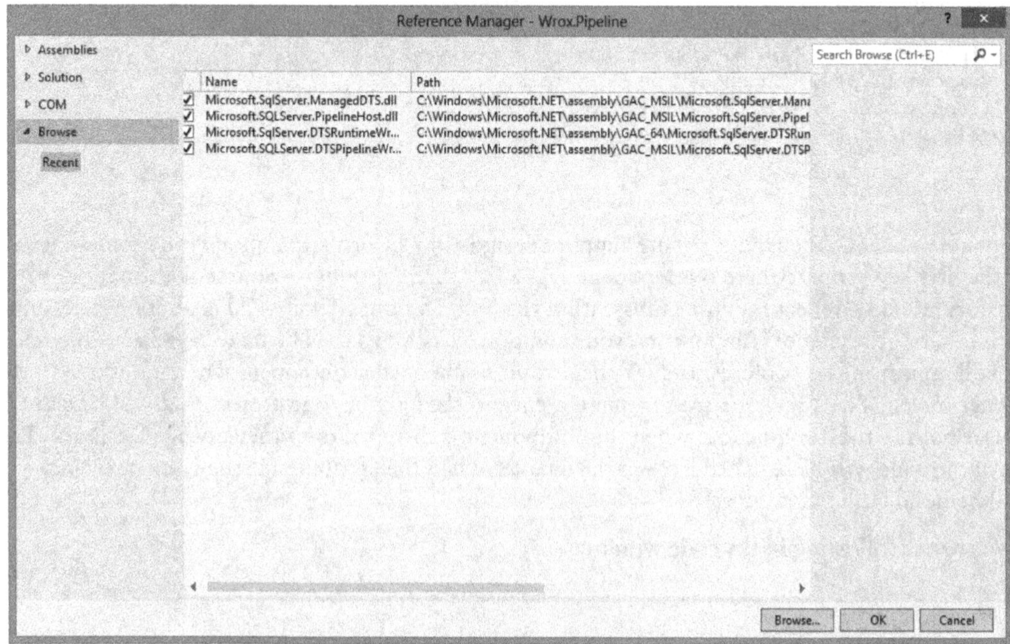

FIGURE 19-2

In a standard installation of SQL Server 2014 Integration Services, these reference files should be available in the directory `C:\Program Files\Microsoft SQL Server\120\SDK\Assemblies\`; 64-bit machines need to look in the x86 program files directory `C:\Program Files (x86)\Program Files\Microsoft SQL Server\120\SDK\Assemblies`.

Once you have those set up, you can start to add the `Using` directives. These directives tell the compiler which libraries you are going to use. Here are the directives you will need to add to the top of the class in the code editor:

```
#region Using directives
using System;
using System.Collections.Generic;
using System.Text;
using System.Globalization;
using System.Runtime.InteropServices;
```

```
using Microsoft.SqlServer.Dts.Pipeline;
using Microsoft.SqlServer.Dts.Pipeline.Wrapper;
using Microsoft.SqlServer.Dts.Runtime.Wrapper;
using Microsoft.SqlServer.Dts.Runtime;
#endregion
```

The first stage in building a component is to inherit from the `PipelineComponent` base class and decorate the class with `DtsPipelineComponent`. From this point on, you are officially working on a Pipeline Component.

```
namespace Wrox.Pipeline
{ [DtsPipelineComponent(
 DisplayName = "Wrox Reverse String",
 ComponentType = ComponentType.Transform,
 IconResource = "Wrox.Pipeline.ReverseString.ico")]
public class ReverseString : PipelineComponent
{
 ...
```

The `DtsPipelineComponent` attribute supplies design-time information about your component, and the first key property here is `ComponentType`. The three options — Source, Destination, or Transformation — reflect the three tabs within the SSIS Designer Toolbox. This option determines which tab, or grouping of components, your component belongs to. The `DisplayName` is the text that will appear in the Toolbox, and it's the default name of the component when it's added to the designer screen. The `IconResource` is the reference to the icon in your project that will be shown to the user both in the Toolbox and when the component is dropped onto the Package Designer. This part of the code will be revisited later in the chapter when the attribute for the User Interface, which you'll be building later, is added.

Now type the following in the code window:

```
public override
```

After you press the space bar after the word "`override`," you'll see a list of all the methods on the base class. You are now free to type away to your heart's content and develop the component.

We cover development of the components a little later in the chapter, but for now we focus on how you deploy it into the SSIS environment once it is ready. In addition to being built, the component also needs a few other things to happen to it. If you are a seasoned developer, then this section will be old hat to you, but for anyone else, it's important to understand what needs to happen for the components to work:

- Provide a strong name key for signing the assembly.
- Set the build output location to the `PipelineComponents` folder.
- Use a post-build event to install the assembly into the GAC.
- Set assembly-level attributes in the `AssemblyInfo.cs` file.

SSIS needs the GAC because components can be executed from within the SQL Server Data Tools, SQL Server Agent, or DTExec, all which reside in different directories. Strong names are a consequence of this requirement. The `PipelineComponents` folder allows the designer to discover the component and put it in the Toolbox. Additional assembly-level metadata from your component is a consequence of the fact that the strong name, including version, is persisted in the package, which causes all your packages to break if you rebuild the component unless you stop incrementing the `AssemblyVersion` attribute of the component.

To sign the project, right-click your C# project and choose Properties from the context menu. You are not going to look at all the tabs on the left side of the screen, only those that are relevant to what you are doing here. Figure 19-3 shows the Application tab.

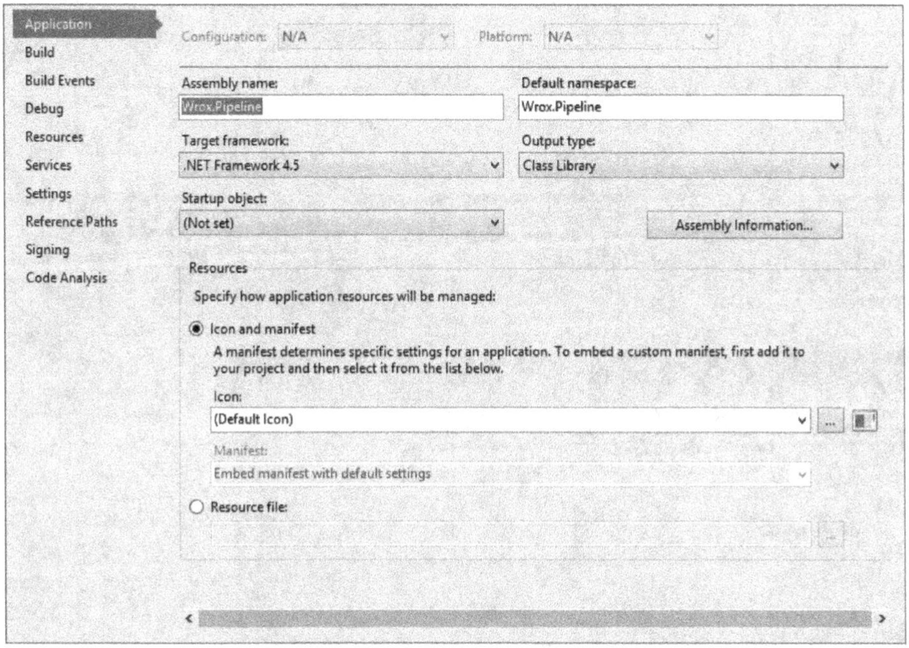

FIGURE 19-3

In this tab, the only thing you really need to do is change the assembly name to be the same as your default namespace.

In order for the SSIS designer to use a component, it must be placed in a defined folder. On a 32-bit (x86) PC, this folder is usually located here:

```
C:\Program Files\Microsoft SQL Server\120\DTS\PipelineComponents
```

If you have a 64-bit (x64) environment, then you should explicitly choose the 64-bit location:

```
C:\Program Files (x86)\Microsoft SQL Server\120\DTS\PipelineComponents
```

For your new component to work correctly, it must be placed in the global assembly cache. To copy the assemblies into the program files directory and install them with the GAC, you're going to use a post-build event on the project. Copying the files into the preceding directories and installing them into the GAC are both required steps. You can do this manually, but it makes for faster development if you do it as part of the build process.

Click the Build Events tab. Then, in the Post-build Command Line dialog, enter the commands that will automatically do these tasks. You can also click on the "Edit Post Build . . ." button, which allows for better readability on the longer command lines. Following is an example post-build event command (see also Figure 19-4). Be sure to include the double quotes in the path statements. If this exact command doesn't work in your development environment, then do a search for `gacutil.exe` on your hard drive and use its path in the manner shown here.

```
"C:\Program Files (x86)\Microsoft SDKs\Windows\v8.1A\Bin\NETFX 4.5.1 Tools\
gacutil.exe"
/u "$(TargetName)"
"C:\Program Files (x86)\Microsoft SDKs\Windows\v8.1A\Bin\NETFX 4.5.1 Tools\
gacutil.exe"
/if "$(TargetPath)"
```

> **NOTE** *Note that the path shown earlier is for Windows 8/2012 machines. The path on older OSs may be slightly different.*

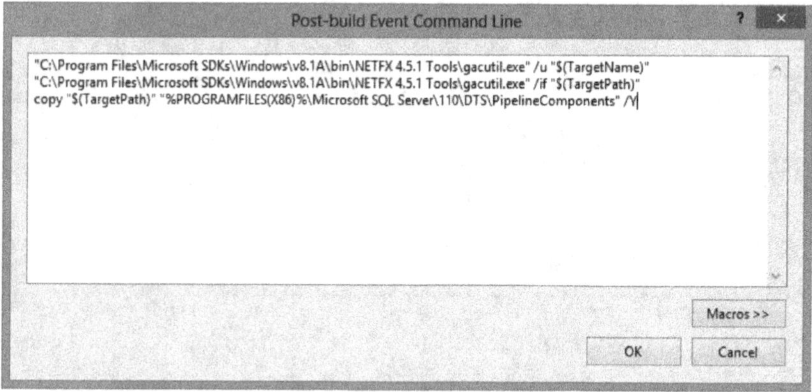

FIGURE 19-4

The SSIS components referenced in this project are built with .NET 4.5. This means you need to verify that you're using the `gacutil.exe` file for .NET 4.5 as well. Otherwise, the `gacutil` steps of the post-build event will fail.

When you compile the code, Visual Studio will expand the macros shown in the preceding snippet into real paths — for instance, the first command shown will expand into the following statement, and Visual Studio will then execute it. Because you have declared the statement in the post-build event, after compiling the code the statement will run automatically and place the new library (`.dll`) into the GAC.

```
"C:\Program Files\Microsoft SDKs\Windows\v8.1A\Bin\NETFX 4.5.1 Tools\gacutil.exe"
/if "C:\SSIS\ProSSIS2014\Wrox.Pipeline\bin\debug\Wrox.Pipeline.dll"
```

The assembly is to be installed in the GAC, so you also need to sign it using a strong name key, which can be specified and created from the Signing page, shown in Figure 19-5.

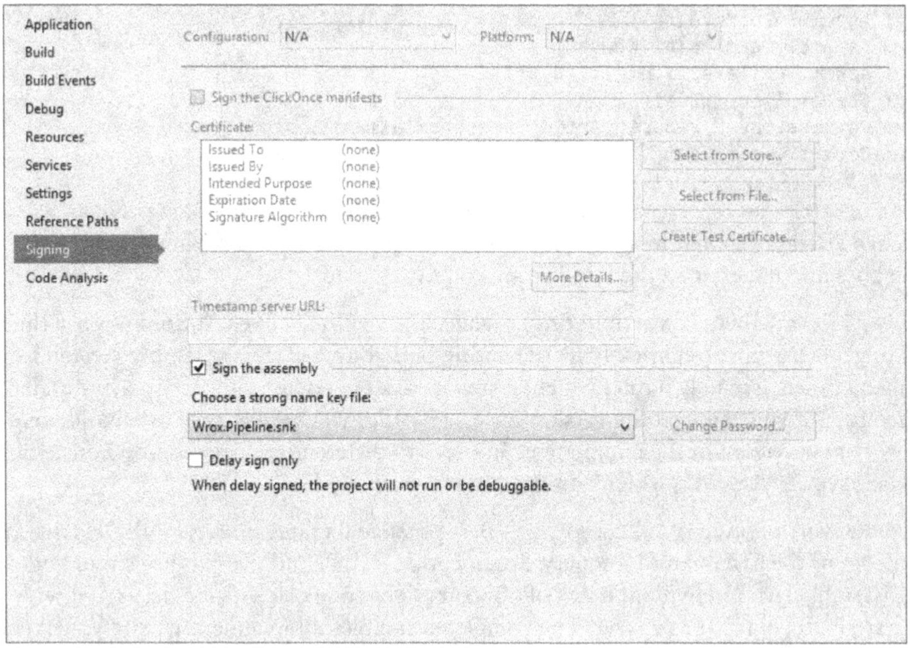

FIGURE 19-5

> **NOTE** *Keep in mind that on some operating systems, such as Windows 7 or 8, you will be required to run the Wrox.Pipeline project in Visual Studio 2013 under the administrator account. That's because the* `gacutil` *utility requires administrator privileges to copy files to the GAC. To run Visual Studio as the administrator, right-click the Visual Studio icon to bring up the context menu and select "Run as administrator."*

That's all you need to do as far as the project's properties are concerned, so now you can move on to handling the `AssemblyInfo` file. While most assembly attributes can be set through the Assembly Information dialog, available from the Application tab of Project Properties (refer to Figure 19-3), you require some additional settings. Shown next is the `AssemblyInfo.cs` file for the example project, which can be found under the `Properties` folder within the Solution Explorer of Visual Studio:

```
#region Using directives
using System;
using System.Security.Permissions;
using System.Reflection;
using System.Runtime.CompilerServices;
using System.Runtime.InteropServices;
#endregion
[assembly: AssemblyTitle("Wrox.Pipeline")]
```

```
[assembly: AssemblyDescription("A reverse string pipeline component from Wrox ")]
[assembly: AssemblyConfiguration("")]
[assembly: AssemblyProduct("Wrox.Pipeline")]
[assembly: AssemblyTrademark("")]
[assembly: AssemblyCulture("")]
[assembly: AssemblyVersion("1.0.0.0")]
[assembly: AssemblyFileVersion("1.0.0.0")]
[assembly: CLSCompliant(true)]
[assembly: PermissionSet(SecurityAction.RequestMinimum)]
[assembly: ComVisible(false)]
```

The first section of attributes represents general information such as company name. The `AssemblyCulture` attribute should be left blank unless you are experienced with working with localized assemblies and understand the implications of any change.

The `AssemblyVersion` attribute is worth noting; because the version is fixed, it does not use the asterisk token to generate an automatically incrementing build number. The assembly version forms part of the fully qualified assembly name, which is how a package references a component under the covers. Therefore, if you changed the version for every build, you would have to rebuild your packages for every new version of the component. In order to differentiate between versions, you should use `AssemblyFileVersion`, which you need to manually update.

The other attribute worth noting is `CLSCompliant`. Best practice dictates that the .NET classes and assemblies conform to the Command Language Specification (CLS), and compliance should be marked at the assembly level. Individual items of noncompliant code can then be decorated with the `CLSCompliant` attribute, marked as `false`. The completed samples all include this, and you can also refer to SQL Server documentation for guidance, as well as follow the simple compiler warnings that are raised when this condition is not met.

The following example shows how to deal with a noncompliant method in your component:

```
[CLSCompliant(false)]
public override DTSValidationStatus Validate()
{
...
```

Building the Source Component

As mentioned earlier, the Source adapter needs to be able to retrieve information from a file and present the data to the downstream component. The file is not your standard-looking file, and while the format is strange, it's consistent. When you design the Destination adapter, you will write the contents of an upstream component to a file in a very similar format. After you have read this chapter, you may want to take the Source adapter and alter it slightly so that it can read a file produced by the sample Destination adapter.

If you're following along with the book and are writing the code manually, right click on the Wrox .Pipeline project in Visual Studio and click "Add ⇨ New Item". Select the "Class" template in the "Add New Item" dialog and create a new file named SimpleFileProcessorSource.cs.

The first method to look at is `ProvideComponentProperties`. This is called almost as soon as you drop the component onto the designer. Here is the method in full (`SimpleFileProcessorSource.cs`) before you look at its parts:

```
public override void ProvideComponentProperties()
{
 ComponentMetaData.RuntimeConnectionCollection.RemoveAll();
 RemoveAllInputsOutputsAndCustomProperties();
 ComponentMetaData.Name = "Wrox Simple File Processor Source Adapter";
 ComponentMetaData.Description = "Our first Source Adapter";
 IDTSRuntimeConnection100 rtc =
 ComponentMetaData.RuntimeConnectionCollection.New();
 rtc.Name = "File To Read";
 rtc.Description = "This is the file from which we want to read";
IDTSOutput100 output = ComponentMetaData.OutputCollection.New();
 output.Name = "Component Output";
 output.Description = "This is what downstream Components will see";
 output.ExternalMetadataColumnCollection.IsUsed = true;
}
```

Now you can break down some of this code. The first thing the preceding code does is remove any runtime connections in the component, which you'll be adding back soon:

```
ComponentMetaData.RuntimeConnectionCollection.RemoveAll();
RemoveAllInputsOutputsAndCustomProperties();
```

You can also remove inputs, outputs, and custom properties. Basically your component is now a clean slate. This is not strictly required for this example; however, it's advantageous to follow this convention because it prevents any unexpected situations that may arise in more complicated components.

The following three lines of code simply help to identify your component when you look in the property pages after adding it to the designer:

```
ComponentMetaData.Name = "Wrox Simple File Processor";
ComponentMetaData.Description = "Our first Source Adapter";
ComponentMetaData.ContactInfo = "www.wrox.com";
```

The only property here that may not be obvious is `ContactInfo`, which simply identifies to the user the developer of the component. If a component throws a fatal error during loading or saving — for example, areas not influenced by the user-controlled settings — then the designer will show the contact information for support purposes.

Next, your component needs a runtime connection from which you can read and get the data:

```
IDTSRuntimeConnection100 rtc =
ComponentMetaData.RuntimeConnectionCollection.New();
rtc.Name = "File To Read";
rtc.Description = "This is the file from which we want to read";
```

You removed any existing connections earlier in the method, so here is where you add it back. Simply give it a name and a description.

Downstream components will see the data by having it presented to them from an output in this component. In other words, the output is the vehicle that the component uses to present data from the input file to the next component downstream. Here you add a new output to the output collection and give it a name and a description:

```
IDTSOutput100 output = ComponentMetaData.OutputCollection.New();
output.Name = "Component Output";
output.Description = "This is what downstream Components will see";
```

The final part of this component is to use `ExternalMetadataColumns`, which enables you to view the structure of the Data Source with no connection:

```
output.ExternalMetadataColumnCollection.IsUsed = true;
```

Here, you tell the output you created earlier that it will use `ExternalMetaData` columns.

The next method to look at is `AcquireConnections`. In this method, you want to ensure that you have a runtime connection available and that it is the correct type. You then want to retrieve the filename from the file itself. Here is the method in full (`SimpleFileProcessorSource.cs`):

```
public override void AcquireConnections(object transaction)
{
 if (ComponentMetaData.RuntimeConnectionCollection["File To
Read"].ConnectionManager != null)
 { ConnectionManager cm =
 Microsoft.SqlServer.Dts.Runtime.DtsConvert.GetWrapper(
 ComponentMetaData.RuntimeConnectionCollection["File To Read"].
 ConnectionManager);
 if (cm.CreationName != "FILE")
 {
 throw new Exception("The Connection Manager is not a FILE Connection Manager");
 }
 else
 {
 _fil = (Microsoft.SqlServer.Dts.Runtime.DTSFileConnectionUsageType)
 cm.Properties["FileUsageType"].GetValue(cm);
 if (_fil != DTSFileConnectionUsageType.FileExists)
 {
 throw new Exception("The type of FILE connection manager must be an
 Existing File");
 }
 else
 {
 _filename = ComponentMetaData.RuntimeConnectionCollection["File To
 Read"].ConnectionManager.AcquireConnection(transaction).
 ToString();
 if (_filename == null || _filename.Length == 0)
 {
 throw new Exception("Nothing returned when grabbing the filename");
 }
 }
 }
 }
 }
```

This method covers a lot of ground and is really quite interesting. The first thing you want to do is find out if you can get a Connection Manager from the runtime connection collection of the component. The runtime connection was defined during `ProvideComponentProperties` earlier. If it is `null`, then the user has not provided a runtime connection:

```
if (ComponentMetaData.RuntimeConnectionCollection["File To
Read"].ConnectionManager
!= null)
```

The next line of code is quite cool. It converts the native `ConnectionManager` object to a managed Connection Manager. You need the managed Connection Manager to determine what type it is and the properties:

```
ConnectionManager cm =
Microsoft.SqlServer.Dts.Runtime.DtsConvert.ToConnectionManager(
ComponentMetaData.RuntimeConnectionCollection["File To Read"].ConnectionManager);
```

Once you have the managed Connection Manager, you can start to look at some of its properties to ensure that it is what you want. All Connection Managers have a `CreationName` property. For this component, you want to ensure that the `CreationName` property is `FILE`, as highlighted here:

```
if (cm.CreationName != "FILE")
```

If the `CreationName` is not `FILE`, then you send an exception back to the component:

```
throw new Exception("The type of FILE connection manager must be an Existing
File");
```

You've established that a connection has been specified and that it is the right type. However, the `FILE` Connection Manager can still have the wrong usage mode specified. To determine whether it has the right mode, you have to look at another of its properties, the `FileUsageType` property. This can return one of four values, defined by the `DTSFileConnectionUsageType` enumeration:

- `DTSFileConnectionUsageType.CreateFile`: The file does not yet exist and will be created by the component. If the file does exist, then you can raise an error, although you may also accept this and overwrite the file. Use this type for components that create new files. This mode is more useful for Destination Components, not sources.
- `DTSFileConnectionUsageType.FileExists`: The file exists, and you are expected to raise an error if this is not the case.
- `DTSFileConnectionUsageType.CreateFolder`: The folder does not yet exist and will be created by the component. If the folder does exist, then you can decide how to handle this situation, as with `CreateFile` earlier. This is also more useful for destinations.
- `DTSFileConnectionUsageType.FolderExists`: The folder exists, and you are expected to raise an error if this is not the case.

The type you want to check for in your component is `DTSFileConnectionUsageType.FileExists` and you do that like this, throwing an exception if the type is not what you want:

```
_fil = (Microsoft.SqlServer.Dts.Runtime.DTSFileConnectionUsageType)cm.Properties
["FileUsageType"].GetValue(cm);
if (_fil != Microsoft.SqlServer.Dts.Runtime.DTSFileConnectionUsageType.FileExists)
{...}
```

You're nearly done checking your Connection Manager now. At this point, you need the filename so you can retrieve the file later when you need to read it for data. You do that like this:

```
_filename = ComponentMetaData.RuntimeConnectionCollection
["File To Read"].ConnectionManager.AcquireConnection(transaction).ToString();
```

That concludes the `AcquireConnections` method, so you can now move straight on to the `Validate` method (`SimpleFileProcessorSource.cs`):

```
[CLSCompliant(false)]
public override DTSValidationStatus Validate()
{
 bool pbCancel = false;
 IDTSOutput100 output = ComponentMetaData.OutputCollection["Component Output"];
if (ComponentMetaData.InputCollection.Count != 0)
{
 ComponentMetaData.FireError(0, ComponentMetaData.Name, "Unexpected input
 found. Source components do not support inputs.", "", 0, out pbCancel);
 return DTSValidationStatus.VS_ISCORRUPT;
}
if (ComponentMetaData.RuntimeConnectionCollection["File To Read"].
 ConnectionManager == null)
{
 ComponentMetaData.FireError(0, "Validate", "No Connection Manager
 Specified.", "", 0, out pbCancel);
 return DTSValidationStatus.VS_ISBROKEN;
}
// Check for Output Columns, if not then force ReinitializeMetaData
if (ComponentMetaData.OutputCollection["Component
 Output"].OutputColumnCollection.Count == 0)
{
 ComponentMetaData.FireError(0, "Validate", "No output columns specified.
 Making call to ReinitializeMetaData.", "", 0, out pbCancel);
 return DTSValidationStatus.VS_NEEDSNEWMETADATA;
}
//What about if we have output columns but we have no ExternalMetaData
// columns? Maybe somebody removed them through code.
if (DoesEachOutputColumnHaveAMetaDataColumnAndDoDatatypesMatch(output.ID)
 == false)
{
 ComponentMetaData.FireError(0, "Validate", "Output columns and metadata
 columns are out of sync. Making call to ReinitializeMetaData.", "",
```

```
  0, out pbCancel);
  return DTSValidationStatus.VS_NEEDSNEWMETADATA;
}
return base.Validate();
}
```

The first thing this method does is check for an input. If it has an input, it raises an error back to the component using the `FireError` method and returns `DTSValidationStatus.VS_ISCORRUPT`. This is a Source adapter, and there is no place for an input. Because the data rows enter the component from the file, there is no need for a buffer input that would receive data from an upstream component.

```
if (ComponentMetaData.InputCollection.Count != 0)
```

Next, you check whether the user has specified a Connection Manager for your component. If not, then you return to the user a message indicating that a Connection Manager is required. You do this through the `FireError` method again. If no Connection Manager is specified, then you tell the component it is broken. Remember that you must perform the validation of any Connection Manager specified in `AcquireConnections()`.

```
if (ComponentMetaData.RuntimeConnectionCollection["File To
Read"].ConnectionManager == null)
{
  ComponentMetaData.FireError(0, "Validate", "No Connection Manager Specified.",
  "", 0, out pbCancel);
  return DTSValidationStatus.VS_ISBROKEN;
}
```

Now you need to check whether the output has any columns. For the initial drop onto the designer, the output will have no columns. If this is the case, the `Validate()` method will return `DTSValidationStatus.VS_NEEDSNEWMETADATA`, which in turn calls `ReinitializeMetaData`. You will see later what happens in that method.

```
if (ComponentMetaData.OutputCollection["Component
Output"].OutputColumnCollection.Count == 0)
{
  ComponentMetaData.FireError(0, "Validate", "No output columns specified. Making
  call to ReinitializeMetaData.", "", 0, out pbCancel);
return DTSValidationStatus.VS_NEEDSNEWMETADATA;
}
```

If the output has output columns, then one of the things you want to check is whether the output columns have an `ExternalMetaDataColumn` associated with them. Recall that for `ProvideComponentProperties`, it was stated that you would use an `ExternalMetadataColumnCollection`. Therefore, for each output column, you need to ensure that there is an equivalent external metadata column and that the data type properties also match:

```
if (DoesEachOutputColumnHaveAMetaDataColumnAndDoDatatypesMatch(output.ID) ==
false)
```

```
{
 ComponentMetaData.FireError(0, "Validate", "Output columns and metadata columns
are out of sync. Making call to ReinitializeMetaData.", "",
 0, out pbCancel);
 return DTSValidationStatus.VS_NEEDSNEWMETADATA;
}
```

The next method is used to validate some properties of the component. This is not a method provided by Microsoft that you are overriding; rather, it is completely custom code used to help you do some common work, which is why such functions are sometimes called *helper methods*. This rather long-named helper method, `DoesEachOutputColumnHaveAMetaDataColumnAndDoDatatypesMatch`, accepts as a parameter the ID of an output, so you pass in the output's ID. This method has to do two things. First, it has to confirm that each output column has an `ExternalMetadataColumn` associated with it; second, it has to ensure that the two columns have the same column data type properties. Here is the method in full (`SimpleFileProcessorSource.cs`):

```
private bool DoesEachOutputColumnHaveAMetaDataColumnAndDoDatatypesMatch(int
outputID)
{
 IDTSOutput100 output =
ComponentMetaData.OutputCollection.GetObjectByID(outputID);
IDTSExternalMetadataColumn100 mdc;
bool rtnVal = true;
foreach (IDTSOutputColumn100 col in output.OutputColumnCollection)
{
 if (col.ExternalMetadataColumnID == 0)
 {
 rtnVal = false;
 }
 else
 {
 mdc = output.ExternalMetadataColumnCollection.GetObjectByID
(col.ExternalMetadataColumnID);
 if (mdc.DataType != col.DataType || mdc.Length != col.Length ||
 mdc.Precision != col.Precision || mdc.Scale != col.Scale ||
 mdc.CodePage != col.CodePage)
 {
 rtnVal = false;
 }
 }
 }
return rtnVal;
}
```

The first thing this method does is translate the ID passed in as a parameter to the method into an output:

```
IDTSOutput100 output = ComponentMetaData.OutputCollection.GetObjectByID(outputID);
```

Once you have that, the code loops over the output columns in that output to determine whether the ExternalMetadataColumnID associated with that output column has a value of 0 (that is, there is no value). If the code finds an instance of a value, then it sets the return value from the method to be false:

```
foreach (IDTSOutputColumn100 col in output.OutputColumnCollection)
{
 if (col.ExternalMetadataColumnID == 0)
 {
 rtnVal = false;
 }
...
```

If all output columns have a nonzero ExternalMetadataColumnID, then you move on to the second test:

```
mdc = output.ExternalMetadataColumnCollection.GetObjectByID
(col.ExternalMetadataColumnID);
if (mdc.DataType != col.DataType || mdc.Length != col.Length || mdc.Precision !=
 col.Precision || mdc.Scale != col.Scale || mdc.CodePage != col.CodePage)
{
 rtnVal = false;
}
```

In this part of the method, you are checking whether all the attributes of the output column's data type match those of the corresponding ExternalMetadataColumn. If they do not, then again you return false from the method, which causes the Validate() method to call ReinitializeMetaData. Notice that you use the ID rather than a name, as names can be changed by the end user.

ReinitializeMetaData is where a lot of the work happens in most components. In this component, it fixes up the output columns and the ExternalMetadataColumns. Here's the method (SimpleFileProcessorSource.cs):

```
public override void ReinitializeMetaData()
{
 IDTSOutput100 _profoutput = ComponentMetaData.OutputCollection["Component
Output"];
 if (_profoutput.ExternalMetadataColumnCollection.Count > 0)
 {
 _profoutput.ExternalMetadataColumnCollection.RemoveAll();
}
if (_profoutput.OutputColumnCollection.Count > 0)
{
 _profoutput.OutputColumnCollection.RemoveAll();
}
 CreateOutputAndMetaDataColumns(_profoutput);
}
```

This is a really simple way of doing things. Basically, you are removing all the ExternalMetaDataColumns and then removing the output columns. You will then add them back using the CreateOutputAndMetaDataColumns helper method.

> **NOTE** *As an exercise, you may want to see if you can determine which columns actually need fixing, instead of just dropping and recreating them all.*

`CreateOutputAndMetaDataColumns` is a helper method that creates the output's output columns and the `ExternalMetaData` columns to go with them (`SimpleFileProcessorSource.cs`). This implementation is very rigid, and it presumes that the file you get will be in one format only:

```
private void CreateOutputAndMetaDataColumns(IDTSOutput100 output)
{
 IDTSOutputColumn100 outName = output.OutputColumnCollection.New();
 outName.Name = "Name";
 outName.Description = "The Name value retrieved from File";
 outName.SetDataTypeProperties(DataType.DT_STR, 50, 0, 0, 1252);
CreateExternalMetaDataColumn(output.ExternalMetadataColumnCollection, outName);
 IDTSOutputColumn100 outAge = output.OutputColumnCollection.New();
 outAge.Name = "Age";
 outAge.Description = "The Age value retrieved from File";
 outAge.SetDataTypeProperties(DataType.DT_I4, 0, 0, 0, 0);
 //Create an external metadata column to go alongside with it
 CreateExternalMetaDataColumn(output.ExternalMetadataColumnCollection, outAge);
 IDTSOutputColumn100 outMarried = output.OutputColumnCollection.New();
 outMarried.Name = "Married";
 outMarried.Description = "The Married value retrieved from File";
 outMarried.SetDataTypeProperties(DataType.DT_BOOL, 0, 0, 0, 0);
 //Create an external metadata column to go alongside with it
CreateExternalMetaDataColumn(output.ExternalMetadataColumnCollection, outMarried);
 IDTSOutputColumn100 outSalary = output.OutputColumnCollection.New();
 outSalary.Name = "Salary";
 outSalary.Description = "The Salary value retrieved from File";
 outSalary.SetDataTypeProperties(DataType.DT_DECIMAL, 0, 0, 10, 0);
 //Create an external metadata column to go alongside with it
CreateExternalMetaDataColumn(output.ExternalMetadataColumnCollection,
 outSalary);
}
```

This code follows the same pattern for every column you want to create, so you'll just look at one example here because the rest are variations of the same code. In `CreateOutputAndMetaDataColumns`, you first need to create an output column and add it to the `OutputColumnCollection` of the output, which is a parameter to the method. You give the column a name, a description, and a data type, along with details about the data type:

> **NOTE** `SetDataTypeProperties` *takes the name, the length, the precision, the scale, and the code page of the data type. A list of what is required for these fields can be found in Books Online.*

```
IDTSOutputColumn100 outName = output.OutputColumnCollection.New();
 outName.Name = "Name";
 outName.Description = "The Name value retrieved from File";
 outName.SetDataTypeProperties(DataType.DT_STR, 50, 0, 0, 1252);
```

Note that if you decided to use Unicode data, which does not require a code page, then the same call would have looked like this:

```
outName.SetDataTypeProperties(DataType.DT_WSTR, 50, 0, 0, 0);
```

You now create an `ExternalMetaDataColumn` for the `OutputColumn`, and you do that by calling the helper method called `CreateExternalMetaDataColumn`. This method takes as parameters the `ExternalMetaDataColumnCollection` of the output and the column for which you want to create an `ExternalMetaDataColumn`:

```
CreateExternalMetaDataColumn(output.ExternalMetadataColumnCollection, outName);
```

The first thing you do in the method is create a new `ExternalMetaDataColumn` in the `ExternalMetaDataColumnCollection` that was passed as a parameter. You then map the properties of the output column that was passed as a parameter to the new `ExternalMetaDataColumn`. Finally, you create the relationship between the two by assigning the ID of the `ExternalMetaDataColumn` to the `ExternalMetadataColumnID` property of the output column:

```
IDTSExternalMetadataColumn100 eColumn = externalCollection.New();
eColumn.Name = column.Name;
eColumn.DataType = column.DataType;
eColumn.Precision = column.Precision;
eColumn.Length = column.Length;
eColumn.Scale = column.Scale;
eColumn.CodePage = column.CodePage;
column.ExternalMetadataColumnID = eColumn.ID;
```

At this point, the base class will call the `MapOutputColumn` method. You can choose to override this method to ensure that the external columns and the output column match and that you want to allow the mapping to occur, but in this case you should leave the base class to simply carry on.

Now it's time to look at the runtime methods. `PreExecute` is the usual place to start for most components, but it is done slightly differently here. Normally you would enumerate the output columns and enter them into a *struct*, so you could easily retrieve them later. For illustration purposes, you're not going to do that here (but you do this in the Destination adapter, so you could port what you do there into this adapter as well). The only method you are interested in with this adapter is `PrimeOutput`. Here is the method in full:

```
public override void PrimeOutput(int outputs, int[] outputIDs, PipelineBuffer[]
buffers)
{
 ParseTheFileAndAddToBuffer(_filename, buffers[0]);
buffers[0].SetEndOfRowset();
}
```

On the face of it, this method looks really easy, but as you can see, all the work is being done by the helper method called `ParseTheFileAndAddToBuffer`. To that procedure you need to pass the filename you retrieved in `AcquireConnections`, and the buffer is `buffers[0]` because there is only one buffer and the collection is zero-based. You'll look at the `ParseTheFileAndAddToBuffer` method in a moment, but the last thing you do in this method is call `SetEndOfRowset` on the buffer. This basically tells the downstream component that there are no more rows to be retrieved from the adapter.

Now consider the `ParseTheFileAndAddToBuffer` method in a bit more detail (`SimpleFileProcessorSource.cs`):

```
private void ParseTheFileAndAddToBuffer(string filename, PipelineBuffer buffer)
{
 TextReader tr = File.OpenText(filename);
 IDTSOutput100 output = ComponentMetaData.OutputCollection["Component Output"];
 IDTSOutputColumnCollection100 cols = output.OutputColumnCollection;
 IDTSOutputColumn100 col;
 string s = tr.ReadLine();
 int i = 0;
 while (s != null)
 {
 if (s.StartsWith("<START>"))
 buffer.AddRow();
 if (s.StartsWith("Name:"))
 {
 col = cols["Name"];
 i = BufferManager.FindColumnByLineageID(output.Buffer, col.LineageID);
 string value = s.Substring(5);
 buffer.SetString(i, value);
 }
 if (s.StartsWith("Age:"))
 {
 col = cols["Age"];
 i = BufferManager.FindColumnByLineageID(output.Buffer, col.LineageID);
 Int32 value;
 if (s.Substring(4).Trim() == "")
 value = 0;
 else
 value = Convert.ToInt32(s.Substring(4).Trim());
 buffer.SetInt32(i, value);
 }
 if (s.StartsWith("Married:"))
 {
 col = cols["Married"];
 bool value;
 i = BufferManager.FindColumnByLineageID(output.Buffer, col.LineageID);
 if (s.Substring(8).Trim() == "")
 value = true;
 else
 value = s.Substring(8).Trim() != "1" ? false : true;
 buffer.SetBoolean(i, value);
 }
```

```
if (s.StartsWith("Salary:"))
{
col = cols["Salary"];
Decimal value;
i = BufferManager.FindColumnByLineageID(output.Buffer, col.LineageID);
if (s.Substring(7).Trim() == "")
value = 0M;
else
value = Convert.ToDecimal(s.Substring(8).Trim());
buffer.SetDecimal(i, value);
}
s = tr.ReadLine();
}
tr.Close();
}
```

Because this is not a lesson in C# programming, we will simply describe the points relevant to SSIS programming in this component. You start off by getting references to the output columns collection in the component:

```
IDTSOutput100 output = ComponentMetaData.OutputCollection["Component Output"];
IDTSOutputColumnCollection100 cols = output.OutputColumnCollection;
IDTSOutputColumn100 col;
```

The `IDTSOutputColumn100` object will be used when you need a reference to particular columns. At this point, the columns in the file are actually in rows, so you need to pivot them into columns. First, you read a single line from the file using this code:

```
string s = tr.ReadLine();
```

For this specific source file format, you can determine that you need to add a new row to the buffer if when reading a line of text from the file it begins with the word `<START>`. You do that in the code shown here (remember that the variable `s` is assigned a line of text from the file):

```
if(s.StartsWith("<START>"))
 buffer.AddRow();
```

Here, you have added a row to the buffer, but the row is empty (contains no data yet). As you read lines in the file, you test the beginning of each line. This is important because you need to know this in order to be able to grab the right column from the output columns collection and assign it the value from the text file. The first column name you test for is the `"Name"` column:

```
if (s.StartsWith("Name:"))
{
 col = cols["Name"];
 i = BufferManager.FindColumnByLineageID(output.Buffer, col.LineageID);
 string value = s.Substring(5);
 buffer.SetString(i, value);
}
```

The first thing you do here is check what the row begins with. In the preceding example, it is "Name:". Next, you set the IDTSColumn100 variable column to reference the Name column in the OutputColumnCollection. You need to be able to locate the column in the buffer, and to do this you need to look at the Buffer Manager. This has a method called FindColumnByLineageID that returns the integer location of the column. You need this to assign a value to the column.

To this method, you pass the output's buffer and the column's LineageID. Once you have that, you can use the SetString method on the buffer object to assign a value to the column by passing in the buffer column index and the value to which you want to set the column. Now you no longer have an empty row; it has one column populated with a real data value.

You pretty much do the same with all the columns for which you want to set values. The only variation is the method you call on the buffer object. The buffer object has a set<datatype> method for each of the possible data types. In this component, you need a SetInt32, a SetBoolean, and a SetDecimal method. They do not differ in structure from the SetString method at all. You can also set the value in a non-type-safe manner by using buffer[i] := value, though as a best practice this is not advised.

You can now compile the project. Assuming there are no syntax errors, the project should output the .dll in the specified folder and register it in the GAC. When SQL Server Data Tools is opened, the component should show up in the SSIS Toolbox toolbar as well.

Building the Transformation Component

In this section, you build the transformation that is going to take data from the upstream Source adapter. After reversing the strings, it will pass the data to the downstream component. In this example, the downstream component will be the Destination adapter, which you'll write after you're done with the transformation. The component needs a few things prepared in advance in order to execute efficiently during its lifetime (ReverseString.cs):

```
private ColumnInfo[] _inputColumnInfos;
const string ErrorInvalidUsageType = "Invalid UsageType for column '{0}'";
const string ErrorInvalidDataType = "Invalid DataType for column '{0}'";
CLSCompliant(false)]
public struct ColumnInfo
{
 public int bufferColumnIndex;
 public DTSRowDisposition columnDisposition;
 public int lineageID;
}
```

The struct that you create here, called ColumnInfo, is something you use in various guises repeatedly in your components. It is very useful for storing details about columns that you will need later in the component. In this component, you will store the BufferColumnIndex, which indicates where the column is in the buffer, so that you can retrieve the data. You'll store how the user wants the row to be treated in an error, and you'll store the column's LineageID, which helps to retrieve the column from the InputColumnCollection.

Design-Time Methods

Logically, it would make sense to code the component beginning with the design time, followed by the runtime. When your component is dropped into the SSIS Package Designer surface, it first makes a call to `ProvideComponentProperties`. In this component, you want to set up an input and an output, and you need to tell your component how it should handle data — as in whether it is a synchronous or an asynchronous transformation, as discussed earlier in the chapter. Just as you did with the Source adapter, we'll look at the whole method first and then examine parts of the method in greater detail. Here is the method in full (`ReverseString.cs`):

```
public override void ProvideComponentProperties()
{
 ComponentMetaData.UsesDispositions = true;
 IDTSInput100 ReverseStringInput = ComponentMetaData.InputCollection.New();
 ReverseStringInput.Name = "RSin";
 ReverseStringInput.ErrorRowDisposition = DTSRowDisposition.RD_FailComponent;
 IDTSOutput100 ReverseStringOutput = ComponentMetaData.OutputCollection.New();
 ReverseStringOutput.Name = "RSout";
 ReverseStringOutput.SynchronousInputID = ReverseStringInput.ID;
 ReverseStringOutput.ExclusionGroup = 1;
 AddErrorOutput("RSErrors", ReverseStringInput.ID,
 ReverseStringOutput.ExclusionGroup);
}
```

Breaking it down, you first tell the component to use dispositions:

```
ComponentMetaData.UsesDispositions = true;
```

In this case, you're telling the component that it can expect an error output. Now you move on to adding an input to the component:

```
// Add a new Input, and name it.
IDTSInput100 ReverseStringInput = ComponentMetaData.InputCollection.New();
ReverseStringInput.Name = "RSin";
// If an error occurs during data movement, then the component will fail.
ReverseStringInput.ErrorRowDisposition = DTSRowDisposition.RD_FailComponent;
```

Next, you add the output to the component:

```
// Add a new Output, and name it.
IDTSOutput100 ReverseStringOutput = ComponentMetaData.OutputCollection.New();
ReverseStringOutput.Name = "RSout";
// Link the Input and Output together for a synchronous behavior
ReverseStringOutput.SynchronousInputID = ReverseStringInput.ID;
```

This is similar to adding the input, except that you specify that this is a synchronous component by setting the `SynchronousInputID` on the output to the ID of the input you created earlier. If you were creating an asynchronous component, you would set the `SynchronousInputID` of the output to be `0`, like this:

```
ReverseStringOutput.SynchronousInputID = 0
```

This tells SSIS to create a buffer for the output that is separate from the input buffer. This is not an asynchronous component, though; you will revisit some of the subtle differences later.

`AddErrorOutput` creates a new output on the component and tags it as being an error output by setting the `IsErrorOut` property to `true`. To the method, you pass the name of the error output you want, the input's `ID` property, and the output's `ExclusionGroup`. An `ExclusionGroup` is needed when two outputs use the same synchronous input. Setting the exclusion group enables you to direct rows to the correct output later in the component using `DirectRow`.

```
AddErrorOutput("RSErrors",
ReverseStringInput.ID,ReverseStringOutput.ExclusionGroup);
ReverseStringOutput.ExclusionGroup = 1;
```

That's it for `ProvideComponentProperties`.

Now you'll move on to the `Validate` method. As mentioned earlier, this method is called on numerous occasions, and it is your opportunity within the component to check whether what has been specified by the user is allowable by the component.

Here is your completed `Validate` method (`ReverseString.cs`):

```
[CLSCompliant(false)]
public override DTSValidationStatus Validate()
{
 bool Cancel;
 if (ComponentMetaData.AreInputColumnsValid == false)
 return DTSValidationStatus.VS_NEEDSNEWMETADATA;
 foreach (IDTSInputColumn100 inputColumn in
ComponentMetaData.InputCollection[0].InputColumnCollection) \
{
 if (inputColumn.UsageType != DTSUsageType.UT_READWRITE)
 {
 ComponentMetaData.FireError(0, inputColumn.IdentificationString,
 String.Format(ErrorInvalidUsageType, inputColumn.Name), "",
 0, out Cancel);
 return DTSValidationStatus.VS_ISBROKEN;
 }
 if (inputColumn.DataType != DataType.DT_STR && inputColumn.DataType !=
 DataType.DT_WSTR)
 {
 ComponentMetaData.FireError(0, inputColumn.IdentificationString,
 String.Format(ErrorInvalidDataType, inputColumn.Name), "",
 0, out Cancel);
 return DTSValidationStatus.VS_ISBROKEN;
 }
}
return base.Validate();
}
```

This method will return a validation status to indicate the overall result and may cause subsequent methods to be called. Refer to the SQL Server documentation for a complete list of values (see `DTSValidationStatus`).

Now, to break down the Validate method. A user can easily add and remove an input from the component at any stage and later add it back. It may be the same one, but it may be a different one, presenting the component with an issue. When an input is added, the component stores the LineageIDs of the input columns. If that input is removed and another is added, those LineageIDs may have changed because something such as the query used to generate those columns may have changed. Therefore, you are presented with different columns, so you need to determine whether that has happened; if so, you need to invalidate the LineageIDs. If that's the case, the component will call ReinitializeMetaData.

```
if (ComponentMetaData.AreInputColumnsValid == false)
{ return DTSValidationStatus.VS_NEEDSNEWMETADATA; }
```

Next, you should ensure that each of the columns in the InputColumnCollection chosen for the component has been set to READ WRITE. This is because you will be altering them in place — in other words, you will read a string from a column, reverse it, and then write it back over the old string. If they are not set to READ WRITE, you need to feed that back by returning VS_ISBROKEN. You can invoke the FireError method on the component, which results in a red cross displayed on the component, along with tooltip text indicating the exact error:

```
if (RSincol.UsageType != DTSUsageType.UT_READWRITE)
{
 ComponentMetaData.FireError(0, inputColumn.IdentificationString,
 String.Format(ErrorInvalidUsageType, inputColumn.Name), "",
 0, out Cancel);
 return DTSValidationStatus.VS_ISBROKEN;
}
```

The last thing you do in Validate is verify that the columns selected for the component have the correct data types:

```
if (inputColumn.DataType != DataType.DT_STR && inputColumn.DataType !=
 DataType.DT_WSTR)
...
```

If the data type of the column is not in the list, then you again fire an error and set the return value to VS_ISBROKEN.

Now you will look at the workhorse method of so many of your components: ReinitializeMetaData. Here is the method in full (ReverseString.cs):

```
public override void ReinitializeMetaData()
{
 if (!ComponentMetaData.AreInputColumnsValid)
 {
 ComponentMetaData.RemoveInvalidInputColumns();
 }
 base.ReinitializeMetaData();
}
```

Remember that if `Validate` returns `VS_NEEDSNEWMETADATA`, then the component internally automatically calls `ReinitializeMetaData`. The only time you do that for this component is when you have detected that the `LineageIDs` of the input columns are not quite as expected — that is to say, they do not exist on any upstream column and you want to remove them:

```
if (!ComponentMetaData.AreInputColumnsValid)
{
 ComponentMetaData.RemoveInvalidInputColumns(); }
```

You finish by calling the base class's `ReinitializeMetaData` method as well. Earlier, we referred to this method as the workhorse of your component because you can perform all kinds of triage on it to rescue the component from an aberrant user.

The `SetUsageType` method (`ReverseString.cs`) is called when the user is manipulating how the column on the input will be used by the component. In this component, this method validates the data type of the column and whether the user has set the column to be the correct usage type. The method returns an `IDTSInputColumn`, and this is the column being manipulated:

```
[CLSCompliant(false)]
public override IDTSInputColumn100 SetUsageType(int inputID, IDTSVirtualInput100
virtualInput, int lineageID, DTSUsageType usageType)
{
 IDTSVirtualInputColumn100 virtualInputColumn =
virtualInput.VirtualInputColumnCollection.GetVirtualInputColumnByLineageID(
 lineageID);
 if (usageType == DTSUsageType.UT_READONLY)
 throw new Exception(String.Format(ErrorInvalidUsageType,
 virtualInputColumn.Name));
 if (usageType == DTSUsageType.UT_READWRITE)
 {
 if (virtualInputColumn.DataType != DataType.DT_STR &&
 virtualInputColumn.DataType != DataType.DT_WSTR)
 {
 throw new Exception(String.Format(ErrorInvalidDataType,
 virtualInputColumn.Name));
 }
}
return base.SetUsageType(inputID, virtualInput, lineageID, usageType);
}
```

The first thing the method does is get a reference to the column being changed, from the virtual input, which is the list of all upstream columns available.

You then perform the tests to ensure the column is suitable, before proceeding with the request through the base class. In this case, you want to ensure that the user picks only columns of type `string`. Note that this method looks a lot like the `Validate` method. The only real difference is that the `Validate` method, obviously, returned a different object, but it also reported errors back to the component. `Validate` uses the `FireError` method, but `SetUsageType` throws an exception; in `SetUsageType` you are checking against the `VirtualInput`, and in `Validate()` you check against the `Input100`. (We used to use `FireError` here, but the results bubbled back to the user weren't as predictable, and we were advised that the correct behavior is to throw a new exception.) This method along with others such as `InsertOutput`, `DeleteInput`, `InsertInput`, `OnInputAttached`, and so on are important because they are the key verification methods you can use that enable you to validate in real time a change that is made to your component, and prevent it if necessary.

The `InsertOutput` design-time method is called when a user attempts to add an output to the component. In this component, you want to prohibit that, so if the user tries to add an output, you should throw an exception indicating that it is not allowed:

```
[CLSCompliant(false)]
public override IDTSOutput100 InsertOutput(DTSInsertPlacement insertPlacement, int
outputID)
{
 throw new Exception("You cannot insert an output (" +
 outputID.ToString() + ")");
}
```

You do the same when the user tries to add an input to your component in the `InsertInput` method:

```
[CLSCompliant(false)]
public override IDTSInput100 InsertInput(DTSInsertPlacement insertPlacement, int
inputID)
{
 throw new Exception("You cannot insert an input (" +
 inputID.ToString() + ")");
}
```

Notice again how in both methods you throw an exception in order to tell users that what they requested is not allowed.

If the component were asynchronous, you would need to add columns to the output yourself. You have a choice of methods in which to do this. If you want to add an output column for every input column selected, then the `SetUsageType` method is probably the best place to do that. This is something about which Books Online agrees. Another method for doing this might be `OnInputPathAttached`.

The final two methods you'll look at for the design-time methods are the opposite of the previous two. Instead of users trying to add an output or an input to your component, they are trying to remove one of them. You do not want to allow this either, so you can use the `DeleteOutput` and the `DeleteInput` methods to tell them. Here are the methods as implemented in your component.

First the `DeleteInput` method (`ReverseString.cs`):

```
[CLSCompliant(false)]
public override void DeleteInput(int inputID)
{
 throw new Exception("You cannot delete an input");
}
```

Now the DeleteOutput method:

```
[CLSCompliant(false)]
public override void DeleteOutput(int outputID)
{
 throw new Exception("You cannot delete an output");
}
```

That concludes the code for the design-time part of your Transformation Component.

Runtime Methods

The first runtime method you'll be using is the PreExecute method. As mentioned earlier, this is called once in your component's life, and it is where you typically do most of your setup using the state-holding struct mentioned at the top of this section. It is the first opportunity you get to access the Buffer Manager, providing access to columns within the buffer, which you will need in ProcessInput as well. Keep in mind that you will not be getting a call to PrimeOutput, because this is a synchronous component, and PrimeOutput is not called in a synchronous component. Here is the PreExecute method in full (ReverseString.cs):

```
public override void PreExecute()
{
 // Prepare array of column information. Processing requires
 // lineageID so we can do this once in advance.
 IDTSInput100 input = ComponentMetaData.InputCollection[0];
 _inputColumnInfos = new ColumnInfo[input.InputColumnCollection.Count];
 for (int x = 0; x < input.InputColumnCollection.Count; x++)
 {
 IDTSInputColumn100 column = input.InputColumnCollection[x];
 _inputColumnInfos[x] = new ColumnInfo();
 _inputColumnInfos[x].bufferColumnIndex =
 BufferManager.FindColumnByLineageID(input.Buffer, column.LineageID);
 _inputColumnInfos[x].columnDisposition = column.ErrorRowDisposition;
 _inputColumnInfos[x].lineageID = column.LineageID;
 }
}
```

This method first gets a reference to the input collection. The collection is zero-based, and because you have only one input, you have used the indexer and not the name, though you could have used the name as well:

```
IDTSInput100 input = ComponentMetaData.InputCollection[0];
```

At the start of this section was a list of the things your component would need later. This included a struct that you were told you would use in various guises, and it also included an array of these structs. You now need to size the array, which you do here by setting it to the count of columns in the InputColumnCollection for your component:

```
_inputColumnInfos = new ColumnInfo[input.InputColumnCollection.Count];
```

Now you loop through the columns in the `InputColumnCollection`. For each of the columns, you create a new instance of a column and a new instance of the struct:

```
IDTSInputColumn100 column = input.InputColumnCollection[x];
_inputColumnInfos[x] = new ColumnInfo();
```

You then read from the column the details you require and store them in the `ColumnInfo` object. The first thing you want to retrieve is the column's location in the buffer. You cannot simply do this according to the order that you added them to the buffer. Though this would *probably* work, it is likely to catch you out at some point. You can find the column in the buffer by using a method called `FindColumnByLineageID` on the `BufferManager` object. This method takes the buffer and the `LineageID` of the column that you wish to find as arguments:

```
_inputColumnInfos[x].bufferColumnIndex =
BufferManager.FindColumnByLineageID(input.Buffer, column.LineageID);
```

You now need only two more details about the input column: the `LineageID` and the `ErrorRowDisposition`. Remember that `ErrorRowDisposition` tells the component how to treat an error:

```
_inputColumnInfos[x].columnDisposition = column.ErrorRowDisposition;
_inputColumnInfos[x].lineageID = column.LineageID;
```

When you start to build your own components, you will see how useful this method really is. You can use it to initialize any counters you may need or to open connections to Data Sources as well as anything else you think of.

The final method to look at for this component is `ProcessInput`. Recall that this is a synchronous transformation as dictated in `ProvideComponentProperties`, and this is the method in which the data is moved and manipulated. This method contains a lot of information that will help you understand the buffer and what to do with the columns in it when you receive them. It is called once for every buffer passed.

Here is the method in full (`ReverseString.cs`):

```
public override void ProcessInput(int inputID, PipelineBuffer buffer)
{
int errorOutputID = -1;
int errorOutputIndex = -1;
int GoodOutputId = -1;
IDTSInput100 inp = ComponentMetaData.InputCollection.GetObjectByID(inputID);
#region Output IDs
GetErrorOutputInfo(ref errorOutputID, ref errorOutputIndex);
// There is an error output defined
errorOutputID = ComponentMetaData.OutputCollection["RSErrors"].ID;
GoodOutputId = ComponentMetaData.OutputCollection["ReverseStringOutput"].ID;
#endregion
while (buffer.NextRow())
{
// Check if we have columns to process
if (_inputColumnInfos.Length == 0)
```

```
{
// We do not have to have columns. This is a Sync component so the
// rows will flow through regardless. Could expand Validate to check
// for columns in the InputColumnCollection
buffer.DirectRow(GoodOutputId);
}
else
{
try
{
for (int x = 0; x < _inputColumnInfos.Length; x++)
{
ColumnInfo columnInfo = _inputColumnInfos[x];
if (!buffer.IsNull(columnInfo.bufferColumnIndex))
{
// Get value as character array
char[] chars =
buffer.GetString(columnInfo.bufferColumnIndex)
.ToString().ToCharArray();
// Reverse order of characters in array
Array.Reverse(chars);
// Reassemble reversed value as string
string s = new string(chars);
// Set output value in buffer
buffer.SetString(columnInfo.bufferColumnIndex, s);
}
}
buffer.DirectRow(GoodOutputId);
}
catch(Exception ex)
{
switch (inp.ErrorRowDisposition)
{
case DTSRowDisposition.RD_RedirectRow:
buffer.DirectErrorRow(errorOutputID, 0, buffer.CurrentRow);
break;
case DTSRowDisposition.RD_FailComponent:
throw new Exception("Error processing " + ex.Message);
case DTSRowDisposition.RD_IgnoreFailure:
buffer.DirectRow(GoodOutputId);
break;
}
}
}
}
}
```

There is a lot going on in this method, so we'll break it down to make it more manageable. The first thing you do is find out from the component the location of the error output:

```
int errorOutputID = -1;
int errorOutputIndex = -1;
int GoodOutputId = -1;
#region Output IDs
```

```
GetErrorOutputInfo(ref errorOutputID, ref errorOutputIndex);
errorOutputID = ComponentMetaData.OutputCollection["RSErrors"].ID;
GoodOutputId = ComponentMetaData.OutputCollection["ReverseStringOutput"].ID;
#endregion
```

The method `GetErrorOutput` returns the output ID and the index of the error output. Remember that you defined the error output in `ProvideComponentProperties` with the `AddErrorOutput` function.

Because you could have many inputs to a component, you want to isolate the input for this component. You can do that by finding the output that is passed into the method:

```
IDTSInput100 inp = ComponentMetaData.InputCollection.GetObjectByID(inputID);
```

You need this because you want to know what to do with the row if you encounter an issue. You provided a default value for the `ErrorRowDisposition` property of the input in `ProvideComponentProperties`, but this can be overridden in the UI.

Next, you want to check that the upstream buffer has not called `SetEndOfRowset`, which would mean that it has no more rows to send after the current buffer; however, the current buffer might still contain rows. You then loop through the rows in the buffer like this:

```
while (buffer.NextRow())
...
```

You then check whether the user asked for any columns to be manipulated. Because this is a synchronous component, all columns and rows are going to flow through even if you do not specify any columns for the component. Therefore, you specify that if there are no input columns selected, the row should be passed to the normal output. You do this by looking at the size of the array that holds the collection of `ColumnInfo` struct objects:

```
if (_inputColumnInfos.Length == 0)
{
buffer.DirectRow(GoodOutputId);
}
```

If the length of the array is not zero, then the user has asked the component to perform an operation on the column. In turn, you need to grab each of the `ColumnInfo` objects from the array so you can look at the data. Here you begin your loop through the columns, and for each column you create a new instance of the `ColumnInfo` struct:

```
for (int x = 0; x < _inputColumnInfos.Length; x++)
{
ColumnInfo columnInfo = _inputColumnInfos[x];
...
```

You now have a reference to that column and are ready to start manipulating it. You first convert the column's data into an array of chars:

```
char[] chars =
buffer.GetString(columnInfo.bufferColumnIndex).ToString().ToCharArray();
```

The interesting part of this line is the method `GetString()` on the buffer object. It returns the string data of the column and accepts as an argument the index of the column in the buffer. This is really easy, because you stored that reference earlier in the `PreExecute` method.

Now that you have the char array, you can perform some operations on the data. In this case, you want to reverse the string. This code is not particular to SSIS, and it's a trivial example of string manipulation, but you can imagine doing something more useful here such as encryption, cleaning, or formatting:

```
Array.Reverse(chars);
string s = new string(chars);
```

Now you reassign the changed data back to the column using the `SetString()` method on the buffer:

```
buffer.SetString(columnInfo.bufferColumnIndex, s);
```

Again, this method takes as one of the arguments the index of the column in the buffer. It also takes the string you want to assign to that column. You can see now why it was important to ensure that this column is read/write. If there was no error, you point the row to the good output buffer:

```
buffer.DirectRow(GoodOutputId);
```

If you encounter an error, you want to redirect this row to the correct output or alternately throw an error. You do that in the `catch` block:

```
catch(Exception ex)
{
switch (inp.ErrorRowDisposition)
{
case DTSRowDisposition.RD_RedirectRow:
buffer.DirectErrorRow(errorOutputID, 0, buffer.CurrentRow);
break;
case DTSRowDisposition.RD_FailComponent:
throw new Exception("Error processing " + ex.Message);
case DTSRowDisposition.RD_IgnoreFailure:
buffer.DirectRow(GoodOutputId);
break;
}
}
```

The code is mostly self-explanatory. If the input was configured by the user to redirect the row to the error output, then you do that. If it was told to fail the component or the user did not specify anything, then you throw an exception. Otherwise, the component is asked to just ignore the errors and allow the error row to flow down the normal output.

How would this have looked had it been an asynchronous transformation? You would get a buffer from both `PrimeOutput` and `ProcessInput`. The `ProcessInput` method would contain the data and structure that came into the component, and `PrimeOutput` would contain the structure that the component expects to pass on. The trick here is to get the data from one buffer into the other. Here is one way you can approach it.

At the class level, create a variable of type `PipelineBuffer`, something like this:

```
PipelineBuffer _pipelinebuffer;
```

In `PrimeOutput`, assign the output buffer to this buffer:

```
public override void PrimeOutput(int outputs, int[] outputIDs, PipelineBuffer[]
buffers)
{
_pipelinebuffer = buffers[0];
}
```

You now have a cached version of the buffer from `PrimeOutput`, and you can go straight over to `ProcessInput` and use it. Books Online has a great example of doing this in an asynchronous component: navigate to "asynchronous outputs."

> **NOTE** *Don't hesitate to look through Books Online. Microsoft has done a fantastic job of including content that offers good, solid examples. Also search for the SSIS component samples on* `http://msdn.microsoft.com/en-us/`. *Visit* `http://sqlsrvintegrationsrv.codeplex.com/` *for some open-source components that you can download, change, and use. The projects here are also a great learning tool because the authors are usually expert SSIS developers.*

Building the Destination Adapter

The requirement for the Destination adapter is that it accepts an input from an upstream component of any description and converts it to a format similar to that seen in the Source adapter. The component will use a `FILE` Connection Manager, and as shown in earlier components, this involves a significant amount of validation. You also need to validate whether the component is structurally correct; if it isn't, you need to correct things.

If you're following along with the book and are writing the code manually, right-click on the Wrox. Pipeline project in Visual Studio and click "Add ➪ New Item". Select the "Class" template in the "Add New Item" dialog and create a new file named ProfSSISDestAdapter.cs.

The first thing you always need to do is declare some variables that will be used throughout the component (`ProfSSISDestAdapter.cs`). You also need to create the very valuable state-information struct that is going to store the details of the columns, which will be needed in `PreExecute` and `ProcessInput`:

```
#region Variables
private ArrayList _columnInfos = new ArrayList();
private Microsoft.SqlServer.Dts.Runtime.DTSFileConnectionUsageType _fil;
private string _filename;
FileStream _fs;
StreamWriter _sw;
#endregion
```

You should quickly run through the meaning of these variables and when they will be needed. The `_columnInfos variable` is used to store `ColumnInfo` objects, which describe the columns in the `InputColumnCollection`. The `_fil` variable is used to validate the type of `FILE` Connection Manager the user has assigned to your component. `_filename` stores the name of the file that is retrieved from the `FILE` Connection Manager. The final two variables, `_fs` and `_sw`, are used when you write to the text file in `ProcessInput`. Now take a look at the `ColumnInfo` struct:

```
#region ColumnInfo
private struct ColumnInfo
{
public int BufferColumnIndex;
public string ColumnName;
}
#endregion
```

The struct is used to store the index number of the column in the buffer and the name of the column.

At this point, it is time to look at the `ProvideComponentProperties` method, which is where you set up the component and prepare it for use by an SSIS package, as in the other two components. Here's the method in full (`ProfSSISDestAdapter.cs`):

```
public override void ProvideComponentProperties()
{
ComponentMetaData.RuntimeConnectionCollection.RemoveAll();
RemoveAllInputsOutputsAndCustomProperties();
ComponentMetaData.Name = "Wrox SSIS Destination Adapter";
ComponentMetaData.Description = "Our first Destination Adapter";
ComponentMetaData.ContactInfo = "www.wrox.com";
IDTSRuntimeConnection100 rtc =
ComponentMetaData.RuntimeConnectionCollection.New();
rtc.Name = "File To Write";
rtc.Description = "This is the file to which we want to write";
IDTSInput100 input = ComponentMetaData.InputCollection.New();
input.Name = "Component Input";
input.Description = "This is what we see from the upstream component";
input.HasSideEffects = true;
}
```

The first part of the method gets rid of any runtime Connection Managers that the component may have and removes any custom properties, inputs, and outputs it may contain. This makes the component a clean slate to which you can now add back anything it may need:

```
ComponentMetaData.RuntimeConnectionCollection.RemoveAll();
RemoveAllInputsOutputsAndCustomProperties();
```

The component requires one connection, defined as follows:

```
IDTSRuntimeConnection100 rtc = ComponentMetaData.RuntimeConnectionCollection.New();
rtc.Name = "File To Write";
rtc.Description = "This is the file to which we want to write";
```

The preceding piece of code gives the user the opportunity to specify a Connection Manager for the component. This will be the file to which you write the data from upstream.

Next, you add back the input:

```
IDTSInput100 input = ComponentMetaData.InputCollection.New();
input.Name = "Component Input";
input.Description = "This is what we see from the upstream component";
```

This is what the upstream component will connect to, and through which you will receive the data from the previous component. You need to ensure that the `IDTSInput100` object of the component remains in the execution plan, regardless of whether it is attached, by setting the `HasSideEffects` property to `true`. This means that at runtime, the SSIS execution engine is smart enough to "prune" from the package any components that are not actually doing any work. You need to explicitly tell SSIS that this component is doing work (external file writes) by setting this property:

```
input.HasSideEffects = true;
```

After completing the `ProvideComponentProperties` method, you can move on to the `AcquireConnections` method (`ProfSSISDestAdapter.cs`). This method is not really any different from the `AcquireConnections` method you saw in the Source adapter; the method is shown in full but without being described in detail. If you need line-by-line details about what's happening, you can refer back to the Source adapter. This method accomplishes the following tasks:

- Checks whether the user has supplied a Connection Manager to the component.
- Checks whether the Connection Manager is a `FILE` Connection Manager.
- Ensures that the `FILE` Connection Manager has a `FileUsageType` property value of `DTSFileConnectionUsageType.CreateFile`. (This is different from the Source, which required an existing file.)
- Gets the filename from the Connection Manager.

```
public override void AcquireConnections(object transaction)
{
bool pbCancel = false;
if (ComponentMetaData.RuntimeConnectionCollection["File To
Write"].ConnectionManager != null)
{
ConnectionManager cm =
Microsoft.SqlServer.Dts.Runtime.DtsConvert.GetWrapper(
ComponentMetaData.RuntimeConnectionCollection["File To Write"]
.ConnectionManager);
if (cm.CreationName != "FILE")
{
ComponentMetaData.FireError(0, "Acquire Connections", "The Connection
Manager is not a FILE Connection Manager", "", 0, out pbCancel);
throw new Exception("The Connection Manager is not a FILE Connection
Manager");
}
else
```

```
{
_fil = (DTSFileConnectionUsageType)cm.Properties["FileUsageType"]
.GetValue(cm);
if (_fil != DTSFileConnectionUsageType.CreateFile)
{
ComponentMetaData.FireError(0, "Acquire Connections",
"The type of FILE connection manager must be Create File", "",
0, out pbCancel);
throw new Exception("The type of FILE connection manager must be
Create File");
}
else
{
_filename = ComponentMetaData.RuntimeConnectionCollection
["File To Read"].ConnectionManager.AcquireConnection(transaction)
.ToString();
if (_filename == null || _filename.Length == 0)
{
ComponentMetaData.FireError(0, "Acquire Connections", "Nothing
returned when grabbing the filename", "", 0, out pbCancel);
throw new Exception("Nothing returned when grabbing the filename");
}
}
}
}
}
```

A lot of ground is covered in the `AcquireConnections` method. Much of this code is covered again in the `Validate` method, which you will visit now. The `Validate` method also checks whether the input to the component is correct; if it isn't, you try to fix what is wrong by calling `ReinitializeMetaData`. Here is the `Validate` method (`ProfSSISDestAdapter.cs`):

```
[CLSCompliant(false)]
public override DTSValidationStatus Validate()
{
bool pbCancel = false;
if (ComponentMetaData.OutputCollection.Count != 0)
{
ComponentMetaData.FireError(0, ComponentMetaData.Name,
"Unexpected Output
Found. Destination components do not support outputs.", "",
0, out pbCancel);
return DTSValidationStatus.VS_ISCORRUPT;
}
if (ComponentMetaData.RuntimeConnectionCollection["File To Write"]
.ConnectionManager == null)
{
ComponentMetaData.FireError(0, "Validate", "No Connection Manager returned",
"", 0, out pbCancel);
return DTSValidationStatus.VS_ISCORRUPT;
}
```

```
if (ComponentMetaData.AreInputColumnsValid == false)
{
ComponentMetaData.InputCollection["Component Input"]
InputColumnCollection.RemoveAll();
return DTSValidationStatus.VS_NEEDSNEWMETADATA;
}
return base.Validate();
}
```

The first check in the method ensures that the component has no outputs:

```
bool pbCancel = false;
if (ComponentMetaData.OutputCollection.Count != 0)
{
ComponentMetaData.FireError(0, ComponentMetaData.Name, "Unexpected Output found.
Destination components do not support outputs.", "", 0, out pbCancel);
return DTSValidationStatus.VS_ISCORRUPT;
}
```

You now want to ensure that the user specified a Connection Manager. Remember that you are only validating the fact that a Connection Manager is specified, not whether it is a valid type. The extensive checking of the Connection Manager is done in `AcquireConnections()`.

```
if (ComponentMetaData.RuntimeConnectionCollection["File To
Write"].ConnectionManager == null)
{
ComponentMetaData.FireError(0, "Validate", "No Connection Manager returned", "",
0, out pbCancel);
return DTSValidationStatus.VS_ISCORRUPT;
}
```

The final thing you do in this method is to check whether the input columns are valid. *Valid* in this instance means that the columns in the input collection reference existing columns in the upstream component. If this is not the case, you call the trusty `ReinitializeMetaData` method.

```
if (ComponentMetaData.AreInputColumnsValid == false)
{
ComponentMetaData.InputCollection["Component Input"]
.InputColumnCollection.RemoveAll();
return DTSValidationStatus.VS_NEEDSNEWMETADATA;
}
```

The return value `DTSValidationStatus.VS_NEEDSNEWMETADATA` means that the component will now call `ReinitializeMetaData` to try to sort out the problems with the component. Here is that method in full:

```
public override void ReinitializeMetaData()
{
IDTSInput100 _profinput = ComponentMetaData.InputCollection["Component Input"];
_profinput.InputColumnCollection.RemoveAll();
```

```
IDTSVirtualInput100 vInput = _profinput.GetVirtualInput();
foreach (IDTSVirtualInputColumn100 vCol in vInput.VirtualInputColumnCollection)
{
this.SetUsageType(_profinput.ID, vInput, vCol.LineageID,
DTSUsageType.UT_READONLY);
}
}
```

> **NOTE** *Notice that the columns are blown away in* `ReinitializeMetaData` *and built again from scratch. A better solution is to test what the invalid columns are and try to fix them. If you cannot fix them, you could remove them, and then the user could reselect at leisure. Books Online has an example of doing this.*

The `IDTSVirtualInput` and `IDTSVirtualInputColumnCollection` in this component need a little explanation. There is a subtle difference between these two objects and their input equivalents. The "virtual" objects are what your component could have as inputs — that is to say, they are upstream inputs and columns that present themselves as available to your component. The inputs themselves are what you have chosen for your component to have as inputs from the virtual object. In the `ReinitializeMetaData` method, you start by removing all existing input columns:

```
IDTSInput100 _profinput = ComponentMetaData.InputCollection["Component Input"];
_profinput.InputColumnCollection.RemoveAll();
```

You then get a reference to the input's virtual input:

```
IDTSVirtualInput100 vInput = _profinput.GetVirtualInput();
```

Now that you have the virtual input, you can add an input column to the component for every virtual input column you find:

```
foreach (IDTSVirtualInputColumn100 vCol in vInput.VirtualInputColumnCollection)
{
this.SetUsageType(_profinput.ID, vInput, vCol.LineageID,
DTSUsageType.UT_READONLY);
}
```

The `SetUsageType` method simply adds an input column to the input column collection of the component, or removes it depending on your `UsageType` value. When a user adds a connector from an upstream component that contains its output to this component and attaches it to this component's input, the `OnInputAttached` method is called. This method has been overridden in the component herein:

```
public override void OnInputPathAttached(int inputID)
{
IDTSInput100 input = ComponentMetaData.InputCollection.GetObjectByID(inputID);
IDTSVirtualInput100 vInput = input.GetVirtualInput();
```

```
foreach (IDTSVirtualInputColumn100 vCol in vInput.VirtualInputColumnCollection)
{
this.SetUsageType(inputID, vInput, vCol.LineageID, DTSUsageType.UT_READONLY);
}
}
```

This method is the same as the `ReinitializeMetaData` method except that you don't need to remove the input columns from the collection. This is because if the input is not mapped to the output of an upstream component, there can be no input columns.

That completes the design-time methods for your component. You can now move on to look at the runtime methods. You are going to be looking at only two methods: `PreExecute` and `ProcessInput`.

`PreExecute` is executed only once in this component (`ProfSSISDestAdapter.cs`), so you want to do as much preparation work as you can in this method. It is also the first opportunity in the component to access the Buffer Manager, which contains the columns. In this component, you use it for two things: getting the information about the component's input columns and storing essential details about them:

```
public override void PreExecute()
{
IDTSInput100 input = ComponentMetaData.InputCollection["Component Input"];
foreach (IDTSInputColumn100 inCol in input.InputColumnCollection)
{
ColumnInfo ci = new ColumnInfo();
ci.BufferColumnIndex = BufferManager.FindColumnByLineageID(input.Buffer,
inCol.LineageID);
ci.ColumnName = inCol.Name;
_columnInfos.Add(ci);
}
// Open the file
_fs = new FileStream(_filename, FileMode.OpenOrCreate, FileAccess.Write);
_sw = new StreamWriter(_fs);
}
```

First you get a reference to the component's input:

```
IDTSInput100 input = ComponentMetaData.InputCollection["Component Input"];
```

Then you loop through the input's `InputColumnCollection`:

```
foreach (IDTSInputColumn100 inCol in input.InputColumnCollection)
{
```

For each input column you find, you need to create a new instance of the `ColumnInfo` struct. You then assign to the struct values you can retrieve from the input column itself and the Buffer

Manager. You assign these values to the struct and finally add them to the array that is holding all the `ColumnInfo` objects:

```
ColumnInfo ci = new ColumnInfo();
ci.BufferColumnIndex = BufferManager.FindColumnByLineageID(input.Buffer,
inCol.LineageID);
ci.ColumnName = inCol.Name;
_columnInfos.Add(ci);
```

Doing things this way will enable you to move more quickly through the `ProcessInput` method. The last thing you do in the `PreExecute` method is get a reference to the file to which you want to write:

```
_fs = new FileStream(_filename, FileMode.OpenOrCreate, FileAccess.Write);
_sw = new StreamWriter(_fs);
```

You will use this in the next method, `ProcessInput` (`ProfSSISDestAdapter.cs`). `ProcessInput` is where you are going to keep reading the rows that are coming from the upstream component. While there are rows, you write those values to a file. This is a very simplistic view of what needs to be done, so you should have a look at how to make that happen.

```
public override void ProcessInput(int inputID, PipelineBuffer buffer)
{
while (buffer.NextRow())
{
_sw.WriteLine("<START>");
for (int i = 0; i < _columnInfos.Count; i++)
{
ColumnInfo ci = (ColumnInfo)_columnInfos[i];
if (buffer.IsNull(ci.BufferColumnIndex))
{
_sw.WriteLine(ci.ColumnName + ":");
}
else
{
_sw.WriteLine(ci.ColumnName + ":" +
buffer[ci.BufferColumnIndex].ToString());
}
}
_sw.WriteLine("<END>");
}
if (buffer.EndOfRowset) _sw.Close();
}
```

The first thing you do is check whether there are still rows in the buffer:

```
while (buffer.NextRow())
{
...
```

You now need to loop through the array that is holding the collection of `ColumnInfo` objects that were populated in the `PreExecute` method:

```
for (int i = 0; i < _columnInfos.Count; i++)
```

For each iteration, you create a new instance of the `ColumnInfo` object:

```
ColumnInfo ci = (ColumnInfo)_columnInfos[i];
```

You now need to retrieve from the buffer object the value of the column whose index you will pass in from the `ColumnInfo` object. If the value is not null, you write the value of the column and the column name to the text file. If the value is null, you write just the column name to the text file. Again, because you took the time to store these details in a `ColumnInfo` object earlier, retrieving these properties is easy.

```
if (buffer.IsNull(ci.BufferColumnIndex))
{
_sw.WriteLine(ci.ColumnName + ":");
}
else
{
_sw.WriteLine(ci.ColumnName + ":" + buffer[ci.BufferColumnIndex].ToString());
}
```

Finally, you check whether the upstream component has called `SetEndOfRowset`; if so, you close the file stream:

```
if (buffer.EndOfRowset) _sw.Close();
```

Having concluded your look at the Destination adapter, you are ready to learn how you get SSIS to recognize your components and what properties you need to assign to them.

USING THE COMPONENTS

In this section you install the components you have created into the SSIS design environment so you can use them to build packages. You then learn how to debug the components so you can troubleshoot any coding issues they contain.

Installing the Components

Unlike previous versions of BIDS pre SQL Server 2012, there is no Choose Items dialog for SQL Server Data Tools SSIS components. To add a component to the SSIS Toolbox:

1. Open SQL Server Data Tools and then create or open an SSIS solution.
2. Create a new Data Flow Task and then double-click it to enter the Data Flow panel. The Wrox.Pipeline components will automatically appear in the SSIS Toolbox (see Figure 19-6).

The components show up automatically because they are copied to the `%PROGRAMFILES%\Microsoft SQL Server\120\DTS\PipelineComponents` directory in your project's post-build event.

If the components are not displayed in the SSIS Toolbox, ensure that you are referencing the SQL Server 2014 versions of the references, not any of the previous versions of SQL Server, and that the post-build event in your project is copying the files to the correct directory for your installation of Integration Services.

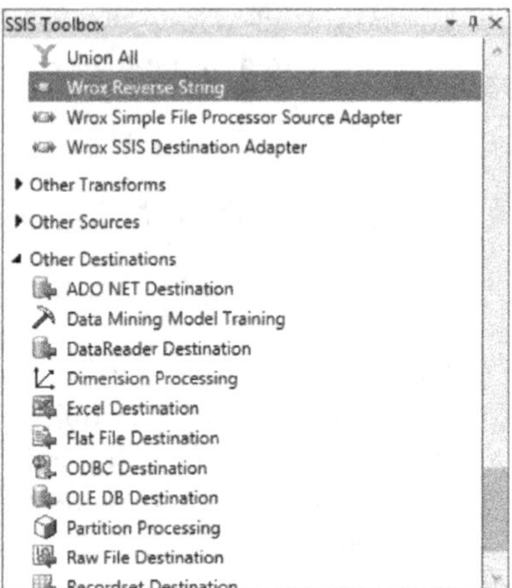

FIGURE 19-6

Debugging Components

Debugging components is a really great feature of SSIS. If you are a Visual Studio.NET developer, you should easily recognize the interface. If you're not familiar with Visual Studio, this section explains what you need to know to become proficient in debugging your components.

There are two phases for debugging. The design time can be debugged only while you're developing your package, so it makes sense that you need to use SQL Server Data Tools to do this. The second phase, which is the runtime experience, is slightly different. You can still use SQL Server Data Tools, though, and when your package runs, the component will stop at breakpoints you designate. You need to set up a few things first, though. You can also use DTExec to fire the package straight from Visual Studio. The latter method saves you the cost of invoking another instance of Visual Studio. The component you are going to debug is the Reverse String Transformation.

Design Time

This section describes the process of debugging the component at design time. Open the Visual Studio Wrox.Pipeline C# project and set a C# breakpoint at ProvideComponentProperties (SSIS also has breakpoints, which are discussed further in Chapter 18). Now create a new SSIS project in SQL Server Data Tools. In the package, add a Data Flow Task and double-click it. If your component is not in the Toolbox already, add it now.

You need to create a full pipeline in this package because you'll be using it later when you debug the runtime. Therefore, get an OLE DB or ADO.NET Connection Manager and point it to the AdventureWorks database. Now add an OLE DB or ADO.NET Source adapter to the design surface and configure it to use the Connection Manager you just created. Point the source to one of the tables in AdventureWorks — perhaps `Person.Person` — and select the columns you want to use.

Before adding your new components to the designer, you need to attach to the SQL Server Data Tools instance (DevEnv.exe) from the Wrox.Pipeline project you're working in so that it can receive the methods fired by the component. To do that, in the Visual Studio Wrox.Pipeline C# project, select Debug ⇨ Attach to Process. The Attach to Process dialog opens (see Figure 19-7), where you can choose what you want to debug, as well as which process.

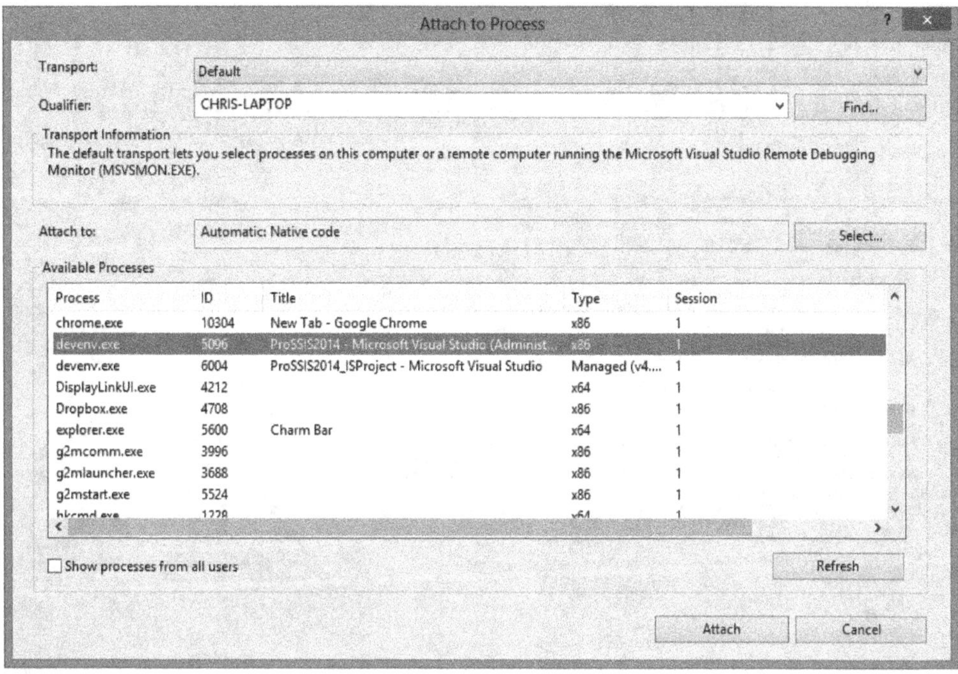

FIGURE 19-7

The process you're interested in is the package you're currently building. This shows up in the Available Processes list as ProSSIS2014_ISProject – Microsoft Visual Studio (the name you see may differ). Just above this window is a small box containing the words "Managed (v4.0) code." This tells the debugger what you want to debug in the component. Three options are available, which you can view by clicking the Select button to the right of the label: Managed, Native, and Script.

Highlight the process for your package and click Attach. If you look down now at the status bar in your component's design project, you should see a variety of debug symbols being loaded. Go back to the SSIS package and drop the Reverse String Transformation onto the design surface. Because one of the first things a component does after it is dropped into a package is call `ProvideComponentProperties`, you should immediately see your component break into the code in its design project, as shown in Figure 19-8.

As you can see, the breakpoint on `ProvideComponentProperties` in the component's design project has been hit. This is indicated by a yellow arrow inside the red breakpoint circle on the left. You are now free to debug the component as you would any other piece of managed code in Visual Studio.NET. If you're familiar with debugging, a number of windows appear at this point at the bottom of the IDE, such as Locals, Autos, and Call Stack. These can help you get to the root of any debugging problems, but you don't need to use them now.

To leave debugging mode, return to Visual Studio and select Debug ⇨ Stop Debugging.

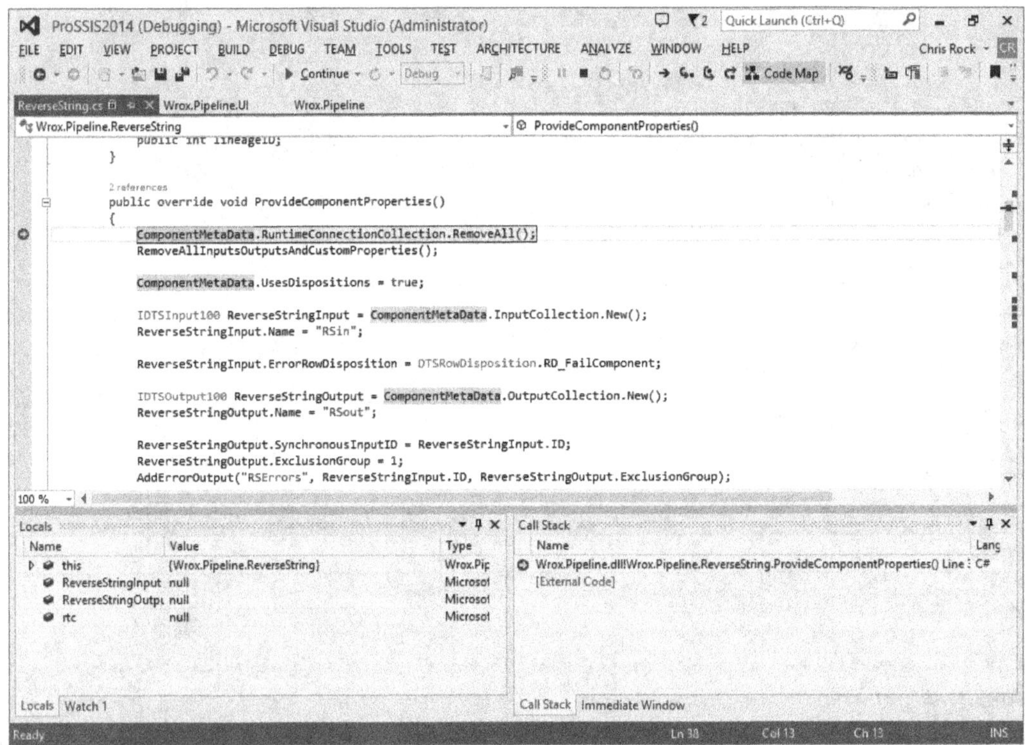

FIGURE 19-8

Building the Complete Package

Because the package already has a source and Transformation Component on it, you just need to add a destination. First make sure you have both configured the Reverse String Transformation to reverse some of the columns by double-clicking it and selected the required columns in the custom UI (or the Advanced UI if you have not built the custom UI yet, which is discussed in Chapter 20).

In the SSIS Connections pane, create a new File Connection Manager, setting the Usage Type to Create File. Enter a filename in a location of your choice, and then close the Connection Manager dialog.

Drop the Destination Component you have just built onto the design surface and connect the output of the Reverse String Transformation to the input of the destination. Open the destination's editor, and on the first tab of the Advanced Editor, set the File to Write property value to the name of the connection you just created. Flip over to the Input Columns tab in the editor, and select which columns you want to write to the output file.

Runtime Debugging

As promised, in this section you are going to look at two ways of debugging. As with design-time debugging, the first is through the SQL Server Data Tools designer. The other is by using `DTExec` and the package properties. Using SQL Server Data Tools is similar to the design-time method with a subtle variation.

You should now have a complete pipeline with the Reverse String Transformation in the middle. If you don't, quickly create a pipeline like the one shown in Figure 19-9.

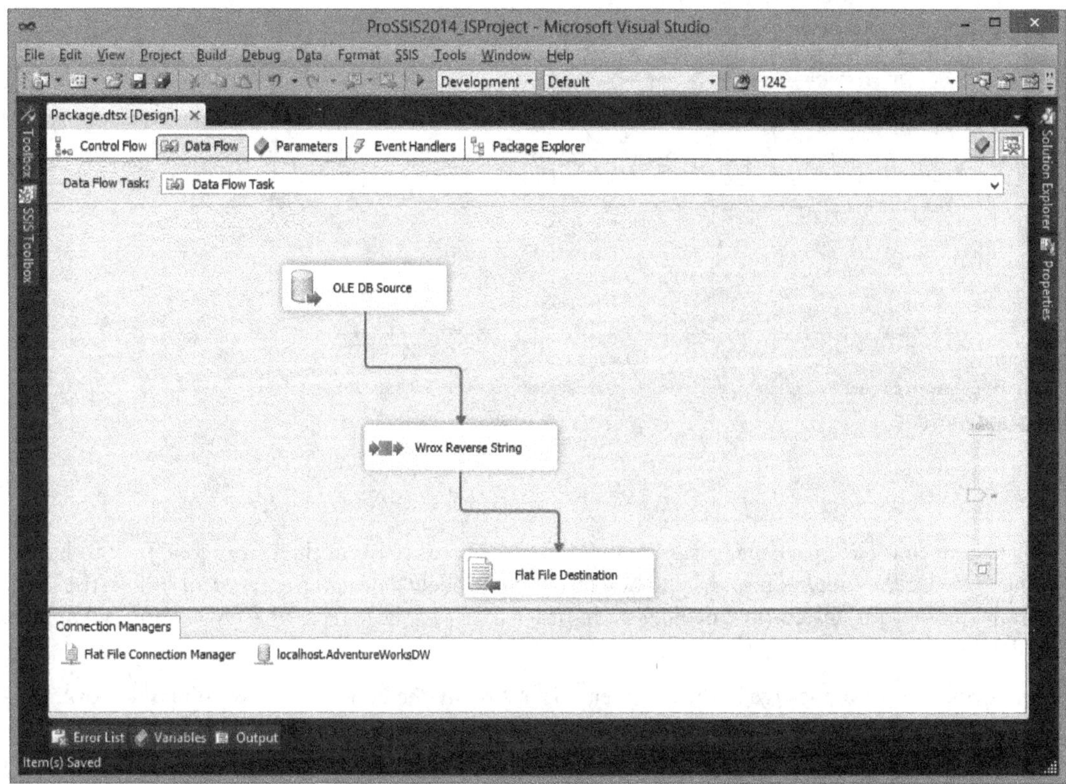

FIGURE 19-9

> **NOTE** *Instead of a real destination that writes to a file or database, it is often useful to write to a so-called* trash destination. *You can use a Row Count Transformation or Union All Transformation for this purpose.*

You now need to add a breakpoint to the Data Flow Task that is hit when the Data Flow Task hits the `OnPreExecute` event. You need to do this so that you can attach your debugger to the correct process at runtime. Right-click the Data Flow Task itself and select Edit Breakpoints. The Set Breakpoints dialog will appear, as shown in Figure 19-10.

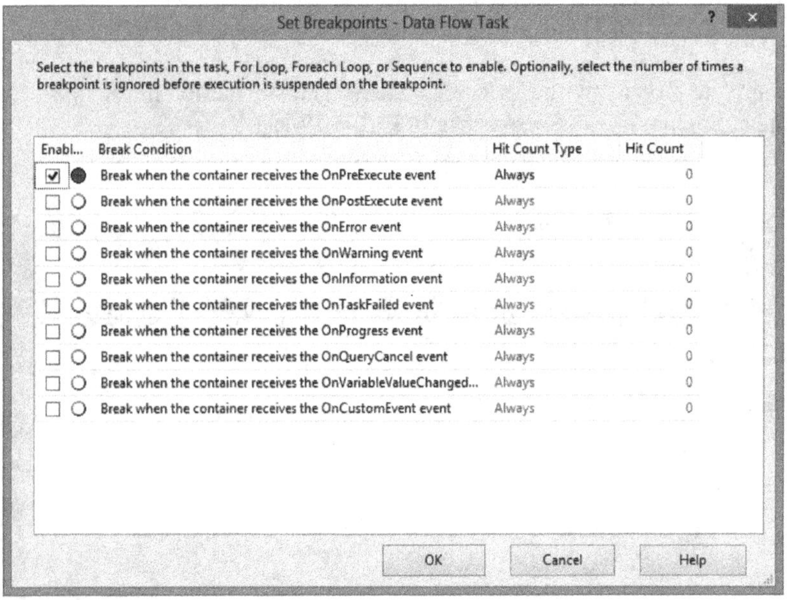

FIGURE 19-10

To execute your SSIS package, press F5 and allow the breakpoint in the Data Flow Task to be hit. When you hit the breakpoint, switch back to the component's design process and follow the steps detailed earlier for design-time debugging in order to get to the screen where you chose what process to debug.

When you execute a package in the designer, it is not really the designer that is doing the work. It hands off the execution to a process called `DtsDebugHost.exe`. This is the package that you want to attach to, as shown in Figure 19-11. You will probably see two of these processes listed; the one you want has Managed listed under the Type column (don't attach to the process showing x86 as the type).

Click Attach and watch the debug symbols being loaded by the project. Before returning to the SSIS package, you need to set a breakpoint on one of the runtime methods used by your component, such as `PreExecute`. Return to the SSIS project and press F5 again. This will release the package from its suspended state and allow the package to flow on. Now when the Reverse String Component hits its `PreExecute` method, you should be able to debug what it is doing. In Figure 19-12, this user put a breakpoint on a line of code that enables him or her to look at the "input" variable in the Locals window.

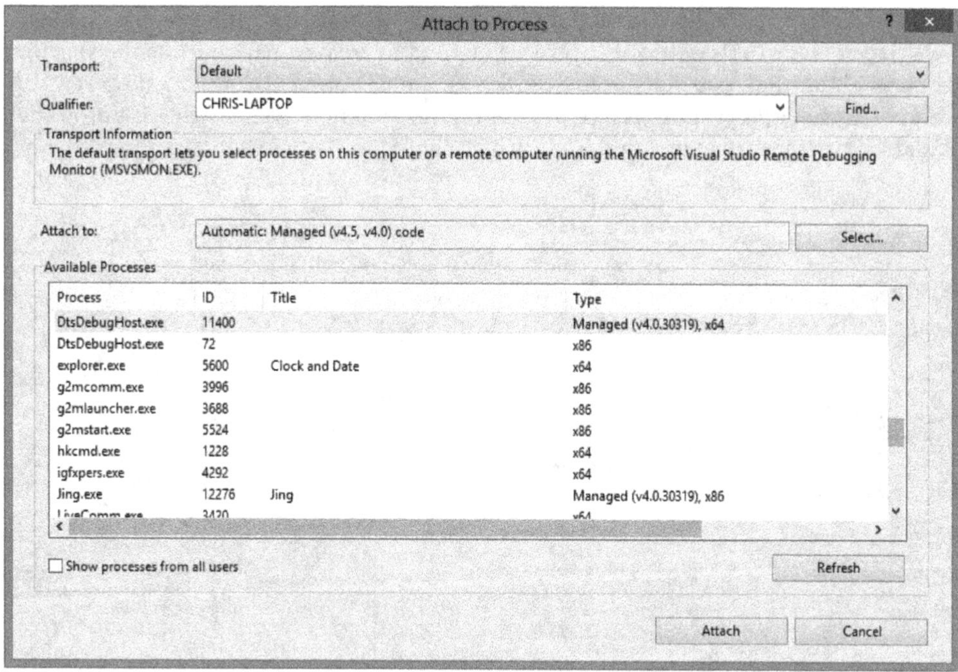

FIGURE 19-11

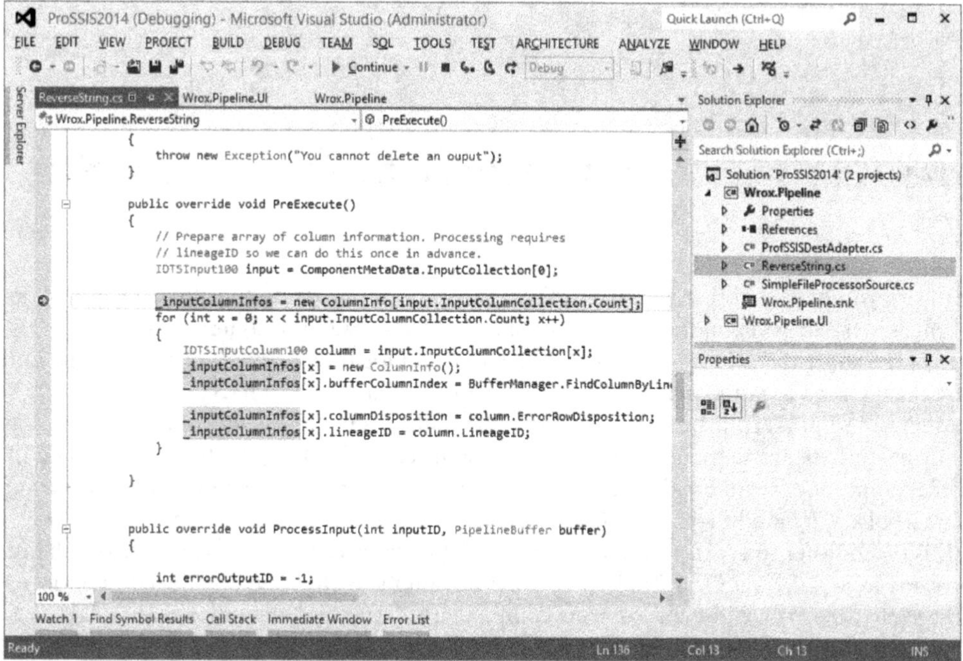

FIGURE 19-12

That concludes your look at the first method for debugging the runtime. The second method involves SQL Server Data Tools indirectly because you need to create a package like this one that you can call later. After that, you don't need SQL Server Data Tools at all. You do, however, still need the component's design project open. Open your Visual Studio Reverse String C# project's properties and look at the Debug tab on the left, which should look similar to Figure 19-13.

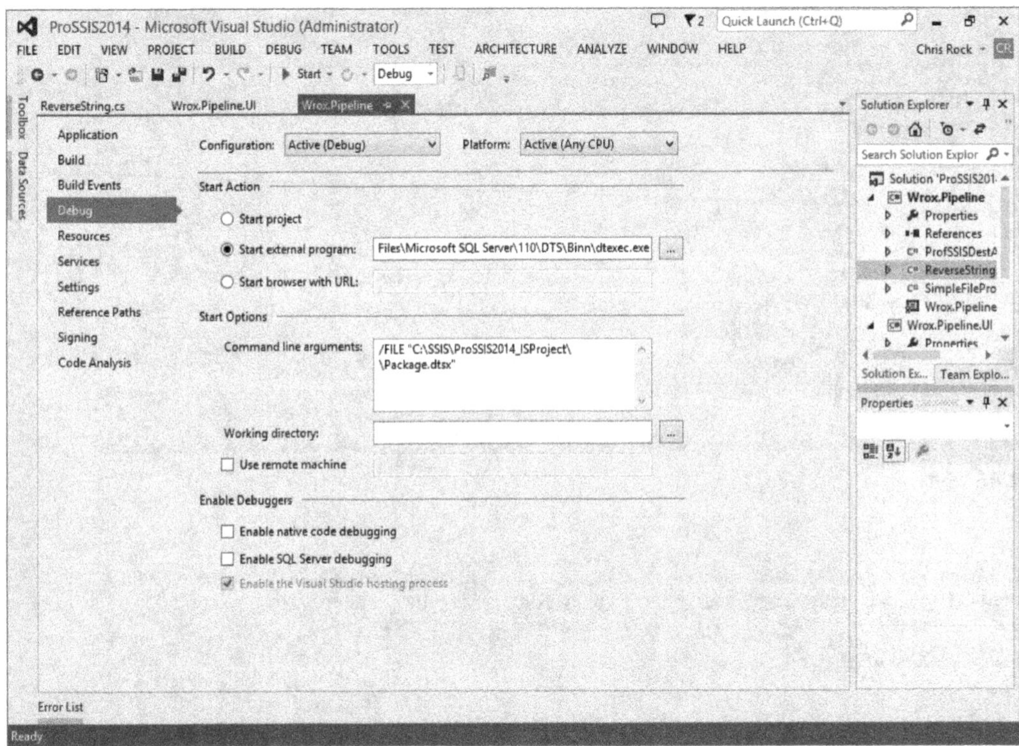

FIGURE 19-13

As you can see, you have said that you want to start an external program to debug. That program is `DTExec`, which is the new and more powerful version of `DTSRun`. On the command line, you pass a parameter `/FILE` to `DTExec`. This tells `DTExec` the name and location of the package you just built. Make sure the file path to your package is valid, and ensure that you still have a C# breakpoint set on `PreExecute`, and press F5 in your project. A DOS window will appear where you will see some messages fly past; these are the same messages you would see in the designer. Eventually you will get to your breakpoint, and it will break in exactly the same way that it did when you were using SQL Server Data Tools. Why might you use one approach over the other? The most obvious answer is speed. It is much faster to get to where you want to debug your component using `DTExec` than it is doing the same in SQL Server Data Tools. The other advantage is that you don't need two tools open at the same time. You can focus on your component's design project and not worry about SQL Server Data Tools at all.

UPGRADING TO SQL SERVER 2014

If you already built components in SQL Server 2008 and you want to use them in SQL Server 2014, you have to update the references and recompile the components. There weren't any significant changes to SSIS from 2012, and all components compiled to run against 2012 will automatically work in 2014.

Microsoft has retained the same interface names used in SQL Server 2008 (for example, `IDTSInput100`) so the upgrade process is straightforward. To upgrade, simply open your old Visual Studio 2008 project in Visual Studio 2010, 2012 or 2013. The project will upgrade automatically to the new Visual Studio format. You then need to update the references to the latest SQL Server 2014 Integration Services components referenced in the beginning of the chapter. Most of the code should be the same, as the interfaces haven't changed that much between SQL Server 2008, 2012, and 2014 in reference to the SSIS interfaces. Everything should compile, and you should be able to run your components in the SQL Server 2014 SQL Server Data Tools environment.

SUMMARY

In this chapter, you have built Pipeline Components. Although designing your own components isn't exactly like falling off a log, once you get a handle on what methods do what, when they are called, and what you can possibly use them for, you can certainly create new components with only a moderate amount of programming knowledge. After you learn the basic patterns, it is simple to develop your second, third, and tenth components. The components you designed here are very simple in nature, but it is hoped that this chapter provided you with the confidence to experiment with some of your own unique requirements. In Chapter 20, you learn how to create custom user interfaces for your components. While this is not a necessary step (because SSIS provides a default UI for custom components), it can make your components more user-friendly, especially if they are tricky to configure.

> **NOTE** *One area that we weren't able to cover in this chapter is how to build a custom Connection Manager. For more help on building a Connection Manager you can visit* `http://msdn.microsoft.com/en-us/library/ms403359.aspx`.

20

Adding a User Interface to Your Component

WHAT'S IN THIS CHAPTER?

- Outlining key steps to create a UI for your component
- Using the IDtsComponentUI interface
- Creating your first custom user UI

WROX.COM DOWNLOADS FOR THIS CHAPTER

You can find the wrox.com code downloads for this chapter at `www.wrox.com/go/prossis2014` on the Download Code tab.

Now that you have learned how to extend the pipeline with your own custom components, the next step is to improve the user experience and efficiency by adding a user interface (UI). This will be demonstrated using the Reverse String example from the previous chapter.

Pipeline Components do not require the developer to provide a user interface, because the components ship with a default interface called the Advanced Editor. Although this saves time and resources, the overall user experience can be poor. It can increase package development time and requires the user to have an intimate knowledge of the component in order to be able to correctly set the required columns and properties. Using the default interface can lead to data integrity problems, because the more complex the configuration required, the more acute the lack of suitable prompts and real-time validation becomes, making configuration tedious and error prone. For simple components, however, the built-in Advanced Editor, used by several stock components, is perfectly acceptable. For complex components with multiple inputs, the Advanced Editor will not be suitable.

If you want to add that extra style and guidance for the end user, though, this chapter is for you. You will learn how to add a user interface to a component, looking in detail at each of the stages. By the end of this chapter, you will be ready to apply these techniques to your own components.

> **NOTE** *Note that this chapter deals exclusively with managed components, that is, components written in .NET code.*

THREE KEY STEPS FOR DESIGNING THE UI: AN OVERVIEW

There are three steps to adding a user interface to any component, and each will be examined in detail. However, it is essential that you build the actual component first; get the functionality working properly, iron out any problems, tweak the performance, and make sure it installs properly. Once those core tasks are complete, you can add the polish to the solution by designing the UI. Trying to build anything other than a simple UI at the same time you are building the component can create unnecessary overhead in keeping the two projects working well in tandem. With that said, here's a summary of each of the three key UI steps.

1. The first step is to add a class that implements the `IDtsComponentUI` interface. This defines the methods needed for the designer to interact with your user interface class. This class is not the visible UI itself; rather, it provides a way for the designer to request what it needs when it needs it and exposes several methods that enable you to hook into the life cycle of your UI. For example, you have a `New` method, which is called when a component is first added to a package, and an `Edit` method, which is called when you open an existing component inside your package. The interface is expanded on in the following paragraphs.
2. The second step is to actually build the visible interface, normally a Windows Form. The form is invoked from the `IDtsComponentUI.Edit` method; by customizing the constructor, you can pass through references to the base component and supporting services. The form then displays details such as component properties or data-handling options, including inputs, outputs, and columns within each.
3. The final stage is to update the component itself to tell the designer that you have provided a user interface and where to find it, or specifically where to find the `IDtsComponentUI` implementation. You do this through the `UITypeName` property of the `DtsPipelineComponent` attribute, which decorates the component, your existing `PipelineComponent` inheriting class. The `UITypeName` is the fully qualified name of the class implementing your user interface, enabling the designer to find the assembly and class to invoke the user interface when required through the interface methods mentioned previously.

In summary, you need a known interface with which the designer can interact along with a form that you display to the user through the relevant interface method; the component also needs to advertise that it has a user interface and provide instructions about where to find the UI when required.

BUILDING THE USER INTERFACE

Now that the key stages have been explained, you can examine each of them in detail. This guide makes very few assumptions about your current level of development experience, explaining all the actions required, so as long as you can open Visual Studio on your own, you should be able to follow these steps and, perhaps more important, understand why you are performing each one.

Adding the Project

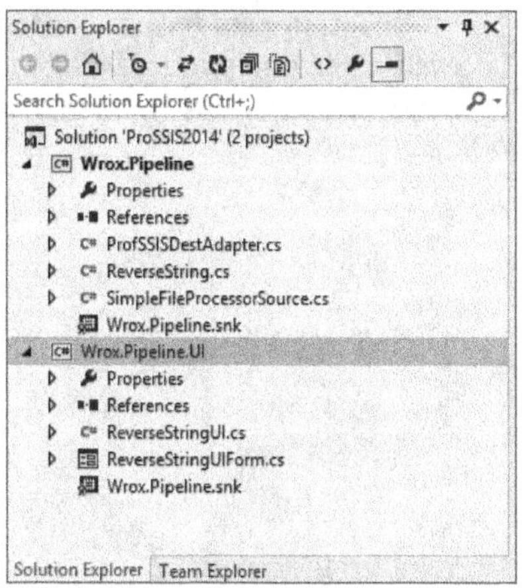

FIGURE 20-1

If you followed the example in the previous chapter, you currently have an existing solution in Visual Studio that contains the Pipeline Component project (Wrox.Pipeline). Therefore, your first step is to add a new Class Library project to host the UI, as shown in Figure 20-1. Although the UI can be implemented within the Pipeline Component project, for performance reasons this is not the recommended approach. Because SSIS has distinct runtime versus design-time elements, combining the two functions leads to a larger assembly, which requires more memory and consequently results in lower runtime performance. When you deploy your components in production, the component UI is never shown, so it is important that your components can operate without a UI. To support this use, you should ensure the core component code does not have any dependencies on UI code. The practice of separating the UI and component projects allows for easier code development and maintenance, reducing confusion and conflicts within the areas of code.

As you start with the empty project, the first task is to configure any project properties, so you need to set the Assembly Name and Default Namespace to be consistent with your development practices, as shown in Figure 20-2.

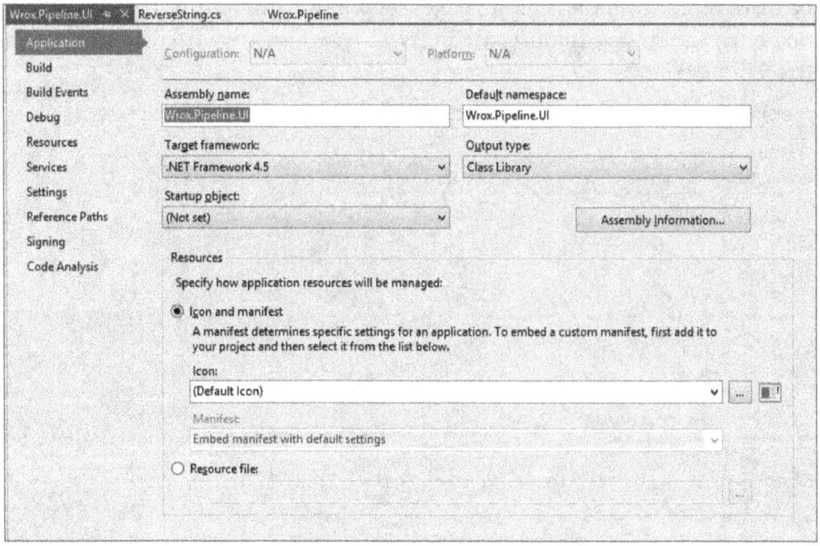

FIGURE 20-2

The user interface assembly does not need to be placed in a defined location like components and tasks (`%Program Files%\Microsoft SQL Server\120\DTS\PipelineComponents` or `%Program Files%\Microsoft SQL Server\120\DTS\Tasks`, respectively), but it does need to be installed within the global assembly cache (GAC). Therefore, within the project properties, you can leave the build output path location as the default value, but for ease of development you can add a post-build event command on the Build Events page, as shown in Figure 20-3. Refer to Chapter 19 for more details on what this command should look like.

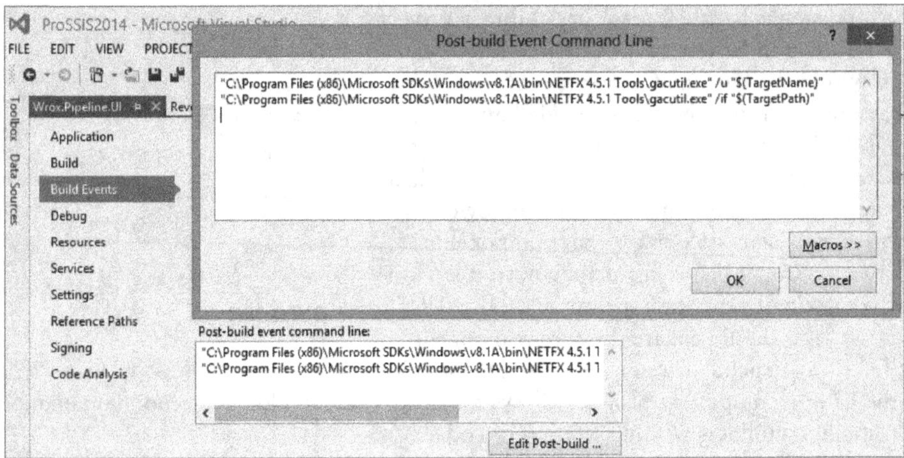

FIGURE 20-3

Because the assembly will be installed in the GAC, you need to sign the assembly using a strong name key, which can be configured from the Signing page, shown in Figure 20-4. For more information about strong names and their importance in .NET, see "Security Briefs: Strong Names and Security in the .NET Framework":

```
http://msdn.microsoft.com/en-us/library/aa302416.aspx
```

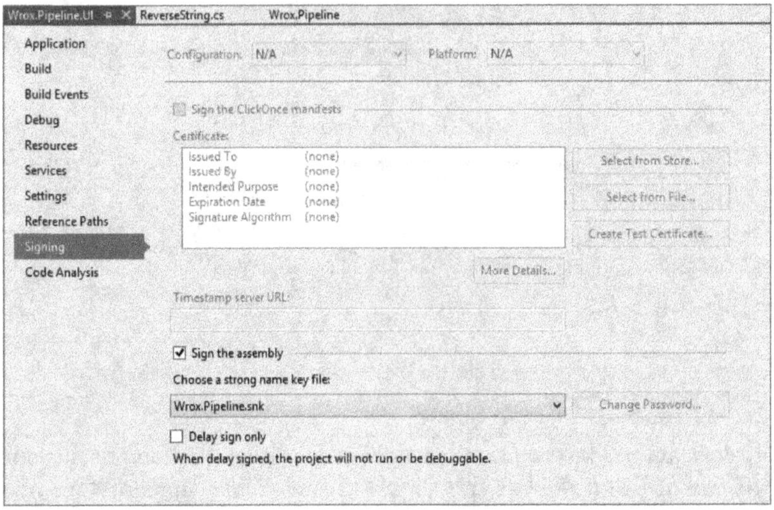

FIGURE 20-4

Although most assembly attributes can now be set through the Assembly Information dialog, accessed from the Application page of Project Properties, you still need to manually edit `AssemblyInfo.cs` (`AssemblyInfo.cs` file of the `Wrox.Pipeline.UI` project), which can be seen by clicking on the arrow next to Properties in the Solution Explorer, adding the `CLSCompliant` attribute, as described in Chapter 19 and shown here:

```
#region Using directives
using System;
using System.Security.Permissions;
using System.Reflection;
using System.Runtime.CompilerServices;
using System.Runtime.InteropServices;
#endregion
[assembly: AssemblyTitle("Wrox.Pipeline.UI")]
[assembly: AssemblyDescription("UI for Wrox.Pipeline")]
[assembly: AssemblyConfiguration("")]
[assembly: AssemblyProduct("Wrox.Pipeline")]
[assembly: AssemblyTrademark("")]
[assembly: AssemblyCulture("")]
[assembly: AssemblyVersion("1.0.0.0")]
[assembly: AssemblyFileVersion("1.0.0.0")]
[assembly: CLSCompliant(true)]
[assembly: PermissionSet(SecurityAction.RequestMinimum)]
[assembly: ComVisible(false)]
```

> **NOTE** *The* `AssemblyVersion` *will form part of the* `UITypeName` *property, described later in this chapter; therefore, it is important that this is not allowed to auto-increment using the * token, because this will break the linkage between the component and its user interface.*

You also need a Windows Form to actually display your component's interface to the user in addition to the default class you have in your project, so one will be added at this stage.

The final preparatory task is to add some additional references to your project. The recommended five are listed here:

- `Microsoft.SqlServer.Dts.Design`
- `Microsoft.SqlServer.DTSPipelineWrap`
- `Microsoft.SQLServer.ManagedDTS`
- `System.Windows.Forms`
- `Microsoft.SqlServer.DTSRuntimeWrap`

Implementing IDtsComponentUI

You now have the empty framework for the UI assembly, and you can start coding. The first step is to implement the `Microsoft.SqlServer.Dts.Pipeline.Design.IDtsComponentUI` interface. Using the default class in the project, you can add the interface declaration and take advantage of the Visual Studio context menu features, as well as use the Implement Interface command to quickly generate the five method stubs, saving you from manually typing them out.

The methods are documented in detail in the following sections; however, it is useful to understand the scenarios in which each method is called, highlighting how the `Initialize` method is usually called before the real action method:

- Adding a new component to the package:
  - Initialize
  - New
- Editing the component, either through a double-click or by selecting Edit from the context menu:
  - Initialize
  - Edit
- Deleting the component, through the Delete key or by selecting Delete from the context menu:
  - Delete

The following sections describe each method in more detail and demonstrate how they are implemented in the example.

IDtsComponentUI.Delete

The `Delete` method is called when a component is deleted from the SSIS designer. It enables you to perform any cleaning operations that may be required or warn users of the consequences. This is not normally required, because the consequences should be fairly obvious, but the opportunity is available. For this example, simply remove the placeholder exception, leaving an empty method.

IDtsComponentUI.Help

The `Help` method has not been implemented in SQL Server 2014. For this example, simply remove the placeholder exception. The method will not be called, but this should prevent any surprises in case of a service pack introducing the functionality, although this is unlikely.

IDtsComponentUI.New

The `New` method is called when a component is first added to your package through the SSIS designer. Use this method to display a user interface specific to configuring the component for the first time, such as a wizard to help configure the component, or an option dialog that gathers some information that will influence the overall use of the component. The Script Transformation uses this method to display a dialog asking for the type, source, destination, or transformation.

The `New` method is not widely used, because configuration of the component usually requires you to have wired up the Data Flow paths for the component. In addition, most people start by laying out the package and adding most or all of the components together, enabling them to visualize and validate their overall Data Flow design before configuring each component in detail, but in specialized circumstances you have this option.

For this example, simply remove the placeholder exception, leaving an empty method.

IDtsComponentUI.Initialize

`Initialize` is the first method to be called when adding or editing a component; although you do not actually perform any actions at this stage, the parameters provided are normally stored in private member variables for later use. At a minimum, you will store the `IDTSComponentMetaData100` reference, because a UI always needs to interact with the underlying component, and this is done through the `IDTSComponentMetaData100` reference.

For components that use connections or variables, you would also store a reference to `IServiceProvider`. This enables you to access useful services, like the connection service (`IDtsConnectionService`) and the variable service (`IDtsVariableService`). These designer services enable you to create new connections and variables, respectively. For connections, the service will invoke the Connection Manager user interface, provided by the connection author; for variables, you use the dialog built into the SSIS designer. This is a good example of how Microsoft has made life easier for component developers, offering access to these services, saving you time and effort. Two other services are available: `IErrorCollectionService` for retrieving error and warning event messages, and `IDtsClipboardService`, which enables component developers to determine whether a component was created by a copy-and-paste operation.

In the Wrox.Pipeline example, these services are not required, but you would follow the same pattern as you do with `IDTSComponentMetaData100` here (`ReverseStringUI.cs` file of the `Wrox.Pipeline.UI` project):

```
private IDTSComponentMetaData100 _dtsComponentMetaData;
[CLSCompliant(false)]
public void Initialize(IDTSComponentMetaData100 dtsComponentMetadata,
IServiceProvider serviceProvider)
{
// Store ComponentMetaData for later use
_dtsComponentMetaData = dtsComponentMetadata;
}
```

IDtsComponentUI.Edit

The `Edit` method is called by the designer when you edit the component, and this is the place where you actually display the visible window or form of the user interface component. The purpose of the `Edit` method is to display the form, passing through any references you need, stored in private variables during `Initialize`. The `Edit` method also has a Boolean return value that notifies the designer whether changes have been made.

This is perhaps one of the most useful features of the component UI pattern, as it enables you to make changes directly to the component, but they are persisted only if the return value is `true`. In other words, users can make as many changes as they want in the custom UI, but none of those changes are saved into the component unless the return value is true. You get commit or rollback functionality free, rather than having to write additional code to cache changes within the UI, and apply them only when a user clicks the OK button.

It also enables you to benefit from validation routines you have written into the component itself. For example, the ReverseString.SetUsageType method checks data types and the UsageType property for the column being selected, because this component supports only string types. Putting the validation into the component, rather than the UI, ensures that if a user bypasses your UI and uses the built-in Advanced Editor or the Visual Studio Properties instead, the same validation takes place.

Therefore, your UI should focus on the display side and leave as much validation as possible to the component. Inevitably, some validation will be implemented in the UI, but always bear in mind that you can use the existing component code in a modularized manner, saving time and simplifying maintenance through reuse.

For ease of implementation, you can use the DialogResult functionality of the form to indicate the return value for the form. This is illustrated in the example implementation of Edit (ReverseStringUI.cs file of the Wrox.Pipeline.UI project):

```
public bool Edit(IWin32Window parentWindow, Variables variables,
Connections connections)
{
Try
{
// Create UI form and display
ReverseStringUIForm ui = new ReverseStringUIForm(_dtsComponentMetaData);
DialogResult result = ui.ShowDialog(parentWindow);
// Set return value to represent DialogResult. This tells the
// managed wrapper to persist any changes made
// on the component input and/or output, or properties.
If
(result == DialogResult.OK)
{
return true;
}
}
catch (Exception ex)
{
MessageBox.Show(ex.ToString());
}
return false;
}
```

The Edit method also provides references to the Variables and Connections collections, which you can use to list the available variables and connections. The Variables collection is already limited to those in scope for the current Data Flow Task.

If your component uses connections or variables, you would modify the form constructor to accept these, as well as the System.IServiceProvider reference you captured during Initialize. This enables you to offer the option of selecting an existing item or creating a new one as needed. These are not required for the Reverse String Component, but an example of an `Edit` method implementation using them is shown here (`ReverseStringUI.cs` file of the `Wrox.Pipeline.UI` project):

```
public bool Edit(IWin32Window parentWindow,
Variables variables, Connections connections)
{
Try
{
TraceSourceUIForm ui = new TraceSourceUIForm(_dtsComponentMetaData,
variables, connections, _serviceProvider);
DialogResult result = ui.ShowDialog(parentWindow);
if (result == DialogResult.OK)
{
return true;
}
}
catch (Exception ex)
{
Konesans.Dts.Design.ExceptionDialog.Show(ex);
}
return false;
}
```

Setting the UITypeName

This section deals with changes to the Reverse String Component itself, rather than the user interface project. This is listed as the last of the three key steps for providing a user interface, but it is generally done fairly early on, because once it is complete, you can actually test your UI in the designer itself.

You need to tell the designer that your component has a user interface, in effect overriding the Advanced Editor dialog provided by default. To do this, set the `UITypeName` property of the `DtsPipelineComponentAttribute`, which already decorates the component class in the transformation project. The required format of the property value is as follows:

```
<Full Class Name>,
<Assembly Name>,
Version=<Version>,
PublicKeyToken=<Token>
```

> **NOTE** *You may recognize the format as being very similar to an assembly strong name, because apart from the additional* `<Full Class Name>` *at the beginning, it is the assembly strong name. Using the strong name, the designer can find and load the assembly, and then using the class name, it knows exactly where to go for its entry point, the* `IDTSComponentUI` *implementation.*

Setting this property often causes developers problems, but if you know where to look, it is quite easy:

```
...
namespace Wrox.Pipeline.UI
{
public class ReverseStringUI : IDtsComponentUI
{
...
```

This code snippet from the main UI class file shows the namespace and the class name, so the first token on the `UITypeName` is `Wrox.Pipeline.UI.ReverseStringUI`.

The remainder is just the strong name of the assembly. The simplest way to obtain this is to compile the project; if you set the post-build events as described previously, your assembly will have been installed in the GAC. Open a command window and run the command `gacutil /l Wrox.Pipeline.UI` to get the full string name of the assembly. Figure 20-5 shows the full path on my machine.

The GACUTIL executable should be available in the `%programfiles%\Microsoft SDKs\Windows\v8.1A\Bin\NETFX 4.5.1 Tools\` directory.

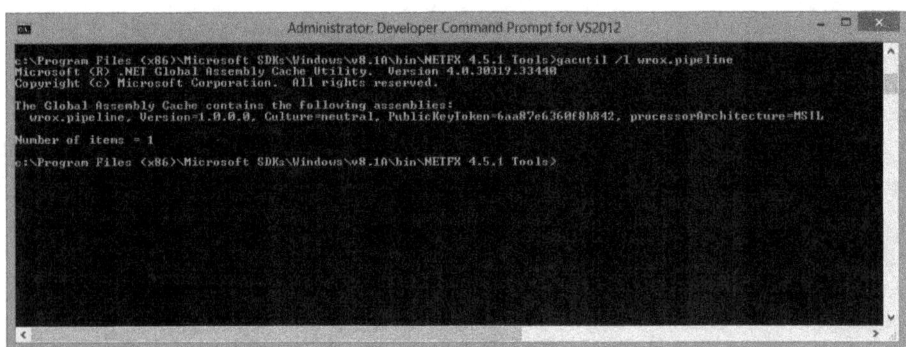

FIGURE 20-5

If the `gacutil` call fails, make sure you change directory (CD) into the NETFX 4.5.1 Tools directory that contains the `gacutil` executable. Now that you can see the `PublicKeyToken` property, the `UITypeName` property can be set.

If you make a mistake when setting this property, you will get an error such as the following when you use the component UI:

```
Could not load file or assembly 'Wrox.Pipeline.UI.ReverseStringUI,
Version=2.0.0.0, Culture=neutral, PublicKeyToken=b8351fe7752642cc' or one of its
dependencies. The system cannot find the file specified. (mscorlib)
```

The completed attribute for the `Wrox.Pipeline` Component, referencing the `ReverseStringUI` assembly, is illustrated as follows (`ReverseString.cs` file of the `Wrox.Pipeline.UI` project):

```
[DtsPipelineComponent(
DisplayName = "Wrox Reverse String",
ComponentType = ComponentType.Transform,
UITypeName = "Wrox.Pipeline.UI.ReverseStringUI,
Wrox.Pipeline.UI, Version=1.0.0.0, Culture=neutral,
PublicKeyToken=6aa87e6360f8b842")]
public class ReverseString : PipelineComponent
...
```

Building the Form

The final development stage is building the form itself, enabling it to capture the user input and apply the selections to the component. Before you start building the form, however, review the following summary of the progress so far.

You have implemented `IDTSComponentUI`, providing the methods required by the designer to support a custom user interface. The `IDTSComponentUI.Edit` method is used to display the form, passing through a reference to the base component (`IDTSComponentMetaData100`). This was gained using the `IDTSComponentUI.Initialize` method and stored in a private class-level variable.

Finally, you have updated the component itself to include the `UITypeName` property for the `DtsPipelineComponentAttribute`. This enables the designer to detect and then find your user interface class, thereby calling the `IDTSComponentUI` methods you have now implemented, leading to the display of the form.

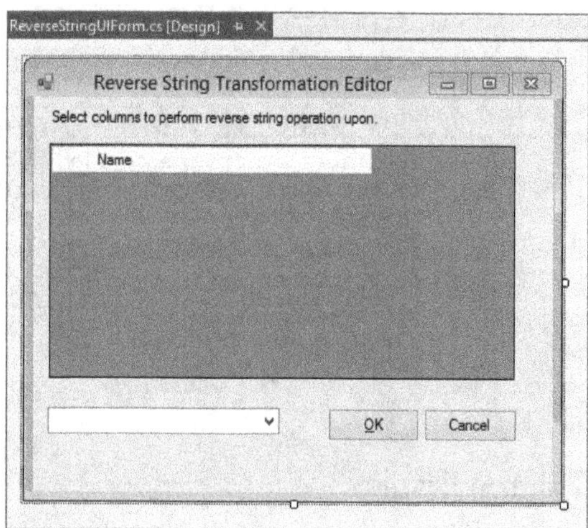

FIGURE 20-6

The sample form for the user interface is shown in Figure 20-6.

Modifying the Form Constructor

As previously mentioned, the default form constructor is modified to accept the references you will need, such as the component and support objects, variables, and connections. For this example, you just have the component reference, `IDTSComponentMetaData100`. You should store these constructor parameters in private member variables for later use elsewhere in the form, as well as use the member variables directly in the constructor itself.

The commit and rollback feature discussed in the "IDtsComponentUI.Edit" section has one specific requirement: any changes made must be done through a wrapper class, rather than applied directly to the IDTSComponentMetaData100 reference. This wrapper, the IDTSDesigntimeComponent100 design-time interface, is created within the constructor and stored in a private member variable for later use.

Changes can be made directly to IDTSComponentMetaData100, but they will be permanent; so even if you return false from IDtsComponentUI.Edit, the changes will persist. Users like recognizable and intuitive user interfaces, and the capability to recover from a mistake using the Cancel button is a design pattern that all users have been grateful for on numerous occasions. Writing code to implement this yourself would be a considerable amount of work, so make sure you issue changes only through the design-time interface.

The complete form constructor is shown as follows (ReverseStringUIForm.cs file of the Wrox .Pipeline.UI project), including the call to the SetInputVirtualInputColumns method, covered later in the chapter:

```
private IDTSComponentMetaData100 _dtsComponentMetaData;
private IDTSDesigntimeComponent100 _designTimeComponent;
private IDTSInput100 _input;
public ReverseStringUIForm(IDTSComponentMetaData100 dtsComponentMetaData)
{
InitializeComponent();
// Store constructor parameters for late
_dtsComponentMetaData = dtsComponentMetaData;
// Get design-time interface for changes and validation
_designTimeComponent = _dtsComponentMetaData.Instantiate();
// Get Input
_input = _dtsComponentMetaData.InputCollection[0];
// Set any form controls that host component properties or connections here
// None required for ReverseString component
// Populate DataGridView with columns
SetInputVirtualInputColumns();
}
```

Column Display

Once all the constructor parameters have been stored and the initial preparation is complete, you can begin to interrogate the component and other objects that may have been supplied on the constructor to populate the form controls.

The Reverse String Transformation will operate on any column the user selects, so the user interface will simply consist of a way to allow columns to be selected. For this example, you should use a DataGridView control. Using the control designer, you'll preconfigure two columns: a checkbox column for the selection state (DataGridViewCheckBoxColumn) and a text column for the column name (DataGridViewTextBoxColumn). The individual form controls are not covered in detail; rather, the focus is on their use and interaction with the component, because the choice of control is entirely up to you as the user interface developer.

> **NOTE** *To see exactly how the controls have been configured, review the completed project available at* `www.wrox.com/go/prossis2014`.

Because you allow users to select columns, the initial requirement is to enumerate the columns and determine their current selection state. To do this, you need to understand the architecture of a component in relation to data movement. For a simple synchronous transformation such as this one, you have a single input. The input has a collection of input columns, which at runtime hold the data provided in the pipeline buffer, so the transformation itself operates on these columns.

> **NOTE** *For more details on pipeline architecture, see Chapter 16.*

In the Reverse String Component, the presence of an input column means that the user wants the operation to be performed on that column. By default, the input contains no columns, because no columns have been selected for transformation. To select a column, you set the column usage type to something other than `DTSUsageType.UT_IGNORED`. For this component, because you do an in-place transformation on the column value, you require both read and write access as indicated by `DTSUsageType.UT_READWRITE`. This allows you to read the column value and reverse it before writing it back into the buffer.

> **NOTE** *It is important that you select only those columns that are required for any transformation and minimize excess columns through all stages of the pipeline for performance reasons. The designer will display a warning like this when it detects unused columns:*
>
> ```
> [DTS.Pipeline] Warning: The output column "ProductPrice"; (36) on
> output
> "OLE DB Source Output" (10) and component "Products" (1) is not
> subsequently used in the Data Flow task. Removing this unused
> output
> column can increase Data Flow task performance.
> ```

Because the input column collection is empty by default, you actually work on the virtual input column collection instead. The virtual input represents all the upstream columns available to the transformation, enabling you to enumerate columns, as well as interrogate the virtual input column's `UsageType` property.

Calling `GetVirtualInput` to get the collection of virtual columns is a potentially expensive operation, depending on the number of upstream columns. You should therefore call it only once and cache the result for later use in other methods. You should also be aware that because a virtual input is very much a snapshot of current state, it can become invalid. Simple changes to the current component do not affect the virtual columns, but deeper changes like `ReinitializeMetaData` can invalidate it. You should therefore plan the lifetime of the cached reference and periodically refresh it after major changes.

The use of the virtual input and the column usage type is the basis for the `SetInput VirtualInputColumns` helper method included in the form. This populates the `DataGridView` with a list of columns and their current selection state. This method is the final call in the form constructor and completes the initialization of the form (`ReverseStringUIForm.cs` file of the `Wrox.Pipeline.UI` project). As a separate exercise you may wish to augment this procedure with logic to hide (or gray-out) nonstring columns, so that users do not inadvertently try to reverse numeric values.

```
private void SetInputVirtualInputColumns()
{
_virtualInput = _input.GetVirtualInput();
IDTSVirtualInputColumnCollection100 virtualInputColumnCollection =
_virtualInput.VirtualInputColumnCollection;
IDTSInputColumnCollection100 inputColumns =
_input.InputColumnCollection;
int columnCount = virtualInputColumnCollection.Count;
for (int i = 0; i Đ columnCount; i++)
{
IDTSVirtualInputColumn100 virtualColumn = virtualInputColumnCollection[i];
int row;
if (virtualColumn.UsageType == DTSUsageType.UT_READONLY ||
virtualColumn.UsageType == DTSUsageType.UT_READWRITE)
{
row = this.dgColumns.Rows.Add( new object[]
{CheckState.Checked, " " + virtualColumn.Name });
}
Else
{
row = this.dgColumns.Rows.Add(new object[]
{
CheckState.Unchecked, " " + virtualColumn.Name });
}
this.dgColumns.Rows[rowIndex].Tag = i;
DataGridViewCheckBoxCell cell =
(DataGridViewCheckBoxCell)dgColumns.Rows[row].Cells[0];
cell.ThreeState = false;
}
}
```

The pipeline engine is implemented in native code for performance, so calls to pipeline objects normally use a wrapper class and incur the overhead of COM Interop. You should therefore minimize such calls through efficient coding practices. In the preceding example, the count from the virtual input column collection is retrieved only once, as opposed to being interrogated within the `for` loop test itself.

Column Selection

The next task to complete in building the user interface is to react to user input and reflect any changes back to the component. In this example, the only option offered is the selection of columns, made through the `DataGridView`, as captured through the `CellContentClick` event. You use this event, rather than one of the others available such as `CellValueChanged`, because this is raised immediately and you can give timely feedback to the user.

Through the `DataGridViewCellEventArgs`, you can obtain the row and column indices for the cell. This is first used to validate that the row exists and that the column is the first column, because this column contains the checkboxes used for managing selection. You then use the virtual input again and set the usage type as indicated by the checkbox or cell value.

Because the example component includes validation within the overridden `SetUsageType` method, you need to ensure that you catch any exceptions thrown and can react and provide feedback to the component user, as shown here (`ReverseStringUIForm.cs` file of the `Wrox.Pipeline.UI` project):

```
private void dgColumns_CellContentClick(object sender, DataGridViewCellEventArgs e)
{
if (e.ColumnIndex == 0 && e.RowIndex > = 0)
{
// Get current value and flip boolean to get new value
bool newValue = !Convert.ToBoolean(dgColumns.CurrentCell.Value);
// Get the virtual column to work with
IDTSVirtualInputColumn100 virtualColumn =
_virtualInput.VirtualInputColumnCollection[e.RowIndex];
Try
{
// Set the column UsageType to indicate the column is selected or not
if (newValue)
_designTimeComponent.SetUsageType(_input.ID, _virtualInput,
virtualColumn.LineageID,
DTSUsageType.UT_READWRITE);
Else
_designTimeComponent.SetUsageType(_input.ID, _virtualInput,
virtualColumn.LineageID, DTSUsageType.UT_IGNORED);
}
catch(Exception ex)
{
// Catch any error from base class SetUsageType here.
// Display simple error message from exception
MessageBox.Show(ex.Message, "Invalid Column", MessageBoxButtons.OK,
 MessageBoxIcon.Error);
// Rollback UI selection
dgColumns.CancelEdit();
}
}
}
```

To complete the description of the user interface example, there are two button controls on the form, OK and Cancel, each with its respective `DialogResult` property values set. By using the dialog results in this way, you do not need any event handler bound to the `click` event, and no additional code is required to close the form. The dialog result is then used within `IDTSComponentUI.Edit` to commit or roll back any changes made to the component wrapper, as shown previously.

This concludes the example; if you have been building the UI as you read, the only remaining task is to compile the project. If you configured the build events that were described at the beginning, the assemblies should be in the correct locations ready for use.

You need to start a new instance of Visual Studio and open an SSIS project. Before you can use the component, you need to verify the new components are part of the SSIS Toolbox tab. The components are added automatically after they are copied to the DTS directories, as explained in the "Installing the Components" section of Chapter 19. If the components are not present in the SSIS Toolbox, this is usually a sign that the assemblies have not been copied to those directories.

> **NOTE** *The completed example is available for download from* `www.wrox.com/go/prossis2014`.

EXTENDING THE USER INTERFACE

The simple component that was used in the preceding example lacks some of features you may require in your project. For example, components can use runtime connections or have properties. These would generally be represented through additional form controls, and their values would be interrogated, and controls initialized in the form constructor. You will now look at these other methods in greater detail.

Runtime Connections

As previously discussed, components can use connections and the `System.IServiceProvider` from `IDtsComponentUI.Initialize` and the `Connections` collection from `IDtsComponentUI.Edit` enable you to provide meaningful UI functions around them. You have seen examples of passing these as far as the form constructor, so now you will be shown what you do with them. This example shows a modified constructor that accepts the additional connection-related parameters, performs some basic initialization, and stores them for later use. You would perform any column- or property-related work as shown in the previous examples, but for clarity none are included here. The final task is to initialize the combo box that will list the runtime connections.

For this example, you will presume that the component accepts one connection, which would have been defined in the `ProvidedComponentProperties` method of the component. You will use a `ComboBox` control to offer the selection options, as well as the capability to create a new connection through the `IDtsConnectionService`. The component expects an ADO.NET SqlClient connection, so the list will be restricted to this, and the current connection, if any, will be preselected in the list. The preparatory work for this is all shown here (`ReverseStringUIForm.cs` file of the `Wrox.Pipeline.UI` project):

```
private IDTSComponentMetaData100 _dtsComponentMetaData;
private IDTSDesigntimeComponent100 _designTimeComponent;
private IDtsConnectionService _dtsConnectionService;
private Microsoft.SqlServer.Dts.Runtime.Connections _connections;
// Constant to define the type of connection we support and wish to work with
 private const string Connection_Type =
"ADO.NET:System.Data.SqlClient.SqlConnection, System.Data, Version=2.0.0.0,
Culture=neutral, PublicKeyToken=b77a5c561934e089";
public ConnectionDemoUIForm(IDTSComponentMetaData100 dtsComponentMetaData,
IServiceProvider serviceProvider, Connections connections)
```

```
{
InitializeComponent();
// Store constructor parameters for later.
_dtsComponentMetaData = dtsComponentMetaData;
connections = connections;
// Get IDtsConnectionService and store.
IDtsConnectionService dtsConnectionService =
serviceProvider.GetService(typeof(IDtsConnectionService))
as IDtsConnectionService;
_dtsConnectionService = dtsConnectionService;
// Get design-time interface for changes and validation.
_designTimeComponent = _dtsComponentMetaData.Instantiate();
// Perform any other actions, such as column population or
// component property work.
// Get Connections collection, and get name of currently selected connection.
string connectionName = "";
if (_dtsComponentMetaData.RuntimeConnectionCollection[0] != null)
{
IDTSRuntimeConnection100 runtimeConnection =
_dtsComponentMetaData.RuntimeConnectionCollection[0];
if (runtimeConnection != null
&& runtimeConnection.ConnectionManagerID.Length> 0
&&connections.Contains(runtimeConnection.ConnectionManagerID))
{
connectionName = _connections[runtimeConnection.ConnectionManagerID].Name;
}
}
// Populate connections combo.
PopulateConnectionsCombo(this.cmbSqlConnections, Connection_Type,
connectionName);
}
```

The final command in the constructor is to call your helper function, `PopulateConnectionsCombo`, to populate the combo box. The parameters for this are quite simple: the combo box to populate, the type of connection you wish to list, and the name of the currently selected connection. Using these three items, you can successfully populate the combo box as shown here (`ReverseStringUIForm.cs` file of the `Wrox.Pipeline.UI` project):

```
private void PopulateConnectionsCombo(ComboBox comboBox,
string connectionType, string selectedItem)
{
// Prepare combo box by clearing, and adding the new connection item.
comboBox.Items.Clear();
comboBox.Items.Add("<New connection…>");
// Enumerate connections, but for type supported.
foreach (ConnectionManager connectionManager in
_dtsConnectionService.GetConnectionsOfType(connectionType))
{
comboBox.Items.Add(connectionManager.Name);
}
// Set currently selected connection
comboBox.SelectedItem = selectedItem;
}
```

The ADO.NET connection is slightly different from most connections in that it has what can be thought of as subtypes. Because you need a specific subtype, the `System.Data.SqlClient.SqlConnection`, you must use the full name of the connection, as opposed to the shorter creation name moniker, ADO.NET, which you may see elsewhere and which is the pattern used for other simpler types of Connection Managers.

If you have any problems with this sample code, perhaps because you have different versions of SQL Server on the same box, then change the relevant line of the preceding code to the following. This alternative code lists any Connection Manager in the combo box (`ReverseStringUIForm.cs` file of the `Wrox.Pipeline.UI` project):

```
// Enumerate connections, but for any connection type.
foreach (ConnectionManager connectionManager in
_dtsConnectionService.GetConnections())
{
comboBox.Items.Add(connectionManager.Name);
}
```

Now that you have populated the combo box, you need to handle the selection of an existing connection or the creation of a new connection. When you author a Connection Manager yourself, you can provide a user interface by implementing the `IDtsConnectionManagerUI`, which is analogous to the way you have implemented `IDtsComponentUI` to provide a user interface for your component. The connection service will then display this user interface when you call the `CreateConnection` method.

The following example (`ReverseStringUIForm.cs` file of the `Wrox.Pipeline.UI` project) shows the event handler for the connections combo box, which supports new connections and existing connections and ensures that the selection is passed down to the component:

```
private void cmbSqlConnections_SelectedValueChanged(object sender, EventArgs e)
{
ComboBox comboxBox = (ComboBox)sender;
// Check for index 0 and <New Item...>
if (comboxBox.SelectedIndex == 0)
{
// Use connection service to create a new connection.
ArrayList newConns = _dtsConnectionService.CreateConnection(Connection_Type);
if (newConns.Count > 0)
{
// A new connection has been created, so populate and select
ConnectionManager newConn = (ConnectionManager)newConns[0];
PopulateConnectionsCombo(comboxBox, Connection_Type, newConn.Name);
}
Else
{
// Create connection has been cancelled
comboxBox.SelectedIndex = -1;
}
}
// An connection has been selected. Verify it exists and update component.
if (_connections.Contains(comboxBox.Text))
{
// Get the selected connection
ConnectionManager connectionManager = _connections[comboxBox.Text];
```

```
// Save selected connection
_dtsComponentMetaData.RuntimeConnectionCollection[0].ConnectionManagerID =
_connections[comboxBox.Text].ID;
_dtsComponentMetaData.RuntimeConnectionCollection[0].ConnectionManager =
DtsConvert.ToConnectionManager100(_connections[comboxBox.Text]);
}
}
```

By following the examples shown here, you can manage connections from within your user interface, allowing the user to create a new connection or select an existing one, and ensure that the selection is persisted through to the component's `RuntimeConnectionCollection`, thereby setting the connection.

You can also use variables within your UI. Normally, the selected variable is stored in a component property, so by combining the property access code from the component properties section and following the pattern for runtime connections, substituting the `IDtsVariableService` instead, you can see how this can be done.

Component Properties

As an example of displaying and setting component-level properties, you may have a string property that is displayed in a simple `TextBox` control and an enumeration value that is used to set the selected index for a `ComboBox` control. The following example assumes that the two component properties, `StringProp` and `EnumProp`, have been defined in the overridden `ProvideComponentProperties` method of your component class. You would then extend the form constructor to include some code to retrieve the property values and display them in the form controls. This assumes that you have added two new form controls, a `TextBox` control called `MyStringTextBox`, and a `ComboBox` called `MyEnumValComboBox`. An example of the additional form constructor code is shown here (`ReverseStringUIForm.cs` file of the `Wrox.Pipeline.UI` project):

```
MyStringTextBox.Text =
_dtsComponentMetaData.CustomPropertyCollection["StringProp"].Value.ToString();
MyEnumValComboBox.SelectedIndex =
Convert.ToInt32(_dtsComponentMetaData.CustomPropertyCollection["EnumProp"].Value);
```

The appropriate events for each control would then be used to set the property value of the component, ensuring that this is done through the design-time interface. A variety of events could be used to capture the value change within the Windows Form control, depending on the level of validation you wish to apply within the form or whether you wish to rely solely on validation routines within an overridden `SetComponentProperty` method in your component class. Capturing these within the control's validating event would then enable you to cancel the change in the form, as well as display information to the user. A simple example is shown here for the two properties (`ReverseStringUIForm.cs` file of the `Wrox.Pipeline.UI` project):

```
private void MyStringTextBox_Validating(object sender, CancelEventArgs e)
{
// Set the property, and capture any validation errors
// thrown in SetComponentProperty try
{
_designTimeComponent.SetComponentProperty("StringProp",
MyStringTextBox.Text);
```

```
}
catch(Exception ex)
{
// Display exception message
MessageBox.Show(ex.Message);
// Cancel event due to error
e.Cancel = true;
}
private voidMyEnumValComboBox_SelectedIndexChanged(object sender, EventArgs e)
{
Try
{
_designTimeComponent.SetComponentProperty("EnumProp ",
((ComboBox)sender).SelectedIndex);
}
catch(Exception ex)
{
// Display exception message
MessageBox.Show(ex.Message);
// Cancel event due to error
e.Cancel = true;
}
}
```

Providing an overridden `SetComponentProperty` is a common requirement. The most obvious reason is that component properties are stored through the object type, but you may require a specific type, such as integer, so the type validation code would be included in `SetComponentProperty`. A simple example of this is shown here (`ReverseStringUIForm.cs` file of the `Wrox.Pipeline.UI` project), where the property named `IntProp` is validated to ensure that it is an integer:

```
public override IDTSCustomProperty100 SetComponentProperty(string propertyName,
object propertyValue)
{
int result; if (propertyName == "IntProp" &&
int.TryParse(propertyValue.ToString(), out result) == false)
{
bool cancel;
ComponentMetaData.FireError(0, ComponentMetaData.Name, "The IntProp property
is required to be a valid integer.", "", 0, out cancel);
throw new ArgumentException("The value you have specified for IntProp is not
a numeric value");
}
return base.SetComponentProperty(propertyName, propertyValue);
}
```

In the next section, you build on this example by learning how to handle the exceptions and events.

Handling Errors and Warnings

The previous example and the column selection method in the main example both demonstrated how you can catch exceptions thrown from the base component when you apply settings. Although it is recommended that you use managed exceptions for this type of validation and feedback, you may also wish to use the component events such as `FireError` or `FireWarning`. In Chapter 19 you saw an example of the FireError method in the Validation function. The example below gives an overview of how the FireError method is called. Usually, these would be called immediately prior to the exception and used to provide additional information in support of the exception. Alternatively, you could use them to provide the detail and throw the exception only as a means of indicating that an event has been raised. To capture the event information, you can use the IErrorCollectionService. This service can be obtained through System.IServiceProvider, and the preparatory handling is identical to that of IDtsConnectionService, as illustrated in the previous example. For the following examples, assume that a class-level variable containing the IErrorCollectionService has been declared, _errorCollectionService, and populated in the form constructor.

```
ComponentMetaData.FireError(ERROR_NUMBER, "Where did the error occur?", "What error
 occurred?", "Where is the help file location?", HELP_FILE_INDEX,
CANCEL_EXECUTION?);
```

In the example above, ERROR_NUMBER references an error number if one is available. HELP_FILE_INDEX references the index of where the help topic for this error can be found in the help file. CANCEL_EXECUTION is a Boolean value that can be used to tell the SSIS Engine to stop execution of the package.

The following example (ReverseStringUIForm.cs file of the Wrox.Pipeline.UI project) demonstrates how you can use the GetErrorMessage method of the IErrorCollectionService to retrieve details about an event. This will also include details about any exception thrown. The validating method of a TextBox control is illustrated, and SetComponentProperty is based on the overridden example shown previously, to validate that the property value is an integer:

```
private void txtIntPropMessage_Validating(object sender, CancelEventArgs e)
{
// Clear any existing errors in preparation for setting property
_errorCollectionService.ClearErrors();
Try
{
// Set property through IDTSDesigntimeComponent100
_designTimeComponent.SetComponentProperty("IntProp",
this.txtIntPropMessage.Text);
}
Catch
{
// Display message
MessageBox.Show(_errorCollectionService.GetErrorMessage());
// Cancel event due to error
e.Cancel = true;
}
}
```

If a noninteger value is entered, the following message is displayed:

```
Error at Data Flow Task [ReverseString]: The IntProp property is required to be a
valid integer.
```

```
Error at Data Flow Task [ReverseString [84]]: System.ArgumentException: The value
you have specified for IntProp is not a numeric value
at Wrox.Pipeline.ReverseString.ReverseString.SetComponentProperty(String
propertyName, Object propertyValue)
at Microsoft.SqlServer.Dts.Pipeline.ManagedComponentHost.HostSetComponentProperty(
IDTSDesigntimeComponent100 wrapper,
String propertyName, Object propertyValue)
```

The following example (`ReverseStringUIForm.cs` file of the `Wrox.Pipeline.UI` project) demonstrates the `GetErrors` method and how to enumerate through the errors captured by the service individually:

```
private void txtIntPropErrors_Validating(object sender, CancelEventArgs e)
{
// Clear any existing errors in preparation for setting property
_errorCollectionService.ClearErrors();
Try
{
// Set property through IDTSDesigntimeComponent100
_designTimeComponent.SetComponentProperty("IntProp",
this.txtIntPropErrors.Text);
}
Catch
{
// Get ICollection of IComponentErrorInfo and cast into
// IList for accessibility
IList<IComponentErrorInfo> errors =
_errorCollectionService.GetErrors() as IList<IComponentErrorInfo>;
// Loop through errors and process into message
string message = "";
for (int i = 0; i < errors.Count; i++)
{
IComponentErrorInfo errorInfo = errors[i] as IComponentErrorInfo;
message += "Level: " + errorInfo.Level.ToString() + Environment.NewLine
"Description : " +
Environment.NewLine + errorInfo.Description + Environment.NewLine +
Environment.NewLine;
}
// Display message
MessageBox.Show(message);
// Cancel event due to error
e.Cancel = true;
}
}
```

If a noninteger value is entered, the following message is displayed:

```
Level: Error
Description :
The IntProp property is required to be a valid integer.
Level: Error
Description :
System.ArgumentException:
```

```
The value you have specified for IntProp is not a numeric value
at Wrox.Pipeline..ReverseString.ReverseString.SetComponentProperty
(String propertyName, Object propertyValue)
at Microsoft.SqlServer.Dts.Pipeline.ManagedComponentHost.HostSetComponentProperty(
IDTSDesigntimeComponent100 wrapper, String propertyName, Object propertyValue)
```

As you can see, both the event and the exception information are available through the `IErrorCollectionService`. This example also demonstrates the use of the `Level` property, which can be useful for differentiating between errors and warnings. For a complete list of `IComponentErrorInfo` properties, please refer to the SQL Server documentation.

Column Properties

When you require column-level information, beyond the selection state of a column, it is a best practice to store this as a custom property on the column. This applies to all column types. An example of this can be seen with the stock Character Map Transformation. If you select a column and perform an in-place operation, such as the Lowercase operation, this is stored as a custom property on that input column. To confirm this, select a column as described and view the component through the Advanced Editor (to open the Advanced Editor, right-click the Character Map Transformation and select Show Advanced Editor). If you then navigate to the Input and expand to select the column, you will see a custom property called `MapFlags`. This stores the operation enumeration, as shown in Figure 20-7.

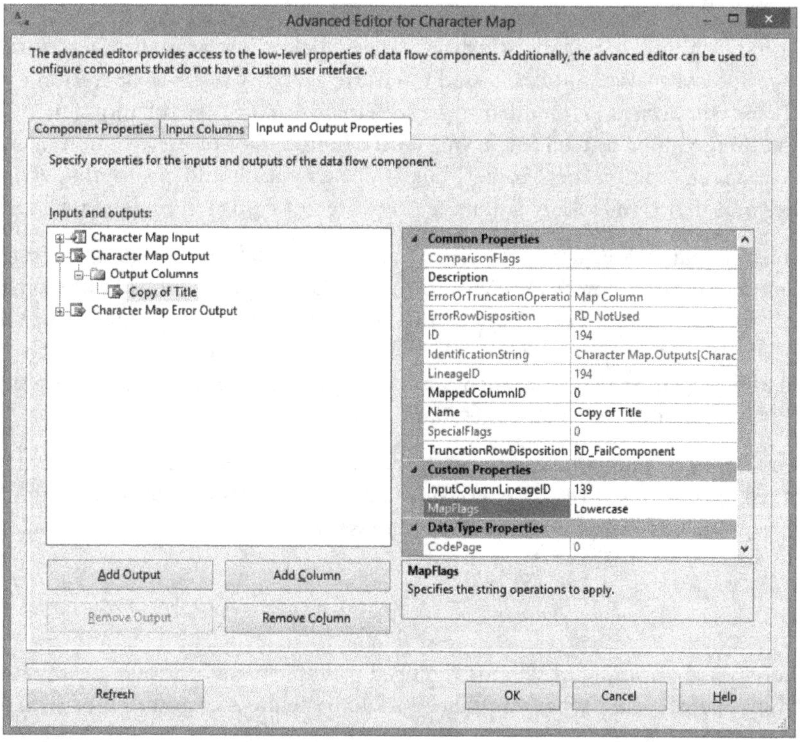

FIGURE 20-7

If your component uses custom column properties in this way, these are perhaps the best candidates for a custom user interface. Using the Advanced Editor to navigate columns and set properties correctly carries a much higher risk of error and is more time-consuming for the user than a well-designed user interface. Unfortunately, this does raise the complexity of the user interface somewhat, particularly from the Windows Forms programming perspective, as the effective use of form controls is what determines the success of such a UI. However, if you are still reading this chapter, you are probably comfortable with such challenges.

To persist these column-level properties, simply call the appropriate `SetColumnTypeProperty` method on the design-time interface, `IDTSDesigntimeComponent100`. Obviously, you want to ensure that you previously created the actual properties. For example, in the following code, a property is being set on an input column:

```
IDTSInput100 _input = ComponentMetadata.InputCollection[0];
IDTSInputColumn100 inputColumn = _input.InputColumnCollection.GetByColumnName("",
"MyColumnName");
_designTimeComponent.SetInputColumnProperty(_input.ID, inputColumn.ID,
"PropertyName", propertyValue);
```

OTHER UI CONSIDERATIONS

Any good user interface should be designed with usability, accessibility, localization, and other such principles in mind. That means that the user interface should not require a mouse to be configured — the user should be able to navigate using only the keyboard just as easily. Descriptions should be clear, and strings and controls should be tested to ensure that any resizing operation does not truncate them. If the component is intended to be sold to customers, localization (and globalization) may be something you want to think about. You can find a lot of information on `http://msdn.microsoft.com/en-us/` on these topics, but as a start you should ensure that string literals live in resource files and that right-to-left language users are not confused by the interface.

Test the component and ensure that it does not crash when receiving invalid input, that any error messages are descriptive, and that exception recovery is graceful. Also keep in mind that users may intentionally or mistakenly use the default UI (Advanced Editor) for the component and corrupt the state that may otherwise have been protected by your UI. If the component is designed correctly, validation is modularized and shared by the component and its UI; however, if this is not possible, then try to ensure that the UI does not break if the metadata is corrupt.

Remember that both the component and its UI may need to be deployed together to other machines (depending on their intended use). If this is the case, consider building an installation script to place the files in the right folders and install them in the GAC as necessary.

SUMMARY

You should now have a good understanding of what is required to implement your own custom user interface for a Pipeline Component. Here's what you'll need to do to create a custom UI for your component:

- Build a form that will be used as the UI.
- Add a UI class that implements the `IDTSComponentUI` interface. This class will instantiate and display the custom UI.
- Add the `UITypeName` attribute to your custom component that points to the UI class in Step 2, for example: `UITypeName=Wrox.Pipeline.UI.ReverseStringUI,Wrox.Pipeline.UI, Version=1.0.0.0, Culture=neutral,PublicKeyToken=6aa87e6360f8b842".`
- Write the necessary code to interact with the MetaData and Runtime Connections for your component.

With the lessons learned in this chapter, you should now have the knowledge to apply this guidance for yourself and, perhaps more important, should understand why certain practices are to be followed, enabling you to confidently develop your own components. The functionality described in this chapter enables you to truly exploit the power and extensibility of SQL Server Integration Services.

21

External Management and WMI Task Implementation

WHAT'S IN THIS CHAPTER?

- Managing SSIS in SQL Server 2014
- The Managed Object Model code library
- Using the `Project` class
- Using the `Application` and `Package` classes
- WMI operations

WROX.COM DOWNLOADS FOR THIS CHAPTER

You can find the wrox.com code downloads for this chapter at `www.wrox.com/go/prossis2014` on the Download Code tab.

Throughout this book, you've been exposed to different ways to manage the development and administration of SSIS packages using the Visual Studio IDE and SQL Server Management Studio. This chapter expands on those operations by providing an overview of the ways in which you perform these same management and administrative functions programmatically through managed code. You learn how to use the `Project` and `Parameter` classes that have been added to the `Microsoft.SqlServer.Dts.Runtime` class, as well as the `Microsoft.SqlServer.Management.IntegrationServices` class also known as the Managed Object Model. You will also learn how to perform legacy package management operations using the managed `Application` and `Package` classes exposed in the dynamic-linked library `Microsoft.SQLServer.ManagedDTS.dll` by the .NET `Microsoft.SqlServer.Dts.Runtime` namespace.

The second half of this chapter details the capabilities of the WMI Data Reader Task and the WMI Event Watcher Task. These tasks provide access to system information via the Windows Management Interface model, better known as WMI. Through a query-based language called

WQL, similar to SQL in structure and syntax, you can obtain information about a wide variety of system resources to assist you in your SQL Server administrative responsibilities. With WMI, you can mine system-based metrics to look for hardware and operating system trends. In SSIS, using WMI, you can also work more proactively to monitor a Windows-based system for notable events that occur in the system, and even trigger responsive actions.

EXTERNAL MANAGEMENT OF SSIS WITH MANAGED CODE

The SSIS development team has exposed a robust architecture to manage SSIS through managed code. Managed code in this case refers to the use of the .NET Framework Common Language Runtime (CLR), which hosts code written in C# or VB.NET.

Through a rich object model, you can customize your applications to control almost every aspect of managing an SSIS project and package. This section provides a brief overview of the SSIS programming model as it applies to externally managing SSIS projects and packages.

Setting Up a Test SSIS Package for Demonstration Purposes

For this chapter, we'll be adding a new SSIS package to the project created in Chapter 19 named ProSSIS2014_SSIS. Note that all the code in this chapter can be downloaded from `www.wrox.com/go/prossis2014`. The package you will set up for this chapter is designed specifically to highlight some of the capabilities of using the managed code libraries.

To start, open the ProSSIS2014_SSIS and add a new package. Name the package **package.dtsx**. This package will contain a simple Script Task that runs for 10 seconds.

Add two variables to the package as follows:

VARIABLE NAME	TYPE	VALUE	EXPRESSION
MyExpression	String		@[System::PackageName]
MyVariable	String	Hello World	

Now drop a Script Task on the Control Flow surface. For the Script Task, set the script language to C# and set the code like this (see the testSSISPackage project):

```
public void Main()
{
bool ret = false;
Dts.Events.FireInformation(0, "TestPackage",
"Running C# Script Task" " + Dts.Variables[0].Value.ToString(),
"", 0, ref ret);
System.Threading.Thread.Sleep(10000);
Dts.TaskResult = (int)ScriptResults.Success;
}
```

Test the package to ensure that everything is working correctly. Your results should resemble Figure 21-1.

Now that you have a working test package, you can use it to examine the management capabilities of the DTS runtime managed code library.

FIGURE 21-1

The Managed Object Model Code Library

To start with the external management examples in this chapter, you need to have SQL Server installed (with SSIS). You also need the Visual Studio project templates for developing console, windows, and web applications. The code is simple enough to follow along, and as always you can download it from `www.wrox.com/go/prossis2014`. If you have installed SSIS, you will find a DLL registered in the global assembly cache (GAC) named `Microsoft.SQLServer.Management.IntegrationServices.dll` (version 11 or higher). In this DLL is a namespace called `Microsoft.SqlServer.Management.IntegrationServices` nicknamed "MOM," which stands for Managed Object Model. To access the classes in this namespace, you must first create a project in Visual Studio and then add a reference to the namespace for `Microsoft.SQLServer.Management.IntegrationService.dll`. To avoid typing the full namespace reference, you'll want to add either an `Imports` or a `Using` statement to include the namespace in your code classes like this:

C#

```
using Microsoft.SqlServer.Management.IntegrationServices;
```

VB

```
Imports Microsoft.SqlServer.Management.IntegrationServices
```

The Managed Object Model relies on the use of SMO (Server Management Objects), which means you will need to reference the `Microsoft.SqlServer.Smo.dll`, `Microsoft.SqlServer.ConnectionInfo.dll`, and `Microsoft.SqlServer.Management.Sdk.Sfc.dll`. All of these assemblies can be found in the GAC. If you try to compile a project without these references, you will receive an error stating the references will need to be added. For the Managed Object Model examples you will also need to add the `Imports` or `Using` statement for SMO like this:

C#

```
using Microsoft.SqlServer.Management.SMO;
```

VB

```
Imports Microsoft.SqlServer.Management.SMO
```

The Managed Object Model contains the classes used to manage SSIS server instances for SQL Server 2014. This includes managing SSIS catalogs, projects, packages, parameters, environments, and operations.

The `IntegrationServices` class is the gateway to a SQL Server 2014 SSIS instance. Its primary feature is to be used as the programmatic reference to an SSIS instance.

The `Catalog` class is used to create and manage the single catalog allowed in SQL Server 2014. The following are typical operations of the `Catalog` class:

- Create, manage, and remove an SSIS catalog.
- Provide the `Folders` property, which contains a collection of `CollectionFolder` objects.

- Provide the `Operations` property, which contains a collection of `Operation` objects. Operations include log messages, validation results, and so on.
- Provide the `Executions` property, which contains a collection of `ExecutionOperation` objects. Executions are log events of when a package executed or will show that a package is executing.

The `CatalogFolder` class represents a folder that belongs to a catalog. Typical operations performed by the `CatalogFolder` are:

- Create, manage, and remove folders
- Deploy and remove projects
- Manage permissions to folders
- Create, manage, and remove environments
- Provide the `Projects` property, which is a collection of projects for the folder

Now that you've been introduced to the core classes you'll be using, it's time to go ahead and write some code.

Catalog Management

Our first example (from the MomDemo project) is simply connecting to the local instance of SQL Server 2014 and creating a new catalog. Even though the Managed Object Model provides a `CatalogCollection` class, there can be only one catalog in an SSIS instance. A side effect of having only one catalog is that if you try to execute the code example that follows more than once against an SSIS instance, you will receive an error stating that SSIS supports only one catalog.

```
// create an SMO Server instance to the local sql server instance
Server server = new Server("localhost");

// create an instance of the "MOM" class and initialize it with the SMO Server
IntegrationServices isServer = new IntegrationServices(server);

// create an instance of the Catalog class. The parameters are (server, name of
catalog, password for catalog)

Catalog catalog = new Catalog(isServer, "SSISDB", "password");

// now call create
catalog.Create();
```

As mentioned previously, the `IntegrationServices` class represents an instance of SSIS in SQL Server 2014. One of the benefits of the `IntegrationServices` class is it has more than one constructor that allows you to pass in an SMO `Server` object, a `SqlConnection` object, or a `SqlStoreConnection` object from the `Microsoft.SqlServer.Management.Sdk.Sfc` class. This flexibility allows the management of the SSIS instance from a variety of different project types.

After the example is executed, you should see the new SSISDB catalog in SSMS under the Integration Services Catalogs folder (see Figure 21-2).

To remove a catalog from an SSIS instance, you would call the `Drop` method on a `Catalog` class. However, because there is only one instance of a catalog, the `Drop` method shouldn't be used unless you want to recreate your whole catalog.

FIGURE 21-2

Folder Management

In this next example (from the MomDemo project) you are going to create a folder in the newly created catalog by using the `CatalogFolder` class. The `CatalogFolder` class allows you to create and manage folders that belong to an SSIS catalog. The catalog created in the last example is being retrieved by using the `CatalogCollection` class.

```
// create an SMO Server instance to the local sql server instance
Server server = new Server("localhost");

// create an instance of the "MOM" class and initialize it with the SMO Server
IntegrationServices isServer = new IntegrationServices(server);

// retrieve the catalog we created in the last example
Catalog catalog = isServer.Catalogs["SSISDB"];

// create an instance of the Folder class passing in the catalog, name of the
folder and description of the folder

CatalogFolder folder = new CatalogFolder(catalog, "ProSSIS", "Description");

// now call create
folder.Create();
```

You saw in this example that you're able to access the `CatalogCollection` class by using the `Catalogs` property that is part of the `IntegrationServices` class. To retrieve an instance of the `Catalog` class, you have to either know the name of the catalog or iterate through the collection in the `Catalogs` property. If you don't know the name, you will iterate through the collection and grab the first (and only) catalog in the `Catalogs` property like this:

```
Catalog catalog = null;

foreach(Catalog c in isServer.Catalogs)
        catalog = c;
```

After running the preceding example, you should have a ProSSIS folder underneath the SSISDB catalog in SSMS (see Figure 21-3).

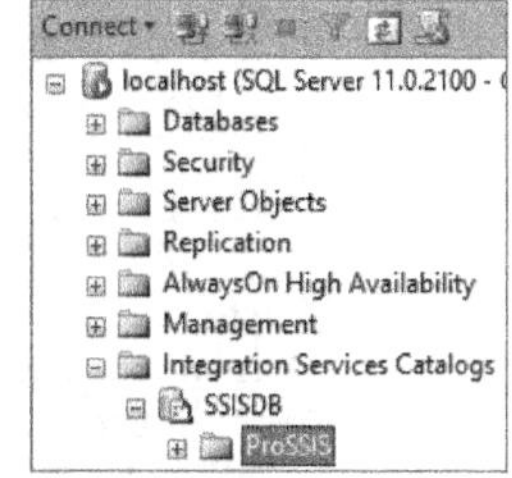

FIGURE 21-3

If you're copying the examples from the book and not using the examples downloaded from www.wrox.com/go/prossis2014, you need to be aware of an issue when calling `Create` on the `CatalogFolder` class that you may run into. You may receive an error stating "Mixed mode assembly is built against version 'v.2.0.50727' of the runtime and cannot be loaded in the 4.0 runtime without additional configuration information." If you receive this error, then you will need to add the following section to the App.Config of your project:

```
<startup useLegacyV2RuntimeActivationPolicy="true">
      <supportedRuntime="v4.0" />
</startup>
```

Environments

Environments are containers that store parameters to be used in your packages deployed to an SSIS catalog. They are covered more extensively in Chapter 22. Imagine you have a project that runs on a schedule. On weekdays, the packages in the project need to run with a certain set of parameter values, but on weekends, they need a different set of values. This is a project with several packages, and each package has several parameters. All the packages in the project need to use the same parameter values when they run. Environments make it easy to run these packages with different sets of parameter values.

The next example (from the MomDemo project) will show you how to retrieve a catalog folder by name, create an environment, and add variables to the environment by using the `EnvironmentInfo` and `EnvironmentVariables` classes.

```
// create an SMO Server instance to the local sql server instance
Server server = new Server("localhost");

// create an instance of the "MOM" class and initialize it with the SMO Server
IntegrationServices isServer = new IntegrationServices(server);

// retrieve the catalog we created in the last example
Catalog catalog = isServer.Catalogs["SSISDB"];

// grab the "ProSSIS" folder. You will need to

CatalogFolder folder = catalog.Folders["ProSSIS"];

// create a new Environment
EnvironmentInfo env = new EnvironmentInfo(folder, "Environment1", "Description");
env.Create();

// create a non sensitive, integer variable
// the add function parameters are (name of variable, type code, value, is
sensitive, description)

e.Variables.Add("IntVar1", TypeCode.Int32, 1, false, "Description of IntVar1");

// create a sensitive (secure), string variable
e.Variables.Add("SecureVar1", TypeCode.String, "securevalue", true,
"Description of SecureVar1");

// now call alter to save the environment
env.Alter();
```

After the example is run, a new SSIS environment will be created under the ProSSIS folder with two variables, as seen in Figure 21-4.

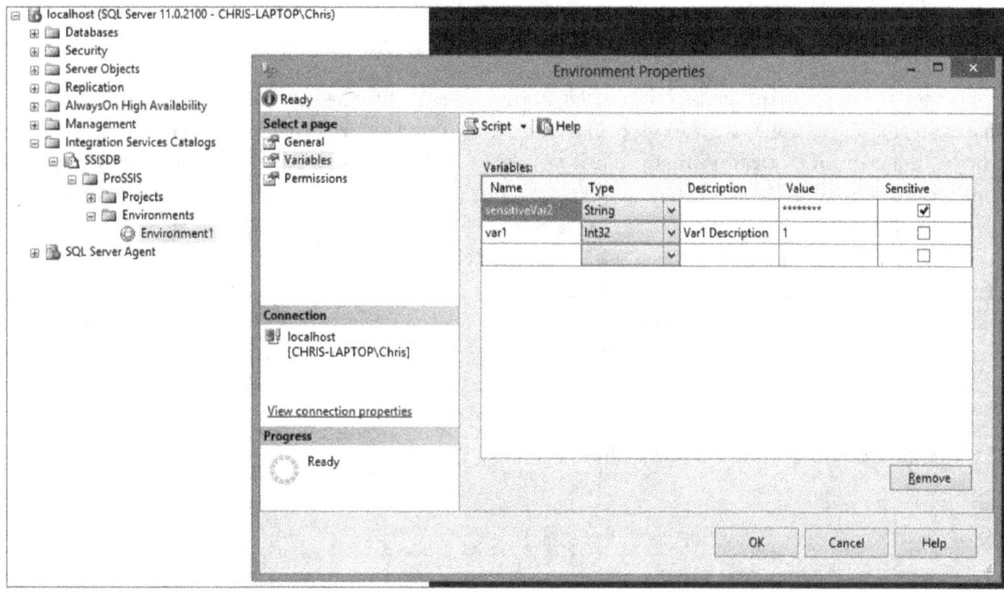

FIGURE 21-4

Environments can be used when executing packages on the server to inject parameter values into a package. This is especially useful when your package needs to be executed against different environments like development and production environments.

To remove a folder you'd simply call the `Drop` method and the folder. If the folder contains any projects or environments, those projects and environments have to be removed before dropping the folder. The next example (from the MomDemo project) shows how to iterate through any folder contents and remove them before dropping the folder from the catalog.

```
CatalogFolder folder = catalog.Folders["Test"];

// must use ToArray() to avoid an error for "Collection was modified after
enumeration"
foreach(EnvironmentInfo env in folder.Environments.ToArray())
{
        env.Drop();
}

foreach(ProjectInfo p in folder.Projects.ToArray())
{
        p.Drop();
}

folder.Drop();
```

This section covered the basics of the Managed Object Model that can be used to manipulate SSIS server instances. At this point you need to be introduced to the DTS Runtime library that will be used to create projects that can be deployed using the Managed Object Model.

The DTS Runtime Managed Code Library

Now that you've been introduced to the server management libraries, the next step is to learn about the classes in the `Microsoft.SqlServer.Dts.Runtime` namespace. For this section you need to have the SQL Server SDK or SSIS installed. If you have installed the SQL Server SDK or SSIS, you will find a DLL registered in the global assembly cache named `Microsoft.SQLServer.ManagedDTS.dll` (version 11 or higher). In this DLL is a namespace called `Microsoft.SqlServer.Dts.Runtime`. To access the classes in this namespace, you must first create a project in Visual Studio and then add a reference to the namespace for `Microsoft.SQLServer.ManagedDTS.dll`. To avoid having to type the full namespace reference, you'll want to add either an `Imports` or a `Using` statement to include the namespace in your code classes like this:

C#

```
using Microsoft.SqlServer.Dts.Runtime;
```

VB

```
Imports Microsoft.SqlServer.Dts.Runtime
```

SSIS Deployment Projects

Prior to SQL Server 2012, an SSIS project was only a basic container in BIDS to store all of your single packages and configurations in a logical group on your development system. The concept of a development environment project did not go away with SQL Server 2012, but the deployment project model alleviates some of the headaches that went along with the deployment of SSIS packages. Chapter 22 covers the deployment model, but this chapter covers how to create the new project files programmatically.

The deployment package is created automatically when you build an Integration Services project in SQL Server Data Tools (SSDT). The type of file that is created is known as an `.ispac` file. An `.ispac` file is basically a zip file with an `.ispac` extension that stores all of the packages, parameters, project configurations, and so on for easy portability. Because the file is stored in zip format, the only way to create an `.ispac` file is by either using the SQL Server Data Tools to build the file or creating the file using the `Project` class.

The `Project` class was created to allow you to manipulate SSIS deployment projects. The following are typical operations that can be performed with the `Project` class.

- Create, open, and save SSIS deployment project files
- Add and remove packages to SSIS project files
- Set project level properties like `ProtectionLevel` and `Password`
- Add parameters to and remove parameters from projects

The following is a simple example (from the MomDemo project) of how to create an SSIS deployment project, add a SSIS package, and then save it as an `.ispac` file. I copied the `Package.dtsx` file from the testSSISProject to the MomDemo project for the following example.

```
string projectFileName = @"c:\ssis\MOMDemo\myproject.ispac";

//Create a new project and specify the project file name as the project storage
using (Project project = Project.CreateProject(projectFileName))
{
    project.Name = "My ProSSIS Project";

    //Set the project property
    project.Description = "This is a new project";

    //Add a package to the project
    project.PackageItems.Add(new Package(), "package.dtsx"); // copies from
        testSSISproject

    //Get the package and modify its description property
    project.PackageItems[0].Package.Description = "Package description ";

    //Save the project
    project.Save();
}
```

The `CreateProject` method can be used like it is in the preceding example by passing in a path to a file or by passing in a `System.IO.Stream` object. A package is added to the project by calling the `PackageItems.Add` method.

The first parameter accepts a `Microsoft.SqlServer.Dts.Runtime.Package` object. Because `"package.dtsx"` already existed on the local machine, instantiating an empty `Package` class (new `Package()`) is done to simply create a placeholder object. If you're creating packages programmatically using the `Microsoft.SqlServer.Dts.Runtime.Package` class, those packages can be passed into the first parameter instead of the placeholder.

The second parameter is the name of the package being added to the project. In the example the path of an existing SSIS package was passed into the `Add` method (`package.dtsx`).

Parameter Objects

Chapter 5 earlier in the book introduces parameters. Parameters were added to the SQL Server 2012 version of SSIS to be used in expressions throughout your project and packages. Because project level parameters are supported, this makes it very easy for a single value to be used across your whole project in several packages.

This is an important feature that was added to allow the reuse of packages across several environments with just a simple change to the parameter. For instance, you could pass in the connection string for an OLE DB connection using a parameter and reuse the same package to execute against your development and production servers.

This next example (from the MomDemo project) takes part of the last example and expands on it by adding a few package parameters and setting the parameter values, as well as saving the project after all the package settings have been added.

```
using (Project project = Project.CreateProject())
{

    project.Name = "My ProSSIS Project";

    //Add a package to the project
    project.PackageItems.Add(new Package(), "package.dtsx");
    Package package = project.PackageItems[0].Package;

    //Add a package parameter with name "PackageParameter1" and type string
    package.Parameters.Add("PackageParameter1", TypeCode.String);

    //Add a project parameter with name "ProjectParameter2" and type String
    project.Parameters.Add("ProjectParameter2", TypeCode.String);

    //Get parameter by name
    package.Parameters["PackageParameter1"].Value = "Value for a package
        parameter";

    //Get parameter by index
    project.Parameters[0].Value = " Value for a project parameter ";

    //Use parameters in expression
    package.Properties["Description"].SetExpression(package,
        "@[$Project::ProjectParameter2]");

    project.Save();

}
```

In this example you saw how to add parameters to both the SSIS project and the package that was added to the project. When you are creating parameters, both the name of the parameter and the data type need to be specified. Most data types are supported, but the following data types cannot be used for parameters: Object, DBNull, Char, and UInt16. Ideally the parameters should have unique names, but the same parameter name can be used in both a project and a package level parameter, meaning you could have a project parameter named “Connection” and a package level parameter named “Connection.”

The line of code in the preceding example above that calls `SetExpression` shows you how to access the `$Project` parameter object that is used to access project level parameters when using SSIS expressions. Both the project and the package level parameters can be accessed through namespace objects, which are named `$Project` and `$Package`, respectively.

Any of the parameters, whether they are stored on the project and parameter level, can be accessed using the `$Namespace::ParameterName` format (for example, `$Package::PackageParameter1` or `$Project::ProjectParameter2`).

Server Deployment

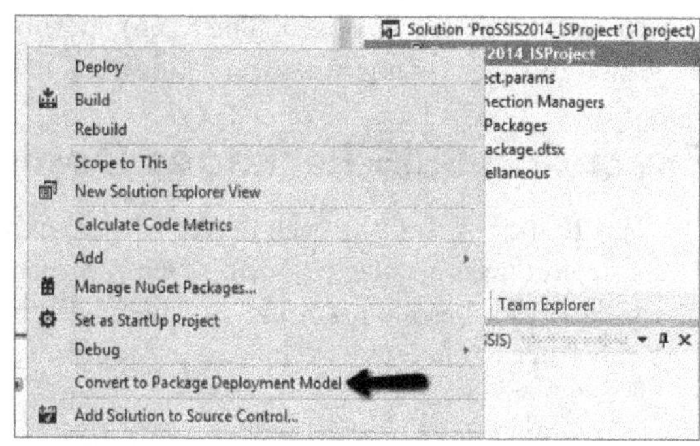

FIGURE 21-5

As mentioned earlier in the chapter, deployment in SQL Server 2012 changed from a single package deployment to a project deployment model. You can still use the previous deployment model by right-clicking on the SSIS project in SQL Server Data Tools and clicking the "Convert to Package Deployment Model" (see Figure 21-5), which will revert the deployment model to the pre-2012 model of storing the packages in the MSDB database or Integration Services store. Keep in mind that if you're using project or package level parameters in your packages or any task like the Execute Package Task that uses project references, you cannot use the package deployment model.

The next example (from the MomDemo project) opens the project created in the previous example (`myproject.ispac`) and deploys it to the ProSSIS folder in the SSIS catalog on the local SQL Server 2014 server.

```
// create an SMO Server instance to the local sql server instance
Server server = new Server("localhost");

// create an instance of the "MOM" class and initialize it with the SMO Server
IntegrationServices isServer = new IntegrationServices(server);

// retrieve the catalog we created in the last example
Catalog catalog = isServer.Catalogs["SSISDB"];

// grab the prossis folder
CatalogFolder folder = catalog.Folders["ProSSIS"];

string projectFileName = "C:\ssis\ExtMgt\MomDemo\myproject.ispac";

using (Project project = Project.OpenProject(projectFileName))
{
    // deploy the project
    folder.DeployProject(project);

    // call "Alter" to save the project to the folder
    folder.Alter();
}
```

In the preceding example `DeployProject` was called using the `CatalogFolder` class. When you are deploying a project to a catalog, a folder must be used to store the project. In this case the

"ProSSIS" folder was used. The Alter method was called to save the changes made to the folder, which in this example was simply adding a new project.

Executing SSIS Packages Deployed to the SSIS Catalog

Now that a project has been deployed, you can execute a package on the server and grab the execution messages (see the MomDemo project). This is a powerful way of executing a package on the server and easily grabbing any messages that were outputted during execution. We are assuming a reference to the "ProSSIS" catalog folder was already obtained.

```
// folder was obtained already
ProjectInfo p = folder.Projects["My ProSSIS Project"];

// get a reference to the package.dtsx package store in the project
PackageInfo pkg = p.Packages["package.dtsx"];

// execute the project. The parameters are (run as 64 bit, Environment reference)
// Environment reference can be used to tell the package to use an environment
created
// in the current catalog
// We're grabbing the "operation id" for this execution

long operationId = pkg.Execute(false, null);

// refresh the operations in the catalog. This will assure we are getting the
messages for our package execution
catalog.Operations.Refresh();

StringBuilder messages = new StringBuilder();

// iterate through each operation.
foreach (Operation op in catalog.Operations)
{
    // make sure we're only looking at the operation for this execution
    if (operationId == op.Id)
    {
                op.Refresh();

                foreach (OperationMessage msg in op.Messages)
                {

                messages.AppendLine(msg.Message);

                }
    }

}

LogFileTextbox.Text = "Package executed: " + messages.ToString();
```

When calling the `Execute` method from the `PackageInfo` class, you're able to object the `Id` of the operation by assigning it to the `operationId` variable. This is later used in the method when iterating through the `Operations` property of the `Catalog` class to retrieve only the `OperationMessage` references for the package that was just executed.

At the end of the example, we used the `Message` property of the `OperationMessage` class to build the messages string builder.

Environment References

We mentioned earlier in the chapter that environments can be used when executing a package stored in an SSIS catalog. The second parameter of `PackageInfo.Execute` method accepts an `EnvironmentReference` object, not an `EnvironmentInfo` object that was used to create the environment. To use an environment you must add an environment reference to the project either in SSMS (see Chapter 22) or programmatically using the `ProjectInfo.References.Add` method. An environment reference is basically a pointer to an existing environment.

This next example (from the MomDemo project) expands on an earlier example where an environment was added to a project by adding an environment reference to a project.

```
CatalogFolder folder = catalog.Folders["ProSSIS"];

// create a new Environment
EnvironmentInfo env = new EnvironmentInfo(folder, "Environment1", "Description");
env.Create();

// create a non sensitive, integer variable
// the add function parameters are (name of variable, type code, value, is
sensitive, description)

e.Variables.Add("IntVar1", TypeCode.Int32, 1, false, "Description of IntVar1");

// create a sensitive (secure), string variable
e.Variables.Add("SecureVar1", TypeCode.String, "securevalue", true,
    "Description of SecureVar1");

// now call alter to save the environment
env.Alter();

ProjectInfo p = folder.Projects["My ProSSIS Project"];

// add the reference. Parameters are: name of environment, folder where
environment is stored.

p.References.Add("Environment1", folder.Name);
p.Alter(); // save the project
```

The last few lines of code in this example show you how to add a reference to an environment by utilizing the `EnvironmentReference.Add` method. Now that a reference has been added, you can use it when executing a package on the server. This next example (from the MomDemo project) shows you how to retrieve an `EnvironmentReference` object and pass it into the `Package.Execute` method.

```
ProjectInfo p = folder.Projects["My ProSSIS Project"];

PackageInfo pkg = p.Packages["package.dtsx"];

// you must use the name of the Environment and foldername to get the reference
EnvironmentReference reference = p.References["Environment1", folder.Name];
reference.Refresh();

pkg.Execute(false, reference);
```

PACKAGE OPERATIONS

The `Application` object is the core class that exposes methods used to connect to and interface with an SSIS service instance for pre-SQL 2012 instances of SQL Server or when the deployment model of your SSIS project is set to use the package deployment model. The following are typical management operations that can be performed using this class:

- Load, save, and delete SSIS packages on the Windows files system, SQL Server, or Integration Services repository
- Construct and execute packages either from a storage facility or in memory
- Add, remove, and rename folders in SQL Server or Integration Services repository folders
- Control package permissions stored within a SQL Server
- Obtain state information and status regarding the execution of packages in SQL Server or the SSIS package repository

The `Package` object represents an instance of a single SSIS package. Although this object exposes many methods that enable you to control every aspect of a package, this chapter deals only with functionality that applies to maintenance-type operations. Here are the maintenance-based operations that the `Package` object exposes:

- Configuring log providers
- Managing package configurations
- Managing Connection Managers in SQL Server and Integration Services

Now that you have an overview of the managed class library for the DTS runtime, the following sections dig deeper into each of the primary classes and demonstrate some useful examples.

APPLICATION OBJECT MAINTENANCE OPERATIONS

SSIS packages can be stored on either the Windows file system or the SSIS catalog. For pre-2012 SQL Server instances and SSIS 2014 projects using the package deployment model, packages can also be stored in the SSIS package store or within SQL Server. The methods of the `Application` object enable you to manage SSIS packages in each of these storage scenarios excluding the SSIS catalog, including management of packages in other server instances. Once the package is loaded or constructed in the `Application` object, it may be run or executed. The flexibility to store, load, and run packages in separate machine spaces expands the scaling capabilities of SSIS packages.

The convention that the SSIS team chose to employ in naming the methods on this `Application` class is to use `DtsServer` in their names when the operation applies to packages in the SSIS package store and `SqlServer` in their names when storage is in SQL Server. If you don't see either of these in the method name, typically this means that the operation is for packages stored in the file system.

In terms of the operations that the `Application` object supports, you'll find methods for general package, folder, and role maintenance.

Package Operations

The `Application` object exposes the following methods to manage packages in the Windows file system, the SSIS package store, and the SQL Server database instance. The SSIS package store has been replaced by the SSIS catalog, so any of the `LoadFrom...` and `SaveTo...` methods (with exception of `SaveToXML`) are now obsolete if you're using the SSIS catalog. These methods can still be used if you prefer to use the pre-SQL Server 2012 storage methods, which are still supported in SQL Server 2014.

- `LoadPackage`: Loads a package from the file system
- `LoadFromDtsServer`: Loads a package from the specified SSIS package store
- `LoadFromSqlServer`: Loads a package from the specified SQL Server instance
- `LoadFromSqlServer2`: Loads a package from the specified SQL Server instance by supplying a valid connection object
- `SaveToXML`: Saves a package object to the file system with a `dtsx` file extension
- `SaveToDtsServer`: Saves a package to the SSIS package store
- `SaveToSqlServer`: Saves a package to the specified SQL Server instance
- `SaveToSqlServerAs`: Saves a package as a different name to the specified SQL Server instance
- `RemoveFromDtsServer`: Removes a package from the SSIS package store
- `RemoveFromSqlServer`: Removes a package from the specified SQL Server instance
- `ExistsOnDtsServer`: Indicates whether a specified package already exists in the SSIS package store at the specified path
- `ExistsOnSqlServer`: Indicates whether a specified package already exists on a specified SQL Server

Now armed with the basic capabilities of the `Application` class, you can put together some real-world examples. First you'll put together an example that examines the variables in a package, and then you'll look at how you can programmatically deploy packages to a DTS package store.

A Package Maintenance Example

At the most basic level, you need to understand how to access a package programmatically to examine its internals. This is where the `Package` object class is used. This class mirrors the structure of the SSIS packages and allows them to be loaded into a navigable object model. Once the package is deep copied into this `Package` structure, you can look at anything in the package. The following C# code snippet is just a partial example of how to load your demonstration package into a `Package` object variable from the file system. Notice that because the package exists on the file system, you are using the `LoadPackage` method of the `Application` object instead of the methods that apply to DTS or SQL Server package stores. Note that this snippet assumes you have the references to `Microsoft.SQLServer.ManagedDTS.dll`. Code can be found in the ExtMgt folder in the CSharp_LoadPackage or vb_LoadPackage.

C#

```
using Microsoft.SqlServer.Dts.Runtime;
public void LoadPackage()
{
Application dtsApp = new Application();
string TestPackageFullPath =
@"C:\SSIS\extmgt\TestSSISPackage\TestSSISPackage\Package.dtsx";
Package pac = dtsApp.LoadPackage(TestPackageFullPath, null);
...
}
```

VB

```
Imports Microsoft.SqlServer.Dts.Runtime
Public Sub LoadPackage()
Dim dtsApp as new Application()
Dim TestPackageFullPath as String = _
"C:\SSIS\extmgt\TestSSISPackage\TestSSISPackage\Package.dtsx"
Dim package As Package = dtsApp.LoadPackage(TestPackageFullPath, Nothing)
...
End Sub
```

Once the `Application` class is created and the `Package` object is loaded, you can interrogate the `Package` object to perform many different tasks. A useful example involves examining the variables within a package. You can do this easily by iterating the variables collection to look for user variables or system variables. The following code snippet (from the ExtMgt folder in CSharp_LoadPackage or vb_LoadPackage) is in the form of a function that you can add to your solution to perform this task:

C#

```
private static void DisplayFilePackageVariables(string FullPath,
bool ShowOnlyUserVariables)
{
Application app = new Application()
Package package = app.LoadPackage(FullPath, null);
string sMsg = "Variable:[{0}] Type:{1} Default Value:{2}
```

```
IsExpression?:{3}\n";
foreach(Variable var in package.Variables)
{
if ((var.Namespace != "System") &&
ShowOnlyUserVariables) ||
!ShowOnlyUserVariables)
{
Console.WriteLine(String.Format(sMsg, var.Name,
var.DataType.ToString(),
var.Value.ToString(),
var.EvaluateAsExpression.ToString()));
}
}
}
```

VB

```
Private Sub DisplayFilePackageVariables(ByVal FullPath As String, ByVal
ShowOnlyUserVariables As Boolean)
Dim app As New Application()
Dim package As Package = app.LoadPackage(FullPath, Nothing)
Dim sMsg As String
sMsg = "Variable:[{0}] Type:{1} Default Value:{2} IsExpression?:{3}"
+ vbCrLf
For Each Variable In package.Variables
If ((Variable.Namespace <> "System" And _
ShowOnlyUserVariables = True) Or _
ShowOnlyUserVariables = False) Then
Console.WriteLine(String.Format(sMsg, Variable.Name, _
Variable.DataType.ToString(), _
Variable.Value.ToString(), _
Variable.EvaluateAsExpression.ToString()))
End If
Next
End Sub
```

If you run this code using the full file path of the demonstration SSIS package and set the option to show only the user variables, the console results will look like Figure 21-6.

FIGURE 21-6

You can see in the console that this correctly shows the two user variables that you set up earlier in the Test SSIS package at the start of this chapter. The results also correctly show that the `myExpression` variable is an expression-based variable using the `EvaluateAsExpression` property. The power of the application and package objects don't stop there. You can also move packages from one store to another, as shown in this next example.

Package Monitoring

You saw an example earlier how the `Catalog` class exposes a property named `Executions`, which is a collection of `ExecutionOperation` objects. You can iterate through the `ExecutionOperation` objects to get a list of the packages that previously ran or a list of currently running packages. The `ExecutionOperation` class has properties that give you the details of the execution operation such as the package name, the project name, when the package starting running, whether or not the package is completed, when the package completed running, and other useful information about the execution.

The following example (from the MomDemo folder) shows you how to list the packages that are currently running in an SSIS catalog.

```
Catalog catalog = isServer.Catalogs["SSISDB"];

StringBuilder messages = new StringBuilder();

foreach(ExecutionOperation exec in catalog.Executions)
{
    catalog.Executions.Refresh();
    if (!exec.Completed)
    {
    messages.AppendLine("Package " + exec.PackageName " is running.
      The project name is " + exec.ProjectName);
    }
}

LogFileTextbox.Text = messages.ToString();
```

For previous versions of SQL Server or if you're using the package deployment model, the `Application` class exposes a method to enumerate all the packages that are currently being executed on an SSIS server. By accessing a running package, you can view some general properties of the package's execution status, and you can even stop a package's execution status. The following methods can be used:

- `GetRunningPackages`: Returns a `RunningPackages` object that enumerates all the packages currently running on a server
- `RunningPackages`: A collection of `RunningPackage` objects
- `RunningPackage`: An informational object that includes such information as package start time and current running duration

The following code (from the ExtMgt folder in CSharp_GetRunningPkgs or vb_GetRunningPkgs) uses the `GetRunningPackage` object to enumerate information about each running package, such as the package's start time and running duration.

C#

```
private static void GetRunningPackageInformation(string Server)
{
Application app = new Application();
RunningPackages runPkgs = app.GetRunningPackages(Server);
Console.WriteLine("Running Packages Count is {0}", runPkgs.Count);
foreach(RunningPackage pkg in runPkgs)
{
Console.WriteLine("Instance ID: {0}", pkg.InstanceID);
Console.WriteLine("Package ID: {0}", pkg.PackageID);
Console.WriteLine("Package Name: {0}", pkg.PackageName);
Console.WriteLine("User Name Running Package: {0}", pkg.UserName);
Console.WriteLine("Execution Start Time: {0}",
pkg.ExecutionStartTime.ToString());
Console.WriteLine("Execution Duration: {0} secs",
pkg.ExecutionDuration.ToString());
}
}
```

VB

```
Private Sub GetRunningPackageInformation(ByVal Server As String)
Dim app As New Application()
Dim runPkgs As RunningPackages = app.GetRunningPackages(Server)
Console.WriteLine("Running Packages Count is {0}", runPkgs.Count)
For Each RunningPackage In runPkgs
Console.WriteLine("Instance ID: {0}", RunningPackage.InstanceID)
Console.WriteLine("Package ID: {0}", RunningPackage.PackageID)
Console.WriteLine("Package Name: {0}",-
RunningPackage.PackageName)
Console.WriteLine("User Name Running Package: {0}", _
RunningPackage.UserName)
Console.WriteLine("Execution Start Time: {0}", _
RunningPackage.ExecutionStartTime.ToString())
Console.WriteLine("Execution Duration: {0} secs", _
RunningPackage.ExecutionDuration.ToString())
Next
End Sub
```

To see this in action, run your SSIS package, and then run this code to see any package that is currently running. This type of code can be useful for monitoring your server to determine whether any packages are running prior to shutting down the server. For example, you may need to get an inventory of the packages on a server. If so, you'll want to review the next section, which shows you how to do that programmatically.

Project, Folder, and Package Listing

When you want to see a listing of the projects, folders, and packages for a catalog, this is easily achieved by iterating through a few collection classes. The first `Collection` class that you need to iterate through is the `FolderCollection` class, which is accessed through the `Folders` property on the `Catalog` class. Next, you will iterate through the `ProjectsCollection` class that is accessed through the `Projects` property on the `Folder` class. Finally you'll iterate through the `PackageCollection` class, which is accessed through the `Packages` property on the `Project` class. This is useful for taking an inventory of all the packages that exist on a server. Here is the code (from the MomDemo folder) that will do this for a catalog on a 2014 SSIS Instance by adding the catalog, catalog folders, projects, and packages to a TreeView.

```
Server server = new Server(@"localhost");

IntegrationServices isServer = new IntegrationServices(server);
Catalog catalog = null;

// we're assuming we don't know the name of the catalog here
foreach (Catalog c in isServer.Catalogs)
        catalog = c;


TreeNode catalogNode = new TreeNode("Catalog: " + catalog.Name);
treeView1.Nodes.Add(catalogNode);

foreach (CatalogFolder f in catalog.Folders)
{

        TreeNode folderNode = new TreeNode("Folder: " + f.Name);
        catalogNode.Nodes.Add(folderNode);

        foreach (ProjectInfo p in f.Projects)
        {

                TreeNode projectNode = new TreeNode("Project: " + p.Name);
                folderNode.Nodes.Add(projectNode);

                foreach (Microsoft.SqlServer.Management.IntegrationServices
                    .PackageInfo pkg in p.Packages)
                {
                        TreeNode packageNode = new TreeNode("Package: " +
                            pkg.Name);
                        projectNode.Nodes.Add(packageNode);
                }
        }
}
```

The result is information about the packages stored on the server instance, as shown in Figure 21-7.

This is only the tip of the iceberg in terms of what you can do with the DTS runtime libraries. To get an idea of what you can do using this library, in the next section you build a simple UI that enables you to use some of the code techniques described so far.

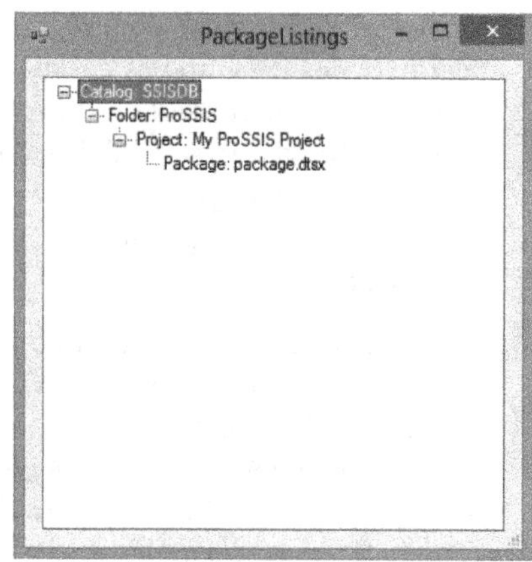

FIGURE 21-7

A Package Management Example

The following example demonstrates how to incorporate package management operations in a web-based application. It shows how to enumerate the catalog, folder, and project structure of a SQL Server SSIS instance; enumerate the packages that are contained in a selected project; and then execute a package from the web page itself. This chapter demonstrates with a C# version of the project. However, you can download a VB.NET version of the project, as well as the source shown in this chapter, from `www.wrox.com/go/prossis2014`.

To start, first create a new web project in Visual Studio. Launch Visual Studio and select File ➪ New ➪ Web Site. In the New Web Site dialog (see Figure 21-8), select ASP.NET Web Forms Site and then choose Visual C# or Visual Basic as the language. Leave the rest of the fields as shown.

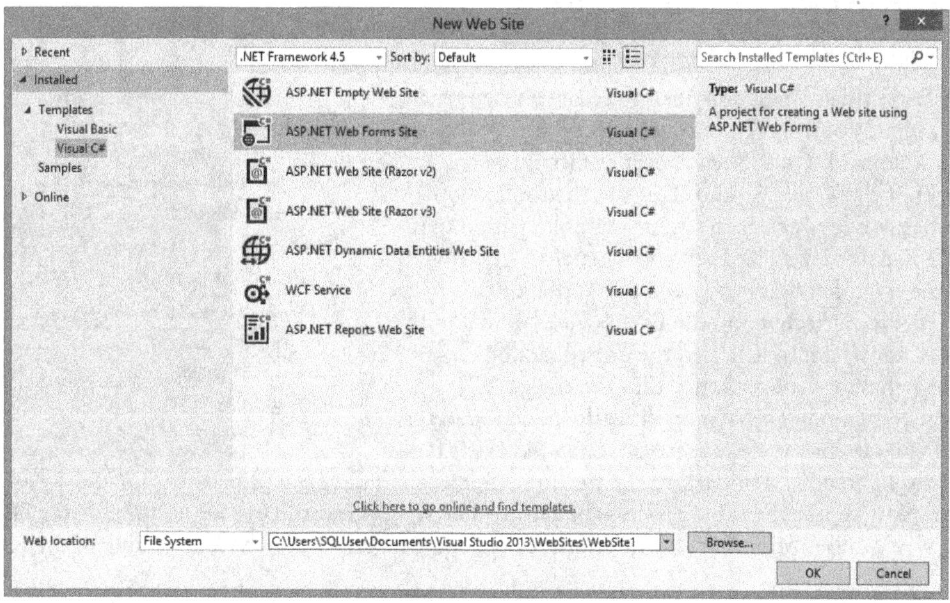

FIGURE 21-8

Click the OK button, and the Web Site project will be initialized. By default, the `Default.aspx` page is created and displayed automatically. Now you can start building the page that will display the information you want. First, you must add the web controls to the page.

To do this, select the Design view from the bottom-left corner of the Default.aspx tab. This puts the interface into graphics designer mode. From the Toolbox on the left-hand side of the window, drag a TreeView control onto the page. The TreeView control is in the Navigation group of the Toolbox. Now drag a GridView control onto the page. The GridView is located in the Data group of the Toolbox. Finally, drag over a Button control from the Toolbox. The Button control can be found in the Standard group. Click the Button control, and in the Properties tab change the Text property to the word "Refresh."

Now you need to add some supporting HTML in the source view of the page to configure the columns of the GridView control. To do so, click the Source button on the bottom left of the Default.aspx tab. This switches the view to show you the HTML code that defines this page. Add the following HTML code between the <asp:GridView1> elements. The <asp:BoundField> elements you're adding configure the GridView to display three data columns and a button column. You could do this through the Design interface, but this is a bit quicker for your purposes:

```
<Columns>
<asp:BoundField DataField="PackageName" HeaderText="Name" />
<asp:BoundField DataField="PackageFolder" HeaderText="Folder" />
<asp:BoundField DataField="Status" HeaderText="Status" />
<asp:ButtonField Text="Execute" ButtonType=Button/>
</Columns>
```

Select GridView1 in design mode to show the properties. If your properties bar isn't visible, press F4. Now set the "AutoGenerateColumns" property of GridView1 to false.

The page should now look like Figure 21-9.

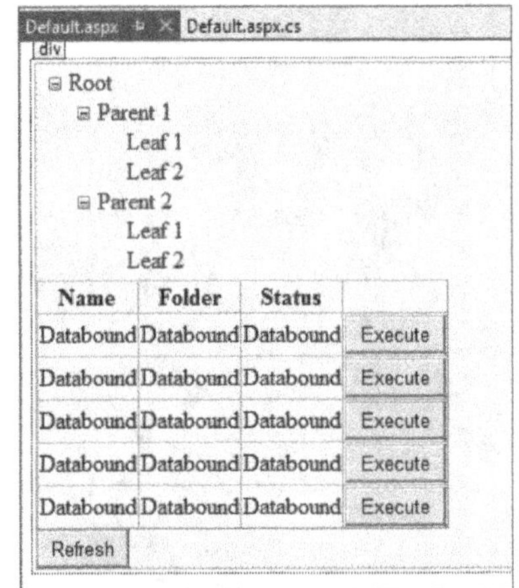

FIGURE 21-9

Before you leave this screen, you need to create a few event handlers on these controls. To do this, select the TreeView control. Go to the Properties tab in the bottom right of the Visual Studio IDE. On the toolbar of the Properties window, select the lightning bolt symbol that signifies the Events view. The Events view enables you to configure the event handlers you need to handle for this page. With the TreeView selected and the Events view shown in the Properties window, double-click in the SelectedNodeChanged event in the Behavior group. Notice that the Default .aspx.cs code-behind page is automatically loaded, and the event handler code for the SelectedNodeChanged event is automatically created. Switch back to the Default.apsx tab and do the same thing for the TreeView Load event. Now repeat the same process for the GridView RowCommand event and the Button Click events. To view a description of what these events do, you can search for the event name in the Help screen.

The full HTML code of the page (see the CSharp_Website2014 project) should now look something like this:

```
<%@ Page Language="C#" AutoEventWireup="true" CodeFile="Default.aspx.cs"
Inherits="_Default2" %>
<!DOCTYPE html PUBLIC "-//W3C//DTD XHTML 1.1//EN"
"http://www.w3.org/TR/xhtml11/DTD/xhtml11.dtd">
<html xmlns="http://www.w3.org/1999/xhtml">
<head runat="server">
<title>Untitled Page</title>
</head>
<body>
<form id="form1" runat="server">
<div>
<asp:TreeView ID="TreeView1" runat="server" ShowLines="True"
OnLoad="TreeView1_Load" OnSelectedNodeChanged=
"TreeView1_SelectedNodeChanged">
</asp:TreeView>
<br />
<asp:GridView ID="GridView1" runat="server" AutoGenerateColumns=False
OnRowCommand="GridView1_RowCommand">
<Columns>
<asp:BoundField DataField="PackageName" HeaderText="Name" />
<asp:BoundField DataField="PackageFolder" HeaderText="Folder" />
<asp:BoundField DataField="Status" HeaderText="Status" />
<asp:ButtonField Text="Execute" ButtonType=Button/>
</Columns>
</asp:GridView>
 <br />
<asp:Button ID="Button1" runat="server" OnClick="Button1_Click"
Text="Refresh" />
</div>
</form>
</body>
</html>
```

Now you need to start adding the code behind the page that makes this page work. For this example, you will be creating a few custom classes to support code you will be writing in the code-behind page of the Web Form. First, you need to add two new class files. To do this, select File ⇨ New ⇨ File from the main menu. In the Add New File dialog that appears, select a new Class object and name it `PackageGroup.cs`. The `PackageGroup` object will be used to wrap a `PackageInfo` object and enhance its functionality. Next, add another Class object and call this one `PackageGroupCollection.cs`. Notice that these two files have been added to the App_Code directory of the solution. In Visual Studio, your code external modules are stored in the App_Code directory. Add the following references to your project:

```
Microsoft.SQLServer.ManagedDTS.dll
Microsoft.SqlServer.Management.IntegrationServices.dll
Microsoft.SqlServer.Smo.dll
Microsoft.SqlServer.ConnectionInfo.dl
Microsoft.SqlServer.Management.Sdk.Sdf.dll
```

Next, open the `PackageGroup.cs` file and add the following code to it (see the CSharp_Website2014 project). You can overwrite the code that was automatically generated with this code:

```
using System;
using System.Data;
using System.Configuration;
using System.Web;
using System.Web.Security;
using System.Web.UI;
using System.Web.UI.WebControls;
using System.Web.UI.WebControls.WebParts;
using System.Web.UI.HtmlControls;
using Microsoft.SqlServer.Management.IntegrationServices ;
using Microsoft.SqlServer.Management.Smo;
///

<summary>
///

Summary description for PackageGroup
///

</summary>
///

public

class PackageGroup
{

public PackageGroup(PackageInfo packageInfo, string server, string catalog,
string folder, string project)
{

_packageinfo = packageInfo;
_server = server;
_folder = folder;
_catalog = catalog;
_project = project;
}

private PackageInfo _packageinfo;
private string _server;
private string _catalog;
private string _folder;
private string _project;

public string PackageName
{
get { return _packageinfo.Name; }
}

public string PackageCatalog
{
get { return _catalog; }
```

```
}

public string PackageFolder
{
get { return _folder; }
}

public string PackageProject
{
get { return _project; }
}

public string Status
{
get { return GetPackageStatus(); }
}

public void ExecPackage()
{
Server server = new Server(_server);
IntegrationServices service = new IntegrationServices(server);
Catalog catalogObject = service.Catalogs[_catalog];
CatalogFolder folderObject = catalogObject.Folders[_folder];
ProjectInfo projectObject = folderObject.Projects[_project];
PackageInfo p = projectObject.Packages[_packageinfo.Name];

p.Execute(false, null);
}

private string GetPackageStatus()
{
Server server = new Server(_server);
IntegrationServices service = new IntegrationServices(server);
Catalog catalog = service.Catalogs[_catalog];

foreach (ExecutionOperation exec in catalog.Executions)
{

if (exec.FolderName == _folder && exec.PackageName == _packageinfo.Name)
{
catalog.Executions.Refresh();

if (!exec.Completed)
{
return "Executing";
}
}

}

return "Sleeping";

}
```

As you can see, this object stores the information about a package and wraps a `PackageInfo` object. You could just link the `PackageInfo` objects to the GridView, but this method codes a wrapper with additional functionality to determine a package's execution status and execute a package. The `ExecutePackage` method can be called to execute the package, and the `GetPackageStatus` method searches the currently running packages on the server and returns an execution status to the calling object.

To store information about multiple packages, you need to roll all the `PackageGroup` objects you create into a collection object. To do this, you created a strongly typed collection class called `PackageGroupCollection` to house very concrete `PackageGroup` objects. Open the `PackageGroupCollection` file and add the following code (see the CSharp_Website2014 project). Once again, you can overwrite the code that was automatically created when the file was created with this example code:

```
using System;
using System.Data;
using System.Configuration;
using System.Web;
using System.Web.Security;
using System.Web.UI;
using System.Web.UI.WebControls;
using System.Web.UI.WebControls.WebParts;
using System.Web.UI.HtmlControls;

///<summary>
///Summary description for PackageGroupCollection
///</summary>
///

Public class PackageGroupCollection : System.Collections.CollectionBase
{

public PackageGroupCollection()
{

}

public void Add(PackageGroup aPackageGroup)
{
List.Add(aPackageGroup);
}

public void Remove(int index)
{
if (index > Count - 1 || index < 0)
{
throw new Exception("Index not valid!");
}

else
{
List.RemoveAt(index);
```

```
}
}

public PackageGroup Item(int Index)
{
return (PackageGroup)List[Index];
}

}
```

This class simply inherits from the `System.CollectionBase` class to implement a basic `IList` interface. To learn more about strongly typed collections and the `CollectionBase` class, search the Help files. Next you will add the code-behind page of the `Default.aspx` page. Select the `Default.aspx.cs` tab and add the following code (see the CSharp_Website2014 project) to this page:

```
using System;
using System.Data;
using System.Data.SqlClient;
using System.Configuration;
using System.Web;
using System.Web.Security;
using System.Web.UI;
using System.Web.UI.WebControls;
using System.Web.UI.WebControls.WebParts;
using System.Web.UI.HtmlControls;
using System.Threading;
using Microsoft.SqlServer.Dts.Runtime;
using Microsoft.SqlServer.Management.IntegrationServices;
using Microsoft.SqlServer.Management.Smo;

public partial class _Default : System.Web.UI.Page
{
    PackageGroupCollection pgc;
    string ssisServer = @"localhost ";
    protected void Page_Load(object sender, EventArgs e)
    {

    }

    protected void TreeView1_Load(object sender, EventArgs e)
    {

        //Clear TreeView and Load root node
        //Load the SqlServer SSIS catalog, folder and project structure into
        tree view and show all
        //nodes
        TreeView1.Nodes.Clear();

        Server server = new Server(ssisServer);
        IntegrationServices isServer = new IntegrationServices(server);
        Catalog catalog = null;

        foreach (Catalog c in isServer.Catalogs)
```

```
            catalog = c;

        LoadTreeView(catalog);

        TreeView1.ExpandAll();

    }

    protected void TreeView1_SelectedNodeChanged(object sender, EventArgs e)
    {
        // does the current node have 2 / slashes in the valuepath
        // (e.g. SSISDB/ProSSIS/My ProSSIS Project)

        System.Text.RegularExpressions.Regex regEx = new
            System.Text.RegularExpressions.Regex(@"\/");
        if (regEx.Matches(TreeView1.SelectedNode.ValuePath).Count == 2)
        {
            // were in a project node
            PackageGroupCollection pgc = BuildPackageGroupCollection
                (TreeView1.SelectedNode.ValuePath);
            LoadGridView(pgc);
            Session.Add("pgc", pgc);
        }
    }

    protected void GridView1_RowCommand(object sender, GridViewCommandEventArgs e)
    {
        if (e.CommandName == "Execute")
        {
        pgc = (PackageGroupCollection)Session["pgc"];
        PackageGroup pg = pgc.Item(Convert.ToInt32(e.CommandArgument));
        Thread oThread = new System.Threading.Thread(new
            System.Threading.ThreadStart(pg.ExecPackage));

        oThread.Start();

        LoadGridView(pgc);
        }
    }

    protected void LoadTreeView(Catalog catalog)
    {

        TreeNode catalogNode = new TreeNode(catalog.Name);
        TreeView1.Nodes.Add(catalogNode);

        foreach (CatalogFolder f in catalog.Folders)
        {

        TreeNode folderNode = new TreeNode(f.Name);
        catalogNode.ChildNodes.Add(folderNode);

        foreach (ProjectInfo p in f.Projects)
```

```
            {

            TreeNode projectNode = new TreeNode( p.Name);
            folderNode.ChildNodes.Add(projectNode);
            }

            }
        }

        protected void LoadGridView(PackageGroupCollection pgc)
        {
            GridView1.DataSource = pgc;
            GridView1.DataBind();
        }

        protected PackageGroupCollection BuildPackageGroupCollection(string
            pathToProject)
        {

            // split the ValuePath by /
            string[] path = pathToProject.Split('/');
            string catalog = path[0];
            string folder = path[1];
            string project = path[2];

            Server server = new Server(ssisServer);
            IntegrationServices service = new IntegrationServices(server);
            Catalog catalogObject = service.Catalogs[catalog];
            CatalogFolder folderObject = catalogObject.Folders[folder];
            ProjectInfo projectObject = folderObject.Projects[project];
            PackageGroupCollection collection = new PackageGroupCollection();

            foreach (Microsoft.SqlServer.Management.IntegrationServices.PackageInfo
                p in projectObject.Packages)
            {
            PackageGroup g = new PackageGroup(p, server.Name, catalog, folder,
                project);
            collection.Add(g);
            }

            return collection;
        }

        // refresh button
        protected void Button1_Click(object sender, EventArgs e)
        {
            LoadGridView((PackageGroupCollection)Session["pgc"]);
        }
    }
```

When the page is processed, several additional methods are called. The `TreeView_Load` method is called, which in turn calls the `LoadTreeView` method, which accepts a `Catalog` collection.

The folders and projects of the catalog are iterated, and each folder and project is added to the TreeView. When the page is first loaded, just the TreeView is displayed. By selecting a project in the TreeView, the page is posted back to the server, and the `TreeView1_SelectedNodeChanged` method is called. This method calls another method in this page called `BuildPackageGroupCollection`, which accepts a string value that contains the `ValuePath` of the selected tree node. The string is split by a forward slash, which stores the value of the catalog, folder, and project. Before iterating through the collection of packages, the `IntegrationServices`, `Catalog`, `CatalogFolder`, and `ProjectInfo` objects are instantiated. Then the `Packages` property of the `ProjectInfo` class is iterated to list the packages stored in the selected project. Once the collection is built, the `LoadGridView` method is called to link the `PackageGroupCollection` to the GridView. In the `LoadGridView` method, the collection is bound to the GridView object. This action automatically loads all the objects in the `PackageGroupCollection` into the GridView.

How does the GridView know which columns to display? Remember back in the beginning of this example when you added the `«asp:BoundColumn»` elements to the GridView object. Notice that the `DataField` attributes are set to the properties of the `PackageGroup` objects in the `PackageGroupCollection` object. Therefore, in your walkthrough of the code, the page is basically finished processing, and the results would be displayed to the user in the web page. Try it and inspect what you have so far. Go ahead and build and then run the project. Figure 21-10 shows a sample of what you may see when you run the web page. Your results may vary depending on the folders and packages you have configured in your server.

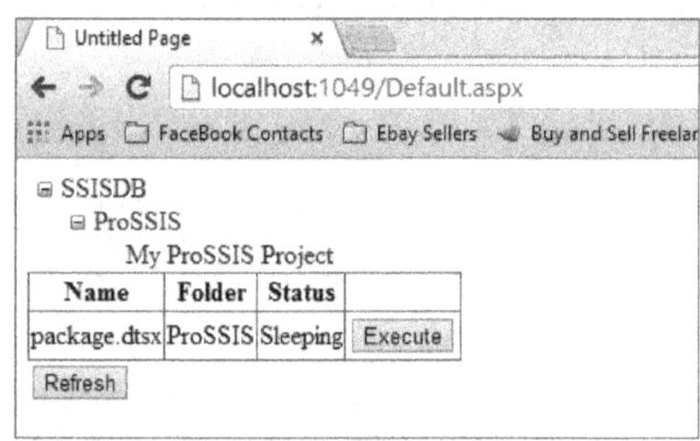

FIGURE 21-10

> **NOTE** *You'll need to click the My ProSSIS Project node to see the packages in the grid.*

Now take a look at how the status field and Execute button work. When the GridView is loaded with `PackageGroup` objects, the `status` property of the `PackageGroup` class is called. Look in the `PackageGroup.cs` file and you will see that when the `status` property is called, the code iterates through a collection of `ExecutionOperation` objects to determine whether a package is currently running or not. The `ExecutionOperation` stores the name of the folder and package, and those two properties are compared to the internal `_folder` and `_packageInfo.Name` values of the current `PackageGroup` object. If a match is found, the `Completed` property of the `ExecutionOperation` object is checked for a value of False. If False is returned from the `Completed` property, a string value of "Executing" is returned to the GridView. If the `Completed` property returns True or nothing is found in the iteration of the `ExecutionOperationCollection` object, the value of "Sleeping" is returned. The Execute button works in a similar fashion.

When the Execute button is clicked, the `GridView1_RowCommand` method is called in the page's code-behind file. This method re-instantiates the `PackageGroup` object from the page's viewstate cache. When found, the package is executed by calling the `Execute` method of the `PackageGroup` object. Notice that this call is done in a newly created thread. By design, a web page is processed synchronously. This means that if the package were executed in the same thread, the `Execute` method would not return until the package was finished executing. Therefore, by starting the package in a new thread, the page can return, and the status of the package can be displayed in the GridView. Give it a try. Make sure your package runs long enough for you to refresh the web page and see the status value change.

That's just a basic implementation of some of the functionality exposed by the `Microsoft.SqlServer.Dts.Runtime` and `Microsoft.SqlServer.Management.Integration` namespaces to manage your SSIS packages through managed code. You saw how to obtain a collection of `PackageInfo` objects and how to leverage the functionality of the objects in an application. In addition, you learned how to run a package and determine which packages are currently running. Obviously, this is a simple application and could stand to be greatly improved with error handling and additional functionality. For example, you could add functionality to cancel a package's execution, load or delete package files to SQL Server through the website, or modify the code to support the viewing of packages in the SSIS file storage hierarchy.

PACKAGE LOG PROVIDERS

Log providers are used to define the destination for the log information that is generated when a package executes. For instance, if you require a record of the execution of your package, a log provider could persist the events and actions that had transpired into a log file, recording not only the execution but also, if required, the values and results of the execution.

Defining what should be logged during a package's execution is a two-step process. First, you must define which log providers to use. You can define multiple providers in a single package. Second, you need to define what information should be sent to the defined log providers.

Keep in mind that if you're executing a package store in a SQL Server 2014 catalog that the logging of events is done automatically and can be seen in the catalog.executions, catalog.operations, and catalog.operationmessages tables. To programmatically retrieve the logs, you will use the `Executions` and `Operations` properties of the `Catalog` class. We will see an example of that in this section.

To demonstrate how you would do this using the UI, open the MomDemo project and make sure package.dtsx is loaded. Then to configure logging for the test SSIS package you'll select SSIS ➪ Logging from the menu. The Configure SSIS Logs dialog that is displayed shows all the containers that currently exist in the package. The first step is completed by configuring SSIS Log Providers on the Providers and Logs tab, shown in Figure 21-11.

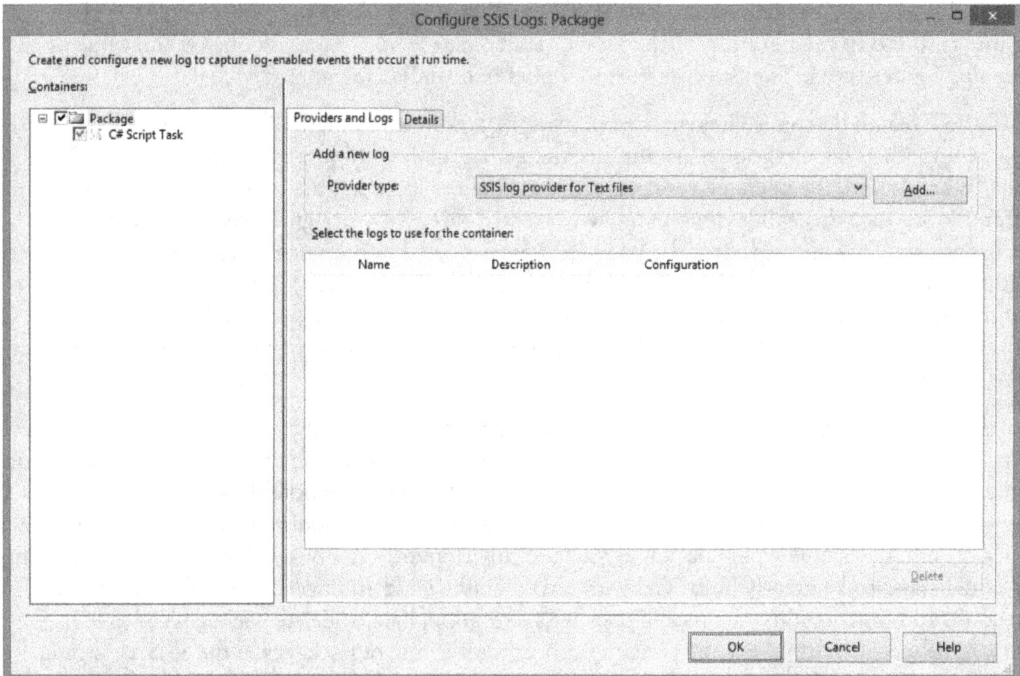

FIGURE 21-11

SQL Server Integration Services includes several default log providers. These providers are selected in the Provider Type combo box and are defined as follows:

- **SSIS Log Provider for Text Files:** Used to store log information to a CSV file on the file system. This provider requires you to configure a File Connection object that defines the location of the file. Storing log information in a text file is the easiest way to persist a package's execution. Text files are portable, and the CSV format is a simple-to-use industry-wide standard.
- **SSIS Log Provider for SQL Profiler:** This provider produces a SQL Provider trace file. The file must be specified with a `trc` file extension so that you can open it using the SQL Profiler diagnostic tool. Using SQL Profiler trace files is an easy way for DBAs to view log information. Using Profiler, you could view the execution of the package step-by-step, even replaying the steps in a test environment.
- **SSIS Log Provider for SQL Server:** This provider sends package log events to a table in the specified SQL Server database. The database is defined using an OLE DB connection. The first time this package is executed, a table called sysssislog is created automatically. Storing log information in a SQL Server database inherits the benefits of persisting information in a relational database system. You could easily retrieve log information for analysis across multiple package executions.

- **SSIS Log Provider for Windows Event Log:** This provider sends log information to the Application event store. The entries created are under the Source name SQLISPackage. No additional configuration is required for this provider. Logging package execution to the Windows Event Log is possibly the easiest way to store log events. The Windows Event Log is easy to view and can be viewed remotely if required.
- **SSIS Log Provider for XML Files:** This provider stores log information in a specified XML file on the file system. The file is specified through a File Connection object. Make sure you save the file with an `xml` file extension. Logging events to XML inherits the advantages of the XML specification. XML files are very portable across systems and can be validated against a Schema definition.

Specifying Events to Log

Once you have configured the log providers you wish to employ, you must define what events in the package to log. This is done in the Details tab (see Figure 21-12) of the log configuration dialog. To enable an event to be logged, check the box next to its name. For instance, in Figure 21-12, the `OnError` event for the package has been selected for logging. By selecting other containers on the left-hand side of the dialog, additional events can be selected, down to an individual task or Data Flow event level. To select all events at once, check the box in the header row of the table. By selecting individual containers in the tree view on the left, you can configure the logging of events on an individual task level. By configuring logging at the task level, the special events exposed by a task can additionally be included in the log.

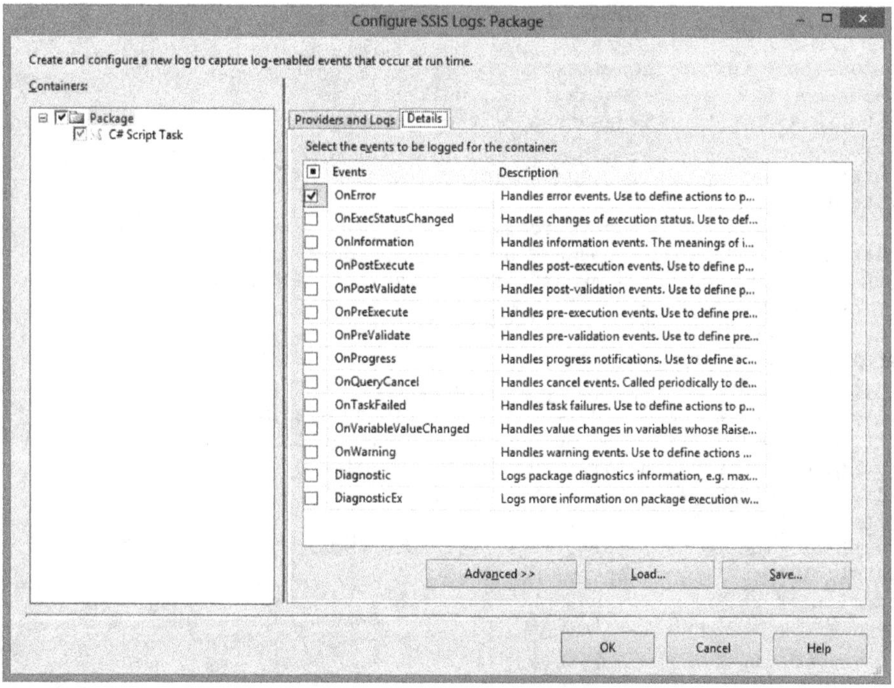

FIGURE 21-12

This is the way to set up a log file using the UI. The next section describes how to examine log providers programmatically.

Programming to Log Providers

The `Package` object exposes the `LogProviders` collection object, which contains the configured log providers in a package. The `LogProvider` object encapsulates a provider's configuration information.

The `LogProvider` object exposes the following key properties:

- `Name`: This is a descriptive name for the log provider.
- `ConfigString`: This is the name of a valid `Connection` object within the package that contains information about how to connect to the destination store.
- `CreationName`: This is the `ProgID` of the log provider. This value is used in the creation of log providers dynamically.
- `Description`: This describes the type of provider and optionally the destination to which it points.

The next two examples (see the CSharp_GetPkgLogs folder) enumerate all the log providers that have been configured in a package and write the results to the console window. To get extra mileage out of these examples, the C# version loads the package from a file; the VB.NET version loads the package from an Integration Server:

C#

```
private static void GetPackageLogsForPackage(string PackagePath)
{
Application dtsapp = new Application();
Package p = dtsapp.LoadPackage(PackagePath, null);
Console.WriteLine("Executing Package {0}", PackagePath);
p.Execute();
Console.WriteLine("Package Execution Complete");
Console.WriteLine("LogProviders");
LogProviders logProviders = p.LogProviders;
Console.WriteLine("LogProviders Count: {0}", logProviders.Count);
LogProviderEnumerator logProvidersEnum = logProviders.GetEnumerator();
while (logProvidersEnum.MoveNext())
{
LogProvider logProv = logProvidersEnum.Current;
Console.WriteLine("ConfigString: {0}", logProv.ConfigString);
Console.WriteLine("CreationName {0}", logProv.CreationName);
Console.WriteLine("DelayValidation {0}", logProv.DelayValidation);
Console.WriteLine("Description {0}", logProv.Description);
Console.WriteLine("HostType {0}", logProv.HostType);
Console.WriteLine("ID {0}", logProv.ID);
Console.WriteLine("InnerObject {0}", logProv.InnerObject);
Console.WriteLine("Name {0}", logProv.Name);
Console.WriteLine("------------------");
}
}
```

You can, of course, dynamically configure a package's log providers. To do so, a valid connection must initially be created to support the communications to the database. In the following code (see the CSharp_GetPkgLogs folder), first a package is loaded into memory. Then the connection is created for the `mytext.xml` file and named. This name is used later as the `ConfigString` for the log provider to connect the output to the file Connection Manager.

C#

```
public static void CreatePackageLogProvider(string PackagePath)
{
Application dtsapp = new Application();
Package p = dtsapp.LoadPackage(PackagePath, null);
ConnectionManager myConnMgr = p.Connections.Add("FILE");
myConnMgr.Name = "mytest.xml";
myConnMgr.ConnectionString = "c:\\ssis\\mytest.xml";
LogProvider logProvider = p.LogProviders.Add("DTS.LogProviderXMLFile.2");
logProvider.ConfigString = "mytest.xml";
p.LoggingOptions.SelectedLogProviders.Add(logProvider);
p.LoggingOptions.EventFilterKind = DTSEventFilterKind.Inclusion;
p.LoggingOptions.EventFilter = new string[] { "OnError", "OnWarning",
"OnInformation" };
p.LoggingMode = DTSLoggingMode.Enabled;
logProvider.OpenLog();
p.Execute();
}
```

Next, the log provider is instantiated by passing the `ProgID` of the provider you wish to create. The following is a list of the `ProgIDs` for each type of log provider available:

- **Text File Log Provider:** `DTS.LogProviderTextFile.3`
- **SQL Profiler Log Provider:** `DTS.LogProviderSQLProfiler.3`
- **SQL Server Log Provider:** `DTS.LogProviderSQLServer.3`
- **Windows Event Log Provider:** `DTS.LogProviderEventLog.3`
- **XML File Log Provider:** `DTS.LogProviderXMLFile.3`

SQL Server 2014 Operation Logs

As mentioned earlier in the chapter, the execution log and messages for packages executed on a SQL Server 2014 server within a catalog are automatically stored to log tables in the catalog database (for example, SSISDB). To retrieve the execution logs and message, you can either query the table via views or use the properties available within the `Catalog` class.

If you'd like to see the execution results and message, you can query the following views in the catalog table:

- **catalog.executions:** This view retrieves the execution logs of any package executed on the catalog. The Id column from this view is also stored with the operation messages. The other key columns are project, packagename, and folder.

- **catalog.operations:** This view stores all of the operations performed for a project or execution. The operation_type column stores the operation performed for the record. Some of the most common operations are
  - **101:** Deploy project
  - **200:** Create execution or start execution
  - **201:** Validate package
  - **202:** Stop operation

  The Id column in the catalog.operations will match the Id column from the catalog.executions view if the operation is from an execution of a package.
- **catalog.operationmessages:** This view stores all of the operational messages from an operation. For execution this includes the common messages you're used to seeing when executing a package, like "Validation has started."

In the example that follows (see the MomDemo folder), you're going to retrieve the execution results of packages programmatically. To do so you will iterate the `Executions` property of the `Catalog` class. The `Executions` property is a collection of `ExecutionOperation` objects. Then, you will use a LINQ query on the `Operations` property to match the `Id` property from the `ExecutionOperation` class to the `Id` property of the `Operation` class. Finally, you will iterate through the `Messages` property of the `Operation` class to show the logged messages of the package execution.

```
Catalog catalog = isServer.Catalogs["SSISDB"];
CatalogFolder folder = catalog.Folders["ProSSIS"];
ProjectInfo p = folder.Projects["My ProSSIS Project"];

catalog.Operations.Refresh();

StringBuilder messages = new StringBuilder();
foreach(ExecutionOperation exec in catalog.Executions)
{
    // execution complete?
    if (exec.Completed)
    {

    messages.AppendLine(exec.PackageName + " completed " +
        exec.EndTime.ToString());

     // query the operations property using the
     // Id property and match it to the exec.Id
     var ops = from a in catalog.Operations where a.Id == exec.Id select a;

     foreach(Operation op in ops)
     {

     op.Refresh();

     foreach (OperationMessage msg in op.Messages)
```

```
            {
            messages.AppendLine("\t" + msg.Message);
            }
            }
    }
    }
    LogFileTextbox.Text = messages.ToString();
```

After running this example you should see a window similar to Figure 21-13.

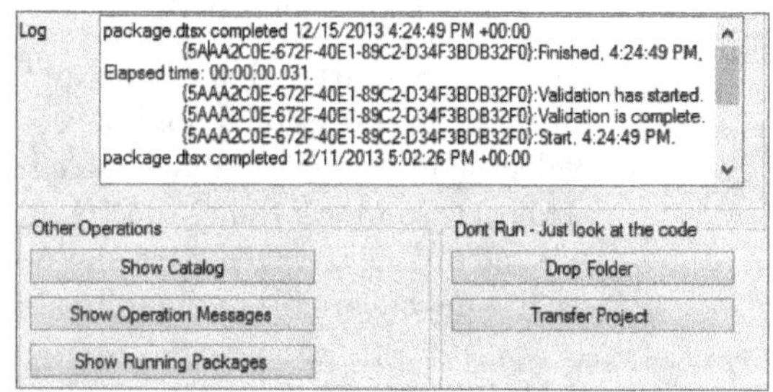

FIGURE 21-13

PACKAGE CONFIGURATIONS

Prior to SQL Server 2012 a package configuration was the optimal method to store configurable values that could be used in your package without altering the package. The introduction of parameters, which you can read about in Chapter 5 and see in the earlier examples in this chapter, means they are now the preferred method of storing configurable values that can be injected into packages at runtime.

Package configurations are still a valid way to store configurable values in other locations where parameters cannot be stored, such as XML files, SQL Server tables, and registry entries.

Package configurations are a flexible method of dynamically configuring a package at runtime. This gives you a high degree of flexibility in the execution of SSIS packages, enabling you to design the package to run in different environments without having to modify the package file itself. When a package is written, not all operational parameters may be known, such as the location of a file or the value of a variable. By supplying this information at runtime, the user does not have to hardcode these values into a package. When a package is run, the values stored in the specified configuration store are loaded for use during the package's execution. The configuration capabilities of SSIS support the storage of data in five different data stores. The following list describes each type of data store and its capabilities:

- **XML File Configuration:** The XML File Configuration option stores package information in an XML file on the file system. This configuration provider enables you to store multiple configuration settings in a single file. As an alternative to hardcoding the path to the XML file, the path can be stored in a user-defined environment variable. Using this option, you can easily both modify the XML file and distribute the configuration with the package.
- **Environment Variable:** This option enables you to store a configuration value in an environment variable. Using this option, you are allowed to save only a single configuration parameter. By specifying an environment variable that is available on each machine on

which the package will run, you can ensure that the package configuration is valid for each environment. Also, setup of the environment variable can be done once during initial setup of the package's environment.

- **Registry Entry:** This option allows you to store a configuration value in a registry value. Only a single value can be specified. Optionally, you can specify an environment variable that contains a registry key where the value is stored. Configuration entries in the registry are a secure and reliable way to store configuration values.
- **Parent Package Variable:** This option enables you to specify a fully qualified variable in a different package as the source for the configuration value. Only a single value can be stored in a specified configuration store. This is a good way to link packages and pass values between packages at runtime. When one package depends on the results from another package, this option is perfect.
- **SQL Server:** This option creates an SSIS Configuration table in a database that you specify. Because this table could hold the configurations for multiple packages, a configuration filter value should be specified to enable the system to return the correct configuration values. This option allows you to specify multiple configuration values that will be stored under the filter name specified. Optionally, you can specify the database, table, and filter in an environment variable in the following format:

```
<database connection>;<configuration table>;<filter>;
```

For example:

```
VSTSB2.WroxTestDB;[dbo].[SSIS Configurations];Package1;
```

Creating a Configuration

To create a configuration for a package, select SSIS ⇨ Package Configurations. In the dialog that is displayed, select the "Enable package configurations" checkbox. From here, you must define which package configuration provider to use. This can be accomplished through the Package Configuration Wizard that is started when you click the Add button.

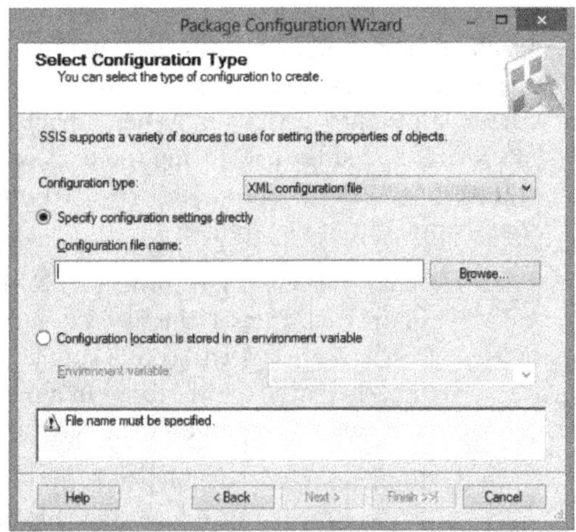

FIGURE 21-14

On the first page of the wizard, shown in Figure 21-14, you must specify which configuration provider you wish to use to store the configuration information. For this example, choose the XML File Configuration option. Now specify the path where the configuration file will reside. Having a standard location to store your configuration files helps to ensure that as a package is moved from environment to environment, the links to the configuration are not broken. If the path to the configuration is not standard, you can store the path to the configuration file in an environment variable and then reference the environment variable in the package wizard. Remember that if you have recently added the environment variable to your system, you may need to reboot in order for it to be available for use in your package.

After you have chosen a configuration storage provider, the next step is to specify the properties to save in the configuration store, as shown in Figure 21-15. You can either select a single value from the property tree view or select multiple values at one time. Because you selected the XML File Configuration provider, you can select multiple values to store.

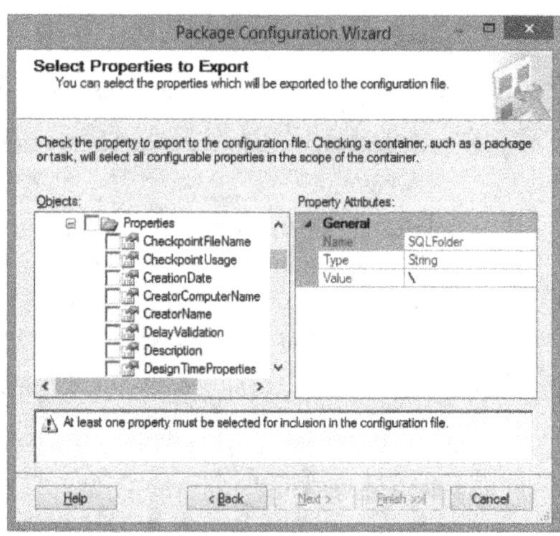

FIGURE 21-15

Notice that not only can you store default values to load at the time the package is executed, but you can also load entire object definitions at runtime. This is useful if you just want to load a variable's value or actually specify an entire variable configuration at runtime. For example, you may want to configure the actual properties of a variable. Almost every aspect of a package can be persisted to a configuration store, including package properties, configured values in defined tasks, configuration information for log providers, and Connection Manager information. About the only thing you can't store in a package configuration store is specific data about the package configurations.

When it is complete, the package configuration information is stored in the package. When the package is executed, the configuration providers load the values from the specified data stores and substitute the values found for the default values saved in the package.

Programming the Configuration Object

You can also programmatically configure a package's configuration through the `Configuration` object. This is useful if you would like to configure a package through managed code as shown at the beginning of this chapter. All package configurations can be accessed through the `Configurations` collection of the package object.

The `Configuration` object exposes functionality to dynamically configure a package's configuration settings. This enables you to programmatically configure a package based on the environment in which it will run. Because a package can contain multiple configuration sources, you can discover all the configurations in a package by enumerating the `Configuration` objects contained in a `Package.Configurations` property.

Configuration Object

The `Configuration` object exposes the following members:

- `ConfigurationString`: This is the path describing where the physical configuration store is located.
- `ConfigurationType`: This sets the configuration provider to be used to interface to the configuration data store. The configuration type is referenced from the `DTSConfigurationType` enumeration. Note that a `DTSConfigurationType` that starts with an "I" denotes that the `configurationstring` is stored in an environment variable.
- `Name`: This is the unique name for the configuration object in the package.
- `PackagePath`: This defines the path of the actual data that is being accessed.

The following example (see the CSharp_ConfigPkg folder) details how to add an existing configuration store to a package. First, the `EnableConfiguration` property is set to true. Then, an empty configuration object is added to the package. The configuration object is then set to the Config File type, which directs the configuration to expect a valid `dtsconfig` file to be specified in the `configurationstring` property. Finally, the path to the configuration information is supplied, and the package's path is stored. The package is then saved, thus persisting the configuration setup to the package file.

```
private static void CreatePackageConfig(string PackagePath)
{
Application app = new Application();
Package pkg = app.LoadPackage(PackagePath, null);
Variable var = pkg.Variables.Add("myConfigVar", false, "", "Test");
string packagePathToVariable = var.GetPackagePath();
pkg.EnableConfigurations = true;
Configuration config = pkg.Configurations.Add();
config.ConfigurationString = "ConfigureMyConfigVar";
config.ConfigurationType = DTSConfigurationType.EnvVariable;
config.Name = "ConfigureMyConfigVar";
config.PackagePath = packagePathToVariable;
app.SaveToXml(@"C:\SSIS\extmgt\TestSSISPackage\TestSSISPackage\" +
"myTestSSISPackageConfig.xml", pkg, null);
Console.WriteLine("Configuration Created and Saved");
}
```

If you run this code against the Test SSIS package for this chapter, you'll see a new `myTestSSISPackageConfig.xml` file in the TestSSISPackage directory with the additional variable that was added and a configuration for the variable.

This section has described how you can use the DTS runtime code library to perform many of your mundane administrative tasks programmatically. The next section looks at another feature of SSIS that you can use in your administrative Toolbox — Windows Management Instrumentation.

WINDOWS MANAGEMENT INSTRUMENTATION TASKS

SSIS includes two special tasks that enable you to query system information and monitor system events: the WMI Data Reader Task and the WMI Event Watcher Task. These tasks are especially useful for system management, as you will discover with examples later in this chapter. WMI uses a specialized query language known as WQL, which is similar to SQL, to obtain information about a Windows system. WMI has many features and capabilities, so we won't be able to cover all of them, but here are a few common uses:

- You can get information about files and directories, such as file size, or enumerate the files in a folder. You can also monitor the file system for events, such as whether a file has been modified recently. This could be required in a package if your package is importing data from a CSV or XML file. A change in the file could trigger tasks to fire in your package.
- You can determine whether an application is currently running. In addition, you can find out how much memory that application is using or how much processor time it has used. This is useful if your package needs to know whether a companion process is running before creating some sort of output result.
- You can obtain information about users in Active Directory, such as whether a user is active or has certain permissions to a resource. This is useful in a package if information about a user or machine on the network is required for your package's execution.
- You can control services that are running on a computer system and actually start and stop them as required. This is useful if your package needs to stop a service during a data transfer.

This is just a small sample of the information you can glean from a computer system. You can obtain information not only about the current system but also about remote systems. As you can see, this gives you access to a great deal of information that could be used in the execution of an SSIS package. For example, you could determine if enough disk space existed on a drive before copying a backup file from a remote system to the current system. You could also monitor a file for updates and automatically import the changes into a database table. Later in this chapter you will see how to actually implement these two examples. For more information on the WMI system, visit `http://msdn.microsoft.com/en-us/library/windows/desktop/aa394582(v=vs.85).aspx`.

WMI Reader Task Explained

The WMI Data Reader Task has the following parameters that must be configured properly for the task object to work:

- `WmiConnection`: This is a configured WMI Connection object.
- `WqlQuerySourceType`: This setting specifies where the WQL query is referenced. The query can be manually typed in or stored in a file or a variable.
- `WqlQuerySource`: This field sets the actual source of the WQL query source selected in the `WqlQuerySourceType`.

- `OutputType`: This parameter sets the structure in which the results of the WQL query are stored after execution.
- `Overwrite Destination`: This determines whether the previous results are retained or overwritten when the task is executed.
- `Destination Type`: This enables you to specify how the results will be stored.
- `Destination`: This enables you to specify the location of the destination type.

To start configuration of the WMI Data Reader Task, you must first create a WMI Connection Manager object. The WMI Connection Manager specifies the WMI namespace that the query will run against. The WMI class used in the query must be contained within that namespace. The standard namespace for most machines is the `\root\cimv2` namespace. This namespace contains the majority of WMI classes that can be called to get system information. The connection object specifies the target computer system that the query will be run against. By default, the SSIS WMI Connection points to the localhost machine, but remote systems can be specified as well by using the NetBIOS, IP address, or DNS name of the remote machine. Because security is always an issue, the WMI Connection object specifies the user that the query will be run against. Whether it is Windows Authentication or a specified user, the user must have permissions to query the WMI repository on the system for it to work.

Next, the WQL query must be designed. Because WMI is so extensive a subject, this chapter can't explain the intricacies of the model. We suggest that you locate a good book on WMI scripting to learn the details of how WMI works. Another resource for free WMI tools is the MSDN downloads site. Two applications that are helpful for WQL query generation are the Scriptomatic V2 application available at `http://www.microsoft.com/download/en/details.aspx?id=12028`, which enables you to browse the classes in WMI namespace and generate WMI queries in several different scripting formats, and the WMI Administrative tools package available at `http://www.microsoft.com/download/en/details.aspx?id=24045`. This package includes several sample apps to enumerate the classes in various namespaces and monitor WMI filter events, among other useful features. These two tools can help you derive WMI queries quickly and easily.

Once you have figured out the structure of your query, you must decide into which object type to store your query results. The WMI Data Reader Task object gives you basically two options: a string or a data table. Either object can be stored in a user-defined variable or in a file on the file system. When storing the result in a user-defined variable, the variable must be defined as a `String` data type or `Object` data type. This means that when you're obtaining numeric information from the system, you must convert the resultant string to the appropriate data type for use in a mathematical expression. The file transfer example suggests one way to accomplish this transformation, but this is not the only way. When storing a data table to file, the result is a basic comma-separated file with the properties listed in the first row and the actual values returned in the second row.

WMI Data Reader Example

The best way to explain the WMI Data Reader Task is to see an example of it in action. The idea of this example is to query the file system for the size of a database file and the amount of free space on a drive. With this information, you can then determine if the drive has enough space to handle the new file. For simplicity, this example will copy from directories on the same drive. At the end of the example, you will learn how to modify the WMI queries to query the same information from remote systems.

To set up this example, you must first create a file you would like to copy. This example uses a backup of the AdventureWorks database (but any large file will do). If you don't know how to create a backup of the AdventureWorks database, you can create any large file or use a file from one of many examples in this book. If you do use the AdventureWorks backup, it will tie into the WMI Event Watcher Task example later in this chapter. As always, you can also download the complete samples for this chapter from `www.wrox.com/go/prossis2014`.

Open a new Integration Services project and call it **WMI_DataReader**. Drag a new WMI Data Reader Task object from the Toolbox to the Control Flow page of the package. First, give this task a unique name; in this case, call it "WMI Data Reader Task - Read Free Space on C." Now, right-click the task and select Edit from the pop-up menu to bring up the WMI Data Reader Task Editor. Click the WMI Options tab to render the editor, as shown in Figure 21-16.

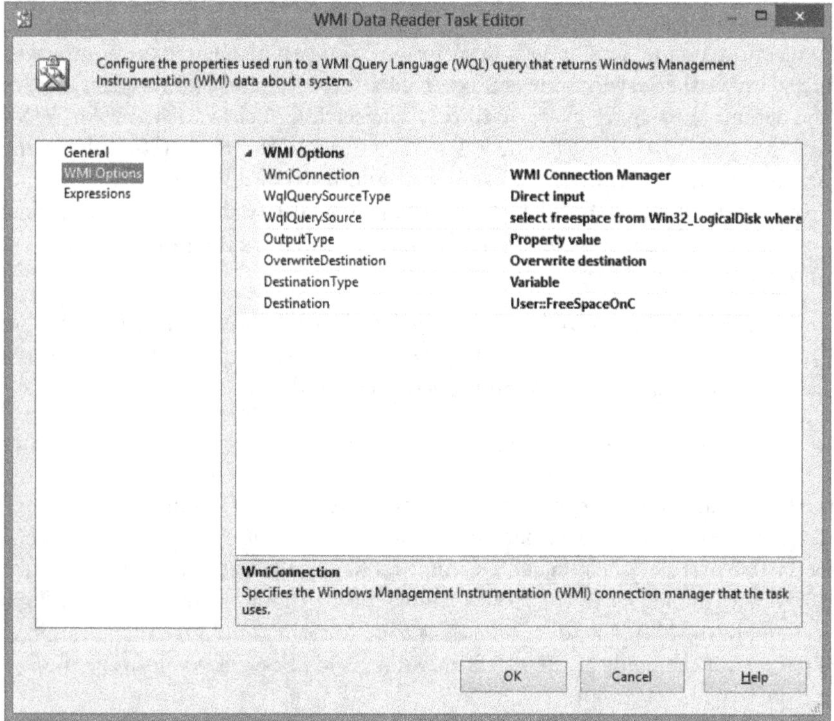

FIGURE 21-16

Click in the WmiConnection parameter field and select the button to the right. Select <New WMI Connection . . . > from the dropdown list. The dialog shown in Figure 21-17 will be displayed.

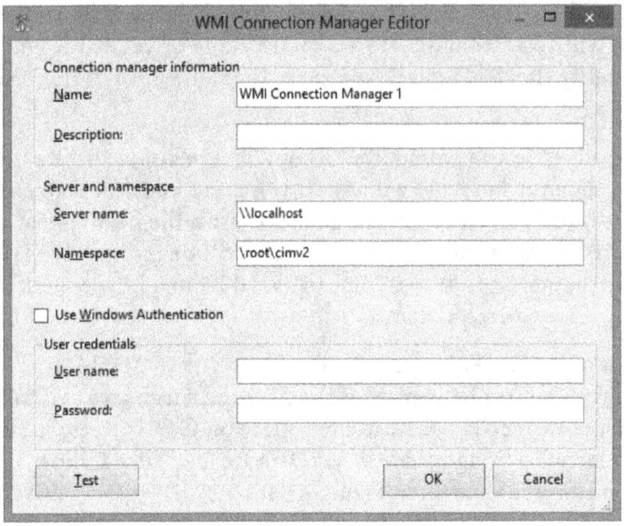

FIGURE 21-17

Give the new WMI connection a name and enter a description. You can also enter the computer system you wish to query. Leave the server name set to the default of \\LocalHost to query the local computer, and leave the default namespace as \root\cimv2. The setting of cimv2 is the main WMI repository that contains the core WMI classes to access information on the system. Finally, check the box to use Windows Authentication or enter a user name and password that has rights to query the CIM repository on this computer. Click the Test button to verify the settings, and then click OK to close the dialog. This completes the WMI connection and adds it automatically to the WMIConnection property in the editor.

Back in the WMI Data Reader Task Editor dialog, leave the WqlQuerySourceType as DirectInput. Next, select the WqlQuerySource field and click the ellipsis button on the right. In the dialog that appears, enter the following WQL query in the WqlQuerySource window:

```
SELECT FreeSpace FROM Win32_LogicalDisk Where DeviceID ='C:'
```

This query will return the amount of free space that exists on drive C. Next, change the OutputType to Property Value and leave the OverwriteDestination field set to Overwrite Destination. Set the DestinationType property to Variable. Click in the Destination field and choose the ellipsis button to the right and select <New variable...>. In the Add Variable dialog that appears (shown in Figure 21-18), enter FreeSpaceOnC in the Name field, set the data type to string, and give the variable a default of zero. Leave the rest of the fields at their default values and click OK to close the dialog. We'll explain the string data type in a minute.

Now you'll add another WMI Data Reader Task and configure it to return the size of the AdventureWorks backup file. Call this task "WMI Data Reader Task - Read DB File Size." Open the WMI Data Reader Task dialog for this new task. Click in the WMI Connector field and choose the WMI Connection Manager connection. Because the CIM class you will be using to obtain the file size of the backup file is in the same CIM namespace, you can reuse the same WMI Connection object.

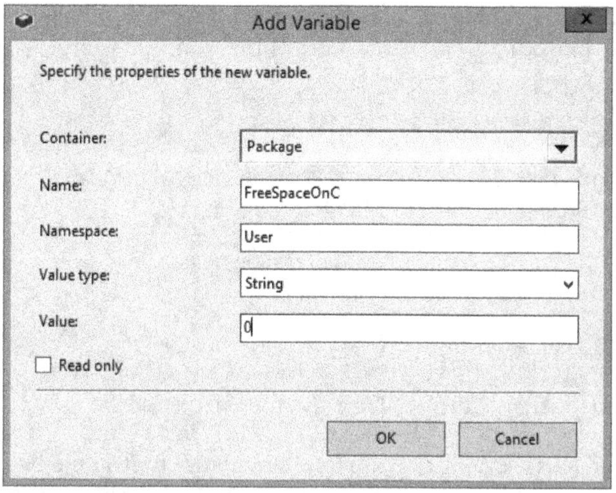

FIGURE 21-18

Leave the WqlQuerySourceType as DirectInput. Now, click the SqlQuerySource field and click the ellipsis to the right to open the query editor dialog. Enter the following query:

```
Select FileSize FROM CIM_Datafile WHERE Name =
"C:\\SSIS\\EXTMGT\\WMI_DataReader\\AdventureWorks.bak"
```

In the OutputType field, choose Property Value. In the DestinationType field, choose Variable, and then click in the Destination field and choose <New variable...>. Call the new variable **DBBackupFileSize**, with a data type of string and an initial value set to zero (0).

That's all there is to configuring the tasks themselves. Hook them together so that you can add some logic to handle the data the WQL query will return. It was stated previously that the WMI Data Reader could only write to strings and Data Table objects. Well, when a string is returned, it has several extraneous characters at the end that cause a data conversion from String to Integer to fail. You can see these characters by setting a breakpoint on the `PostExecute` event of one of the WMI Data Reader Tasks and running the package. When the task turns green, go to the Variables tab and look at the data in the two user-defined variables. The value looks like this: "FileSize\r\n45516800\r\n."

To massage this data into a usable form suitable for conversion to an Integer data type, you will create a Script Task to strip the extra characters from the string, leaving just numeric digits. To start, click the Event Handler tab of the package. In the Executables dropdown box, choose the WMI Data Reader Task called "WMI Data Reader Task - Read Free Space on C." Next, select the `OnPostExecute` event handler and click the hyperlink in the middle of the page to create the event. Drag a Script Task object from the Toolbox onto the page. Change the name of the object to "FileSizeOnC Data Massage." Right-click the task and select Edit from the pop-up menu. On the left-hand side of the Script Editor dialog, choose the Script page. In the ReadWriteVariables property, select the variable User::FreeSpaceOnC. This will give you read/write access to the variable from within the Script Task.

Now, click the Edit Script button in the bottom-right corner of the window. In the Script Host editor that appears, add the following code immediately after the start of the Main subroutine (see the WMI_DataReader folder):

C#

```
string s = System.Convert.ToString(Dts.Variables["User::FreeSpaceOnC"].Value);
s = System.Text.RegularExpressions.Regex.Replace(s, "\\D", "");
Dts.Variables["User::FreeSpaceOnC"].Value = Int64.Parse(s);
```

VB

```
Dim s As String
s = CType(Dts.Variables("User::FreeSpaceOnC").Value, String)
s = System.Text.RegularExpressions.Regex.Replace(s, "\\D", "")
Dts.Variables("User::FreeSpaceOnC").Value = Int64.Parse(s).ToString()
```

As you can see, this code parses the string and uses the `RegularExpressions` library to strip the characters from the returned value. Then the cleaned-up string is cast to return an Int64 value as a string. In short, this code will strip all the extraneous characters from the string and return a numerical result into the same variable. As a result, the contents of the string are ready to be used in a mathematical expression. To finish, close the Script Host windows and click OK to close the Script Task Editor dialog. Repeat this same setup for the ReadDBFileSize Task, making sure to change the variable references to the appropriate variable names.

You're now in the home stretch of this example. The final steps are to set up the file transfer and add the precedence constraint that ensures you have enough space on the drive before you initiate the transfer. First, drag a File System Task onto the Control Flow page. Name this task **Copy Db File**. Right-click the task and click Edit in the pop-up menu. In the File System Task Editor, set the following properties as shown in Figure 21-19.

In the Parameters tab of the package, create two new parameters with a string data type called `DBFile_Source` and `DBFile_Destination`. Set the `DBFile_Source` parameter to the AdventureWorks backup file. If you are using the file structure from the download files, this will be `c:\ssis\extmgt\WMI_DataReader\AdventureWorks.bak`. In the `DBFile_Destination` parameter, enter the backup folder or `c:\ssis\extmgt\WMI_DataReader\Backup\AdventureWorks.bak`. Set the DestinationVariable value to the `DBFile_Destination` parameter (`$Package::DBFile_Destination`) and set the SourceVariable to the `DBFile_Source` parameter (`$Package::DBFile_Source`). Click OK to close the dialog. If you are not using the download sample files, make sure you create the directory in which you intend to back up the file. The File System Task will not create the directory automatically.

The final step is to link these tasks with precedence constraints. Link the tasks as shown in Figure 21-20.

After adding the links, right-click the constraint between the Read DB File Size Task and the Copy Db File Task. Click the Edit option in the pop-up menu to open the Precedence Constraint Editor. Set the Evaluation option to Expression and Constraint and then enter the following line of code in the Expression field:

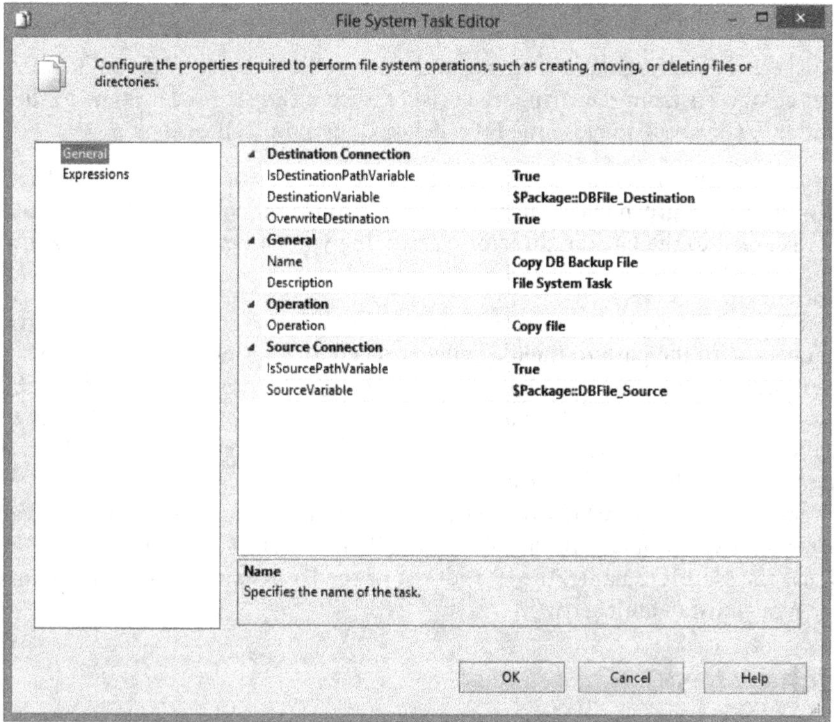

FIGURE 21-19

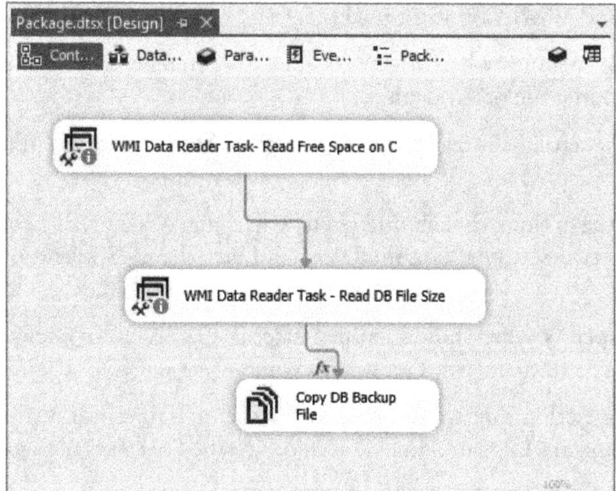

FIGURE 21-20

```
(DT_I8)@FreeSpaceOnC > (DT_I8)@DBBackupFileSize
```

As you can see, this is where the massaging of the data in the Script Task pays off. If you had not stripped the extraneous characters from the string, then the cast from the String data type to the Integer data type would fail. Click OK to close the Precedence Constraint Editor dialog.

Now you are ready for the moment of truth: running the package. If all went well, all the tasks should run successfully and have a green check mark icon on the top-right corner of the task, and the file should have been copied to the backup directory (assuming you had enough space available on the drive).

We mentioned earlier about ways you could improve this example. It seems a waste that you have to hardcode the WQL query with the path to the file being checked for size, especially since the path to the file is already stored in the `DBFile_Source` parameter. One option is to build the WQL query on the fly with a Script Task. This would enable you to construct the path in the WQL in the proper format — namely, changing the single backslash in the path to double backslashes. Also, in a more advanced scenario, the file could be located on another computer system. This could easily be handled by creating a separate WMI Connection object pointing to the second system and assigning it to the `WmiConnection` property in the WMI Data Reader Task - Read DB File Size Task. For remote machines, use the NetBIOS name, the IP address, or the DNS name in the ServerName property instead of the \\localhost default setting.

WMI Event Watcher Task

As outlined earlier, not only can WMI obtain information about a computer system, it can also monitor that system for certain events to occur. This capability enables you to monitor the file system for a change in a file or monitor the Windows system for the start of an application. The WMI Event Watch Task has the following options to configure:

- `WmiConnection`: This is a configured WMI Connection Manager.
- `WqlQuerySourceType`: This setting specifies where the WQL query is referenced. The query can be manually typed in or stored in a file or a variable.
- `WqlQuerySource`: This field sets the actual source of the WQL Query Source selected in the `WqlQuerySourceType`.
- `ActionAtEvent`: This option sets the actions that should occur when the WMI event being monitored occurs. This option has two settings: Log the Event and Fire the SSIS Event, or just Log the Event.
- `AfterEvent`: This field is used to specify what should happen after the WMI event occurs. The options are Return with Success, Return with Failure, or Watch for the Event Again.
- `ActionAtTimeout`: This defines the action that should be taken if the task times out waiting for the WMI event to occur. Options are Log the Time-Out and Fire the SSIS event, or just Log the Time-Out.
- `AfterTimeout`: This defines what action should be taken after the task times out. This option sets what should happen after the `ActionAtTimeout` occurs. The options are Return with Failure, Return with Success, or Watch for the Event Again.

- `NumberOfEvents`: This option specifies how many events must occur before the specified action is taken.
- `Timeout`: This sets how long the task should wait, in seconds, before the specified time-out action is taken. A setting of zero (0) denotes that the task will never time-out.

The WMI Event Watcher Task is similar to the WMI Data Reader Task in that the basic query setup is the same in both cases. You must define a WMI Connection object and create a WMI query to monitor for an event. The specific options available in this task define how the task reacts when the event occurs.

There are two basic types of actions: what should happen when the event actually occurs, and what should happen if the event does not occur within a specified time. Both these actions can either log the event to the package log or, in addition to logging the event, fire an event that can be used to perform additional specified tasks. Also, both actions can dictate what happens after the event occurs or the task times out. These after-events can be passing to subsequent tasks a success or failure of the WMI Event Watcher Task or simply continuing to monitor for the event to occur again.

WMI Event Watcher Task Example

In the WMI Data Reader example, you used WMI to check the size of a file before you copied it to the drive. You would most likely perform this type of task after some other process created the backup of the database. In some cases, you can execute the package manually when you are ready to perform the actions in the package. However, if you need certain tasks to be performed in response to an event like the backup file being created, then use the WMI Event Watcher Task. This task can monitor any system event, including the creation of a file like the backup file you used in the WMI reader example.

In this example, you'll use the WMI Event Watcher Task to look for the file, and then kick off the WMI Data Reader package created earlier. You could also use this example to look for incoming data files that need to be processed. You can see an example of this use of the WMI Task in Chapter 3.

To use this task to determine when the backup has completed from our first WMI example, create a new SSIS package called **WMI Event Watcher Package**. Add a WMI Event Watcher Task to the Control Flow page of the package. Name this task "WMI Event Watcher Task - Monitor DB File." Right-click the task and select Edit from the pop-up menu. You are now presented with the WMI Event Watcher Task Editor. Select WMI Options from the pane on the left and configure the properties as outlined in this section.

First, create a `WmiConnection` pointing to the machine where the backup file would normally be created. In this example that will be the root directory of the WMI_DataReader project. You can use the same connection properties as outlined in the previous example. Next, enter the WqlQuerySource that will monitor the file system for changes to the `AdventureWorks.bak` file:

```
Select * from __InstanceModificationEvent within 30 where targetinstance isa
"CIM_DataFile" and targetinstance.name =
"C:\\SSIS\\extmgt\\WMI_DataReader\\AdventureWorks.bak"
```

As you can see, this query monitors the `AdventureWorks.bak` file for changes every 30 seconds.

The rest of the properties are specific to the WMI Event Watcher Task. Set the `ActionAtEvent` property to Log the Event and Fire the SSIS Event. As you'll see in a moment, this event is used to launch the "Db Data File Copy" package created in the previous example. Next, set the `AfterEvent` property to Watch for this Event Again. This setting essentially sets up a monitoring loop that perpetually watches the file for changes as long as the package is running. Because you don't care if the task times out, leave the time-out settings at their default values. The editor should look like Figure 21-21. Click the OK button to close the dialog.

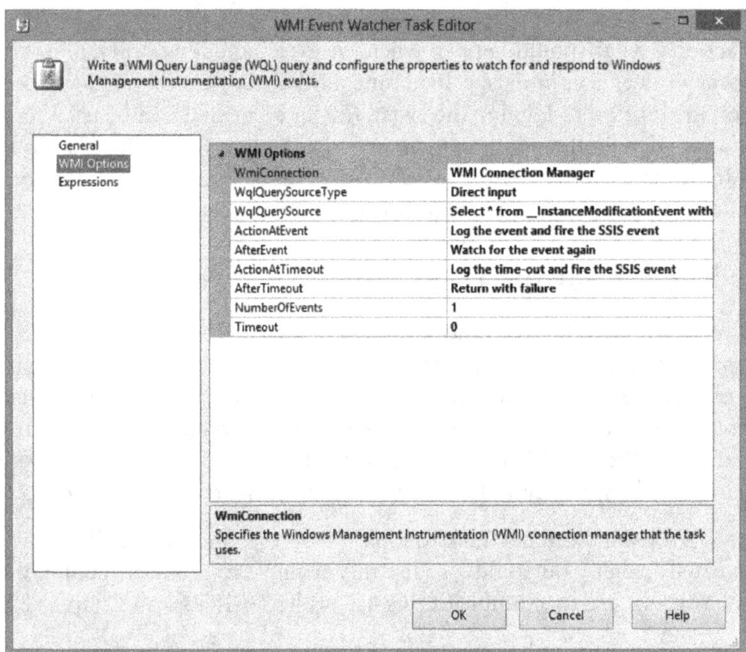

FIGURE 21-21

Now that the task is configured, you need to configure the event handler that will be fired when a file change is detected. Click the Event Handler tab and select the WMI Event Watcher Task - Monitor DB File in the executable combo box, and then the WMIEventWatcherEventOccurred in the Event Handlers combo box. Click the hyperlink in the middle of the page to create this event. Now drag an Execute Package Task from the Toolbox to the event page. Rename this task **Execute WMI Data Reader Package**. The Execute Package Task event handler should look like Figure 21-22.

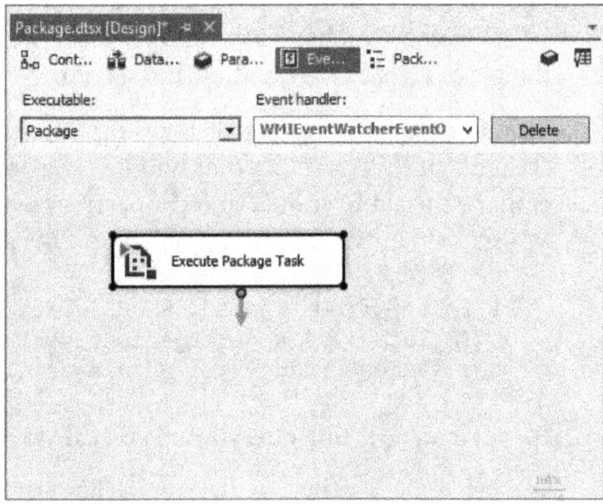

FIGURE 21-22

Right-click the task and select Edit from the pop-up menu. In the Execute Package Task Editor dialog, click the Package item in the listbox. For this example, you will be referencing the package via the file system, but in real life you would probably be calling a package that had been deployed to a SQL Server instance. For demonstration purposes, the WMI Data Reader Package file will be referenced so that you can see the package execute in the Visual Studio IDE. Therefore, in the Location property, choose File System. In the Connection property, create a new file connection pointing to the WMI Data Reader `Package.dtsx` file. Leave the rest of the properties at their default values. The Execute Package Task Editor should look like Figure 21-23. Click OK to finish configuration of this example.

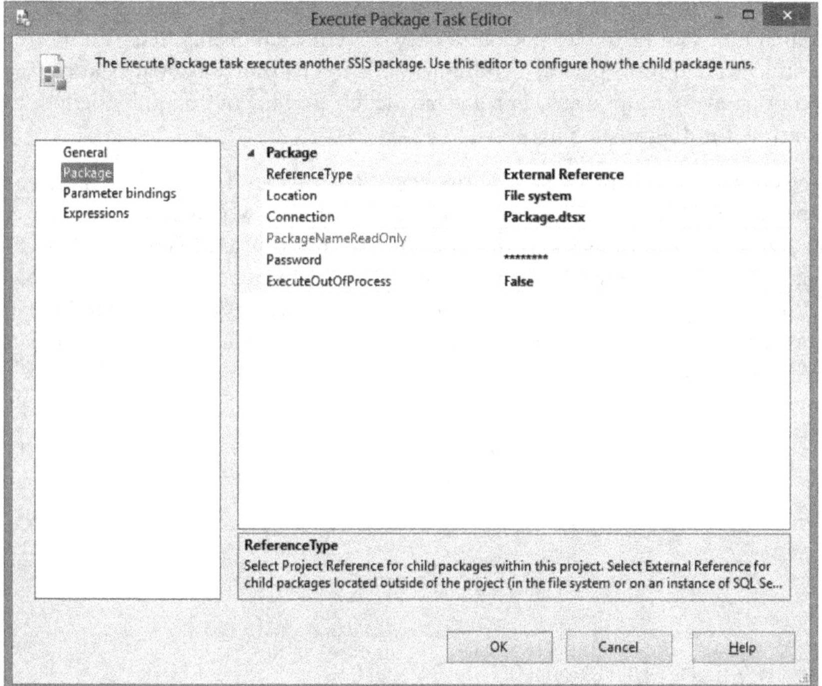

FIGURE 21-23

Now test out your new package by first removing the `AdventureWorks.bak` backup file from the `c:\ssis\extmgt\WMI_DataReader` directory. Then run the WMI Event Watcher Package. The WMI Event Watcher Task should turn yellow. The WMI Event Watcher is now monitoring the file location where it expects to find the `AdventureWorks.bak` file for changes. Next, copy the `AdventureWorks.bak` file into the root `WMI_DataReader` directory to simulate the SQL Server process of creating a backup of the AdventureWorks database. In fact, you can also test this package by going into SSMS and creating a backup in this root directory. At some point during the backup process, you should see the WMI Data Reader Package kick off and copy the backup file to the `c:\ssis\extmgt\WMI_DataReader\Backup` directory.

When the copy is complete, the package will continue to monitor the backup file for change. When the next backup is found in the root WMI_DataReader directory, the package will initiate another file copy of the backup. The package is responding to WMI events that detect the change to the directory to copy the file. As you can see, these WMI features provide an extremely powerful capability that SSIS does a great job of abstracting for you in these WMI Tasks.

SUMMARY

This chapter has provided you with the basic information you need to manage and administer your SSIS packages in both the SSIS catalog and the pre-2012 storage model. You were exposed to the DTS runtime libraries, and you have seen how easy it is to manipulate package information, make changes programmatically, and transfer packages between your environments. You have also learned how to create and maintain package configurations to customize packages at runtime. In addition, you now know how to configure log providers, which enable you to apply logging to existing packages at runtime for diagnostic purposes.

In the second half of the chapter, you learned how to use the WMI Reader Task and WMI Event Watcher Task in your packages. Using these two tasks, you discovered how you can gain access to a huge amount of system information to use in your packages. With the WMI Event Watcher, you learned how to monitor the system for events that occur and then perform actions in your SSIS package in response. With both the DTS runtime libraries and the WMI Tasks, you should be able to enhance your system administrative capabilities working with SSIS. In Chapter 22, you'll learn more about administering SSIS packages.

22

Administering SSIS

WHAT'S IN THIS CHAPTER?

- Using the SSIS catalog
- Choosing and using the different deployment models
- Using T-SQL with SSIS
- Managing security in SSIS
- Scheduling and monitoring packages

WROX.COM DOWNLOADS FOR THIS CHAPTER

You can find the wrox.com code downloads for this chapter at `www.wrox.com/go/prossis2014` on the Download Code tab.

Welcome to the most exciting chapter in this book, the administration chapter. Okay, it is probably the most dreaded chapter, as administration tends to be a dry subject, but this chapter is a must read for anyone who needs to execute, manage, and administer SSIS packages. You will learn how to parameterize, deploy, and administer the SSIS service. You will see the SSIS catalog and how it will make executing packages much easier. You will also learn how to create a standalone ETL server, about some of the command-line utilities, and the T-SQL commands you can use to make your job easier. After reading this chapter, you'll be able to create a package that doesn't require any effort to migrate from development to production after the first deployment.

USING THE SSIS CATALOG

The SSIS catalog was introduced in SQL Server 2012. It is the central storage location for SSIS. Here you will administer projects, packages, parameters, and environments. Log in to the database engine in SSMS to work with the SSIS catalog, which is shown in Figure 22-1.

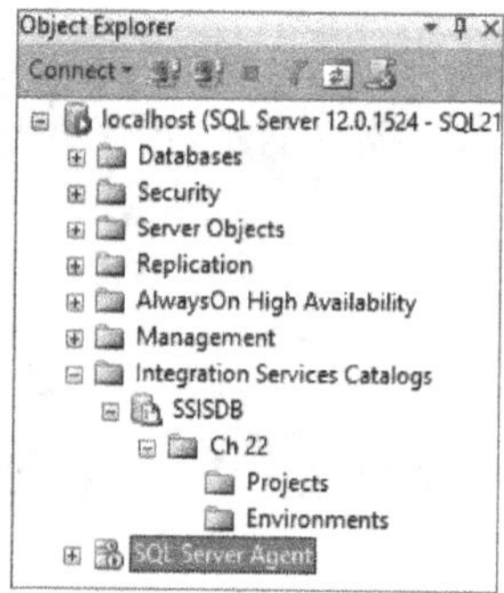

FIGURE 22-1

When you first install Integration Services, the SSIS catalog will need to be created. Create it manually by right-clicking on the Integration Services folder in the Database Engine in SSMS and selecting Create Catalog. The Create Catalog prompt will ask for a password. This password creates a database master key, and the master key encrypts sensitive data in the catalog.

The SSIS catalog is implemented as a SQL Server database named SSISDB. This database contains tables, views, stored procedures, and other objects. Queries can be written to the SSISDB just as you would to any other SQL database. In the SSIS catalog, every object is stored in a folder. Folders can be used to set up security that controls which users can see the objects in the catalog folders. For example, if you want users to have administrative rights over the folders, then grant them `MANAGE_OBJECT_PERMISSIONS` in the SSISDB. The SSISDB is the storage location for all Integration Services objects. The SSIS catalog is used to administer this database. Security is covered in depth later in this chapter.

Setting the SSIS Catalog Properties

The SSIS catalog has several properties that you can modify to change its behavior. Right-click on the SSISDB under the Integration Services Catalogs folder and select Properties. Figure 22-2 shows this Catalog Properties window.

The SSIS catalog holds the information about all of your package executions, whether the package failed or succeeded. It contains a list of all the packages in your catalog and the executable tasks in those packages. Parameters and their values are stored in the SSIS catalog. Just about any object or property associated with your SSIS packages is housed in the SSIS catalog. The stored procedures are the tools used to control and manage the SSIS catalog. There is also a library of views that make it easier to view the information in the SSISDB. It will make the information in this chapter easier to understand if you take a few minutes to look at some of the views and the tables in the SSISDB. Go to SSMS and browse through the tables and views to become familiar with the objects in the SSISDB.

When you execute a package, the package execution is written to the SSISDB. In fact just about anything you do to the SSIS catalog is going to write or at least alter data in the SSISDB. There are even built-in reports now that query from the executions saved in the SSISDB. The properties of the SSIS catalog are stored in the SSISDB also.

You can alter the SSIS catalog properties using the catalog's built-in stored procedures. To view the properties, run the stored procedure `catalog.catalog_property`. To change the properties, run the stored procedure `catalog.configure_catalog`. However, note that the properties shown in Figure 22-2 have different names than the properties used by the stored procedure. Table 22-1 resolves these differences.

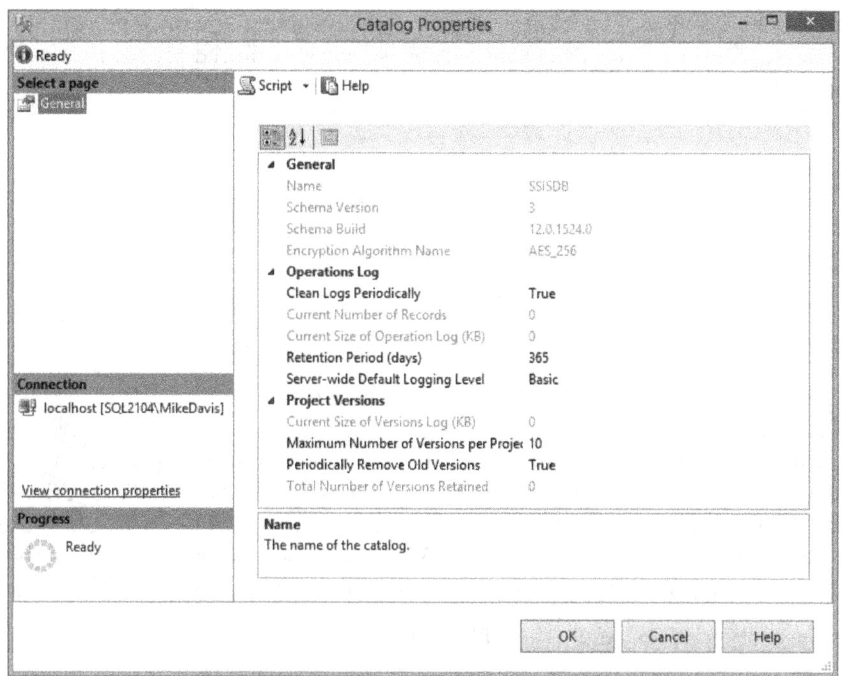

FIGURE 22-2

TABLE 22-1: SSIS Catalog Properties

PROPERTY NAME (PROPERTIES WINDOW)	PROPERTY NAME (STORED PROCEDURES)
Encryption Algorithm Name	ENCRYPTION_ALGORITHM
Clean Logs Periodically	OPERATION_CLEANUP_ENABLED
Retention Period (days)	RETENTION_WINDOW
Periodically Remove Old Versions	VERSION_CLEANUP_ENABLED
Maximum Number of Versions per Project	MAX_PROJECT_VERSIONS
Validation Timeout (Seconds)	VALIDATION_TIMEOUT

That is right; you can now use T-SQL to control the SSIS environment. The SSIS catalog includes a wide range of stored procedures that represent a T-SQL API for managing the SSIS server. In fact, this chapter has an entire section on using T-SQL with SSIS. Here is an example of running the stored procedure to set the cleanup property to false:

```
EXEC [SSISDB].[catalog].[configure_catalog]
@property_name=N'OPERATION_CLEANUP_ENABLED', @property_value=N'FALSE'
```

Parameters can be encrypted in the SSIS catalog. This enables you to store connection strings with a password without any fear of a plain-text password, unlike previous versions. To set the encryption algorithm, use the `Encrypt_Algorithm` property. To do so, first you must put the catalog in single-user mode. Then run the `catalog.configure_catalog` stored procedure to set the algorithm to one of the following options:

- DES
- TRIPLE_DES
- TRIPLE_DES_3KEY
- DESX
- AES_128
- AES_192
- AES_256 (default)

The encryption algorithm AES_256 is the default level. No one encryption level is perfect for all situations. AES stands for Advanced Encryption Standard, and DES stands for Data Encryption Standard. DES was the standard since 1977, and now AES has been the standard since 2001. AES is generally the faster encryption. A thorough encryption explanation is beyond the scope of this book; in fact, there are entire books on just encryption. However, here are some basics to keep in mind:

- The stronger the encryption, the more the CPU is used.
- Longer keys give better encryption than shorter keys.
- Long passwords are stronger than short passwords.

Executing and deploying packages writes data to the SSISDB, and as you can imagine, after many package deployments and executions there will be a lot of data stored in the SSISDB. This data will need to be cleaned up. A SQL Agent job is run to clean up old data from package executions and project deployments. Two properties are used to control this operation:

- `Operation_Cleanup_Enabled`: Setting this to true enables the operation job.
- `Retention_Window`: Set this to specify the maximum number of days to keep data.

You can control some operations using stored procedures like `catalog.operations` and `catalog.extended_operations_info`.

Another great feature of SSIS is project versioning. Gone are the days of deploying a project and overwriting packages and losing them forever. Now when you deploy a project there is a version number assigned, and you can retrieve old versions of projects.

After you have deployed a project dozens of times, you will want to clean up the old versions. The version cleanup job deletes old versions of your projects. Two properties control the behavior of the version cleanup job:

- `Version_Cleanup_Enabled`: Set this to true to enable the version cleanup job.
- `Max_Project_Versions`: Set this to specify the maximum number of versions to keep in history.

You can use the stored procedure `catalog.object_version` to view versioning information. You can also right-click on a project in the catalog and select Versions to see the versions of a particular project (see Figure 22-3). Toward the bottom-right corner of this window is a button for restoring old versions of projects.

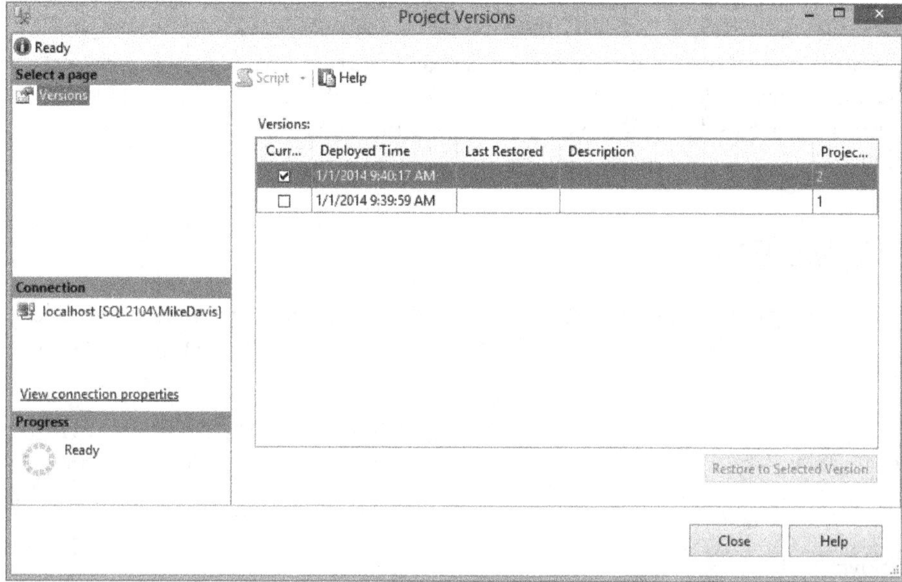

FIGURE 22-3

Another property of the SSIS catalog is the validation timeout. Validation is the process of checking the connections in an SSIS package. The time it takes to run this validation varies according to your servers. Validation runs asynchronously and has a timeout property that controls how long the service will wait for a response. Packages with more connections take longer to validate. The `Validation_Timeout` property is set in seconds, with a default of 300 seconds (5 minutes). You can also run validation on a project by running the stored procedure `catalog.validate_project` or on a package by running `catalog.validate_package`. Alternately, you can right-click on a project or package in SQL Server Management Studio and select Validate.

SSISDB

When you install Integration Services 2014, it will not automatically install the database named SSISDB. To create this database you will need to right-click on the SSIS catalog in SSMS and select Create Catalog. Figure 22-4 shows an image of this database and some of its tables.

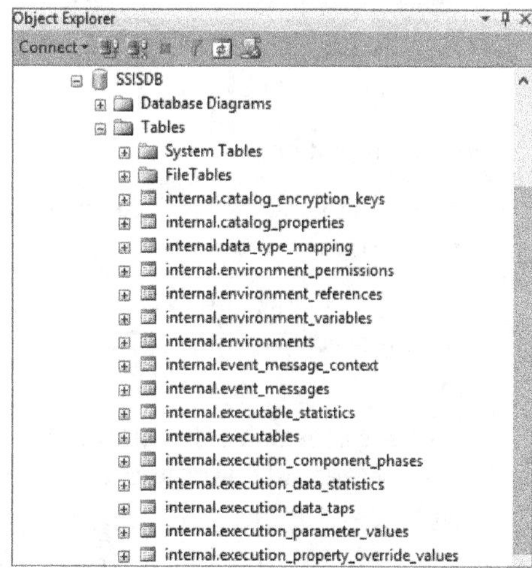

FIGURE 22-4

This database contains all the information and objects for the SSIS catalog. You will administer Integration Services using the SSIS catalog, but your DBA will back up and secure the SSISDB just like any other database. Because of the encryption key specified when creating the catalog, backup and restoring, particularly restoring to a different server, is more involved than a typical database.

There are several tables and stored procedures in the SSISDB. When you execute a package, deploy a project (in the project deployment model), delete a project, or do any other work with Integration Services, you are making changes to the SSISDB. Therefore, you can control your Integration Services instance using T-SQL. This is discussed in more detail in the "Using T-SQL with SSIS" section.

DEPLOYMENT MODELS

You can deploy packages using the project deployment model or the package deployment model. The project deployment model, enables you to use the parameters and deploy to the Integration Services catalog.

There are several differences between the project deployment model and the package deployment model, as shown in Table 22-2.

TABLE 22-2: Deployment Models

PROJECT DEPLOYMENT MODEL	PACKAGE DEPLOYMENT MODEL
Project is deployed.	Package is deployed.
Project uses parameters.	Package uses configuration files/tables.
Project is located in an `.ispac` file and packages have `.dtsx` extensions.	Packages have a `.dtsx` extension.
Project is deployed to Integration Services Catalog.	Packages are deployed to the MSDB or file system.
CLR integration is required.	CLR integration is not required.
New environments in the SSIS catalog can be used with parameters.	System environment variables can be used with configurations.
Projects and packages can be validated before execution with T-SQL or managed code.	Packages are validated just before execution and can be validated with dtexec or managed code.
Packages are executed with T-SQL. Parameters and environments can be set with T-SQL.	Packages are executed with dtexe and dtexecui. Command parameters can be passed to the command prompt.
Robust logging is built in with several reports.	Logging is built in with no reports.

Project Deployment Model

In previous versions of SSIS, you deployed packages to either a server or a file system. Those options are still available but are not the recommended practice since SQL Server 2012. The project deployment model is the standard and makes deployment much easier, as you will see in this chapter. Parameters and environments are great features also and will be the standard for your SSIS development replacing configuration files and tables. The old configuration methods are still available though not recommended. This project deployment method along with the parameters and environments is a big change in the way you think about SSIS package deployments. You will now consider deploying projects as a group of work not individual packages. Think of a project as a body of work that needs to be completed together. This may include just one package or several. This section will cover the project deployment model.

When choosing a deployment model, you should consider the administration options and the deployment options. The project deployment model provides some development features, such as parameters and environments.

The Integration Services catalog is the location where packages and all SSIS objects are stored in SQL Server 2014 if the project deployment model is selected. An instance of SQL Server can have one catalog, and a catalog can contain folders for organizing your instance. Folders hold the SSIS projects and environments. As mentioned earlier, the folders in the catalog can also be used for security.

Parameters are covered briefly in Chapter 2. In this chapter you will learn how they work from the administration side. When you create a parameter, you can scope it to either the package level or the project level. Parameters work much like variables. They can be used in expressions and tasks. You can assign parameters at runtime with T-SQL or let the package use the default value set during development.

Once you have a package deployed with numerous parameters, you may want to control them with different sets of values. Environments give you this capability. Environments store a set of variable values that can be referenced during package execution. You can store values for different runtimes. For example, you might have different values for weekend runtimes versus weekday runtimes. By storing all the parameter values in an environment, you can execute your package and point it to the correct set of parameter values, rather than set each value individually.

After you have completed your package development, you are ready to deploy the project to the SSIS catalog. In this example you have a package that contains an Execute SQL Task. You will have one parameter on the package, and deploy the package to the SSIS catalog and set up an environment. This sample package is available with the code download for this book.

In this example package you will simply use the Execute SQL Task to write a row to a table in AdventureWorks. Use the following code to create this example table:

```
USE [AdventureWorks]
GO
CREATE TABLE [dbo].[InsertTest](
        [StringCol] [varchar](50) NULL
) ON [PRIMARY]
GO
```

> **NOTE** *All code samples in this chapter are available as part of the Chapter 22 code download for the book at* www.wrox.com/go/prossis2014.

The SQL statement in the Execute SQL Task in the package is as follows:

```
INSERT INTO [dbo].[InsertTest]
           ([StringCol])
     VALUES
           (?)
```

The project will contain one package with an Execute SQL Task that will write a value to the InsertTest table. The value that is inserted into this table is the parameter value. This parameter value will be changed using the environments. This first example uses a package level parameter. The example package has a package level parameter on it named `strInput` with a data type of `String` and a value of `PackageParam`, as shown in Figure 22-5.

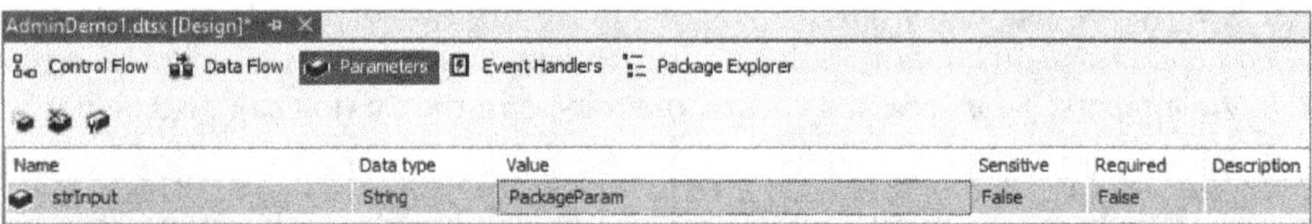

FIGURE 22-5

Now that you are familiar with the package, you are going to deploy it to the SSIS catalog.

1. To start the deployment, right-click on the project name in Solution Explorer in SQL Server Data Tools, and select Deploy (see Figure 22-6). In the middle of this menu you should see the option Convert to Package Deployment Model. If you instead see Convert to Project Deployment Model, then your project is in the package deployment model, and you will need to click this option to convert it to the project deployment model.

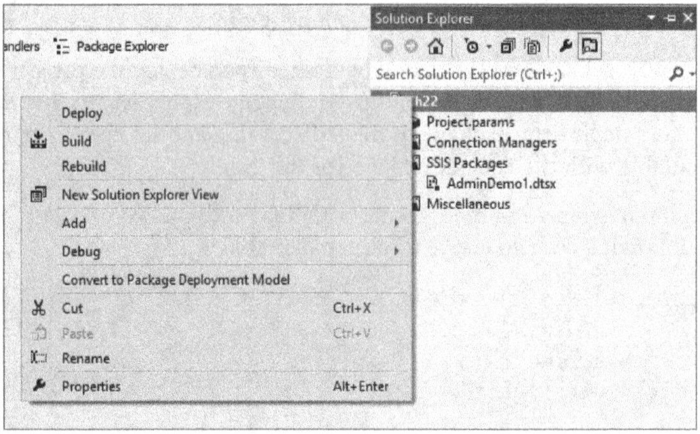

FIGURE 22-6

2. The first window of the SSIS Deployment Wizard is the basic information screen. Read this and then click the checkbox at the bottom to hide the screen in the future, and then click Next.
3. The next window asks for the server name and the path. Enter your server name. This example uses LocalHost as the server name.
4. Now click the Browse button next to Path and select a folder into which the package should be deployed. You can create a new folder by clicking the New Folder button at the bottom of the window. You must deploy the project into a folder; you cannot put it in the SSISDB root. For this example, use the folder named AdminDemo, as shown in Figure 22-7, and click Next.

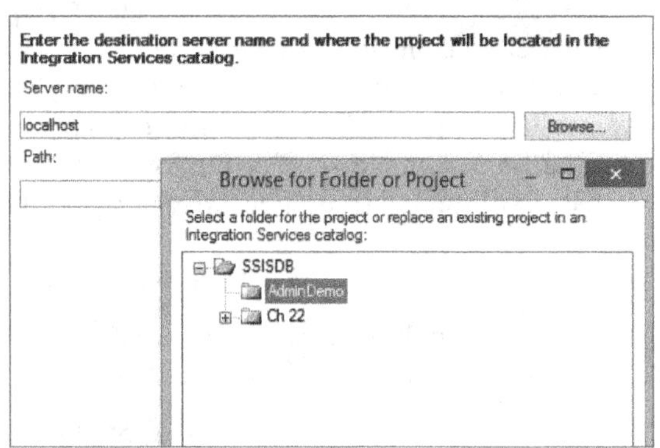

FIGURE 22-7

5. This next window is the Review window. Check the source and destination here to ensure everything is correct, and then click Deploy.
6. The last window is the Results window. You should see a passed result for every step, as shown in Figure 22-8.

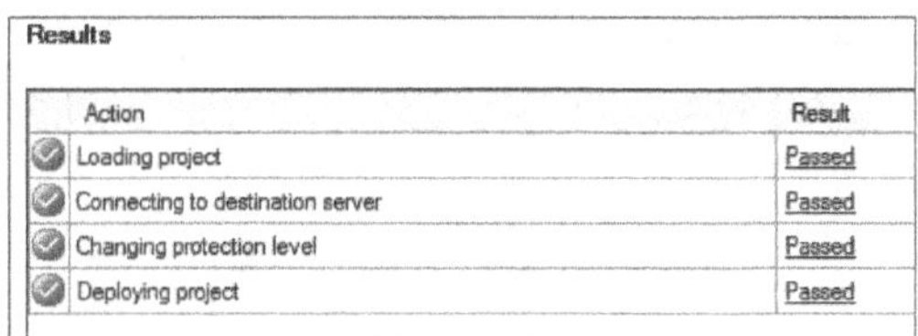

FIGURE 22-8

Congratulations. You have successfully deployed your first project to your SSIS catalog. The next section describes the package deployment model. Then we will return to this project in the T-SQL section of this chapter, where you will learn how to execute the package and set the parameter values and environments.

Package Deployment Model

The package deployment model is the older version of deployment, and you should be changing your methods to take full advantage of the newer method. Because of the fact that some users will still want to use the old model, either because of large frameworks they have in place or just because changing can be difficult, this model is covered in this section.

In the package deployment model, you can create a deployment utility that helps users install your project of packages and any dependencies. This deployment utility is similar to creating a program like InstallShield, and it is for times when you want to pass a set of packages to a customer or a production DBA who may not know how to install SSIS packages manually. When you create a deployment utility, all the files necessary to install the project are copied into a centralized directory, and an `.SSISDeploymentManifest` file is created for the installer to run, which opens the Package Installation Wizard.

Creating the Deployment Manifest

To create a deployment utility, simply right-click the SSIS project in SQL Server Data Tools and select Properties. In the Property Pages dialog, go to the Deployment Utility page and change the CreateDeploymentUtility property to True, as shown in Figure 22-9. This is set to False by default. The AllowConfigurationChanges property is a key setting as well, and when set to True, it asks installers whether they would like to change any settings that may be exposed via a configuration file at installation time. The DeploymentOutputPath property specifies where the deployment utility will be outputted to underneath the project folder.

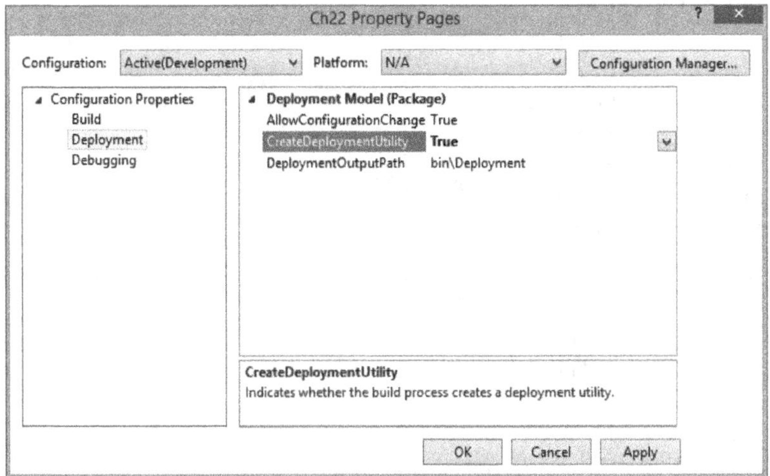

FIGURE 22-9

Next, under the Build menu, select Build <*Project Name*>, where <*Project Name*> represents your project's name. You should see "(package deployment model)" next to the package name, as shown in Figure 22-10. If you don't see this, then you are in project deployment model. If so, right-click on the project in Solution Explorer to convert to the package deployment model.

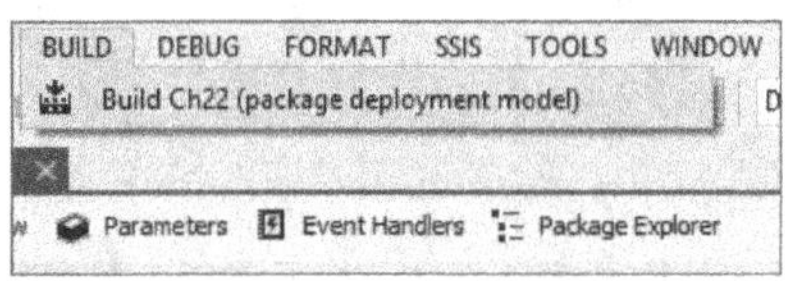

FIGURE 22-10

Clicking Build will open each package and build the project. If there are any errors in the package, you will see them at this point. As it builds the project, each package, and the project's `.SSISDeploymentManifest` file, is validated and then outputted into the `\bin\deployment` directory under your project's folder.

> **NOTE** *After building the deployment utility, you should change the CreateDeploymentUtility option to False again. Otherwise, each time you click the Play button to execute the package, each package will be validated and executed, which could take an enormous amount of time for a large project. Instead of using the green debug arrow at the top of SQL Server Data Tools, the best practice is to right-click on the package in Solution Explorer and then click Execute package. This ensures that only the package is executed.*

The Package Deployment Wizard

Now that you have created a deployment `.SSISDeploymentManifest` file, you're ready to send the contents of the `«project location»\bin\deployment` folder to the installation person. The installation person would then need to copy the contents of the folder to the server he or she wishes to deploy to and double-click the `.SSISDeploymentManifest` file. The installer could also run it remotely, but it is recommended that you run it on the same server as the target deployment server to simplify the installation. You can also modify the `.SSISDeploymentManifest` file in your favorite XML editor to specify which packages should be deployed. If the wizard does not open on double-clicking the mainfest file, choose dtsinstall found in program files as the program to open it.

After the introduction screen, you are asked where you want to deploy the packages, as shown in Figure 22-11. You can choose either a file system deployment or a SQL Server deployment. A file system deployment just copies the packages, which are the `.dtsx` files, to a directory on the server. A SQL Server deployment stores the packages in the MSDB database on the target server. Select the SQL Server deployment option if you are following this example, and then click Next. You can also have the wizard validate each package after you install it. This ensures that the package delivered to you is valid on your machine, including the Data Sources.

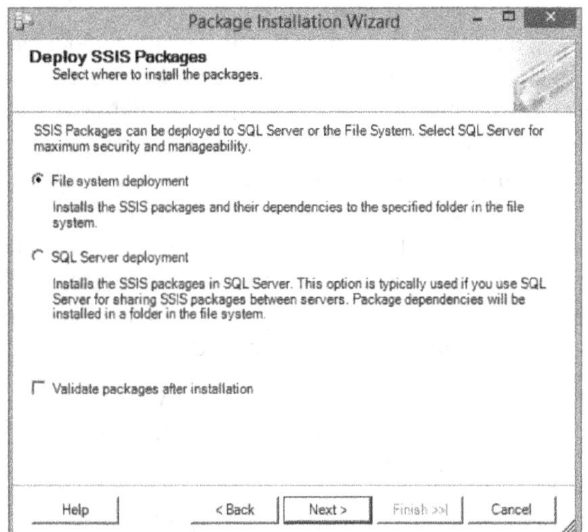

FIGURE 22-11

The following table lists the pros and cons of the MSDB versus File System Deployment. Security is usually the defining factor here.

FUNCTIONALITY	BEST IN FILE SYSTEM	BEST IN MSDB
Security		✓
Backup and recovery	✓	
Deployment	✓	
Troubleshooting	✓	
Availability	✓	
Execution speed	✓	✓

If you selected SQL Server deployment, the next screen prompts you for the SQL Server 2014 instance to which you wish to deploy the packages. Additionally type "/" (without the quotes) for the Package Path property. This specifies that the packages will be installed into the root path. If you had selected a file system deployment, the next screen prompts you for the file path to which you wish to deploy the packages. The last option in the SQL Server deployment screen enables you to specify whether you want to rely on the SQL Server to protect the package by encrypting it. This is the recommended option, and it will change the ProtectionLevel package property to ServerStorage as it installs each package. You'll learn more about the ProtectionLevel property later in this chapter.

Even though you selected a SQL Server deployment, you may still need to deploy files such as configuration files and readme files. The next screen enables you to specify where you want these files. Generally, they'll be located in a subfolder named after the project under the `C:\Program Files\Microsoft SQL Server\120\DTS\Packages` folder.

After you click Next, the packages will be installed in the package store on the server. After the packages are installed, if the developer selected True for the AllowConfigurationChanges option in SQL Server Data Tools (refer to Figure 22-9), then an additional screen appears, giving you, as installer, a chance to edit the values in the configuration file at deployment time. This is shown in Figure 22-12, and you can click the dropdown menu to see multiple configuration files. Unfortunately, it does not show the packages to which these files are associated.

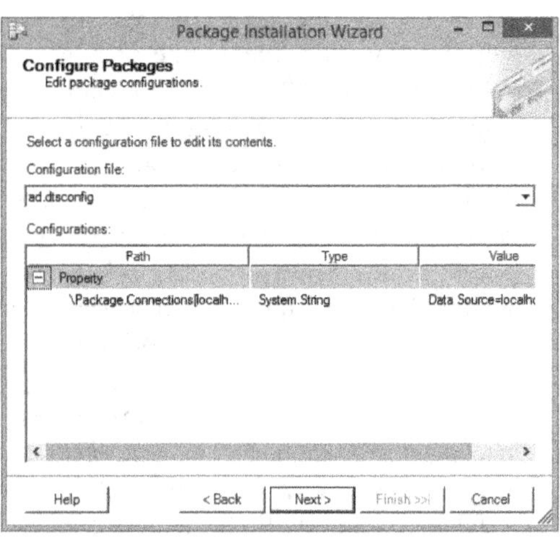

FIGURE 22-12

The only other additional screen you might see is a pop-up if there were a user password on any package.

After the packages have been deployed, they are validated, as shown in Figure 22-13. Any problems will appear in this Packages Validation screen, and you can redeploy after correcting the problem. The last screen is a summary screen to complete the wizard.

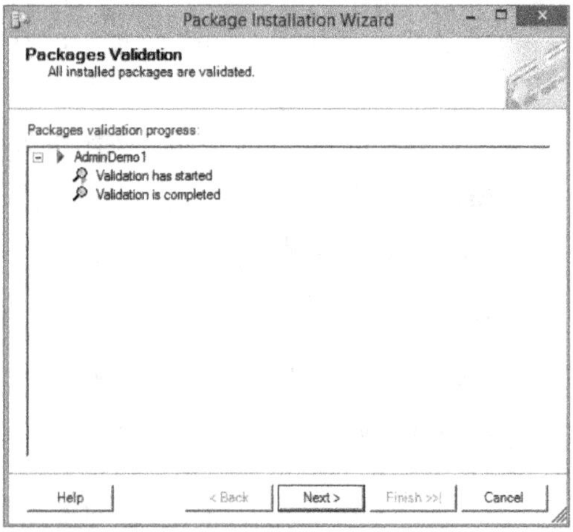

FIGURE 22-13

If you wish to deploy a package in Management Studio, as shown later in this chapter, you have to do it one package at a time. The file system, however, is much easier. With this method of storage, you can just copy the `.dtsx` and supporting files manually into a directory that is monitored by the SSIS service, and the packages can be seen immediately from Management Studio.

The main point to remember about using the deployment utility is that every package and all project dependencies are deployed. If you don't want to deploy that many packages, you can edit the `.SSISDeploymentManifest` file in a text editor to remove any extra files you don't want to migrate. Some find it useful to create a project in the same solution that contains a subset of the packages that they wish to deploy, if deploying all packages and dependencies is too aggressive for them.

If you did want to edit the `.SSISDeploymentManifest` XML file before sending the folder to a client, you could just remove one of the `<Package>` lines, as shown in the following XML example. The header of the XML file indicates who created the deployment tool and when. This information is useful if the project doesn't install correctly. If you don't wish to deploy a configuration file with the wizard, you can remove the `<ConfigurationFile>` line in order to prevent the configuration file from overwriting the older configuration files that may already be on the server file.

```
<?xml version="1.0" ?>
<DTSDeploymentManifest GeneratedBy="MikeDavis\MDavis"
GeneratedFromProjectName="Pro SSIS"
GeneratedDate="2011-10-15T23:39:54.7343750-05:00"
AllowConfigurationChanges="true">
<Package>EventHandler.dtsx</Package>
<Package>Package1.dtsx</Package>
<Package>Restartability.dtsx</Package>
<Package>ConfigFiles.dtsx</Package>
<Package>Chapter1.dtsx</Package>
<Package>RawFile.dtsx</Package>
<Package>DBSnapshots.dtsx</Package>
<Package>Logging.dtsx</Package>
<Package>FileWatcher.dtsx</Package>
<Package>ConfigRepository.dtsx</Package>
<ConfigurationFile>configuration.xml</ConfigurationFile>
</DTSDeploymentManifest>
```

Using the SSIS Package Store

The other option for deploying your packages is the SSIS Package Store. This is the older option now, and you should be moving your packages to the SSIS catalog to take advantage of features like parameters and environments. In some cases, the Package Store will actually physically store the package, such as the MSDB database option. If you're using file system storage, the Package Store just keeps a pointer to the top-level directory and enumerates through the packages stored underneath that directory. In order to connect to the Package Store, the SSIS service must be running. This service is called SQL Server Integration Services, or MSDTSServer120. There is only one instance of the service per machine or per set of clustered machines.

You can configure the SSIS service in the Services applet (select Control Panel ⇨ Administrative Tools ⇨ Services). Double-click SQL Server Integration Services. The service is set to automatically start by default, under the NT AUTHORITY\NetworkService account. In the Recovery tab, you can specify that the service should automatically start up again in the event of a failure, as shown in Figure 22-14. You can specify what action should be taken if the service fails the first, second, and subsequent times. In this case, the service has been changed to restart if a failure occurs two times. The failure count is also reset after two days.

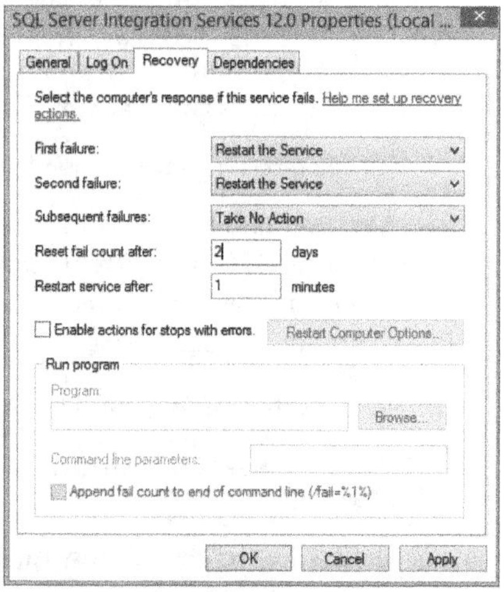

FIGURE 22-14

Although you can run and stop packages programmatically without the service, the service makes running packages more manageable. For example, if you have the service run the package, it tracks package execution, and users with the proper permission can interrogate the service to find out which packages are running. Those who are in the Windows Administrators group can stop all running packages. Otherwise, you can stop only packages that you have started. It can also aid in importing and exporting packages into the Package Store. We cover other uses for the service throughout this chapter, but another benefit is that it enables you to create a centralized ETL server to handle the execution of your packages throughout your enterprise.

The MSDTSServer120 service is configured through an XML file that is located by default in the following path: `C:\Program Files\Microsoft SQL Server\120\DTS\Binn\MsDtsSrvr.ini.xml`. This path varies if your servers are in a cluster. If you cannot find the path, go to the `HKEY_LOCAL_MACHINE\SOFTWARE\Microsoft\Microsoft SQL Server\120\SSIS\ServiceConfigFile` registry key. By default, the XML file should look like the following:

```
<?xml version="1.0" encoding="utf-8" ?>
- <DtsServiceConfiguration xmlns:xsd=http://www.w3.org/2001/XMLSchema"
xmlns:xsi=http://www.w3.org/2001/XMLSchema-instance>
<StopExecutingPackagesOnShutdown>true</StopExecutingPackagesOnShutdown>
- <TopLevelFolders>
-<Folder xsi:type="SqlServerFolder">
<Name>MSDB</Name>
<ServerName>.</ServerName>
</Folder>
- <Folder xsi:type="FileSystemFolder">
- <Name>File System</Name>
<StorePath>..\Packages</StorePath>
</Folder>
</TopLevelFolders>
</DtsServiceConfiguration>
```

There isn't much to really configure in this file, but it does have some interesting uses. The first configuration line tells the packages how to react if the service is stopped. By default, packages that the service is running will stop if the service stops or fails over. You could also configure the packages to continue to run until they complete after the service is stopped by changing the `StopExecutingPackagesOnShutdown` property to False, as shown here:

```
<StopExecutingPackagesOnShutdown>false</StopExecutingPackagesOnShutdown>
```

The next configuration sections are the most important. They specify which paths and servers the MSDTSServer120 service will read from. Whenever the service starts, it reads this file to determine where the packages are stored. The default file contains a single entry for a SQL Server that looks like the following `SqlServerFolder` example:

```
<Folder xsi:type="SqlServerFolder">
<Name>MSDB</Name>
<ServerName>.</ServerName>
</Folder>
```

The «`Name`» line represents how the name will appear in Management Studio for this set of packages. The «`ServerName`» line represents where the connection will point to. There is a problem, however: if your SQL Server is on a named instance, this file will still point to the default non-named instance (.). If you do have a named instance, simply replace the period with your instance name.

The next section shows you where your file system packages will be stored. The «StorePath» property specifies the folder from which all packages will be enumerated. The default path is `C:\program files\microsoft sql server\120\dts\Packages`, which is represented as `..\Packages` in the default code that follows. That part of the statement goes one directory below the SSIS service file and then into the Packages folder.

```
<Folder xsi:type="FileSystemFolder">
<Name>File System</Name>
<StorePath>..\Packages</StorePath>
</Folder>
```

Everything in the Packages folder, and below that folder, will be enumerated. You can create subdirectories under this folder, and they will immediately show up in Management Studio; you don't have to modify the service configuration file. Each time you make a change to the `MsDtsSrvr.ini.xml` file, you must stop and start the MSDTSServer120 service.

In this section you learned how to use the SSIS Package store. Again keep in mind that this is an older method that you should move away from. Using the SSIS catalog and SSISDB gives you the ability to take advantage of the features like versioning, parameters, and environments.

USING T-SQL WITH SSIS

One of the most exciting features of SSIS is the fact that you can use T-SQL to interact with your packages and projects natively (if you are using the project deployment model). You can write stored procedures or just open SSMS and type in the T-SQL code you need to execute or validate your packages. In this section you will be using the project from the "Project Deployment Model" section earlier in this chapter. The code and projects can be downloaded from the book's website at `www.wrox.com/go/prossis2014`.

Executing Packages

This first item to learn in the world of T-SQL and SSIS is how to execute a package using T-SQL. If you right-click on the package in the SSIS catalog and click the script button at the top of the execution window, you can copy the script into a new query window. The script window has been available for other SQL commands in past versions of SQL Server, but now you can use this same feature in the SSIS catalog. In just about all of the SSIS windows you see in the catalog, you will have this automatic scripting option. This can do two things for you: speed up your writing of the T-SQL you need and help you learn the T-SQL commands used in this version of SSIS. By scripting out commands and looking at the names of the stored procedures, you can start noting procedures you will use frequently. The following script is an example of this code:

```
Declare @execution_id bigint
EXEC [SSISDB].[catalog].[create_execution] @package_name=N'AdminDemo1.dtsx',
@execution_id=@execution_id OUTPUT,
@folder_name=N'AdminDemo',
@project_name=N'Ch22',
@use32bitruntime=False,
```

```
@reference_id=Null
Select @execution_id
EXEC [SSISDB].[catalog].[start_execution] @execution_id
GO
```

You need to understand four sections of this code. The first line is a simple variable declaration that is used to hold the execution ID that you will create in the next section of the T-SQL code.

The next section of the code is the meat of the work. You are using the `EXEC` command to call the stored procedure in the SSISDB named `Catalog.Create_Execution`. This command creates an execution ID, which is a unique ID for executing the package. The execution ID is saved in a table in the SSISDB. You won't usually need to manually touch the internal table in the SSISDB; management should be done from the SSIS catalog using T-SQL, but because this is a professional-level SSIS book, you will get to see some of the work done by the stored procedure on the SSISDB.

The stored procedure that creates the execution inserts a row on the `internal.operations` table. Keep in mind that the stored procedures work like any other, so with proper permissions you can read through them. If you look at the `create_execution` stored procedure, you will see it calls another stored procedure named `internal.insert_operation`, which does the actual inserting of the row into the internal.operations table.

In the preceding execution code, the `catalog.create_execution` stored procedure takes a few parameters: the package name, an output parameter with the execution ID, the folder name in which the package resides, the project name of the package, whether the package should be executed in 32-bit mode, and a reference ID.

The next line of the code is a `SELECT` statement. This is included just to show you the execution ID in the results pane. You can run the execution without this line.

The last line executes the package by calling another stored procedure: `catalog.start_execution`. This stored procedure calls another stored procedure named `internal.start_execution_internal`. As shown in Figure 22-15, this stored procedure has a small icon of a lock on it in the SSISDB. This indicates that the stored procedure is a SQL CLR stored procedure. If you right-click on the stored procedure, you will see that the modify option is grayed out. As mentioned earlier, you are probably never going to alter these stored procedures. They are calling the internal workings of the SSIS catalog. You can see the code in this stored procedure by right-clicking on it and selecting "Script Stored Procedure as" ➪ "Alter to" ➪ "New Query Editor Window." This shows you the API call to the internal SSIS code.

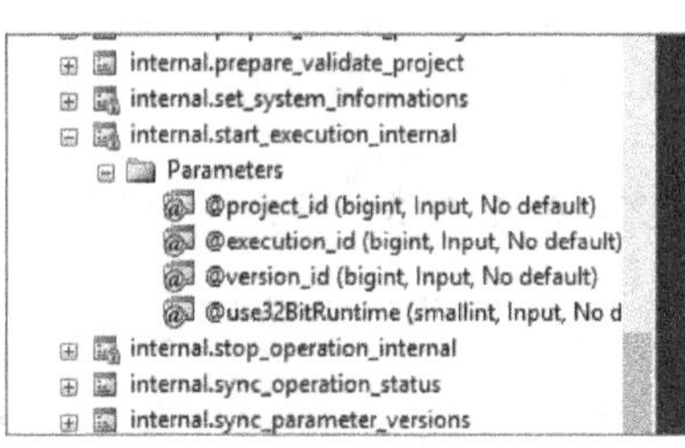

FIGURE 22-15

Executing the preceding code will insert a row into the InsertTest table. The value inserted will be PackageParam, which is the default value of the package parameter saved in the package. The next section demonstrates how to change the value of this parameter.

Using Parameters

Now that you have the AdminDemo package deployed to the SSIS catalog, you are ready to set the parameter value and execute the package using T-SQL. The previous section showed the execution query, but it was incomplete because the AdminDemo package has a parameter whose value you want to set. To do so, just add the following lines to the execution query:

```
Declare @execution_id bigint

EXEC [SSISDB].[catalog].[create_execution] @package_name=N'AdminDemo1.dtsx',
 @execution_id=@execution_id OUTPUT, @folder_name=N'AdminDemo',
  @project_name=N'Ch22', @use32bitruntime=False, @reference_id=Null

Select @execution_id

DECLARE @var0 sql_variant = N'PackageParam'

EXEC [SSISDB].[catalog].[set_execution_parameter_value] @execution_id,
@object_type=30,
@parameter_name=N'strInput',
@parameter_value=@var0

EXEC [SSISDB].[catalog].[start_execution] @execution_id
GO
```

The two new lines in the query are the variable declaration, which holds the value of the parameter, and the stored procedure to set the parameter value. The `DECLARE` creates a variable and sets the value to a string value — in this case, `PackageParam`.

The next line calls the stored procedure named `catalog.set_execution_parameter_value`. This stored procedure has a few parameters: the execution ID of the package created in the create execution procedure, the object type, the parameter name, and the parameter value, which is set to the previously created variable. The object type is set to either 20 (for a project parameter) or 30 (for a package parameter).

If you run the preceding script and then query the InsertTest table in AdventureWorks, you will see a new row added to the table. To ensure that the parameter is working, change the parameter value in the script from `PackageParam` to `Changed with T-SQL`. Then run the script again. You should see this row added to the table.

Querying Tables for Parameter Values

The T-SQL statements work great for changing the default value of a parameter for a package execution. The value is still basically hardcoded into a script. It would be nice if you could query a table and set the value of a parameter based on the results of the query.

The next bit of code shows how to do that. It's very similar to the previous T-SQL. The only difference is that the value is selected from a table from AdventureWorks.

```
Declare @execution_id bigint
EXEC [SSISDB].[catalog].[create_execution] @package_name=N'AdminDemo1.dtsx',
@execution_id=@execution_id OUTPUT,
@folder_name=N'AdminDemo',
@project_name=N'Ch22',
@use32bitruntime=False,
```

```
@reference_id=Null
Select @execution_id
DECLARE @var0 sql_variant = (
  Select top(1) FirstName from
  [AdventureWorks].[Person].[Contact]
  Order by LASTNAME
  )
EXEC [SSISDB].[catalog].[set_execution_parameter_value] @execution_id,
@object_type=30,
@parameter_name=N'strInput',
@parameter_value=@var0
EXEC [SSISDB].[catalog].[start_execution] @execution_id
GO
```

On the line where the parameter value is set, the hardcoded value of `PackageParam` has been replaced with a query from AdventureWorks, as shown here:

```
Select top(1) FirstName from
  [AdventureWorks].[Person].[Contact]
  Order by LASTNAME
```

This query returns the results of someone's first name — in this case, "Syed." You can run this query separately from the package execution to see if your results differ.

> **NOTE** *Note that Microsoft may have altered the AdventureWorks sample database after publication of this book.*

Now you have the tools to set parameter values using queries. This can be very useful in terms of controlling many packages, even in different projects or on different machines. You can update a table, and all the package executions querying the table to set their parameters will be altered, but if you want to change sets of parameter values easily, then you will want to use environments.

Using Environments

Imagine you have a project that runs on a schedule. On weekdays, the packages in the project need to run with a certain set of parameter values, but on weekends, they need a different set of values. This is a project with several packages, and each package has several parameters. All the packages in the project need to use the same parameter values when they run. Environments make it easy to run these packages with different sets of parameter values.

This example project, named EnvironmentDemo, contains three packages: EnvironDemo1, EnvironDemo2, and EnvironDemo3. The project has two project level parameters. You can download this project from the website for this book at `www.wrox.com/go/prossis2014`.

Creating and Configuring Project Level Parameters

If you want to create project level parameters, double-click on Project.params under the project in SQL Server Data Tools in Solution Explorer, as shown in Figure 22-16. Here, you can see the two project level parameters that already exist in this project: strRunType and intNumber. Each has a default value set, but you do not want to use the default value.

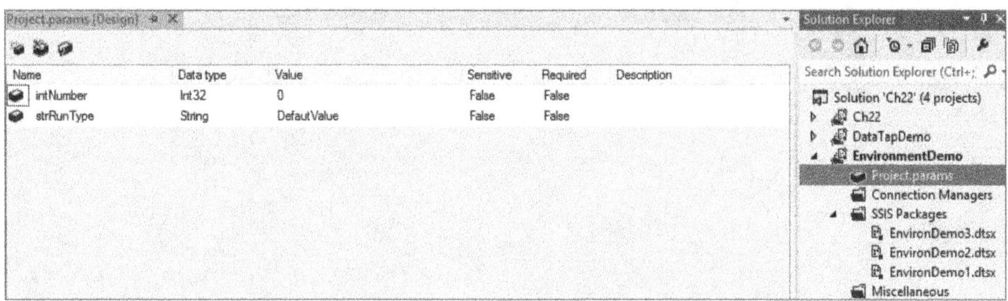

FIGURE 22-16

This package will simply write the two parameter values to a table named EnvironmentDemo in AdventureWorks. Following is the script to create this table. Deploy this project to a folder named EnvironmentDemo in the SSIS catalog.

```
CREATE TABLE [dbo].[EnvironmentDemo](
       [RunType] [varchar](50) NULL,
      [IntParamValue] [nchar](10) NULL
) ON [PRIMARY]
```

Setting Up Your Environments

Now deploy your project using the project deployment model as described in the "Project Deployment Model" section earlier in this chapter. After the project is deployed, you are ready to set up your environments. In the SSIS catalog, right-click on the Environments folder and click Create Environment. Name the first environment **Week Days** and then create a second environment and name it **Weekends**. When you are done, you should see two environments in the EnvironmentDemo folder, as shown in Figure 22-17.

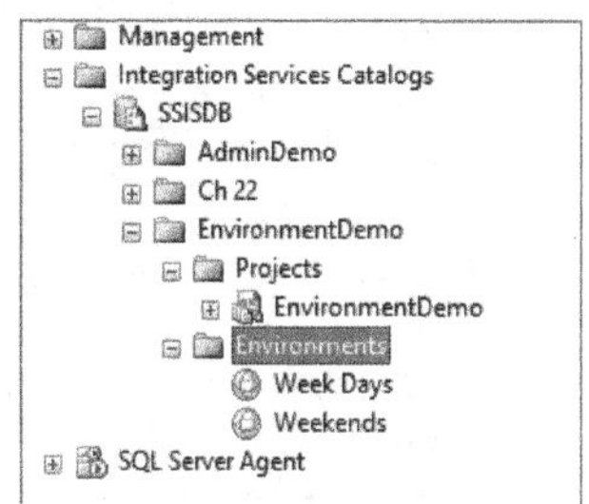

FIGURE 22-17

To set variable values in the environments, you can right-click on the environment and select Properties. Then click the Variables option on the left. Set the name, type, and value of the variables as shown in Figure 22-18.

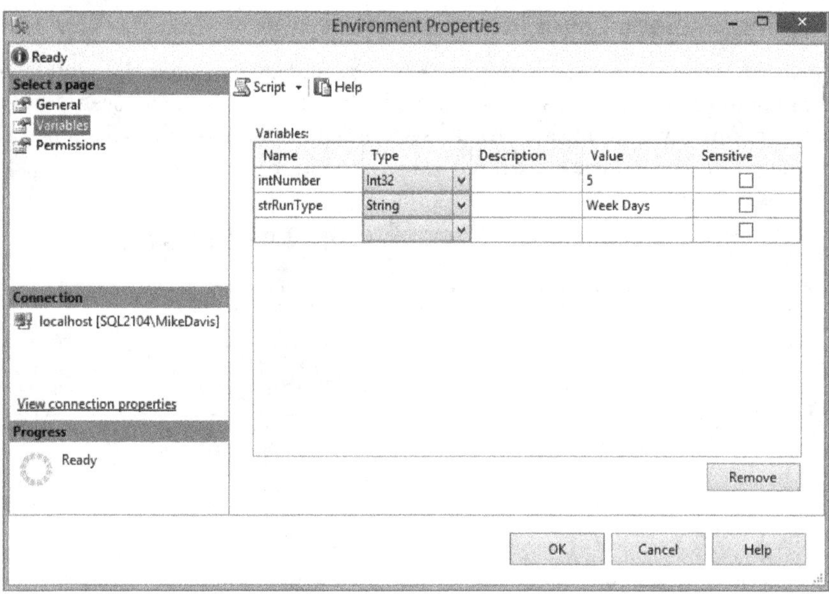

FIGURE 22-18

You can also set the value of the environments using T-SQL queries. The following code shows how this is done. The stored procedure named `catalog.create_environment_variable` creates a variable in the environment. This stored procedure takes six parameters: variable name, whether the variable is sensitive and therefore needs to be encrypted, the name of the environment, the folder name where the project is found, the value of the variable, and the data type.

```
DECLARE @var int = N'2'
EXEC [SSISDB].[catalog].[create_environment_variable] @variable_
name=N'intNumber',
@sensitive=False,
@description=N'',
@environment_name=N'Weekends',
@folder_name=N'EnvironmentDemo',
@value=@var,
@data_type=N'Int32'
GO
DECLARE @var sql_variant = N'Weekends'
EXEC [SSISDB].[catalog].[create_environment_variable] @variable_
name=N'strRunType',
@sensitive=False,
@description=N'',
@environment_name=N'Weekends',
@folder_name=N'EnvironmentDemo',
@value=@var,
@data_type=N'String'
GO
```

Once you have the variables created in the environments, ensure that the values are set.

Configuring the Project to Use Environments

The next step is to configure the SSIS project to use the environments you just created. Right-click on the EnvironDemo1 package and select Configure. In the Scope dropdown menu, select EnvironmentDemo, which is the project. You could create package level parameters and use the package level scope here, but because you want all your packages to use the same value, you will use the project scope.

Click the References option on the right. Then click Add at the bottom and select the Week Days environment. Add the Weekends environment the same way. When you are done, your window should look like Figure 22-19. Click OK to close the window.

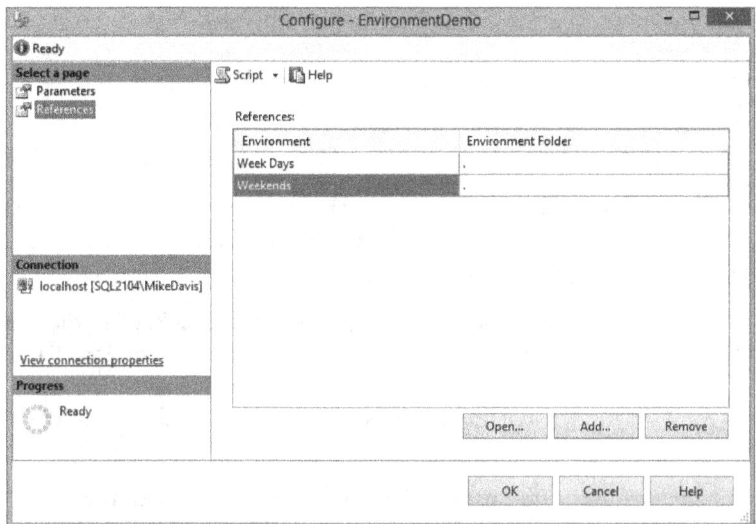

FIGURE 22-19

Now that the packages have references to the environments, you need to configure the project to use the variables from the environments. Right-click on the EnvironmentDemo project and then click configure. Ensure that the scope is set to All Packages and Project. Click the ellipses next to the intNumber variable. This will open the Set Parameter Value dialog. At the bottom are three options: Edit value, Use default value from package, and Use environment variable. Select the third option and choose the intNumber variable from the dropdown menu, as shown in Figure 22-20. Repeat the same steps for the strRunType variable.

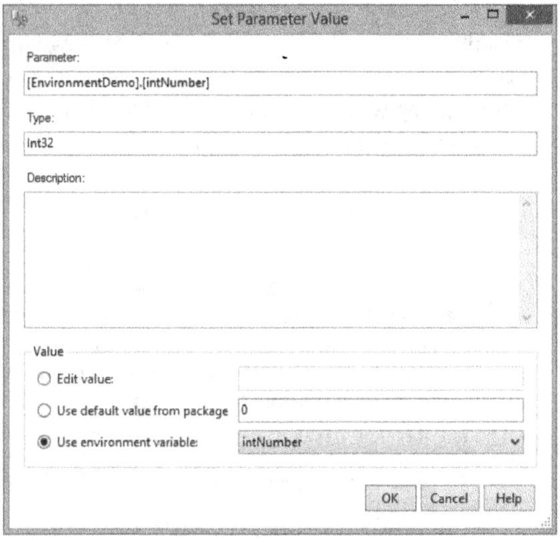

FIGURE 22-20

As stated before, all this work in the GUI can be done with T-SQL. If you click the script button before clicking OK and send the script to a new query window, you will see the following code (the stored procedure used here is `catalog.set_object_parameter_value`):

```
EXEC [SSISDB].[catalog].[set_object_parameter_value] @object_type=20,
@parameter_name=N'intNumber',
@object_name=N'EnvironmentDemo',
@folder_name=N'EnvironmentDemo',
@project_name=N'EnvironmentDemo',
@value_type=R,
@parameter_value=N'intNumber'
GO
EXEC [SSISDB].[catalog].[set_object_parameter_value] @object_type=20,
@parameter_name=N'strRunType',
@object_name=N'EnvironmentDemo',
@folder_name=N'EnvironmentDemo',
@project_name=N'EnvironmentDemo',
@value_type=R,
@parameter_value=N'strRunType'
GO
```

The only new parameter here is `value_type`, which is set to `R` in this example. This indicates that the parameter value is a referenced value and is using an environment variable. You can also set the `value_type` parameter to `V`, to indicate the parameter is a literal value.

Now you are ready to execute the package. Right-click on the EnvironDemo1 package in the SSMS Object Explorer window and select Execute. At the bottom of the Execute Package dialog is an environment option. Place a check next to Environment and select Week Days from the dropdown. Click OK to execute the package. When a message box appears asking if you would like to open the overview report, click No.

Query the EnvironmentDemo table in AdventureWorks and you will see the row with the value of Week Days and the number 5. You can truncate or delete from this table if you prefer. Now repeat the same steps to execute the EnvironDemo2 package. Another row with the same values will be inserted.

Right-click on the EnvironDemo3 package and select Execute. Select the Weekends environment this time. Instead of letting the GUI execute the package, click the script button and send the script to a new query window. Click Cancel to close the Execute window. In the newly created query window you will see the following code:

```
Declare @execution_id bigint

EXEC [SSISDB].[catalog].[create_execution]
@package_name=N'EnvironDemo3.dtsx',
 @execution_id=@execution_id OUTPUT,
 @folder_name=N'EnvironmentDemo',
  @project_name=N'EnvironmentDemo',
  @use32bitruntime=False,
 @reference_id=5

Select @execution_id

EXEC [SSISDB].[catalog].[start_execution] @execution_id
GO
```

The new parameter in this code is the `reference_id`. This is an internal reference to the environment. The only way to find this ID is to create the script as you just did.

> **NOTE** *Note that there is an identifier number on each environment. This is not the same as the* `reference_id`*, even though they might match by coincidence sometimes.*

Setting Environment References

When you create an environment, you may want to use it so that if the package is moved it still points to the same environment. This can be accomplished by creating an *absolute* environment reference. Basically, environment references can be set to either relative or absolute.

- **Absolute references** always point to the same environment, no matter where the project or package is moved.
- **Relative references** point to the place to which a project or package is moved.

Right-click on the EnvironmentDemo project and select Configure. Click the Reference option on the left, and then click the Add button at the bottom. Note that the Browse Environments window contains a local folder and a duplicate beneath it. In this case the local folder is the EnvironmentDemo folder, as shown in Figure 22-21. If you select the local folder environment, the reference is set as a *relative* reference. If you select the folder below, the reference is set to absolute.

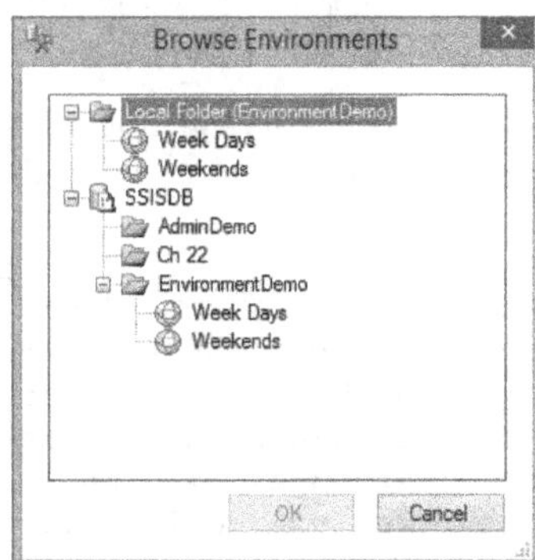

FIGURE 22-21

In most situations you will use relative references so that packages moved from development to production will use the environments in production. Absolute references are useful when you have several packages using the same set of parameters in an environment. You can point different projects to the same environments using absolute references.

Using Data Taps

Data viewers are great tools to use while working in SQL Server Data Tools to view data in a Data Flow. In this release of SQL Server Integration Services you can now place a *data tap* in a package executing on the server. A data tap acts like a data viewer from SQL Server Data Tools because it lets you see data in a Data Flow, although with different methods. It enables you to see a sample of the rows moving through a Data Flow sent to a file for review.

The sample code included with this book at `www.wrox.com/go/prossis2014` contains a project named DataTapDemo. Deploy this project to a folder named DataTapDemo on the SSIS catalog. Once you have the project deployed to the server, you are ready to execute and add a data tap to the package.

The code to add a data tap is just like all the other commands discussed already; it uses a stored procedure. The stored procedure to add the data tap is `catalog.add_data_tap`. The following code shows how to add a data tap to the sample package:

```
exec [SSISDB].[catalog].[add_data_tap]
    @execution_id= @execution_id,
     @task_package_path = '\Package\Get Person Data',
     @dataflow_path_id_string = 'Paths[Person Source.OLE DB Source Output]',
     @data_filename = datatap.csv'
```

The preceding code adds a data tap to the Data Flow in the package. The parameters are those you will probably need to retrieve while you have the package open in SQL Server Data Tools. The execution ID comes from the execution creation, which is done before this code. The task package path is the path of the Data Flow in the package. To find this, open the package in SQL Server Data Tools, right-click on the Data Flow, and select Properties. The package path is the property you need.

The Data Flow path ID is found in the Data Flow. Open the Data Flow of the package in SQL Server Data Tools. Then right-click on the Data Flow line where you want to add the data tap and select Properties. The `IdentificationString` property is the property you need for the Data Flow `path_id_string` parameter. The last parameter is the filename where you want the rows written. The file path cannot be changed; the data tap files are always created in the data dumps folder in the SQL Server install directory.

The following example shows the complete execution code to run a package with a data tap. There is no GUI interface to create data taps. Creating data taps is a manual process.

```
Declare @execution_id bigint
EXEC [SSISDB].[catalog].[create_execution] @package_name=N'DataTap1.dtsx',
@execution_id=@execution_id OUTPUT,
@folder_name=N'DataTapDemo',
@project_name=N'DataTapDemo',
@use32bitruntime=False,
@reference_id=Null

Select @execution_id

exec [SSISDB].[catalog].[add_data_tap]
    @execution_id= @execution_id,
     @task_package_path = '\Package\Get Person Data',
     @dataflow_path_id_string = 'Paths[Person Source.OLE DB Source Output]',
     @data_filename = 'Cdatatap.csv'

EXEC [SSISDB].[catalog].[start_execution] @execution_id
GO
```

CREATING A CENTRAL SSIS SERVER

This is another section that applies only to the package deployment model. If you can, you should be changing your SSIS methods to take advantage of the project deployment model.

Many enterprises have so many packages that they decide to separate the service from SQL Server and place it on its own server. When you do this, you must still license the server just as if it were running SQL Server. The advantages of this separation are that your SSIS packages will not suffocate the SQL Server's memory during a large load and you have a central management location. The disadvantages are that you must license the server separately and you add an added layer of complexity when you're debugging packages. You have a fantastic way to easily scale packages by adding more memory to your central server, but you also create an added performance hit because all remote data must be copied over the network before entering the Data Flow buffer.

To create a centralized SSIS hub, you only need to modify the `MsDtsSrvr.ini.xml` file and restart the service. The service can read a UNC path like `\\ServerName\Share`, and it can point to multiple remote servers. In the following example, the service enumerates packages from two servers, one that is local and another that is a named instance. After restarting the service, you will see a total of six folders to expand in Management Studio. We cover the Management Studio aspect of SSIS in much more detail later in this chapter.

```
<? xml version="1.0" encoding="utf-8" ?>
<DtsServiceConfiguration xmlns:xsd="http://www.w3.org/2001/XMLSchema" xmlns:xsi=
"http://www.w3.org/2001/XMLSchema-instance">
<StopExecutingPackagesOnShutdown<true</StopExecutingPackagesOnShutdown>
<TopLevelFolders>
<Folder xsi:type="SqlServerFolder">
<Name>Server A MSDB</Name>
<ServerName>localhost</ServerName>
</Folder>
<Name>Server B MSDB</Name>
<ServerName>SQLServerB</ServerName>
</Folder>
<Name>Server C MSDB</Name>
<ServerName>SQLServerC\NamedInstance</ServerName>
</Folder>
<Folder xsi:type="FileSystemFolder">
<Name>Server A File System</Name>
<StorePath>P:\Packages</StorePath>
</Folder>
<Folder xsi:type="FileSystemFolder">
<Name<Server B File System</Name>
<StorePath>\\SQLServerB\Packages</StorePath>
</Folder>
<Folder xsi:type="FileSystemFolder">
<Name>Server C File System</Name>
<StorePath>\\SQLServerC\Packages</StorePath>
</Folder>
</TopLevelFolders>
</DtsServiceConfiguration>
```

To schedule packages when using a centralized SSIS hub as in this example, you have two options. You can schedule your packages through SQL Server Agent or through a scheduling system like Task Scheduler from Windows. Because you're already paying for a SQL Server license, it's better to install SQL Server on your server and use Agent, because it gives you much more flexibility, as you will see later in this chapter. Keep in mind that packages run from the machine that executes the package. Therefore, if you have a package stored on Server A but execute it from Server B, it will use Server B's resource. You can also store configuration tables and logging tables on this SQL Server to centralize its processing as well. Both scheduling mechanisms are covered later in this chapter.

CLUSTERING SSIS

This is another section that applies only to the package deployment model. If you can, you should be changing your SSIS methods to take advantage of the project deployment model.

Unfortunately, SSIS is not a clustered service by default. Microsoft does not recommend that you cluster SSIS, because it can lead to unpredictable results. For example, if you place SSIS in the same cluster group as SQL Server and the SQL Server fails over, it would cause SSIS to fail over as well. Even though it does not cluster in the main SQL Server setup, it can still be clustered manually through a series of relatively easy steps. If you decide you must cluster SSIS, this section walks you through those steps, but it assumes that you already know how to use Windows clustering and understand the basic clustering architecture. Essentially, the steps to setting up SSIS as a clustered service are as follows:

1. Install SSIS on the other nodes that can own the service.
2. Create a new cluster group (optionally).
3. If you created a new group, create a virtual IP, name, and drive as clustered resources.
4. Copy over the `MsDtsSrvr.ini.xml` file to the clustered drive.
5. Modify the `MsDtsSrvr.ini.xml` file to change the location of the packages.
6. Change the registry setting to point to the `MsDtsSrvr.ini.xml` file.
7. Cluster the MSDTSServer120 service as a generic service.

You need to make a minor decision prior to clustering. You can choose to cluster the MSDTSServer120 service in the main SQL Server cluster group for a given instance or you can create its own cluster group. You will find that while it's easier to piggyback the main SQL Server service, it adds complexity to management.

The SSIS service has only a single instance in the entire Windows cluster. If you have a four-instance SQL Server cluster, where would you place the SSIS service then? This is one scenario that demonstrates why it makes the most sense to move the SSIS service into its own group. The main reason, though, is manageability. If you decided that you needed to fail over the SSIS service to another node, you would have to fail over the SQL Server as well if they shared a cluster group, which would cause an outage. Moving the SSIS service into its own cluster group ensures that only the SSIS service fails over and does not cause a wider outage.

Placing the service in its own group comes at a price, though. The service will now need a virtual IP address, its own drive, and a name on the network. Once you meet those requirements, however, you're ready to go ahead and cluster. If you decided to place SSIS into its own group, you would not need the drive, IP, or name.

The first step to clustering is installing SSIS on all nodes in the Windows cluster. If you installed SSIS as part of your SQL Server install, you'll see that SSIS installed only on the primary node. You now need to install it manually on the other nodes in the cluster. Make the installation simple by installing SSIS on the same folder on each node.

If you want to have the SSIS service in a different group than the database engine, you first have to create a new group called SSIS in Cluster Administrator for the purpose of this example (although it can be called something else). This group needs to be shared by whichever nodes you would like to participate in the cluster. Then, add to the group a physical drive that is clustered, an IP address, and a network name. The IP address and network name are virtual names and IPs.

From whichever node owns the SSIS group, copy the `MsDtsSrvr.ini.xml` file to the clustered physical drive that's in the SSIS cluster group. We generally create a directory called `«Clustered Drive Letter»\SSISSetup` for the file. Make a note of wherever you placed the file for a later configuration step. You'll also want to create a folder called Packages on the same clustered drive for storing your packages. This directory will store any packages and configuration files that will be stored on the file system instead of the SSIS catalog database.

Next, open the Registry editing tool and change the `HKEY_LOCAL_MACHINE\SOFTWARE\Microsoft\Microsoft SQL Server\120\SSIS\ServiceConfigFile` key to point to the new location (including the filename) for the `MsDtsSrvr.ini.xml` file. Make sure you backup the registry before making this change.

After that, you're ready to cluster the MSDTSServer120 service. Open Cluster Administrator again and right-click the SSIS cluster group (if you're creating it in its own group) and select New ➪ Resource. This will open the Resource Wizard, which clusters nearly any service in Windows. On the first screen, type **Integration Services** for the name of the clustered resource, and select Generic Service. This name is a logical name that is going to be meaningful only to the administrator and you.

Next, on the Possible Owner screen, add any node that you wish to potentially own the SSIS service. On the Dependencies page, add the group's Network Name, IP Address, and Drive as dependencies. This ensures that the SSIS service won't come online before the name and drives are online. Also, if the drive fails, the SSIS service will also fail.

The next screen is Generic Service Parameters, where you should enter **MSDTSServer120** for the service to cluster. The last screen in the wizard is the Registry Replication screen, where you want to ensure that the `SOFTWARE\Microsoft\Microsoft SQL Server\120\SSIS\ServiceConfigFile` key is replicated. If a change is made to this registry key, it will be replicated to all other nodes. After you finish the wizard, the SSIS service is almost ready to come online and be clustered.

The final step is to move any packages that were stored on the file system over to the clustered drive in the `Packages` folder. The next time you open Management Studio, you should be able to see all the packages and folders. You also need to edit the `MsDtsSrvr.ini.xml` file to change the SQL Server to point to SQL Server's virtual name, not the physical name, which allows failovers of the database engine. In the same file, you need to change the path in the StorePath to point to the `«Clustered Drive»:\Packages` folder you created earlier as well. After this, you're ready to bring the service online in Cluster Administrator.

Now that your SSIS service is clustered, you will no longer connect to the physical machine name to manage the packages in Management Studio. Instead, you will connect to the network name that you created in Cluster Administrator. If you added SSIS as a clustered resource in the same group as SQL Server, you would connect to the SQL Server's virtual network name.

PACKAGE CONFIGURATION

This section covers older configurations. You will need this information if you decide to run your packages with the package model and use configuration files or tables, rather than upgrade your packages to use parameters and environments in the project deployment model.

Now that you have a set of packages complete, the challenge is trying to deploy those packages to your testing environment or production without having to manually configure the packages for that environment. For example, your production server may not have the same directory to pull extract files from or the same user name for connecting to the database. Configuration files and tables help you make the migrations seamless and automated to reduce your risk of errors. In this section you'll see how to create a configuration repository for files and how to set up a configuration table.

The SSIS Package Configuration option allows you to write any SSIS property for the package, connection, container, variable, or any task into an XML file or a table, for example, and then read the setting at runtime. You could deploy the configuration file to multiple servers and point the setting inside the file to a new SQL Server database on the second server, and when the package runs, it will automatically shift its connection to the new database. Configurations also come in handy later when you deploy the packages to production using the deployment utility.

The following short example demonstrates the strengths and weaknesses of package configurations. In this example, you're going to create a simple package with a Script Task that will pop up a message with the configuration value instead of its normal, hardcoded value. You'll then create multiple configuration files and see which configuration file is used by the package.

First, create a new package called **ConfigFiles.dtsx** in a project set to package deployment model. Drag a new Script Task onto the Control Flow tab in the newly created package and name the task **Popup Value**. Next, create a new string variable called `strMessage` that is scoped to the package, not the Script Task. Seed a default value of "Hard Coded Value" for the string variable.

Double-click the Script Task to configure it. In the Script page, type **strMessage** for the ReadOnlyVariables property. Change the ScriptLanguage property to Microsoft Visual Basic 2012. Click Edit Script to add your code to the task. Double-click the `ScriptMain.vb` file in the Project Explorer window if it isn't already open. The code you're going to add will pop up the value from the `strMessage` variable by using the following code in the `Main()` subroutine:

```
Public Sub Main()
'
'Add your code here
MsgBox(Dts.Variables("strMessage").Value)
Dts.TaskResult = ScriptResults.Success
End Sub
```

> **NOTE** *For more information about the Script Task, see Chapter 9.*

Close the task. If you execute the package at this point, you should see a pop-up dialog that states "Hard Coded Value." If so, you're now ready to set this variable from a configuration file instead.

Select Package Configurations either from the SSIS menu or by right-clicking in the background of the Control Flow tab. This opens the Package Configurations Organizer, where you will create and arrange the priority of your package configurations. Click Enable Package Configurations to enable this feature.

To add your first package configuration, click Add. This will open the Package Configuration Wizard. You can set your package configuration to use an XML file, a SQL Server table, an environment variable, or a registry setting or to read a variable from a parent package. Most people choose to use XML files or a SQL Server table. XML files are generally easier to implement because the files are portable and easy to transport from environment to environment. In this example, you'll use an XML file. Type `C:\ProSSIS\Data\Ch22\Configuration.xml` for the Configuration File name property. The default extension for configuration XML files is `.dtsConfig`, but we prefer to use an XML extension so it is easily registered to most XML editors.

You can even make the path and filename of the XML file dynamic by reading it from an environment variable. Otherwise, the file must be in the `C:\ProSSIS\Data\Ch22\` folder on each server to which you want to deploy the package, which may not be allowed in your production environment. You can also change this later during deployment, as discussed earlier in the "Package Deployment Model" section.

Click Next to go to the Select Properties to Export screen of the wizard. If the `C:\ProSSIS\Data\Ch22\configuration.xml` file already existed on your server, you would be prompted to specify whether you wish to reuse the existing file or overwrite the file. If you choose to reuse an existing file, the next screen is the final summary screen. This option is fantastic if you want all the packages in your project to reuse the same configuration file, but to do this the property names have to match exactly.

In this screen, you can check any property that you wish to have read from the configuration file. In this case, you want to drill down to Variables ➪ strMessage ➪ Properties and check the Value option (as shown in Figure 22-22). Click Next to proceed to the next screen.

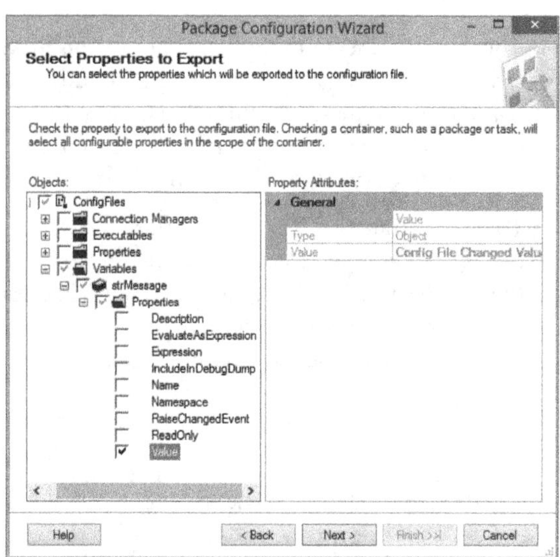

FIGURE 22-22

You are then taken to the summary screen, where you should name the configuration **strMessage** and click Finish, which takes you back to the Package Configurations Organizer. Click Close to exit the organizer and execute the package. If you run the package again, you'll see that the pop-up still has the same old message. The configuration file now has been created and contains the same value as the package.

Open the `configuration.xml` file in your favorite XML editor or Notepad, and replace the old variable value of "Hard Coded Value" with a new value of "Config File Changed Value," as shown in the following code. The other pieces of the configuration file contain a lot of metadata about who created the configuration file and from what package.

```
<?xml version="1.0"?>
<DTSConfiguration>
<DTSConfigurationHeading>
<DTSConfigurationFileInfo GeneratedBy="SSISMVP\MVP" GeneratedFromPackageName=
"ConfigFiles"
GeneratedFromPackageID=
"{D1A65B15-5EB7-486D-B396-B204B0D2CB42}"
GeneratedDate=
"9/26/2011 12:24:09 PM"/>
</DTSConfigurationHeading>
<Configuration ConfiguredType="Property"
Path=
"\Package.Variables[User::strMessage].Properties[Value]"
 ValueType="String">
<ConfiguredValue>Config File Changed Value</ConfiguredValue
></Configuration>
</DTSConfiguration>
```

When you execute the package again, notice this time the message has changed to "Config File Changed Value."

You can also create multiple configuration files. For example, you may want a configuration file that contains your corporate logging database for all of your packages to use, and then another configuration file for the individual package. As you add more package configurations, they stack on top of each other in the Configurations Organizer screen. At runtime, if there is a conflict between two configurations, the last configuration on the bottom will win.

To demonstrate this, create one additional configuration. This time, when you're asked for the configuration type, select SQL Server. For the Connection property, select New and point the connection to the AdventureWorks database, which will create a Connection Manager. Lastly, click New for the Configuration Table property. The table can be called whatever you'd like as long as you have the core four columns. Name the table `ctrlConfigurations`, as shown in the following script:

```
CREATE TABLE [dbo].[ctrlConfigurations]
(
ConfigurationFilter NVARCHAR(255) NOT NULL,
ConfiguredValue NVARCHAR(255) NULL,
PackagePath NVARCHAR(255) NOT NULL,
ConfiguredValueType NVARCHAR(20) NOT NULL
)
```

Type **Development** for the Configuration Filter. When the package reads from the `ctrlConfigurations` table, it will read all the properties where the ConfigurationFilter column is equal to "Development," as shown in Figure 22-23. Typically, you would want to set this filter to either the package name or the group of packages that you wish to share the same configuration settings. This is because all configurations in SQL Server are stored in the same table.

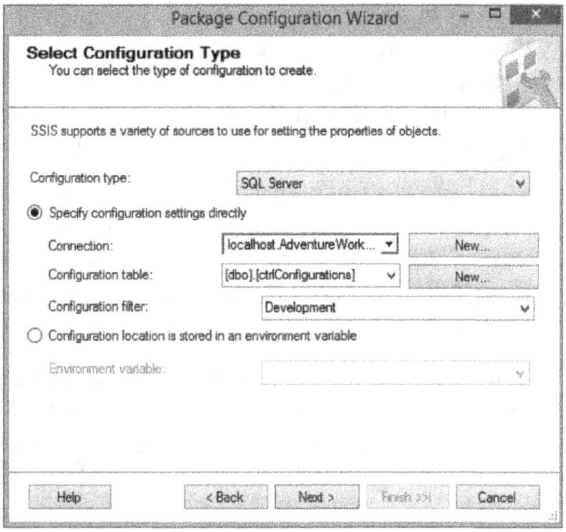

In the next screen, select the value property of the strMessage variable. Click Next to go to the next screen and name this configuration "SQL Server Config." You should now have two package configurations, as shown in Figure 22-24. Set the variable's value by going to the ctrlConfigurations table in the AdventureWorks database and setting the ConfiguredValue column to "SQL Server Config Value," as shown in the following query:

FIGURE 22-23

```
Update ctrlConfigurations
SET ConfiguredValue = 'SQL Server Config Value'
where ConfiguredValue = 'Hard Coded Value'
```

When you execute the package, notice that the value that pops up now is "SQL Server Config Value." This is because even though there were two configurations that set the same variable, the one at the bottom (see Figure 22-24) set the value last.

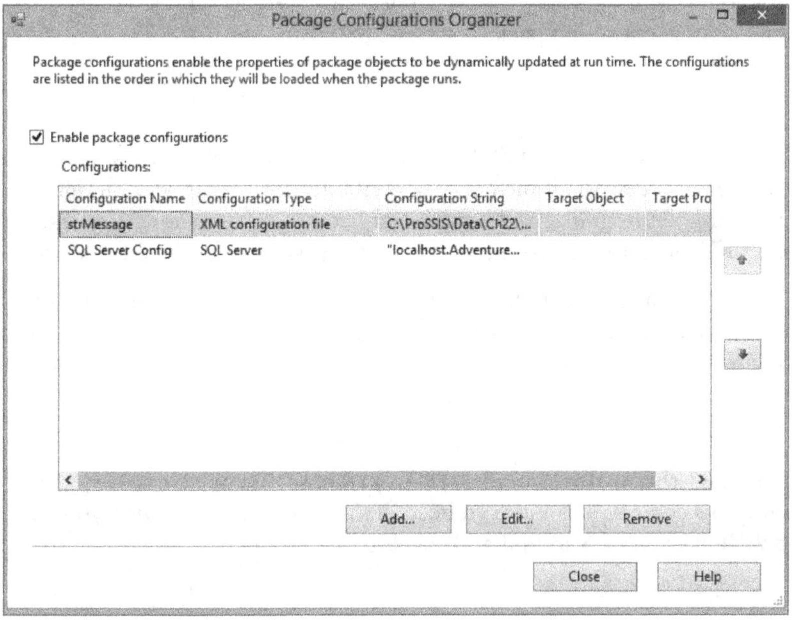

FIGURE 22-24

Package configurations make it easy to migrate a package from environment to environment. For the most part, it's going to be easier to store your configurations in the SQL Server because you can write some sort of front-end to modify the settings, and you can create reports to view the settings. The main problem with package configurations is that data is not encrypted, so you should not store anything that must be secure inside package configurations.

There are a few methodologies you can employ when you use configuration files. One is to group all the like configuration properties together into files or with filters if you choose to store the settings in a table. The other option, which many prefer, is to store each property in its own file or with its own filter. The latter option requires more work in terms of creating your package because you may have to create dozens of files, but it enables you to pick which settings you like and reuse them repeatedly.

In this section you learned how to use configuration files and configuration tables to make deployment easier in the older package deployment model. However, at the risk of my sounding like a broken record, I'll say that you should be updating your methods to take full advantage of the SSIS catalog features.

COMMAND-LINE UTILITIES

The SSIS command-line tools are still available, but you should be using the T-SQL functions to execute and manage your packages. However, DTExec and DTUtil have been updated to work with the SSIS catalog.

So far, the bulk of this chapter has focused on the GUI tools you can use to administer SSIS. There is also a set of tools that can be used from a command line that serves as a Swiss Army knife to an SSIS administrator: `DTExec.exe` and `DTUtil.exe`. DTExec is a tool you use to execute your packages from a command line, and DTUtil can help you migrate a package or change the security of a package, just to name a couple of its functions. In this release of SQL Server, the command-line tools have been enhanced to support executing packages in the SSIS catalog.

DTExec

DTExec is a command-prompt tool included with SQL Server. This command is used to configure and execute SSIS packages. It gives access to all the package configuration and execution options, like connections, properties, variables, logging, and progress indicators. It also supports packages from three different sources: SQL Server databases, the SSIS package store, and the file system.

DTExecUI is a powerful tool that wraps the command-line utility DTExec. A shortcut here is to use DTExecUI to create the command for you. You can see the list of switches, minus three optional switches, for this utility by typing the following:

```
dtexec.exe /?
```

For example, to execute a package that is stored in the MSDB database on your localhost, you could use the following command. This command is more verbose than is required. In reality, you only need to type the `/DTS` and `/SERVER` switches to find and execute the package.

```
DTExec.exe /DTS "\MSDB\DBSnapshots" /SERVER localhost /MAXCONCURRENT " -1 "
/CHECKPOINTING OFF /REPORTING V
```

Table 22-3 describes three optional arguments not included in the command-line list you generated previously for DTExec. You can see these include the parameters and environments. A complete list of all the arguments can be found on Microsoft's Books Online.

TABLE 22-3: DTEXEC Options

OPTION	DESCRIPTION
`/ISServer package_path`	(Optional) Loads a package that is on an SSIS server. The `package_path` points to the path and filename of the package.
`/Par[ameter] parameter_name (Type);Value`	(Optional) Sets a parameter value. This can be a project level or package level parameter.
`/Envreference reference_id`	(Optional) Sets the environment to be used by the package.

DTExecUI

In older versions of SQL Server, the primary way to execute a package was with `DTExecUI.exe`. With the integration of T-SQL to execute the packages, these tools will not be needed as often. This utility is a graphical wrapper for `DTExec.exe`, and it provides an easier way to produce the necessary switches to execute the package. You can open the utility by selecting Start ➪ Run and typing **DTExecui.exe**.

Before we begin working with this utility, note that it's a 32-bit utility. It will run on a 64-bit machine, but it will wrap the 32-bit version of `DTExec.exe`. In the "64-Bit Issues" section later in this chapter, you will learn some tricks to use to run the package in 64-bit mode.

The first screen in DTExecUI is shown in Figure 22-25. Here you point to the package you wish to execute and specify where the package is located. If you select the Package Store to connect to from the Package Source dropdown menu, you can view all the packages stored on the server. Notice you do not have an option for SSIS catalog. The SSIS catalog is not supported by the command-line tool DTExecUI. There are windows in SSMS for running the packages in the catalog. Your other options are SQL Server or the File System. With the SQL Server option, you will see only packages stored in the MSDB of the server that you name. The File System option allows you to point to a `.dtsx` file to execute.

The next page in the Execute Package Utility is the Configurations page. Here, you can select additional configuration files that you wish to include for this execution of the package. If you don't select an additional configuration file, any configuration files already on the server will be used. You will not be able to see existing configuration files that are being used in the package.

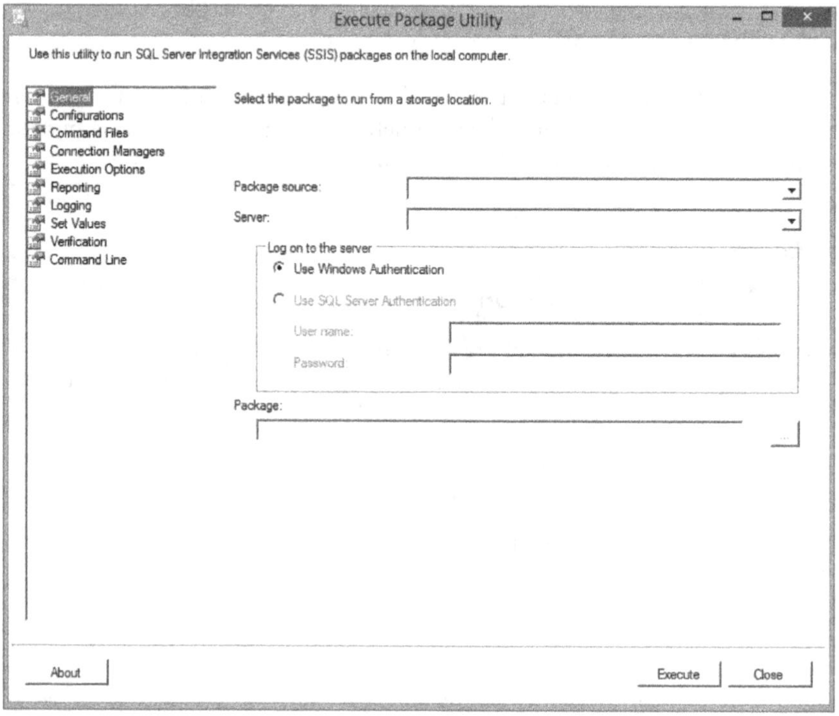

FIGURE 22-25

The Command Files page provides links to files that contain a series of additional switches you can use during execution. Remember that this tool wraps DTExec, which is a command-line utility. With a command file, you can place part of the standard DTExec switches in a file and then reuse them repeatedly for every package.

The Connection Managers page shows the power of Connection Managers. This page allows you to change the Connection Manager settings at runtime to a different setting than what the developer originally intended. For example, perhaps you'd like to move the destination connection for a package to a production server instead of a QA server (see Figure 22-26). Another typical example is when the drive structure differs between production and development, and you need to move the Connection Manager to a different directory.

The Execution Options page (shown in Figure 22-27) provides advanced settings for the package execution. For example, you can force the package to fail upon the first package warning, which would normally be ignored. You can also simply validate the package without executing it. An especially powerful setting in this page is the Maximum Concurrent Executables option, which simply controls how many concurrent tasks will run in parallel. For example, it is common to migrate a package to a different environment with fewer processors, which could cause performance issues until you lower this setting. The setting of -1 means that two tasks plus the number of CPUs will run concurrently. You can use the last set of options on this page to enable checkpoints on the package, if they are not already enabled, by checking the Enable Package Checkpoints option and specifying a name.

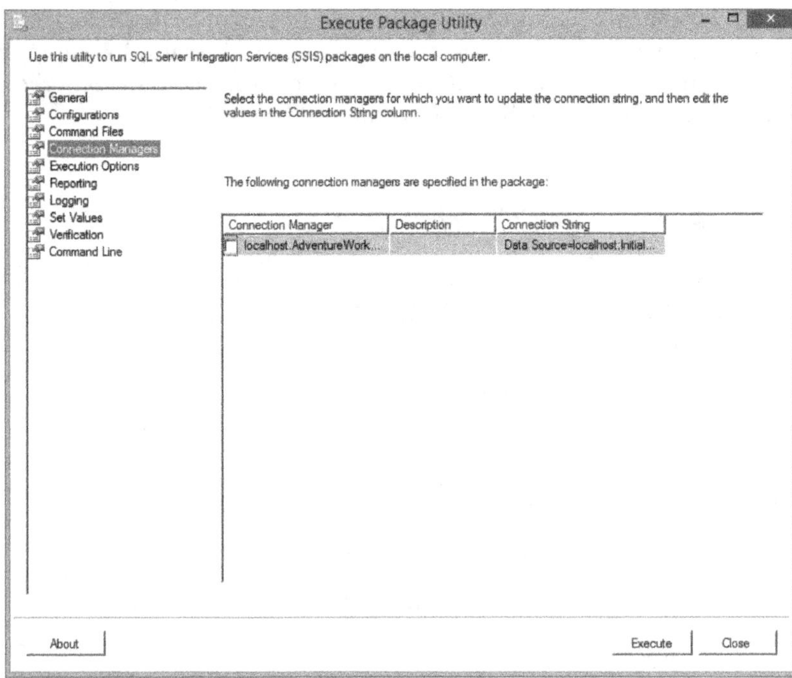

FIGURE 22-26

FIGURE 22-27

The Reporting page (shown in Figure 22-28) controls the amount of detail shown in the console. The default option is Verbose, which may be too detailed for you. You may decide that you want to see only errors and warnings, for example, which allows slightly better performance than the verbose setting. You can also control which columns will be displayed in the console.

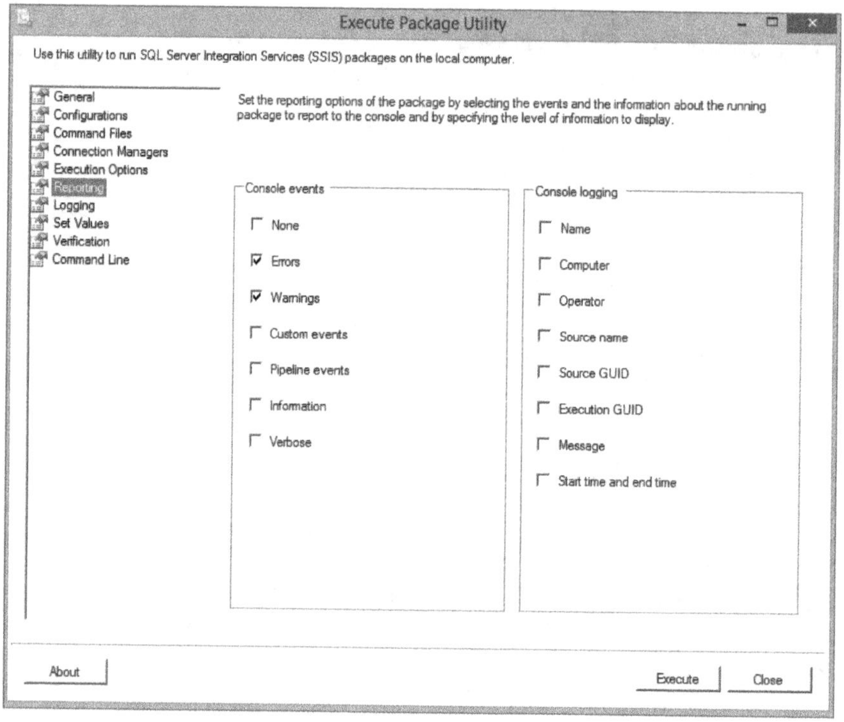

FIGURE 22-28

Another powerful page is the Set Values page (shown in Figure 22-29). This page allows you to override nearly any property you wish by typing the property path for the property. The most common use for this would be to set the value of a variable. To do this, you would use a property path that looked like this: `\Package.Variables[`*`VariableName`*`].Value`. Then type the value for the variable in the next column. This page also provides a workaround for properties that can't be set through expressions. With those properties, you generally can access them through the property path.

In the Verification page (shown in Figure 22-30), you can ensure that you execute only those packages that meet your criteria. For example, you may want to ensure that you execute only signed packages or packages with a certain build number. This could be handy for Sarbanes-Oxley compliance, for which you must guarantee that you don't execute a rogue package.

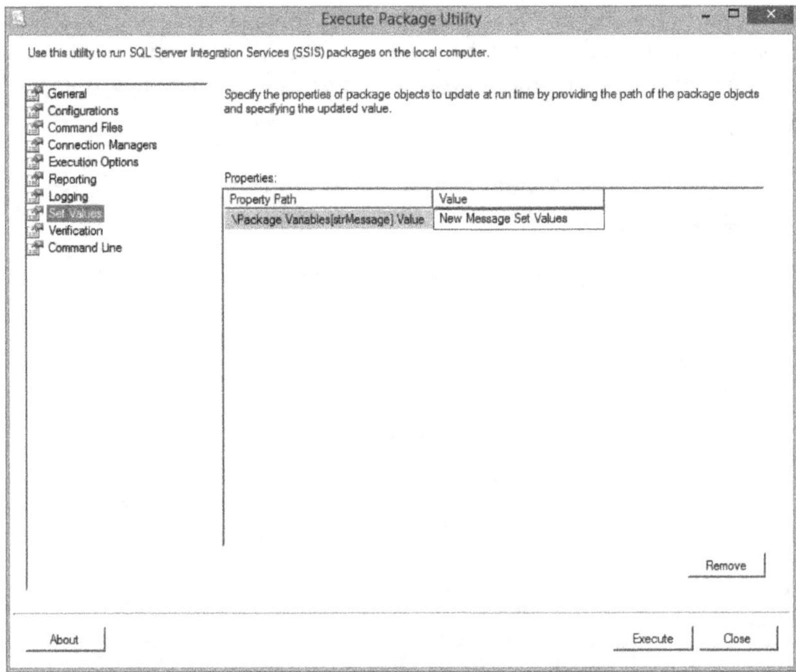

FIGURE 22-29

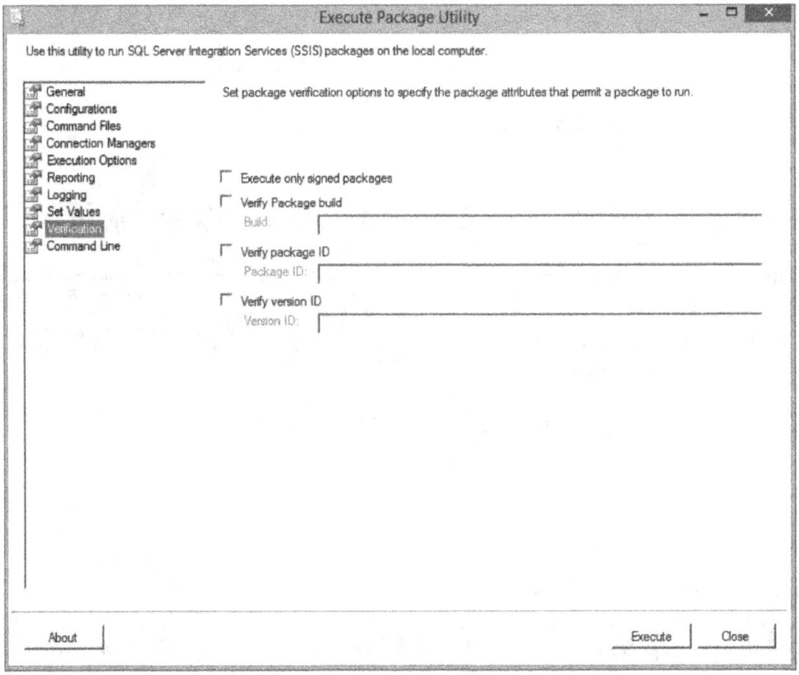

Execute Package Utility

Use this utility to run SQL Server Integration Services (SSIS) packages on the local computer.

General
Configurations
Command Files
Connection Managers
Execution Options
Reporting
Logging
Set Values
Verification
Command Line

Set package verification options to specify the package attributes that permit a package to run.

Execute only signed packages
Verify Package build
Build:
Verify package ID
Package ID:
Verify version ID
Version ID:

About
Execute
Close

FIGURE 22-30

The Command Line page (shown in Figure 22-31) is one of the most important pages. This page shows you the exact `DTExec.exe` command that will be executing. You can also edit the command here. When you have the command you want, you can copy and paste it in a command prompt after the command `DTExec.exe`.

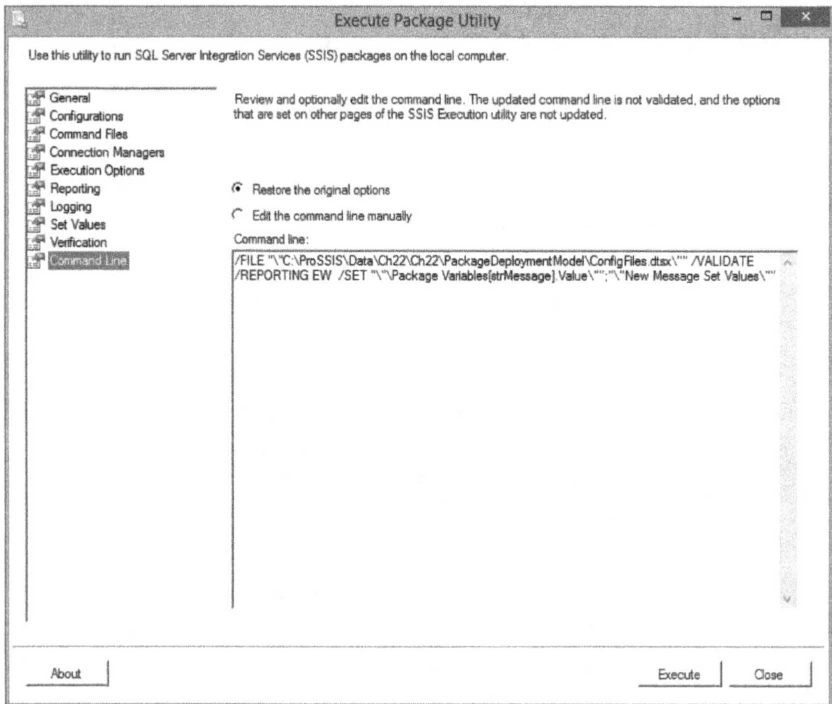

FIGURE 22-31

You can also execute the package by clicking the Execute button at any time from any page. After you click the Execute button, you will see the Package Execution Progress window, which displays any warnings, errors, and informational messages, as shown in Figure 22-32. In some cases, you'll see only a fraction of the message; just hover the cursor over the text to see the full message.

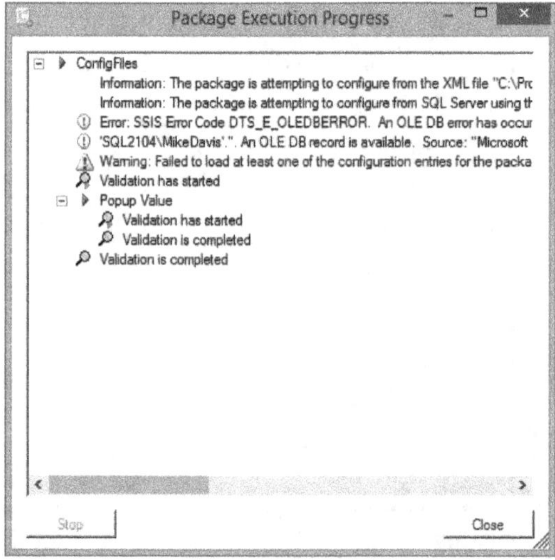

FIGURE 22-32

DTUtil

One of the best undiscovered command-line tools in your administrator kit is DTUtil.exe. This is also a good tool for developers. It performs a number of functions, including moving packages, renumbering the PackageID, re-encrypting a package, and digitally signing a package. To see everything this tool can do, type the following command from a command prompt:

```
DTUtil.exe /?
```

Essentially, this tool can be used to do many of the things that you do in Management Studio, and to a lesser extent in SQL Server Data Tools. The next sections describe creative ways to use DTUtil.exe.

Re-encrypting All Packages in a Directory

By default, SSIS files in development are encrypted to prevent an unauthorized person from seeing your SSIS package. The type of encryption is seamless behind the scenes and is applied at a workstation and user level. Earlier in development you can set the ProtectionLevel property to EncryptSensitiveWithUserKey (default option) to lock down password information in Connection Managers and other sensitive data. You can also set a password on the package by changing the ProtectionLevel property to EncryptSensitiveWithPassword.

By default, if you were to send a package that you're developing to another developer on your team, he or she would not be able to open it. The same would apply if you logged in with a different user account. You would receive the following error:

```
There were errors while the package was being loaded. The package might be
corrupted. See the Error List for details.
```

This error message is very misleading. In truth, you can't open the package, because the originating user encrypted it, whether intentionally or not. To fix this, the owner of the package can open it and select a different option in the Properties pane (like a package password) for the ProtectionLevel option. The default option is EncryptSensitiveWithUserKey. To protect the entire package with a password, select the EncryptAllWithPassword option.

Another useful option enables SSIS designers to encrypt all packages with the default option, and when it is time to send them to production, they can develop a batch file to loop through a directory's `.dtsx` file and set a password. The batch file would use DTUtil.exe and look like this:

```
for %%f in (*.dtsx) do Dtutil.exe /file %%f /encrypt file;%%f;3;newpassword
```

This would loop through each `.dtsx` file in your directory and assign the password of `newpassword`. The production support group could then use the same batch file to reset the password to a production password. The number `3` before the word `newpassword` sets the ProtectionLevel property of the package to EncryptAllWithPassword.

Handling a Corrupt Package

Occasionally when you copy objects in and out of a container, you may corrupt a given task in the package. In that case, you can't delete the task or move it outside the container or link it in the container. This doesn't happen often, but when you suspect you have a corrupt package or object, you can use DTUtil.exe to regenerate the package's XML. To do so, you can use the `-I` switch to generate a new PackageID and regenerate the XML, like this:

```
DTUtil.exe -I -File dbsnapshots.dtsx
```

After you do this, the package may look different when you open it because the XML has been regenerated. For example, some of your containers may be smaller than they were originally and placed in areas they weren't originally located. You can also use this command to generate a new PackageID when you find that the developer has copied and pasted the package in SQL Server Data Tools.

You can also create a batch file to loop through the directory and regenerate the ID for every package in the directory. The batch file will loop through every `.dtsx` file and execute DTUtil.exe. The batch file looks like this:

```
for %%f in (*.dtsx) do dtutil.exe /I /FILE "%%f"
```

SECURITY

The security of SSIS packages has changed because of the architecture changes in Integration Services. In the previous version of SSIS you could deploy to the MSDB or the file system. These options are still available but are older techniques that should be changed to use the project deployment model to take advantage of the security options. The SSIS catalog can be found in the standard database connection in SSMS, as shown in Figure 22-33. At the top you can see the SSIS catalog and the folder structure. The bottom section of the figure shows the Integration Services connection and the packages in the MSDB. You can also see the file system folder here.

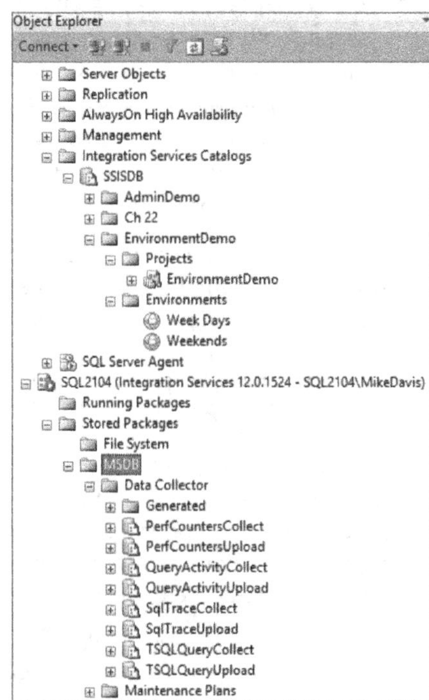

FIGURE 22-33

Securing the SSIS Catalog

It is easy to set and control security in the SSIS catalog either with the GUI interface or using T-SQL. The types of authentication supported by SSIS are Windows Authentication and SQL Server Authentication.

The SQL Server Integration Services administration role is named ssis_admin. This role has permission to view and modify all the objects in the SSIS catalog. Members of this role can create folders, move objects, delete objects, create and modify environments, and perform configuration changes to the catalog.

The SSIS catalog separates all the projects and objects into folders. Although these folders are great for organizing SSIS objects, they are also securable objects. You can grant users permission to a folder without adding them to the ssis_admin role. To give a user access to a folder, grant the user Manage_Object_Permissions on the appropriate folder.

Managing Security with the GUI

You can control the security of the folder in the SSIS catalog using the SSMS GUI. If you have been following along with the previous examples in this chapter, you should have at least two folders in the SSIS catalog, one named AdminDemo and the other named DataTapDemo.

Right-click on the DataTapDemo folder and select Properties. Click the Permissions option on the left side. In the top-right corner, click Browse and select the user or role to whom you want to give access to the folder. In the bottom section you can control the permissions at a granular level, as shown in Figure 22-34. Users and roles can be added at the top of this dialog. If you want to grant a group of users in a role access to the folder, you can do it here. Place a check next to all the permissions you want to grant or deny for the user or role.

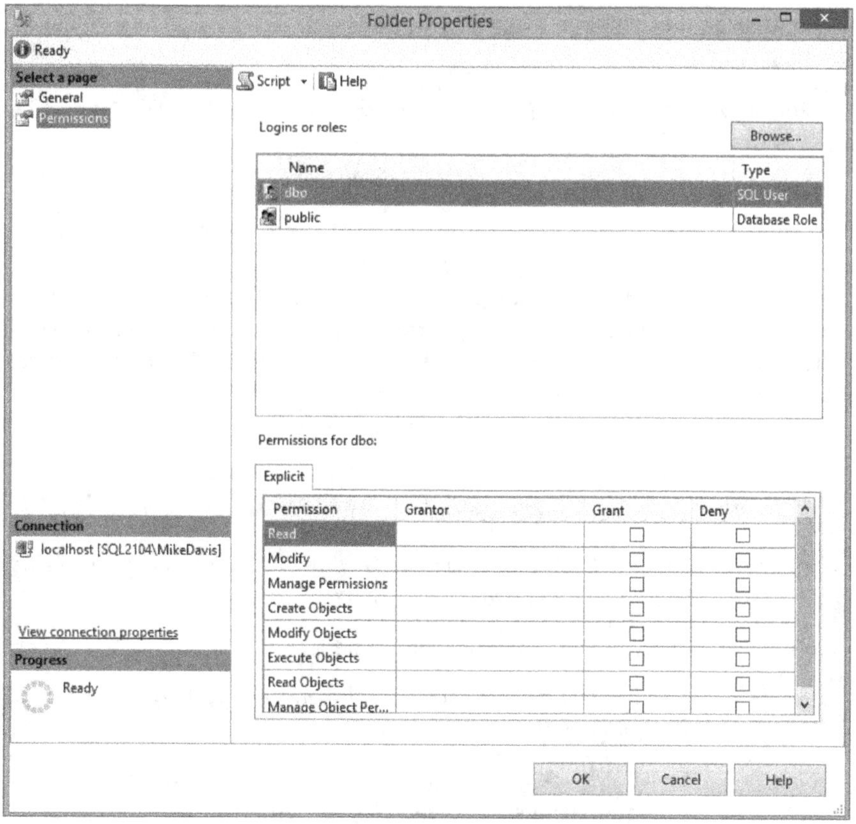

FIGURE 22-34

The permissions available at the bottom of the dialog are explained in Table 22-4.

TABLE 22-4: SSIS Catalog Permissions

PERMISSION	ALLOW DESCRIPTION	SUPPORTED OBJECT TYPES	VALUE
Read	Read information, such as properties	Folder, Project, Environment, Operation	1
Modify	Change information in the object, such as properties	Folder, Project, Environment, Operation	2
Execute	Run the packages in the project	Project	3
Manage Permissions	Change permissions of an object	Folder, Project, Environment, Operation	4
Create Objects	Create objects in a folder	Folder	100
Read Objects	Read every object in a folder	Folder	101
Modify Objects	Make changes to objects in a folder	Folder	102
Execute Objects	Run all packages in all projects in a folder	Folder	103
Manage Object Permissions	Change permissions on all objects in a folder	Folder	104

There are only five securable objects in the SSIS catalog (see Table 22-5). The permissions in the preceding table can be applied to these objects. The Supported Object Types column shows which objects can receive which permissions. The following table contains the list of objects, their types, and a description of the permissions it controls.

TABLE 22-5: SSIS Catalog Object Security

OBJECT	TYPE	PERMISSION DESCRIPTION
Folder	Container	This holds permissions for itself and the objects inside. Objects in the folder can have independent security.
Project	Object	This holds permissions for the project and objects in the project.
Environment	Object	This holds the permissions for the environment and the variables contained within it.
Operation	Object	This holds the permissions for instances of executions, operational messages, and all other operations. There is no GUI, so this must be managed with T-SQL.
Catalog	Container	The ssis_admin role is required.

Encryption of the catalog is handled with a master key. The SSISDB is just like any other database and therefore uses a master key, which is created when the catalog is created. This was covered in the "Setting the SSIS Catalog Properties" section earlier in this chapter.

Package level and project level parameters have a Boolean-sensitive property. When this property is set to true, the parameter value is encrypted in the SSISDB. When you query a sensitive parameter, it will show a null value. Other than this, the parameters behave like any nonsensitive parameters. The sensitive parameters work great for storing passwords or entire connection strings.

Managing Security with T-SQL

Five stored procedures can be used to manage security in the SSIS catalog. If you prefer running T-SQL, or you have a custom application you want to use to manage security, then scripting out your security changes is the way to go. Table 22-6 shows the five stored procedures used to manage security.

TABLE 22-6: SSIS Catalog Security Stored Procedures

STORED PROCEDURE NAME	DESCRIPTION
catalog.effective_object_permissions	Shows the effective permissions for all objects
catalog.explicit_object_permissions	Shows only explicitly set permissions
catalog.grant_permission	Grants permission to an object
catalog.deny_permission	Denies permission to an object
catalog.revoke_permission	Removes a permission on an object

Legacy Security

If you decide to deploy your packages to the MSDB or file system, then you are using the package deployment model and the older version of security. The only login option for connecting to the SSIS service is to use your Active Directory account. Once you connect, you'll see only the packages that you are allowed to see. This protection is accomplished based on package roles. Package roles are available only on packages stored in the MSDB database. Packages stored on the file system must be protected with a password.

Package roles can be accessed in Management Studio by right-clicking a package that you wish to protect and selecting Package Roles. The Package Roles dialog, shown in Figure 22-35, enables you to choose the MSDB role that will be in the writer role and reader role. The writer role can perform administrative-type functions such as overwriting a package with a new version, deleting a package, managing security, and stopping the package from running. The reader role can execute packages, view packages, and export packages from Management Studio.

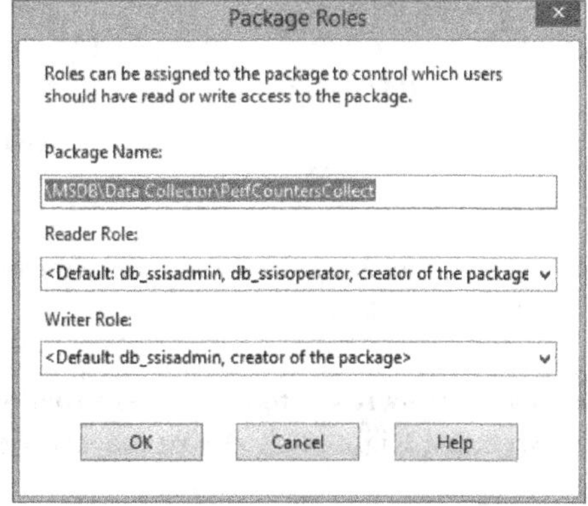

FIGURE 22-35

Package roles use database roles from the MSDB database. By default, the creator of the package and people who are in the db_dtsadmin or db_dtsoperator database roles can be a reader. The writer role is held by members of the db_dtsadmin database role or the creator of the package by default. When you select the dropdown box in the Package Roles dialog, you can change the package role from the default to another customized role from the MSDB database.

You may want to assign a group of people to a customized role to ensure that they are the only ones who can execute a set of packages. For instance, the following short example secures a package to a role called Accounting for the writer and reader package role.

First, open Management Studio and connect to your development or local database engine instance. Then, expand System Databases ➪ MSDB ➪ Security and right-click Roles, selecting New Role. This opens the New Database Role dialog (shown in Figure 22-36). Of course, you need the appropriate security to create a new database role.

Name the role **AccountingRole** and make your own login a member of the role by clicking the Add button. Additionally, make your own user name an owner of the role. You may have to add your login as a user to the MSDB database prior to adding the role if it isn't there already.

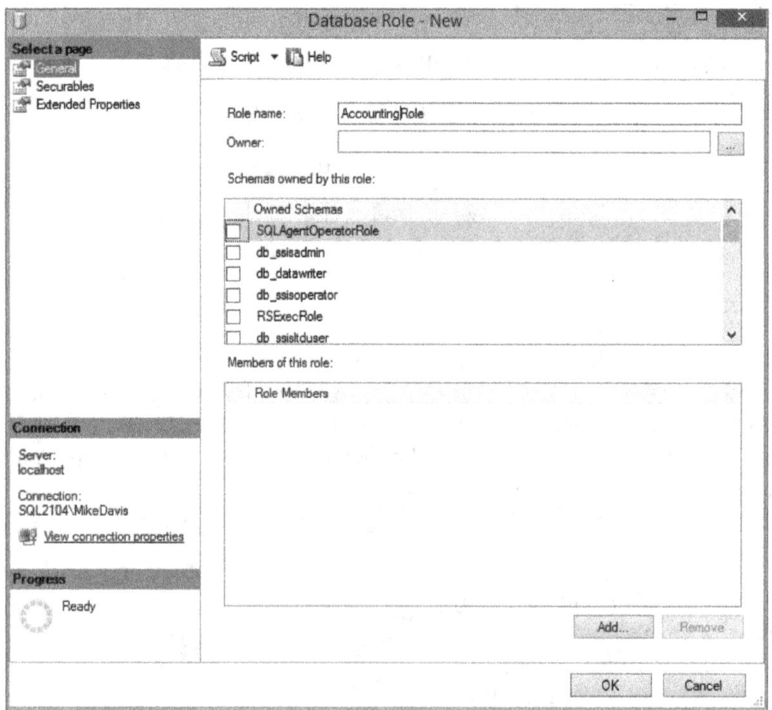

FIGURE 22-36

You're now ready to tie this role to a package. In Management Studio, connect to Integration Services. Right-click any package stored in the MSDB database and select Package Role to secure the package. For the writer and reader roles, select the newly created AccountingRole role and click OK. Now, packages of the AccountingRole role will be able to perform actions on the package. If you're a member of the sysadmin role for the server, you will be able to perform all functions in SSIS, such as execute and update any package, and bypass the package role.

If your packages are stored on the file system, you must set a package password on the package to truly secure it. You can also enforce security by protecting the directory with Windows Active Directory security on the file or folder where your packages are stored. To set a package password in SQL Server Data Tools, set the ProtectionLevel property to EncryptSensitiveWithPassword and type a password for the PackagePassword property. You can also set a package password using a utility called DTUtil.exe, which was covered in the "Command-Line Utilities" section earlier in this chapter.

To connect to a package store, the SSIS service must be started on the given server. Additionally, you must have TCP/IP port 135 open between your machine and the server. This is a common port used for DCOM, and many network administrators will not have this open by default. You also need to have the SQL Server database engine port open (generally TCP/IP port 1433) to connect to the package store in the MSDB database.

SCHEDULING PACKAGES

Now you have your packages deployed and are ready to set up a schedule to run them on a regular basis. The typical tool used is the SQL Server Agent. Although you can use other third-party tools instead of the SQL Server Agent, discussing them is beyond the scope of this book.

SQL Server Agent

The primary way to schedule packages in SSIS is with SQL Server Agent, which ships with the SQL Server database engine. If you don't have a database engine in your environment, then you must use something like Task Scheduler, which ships with Windows. Scheduling a package with SQL Server Agent is much simpler and gives you much more flexibility.

The first step to scheduling a package is to connect to the database engine. Ensure that the SQL Server Agent service is started. Right-click Jobs under the SQL Server Agent tree and select New Job. The New Job dialog will open.

On the General page, name your job **Execute Package**. On the Steps page, click New, which opens the New Job Step dialog. Type **Execute Sample Package** for the Step Name property in the General page, as shown in Figure 22-37. Then, select SQL Server Integration Services Package as the type of step. For the time being, use the default SQL Agent Service Account as the Run As account. This means that the account that starts SQL Server Agent will execute the package, and sources and destinations in your package will use Windows Authentication with that account if they are set up to do so.

For the Package Source, select the SSIS catalog and point to a valid SSIS server. Pick any test package that won't have an impact on production by clicking the ellipsis button. When you click the ellipsis button, you'll see all the folders in the SSIS catalog. You still have the older options of File System, SSIS Package Store, and SQL Server for those using the package deployment model.

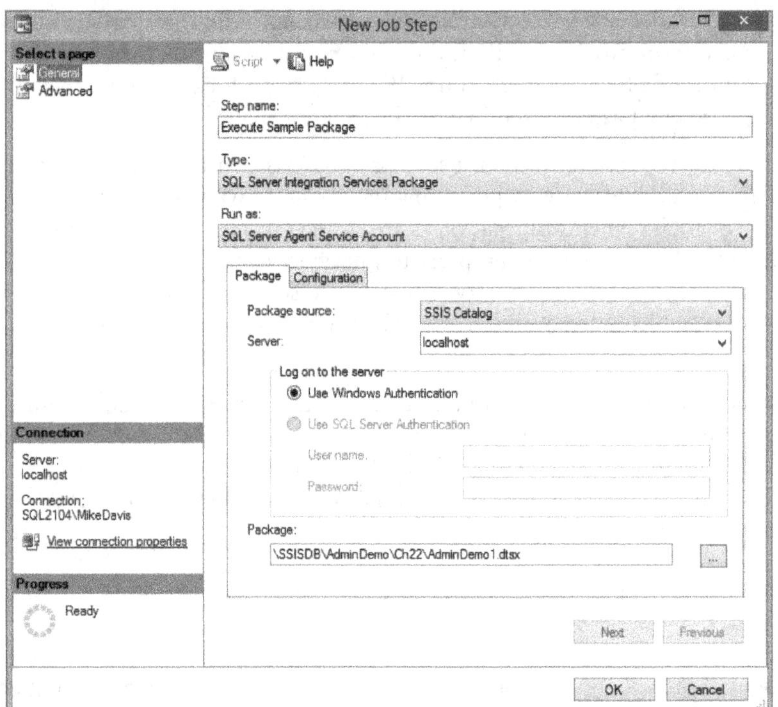

FIGURE 22-37

Under Package Source is the SSIS Package Store. This is the older location, and it is where you would find the packages that you may have deployed to the MSDB or file system.

If you select the SSIS Package Store and choose a package there, the rest of the options are identical to those shown earlier in DTExecUI.exe, with the exception of the Reporting tab because there is no console to report to from a job. You can also optionally go to the Advanced page to set the Include Step Output in History option to get more information about the job when it succeeds or fails. Click OK to go back to the New Job dialog. You can then go to the Schedules page to configure when you want the job to run. Click OK again to go back to the main Management Studio interface.

After you have the SSIS catalog selected and a package selected, you can click the Configurations tab and make changes to any parameters or select an environment. You can also make changes to any Connection Managers by selecting the Connection Managers tab. The Advanced tab allows you to add any other package properties, but these should have been handled with parameters during development. If you need to run the package in 32-bit mode, there is an option for that also.

With the job now scheduled, right-click the newly created job and select Start Job at Step. A status box will open that starts the job. When you see a success message, it does not mean the job passed or failed; it just means that the job was started successfully. You can right-click the job and select View History to see if it was successful. This opens the Log File Viewer, which shows you each execution of the package. You can drill into each execution to see more details about the steps in the job. The information this step gives you is adequate to help you identify a problem, but you may need package logs to truly diagnose the problem.

Proxy Accounts

A classic problem in SSIS and DTS is that a package may work in the design environment but not work once scheduled. Typically, this is because you have connections that use Windows Authentication. At design time, the package uses your credentials, and when you schedule the package, it uses the SQL Server Agent service account by default. This account may not have access to a file share or database server that is necessary to successfully run the package. Proxy accounts in SQL Server enable you to circumvent this problem.

With a proxy account, you can assign a job to use an account other than the SQL Server Agent account. Creating a proxy account is a two-step process. First, you must create a credential that allows a user to use an Active Directory account that is not his or her own, and then you specify how that account may be used.

To create a credential, open Management Studio and right-click Credentials under the Security tree and select New Credential. For this example, you'll create a credential called AdminAccess (see Figure 22-38). The credential will allow users to temporarily gain administrator access. For the Identity property, type the name of an administrator account or an account with higher rights. Lastly, type the password for the Windows account, and click OK.

> **NOTE** *As you can imagine, because you're typing a password here, be aware of your company's password expiration policies. Credential accounts should be treated like service accounts.*

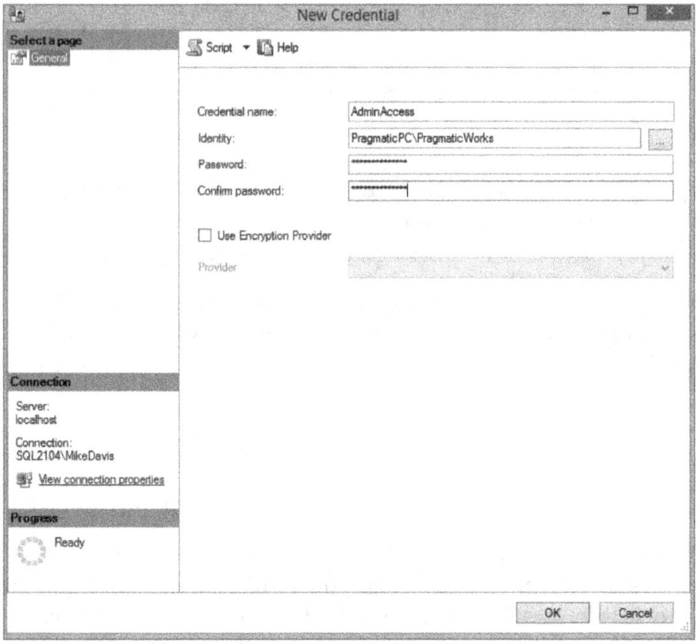

FIGURE 22-38

The next step is to specify how the credential can be used. Under the SQL Server Agent tree, right-click Proxies and select New Proxy, which opens the New Proxy Account dialog (shown in Figure 22-39). Type **Admin Access Proxy** for the Proxy Name property, and **AdminAccess** as the Credential Name. Check SQL Server Integration Services Package for the subsystem type allowed to use this proxy.

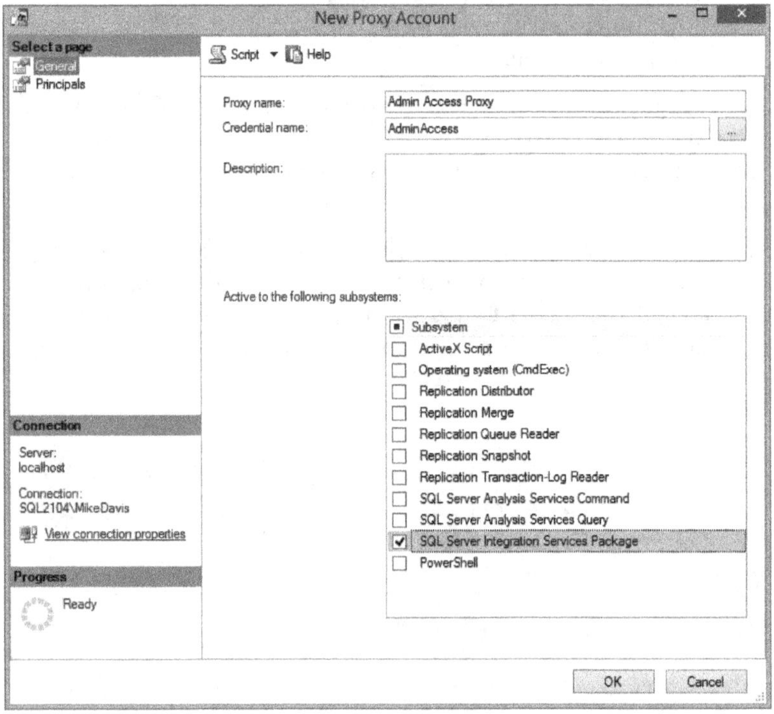

FIGURE 22-39

Optionally, you can go to the Principals page in the New Proxy Account dialog to specify which roles or accounts can use your proxy from SSIS. You can explicitly grant server roles, specific logins, or members of given MSDB roles rights to your proxy. Click Add to grant rights to the proxy one at a time.

Click OK to save the proxy. Now if you create a new SSIS job step as shown earlier, you'll be able to use the new proxy by selecting the Admin Access Proxy from the Run As dropdown box. Any connections that use Windows Authentication will then use the proxy account instead of the standard account.

64-BIT ISSUES

As mentioned before, DTExecUI.exe is a 32-bit application. Therefore, whenever you execute a package from DTExecUI.exe, it will execute in 32-bit mode and potentially take longer to execute than if you were executing it on your development machine. Much of the reason for this is data must be marshaled back and forth between 32-bit mode and 64-bit mode, and the amount of memory available differs. Also, Visual Studio is a 32-bit process, so you will need to run your packages out of the Visual Studio debug mode to get a true 64-bit run. To get around this problem, you can go to the Command Line page of this tool, copy the command out of the window, and paste it into a command prompt, prefixing `dtexec.exe` in front of it.

DTExec comes in two flavors: 32-bit and 64-bit. The 32-bit version is stored in the `\Program Files (x86)` directory, and the 64-bit version is stored in the main `\Program Files` directory. Occasionally, we have seen issues where the environment variables used in configurations have issues and point to the wrong `C:\Program Files\Microsoft SQL Server\100\DTS\Binn\` directory. You can fix this issue by right-clicking My Computer from your desktop and selecting Properties. From the Advanced tab, select Environment Variables. In the System Variables window, select the Path variable and click Edit. In the window that appears, you will see the path to the `Binn` directory. Ensure that the path is set to `\Program Files` and not `\Program Files (x86)`, and click OK. After doing that, you can feel confident when typing **DTExec** at a command prompt that you're executing the 64-bit version (the version of DTExec is shown in the first few lines of package execution). Note that this applies only to 64-bit machines.

A particularly annoying quirk (at the time of publication) is the lack of an MDAC driver for the 64-bit architecture. The impact of this is that you can't execute packages in 64-bit mode if they refer to anything that uses a Jet driver, in particular Access and Excel. If you need to do this, you can execute the package using the 32-bit version of DTExec.exe. Another option in SQL Server Data Tools is to right-click the project, select Properties, and set the Run64BitRuntime to false in the Debugging page. This will set packages inside the project to run in 32-bit mode when debugging.

Aside from the few quirks of the 64-bit architecture and SSIS, the benefits are incredible. Keep in mind that SSIS is very memory intensive. If you're able to scale up the memory on demand with a 64-bit architecture, you have a truly compelling reason to upgrade. Even though tools like DTExecUI are not 64-bit ready, scheduled packages will run under 64-bit mode. If you want a package to run under 32-bit mode, you have to add the step to run the 32-bit DTExec from the scheduled job by going to the runtime option in the Execution Options tab in SQL Server Agent.

MONITORING PACKAGE EXECUTIONS

Auditing SSIS packages in the previous version of SQL Server is a pain. If you don't have a third-party tool like BI xPress from Pragmatic Works, you have to manually set up auditing or use the built-in logging, which is very limited. Reporting is built into the SSIS catalog in SQL Server. You don't need to create any reports at all — that is, unless you want a custom report from the SSIS catalog or want a central SSIS auditing database. The auditing built into SSIS is on the SSIS server where SSIS is running, so if you have ten different SSIS servers, you will need to look at each server to read the reports. This reporting is a part of the project deployment model. If you use the older package deployment model, you will need to use the older logging methods.

Built-in Reporting

Several reports are built into SSMS and query the SSIS catalog. The easiest way to view the reports for a package is to right-click on the package and select Reports ➪ Standard Reports ➪ All Executions (see Figure 22-40).

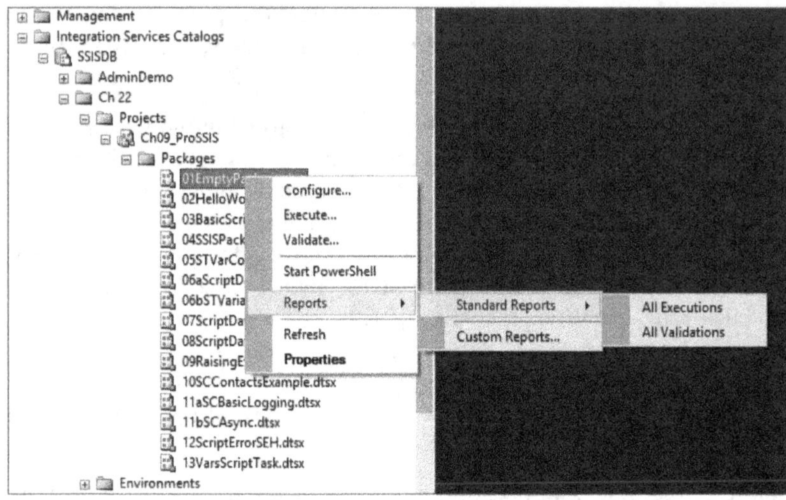

FIGURE 22-40

The All Executions report shows the package execution history. This report includes the execution ID, whether it succeeded or failed, the folder in which the package is located, project name, package name, start time, end time, and duration of the package, in seconds. An example is shown in Figure 22-41.

All Executions

on SQL2104 at 1/1/2014 11:22:21 AM

This report provides information about the Integration Services package executions that have been performed on the connected SQL Server instance.

Filter: Start time range: 12/26/2013 - 1/1/2014; Status: All; (4 more)

Execution Information

0	0	0	4
Failed	Running	Succeeded	Others

ID	Status	Report			Folder Name	Project Name	Package Name	Start Time
8	Pending Execution	Overview	All Messages	Execution Performance	Ch 22	Ch09_ProSSIS	01EmptyPackage.dtsx	1/1/2014 11:21
7	Pending Execution	Overview	All Messages	Execution Performance	Ch 22	Ch09_ProSSIS	01EmptyPackage.dtsx	1/1/2014 11:21
6	Pending Execution	Overview	All Messages	Execution Performance	Ch 22	Ch09_ProSSIS	01EmptyPackage.dtsx	1/1/2014 11:21
5	Pending Execution	Overview	All Messages	Execution Performance	Ch 22	Ch09_ProSSIS	01EmptyPackage.dtsx	1/1/2014 11:21

FIGURE 22-41

One of the nicest features of the SSIS reports is the capability to drill through to more detailed reports using the hyperlinks. The first link in the All Executions report is the Overview link. Clicking this link opens the Overview report, which provides a summary of the package's execution. This report shows each task in the package, including its duration. After drilling down for more detailed information, you can click the back link in the top-left corner of a report to return to the previous report (see Figure 22-42).

Overview
on SQL2104 at 1/1/2014 11:24:18 AM
This report provides an overview of the package tasks and parameters, including execution or validation information.
View Messages
View Performance

Execution Information

Operation ID	8	Duration (sec)	48.298
Package	Ch 22\Ch09_ProSSIS\01EmptyPackage.dtsx	Start Time	1/1/2014 11:21:37 AM
Environment	-	End Time	1/1/2014 11:22:26 AM
Status	Failed	Caller	SQL2104\MikeDavis

Execution Overview
Filter: Result: All; (3 more)

Result	Duration (sec)	Package Name	Task Name	Execution Path
No task information is available. One or more filters have been set, or one or more errors occurred during pre-execution. For information about the error messages, click View Messages to open the Messages report.				

Parameters Used

Name	Value	Da
CALLER_INFO		String
DUMP_EVENT_CODE	0	String
DUMP_ON_ERROR	False	Boolean
DUMP_ON_EVENT	False	Boolean

FIGURE 22-42

The Overview report has two links at the top that you can use to drill down for more detailed information. The first is the View Messages report, which includes details about the package down to the event level. The Messages report is great for troubleshooting a package that has errors. The other link on the Overview report is View Performance. This link opens the Execution Performance report, which shows the trending of the package in terms of duration. You can see this report in Figure 22-43.

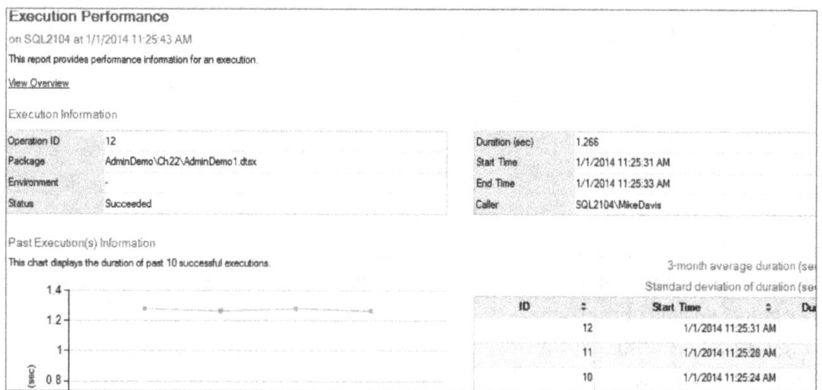

FIGURE 22-43

If you return to the All Executions report, you will see that the message and execution performance links are also on this report. Therefore, you can drill through from this report directly to those reports, without going through the Overview report.

A Dashboard report is available also. To open it, right-click on the SSISDB in the SSIS catalog and navigate to Reports ➪ Standard Reports ➪ Integration Services Dashboard, as shown in Figure 22-44.

This Dashboard report provides a high-level overview of the entire SSIS catalog. Using this report, you can quickly see the number of packages failed, running, or succeeded, and other status information. You can drill through to the detail reports by clicking the links on the right, as shown in Figure 22-45.

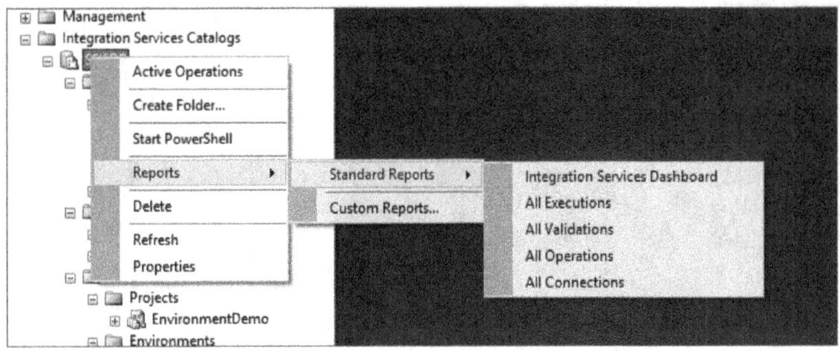

FIGURE 22-44

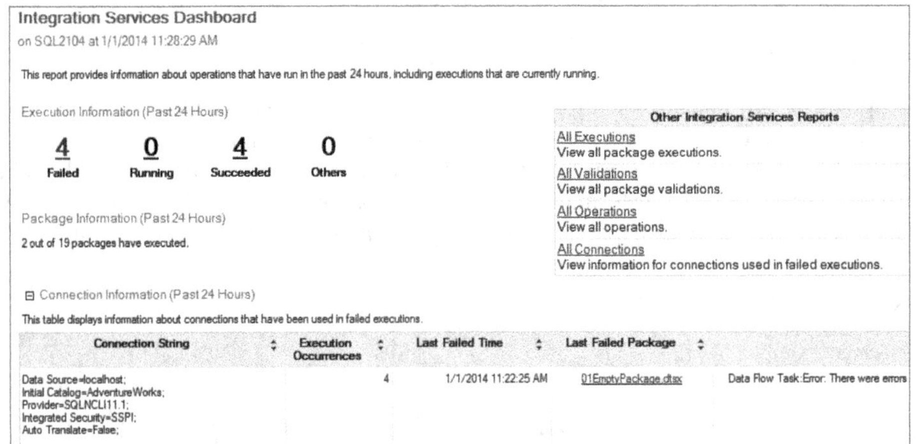

FIGURE 22-45

Four report options are available: All Executions, All Validations, All Operations, and All Connections. The names of these reports are self-explanatory, with each report showing details for that item. For example, if you run validation on a package, it will be displayed on the All Validations report. The All Connections report shows all connections used in the package executions or validations. The All Operations report shows any operation performed on the SSIS catalog, such as executing packages, deploying, and server start-up. Each report also has a filter link, which enables you to filter information based on date, status, package name, project name, ID, and folder name. You can see the Filter Settings dialog in Figure 22-46.

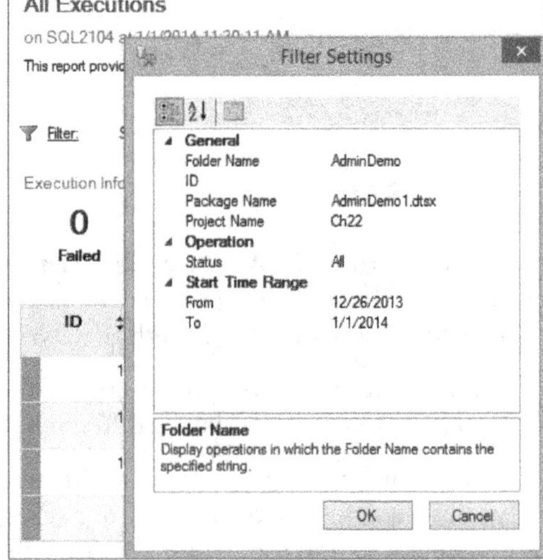

FIGURE 22-46

When you right-click on SSIS packages you will notice there is an option for custom reports. You can develop your own custom reports in Reports Services based on the SSISDB.

Custom Reporting

The reporting built into the SSIS catalog gives you an opportunity to view the execution results of your packages. It even gives you trending reports to compare current package runtimes to previous runtimes. Sometimes, however, you might want a report that isn't provided by the SSIS catalog. In that case, you can either create your own report in Reporting Services or download an already existing report.

CodePlex.com offers a report pack containing a set of useful reports. You can download these reports at `http://ssisreportingpack.codeplex.com/`. Keep in mind that this is an open-source product, so it is not supported by Microsoft or any other vendor.

First download the SSIS Reporting Pack.msi from CodePlex.com. Install the report pack by double-clicking on the install file you downloaded. The default install directory is `c:\SSIS Reporting Pack`. You can change this location during the install.

After downloading the reports, you need to point them to your SSISDB. To do this, you must open them in a SSRS project in SQL Server Data Tools and adjust the Data Source. Then save the reports to a location you can access from the SSISDB. Now you can right-click on an object in the SSIS catalog and select Custom Reports. Browse to the location where you saved the reports, and you should be able to view them. When you receive a warning that you are about to run a custom report that could contain malicious queries, click Run to run the report. Keep in mind that if you receive an error, there is no support for these reports.

You can also run these reports outside of the SSIS catalog in Reporting Services. You can even schedule the reports to run on a subscription basis, to be delivered to the person responsible for monitoring package executions in your environment. In fact, this option is probably a better idea in terms of reporting. By having the reports delivered outside of SSMS, you don't need to have access to the SSIS catalog to view the package history. This will be critical when developers need to monitor packages in a production environment and don't have rights to the production SSIS catalog.

PERFORMANCE COUNTERS

There are a few key performance counters to watch when you're trying to monitor the performance of your SSIS package. These counters greatly help you troubleshoot issues, if you have memory contention or you need to tweak your SSIS settings. Inside the System Monitor (also known to old-school administrators as *perfmon*) is a performance object called SQLServer: SSIS Pipeline. (There are quite a few other objects as well, but they are not useful enough to describe here.)

If you're trying to benchmark how many rows are being read and written, you can use the Rows Read and Rows Written counters. These counters show you the number of rows since you starting monitoring the packages. It sums all rows in total across all packages and does not allow you to narrow the results down to a single package.

The most important counters are the buffer counters. The Buffer Memory counter shows you the amount of memory, in total, being used by all the packages. The Buffers In Use counter indicates how many buffers are actually in use. The critical counter here, though, is Buffers Spooled. This shows you how many buffers have been written from memory to disk. This is critical for the performance of your system. If you have buffers being spooled, you have a potential memory contention, and you may want to consider increasing the memory or changing your buffer settings in your package. This is covered in more detail in Chapter 16, but you should never see this number creep above a 5, if not 0.

SUMMARY

This chapter covered many aspects of the Integration Services 2014 release. From the SSIS catalog to parameters and environments, you should become familiar with the features. This is especially true if you are going to be administrating Integration Services. With the T-SQL tools and GUI tools, you have a massive amount of control over your Integration Services instance. The capability to use T-SQL and the built-in stored procedures enables you to create scripts and then reuse them, making administration a lot easier. Integration Services administration always seems like a daunting task, but if you become familiar with the items described in this chapter, you can rest assured that you have the right tools for the job.

SSIS Crib Notes

In this appendix you find a list of the most commonly used expressions, tasks, and transforms in SSIS with a description of when to use them. Reference these tables when you have a package to build in SSIS, and you are not sure which SSIS component to use to perform the needed actions.

WHEN TO USE CONTROL FLOW TASKS

TASKS	WHEN TO USE
Data Flow Task	Use this task when you need to pass data from a source to a destination. The source and destination can be a flat file, an OLE DB Connection, or any other connections supported in the connection manager.
Execute Package Task	Use this task when you need to call another package from within a package. The package performing the call is the parent package. The called package is the child package. Information can be passed from the parent package to the child package with configurations.
Execute Process Task	Use this task to call an executable. The executable can be a batch file or an application. This task can call applications to perform functions on the files in SSIS, such as compressing a file. This task is commonly used to call third-party programs like compression or FTP tools.
Execute SQL Task	Use this task to perform any T-SQL operation. The SQL can be saved directly in the task, in a file, or in a variable. This task is commonly used to call stored procedures.
File System Task	Use this task to manipulate files. This task can move, rename, copy, and delete files and directories. You can also change the attributes of a file. A common use is archiving files after loading them.

continues

(continued)

TASKS	WHEN TO USE
FTP Task	Use this task to send or receive a file via the FTP protocol. You must have a valid FTP connection to perform this task. This task is commonly used to receive files from an FTP host for loading in a database.
Message Queue Task	Use this task to send or receive messages to a message queue. You must have a valid MSMQ connection to perform this task.
Script Task	Use this task to perform complex tasks that are not available in SSIS. This task allows you to leverage the .NET Framework to perform just about any task. Checking for the existence of a file is common use of this task.
Send Mail Task	Use this task to send e-mail via SMTP. You must have a valid SMTP server connection to use this task. You can use this task to send notification of the package information to recipients. You can also send files via the attachments on the e-mail.
Web Service Task	Use this task to call a web service. You need a valid web service URL to perform this task.
XML Task	Use this task to perform XML functions. This task can perform common XML tasks such as Diff, used to compare two XML files and find the differences.

WHEN TO USE DATA FLOW TRANSFORMS

TRANSFORMS	WHEN TO USE
Aggregate	Use this transform to perform grouping and summing of data. This is similar to the `Group By` function in T-SQL.
Audit	Use this transform to add a column to a Data Flow with package information. You can add items like the package name and user name as a new column in the Data Flow.
Conditional Split	Use this transform to divide data into different paths based on a Boolean expression. You can use all the paths from the split or ignore some outputs. This transform equates to a `CASE` statement in T-SQL.
Copy Column	Use this transform to create a new column in the Data Flow that is an exact copy of another column.
Data Conversion	Use this transform to convert data from one data type to another. For example, you can change Unicode to non-Unicode or change a string to an integer.

Derived Column	This is the most important transform. Use this transform to create or replace a column in the Data Flow with a column created by an expression. You can combine columns or use functions like `getdate` to create new data.
Export Column	Use this transform to send a column in a Data Flow to a file. The data types can be `DT_TEXT`, `DT_NTEXT`, and `DT_IMAGE`.
Fuzzy Grouping	Use this transform to group data together based on a percentage match. In this transform the data does not have to be an exact match to be grouped together. You can control the percentage of matching needed to group the data.
Fuzzy Lookup	Use this transform to find matching data in a table. The data does not have to match exactly. You can control the percentage of matching needed to group the data.
Import Column	Use this transform to import data from files into rows in a data set.
Lookup	Use this transform to compare data in a Data Flow to a table. This will find exact matches in the date and give you a match and no-match output from the transform. This transform equates to an `INNER JOIN` statement in T-SQL.
Merge	Use this transform to combine two sets of data in a way similar to a Union All. This transform requires both inputs to be sorted.
Merge Join	Use this transform to combine two sets of data in a way similar to a left outer join. This transform requires both inputs to be sorted.
Multicast	Use this transform to clone the data set and send it to different locations. This transform does not alter the data.
OLE DB Command	Use this transform to send T-SQL commands to a database. This can be used to insert data into a table using the T-SQL `Insert` command.
Percentage Sampling	Use this transform to select a percentage of the rows in a Data Flow. The rows are randomly selected. You can set a seed to select the same rows on every execution of the transform. The unselected rows will follow a different path in the Data Flow.
Pivot	Use this transform to convert normalized data to denormalized data. This transform changes the rows into columns.
Row Count	Use this transform to write the row count in a Data Flow to a variable.
Row Sampling	Use this transform to select a number of rows in the Data Flow. The number of rows is set in the transform. The unselected rows will follow a different path in the Data Flow.

continues

(continued)

TRANSFORMS	WHEN TO USE
Script Component	Use this transform to perform complex transforms that are not available in SSIS. This transform allows you to leverage the .NET Framework to perform just about any transform.
Slowly Changing Dimension	Use this transform to create a dimension load for a data warehouse. This is a wizard that will walk you through all the decision making in setting up a dimensional load.
Sort	Use this transform to order the data by a column or more than one column. This is similar to an "order by" command in T-SQL.
Term Extraction	Use this transform to find words in a Data Flow and create an output with the words listed and a score.
Term Lookup	Use this transform to compare to data in a Data Flow and determine if a word exists in the data.
Union All	Use this transform to combine two sets of data on top of each other. This is similar to the `Union` command in T-SQL.
Unpivot	Use this transform to convert denormalized data to normalized data. This transform changes the columns into rows.

COMMON EXPRESSIONS AND SCRIPTS

PROBLEM	QUICK SOLUTION
Loop over a list of files and load each one.	**Tasks Required:** Foreach Loop, Data Flow Task **Solution:** Configure the Foreach Loop to loop over any particular directory of files. The loop should be configured to output to a given variable. Map the given variable to a connection manager by using expressions. More of this can be found in Chapter 6.
Conditionally executing tasks	**Solution:** Double-click the precedence constraint and set the Evaluation property to Expression and Constraint. Type the condition that you want to evaluate in the Expression box.

Move and rename the file at the same time.	**Tasks Required:** File System Task **Solution:** Set the File System Task to rename the file and point to the directory you'd like to move it to. This enables you to rename and move the file in the same step. More on this can be found in Chapter 3.
Loop over an array of data in a table and perform a set of tasks for each row.	**Tasks Required:** Execute SQL Task, Foreach Loop **Solution:** Use an Execute SQL Task to load the array and send the data into an object variable. Loop over the variable in a Foreach Loop by using an ADO Enumerator. More of this can be found in Chapter 6.
Perform an incremental load of data.	**Tasks Required:** Two Execute SQL Tasks, Data Flow Task **Solution:** Have the first Execute SQL Task retrieve a date from a control table of when the target table was last loaded and place that into a variable. In the Data Flow Task, create a date range on your query using the variable. Then, update the control table using a second Execute SQL Task to specify when the table was last updated. You can also use the Change Data Capture (CDC) components built into SQL Server and SSIS to simplify this if you have Enterprise Edition of SQL Server installed. More on this can be found in Chapter 11.
Perform a conditional update and insert.	**Components Required:** Data Flow Task, Conditional Split, Lookup Transform or Merge Join, OLE DB Command Transform **Solution:** Use the Lookup Transform or Merge Join to determine if the row exists on the destination and ignore a failed match. If the row yields blank on the key, then you know the row should be inserted into target (by a Conditional Split). Otherwise, the row is a duplicate or an update. Determine if the row is an update by comparing the source value to the target value in the Conditional Split. The update can be done by an OLE DB Command Transform or by loading the data into a staging table. More of this can be found in Chapter 13.

continues

(continued)

PROBLEM	QUICK SOLUTION

Create a file name with today's date.	**Expression on the Flat File or File Connection Manager:**
	`"C:\\Projects\\MyExtract" + (DT_WSTR, 30) (DT_DBDATE) GETDATE() + ".csv"`
	
	Results in:
	`C:\Projects\MyExtract2014-03-20.csv`

Use a two-digit date. For example, retrieve a month in two-digit form (03 for March instead of 3).	`RIGHT("0"+(DT_WSTR,4)MONTH(Getdate()),2)` **Results in:** 03 (if the month is March)
Multiple condition if statement. In this example, the statement determines that if the `ColumnName` column is blank or null, it will be set to unknown. To make a Logical AND condition, use `&&` instead of the `||` operator.	`ISNULL(ColumnName) || TRIM(ColumnName)== "" ? "Unknown" : ColumnName`
Return the first five characters from a zip code.	**Derived Column Transform in the Data Flow:** `SUBSTRING(ZipCodePlus4,1,5)`
Remove a given character from a string (example shows how to remove dashes from a Social Security number).	**Derived Column Transform in the Data Flow:** `REPLACE(SocialSecurityNumber, "-","")`
Uppercase data	**Derived Column Transform in the Data Flow:** `UPPER(ColumnName)`

Replace NULL with another value.	**Derived Column Transform in the Data Flow:** `ISNULL(ColumnName) ? "New Value": ColumnName`
Replace blanks with NULL values.	**Derived Column Transform in the Data Flow:** `TRIM(ColumnName) == "" ? (DT_STR,4,1252)NULL(DT_STR,4,1252) : ColumnName`

Remove any non-numeric data from a column.	**Script Transform in the Data Flow Task with the code as follows:**
	`Imports System.Text.RegularExpressions`
	`Public Overrides Sub Input0_ProcessInputRow(ByVal Row As Input0Buffer)`
	` If Row.ColumnName_IsNull = False Or Row.ColumnName = "" Then`
	`    Dim pattern As String = String.Empty`
	`    Dim r As Regex = Nothing`
	`    pattern = "[^0-9]"`
	`   r = New Regex(pattern, RegexOptions.Compiled)`
	` Row.ColumnName = Regex.Replace(Row.ColumnName, pattern, "")`
	`    End If`
	`End Sub`

Convert text to proper case (first letter in each word uppercase).	**Script Transform with the line of partial code as follows (note that this code should go on one line):** `Row.OutputName = StrConv(Row.InputName, VbStrConv.ProperCase)`

B

SSIS Internal Views and Stored Procedures

In this appendix you find an abbreviated table of some of the stored procedures and views that may be helpful for an administrator when hacking the SSISDB catalog. For the most part, you want to use the views instead of the underlying tables since the tables may change during service packs or new versions of SQL Server. It is for this reason the tables are not in the appendix. This list is not comprehensive but focuses on the commonly used ones when you want to hack the SSIS catalog.

VIEWS

VIEW	USE
catalog.catalog_properties	Contains all the properties of the SSIS catalog.
catalog.environment_variables	Lists all the variables used by a set of environments.
catalog.environments	Contains a list of SSIS environments in folders. You may need to reference this view to see what potential environments you have when running a package through T-SQL.
catalog.executions	Each time you execute a package, a row is shown here. Shows the amount of resources being allocated to the package. Shows the duration of the package runtime, who ran the package, and from what machine.

continues

(continued)

VIEW	USE
`catalog.event_messages`	As a package runs, several rows are shown here for each successful run of a step.
`catalog.folders`	Contains a list of folders in the catalogs.
`catalog.execution_data_statistics`	When the package runs in verbose mode, the package shows the statistics about the package runtime and rows sent.
`catalog.object_parameters`	Shows a list of all the parameters by package and project.
`catalog.projects`	Lists all the projects installed in the SSIS catalog.
`catalog.packages`	Contains a list of all the packages in SSIS projects and folders.

STORED PROCEDURES

STORED PROCEDURE ALL IN THE CATALOG SCHEMA	USE
`create_folder`	Creates an SSIS folder in the catalog. `create_folder [ @folder_name = ] folder_name, [ @folder_id = ] folder_id OUTPUT`

`create_environment`	Create a new environment.
	
	`create_environment [ @folder_name = ] folder_name`
	`, [ @environment_name = ] environment_name`
	`[ , [ @environment_description = ] environment_description ]`

`create_environment_reference`	Maps an environment to a project.
	
	`create_environment_reference [ @folder_name = ] folder_name`
	`, [ @project_name = ] project_name`
	`, [ @environment_name = ] environment_name`
	`, [ @reference_location = ] reference_location`
	`[ , [ @environment_folder_name = ] environment_folder_name ]`
	`[ , [ @reference_id = ] reference_id OUTPUT ]`

`create_execution`	Instantiates a package before execution.
	
	`create_execution [ @folder_name = folder_name`
	`    , [ @project_name = ] project_name`
	`    , [ @package_name = ] package_name`
	`  [ , [ @reference_id = ] reference_id ]`
	`  [ , [ @use32bitruntime = ] use32bitruntime ]`
	`    , [ @execution_id = ] execution_id OUTPUT`

`start_execution`	Starts the package execution and is run directly after `create_execution`. `start_execution [ @execution_id = ] execution_id`

`set_execution_parameter_value`	Sets parameters values for a given execution prior to the run of the package. Used after the `create_execution` stored procedure but before the `start_execution` stored procedure.
	
	`set_execution_parameter_value [ @execution_id = execution_id`
	`    , [ @object_type = ] object_type`
	`    , [ @parameter_name = ] parameter_name`
	`    , [ @parameter_value = ] parameter_value`

`stop_operation`	Stops a package run with an `operation_id`. `stop_operation [ @operation_id = ] operation_id`

Interviewing for an ETL Developer Position

This appendix should be used as a preparation guide for interview questions you may encounter when interviewing for an ETL Developer position. This is not an all-encompassing list of what you may be asked, but it does provide a good sample of common questions. These questions also only focus on the technical aspects of interviewing and do not offer guidance for personality and work behavior, which are likely questions to occur during an interview. Each question includes a chapter reference to guide you on where you can read more details on the topic.

Oftentimes in technical interviews you will be asked to demonstrate skills or whiteboard concepts. So be prepared to not only answer questions verbally but also visualize processes to the interviewer. You should anticipate the interviewer requesting you to do this, so practice whiteboarding common ETL concepts.

QUESTIONS

1. Discuss why you would use checkpoints and how they affect the execution of an SSIS package (See Chapter 15).
2. If you have a package that runs fine in SQL Server Data Tools (SSDT) but fails when running from a SQL Agent Job what would be your first step in troubleshooting the problem (See Chapter 22)?
3. Discuss why you would use transactions and how they affect the execution of an SSIS package (See Chapter 15).
4. What techniques would you consider to add notification to your packages? You're required to send e-mails to essential staff members immediately after a package fails (See Chapter 22).
5. Explain what breakpoints are and how you would use them (See Chapter 18).

6. Discuss what method you would use for looping over a folder of files and loading the file contents into a database (See Chapter 6).
7. What techniques would you consider when adding auditing to your packages? You're required to log when a package fails and how many rows were extracted and loaded in your sources and destinations (See Chapter 22).
8. In the SSIS Data Flow what is the difference between synchronous (non-blocking) transformations and asynchronous (blocking) transformations (See Chapter 16)?
9. How can you configure your SSIS package to run in 32-bit mode on a 64-bit machine when using some data providers which are only available on the 32-bit machines (See Chapter 14)?
10. How is a Data Flow path different from a precedence constraint (See Chapter 1)?
11. What are annotations and why should they be used in your package development (Chapter 2)?
12. What feature in SSIS can be used to make a package reconfigure itself at runtime to add the current date to the end of a file name (Chapter 5)?
13. Which task allows you to perform common file operations and name one limitation it has (Chapter 3)?
14. Name one reason why you would have to choose a Merge Join over a Lookup Transformation (Chapter 7)?
15. Explain what buffers are and how the SSIS Data Flow uses them (Chapter 4)?
16. How can Data Quality Services be used with SSIS to clean incoming address data with known issues (Chapter 11)?
17. What is Team Foundation Server and how can it integrate with SSIS (Chapter 17)?
18. In what scenarios would you potentially utilize a Script Component in your SSIS Data Flow design (Chapter 9)?
19. You need to run a SQL Server stored procedure inside your SSIS package to start an update process. How can you run a stored procedure in the Control Flow and also pass values into any parameters it may have (Chapter 3)?
20. What does the FastParse do and which Data Flow components can it be enabled on (Chapter 4)?

ANSWERS

1. When checkpoints are enabled on a package, if the package fails it will save the point at which the package fails. This way you can correct the problem and then rerun from the point that it failed instead of rerunning the entire package. The obvious benefit to this is if you load a million record file just before the package fails you don't have to load it again.
2. The account that runs SQL Agent Jobs likely doesn't have the needed permissions for one of the connections in your package. Either elevate the account permissions or create a

proxy account. To create a proxy account you need to first create new credentials with the appropriate permissions. Next, assign those credentials to a proxy account. When you run the job now, you will select Run As the newly created proxy account.

3. If transactions are enabled on your package and tasks, then when the package fails it will rollback everything that occurred during the package. First make sure MSDTC (Microsoft Distributed Transaction Coordinator) is enabled in the Control Panel ➪ Administrative Tools ➪ Component Services. Transactions must be enabled not only on the package level but also on each task you want included as part of the transaction. To have the entire package in a transaction, set TransactionOption at the package level to Required and each task to Supported.

4. This could either be set in a SQL Agent Job when the package runs or actually inside the package itself with a Send Mail Task in the Event Handlers to notify when a package fails. You could also recommend third-party tools to accomplish this.

5. Breakpoints put pauses in your package. It's a great tool for debugging a package because you can place a breakpoint on a task and it will pause the package based on execution events. A situation where I have used breakpoints is when I have a looping container and I want to see how my variables are changed by the loop. You can place a watch window on the package and type the variable name in. Set a breakpoint on the container and then stop after each iteration of the loop.

6. This would require a Foreach Loop using the Foreach File Enumerator. Inside the Foreach Loop Editor you need to set a variable to store the directory of the files that will be looped through. Next, select the connection manager used to load the files and add an expression to the connection string property that uses the variable created in the Foreach Loop.

7. This could be done by creating a database that is designated for package auditing. Track row counts coming from a source and which actually make it to a destination. Row counts and package execution should be all in one location and then optionally report off that database. This reporting database could allow you to see package execution trends and calculate other interesting metrics about package executions. There are also third-party tools that can accomplish this for you.

8. A synchronous transformation is one in which the buffers are immediately handed off to the next downstream transformation at the completion of the transformation logic. A common example of a synchronous component is a Derived Column Transformation.

   A transformation output is asynchronous if the buffers used in the input are different from the buffers used in the output. An asynchronous transform is blocking because it must first consume all the data flow rows first prior to sending any to the next task. A common example of an asynchronous component is an Aggregate Transformation.

9. In order to run an SSIS package in Visual Studio in 32-bit mode, the SSIS project property Run64BitRuntime needs to be set to False. The default configuration for this property is True. This configuration is an instruction to load the 32-bit runtime environment rather than 64-bit, and your packages will still run without any additional changes. The property can be found under SSIS Project Property Pages ➪ Configuration Properties ➪ Debugging. When running a package from a SQL Server Agent job, you must check the property "Use 32 bit runtime" on the Execution Options tab of the job.

10. Precedence constraints are used to control the order of operations of task execution in the Control Flow. These constraints can run a task based on the success, failure, or completion of the previous task. They can also be made dynamic with the evaluation of an SSIS expression. A Data Flow path controls the direction of data movement inside the Data Flow. These allow for the developer to send error rows down special paths, while successful rows may be loaded into a table.

11. An annotation is a comment that you place in your package to help others and yourself understand what is happening in the package. Often annotations are used for identifying the version number of a package and a list of changes that have been made in the package. Using annotations can help clearly define what the package is intended for, who developed it, and what changes have been made.

12. This can be done with SSIS expressions and variables. Concatenating the `GETDATE()` with a filename will produce this result. This also requires a casting function to bring together a datetime value with the string value of the filename.

13. The File System Task is capable of copying, deleting, moving, and renaming directories or files. One limitation that this task has is that it does not participate in transactions. So if you turn on a transaction on the entire package with a File System Task that deletes a file, you will not recover that file during a rollback.

14. The Lookup Transformation can only join data from OLE DB connections, so if you need to join data from a Flat File, then you must use a Merge Join Transformation to accomplish this.

15. Consider buffers like buckets of memory resources that can be used by SSIS. Data flows out of a source in memory buffers that are 10 megabytes in size or 10,000 rows (whichever comes first) by default. As the first transformation is working on those 10,000 rows, the next buffer of 10,000 rows is being processed at the source.

16. Data Quality Services requires that you define a Knowledge Base that can define what makes a good address value and what makes a bad address value. Once the Knowledge Base is set up you can integrate it into SSIS using the DQS Cleansing Transformation in the Data Flow of your package. Incoming rows will be evaluated by DQS and output corrected records that will be sent to a destination.

17. Team Foundation Server (TFS) is an enterprise software development life cycle suite and project management repository consisting of collaborative services, integrated functionality, and an extensible application programming interface (API). TFS allows developers to easily manage code developed and to work together on solutions through a process of checking in and checking out files while they are under development. TFS tightly integrates with Visual Studio, making it easy for developers to manage their code in the same application they use for developing SSIS packages.

18. The Script Component in the SSIS Data Flow can be used as a custom Source, Transformation, or Destination. You may need to use a Script Source when you are loading unusual file formats. For example, the data does not follow standard column and row formats. You may use a Script Transformation if the native transformations that are provided to you don't solve the data extraction problem you have. For example, the Script Transformation may be used to apply regular expression formatting to your data being

extracted. You may need to use the Script Destination if your required output of data does not follow traditional column and row formats. For example, your business is requiring a file sent to customers that has summary rows after each category of data that would cause a break in the traditional row and column format of the source data.

19. Using the Execute SQL Task you can run SQL Server stored procedures. If the stored procedure has parameters, those are identified in SSIS with a question mark. You can then pass values into the question mark(s) using the Parameter Mappings page of the Execute SQL Task Editor.

20. The FastParse property can be turned on to skip validation steps that SSIS does when evaluated date, time or numeric data. Turning this property on can in some cases significantly help performance. FastParse can be enabled on either the Flat File Source or the Data Conversion Transformation. It is turned on at a column level, so for each column of the appropriate data types you must change the FastParse property to TRUE.

INDEX

D

E

F

G

H

I

M

N

O

P

Q

R

S

T

U

V